PEÑÍNGUIDE

TO SPANISH WINE

2016

www.guiapenin.com

MORE THAN **11.200** SAMPLES TASTED ~ MORE THAN **2.100** WINERIES WITH ALL THEIR ESSENTIAL INFORMATION ~ **ECOLOGICAL WINES** ~ DIRECT ACCESS TO ALL WINES VIA OUR **webpage**

Team:

Director: Carlos González
Editor in Chief: Javier Luengo
Tasting team: Carlos González, Javier Luengo and Pablo Vecilla
Texts: Javier Luengo and Carlos González
Database manager: Erika Laymuns
Advertising: Mª Carmen Hernández
Cover design, layout and desktop publishing: Flying Donkey, Luis Salgado and Jose Antonio Sánchez
External advisor: José Peñín

PUBLISHED BY: PI&ERRE
Gran Vía, 16 – 3º centro
28013 Madrid
SPAIN
Tel.: 914 119 464 - Fax: 915 159 499
comunicacion@guiapenin.com
www.guiapenin.com

ISBN: 978-84-95203-45-8
Copyright library: M-29360-2015
Translation: John Mullen Connelly
Printed by: Villena Artes Gráficas

DISTRIBUTED BY: GRUPO COMERCIAL ANAYA
Juan Ignacio Luca de Tena, 15
Tel: 0034 913 938 800
28027 MADRID
SPAIN

DISTRIBUTED BY: ACC PUBLISHING GROUP
Antique Collector's Club Ltd.
Sandy Jane, Old Martlesham
Woodbridge, Suffolk
IP12 45D, United Kingdom

CHANGE OF CYCLE FOR WINE IN SPAIN

11,200 Spanish wines tasted in one year is such an astonishingly high figure that, to date, no professional or opinion leader has been able to provide an analysis and description of Spanish wines as complete as the one you have in your hands.

This tasting figure is a landmark for this firm. This complete manual of Spanish wines deals with approximately one thousand new wines and almost 307 new wineries. Moreover, it has an updated photograph of Spanish wine at a determined time, 2016.

Some years stand out in our memories as unusually different. At the time, we know that something is happening but we fail to pinpoint the relevance of the change until time inexorably moves forward. This happened in 1990 with the progress of technology and its global adaptation in our wineries, in 2000 with the restructuring of the vineyards in order to favour of our own varieties and in 2010 with the plot concept of wine through sensible work centred on the vineyard. This is what is happening today. For three years, we at the Guía Peñín have been observing and informing on the arrival of young wine growers, and we stress the expression "wine growers" as their central focus is the vineyard and not the winery. Until a short time ago, the higher quality wines were limited to wineries with long pedigrees, historical wine making families who have written a substantial part of the history of wine generation after generation. However, for some time, younger persons are demanding a place among the greats. It has become more and more normal to find a recently created wine whose first harvest easily enters the kingdom of the wines with more than 90 points. Luck? It could be luck if these were very isolated cases, however, this has now become a tendency.

In order to understand the capacity for growth, we must take several factors into account. In the first place, frontiers are no longer an impediment to getting to know the wines which are produced in other countries. Something that was so simple but not very normal in the recent past such as tasting and describing new wines of the world is now an essential exercise for many of these promising young people. Hardly a year passes in which they save a little money to fill their cars and start off on a visit to our French neighbours in order to get to know the magnificence and uniqueness of their land. It is also unlikely that the car boots return empty, instead they return filled with bottles acquired due to their uniqueness or to the emotion which the wine has brought about in the buyer. Thus, our young people try many wines, ladies and gentlemen, and this provides them with extra knowledge and a wider view of the horizon which lies before them. This adventurous and travel loving spirit is important as is the attitude with which they address their projects. This young breed tackles wine with a firm, confident approach, unafraid of error, with the sole intention to understand and interpret the vineyard as simply and naturally as possible. They are supported by the experience of the older growers, by the popular wisdom of traditional tillage and, based on this experience, they construct a new way to make wines. Finally, the exchange of knowledge is undoubtedly another of its strengths. In the past it was strange to find someone who shared his experience with his neighbour due to the fear that the neighbour might make better wines. This change is due to a great extent to the appearance of the new technologies, and in part to the situation of abandonment in which our young people found themselves during the evolution and culmination of the latest severe crisis in our country. The channels through which information travels are accessible and immediate. There are no longer distances which obstruct communication with the most distant neighbour and the wine growers use this technology which formerly was unthinkable for country people.

NEW PROJECTS AND STYLES IN UNDERDEVELOPED AREAS

The most marvellous aspect of this change we are witnessing is that many of these new projects are proliferating in underdeveloped areas. It is no longer necessary to resort to a recognised area. Apart from the fact that it is economically more complicated, the new generation of wine producers have decided to try to make a success of their places of origin, initially with small plots on which they attempt to attain the maximum prestige of limited productions amounting to scarcely 2,000 bottles. This year, the Valle de la Orotava, Empordà, Ribeiro and Ycoden-Daute-Isora are some of the zones where new and surprising work has been carried out. In the Canary Islands, the innovations came from two wineries, Suertes de Marqués (Valle de la Orotava) with an excellent vintage 2010 sweet wine and Borja Pérez González (Ycoden-Daute-Isora) with its Ignios Origenes Vijariego Negro 2013 red. In Cigales, which is mistakenly called the "little sister of Ribera del Duero", we located one of the finest examples of tempranillo cigaleño, named 50 Vendimias de Sinforiano 2009, a homage to the 50 grape harvests its founder had participated in and whose grapes come from vineyards aged from 90 to 110 years, a treasure in a bottle. In the Empordà, Espelt Viticultores wished to pay homage to one of their own special varieties, the LLedoner Roig (red garnacha), a red variety which is produced as a white wine and, in the Espelt Lledoner Roig 2013 wine, it achieves extraordinary expressivity and balance. At the other end of the map, El Paraguas wineries surprised us with a very limited production of treixadura, godello and albariño, Fai un Sol de Carallo 2013, a vindication of the long lived, complex white wines. With its first harvest it became one of the most highly valued Ribeiro white wines.

The Dominio del Águila winery of Jorge Monzón and Isabel Rodero merits special attention since, with the second harvest of its Dominio del Águila 2011, a mixture of tempranillo, garnacha, bobal and the local white grape (albillo) of the oldest vineyards of La Aguilera, in Burgos, it managed to become one of the best red wines of the year, sharing a position with authentic heavyweights of oenology and wine growing. Moreover, at long last, someone decided to salvage a type of wine which had been left forgotten in the bottom drawer, the Rueda Dorado. Bodega de Alberto recovered this type of wine with supreme mastery, providing us with an excellent example of a Rueda Dorado.

It is striking how the large wineries are paying special attention to these wineries and their way of working. They also note how the most dynamic of these are making a slight change of direction in order to focus on the development of the style of each variety, which means that more and improved examples of responsible wine growing are appearing, as well as, curiously, a greater number of single variety wines.

However, one area that has thrilled us this year has been Priorat, with its spectacular 2013 harvest, responsible for some of the best wines of the year such as L'Ermita, Clos Erasmus and Finca Dofí. The freshness of the harvest in these areas made it possible for the wines to be expressed in all their splendour, converting the denomination of origin in the zone with the second best scoring, only surpassed by the inimitable Jerez, Xèrés, Sherry and Manzanilla de Sanlúcar de Barrameda.

Spanish wine does not come to a standstill, it continues to make progress in its expansion in international markets as a natural, compulsory outlet for the infinite number of brands. The large wineries now have expert knowledge of the most relevant markets for Spanish wine, while the small wineries little by little take tentative steps forward in order to approach these markets. Guía Peñín is aware of this situation and has spent years arranging highly successful professional encounters and fairs in cities such as New York, Moscow, Mexico City, Düsseldorf and Tokyo, and will continue to do so throughout 2016, an efficient way to bring together the wine growing riches of Spain and the international markets.

There is no doubt that we are experiencing the stage of greatest diversity of Spanish wine and again Guía Peñín is witnessing the change. The concept of micro-productions has been implemented in France for years, it is now time for this new stage to begin in Spain.

TEAM

Born in Avila in 1979, Agricultural Engineer, with Masters in Enology and Viticulture and a Masters in Wine Business Management. He has worked in several different areas of the world of wine including holding posts ranging from oenologist and vineyard technician toTechnical Manager of a wine importer and distributor. For the last nine years he has headed the Technical Department of the Peñin Guide, responsible for the coordination of staff assignments and development of wine tastings that appear in the various guides under the Peñin group.

Carlos González Sáez
Director
cgonzalez@guiapenin.com

Born in Castellón de la Plana in 1976, graduated with a degree in Journalism from the Universidad Complutense of Madrid and is also qualified in Integral Communications, University Francisco de Vitoria. After working as a journalist in different media agencies and publications, he joined the communication department of PI & ERRE as account director. Javier has been a professional taster for the Peñin team for seven years, both wines and distillates. He is currently responsible for the different editorial publishing products covered by the Peñin Guide.

Javier Luengo
Editor in Chief and Taster
jluengo@guiapenin.com

Born in Villacañas, he has been responsible for wines of the Cultural Association of La Carrasca, a promotor of wine in the university area. He was also President of this Association in 2008 and 2009. Pablo became part of the tasting team in 2010. Currently he is responsible for the training courses carried out through the Peñín Tasting School.

Pablo Vecilla
Taster
pvecilla@guiapenin.com

ACKNOWLEDGMENT

All regulatory councils that have worked effectively providing facilities and staff for logistics tasting . In some cases the tasting could not be carried out at its headquarters for reasons of our own organization. Also, special thanks to Jose Matas Enoteca Casa Bernal in El Palmar (Murcia) ; Juan Luis Perez de Eulate La Vinoteca Store in Palma de Mallorca ; Quim Vila Vila Viniteca shop in Barcelona ; Casa del Vino La Baranda El Sauzal , in the person of Jorge Miguel Garcia , in addition to the Casa del Vino de Gran Canaria ; Wine Technology Park (VITEC) in Falset (Tarragona) .

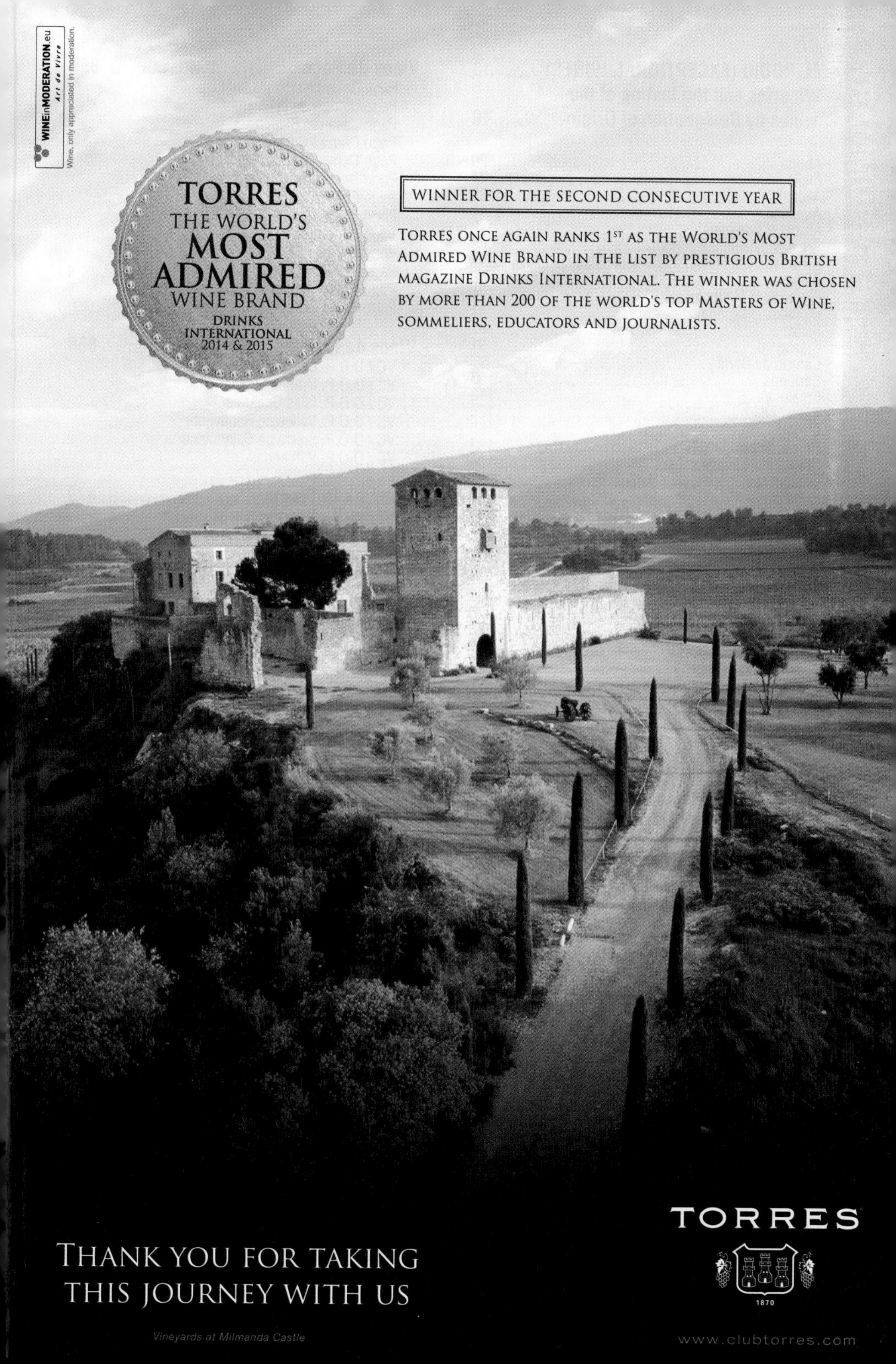

Vineyards at Milmanda Castle

SUMMARY

EXCEPTIONAL WINES

Each year, the tasting of more than 11,000 wines provides us with a select group of brands which, due to their high scores, become part of the "exceptional wines" (Page 19) of the Guía Peñín. These are the wines which achieve 95 points and more, which come near to sensorial perfection and become essential references for those seeking wines throughout the world.

Each one of these wines can be considered to be the portrait of a specific moment in time, from a particular soil, just like enclosing a moment in time in a bottle in order to enjoy it years later. The approximately 170 highest scoring wines on this Podium have passed a double "exam" each year. One was the tasting of the wine carried out by each Regulating Board together with similar wines. The other process is the so-called Second Tasting of the Guía Peñín. This second tasting is now a ritual in this firm and is repeated annually in the month of July as a failsafe counter-analysis. I is carried out behind closed doors and our tasters hone the scoring of the wines, which, above 94 points, becomes a task involving millimetres.

The wines are positioned by score, style, variety, harvest and zones over a number of month. Each one of these wines has its glass in front so that after an organoleptic examination and a comparison with wines which have a similar style and scoring, it is possible determine whether the wine in question may rise, keep its initial score or drop if its quality does not settle at the level of the others. The possible improvement of the wine is the result of it improving over the possible tables, 94, 95, 96, 97, 98 in order to guarantee its splendid qualities as regards wines with higher scores so that it it finally perfectly fits one of these tables and obtains a definitive score. This is the fairest and most analytic way for a wine to achieve a high score.

Therefore, we invite you to let yourself be seduced by this exquisite world of grand Spanish wines, a podium which shows what a grand wine can achieve in each of its types. The triumph of the soil and the vine over technological wines. The knowledge transmitted from grandparents to parents and from these to their children and so on.

PODIUM

EXCEPTIONAL WINES (RED & SWEET RED WINES)

POINTS	WINE	DO	PAGE
98 POINTS	Alabaster 2013	Toro	786
	L'Ermita 2013	Priorat	430
	La Nieta 2012	Rioja	680
	Recóndita Armonía 1978 Dulce	Vinos de Mesa	955
97 POINTS	Artadi Viña El Pisón 2013	Rioja	638
	Avrvs 2010	Rioja	650
	Clos Erasmus 2013 Barrica	Priorat	440
	Dominio del Aguila 2011 Reserva	Ribera del Duero	547
	Finca Dofí 2013 Crianza	Priorat	430
	Las Beatas 2012	Rioja	645
	Les Manyes 2012	Priorat	448
	Termanthia 2012	Toro	770
	Vega Sicilia Reserva Especial 96/98/02	Ribera del Duero	532
	Victorino 2012	Toro	786
96 POINTS	1902 Cariñena Centenaria 2010	Priorat	436
	Alabaster 2012	Toro	786
	Aquilón 2012	Campo de Borja	98
	Artadi El Carretil 2013	Rioja	638
	Artuke La Condenada 2013	Rioja	578
	Bosque de Matasnos Edición Limitada 2011	Ribera del Duero	541
	Cirsion 2010	Rioja	628
	Clos Mogador 2011	Priorat	440
	Dalmau 2011 Reserva	Rioja	661
	Dominio de Atauta Llanos del Almendro 2010	Ribera del Duero	546
	El Reventón 2013	VT Castilla y León	928
	Ferratus Sensaciones Décimo 2003	Ribera del Duero	512
	Finca El Bosque 2012	Rioja	682
	Finca Villacreces Nebro 2011 Crianza	Ribera del Duero	549
	La Rioja Alta Gran Reserva 890 Selección Especial 2001	Rioja	659
	Numanthia 2012	Toro	769
	Pago de Carraovejas "Cuesta de las Liebres" Vendimia Seleccionada 2011 Reserva	Ribera del Duero	553
	Recóndita Armonía 1979 Dulce	Vinos de Mesa	955
	Remelluri 2010 Reserva	Rioja	669
	San Vicente 2012	Rioja	671
	Terreus 2012	VT Castilla y León	924
	Valbuena 5º 2011	Ribera del Duero	532
95 POINTS	Aalto PS 2012	Ribera del Duero	497
	Alto Moncayo 2012	Campo de Borja	98
	Amancio 2012	Rioja	682
	Arbossar 2012	Priorat	448
	Arínzano Gran Vino 2008	Pago Señorío de Arinzano	867
	Artadi La Poza de Ballesteros 2013	Rioja	638
	Artadi Valdeginés 2013	Rioja	638
	As Caborcas 2012	Valdeorras	808
	Calvario 2011	Rioja	651
	Cantos del Diablo 2013	Méntrida	330

95 POINTS

WINE	DO	PAGE
Celsus 2013	Toro	776
Contino Viña del Olivo 2011	Rioja	681
Cortijo Los Aguilares Tadeo 2012	Málaga y Sierras de Málaga	315
Cosme Palacio 1894 2012	Rioja	621
Domaines Lupier La Dama 2012	Navarra	381
Dominio de Atauta Valdegatiles 2010	Ribera del Duero	546
Dominio de Es La Diva 2013	Ribera del Duero	546
Dominio de Es Viñas Viejas de Soria 2013	Ribera del Duero	546
Dominio do Bibei 2011	Ribeira Sacra	480
El Cf de Chozas Carrascal 2014	Vino de Pago Chozas Carrascal	862
El Nido 2012	Jumilla	266
El Puntido 2012	Rioja	680
El Sequé 2013	Alicante	38
Finca El Rincón de Clunia 2011	VT Castilla y León	927
Flor de Pingus 2013	Ribera del Duero	547
Gran Reserva 904 Rioja Alta 2005	Rioja	659
Hacienda Monasterio 2010 Reserva	Ribera del Duero	516
La Creu Alta 2012	Priorat	431
Lacima 2012	Ribeira Sacra	480
Les Terrasses Velles Vinyes 2013	Priorat	430
Luis Cañas Hiru 3 Racimos 2007	Rioja	610
Macán 2012	Rioja	586
Milagros de Figuero 2010	Ribera del Duero	566
Moncerbal 2013	Bierzo	66
Pago de Carraovejas 2012 Reserva	Ribera del Duero	553
Pago La Jara 2011	Toro	778
Pegaso "Barrancos de Pizarra" 2012	VT Castilla y León	928
Pingus 2013	Ribera del Duero	547
Recóndita Armonía 1987	Vinos de Mesa	955
Recóndita Armonía Dulce 1985	Vinos de Mesa	955
Regina Vides 2012	Ribera del Duero	517
Reserva Real 2010	Penedès	394
San Vicente 2011	Rioja	671
Sierra Cantabria Colección Privada 2012	Rioja	682
Somni Magnum 2012	Priorat	439
St. Antoni de Scala Dei 2012	Priorat	438
Torroja Vi de la Vila 2013	Priorat	448
Valtuille La Cova de la Raposa 2010	Bierzo	62
Viña Sastre Pesus 2012	Ribera del Duero	517

PODIUM
EXCEPTIONAL WINES (WHITE & SWEET WHITE WINES)

	WINE	TYPE	DO	PAGE
98 POINTS	Casta Diva Reserva Real Dulce 2002	B Reserva Dulce	Vinos de Mesa	955
97 POINTS	Albariño de Fefiñanes III año 2012	B	Rias Baixas	458
	Molino Real 2012	B Dulce	Málaga y Sierras de Málaga	314
96 POINTS	Jorge Ordóñez & Co. Nº3 Viñas Viejas Naturalmente Dulce 2011	B Dulce	Málaga y Sierras de Málaga	316
	Mártires 2013	B	Rioja	651
	Mártires 2014	B	Rioja	651
	MR Dulce 2012	B Dulce	Málaga y Sierras de Málaga	314
	Pazo Señorans Selección de Añada 2007	B	Rias Baixas	468
	Tenequía Malvasía Dulce Estelar Naturalmente Dulce 1996	B Gran Reserva Dulce	La Palma	300
95 POINTS	Advent Samsó Dulce Natural 2010	B Dulce	Penedès	406
	Allende Dulce 2011	B Dulce	Rioja	650
	Branco de Santa Cruz 2012	B	Valdeorras	808
	Chivite Colección 125 2012	BFB	Navarra	383
	Jorge Ordóñez & Co Nº 2 Victoria Naturalmente Dulce 2014	B	Málaga y Sierras de Málaga	316
	La Bota de Florpower nº57 MMXII 2012	B	Vinos de Mesa	962
	La Val Crianza sobre Lías 2007	BC	Rias Baixas	459
	Matias i Torres Malvasía Aromática Naturalmente Dulce 2011	B	La Palma	298
	Nisia 2014	B	Rueda	701
	Pezas da Portela 2012	BFB	Valdeorras	810
	Remelluri 2012	B	Rioja	669
	Suertes del Marqués Dulce 2010	B Dulce	Valle de la Orotava	839
	Trossos Tros Blanc 2013	B	Montsant	347
	Trossos Tros Blanc Magnum 2007	B	Montsant	347
	Vi de Glass Gewürztraminer 0,75 2008	BC Dulce	Penedès	406
	Vid Sur Dulce 2008	B B Dulce	La Palma	298
	Navazos Niepoort 2014	B	Vinos de Mesa	962

PODIUM
EXCEPTIONAL FORTIFIED WINES

	WINE	TYPE	DO	PAGE
98 POINTS	La Bota de Manzanilla Pasada Nº59 "Capataz Rivas"	MZ	Jerez	249
	La Bota de Pedro Ximenez nº56 Bota NO	PX	Jerez	249
97 POINTS	Alvear Solera 1830	PX Reserva	Montilla - Moriles	340
	Don P.X. Selección 1946	PX	Montilla - Moriles	344
	Don P.X. Selección 1965	PX	Montilla - Moriles	344
	La Bota de Amontillado nº 61 "Bota NO"	AM	Jerez	249
	La Bota de Manzanilla Pasada Nº60 "Bota Punta"	MZ	Jerez	249
	Osborne Solera BC 200	OL	Jerez	247
	Venerable VORS	PX	Jerez	248
96 POINTS	Barbadillo Amontillado VORS	AM	Jerez	244
	Don Gonzalo VOS	OL	Jerez	257
	Don P.X. Convento Selección 1955	PX	Montilla - Moriles	344
	Fino Cuatro Palmas	FI	Jerez	252
	La Cañada	PX	Montilla - Moriles	343
	Oloroso Tradición VORS	OL	Jerez	248
	Osborne Solera AOS	AM	Jerez	247
	Osborne Solera PAP	PC	Jerez	248
	Sacristía AB	AM	Jerez	258
	Solear en Rama	MZ	Jerez	245
	Solera de su Majestad VORS 37,5 cl.	OL	Jerez	258
95 POINTS	Amontillado 51-1ª VORS	AM	Jerez	247
	Añada Millennium	OL	Jerez	252
	De Muller Garnacha Solera 1926	Solera	Tarragona	742
	Dom Joan Fort 1865	Rancio	Priorat	440
	El Grifo Canari Dulce de Licor		Lanzarote	307
	El Tresillo 1874 Amontillado Viejo	AM	Jerez	254
	Fernando de Castilla "P.X. Antique"	PX	Jerez	250
	Fernando de Castilla "Palo Cortado Antique"	PC	Jerez	250
	Fino Dos Palmas	FI	Jerez	252
	Fino en Rama Navazos, Saca Mayo 2015	FI	Jerez	249
	Fino Tres Palmas	FI	Jerez	252
	Garvey VORS	PX	Jerez	251
	Jauna	PC	Jerez	251
	La Bota de Amontillado nº 58 Navazos	AM	Jerez	249
	La Bota de Manzanilla nª 55	MZ	Jerez	249
	La Ina	FI	Jerez	255
	La Panesa Especial Fino	FI	Jerez	254
	Lyric Vino de Licor Dulce	Vino de Licor Gran Reserva	Vinos de Mesa	963
	Noé VORS	PX	Jerez	253
	Osborne Pedro Ximénez Viejo VORS	PX	Jerez	247
	Osborne Solera India	OL	Jerez	248
	Sacristía AB	MZ	Jerez	258
	Sibarita VORS	OL	Jerez	248
	Tío Pepe en Rama	FI	Jerez	253

PODIUM
EXCEPTIONAL WINES SPARKLING WINES

POINTS	WINE	TYPE	DO	PAGE
98 POINTS	Gramona Enoteca 2001	BN Gran Reserva	Cava	147
97 POINTS	Enoteca Personal Manuel Raventos 20 Anys 1996	ESP	Vinos Espumosos	971
	Gramona Enoteca 2001	BR Gran Reserva	Cava	147
96 POINTS	Enoteca Personal Manuel Raventos 1998	White	Vinos Espumosos	970
	Enoteca Personal Manuel Raventos 1999	White	Vinos Espumosos	970
	Enoteca Personal Manuel Raventos 2000	White	Vinos Espumosos	971
	Enoteca Personal ManuelRaventos Magnum 2002	White	Vinos Espumosos	971
	Gramona Celler Batlle 2005	BR Gran Reserva	Cava	147
	Recaredo Reserva Particular 2004	BN Gran Reserva	Cava	175
	Turo d'en Mota 2003	White	Cava	175
95 POINTS	Juvé & Camps Milesimé Chardonnay 2008	BN Reserva	Cava	163
	Juvé & Camps Viña La Capella 2005	BN Gran Reserva	Cava	164
	Recaredo Terrers 2008	BN Gran Reserva	Cava	175

WINERIES AND TASTING OF THE WINES BY DESIGNATED OF ORIGIN

SCORING SYSTEM

95-100 EXCEPTIONAL

The wine excels among those of the same type, vintage and origin. It is in every sense extraordinary. It is full of complexity, with abundant sensory elements both on the nose and on the palate that arise from the combination of soil, grape variety, winemaking and ageing methods; elegant and utterly outstanding, it exceeds average commercial standards and in some cases it may still be unknown to the general public.

90-94 EXCELLENT

A wine with the same attributes as those indicated above but with less exceptional or significant characteristics.

85-89 VERY GOOD

The wine stands out thanks to features acquired through great winemaking and/or ageing standards, or an exceptional varietal character. It is a wine with unique features, although it may lack soil or terroir expression.

80-84 GOOD

Although not as distinctive, the wine expresses the basic characteristics of both its type and region of origin.

70-79 AVERAGE

The wine has no defects, but no virtues either.

60-69 NOT RECOMMENDED

It is a non-acceptable wine in which some faults are evident, although they may not spoil the overall flavour.

50-59 FAULTY

A non-acceptable wine from a sensory point of view that may be oxidised or have defects due to bad ageing or late racking; it may be an old wine past its best or a young wine with unfavourable fermentation off-odours.

ABBREVIATIONS

B	WHITE	PCR	PALE CREAM	TGR	RED AGED (GRAN RESERVA)	SS	SEMI-DRY
AM	AMONTILLADO	RD	ROSÉ	BR	BRUT	OLV	OLOROSO VIEJO (OLD OLOROSO)
BC	AGED WHITE	CR	CREAM	FI	FINO	S/C	SIN COSECHA (NON-VINTAGE)
PX	PEDRO XIMÉNEZ (SWEET)	TC	RED AGED (CRIANZA)	BN	BRUT NATURE	SC	SIN CALIFICAR
BFB	BARREL-FERMENTED WHITE	GE	GENEROSO (FORTIFIED)	MZ	MANZANILLA		
PC	PALO CORTADO	TR	RED AGED (RESERVA)	SC	DRY		
T	RED	ESP	SPARKLING	OL	OLOROSO		

ORGANIC WINES

D.O.P. DENOMINACIÓN DE ORIGEN PROTEGIDA

I.G.P. INDICACIÓN GEOGRÁFICA PROTEGIDA

S.C. UNRATED

DO. ABONA

CONSEJO REGULADOR

Martín Rodríguez, 9
38588 Porís de Abona - Arico (Santa Cruz de Tenerife)
☎:+34 922 164 241 - Fax: +34 922 164 135
@: vinosdeabona@vinosdeabona.com
www.vinosdeabona.com

LOCATION:

In the southern area of the island of Tenerife, with vineyards which occupy the slopes of the Teide down to the coast. It covers the municipal districts of Adeje, Arona, Vilaflor, San Miguel de Abona, Granadilla de Abona, Arico and Fasnia.

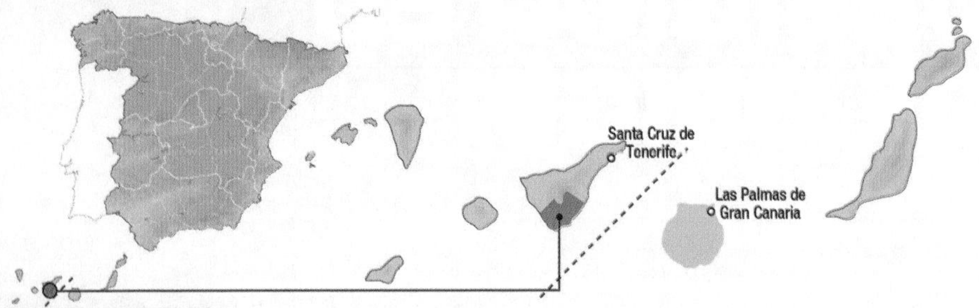

GRAPE VARIETIES:

WHITE: albillo, marmajuelo, forastera blanca, güal, malvasía, moscatel alejandría, sabro, verdello, vijariego, baboso blanco, listán blanco, pedro ximénez and torrontés.
RED: castellana negra, listán negro, malvasía rosada, negramoll, tintilla, baboso negro, cabernet sauvignon, listán prieto, merlot, moscatel negro, pinot noir, ruby cabernet, syrah, tempranillo and vijariego negro.

FIGURES:

Vineyard surface: 951 – **Wine-Growers:** 1,237 – **Wineries:** 19 – **2014 Harvest rating:** Very Good – **Production 2014:** 1,070,000 L. – **Market percentages:** 100% National.

SOIL:

Distinction can be made between the sandy and calcareous soil inland and the more clayey, well drained soil of the higher regions, seeing as they are volcanic. The so-called 'Jable' soil is very typical, and is simply a very fine whitish volcanic sand, used by the local winegrower to cover the vineyards in order to retain humidity in the ground and to prevent weeds from growing. The vineyards are located at altitudes which range between 300 and 1,750 m (the better quality grapes are grown in the higher regions), which determines different grape harvesting dates in a period spanning the beginning of August up to October.

CLIMATE:

Mediterranean on the coastal belt, and gradually cools down inland as a result of the trade winds. Rainfall varies between 350 mm per year on the coast and 550 mm inland. In the highest region, Vilaflor, the vineyards do not benefit from these winds as they face slightly west. Nevertheless, the more than 200 Ha of this small plateau produce wines with an acidity of 8 g/l due to the altitude, but with an alcohol content of 13%, as this area of the island has the longest hours of sunshine.

VINTAGE RATING

PEÑÍNGUIDE

2010	2011	2012	2013	2014
EXCELLENT	VERY GOOD	VERY GOOD	GOOD	GOOD

ALTOS DE TR3VEJOS

La Iglesia, 1
San Miguel de Abona
(Santa Cruz de Tenerife)
☎: +34 650 937 340
trevejos@altosdetrevejos.com
www.altosdetrevejos.com

Altos de Tr3vejos BN
81

Altos de Tr3vejos 2014 B
85

Altos de Tr3vejos 2014 T
85

Altos de Tr3vejos Baboso Negro 2014 T
86

Altos de Tr3vejos Rosado 2013 BN
87

Colour: rose. Nose: floral, red berry notes, ripe fruit, fragrant herbs. Palate: powerful, balanced, flavourful.

Altos de Tr3vejos Vijariego Negro 2014 T
88

Colour: cherry, garnet rim. Nose: mineral, expressive, spicy, ripe fruit. Palate: flavourful, ripe fruit, long, good acidity, balanced.

La Jirafa Afrutada 2014 B
88

Colour: bright straw. Nose: white flowers, fine lees, dried herbs. Palate: flavourful, fruity, good acidity.

Tr3vejos Viñas Viejas 2014 B
listán blanco, malvasía

87

Colour: bright straw. Nose: white flowers, fine lees, dried herbs, mineral, sweet spices. Palate: flavourful, fruity, good acidity, round.

BODEGA REVERÓN

Ctra. Gral. Vilaflor, 8
38620 Los Quemados
(Santa Cruz de Tenerife)
☎: +34 922 725 044
bodegasreveron@hotmail.com
www.bodegareveron.com

Los Quemados Albillo Criollo 2014 BFB
100% albillo

86

Los Quemados Albillo Criollo Clásico 2014 B
100% albillo

87

Colour: bright straw. Nose: white flowers, fresh fruit, fragrant herbs. Palate: flavourful, fruity, balanced.

Los Quemados Moscatel Semiseco 2014 B
moscatel

84

Los Quemados Vendimia Seleccionada 2013 T
syrah

84

Pago Reverón Ecológico 2014 T
listán negro, castellana, tempranillo

85 ♣

Pagos Reverón 2011 TC
syrah

88

Colour: cherry, garnet rim. Nose: smoky, spicy, overripe fruit. Palate: flavourful, smoky aftertaste, ripe fruit.

Pagos Reverón 2014 B
100% listán blanco

86 ♣

Pagos Reverón Afrutado 2014 B
listán blanco

84

Pagos Reverón Afrutado 2014 RD
listán negro

85

Pagos Reverón Naturalmente Dulce 2012 B
listán blanco, moscatel

87

Colour: golden. Nose: powerfull, honeyed notes, candied fruit, fragrant herbs, dry nuts. Palate: flavourful, sweet, fresh, fruity, good acidity, long.

BODEGA SAN MIGUEL

Ctra. General del Sur, 5
38620 San Miguel de Abona
(Santa Cruz de Tenerife)
☎: +34 922 700 300
Fax: +34 922 700 301
bodega@casanmiguel.com

Chasnero 2014 B
84

Marqués de Fuente 2012 TC

87

Colour: cherry, garnet rim. Nose: fine reductive notes, wet leather, aged wood nuances, overripe fruit. Palate: spicy, long, toasty.

BODEGA VENTO

Quezal, nº 36, Piso A-3
38632 El Palm-Mar
(Santa Cruz de Tenerife)
☎: +34 638 156 728
bodegavento@hotmail.com

Vento 2014 T

castellana, vijariego negro

84

Vento Afrutado 2014 B

listán blanco

84

Vento Seco 2014 B

listán blanco

82

MENCEY CHASNA

Marta, 3 Chimiche
38594 Granadilla de Abona
(Santa Cruz de Tenerife)
☎: +34 922 777 285
Fax: +34 922 777 259
ventas@menceychasna.com
www.menceychasna.es

Los Tableros 2014 B Barrica

malvasía, listán blanco

86

Los Tableros 2014 T Barrica

vijariego negro, syrah

86

Los Tableros Ecológico 2014 B

listán blanco

85

Mencey Chasna 2014 T

listán negro, tempranillo, ruby cabernet

84

Mencey Chasna Afrutado 2014 B

listán blanco

86

Mencey Chasna Seco 2014 B

listán blanco

85

Mencey de Chasna Vijariego Negro 2014 T

vijariego negro

84

SOC. COOP. CUMBRES DE ABONA

Camino del Viso, s/n Teguedite
38580 Arico (Santa Cruz de Tenerife)
☎: +34 922 768 604
Fax: +34 922 768 234
bodega@cumbresdeabona.es
www.cumbresdeabona.es

Flor de Chasna 2014 T Barrica

100% syrah

87

Colour: cherry, purple rim. Nose: ripe fruit, woody, roasted coffee. Palate: flavourful, spicy, powerful.

Flor de Chasna Naturalmente Dulce 2011 T

70% syrah, 30% tempranillo

80

Flor de Chasna Seco 2014 B

listán blanco

87

Colour: straw. Nose: medium intensity, ripe fruit, floral, grassy. Palate: correct, easy to drink.

Flor de Chasna Tradición 2014 T

30% merlot, 30% tempranillo, 30% ruby, 10% baboso negro

88

Colour: deep cherry, purple rim. Nose: creamy oak, toasty, ripe fruit, balsamic herbs, earthy notes. Palate: balanced, spicy, long.

Testamento Malvasía 2014 BFB

100% malvasía

89

Colour: bright straw. Nose: white flowers, fresh fruit, fragrant herbs, expressive. Palate: flavourful, fruity, good acidity, balanced.

Testamento Malvasía Dulce 2014 B

malvasía

88

Colour: bright yellow. Nose: balsamic herbs, honeyed notes, floral, sweet spices. Palate: rich, fruity, powerful, flavourful.

Testamento Malvasía Esencia Dulce 2009 B

100% malvasía

91

Colour: golden. Nose: powerfull, honeyed notes, candied fruit, fragrant herbs, acetaldehyde. Palate: flavourful, sweet, fresh, fruity, good acidity, long.

TIERRA DE FRONTOS

Lomo Grande, 1- Los Blanquitos
38600 Granadilla de Abona
(Santa Cruz de Tenerife)
☎: +34 922 777 253
Fax: +34 922 777 246
bodega@frontos.es
www.frontos.es

Tierra de Frontos 2014 B
verdello, marmajuelo, albillo, malvasía

85

Tierra de Frontos Dulce 2010 T
100% baboso negro

85

Tierra Frontos Blanco Seco Ecológico 2014 B
listán blanco

86

DO. ALELLA

CONSEJO REGULADOR

Avda. San Mateu, 2 - Masía Can Magarola
08328 Alella (Barcelona)
☎:+34 935 559 153 - Fax: +34 935 405 249
@: doalella@doalella.org
www.doalella.org

LOCATION:

It extends over the regions of El Maresme and el Vallès in Barcelona. It covers the municipal districts of Alella, Argentona, Cabrils, El Masnou, La Roca del Vallès, Martorelles, Montornès del Vallès, Montgat, Orrius, Premià de Dalt, Premià de Mar, Santa Mª de Martorelles, Sant Fost de Campsentelles, Teià, Tiana, Vallromanes, Vilanova del Vallès and Vilasar de Salt. The main feature of this region is the urban environment which surrounds this small stretch of vineyards; in fact, one of the smallest DO's in Spain.

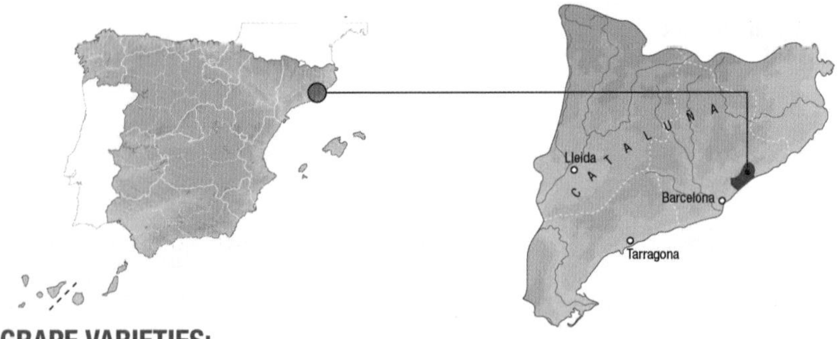

GRAPE VARIETIES:

WHITE: Pansa Blanca (similar to the Xarel·lo from other regions in Catalonia), Garnatxa Blanca, Pansa Rosada, Picapoll, Malvasía, Macabeo, Parellada, Chardonnay, Sauvignon Blanc and Chenin Blanc.

RED (MINORITY): Garnatxa Negra, Ull de Llebre (Tempranillo), Merlot, Pinot Noir, Syrah, Monastrell, Cabernet Sauvignon, Sumoll and Mataró.

FIGURES:

Vineyard surface: 224 – **Wine-Growers:** 60 – **Wineries:** 8 – **2014 Harvest rating:** Very Good – **Production 14:** 244,445 L. – **Market percentages:** 86% National - 14% International.

SOIL:

Distinction can be made between the clayey soils of the interior slope of the coastal mountain range and the soil situated along the coastline. The latter, known as Sauló, is the most typical. Almost white in colour, it is renowned for it high permeability and great capacity to retain sunlight, which makes for a better ripening of the grapes.

CLIMATE:

A typically Mediterranean microclimate with mild winters and hot dry summers. The coastal hills play an important role, as they protect the vines from cold winds and condense the humidity from the sea.

VINTAGE RATING

PEÑÍNGUIDE

2010	2011	2012	2013	2014
VERY GOOD	VERY GOOD	VERY GOOD	VERY GOOD	GOOD

ALELLA VINÍCOLA

Avda. Angel Guimerà, 62
08328 Alella (Barcelona)
☎: +34 935 403 842
xavi@alellavinicola.com
www.alellavinicola.com

Ivori 2013 B
60% garnacha blanca, 40% pansa blanca

87

Colour: bright straw. Nose: dried herbs, faded flowers, ripe fruit, slightly evolved. Palate: ripe fruit, spicy, long.

Ivori Negre 2010 T
50% garnacha, 30% syrah, 20% cabernet sauvignon

91

Colour: cherry, garnet rim. Nose: ripe fruit, wild herbs, earthy notes, balsamic herbs, fine reductive notes. Palate: balanced, flavourful, long, balsamic.

Marfil 2010 BN
100% pansa blanca

89

Colour: bright golden. Nose: fine lees, fragrant herbs, complex. Palate: powerful, flavourful, good acidity, fine bead.

Marfil 2012 TC
50% garnacha, 30% cabernet sauvignon, 20% syrah

86

Marfil Blanc de Noirs 2010 BR Reserva
100% garnacha

89

Colour: bright straw. Nose: fresh fruit, dried herbs, fine lees, floral. Palate: fresh, fruity, flavourful, good acidity.

Marfil Blanco Seco 2014 B
90% pansa blanca, 10% garnacha blanca

88

Colour: bright straw. Nose: white flowers, fresh fruit, fragrant herbs, dry stone. Palate: flavourful, fruity, good acidity.

Marfil Clàssic 2014 B
60% pansa blanca, 40% garnacha

90

Colour: bright straw. Nose: white flowers, dried herbs, ripe fruit, citrus fruit. Palate: flavourful, fruity, good acidity, elegant.

Marfil Generoso Seco Solera 1976 B
100% pansa blanca

94

Colour: dark mahogany. Nose: candied fruit, fruit liqueur notes, spicy, varnish, acetaldehyde, dry nuts. Palate: fine solera notes, spirituous, balanced, elegant.

Marfil Generoso Semi Solera 1976 PX
100% pansa blanca

94

Colour: mahogany. Nose: caramel, creamy oak, fruit liqueur notes, sweet spices. Palate: sweetness, spirituous, complex, balanced.

Marfil Molt Dolç 2003 AM
100% pansa blanca

92

Colour: mahogany. Nose: complex, fruit liqueur notes, dried fruit, pattiserie, toasty, sweet spices. Palate: sweet, rich, unctuous, long, round, balanced, elegant.

Marfil Moscatel Dulce 2010 ESP
100% moscatel grano menudo

90

Colour: bright straw. Nose: floral, fragrant herbs, candied fruit. Palate: fresh, fruity, flavourful, sweet.

Marfil Rosat 2014 RD
100% garnacha

87

Colour: onion pink. Nose: elegant, red berry notes, floral, fragrant herbs. Palate: light-bodied, flavourful, good acidity.

Marfil Violeta Dulce Natural 2003 T
100% garnacha

90

Colour: bright cherry, garnet rim. Nose: acetaldehyde, varnish, candied fruit, sweet spices, toasty. Palate: fruity, flavourful, sweet, correct.

Vallmora 2012 T
100% garnacha

88

Colour: bright cherry. Nose: ripe fruit, sweet spices, creamy oak, wild herbs. Palate: flavourful, fruity, toasty.

ALTA ALELLA - PRIVAT

Camí Baix de Tiana s/n
08328 Alella (Barcelona)
☎: +34 934 693 720
info@altaalella.cat
www.altaalella.cat

AA Blanc de Neu Dulce 2014 BFB
pansa blanca, otras

89

Colour: bright straw. Nose: floral, honeyed notes. Palate: rich, fruity, balanced, easy to drink.

AA Dolç Mataró 2012 T
mataró

91

Colour: cherry, garnet rim. Nose: fruit preserve, spicy, warm, fruit liqueur notes. Palate: powerful, flavourful, sweet, rich, balanced.

AA Lanius 2013 BFB
pansa blanca, otras

91

Colour: bright yellow. Nose: ripe fruit, spicy, creamy oak, wild herbs, citrus fruit. Palate: powerful, flavourful, rich, round.

AA Merla sin Sulfitos 2014 T
mataró

88

Colour: ruby red. Nose: ripe fruit, fruit preserve, balsamic herbs, earthy notes. Palate: powerful, flavourful, spicy, good finish.

AA Orbus 2011 T
syrah

90

Colour: cherry, garnet rim. Nose: ripe fruit, wild herbs, earthy notes, spicy, balsamic herbs. Palate: balanced, flavourful, long, balsamic.

AA Parvus Chardonnay 2014 B
chardonnay

88

Colour: bright yellow. Nose: expressive, dried herbs, ripe fruit, spicy. Palate: flavourful, fruity, good acidity, balanced.

AA Parvus Rosé 2014 RD
cabernet sauvignon, syrah

83

AA Parvus Syrah 2013 T
syrah

88

Colour: cherry, garnet rim. Nose: ripe fruit, fragrant herbs, floral, spicy. Palate: powerful, flavourful, good finish.

AA PS Xtrem 2012 TC
syrah

88

Colour: very deep cherry, garnet rim. Nose: complex, mineral, balsamic herbs, ripe fruit. Palate: full, flavourful, round tannins.

AA Puput sin Sulfitos 2013 T
mataró

91

Colour: cherry, garnet rim. Nose: dry stone, wild herbs, ripe fruit, candied fruit. Palate: rich, long, correct.

AA Tallarol 2014 B
pansa blanca

84

Alta Alella GX 2014 T
garnacha

86

Alta Alella PB 2014 B
pansa blanca

86

BODEGAS CASTILLO DE SAJAZARRA

Del Río, s/n
26212 Sajazarra (La Rioja)
☎: +34 941 320 066
Fax: +34 941 320 251
bodega@castillodesajazarra.com
www.castillodesajazarra.com

In Vita Kosher 2013 B
pansa blanca, sauvignon blanc

89

Colour: yellow. Nose: ripe fruit, citrus fruit, fragrant herbs, spicy. Palate: flavourful, balanced, fresh, fruity.

In Vita Kosher 2014 B
60% pansa blanca, 40% sauvignon blanc

87

Colour: bright straw. Nose: ripe fruit, wild herbs, balanced. Palate: rich, fruity, ripe fruit, fine bitter notes, good acidity.

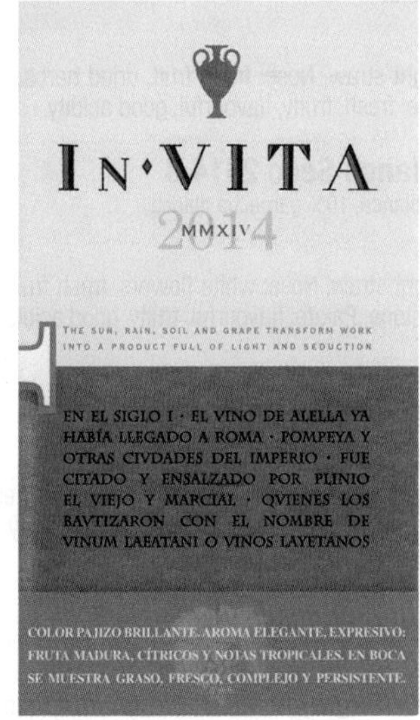

BODEGAS ROURA

Valls de Rials, s/n
08328 Alella (Barcelona)
☎: +34 663 235 353
Fax: +34 933 524 339
roura@roura.es
www.roura.es

Roura Coupage 2012 T
merlot, garnacha, cabernet sauvignon, syrah

87
Colour: cherry, garnet rim. Nose: ripe fruit, spicy, creamy oak, complex. Palate: flavourful, toasty, round tannins.

Roura Crianza Tres Ceps 2010 TC
merlot, cabernet sauvignon, syrah

86

Roura Garnatxa 2014 T
100% garnacha

85

Roura Merlot 2010 T
100% merlot

85

Roura Merlot 2014 RD
100% merlot

84

Roura Sauvignon Blanc 2014 B
100% sauvignon blanc

86

Roura Xarel.lo 2014 B
100% xarel.lo

88
Colour: bright straw. Nose: white flowers, fresh fruit, fragrant herbs, expressive. Palate: flavourful, fruity, good acidity, balanced.

BOUQUET D'ALELLA

Carrer Sant Josep de Calassanç, 8
08328 Alella (Barcelona)
☎: +34 935 556 997
bouquetda@bouquetdalella.com
www.bouquetdalella.com

Bouquet D'A Blanc + 2014 BFB
pansa blanca, garnacha blanca

90 ♣
Colour: bright yellow. Nose: ripe fruit, powerfull, toasty, aged wood nuances, pattiserie. Palate: flavourful, fruity, spicy, toasty, long.

Bouquet D'A Blanc 2014 B
pansa blanca, garnacha blanca

85 ♣

Bouquet D'A Garnatxa Negra 2014 T
garnacha

89 ♣
Colour: light cherry. Nose: red berry notes, floral, balsamic herbs. Palate: powerful, fresh, fruity, easy to drink.

Bouquet D'A Syrah 2012 T
syrah

86 ♣

MARQUÉS DE ALELLA

Masia Can Matons
08106 Santa Maria de Martorelles
(Barcelona)
☎: +34 935 153 100
info@parxet.es
www.marquesdealella.com

Galactica 2012 B
100% pansa blanca

91 ♣
Colour: bright yellow. Nose: ripe fruit, powerfull, toasty, pattiserie. Palate: flavourful, fruity, spicy, toasty, long, balanced.

Marqués de Alella Allier 2011 BFB
100% chardonnay

92 ♣
Colour: bright yellow. Nose: ripe fruit, powerfull, toasty, aged wood nuances, pattiserie. Palate: flavourful, fruity, spicy, toasty, long, balanced, elegant.

Marqués de Alella Pansa Blanca 2013 B
100% pansa blanca

90
Colour: bright straw. Nose: white flowers, fine lees, dried herbs, ripe fruit, candied fruit, citrus fruit. Palate: flavourful, fruity, good acidity, elegant.

Marqués de Alella Viognier 2013 B
100% viognier

87 ♣
Colour: bright yellow. Nose: expressive, dried herbs, ripe fruit, spicy. Palate: flavourful, fruity, good acidity, balanced.

Perfum de Pansa Blanca 2010 B
100% pansa blanca

89 ♣
Colour: bright yellow. Nose: ripe fruit, dry nuts, dried herbs. Palate: spicy, long, balsamic, ripe fruit.

Sepo 2013 B
100% pansa blanca

90 ♣

Colour: bright straw. Nose: white flowers, fresh fruit, fragrant herbs, expressive. Palate: flavourful, fruity, good acidity, balanced.

TESTUAN
Carrer dels Roures, 3
08348 Cabrils (Barcelona)
☎: +34 679 448 722
info@testuan.com
www.testuan.com

3 de Testuan 2014 B
70% pansa blanca, 30% garnacha blanca

87

Colour: bright yellow. Nose: ripe fruit, powerfull, toasty. Palate: flavourful, fruity, spicy.

DO. ALICANTE

CONSEJO REGULADOR

Monjas, 6
03002 Alicante
☎:+34 965 984 478 - Fax: +34 965 229 295
@: info@vinosdealicantedop.org
www.vinosdealicantedop.org

LOCATION:

In the province of Alicante (covering 51 municipal districts), and a small part of the province of Murcia. The vineyards extend over areas close to the coast (in the surroundings of the capital city of Alicante, and especially in the area of La Marina, a traditional producer of Moscatel), as well as in the interior of the province.

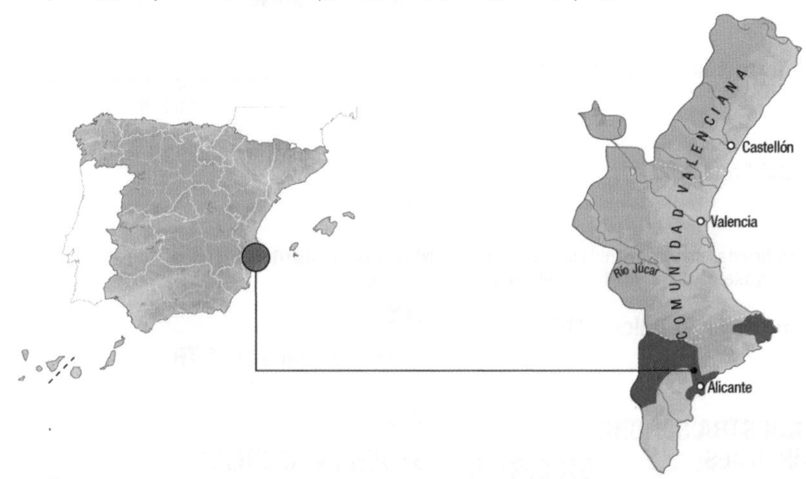

GRAPE VARIETIES:

WHITE: Merseguera, Moscatel de Alejandría, Macabeo, Planta Fina, Verdil, Airén, Chardonnay and Sauvignon Blanc.
RED: Monastrell, Garnacha Tinta (Alicante or Giró), Garnacha Tintorera, Bobal, Tempranillo, Cabernet Sauvignon, Merlot, Pinot Noir, Syrah and Petit Verdot.

FIGURES:

Vineyard surface: 9,515 – **Wine-Growers:** 1,996 – **Wineries:** 35 – **2014 Harvest rating:** Very Good – **Production 14:** 10,962,900 litres – **Market percentages:** 75% National - 25% International.

SOIL:

In general, the majority of the soils in the region are of a dun limestone type, with little clay and hardly any organic matter.

CLIMATE:

Distinction must be made between the vineyards situated closer to the coastline, where the climate is clearly Mediterranean and somewhat more humid, and those inland, which receive continental influences and have a lower level of rainfall.

VINTAGE RATING

PEÑÍNGUIDE

2010	2011	2012	2013	2014
VERY GOOD	VERY GOOD	VERY GOOD	VERY GOOD	GOOD

BODEGA COOP, DE ALGUEÑA COOP. V.

Ctra. Rodriguillo, km. 29,5
03668 Algueña (Alicante)
☎: +34 965 476 113
Fax: +34 965 476 229
bodega@vinosdealguenya.es
www.vinosdealguenya.com

Alhenia 2011 T
monastrell

85

Casa Jiménez 2012 TC
monastrell

84

Dominio de Torreviñas Doble Pasta 2013 T
monastrell

84

Fondillón 1980 Fondillón
monastrell

90

Colour: mahogany. Nose: acetaldehyde, fruit preserve, varnish, complex, dry nuts. Palate: flavourful, full, fine bitter notes.

Fondonet Vino de Licor Dulce 2010 T
monastrell

85

BODEGA NUESTRA SEÑORA DE LAS VIRTUDES

Ctra. de Yecla, 9
03400 Villena (Alicante)
☎: +34 965 802 187
coopvillena@coopvillena.com
www.coopvillena.com

Vinalopó 2010 TR
50% monastrell, 50% cabernet sauvignon

82

Vinalopó 2011 TC
50% monastrell, 50% cabernet sauvignon

86

Vinalopó 2014 RD
100% monastrell

86

Vinalopó 2014 T
100% monastrell

84

Vinalopó Esencia del Mediterráneo 2014 B
50% sauvignon blanc, 50% moscatel

84

Vinalopó Selección 2013 T Barrica
50% monastrell, 50% syrah

84

BODEGA SANTA CATALINA DEL MAÑÁN COOP. V.

Ctra. Monóvar-Pinoso, Km. 10,5
03649 Mañán Monóvar (Alicante)
☎: +34 966 960 096
Fax: +34 966 960 096
bodegamanan@gmail.com
www.vinoselmana.wordpress.com

Gran Mañán Moscatel
moscatel

87

Colour: bright yellow. Nose: balsamic herbs, honeyed notes, floral, sweet spices. Palate: rich, fruity, powerful, flavourful.

Mañá 3 Meses Barrica 2013 T
monastrell, merlot

86

Mañá Chardonnay 2013 B
chardonnay

86

Torrent del Mañá 2011 TR
monastrell, cabernet sauvignon

85

BODEGA VINESSENS

Ctra. de Caudete, Km. 1
03400 Villena (Alicante)
☎: +34 965 800 265
Fax: +34 965 800 265
comercial@vinessens.es
www.vinessens.es

El Telar 2011 TR
90% monastrell, 10% cabernet sauvignon

92

Colour: cherry, garnet rim. Nose: mineral, spicy, toasty, scrubland. Palate: flavourful, ripe fruit, long, good acidity, balanced.

Essens 2014 BFB
100% chardonnay

89

Colour: bright yellow. Nose: expressive, dried herbs, ripe fruit, spicy. Palate: fruity, good finish.

Sein 2012 TC
60% monastrell, 40% syrah

90

Colour: cherry, garnet rim. Nose: creamy oak, balanced, fruit preserve. Palate: flavourful, spicy, elegant, round tannins.

BODEGAS ANTONIO LLOBELL

Avda. Santa Catalina, 82
03725 Teulada (Alicante)
☎: +34 667 964 751
info@misteladeteulada.com
www.misteladeteulada.com

Bouquet Semiseco 2014 B
moscatel

82

Cap d'Or Vendimia Seleccionada 2014 Vino de licor
moscatel

88

Colour: golden. Nose: powerfull, honeyed notes, candied fruit. Palate: flavourful, sweet, fresh, long.

Cims del Mediterrani 2014 Vino de licor
moscatel

90

Colour: old gold. Nose: candied fruit, pattiserie, expressive, fruit liqueur notes, honeyed notes. Palate: rich, flavourful, balanced.

BODEGAS BERNABÉ NAVARRO

Ctra. Villena-Cañada, Km. 3
03400 Villena (Alicante)
☎: +34 966 770 353
Fax: +34 966 770 353
info@rafabernabe.com
www.rafabernabe.com

Beryna 2012 TC
90% monastrell, 10% garnacha

91

Colour: bright cherry. Nose: ripe fruit, sweet spices, creamy oak, expressive. Palate: flavourful, fruity, toasty, round tannins.

Casa Balaguer 2012 T
monastrell, otras

92

Colour: dark-red cherry. Nose: expressive, complex, mineral, balsamic herbs, spicy, ripe fruit. Palate: full, flavourful, round tannins, balanced, elegant.

Curro 2010 T
60% cabernet sauvignon, 40% monastrell

94

Colour: cherry, garnet rim. Nose: ripe fruit, wild herbs, earthy notes, spicy, balsamic herbs. Palate: balanced, flavourful, long, balsamic, elegant.

Cuvee J Padilla Magnum 2012 TC
monastrell

93

Colour: cherry, garnet rim. Nose: mineral, spicy, scrubland, ripe fruit, expressive. Palate: flavourful, ripe fruit, long, good acidity, balanced.

El Carro BC
moscatel

90

Colour: bright golden. Nose: complex, expressive, pungent, saline, dried herbs, faded flowers, dry nuts, spicy. Palate: powerful, fresh, fine bitter notes.

Morrón 2013 T
garnacha

92

Colour: light cherry. Nose: fruit expression, fruit liqueur notes, fragrant herbs, spicy, creamy oak. Palate: balanced, elegant, spicy, long, toasty.

Ramblis del Arco 2013 T

91

Colour: light cherry. Nose: ripe fruit, wild herbs, floral, mineral, elegant. Palate: flavourful, fresh, balanced, good acidity.

Ramblis Monastrell 2013 T
monastrell

93

Colour: deep cherry, garnet rim. Nose: red berry notes, fruit liqueur notes, floral, fragrant herbs, spicy, balanced. Palate: fresh, fruity, complex, spicy, balsamic, elegant.

Tragolargo 2013 T
monastrell

87

Colour: deep cherry. Nose: ripe fruit, fruit preserve, wild herbs, spicy. Palate: flavourful, long, balsamic.

BODEGAS BOCOPA

Paraje Les Pedreres, Autovía A-31, km. 200 - 201
03610 Petrer (Alicante)
☎: +34 966 950 489
Fax: +34 966 950 406
info@bocopa.com
www.bocopa.com

Alcanta 2012 TC
monastrell, tempranillo

89

Colour: bright cherry. Nose: ripe fruit, sweet spices, expressive, dark chocolate. Palate: flavourful, fruity, toasty, round tannins.

Alcanta 2014 T
monastrell, tempranillo

90

Colour: bright cherry. Nose: ripe fruit, sweet spices, creamy oak, expressive. Palate: flavourful, fruity, round tannins.

Castillo de Alicante 2014 T
tempranillo, cabernet sauvignon, monastrell

89

Colour: cherry, purple rim. Nose: powerfull, ripe fruit, spicy. Palate: powerful, fruity.

Dulcenegra Vino de Licor T
monastrell

88

Colour: cherry, garnet rim. Nose: fruit preserve, spicy, warm, fruit liqueur notes. Palate: powerful, flavourful, sweet, rich.

Fondillón Alone 1987 Fondillón
monastrell

90

Colour: iodine, amber rim. Nose: powerfull, complex, dry nuts, creamy oak, varnish. Palate: rich, long, spicy.

Laudum 2011 TR
monastrell, merlot, cabernet sauvignon

89

Colour: very deep cherry, garnet rim. Nose: expressive, complex, mineral, balsamic herbs, balanced. Palate: full, flavourful, round tannins.

Laudum 2012 TC
monastrell, merlot, cabernet sauvignon

87

Colour: cherry, purple rim. Nose: ripe fruit, roasted coffee. Palate: flavourful, spicy, powerful.

Laudum Barrica Especial 2013 T Barrica
monastrell, merlot, cabernet sauvignon

88

Colour: deep cherry, purple rim. Nose: creamy oak, ripe fruit, balsamic herbs. Palate: balanced, spicy, long.

Laudum Chardonnay 2014 BFB
chardonnay

84

Laudum Nature 2014 T
monastrell, tempranillo, cabernet sauvignon

86

Laudum Petit Verdot 2014 T
petit verdot

87

Colour: cherry, purple rim. Nose: powerfull, ripe fruit, spicy. Palate: powerful, fruity, unctuous.

Marina Alta 2014 B
moscatel de alejandría

89

Colour: bright straw. Nose: white flowers, fresh fruit, fragrant herbs, expressive, varietal. Palate: flavourful, fruity, good acidity, balanced.

Marina Espumante B
moscatel de alejandría

87

Colour: straw. Nose: ripe fruit, floral. Palate: correct, easy to drink.

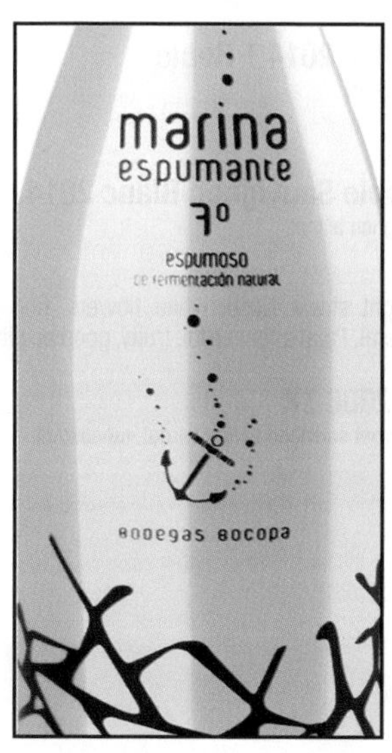

Marina Espumante BR
chardonnay, merseguera, macabeo

84

Marina Espumante RD
monastrell

86

Marina Espumante T
monastrell

87

Colour: cherry, purple rim. Nose: fresh fruit, red berry notes. Palate: flavourful, fruity, good acidity, sweetness.

Señorío de Benidorm 2014 T Roble

88

Colour: deep cherry, purple rim. Nose: creamy oak, toasty, ripe fruit, balsamic herbs. Palate: balanced, spicy, long.

Sol de Alicante Moscatel B
moscatel

92

Colour: golden. Nose: powerfull, honeyed notes, candied fruit, fragrant herbs, acetaldehyde. Palate: flavourful, sweet, fresh, fruity, good acidity, long.

BODEGAS CASA CORREDOR

Autovía Alicante/Albacete,
salida 168 La Encina
03400 Villena (Alicante)
☎: +34 966 842 064
jverdugo@fincalalagunilla.com
www.mgwinesgroup.com

Casa Corredor T&S 2013 T
tempranillo, syrah

85

Semsum 2 2014 B
macabeo, moscatel

80

BODEGAS E. MENDOZA

Partida El Romeral, s/n
03580 Alfaz del Pi (Alicante)
☎: +34 965 888 639
Fax: +34 965 889 232
bodegas-mendoza@bodegasmendoza.com
www.bodegasmendoza.com

Enrique Mendoza Cabernet - Shiraz 2012 TC
30% syrah, 70% cabernet sauvignon

92

Colour: deep cherry, purple rim. Nose: creamy oak, toasty, ripe fruit, balsamic herbs. Palate: balanced, spicy, long.

Enrique Mendoza Cabernet Monastrell 2013 TC
50% cabernet sauvignon, 50% monastrell

89

Colour: deep cherry, purple rim. Nose: creamy oak, toasty, ripe fruit, balsamic herbs. Palate: balanced, spicy, long.

Enrique Mendoza Chardonnay 2014 B
100% chardonnay

90

Colour: bright yellow. Nose: expressive, dried herbs, ripe fruit, spicy. Palate: flavourful, fruity, good acidity, balanced.

Enrique Mendoza Merlot Monastrell 2013 T
50% merlot, 50% monastrell

91

Colour: cherry, garnet rim. Nose: red berry notes, ripe fruit, fragrant herbs, spicy, toasty, creamy oak, mineral. Palate: powerful, flavourful, balsamic, balanced.

Enrique Mendoza Petit Verdot 2012 TC
100% petit verdot

90

Colour: cherry, garnet rim. Nose: roasted coffee, smoky, spicy, ripe fruit. Palate: flavourful, smoky aftertaste, ripe fruit.

Enrique Mendoza Santa Rosa 2011 T
70% cabernet sauvignon, 15% merlot, 15% syrah

93

Colour: cherry, garnet rim. Nose: mineral, expressive, spicy. Palate: flavourful, ripe fruit, long, good acidity, balanced.

Enrique Mendoza Shiraz 2012 TC
100% syrah

91

Colour: bright cherry. Nose: ripe fruit, sweet spices, creamy oak, expressive, mineral. Palate: flavourful, fruity, toasty, round tannins.

Estrecho Monastrell 2011 TC
100% monastrell

93

Colour: cherry, garnet rim. Nose: mineral, expressive, spicy. Palate: flavourful, ripe fruit, long, good acidity, balanced.

BODEGAS FAELO

Cº de los Coves, Partida
de Matola, Pol. 3 Nº 18
03296 Elche (Alicante)
☎: +34 655 856 898
info@vinosladama.com
www.vinosladama.com

L'Alba de Faelo 2014 RD
syrah

86

L'Alba del Mar 2014 B
chardonnay

84

La Dama 2012 TC
40% monastrell, 60% cabernet sauvignon

89

Colour: bright cherry. Nose: ripe fruit, sweet spices, creamy oak, expressive, wild herbs. Palate: flavourful, fruity, toasty, round tannins.

Palma Blanca Dulce 2014 B
moscatel

88

Colour: bright straw. Nose: medium intensity, varietal, white flowers. Palate: flavourful, ripe fruit.

BODEGAS FRANCISCO GÓMEZ

Paraje Finca La Serrata Ctra.
Villena - Pinoso, Km. 8,8
03400 Villena (Alicante)
☎: +34 965 979 195
info@bodegasfranciscogomez.es
www.bodegasfranciscogomez.es

Boca Negra 2008 TC
100% monastrell

90

Colour: pale ruby, brick rim edge. Nose: spicy, fine reductive notes, wet leather, aged wood nuances, fruit liqueur notes. Palate: spicy, fine tannins, balanced.

Fruto Noble 2008 TC
monastrell, cabernet sauvignon, syrah

86

Fruto Noble 2014 T Roble
monastrell, syrah

83

Fruto Noble Sauvignon Blanc 2014 B
100% sauvignon blanc

89

Colour: bright straw. Nose: white flowers, fine lees, dried herbs, mineral. Palate: flavourful, fruity, good acidity, round.

Serrata 2008 TR
merlot, cabernet sauvignon, petit verdot, monastrell

84

BODEGAS MURVIEDRO

Ampliación Pol. El Romeral, s/n
46340 Requena (Valencia)
☎: +34 962 329 003
Fax: +34 962 329 002
murviedro@murviedro.es
www.murviedro.es

Cueva del Perdón 2011 TC
60% monastrell, 40% syrah

91

Colour: bright cherry. Nose: ripe fruit, sweet spices, creamy oak, expressive. Palate: flavourful, fruity, toasty, round tannins.

DNA Murviedro Classic Monastrell 2014 T
monastrell

86

DNA Murviedro Signature Eko 2012 T
monastrell

90

Colour: cherry, garnet rim. Nose: creamy oak, red berry notes, balanced, elegant, wild herbs. Palate: flavourful, spicy, elegant.

BODEGAS PARCENT

Avda. Denia, 15
03792 Parcent (Alicante)
☎: +34 636 536 693
Fax: +34 966 405 173
armando@bodegasparcent.com
www.bodegasparcent.com

Auro 2014 B
chardonnay, moscatel

84

Comtat de Parcent 2012 TC
merlot, cabernet sauvignon

84

Dolç D'Art Selección de Licor 2013 B
moscatel de alejandría

90

Colour: bright yellow. Nose: balsamic herbs, floral, sweet spices, expressive, varietal. Palate: rich, fruity, powerful, flavourful, elegant.

Grà D'Or Blanco Seco 2014 B
moscatel

85

Rosat 2014 RD
syrah

83

BODEGAS SIERRA DE CABRERAS

La Molineta, s/n
03638 Salinas (Alicante)
info@carabibas.com
www.carabibas.com

Carabibas 21 meses 2011 TR
cabernet sauvignon, merlot, monastrell

93

Colour: cherry, garnet rim. Nose: mineral, expressive, spicy. Palate: flavourful, ripe fruit, long, good acidity, balanced.

Carabibas La Viña del Carpintero 2013 T
monastrell, merlot

89

Colour: bright cherry. Nose: ripe fruit, sweet spices, creamy oak, earthy notes. Palate: flavourful, fruity, toasty, round tannins.

Carabibas VS 2013 TC
cabernet sauvignon, merlot, monastrell

91

Colour: cherry, garnet rim. Nose: mineral, expressive, spicy. Palate: flavourful, ripe fruit, long, good acidity, balanced.

BODEGAS SIERRA SALINAS

Ctra. Villena-Pinoso, CV 813 km. 18
30400 Villena (Alicante)
☎: +34 965 979 786
joseramon@sierrasalinas.com
www.mgwinesgroup.com

1237 Salinas 2010 T
monastrell, cabernet sauvignon, petit verdot, garnacha tintorera

92

Colour: cherry, garnet rim. Nose: mineral, expressive, spicy. Palate: flavourful, ripe fruit, long, good acidity, balanced.

Mira Salinas 2010 T
monastrell, cabernet sauvignon, garnacha tintorera

92

Colour: deep cherry, garnet rim. Nose: scrubland, spicy, ripe fruit, balanced. Palate: flavourful, good structure, balsamic, long.

Mira Salinas 2011 T
monastrell, cabernet sauvignon, garnacha tintorera, petit verdot

90

Colour: cherry, garnet rim. Nose: smoky, spicy, ripe fruit, aromatic coffee. Palate: flavourful, smoky aftertaste, ripe fruit.

Mo Salinas 2012 T
monastrell, cabernet sauvignon, garnacha tintorera

89

Colour: very deep cherry, garnet rim. Nose: expressive, balsamic herbs, balanced. Palate: full, flavourful, round tannins.

Puerto Salinas 2010 T
monastrell, cabernet sauvignon, garnacha tintorera, petit verdot

92

Colour: cherry, garnet rim. Nose: smoky, spicy, ripe fruit, toasty. Palate: flavourful, smoky aftertaste, ripe fruit.

Puerto Salinas 2011 T
monastrell, cabernet sauvignon, garnacha tintorera

92

Colour: cherry, garnet rim. Nose: expressive, spicy, wild herbs. Palate: flavourful, ripe fruit, long, good acidity, balanced.

Puerto Salinas Moscatel Chardonnay 2013 BFB
chardonnay, moscatel

86

BODEGAS VICENTE GANDÍA

Ctra. Cheste a Godelleta, s/n
46370 Chiva (Valencia)
☎: +34 962 524 242
Fax: +34 962 524 243
info@vicentegandia.com
www.vicentegandia.es

El Miracle Art 2013 T
25% monastrell, 20% pinot noir, 20% syrah, 20% merlot, 15% tempranillo

87

Colour: bright cherry. Nose: ripe fruit, sweet spices, creamy oak. Palate: flavourful, fruity, toasty.

El Miracle Planet Organic Wine 2013 T
100% monastrell

84 ♣

Puerto Alicante Chardonnay 2014 B
100% chardonnay

86

Puerto Alicante Syrah 2013 T
100% syrah

87

Colour: bright cherry. Nose: ripe fruit, sweet spices, grassy. Palate: flavourful, fruity, spicy.

BODEGAS VIVANZA

Ctra. Jumilla Pinoso , Km. 13
30520 Jumilla (Murcia)
☎: +34 966 078 686
vivanza@vivanza.es
www.vivanza.es

Vivanza 2012 TC
monastrell, syrah, pinot noir

87

Colour: cherry, garnet rim. Nose: smoky, spicy, ripe fruit. Palate: flavourful, smoky aftertaste, ripe fruit.

Vivanza 2013 T
cabernet sauvignon, merlot

89

Colour: cherry, garnet rim. Nose: smoky, spicy, ripe fruit, toasty, mineral. Palate: flavourful, smoky aftertaste, ripe fruit.

Vivanza 2014 B
sauvignon blanc, chardonnay

85

BODEGAS VOLVER

Ctra de Pinoso a Fortuna
03650 Pinoso (Alicante)
☎: +34 965 978 603
export@bodegasvolver.com
www.bodegasvolver.com

Meleta 2012 TC
100% monastrell

90

Colour: cherry, garnet rim. Nose: creamy oak, balanced, ripe fruit. Palate: flavourful, spicy, elegant.

Meleta 2014 T Roble
monastrell

88

Colour: bright cherry. Nose: ripe fruit, sweet spices, creamy oak, smoky. Palate: flavourful, fruity, toasty, round tannins.

Tarima ESP
moscatel

88

Colour: bright straw. Nose: floral, fragrant herbs, candied fruit. Palate: fresh, fruity, flavourful, sweet.

Tarima 2014 B
macabeo, merseguera, moscatel

90

Colour: bright yellow. Nose: expressive, dried herbs, floral, candied fruit. Palate: flavourful, fruity, good acidity, balanced.

Tarima Hill 2013 T
monastrell

93

Colour: cherry, garnet rim. Nose: roasted coffee, smoky, ripe fruit, fruit liqueur notes. Palate: flavourful, smoky aftertaste, ripe fruit.

Tarima Monastrell 2012 T
monastrell

92 ♣

Colour: cherry, garnet rim. Nose: creamy oak, red berry notes, fresh fruit, balanced. Palate: flavourful, spicy.

Tarima Monastrell 2014 T
monastrell

89

Colour: deep cherry. Nose: creamy oak, ripe fruit, balsamic herbs. Palate: balanced, spicy, long.

Triga 2012 T
monastrell, cabernet sauvignon

94

Colour: cherry, garnet rim. Nose: mineral, expressive, spicy. Palate: flavourful, ripe fruit, long, good acidity, balanced.

BODEGAS XALÓ

Ctra. Xaló Alcalali, s/n
03727 Xaló (Alicante)
☎: +34 966 480 034
Fax: +34 966 480 808
comercial@bodegasxalo.com
www.bodegasxalo.com

1962 2012 T
100% giró

90

Colour: cherry, garnet rim. Nose: fine reductive notes, aged wood nuances, tobacco, ripe fruit. Palate: spicy, long, toasty, flavourful.

Bahía 2012 BN
moscatel

85

Bahía de Denia 2014 B Joven
moscatel

88

Colour: bright straw. Nose: white flowers, fresh fruit, fragrant herbs, varietal. Palate: flavourful, fruity, good acidity, balanced.

Castell D'Aixa 2014 B
moscatel

87

Colour: bright straw. Nose: fresh fruit, fragrant herbs, floral. Palate: flavourful, good acidity, balanced.

Riu Rau Dulce 2013 Mistela
moscatel

90

Colour: golden. Nose: powerfull, honeyed notes, candied fruit, fragrant herbs, acetaldehyde. Palate: flavourful, sweet, long.

Serra de Bernia 2013 T Roble
garnacha, tempranillo

83

Vall de Xaló 2013 T
garnacha

84

Vall de Xaló 2014 B
moscatel

85

Vall de Xaló 2014 RD
garnacha

85

Vall de Xaló Moscatel 2013 Mistela
moscatel

87

Colour: bright yellow. Nose: balsamic herbs, honeyed notes, floral, sweet spices, varietal. Palate: rich, fruity, powerful, flavourful, elegant.

Vall de Xalón Mistela Giró Dulce T
giró

88

Colour: cherry, garnet rim. Nose: fruit preserve, spicy, warm, fruit liqueur notes. Palate: powerful, flavourful, sweet, rich.

BODEGAS Y VIÑEDOS EL SEQUÉ

Casas de El Sequé, 59
03650 Pinoso (Alicante)
☎: +34 945 600 119
Fax: +34 945 600 850
elseque@artadi.com
www.artadi.com/seque

PODIUM

El Sequé 2013 T
100% monastrell

95

Colour: deep cherry, purple rim. Nose: creamy oak, toasty, ripe fruit, balsamic herbs. Palate: balanced, spicy, long, elegant.

COMERCIAL GRUPO FREIXENET

Joan Sala, 2
08770 Sant Sadurní D'Anoia (Barcelona)
☎: +34 938 917 000
Fax: +34 938 183 095
freixenet@freixenet.es
www.freixenet.es

Nauta 2011 TC
monastrell

87

Colour: bright cherry. Nose: ripe fruit, sweet spices, creamy oak, expressive. Palate: flavourful, fruity, toasty, round tannins

FINCA COLLADO

Ctra. de Salinas a Villena, s/n
03638 Salinas (Alicante)
☎: +34 607 510 710
Fax: +34 962 878 818
info@fincacollado.com
www.fincacollado.com

Delit 2012 TC
100% monastrell

92

Colour: cherry, garnet rim. Nose: mineral, expressive, spicy. Palate: flavourful, ripe fruit, long, good acidity, balanced.

Finca Collado Chardonnay Moscatel 2014 B
chardonnay, moscatel

84

HAMMEKEN CELLARS

Calle de la Muela, 16
03730 Jávea (Alicante)
☎: +34 965 791 967
Fax: +34 966 461 471
cellars@hammekencellars.com
www.hammekencellars.com

Montgó Monastrell 2012 T
100% monastrell

88

Colour: deep cherry, purple rim. Nose: creamy oak, toasty, ripe fruit, balsamic herbs. Palate: balanced, spicy, long.

Radio Boca Rosé 2013 RD
100% monastrell

87

Colour: rose, purple rim. Nose: red berry notes, floral, expressive. Palate: powerful, fruity, fresh.

HERETAT ANTIGUA, CASA SICILIA 1707

Paraje Alcaydias, 4
03660 Novelda (Alicante)
☎: +34 965 605 385
Fax: +34 965 604 763
administracin@casasicilia1707.es
www.casacesilia.com

Casa Cesilia 2010 TC
monastrell, cabernet sauvignon, petit verdot

87

Colour: cherry, garnet rim. Nose: roasted coffee, smoky, spicy, ripe fruit. Palate: flavourful, smoky aftertaste, ripe fruit.

Casa Cesilia 2014 B
sauvignon blanc, macabeo

87

Colour: bright yellow. Nose: dried herbs, ripe fruit, spicy. Palate: flavourful, fruity, good acidity.

Cesilia Blanc 2014 B
moscatel, malvasía

86

Cesilia Rosé 2014 RD
merlot, syrah

88

Colour: salmon. Nose: floral, wild herbs, fruit expression, expressive. Palate: flavourful, balanced, elegant.

IBERICA BRUNO PRATS

CV 830, km. 3,2
03640 Monovar (Alicante)
☎: +34 645 963 122
stephanepoint@hotmail.com
www.fidelisalliance.com

Alfynal 2011 T
100% monastrell

90

Colour: cherry, garnet rim. Nose: smoky, ripe fruit, aromatic coffee. Palate: flavourful, smoky aftertaste, ripe fruit.

Mosyca 2011 T
monastrell, syrah, cabernet sauvignon, otras

87

Colour: cherry, garnet rim. Nose: smoky, spicy, ripe fruit, old leather, tobacco. Palate: flavourful, ripe fruit, long.

LA BODEGA DE PINOSO

Paseo de la Constitución, 82
03650 Pinoso (Alicante)
☎: +34 965 477 040
Fax: +34 966 970 149
labodega@labodegadepinoso.com
www.labodegadepinoso.com

Pinoso Clásico 2011 TC
monastrell

84

Pontos 1932 2011 TC
monastrell

87

Colour: deep cherry, purple rim. Nose: creamy oak, toasty, ripe fruit, balsamic herbs. Palate: balanced, spicy, long.

Pontos Cepa 50 2013 T
monastrell

87

Colour: bright cherry. Nose: ripe fruit, sweet spices, creamy oak. Palate: flavourful, fruity, toasty, round tannins.

Torre del Reloj 2014 B
airén, macabeo

82

Torre del Reloj 2014 RD
monastrell, tempranillo, syrah

84

Torre del Reloj Monastrell 2013 T
monastrell

84

Vergel 2010 TC
monastrell, syrah, merlot

90

Colour: bright cherry. Nose: ripe fruit, sweet spices, creamy oak, expressive. Palate: flavourful, fruity, toasty, round tannins.

Vergel 2013 T
alicante bouschet, merlot, monastrell

88

Colour: bright cherry. Nose: ripe fruit, sweet spices, creamy oak. Palate: flavourful, fruity, toasty, round tannins.

Vermador 2014 B
macabeo

82

Vermador 2014 RD
monastrell

88 ♣

Colour: rose, purple rim. Nose: red berry notes, floral, expressive. Palate: powerful, fruity, fresh.

Vermador Monastrell Petit Verdot 2013 T
monastrell, petit verdot

81 ♣

Vermador Monastrell Syrah 2013 T Roble
monastrell, syrah

86 ♣

PRIMITIVO QUILES

Mayor, 4
03640 Monóvar (Alicante)
☎: +34 965 470 099
Fax: +34 966 960 235
info@primitivoquiles.com
www.primitivoquiles.com

Primitivo Quiles Fondillón 1948 Fondillón
100% monastrell

93

Colour: light mahogany. Nose: powerfull, complex, dry nuts, toasty, acetaldehyde. Palate: rich, long, fine solera notes, spicy, round.

Primitivo Quiles Gran Imperial Solera
100% moscatel

93

Colour: dark mahogany. Nose: powerfull, aromatic coffee, spicy, acetaldehyde, dry nuts. Palate: balanced, elegant, fine solera notes, toasty, long.

Primitivo Quiles Monastrell-Merlot 2012 T Roble
60% monastrell, 40% merlot

81

Primitivo Quiles Moscatel Extra Vino de licor
100% moscatel

90

Colour: dark mahogany. Nose: candied fruit, dried fruit, pattiserie, sweet spices. Palate: balanced, good acidity, long.

Primitivo Quiles Moscatel Laurel de Licor B
100% moscatel

87

Colour: golden. Nose: powerfull, honeyed notes, candied fruit. Palate: flavourful, fresh, fruity, good acidity, long.

Primitivo Quiles Raspay 2008 TR
100% monastrell

83

VINS DEL COMTAT

Turballos, 11
03820 Cocentaina (Alicante)
☎: +34 965 593 194
Fax: +34 965 593 590
vinsdelcomtat@gmail.com
www.vinsdelcomtat.com

Cristalí Dulce 2013 B
100% moscatel de alejandría

91

Colour: bright yellow. Nose: honeyed notes, floral, expressive. Palate: fruity, powerful, flavourful, elegant, full.

M Monastrell 2011 T
monastrell

88

Colour: very deep cherry, garnet rim. Nose: expressive, complex, balsamic herbs, balanced, varietal. Palate: full, flavourful, round tannins.

Maigmó Dulce Natural 2011 T
monastrell

88

Colour: cherry, garnet rim. Nose: fruit preserve, spicy, warm, fruit liqueur notes. Palate: powerful, flavourful, sweet, rich.

Montcabrer 2011 TR
100% cabernet sauvignon

89

Colour: very deep cherry, garnet rim. Nose: expressive, complex, balsamic herbs, balanced. Palate: full, flavourful, round tannins.

Penya Cadiella Selecció 2011 T
monastrell, cabernet sauvignon, merlot, syrah

90

Colour: cherry, garnet rim. Nose: smoky, spicy, ripe fruit. Palate: flavourful, smoky aftertaste, ripe fruit.

Peña Cadiella 2011 TC
monastrell, cabernet sauvignon, merlot

86

Santa Bárbara 2013 T Roble
80% monastrell, 20% cabernet sauvignon

87

Colour: deep cherry, purple rim. Nose: creamy oak, toasty, ripe fruit, balsamic herbs. Palate: balanced, spicy, long.

Serrella 2011 T
monastrell, merlot

89

Colour: dark-red cherry, garnet rim. Nose: dried herbs, ripe fruit, tobacco. Palate: flavourful, balanced, round tannins, good acidity.

Tabarca 2014 B

87

Colour: bright straw. Nose: white flowers, fine lees, dried herbs. Palate: flavourful, fruity, good acidity.

Verdeval 2014 B
60% moscatel de alejandría, 20% macabeo, 20% chardonnay

88

Colour: bright straw. Nose: white flowers, fresh fruit, varietal. Palate: flavourful, fruity, good acidity, balanced.

Vins del Comtat Rosado 2013 RD

82

DO. ALMANSA

CONSEJO REGULADOR

Avda. Carlos III (Apdo. 158)
02640 Almansa (Albacete)
☎:+34 967 340 258 - Fax: +34 967 310 842
@: info@vinosdealmansa.com
www.vinosdealmansa.com

LOCATION:

In the South East region of the province of Albacete. It covers the municipal areas of Almansa, Alpera, Bonete, Corral Rubio, Higueruela, Hoya Gonzalo, Pétrola and the municipal district of El Villar de Chinchilla.

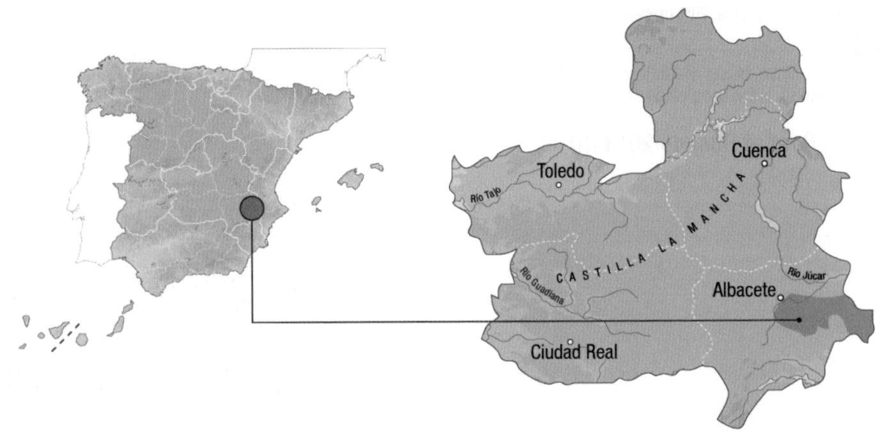

GRAPE VARIETIES:

WHITE: Chardonnay, moscatel de grano menudo, Verdejo and Sauvignon Blanc.
RED: Garnacha Tintorera (most popular), Cencibel (Tempranillo), Monastrell (second most popular), Syrah, cabernet sauvignon, merlot, granacha, petit verdot and pinot noir.

FIGURES:

Vineyard surface: 7,200 – **Wine-Growers:** 760 – **Wineries:** 12 – **2014 Harvest rating:** Very Good – **Production 14:** 5,828,000 litres – **Market percentages:** 20% National - 80% International.

SOIL:

The soil is limy, poor in organic matter and with some clayey areas. The vineyards are situated at an altitude of about 700 m.

CLIMATE:

Of a continental type, somewhat less extreme than the climate of La Mancha, although the summers are very hot, with temperatures which easily reach 40 °C. Rainfall, on the other hand, is scant, an average of about 350 mm a year. The majority of the vineyards are situated on the plains, although there are a few situated on the slopes.

VINTAGE RATING

PEÑÍNGUIDE

2010	2011	2012	2013	2014
GOOD	VERY GOOD	VERY GOOD	VERY GOOD	GOOD

BODEGA SANTA CRUZ DE ALPERA

Cooperativa, s/n
02690 Alpera (Albacete)
☎: +34 967 330 108
Fax: +34 967 330 903
comercial@bodegasantacruz.com
www.bodegasantacruz.com

Albarroble 2012 TC
70% garnacha tintorera, 30% syrah

86

Albarroble 2013 T Roble
syrah

85

Albarroble Selección 2012 TC
garnacha tintorera

90

Colour: cherry, garnet rim. Nose: creamy oak, balanced, ripe fruit. Palate: flavourful, spicy, full, good structure.

Rupestre de Alpera 2012 TR
garnacha tintorera

90

Colour: dark-red cherry, purple rim. Nose: ripe fruit, characterful, wild herbs, dry stone, warm. Palate: powerful, balanced, spirituous.

Santa Cruz de Alpera 2013 BFB
verdejo

87

Colour: bright yellow. Nose: ripe fruit, powerfull, aged wood nuances, pattiserie. Palate: flavourful, fruity, spicy, long.

Santa Cruz de Alpera 2014 B
verdejo

85

Santa Cruz de Alpera 2014 RD
syrah

88

Colour: rose, purple rim. Nose: red berry notes, floral, expressive. Palate: powerful, fruity, fresh.

Santa Cruz de Alpera 2014 T Maceración Carbónica
30% garnacha tintorera, 70% syrah

87

Colour: cherry, purple rim. Nose: expressive, red berry notes, floral, lactic notes. Palate: flavourful, fruity, good acidity.

Santa Cruz de Alpera 2014 T Roble
garnacha tintorera

88

Colour: very deep cherry, purple rim. Nose: powerfull, characterful, smoky, toasty. Palate: fruity, spicy.

Santa Cruz de Alpera Blend 2014 T
garnacha tintorera

86

Santa Cruz de Alpera Mosto Parcialmente Fermentado 2014 B
verdejo

83

Santa Cruz de Alpera Mosto Parcialmente Fermentado 2014 RD
syrah

87

Colour: rose, purple rim. Nose: red berry notes, floral, lactic notes. Palate: fruity, fresh, easy to drink.

BODEGAS ALMANSEÑAS

Ctra. de Alpera, CM 3201 Km. 98,6
02640 Almansa (Albacete)
☎: +34 967 098 116
Fax: +34 967 098 121
adaras@ventalavega.com
www.ventalavega.com

Adaras 2010 T
garnacha tintorera

92

Colour: cherry, garnet rim. Nose: ripe fruit, spicy, creamy oak, complex, mineral. Palate: flavourful, toasty.

Aldea de Adaras 2014 T
80% monastrell, 20% garnacha tintorera

88 ♣

Colour: cherry, purple rim. Nose: powerfull, ripe fruit, spicy, grassy. Palate: powerful, fruity, unctuous.

Calizo de Adaras 2014 T
garnacha tintorera, monastrell

88 ♣

Colour: light cherry. Nose: fruit expression, fruit liqueur notes, fragrant herbs, spicy, dry stone. Palate: long, balsamic, balanced.

La Huella de Adaras 2013 T
garnacha tintorera

91 ♣

Colour: ruby red. Nose: scrubland, ripe fruit, fruit liqueur notes, spicy, expressive, mineral. Palate: powerful, flavourful, spicy, long, balsamic.

La Huella de Adaras 2014 B
verdejo, sauvignon blanc

85

Sarada Selección 2013 T
garnacha tintorera, monastrell

90

Colour: light cherry. Nose: fruit liqueur notes, scrubland, earthy notes. Palate: balsamic, ripe fruit, correct.

Sargentillo 2014 T
garnacha tintorera, monastrell

90

Colour: deep cherry, purple rim. Nose: ripe fruit, balsamic herbs, wild herbs, spicy, earthy notes. Palate: balanced, long, balsamic.

Viña Venta la Vega Very Old Vine 2013 T
monastrell

91

Colour: light cherry. Nose: ripe fruit, wild herbs, spicy, earthy notes, expressive. Palate: fresh, flavourful, spicy, long, balsamic.

BODEGAS ATALAYA

Ctra. Almansa - Ayora, Km. 1
02640 Almansa (Albacete)
☎: +34 968 435 022
Fax: +34 968 716 051
info@orowines.com
www.orowines.com

Alaya Tierra 2013 T
100% garnacha tintorera

91

Colour: cherry, purple rim. Nose: fruit preserve, wild herbs, creamy oak, toasty. Palate: powerful, flavourful, concentrated.

Atalaya 2012 T
85% garnacha tintorera, 15% monastrell

90

Colour: cherry, garnet rim. Nose: fruit preserve, scrubland, spicy, toasty. Palate: powerful, flavourful, spicy, long, toasty, concentrated.

La Atalaya del Camino 2013 T
85% garnacha tintorera, 15% monastrell

91

Colour: cherry, garnet rim. Nose: red berry notes, ripe fruit, spicy, creamy oak, complex. Palate: flavourful, toasty, round tannins.

Laya 2013 T
70% garnacha tintorera, 30% monastrell

87

Colour: cherry, garnet rim. Nose: ripe fruit, toasty, herbaceous, fruit preserve. Palate: powerful, toasty.

Laya 2014 T
70% garnacha tintorera, 30% monastrell

89

Colour: cherry, purple rim. Nose: ripe fruit, roasted coffee, aromatic coffee. Palate: flavourful, spicy, powerful.

BODEGAS PIQUERAS

Zapateros, 11
02640 Almansa (Albacete)
☎: +34 967 341 482
info@bodegaspiqueras.es
www.bodegaspiqueras.es

Castillo de Almansa 2011 TR

89

Colour: cherry, garnet rim. Nose: ripe fruit, spicy, creamy oak, complex. Palate: flavourful, toasty, round tannins.

Castillo de Almansa 2012 TC

87

Colour: cherry, garnet rim. Nose: ripe fruit, spicy, creamy oak, complex. Palate: flavourful, toasty.

Castillo de Almansa Verdejo Sauvignon 2014 B
verdejo, sauvignon blanc

83

Valcanto 2012 T
monastrell

87

Colour: cherry, garnet rim. Nose: spicy, toasty, fruit preserve. Palate: toasty, powerful, flavourful.

Valcanto Syrah 2012 T Roble

86

SOC. COOP. AGRARIA SANTA QUITERIA, BODEGA TINTORALBA

Baltasar González Sáez, 34
02694 Higueruela (Albacete)
☎: +34 967 287 012
Fax: +34 967 287 031
direccion@tintoralba.com
www.tintoralba.com

Tintoralba 2014 T Roble
70% garnacha tintorera, 30% syrah

87

Colour: bright cherry. Nose: ripe fruit, sweet spices, creamy oak, toasty. Palate: flavourful, fruity.

Tintoralba Ecológico Selección 2013 T
100% garnacha tintorera

87

Colour: cherry, garnet rim. Nose: ripe fruit, wild herbs, earthy notes, spicy, balsamic herbs. Palate: flavourful, long, balsamic.

Tintoralba Garnacha Tintorera 2014 T

100% garnacha tintorera

88

Colour: cherry, purple rim. Nose: red berry notes, floral, wild herbs. Palate: powerful, fruity, concentrated.

Tintoralba Selección 2011 T

70% garnacha tintorera, 35% syrah

89

Colour: cherry, garnet rim. Nose: ripe fruit, spicy, creamy oak, complex. Palate: flavourful, toasty, spicy.

Tintoralba Syrah 2014 RD

100% syrah

87

Colour: rose, purple rim. Nose: red berry notes, floral, expressive. Palate: powerful, fruity, fresh.

DO. ARABAKO TXAKOLINA

CONSEJO REGULADOR
Dionisio Aldama, 7- 1ºD Apdo. 36
01470 Amurrio (Álava)
☎ :+34 656 789 372 - Fax: +34 945 891 211
@: merino@txakolidealava.com
www.txakolidealava.com

LOCATION:

It covers the region of Aiara (Ayala), situated in the north west of the province of Alava on the banks of the Nervion river basin. Specifically, it is made up of the municipalities of Amurrio, Artziniega, Aiara (Ayala), Laudio (Llodio) and Okondo.

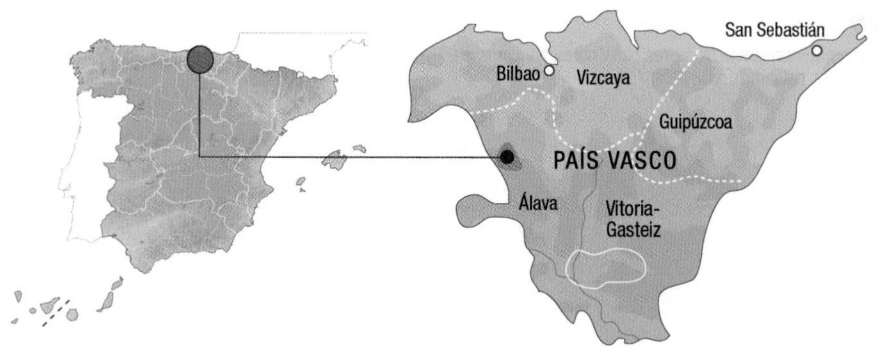

GRAPE VARIETIES:

MAIN: Hondarrabi Zuri (80%).
AUTHORIZED: Petit Manseng, Petit Corbu and Gross Manseng.

FIGURES:

Vineyard surface: 100 – **Wine-Growers:** 50 – **Wineries:** 8 – **2014 Harvest rating:** Very Good – **Production 14:** 328,520 litres – **Market percentages:** 85% National - 15% International.

SOIL:

A great variety of formations are found, ranging from clayey to fundamentally stony, precisely those which to date are producing the best results and where fairly stable grape ripening is achieved.

CLIMATE:

Similar to that of the DO Bizkaiko Txakolina, determined by the influence of the Bay of Biscay, although somewhat less humid and slightly drier and fresher. In fact, the greatest risk in the region stems from frost in the spring. However, it should not be forgotten that part of its vineyards borders on the innermost plantations of the DO Bizkaiko Txakolina.

VINTAGE RATING

PEÑÍNGUIDE

2010	2011	2012	2013	2014
N/A	N/A	EXCELLENT	VERY GOOD	UNRATED

BODEGA SEÑORÍO DE ASTOBIZA

Caserío Aretxabala, Bº Jandiola 16
01409 Okondo (Araba)
☎: +34 945 898 516
Fax: +34 945 898 447
comercial@senoriodeastobiza.com
www.senoriodeastobiza.com

Astobiza 2014 B

90% hondarrabi zuri, 10% hondarrabi zuri zerratie

88

Colour: bright straw. Nose: fresh fruit, dried herbs, floral. Palate: flavourful, fruity, good acidity, balanced.

Malkoa Txakoli Edición Limitada 2014 B

89

Colour: bright straw. Nose: fresh fruit, citrus fruit, wild herbs. Palate: correct, easy to drink, fine bitter notes, fresh.

GOIANEA KOOP E.

Pol. Ind. Kalzadako, 10 Pab. 3B
01470 Saratxo Amurrio (Alava)
☎: +34 656 714 709
Fax: +34 945 892 141
info@txakoliuno.com
www.txakoliuno.com

Uno 2013 B

50% hondarrabi zuri, 50% hondarrabi zuri zerratia

90

Colour: bright yellow. Nose: expressive, dried herbs, ripe fruit, spicy. Palate: flavourful, fruity, good acidity, balanced.

Uno 2014 B

50% hondarrabi zuri, 50% hondarrabi zuri zerratia

90

Colour: bright straw. Nose: medium intensity, floral, balanced. Palate: balanced, fine bitter notes, good acidity, long.

Urtaran 2014 B

hondarrabi zuri

91

Colour: bright straw. Nose: white flowers, fine lees, dried herbs, ripe fruit, citrus fruit. Palate: flavourful, fruity, good acidity, elegant, balanced.

DO. ARLANZA

CONSEJO REGULADOR

Ronda de la Cárcel, 4 - Edif. Arco de la Cárcel
09340 Lerma (Burgos)
☎:+34 947 171 046 - Fax: +34 947 171 046
@: info@arlanza.org
www.arlanza.org

LOCATION:

With the medieval city of Lerma at the core of the region, Arlanza occupies the central and southern part of the province of Burgos, on the river valleys of the Arlanza and its subsidiaries, all the way westwards through 13 municipal districts of the province of Palencia until the Pisuerga River is reached.

GRAPE VARIETIES:

WHITE: Albillo and Viura.
RED: Tempranillo, Garnacha and Mencía.

FIGURES:

Vineyard surface: 400 – **Wine-Growers:** 290 – **Wineries:** 16 – **2014 Harvest rating:** Very Good – **Production 14:** 900,000 litres – **Market percentages:** 80% National - 20% International.

SOIL:

Soil in the region is not particularly deep, with soft rocks underneath and good humidity levels. The landscape is one of rolling hills where vines are planted on varied soils, from limestone to calcareous, with abundant granite on certain areas.

CLIMATE:

The climate of this wine region is said to be one of the harshest within Castilla y León, with lower temperatures towards the western areas and rainfall higher on the eastern parts, in the highlands of the province of Soria.

VINTAGE RATING

PEÑÍNGUIDE

2010	2011	2012	2013	2014
VERY GOOD	VERY GOOD	VERY GOOD	GOOD	N/A

ALONSO ANGULO

Mayor 14
09348 Castrillo de Solarana (Burgos)
☎: +34 647 628 148
info@alonsoangulo.com
www.alonsoangulo.com

Flor de Sanctus 2012 T
100% tempranillo

87

Colour: cherry, garnet rim. Nose: creamy oak, toasty, ripe fruit, balsamic herbs. Palate: balanced, spicy, long.

Sanctus 2012 T
tempranillo, garnacha, mencía, albillo, viura

90

Colour: cherry, garnet rim. Nose: ripe fruit, wild herbs, earthy notes, spicy, balsamic herbs. Palate: balanced, flavourful, long, balsamic.

ARLESE NEGOCIOS (BODEGAS Y VIÑEDOS)

Pol. Ind. de Villamanzo Parcela 109
09390 Villalmanzo (Burgos)
☎: +34 947 172 866
info@bodegasarlese.com
www.bodegasarlese.com

Almanaque 2011 TC
100% tempranillo

87

Colour: cherry, garnet rim. Nose: red berry notes, ripe fruit, spicy, creamy oak. Palate: flavourful, toasty.

Almanaque 2012 T Roble
100% tempranillo

84

Almanaque 2014 RD
100% tempranillo

88

Colour: rose, purple rim. Nose: red berry notes, floral, expressive. Palate: powerful, fruity, fresh.

Señorío de Aldaviña 2010 TC
100% tempranillo

85

BODEGA ESTEBAN ARAUJO

Diseminados s/n
34230 Torquemada (Palencia)
☎: +34 620 479 142
bodegaestebanaraujo@gmail.com
www.bodegaestebanaraujo.com

El Monjío 2012 TC
tempranillo

87

Colour: cherry, garnet rim. Nose: ripe fruit, spicy, creamy oak. Palate: flavourful, toasty.

El Monjío 2013 T Roble
tempranillo

85

El Monjío 2014 RD
tempranillo

83

BODEGAS CARRILLO DE ALBORNOZ

09345 Avellanosa de Muñó (Burgos)
☎: +34 626 412 222
bodegascda@bodegascda.com
www.bodegascda.com

Albor 2013 T Roble
tempranillo

87

Colour: cherry, garnet rim. Nose: creamy oak, red berry notes, ripe fruit, balsamic herbs. Palate: flavourful, spicy.

BODEGAS LERMA

Ctra. Madrid-Irún, Km. 202,5
09340 Lerma (Burgos)
☎: +34 947 177 030
Fax: +34 947 177 004
info@tintolerma.com
www.tintolerma.com

Gran Lerma Vino de Autor 2011 T
100% tempranillo

91

Colour: cherry, garnet rim. Nose: ripe fruit, wild herbs, earthy notes, spicy, balsamic herbs. Palate: balanced, flavourful, balsamic.

Lerma Selección 2011 TR
100% tempranillo

90

Colour: cherry, garnet rim. Nose: red berry notes, ripe fruit, spicy, creamy oak, complex. Palate: flavourful, toasty, spicy.

Risco 2014 RD
95% tempranillo, 5% garnacha, albillo

86

Tinto Lerma 2012 TC
100% tempranillo

86

BODEGAS MONTE AMÁN

Ctra. Santo Domingo de Silos, 5
09348 Castrillo de Solarana (Burgos)
☎: +34 947 173 304
bodegas@monteaman.com
www.monteaman.com

Monte Amán 2009 TC
100% tempranillo

86

Monte Amán 2014 RD
100% tempranillo

83

Monte Amán 2014 T
100% tempranillo

86

Monte Amán 5 meses de barrica 2013 T Roble
100% tempranillo

87

Colour: bright cherry. Nose: ripe fruit, sweet spices, creamy oak. Palate: flavourful, fruity, toasty, round tannins.

BUEZO

Paraje Valdeazadón, s/n
09342 Mahamud (Burgos)
☎: +34 947 616 899
Fax: +34 947 616 885
info@buezo.com
www.buezo.com

Buezo Nattan 2005 TR
tempranillo

91

Colour: pale ruby, brick rim edge. Nose: spicy, fine reductive notes, wet leather, aged wood nuances, fruit liqueur notes. Palate: spicy, fine tannins, balanced.

Buezo Petit Verdot Tempranillo 2005 TR
petit verdot, tempranillo

87

Colour: pale ruby, brick rim edge. Nose: elegant, spicy, fine reductive notes, tobacco, balsamic herbs. Palate: spicy, fine tannins, long.

Buezo Tempranillo 2006 TR
tempranillo

85

Buezo Varietales 2006 TR
cabernet sauvignon, merlot, tempranillo

87

Colour: cherry, garnet rim. Nose: ripe fruit, spicy, balsamic herbs, fine reductive notes. Palate: flavourful, long, balsamic.

OLIVIER RIVIÈRE VINOS

Breton de los Herreros, 14 Entreplanta
26001 Logroño (La Rioja)
☎: +34 690 733 541
olivier@olivier-riviere.com
www.olivier-riviere.com

El Cadastro 2012 T
95% tempranillo, 5% garnacha

94

Colour: cherry, garnet rim. Nose: balanced, complex, ripe fruit, spicy, balsamic herbs, mineral. Palate: good structure, flavourful, round tannins, balanced, elegant.

PAGOS DE NEGREDO VIÑEDOS

N-622, Km 85
34257 Palenzuela (Palencia)
☎: +34 979 700 450
Fax: +34 979 702 171
ventas@pagosdenegredo.com
www.pagosdenegredo.com

Pagos de Negredo 2014 RD
100% tempranillo

87

Colour: light cherry, bright. Nose: balanced, fruit expression, floral. Palate: fruity, easy to drink, good finish.

Pagos de Negredo Cuvee 2014 T
100% tempranillo

86

SABINARES Y VIÑAS

Vista Alegre, 19
09340 Lerma (Burgos)
☎: +34 983 406 212
info@sabinares.com
www.vinoval.es

Sabinares Blanco de Guarda 2013 B
viura, albillo, malvasía, rojaal, casselas

90

Colour: bright straw. Nose: white flowers, fine lees, dried herbs, ripe fruit, candied fruit, citrus fruit. Palate: flavourful, fruity, good acidity, elegant.

Sabinares El Confin 2012 T
tempranillo, garnacha, mencía, otras

93

Colour: cherry, garnet rim. Nose: balanced, complex, ripe fruit, spicy, mineral. Palate: good structure, flavourful, round tannins, balanced.

Sabinares El Temido 2012 T
tempranillo, garnacha, mencía, otras

92

Colour: cherry, garnet rim. Nose: red berry notes, ripe fruit, spicy, creamy oak, complex. Palate: flavourful, toasty, balanced.

SEÑORÍO DE VALDESNEROS

Avda. La Paz, 4
34230 Torquemada (Palencia)
☎: +34 979 800 545
Fax: +34 979 800 545
sv@bodegasvaldesneros.com
www.bodegasvaldesneros.com

Eruelo 2009 TC
tempranillo

86

Señorío de Valdesneros 2014 RD
tempranillo

86

Señorío de Valdesneros 6 meses 2012 T Roble
tempranillo

86

Señorío de Valdesneros Selección 2009 TC
tempranillo

88

Colour: cherry, garnet rim. Nose: ripe fruit, spicy, creamy oak, complex. Palate: flavourful, toasty, round tannins.

DO. ARRIBES

CONSEJO REGULADOR

Arribes del Duero, 1
37175 Pereña de la Ribera (Salamanca)
☎:+34 923 573 413
@: info@doarribes.es / directortecnico@doarribes.es
www.doarribes.es

LOCATION:

In Las Arribes National Park, it comprises a narrow stretch of land along the southwest of Zamora and northeast of Salamanca. The vineyards occupy the valleys and steep terraces along the river Duero. Just a single municipal district, Fermoselle, has up to 90% of the total vineyard surface.

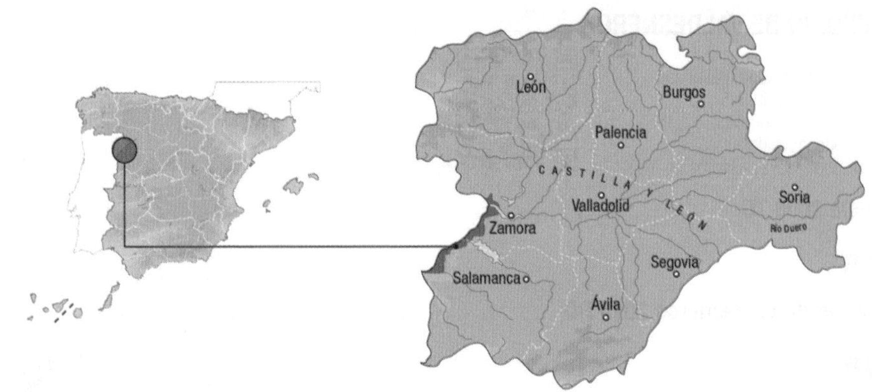

GRAPE VARIETIES:

WHITE: Malvasía, Verdejo and Albillo.
RED: Bruñal, Juan García, Rufete, Tempranillo (preferential); Mencía, Garnacha (authorized).

FIGURES:

Vineyard surface: 337 – **Wine-Growers:** 267 – **Wineries:** 14 – **2014 Harvest rating:** Very Good – **Production 14:** 807,810 litres – **Market percentages:** 80% National - 20% International.

SOIL:

The region has shallow sandy soils with abundant quartz and stones, even some granite found in the area of Fermoselle. In the territory which is part of the province of Salamanca it is quite noticeable the presence of slate, the kind of rock also featured on the Portuguese part along the Duero, called Douro the other side of the border. The slate subsoil works a splendid thermal regulator capable of accumulating the heat from the sunshine during the day and to slowly release it during the night time.

CLIMATE:

This wine region has a strong Mediterranean influence, given the prominent decrease in altitude that the territory features from the flat lands of the Sáyago area along the Duero valley until the river reaches Fermoselle, still in the province of Zamora. Rainfall is low all through the year, even during the averagely hot summer.

VINTAGE RATING

PEÑÍNGUIDE

2010	2011	2012	2013	2014
VERY GOOD	EXCELLENT	VERY GOOD	N/A	GOOD

BODEGA ARRIBES DEL DUERO

Ctra. Masueco, s/n
37251 Corporario - Aldeadavila
(Salamanca)
☎: +34 923 169 195
Fax: +34 923 169 195
secretaria@bodegasarribesdelduero.com
www.bodegasarribesdelduero.com

Arribes de Vettonia 2008 BFB
malvasía

90

Colour: bright yellow. Nose: ripe fruit, powerfull, toasty, aged wood nuances, pattiserie. Palate: flavourful, fruity, spicy, toasty, long.

Arribes de Vettonia 2011 TR
juan garcía

90

Colour: light cherry. Nose: fine reductive notes, aged wood nuances, toasty. Palate: spicy, toasty, flavourful.

Arribes de Vettonia 2012 TC
juan garcía

87

Colour: cherry, garnet rim. Nose: fine reductive notes, wet leather, aged wood nuances, ripe fruit. Palate: spicy, long, toasty.

Arribes de Vettonia 2013 T Roble

78

Arribes de Vettonia 2014 B
malvasía

88

Colour: straw. Nose: medium intensity, ripe fruit, floral. Palate: correct, easy to drink.

Arribes de Vettonia 2014 RD
juan garcía

85

Arribes de Vettonia Vendimia Selecionada 2011 T Roble
bruñal

90

Colour: cherry, garnet rim. Nose: fine reductive notes, wet leather, aged wood nuances, ripe fruit. Palate: spicy, long, toasty.

Secreto del Vetton 2009 T
bruñal

91

Colour: cherry, garnet rim. Nose: old leather, tobacco, sweet spices. Palate: correct, flavourful, spicy, good acidity.

BODEGA COOP. VIRGEN DE LA BANDERA

Avda. General Franco, 24
49220 Fermoselle (Zamora)
☎: +34 692 682 682
vinosborbon@vinosborbon.com

Viña Borbon 2011 TC

87

Colour: cherry, garnet rim. Nose: roasted coffee, spicy, ripe fruit. Palate: flavourful, smoky aftertaste, ripe fruit.

Viña Borbon 2014 T

86

BODEGA LA FONTANICAS

Requejo 222
49220 Fermoselle (Zamora)
☎: +34 629 548 774
info@arribesduero.com

Fontanicas 2012 TC

88

Colour: bright cherry. Nose: ripe fruit, sweet spices, creamy oak. Palate: flavourful, fruity, toasty, round tannins.

BODEGA PEÑOS MARTIN MARCOS

San Juan, 21
49220 Fermoselle (Zamora)
☎: +34 639 124 635
jpenos@elecnor.es

Romanorum 2013 TC

87

Colour: cherry, garnet rim. Nose: roasted coffee, smoky, spicy, ripe fruit. Palate: flavourful, smoky aftertaste, ripe fruit.

Romanorum 2014 T

88

Colour: cherry, purple rim. Nose: ripe fruit, woody. Palate: flavourful, spicy, powerful.

BODEGA QUINTA LAS VELAS

Humilladero, 44
37248 Ahigal de los Aceiteros
(Salamanca)
☎: +34 619 955 735
Fax: +34 923 120 674
enrique@esla.com
www.quintalasvelas.com

Quinta las Velas 2012 TC
tempranillo

87

Colour: bright cherry. Nose: ripe fruit, sweet spices, creamy oak. Palate: flavourful, fruity, toasty, round tannins.

Quinta las Velas Selección Especial Bruñal 2012 T
bruñal

90

Colour: cherry, garnet rim. Nose: creamy oak, red berry notes, fresh fruit, balanced. Palate: flavourful, spicy, elegant.

BODEGAS PASTRANA
Toro, 9
49018 (Zamora)
☎: +34 664 546 131
info@bodegaspastrana.es
www.bodegaspastrana.es

Paraje de los Bancales 2011 T
92

Colour: cherry, garnet rim. Nose: mineral, expressive, spicy. Palate: flavourful, ripe fruit, long, good acidity, balanced.

BODEGAS RIBERA DE PELAZAS
Camino de la Ermita, s/n
37175 Pereña de la Ribera (Salamanca)
☎: +34 902 108 031
Fax: +34 987 218 751
bodega@bodegasriberadepelazas.com
www.bodegasriberadepelazas.com

Abadengo 2008 TR
87

Colour: cherry, garnet rim. Nose: old leather, tobacco, candied fruit, warm. Palate: correct, flavourful, spicy.

Abadengo 2010 TC
90

Colour: cherry, garnet rim. Nose: smoky, sweet spices. Palate: flavourful, smoky aftertaste, ripe fruit.

Abadengo Selección Especial 2004 T
85

Gran Abadengo 2008 TR
89

Colour: light cherry. Nose: fine reductive notes, aged wood nuances, toasty, fruit liqueur notes. Palate: spicy, toasty, flavourful.

BODEGAS VIÑA ROMANA
37160 Villarino de los Aires
(Salamanca)
☎: +34 629 756 328
joseluis@vinaromana.com
www.vinaromana.com

Harley Design Wine 2010 T
juan garcía, bruñal

91

Colour: very deep cherry, garnet rim. Nose: complex, mineral, balsamic herbs, fine reductive notes. Palate: full, flavourful, round tannins.

Heredad del Viejo Imperio Homenaje Selección 2010 T
bruñal

93

Colour: cherry, garnet rim. Nose: fine reductive notes, aged wood nuances, ripe fruit, earthy notes, mineral. Palate: spicy, long, toasty.

GALLO VISCAY
Avda. San Amaro, 52
37160 Villarino de los Aires
(Salamanca)
☎: +34 659 159 218
galloviscay@gmail.com
www.galloviscay.com

Eighteen 18 2010 T
89

Colour: cherry, garnet rim. Nose: fine reductive notes, aged wood nuances, ripe fruit. Palate: spicy, long, toasty.

HACIENDA ZORITA MARQUÉS DE LA CONCORDIA FAMILY OF WINES
Crta Zamora-Fermoselle, Km 56
37115 Fermoselle (Zamora)
☎: +34 980 613 163
abasilio@unitedwineries.com
www.the-haciendas.com

Hacienda Zorita 2010 TC
100% tempranillo

88

Colour: cherry, purple rim. Nose: ripe fruit, woody, roasted coffee. Palate: flavourful, spicy, powerful.

LA SETERA

Calzada, 7
49232 Fornillos de Fermoselle (Zamora)
☎: +34 980 612 925
Fax: +34 980 612 925
lasetera@lasetera.com
www.lasetera.com

La Setera 2009 TC
juan garcía

88

Colour: light cherry. Nose: fine reductive notes, aged wood nuances, toasty, wet leather. Palate: spicy, toasty, flavourful.

La Setera 2010 TC
juan garcía

88

Colour: cherry, garnet rim. Nose: fine reductive notes, wet leather, aged wood nuances, ripe fruit. Palate: spicy, long, toasty, fine bitter notes.

La Setera 2014 B
malvasía

87

Colour: bright straw. Nose: fresh fruit, fragrant herbs, varietal. Palate: flavourful, fruity, good acidity, balanced.

La Setera 2014 T
juan garcía

88

Colour: cherry, purple rim. Nose: expressive, fresh fruit, red berry notes, floral. Palate: flavourful, fruity, grainy tannins.

La Setera Mencía 2011 TC
mencía

87

Colour: bright cherry. Nose: ripe fruit, sweet spices, creamy oak, warm. Palate: flavourful, toasty, round tannins.

La Setera Selección Especial 2011 T Roble
touriga

92

Colour: very deep cherry, garnet rim. Nose: expressive, complex, mineral, balsamic herbs. Palate: full, flavourful, round tannins.

La Setera Tinaja Varietales 2011 T Roble
juan garcía, mencía, rufete, bastardillo, bruñal, tinta madrid

92

Colour: very deep cherry, garnet rim. Nose: complex, mineral, balsamic herbs, warm. Palate: full, flavourful, round tannins, mineral.

La Setera Tinaja Varietales 2012 T Roble
juan garcía, mencía, rufete, bastardillo, bruñal, tinta madrid

91

Colour: very deep cherry, garnet rim. Nose: complex, mineral, balsamic herbs, balanced, ripe fruit. Palate: full, flavourful, round tannins.

OCELLUM DURII

San Juan 56 - 58
49220 Fermoselle (Zamora)
☎: +34 983 390 606
ocellumdurii@hotmail.com
www.bodegasocellumdurii.es

Condado de Fermosel 2010 T
juan garcía, tempranillo, rufete, bruñal, garnacha, malvasía

92

Colour: cherry, garnet rim. Nose: creamy oak, red berry notes, fresh fruit. Palate: flavourful, spicy, elegant.

Condado de Fermosel 2012 T
juan garcía, tempranillo, rufete, bruñal, garnacha tintorera

92

Colour: cherry, garnet rim. Nose: creamy oak, red berry notes, fresh fruit, balanced. Palate: flavourful, spicy, elegant.

Transitium Durii 2007 T
juan garcía, tempranillo, rufete, bruñal

87

Colour: pale ruby, brick rim edge. Nose: spicy, ripe fruit. Palate: spicy, toasty.

Transitium Durii 2008 T
juan garcía, tempranillo, rufete, garnacha

87 ♣

Colour: cherry, garnet rim. Nose: creamy oak, ripe fruit. Palate: toasty, lacks balance.

Transitium Durii Ocila 2007 T
juan garcía, tempranillo, rufete, bruñal, garnacha tintorera

89

Colour: cherry, garnet rim. Nose: ripe fruit, spicy, creamy oak. Palate: flavourful, toasty, round tannins.

Transitium Durii Ocila 2008 TR
juan garcía, tempranillo, rufete, bruñal, garnacha tintorera

91

Colour: light cherry. Nose: fine reductive notes, aged wood nuances, toasty, ripe fruit. Palate: spicy, toasty, flavourful.

DO. BIERZO

CONSEJO REGULADOR

Mencía, 1
24540 Cacabelos (León)
☎ :+34 987 549 408 - Fax: +34 987 547 077
@: info@crdobierzo.es
www.crdobierzo.es

LOCATION:

In the north west of the province of León. It covers 23 municipal areas and occupies several valleys in mountainous terrain and a flat plain at a lower altitude than the plateau of León, with higher temperatures accompanied by more rainfall. It may be considered an area of transition between Galicia, León and Asturias.

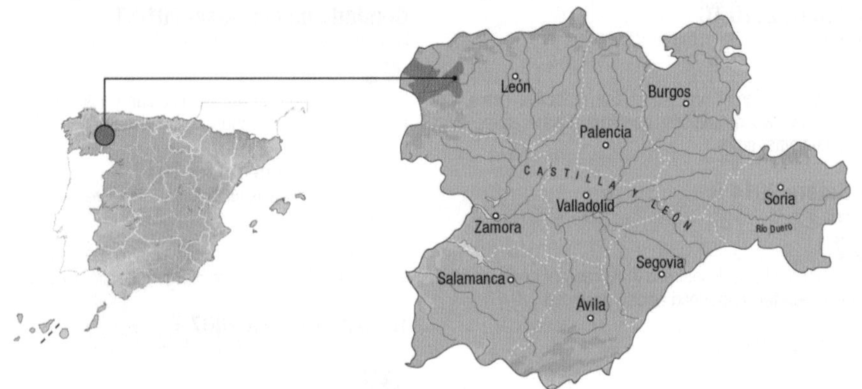

GRAPE VARIETIES:

WHITE: Godello, Palomino, Dona Blanca and Malvasia.
RED: Mencía or Negra and Garnacha Tintorera.

FIGURES:

Vineyard surface: 3,018 – **Wine-Growers:** 2,419 – **Wineries:** 75 – **2014 Harvest rating:** Excellent – **Production 14:** 9,749,094 litres – **Market percentages 2013:** 72% National - 28% International.

SOIL:

In the mountain regions, it is made up of a mixture of fine elements, quartzite and slate. In general, the soil of the DO is humid, dun and slightly acidic. The greater quality indices are associated with the slightly sloped terraces close to the rivers, the half - terraced or steep slopes situated at an altitude of between 450 and 1,000 m.

CLIMATE:

Quite mild and benign, with a certain degree of humidity due to Galician influence, although somewhat dry like Castilla. Thanks to the low altitude, late frost is avoided quite successfully and the grapes are usually harvested one month before the rest of Castilla. The average rainfall per year is 721 mm.

VINTAGE RATING

PEÑÍNGUIDE

2010	2011	2012	2013	2014
EXCELLENT	GOOD	VERY GOOD	VERY GOOD	VERY GOOD

AKILIA

Ctra. LE-142, PK. 54,7
24401 Ponferrada (León)
☎: +34 625 535 807
info@akiliawines.com
www.akiliawines.com

Akilia "Villa de San Lorenzo" 2013 T
100% mencía

88

Colour: cherry, purple rim. Nose: varietal, fresh fruit, woody. Palate: balsamic, fruity, harsh oak tannins.

ALMÁZCARA MAJARA

Calle de Las Eras, 5
24395 Almázcara (León)
☎: +34 609 322 194
javier.alvarez@es.coimgroup.com
www.almazcaramajara.com

Almázcara Majara 2012 T Roble

90

Colour: dark-red cherry. Nose: fresh fruit, red berry notes, smoky, spicy, creamy oak, cedar wood. Palate: flavourful, powerful, fruity, good structure, creamy.

Amphora de Cobija del Pobre 2013 T
mencía

88

Colour: dark-red cherry, orangey edge. Nose: damp earth, undergrowth, fresh fruit, medium intensity. Palate: balsamic, fruity, fresh fruit tannins.

Cobija del Pobre 2014 B
godello

88

Colour: straw. Nose: medium intensity, fresh fruit, dried herbs, slightly evolved. Palate: correct, fresh, smoky aftertaste.

Demasiado Corazón 2013 B
godello

90

Colour: bright straw. Nose: white flowers, fine lees, dried herbs, mineral. Palate: flavourful, fruity, good acidity, round.

Jarabe de Almázcara 2013 T
mencía

87

Colour: dark-red cherry. Nose: red berry notes, fresh, varietal, damp undergrowth. Palate: good acidity, fresh, fruity, dry, harsh oak tannins.

ÁLVAREZ DE TOLEDO VIÑEDOS Y GRUPO BODEGAS

Río Selmo, 8
24560 Toral de los Vados (León)
☎: +34 987 563 551
Fax: +34 987 563 532
admon@bodegasalvarezdetoledo.com
www.bodegasalvarezdetoledo.com

Álvarez de Toledo Godello 2014 B
100% godello

86

Álvarez de Toledo Mencía 2013 T Roble
100% mencía

88

Colour: dark-red cherry, garnet rim. Nose: medium intensity, balsamic herbs, ripe fruit. Palate: spicy, balsamic, easy to drink.

ARTURO GARCÍA VIÑEDOS Y BODEGAS

La Escuela, 2 Perandones
24516 Villafranca del Bierzo (León)
☎: +34 987 553 000
Fax: +34 987 553 001
info@solardesael.es
www.bodegasrturo.es

Hacienda Elsa Godello 2014 B
godello

89

Colour: straw. Nose: fine lees, grassy, fresh fruit. Palate: elegant, fruity, flavourful, mineral.

Hacienda Elsa Mencía 2014 T
mencía

88

Colour: dark-red cherry, garnet rim. Nose: fruit expression, red berry notes, fresh, varietal. Palate: good acidity, fresh, fruity, flavourful.

Hacienda Sael Mencía 2014 T
mencía

89

Colour: cherry, purple rim. Nose: expressive, fresh fruit, red berry notes, scrubland. Palate: flavourful, fruity, good acidity.

Solar de Sael Mencía 2012 TC
mencía

90

Colour: deep cherry. Nose: ripe fruit, powerfull, varietal, aromatic coffee. Palate: balsamic, creamy, good structure, powerful, flavourful, ripe fruit.

Valderica 2014 B
dona blanca, palomino

86

Valderica Mencía 2014 T
mencía

86

AURELIO FEO VITICULTOR

El Oteiro, 7 San Andrés de Montejos
24491 Ponferrada (León)
☎: +34 987 401 865
Fax: +34 987 401 865
bodega@bodegafeo.es
www.bodegafeo.es

Buencomiezo 2012 T
mencía

88

Colour: very deep cherry, garnet rim. Nose: expressive, mineral, balsamic herbs, balanced. Palate: flavourful, round tannins.

Cruz de San Andrés 2013 T
mencía

86

Montelios 2011 T
mencía

91

Colour: deep cherry. Nose: complex, elegant, expressive, ripe fruit. Palate: good structure, powerful, full, fruity, mineral, creamy.

BODEGA DEL ABAD

Ctra. N-VI, km. 396
24549 Carracedelo (León)
☎: +34 987 562 417
Fax: +34 987 562 428
info@bodegadelabad.com
www.bodegadelabad.com

Abad Dom Bueno Godello 2014 B
godello

89

Colour: straw. Nose: medium intensity, ripe fruit, floral, grassy, citrus fruit, fine lees. Palate: correct, easy to drink, rich, fruity.

Abad Dom Bueno Godello 2014 BFB
godello

88

Colour: bright yellow. Nose: ripe fruit, toasty. Palate: flavourful, fruity, spicy, toasty, long.

Abad Dom Bueno Mencía 2013 T
mencía

89

Colour: deep cherry, purple rim. Nose: creamy oak, toasty, ripe fruit, balsamic herbs. Palate: balanced, spicy, long.

Abad Dom Bueno Mencía 2014 T
100% mencía

87

Colour: cherry, purple rim. Nose: red berry notes, floral, balsamic herbs. Palate: powerful, fresh, fruity.

Abad Dom Bueno Señorío de Valcarce 2012 T Roble
mencía

89

Colour: very deep cherry, garnet rim. Nose: balsamic herbs, balanced, ripe fruit. Palate: full, flavourful, round tannins.

Carracedo 2012 TR
mencía

89

Colour: cherry, garnet rim. Nose: smoky, spicy, ripe fruit. Palate: flavourful, smoky aftertaste, ripe fruit.

Gotín del Risc Essencia 2008 TR
mencía

90

Colour: dark-red cherry. Nose: red clay notes, balanced, ripe fruit, smoky, cocoa bean. Palate: flavourful, fruity, powerful, creamy, spicy.

Gotín del Risc Godello 2014 B
godello

90

Colour: bright yellow. Nose: neat, characterful, varietal, ripe fruit, floral. Palate: fruity, good acidity, flavourful.

Gotín del Risc Mencia 2013 T
mencía

90

Colour: deep cherry. Nose: red berry notes, cocoa bean, spicy. Palate: fruity, good structure, flavourful, mineral.

San Salvador Godello 2012 B
godello

92

Colour: bright yellow. Nose: expressive, dried herbs, ripe fruit, spicy. Palate: flavourful, fruity, good acidity, balanced.

Tesín de la Campana 2013 T

93

Colour: cherry, garnet rim. Nose: balanced, complex, ripe fruit, spicy, balsamic herbs. Palate: good structure, flavourful, round tannins, balanced.

BODEGA MARTÍNEZ YEBRA

San Pedro, 96
24530 Villadecanes (León)
☎: +34 987 562 082
info@bodegamartinezyebra.es
www.bodegamartinezyebra.es

Canes 2014 T
100% mencía

86

Tres Racimos 2012 T
100% mencía

90

Colour: dark-red cherry. Nose: complex, varietal, cocoa bean, spicy, powerfull, fruit expression. Palate: fruity, flavourful, spicy.

Viñadecanes 2009 TC
100% mencía

90

Colour: cherry, garnet rim. Nose: creamy oak, balanced, cocoa bean, ripe fruit. Palate: flavourful, spicy, round tannins.

BODEGA Y VIÑEDOS LUNA BEBERIDE

Ant. Ctra. Madrid - Coruña, Km. 402
24540 Cacabelos (León)
☎: +34 987 549 002
Fax: +34 987 549 214
info@lunabeberide.es
www.lunabeberide.es

Art Luna Beberide 2012 TC
100% mencía

88

Colour: deep cherry. Nose: roasted coffee, short. Palate: correct, flavourful, spicy, ripe fruit.

Finca La Cuesta Luna Beberide 2012 TC
100% mencía

92

Colour: cherry, garnet rim. Nose: creamy oak, red berry notes, balanced, ripe fruit, balsamic herbs. Palate: flavourful, spicy.

Godello Luna Beberide 2014 B
100% godello

89

Colour: bright yellow. Nose: ripe fruit, dried flowers, faded flowers. Palate: balanced, fine bitter notes, fruity.

Mencía Luna Beberide 2014 T
100% mencía

89

Colour: cherry, purple rim. Nose: expressive, fresh fruit, red berry notes, floral. Palate: flavourful, fruity, good acidity.

BODEGAS ADRIÁ

Antigua Ctra. Madrid - Coruña, Km. 408
24500 Villafranca del Bierzo (León)
☎: +34 987 540 907
Fax: +34 911 982 996
paco@bodegasadria.com
www.bodegasadria.com

Vega Montán Adriá 2012 T
mencía

89

Colour: deep cherry. Nose: powerfull, smoky, cedar wood, macerated fruit. Palate: good structure, astringent, oaky, fruity.

Vega Montán Godello 2014 B
godello

90

Colour: bright straw. Nose: undergrowth, fresh fruit, fragrant herbs. Palate: fresh, light-bodied, flavourful, fruity.

Vega Montán Mencía 2014 T
mencía

87

Colour: bright cherry. Nose: fresh, neat, fresh fruit. Palate: balanced, correct, light-bodied, flavourful.

BODEGAS BERNARDO ÁLVAREZ

San Pedro, 75
24530 Villadecanes (León)
☎: +34 987 562 129
Fax: +34 987 562 129
vinos@bodegasbernardoalvarez.com
www.bodegasbernardoalvarez.com

Campo Redondo 2013 T Roble
100% mencía

88

Colour: bright cherry. Nose: ripe fruit, sweet spices, creamy oak, expressive. Palate: flavourful, fruity, round tannins.

Campo Redondo Godello 2014 B
100% godello

88

Colour: bright straw. Nose: complex, elegant, fresh, varietal. Palate: balsamic, good acidity, fruity, fresh, light-bodied, flavourful.

Viña Migarrón 2012 TC
100% mencía

87

Colour: deep cherry. Nose: balsamic herbs, balanced, ripe fruit, dried herbs. Palate: round tannins, fruity.

Viña Migarrón 2013 T
100% mencía

86

Viña Migarrón 2014 B
dona blanca, jerez, godello

89

Colour: yellow. Nose: wild herbs, dried flowers, balanced. Palate: correct, fine bitter notes, flavourful.

Viña Migarrón 2014 RD
100% mencía

87

Colour: light cherry, bright. Nose: red berry notes, ripe fruit, floral, powerfull. Palate: correct, flavourful, ripe fruit.

BODEGAS CUATRO PASOS

Santa María, 43
24540 Cacabelos (León)
☎: +34 987 548 089
bierzo@martincodax.com
www.cuatropasos.es

Cuatro Pasos 2012 T
100% mencía

90

Colour: deep cherry. Nose: neat, expressive, varietal, mineral, fresh fruit, wild herbs. Palate: complex, good structure, powerful, flavourful.

Cuatro Pasos 2014 RD
100% mencía

88

Colour: light cherry, bright. Nose: red berry notes, floral, expressive, fragrant herbs, varietal. Palate: powerful, fruity, fresh.

Cuatro Pasos Black 2011 T
100% mencía

92

Colour: cherry, garnet rim. Nose: expressive, spicy, mineral, varietal. Palate: flavourful, ripe fruit, long, good acidity, balanced.

Pizarras de Otero 2014 T
100% mencía

90

Colour: cherry, purple rim. Nose: red berry notes, floral, balsamic herbs, expressive, balanced. Palate: powerful, fresh, fruity.

BODEGAS GODELIA

Antigua Ctra. N-VI, NVI, Km. 403,5
24547 Pieros-Cacabelos (León)
☎: +34 987 546 279
Fax: +34 987 548 026
www.godelia.es

Godelia 2011 TC
100% mencía

90

Colour: deep cherry, garnet rim. Nose: ripe fruit, spicy. Palate: good structure, flavourful, full.

Godelia 2013 B
80% godello, 20% dona blanca

91

Colour: yellow, greenish rim. Nose: white flowers, fine lees, dried herbs. Palate: flavourful, fruity, good acidity, round.

Godelia 2014 RD
100% mencía

89

Colour: raspberry rose. Nose: candied fruit, macerated fruit. Palate: elegant, balanced, fruity, fresh, flavourful.

Godelia Blanco Selección 2012 B
100% godello

90

Colour: bright straw. Nose: complex, medium intensity, macerated fruit. Palate: round, balanced, elegant, fruity, creamy.

Godelia Tinto Selección 2011 T
100% mencía

91

Colour: deep cherry. Nose: red clay notes, undergrowth, ripe fruit, animal reductive notes, fine reductive notes. Palate: good acidity, balanced, fruity, powerful.

Pilgrim 2013 B
80% godello, 20% dona blanca

90

Colour: bright straw. Nose: white flowers, fresh fruit, fragrant herbs. Palate: flavourful, fruity, good acidity, balanced, rich.

Pilgrim Mencía 2011 TC
100% mencía

86

Pilgrim Mencía 2014 T
100% mencía

85

Viernes 2014 T
100% mencía

88

Colour: bright cherry, purple rim. Nose: fresh fruit, balanced, wild herbs. Palate: balanced, good acidity.

BODEGAS ORDÓÑEZ

Julio Romero de Torres, 12
29700 Vélez- Málaga (Málaga)
☎: +34 952 504 706
Fax: +34 951 284 796
info@jorgeordonez.es
www.grupojorgeordonez.com

Tritón Mencía 2014 T
100% mencía

91

Colour: cherry, purple rim. Nose: powerfull, ripe fruit, spicy, red berry notes. Palate: powerful, fruity, unctuous.

BODEGAS PEIQUE

El Bierzo, s/n
24530 Valtuille de Abajo (León)
☎: +34 987 562 044
Fax: +34 987 562 044
bodega@bodegaspeique.com
www.bodegaspeique.com

Luis Peique 2010 T
mencía

90

Colour: bright cherry. Nose: ripe fruit, fruit preserve, cocoa bean. Palate: good structure, flavourful, full, long, spicy.

Peique 2014 RD
mencía

86

Peique Godello 2014 B
godello

89

Colour: bright straw. Nose: balanced, ripe fruit. Palate: rich, flavourful, fine bitter notes, long.

Peique Ramón Valle 2013 T
mencía

89

Colour: bright cherry. Nose: macerated fruit, damp earth. Palate: fresh, fruity, powerful, flavourful, balsamic.

Peique Selección Familiar 2010 T
mencía

92

Colour: cherry, garnet rim. Nose: balanced, complex, ripe fruit, spicy, fine reductive notes. Palate: good structure, flavourful, round tannins, balanced.

Peique Tinto Mencía 2014 T
mencía

89

Colour: dark-red cherry. Nose: closed, varietal, ripe fruit. Palate: balsamic, fruity, flavourful, dry.

Peique Viñedos Viejos 2011 T Roble
mencía

91

Colour: bright cherry, garnet rim. Nose: mineral, ripe fruit, fruit preserve, sweet spices. Palate: balsamic, good structure.

BODEGAS TENOIRA GAYOSO

24500 Villafranca del Bierzo (León)
☎: +34 987 540 307
export@tenoiragayoso.com
www.tenoiragayoso.com

Tenoira Gayoso 2010 T Barrica
100% mencía

90

Colour: cherry, garnet rim. Nose: ripe fruit, wild herbs, earthy notes, spicy, balsamic herbs. Palate: balanced, flavourful, long, balsamic.

Tenoira Gayoso Godello 2014 B
100% godello

87

Colour: bright straw. Nose: white flowers, fresh fruit, fragrant herbs, expressive. Palate: flavourful, fruity, good acidity, balanced.

Tenoira Gayoso Mencía 2014 T
100% mencía

88

Colour: cherry, purple rim. Nose: powerfull, ripe fruit, spicy. Palate: powerful, fruity, unctuous.

BODEGAS VIÑAS DE VIÑALES

Calle del Campo, s/n
24319 Viñales - Bembibre (León)
☎: +34 609 652 058
bodegasvinasdevinales@gmail.com
www.bodegasvinasdevinales.com

Interamnum Catorce 2014 T
mencía

86

Interamnum Doce 2012 T Roble
mencía

87

Colour: deep cherry, purple rim. Nose: toasty, ripe fruit, balsamic herbs, dried herbs. Palate: balanced, spicy.

Interamnum Doce 2012 TC
mencía

89

Colour: cherry, garnet rim. Nose: creamy oak, balanced, ripe fruit, wild herbs, dried herbs. Palate: flavourful, spicy.

Interamnum Trece 2013 T Roble
mencía

87

Colour: deep cherry, purple rim. Nose: toasty, balsamic herbs, damp undergrowth. Palate: balanced, spicy, long.

BODEGAS Y VIÑEDOS CASTROVENTOSA

Finca El Barredo
24530 Valtuille de Abajo (León)
☎: +34 987 562 148
Fax: +34 987 562 191
info@castroventosa.com
www.castroventosa.com

Castro Ventosa 2014 T
mencía

89

Colour: deep cherry, purple rim. Nose: balanced, red berry notes, ripe fruit, varietal. Palate: correct, balsamic, easy to drink.

Castro Ventosa"Vintage" 2012 T

88

Colour: dark-red cherry, garnet rim. Nose: ripe fruit, expressive, balanced, wild herbs. Palate: correct, balanced.

El Castro de Valtuille 2011 T

92

Colour: cherry, garnet rim. Nose: ripe fruit, wild herbs, earthy notes, spicy, balsamic herbs. Palate: balanced, flavourful, long, balsamic.

El Castro de Valtuille Joven 2014 T

91

Colour: cherry, purple rim. Nose: red berry notes, floral, balsamic herbs, varietal. Palate: powerful, fresh, fruity, elegant.

Valtuille Cepas Centenarias 2012 T

93

Colour: deep cherry, garnet rim. Nose: wild herbs, dried herbs, mineral, ripe fruit, neat. Palate: good structure, flavourful, round tannins.

PODIUM

Valtuille La Cova de la Raposa 2010 T

95

Colour: deep cherry, garnet rim. Nose: neat, expressive, varietal, wild herbs, complex, ripe fruit. Palate: full, complex, fruity, fine tannins.

Valtuille Villegas 2010 T Barrica

94

Colour: deep cherry, garnet rim. Nose: balsamic herbs, scrubland, fruit expression, cocoa bean, creamy oak. Palate: elegant, flavourful, powerful, fruity, slightly dry, soft tannins.

BODEGAS Y VIÑEDOS GANCEDO

Vistalegre, s/n
24548 Quilós (León)
☎: +34 987 134 980
info@bodegasgancedo.com
www.bodegasgancedo.com

Capricho Val de Paxariñas 2014 B
85% godello, 15% dona blanca

94

Colour: bright straw. Nose: white flowers, fine lees, dried herbs, ripe fruit, wild herbs. Palate: flavourful, fruity, good acidity, elegant.

Gancedo 2012 T
mencía

91

Colour: deep cherry. Nose: creamy oak, toasty, ripe fruit, balsamic herbs. Palate: balanced, spicy, long.

Herencia del Capricho 2008 BFB
90% godello, 10% dona blanca

92

Colour: bright golden. Nose: ripe fruit, balsamic herbs, creamy oak, sweet spices. Palate: rich, powerful, flavourful, spicy, long.

Ucedo Mencía 2008 T
100% mencía

90

Colour: cherry, garnet rim. Nose: ripe fruit, wild herbs, earthy notes, spicy, balsamic herbs. Palate: balanced, flavourful, long, balsamic.

Xestal 2009 T
100% mencía

90

Colour: deep cherry. Nose: expressive, complex, mineral, balsamic herbs, ripe fruit. Palate: full, flavourful, round tannins.

BODEGAS Y VIÑEDOS JOSE ANTONIO GARCIA

El Puente s/n
24530 Valtuille de Abajo (León)
☎: +34 987 562 223
Fax: +34 987 562 223
jose@g2wines.com

Aires de Vendimia 2012 T
mencía

92

Colour: very deep cherry, garnet rim. Nose: expressive, complex, mineral, balsamic herbs, balanced. Palate: full, flavourful, round tannins.

Aires de Vendimia Godello 2013 B
godello

89

Colour: bright yellow. Nose: white flowers, fine lees, dried herbs, sweet spices. Palate: flavourful, fruity, good acidity, round, rich.

El Chuqueiro 2014 B
godello

89

Colour: bright straw. Nose: fresh fruit, citrus fruit, faded flowers, expressive. Palate: balanced, fine bitter notes, good acidity.

Unculin 2014 T
mencía

84

BODEGAS Y VIÑEDOS LA SENDA

24530 Valtuille de Abajo (León)
☎: +34 674 608 232
contacto@bodegalasenda.es
www.bodegalasenda.es

1984 2014 T
mencía

89

Colour: cherry, purple rim. Nose: red berry notes, floral, scrubland. Palate: powerful, fresh, fruity, balanced, balsamic.

BODEGAS Y VIÑEDOS MENGOBA

Avda. del Parque, 7
24544 San Juan de Carracedo (León)
☎: +34 649 940 800
gregory@mengoba.com
www.mengoba.com

Brezo 2014 RD
85

Brezo 2014 T
88

Colour: deep cherry, purple rim. Nose: scrubland, varietal, ripe fruit. Palate: correct, balanced.

Brezo Godello y Doña Blanca 2014 B
90

Colour: bright straw. Nose: fresh fruit, fragrant herbs, expressive, dried flowers. Palate: flavourful, fruity, good acidity, balanced.

Flor de Brezo 2013 T
88

Colour: cherry, garnet rim. Nose: ripe fruit, spicy, grassy, wild herbs. Palate: easy to drink, ripe fruit, correct.

Mengoba 2013 T
mencía

90

Colour: bright cherry, garnet rim. Nose: balanced, wild herbs, varietal. Palate: flavourful, fruity, balsamic, balanced.

Mengoba Godello sobre lías 2013 B
92

Colour: bright yellow. Nose: medium intensity, ripe fruit, floral, fine lees. Palate: rich, flavourful, complex, fine bitter notes, long.

Mengoba La Vigne de Sancho Martín 2012 T
94

Colour: deep cherry. Nose: expressive, macerated fruit, fruit expression, cocoa bean, elegant, powerfull. Palate: elegant, good structure, fruity, powerful, flavourful.

BODEGAS Y VIÑEDOS MERAYO

Ctra. de la Espina, km. 3
Finca Miralmonte
24491 San Andrés de Montejos (León)
☎: +34 987 057 925
info@byvmerayo.com
www.bodegasmerayo.com

Aquiana 2012 T
mencía

91

Colour: cherry, garnet rim. Nose: ripe fruit, wild herbs, earthy notes, spicy, balsamic herbs. Palate: balanced, flavourful, long, balsamic.

La Galbana 2012 T
mencía

90

Colour: deep cherry. Nose: spicy, aged wood nuances, ripe fruit. Palate: slightly tart, flavourful, fruity, spicy, ripe fruit, sweetness.

Merayo 2014 RD
mencía

87

Colour: rose, purple rim. Nose: powerfull, fresh, ripe fruit, raspberry. Palate: balsamic, ripe fruit, flavourful.

Merayo Godello 2014 B
godello

90

Colour: bright straw. Nose: white flowers, fresh fruit, fragrant herbs, expressive. Palate: flavourful, fruity, good acidity, balanced.

Merayo Mencía 2014 T
mencía

91

Colour: cherry, purple rim. Nose: expressive, fresh fruit, red berry notes, floral. Palate: flavourful, fruity, good acidity, fruity aftestaste.

Tres Filas 2014 T Roble
mencía

90

Colour: cherry, purple rim. Nose: red berry notes, floral, balsamic herbs, spicy. Palate: powerful, fresh, fruity, balanced.

BODEGAS Y VIÑEDOS PAIXAR

Ribadeo, 56
24500 Villafranca del Bierzo (León)
☎: +34 987 549 002
Fax: +34 987 549 214
info@lunabeberide.es

Paixar Mencía 2012 T
100% mencía

92

Colour: deep cherry. Nose: expressive, characterful, powerfull, varietal, dried herbs. Palate: good structure, full, flavourful.

CAMINO DEL NORTE, COMPAÑÍA DE VINOS

Avenida de Galicia 12
24540 Cacabelos (León)
☎: +34 658 617 390
info@caminodelnortevinos.com
www.caminodelnortevinos.com

El Tesón Mencía 2012 T
mencía

93

Colour: light cherry, purple rim. Nose: fruit expression, fruit liqueur notes, fragrant herbs, spicy, creamy oak. Palate: balanced, elegant, spicy, long.

Soradal Mencía 2012 T
mencía

91

Colour: cherry, garnet rim. Nose: ripe fruit, wild herbs, spicy, balsamic herbs. Palate: balanced, flavourful, long, balsamic.

CASAR DE BURBIA

Travesía la Constitución, s/n
24549 Carracedelo (León)
☎: +34 987 562 850
Fax: +34 987 562 850
info@casardeburbia.com
www.casardeburbia.com

Casar de Burbia 2013 T
mencía

93

Colour: cherry, garnet rim. Nose: creamy oak, balanced. Palate: flavourful, spicy, good acidity.

Casar Godello 2013 BFB
godello

91

Colour: bright yellow. Nose: powerfull, toasty, aged wood nuances, pattiserie, candied fruit. Palate: flavourful, fruity, spicy, toasty, long.

Casar Godello 2014 B
godello

89

Colour: bright straw. Nose: white flowers, fragrant herbs, ripe fruit. Palate: flavourful, fruity, good acidity.

Hombros 2013 T

93

Colour: bright cherry. Nose: sweet spices, creamy oak, overripe fruit. Palate: flavourful, toasty, round tannins.

Tebaida 2012 T
mencía

92

Colour: bright cherry. Nose: sweet spices, creamy oak, overripe fruit. Palate: flavourful, fruity, round tannins.

Tebaida Nemesio 2012 T
mencía

94

Colour: cherry, garnet rim. Nose: smoky, spicy, ripe fruit, earthy notes, mineral. Palate: flavourful, smoky aftertaste, ripe fruit.

CEPAS DEL BIERZO

Ctra. de Sanabria, 111
24401 Ponferrada (León)
☎: +34 987 412 333
Fax: +34 987 412 912
coocebier@coocebier.e.telefonica.net

Don Osmundo 2009 T Barrica
100% mencía

86

Don Osmundo 2010 T Barrica
mencía

86

Don Osmundo 2011 T Barrica
mencía

88

Colour: cherry, garnet rim. Nose: smoky, spicy, ripe fruit. Palate: flavourful, smoky aftertaste, ripe fruit.

Don Osmundo 2012 T
100% mencía

85

Escaril 2013 B
palomino, valenciana

81

Faneiro 2012 RD
mencía, palomino

83

COBERTIZO DE VIÑA RAMIRO

Promadelo Pol. 33 Parcela 407
24530 Valtuille de Abajo (León)
☎: +34 987 562 157
Fax: +34 987 562 157
vinos@bodegacobertizo.com
www.bodegacobertizo.com

Cobertizo 2013 T

83

Cobertizo s/c B

88

Colour: bright yellow, greenish rim. Nose: faded flowers, ripe fruit, fine lees. Palate: flavourful, balanced, fine bitter notes.

Cobertizo Selección 2011 T Roble

84

DESCENDIENTES DE J. PALACIOS

Avda. Calvo Sotelo, 6
24500 Villafranca del Bierzo (León)
☎: +34 987 540 821
Fax: +34 987 540 851
info@djpalacios.com

Las Lamas 2013 T

98% mencía, 2% alicante bouschet

94

Colour: cherry, garnet rim. Nose: elegant, red berry notes, balsamic herbs, complex, varietal. Palate: ripe fruit, long, elegant, balanced, balsamic.

PODIUM

Moncerbal 2013 T

98% mencía, 2% uva blanca

95

Colour: cherry, garnet rim. Nose: cocoa bean, scrubland, complex. Palate: long, balanced, round, round tannins, balsamic.

Pétalos del Bierzo 2013 T

95% mencía, 3% uva blanca, 2% alicante bouschet, otras

92

Colour: deep cherry, purple rim. Nose: ripe fruit, balsamic herbs, cocoa bean. Palate: balanced, spicy, long, good acidity.

Villa de Corullón 2013 T

97% mencía, 3% uva blanca

93

Colour: cherry, garnet rim. Nose: ripe fruit, fragrant herbs, spicy, toasty, creamy oak, mineral. Palate: powerful, flavourful, balsamic, balanced.

DOMINIO DE LOS CEREZOS

Camino de las Salgueras, s/n
24413 Molinaseca (León)
☎: +34 639 202 403
Fax: +34 987 405 779
mariazv.bierzo@gmail.com
www.dominiodeloscerezos.com

Van Gus Vana 2010 T

mencía

92

Colour: cherry, garnet rim. Nose: creamy oak, red berry notes, balanced, ripe fruit, scrubland. Palate: flavourful, spicy, elegant.

Van Gus Vana 2011 T

mencía

92

Colour: cherry, garnet rim. Nose: mineral, expressive, spicy, toasty. Palate: flavourful, ripe fruit, long, good acidity, balanced.

Van Gus Vana 2012 T

mencía

90

Colour: cherry, garnet rim. Nose: varietal, dried herbs, faded flowers. Palate: good structure, flavourful, ripe fruit.

DOMINIO DE TARES

P.I. Bierzo Alto, Los Barredos, 4
24318 San Román de Bembibre (León)
☎: +34 987 514 550
Fax: +34 987 514 570
info@dominiodetares.com
www.dominiodetares.com

Baltos 2012 T

100% mencía

89

Colour: bright cherry. Nose: ripe fruit, sweet spices, creamy oak, expressive. Palate: flavourful, fruity, round tannins.

Bembibre 2009 T

100% mencía

91

Colour: cherry, garnet rim. Nose: ripe fruit, old leather, tobacco. Palate: correct, flavourful, spicy, full, long.

Dominio de Tares Cepas Viejas 2012 TC

100% mencía

92

Colour: deep cherry, garnet rim. Nose: aged wood nuances, ripe fruit, sweet spices, balanced. Palate: good structure, round tannins.

Dominio de Tares Godello 2014 BFB
godello

90

Colour: bright straw. Nose: fresh fruit, fine lees, powerfull, expressive. Palate: good acidity, elegant, powerful, fruity, fresh.

Tares P. 3 2009 T Roble
100% mencía

92

Colour: very deep cherry, garnet rim. Nose: expressive, balsamic herbs, balanced, fruit preserve. Palate: full, flavourful, round tannins.

EL SECRETO DEL ÉXITO

Ctra. de Ribes, 137
08520 Les Franqueses del Valles
(Barcelona)
☎: +34 609 322 194
javier.alvarez@es.coimgroup.com

L'Aphrodisiaque 2013 T
mencía

86

L'Aphrodisiaque 2014 B
godello

87

Colour: pale. Nose: grassy, balsamic herbs, fresh fruit, medium intensity. Palate: correct, balanced, fruity, flavourful.

ENCIMA WINES

Ctra. de Lombillo
24413 Molinaseca (León)
☎: +34 659 954 908
info@vinosboton.com
www.vinosboton.com

Para Muestra un Botón 2013 B
godello

89

Colour: bright yellow. Nose: balanced, white flowers, fine lees, expressive. Palate: balanced, fine bitter notes, good acidity.

Para Muestra un Botón 2013 TR
mencía

84

ESTEFANÍA

Ctra. de Dehesas - Posada del Bierzo, s/n
24540 Ponferrada (León)
☎: +34 987 420 015
Fax: +34 987 420 015
info@tilenus.com
www.tilenus.com

Tilenus "La Florida" 2008 TC
100% mencía

91

Colour: dark-red cherry, orangey edge. Nose: expressive, balsamic herbs, balanced, spicy, old leather. Palate: full, flavourful, round tannins, balanced.

Tilenus 2011 T Roble
100% mencía

89

Colour: dark-red cherry, garnet rim. Nose: varietal, balanced, powerfull, ripe fruit, dried herbs. Palate: good structure, long, balsamic, round tannins.

Tilenus 2013 T
mencía

89

Colour: cherry, purple rim. Nose: red berry notes, balsamic herbs, floral, mineral. Palate: flavourful, fresh, fruity.

Tilenus Godello 2014 B
100% godello

90

Colour: bright yellow. Nose: dried herbs, faded flowers, ripe fruit, fine lees. Palate: flavourful, spicy.

Tilenus Pagos de Posada 2006 T
100% mencía

91

Colour: deep cherry, brick rim edge. Nose: elegant, spicy, fine reductive notes, tobacco, balsamic herbs. Palate: spicy, fine tannins, elegant, long, balanced.

Tilenus Pieros 2007 T
100% mencía

92

Colour: cherry, garnet rim. Nose: complex, ripe fruit, spicy, fine reductive notes, mineral. Palate: good structure, flavourful, round tannins, balanced.

Tilenus Vendimia 2014 T
100% mencía

89

Colour: bright cherry, purple rim. Nose: expressive, varietal, scrubland. Palate: balanced, ripe fruit, balsamic.

HAMMEKEN CELLARS

Calle de la Muela, 16
03730 Jávea (Alicante)
☎: +34 965 791 967
Fax: +34 966 461 471
cellars@hammekencellars.com
www.hammekencellars.com

Aventino Mencía 6 Months in Barrel 2012 T
mencía

89

Colour: very deep cherry, garnet rim. Nose: balsamic herbs, smoky, toasty, ripe fruit. Palate: flavourful, round tannins, smoky aftertaste.

Viña Altamar 2014 T
mencía

88

Colour: cherry, purple rim. Nose: balanced, red berry notes, ripe fruit, balsamic herbs. Palate: fruity, flavourful, easy to drink.

Viña Altamar Mencía Barrel Select 2012 T
mencía

88

Colour: dark-red cherry, garnet rim. Nose: earthy notes, mineral, cedar wood, smoky. Palate: correct, fruity, flavourful, oaky.

LOSADA VINOS DE FINCA

Ctra. a Villafranca LE-713, Km. 12
24540 Cacabelos (León)
☎: +34 987 548 053
Fax: +34 987 548 069
bodega@losadavinosdefinca.com
www.losadavinosdefinca.com

Altos de Losada 2011 T
100% mencía

92

Colour: very deep cherry, garnet rim. Nose: complex, mineral, balsamic herbs, balanced. Palate: full, flavourful, round tannins.

La Bienquerida 2013 T
95% mencía, 5% otras

92

Colour: deep cherry. Nose: ripe fruit, fruit expression, undergrowth, aromatic coffee, caramel, creamy oak. Palate: creamy, balsamic, flavourful, complex.

Losada 2012 TC
100% mencía

91

Colour: very deep cherry. Nose: earthy notes, damp earth, macerated fruit, aromatic coffee, smoky, creamy oak. Palate: good structure, powerful, ripe fruit, mineral.

Losada 2013 T
100% mencía

92

Colour: cherry, garnet rim. Nose: creamy oak, red berry notes, fresh fruit, balanced, sweet spices. Palate: flavourful, spicy, elegant.

MÁQUINA & TABLA

Villalba de los Alcores, 2-3 B
47008 Valladolid (Valladolid)
☎: +34 609 885 083
hola@maquina-tabla.com
www.maquina-tabla.com

Laderas de Leonila 2013 T
mencía

92

Colour: light cherry. Nose: fruit liqueur notes, spicy, creamy oak, wild herbs. Palate: balanced, elegant, spicy, long.

MAS ASTURIAS

Avda. de Madrid, s/n
24500 Villafranca del Bierzo (León)
☎: +34 650 654 492
jose_mas_asturias@hotmail.com
www.bodegamasasturias.com

Massuria 2011 T
mencía

90

Colour: cherry, garnet rim. Nose: balanced, ripe fruit, sweet spices, smoky. Palate: flavourful, spicy.

OTERO SANTÍN

Ortega y Gasset, 10
24402 Ponferrada (León)
☎: +34 987 410 965
adela@vinotecabenitootero.com

Otero Santín 2012 TC
mencía

89

Colour: deep cherry. Nose: sweet spices, smoky, ripe fruit. Palate: creamy, good structure, full, flavourful.

Otero Santín 2014 RD
mencía

88

Colour: rose, purple rim. Nose: complex, neat, fresh, powerfull, fresh fruit, red berry notes. Palate: fine bead, sweetness, fresh, fruity, flavourful.

Otero Santín Godello 2014 B
godello

88

Colour: bright straw, greenish rim. Nose: fresh fruit, dried flowers, fragrant herbs, balanced. Palate: flavourful, fruity, easy to drink.

Otero Santín Mencía s/c T
mencía

86

Valdecampo 2013 T Roble
mencía

86

PALACIO DE CANEDO

La Iglesia, s/n
24546 Canedo (León)
☎: +34 987 563 366
Fax: +34 987 567 000
info@pradaatope.es
www.pradaatope.es

Curia Plena 2010 T
mencía

88

Colour: deep cherry. Nose: ripe fruit, wild herbs, earthy notes, spicy, balsamic herbs. Palate: balanced, flavourful, long, balsamic.

Palacio de Canedo 2009 TR
mencía

88

Colour: dark-red cherry, garnet rim. Nose: fruit preserve, cocoa bean. Palate: balanced, flavourful, good structure, ripe fruit.

Palacio de Canedo 2014 RD
mencía

87

Colour: light cherry, bright. Nose: red berry notes, floral, expressive. Palate: powerful, fruity, fresh.

Palacio de Canedo 2014 T Maceración Carbónica
mencía

88

Colour: cherry, garnet rim. Nose: balsamic herbs, fresh fruit. Palate: green, balsamic, flavourful, dry.

Palacio de Canedo Godello 2014 B
godello

90

Colour: bright straw. Nose: balanced, neat, fresh, varietal. Palate: complex, rich, fruity, fresh, flavourful.

Palacio de Canedo Mencía 2009 TC

mencía

88 ♣

Colour: dark-red cherry. Nose: spicy, creamy oak, ripe fruit. Palate: creamy, spicy, sweetness, powerful, flavourful.

Palacio de Canedo Mencía 2014 T

mencía

87 ♣

Colour: cherry, garnet rim. Nose: scrubland, ripe fruit, candied fruit. Palate: balanced.

Picantal 2010 T Barrica

mencía

90 ♣

Colour: deep cherry. Nose: balanced, characterful, fruit expression, earthy notes. Palate: creamy, spicy, powerful, flavourful, fruity, sweet tannins.

PÉREZ CARAMÉS

Peña Picón, s/n
24500 Villafranca del Bierzo (León)
☎: +34 987 540 197
enoturismo@perezcarames.com
www.perezcarames.com

El Vino de Los Cónsules de Roma 2014 T

mencía

85

Valdaiga X 2014 T

mencía

86 ♣

REAL MERUELO

Alto de Urba. Patricia
24400 Ponferrada (León)
☎: +34 616 429 253
donmeruelo@hotmail.com

Don Meruelo 2006 TR

mencía

86

Don Meruelo 2012 B

godello

87

Colour: bright yellow. Nose: faded flowers, ripe fruit. Palate: correct, spicy, long.

RIBAS DEL CÚA

Finca Robledo A.C. 83
24540 Cacabelos (León)
☎: +34 987 971 018
Fax: +34 987 971 016
bodega@ribasdelcua.com
www.ribasdelcua.com

Ribas del Cúa Privilegio 2010 T

100% mencía

88

Colour: deep cherry. Nose: undergrowth, damp earth, ripe fruit, wet leather, animal reductive notes. Palate: lacks balance, good acidity, fine bitter notes, fruity.

RODRÍGUEZ SANZO

Manuel Azaña, 11
47014 (Valladolid)
☎: +34 983 150 150
Fax: +34 983 150 151
comunicacion@valsanzo.com
www.rodriguezsanzo.com

Sauron 2014 T Roble

87

Colour: cherry, purple rim. Nose: ripe fruit, roasted coffee. Palate: flavourful, spicy, powerful.

SILVA BROCO

Paradones
24516 Toral Vados (León)
☎: +34 615 276 894
Fax: +34 987 553 043
antoniosilvabroco@hotmail.com
www.silvabroco.es

Lagar de Caxan 2014 T

mencía

86

SOTO DEL VICARIO

Ctra. Cacabelos- San Clemente,
Pol. Ind. 908 Parcela 155
24547 San Clemente (León)
☎: +34 670 983 534
Fax: +34 926 666 029
sandra.luque@pagodelvicario.com
www.pagodelvicario.com

Go de Godello 2014 BFB

100% godello

89

Colour: bright yellow. Nose: expressive, dried herbs, ripe fruit, spicy. Palate: flavourful, fruity, good acidity, balanced.

Soto del Vicario Altos de San Clemente 2011 T

100% mencía

86

Soto del Vicario Men 2009 T
100% mencía

89

Colour: cherry, garnet rim. Nose: red berry notes, balanced, dried herbs. Palate: flavourful, spicy, fruity aftestaste.

THE PEPE'S WINE CO.
Cl. Doligencia, 6-K, 5º A
28018 Madrid (Madrid)
☎: +34 639 382 528
info@thepepeswine.com

Flor del Sil 2014 B
godello

87

Colour: bright straw. Nose: white flowers, fresh fruit, expressive. Palate: fruity, good acidity, balanced.

VEHEMENCIA S.G.F.
Pza. Ramón Carnicer, 17
24530 Villadecanes (León)
☎: +34 671 943 949
vehe-mencia@hotmail.com
www.vehemencia.com

Vehemencia 2014 T
mencía, alicante

82

VINOS DE ARGANZA
Río Ancares
24560 Toral de los Vados (León)
☎: +34 987 544 831
Fax: +34 987 563 532
admon@vinosdearganza.com
www.vinosdearganza.com

Encanto Charm Selección 2013 T
90

Colour: very deep cherry, garnet rim. Nose: ripe fruit, wild herbs, spicy, mineral. Palate: round tannins, long, balsamic.

Encanto Mencía 2012 T Roble
100% mencía

89

Colour: bright cherry. Nose: ripe fruit, sweet spices, creamy oak. Palate: flavourful, fruity, toasty.

Flavium Mencía Premium 2013 T
mencía

89

Colour: bright cherry, garnet rim. Nose: ripe fruit, wild herbs, spicy. Palate: fresh, fruity, long.

Flavium Selección 2013 T
mencía

90

Colour: cherry, garnet rim. Nose: red berry notes, ripe fruit, fragrant herbs, spicy, mineral. Palate: flavourful, balsamic, balanced.

Legado de Farro Godello 2014 B
godello

88

Colour: bright straw. Nose: white flowers, fresh fruit, fragrant herbs. Palate: flavourful, fruity, good acidity.

Legado de Farro Mencía Selección 2012 T
100% mencía

90

Colour: very deep cherry, garnet rim. Nose: expressive, complex, mineral, balsamic herbs, balanced. Palate: full, flavourful, round tannins.

Século Cepas Viejas 2013 T Roble
100% mencía

90

Colour: deep cherry. Nose: creamy oak, toasty, ripe fruit, balsamic herbs. Palate: balanced, spicy, long.

VINOS GUERRA

Avda. Constitución, 106
24540 Cacabelos (León)
☎: +34 987 546 150
Fax: +34 987 549 236
info@vinosdelbierzo.com
www.vinosguerra.com

Armas de Guerra 2014 B
30% godello, 70% dona blanca

87

Colour: bright straw. Nose: fresh fruit, wild herbs, dried herbs. Palate: flavourful, fruity, good acidity, balanced.

Armas de Guerra 2014 RD
mencía

86

Armas de Guerra Godello 2014 B
godello

88

Colour: bright straw. Nose: white flowers, fresh fruit, fragrant herbs, expressive. Palate: flavourful, fruity, good acidity, balanced.

Armas de Guerra Mencía 2011 TC
mencía

87

Colour: dark-red cherry, garnet rim. Nose: ripe fruit, warm, dried herbs. Palate: spicy, ripe fruit.

Armas de Guerra Mencía 2013 T Roble
mencía

86

Armas de Guerra Mencía 2014 T
mencía

87

Colour: cherry, purple rim. Nose: fresh fruit, red berry notes, floral, spicy. Palate: flavourful, fruity, good acidity.

Guerra 2008 TC
mencía

85

Guerra 2014 B
godello, dona blanca, palomino

85

Guerra 2014 RD
mencía

86

Guerra Mencía 2014 T
mencía

86

Guerra Tradición 2008 TC
100% mencía

86

Señorío del Bierzo Godello Cepas Únicas 2012 B
godello

91

Colour: bright yellow. Nose: balanced, expressive, sweet spices, elegant. Palate: fruity, fine bitter notes, ripe fruit, long.

Señorío del Bierzo Mencía Centenaria 2009 TR
mencía

89

Colour: very deep cherry, garnet rim. Nose: mineral, balsamic herbs, balanced, medium intensity, smoky. Palate: fruity, balanced, easy to drink, spicy.

Vinicio 2008 TC
mencía

85

Vinicio 2014 T
mencía

84

Vinicio Godello 2014 B
godello

85

Viña Oro 2014 B
godello, dona blanca, palomino

87

Colour: bright straw. Nose: closed, medium intensity, grassy. Palate: flavourful, dry, fruity, fresh.

Viña Oro 2014 RD
mencía

85

Viña Oro 2014 T
mencía

86

VINOS VALTUILLE

Promadelo
24530 Valtuille de Abajo (León)
☎: +34 987 562 165
info@vinosvaltuille.com
www.vinosvaltuille.com

Pago de Valdoneje 2014 T
mencía

88

Colour: deep cherry, purple rim. Nose: ripe fruit, wild herbs, floral, powerfull. Palate: flavourful, fruity, balanced.

Pago de Valdoneje 2014 T Roble
mencía

88

Colour: bright cherry. Nose: ripe fruit, sweet spices, expressive, lactic notes. Palate: flavourful, fruity, round tannins.

Pago de Valdoneje Viñas Viejas 2013 TC
mencía

90

Colour: cherry, garnet rim. Nose: fruit expression, red berry notes, varietal, expressive. Palate: balsamic, fruity, flavourful, dry.

VIÑA ALBARES

Camino Real, s/n
24310 Albares de la Ribera (León)
☎: +34 987 519 147
info@quintadelobispo.com
www.quintadelobispo.com

Puerta de Albares 2013 T
mencía

88

Colour: dark-red cherry. Nose: roasted coffee, varietal, red berry notes. Palate: spicy, flavourful, powerful, sweetness.

VIÑAS DEL BIERZO S.COOP.

Ctra. Ponferrada a Cacabelos, s/n
24410 Camponaraya (León)
☎: +34 987 463 009
Fax: +34 987 450 323
vdelbierzo@granbierzo.com
www.granbierzo.com

Fundación 1963 2010 TR
100% mencía

88

Colour: very deep cherry, garnet rim. Nose: mineral, balsamic herbs, balanced. Palate: full, flavourful, fine tannins.

Gran Bierzo 2010 TR
100% mencía

87

Colour: dark-red cherry. Nose: cocoa bean, smoky, ripe fruit. Palate: creamy, balsamic, flavourful, powerful.

Gran Bierzo 2011 TC
100% mencía

87

Colour: deep cherry, garnet rim. Nose: mineral, dry nuts, ripe fruit. Palate: balanced, spicy.

Gran Bierzo Origen 2013 T
100% mencía

90

Colour: dark-red cherry. Nose: cocoa bean, red berry notes, varietal, macerated fruit. Palate: balsamic, green, fruity, dry.

Marqués de Cornatel 2013 T Roble
100% mencía

89

Colour: cherry, garnet rim. Nose: premature reduction notes, ripe fruit, expressive, varietal. Palate: mineral, balsamic, flavourful.

Marqués de Cornatel 2014 B
100% godello

84

Naraya 2014 RD
100% mencía

82

Naraya 2014 T
100% mencía

88

Colour: cherry, garnet rim. Nose: closed, reduction notes, ripe fruit. Palate: fresh, fruity, balsamic, dry.

Valmagaz 2014 B
100% dona blanca

85

Valmagaz Mencía 2014 T
100% mencía

86

VIÑEDOS SINGULARES

Cuzco, 26 - 28, Nave 8 - 9
08030 Barcelona (Barcelona)
☎: +34 934 807 041
Fax: +34 934 807 076
info@vinedossingulares.com
www.vinedossingulares.com

Corral del Obispo 2013 T
mencía

90

Colour: very deep cherry, garnet rim. Nose: balsamic herbs, balanced, ripe fruit, varietal. Palate: full, flavourful, round tannins.

VIÑEDOS Y BODEGAS PITTACUM

De la Iglesia, 11
24546 Arganza (León)
☎: +34 987 548 054
Fax: +34 987 548 028
pittacum@pittacum.com
www.pittacum.com

Petit Pittacum 2014 RD
mencía

88

Colour: raspberry rose. Nose: powerfull, off-odours, candied fruit, fresh fruit, wild herbs. Palate: powerful, fruity, flavourful.

Petit Pittacum 2014 T
100% mencía

88

Colour: deep cherry. Nose: balanced, fresh, varietal, fruit expression, ripe fruit. Palate: elegant, round, sweet, fresh, flavourful.

Pittacum 2009 T Barrica
100% mencía

91

Colour: cherry, garnet rim. Nose: ripe fruit, wild herbs, earthy notes, spicy, balsamic herbs. Palate: balanced, flavourful, long, balsamic.

Pittacum Aurea 2009 TC
100% mencía

93

Colour: bright cherry. Nose: expressive, spicy, ripe fruit, scrubland, varietal. Palate: ripe fruit, long, good acidity, balanced.

VIÑOS DE ENCOSTAS

Florentino López Cuevillas, 6 1ºA
32500 O Carballiño (Ourense)
☎: +34 988 101 733
Fax: +34 988 488 174
miguel@losvinosdemiguel.com
www.xlsebio.es

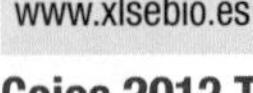

Coios 2012 T
mencía

90

Colour: deep cherry, purple rim. Nose: fruit expression, mineral, red berry notes, spicy. Palate: balanced, ripe fruit, long.

DO. BINISSALEM MALLORCA

CONSEJO REGULADOR

Celler de Rei, 9-1°
07350 Binissalem (Mallorca)
☎:+34 971 512 191 - Fax: +34 971 512 191
@: info@binissalemdo.com
www.binissalemdo.com

LOCATION:

In the central region on the island of Majorca. It covers the municipal areas of Santa María del Camí, Binissalem, Sencelles, Consell and Santa Eugenia.

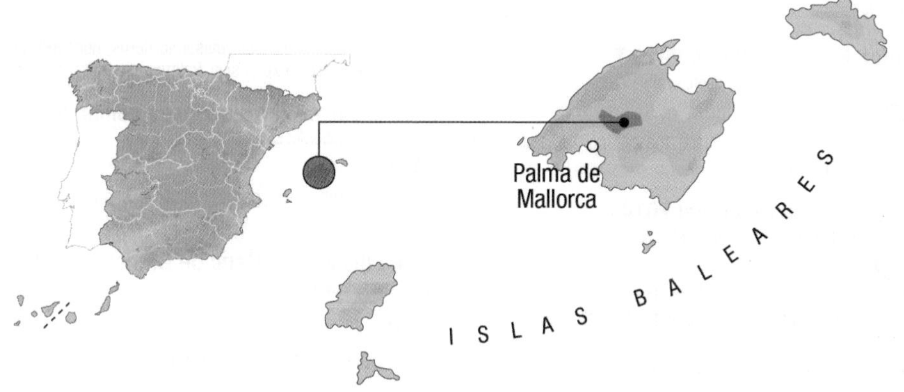

GRAPE VARIETIES:

WHITE: Moll or Prensal Blanc (46 Ha), Macabeo, Parellada, Moscatel and Chardonnay.
RED: Manto Negro, Callet, Tempranillo, Syrah, Monastrell, Cabernet Sauvignon, Gorgollassa, Giró Ros and Merlot.

FIGURES:

Vineyard surface: 605.99 – **Wine-Growers:** 123 – **Wineries:** 15 – **2014 Harvest rating:** N/A – **Production 14:** 1,568,380 litres – **Market percentages:** 80% National - 20% International.

SOIL:

The soil is of a brownish - grey or dun limey type, with limestone crusts on occasions. The slopes are quite gentle, and the vineyards are situated at an altitude ranging from 75 to 200 m.

CLIMATE:

Mild Mediterranean, with dry, hot summers and short winters. The average rainfall per year is around 450 mm. The production region is protected from the northerly winds by the Sierra de Tramuntana and the Sierra de Alfabia mountain ranges.

VINTAGE RATING

PEÑÍNGUIDE

2010	2011	2012	2013	2014
VERY GOOD	VERY GOOD	VERY GOOD	VERY GOOD	GOOD

BODEGA BINIAGUAL

Llogaret de Biniagual, Cami de Muro s/n
07350 Binissalem (Mallorca)
☎: +34 689 183 954
Fax: +34 971 886 108
info@bodegabiniagual.com
www.bodegabiniagual.com

Finca Biniagual Gran Verán 2011 TR
manto negro, syrah

93

Colour: cherry, garnet rim. Nose: balanced, complex, ripe fruit, spicy, tobacco. Palate: good structure, flavourful, round tannins, balanced.

Finca Biniagual Verán 2010 T
manto negro, cabernet sauvignon, syrah

89

Colour: cherry, garnet rim. Nose: toasty, ripe fruit. Palate: balanced, spicy, long.

Memòries de Biniagual 2014 B
prensal, chardonnay, moscatel de alejandría

88

Colour: bright straw. Nose: white flowers, fresh fruit, expressive. Palate: flavourful, fruity, good acidity, balanced.

Memòries de Biniagual 2014 RD
manto negro

85

BODEGAS JOSÉ L. FERRER

Conquistador, 103
07350 Binissalem (Illes Balears)
☎: +34 971 511 050
Fax: +34 971 870 084
info@vinosferrer.com
www.vinosferrer.com

José L. Ferrer 2012 TC
manto negro, cabernet sauvignon, tempranillo, syrah, callet

85

José L. Ferrer 2012 TR
manto negro, cabernet sauvignon, callet

89

Colour: light cherry, garnet rim. Nose: ripe fruit, characterful, warm. Palate: balsamic, balanced, spicy, fruity aftestaste.

José L. Ferrer Veritas 2014 B
moll, chardonnay

87

Colour: bright yellow. Nose: ripe fruit, powerfull, toasty, aged wood nuances, pattiserie. Palate: flavourful, fruity, spicy, toasty, long.

José L. Ferrer Veritas 2007 TR
manto negro, callet, cabernet sauvignon

89

Colour: cherry, garnet rim. Nose: ripe fruit, wild herbs, earthy notes, spicy, balsamic herbs. Palate: balanced, flavourful, long, balsamic.

José L. Ferrer Veritas 2013 BN
moll, otras

84

José L. Ferrer Veritas Dolç 2014 Moscatel
moscatel

88

Colour: bright yellow. Nose: balsamic herbs, honeyed notes, floral, sweet spices, expressive. Palate: rich, fruity, flavourful.

José L. Ferrer Veritas Vinyes Velles 2012 T
manto negro, cabernet sauvignon, syrah, callet

87

Colour: dark-red cherry, garnet rim. Nose: characterful, warm, grassy, scrubland. Palate: correct, ripe fruit, spicy.

José Luis Ferrer Blanc de Blancs 2014 B
moll, chardonnay, moscatel

86

José Luis Ferrer Veritas Roig 2014 RD
manto negro, callet, syrah

87

Colour: light cherry, bright. Nose: white flowers, fresh, red berry notes. Palate: correct, fine bitter notes, easy to drink.

Pedra de Binissalem 2013 T
manto negro, cabernet sauvignon

88 🌱

Colour: light cherry, garnet rim. Nose: balsamic herbs, spicy, ripe fruit, balanced, characterful. Palate: correct, fine bitter notes, easy to drink.

Pedra de Binissalem Rosat 2014 RD
manto negro, cabernet sauvignon

85 🌱

BODEGUES MACIÀ BATLE

Camí Coanegra, s/n
07320 Santa María del Camí
(Illes Balears)
☎: +34 971 140 014
Fax: +34 971 140 086
correo@maciabatle.com
www.maciabatle.com

Dos Marias 2013 T Roble
40% manto negro, 25% cabernet sauvignon, 20% merlot, 15% syrah

86

LLum 2014 B
65% prensal, 35% chardonnay

89

Colour: bright yellow. Nose: white flowers, fragrant herbs, citrus fruit, ripe fruit. Palate: flavourful, fruity, good acidity.

Macià Batle 2012 TC
40% manto negro, 30% merlot, 20% cabernet sauvignon, 10% syrah

88

Colour: deep cherry, purple rim. Nose: toasty, ripe fruit, balsamic herbs, warm. Palate: balanced, spicy, long.

Macià Batle 2013 T
35% manto negro, 35% merlot, 30% cabernet sauvignon

88

Colour: light cherry. Nose: red berry notes, floral, balsamic herbs. Palate: fresh, fruity, light-bodied.

Macià Batle 2014 RD
35% manto negro, 35% merlot, 30% cabernet sauvignon

87

Colour: light cherry. Nose: fragrant herbs, varietal, fresh. Palate: fine bitter notes, balanced, fruity.

Macià Batle Blanc de Blancs 2014 B
55% prensal, 40% chardonnay, 5% moscatel

88

Colour: bright straw. Nose: white flowers, fresh fruit, fragrant herbs, expressive. Palate: flavourful, fruity, good acidity, balanced.

Macià Batle Blanc Dolç 2010 B
85% prensal, 15% moscatel

90

Colour: bright yellow. Nose: balsamic herbs, honeyed notes, sweet spices. Palate: rich, fruity, flavourful, elegant, concentrated.

Macià Batle Margalida Llompart 2014 RD
80% manto negro, 10% merlot, 10% cabernet sauvignon

88

Colour: onion pink. Nose: elegant, red berry notes, fragrant herbs, citrus fruit. Palate: flavourful, good acidity, fine bitter notes.

Macià Batle Negre Dolç 2008 T
85% manto negro, 15% syrah

90

Colour: light cherry, orangey edge. Nose: spicy, fruit preserve, dried herbs. Palate: flavourful, full, good acidity.

Macià Batle Reserva Privada 2011 TR
50% manto negro, 20% merlot, 20% syrah, 10% cabernet sauvignon

89

Colour: dark-red cherry, orangey edge. Nose: toasty, ripe fruit, balsamic herbs, tobacco. Palate: balanced, spicy, long.

P. de Marìa 2010 T
55% manto negro, 20% syrah, 15% cabernet sauvignon, 10% merlot

93

Colour: dark-red cherry, orangey edge. Nose: scrubland, wild herbs, expressive, characterful. Palate: flavourful, spicy, long, good acidity.

P. de Marìa 2011 T
55% manto negro, 25% syrah, 10% cabernet sauvignon, 10% merlot

92

Colour: cherry, garnet rim. Nose: ripe fruit, wild herbs, earthy notes, spicy, balsamic herbs. Palate: balanced, flavourful, long, balsamic.

CA'N VERDURA VITICULTORS

S'Era, 6
07350 Binissalem (Illes Balears)
☎: +34 695 817 038
tomeuverdura@gmail.com

Ca'n Verdura 2014 T
manto negro, monastrell, merlot, cabernet sauvignon

86

Ca'n Verdura Supernova 2013 TC
manto negro

88

Colour: light cherry. Nose: ripe fruit, balsamic herbs, spicy, tobacco. Palate: balanced, spicy, long.

Ca'n Verdura Supernova Blanc 2014 B
moll

89

Colour: bright straw, greenish rim. Nose: expressive, characterful, scrubland, wild herbs. Palate: flavourful, rich, spicy, ripe fruit.

JAUME DE PUNTIRÓ

Pza. Nova, 23
07320 Santa María del Camí
(Illes Balears)
☎: +34 971 620 023
pere@vinsjaumedepuntiro.com
www.vinsjaumedepuntiro.com

Buc 2011 TC
manto negro, cabernet sauvignon

87

Colour: dark-red cherry, orangey edge. Nose: fruit preserve, sweet spices, cocoa bean. Palate: flavourful, good structure.

Daurat 2013 BFB

88

Colour: bright yellow. Nose: ripe fruit, powerfull, toasty. Palate: flavourful, fruity, spicy, toasty, long.

J.P. 2007 TR
manto negro, cabernet sauvignon

90

Colour: cherry, garnet rim. Nose: ripe fruit, old leather, tobacco. Palate: correct, flavourful, spicy, ripe fruit, long.

Jaume de Puntiró Blanc 2014 B
prensal

87

Colour: bright straw. Nose: scrubland, expressive, varietal, dried flowers. Palate: ripe fruit, flavourful.

Jaume de Puntiró Carmesí 2012 T
manto negro, callet, syrah, cabernet sauvignon

90

Colour: dark-red cherry. Nose: wild herbs, earthy notes, spicy, ripe fruit, fruit preserve. Palate: balanced, flavourful, long.

Jaume de Puntiró Moscatel Dolç 2012 B
moscatel

85

Porprat 2012 T
merlot, manto negro

87

Colour: cherry, garnet rim. Nose: fine reductive notes, wet leather, aged wood nuances. Palate: spicy, long, toasty.

TIANNA NEGRE

Cami des Mitjans, Parcel·la 67 – Pol. 7
07350 Binissalem (Illes Balears)
☎: +34 971 886 826
Fax: +34 971 226 201
info@tiannanegre.com
www.tiannanegre.com

El Columpio 2014 T
manto negro, merlot, syrah, callet, cabernet sauvignon

88

Colour: bright cherry. Nose: ripe fruit, sweet spices, creamy oak, expressive. Palate: flavourful, fruity, round tannins, smoky aftertaste, toasty.

El Columpio Blanc 2014 B
prensal, chardonnay, sauvignon blanc

87

Colour: bright straw. Nose: white flowers, expressive, ripe fruit, balanced. Palate: flavourful, fruity, good acidity, balanced.

Ses Nines Blanc 2014 B Barrica
prensal, chardonnay, moscatel

89

Colour: bright yellow. Nose: ripe fruit, powerfull, toasty, pattiserie, sweet spices. Palate: flavourful, fruity, spicy, toasty, long.

Ses Nines Negre 2014 T
manto negro, merlot, syrah, callet, cabernet sauvignon

90

Colour: cherry, purple rim. Nose: expressive, red berry notes, floral, ripe fruit, earthy notes. Palate: flavourful, fruity, good acidity.

Ses Nines Selecció 2013 T
manto negro, cabernet sauvignon, callet, syrah, merlot

91

Colour: light cherry, garnet rim. Nose: ripe fruit, dried herbs, characterful. Palate: balanced, spicy, fruity.

Tianna Bocchoris Negre 2013 T

90

Colour: very deep cherry, garnet rim. Nose: complex, balsamic herbs, balanced, earthy notes. Palate: full, flavourful, round tannins.

Tianna Negre 2013 T
manto negro, callet, cabernet sauvignon, syrah

91

Colour: cherry, garnet rim. Nose: ripe fruit, wild herbs, earthy notes, spicy, balsamic herbs. Palate: balanced, flavourful, long, balsamic.

Velorosé 2014 RD
100% manto negro

89

Colour: salmon, bright. Nose: floral, wild herbs, fruit expression, expressive. Palate: flavourful, complex, balanced, elegant.

VINS NADAL

Ramón Llull, 2
07350 Binissalem (Illes Balears)
☎: +34 971 511 058
Fax: +34 971 870 150
albaflor@vinsnadal.es
www.vinsnadal.es

Albaflor 2009 TR
manto negro, cabernet sauvignon, merlot

87

Colour: cherry, garnet rim. Nose: fine reductive notes, wet leather, aged wood nuances. Palate: spicy, long, toasty.

Albaflor 2010 TC
manto negro, cabernet sauvignon, merlot

87

Colour: dark-red cherry. Nose: sweet spices, fruit preserve. Palate: flavourful, fruity, toasty, round tannins, balsamic.

Albaflor 2014 B
prensal, macabeo, moscatel

83

Albaflor 2014 RD
merlot, manto negro, cabernet sauvignon, syrah

88

Colour: rose, purple rim. Nose: floral, expressive, red berry notes, ripe fruit. Palate: powerful, fruity, fresh.

VINYA TAUJANA

Balanguera, 40
07142 Santa Eugenia (Illes Balears)
☎: +34 971 144 494
Fax: +34 971 144 494
vinyataujana@gmail.com
www.vinyataujana.es

Torrent Fals 2012 TC
47% manto negro, 41% syrah, 12% merlot

87

Colour: cherry, garnet rim. Nose: ripe fruit, fruit preserve, cocoa bean, dried herbs. Palate: fruity, correct, easy to drink.

Vinya Taujana Blanc de Blanc 2014 B
100% prensal

86

Vinya Taujana Rosat 2014 RD
100% manto negro

84

VINYES I VINS CA SA PADRINA

Camí dels Horts, s/n
07140 Sencelles (Illes Balears)
☎: +34 660 211 939
Fax: +34 971 874 370
cellermantonegro@gmail.com

Mollet Suñer Bibiloni 2014 B Joven
prensal, chardonnay

90

Colour: bright yellow. Nose: white flowers, expressive, ripe fruit. Palate: fruity, good acidity, balanced.

Montenegre 2014 T Roble
manto negro, merlot, syrah, cabernet sauvignon

89

Colour: bright cherry. Nose: ripe fruit, sweet spices, creamy oak, expressive, warm. Palate: flavourful, fruity, toasty, round tannins.

Rossat De Ca Sa Padrina 2014 RD
manto negro, merlot

84

DO. BIZKAIKO TXAKOLINA

CONSEJO REGULADOR

B° Mendibile, 42
48940 Leioa (Bizkaia)
☎ :+34 946 076 071 - Fax: +34 946 076 072
@: info@bizkaikotxacolina.org
www.bizkaikotxakolina.org

LOCATION:

In the province of Vizcaya. The production region covers both coastal areas and other areas inland.

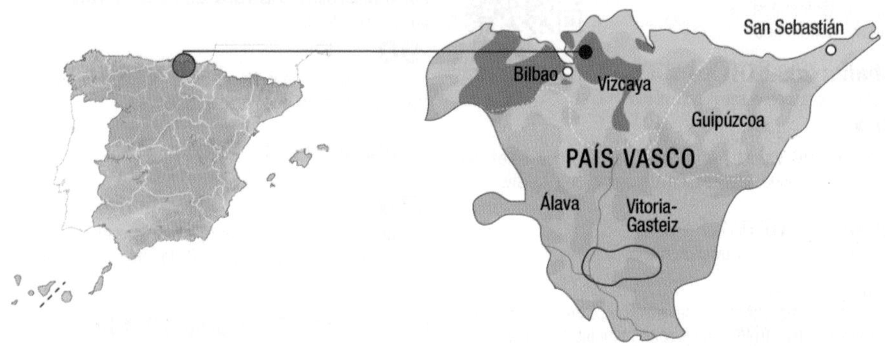

GRAPE VARIETIES:

WHITE: Hondarrabi Zuri, Folle Blanche.
RED: Hondarrabi Beltza.

FIGURES:

Vineyard surface: 383 – **Wine-Growers:** 210 – **Wineries:** 45 – **2014 Harvest rating:** Excellent – **Production 14:** 1,569,634 litres – **Market percentages:** 96.96% National - 3.04% International.

SOIL:

Mainly clayey, although slightly acidic on occasions, with a fairly high organic matter content.

CLIMATE:

Quite humid and mild due to the influence of the Bay of Biscay which tempers the temperatures. Fairly abundant rainfall, with an average of 1,000 to 1,300 mm per year.

VINTAGE RATING

PEÑÍNGUIDE

2010	2011	2012	2013	2014
EXCELLENT	EXCELLENT	EXCELLENT	VERY GOOD	VERY GOOD

ABIO TXAKOLINA

Barrio Elexalde, 5 Caserío Basigo
48130 Bakio (Bizkaia)
☎: +34 657 794 754
www.abiotxakolina.com

Abio Txakolina 2014 B

88

Colour: bright straw. Nose: white flowers, fragrant herbs, expressive. Palate: flavourful, fruity, good acidity, balanced.

Gorena 2014 B

86

AMEZKETAKO TXAKOLINA

Santa Marina, 4
48215 Iurreta (Vizcaya)
☎: +34 946 813 800

Amezketa 2014 B

86

AXPE (JOSE A. BILBAO)

Bº Atxondoa, Cº Axpe, 13
48300 Markina - Xemein (Bizkaia)
☎: +34 946 168 285
Fax: +34 946 168 285
www.axpesagardotegia.com

Axpe 2014 B

hondarrabi zuri, hondarribi Zerratia, sauvignon blanc

89

Colour: bright straw. Nose: white flowers, fresh fruit, fragrant herbs, expressive. Palate: flavourful, fruity, good acidity, balanced.

BASALBEITIKO TXAKOLINA

Barrio Goitioltza, 37 Caserío Basalbeiti
48196 Lezama
☎: +34 944 556 146

Basalbeitiko 2014 B

85

BIZKAIBARNE

Bº Murueta s/n
48410 Orozko (Bizkaia)
☎: +34 636 277 207
bizkaibarne@gmail.com
www.bizkaibarne.com

Egiaenea 2013 B

100% hondarrabi zuri zerratia

90

Colour: bright straw. Nose: faded flowers, fine lees, expressive. Palate: full, flavourful, long.

Egiaenea 2014 B

100% hondarrabi zuri zerratia

90

Colour: bright straw. Nose: grassy, wild herbs, white flowers, expressive. Palate: balanced, fine bitter notes, good acidity.

Egiaenea sobre Lías 2012 B

100% hondarrabi zuri zerratia

92

Colour: yellow. Nose: fine lees, dried herbs, ripe fruit, candied fruit, citrus fruit, dried flowers. Palate: flavourful, good acidity, fine bitter notes.

Marko 2014 B

100% hondarrabi zuri zerratia

91

Colour: bright straw. Nose: white flowers, fragrant herbs, expressive, fine lees, ripe fruit. Palate: flavourful, fruity, good acidity, balanced.

Mendiolagan 2014 B

100% hondarrabi zuri

89

Colour: bright straw. Nose: saline, fresh fruit, balanced, floral, expressive. Palate: balanced, fine bitter notes, long.

Otxanduri 2014 B

100% hondarrabi zuri

89

Colour: bright straw. Nose: medium intensity, white flowers, ripe fruit. Palate: flavourful, balsamic, good acidity, fine bitter notes.

BODEGA ADOS BASARTE

Urkitzaurrealde, 4
48130 Bakio (Bizkaia)
☎: +34 605 026 115
basarte@basarte.net
www.basarte.net

Ados 2014 B

100% hondarrabi zuri

90

Colour: bright straw. Nose: saline, fresh, white flowers, expressive, balanced. Palate: full, flavourful, long, fine bitter notes.

BODEGA BERROJA

Ctra. de Zugastieta al Balcón
de Bizkaia. Ajuria
48392 Muxika (Bizkaia)
☎: +34 944 106 254
Fax: +34 946 309 390
txakoli@bodegaberroja.com
www.bodegaberroja.com

Txakoli Aguirrebeko 2014 B

85% hondarrabi zuri, 10% riesling, 5% folle blanch

87

Colour: straw. Nose: medium intensity, ripe fruit, floral, wild herbs. Palate: correct, easy to drink, good acidity.

Txakoli Berroja 2013 B

80% hondarrabi zuri, 20% riesling

91

Colour: bright yellow. Nose: wild herbs, dried herbs, dried flowers, ripe fruit. Palate: rich, full, long.

BODEGA ELIZALDE

Barrio Mendraka, 1
48230 Elorrio (Bizkaia)
☎: +34 946 820 000
Fax: +34 946 820 000
kerixa@gmail.com
www.mendraka.eus

Mendraka 2014 B

hondarrabi zuri zerratu

90

Colour: bright yellow. Nose: faded flowers, balanced, expressive, ripe fruit. Palate: full, flavourful, good acidity, fine bitter notes.

BODEGA ERDIKOETXE

Goitioltza, 38
48196 Lezama (Bizkaia)
☎: +34 625 700 554
erdikoetxelandetxea@hotmail.com
bizkaikotxakolina.eus/bodegas/bodega-erdikoetxe

Erdikoetxe 2014 B

hondarrabi zuri, gross manseng

86

Erdikoetxe 2014 T

hondarrabi beltza

84

BODEGA HARIZPE

Eguidazu Kaia, 19
48700 Ondarroa (Bizkaia)
☎: +34 615 730 615
txakoliharizpe@gmail.com
www.harizpe.com

Harizpe 2014 B

50% hondarrabi zuri, 45% petit corbu, 5% riesling

88

Colour: bright straw. Nose: fresh fruit, fragrant herbs, expressive. Palate: flavourful, fruity, good acidity, balanced.

BODEGA TALLERI

Barrio Erroteta s/n
48115 Morga (Bizkaia)
☎: +34 944 651 689
info@bodegatalleri.com
www.bodegatalleri.com

Bitxia 2014 B

hondarrabi zuri, hondarrabi zuri zerratia

87

Colour: bright straw. Nose: grassy, fresh, citrus fruit. Palate: good acidity, fine bitter notes, easy to drink.

Bitxia Oilar Begi 2014 RD

hondarrabi beltza

84

Bitxia Selección 2014 B

hondarrabi zuri

88

Colour: bright straw. Nose: sweet spices, ripe fruit, white flowers. Palate: rich, flavourful, ripe fruit, long.

TX 16 2014 B

hondarrabi zuri

91

Colour: bright straw. Nose: white flowers, fine lees, dried herbs, ripe fruit, citrus fruit, spicy. Palate: flavourful, fruity, good acidity, elegant, rich, full.

BODEGA TXAKOLI URIARTE

Bº Acillcona-Cº Eguskiza
48113 Fika (Bizkaia)
☎: +34 946 153 140
Fax: +34 946 153 535
info@txakoli-uriarte.com
www.txakoli-uriarte.com

Uriarte 2014 B

87

Colour: bright straw. Nose: fresh fruit, wild herbs, fresh. Palate: fruity, good acidity, easy to drink.

Uriarte Especial Berezia 2014 B

88

Colour: bright straw. Nose: white flowers, citrus fruit. Palate: correct, easy to drink, good finish, fruity, fresh, good acidity.

BODEGA ULIBARRI

Caserío Isuskiza Handi, 1 Barrio Zaldu
48192 Gordexola (Bizkaia)
☎: +34 665 725 735
ulibarriartzaiak@gmail.com

Artzai 2012 BFB

86

Artzai 2013 B

87

Colour: yellow, pale. Nose: citrus fruit, faded flowers, dried flowers, spicy, toasty. Palate: flavourful, fruity, ripe fruit, correct, fine bitter notes.

Ulibarri 2013 B

87

Colour: yellow, pale. Nose: medium intensity, ripe fruit, dried flowers. Palate: correct, easy to drink, fine bitter notes.

BODEGAS DE GALDAMES S.L.

El Bentorro, 4
48191 Galdames (Bizkaia)
☎: +34 627 992 063
Fax: +34 946 100 107
info@vinasulibarria.com
www.vinasulibarria.com

Torre de Loizaga Bigarren 2014 B

86

BODEGAS GORKA IZAGIRRE

Barrio Legina, s/n
48195 Larrabetzu (Bizkaia)
☎: +34 946 742 706
Fax: +34 946 741 221
txakoli@gorkaizagirre.com
www.gorkaizagirre.com

42 By Eneko Atxa 2013 B

100% hondarrabi zerratia

91

Colour: bright yellow. Nose: white flowers, fine lees, dried herbs, ripe fruit, citrus fruit, faded flowers. Palate: flavourful, good acidity, spicy.

Aretxondo 2014 B

50% hondarrabi zuri, 45% hondarrabi zerratia, 5% mune mahatsa

90

Colour: bright straw. Nose: expressive, balanced, wild herbs, fresh fruit, floral. Palate: good acidity, balanced, fresh.

Arima de Gorka Izagirre Vendimia Tardía 2013 B

100% hondarrabi zerratia

90

Colour: bright yellow. Nose: citrus fruit, faded flowers, ripe fruit, honeyed notes, sweet spices. Palate: rich, flavourful, good acidity, balanced.

E-Gala 2014 B

65% hondarrabi zuri, 35% hondarrabi zerratia

88

Colour: bright straw. Nose: medium intensity, ripe fruit, floral, grassy, fresh. Palate: correct, easy to drink.

G22 de Gorka Izagirre 2012 B

100% hondarrabi zerratia

91

Colour: yellow, pale. Nose: faded flowers, ripe fruit, complex, powerfull, expressive. Palate: good structure, flavourful, full.

Garena 2014 B

80% hondarrabi zerratia, 20% hondarrabi zuri

90

Colour: bright straw. Nose: white flowers, fine lees, dried herbs, ripe fruit, citrus fruit. Palate: flavourful, fruity, good acidity, elegant, long.

Garitza 2014 B

75% hondarrabi zerratia, 25% hondarrabi zuri

90

Colour: bright straw. Nose: white flowers, fresh fruit, fragrant herbs, expressive. Palate: flavourful, fruity, good acidity, balanced.

Gorka Izagirre 2014 B
50% hondarrabi zuri, 50% hondarrabi zerratia

90

Colour: yellow. Nose: white flowers, faded flowers, citrus fruit, ripe fruit, balanced. Palate: rich, flavourful, long.

Munetaberri 2014 B

87

Colour: bright straw. Nose: white flowers, expressive, ripe fruit, dried herbs. Palate: fruity, good acidity, balanced.

Saratsu 2014 B
100% hondarrabi zerratia

89

Colour: bright yellow. Nose: faded flowers, powerfull, ripe fruit. Palate: fresh, flavourful, good acidity, fine bitter notes.

Uixar 2014 B
100% hondarrabi zerratia

89

Colour: bright straw. Nose: dried herbs, ripe fruit. Palate: flavourful, fruity, good acidity, balanced.

BODEGAS ITSAS MENDI

Barrio Arane, 3
48300 Gernika (Bizkaia)
☎: +34 946 270 316
Fax: +34 946 251 032
info@bodegasitsasmendi.com
www.bodegasitsasmendi.com

Eklipse Itsas Mendi 2012 T
65% pinot noir, 35% hondarrabi beltza

90

Colour: dark-red cherry, garnet rim. Nose: dried flowers, scrubland, ripe fruit, spicy. Palate: balanced, good acidity, flavourful.

Itsas Artizar 2011 B
hondarrabi zuri

90

Colour: yellow. Nose: spicy, toasty, fine lees, faded flowers, complex. Palate: flavourful, balanced, ripe fruit, long, rich.

Itsas Artizar 2012 B
hondarrabi zuri

89

Colour: yellow. Nose: faded flowers, sweet spices, ripe fruit. Palate: rich, flavourful, spicy, ripe fruit.

Itsas Mendi Urezti Dulce Natural 2011 B
90% hondarrabi zuri zerratie, 10% izkiriot handi

93

Colour: bright yellow. Nose: fine lees, citrus fruit, honeyed notes, faded flowers, complex. Palate: flavourful, fruity, good acidity, elegant.

Itsasmendi 2014 B
hondarrabi zuri, hondarrabi zuri zerratie

88

Colour: straw. Nose: floral, fresh, grassy, dried flowers, saline. Palate: correct, easy to drink, flavourful, fine bitter notes.

Itsasmendi nº 7 2013 B
80% hondarrabi zuri zerratie, 20% riesling

89

Colour: bright yellow. Nose: fresh, fragrant herbs, citrus fruit, balanced. Palate: balanced, fine bitter notes, good acidity.

Itsasmendi nº 7 Magnum 2012 B
80% hondarrabi zuri zerratie, 20% riesling

93

Colour: bright yellow. Nose: complex, expressive, ripe fruit, fine lees, faded flowers. Palate: elegant, balsamic, spicy, good structure, full.

DONIENE GORRONDONA TXAKOLINA

Gibelorratzagako San Pelaio, 1
48130 Bakio (Bizkaia)
☎: +34 946 194 795
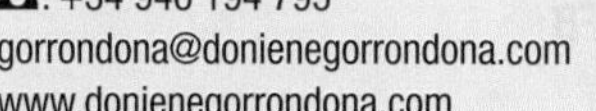
gorrondona@donienegorrondona.com
www.donienegorrondona.com

Artxanda 2014 B
hondarrabi zuri

87

Colour: bright straw. Nose: medium intensity, fresh fruit, fresh. Palate: balanced, correct, good finish.

Doniene 2012 BFB
100% hondarrabi zuri

89

Colour: yellow, pale. Nose: creamy oak, sweet spices, lees reduction notes. Palate: rich, flavourful, ripe fruit, long, smoky aftertaste.

Doniene 2014 B
100% hondarrabi zuri

90

Colour: bright straw. Nose: white flowers, fresh fruit, fragrant herbs, expressive. Palate: flavourful, fruity, good acidity, balanced.

Gorrondona 2014 B
hondarrabi zuri

89

Colour: bright straw. Nose: fresh fruit, fragrant herbs, expressive, saline. Palate: flavourful, fruity, good acidity, balanced, long.

Gorrondona 2014 T
hondarrabi beltza

87

Colour: deep cherry, purple rim. Nose: herbaceous, grassy, red berry notes. Palate: flavourful, fruity, balsamic.

GARKALDE TXAKOLINA

Barrio Goitioltza, 8 - Caserio Garkalde
48196 Lezama
☎: +34 944 556 412
garkaldetxakolina@hotmail.com

Garkalde Txakolina 2014 B

87

Colour: bright straw. Nose: expressive, fresh fruit, wild herbs, dried flowers. Palate: balanced, fine bitter notes, good acidity.

GURE AHALEGINAK

Barrio Ibazurra, 1
48460 Orduña (Bizkaia)
☎: +34 945 384 126
Fax: +34 945 384 126
a_larrazabal@hotmail.com
www.gureahaleginak.com

Filoxera 2013 T
hondarrabi beltza

82

Gure Ahaleginak 2014 B
hondarrabi zuri

86

JOSÉ ETXEBARRÍA URRUTIA

Txonebarri-C. Igartua, s/n
48110 Gatika (Bizkaia)
☎: +34 946 742 010

Txakoli Etxebarría 2014 B

86

KANDI

48392 Muxika (Bizcaia)
☎: +34 946 258 040
kandisat@kandisat.e.telefonica.net

Kandi 2014 B

87

Colour: bright straw. Nose: fine lees, dried herbs, powerfull. Palate: flavourful, ripe fruit, long, fine bitter notes.

MAGALARTE LEZAMA

B. Garaioltza, 92 B
48196 Lezama (Bizkaia)
☎: +34 636 621 455
Fax: +34 944 556 508
www.magalartelezamatxakolina.com

Magalarte Iñaki Aretxabaleta 2014 BFB

88

Colour: bright yellow. Nose: ripe fruit, toasty, sweet spices. Palate: flavourful, fruity, spicy, toasty, long.

Magalarte Iñaki Aretxabaleta 2014 B

88

Colour: yellow. Nose: ripe fruit, floral, wild herbs. Palate: balanced, fine bitter notes, good acidity.

Sagastibeltza Karrantza 2014 B

88

Colour: bright yellow. Nose: expressive, dried herbs, ripe fruit, spicy. Palate: flavourful, fruity, good acidity, balanced.

MAGALARTE ZAMUDIO

Arteaga Auzoa, 107
48170 Zamudio (Bizkaia)
☎: +34 630 109 686
Fax: +34 944 521 431
magalarte@gmail.com

Artebakarra 2014 B
hondarrabi zuri, petit corbu, petit manseng

86

Magalarte Zamudio 2014 B
hondarrabi zuri, petit corbu, riesling

88

Colour: bright straw. Nose: medium intensity, fresh fruit, grassy, saline. Palate: fine bitter notes, easy to drink, good acidity.

Zabalondo 2014 B
hondarrabi zuri, petit corbu, riesling, petit manseng

87

Colour: straw. Nose: medium intensity, floral, fresh fruit, citrus fruit. Palate: correct, easy to drink, fine bitter notes.

MERRUTXU

Caserio Merrutxu, Bº Arboliz
48311 Ibarrangelu (Bizkaia)
☎: +34 946 276 435
info@merrutxu.com
www.txakolibizkaia.com

Merrutxu 2014 B
hondarrabi zuri, chardonnay

87

Colour: bright straw. Nose: fresh fruit, wild herbs, balanced. Palate: correct, fine bitter notes, good acidity.

TXAKOLI AMUNATEGI

San Bartolomé, 57
48350 Busturia (Bizkaia)
☎: +34 685 737 398
anton.aranburu@gmail.com
www.amunategi.eu

Amunategi 2014 B

hondarrabi zuri

88

Colour: bright straw. Nose: medium intensity, fresh, saline, dried flowers. Palate: good acidity, balanced, fine bitter notes.

TXAKOLI LARRABE

Barrio Garaioltza, 103 - Caserío Usategi
48196 Lezama (Bizkaia)
☎: +34 944 556 491

Txakoli Larrabe 2014 B

87

Colour: bright yellow. Nose: white flowers, ripe fruit, balanced, powerfull. Palate: good acidity, fine bitter notes, fruity.

TXAKOLI OXINBALTZA

Barrio Magunas, 27
48391 Muxika (Bizkaia)
☎: +34 686 345 131
oxinbaltza@oxinbaltza.com
www.oxinbaltza.com

Katan 2014 B

hondarrabi zuri

88

Colour: bright straw. Nose: faded flowers, fine lees, spicy. Palate: flavourful, balsamic, long.

TXAKOLI SASINES

Barrio Bersonaga, 33 - Caserio Sasines
48195 Larrabetzu
☎: +34 944 558 196

Sasine 2014 B

89

Colour: bright straw. Nose: white flowers, fresh fruit. Palate: flavourful, fruity, good acidity, balanced.

TXAKOLI TXABARRI

Juan Antonio del Yermo no1 4ºC
48860 Zalla (Bizkaia)
☎: +34 625 708 114
Fax: +34 946 390 947
txabarri@txakolitxabarri.com
www.txakolitxabarri.com

Abeitxa 2014 B

87

Colour: bright straw. Nose: balanced, saline, fresh fruit, wild herbs. Palate: good acidity, balanced, correct, fine bitter notes.

Txabarri 2014 RD

83

Txabarri 2014 T

84

Txakoli Txabarri 2014 B

85

Txakoli Txabarri Extra 2014 B

87

Colour: straw. Nose: medium intensity, ripe fruit, floral, wild herbs. Palate: correct, easy to drink, flavourful.

TXOÑE

Iguatua, 25
48110 Gatika
☎: +34 646 514 154
kepa@larrabeiti.com

Butroi 2014 B

87

Colour: straw. Nose: medium intensity, ripe fruit, grassy. Palate: correct, easy to drink.

VIRGEN DE LOREA

Barrio de Lorea s/n
48860 Otxaran-Zalla (Bizkaia)
☎: +34 944 242 680
Fax: +34 946 670 521
virgendelorea@spankor.com
www.bodegasvirgendelorea.com

Aretxaga 2014 B

hondarrabi zuri, folle blanch

89

Colour: bright yellow. Nose: ripe fruit, dried flowers, fine lees, powerfull. Palate: rich, flavourful, long.

Señorío de Otxaran 2014 B

90

Colour: bright yellow. Nose: expressive, dried herbs, ripe fruit, spicy, faded flowers. Palate: flavourful, fruity, good acidity, balanced.

DO. BULLAS

CONSEJO REGULADOR

Balsa, 26
30180 Bullas (Murcia)
☎ :+34 968 652 601 - Fax: +968 652 601
@: consejoregulador@vinosdebullas.es
www.vinosdebullas.es

LOCATION:

In the province of Murcia. It covers the municipal areas of Bullas, Cehegín, Mula and Ricote, and several vineyards in the vicinity of Calasparra, Moratalla and Lorca.

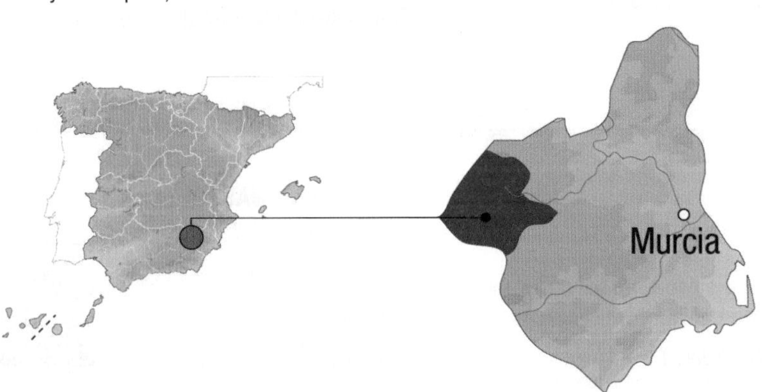

GRAPE VARIETIES:

WHITE: Macabeo (main), Airén, Chardonnay, Malvasía, Moscatel de Grano Menudo and Sauvignon Blanc.
RED: Monastrell (main), Petit Verdot, Tempranillo, Cabernet Sauvignon, Syrah, Merlot and Garnacha.

FIGURES:

Vineyard surface: 1,793 – **Wine-Growers:** 401 – **Wineries:** 10 – **2014 Harvest rating:** Very Good – **Production 14:** 1,450,558 litres – **Market percentages:** 62.9% National - 37.1% International.

SOIL:

Brownish - grey limey soil, with limestone crusts, and alluvial. The terrain is rugged and determined by the layout of the little valleys, each with their own microclimate. Distinction can be made between 3 areas: one to the north north - east with an altitude of 400 – 500 m; another in the central region, situated at an altitude of 500 – 600 m; and the third in the western and north - western region, with the highest altitude (500 – 810 m), the highest concentration of vineyards and the best potential for quality.

CLIMATE:

Mediterranean, with an average annual temperature of 15.6 °C and low rainfall (average of 300 mm per year). The heavy showers and storms which occur in the region are another defining element.

VINTAGE RATING

PEÑÍNGUIDE

2010	2011	2012	2013	2014
VERY GOOD	N/A	GOOD	GOOD	VERY GOOD

BODEGA BALCONA

Calle Democracia, 7
30180 Bullas (Murcia)
☎: +34 968 652 891
info@partal-vinos.com
www.partal-vinos.com

37 Barricas 2006 TC
60% monastrell, 20% syrah, 10% tempranillo, 10% cabernet sauvignon

87

Colour: cherry, garnet rim. Nose: fine reductive notes, wet leather, aged wood nuances. Palate: spicy, long, toasty.

Mabal 2013 T
100% monastrell

87

Colour: bright cherry. Nose: sweet spices, creamy oak, warm. Palate: flavourful, fruity, toasty.

Mabal 2014 T
100% monastrell

90

Colour: cherry, purple rim. Nose: red berry notes, floral, balsamic herbs. Palate: powerful, fresh, fruity.

Partal de Autor 2006 T
50% monastrell, 25% syrah, 15% merlot, 10% cabernet sauvignon

88

Colour: light cherry. Nose: fine reductive notes, aged wood nuances, toasty, fruit liqueur notes. Palate: spicy, toasty, flavourful.

BODEGA COOPERATIVA VINÍCOLA AGRARIA SAN ISIDRO

Pol. Ind. Marimingo, Altiplano, s/n
30180 Bullas (Murcia)
☎: +34 968 654 991
Fax: +34 968 652 160
administracion@bodegasanisidrobullas.com

Cepas del Zorro 2011 TC
80% monastrell, 20% syrah

89

Colour: cherry, garnet rim. Nose: creamy oak, balanced, ripe fruit. Palate: flavourful, spicy.

Cepas del Zorro 2013 T
100% monastrell

88

Colour: bright cherry. Nose: ripe fruit, sweet spices, creamy oak. Palate: flavourful, fruity, toasty.

Cepas del Zorro 2014 RD
80% monastrell, 20% garnacha

87

Colour: rose, purple rim. Nose: red berry notes, floral, expressive. Palate: powerful, fruity, fresh.

Cepas del Zorro 2014 T
80% monastrell, 20% syrah

89

Colour: cherry, purple rim. Nose: powerfull, ripe fruit, spicy, violet drops. Palate: powerful, fruity, spicy.

Cepas del Zorro Macabeo 2014 B
100% macabeo

88

Colour: bright straw. Nose: white flowers, fresh fruit, fragrant herbs, expressive. Palate: flavourful, fruity, good acidity, balanced.

BODEGA MONASTRELL

Ctra. Bullas-Avilés, km. 9,3
"Valle Aceniche"
30180 Bullas (Murcia)
☎: +34 968 654 925
Fax: +34 968 654 925
info@bodegamonastrell.com
www.bodegamonastrell.com

Almudí 2012 T
90% monastrell, 5% tempranillo, 5% petit verdot

90 ♣

Colour: cherry, garnet rim. Nose: smoky, spicy, ripe fruit, earthy notes. Palate: flavourful, smoky aftertaste, ripe fruit.

Chaveo 2011 TC
100% monastrell

90 ♣

Colour: cherry, garnet rim. Nose: roasted coffee, smoky, spicy, ripe fruit. Palate: flavourful, smoky aftertaste, ripe fruit.

Valché 2010 TC
100% monastrell

90 ♣

Colour: cherry, garnet rim. Nose: smoky, spicy, ripe fruit. Palate: flavourful, smoky aftertaste, ripe fruit.

BODEGA TERCIA DE ULEA

Paraje Tercia de Ulea, s/n
(Ctra. B-35, km. 7,5)
30440 Moratalla (Murcia)
☎: +34 968 433 213
info@terciadeulea.com
www.terciadeulea.com

Cañadas de Moratalla 2014 TC
80% monastrell, 20% tempranillo

82

Rambla de Ulea 2014 T
100% monastrell

89

Colour: cherry, purple rim. Nose: powerfull, ripe fruit, spicy, grassy. Palate: powerful, fruity.

Rebeldía 2014 RD
100% monastrell

85

Travesura 2014 T
monastrell

91

Colour: deep cherry, purple rim. Nose: creamy oak, toasty, ripe fruit, balsamic herbs. Palate: balanced, spicy, long.

Viña Botial 2014 T
100% monastrell

92

Colour: bright cherry. Nose: ripe fruit, sweet spices, creamy oak, wild herbs. Palate: flavourful, fruity, round tannins.

BODEGAS CARREÑO

Ginés de Paco, 22
30430 Cehegín (Murcia)
☎: +34 968 740 004
Fax: +34 968 740 004
info@bodegascarreno.com
www.bodegascarreno.com

Begastri 2011 T
60% monastrell, 40% petit verdot

85

Begastri 2013 T
65% monastrell, 20% petit verdot, 15% syrah

86

Begastri 2013 T
70% monastrell, 30% petit verdot

83

Begastri Monastrell 2013 T
100% monastrell

82 ♣

Marmallejo 2011 TC
60% monastrell, 40% petit verdot

87

Colour: cherry, garnet rim. Nose: roasted coffee, smoky, spicy, ripe fruit. Palate: flavourful, smoky aftertaste, ripe fruit.

BODEGAS CONTRERAS

Los Ríos, 1
30800 Avilés de Lorca (Murcia)
☎: +34 685 874 594
info@bodegas-contreras.com
www.bodegas-contreras.com

Sortius Monastrell 2013 T
monastrell

83

Sortius Syrah 2013 T Roble
syrah

85

BODEGAS DEL ROSARIO

Avda. de la Libertad, s/n
30180 Bullas (Murcia)
☎: +34 968 652 075
Fax: +34 968 653 765
info@bodegasdelrosario.com
www.bodegasdelrosario.es

Las Reñas 2012 TC
monastrell, syrah

89

Colour: bright cherry. Nose: sweet spices, creamy oak, ripe fruit. Palate: flavourful, fruity, toasty.

Las Reñas Barrica 2013 T
monastrell

89

Colour: bright cherry. Nose: ripe fruit, sweet spices, creamy oak, expressive. Palate: flavourful, fruity, toasty, round tannins.

Las Reñas Macabeo 2014 B
macabeo, malvasía

87

Colour: straw. Nose: medium intensity, ripe fruit, floral. Palate: correct, easy to drink.

Las Reñas Monastrell 2014 T
monastrell

89

Colour: cherry, purple rim. Nose: powerfull, ripe fruit, spicy. Palate: powerful, fruity.

Las Reñas Selección 2012 TC
monastrell, syrah

91

Colour: cherry, garnet rim. Nose: mineral, expressive, spicy. Palate: flavourful, ripe fruit, long, good acidity, balanced.

Lorca Selección 2013 T
monastrell

88

Colour: cherry, purple rim. Nose: ripe fruit, aromatic coffee, caramel, dark chocolate, toasty. Palate: flavourful, spicy, powerful.

Niño de las Uvas 2013 T
monastrell

91

Colour: deep cherry, purple rim. Nose: creamy oak, toasty, ripe fruit, balsamic herbs. Palate: balanced, spicy, long.

Niño de las Uvas 2014 RD
100% monastrell

90

Colour: salmon. Nose: elegant, red berry notes, floral, fragrant herbs. Palate: light-bodied, flavourful, good acidity, long, spicy.

Señorío de Bullas 2011 TR
monastrell, syrah

86

BODEGAS LAVIA

Paraje Venta del Pino, Parcela 38
30430 Cehegin (Murcia)
☎: +34 638 046 694
lavia@bodegaslavia.com
www.mgwinesgroup.com

Lavia+ 2010 TC
monastrell

93

Colour: very deep cherry, garnet rim. Nose: expressive, complex, mineral, balsamic herbs, candied fruit. Palate: full, flavourful, spicy, long.

Lavia+ Paso Malo 2012 TC
monastrell

93

Colour: very deep cherry, garnet rim. Nose: expressive, complex, mineral, balsamic herbs, balanced. Palate: full, flavourful, round tannins.

CARRASCALEJO

Finca Carrascalejo, s/n
30180 Bullas (Murcia)
☎: +34 968 652 003
Fax: +34 968 652 003
carrascalejo@carrascalejo.com
www.carrascalejo.com

Carrascalejo 2012 TC
80% monastrell, 10% syrah, 10% cabernet sauvignon

86

Carrascalejo 2014 RD
100% monastrell

87

Colour: rose, purple rim. Nose: powerfull, fruit preserve, warm. Palate: powerful, flavourful, round.

Carrascalejo 2014 T
100% monastrell

86

Rosmarinus 2012 T
80% monastrell, 10% tempranillo, 10% syrah

83

Rosmarinus 2012 T Roble
80% monastrell, 20% syrah

88

Colour: bright cherry. Nose: ripe fruit, sweet spices, creamy oak. Palate: flavourful, fruity, toasty, round tannins.

Rosmarinus 2014 RD
80% monastrell, 20% garnacha

87

Colour: rose, purple rim. Nose: powerfull, fruit preserve, fragrant herbs. Palate: powerful, flavourful, round.

DO. CALATAYUD

CONSEJO REGULADOR

Ctra. de Valencia, 8
50300 Calatayud (Zaragoza)
☎ :+34 976 884 260 - Fax: +34 976 885 912
@: administracion@docalatayud.com
www.docalatayud.com

LOCATION:

It is situated in the western region of the province of Zaragoza, along the foothills of the Sistema Ibérico, outlined by the network of rivers woven by the different tributaries of the Ebro: Jalón, Jiloca, Manubles, Mesa, Piedra and Ribota, and covers 46 municipal areas of the Ebro Valley.

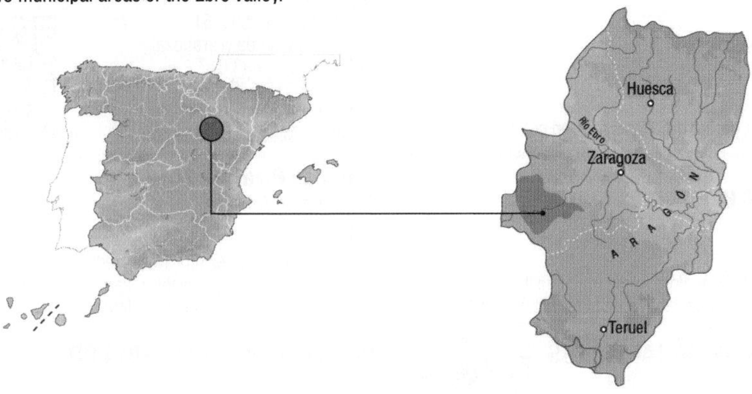

GRAPE VARIETIES:

WHITE: PREFERRED: Macabeo (25%) and Malvasía.
AUTHORIZED: Moscatel de Alejandría, Garnacha Blanca, Sauvignon Blanc, Gewurztraiminer and Chardonnay.
RED: PREFERRED: Garnacha Tinta (61.9%), Tempranillo (10%) and Mazuela.
AUTHORIZED: Monastrell, Cabernet Sauvignon, Merlot, Bobal and Syrah.

FIGURES:

Vineyard surface: 3,200 – **Wine-Growers:** 900 – **Wineries:** 16 – **2014 Harvest rating:** Very Good – **Production 14:** 7,801,500 litres – **Market percentages:** 15% National - 85% International.

SOIL:

In general, the soil has a high limestone content. It is formed by rugged stony materials from the nearby mountain ranges and is on many occasions accompanied by reddish clay. The region is the most rugged in Aragón, and the vineyards are situated at an altitude of between 550 and 880 m.

CLIMATE:

Semi - arid and dry, although somewhat cooler than Cariñena and Borja, with cold winters, an average annual temperature which ranges between 12 and 14 °C, and a period of frost of between 5 and 7 months which greatly affects the production. The average rainfall ranges between 300 – 550 mm per year, with great day/night temperature contrasts during the ripening season.

VINTAGE RATING

PEÑÍNGUIDE

2010	2011	2012	2013	2014
VERY GOOD	VERY GOOD	VERY GOOD	VERY GOOD	GOOD

AGUSTÍN CUBERO

La Charluca, s/n
50300 Calatayud (Zaragoza)
☎: +34 976 882 332
Fax: +34 976 886 606
calatayud@bodegascubero.com
www.bodegascubero.com

Stylo 4 meses 2014 T
garnacha

88

Colour: deep cherry, purple rim. Nose: characterful, powerfull, ripe fruit, spicy. Palate: balanced, round tannins, flavourful, good structure.

Stylo 8 meses 2012 T
garnacha

88

Colour: cherry, garnet rim. Nose: roasted coffee, smoky, spicy, aromatic coffee. Palate: flavourful, smoky aftertaste, ripe fruit.

Unus 2014 B
macabeo

87

Colour: bright yellow. Nose: medium intensity, ripe fruit, floral. Palate: correct, easy to drink, fine bitter notes, balanced.

ALIANZA DE GARAPITEROS

Plaza España, 6 Planta 1ª Of. B
50001 Zaragoza (Zaragoza)
☎: +34 976 094 033
Fax: +34 976 094 033
www.alianzadegarapiteros.es

Alquéz Garnacha Viñas Viejas 2012 T
garnacha

88

Colour: cherry, garnet rim. Nose: roasted coffee, smoky, spicy, ripe fruit. Palate: flavourful, smoky aftertaste, ripe fruit.

Alquéz Garnacha Viñas Viejas 2013 T
garnacha

88

Colour: cherry, garnet rim. Nose: roasted coffee, smoky, spicy, ripe fruit. Palate: flavourful, smoky aftertaste, ripe fruit.

Lamin 2011 T
garnacha

90

Colour: cherry, garnet rim. Nose: mineral, expressive, spicy, fruit preserve, toasty. Palate: flavourful, ripe fruit, long, good acidity, balanced.

Nietro Garnacha Viñas Viejas 2014 T
garnacha

90

Colour: deep cherry, purple rim. Nose: toasty, ripe fruit, balsamic herbs. Palate: balanced, spicy, long, flavourful.

Nietro Macabeo Viñas Viejas 2014 B
macabeo

88

Colour: bright yellow. Nose: expressive, dried herbs, ripe fruit, spicy. Palate: flavourful, fruity, good acidity, balanced.

BODEGA CASTILLO DE MALUENDA

Avda. José Antonio, 61
50340 Maluenda (Zaragoza)
☎: +34 976 893 017
Fax: +34 976 546 969
info@castillodemaluenda.com
www.castillodemaluenda.com

Alto Las Pizarras 2013 T
95% garnacha, 5% syrah

90

Colour: cherry, garnet rim. Nose: red berry notes, ripe fruit, fragrant herbs, spicy, toasty, creamy oak, mineral. Palate: powerful, flavourful, balsamic, balanced.

Castillo de Maluenda 2014 RD
100% garnacha

83

Claraval 2014 B
100% viura

84

Claraval Garnacha 2013 T
100% garnacha

87

Colour: bright cherry. Nose: ripe fruit, sweet spices, characterful. Palate: flavourful, fruity, round tannins.

Claraval Selección Cuvée 2011 T
85% garnacha, 10% syrah, 5% tempranillo

89

Colour: deep cherry, garnet rim. Nose: powerfull, fruit expression, fragrant herbs. Palate: flavourful, round tannins.

Claraval Syrah 2013 T
100% syrah

87

Colour: cherry, purple rim. Nose: powerfull, ripe fruit, spicy, characterful. Palate: powerful, fruity, unctuous.

Claraval Tempranillo 2013 T
100% tempranillo

88

Colour: cherry, purple rim. Nose: expressive, fresh fruit, red berry notes, floral, spicy. Palate: flavourful, fruity, good acidity.

La Dolores 2012 TC
70% tempranillo, 30% syrah

84

La Dolores 2014 T
60% tempranillo, 40% syrah

83

La Dolores Delux 2011 T
85% garnacha, 10% syrah, 5% tempranillo

85

Las Pizarras 2013 T
95% garnacha, 5% syrah

90

Colour: cherry, garnet rim. Nose: mineral, expressive, spicy. Palate: flavourful, ripe fruit, long, good acidity, balanced.

Las Pizarras Collection Fabla Garnacha 2013 T
100% garnacha

90

Colour: deep cherry, garnet rim. Nose: powerfull, characterful, ripe fruit, varietal. Palate: good structure, flavourful, round tannins.

Las Pizarras Collection Siosy Syrah 2013 T
100% syrah

87

Colour: deep cherry, purple rim. Nose: ripe fruit, violets, sweet spices. Palate: flavourful, ripe fruit.

Las Pizarras Collection Volcán Tempranillo 2013 T
100% tempranillo

89

Colour: cherry, garnet rim. Nose: expressive, fresh fruit, red berry notes, floral. Palate: flavourful, fruity, good acidity.

BODEGA SAN GREGORIO

Ctra. Villalengua, s/n
50312 Cervera de la Cañada (Zaragoza)
☎: +34 976 899 206
Fax: +34 976 896 240
tresojos@bodegasangregorio.com
www.bodegasangregorio.com

Armantes 2008 TR
70% garnacha, 22% tempranillo, 8% syrah, merlot, cabernet sauvignon

88

Colour: cherry, garnet rim. Nose: ripe fruit, wild herbs, spicy, balsamic herbs. Palate: balanced, flavourful, long.

Armantes 2011 TC
60% garnacha, 22% tempranillo, 9% syrah, 9% merlot

87

Colour: dark-red cherry, garnet rim. Nose: ripe fruit, spicy, dried herbs, toasty. Palate: balanced, easy to drink.

Armantes 2012 TC
78% tempranillo, 22% syrah

87

Colour: cherry, garnet rim. Nose: balanced, ripe fruit, sweet spices. Palate: flavourful, spicy.

Armantes 2013 BFB
macabeo

87

Colour: bright yellow. Nose: ripe fruit, powerfull, toasty, aged wood nuances, pattiserie. Palate: flavourful, fruity, spicy, toasty, long.

Armantes 2014 B
macabeo

85

Armantes 2014 RD
50% garnacha, 50% tempranillo

85

Armantes 2014 T
50% garnacha, 50% tempranillo

87

Colour: cherry, purple rim. Nose: powerfull, ripe fruit, spicy. Palate: powerful, fruity, unctuous.

Armantes Carmesí 2012 T
85% garnacha, 15% tempranillo

84

Armantes Vendimia Seleccionada 2012 T
70% garnacha, 22% tempranillo, 8% syrah

91

Colour: very deep cherry, garnet rim. Nose: mineral, balsamic herbs, balanced, ripe fruit. Palate: full, flavourful, round tannins, fruity aftestaste.

Tres Ojos Garnacha 2013 T
garnacha

84

Tres Ojos Tempranillo 2013 T
tempranillo

84

BODEGA VIRGEN DE LA SIERRA

Avda. de la Cooperativa, 21-23
50310 Villarroya de la Sierra (Zaragoza)
☎: +34 976 899 015
Fax: +34 976 899 132
oficina@bodegavirgendelasierra.com
www.bodegavirgendelasierra.com

Albada 2013 T
100% garnacha

87

Colour: cherry, garnet rim. Nose: ripe fruit, fruit preserve, wild herbs, spicy. Palate: powerful, flavourful, toasty.

Albada 2014 B
100% macabeo

88

Colour: bright straw. Nose: white flowers, fresh fruit, fragrant herbs, expressive. Palate: flavourful, fruity, good acidity, balanced.

Albada Finca V4 2012 T
100% garnacha

91

Colour: deep cherry, garnet rim. Nose: mineral, characterful, ripe fruit. Palate: balanced, spicy, round tannins.

Albada Finca V5 2012 T
100% garnacha

90

Colour: deep cherry, garnet rim. Nose: expressive, mineral, fruit preserve, spicy. Palate: balanced, long, round tannins.

Cruz de Piedra 2014 B
100% macabeo

86

Cruz de Piedra 2014 RD
100% garnacha

87

Colour: rose, bright. Nose: floral, wild herbs, fruit expression, expressive. Palate: flavourful, balanced, elegant.

Cruz de Piedra 2014 T
100% garnacha

86

Cruz de Piedra Selección Especial 2013 T
100% garnacha

89

Colour: bright cherry. Nose: ripe fruit, sweet spices, creamy oak. Palate: flavourful, fruity, toasty.

BODEGAS ATECA

Ctra. N-II, s/n
50200 Ateca (Zaragoza)
☎: +34 968 435 022
Fax: +34 968 716 051
info@orowines.com
www.orowines.com

Atteca 2012 T
100% garnacha

92

Colour: cherry, garnet rim. Nose: balanced, complex, ripe fruit, spicy, mineral. Palate: good structure, flavourful, round tannins, balanced.

Atteca 2013 T
100% garnacha

91

Colour: very deep cherry, purple rim. Nose: ripe fruit, toasty, mineral, dried herbs, characterful. Palate: good structure, flavourful.

Atteca Armas 2011 T
100% garnacha

92

Colour: cherry, garnet rim. Nose: mineral, expressive, spicy, characterful, cocoa bean. Palate: flavourful, ripe fruit, long, balanced.

Honoro Vera Garnacha 2014 T
100% garnacha

88

Colour: bright cherry. Nose: ripe fruit, creamy oak. Palate: flavourful, fruity, toasty.

BODEGAS AUGUSTA BILBILIS

Carramiedes, s/n
50331 Mara (Zaragoza)
☎: +34 677 547 127
bodegasaugustabilbilis@hotmail.com
www.bodegasaugustabilbilis.com

Samitier 2013 T Roble
100% garnacha

92

Colour: bright cherry. Nose: ripe fruit, sweet spices, creamy oak. Palate: flavourful, toasty, round tannins, ripe fruit.

Samitier MACABEO 2013 B
100% macabeo

91

Colour: bright straw. Nose: white flowers, dried herbs, mineral. Palate: flavourful, fruity, round.

Samitier Syrah 2013 T
100% syrah

93

Colour: cherry, garnet rim. Nose: mineral, spicy. Palate: flavourful, ripe fruit, good acidity, balanced.

BODEGAS BRECA

Ctra. Monasterio de Piedra, s/n
50219 Munébrega (Zaragoza)
☎: +34 952 504 706
Fax: +34 951 284 796
breca@jorgeordonez.es
www.grupojorgeordonez.com

Breca 2013 T Fermentado en Barrica
100% garnacha

92

Colour: cherry, garnet rim. Nose: creamy oak, ripe fruit. Palate: spicy, sweetness.

BODEGAS LANGA

Ctra. Nacional II, Km. 241,700
50300 Calatayud (Zaragoza)
☎: +34 976 881 818
Fax: +34 976 884 463
info@bodegas-langa.com
www.bodegas-langa.com

Langa Organic 2013 T
merlot, syrah, garnacha

89

Colour: bright cherry. Nose: ripe fruit, sweet spices, creamy oak, expressive. Palate: flavourful, fruity, round tannins.

Langa Pasión 2013 T
garnacha

88

Colour: cherry, garnet rim. Nose: creamy oak, red berry notes, fresh fruit, balanced, toasty. Palate: flavourful, spicy, elegant.

Langa Tradición 2012 T
garnacha

89

Colour: cherry, garnet rim. Nose: red berry notes, ripe fruit, spicy, creamy oak. Palate: flavourful, toasty.

Real de Aragón Centenaria 2012 T
garnacha

89

Colour: cherry, garnet rim. Nose: creamy oak, red berry notes, fresh fruit, balanced. Palate: flavourful, spicy, elegant, toasty.

BODEGAS SAN ALEJANDRO

Ctra. Calatayud - Cariñena, Km. 16,4
50330 Miedes de Aragón (Zaragoza)
☎: +34 976 892 205
Fax: +34 976 890 540
contacto@san-alejandro.com
www.san-alejandro.com

Baltasar Gracián 2012 TC
60% garnacha, 40% syrah

90

Colour: very deep cherry, garnet rim. Nose: mineral, balsamic herbs, balanced, characterful. Palate: full, flavourful, round tannins.

Baltasar Gracián 2011 TR
70% garnacha, 30% syrah

90

Colour: cherry, garnet rim. Nose: balanced, complex, ripe fruit, spicy, fine reductive notes. Palate: good structure, flavourful, round tannins, balanced.

Baltasar Gracián Garnacha 2014 RD
100% garnacha

87

Colour: rose, bright. Nose: red berry notes, floral, expressive. Palate: fruity, fresh, easy to drink, good finish.

Baltasar Gracián Garnacha 2014 T
100% garnacha

89

Colour: cherry, purple rim. Nose: red berry notes, floral, balsamic herbs, mineral. Palate: powerful, fresh, fruity.

Baltasar Gracián Garnacha Nativa 2012 T
100% garnacha

92

Colour: cherry, garnet rim. Nose: ripe fruit, fruit preserve, spicy, creamy oak. Palate: powerful, flavourful, balsamic, long.

Baltasar Gracián Garnacha Viñas Viejas 2013 T
100% garnacha

90

Colour: very deep cherry, purple rim. Nose: spicy, ripe fruit, powerfull, wild herbs, balanced, sweet spices. Palate: good structure, fruity.

Baltasar Gracián Macabeo 2014 B
100% macabeo

86

Las Rocas Garnacha 2013 T
100% garnacha

91

Colour: deep cherry, purple rim. Nose: creamy oak, toasty, ripe fruit, balsamic herbs, mineral. Palate: balanced, spicy, long.

Las Rocas Garnacha Viñas Viejas 2013 T
100% garnacha

92

Colour: cherry, garnet rim. Nose: ripe fruit, wild herbs, spicy, balsamic herbs, mineral. Palate: balanced, flavourful, long, balsamic.

FLORIS LEGERE
Hecho 2, Bloque 2, Bajo B
50410 Cuarte de Huerva (Zaragoza)
☎: +34 608 974 809
contact@florislegere.com
www.florislegere.com

Alaviana 2013 T
80% garnacha, 20% syrah

93

Colour: deep cherry, purple rim. Nose: ripe fruit, wild herbs, spicy, mineral. Palate: good structure, long, round tannins, balsamic.

Atractylis 2013 T
100% syrah

92

Colour: very deep cherry, garnet rim. Nose: expressive, complex, earthy notes. Palate: full, flavourful, round tannins, elegant.

GALGO WINES SAN GREGORIO
Calle Tomás Tapia, 2
13600 Alcázar de San Juan
(Ciudad Real)
☎: +34 913 190 401
info@galgowines.com
www.galgowines.com

Místicos 2012 T
70% garnacha, 22% tempranillo, 8% syrah

89

Colour: ruby red. Nose: complex, mineral, balsamic herbs, ripe fruit, creamy oak. Palate: full, flavourful, round tannins.

NIÑO JESÚS
Las Tablas, s/n
50313 Aniñón (Zaragoza)
☎: +34 976 899 150
Fax: +34 976 896 160
produccion@satninojesus.com
www.satninojesus.com

Estecillo 2014 B
macabeo

85

Estecillo 2014 T
garnacha, tempranillo

83

Estecillo Legado Garnacha 2014 T
garnacha

85

Estecillo Legado Garnacha Syrah 2014 T
garnacha, syrah

85

Estecillo Legado Macabeo 2014 BFB
macabeo

86

PAGOS ALTOS DE ACERED
Monasterio San Juan de la Peña,
Nº 1, Escalera 4, Bajo D.
50410 Cuarte de Huerva (Zaragoza)
☎: +34 636 474 723
manuel@lajas.es
www.lajas.es

Lajas "Finca el Peñiscal" 2012 T
garnacha

93

Colour: cherry, garnet rim. Nose: balanced, complex, ripe fruit, spicy, mineral. Palate: good structure, flavourful, round tannins, balsamic.

Lajas "Finca el Peñiscal" 2013 T
garnacha

92

Colour: cherry, garnet rim. Nose: red berry notes, ripe fruit, fragrant herbs, spicy, dry stone. Palate: powerful, flavourful, balsamic, balanced.

DO. CAMPO DE BORJA

CONSEJO REGULADOR

Subida de San Andrés, 6
50570 Ainzón (Zaragoza)
☎:+34 976 852 122 - Fax: +34 976 868 806
@: vinos@docampodeborja.com
www.docampodeborja.com

LOCATION:

The DO Campo de Borja is made up of 16 municipal areas, situated in the north west of the province of Zaragoza and 60 km from the capital city, in an area of transition between the mountains of the Sistema Ibérico (at the foot of the Moncayo) and the Ebro Valley: Agón, Ainzón, Alberite, Albeta, Ambel, Bisimbre, Borja, Bulbuente, Burueta, El Buste, Fuendejalón, Magallón, Malejan, Pozuelo de Aragón, Tabuenca and Vera del Moncayo.

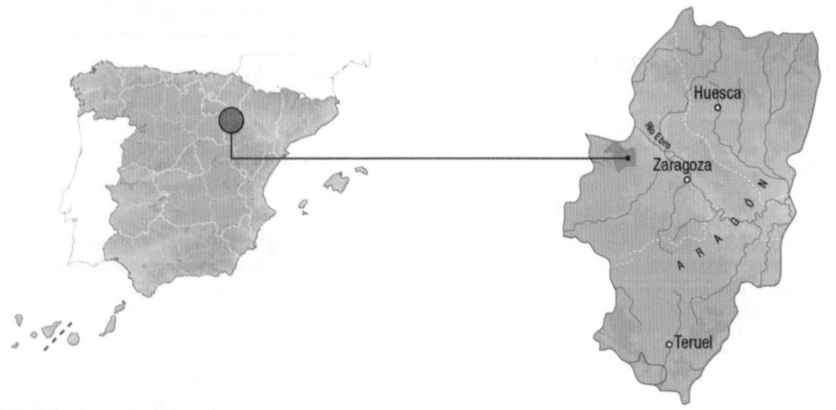

GRAPE VARIETIES:

WHITE: Macabeo, Garnacha Blanca, Moscatel, Chardonnay, Sauvignon Blanc and Verdejo.
RED: Garnacha (majority with 75%), Tempranillo, Mazuela, Cabernet Sauvignon, Merlot and Syrah.

FIGURES:

Vineyard surface: 6,661 – **Wine-Growers:** 1,151 – **Wineries:** 18 – **2014 Harvest rating:** Good – **Production 14:** 20,863,214 litres – **Market percentages:** 39% National - 61% International.

SOIL:

The most abundant are brownish - grey limey soils, terrace soils and clayey ferrous soils. The vineyards are situated at an altitude of between 350 and 700 m on small slightly rolling hillsides, on terraces of the Huecha river and the Llanos de Plasencia, making up the Somontano del Moncayo.

CLIMATE:

A rather extreme continental climate, with cold winters and dry, hot summers. One of its main characteristics is the influence of the 'Cierzo', a cold and dry north - westerly wind. Rainfall is rather scarce, with an average of between 350 and 450 mm per year.

VINTAGE RATING

PEÑÍNGUIDE

2010	2011	2012	2013	2014
VERY GOOD	VERY GOOD	VERY GOOD	GOOD	GOOD

ARTIGA FUSTEL

Progres, 21
08720 Vilafranca del Penedès
(Barcelona)
☎: +34 938 182 317
Fax: +34 938 924 499
info@artiga-fustel.com
www.artiga-fustel.com

Artiga Garnacha 2014 T
100% garnacha

86

Castillo de la Peña 2008 TGR
60% garnacha, 40% cabernet sauvignon

86

Ermita de San Lorenzo 2008 TGR
60% garnacha, 40% cabernet sauvignon

85

AXIAL

Castillo de Capua Nº 10 nave 7
50197 Zaragoza (Zaragoza)
☎: +34 976 780 136
Fax: +34 976 303 035
info@axialvinos.com
www.axialvinos.com

Penélope Sánchez 2014 T
85% garnacha, 15% syrah

88

Colour: deep cherry, purple rim. Nose: ripe fruit, balsamic herbs, spicy. Palate: balanced, spicy, long, concentrated.

BODEGA PICOS

Ctra. Nacional 122, Km. 55'400
50520 Magallón (Zaragoza)
☎: +34 976 863 006
info@bodegapicos.com
www.bodegapicos.com

Gran Gregoriano 2013 T
garnacha, merlot

82

Gregoriano 2013 T Roble
garnacha, tempranillo, merlot, syrah

84

Gregoriano Blanco de Hielo 2014 B
moscatel, macabeo

80

BODEGAS ALTO MONCAYO

Ctra. Borja - El Buste, CV-606 Km. 1,700
50540 Borja (Zaragoza)
☎: +34 976 868 098
Fax: +34 976 867 807
info@bodegasaltomoncayo.com
www.bodegasaltomoncayo.com

PODIUM

Alto Moncayo 2012 T
100% garnacha

95

Colour: bright cherry, garnet rim. Nose: expressive, complex, cocoa bean, varietal, neat. Palate: full, flavourful, good structure, complex, balanced, round tannins.

Alto Moncayo Veratón 2012 T
100% garnacha

94

Colour: cherry, garnet rim. Nose: mineral, expressive, spicy, ripe fruit. Palate: flavourful, ripe fruit, long, good acidity, balanced.

PODIUM

Aquilón 2012 T
100% garnacha

96

Colour: very deep cherry, bright cherry. Nose: ripe fruit, dried herbs, cocoa bean, varietal. Palate: good structure, complex, round tannins.

BODEGAS ARAGONESAS

Ctra. Magallón, s/n
50529 Fuendejalón (Zaragoza)
☎: +34 976 862 153
Fax: +34 976 862 363
www.bodegasaragonesas.com

Aragonia Selección Especial 2012 T
100% garnacha

90

Colour: cherry, garnet rim. Nose: roasted coffee, smoky, spicy, ripe fruit, wild herbs, dried herbs. Palate: flavourful, smoky aftertaste, ripe fruit.

Aragus Ecológico 2014 T
100% garnacha

86

Aragus Garnacha Cabernet 2014 T
85% garnacha, 15% cabernet sauvignon

87

Colour: cherry, purple rim. Nose: powerfull, red berry notes, ripe fruit, spicy. Palate: correct, powerful, balsamic.

Aragus Syrah 2014 T
100% syrah

87

Colour: cherry, purple rim. Nose: fresh fruit, red berry notes, floral, spicy. Palate: flavourful, fruity, good acidity.

Coto de Hayas 2012 TC
60% garnacha, 40% tempranillo

87

Colour: cherry, garnet rim. Nose: ripe fruit, spicy, creamy oak. Palate: flavourful, toasty, round tannins.

Coto de Hayas 2014 RD
90% garnacha, 10% cabernet sauvignon

87

Colour: light cherry, bright. Nose: red berry notes, expressive, scrubland. Palate: powerful, fruity, fresh.

Coto de Hayas Chardonnay 2014 B
100% chardonnay

85

Coto de Hayas Garnacha Centenaria 2014 T
100% garnacha

90

Colour: deep cherry, purple rim. Nose: creamy oak, ripe fruit, balsamic herbs, roasted coffee. Palate: balanced, spicy, long, toasty.

Coto de Hayas Garnacha Syrah 2014 T
85% garnacha, 15% syrah

87

Colour: cherry, purple rim. Nose: powerfull, ripe fruit, spicy. Palate: powerful, fruity, unctuous.

Coto de Hayas Mistela 2014 Vino dulce Natural
100% garnacha

90

Colour: cherry, garnet rim. Nose: fruit expression, fruit preserve, spicy, toasty, creamy oak. Palate: powerful, flavourful, balanced.

Coto de Hayas Moscatel Dulce Natural 2014 B
100% moscatel grano menudo

88

Colour: bright yellow. Nose: powerfull, candied fruit, dried herbs, honeyed notes. Palate: flavourful, sweet, ripe fruit, good acidity.

Coto de Hayas Tempranillo Cabernet 2014 T Roble
70% tempranillo, 30% cabernet sauvignon

87

Colour: dark-red cherry, purple rim. Nose: smoky, spicy, characterful, ripe fruit. Palate: flavourful, fruity.

Coto de Hayas Viñas del Cierzo 2011 T
85% garnacha, 10% syrah, 5% mazuelo

86

Don Ramón 2013 T Barrica
75% garnacha, 25% tempranillo

87

Colour: cherry, purple rim. Nose: sweet spices, smoky, ripe fruit. Palate: correct, easy to drink, good finish, balsamic.

Don Ramón Garnacha Imperial 2013 T Roble
100% garnacha

88

Colour: cherry, garnet rim. Nose: toasty, ripe fruit, balsamic herbs. Palate: balanced, spicy, long.

Ecce Homo 2014 T
100% garnacha

86

Ecce Homo Selección 2011 T
100% garnacha

89

Colour: dark-red cherry, garnet rim. Nose: ripe fruit, powerfull, varietal, balsamic herbs. Palate: balanced, good structure, round tannins.

Fagus de Coto de Hayas 2013 T
100% garnacha

90

Colour: cherry, garnet rim. Nose: roasted coffee, smoky, spicy, ripe fruit. Palate: flavourful, smoky aftertaste, ripe fruit.

Fagus de Coto de Hayas Magnum 2011 T
100% garnacha

92

Colour: cherry, garnet rim. Nose: ripe fruit, spicy, creamy oak, complex. Palate: flavourful, toasty, round tannins, long, balanced.

Galiano 2007 T
100% garnacha

92

Colour: pale ruby, brick rim edge. Nose: elegant, spicy, fine reductive notes, tobacco, ripe fruit. Palate: spicy, fine tannins, elegant, long.

Oxia 2010 TC
100% garnacha

91

Colour: deep cherry, orangey edge. Nose: fine reductive notes, wet leather, aged wood nuances. Palate: spicy, long, toasty, classic aged character.

Oxia 2011 T
100% garnacha

90

Colour: ruby red. Nose: spicy, fine reductive notes, wet leather, aged wood nuances, fruit liqueur notes, fruit preserve. Palate: spicy, fine tannins, balanced.

Solo Centifolia 2014 RD
100% garnacha

89

Colour: onion pink. Nose: elegant, red berry notes, floral, fragrant herbs. Palate: light-bodied, flavourful, good acidity, long, spicy, elegant.

Solo Tiólico 2014 B
100% moscatel de alejandría

87

Colour: bright yellow. Nose: white flowers, varietal, ripe fruit. Palate: flavourful, easy to drink.

Solo Tirio Syrah 2014 T
100% syrah

85

Viña Temprana 2014 B
100% macabeo

85

Viña Temprana 2014 RD
100% garnacha

86

Viña Temprana O.V.G. 2014 T
100% garnacha

85

BODEGAS BORSAO
Ctra. N-122, Km. 63
50540 Borja (Zaragoza)
☎: +34 976 867 116
Fax: +34 976 867 752
info@bodegasborsao.com
www.bodegasborsao.com

Borsao Berola 2011 T
80% garnacha, 20% syrah

91

Colour: very deep cherry, garnet rim. Nose: balsamic herbs, balanced, aged wood nuances, creamy oak. Palate: full, flavourful.

Borsao Bole 2012 T
70% garnacha, 30% syrah

89

Colour: very deep cherry, garnet rim. Nose: expressive, complex, balsamic herbs, fruit preserve. Palate: full, flavourful.

Borsao Selección 2012 TC
60% garnacha, 20% merlot, 20% tempranillo

88

Colour: cherry, garnet rim. Nose: creamy oak, red berry notes, ripe fruit. Palate: flavourful, spicy, toasty.

Borsao Selección 2014 B
100% macabeo

85

Borsao Selección 2014 RD
100% garnacha

87

Colour: coppery red, bright. Nose: wild herbs, red berry notes, ripe fruit, floral. Palate: fruity, fine bitter notes.

Borsao Selección 2014 T
70% garnacha, 20% syrah, 10% tempranillo

87

Colour: cherry, purple rim. Nose: expressive, fresh fruit, red berry notes, floral. Palate: flavourful, fruity, good acidity.

Borsao Tres Picos 2013 T
100% garnacha

92

Colour: deep cherry, garnet rim. Nose: aromatic coffee, toasty, smoky, ripe fruit, balsamic herbs, varietal. Palate: flavourful, smoky aftertaste.

BODEGAS CARLOS VALERO
Castillo de Capúa, 10
Nave 1 Pol. PLA-ZA
50197 Zaragoza (Zaragoza)
☎: +34 976 180 634
Fax: +34 976 186 326
info@bodegasvalero.com
www.bodegasvalero.com

Heredad Garnacha Blanca y Radiante 2014 B
100% garnacha

87

Colour: bright straw, greenish rim. Nose: white flowers, fresh fruit, fragrant herbs, expressive. Palate: flavourful, fruity, good acidity, balanced.

Heredad H Carlos Valero 2012 T
100% garnacha

86

Heredad Red Carlos Valero 2012 T
100% garnacha

91

Colour: cherry, garnet rim. Nose: red berry notes, ripe fruit, spicy, creamy oak, complex. Palate: flavourful, toasty, round tannins, balanced.

BODEGAS ROMÁN

Ctra. Gallur - Agreda, 1
50546 Balbuente (Zaragoza)
☎: +34 976 852 936
info@bodegasroman.es
www.bodegasroman.es

Portal de Moncayo Selección 2014 T
garnacha

87

Colour: bright cherry, purple rim. Nose: balanced, ripe fruit, scrubland. Palate: fruity, flavourful, spicy.

Portal del Moncayo Selección 2012 T Barrica
garnacha

88

Colour: deep cherry, purple rim. Nose: creamy oak, toasty, ripe fruit, balsamic herbs. Palate: balanced, spicy, long.

Román Cepas Viejas 2011 T
garnacha

91

Colour: cherry, garnet rim. Nose: expressive, spicy, dark chocolate, balsamic herbs, fruit preserve. Palate: flavourful, ripe fruit, long, good acidity, balanced.

Senda de Hoyas 2014 T
garnacha

84

BODEGAS RUBERTE

50520 Magallón (Zaragoza)
☎: +34 976 858 106
Fax: +34 976 858 475
info@bodegasruberte.com
www.gruporuberte.com

Ruberte 2014 T
garnacha

86

Ruberte 2014 T
garnacha

84

Ruberte 2014 B
moscatel de alejandría

86

Ruberte 2014 RD
garnacha

86

Ruberte Macabeo 2014 B
macabeo

84

Ruberte Tresor 2013 T
garnacha

86

BODEGAS SANTO CRISTO

Ctra. Tabuenca, s/n
50570 Ainzón (Zaragoza)
☎: +34 976 869 696
Fax: +34 976 868 097
bodegas@bodegas-santo-cristo.com
www.bodegas-santo-cristo.com

Cayus Selección 2013 T Roble
100% garnacha

91

Colour: deep cherry, purple rim. Nose: creamy oak, toasty, ripe fruit, balsamic herbs. Palate: balanced, spicy, long.

Flor de Añon Verdejo 2014 B
verdejo

84

Moscatel Ainzón 90 días de Licor B Barrica
100% moscatel grano menudo

91

Colour: bright yellow. Nose: honeyed notes, floral, sweet spices, fruit liqueur notes. Palate: rich, fruity, powerful, flavourful.

Moscatel Ainzón de Licor B
100% moscatel grano menudo

90

Colour: bright yellow. Nose: balsamic herbs, honeyed notes, floral, sweet spices, expressive. Palate: rich, fruity, powerful, flavourful, elegant.

Terrazas del Moncayo Garnacha 2012 T Roble
100% garnacha

93

Colour: very deep cherry, garnet rim. Nose: expressive, complex, mineral, balsamic herbs, balanced. Palate: full, flavourful, round tannins.

Viña Ainzón 2011 TC
70% garnacha, 30% tempranillo

85

Viña Collado 2014 B
100% macabeo

85

Viña Collado 2014 RD
100% garnacha

86

Viña Collado 2014 T
garnacha, syrah

85

PAGOS DEL MONCAYO

Ctra. Z-372, Km. 1,6
50580 Vera de Moncayo (Zaragoza)
☎: +34 976 900 256
info@pagosdelmoncayo.com
www.pagosdelmoncayo.com

Pagos del Moncayo Garnacha 2013 T
100% garnacha

91

Colour: very deep cherry, garnet rim. Nose: expressive, complex, balsamic herbs, balanced. Palate: full, flavourful, round tannins.

Pagos del Moncayo Garnacha Syrah 2014 T
65% garnacha, 35% syrah

88

Colour: deep cherry, purple rim. Nose: roasted coffee, smoky, ripe fruit. Palate: flavourful, ripe fruit, smoky aftertaste.

Pagos del Moncayo Prados 2013 T
100% syrah

90

Colour: very deep cherry, purple rim. Nose: aged wood nuances, creamy oak, ripe fruit. Palate: good structure, flavourful, round tannins, toasty.

Pagos del Moncayo Syrah 2013 T
100% syrah

89

Colour: bright cherry. Nose: ripe fruit, sweet spices, creamy oak, roasted coffee. Palate: flavourful, fruity, toasty, round tannins.

SPANISH STORY

Espronceda, 27 1ºD
28003 Madrid (Madrid)
☎: +34 915 356 184
Fax: +34 915 363 796
info@spanish-story.com
www.spanish-story.com

Spanish Story Garnacha Campo de Borja 2013 T
100% garnacha

86

DO. CARIÑENA

CONSEJO REGULADOR

Camino de la Platera, 7
50400 Cariñena (Zaragoza)
☎ :+34 976 793 143 / +34 976 793 031 - Fax: +34 976 621 107
@: consejoregulador@elvinodelaspiedras.es
@: secretaria@elvinodelaspiedras.es
www.elvinodelaspiedras.es

LOCATION:

In the province of Zaragoza, and occupies the Ebro valley covering 14 municipal areas: Aguarón, Aladrén, Alfamén, Almonacid de la Sierra, Alpartir, Cariñena, Cosuenda, Encinacorba, Longares, Mezalocha, Muel, Paniza, Tosos and Villanueva de Huerva.

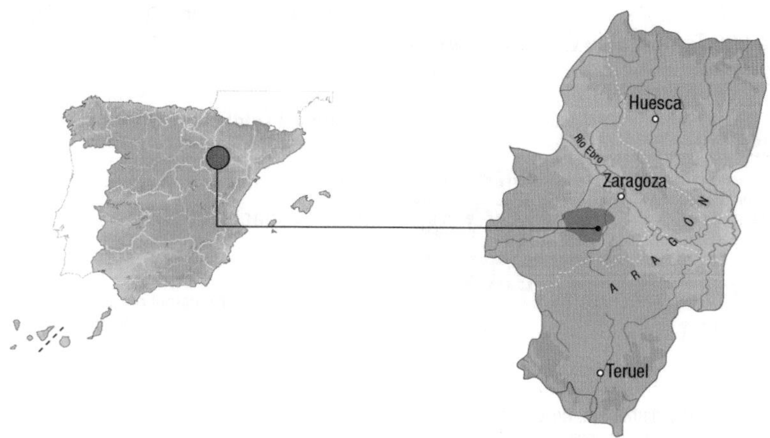

GRAPE VARIETIES:

WHITE: PREFERRED: Macabeo (majority 20%).
AUTHORIZED: Garnacha Blanca, Moscatel Romano, Parellada and Chardonnay.
RED: PREFERRED: Garnacha Tinta (majority 55%), Tempranillo, Mazuela (or Cariñena).
AUTHORIZED: Juan Ibáñez, Cabernet Sauvignon, Syrah, Monastrell, Vidadillo and Merlot.

FIGURES:

Vineyard surface: 14,438 – **Wine-Growers:** 1,587– **Wineries:** 32 – **2014 Harvest rating:** Very Good – **Production 14:** 64,649,239 litres – **Market percentages:** 30% National - 70% International.

SOIL:

Mainly poor; either brownish - grey limey soil, or reddish dun soil settled on rocky deposits, or brownish - grey soil settled on alluvial deposits. The vineyards are situated at an altitude of between 400 and 800 m.

CLIMATE:

A continental climate, with cold winters, hot summers and low rainfall. The viticulture is also influenced by the effect of the 'Cierzo'.

VINTAGE RATING

PEÑÍNGUIDE

2010	2011	2012	2013	2014
GOOD	GOOD	GOOD	GOOD	GOOD

AXIAL

Castillo de Capua Nº 10 nave 7
50197 Zaragoza (Zaragoza)
☎: +34 976 780 136
Fax: +34 976 303 035
info@axialvinos.com
www.axialvinos.com

La Granja 360 Garnacha Syrah 2014 T
garnacha, syrah

85

La Granja 360 Tempranillo 2014 T
100% tempranillo

84

La Granja 360 Tempranillo Garnacha 2014 T
tempranillo, garnacha

85

BIOENOS

Mayor, 88
50400 Cariñena (Zaragoza)
☎: +34 976 620 045
Fax: +34 976 622 082
bioenos@bioenos.com
www.bioenos.com

Pulchrum 2011 T
vidadilo

92

Colour: very deep cherry, garnet rim. Nose: expressive, complex, mineral, balsamic herbs, balanced, fruit expression. Palate: full, flavourful, round tannins.

Pulchrum 2012 T
vidadillo

90

Colour: black cherry, purple rim. Nose: ripe fruit, fruit preserve, sweet spices, creamy oak, balsamic herbs. Palate: good structure, flavourful.

Pulchrum 2013 T
vidadillo

91

Colour: very deep cherry, garnet rim. Nose: expressive, complex, mineral, balsamic herbs, balanced, wild herbs. Palate: full, flavourful, round tannins.

BODEGA PAGO AYLÉS

Finca Aylés. Ctra. A-1101, Km. 24
50152 Mezalocha (Zaragoza)
☎: +34 976 140 473
Fax: +34 976 140 268
pagoayles@pagoayles.com
www.pagoayles.com

Aldeya de Aylés Garnacha 2014 T
garnacha

88

Colour: cherry, purple rim. Nose: expressive, fresh fruit, red berry notes, floral, spicy. Palate: fruity, good acidity, easy to drink.

Aldeya de Aylés Tinto Barrica 2012 T
tempranillo, syrah, merlot

86

Dorondón Chardonnay de Aylés 2014 B
chardonnay

86

Reula Garnacha 2013 T
100% garnacha

87

Colour: dark-red cherry, garnet rim. Nose: ripe fruit, powerfull, toasty, sweet spices. Palate: easy to drink, correct, ripe fruit.

Reula Garnacha 2014 T
garnacha

88

Colour: bright cherry. Nose: ripe fruit, sweet spices, creamy oak. Palate: flavourful, fruity, toasty.

Serendipia Chardonnay de Aylés 2014 B
chardonnay

89

Colour: bright straw. Nose: dried herbs, ripe fruit, spicy. Palate: flavourful, fruity, good acidity, balanced.

Serendipia Syrah 2012 T
syrah

90

Colour: cherry, garnet rim. Nose: creamy oak, balanced, ripe fruit, spicy, smoky. Palate: flavourful, spicy.

BODEGAS AÑADAS

Ctra. Aguarón, km 47,100
50400 Cariñena (Zaragoza)
☎: +34 976 793 016
Fax: +34 976 620 448
bodega@carewines.com
www.carewines.com

Care 2014 T

garnacha, syrah

87

Colour: cherry, purple rim. Nose: red berry notes, ripe fruit, fragrant herbs. Palate: fresh, fruity, easy to drink.

Care 2013 TC

tempranillo, merlot

89

Colour: cherry, garnet rim. Nose: creamy oak, red berry notes, fresh fruit, balanced. Palate: flavourful, spicy, elegant.

Care 2014 RD

tempranillo, cabernet sauvignon

84

Care 2014 T Roble

garnacha, syrah

87

Colour: cherry, purple rim. Nose: ripe fruit, roasted coffee. Palate: flavourful, spicy, powerful.

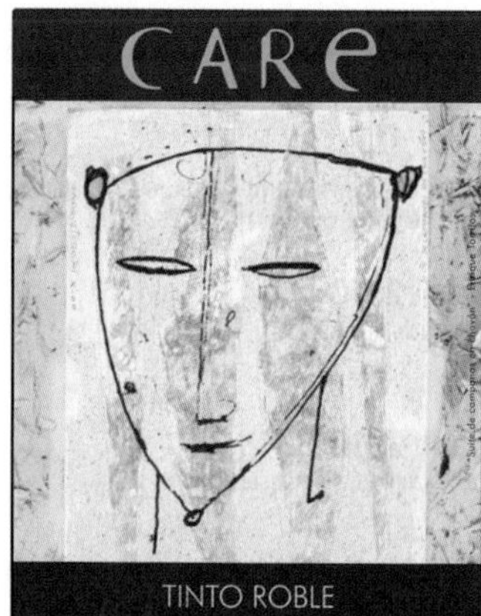

Care Chardonnay 2014 B

chardonnay

88

Colour: bright yellow. Nose: white flowers, mineral, ripe fruit. Palate: flavourful, fruity, good acidity, round, long.

Care Finca Bancales 2012 TR

garnacha

90

Colour: cherry, garnet rim. Nose: balanced, complex, ripe fruit, spicy. Palate: good structure, flavourful, round tannins, balanced.

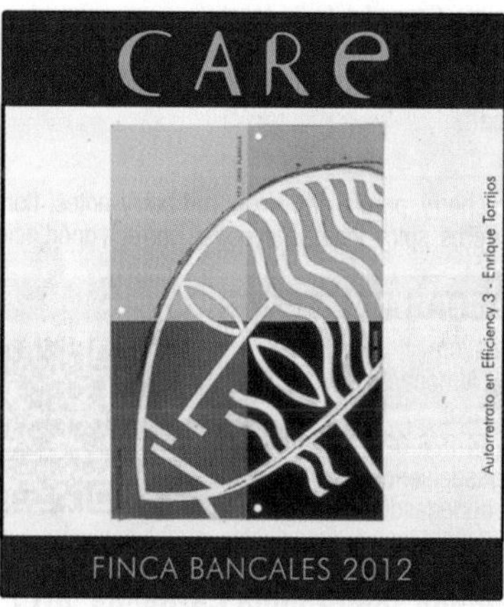

Care Macabeo Chardonnay 2014 B

macabeo, chardonnay

86

Care XCLNT 2011 T

syrah, garnacha, cabernet sauvignon

89

Colour: very deep cherry, garnet rim. Nose: balsamic herbs, fine reductive notes, fruit preserve. Palate: full, flavourful, round tannins.

BODEGAS CARLOS VALERO

Castillo de Capúa, 10
Nave 1 Pol. PLA-ZA
50197 Zaragoza (Zaragoza)
☎: +34 976 180 634
Fax: +34 976 186 326
info@bodegasvalero.com
www.bodegasvalero.com

Heredad X Carlos Valero 2013 T
100% garnacha

88

Colour: bright cherry. Nose: ripe fruit, sweet spices, creamy oak. Palate: flavourful, fruity, toasty.

Heredad X Carlos Valero 2014 T
garnacha

89

Colour: cherry, purple rim. Nose: red berry notes, floral, balsamic herbs, spicy. Palate: flavourful, correct, good acidity.

BODEGAS DEL SEÑORÍO

Afueras, s/n
50108 Almonacid de la Sierra
(Zaragoza)
☎: +34 976 627 225
bodegasdelsenorio@gmail.com
www.bodegasdelsenorio.com

Viña Velerma Coupage de Cabernet Sauvignon Tempranillo Garnacha 2013 TR
cabernet sauvignon, tempranillo, garnacha

82

Viña Velerma Garnacha 100% 2013 T
100% garnacha

84

BODEGAS ESTEBAN MARTÍN

Camino Virgen de Lagunas, s/n
50461 Alfamén (Zaragoza)
☎: +34 976 628 490
Fax: +34 976 628 488
carlosarnal@estebanmartin.es
www.estebanmartin.com

Esteban Martín 2010 TR
garnacha, cabernet sauvignon

85

Esteban Martín 2011 TC
garnacha, syrah

87

Colour: very deep cherry, garnet rim. Nose: expressive, balsamic herbs, balanced. Palate: flavourful, round tannins, easy to drink.

Esteban Martín 2014 B
chardonnay, macabeo

83

Esteban Martín 2014 RD
garnacha

83

Esteban Martín 2014 T
garnacha, syrah

85

Esteban Martín Syrah 2010 T Roble
syrah

84

BODEGAS GABARDA S.L.

Ctra. Valencia, km. 459
50460 Longarés (Zaragoza)
☎: +34 976 621 129
administracion@gabardawines.com
www.gabardawines.com

Gabarda Chardonnay 2014 B
chardonnay

85

Gabarda I 2014 T
garnacha, tempranillo

86

Gabarda II 2014 T
garnacha, tempranillo, syrah

87

Colour: bright cherry. Nose: ripe fruit, sweet spices, creamy oak. Palate: flavourful, fruity.

Gabarda III 2010 T
garnacha, mazuelo, merlot

85

Gabarda IV 2010 TGR
tempranillo, mazuelo, cabernet sauvignon

85

BODEGAS IGNACIO MARÍN

San Valero, 1
50400 Cariñena (Zaragoza)
☎: +34 976 621 129
Fax: +34 976 621 031
comercial@ignaciomarin.com
www.ignaciomarin.com

Ballad 2012 T
garnacha

89

Colour: cherry, garnet rim. Nose: smoky, ripe fruit, sweet spices. Palate: flavourful, smoky aftertaste, ripe fruit, balsamic.

Barón de Lajoyosa 2008 TGR
garnacha, tempranillo, cariñena

85

Campo Marín 2009 TR
tempranillo, garnacha, cariñena

86

Campo Marín 2014 T
tempranillo, garnacha

86

Castillo Mayor 2008 TGR
tempranillo, garnacha, cariñena

80

Duque de Medina 2014 T
garnacha, tempranillo, cariñena

85

Marín Garnacha 2010 T
garnacha

85

BODEGAS LALAGUNA

Ctra. Comarcal A-1304 de Longares
a Alfamés, Km. 1,28
50460 Longares (Zaragoza)
☎: +34 657 804 783
Fax: +34 976 369 980
bodegaslalaguna@bodegaslalaguna.com
www.bodegaslalaguna.com

Lalaguna 2011 TC
tempranillo, garnacha

85

Lalaguna 2014 B
macabeo

83

Lalaguna 2014 RD
garnacha

83

Lalaguna 2014 T
tempranillo, garnacha

83

BODEGAS PANIZA, S. COOP.

Ctra. Zaragoza - Valencia, Km. 53
50014 Paniza (Zaragoza)
☎: +34 976 622 515
Fax: +34 976 622 958
info@bodegaspaniza.com
www.bodegaspaniza.com

Artigazo 2008 T
40% garnacha, 30% syrah, 30% cabernet sauvignon

87

Colour: cherry, garnet rim. Nose: roasted coffee, smoky, spicy, ripe fruit. Palate: flavourful, smoky aftertaste, ripe fruit.

Jabalí Garnacha & Cabernet 2014 RD
90% garnacha, 10% cabernet sauvignon

86

Jabalí Garnacha & Syrah 2014 T
50% garnacha, 50% syrah

88

Colour: cherry, purple rim. Nose: expressive, fresh fruit, red berry notes, floral. Palate: flavourful, fruity, good acidity.

Jabalí Tempranillo & Cabernet 2014 T
50% tempranillo, 50% cabernet sauvignon

88

Colour: cherry, purple rim. Nose: floral, balsamic herbs, ripe fruit, sweet spices, characterful. Palate: powerful, fruity, long.

Jabalí Viura & Chardonnay 2014 B
60% viura, 40% chardonnay

85

Paniza 2009 TGR
30% tempranillo, 10% garnacha, 60% cabernet sauvignon

87

Colour: pale ruby, brick rim edge. Nose: spicy, fine reductive notes, wet leather, aged wood nuances, fruit liqueur notes. Palate: spicy, fine tannins, balanced.

Paniza 2011 TR
80% tempranillo, 5% garnacha, 15% cabernet sauvignon

88

Colour: cherry, garnet rim. Nose: complex, ripe fruit, spicy, fine reductive notes. Palate: good structure, flavourful, round tannins, balanced.

Paniza 2012 TC
60% tempranillo, 20% garnacha, 20% cabernet sauvignon

87

Colour: very deep cherry, garnet rim. Nose: balanced, dried herbs. Palate: flavourful, round tannins.

Paniza Garnacha 2014 RD
100% garnacha

87

Colour: onion pink. Nose: elegant, red berry notes, floral, fragrant herbs. Palate: light-bodied, flavourful, good acidity, long.

Paniza Garnacha 2014 T
100% garnacha

86

Paniza Viura & Chardonnay 2014 B
50% viura, 50% chardonnay

84

Val de Paniza 2014 RD
100% garnacha

87

Colour: rose, purple rim. Nose: red berry notes, floral, expressive. Palate: powerful, fruity, fresh.

Viñas Viejas de Paniza 2012 T
100% garnacha

88

Colour: very deep cherry, garnet rim. Nose: expressive, complex, balsamic herbs, balanced. Palate: full, flavourful, sweet tannins.

BODEGAS SAN VALERO

Ctra. N-330, Km. 450
50400 Cariñena (Zaragoza)
☎: +34 976 620 400
Fax: +34 976 620 398
bsv@sanvalero.com
www.sanvalero.com

Marqués de Tosos 2010 TR
tempranillo, garnacha, cabernet sauvignon

88

Colour: cherry, garnet rim. Nose: red berry notes, ripe fruit, spicy, creamy oak, complex. Palate: flavourful, toasty.

ORIGIUM 2014 B
macabeo, chardonnay

84

Origium 2014 RD

84

Origium 2014 T
garnacha

84

Origium Roble 2013 T Roble

85

Particular Cariñena 2013 T
cariñena

86

Particular Chardonnay 2014 B Barrica
chardonnay

87

Colour: bright yellow. Nose: ripe fruit, powerfull, toasty, aged wood nuances, pattiserie. Palate: flavourful, fruity, spicy, toasty, long.

Particular Garnacha 2014 T
garnacha

84

Particular Garnacha Old Vine 2012 T
garnacha

85

Particular Viñas Centenaria 2011 T
garnacha

89

Colour: cherry, garnet rim. Nose: ripe fruit, wild herbs, earthy notes, spicy, balsamic herbs, old leather. Palate: balanced, flavourful, long, balsamic.

Sierra de Viento Moscatel Dulce 2013 B
moscatel de alejandría

94

Colour: golden. Nose: powerfull, honeyed notes, candied fruit, fragrant herbs, acetaldehyde. Palate: flavourful, sweet, fresh, fruity, good acidity, long.

CAMPOS DE LUZ

Avda. Diagonal, 590, 5º - 1
08021 (Barcelona)
☎: +34 660 445 464
vinergia@vinergia.com
www.vinergia.com

Campos de Luz 2010 TR
85% garnacha, 15% cabernet sauvignon

89

Colour: cherry, garnet rim. Nose: varietal, scrubland, ripe fruit. Palate: balanced, good acidity, spicy, easy to drink.

Campos de Luz 2014 B
viura, chardonnay, moscatel

85

Campos de Luz 2014 RD
100% garnacha

87

Colour: raspberry rose. Nose: red berry notes, floral, fragrant herbs. Palate: light-bodied, flavourful, easy to drink.

Campos de Luz Garnacha 2011 TC
100% garnacha

87

Colour: cherry, garnet rim. Nose: balsamic herbs, balanced, ripe fruit. Palate: flavourful, round tannins, easy to drink.

Campos de Luz Garnacha 2014 T
100% garnacha

86

COVINCA (COMPAÑÍA VITIVINÍCOLA)

Ctra, Valencia, s/n
50460 Cariñena (Zaragoza)
☎: +34 976 142 653
Fax: +34 976 142 402
www.covinca.es

Terrai C11 2011 T Roble
100% cariñena

85

Terrai OVG 2014 T
100% garnacha

88

Colour: bright cherry. Nose: ripe fruit, sweet spices, creamy oak. Palate: flavourful, fruity, toasty, round tannins.

Torrelongares 2011 TR
garnacha, tempranillo, syrah

85

Torrelongares 2012 TC
garnacha, tempranillo, syrah

85

Torrelongares 2014 B
macabeo

83

Torrelongares 2014 RD
garnacha

85

Torrelongares Garnacha 2014 T
100% garnacha

85

Torrelongares Syrah 2013 T
100% syrah

84

Viña Oria 2012 TC
garnacha, tempranillo

84

Viña Oria 2014 B
macabeo

82

Viña Oria 2014 RD
garnacha, tempranillo

84

Viña Oria Garnacha 2014 T
100% garnacha

81

Viña Oria Tempranillo 2014 T
100% tempranillo

83

GRANDES VINOS

Ctra. Valencia Km 45,700
50400 Cariñena (Zaragoza)
☎: +34 976 621 261
Fax: +34 976 621 253
info@grandesvinos.com
www.grandesvinos.com

Anayón Cariñena 2012 T
cariñena

90

Colour: cherry, garnet rim. Nose: mineral, expressive, spicy, ripe fruit. Palate: flavourful, ripe fruit, long, good acidity, balanced.

Anayón Chardonnay 2014 B Barrica

87

Colour: bright yellow. Nose: ripe fruit, powerfull, toasty, sweet spices. Palate: flavourful, fruity, spicy, toasty, long.

Anayón Garnacha 2012 T
garnacha

90

Colour: cherry, garnet rim. Nose: ripe fruit, wild herbs, earthy notes, spicy, balsamic herbs. Palate: balanced, flavourful, long, balsamic.

Anayón Moscatel de Licor B
moscatel de alejandría

87

Colour: bright yellow. Nose: honeyed notes, floral, candied fruit. Palate: fruity, powerful, flavourful, unctuous.

Anayón Selección 2012 T
tempranillo, cabernet sauvignon, syrah

89

Colour: cherry, garnet rim. Nose: creamy oak, red berry notes, balanced. Palate: flavourful, spicy, elegant.

Beso de Vino Garnacha 2014 RD
garnacha

86

Beso de Vino Macabeo 2014 B
macabeo

84

Beso de Vino Old Vine Garnacha 2014 T
garnacha

85

Beso de Vino Selección 2014 T
syrah, garnacha

87

Colour: cherry, purple rim. Nose: powerfull, ripe fruit, spicy. Palate: powerful, fruity, unctuous.

Corona de Aragón 2011 TC
garnacha, tempranillo, cabernet sauvignon, cariñena

87

Colour: cherry, garnet rim. Nose: smoky, spicy, ripe fruit. Palate: flavourful, smoky aftertaste, ripe fruit.

Corona de Aragón 2009 TR
garnacha, tempranillo, cabernet sauvignon, cariñena

87

Colour: cherry, garnet rim. Nose: ripe fruit, wild herbs, spicy, balsamic herbs. Palate: balanced, flavourful, balsamic.

Corona de Aragón Garnacha 2014 T
garnacha

83

Corona de Aragón Garnacha Cabernet Sauvignon 2014 RD
garnacha, cabernet sauvignon

85

Corona de Aragón Macabeo Chardonnay 2014 B
macabeo, chardonnay

85

Corona de Aragón Old Vine Garnacha 2014 T
garnacha

86

Corona de Aragón Special Selection 2013 T
garnacha, cariñena

87

Colour: bright cherry. Nose: ripe fruit, sweet spices, creamy oak. Palate: flavourful, fruity, toasty.

El Circo Cabernet Sauvignon 2014 T
cabernet sauvignon

85

El Circo Cariñena 2014 T
cariñena

85

El Circo Chardonnay 2014 B
chardonnay

84

El Circo Director 2012 T
garnacha, cariñena

85

El Circo Garnacha 2014 RD
garnacha

85

El Circo Garnacha 2014 T
garnacha

84

El Circo Macabeo 2014 B
macabeo

84

El Circo Merlot 2014 T
merlot

86

El Circo Syrah 2014 T
syrah
85

El Circo Tempranillo 2014 T
tempranillo
85

Hoy Celebration 2013 TR
garnacha, tempranillo, cariñena
84

Hoy Chef 2011 T Roble
garnacha, cariñena
83

Hoy Friends 2014 T
garnacha, tempranillo
84

Hoy Love s/c T
garnacha, tempranillo, cariñena
84

Hoy Party 2014 B
macabeo
85

Hoy Relax 2014 RD
garnacha
84

Monasterio de las Viñas 2010 TC
garnacha, tempranillo, cariñena, cabernet sauvignon
84

Monasterio de las Viñas 2014 B
macabeo
84

Monasterio de las Viñas 2007 TGR
garnacha, tempranillo, cariñena
86

Monasterio de las Viñas 2008 TR
garnacha, tempranillo, cariñena
86

Monasterio de las Viñas 2014 RD
garnacha
87
Colour: light cherry. Nose: floral, wild herbs, fruit expression, expressive. Palate: flavourful, balanced, fine bitter notes.

Monasterio de las Viñas Garnacha Tempranillo 2014 T
garnacha, tempranillo
83

Taoz 2011 T
85

HACIENDA MOLLEDA

Ctra. Cariñena-Belchite, 29,3
(A-220, km 29,3)
50154 Tosos (Zaragoza)
☎: +34 976 620 702
Fax: +34 976 620 702
hm@haciendamolleda.com
www.haciendamolleda.com

Finca La Matea Garnacha 2012 T
100% garnacha
89
Colour: very deep cherry, garnet rim. Nose: expressive, complex, mineral, balsamic herbs, balanced. Palate: full, flavourful, round tannins.

Finca La Matea T + G 2011 TC
tempranillo, garnacha
89
Colour: cherry, garnet rim. Nose: ripe fruit, expressive, scrubland, spicy. Palate: spicy, long, fruity aftestaste.

GHM C + C Gran Hacienda Molleda Cariñena + Cariñena 2011 T Roble
100% cariñena
86

GHM C + G Gran Hacienda Molleda Cariñena + Garnacha 2011 T Roble
50% cariñena, 50% garnacha
85

GHM G + G Gran Hacienda Molleda Garnacha + Garnacha 2010 TC
100% garnacha
88
Colour: cherry, garnet rim. Nose: red berry notes, ripe fruit, spicy, creamy oak, complex. Palate: flavourful, toasty, round tannins.

Hacienda Molleda 2013 T
garnacha, tempranillo
85

Hacienda Molleda 2014 B
100% macabeo
84

Hacienda Molleda 2014 RD
garnacha

85

Hacienda Molleda Garnacha 2013 T Roble
100% garnacha

85

Hacienda Molleda Viñas Garnacha 2010 TC
100% garnacha

88

Colour: cherry, garnet rim. Nose: creamy oak, balanced, ripe fruit. Palate: flavourful, spicy, balanced, easy to drink.

Lleda Coupage 2014 T
garnacha, tempranillo

81

Tierra de Andros 2010 TC
100% garnacha

90

Colour: very deep cherry, garnet rim. Nose: expressive, complex, mineral, balsamic herbs, balanced. Palate: full, flavourful, round tannins.

HAMMEKEN CELLARS

Calle de la Muela, 16
03730 Jávea (Alicante)
☎: +34 965 791 967
Fax: +34 966 461 471
cellars@hammekencellars.com
www.hammekencellars.com

Capa Garnacha 2014 T
garnacha

85

Montgó Garnacha 2012 T
garnacha

87

Colour: cherry, garnet rim. Nose: ripe fruit, spicy, creamy oak, complex. Palate: flavourful, toasty, round tannins.

Radio Boca Garnacha 2014 T
garnacha

85

Colour: bright cherry, garnet rim. Nose: grassy, red berry notes. Palate: fruity, easy to drink, balsamic.

HEREDAD ANSÓN

Camino Eras Altas, s/n
50450 Muel (Zaragoza)
☎: +34 976 141 133
Fax: +34 976 141 133
info@bodegasheredadanson.com
www.bodegasheredadanson.com

Heredad de Ansón 2014 B
macabeo

80

Heredad de Ansón 2014 RD
garnacha

83

Heredad de Ansón Merlot Syrah 2014 T
50% merlot, 50% syrah

84

Legum 2007 T
garnacha

86

Liason Garnacha 2014 T
garnacha

83

JORDÁN DE ASSO

Cariñena, 55
50408 Aguarón (Zaragoza)
☎: +34 976 620 291
Fax: +34 976 230 270
info@jordandeasso.com
www.jordandeasso.com

Jordán de Asso 2008 TR
tempranillo, cabernet sauvignon, syrah

84

Jordán de Asso 2011 TC
garnacha, cariñena, cabernet sauvignon

86

Jordán de Asso Garnacha 2014 T
garnacha

84

Jordán de Asso Tempranillo 2014 T
tempranillo

84

MIRAVINOS ARAGÓN

Plaza de Matute, 12
28012 Madrid (Madrid)
☎: +34 609 079 980
info@miravinos.es
www.miravinos.es

Delito Cariñena 2014 T
100% cariñena

84

Delito Garnacha 2014 T
100% garnacha

87

Colour: bright cherry. Nose: ripe fruit, sweet spices, creamy oak. Palate: flavourful, fruity.

NAVASCUÉS ENOLOGÍA

Avda. Ejército, 32
50400 Cariñena (Zaragoza)
☎: +34 651 845 176
info@navascuesenologia.es
www.cutio.es

Cutio 2014 T
garnacha

91

Colour: bright cherry. Nose: ripe fruit, sweet spices, creamy oak. Palate: flavourful, fruity, round tannins.

SAN NICOLÁS DE TOLENTINO

San José, 8
50108 Almonacid de la Sierra (Zaragoza)
☎: +34 976 627 019
Fax: +34 976 627 240
administracion@san-nicolas.es
www.marquesdealmonacid.com

Marqués de Almonacid 2014 B
100% macabeo

85

Marqués de Almonacid 2010 TR
60% garnacha, tempranillo

85

Marqués de Almonacid 2014 RD
100% garnacha

85

Marqués de Almonacid Garnacha 2014 T
100% garnacha

84

Marqués de Almonacid Vendimia Seleccionada 2012 T
60% garnacha, 40% tempranillo

87

Colour: deep cherry, purple rim. Nose: toasty, ripe fruit, balsamic herbs, smoky. Palate: balanced, spicy.

Taninus 2012 T
100% vidadillo

86

SOLAR DE URBEZO
San Valero, 14
50400 Cariñena (Zaragoza)
☎: +34 976 621 968
Fax: +34 976 620 549
info@solardeurbezo.es
www.solardeurbezo.es

Dance del Mar 2014 T
tempranillo, merlot

86

Urbezo 2008 TGR
84

Urbezo 2009 TR
cabernet sauvignon, merlot, syrah

85

Urbezo Chardonnay 2014 B
100% chardonnay

90

Colour: bright straw. Nose: white flowers, fine lees, dried herbs, ripe fruit, candied fruit, citrus fruit. Palate: flavourful, fruity, good acidity, elegant.

Urbezo Garnacha 2014 T
100% garnacha

90

Colour: cherry, purple rim. Nose: ripe fruit, violets, balanced, sweet spices. Palate: balanced, fruity.

Urbezo Merlot 2014 RD
100% merlot

88

Colour: rose, bright. Nose: powerfull, characterful, ripe fruit, red berry notes, floral. Palate: ripe fruit, long, powerful.

Urbezo Vendimia Seleccionada 2010 T
garnacha, cariñena, syrah, cabernet sauvignon

85

Viña Urbezo 2014 T
garnacha, tempranillo, syrah

90

Colour: cherry, purple rim. Nose: red berry notes, ripe fruit. Palate: flavourful, fruity, good acidity, easy to drink, good finish.

Ysiegas 2009 TR
cabernet sauvignon, merlot, syrah

82

Ysiegas 2012 TC
cabernet sauvignon, merlot, syrah

88

Colour: cherry, garnet rim. Nose: ripe fruit, wild herbs, earthy notes, spicy, balsamic herbs. Palate: balanced, flavourful, long, balsamic.

VIÑAS DE ALADRÉN
Via Universitas, 15
50009 Zaragoza (Zaragoza)
☎: +34 637 809 441
nlosilla@yahoo.com
www.viñasdealadren.com

Solanillo 2012 T
merlot, syrah

83

Solanillo 2013 T
merlot, syrah, cabernet sauvignon

84

Viñas de Aladrén 2013 T
merlot, syrah

83

VIÑEDOS Y BODEGAS PABLO
50108 Almonacid de la Sierra (Zaragoza)
☎: +34 976 627 037
Fax: +34 976 627 102
granviu@granviu.com
www.granviu.com

Algairen 2013 T
tempranillo

85

Gran Víu Cariñena 2012 T
cariñena

87

Colour: black cherry, garnet rim. Nose: wild herbs, ripe fruit, spicy. Palate: balanced, slightly dry, soft tannins.

Gran Víu Garnacha del Terreno 2012 T
garnacha

90

Colour: very deep cherry, garnet rim. Nose: expressive, complex, mineral, balsamic herbs, spicy, creamy oak. Palate: full, flavourful, round tannins.

Gran Víu Selección 2012 T
70% garnacha, 10% cabernet sauvignon, 15% tempranillo, 5% syrah

88

Colour: very deep cherry, garnet rim. Nose: expressive, complex, mineral, balsamic herbs. Palate: full, flavourful, round tannins.

Menguante Garnacha 2014 T
garnacha

85

Menguante Garnacha Blanca 2014 B
garnacha blanca

89

Colour: bright yellow. Nose: expressive, dried herbs, ripe fruit. Palate: flavourful, fruity, good acidity, balanced, long, fine bitter notes.

Menguante Garnacha Selección 2013 T
garnacha

90

Colour: cherry, garnet rim. Nose: creamy oak, toasty, ripe fruit, balsamic herbs. Palate: balanced, spicy, long, round.

Menguante Tempranillo 2014 T Roble
tempranillo

85

Menguante Vidadillo 2012 T
vidadilo

88

Colour: deep cherry, garnet rim. Nose: fruit preserve, balsamic herbs, cocoa bean. Palate: flavourful, balanced.

DO. CATALUNYA

CONSEJO REGULADOR

Edifici de l'Estació Enològica Passeig Sunyer, 4-6 1º
43202 Reus (Tarragona)
☎ :+34 977 328 103 - Fax: +34 977 321 357
@: info@do-catalunya.com
www.do-catalunya.com

LOCATION:

The production area covers the traditional vine - growing Catalonian regions, and practically coincides with the current DOs present in Catalonia plus a few municipal areas with vine - growing vocation.

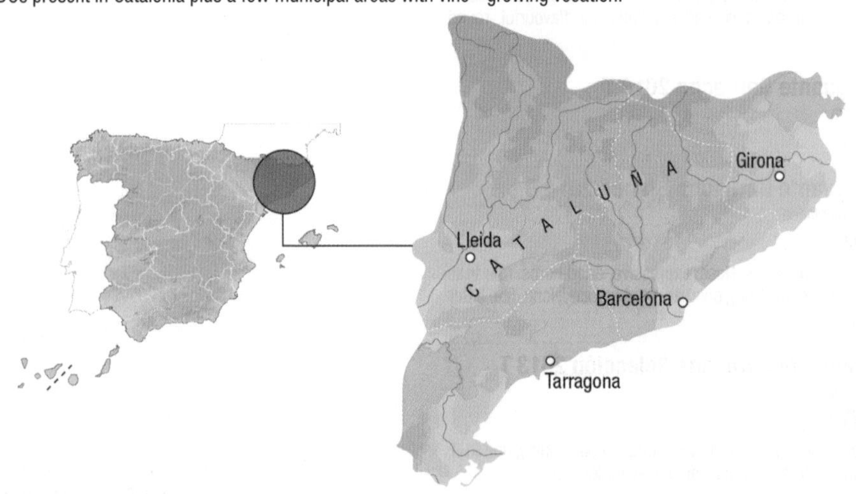

GRAPE VARIETIES:

WHITE: RECOMMENDED: Chardonnay, Garnacha Blanca, Macabeo, Moscatel de Alejandría, Moscatel de Grano Menudo, Parellada, Riesling, Sauvignon Blanc and Xarel·lo.
AUTHORIZED: Gewürztraminer, Subirat Parent (Malvasía), Malvasía de Sitges, Picapoll, Pedro Ximénez, Chenin, Riesling and Sauvignon Blanc
RED: RECOMMENDED: Cabernet Franc, Cabernet Sauvignon, Garnacha, Garnacha Peluda, Merlot, Monastrell, Pinot Noir, Samsó (Cariñena), Trepat, Sumoll and Ull de Llebre (Tempranillo).
AUTHORIZED: Garnacha Tintorera and Syrah.

FIGURES:

Vineyard surface: 44,533 – **Wine-Growers:** 7,614 – **Wineries:** 210 – **2014 Harvest rating:** N/A – **Production 14:** 56,700,377 litres – **Market percentages:** 48% National - 52% International.

CLIMATE AND SOIL:

Depending on the location of the vineyard, the same as those of the Catalonian DO's, whose characteristics are defined in this guide. See Alella, Empordà, Conca de Barberà, Costers del Segre, Montsant, Penedès, Pla de Bages, Priorat, Tarragona and Terra Alta.

VINTAGE RATING — PEÑÍNGUIDE

This denomination of origin, due to the wine-making process, doues not make available single-year wines indicated by vintage, so the following evaluation refers to the overall quality of the wines that were tasted this year.

1898 RAMÓN ROQUETA

Masia Roqueta, s/n
08279 Santa María D'Horta D'Avinyó (Barcelona)
☎: +34 938 743 511
Fax: +34 938 737 204
info@ramonroqueta.com
www.ramonroqueta.com

Mas Oliveras Chardonnay 2014 B
100% chardonnay

86

Mas Oliveras Tempranillo 2014 T
100% tempranillo

84

Ramón Roqueta 2011 TR
60% cabernet sauvignon, 40% tempranillo

85

Ramón Roqueta 2014 T
cabernet sauvignon

85

Vinya Nostra Nit de Tardor 2013 T
90% garnacha, 10% samsó

87

Colour: cherry, garnet rim. Nose: ripe fruit, wild herbs, earthy notes, spicy, balsamic herbs. Palate: balanced, flavourful, long, balsamic.

AGRÍCOLA SANT JOSEP

Estació, 2
43785 Bot (Tarragona)
☎: +34 977 428 352
Fax: +34 977 428 192
info@santjosepwines.com
www.santjosepwines.com

Brau de Bot Blanc Clàssic Bib 3 lt. 2014 B
83

Brau de Bot Negre Clàssic Bib 3 lt. 2014 T
84

Brau de Bot Negre Ull de Llebre Bib 3 lt. 2014 T
ull de llebre

84

Plana d'en Fonoll Blanc 2014 B
75% sauvignon blanc, moscatel de alejandría

88

Colour: bright straw. Nose: white flowers, dried herbs, ripe fruit, citrus fruit. Palate: flavourful, fruity, good acidity, elegant.

Plana d'en Fonoll Cabernet Sauvignon 2013 T
76% cabernet sauvignon, 24% syrah

87

Colour: cherry, garnet rim. Nose: ripe fruit, wild herbs, earthy notes, spicy, balsamic herbs. Palate: balanced, flavourful, long.

Plana d'en Fonoll Selecció Negre Llarga Criança 2006 T
samsó, syrah, cabernet sauvignon

89

Colour: cherry, garnet rim. Nose: balanced, complex, ripe fruit, spicy, fine reductive notes. Palate: good structure, flavourful, round tannins, balanced.

Plana d'en Fonoll Syrah 2012 T
70% syrah, 30% samsó

86

ALBET I NOYA

Can Vendrell de la Codina, s/n
08739 Sant Pau D'Ordal (Barcelona)
☎: +34 938 994 812
Fax: +34 938 994 930
info@albetinoya.cat
www.albetinoya.cat

Albet i Noya La Solana 2012 T
merlot, cabernet sauvignon, syrah, tempranillo

88

Colour: cherry, garnet rim. Nose: ripe fruit, wild herbs, earthy notes, spicy, balsamic herbs, smoky. Palate: balanced, flavourful, long, balsamic.

Albet i Noya Petit Albet 2014 B
xarel.lo, macabeo, chardonnay

86

Albet i Noya Petit Albet Negre 2013 T
ull de llebre, garnacha, cabernet sauvignon

86

Albet i Noya Pla de Morei 2012 T
merlot, syrah, cabernet sauvignon

87

Colour: deep cherry, purple rim. Nose: ripe fruit, balsamic herbs, spicy. Palate: balanced, spicy, long.

BLANCHER CAPDEVILA PUJOL

Plaça Pont Romà, Edificio Blancher
08770 Sant Sadurní D'Anoia
(Barcelona)
☎: +34 938 183 286
Fax: +34 938 911 961
blancher@blancher.es
www.blancher.es

Blancher Parcel.les 2014 B
pansa blanca

84

BODEGAS PUIGGRÒS

Ctra. de Manresa, Km. 13
08711 Odena (Barcelona)
☎: +34 629 853 587
info@bodegaspuiggros.com
www.bodegaspuiggros.com

Exedra 2013 T
garnacha

90

Colour: deep cherry. Nose: creamy oak, toasty, ripe fruit, balsamic herbs, earthy notes. Palate: balanced, spicy, long.

Mestre Vila Vell 2012 T
sumoll

92

Colour: bright cherry. Nose: ripe fruit, sweet spices, creamy oak, wild herbs, earthy notes. Palate: flavourful, fruity, toasty, round tannins.

Sentits Blancs 2014 BFB
garnacha blanca

89

Colour: bright straw, greenish rim. Nose: smoky, sweet spices, ripe fruit. Palate: balanced, spicy, long.

Sentits Negres Garnatxa Negra 2012 T
garnacha

92

Colour: cherry, garnet rim. Nose: balanced, complex, ripe fruit, spicy, dry stone. Palate: good structure, flavourful, balanced.

Signes 2012 T
sumoll, garnacha

90

Colour: very deep cherry, garnet rim. Nose: expressive, complex, mineral, balsamic herbs, balanced, creamy oak. Palate: full, flavourful, round tannins.

BODEGAS TORRES

Miguel Torres i Carbó, 6
08720 Vilafranca del Penedès
(Barcelona)
☎: +34 938 177 400
Fax: +34 938 177 444
mailadmin@torres.es
www.torres.com

Coronas 2012 TC
tempranillo, cabernet sauvignon

86

DeCasta 2014 RD
garnacha, merlot, syrah, cabernet sauvignon, tempranillo

86

Gran Sangre de Toro 2011 TR
garnacha, cariñena, syrah

87

Colour: dark-red cherry, garnet rim. Nose: medium intensity, balsamic herbs, ripe fruit. Palate: correct, round tannins, spicy.

Habitat 2013 B
garnacha blanca, xarel.lo

90

Colour: bright straw. Nose: white flowers, fresh fruit, fragrant herbs, expressive. Palate: flavourful, fruity, good acidity, balanced.

Habitat 2013 T
garnacha, syrah

87

Colour: deep cherry, purple rim. Nose: toasty, ripe fruit, balsamic herbs, spicy. Palate: balanced, spicy, long.

San Valentín Semidulce 2014 B
parellada

85

Sangre de Toro 2013 T
garnacha, merlot, syrah, tempranillo

86

Viña Esmeralda 2014 B
moscatel, gewürztraminer

87

Colour: bright straw. Nose: jasmine, white flowers, expressive, powerfull. Palate: flavourful, fruity, easy to drink, correct, good acidity.

Viña Sol 2014 B
parellada, garnacha blanca

85

BODEGUES VISENDRA

Colón, 22
43815 Les Pobles (Tarragona)
☎: +34 639 338 892
info@bodeguesvisendra.com
www.bodeguesvisendra.com

Visendra 2011 TR
tempranillo, merlot

89

Colour: cherry, garnet rim. Nose: ripe fruit, wild herbs, earthy notes, spicy, balsamic herbs, powerfull, characterful, roasted coffee. Palate: balanced, flavourful, long, balsamic.

CA N'ESTRUC

Finca Ca N'Estruc Ctra. C-1414, Km. 1,05
08292 Esparreguera (Barcelona)
☎: +34 937 777 017
Fax: +34 937 772 268
info@canestruc.com
www.canestruc.com

Ca N'Estruc 2014 RD
garnacha

86

Ca N'Estruc 2014 T
garnacha, syrah, tempranillo

88

Colour: bright cherry, purple rim. Nose: violets, fruit expression, scrubland. Palate: fresh, balanced, fruity.

Ca N'Estruc Blanc 2014 B
xarel.lo, moscatel, garnacha blanca, chardonnay, macabeo

88

Colour: bright straw. Nose: white flowers, jasmine, ripe fruit. Palate: correct, easy to drink, fine bitter notes, good acidity.

Ca N'Estruc Xarel.lo 2014 B
xarel.lo

91

Colour: bright straw. Nose: white flowers, fresh fruit, dried herbs. Palate: flavourful, fruity, good acidity, balanced.

Idoia Blanc 2014 BFB
xarel.lo, garnacha blanca, chardonnay

93

Colour: bright straw. Nose: white flowers, fine lees, dried herbs, mineral. Palate: flavourful, fruity, good acidity, round.

Idoia Negre 2013 T Fermentado en Barrica
syrah, cariñena, garnacha

93

Colour: cherry, garnet rim. Nose: expressive, complex, mineral, balsamic herbs, balanced. Palate: full, flavourful, round tannins, fresh.

L'Equilibrista 2014 B
xarel.lo

93

Colour: bright straw. Nose: white flowers, dried herbs, ripe fruit, citrus fruit, spicy. Palate: flavourful, fruity, good acidity, elegant.

L'Equilibrista Garnatxa 2013 T
garnacha

92

Colour: light cherry. Nose: fruit liqueur notes, spicy, creamy oak, wild herbs. Palate: balanced, elegant, spicy, long.

L'Equilibrista Negre 2013 T
garnacha, syrah, cariñena

93

Colour: very deep cherry, garnet rim, cherry, garnet rim. Nose: complex, mineral, balsamic herbs, characterful. Palate: full, flavourful, round tannins.

CAN GRAU VELL

Can Grau Vell, s/n
08781 Els Hostalets de Pierola
(Barcelona)
☎: +34 676 586 933
Fax: +34 932 684 965
info@grauvell.cat
www.grauvell.cat

Alcor 2010 T
syrah, garnacha, monastrell, marcelan, cabernet sauvignon

93

Colour: cherry, garnet rim. Nose: creamy oak, red berry notes, fresh fruit, balanced. Palate: flavourful, spicy, elegant.

Alcor 2011 T
syrah, garnacha, monastrell, marcelan, cabernet sauvignon

93

Colour: bright cherry. Nose: ripe fruit, sweet spices, creamy oak, earthy notes. Palate: flavourful, fruity, toasty, round tannins.

Tramp 2013 T
syrah, garnacha, monastrell, cabernet sauvignon, marcelan

89

Colour: cherry, purple rim. Nose: expressive, fresh fruit, red berry notes, floral, spicy. Palate: flavourful, fruity, good acidity.

CASTELL D'OR

Mare Rafols, 3- 1ºD
08720 Vilafranca del Penedès
(Barcelona)
☎: +34 938 905 385
Fax: +34 938 905 446
castelldor@castelldor.com
www.castelldor.com

Flama D'Or 2010 TR
cabernet sauvignon, tempranillo

86

Flama D'Or 2012 T
tempranillo

83

Flama D'Or 2014 B
macabeo, xarel.lo, parellada

81

Flama D'Or 2014 RD
trepat

83

Puig de Solivella 2012 T
tempranillo

81

CATALUNYA VINHOS

Carrer La Roca, 3
17750 Capmany (Girona)
☎: +34 629 578 001
rafael@catalunyavinhos.com.br
www.catalunyavinhos.com.br

Clos Catalunya 2014 B
macabeo, garnacha

84

Clos Catalunya 2014 RD
garnacha, samsó

84

Clos Catalunya 2014 T
garnacha, samsó

85

CELLER DE CAPÇANES

Llebaria, 4
43776 Capçanes (Tarragona)
☎: +34 977 178 319
cellercapcanes@cellercapcanes.com
www.cellercapcanes.com

8/X Pinot Noir de Capçanes 2013 T
pinot noir

89

Colour: very deep cherry, garnet rim. Nose: fruit preserve, faded flowers, spicy. Palate: flavourful, balanced, fine tannins.

CELLER REIG-AULET

Can Maura, 2
17468 Parets D'Empordà (Girona)
☎: +34 972 560 214
Fax: +34 972 560 214
972560214@telefonica.net
www.baroniadevilademuls.com

Baronia de Vilademuls 2012 TC
40% cabernet sauvignon, 30% tempranillo, 30% garnacha

85

CELLERS UNIÓ

43206 Reus (Tarragona)
☎: +34 977 330 055
Fax: +34 977 330 070
info@cellersunio.com
www.cellersunio.com

Masia Pubill 2014 RD
ull de llebre

78

Masia Pubill 2014 T
ull de llebre

80

Masia Pubill Blanc 2014 B
macabeo

84

Roca i Mora 2014 B
macabeo, xarel.lo, parellada

84

Roca i Mora 2014 RD
garnacha, ull de llebre

84

Roca i Mora 2014 T
garnacha, sumoll, ull de llebre

82

CLOS D'AGON

Afores, s/n
17251 Calonge (Girona)
☎: +34 972 661 486
Fax: +34 972 661 486
info@closdagon.com
www.closdagon.com

Clos D'Agon 2012 T

58% cabernet franc, 7% cabernet sauvignon, 24% syrah, 11% petit verdot

93

Colour: cherry, garnet rim. Nose: ripe fruit, wild herbs, earthy notes, spicy, balsamic herbs. Palate: balanced, flavourful, long, balsamic.

Clos D'Agon 2013 B

roussanne, marsanne

92

Colour: bright yellow. Nose: expressive, elegant, faded flowers, fresh fruit. Palate: flavourful, rich, spicy, ripe fruit, long.

CLOS MONTBLANC

Ctra. Montblanc-Barbera, s/n
43422 Barberà de la Conca (Tarragona)
☎: +34 977 887 030
Fax: +34 977 887 032
club@closmontblanc.com
www.closmontblanc.com

Clos Montblanc Castell Macabeo Chardonnay 2014 B

macabeo, chardonnay

86

Clos Montblanc Castell Rosat 2014 RD

tempranillo, merlot, syrah

82

Clos Montblanc Castell Tempranillo 2014 T

tempranillo, cabernet sauvignon

85

Clos Montblanc Chardonnay 2014 BFB

chardonnay

88

Colour: bright yellow. Nose: expressive, dried herbs, ripe fruit, spicy. Palate: flavourful, fruity, balanced, long.

Xipella Negre 2012 TC
cariñena, syrah

87

Colour: deep cherry, garnet rim. Nose: red berry notes, ripe fruit, balanced, spicy, toasty. Palate: fruity, round tannins.

COFAMA VINS I CAVES
Casanovas i Bosch 57
08202 Sabadell (Barcelona)
☎: +34 937 220 338
Fax: +34 937 252 385
roger.manyosa@cofamaexport.com
www.cofamaexport.com

Dignitat 2013 T
garnacha, tempranillo

84

Dignitat 2014 B
garnacha blanca

84

Ressó 2013 T
garnacha, tempranillo

83

Ressó 2014 B
garnacha blanca

84

CONDE DE CARALT
Heredad Segura Viudas – Crta.St. Sadurní a St. Pere Riudebitlles, Km.5
08775 Torrelavit (Barcelona)
☎: +34 938 917 070
Fax: +34 938 996 006
condedecaralt@condedecaralt.es
www.condedecaralt.com

Conde de Caralt 2014 B
macabeo, xarel.lo, parellada

84

Conde de Caralt 2014 RD
tempranillo, merlot

84

FERMI BOHIGAS
Finca Can Maciá s/n
08711 Ódena (Barcelona)
☎: +34 938 048 100
Fax: +34 938 032 366
aministracio@bohigas.es
www.bohigas.es

Bohigas 2011 TC
cabernet sauvignon, garnacha

88

Colour: cherry, garnet rim. Nose: red berry notes, ripe fruit, spicy, creamy oak, complex. Palate: flavourful, toasty.

Bohigas Xarel.lo 2014 B
100% xarel.lo

87

Colour: bright straw. Nose: white flowers, fresh fruit, fragrant herbs. Palate: flavourful, fruity, good acidity.

Fermí de Fermí Bohigas 2010 TR
syrah, samsó

89

Colour: cherry, garnet rim. Nose: complex, ripe fruit, spicy, balanced. Palate: good structure, flavourful, round tannins, balanced.

Udina de Fermí Bohigas 2014 B
garnacha blanca, xarel.lo

86

FRANCK MASSARD
Rambla Arnau de Vilanova, 6
08800 Vilanova i La Geltrú (Barcelona)
☎: +34 938 956 541
Fax: +34 938 956 541
info@epicure-wines.com
www.epicure-wines.com

Mas Amor 2014 RD
95% garnacha, 5% cariñena

86

HEREDAD SEGURA VIUDAS
Ctra. Sant Sadurní a St. Pere de Riudebitlles, Km. 5
08775 Torrelavit (Barcelona)
☎: +34 938 917 070
Fax: +34 938 996 006
seguraviudas@seguraviudas.es
www.seguraviudas.com

Viña Heredad Seguras Viudas 2014 RD
tempranillo, merlot

87

Colour: salmon. Nose: elegant, red berry notes, floral, fragrant herbs. Palate: light-bodied, flavourful, good acidity, long, spicy.

JAUME SERRA (J. GARCÍA CARRIÓN)

Ctra. de Vilanova a Vilafranca, Km. 2,5
08800 Vilanova i la Geltru (Barcelona)
☎: +34 938 936 404
Fax: +34 938 147 482
jaumeserra@jgc.es
www.garciacarrion.es

Vinya del Mar Seco 2014 B
40% macabeo, 40% xarel.lo, 20% parellada

79

Viña del Mar 2014 RD
80% tempranillo, 20% cariñena

81

Viña del Mar 2014 T
80% tempranillo, 20% mazuelo

80

Viña del Mar Semidulce 2014 B
60% macabeo, 40% xarel.lo

76

MASET DEL LLEÓ

Ctra. Vilafranca-Igualada C-15 (Km.19)
08792 La Granada (Barcelona)
☎: +34 902 200 250
Fax: +34 938 921 333
info@maset.com
www.maset.com

Maset del LLeó Cabernet Franc 2013 T
cabernet franc

89

Colour: cherry, garnet rim. Nose: toasty, ripe fruit, balsamic herbs. Palate: balanced, spicy, long.

Maset del Lleó Gran Roble 2010 TR
tempranillo

88

Colour: very deep cherry. Nose: ripe fruit, fruit preserve, spicy, dark chocolate. Palate: correct, round tannins, balsamic.

Maset del Lleó Roble 2012 T Roble
tempranillo

87

Colour: cherry, garnet rim. Nose: ripe fruit, wild herbs, earthy notes, spicy. Palate: balanced, flavourful, long.

Maset del LLeó Syrah 2011 TR
syrah

92

Colour: cherry, garnet rim. Nose: expressive, spicy, ripe fruit. Palate: flavourful, ripe fruit, long, good acidity, balanced.

MASIA BACH

Ctra. Martorell Capellades, km. 20,5
08635 Sant Esteve Sesrovires
(Barcelona)
☎: +34 937 714 052
codinfo@codorniu.es
www.grupocodorniu.com

Bach Extrísimo Semidulce 2014 B

85

MASIA VALLFORMOSA

La Sala, 45
08735 Vilobi del Penedès (Barcelona)
☎: +34 938 978 286
Fax: +34 938 978 355
vallformosa@vallformosa.com
www.vallformosagroup.com

Laviña 2014 B
macabeo, garnacha

83

Laviña 2014 RD
tempranillo

85

Laviña Semi Dulce 2014 B
macabeo, garnacha

84

Laviña Tempranillo Merlot 2013 T
tempranillo, merlot

85

PAGO DIANA

Pago Diana, Manso Sant Mateu s/n
17464 Sant Jordi Desvalls (Girona)
☎: +34 666 395 251
info@pagodiana.com
www.pagodiana.com

Clos Diana 2009 T

86

Pago Diana Tempranillo 2010 T
tempranillo

84

Teria 2009 T

86

RENÉ BARBIER

Ctra. Sant Sadurní a St.
Pere Riudebitlles, km. 5
08775 Torrelavit (Barcelona)
☎: +34 938 917 070
Fax: +34 938 996 006
renebarbier@renebarbier.es
www.renebarbier.com

René Barbier Kraliner 2014 B
macabeo, xarel.lo, parellada

85

René Barbier Rosado Tradición 2014 RD
tempranillo, merlot

84

René Barbier Viña Augusta Semidulce 2013 B
macabeo, xarel.lo, parellada, moscatel

84

ROCAMAR

Major, 80
08755 Castellbisbal (Barcelona)
☎: +34 937 720 900
Fax: +34 937 721 495
info@rocamar.net
www.rocamar.net

Blanc de Palangre de Aguja B
macabeo, parellada

81

Masia Ribot 2014 B
macabeo, parellada

80

Masia Ribot 2014 RD
tempranillo, garnacha

82

Masia Ribot 2014 T
tempranillo, garnacha

78

Rosat de Palangre de Aguja RD
trepat

83

ROSELL MIR

Bario El Rebato s/n
08739 Subirats (Barcelona)
☎: +34 938 911 354
infoceller@rosellmir.com
www.rosellmir.com

Masia Posta 2012 T
merlot, cabernet sauvignon

87

Colour: black cherry. Nose: ripe fruit, wild herbs, earthy notes, spicy, balsamic herbs. Palate: balanced, flavourful, long, balsamic.

VINOS PADRÓ

Avda. Catalunya, 56-58
43812 Brafim (Tarragona)
☎: +34 977 620 012
Fax: +34 977 620 486
info@vinspadro.com
www.vinspadro.com

Poesía 2014 RD
tempranillo, merlot

85

Poesía Blanc 2014 B
macabeo, xarel.lo, moscatel

84

Poesía Negre 2014 T
tempranillo, merlot

85

Poesía Tempranillo Merlot 2011 TC
tempranillo, merlot

87

Colour: cherry, garnet rim. Nose: smoky, spicy, ripe fruit. Palate: flavourful, smoky aftertaste, ripe fruit.

VINS DE TALLER

Nou, 5
17469 Siurana d'Empordà (Girona)
☎: +34 972 525 578
Fax: +34 972 525 578
info@vinsdetaller.com
www.vinsdetaller.com

Vins de Taller Baseia 2014 B
viognier

91 ♣

Colour: bright yellow. Nose: floral, wild herbs, mineral, sweet spices, creamy oak. Palate: flavourful, spicy, long, balsamic. Personality.

Vins de Taller Gris 2014 RD
garnacha, syrah

86 ♣

Vins de Taller Merlot Jr. 2014 T
merlot

89 ♣

Colour: deep cherry, purple rim. Nose: balsamic herbs, red berry notes, spicy, wild herbs, dry stone. Palate: spicy, long, balanced.

Vins de Taller Phlox 2014 B
chardonnay, viognier

88 ♣

Colour: bright yellow. Nose: expressive, dried herbs, ripe fruit, spicy, floral. Palate: flavourful, good acidity, balanced.

Vins de Taller Siurà 2011 T
merlot, garnacha, syrah

90

Colour: cherry, garnet rim. Nose: fine reductive notes, aged wood nuances, ripe fruit, mineral, expressive. Palate: spicy, long, toasty.

VINS GRAU

Ctra. C-37, Km. 75,5
D'Igualada a Manresa
08255 Maians-Castellfollit del Boix
(Barcelona)

☎: +34 938 356 002
info@vinsgrau.com
www.vinsgrau.com

Clos del Recó 2014 B
macabeo, xarel.lo, parellada, moscatel

84

Clos del Recó 2014 RD
tempranillo

85

Clos del Recó 2014 T
tempranillo

83

VINYES DE L'ALBÀ

Masia La Vilella, 22
43815 Tarragona (Tarragona)
☎: +34 625 465 895
carles@vinyesdelalba.com

Vinyes de L'Alba Sumoll 2014 T
100% sumoll

89

Colour: light cherry, purple rim. Nose: grassy, citrus fruit, dry stone. Palate: correct, balsamic, good finish.

VIÑA TRIDADO

Noves Tecnologies, Parc.1
Pol.Les Borges I i II
43350 Les Borges del Camp
☎: +34 977 328 512
Fax: +34 977 318 115
vega@reservadelatierra.com

Chirico 2013 B
macabeo, moscatel

84

Chirico 2013 RD

85

Chirico España S/C T
100% tempranillo

85

Chirico S/C T

83

Viña Puerta de Plata S/C T

84

DO. CAVA

CONSEJO REGULADOR

Avinguda Tarragona, 24
08720 Vilafranca del Penedès (Barcelona)
☎:+34 938 903 104 - Fax: +34 938 901 567
@: consejo@crcava.es
www.crcava.es

LOCATION:

The defined Cava region covers the sparkling wines produced according to the traditional method of a second fermentation in the bottle of 63 municipalities in the province of Barcelona, 52 in Tarragona, 12 in Lleida and 5 in Girona, as well as those of the municipal areas of Laguardia, Moreda de Álava and Oyón in Álava, Almendralejo in Badajoz, Mendavia and Viana in Navarra, Requena in Valencia, Ainzón and Cariñena in Zaragoza, and a further 18 municipalities of La Rioja.

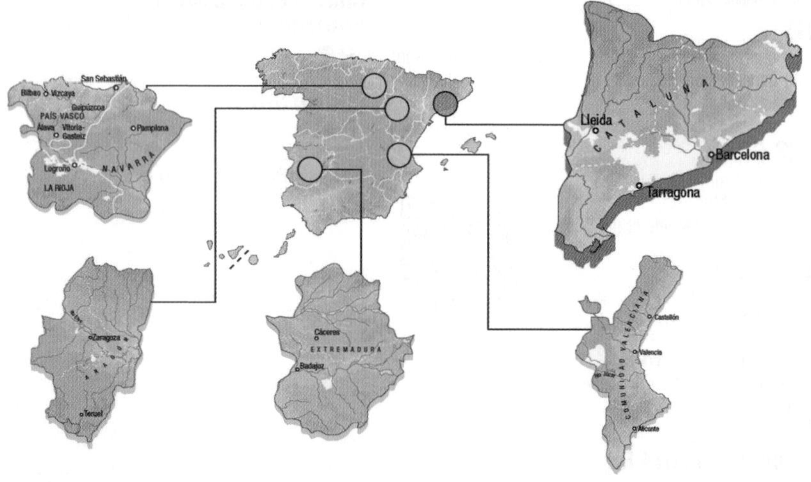

GRAPE VARIETIES:

WHITE: Macabeo (Viura), Xarel.lo, Parellada, Subirat (Malvasía Riojana) and Chardonnay.
RED: Garnacha Tinta, Monastrell, Trepat and Pinot Noir.

FIGURES:

Vineyard surface: 33,352.29 – **Wine-Growers:** 6,335 – **Wineries:** 244 – **2014 Harvest rating:** Good – **Production 14:** 241,000,000 bottles – **Market percentages:** 36% National - 64% International.

SOIL:

This also depends on each producing region.

CLIMATE:

That of each producing region stated in the previous epigraph. Nevertheless, the region in which the largest part of the production is concentrated (Penedès) has a Mediterranean climate, with some production areas being cooler and situated at a higher altitude.

VINTAGE RATING

PEÑÍNGUIDE

This denomination of origin, due to the wine-making process, does not make available single-year wines indicated by vintage, so the following evaluation refers to the overall quality of the wines that were tasted this year.

1 + 1 = 3

Masía Navinés
08736 Font-Rubí (Barcelona)
☎: +34 938 974 069
teresa@umesufan3.com
www.umesufan3.com

1 + 1 = 3 BN Reserva
macabeo, xarel.lo, parellada

90

Colour: bright straw. Nose: fresh fruit, dried herbs, fine lees, floral. Palate: fresh, fruity, flavourful, good acidity.

1 + 1 = 3 BR Reserva
macabeo, xarel.lo, parellada

89

Colour: bright yellow. Nose: fine lees, floral, fragrant herbs. Palate: flavourful, good acidity, fine bead.

1 + 1 = 3 Cygnus BN Reserva
macabeo, xarel.lo, parellada

91

Colour: bright yellow. Nose: fine lees, balanced, dried herbs, fresh fruit. Palate: good acidity, flavourful, ripe fruit, long.

1 + 1 = 3 Especial 2008 BN Gran Reserva
xarel.lo, pinot noir

93

Colour: bright golden. Nose: fine lees, dry nuts, fragrant herbs, complex, toasty. Palate: powerful, flavourful, good acidity, fine bead, fine bitter notes.

1 + 1 = 3 Especial Blanc de Noirs BN Reserva
pinot noir

91

Colour: yellow. Nose: medium intensity, dried herbs, fine lees, ripe fruit, faded flowers. Palate: fresh, fruity, flavourful, good acidity.

1 + 1 = 3 Especial Xarel.lo BN Reserva
xarel.lo

92

Colour: bright straw. Nose: fine lees, dry nuts, fragrant herbs, complex, toasty. Palate: powerful, flavourful, good acidity, fine bead, fine bitter notes.

ADERNATS VINÍCOLA DE NULLES

Raval de Sant Joan, 7
43887 Nulles (Tarragona)
☎: +34 977 602 622
botiga@vinicoladenulles.com
www.adernats.cat

Adernats 2009 BN Gran Reserva
macabeo, xarel.lo, chardonnay

90

Colour: yellow. Nose: fine lees, dry nuts, fragrant herbs, toasty. Palate: powerful, flavourful, good acidity, fine bead, fine bitter notes.

Adernats 2009 BR Gran Reserva
macabeo, xarel.lo, chardonnay

90

Colour: bright yellow. Nose: fine lees, fragrant herbs, ripe fruit, dry nuts. Palate: powerful, flavourful, good acidity, fine bead, fine bitter notes.

Adernats 2012 BR Reserva
macabeo, xarel.lo, parellada

88

Colour: bright straw. Nose: fine lees, floral, fragrant herbs. Palate: flavourful, good acidity, fine bead.

Adernats Dolç 2012 Reserva
macabeo, xarel.lo, parellada

85

Adernats Reserva BN
macabeo, xarel.lo, parellada

87

Colour: bright straw. Nose: medium intensity, fresh fruit, dried herbs, fine lees, floral. Palate: fresh, fruity, flavourful, good acidity.

Adernats Rosat BR Reserva
trepat

86

Adernats XC BN Gran Reserva
xarel.lo

92

Colour: bright golden. Nose: fine lees, dry nuts, fragrant herbs, complex, toasty. Palate: powerful, flavourful, good acidity, fine bead, fine bitter notes, elegant.

AGUSTÍ TORELLÓ MATA

La Serra, s/n
08770 Sant Sadurní D'Anoia
(Barcelona)
☎: +34 938 911 173
Fax: +34 938 912 616
visites@agustitorellomata.com
www.agustitorellomata.com

Agustí Torelló Mata 2010 BN Gran Reserva
macabeo, xarel.lo, parellada

91

Colour: bright yellow. Nose: ripe fruit, fine lees, balanced, dried herbs. Palate: good acidity, flavourful, ripe fruit, long.

Agustí Torelló Mata 2010 BR Gran Reserva
macabeo, xarel.lo, parellada

90

Colour: bright golden. Nose: dry nuts, dried herbs, complex, spicy. Palate: powerful, flavourful, good acidity, fine bead, fine bitter notes.

Agustí Torelló Mata 2011 BR Reserva
macabeo, xarel.lo, parellada

90

Colour: bright straw. Nose: fine lees, floral, fragrant herbs, expressive. Palate: powerful, flavourful, good acidity, fine bead, balanced.

Agustí Torelló Mata Gran Reserva Barrica 2010 BN
macabeo

93

Colour: bright golden. Nose: fine lees, dry nuts, fragrant herbs, complex. Palate: powerful, flavourful, good acidity, fine bead, fine bitter notes.

Agustí Torelló Mata Magnum 2008 BN Gran Reserva
macabeo, xarel.lo, parellada

93

Colour: bright golden. Nose: fine lees, dry nuts, fragrant herbs, complex, spicy. Palate: powerful, flavourful, good acidity, fine bead, fine bitter notes, balanced.

Agustí Torelló Mata Rosat Trepat 2012 BR Reserva
trepat

90

Colour: light cherry. Nose: floral, red berry notes, ripe fruit, fragrant herbs, expressive. Palate: powerful, balanced, flavourful.

Kripta 2008 BN Gran Reserva
macabeo, xarel.lo, parellada

93

Colour: bright yellow. Nose: ripe fruit, fine lees, balanced, dried herbs, sweet spices, cocoa bean. Palate: good acidity, flavourful, ripe fruit, long.

ALSINA & SARDÁ

Barrio Les Tarumbas, s/n
08733 Pla del Penedès (Barcelona)
☎: +34 938 988 671
Fax: +34 938 988 671
gestio@alsinasarda.com
www.alsinasarda.com

Alsina & Sardá BR Reserva
macabeo, xarel.lo, parellada

88

Colour: bright straw. Nose: fine lees, floral, fragrant herbs. Palate: flavourful, good acidity, fine bead, balanced.

Alsina & Sardá 2012 BN Reserva
macabeo, xarel.lo, parellada

87

Colour: bright yellow. Nose: ripe fruit, fine lees, balanced, dried herbs. Palate: good acidity, flavourful, ripe fruit, long.

Alsina & Sardá Gran Cuvée Vestigis 2008 BN Gran Reserva
macabeo, xarel.lo, parellada, pinot noir, chardonnay

89

Colour: bright golden. Nose: fine lees, dry nuts, fragrant herbs, complex. Palate: powerful, flavourful, good acidity, fine bead, fine bitter notes, slightly evolved.

Alsina & Sardá Gran Reserva Especial 2009 BN Gran Reserva
xarel.lo, chardonnay

89

Colour: bright golden. Nose: fine lees, dry nuts, fragrant herbs. Palate: powerful, flavourful, good acidity, fine bead, fine bitter notes.

Alsina & Sarda Pinot Noir Rosado BN Reserva
pinot noir

89

Colour: coppery red. Nose: floral, jasmine, fragrant herbs, candied fruit. Palate: fresh, fruity, flavourful, correct.

Alsina & Sardá Sello 2011 BN Gran Reserva
xarel.lo, macabeo, parellada

87

Colour: bright straw. Nose: medium intensity, fresh fruit, dried herbs, fine lees, floral. Palate: fresh, fruity, flavourful, good acidity.

Mas D'Alsina & Sardá BN Reserva
chardonnay, macabeo, xarel.lo, parellada

89

Colour: bright yellow. Nose: medium intensity, fresh fruit, dried herbs, fine lees. Palate: fresh, fruity, flavourful, good acidity.

ALTA ALELLA - PRIVAT

Camí Baix de Tiana s/n
08328 Alella (Barcelona)
☎: +34 934 693 720
info@altaalella.cat
www.altaalella.cat

AA Bruel 2013 BN
pansa blanca

86

AA Capsigrany 2013 BN
pansa rosada

82

AA Mirgin 2010 BN Gran Reserva
pansa blanca, chardonnay, pinot noir

91

Colour: bright golden. Nose: dry nuts, fragrant herbs, complex, toasty. Palate: powerful, flavourful, good acidity, fine bead, fine bitter notes.

AA Privat 2013 BN
pansa blanca, macabeo, parellada

89

Colour: bright straw. Nose: fine lees, balanced, dried herbs, citrus fruit, fresh. Palate: good acidity, flavourful, ripe fruit, long.

AA Privat 2013 BR
pansa blanca, macabeo, parellada

89

Colour: bright straw. Nose: fine lees, floral, fragrant herbs, citrus fruit. Palate: flavourful, good acidity, fine bead.

AA Privat Chardonnay 2013 BN Reserva
chardonnay

87

Colour: bright straw. Nose: medium intensity, fresh fruit, floral. Palate: fresh, fruity, flavourful, good acidity, easy to drink.

AA Privat Laietà 2011 BN Gran Reserva
pansa blanca, chardonnay, pinot noir

91

Colour: bright yellow. Nose: ripe fruit, fine lees, balanced, dried herbs, elegant. Palate: good acidity, flavourful, ripe fruit, long, balanced.

AA Privat Laietà Rosé 2011 BN Gran Reserva
mataró

90

Colour: coppery red. Nose: floral, jasmine, fragrant herbs, candied fruit. Palate: fresh, fruity, flavourful, correct.

AA Privat Opus Evolutium BN Gran Reserva
pansa blanca, chardonnay, pinot noir

93

Colour: bright golden. Nose: fine lees, dry nuts, fragrant herbs, complex, spicy. Palate: powerful, flavourful, good acidity, fine bead, fine bitter notes.

AA Privat Rosé 2012 BN Reserva
mataró

88

Colour: coppery red. Nose: floral, jasmine, fragrant herbs, candied fruit. Palate: fresh, fruity, flavourful, correct.

AA Privat Rosé 2013 BN Reserva
mataró

86

ARBOLEDA MEDITERRÁNEA

Ctra Sant Sadurni - Piera
08784 La Fortesa (Piera) (Barcelona)
☎: +34 937 279 831
Fax: +34 937 478 891
export@arboledamediterranea.com
www.arboledamediterranean.com

Torrens & Moliner BN Gran Reserva
macabeo, xarel.lo, parellada

89

Colour: bright yellow. Nose: ripe fruit, fine lees, balanced, dried herbs. Palate: good acidity, flavourful, ripe fruit, long.

Torrens & Moliner BR
macabeo, xarel.lo, parellada

87

Colour: bright straw. Nose: fine lees, floral, fragrant herbs. Palate: flavourful, good acidity, fine bead, correct.

Torrens & Moliner Reserva Particular BN Reserva
macabeo, xarel.lo, parellada

88

Colour: bright straw. Nose: medium intensity, fresh fruit, dried herbs, fine lees, floral. Palate: fresh, fruity, flavourful, good acidity.

ARTIUM – CELLER COOPERATIU D'ARTÉS
Cr. Rocafort, 44
08271 Artés (Barcelona)
☎: +34 938 305 325
Fax: +34 938 306 289
artium@cavesartium.com
www.cavesartium.com

Artium 2013 BN Reserva
macabeo, xarel.lo, parellada

87

Colour: yellow. Nose: medium intensity, ripe fruit, fresh, dried herbs. Palate: balanced, correct, good acidity.

Artium 2013 BR Reserva
macabeo, xarel.lo, parellada

86

Artium Rosat BR Reserva
100% trepat

84

Lluís Guitart 2011 BR
macabeo, xarel.lo, parellada

85

AVINYÓ CAVAS
Masia Can Fontanals
08793 Avinyonet del Penedès (Barcelona)
☎: +34 938 970 055
Fax: +34 938 970 691
avinyo@avinyo.com
www.avinyo.com

Avinyó BN Reserva
macabeo, xarel.lo, parellada

88

Colour: bright straw. Nose: medium intensity, fresh fruit, dried herbs, fine lees, floral. Palate: fresh, fruity, flavourful, good acidity.

Avinyó BR Reserva
macabeo, xarel.lo, parellada

85

Avinyó Blanc de Noirs BN Reserva
100% pinot noir

88

Colour: bright straw. Nose: fine lees, floral, fragrant herbs, expressive. Palate: powerful, flavourful, good acidity, fine bead, balanced.

Avinyó Rosé Sublim BR Reserva
100% pinot noir

87

Colour: salmon. Nose: fine lees, floral, fragrant herbs. Palate: flavourful, good acidity, fine bead.

Avinyó Selecció La Ticota 2008 BN Gran Reserva
macabeo, xarel.lo

88

Colour: bright yellow. Nose: ripe fruit, fruit liqueur notes, dried herbs, toasty. Palate: correct, slightly evolved.

AXIAL
Castillo de Capua Nº 10 nave 7
50197 Zaragoza (Zaragoza)
☎: +34 976 780 136
Fax: +34 976 303 035
info@axialvinos.com
www.axialvinos.com

La Granja 360 Cava 2013 BR
70% xarel.lo, 30% parellada

85

BALDÚS
Finca Baldús
08792 Santa Fe del Penedés (Barcelona)
☎: +34 938 988 205
Fax: +34 938 988 205
janesantacana@janesantacana.com

Baldús 2011 BN Gran Reserva
60% xarel.lo, 30% macabeo, 10% parellada

88

Colour: bright yellow. Nose: fine lees, dry nuts, fragrant herbs. Palate: flavourful, good acidity, fine bitter notes.

Baldús 2012 BN Reserva
50% xarel.lo, 30% macabeo, 20% parellada

87

Colour: bright straw. Nose: medium intensity, fresh fruit, dried herbs, fine lees, floral. Palate: fresh, flavourful, easy to drink.

Baldús 2012 BR Reserva
50% xarel.lo, 30% macabeo, 20% parellada

86

BARDINET S.A.

Camí Can Valls, s/n
08790 Gélida (Barcelona)
☎: +34 937 790 125
Fax: +34 937 790 505
bardinet@bardinet.es
www.bardinet.es

Montsarra 2011 BR
macabeo, xarel.lo, parellada

87

Colour: bright yellow. Nose: fine lees, floral, fragrant herbs. Palate: flavourful, good acidity, fine bead.

Montsarra 2011 SS
macabeo, xarel.lo, parellada

85

Montsarra Nature 2011 BN
macabeo, xarel.lo, parellada

86

Xaloc Nature 2011 BN
macabeo, xarel.lo, parellada

85

BLANCHER CAPDEVILA PUJOL

Plaça Pont Romà, Edificio Blancher
08770 Sant Sadurní D'Anoia
(Barcelona)
☎: +34 938 183 286
Fax: +34 938 911 961
blancher@blancher.es
www.blancher.es

Blancher 2009 BN Gran Reserva
xarel.lo, macabeo, parellada

87

Colour: bright straw. Nose: ripe fruit, fine lees, dried herbs. Palate: good acidity, flavourful, ripe fruit, long.

Blancher 2009 BR Reserva Especial
xarel.lo, macabeo, parellada

86

Blancher Rosat 2011 BR Reserva
trepat, garnacha, pinot noir

85

Capdevila Pujol 2010 BN Reserva
xarel.lo, macabeo, parellada

89

Colour: bright yellow. Nose: ripe fruit, fine lees, balanced, dried herbs. Palate: good acidity, flavourful, ripe fruit, long.

Obrac 2009 BR Gran Reserva
macabeo, xarel.lo, parellada

87

Colour: bright yellow. Nose: fine lees, balanced, dried herbs. Palate: good acidity, flavourful, ripe fruit, long.

Teresa Blancher de la Tieta 2008 BN Gran Reserva
macabeo, xarel.lo, parellada, pansa blanca

92

Colour: bright golden. Nose: fine lees, dry nuts, fragrant herbs, complex, toasty. Palate: powerful, flavourful, good acidity, fine bead, fine bitter notes.

BODEGA SANSTRAVÉ

De la Conca, 10
43412 Solivella (Tarragona)
☎: +34 977 892 165
Fax: +34 977 892 073
bodega@sanstrave.com
www.sanstrave.com

Sanstravé 2008 BN Gran Reserva
macabeo, parellada, xarel.lo, chardonnay

88

Colour: bright yellow. Nose: ripe fruit, fine lees, dried herbs. Palate: good acidity, flavourful, ripe fruit, long.

Sanstravé Rosat 2012 BR Reserva
trepat

90

Colour: coppery red. Nose: floral, jasmine, fragrant herbs, candied fruit. Palate: fresh, fruity, flavourful, correct.

BODEGAS ARRAEZ

Arcediano Ros, 35
46321 La Font de la Figuera (Valencia)
☎: +34 962 290 031
info@bodegasarraez.com
www.bodegasarraez.com

A2 2011 BR Reserva
chardonnay, macabeo

87

Colour: bright straw. Nose: fresh fruit, dried herbs, fine lees, floral. Palate: fresh, fruity, flavourful, good acidity.

BODEGAS CAÑALVA

Coto, 54
10136 Cañamero (Cáceres)
☎: +34 927 369 405
Fax: +34 927 369 405
info@bodegascanalva.com
www.bodegascanalva.com

Cava Cañalva S/C BR
macabeo, parellada

83

BODEGAS CAPITÀ VIDAL

Ctra. Villafranca-Igualada, Km. 21
08733 Pla del Penedès (Barcelona)
☎: +34 938 988 630
Fax: +34 938 988 625
capitavidal@capitavidal.com
www.capitavidal.com

Fuchs de Vidal BN Gran Reserva
30% macabeo, 50% xarel.lo, 20% parellada

89

Colour: bright straw. Nose: fine lees, dry nuts, fragrant herbs. Palate: powerful, flavourful, good acidity, fine bead, fine bitter notes.

Fuchs de Vidal Brut Cinco BR
30% macabeo, 40% xarel.lo, 30% parellada

87

Colour: bright straw. Nose: fine lees, floral, fragrant herbs, expressive. Palate: powerful, flavourful, good acidity, fine bead.

Fuchs de Vidal Cuvée BN Reserva
35% macabeo, 40% xarel.lo, 25% parellada

90

Colour: bright straw. Nose: ripe fruit, fine lees, balanced, dried herbs. Palate: good acidity, flavourful, ripe fruit, long, complex.

Fuchs de Vidal Unic BN
50% chardonnay, 35% pinot noir, 15% macabeo, xarel.lo, parellada

90

Colour: bright yellow. Nose: ripe fruit, fine lees, balanced, dried herbs. Palate: good acidity, flavourful, ripe fruit, long.

Gran Fuchs de Vidal BN
macabeo, xarel.lo, parellada

90

Colour: bright straw. Nose: medium intensity, fresh fruit, dried herbs, fine lees, floral. Palate: fresh, fruity, flavourful, good acidity.

Palau Solá BN
35% macabeo, 40% xarel.lo, parellada

84

BODEGAS COVIÑAS

Avda. Rafael Duyos, s/n
46340 Requena (Valencia)
☎: +34 962 300 680
Fax: +34 962 302 651
covinas@covinas.es
www.covinas.es

Enterizo BN
macabeo, xarel.lo

83

Enterizo BR
macabeo, xarel.lo

84

Marqués de Plata BN
macabeo, xarel.lo

85

Marqués de Plata BR
macabeo, xarel.lo

87

Colour: bright straw. Nose: fine lees, floral, fragrant herbs. Palate: good acidity, fine bead.

BODEGAS FAUSTINO

Ctra. de Logroño, s/n
01320 Oyón (Álava)
☎: +34 945 622 500
Fax: +34 945 622 511
info@bodegasfaustino.es
www.bodegasfaustino.com

Cava Faustino BR Reserva
macabeo, chardonnay

85

BODEGAS HISPANO SUIZAS

Ctra. N-322, Km. 451,7
46357 El Pontón (Valencia)
☎: +34 962 349 370
Fax: +34 962 138 318
rafael.roman@bodegashispanosuizas.com
www.bodegashispanosuizas.com

Tantum Ergo Chardonnay Pinot Noir 2013 BN
chardonnay, pinot noir

91

Colour: bright yellow. Nose: white flowers, fresh fruit, fine lees. Palate: complex, flavourful, full, fine bitter notes, good acidity.

Tantum Ergo Pinot Noir Rosé 2012 BN
pinot noir

92

Colour: coppery red. Nose: floral, jasmine, fragrant herbs, candied fruit, expressive, elegant. Palate: fresh, fruity, flavourful, correct, balanced.

Tantum Ergo Vintage 2010 BN
chardonnay, pinot noir

93

Colour: bright yellow. Nose: dry nuts, fragrant herbs, complex, toasty. Palate: powerful, flavourful, good acidity, fine bead, fine bitter notes.

BODEGAS MARCELINO DÍAZ

Mecánica, s/n
06200 Almendralejo (Badajoz)
☎: +34 924 677 548
Fax: +34 924 660 977
bodega@madiaz.com
www.madiaz.com

Puerta Palma BR
macabeo

83

Puerta Palma Selección Van der Linde BN Reserva
80% macabeo, 20% parellada

84

BODEGAS MUGA

Barrio de la Estación, s/n
26200 Haro (La Rioja)
☎: +34 941 311 825
marketing@bodegasmuga.com
www.bodegasmuga.com

Conde de Haro 2012 BR
90% viura, 10% malvasía

88

Colour: yellow. Nose: fine lees, dry nuts, fragrant herbs, complex, toasty, pattiserie. Palate: powerful, flavourful, good acidity, fine bead, fine bitter notes.

Conde de Haro Brut Vintage 2012 BR

89

Colour: bright yellow. Nose: faded flowers, ripe fruit, balanced. Palate: correct, fine bitter notes, good acidity.

Conde de Haro Rosado BR
100% garnacha

89

Colour: raspberry rose. Nose: floral, ripe fruit, fragrant herbs. Palate: balanced, flavourful, fresh.

BODEGAS MURVIEDRO

Ampliación Pol. El Romeral, s/n
46340 Requena (Valencia)
☎: +34 962 329 003
Fax: +34 962 329 002
murviedro@murviedro.es
www.murviedro.es

Expresión Solidarity Cuvée Chardonnay BN
chardonnay

87

Colour: bright yellow. Nose: ripe fruit, dried herbs, tropical fruit. Palate: good acidity, flavourful.

Luna de Murviedro BR
macabeo

85

Luna de Murviedro SS
macabeo

85

Luna de Murviedro Organic BR
90% macabeo, 10% chardonnay

88

Colour: bright straw. Nose: fine lees, floral, fragrant herbs. Palate: flavourful, good acidity, fine bead.

Luna de Murviedro Rosé BR
garnacha

87

Colour: raspberry rose. Nose: floral, red berry notes, ripe fruit, fragrant herbs, expressive. Palate: powerful, balanced, flavourful.

BODEGAS OLARRA

Avda. de Mendavia, 30
26009 Logroño (La Rioja)
☎: +34 941 235 299
Fax: +34 941 253 703
bodegasolarra@bodegasolarra.es
www.bodegasolarra.es

Añares BN
100% viura

86

BODEGAS ONDARRE

Ctra. de Aras, s/n
31230 Viana (Navarra)
☎: +34 948 645 300
Fax: +34 948 646 002
bodegasondarre@bodegasondarre.es
www.bodegasondarre.es

Ondarre BN
100% viura

86

BODEGAS PINORD

Doctor Pasteur, 6
08776 Vilafranca del Penedès
(Barcelona)
☎: +34 938 903 066
pinord@pinord.com
www.pinord.com

Marrugat + Natura 2012 BN Reserva
macabeo, xarel.lo, parellada

84

Marrugat Brut Imperial 2011 BR Reserva
macabeo, xarel.lo, parellada

86

Marrugat Brut Nature Milesime 2009 BN Reserva
macabeo, xarel.lo, parellada

88
Colour: bright straw. Nose: medium intensity, fresh fruit, fine lees, floral. Palate: fresh, fruity, flavourful, good acidity.

Rima 32 2008 BN Reserva
pinot noir, chardonnay

89
Colour: bright golden. Nose: fine lees, dry nuts, faded flowers, toasty. Palate: powerful, flavourful, good acidity, fine bead, fine bitter notes.

Suspirum 2009 BN Gran Reserva
macabeo, xarel.lo, parellada, chardonnay

87
Colour: bright yellow. Nose: ripe fruit, fine lees, balanced, dried herbs. Palate: good acidity, flavourful, ripe fruit, long.

BODEGAS RIOJANAS

08770 Sant Sadurní D'Anoia
(Barcelona)
☎: +34 941 454 050
Fax: +34 941 454 529
bodega@bodegasriojanas.com
www.bodegasriojanas.com

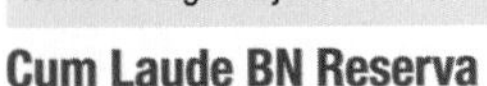

Cum Laude BN Reserva
40% xarel.lo, 30% macabeo, 30% parellada

85

BODEGAS ROURA

Valls de Rials, s/n
08328 Alella (Barcelona)
☎: +34 663 235 353
Fax: +34 933 524 339
roura@roura.es
www.roura.es

Roura BN
70% xarel.lo, 30% chardonnay

85

Roura BR
75% xarel.lo, 25% chardonnay

85

Roura 5 * BN
50% xarel.lo, 50% chardonnay

88
Colour: bright straw. Nose: fine lees, floral, fragrant herbs, expressive. Palate: powerful, flavourful, good acidity, fine bead, balanced.

Roura Rosat BR
100% trepat

83

BODEGAS SAN VALERO SOC. COOP.

Ctra. N-330, Km. 450
50400 Cariñena (Zaragoza)
☎: +34 976 620 400
Fax: +34 976 620 398
bsv@sanvalero.com
www.sanvalero.com

Gran Ducay BN
macabeo, parellada, xarel.lo

83

Gran Ducay 2011 BN Reserva
macabeo, parellada, xarel.lo

86

Gran Ducay Rosé 2012 BN
garnacha

86

BODEGAS VEGAMAR

Garcesa, s/n
46175 Calles (Valencia)
☎: +34 962 109 813
info@bodegasvegamar.com
www.bodegasvegamar.com

Vegamar BN
chardonnay, macabeo

84

Vegamar Rosado BN
garnacha

86

BODEGAS VICENTE GANDÍA

Ctra. Cheste a Godelleta, s/n
46370 Chiva (Valencia)
☎: +34 962 524 242
Fax: +34 962 524 243
info@vicentegandia.com
www.vicentegandia.es

El Miracle BR
chardonnay, macabeo

84

El Miracle Organic BR
chardonnay, macabeo

85

El Miracle Rosado BR
garnacha

84

Hoya de Cadenas BN
macabeo

85

Hoya de Cadenas BR
chardonnay, macabeo

85

Hoya de Cadenas Organic BR
chardonnay, macabeo

85

Hoya de Cadenas Rosado BR
garnacha

84

Vicente Gandía BN
macabeo

86

Vicente Gandía BR
chardonnay, macabeo

86

Vicente Gandía Rosado BR
garnacha

84

BODEGAS Y VIÑEDOS HAYA

Nueva, s/n
46354 Los Cojos (Requena) (Valencia)
☎: +34 678 126 449
Fax: +34 962 335 053
info@bodegashaya.com
www.bodegashaya.com

Publio Elio Adriano 2013 ESP
macabeo, chardonnay

86

BODEGUES CA N'ESTELLA

Masia Ca N'Estella, s/n
08635 Sant Esteve Sesrovires
(Barcelona)
☎: +34 934 161 387
Fax: +34 934 161 620
a.vidal@fincacanestella.com
www.fincacanestella.com

Rabetllat i Vidal 2011 BN Reserva
80% chardonnay, 20% macabeo

88

Colour: bright yellow. Nose: ripe fruit, fine lees, balanced. Palate: good acidity, flavourful, ripe fruit, long.

Rabetllat i Vidal Brut Ca N'Estella 2013 BR
70% macabeo, 30% xarel.lo

88

Colour: bright straw. Nose: fine lees, floral, fragrant herbs. Palate: flavourful, good acidity, fine bead.

Rabetllat i Vidal Gran Reserva de la Finca 2008 BN
88% chardonnay, 12% macabeo

89

Colour: bright golden. Nose: dry nuts, lees reduction notes, toasty. Palate: powerful, flavourful, good acidity, fine bead, fine bitter notes.

Rabetllat i Vidal Rosado 2011 BR
65% trepat, 35% garnacha

85

BODEGUES SUMARROCA

El Rebato, s/n
08739 Subirats (Barcelona)
☎: +34 934 750 125
Fax: +34 934 743 100
amestres@selfoods.es
www.sumarroca.es

Sumarroca BN Gran Reserva
macabeo, parellada, xarel.lo, chardonnay

91

Colour: bright yellow. Nose: fine lees, balanced, dried herbs, fresh fruit. Palate: good acidity, flavourful, ripe fruit, long, fresh.

Sumarroca BR Reserva
macabeo, parellada, xarel.lo, chardonnay

89

Colour: bright straw. Nose: fresh fruit, dried herbs, fine lees, floral. Palate: fresh, fruity, flavourful, good acidity, easy to drink.

Sumarroca Allier BR Gran Reserva
parellada, pinot noir, chardonnay

93

Colour: bright golden. Nose: fine lees, dry nuts, fragrant herbs, spicy. Palate: powerful, flavourful, good acidity, fine bead, fine bitter notes.

Sumarroca Cuvée BN Gran Reserva
chardonnay, parellada

91

Colour: yellow. Nose: fine lees, floral, fragrant herbs, expressive. Palate: flavourful, good acidity, fine bead, balanced.

Sumarroca Ecológic BR Reserva
macabeo, xarel.lo, parellada, chardonnay

86 ♣

Sumarroca Gran Brut Blanc de Negre BR Gran Reserva
parellada, pinot noir, chardonnay

91

Colour: bright yellow. Nose: fine lees, fragrant herbs, characterful, ripe fruit, dry nuts. Palate: powerful, flavourful, good acidity, fine bead, fine bitter notes.

Sumarroca Insitu Extra Brut
macabeo, xarel.lo, parellada

91

Colour: bright straw. Nose: fine lees, floral, fragrant herbs. Palate: flavourful, good acidity, fine bead, balanced.

Sumarroca Núria Claverol BR Gran Reserva
xarel.lo

94

Colour: bright yellow. Nose: fine lees, dry nuts, fragrant herbs, complex, toasty. Palate: flavourful, good acidity, fine bead, fine bitter notes.

Sumarroca Pinot Noir Rosé Brut BR Reserva
pinot noir

91

Colour: coppery red. Nose: floral, jasmine, fragrant herbs, varietal, red berry notes, ripe fruit. Palate: fresh, fruity, flavourful, correct, fine bitter notes.

Sumarroca Rosé BR Reserva
pinot noir

88

Colour: raspberry rose. Nose: floral, red berry notes, fragrant herbs, expressive. Palate: powerful, balanced, flavourful.

BOLET – AGRICULTURA ECOLÓGICA

08732 Castellví de la Marca (Barcelona)
☎: +34 938 918 153
Fax: +34 938 918 153
cavasbolet@cavasbolet.com
www.cavasbolet.com

Bolet 2010 BN Gran Reserva
xarel.lo, macabeo, parellada

86 ♣

Bolet 2011 BN Reserva
xarel.lo, macabeo, parellada

86 ♣

Bolet 2011 BR Reserva
xarel.lo, macabeo, parellada

86 ♣

Bolet Classic 2011 BR
xarel.lo, macabeo, parellada

86 ♣

Bolet Rosat 2012 BR
pinot noir

85 ♣

Bolet Selección Familiar 2010 BN Gran Reserva
xarel.lo, macabeo, parellada

89 ♣

Colour: yellow. Nose: toasty, dry nuts, powerfull. Palate: balanced, fine bitter notes, spicy, long.

CAL SERRADOR

Montserrat, 87
08770 Sant Sadurní D'Anoia
(Barcelona)
☎: +34 938 912 073
comercial@vinuet.com
www.rosellgallart.com

Serra D'Or Chardonnay 2011 BN Reserva
100% chardonnay

81

Serra D'Or Classic 2011 BN
macabeo, xarel.lo, parellada, chardonnay

85

Serra D'Or Pinot Noir 2012 BN Reserva
100% pinot noir

86

Teresa Mata Garriga 2011 BN Reserva
macabeo, xarel.lo, parellada, chardonnay

87

Colour: bright yellow. Nose: fine lees, balanced, dried herbs, dry nuts, fresh fruit. Palate: good acidity, flavourful, ripe fruit, long.

CANALS & MUNNÉ

Ctra. Sant Sadurní a Vilafranca, km 0,5
08770 Sant Sadurní D'Anoia
(Barcelona)
☎: +34 938 910 318
Fax: +34 938 911 945
info@canalsimunne.com
www.canalsimunne.com

1915 by C & M BN Gran Reserva
80% pinot noir, 10% xarel.lo

88

Colour: bright yellow. Nose: fine lees, dried herbs, dry nuts. Palate: good acidity, flavourful, ripe fruit, long.

Canals & Munné BN Gran Reserva
40% macabeo, 30% chardonnay, 30% parellada

88

Colour: bright straw. Nose: fine lees, floral, fragrant herbs, expressive. Palate: powerful, flavourful, good acidity, fine bead, balanced.

Canals & Munné SS Reserva
50% xarel.lo, 30% macabeo, 20% parellada

87

Colour: bright straw. Nose: fine lees, floral, fragrant herbs. Palate: flavourful, sweet.

Canals & Munné 2011 BR Gran Reserva
50% xarel.lo, 30% macabeo, 20% parellada

90

Colour: bright yellow. Nose: ripe fruit, dried herbs, dry nuts. Palate: good acidity, flavourful, ripe fruit, long.

Canals & Munné Dionysus BN Reserva
60% xarel.lo, 30% chardonnay, 10% macabeo

88 ✿

Colour: bright straw. Nose: floral, fragrant herbs. Palate: flavourful, good acidity, correct.

Canals & Munné Insuperable BR Reserva
40% macabeo, 30% xarel.lo, 30% parellada

88

Colour: bright yellow. Nose: balanced, dried herbs, dry nuts. Palate: good acidity, flavourful, ripe fruit, long.

Canals & Munné Insuperable SS Reserva
40% macabeo, 30% xarel.lo, parellada

86

Canals & Munné Pinot Noir SS Reserva
100% pinot noir

87

Colour: light cherry. Nose: fragrant herbs, candied fruit. Palate: fresh, fruity, sweet.

Canals & Munné Pinot Noir Rosé BR Reserva
100% pinot noir

88

Colour: rose. Nose: floral, red berry notes, ripe fruit, fragrant herbs, expressive. Palate: powerful, balanced, flavourful.

Canals & Munné Reserva de L'Avi BN Gran Reserva
50% chardonnay, 20% xarel.lo, 15% macabeo, 15% parellada

90

Colour: bright golden. Nose: dry nuts, fragrant herbs, spicy. Palate: powerful, flavourful, good acidity, fine bead, fine bitter notes.

Eunoia BN Reserva
60% xarel.lo, 30% chardonnay, 10% macabeo

88 ✿

Colour: bright straw. Nose: floral, fragrant herbs, expressive. Palate: powerful, flavourful, good acidity, fine bead.

Gran Duc 2009 BN Gran Reserva
60% chardonnay, 25% xarel.lo, 15% macabeo

90

Colour: bright golden. Nose: fine lees, dry nuts, fragrant herbs. Palate: powerful, flavourful, good acidity, fine bead, fine bitter notes.

CANALS CANALS

Avda. Montserrat, 9
08769 Castellví de Rosanes (Barcelona)
☎: +34 937 755 446
Fax: +34 937 741 719
cava@canalscanals.com
www.canalscanals.com

Canals Canals Reserva Numerada 2012 BN Reserva
xarel.lo, macabeo, parellada

89

Colour: bright yellow. Nose: ripe fruit, fine lees, balanced, dried herbs. Palate: good acidity, flavourful, ripe fruit, long.

Marta 2012 BN Reserva

87

Colour: bright straw. Nose: medium intensity, fresh fruit, dried herbs, fine lees, floral. Palate: fresh, fruity, flavourful, good acidity.

Marta Deluxe 2009 BN Gran Reserva

xarel.lo, macabeo, parellada

91

Colour: bright golden. Nose: fine lees, dry nuts, fragrant herbs, complex, toasty. Palate: powerful, flavourful, good acidity, fine bead, fine bitter notes.

Marta Joia 2011 BR Reserva

xarel.lo, macabeo, parellada

88 ♣

Colour: bright straw. Nose: fine lees, floral, fragrant herbs. Palate: flavourful, good acidity, fine bead.

Marta Magnum BN Gran Reserva

90

Colour: bright yellow. Nose: toasty, dry nuts, fine lees, balanced. Palate: flavourful, long.

Ramón Canals Gran Reserva Limitada 2009 BN Gran Reserva

xarel.lo, macabeo, parellada

91

Colour: bright yellow. Nose: fine lees, dry nuts, fragrant herbs, complex. Palate: powerful, flavourful, good acidity, fine bead, fine bitter notes.

CANALS NADAL

Ponent, 2
08733 El Pla del Penedès (Barcelona)
☎: +34 938 988 081
Fax: +34 938 989 050
cava@canalsnadal.com
www.canalsnadal.com

Antoni Canals Nadal Cupada Selecció 2011 BR Reserva

50% macabeo, 40% xarel.lo, 10% parellada

91

Colour: yellow. Nose: medium intensity, fresh fruit, dried herbs, fine lees, floral. Palate: fresh, fruity, flavourful, good acidity.

Antoni Canals Nadal Cupada Selecció Magnum 2010 BN Reserva

50% macabeo, 40% xarel.lo, 10% parellada

90

Colour: bright yellow. Nose: fine lees, dry nuts, fragrant herbs. Palate: powerful, flavourful, good acidity, fine bead, fine bitter notes.

Antoni Canals Nadal Gran Vintage 2010 BR Reserva

40% chardonnay, 30% macabeo, 30% xarel.lo

90

Colour: bright straw. Nose: fine lees, fragrant herbs. Palate: flavourful, good acidity, fine bead, balanced.

Canals Nadal 2010 BN Gran Reserva

50% macabeo, 40% xarel.lo, 10% parellada

89

Colour: bright straw. Nose: fine lees, floral, fragrant herbs, expressive. Palate: powerful, flavourful, good acidity, fine bead, balanced.

Canals Nadal 2011 BN Reserva

45% macabeo, 40% xarel.lo, 15% parellada

88

Colour: yellow. Nose: medium intensity, fresh fruit, dried herbs, fine lees, floral. Palate: fresh, fruity, flavourful, good acidity.

Canals Nadal 2012 BR Reserva

45% macabeo, 40% xarel.lo, 15% parellada

88

Colour: bright straw. Nose: fine lees, floral, fragrant herbs, expressive. Palate: powerful, good acidity, fine bead, balanced.

Canals Nadal 2013 BR

40% macabeo, 40% xarel.lo, 20% parellada

84

Canals Nadal Magnum 2011 BN Reserva

45% macabeo, 40% xarel.lo, 10% parellada

89

Colour: bright yellow. Nose: fine lees, balanced, dried herbs, fresh fruit. Palate: good acidity, long, fine bitter notes, easy to drink.

Canals Nadal Rosé 2012 BR Reserva

100% trepat

87

Colour: coppery red. Nose: balanced, ripe fruit. Palate: correct, fine bitter notes, easy to drink.

CASTELL D'AGE

Ctra.de Martorell a Capellades, 6-8
08782 La Beguda Baixa (Barcelona)
☎: +34 937 725 181
info@castelldage.com
www.castelldage.com

Castell D'Age Anne Marie 2012 BN Reserva

40% macabeo, 40% xarel.lo, 20% parellada

89 ♣

Colour: bright yellow. Nose: ripe fruit, fine lees, balanced, dried herbs. Palate: good acidity, flavourful, ripe fruit, long.

Castell D'Age Aurèlia 2010 BN Gran Reserva
40% macabeo, 40% xarel.lo, 10% parellada, 10% chardonnay

89

Colour: bright yellow. Nose: ripe fruit, fine lees, balanced, dried herbs. Palate: good acidity, flavourful, ripe fruit, long, elegant.

Castell D'Age Olivia 2009 BN Reserva
100% chardonnay

90

Colour: bright golden. Nose: fine lees, fragrant herbs, characterful, ripe fruit, dry nuts. Palate: powerful, flavourful, good acidity, fine bead, fine bitter notes.

Castell D'Age Rosat 2012 BR
100% pinot noir

87

Colour: rose. Nose: floral, red berry notes, ripe fruit, fragrant herbs. Palate: powerful, flavourful, correct, easy to drink.

Poculum Boni Geni 2006 BN Gran Reserva
50% chardonnay, 50% pinot noir

90

Colour: bright yellow. Nose: fine lees, dry nuts, fragrant herbs, complex, toasty, sweet spices. Palate: powerful, flavourful, good acidity, fine bead, fine bitter notes.

CASTELL D'OR

Mare Rafols, 3- 1ºD
08720 Vilafranca del Penedès
(Barcelona)
☎: +34 938 905 385
Fax: +34 938 905 446
castelldor@castelldor.com
www.castelldor.com

Castell de la Comanda BR
macabeo, parellada

84

Cossetània BN
macabeo, xarel.lo, parellada

87

Colour: bright straw. Nose: fine lees, floral, fragrant herbs, expressive. Palate: powerful, flavourful, good acidity, fine bead, balanced.

Cossetània BR Reserva
30% macabeo, 50% xarel.lo, 20% parellada

87

Colour: bright straw. Nose: fine lees, floral, fragrant herbs. Palate: flavourful, good acidity, fine bead.

Cossetània Rosat BR
trepat

85

Flama D'Or BN
xarel.lo, macabeo, parellada

84

Flama D'Or BR
xarel.lo, macabeo, parellada

85

Francolí BR Reserva
macabeo, parellada

85

Francolí Imperial BR
macabeo, parellada

85

Francoli Rosat BR
trepat

84

L'Arboç 1919 Selecció BR
macabeo, xarel.lo, parellada

85

Puig Solivella BN
macabeo, parellada

84

Pupitre BR
macabeo, xarel.lo, parellada

85

CASTELL SANT ANTONI

Passeig del Parc, 13
08770 Sant Sadurní D'Anoia
(Barcelona)
☎: +34 938 183 099
Fax: +34 938 184 451
cava@castellsantantoni.com
www.castellsantantoni.com

Castell Sant Antoni 37.5 Brut 2010 BR Gran Reserva
xarel.lo, macabeo, parellada, chardonnay

89

Colour: bright yellow. Nose: dried herbs, candied fruit. Palate: good acidity, flavourful, ripe fruit, long.

Castell Sant Antoni 37.5 Brut Nature 2008 BN Gran Reserva
xarel.lo, macabeo, parellada, chardonnay

88

Colour: bright yellow. Nose: ripe fruit, fruit liqueur notes, lees reduction notes, dried herbs. Palate: correct, spirituous.

Castell Sant Antoni Brut de Postre 2010 BR Reserva
xarel.lo, macabeo, parellada, chardonnay

89

Colour: bright straw. Nose: fragrant herbs, candied fruit, pattiserie. Palate: fruity, flavourful, sweet, powerful.

Castell Sant Antoni Camí del Sot BN Reserva
xarel.lo, macabeo, parellada

92

Colour: bright golden. Nose: fine lees, dry nuts, fragrant herbs, complex. Palate: powerful, flavourful, good acidity, fine bead, fine bitter notes.

Castell Sant Antoni Camí del Sot Magnum BN Reserva
macabeo, xarel.lo, parellada

93

Colour: bright yellow. Nose: fresh fruit, dried herbs, fine lees, floral, dry nuts. Palate: fresh, fruity, flavourful, good acidity, balanced.

Castell Sant Antoni Gran Barrica 2007 BN Gran Reserva
chardonnay, xarel.lo, macabeo, parellada

93

Colour: bright golden. Nose: fine lees, dry nuts, fragrant herbs, complex, toasty. Palate: powerful, flavourful, good acidity, fine bead, fine bitter notes.

Castell Sant Antoni Gran Brut 2010 BR Gran Reserva
xarel.lo, macabeo, parellada, chardonnay

92

Colour: bright golden. Nose: fine lees, dry nuts, fragrant herbs, complex, pattiserie. Palate: powerful, flavourful, good acidity, fine bead, fine bitter notes.

Castell Sant Antoni Gran Brut Magnum BR Gran Reserva
xarel.lo, macabeo, parellada, chardonnay

91

Colour: bright straw. Nose: fragrant herbs, pattiserie. Palate: powerful, flavourful, good acidity, fine bead, balanced.

Castell Sant Antoni Gran Reserva 2007 BN Gran Reserva
xarel.lo, macabeo, parellada, chardonnay

93

Colour: bright golden. Nose: fine lees, dry nuts, fragrant herbs, complex, toasty. Palate: powerful, flavourful, good acidity, fine bead, fine bitter notes.

Castell Sant Antoni Gran Reserva Magnum 2006 BN
xarel.lo, macabeo, parellada, chardonnay

92

Colour: bright golden. Nose: dry nuts, fragrant herbs, toasty, lees reduction notes. Palate: powerful, flavourful, good acidity, fine bead, fine bitter notes.

Castell Sant Antoni Gran Rosat Pinot Noir 2008 BN Gran Reserva
100% pinot noir

88

Colour: raspberry rose. Nose: floral, red berry notes, fragrant herbs, expressive, candied fruit. Palate: powerful, balanced, flavourful.

Castell Sant Antoni Primvs BR Reserva
macabeo, xarel.lo, parellada

89

Colour: bright straw. Nose: fine lees, floral, fragrant herbs, dry nuts. Palate: powerful, flavourful, good acidity, fine bead, balanced.

Castell Sant Antoni Primvs Rosat BR Reserva
garnacha, trepat

88

Colour: rose. Nose: floral, red berry notes, ripe fruit, fragrant herbs, expressive. Palate: powerful, balanced, flavourful.

Castell Sant Antoni Primvs Semi-Sec Rosat SS Reserva
garnacha, trepat

87

Colour: light cherry. Nose: floral, fragrant herbs, candied fruit. Palate: fresh, fruity, flavourful, sweet.

Castell Sant Antoni Torre de L'Homenatge 1999 BN Gran Reserva
xarel.lo, macabeo, parellada

92

Colour: bright golden. Nose: dry nuts, dried herbs, complex, spicy, toasty. Palate: powerful, flavourful, good acidity, fine bead, fine bitter notes.

Castell Sant Antoni Torre de L'Homenatge 2003 BN Gran Reserva
xarel.lo, macabeo, parellada

94

Colour: bright golden. Nose: fine lees, dry nuts, fragrant herbs, complex. Palate: powerful, flavourful, good acidity, fine bead, fine bitter notes.

Castell Sant Antoni Torre de L'Homenatge 2005 BN Gran Reserva
xarel.lo, macabeo, parellada

94

Colour: bright golden. Nose: fine lees, dry nuts, fragrant herbs, complex, toasty. Palate: powerful, flavourful, good acidity, fine bead, fine bitter notes.

Castell Sant Antoni Torre de L'Homenatge Magnum 2005 BN Gran Reserva

94

Colour: bright yellow. Nose: fragrant herbs, toasty, fine lees, expressive. Palate: powerful, flavourful, good acidity, fine bead, fine bitter notes.

CASTELLROIG - FINCA SABATÉ I COCA

Ctra. Sant Sadurní a Vilafranca
(c-243a), km. 1
08739 Subirats (Barcelona)
☎: +34 938 911 927
Fax: +34 938 914 055
info@castellroig.com
www.castellroig.com

Castellroig BN Reserva
xarel.lo, macabeo, parellada

88

Colour: bright yellow. Nose: ripe fruit, fine lees, balanced, dried herbs. Palate: good acidity, flavourful, ripe fruit, long.

Castellroig BR
macabeo, xarel.lo, parellada

89

Colour: bright straw. Nose: fresh fruit, dried herbs, fine lees, floral. Palate: fresh, fruity, flavourful, good acidity.

Castellroig 2010 BN Gran Reserva
xarel.lo, macabeo

88

Colour: bright yellow. Nose: fine lees, fragrant herbs, ripe fruit, dry nuts. Palate: powerful, flavourful, good acidity, fine bead, fine bitter notes.

Castellroig Rosat BR
garnacha, trepat

87

Colour: raspberry rose. Nose: floral, jasmine, fragrant herbs, candied fruit. Palate: fresh, fruity, flavourful, correct.

Sabaté i Coca Reserva Familiar 2010 BN Reserva
xarel.lo

91

Colour: bright yellow. Nose: fine lees, dry nuts, fragrant herbs, complex, expressive. Palate: powerful, flavourful, good acidity, fine bead, fine bitter notes.

CASTILLO PERELADA

Avda. Barcelona, 78
08720 Vilafranca del Penedès
(Barcelona)
☎: +34 938 180 676
Fax: +34 938 180 926
perelada@castilloperalada.com
www.perelada.com

Castillo Perelada BR Reserva
macabeo, xarel.lo, parellada

88

Colour: bright straw. Nose: fine lees, floral, fragrant herbs. Palate: flavourful, good acidity, fine bead.

Castillo Perelada 2013 BN
parellada, xarel.lo, macabeo

89

Colour: bright yellow. Nose: ripe fruit, fine lees, balanced, dried herbs. Palate: good acidity, flavourful, ripe fruit, long.

Castillo Perelada Chardonnay 2011 BN
chardonnay

90

Colour: bright straw. Nose: fine lees, floral, fragrant herbs, powerfull. Palate: powerful, flavourful, good acidity, fine bead, balanced.

Castillo Perelada Cuvée Especial 2013 BN
macabeo, parellada, xarel.lo, chardonnay

90

Colour: bright straw. Nose: fine lees, floral, fragrant herbs, expressive. Palate: powerful, flavourful, good acidity, fine bead, balanced.

Castillo Perelada Cuvée Especial Rosado 2012 BR
trepat

90

Colour: coppery red. Nose: floral, jasmine, fragrant herbs, candied fruit. Palate: fresh, fruity, flavourful, correct.

Castillo Perelada Rosé BR
trepat, garnacha, pinot noir

87

Colour: rose. Nose: floral, red berry notes, ripe fruit, fragrant herbs, expressive. Palate: powerful, flavourful.

Gran Claustro Cuvée Especial de Castillo Perelada 2009 BN Gran Reserva
chardonnay, pinot noir, parellada, xarel.lo, macabeo

91

Colour: bright golden. Nose: fine lees, dry nuts, fragrant herbs, complex, toasty. Palate: powerful, flavourful, good acidity, fine bead, fine bitter notes.

Gran Claustro de Castillo Perelada 2011 BN Reserva
chardonnay, pinot noir, parellada, macabeo

90

Colour: bright golden. Nose: fine lees, dry nuts, fragrant herbs, complex, toasty. Palate: powerful, flavourful, good acidity, fine bead, fine bitter notes.

Perelada Stars BR Reserva
macabeo, xarel.lo, parellada

86

Perelada Stars 2013 BN
parellada, xarel.lo, macabeo

89

Colour: bright straw. Nose: medium intensity, fresh fruit, dried herbs, floral. Palate: fresh, fruity, flavourful, good acidity.

Perelada Stars Touch of Rosé 2013 BR
garnacha, pinot noir

88

Colour: coppery red. Nose: floral, jasmine, fragrant herbs, candied fruit. Palate: fresh, fruity, flavourful, correct.

Torre Galatea Rosado BR
garnacha, pinot noir, trepat

84

CAVA & HOTEL MASTINELL

Ctra. de Vilafranca a St. Martí Sarroca, Km. 0,5
08720 Vilafranca del Penedès
(Barcelona)
☎: +34 938 170 586
Fax: +34 938 170 500
info@mastinell.com
www.mastinell.com

MasTinell Brut Real BR Reserva
35% macabeo, 30% xarel.lo, 35% parellada

89

Colour: bright straw. Nose: medium intensity, fresh fruit, dried herbs, fine lees, floral. Palate: fresh, fruity, flavourful, good acidity.

MasTinell Carpe Diem 2007 BN Reserva Especial

30% xarel.lo, 30% parellada, 40% chardonnay

91

Colour: bright yellow. Nose: fine lees, dry nuts, fragrant herbs, complex, toasty. Palate: powerful, flavourful, good acidity, fine bead, fine bitter notes.

MasTinell Cristina 2007 Extra Brut Gran Reserva

10% macabeo, 35% xarel.lo, 35% parellada, 20% chardonnay

89

Colour: bright golden. Nose: fine lees, fragrant herbs, characterful, ripe fruit, dry nuts. Palate: powerful, flavourful, good acidity, fine bead, fine bitter notes.

MasTinell Nature Real 2007 BN Gran Reserva

35% macabeo, 35% xarel.lo, 30% parellada

89

Colour: bright yellow. Nose: ripe fruit, fine lees, balanced, dried herbs. Palate: good acidity, flavourful, ripe fruit, long.

CAVA BERDIÉ

Les Conilleres (La Conillera Gran)
08732 Castellví de la Marca (Barcelona)
☎: +34 902 800 229
Fax: +34 931 980 182
info@cavaberdie.com
www.cavaberdie.com

Berdié 2012 BN Reserva

macabeo, xarel.lo, parellada

86

Berdié Amor Rosado 2012 BR Reserva

macabeo, xarel.lo, parellada, garnacha

87

Colour: coppery red. Nose: floral, jasmine, fragrant herbs, red berry notes. Palate: fresh, fruity, flavourful, correct.

Berdié Fetish Rosado 2011 BR Reserva

monastrell, garnacha

87

Colour: rose. Nose: floral, red berry notes, ripe fruit, fragrant herbs, expressive. Palate: powerful, balanced, flavourful.

Berdié Gran Fetish 2009 BR Gran Reserva

monastrell, garnacha

84

Berdié Gran Nature 2010 BN Gran Reserva

macabeo, xarel.lo, parellada

87

Colour: bright yellow. Nose: ripe fruit, fine lees, balanced, dried herbs. Palate: good acidity, flavourful, ripe fruit, long.

Berdié Rupestre 2012 BR Reserva

macabeo, xarel.lo, parellada

87

Colour: bright yellow. Nose: dry nuts, fine lees, medium intensity. Palate: correct, good acidity, easy to drink.

CAVA CRISTINA COLOMER

Diputació, 58 - 60
08770 Sant Sadurní D'Anoia
(Barcelona)
☎: +34 938 910 804
Fax: +34 938 913 034
info@cavescolomer.com
www.cavescolomer.com

Colomer "er" 2004 BN Gran Reserva

xarel.lo, macabeo, parellada, chardonnay

90

Colour: bright golden. Nose: characterful, ripe fruit, dry nuts, lees reduction notes. Palate: powerful, flavourful, good acidity, fine bead, fine bitter notes, correct.

Colomer 1907 BR Reserva

xarel.lo, macabeo, parellada

88

Colour: bright straw. Nose: fine lees, floral, fragrant herbs. Palate: flavourful, good acidity, fine bead, easy to drink.

Colomer Brut D'Autor Homenatge Gaudí BR Gran Reserva

xarel.lo, macabeo, parellada, chardonnay, pinot noir

89

Colour: bright golden. Nose: fine lees, fragrant herbs, characterful, ripe fruit, dry nuts. Palate: powerful, flavourful, fine bitter notes.

Colomer Costa 2012 BN Reserva

xarel.lo, macabeo, parellada

88

Colour: bright yellow. Nose: ripe fruit, fine lees, balanced, dried herbs. Palate: good acidity, flavourful, ripe fruit, long.

Colomer Costa Magnum 2010 BN Reserva
xarel.lo, macabeo, parellada

88

Colour: bright yellow. Nose: dried herbs, candied fruit. Palate: good acidity, flavourful, ripe fruit.

Colomer Prestige de Dali 2010 BN Gran Reserva
xarel.lo, macabeo, parellada, chardonnay

90

Colour: bright straw. Nose: medium intensity, fresh fruit, dried herbs, fine lees, floral, balanced. Palate: fresh, fruity, flavourful, good acidity, elegant.

CAVA JOSEP M. FERRET GUASCH

Barri L'Alzinar, 68
08736 Font-Rubí (Barcelona)
☎: +34 938 979 037
Fax: +34 938 979 414
ferretguasch@ferretguasch.com
www.ferretguasch.com

Josep M. Ferret Guasch Au79 2014 BR Reserva

87

Colour: bright straw. Nose: balanced, medium intensity, wild herbs, citrus fruit, varietal. Palate: fruity, flavourful, long.

CAVA MARTÍN SOLER

Finca La Serra de Sabanell
08736 Font-Rubí (Barcelona)
☎: +34 938 988 220
info@cavamartinsoler.com
www.cavamartinsoler.com

Margarita de Soler 2011 BN Gran Reserva
macabeo, xarel.lo, parellada

87

Colour: bright golden. Nose: ripe fruit, fine lees, balanced, dried herbs. Palate: good acidity, flavourful, ripe fruit, long.

Martin Soler Masia 1616 2012 Extra Brut Reserva
macabeo, xarel.lo, parellada

85

Martin Soler Rosé 2013 BN
trepat

85

CAVA MESTRES

Plaça Ajuntament, 8
08770 Sant Sadurní D'Anoia
(Barcelona)
☎: +34 938 910 043
Fax: +34 938 911 611
cava@mestres.es
www.mestres.es

Mestres Clos Nostre Senyor 2004 BN Gran Reserva
20% macabeo, 60% xarel.lo, 20% parellada

91

Colour: bright golden. Nose: dry nuts, fragrant herbs, complex, fine lees, macerated fruit, sweet spices, expressive. Palate: powerful, flavourful, good acidity, fine bead, fine bitter notes, elegant.

Mestres Coupage Blue Fin 2009 BR Gran Reserva
30% macabeo, 45% xarel.lo, 25% parellada

90

Colour: bright straw. Nose: fine lees, fragrant herbs, characterful, ripe fruit, dry nuts. Palate: powerful, flavourful, good acidity, fine bead, fine bitter notes.

Mestres Cupage 50 años de "Cava" 2009 BR Gran Reserva
25% macabeo, 50% xarel.lo, 25% parellada

91

Colour: yellow. Nose: fine lees, dry nuts, fragrant herbs, complex. Palate: powerful, flavourful, good acidity, fine bead, fine bitter notes.

Mestres Cupage 80 Aniversario 2008 BR Gran Reserva
25% macabeo, 60% xarel.lo, 15% parellada

90

Colour: bright yellow. Nose: fine lees, dry nuts, fragrant herbs, complex, toasty. Palate: powerful, flavourful, good acidity, fine bead, fine bitter notes.

Mestres Cupage Madrid 2012 BN Reserva
40% macabeo, 30% xarel.lo, 30% parellada

89

Colour: bright yellow. Nose: ripe fruit, fine lees, balanced, dried herbs. Palate: good acidity, flavourful, ripe fruit, long.

Mestres Mas Vía 2000 BR Gran Reserva
15% macabeo, 75% xarel.lo, 10% parellada

94

Colour: bright golden. Nose: dry nuts, dried herbs, complex, spicy, toasty. Palate: powerful, flavourful, good acidity, fine bead, fine bitter notes, elegant.

Mestres Visol 2007 BN Gran Reserva

92

Colour: bright golden. Nose: fine lees, fragrant herbs, ripe fruit, dry nuts. Palate: flavourful, good acidity, fine bead, fine bitter notes, elegant.

CAVA OLIVÉ BATLLORI

Barri Els Casots
08739 Subirats (Barcelona)
☎: +34 938 993 103
info@olivebatllori.com
www.olivebatllori.com

Gran Brut Olive Batllori 2012 BN Reserva

macabeo, xarel.lo, parellada, pinot noir, chardonnay

89

Colour: bright straw. Nose: fine lees, floral, fragrant herbs, expressive. Palate: flavourful, good acidity, balanced.

Olive Batllori 2012 BN Reserva

macabeo, xarel.lo, parellada

87

Colour: bright yellow. Nose: ripe fruit, fine lees, balanced, dried herbs. Palate: good acidity, flavourful, ripe fruit, long.

Olive Batllori Rosado BR

pinot noir

88

Colour: raspberry rose. Nose: floral, jasmine, fragrant herbs, candied fruit. Palate: fresh, fruity, flavourful, correct, easy to drink.

CAVA REVERTÉ

Paseo Tomás García Rebull, 4
43885 Salomó (Tarragona)
☎: +34 630 929 380
Fax: +34 977 629 246
reverte@cavareverte.com
www.cavareverte.com

Cava Reverté "Electe" 2010 BN Reserva

40% xarel.lo, 20% macabeo, 20% parellada, 20% chardonnay

88

Colour: bright straw. Nose: fine lees, floral, fragrant herbs, expressive. Palate: powerful, flavourful, good acidity, fine bead.

Cava Reverté "Electe" Magnum BN Reserva

40% xarel.lo, 20% parellada, 20% chardonnay, 20% macabeo

90

Colour: bright yellow. Nose: fine lees, floral, fragrant herbs, expressive. Palate: powerful, flavourful, good acidity, fine bead, balanced.

Cava Reverté 2009 BN Reserva

60% xarel.lo, 20% macabeo, 20% parellada

87

Colour: bright straw. Nose: fine lees, floral, fragrant herbs, citrus fruit. Palate: flavourful, good acidity, fine bead.

CAVA ROSELL GALLART

Montserrat, 56
08770 Sant Sadurní D'Anoia
(Barcelona)
☎: +34 938 912 073
Fax: +34 938 183 539
info@rosellgallart.com
www.rosellgallart.com

Rosell Gallart 2011 BN Reserva

macabeo, xarel.lo, parellada, chardonnay

86

Rosell Gallart Magnum 2004 BN Gran Reserva

macabeo, xarel.lo, parellada, chardonnay

87

Colour: bright yellow. Nose: ripe fruit, fruit liqueur notes, lees reduction notes, dried herbs, dry nuts, toasty. Palate: correct, flavourful.

Rosell Raventós Cristal 2007 BN Reserva

macabeo, xarel.lo, parellada, chardonnay

80

CAVAS BERTHA

Ctra. de St. Sadurni a Vilafranca, km. 2,4
08739 Subirats (Barcelona)
☎: +34 938 911 091
cavabertha@cavabertha.com
www.cavabertha.com

Bertha 2011 BN Reserva

macabeo, xarel.lo, parellada

89

Colour: bright straw. Nose: medium intensity, fresh fruit, dried herbs, fine lees, floral. Palate: fresh, fruity, flavourful, good acidity.

Bertha Brut 1989 2012 BR Reserva
macabeo, xarel.lo, parellada

88

Colour: bright straw. Nose: fine lees, floral, fragrant herbs, fresh fruit. Palate: flavourful, good acidity, fine bead, fresh, easy to drink.

Bertha Cardús 2009 BN Gran Reserva
macabeo, xarel.lo, parellada

89

Nose: fine lees, fragrant herbs, characterful, ripe fruit, dry nuts. Palate: powerful, flavourful, good acidity, fine bead, fine bitter notes.

Bertha Lounge 2013 BR Gran Reserva
macabeo, xarel.lo, parellada

84

Bertha Lounge Rosé 2013 BR
garnacha, pinot noir

89

Colour: raspberry rose. Nose: floral, jasmine, fragrant herbs, medium intensity. Palate: fresh, fruity, correct, balanced, fine bitter notes, good acidity.

Bertha Max 2006 Gran Reserva
chardonnay, macabeo, xarel.lo, pinot noir

92

Colour: bright yellow. Nose: fine lees, floral, fragrant herbs, expressive, toasty. Palate: powerful, flavourful, good acidity, fine bead, balanced.

Bertha Segle XXI 2006 BN Gran Reserva
macabeo, xarel.lo, parellada, chardonnay

90

Colour: bright yellow. Nose: fine lees, dry nuts, fragrant herbs, complex, ripe fruit. Palate: powerful, flavourful, good acidity, fine bead, fine bitter notes.

Bertha Segle XXI Rosé 2009 BR Gran Reserva
pinot noir

89

Colour: coppery red. Nose: fine lees, floral, fragrant herbs, elegant, dry nuts. Palate: flavourful, good acidity, fine bead, fine bitter notes.

CAVAS FERRET

Avda. de Catalunya, 36
08736 Guardiola de Font-Rubí
(Barcelona)
☎: +34 938 979 148
Fax: +34 938 979 208
comercial@cavasferret.com
www.cavasferret.com

Celia de Ferret Rosado 2010 BN Gran Reserva
80% pinot noir, 20% garnacha

85

Ezequiel Ferret 2007 BN Gran Reserva
50% xarel.lo, 30% macabeo, 20% parellada

88

Colour: bright golden. Nose: fine lees, dry nuts, fragrant herbs, complex. Palate: powerful, flavourful, good acidity, fine bead, fine bitter notes.

Ferret BN Reserva
parellada, xarel.lo, macabeo

90

Colour: bright straw. Nose: medium intensity, fresh fruit, dried herbs, fine lees, floral. Palate: fresh, fruity, flavourful, good acidity.

Ferret BR Reserva
parellada, xarel.lo, macabeo

87

Colour: bright yellow. Nose: ripe fruit, fine lees, balanced, dried herbs. Palate: good acidity, flavourful, ripe fruit, long.

Ferret SS
parellada, xarel.lo, macabeo

86

Ferret 2011 BN Gran Reserva

90

Colour: bright yellow. Nose: ripe fruit, fine lees, balanced, dried herbs, pattiserie. Palate: good acidity, flavourful, ripe fruit, long.

Ferret Barrica 2009 BN Gran Reserva
xarel.lo, parellada, macabeo

87

Colour: bright yellow. Nose: ripe fruit, fine lees, dried herbs. Palate: good acidity, flavourful, ripe fruit, long.

Ferret Magnum BR Reserva
parellada, xarel.lo, macabeo

88

Colour: bright yellow. Nose: medium intensity, fresh fruit, dried herbs, fine lees, floral. Palate: fresh, fruity, flavourful, good acidity.

Ferret Petit BN Reserva

84

CAVAS GRAMONA

Industria, 36
08770 Sant Sadurní D'Anoia
(Barcelona)
☎: +34 938 910 113
Fax: +34 938 183 284
cava@gramona.com
www.gramona.com

Gramona Argent 2010 BR Gran Reserva

100% chardonnay

93

Colour: yellow. Nose: fine lees, dry nuts, fragrant herbs, complex, white flowers, faded flowers. Palate: powerful, flavourful, good acidity, fine bead, fine bitter notes.

Gramona Argent Rosé 2011 BN Gran Reserva

100% pinot noir

90

Colour: bright yellow. Nose: ripe fruit, fine lees, dried herbs, spicy. Palate: powerful, spicy, balanced.

PODIUM

Gramona Celler Batlle 2005 BR Gran Reserva

75% xarel.lo, 25% macabeo

96

Colour: bright golden. Nose: dry nuts, fragrant herbs, complex, fine lees, macerated fruit, sweet spices, expressive. Palate: powerful, flavourful, good acidity, fine bead, fine bitter notes, elegant.

PODIUM

Gramona Enoteca 2001 BN Gran Reserva

75% xarel.lo, 25% macabeo

98

Colour: bright golden. Nose: fine lees, dry nuts, fragrant herbs, complex, pattiserie, sweet spices. Palate: powerful, flavourful, good acidity, fine bead, fine bitter notes, long.

PODIUM

Gramona Enoteca 2001 BR Gran Reserva

75% xarel.lo, 25% macabeo

97

Colour: bright golden. Nose: fine lees, fragrant herbs, characterful, ripe fruit, dry nuts, pattiserie. Palate: powerful, flavourful, good acidity, fine bead, fine bitter notes, sweetness.

Gramona III Lustros 2007 BN Gran Reserva

75% xarel.lo, 25% macabeo

94

Colour: bright golden. Nose: dry nuts, fragrant herbs, complex, expressive, pattiserie, toasty. Palate: powerful, flavourful, good acidity, fine bead, fine bitter notes.

Gramona Imperial 2010 BR Gran Reserva

50% xarel.lo, 40% macabeo, 10% chardonnay

91

Colour: bright yellow. Nose: fine lees, fragrant herbs, characterful, ripe fruit, spicy. Palate: powerful, flavourful, good acidity, fine bead, fine bitter notes.

Gramona Imperial Magnum 2011 BR Gran Reserva

50% xarel.lo, 40% macabeo, 10% chardonnay

92

Colour: bright straw. Nose: fine lees, dry nuts, fragrant herbs, fresh. Palate: flavourful, good acidity, fine bead, fine bitter notes.

CAVAS HILL

Bonavista, 2
08734 Moja-Olérdola (Barcelona)
☎: +34 938 900 588
Fax: +34 938 170 246
cavashill@cavashill.com
www.cavashill.com

Cavas Hill 1887 BR

macabeo, xarel.lo, parellada

86

Cavas Hill 1887 Rosado BR

garnacha, monastrell

83

Cavas Hill Artesanía BN Reserva
macabeo, xarel.lo, chardonnay

87

Colour: bright yellow. Nose: ripe fruit, fine lees, balanced, dried herbs. Palate: good acidity, flavourful, ripe fruit.

Cavas Hill Vintage BR Reserva
macabeo, xarel.lo, chardonnay

87

Colour: bright straw. Nose: fine lees, floral, fragrant herbs, expressive. Palate: powerful, flavourful, good acidity, fine bead, balanced.

Cavas Hill Vintage 2008 BN Gran Reserva
macabeo, xarel.lo, chardonnay

91

Colour: bright golden. Nose: fine lees, fragrant herbs, characterful, ripe fruit, dry nuts. Palate: powerful, flavourful, good acidity, fine bead, fine bitter notes.

CAVES MUSCÀNDIA
Avernó, 4
08770 Sant Sadurní D'Anoia
(Barcelona)
☎: +34 625 632 620
info@cavamuscandia.com
www.muscandia.com

Cava Muscàndia 2009 BN Gran Reserva
80% xarel.lo, 10% macabeo, 10% parellada

87

Colour: bright yellow. Nose: fragrant herbs, characterful, ripe fruit. Palate: powerful, flavourful, good acidity, fine bead, fine bitter notes.

Cava Muscàndia 2012 BR Reserva
60% xarel.lo, 20% macabeo, 20% parellada

86

Cava Muscàndia Magnum 2010 BR Gran Reserva
70% xarel.lo, 30% macabeo

89

Colour: yellow. Nose: fresh fruit, dried herbs, fine lees, floral. Palate: fresh, fruity, flavourful, good acidity.

Cava Muscàndia Rosé 2011 BR Reserva
100% pinot noir

88

Colour: coppery red. Nose: floral, jasmine, fragrant herbs, candied fruit. Palate: fresh, fruity, flavourful, correct.

CAVES NAVERÁN
Masia Can Parellada -
Sant Martí Sadavesa
08775 Torrelavit (Barcelona)
☎: +34 938 988 400
Fax: +34 938 989 027
sadeve@naveran.com
www.naveran.com

Naveran Millesime 2012 BN
30% macabeo, 30% xarel.lo, 30% parellada, 10% chardonnay

91

Colour: yellow. Nose: fine lees, dry nuts, fragrant herbs, complex, dried flowers. Palate: flavourful, good acidity, fine bead, fine bitter notes.

Naverán Odisea 2012 BN
65% chardonnay, 35% parellada

92

Colour: bright straw. Nose: fine lees, dry nuts, fragrant herbs, pattiserie. Palate: powerful, flavourful, good acidity, fine bead, fine bitter notes.

Naveran Perles Blanques 2012 BR
60% pinot noir, 40% chardonnay

92

Colour: yellow. Nose: dry nuts, fragrant herbs, complex, fine lees, expressive. Palate: powerful, flavourful, good acidity, fine bead, fine bitter notes, elegant.

Naveran Perles Blanques Magnum 2010 BR
60% pinot noir, 40% chardonnay

93

Colour: bright golden. Nose: fine lees, dry nuts, fragrant herbs, complex, toasty, faded flowers. Palate: powerful, flavourful, good acidity, fine bead, fine bitter notes.

Naverán Perles Roses Pinot Noir Magnum 2010 BR
100% pinot noir

92

Colour: coppery red. Nose: floral, jasmine, varietal, expressive, fragrant herbs, ripe fruit. Palate: fresh, fruity, flavourful, correct.

Naverán Perles Roses Pinot Noir Rosado 2012 BR
pinot noir

91

Colour: onion pink. Nose: floral, jasmine, fragrant herbs, elegant, white flowers. Palate: fresh, fruity, flavourful, correct.

CAVES VIDAL I FERRÉ

Nou, 2
43815 Les Pobles (Tarragona)
☎: +34 977 638 554
Fax: +34 977 638 554
vidaliferre@vidaliferre.com
www.vidaliferre.com

Vidal i Ferré 2010 BN Gran Reserva
macabeo, xarel.lo, parellada

88

Colour: bright yellow. Nose: ripe fruit, fine lees, balanced, dried herbs. Palate: good acidity, flavourful, ripe fruit, long.

Vidal i Ferré 2011 BN Reserva
macabeo, xarel.lo, parellada

87

Colour: bright straw. Nose: medium intensity, fresh fruit, dried herbs, fine lees, floral. Palate: fresh, fruity, flavourful, good acidity.

Vidal i Ferré 2011 BR Reserva
macabeo, xarel.lo, parellada

87

Colour: bright straw. Nose: fine lees, floral, fragrant herbs, expressive. Palate: powerful, flavourful, good acidity, fine bead, balanced.

Vidal i Ferré 2011 SS Reserva
macabeo, xarel.lo, parellada

84

Vidal i Ferré Rosado 2011 BR Reserva
pinot noir

85

CELLER CARLES ANDREU

Sant Sebastià, 19
43423 Pira (Tarragona)
☎: +34 977 887 404
Fax: +34 977 860 279
celler@cavandreu.com
www.cavandreu.com

Brut Carles Andreu BR
parellada, macabeo

88

Colour: bright straw. Nose: fine lees, floral, fragrant herbs. Palate: powerful, flavourful, good acidity, fine bead.

Brut Nature Carles Andreu BN
parellada, macabeo

86

Carles Andreu Magnum 2012 BN Reserva
parellada, macabeo, chardonnay

89

Colour: bright straw. Nose: fine lees, balanced, dried herbs, fresh fruit. Palate: good acidity, flavourful, ripe fruit, long.

Cava Rosado Trepat Brut Carles Andreu BR
trepat

87

Colour: coppery red. Nose: jasmine, fragrant herbs, candied fruit. Palate: fresh, fruity, flavourful, correct.

Cava Rosado Trepat Reserva Barrica Brut Carles Andreu BR
trepat

90

Colour: coppery red. Nose: floral, jasmine, fragrant herbs, toasty, spicy. Palate: fresh, fruity, flavourful, correct, toasty.

Reserva Barrica Brut Nature Carles Andreu 2011 BN Reserva
parellada, macabeo, chardonnay

92

Nose: fine lees, fragrant herbs, characterful, ripe fruit, dry nuts. Palate: powerful, flavourful, good acidity, fine bead, fine bitter notes, elegant.

Reserva Brut Nature Carles Andreu 2010 BN
parellada, macabeo, chardonnay

90

Colour: bright yellow. Nose: fine lees, dry nuts, fragrant herbs, complex. Palate: powerful, flavourful, good acidity, fine bead, fine bitter notes.

Semiseco Carles Andreu SS
parellada, macabeo

86

CELLER JORDI LLUCH

08777 Sant Quinti de Mediona (Barcelona)
☎: +34 938 988 138
Fax: +34 938 988 138
vinyaescude@vinyaescude.com
www.vinyaescude.com

Vinya Escudé 523 Extra Brut Reserva
macabeo, xarel.lo, parellada

85

Vinya Escudé Rosat BN

84

CELLER VELL CAVA

Partida Mas Solanes, s/n
08770 Sant Sadurní D'Anoia
(Barcelona)
☎: +34 938 910 290
Fax: +34 938 183 246
info@cellervell.com
www.cellervell.com

Celler Vell 2012 BN Reserva
xarel.lo, macabeo, parellada

88

Colour: bright yellow. Nose: ripe fruit, fine lees, balanced, dried herbs. Palate: good acidity, flavourful, ripe fruit, long.

Celler Vell Cuvèe Les Solanes 2010 BN Reserva
xarel.lo, chardonnay, pinot noir

91

Colour: bright yellow. Nose: fine lees, dry nuts, fragrant herbs, complex, toasty. Palate: powerful, flavourful, good acidity, fine bead, fine bitter notes.

Celler Vell Extra Brut 2012 ESP Reserva
xarel.lo, macabeo, parellada

87

Colour: bright straw. Nose: fine lees, fragrant herbs, medium intensity. Palate: flavourful, good acidity, fine bead, easy to drink.

CELLERS CAROL VALLÈS

Can Parellada, s/n - Corral del Mestre
08739 Subirats (Barcelona)
☎: +34 938 989 078
Fax: +34 938 988 413
info@cellerscarol.com
www.cellerscarol.com

Guillem Carol 2010 Extra Brut Gran Reserva
40% parellada, 36% macabeo, 24% chardonnay

87

Colour: bright straw. Nose: medium intensity, fresh fruit, dried herbs, fine lees, floral. Palate: fresh, fruity, flavourful, good acidity.

Guillem Carol 2011 BN Gran Reserva
40% parellada, 40% xarel.lo, 20% chardonnay

89

Colour: yellow. Nose: medium intensity, dried herbs, fine lees, dried flowers. Palate: fresh, fruity, good acidity, good finish.

Guillem Carol Barrica 2008 BN Gran Reserva
50% xarel.lo, 50% chardonnay

90

Colour: bright golden. Nose: fine lees, dry nuts, fragrant herbs, complex, faded flowers. Palate: powerful, flavourful, good acidity, fine bead, fine bitter notes.

Guillem Carol Chardonnay Pinot Noir 2007 BR Reserva
60% chardonnay, 40% pinot noir

88

Colour: bright golden. Nose: fine lees, fragrant herbs, characterful, ripe fruit, dry nuts. Palate: powerful, flavourful, good acidity, fine bead, fine bitter notes.

Guillem Carol Millenium 2006 BR Gran Reserva
30% parellada, 30% xarel.lo, 20% macabeo, 20% chardonnay

90

Colour: bright golden. Nose: fine lees, dry nuts, smoky. Palate: powerful, flavourful, good acidity, fine bead, fine bitter notes.

Guillem Carol Pinot Noir Rosat 2010 BN Reserva
100% pinot noir

84

Parellada i Faura 2012 BN Reserva
60% parellada, 30% macabeo, 10% xarel.lo

87

Colour: bright straw. Nose: floral, fragrant herbs. Palate: powerful, flavourful, good acidity, fine bead, balanced.

Parellada i Faura Millenium 2011 BN Reserva
40% parellada, 40% macabeo, 20% xarel.lo

87

Colour: bright straw. Nose: medium intensity, fresh fruit, dried herbs. Palate: fresh, fruity, flavourful, good acidity.

CELLERS GRAU DÒRIA

Plaza Eliseo Oliver, 4 bis
08811 Canyelles (Barcelona)
☎: +34 938 973 263
Fax: +34 938 973 263
info@graudoria.com
www.graudoria.com

Brut de Grau Dòria 2013 BR
xarel.lo, macabeo, parellada

85

Brut Nature de Grau Dòria 2012 BN

xarel.lo, macabeo, parellada

87

Colour: bright straw. Nose: fine lees, floral, fragrant herbs, expressive. Palate: powerful, flavourful, good acidity, fine bead, balanced.

Grau Dòria Rosado 2013 BR

garnacha, pinot noir

87

Colour: rose. Nose: floral, red berry notes, ripe fruit, fragrant herbs, expressive. Palate: powerful, balanced, flavourful.

Mercè Grau Doria 2007 BN Gran Reserva

xarel.lo, macabeo, chardonnay

88

Colour: bright golden. Nose: fine lees, dry nuts, fragrant herbs, complex. Palate: powerful, flavourful, good acidity, fine bead, fine bitter notes.

Nature Reserva de Grau Dòria 2012 BN Reserva

xarel.lo, macabeo, chardonnay, parellada

88

Colour: bright straw. Nose: medium intensity, dried herbs, fine lees, floral. Palate: fresh, fruity, flavourful, good acidity.

CELLERS PLANAS ALBAREDA

Ctra. Guardiola, Km. 3
08735 Vilobí del Penedès (Barcelona)
☎: +34 938 922 143
Fax: +34 938 922 143
planasalbareda@yahoo.es
www.planasalbareda.com

Planas Albareda 2011 BN Reserva

macabeo, xarel.lo, parellada

87

Colour: bright golden. Nose: fine lees, fragrant herbs, characterful, ripe fruit, dry nuts. Palate: powerful, flavourful, good acidity, fine bead, fine bitter notes.

Planas Albareda 2012 BN

xarel.lo, macabeo, parellada

85

Planas Albareda Reserva de L'Avi 2010 BN Gran Reserva

macabeo, xarel.lo, parellada, chardonnay

88

Colour: bright straw. Nose: medium intensity, dried herbs, floral. Palate: fresh, fruity, flavourful, good acidity.

Planas Albareda Rosat BR

trepat

85

CHOZAS CARRASCAL

Vereda San Antonio
46390 San Antonio de Requena
(Valencia)
☎: +34 963 410 395
chozas@chozascarrascal.es
www.chozascarrascal.es

El Cava de Chozas Carrascal 2012 BN Reserva

50% chardonnay, 50% macabeo

93 ♣

Colour: bright golden. Nose: fine lees, fragrant herbs, complex, floral. Palate: powerful, flavourful, good acidity, fine bead, fine bitter notes.

CODORNÍU

Avda. Jaume Codorníu, s/n
08770 Sant Sadurní D'Anoia
(Barcelona)
☎: +34 938 183 232
codinfo@codorniu.com
www.codorniu.com

Anna de Codorníu BR

70% chardonnay, 15% parellada, 15% macabeo, xarel.lo

86

Anna de Codorníu 20 Cl BR

85

Anna de Codorníu Blanc de Blancs BR Reserva

100% pinot noir

87

Colour: bright straw. Nose: fresh fruit, dried herbs, fine lees, floral. Palate: fresh, fruity, flavourful, good acidity, good finish.

Anna de Codorníu Blanc de Noirs BR

100% pinot noir

87

Colour: bright straw. Nose: fresh fruit, dried herbs, fine lees, floral. Palate: fresh, fruity, flavourful, good acidity.

Anna de Codorníu Rosé BR

70% pinot noir, 30% chardonnay

87

Colour: coppery red. Nose: floral, jasmine, fragrant herbs, candied fruit. Palate: fresh, fruity, flavourful, correct.

CodorNew Frizz 5,5 de Aguja ESP

verdejo

87

Colour: bright straw. Nose: floral, fragrant herbs, candied fruit. Palate: fresh, fruity, flavourful, sweet, easy to drink.

Codorníu Cuvée 1872 BR
macabeo, xarel.lo, parellada

87

Colour: bright straw. Nose: fine lees, floral, fragrant herbs, fresh fruit. Palate: flavourful, good acidity, fine bead, correct.

Codorníu Cuvée 1872 Rosé BR
garnacha, pinot noir

85

Codorníu Ecológica BR
xarel.lo, parellada

87

Colour: bright straw. Nose: floral, lees reduction notes, dried herbs. Palate: flavourful, good acidity, fine bead, easy to drink.

Codorníu Pinot Noir BR
pinot noir

87

Colour: coppery red. Nose: floral, jasmine, fragrant herbs, ripe fruit, lees reduction notes. Palate: fresh, fruity, flavourful, correct.

Codorniu Reina Mª Cristina Blanc de Noirs Vintage 2012 BR Reserva
pinot noir

91

Colour: bright straw. Nose: fine lees, floral, fragrant herbs, expressive. Palate: flavourful, good acidity, fine bead.

Codorniu Reina Mª Cristina Blanc de Noirs Vintage 2013 BR Reserva
pinot noir

92

Colour: bright yellow. Nose: ripe fruit, fine lees, balanced, dried herbs. Palate: good acidity, flavourful, long.

Gran Codorníu Chardonnay BN Reserva
100% chardonnay

90

Colour: bright straw. Nose: medium intensity, fresh fruit, fine lees, white flowers. Palate: fresh, fruity, flavourful, good acidity.

Gran Codorníu Finca El Coster 2009 BR Reserva
100% pinot noir

92

Colour: bright yellow. Nose: fine lees, floral, fragrant herbs, spicy. Palate: flavourful, good acidity, fine bead, fresh, elegant.

Gran Codorníu Finca La Nansa 2009 BR Gran Reserva
100% xarel.lo

94

Colour: bright straw. Nose: fine lees, dry nuts, fragrant herbs, complex, elegant. Palate: flavourful, good acidity, fine bead, fine bitter notes, fresh.

Gran Codorníu Finca la Pleta 2009 BN Gran Reserva
100% chardonnay

93

Colour: yellow. Nose: white flowers, citrus fruit, varietal, balanced. Palate: flavourful, balanced, fine bitter notes, good acidity.

Gran Codorníu Pinot Noir Vintage 2012 BR
100% pinot noir

89

Colour: raspberry rose. Nose: fine lees, raspberry, candied fruit, wild herbs. Palate: fresh, fruity, flavourful, fine bead.

Gran Plus Ultra s/c BN Reserva

89

Colour: bright yellow. Nose: fine lees, floral, fragrant herbs. Palate: flavourful, good acidity, fine bead.

Jaume Codorníu 2010 BR Gran Reserva
pinot noir, chardonnay, xarel.lo

93

Colour: bright yellow. Nose: fine lees, fragrant herbs, characterful, ripe fruit, dry nuts, expressive. Palate: powerful, flavourful, good acidity, fine bead, fine bitter notes.

Codorníu 456 2007 BR Gran Reserva
pinot noir, chardonnay

94

Colour: bright golden. Nose: fine lees, dry nuts, fragrant herbs, complex, toasty. Palate: powerful, flavourful, good acidity, fine bead, fine bitter notes.

COFAMA VINS I CAVES

Casanovas i Bosch 57
08202 Sabadell (Barcelona)
☎: +34 937 220 338
Fax: +34 937 252 385
roger.manyosa@cofamaexport.com
www.cofamaexport.com

Celebrandum BR
macabeo, xarel.lo, parellada

86

Celebrandum BN
xarel.lo, macabeo, parellada

85

Celebrandum Rosado BR
trepat
85

Dignitat BN
xarel.lo, macabeo, parellada
85

Dignitat BR
xarel.lo, macabeo, parellada
85

Dignitat Rosado BR
trepat
84

Grans Moments BN
xarel.lo, macabeo, parellada
86

Mas Bigas BR
xarel.lo, macabeo, parellada
88
Colour: bright straw. Nose: medium intensity, fresh fruit, dried herbs, fine lees, faded flowers. Palate: fresh, fruity, flavourful, good acidity.

Mas Fi BN Reserva
xarel.lo, macabeo, parellada
85

Mas Fi BR
xarel.lo, macabeo, parellada
84

Mas Fi Rosado BR
trepat
85

Mas Geroni BN
xarel.lo, macabeo, parellada
86

Mas Geroni BR
xarel.lo, macabeo, parellada
85

Mas Geroni Rosat BR
trepat
84

COOPERATIVA AGRÍCOLA DE BARBERÀ

Carrer Comerç, 40
43422 Barberà de la Conca (Tarragona)
☎: +34 977 887 035
Fax: +34 977 887 035
cobarbera@doconcadebarbera.com
www.coop-barbera.com

Castell Comanda 2011 BN Reserva
50% macabeo, 50% parellada
87
Colour: bright straw. Nose: ripe fruit, fine lees, balanced, dried herbs. Palate: good acidity, flavourful, ripe fruit, long.

Castell de la Comanda 2011 BR Reserva
50% macabeo, 50% parellada
85

COVIDES VIÑEDOS BODEGAS

Rambla Nostra Senyora, 45 - 1º
08720 Vilafranca del Penedès (Barcelona)
☎: +34 938 172 552
covides@covides.com
www.covides.com

Duc de Foix BR
macabeo, xarel.lo, parellada
85

Duc de Foix BR Reserva Especial
chardonnay, macabeo, xarel.lo, parellada
90
Colour: bright straw. Nose: fine lees, floral, fragrant herbs, citrus fruit. Palate: flavourful, good acidity, fine bead, balanced.

Ferriol Selección BR
macabeo, xarel.lo, parellada
84

CUSCÓ BERGA

Esplugues, 7
08793 Avinyonet del Penedès (Barcelona)
☎: +34 938 970 164
cuscoberga@cuscoberga.com
www.cuscoberga.com

Cuscó Berga 2011 BN Reserva
30% macabeo, 50% xarel.lo, 20% parellada
86

Cuscó Berga 2010 BR Gran Reserva
30% macabeo, 50% xarel.lo, 20% parellada
87
Colour: bright yellow. Nose: fine lees, fragrant herbs, characterful, ripe fruit, dry nuts. Palate: powerful, flavourful, good acidity, fine bead, fine bitter notes.

Cuscó Berga 2011 BR
30% macabeo, 50% xarel.lo, 20% parellada

84

Cuscó Berga lògic 2011 BN Reserva
30% macabeo, 40% xarel.lo, 30% parellada

88

Colour: bright straw. Nose: medium intensity, fresh fruit, dried herbs, fine lees. Palate: fresh, fruity, flavourful, good acidity.

Cuscó Berga Rosé 2012 BR
100% trepat

85

DOMINIO DE LA VEGA
Ctra. Madrid - Valencia, N-III Km. 270
46390 Requena (Valencia)
☎: +34 962 320 570
Fax: +34 962 320 330
dv@dominiodelavega.com
www.dominiodelavega.com

Artemayor BN
chardonnay, macabeo

89

Colour: bright golden. Nose: fine lees, fragrant herbs, characterful, ripe fruit, dry nuts, toasty. Palate: powerful, flavourful, good acidity, fine bitter notes.

Dominio de la Vega BN
macabeo

88

Colour: bright yellow. Nose: ripe fruit, lees reduction notes, dried herbs. Palate: correct, fruity, easy to drink.

Dominio de la Vega BR
macabeo

88

Colour: bright yellow. Nose: fine lees, floral, fragrant herbs, expressive, toasty. Palate: powerful, flavourful, good acidity, fine bead.

Dominio de la Vega 2012 BN Reserva
macabeo, chardonnay

88

Colour: bright straw. Nose: medium intensity, fresh fruit, dried herbs, fine lees, floral. Palate: fresh, fruity, flavourful, good acidity.

Dominio de la Vega Pinot Noir Rosado BR
pinot noir

85

Dominio de la Vega Reserva Especial 2012 BR Reserva
macabeo, chardonnay

88

Colour: yellow. Nose: dry nuts, faded flowers, balanced, spicy. Palate: flavourful, easy to drink, good acidity.

DURAN
Font, 2
08769 Castellví de Rosanes (Barcelona)
☎: +34 937 755 446
info@cavaduran.com
www.cavaduran.com

Duran 2009 BN Gran Reserva
xarel.lo, macabeo, parellada, chardonnay, pinot noir

89

Colour: bright yellow. Nose: ripe fruit, fine lees, balanced, dried herbs. Palate: good acidity, flavourful, ripe fruit, long.

Duran 5V 2009 BR Gran Reserva
xarel.lo, chardonnay, macabeo, parellada, pinot noir

90

Colour: bright golden. Nose: fine lees, fragrant herbs, characterful, ripe fruit, dry nuts. Palate: powerful, flavourful, good acidity, fine bead.

EMENDIS
Barrio de Sant Marçal, 67
08732 Castellet i La Gornal (Barcelona)
☎: +34 938 919 790
Fax: +34 938 918 169
info@emendis.es
www.emendis.es

Emendis 2009 BN Gran Reserva
45% xarel.lo, 20% macabeo, 20% parellada, 15% chardonnay, pinot noir

91

Colour: yellow. Nose: fine lees, dry nuts, fragrant herbs, complex, toasty. Palate: powerful, flavourful, good acidity, fine bead, fine bitter notes.

Emendis 2013 BR
50% xarel.lo, 25% macabeo, 25% parellada

88

Colour: bright straw. Nose: fine lees, floral, fragrant herbs, expressive. Palate: flavourful, good acidity, fine bead, balanced.

Emendis Cabernet Franc 2012 T
100% cabernet franc

88

Colour: light cherry. Nose: fruit expression, fruit liqueur notes, fragrant herbs, spicy. Palate: spicy, long, toasty.

Emendis Imum 2012 BN Reserva
50% xarel.lo, 25% macabeo, 25% parellada

88

Colour: bright straw. Nose: medium intensity, fresh fruit, dried herbs, fine lees, floral. Palate: fresh, good acidity, easy to drink.

Emendis Rosé 2014 BR
100% pinot noir

88

Colour: rose. Nose: floral, red berry notes, ripe fruit, fragrant herbs, expressive. Palate: powerful, balanced, flavourful.

ESTEL D'ARGENT
Font Rubí, 2 Esc. A 4º 1ª
08720 Vilafranca del Penedès
(Barcelona)
☎: +34 677 182 347
cava@esteldargent.com
www.esteldargent.com

Estel D'Argent 2012 BN Reserva
macabeo, xarel.lo, parellada

88

Colour: bright yellow. Nose: fine lees, floral, fragrant herbs, expressive. Palate: powerful, flavourful, good acidity, fine bead, balanced.

Estel D'Argent Especial 2009 Extra Brut Gran Reserva
macabeo, xarel.lo, chardonnay

90

Colour: bright yellow. Nose: fine lees, dry nuts, complex, dried flowers. Palate: powerful, flavourful, good acidity, fine bead, fine bitter notes.

Estel D'Argent Especial 2010 Extra Brut Reserva
macabeo, xarel.lo, chardonnay

89

Colour: bright straw. Nose: medium intensity, fresh fruit, dried herbs, fine lees, floral, expressive. Palate: fresh, fruity, flavourful, good acidity.

Estel D'Argent Rosé 2012 BN Reserva
pinot noir, trepat

84

FERMI BOHIGAS
Finca Can Maciá s/n
08711 Ódena (Barcelona)
☎: +34 938 048 100
Fax: +34 938 032 366
aministracio@bohigas.es
www.bohigas.es

Bohigas BN Reserva
macabeo, xarel.lo, parellada

87

Colour: bright straw. Nose: medium intensity, fresh fruit, dried herbs, fine lees, floral. Palate: fresh, fruity, flavourful, good acidity.

Bohigas BR Reserva
macabeo, xarel.lo, parellada

88

Colour: bright straw. Nose: medium intensity, fresh fruit, dried herbs, fine lees, floral. Palate: fresh, fruity, flavourful, good acidity.

Bohigas 2011 BN Gran Reserva
macabeo, xarel.lo, parellada

89

Colour: bright yellow. Nose: ripe fruit, fine lees, balanced, dried herbs. Palate: good acidity, ripe fruit, easy to drink.

Bohigas Rosat BR
trepat

88

Colour: rose. Nose: floral, red berry notes, ripe fruit, fragrant herbs, expressive. Palate: powerful, balanced, flavourful.

Noa de Fermí Bohigas BN
pinot noir, xarel.lo

91

Colour: bright golden. Nose: fine lees, dry nuts, fragrant herbs, complex, toasty. Palate: powerful, flavourful, good acidity, fine bead, fine bitter notes.

FERRE I CATASUS
Masía Gustems s/n
08792 La Granada del Penedès
(Barcelona)
☎: +34 938 974 558
Fax: +34 938 974 708
eduard@ferreicatasus.com
www.ferreicatasus.com

Ferré i Catasús 2011 BN Reserva
macabeo, xarel.lo, parellada, chardonnay

89

Colour: bright straw. Nose: floral, fragrant herbs. Palate: powerful, flavourful, good acidity, fine bead, balanced.

Ferré i Catasús 2011 BR Reserva
macabeo, xarel.lo, parellada, chardonnay

86

Mas Suau 2012 BN Reserva
macabeo, xarel.lo, parellada

88

Colour: bright yellow. Nose: ripe fruit, fine lees, balanced, dried herbs. Palate: good acidity, flavourful, ripe fruit, long.

FINCA TORREMILANOS
Finca Torremilanos
09400 Aranda de Duero (Burgos)
☎: +34 947 512 852
Fax: +34 947 508 044
reservas@torremilanos.com
www.torremilanos.com

Peñalba-López BN
84 ♣

FINCA VALLDOSERA
Masia Les Garrigues, s/n
08734 Olèrdola (Barcelona)
☎: +34 938 143 047
Fax: +34 938 935 590
general@fincavalldosera.com
www.fincavalldosera.com

Cava MS 4.7 BN Gran Reserva
xarel.lo, macabeo, parellada, subirat parent, chardonnay

90

Colour: bright yellow. Nose: floral, fragrant herbs, expressive, dry nuts. Palate: powerful, flavourful, good acidity, fine bead, balanced.

Subirat Parent BN Gran Reserva
subirat parent

90

Colour: bright yellow. Nose: floral, jasmine, fragrant herbs, wild herbs, tropical fruit. Palate: fresh, fruity, flavourful.

Valldosera BN Reserva
xarel.lo, macabeo, parellada, chardonnay

87

Colour: bright yellow. Nose: ripe fruit, fine lees, dried herbs. Palate: good acidity, flavourful, ripe fruit.

FREIXA RIGAU
Santa Llucía, 15
17750 Capmany (Girona)
☎: +34 972 549 012
Fax: +34 972 549 106
comercial@grupoliveda.com
www.grupoliveda.com

Freixa Rigau Nature Mil.lèssima Reserva Familiar 2011 BN
40% macabeo, 30% xarel.lo, 30% parellada

85

Gran Rigau 2011 BN Reserva
40% macabeo, 30% xarel.lo, 30% parellada

86

Gran Rigau Pinot Noir Rosado BN
100% pinot noir

88

Colour: rose. Nose: floral, red berry notes, ripe fruit, fragrant herbs, expressive. Palate: powerful, balanced, flavourful.

FREIXENET
Joan Sala, 2
08770 Sant Sadurní D'Anoia
(Barcelona)
☎: +34 938 917 000
Fax: +34 938 183 095
freixenet@freixenet.es
www.freixenet.es

Carta Nevada BR
macabeo, xarel.lo, parellada

88

Colour: bright straw. Nose: fine lees, floral, fragrant herbs. Palate: flavourful, good acidity.

Casa Sala 2006 BR Gran Reserva
xarel.lo, parellada

93

Colour: yellow. Nose: fine lees, fragrant herbs, characterful, ripe fruit, dry nuts, toasty. Palate: powerful, flavourful, good acidity, fine bead, fine bitter notes.

Cordón Negro BR
parellada, macabeo, xarel.lo

87

Colour: bright straw. Nose: medium intensity, dried herbs, fine lees, floral. Palate: fresh, fruity, flavourful, good acidity.

Cuvée D.S. 2007 BR Gran Reserva
macabeo, xarel.lo, parellada

90

Colour: bright straw. Nose: fine lees, fragrant herbs, expressive. Palate: powerful, flavourful, good acidity, fine bead, balanced, fine bitter notes.

Elyssia Gran Cuvée BR Reserva
chardonnay, macabeo, parellada, pinot noir

88

Colour: bright straw. Nose: fresh fruit, dried herbs, floral. Palate: fresh, fruity, flavourful, good acidity.

Elyssia Pinot Noir Rosé BR Reserva
pinot noir

88

Colour: raspberry rose. Nose: floral, jasmine, fragrant herbs, candied fruit. Palate: fresh, fruity, flavourful, correct.

Freixenet 2010 BN Gran Reserva
macabeo, xarel.lo, parellada

88

Colour: bright yellow. Nose: ripe fruit, fine lees, balanced, dried herbs. Palate: good acidity, fresh, easy to drink.

Freixenet Malvasía Dulce 2009 BR Gran Reserva
malvasía

87

Colour: bright straw. Nose: floral, fragrant herbs, candied fruit. Palate: fresh, fruity, sweet.

Freixenet Monastrell Xarel.lo 2009 BR Gran Reserva
monastrell, xarel.lo

90

Colour: bright yellow. Nose: ripe fruit, fine lees, balanced, dried herbs. Palate: good acidity, flavourful, ripe fruit, long.

Freixenet Trepat Rosado BR Reserva
trepat

90

Colour: coppery red. Nose: floral, jasmine, fragrant herbs, candied fruit. Palate: fresh, fruity, flavourful, correct.

Meritum BR Gran Reserva
xarel.lo, macabeo, parellada

92

Colour: bright yellow. Nose: ripe fruit, fine lees, dried herbs, expressive. Palate: good acidity, flavourful, ripe fruit, long.

Reserva Real BR Gran Reserva
macabeo, xarel.lo, parellada

93

Colour: bright straw. Nose: fine lees, fragrant herbs, expressive, fresh, wild herbs. Palate: flavourful, good acidity, fine bead.

GASTÓN COTY S.A.
Avernó, 28-30
08770 Sant Sadurní D'Anoia
(Barcelona)
☎: +34 938 183 602
Fax: +34 938 913 461
lorigan@lorigancava.com
www.lorigancava.com

Aire de L'O de L'Origan 2011 BN

91

Colour: bright yellow. Nose: ripe fruit, fine lees, balanced, dried herbs. Palate: good acidity, flavourful, ripe fruit, long.

Aire de L'O de L'Origan Rose 2013 BN

90

Colour: coppery red, bright. Nose: faded flowers, dry nuts, balanced. Palate: balanced, fine bitter notes, good acidity, fine bead.

L'Origan BN

92

Colour: bright golden. Nose: fine lees, dry nuts, fragrant herbs, complex. Palate: powerful, flavourful, good acidity, fine bead, fine bitter notes.

L'Origan Rosat BN

92

Colour: brilliant rose. Nose: fine reductive notes, red berry notes, citrus fruit, dried herbs. Palate: flavourful, fine bitter notes, fine bead.

GIRÓ DEL GORNER
Finca Giró del Gorner
08797 Puigdálber (Barcelona)
☎: +34 938 988 032
gorner@girodelgorner.com
www.girodelgorner.com

Giró del Gorner 2007 BN Gran Reserva
macabeo, xarel.lo, parellada

88

Colour: yellow. Nose: fine lees, dry nuts, fragrant herbs, toasty. Palate: powerful, flavourful, good acidity, fine bead, fine bitter notes.

Giró del Gorner 2007 BR Gran Reserva
macabeo, xarel.lo, parellada

88

Colour: bright yellow. Nose: ripe fruit, fine lees, balanced, dried herbs, citrus fruit. Palate: good acidity, ripe fruit, long, fine bitter notes.

Giró del Gorner 2011 BN Reserva
macabeo, xarel.lo, parellada

88

Colour: bright straw. Nose: fine lees, floral, fragrant herbs, expressive. Palate: powerful, flavourful, good acidity, fine bead.

Giró del Gorner 2011 BR Reserva
macabeo, xarel.lo, parellada

88

Colour: bright straw. Nose: fine lees, floral, fragrant herbs, expressive. Palate: powerful, flavourful, good acidity, fine bead, easy to drink.

Pinot Noir Giró del Gorner Rosado 2013 BR
100% pinot noir

87

Colour: coppery red. Nose: floral, jasmine, red berry notes. Palate: fruity, flavourful, correct, easy to drink, fresh.

GIRÓ RIBOT, S.L.

Finca El Pont, s/n
08792 Santa Fe del Penedès
(Barcelona)
☎: +34 938 974 050
Fax: +34 938 974 311
giroribot@giroribot.es
www.giroribot.es

Giró Ribot Adivinis Magnum 2008 BN Gran Reserva
90% chardonnay, 10% parellada

92

Colour: bright straw. Nose: fresh fruit, varietal, expressive, balanced, fine lees. Palate: balanced, fine bitter notes, good acidity, long.

Giró Ribot Avant Reserva 2010 Fermentado en Barrica
45% xarel.lo, 40% chardonnay, 15% macabeo

92

Colour: bright straw. Nose: fine lees, floral, expressive, white flowers. Palate: powerful, flavourful, good acidity, fine bead, balanced.

Giró Ribot Brut Nature 2011 Gran Reserva
50% macabeo, 30% xarel.lo, 10% parellada, 10% chardonnay

88

Colour: bright yellow. Nose: ripe fruit, fine lees, balanced, dried herbs. Palate: good acidity, flavourful, ripe fruit, long.

Giro Ribot Brut Reserva 2012
50% macabeo, 30% xarel.lo, 10% parellada, 10% chardonnay

86

Giró Ribot Excelsus 100 Magnum 2006 BR Gran Reserva
50% xarel.lo, 30% macabeo, 20% parellada

93

Colour: bright yellow. Nose: ripe fruit, dried herbs, lees reduction notes. Palate: good acidity, flavourful, ripe fruit, long.

Giró Ribot Mare 2008 B Gran Reserva
50% macabeo, 30% xarel.lo, 20% parellada

92

Colour: bright golden. Nose: fine lees, dry nuts, fragrant herbs, complex, toasty. Palate: powerful, flavourful, good acidity, fine bead, fine bitter notes.

Giró Ribot Mare Magnum 2009 B Gran Reserva
50% xarel.lo, 30% macabeo, 20% parellada

92

Colour: bright yellow. Nose: ripe fruit, fine lees, balanced, dried herbs, dried flowers, complex. Palate: good acidity, flavourful, ripe fruit, long.

Giró Ribot Rosé 2013 BR
85% trepat, 15% pinot noir

87

Colour: rose. Nose: floral, red berry notes, ripe fruit, fragrant herbs, expressive. Palate: powerful, flavourful, full.

Giró Ribot Spur 2011 BR Reserva
45% macabeo, 40% xarel.lo, 10% chardonnay, 5% parellada

89

Colour: bright yellow. Nose: ripe fruit, fine lees, balanced, dried herbs. Palate: good acidity, flavourful, long.

Giró Ribot Tendencias 2011 Reserva
40% macabeo, 30% xarel.lo, 15% parellada, 15% chardonnay

86

Giró Ribot Unplugged Rosado 2012 Fermentado en Barrica
pinot noir

93

Colour: coppery red. Nose: floral, jasmine, fragrant herbs, candied fruit. Palate: fresh, fruity, flavourful, correct.

Paul Cheneau 2012 BR Reserva
45% macabeo, 40% xarel.lo, 10% chardonnay, 5% parellada

87

Colour: bright straw. Nose: medium intensity, fresh fruit, dried herbs, fine lees, floral. Palate: fresh, fruity, flavourful, good acidity.

GRIMAU

Masía Torreblanca s/n
08734 Olerdola (Barcelona)
☎: +34 938 918 031
grimau@grimau.com
www.grimau.com

Grimau 2013 BN

macabeo, xarel.lo, parellada

88

Colour: bright yellow. Nose: ripe fruit, fine lees, balanced, dried herbs. Palate: good acidity, flavourful, long.

Grimau 2014 BR

macabeo, xarel.lo, parellada

87

Colour: bright straw. Nose: fine lees, floral, fragrant herbs. Palate: flavourful, good acidity, fine bead.

Grimau Reserva Familiar 2012 BN

macabeo, xarel.lo, parellada

93

Colour: bright golden. Nose: fine lees, dry nuts, fragrant herbs, complex. Palate: powerful, flavourful, good acidity, fine bead, fine bitter notes.

Trencadís 2013 BN

87

Colour: bright straw. Nose: medium intensity, fresh fruit, dried herbs, fine lees, floral. Palate: fresh, fruity, flavourful, good acidity.

Trencadís Rosat 2013 BN

pinot noir, garnacha

84

HAMMEKEN CELLARS

Calle de la Muela, 16
03730 Jávea (Alicante)
☎: +34 965 791 967
Fax: +34 966 461 471
cellars@hammekencellars.com
www.hammekencellars.com

Flor del Montgó BR

35% macabeo, 35% parellada, 30% xarel.lo

86

Picos del Montgó BR

35% macabeo, 35% parellada, 30% xarel.lo

86

HEREDAD SEGURA VIUDAS

Ctra. Sant Sadurní a St. Pere
de Riudebitlles, Km. 5
08775 Torrelavit (Barcelona)
☎: +34 938 917 070
Fax: +34 938 996 006
seguraviudas@seguraviudas.es
www.seguraviudas.com

Aria BN Reserva

macabeo, xarel.lo

87

Colour: yellow. Nose: fresh, fresh fruit, wild herbs. Palate: easy to drink, good finish, good acidity, fine bitter notes.

Conde de Caralt BR Reserva

macabeo, xarel.lo, parellada

85

Conde de Caralt Blanc de Blancs BR Reserva

macabeo, xarel.lo, parellada

91

Colour: bright straw. Nose: fine lees, floral, fragrant herbs. Palate: powerful, flavourful, good acidity, fine bead.

Lavit 2012 BN

macabeo, parellada

88

Colour: bright straw. Nose: fine lees, balanced, dried herbs, fresh fruit. Palate: good acidity, flavourful, ripe fruit, long.

Segura Viudas BR Reserva

macabeo, xarel.lo, parellada

88

Colour: bright straw. Nose: medium intensity, fresh fruit, dried herbs, fine lees, floral. Palate: fresh, fruity, flavourful, good acidity.

Segura Viudas Brut Vintage 2010 BN Gran Reserva

macabeo, parellada

89

Colour: bright yellow. Nose: medium intensity, fresh fruit, dried herbs, fine lees, floral. Palate: fresh, fruity, flavourful, good acidity.

Segura Viudas Reserva Heredad 2010 BR Gran Reserva

macabeo, parellada

92

Colour: bright golden. Nose: fine lees, fragrant herbs, characterful, ripe fruit, dry nuts, elegant. Palate: flavourful, fine bead, fine bitter notes, balanced.

Segura Viudas Rosado BR Reserva
trepat, garnacha

85

HERETAT SABARTÉS

Ctra Santa Oliva, s/n
43711 Banyeres del Penedès
(Tarragona)
☎: +34 934 750 125
amestres@selfoods.es
www.heretatsabartes.com

Heretat Sabartés BN Gran Reserva
macabeo, parellada, xarel.lo, chardonnay

89

Colour: bright golden. Nose: fine lees, fragrant herbs, characterful, ripe fruit. Palate: powerful, flavourful, good acidity, fine bead, fine bitter notes.

Heretat Sabartés BR Reserva
macabeo, parellada, xarel.lo, chardonnay

88

Colour: bright straw. Nose: medium intensity, fresh fruit, dried herbs, fine lees, floral. Palate: fresh, fruity, good acidity.

JANÉ VENTURA

Ctra. Calafell, 2
43700 El Vendrell (Tarragona)
☎: +34 977 660 118
janeventura@janeventura.com
www.janeventura.com

"Do" de Jané Ventura 2009 BN Gran Reserva
macabeo, xarel.lo, parellada

93

Colour: bright golden. Nose: dry nuts, fragrant herbs, complex, toasty, sweet spices. Palate: powerful, flavourful, good acidity, fine bead, fine bitter notes.

"Do" de Jané Ventura 2010 BN Gran Reserva
macabeo, xarel.lo, parellada

91

Colour: bright yellow. Nose: balanced, dried herbs, fresh fruit. Palate: good acidity, flavourful, ripe fruit, long.

"Do" de Jané Ventura Magnum 2008 BN Gran Reserva
macabeo, xarel.lo, parellada

92

Colour: bright golden. Nose: fine lees, dry nuts, fragrant herbs, complex, toasty. Palate: powerful, flavourful, good acidity, fine bead, fine bitter notes.

Cava 1914 de Jané Ventura 2007 BN Gran Reserva
macabeo, xarel.lo, parellada

93

Colour: bright golden. Nose: dry nuts, fragrant herbs, sweet spices, expressive. Palate: powerful, flavourful, good acidity, fine bead, fine bitter notes.

Cava 1914 de Jané Ventura Magnum 2007 BN Gran Reserva
macabeo, xarel.lo, parellada

94

Colour: bright golden. Nose: fine lees, dry nuts, fragrant herbs, complex. Palate: powerful, flavourful, good acidity, fine bead, fine bitter notes.

Jané Ventura Reserva de la Música 2012 BN Reserva
macabeo, xarel.lo, parellada

90

Colour: bright golden. Nose: fine lees, dry nuts, fragrant herbs, complex, toasty. Palate: powerful, flavourful, good acidity, fine bead, fine bitter notes.

Jané Ventura Reserva de la Música 2012 BR Reserva
macabeo, xarel.lo, parellada

89

Colour: bright straw. Nose: fine lees, floral, fragrant herbs, expressive. Palate: powerful, flavourful, good acidity, fine bead, balanced.

Jané Ventura Reserva de la Música Magnum BN

91

Colour: bright yellow. Nose: ripe fruit, fine lees, balanced, dried herbs. Palate: good acidity, flavourful, ripe fruit, long.

Jané Ventura Reserva de la Música Rosé 2012 BR
garnacha

88

Colour: rose. Nose: floral, red berry notes, ripe fruit, fragrant herbs, expressive. Palate: powerful, balanced, flavourful.

JAUME GIRÓ I GIRÓ

Montaner i Oller, 5
08770 Sant Sadurní D'Anoia
(Barcelona)
☎: +34 938 910 165
Fax: +34 938 911 271
cavagiro@cavagiro.com
www.cavagiro.com

Jaume Giró i Giró 2010 BR Reserva
45% xarel.lo, 20% parellada, 20% macabeo, 15% chardonnay

88

Colour: bright straw. Nose: fine lees, floral, fragrant herbs, expressive. Palate: powerful, flavourful, good acidity, fine bead, balanced.

Jaume Giró i Giró Bombonetta 2008 BR Gran Reserva
37% macabeo, 29% xarel.lo, 19% parellada

88

Colour: bright straw. Nose: floral, fragrant herbs, candied fruit. Palate: fresh, fruity, flavourful, sweetness.

Jaume Giró i Giró Elaboración Artesana 2012 BN Reserva
50% xarel.lo, 20% parellada, 20% macabeo, 10% chardonnay

88

Colour: bright straw. Nose: fine lees, floral, fragrant herbs, expressive. Palate: powerful, flavourful, good acidity, fine bead, balanced.

Jaume Giró i Giró Grandalla 2007 BR Gran Reserva
40% parellada, 33% xarel.lo, 22% macabeo, 5% chardonnay

91

Colour: bright golden. Nose: fine lees, dry nuts, fragrant herbs, complex. Palate: powerful, flavourful, good acidity, fine bead, fine bitter notes.

Jaume Giró i Giró Homenatge Cal Rei 2006 BR Gran Reserva
40% parellada, 20% xarel.lo, 25% macabeo, 15% chardonnay

89

Colour: bright golden. Nose: dry nuts, dried herbs, complex, spicy. Palate: powerful, flavourful, good acidity, fine bead, fine bitter notes.

Jaume Giró i Giró Montaner 2008 BN Gran Reserva
40% parellada, 30% xarel.lo, 20% macabeo, 10% chardonnay

90

Colour: bright yellow. Nose: ripe fruit, fine lees, balanced, dried herbs. Palate: good acidity, flavourful, ripe fruit, long.

Jaume Giró i Giró Premium 2006 BN Gran Reserva
40% parellada, 20% xarel.lo, 25% macabeo, 10% chardonnay, 5% pinot noir

89

Colour: bright golden. Nose: fine lees, dry nuts, fragrant herbs. Palate: powerful, flavourful, good acidity, fine bead, fine bitter notes.

Jaume Giró i Giró Rosat de Cal Rei 2011 BR Reserva
100% trepat

85

Jaume Giró i Giró Selecte 2008 BN Gran Reserva
37,5% parellada, 30% xarel.lo, 25% macabeo, 5% chardonnay, 2,5% pinot noir

91

Colour: bright straw. Nose: medium intensity, fresh fruit, dried herbs, fine lees, floral. Palate: fresh, fruity, flavourful, good acidity.

JAUME LLOPART GUELL

Cl. Font Rubí, 9
08736 Font-Rubí (Barcelona)
☎: +34 938 979 133
Fax: +34 938 979 133
info@jaumellopartalemany.com
www.jaumellopartalemany.com

Aina Jaume Llopart Alemany Rosado 2012 BR Reserva
pinot noir

87

Colour: light cherry. Nose: expressive, balsamic herbs, violets, ripe fruit. Palate: flavourful, fruity, easy to drink, good acidity.

Jaume Llopart Alemany BR Reserva
macabeo, xarel.lo, parellada

88

Colour: bright straw. Nose: fine lees, floral, fragrant herbs. Palate: flavourful, good acidity, fine bead.

Jaume Llopart Alemany 2009 BN Gran Reserva
macabeo, xarel.lo, parellada

92

Colour: bright yellow. Nose: fine lees, dry nuts, fragrant herbs, complex, elegant. Palate: powerful, flavourful, good acidity, fine bead, fine bitter notes, balanced.

Jaume Llopart Alemany Rosado BN Reserva
macabeo, xarel.lo, parellada

89

Colour: bright yellow. Nose: ripe fruit, fine lees, balanced, dried herbs. Palate: good acidity, flavourful, ripe fruit, long.

Vinya d'en Ferran Jaume Llopart Alemany 2007 BN Gran Reserva
pinot noir, chardonnay

93

Colour: bright yellow. Nose: fine lees, dry nuts, fragrant herbs, complex. Palate: powerful, flavourful, good acidity, fine bead, fine bitter notes.

JAUME SERRA (J. GARCÍA CARRIÓN)

Ctra. de Vilanova, Km. 2,5
08800 Vilanova i la Geltrú (Barcelona)
☎: +34 938 936 404
Fax: +34 938 147 482
jaumeserra@jgc.es
www.garciacarrion.es

Cristalino Jaume Serra BR
50% macabeo, 35% parellada, 15% xarel.lo

85

Jaume Serra BN
50% macabeo, 25% xarel.lo, 25% parellada

85

Jaume Serra BN Reserva
45% macabeo, 25% parellada, 15% xarel.lo, 15% chardonnay

83

Jaume Serra BR
50% macabeo, 35% parellada, 15% xarel.lo

82

Jaume Serra SS
50% macabeo, 25% xarel.lo, 25% parellada

80

Jaume Serra Chardonnay BR
100% chardonnay

85

Jaume Serra Chardonnay 2011 BN Gran Reserva
100% chardonnay

86

Colour: bright yellow. Nose: ripe fruit, dried herbs, dry nuts, pattiserie. Palate: correct, flavourful.

Jaume Serra Rosado BR
80% trepat, 20% pinot noir

84

Jaume Serra Vintage 2011 BN
25% parellada, 15% xarel.lo, 30% chardonnay

85

Pata Negra BR
40% macabeo, 30% xarel.lo, 30% parellada

84

Pata Negra SS
40% macabeo, 25% xarel.lo, 35% parellada

82

Pata Negra Rosado BR
80% trepat, 20% pinot noir

82

JULIÀ & NAVINÈS (VINDEGOUR)

Av. Catalunya, 28 bajos
08736 Font-Rubi (Barcelona)
☎: +34 938 974 069
teresa@umesufan3.com
www.umesufan3.com

Julià & Navinès BN Reserva
macabeo, xarel.lo, parellada

86

Julià & Navinès BR Reserva
macabeo, xarel.lo, parellada

85

Julià & Navinès Ecológico BN Reserva
macabeo, xarel.lo, parellada

88

Colour: bright yellow. Nose: ripe fruit, fine lees, balanced, dried herbs. Palate: good acidity, flavourful, ripe fruit, long.

JUVÉ & CAMPS

Sant Venat, 1
08770 Sant Sadurní D'Anoia
(Barcelona)
☎: +34 938 911 000
Fax: +34 938 912 100
juveycamps@juveycamps.com
www.juveycamps.com

Essential Xarel.lo 2012 BR Reserva

91

Colour: bright straw. Nose: fine lees, floral, fragrant herbs, expressive. Palate: powerful, flavourful, good acidity, fine bead, balanced.

Gran Juvé Camps 2010 BR Gran Reserva
25% macabeo, 40% xarel.lo, 10% parellada, 25% chardonnay

94

Colour: yellow. Nose: fine lees, dry nuts, fragrant herbs, complex, toasty. Palate: powerful, flavourful, good acidity, fine bead, fine bitter notes, complex.

Gran Juvé Camps Rosé BN Gran Reserva

90

Colour: light cherry. Nose: floral, red berry notes, ripe fruit, fragrant herbs, expressive. Palate: powerful, balanced, flavourful.

Juvé & Camps Blanc de Noirs 2012 BR Reserva
90% pinot noir, 10% xarel.lo

91

Colour: bright straw. Nose: fresh fruit, dried herbs, fine lees, floral, spicy. Palate: fresh, fruity, flavourful, good acidity, balanced, elegant.

Juvé & Camps Cinta Púrpura BR Reserva
33% macabeo, 53% xarel.lo, 14% parellada

89

Colour: bright straw. Nose: fine lees, fragrant herbs, fresh fruit, balanced. Palate: flavourful, good acidity, fine bead.

Juvé & Camps Milesimé Chardonnay 2007 BN Reserva
chardonnay

92

Colour: bright yellow. Nose: powerfull, fruit preserve, candied fruit, spicy. Palate: powerful, spicy, ripe fruit, long.

PODIUM

Juvé & Camps Milesimé Chardonnay 2008 BN Reserva
100% chardonnay

95

Colour: bright golden. Nose: fine lees, dry nuts, fragrant herbs, complex, toasty. Palate: powerful, flavourful, good acidity, fine bead, fine bitter notes.

Juvé & Camps Milesimé Chardonnay 2012 BR Reserva
100% chardonnay

91

Colour: bright straw. Nose: fine lees, dry nuts, complex, floral. Palate: powerful, flavourful, good acidity, fine bead, fine bitter notes.

Juvé & Camps Milesimé Magnum 2011 BR Reserva
100% chardonnay

93

Colour: bright golden. Nose: fine lees, fragrant herbs, characterful, ripe fruit, dry nuts. Palate: powerful, flavourful, good acidity, fine bead, fine bitter notes.

Juvé & Camps Reserva de la Familia 2006 BN Gran Reserva
xarel.lo, macabeo, parellada

93

Colour: bright golden. Nose: fine lees, fragrant herbs, characterful, ripe fruit, dry nuts. Palate: flavourful, good acidity, fine bead, fine bitter notes.

Juvé & Camps Reserva de la Familia 2011 BN Gran Reserva
18% macabeo, 55% xarel.lo, 4% parellada, 24% chardonnay

92

Colour: bright yellow. Nose: fine lees, dry nuts, fragrant herbs, complex, toasty. Palate: powerful, flavourful, good acidity, fine bead, fine bitter notes.

Juvé & Camps Reserva de la Familia Magnum 2011 BN Gran Reserva
18% macabeo, 55% xarel.lo, 4% parellada, 24% chardonnay

93

Colour: bright golden. Nose: dry nuts, fragrant herbs, complex, toasty. Palate: powerful, flavourful, good acidity, fine bead, fine bitter notes.

PODIUM

Juvé & Camps Viña La Capella 2005 BN Gran Reserva
100% xarel.lo

95

Colour: bright golden. Nose: fine lees, dry nuts, fragrant herbs, complex. Palate: powerful, flavourful, good acidity, fine bead, fine bitter notes.

L.B. LACRIMA BACCUS

Finca La Porxada
08729 Sant Marçal (Barcelona)
☎: +34 938 912 202
lavernoya@lavernoya.com
www.lavernoya.com

Lácrima Baccus 2013 BN
xarel.lo, macabeo, parellada

85

Lácrima Baccus 2013 BR
xarel.lo, macabeo, parellada

86

Lácrima Baccus Heretat 2012 BN Reserva
xarel.lo, macabeo, parellada

88

Colour: bright straw. Nose: fine lees, floral, fragrant herbs, expressive. Palate: powerful, flavourful, good acidity, fine bead, balanced.

Lácrima Baccus Primerísimo 2012 BR Reserva
xarel.lo, macabeo, parellada, chardonnay

88

Colour: bright straw. Nose: medium intensity, fresh fruit, dried herbs, fine lees, floral. Palate: fresh, fruity, flavourful, good acidity.

Lácrima Baccus Summum 2012 BN Reserva
xarel.lo, macabeo, parellada, chardonnay

90

Colour: bright golden. Nose: fine lees, dry nuts, fragrant herbs, complex, toasty. Palate: powerful, flavourful, good acidity, fine bead, fine bitter notes.

LLOPART CAVA

Ctra. de Sant Sadurni - Ordal,
Km. 4 Els Casots
08739 Els Casots (Subirats) (Barcelona)
☎: +34 938 993 125
Fax: +34 938 993 038
llopart@llopart.com
www.llopart.com

Cava Llopart 2013 BR Reserva
macabeo, xarel.lo, parellada

88

Colour: bright straw. Nose: fine lees, floral, fragrant herbs, expressive. Palate: powerful, flavourful, good acidity, fine bead, balanced.

Cava Llopart Ex-Vite 2008 BR Gran Reserva
60% xarel.lo, 40% macabeo

94

Colour: bright golden. Nose: dry nuts, fragrant herbs, complex, toasty, fine lees, elegant. Palate: powerful, flavourful, good acidity, fine bead, fine bitter notes.

Cava Llopart Imperial 2011 BR Gran Reserva
40% macabeo, 50% xarel.lo, 10% parellada

90

Colour: bright straw. Nose: fine lees, floral, fragrant herbs, expressive. Palate: flavourful, good acidity, fine bead, balanced.

Cava Llopart Imperial Magnum 2011 BR
40% macabeo, 50% xarel.lo, 10% parellada

92

Colour: bright straw. Nose: fresh fruit, dried herbs, fine lees, floral, balanced. Palate: fresh, fruity, flavourful, good acidity, elegant.

Cava Llopart Integral (375 ml) 2013 BN Reserva
40% parellada, 40% chardonnay, 20% xarel.lo

86

Cava Llopart Integral 2013 BN Reserva
40% parellada, 40% chardonnay, 20% xarel.lo

88

Colour: bright straw. Nose: fine lees, floral, fragrant herbs, expressive. Palate: powerful, flavourful, good acidity, fine bead, balanced.

Cava Llopart Leopardi 2010 BN Gran Reserva
40% macabeo, 40% xarel.lo, 10% parellada, 10% chardonnay

92

Colour: bright golden. Nose: fine lees, dry nuts, fragrant herbs, complex, spicy. Palate: powerful, flavourful, good acidity, fine bead, fine bitter notes, elegant.

Cava Llopart Microcosmos Rosé 2011 BN Reserva
85% pinot noir, 15% monastrell

89

Colour: salmon. Nose: citrus fruit, fresh fruit, fine lees, spicy. Palate: fresh, fruity, flavourful.

Cava Llopart Néctar Terrenal 2012 Semidulce Reserva
50% xarel.lo, 50% parellada

87

Colour: bright straw. Nose: floral, fragrant herbs, candied fruit. Palate: fresh, fruity, flavourful, sweet.

Cava Llopart Original 1887 2009 BN Gran Reserva
50% montónega, 25% macabeo, 25% xarel.lo

93

Colour: bright golden. Nose: fine lees, dry nuts, fragrant herbs, complex, toasty, sweet spices. Palate: powerful, flavourful, good acidity, fine bead, fine bitter notes.

Cava Llopart Rosé (375 ml) 2013 BR Reserva
60% monastrell, 20% garnacha, 20% pinot noir

90

Colour: coppery red. Nose: floral, jasmine, fragrant herbs, candied fruit. Palate: fresh, fruity, flavourful, correct.

Cava Llopart Rosé 2013 BR Reserva
60% monastrell, 20% garnacha, 20% pinot noir

90

Colour: rose. Nose: floral, red berry notes, ripe fruit, fragrant herbs, expressive. Palate: powerful, balanced, flavourful.

LONG WINES

Avda. del Puente Cultural, 8 Bloque B Bajo 7
28702 San Sebastián de los Reyes
(Madrid)
☎: +34 916 221 305
Fax: +34 916 220 029
customer.service@longwines.com
www.longwines.com

Escapada BR
55% macabeo, 40% parellada, 5% chardonnay

86

MARÍA CASANOVAS

Ctra. BV-2242, km. 7,5
08160 Sant Jaume Sesoliveres
(Barcelona)
☎: +34 938 910 812
mariacasanovas@brutnature.com
www.mariacasanovas.com

María Casanovas 2012 BN Gran Reserva
chardonnay, pinot noir, xarel.lo, macabeo, parellada

93

Colour: bright golden. Nose: fragrant herbs, complex, toasty, fine lees. Palate: powerful, flavourful, good acidity, fine bead, fine bitter notes.

María Casanovas Pinot Noir Rosé 2013 BN Reserva
pinot noir, chardonnay

90

Colour: rose. Nose: floral, red berry notes, ripe fruit, fragrant herbs, expressive. Palate: powerful, balanced, flavourful.

MARÍA RIGOL ORDI

Fullerachs, 9
08770 Sant Sadurní D'Anoia
(Barcelona)
☎: +34 686 472 424
Fax: +34 938 910 226
cava@mariarigolordi.com
www.mariarigolordi.com

Maria Rigol Ordi 2008 BN Gran Reserva
macabeo, xarel.lo, parellada

89

Colour: bright golden. Nose: characterful, dry nuts, pattiserie, lees reduction notes, candied fruit. Palate: powerful, flavourful, good acidity, fine bead, fine bitter notes.

María Rigol Ordi 2010 BN Reserva
macabeo, xarel.lo, parellada

88

Colour: bright golden. Nose: fine lees, fragrant herbs, characterful, ripe fruit, dry nuts. Palate: powerful, flavourful, fine bead, fine bitter notes.

María Rigol Ordi 2012 BR
macabeo, xarel.lo, parellada

89

Colour: bright straw. Nose: fresh fruit, dried herbs, fine lees, floral, expressive. Palate: fresh, fruity, flavourful, good acidity.

Maria Rigol Ordi Mil·lenni 2011 BN Reserva
macabeo, xarel.lo, parellada, chardonnay

90

Colour: bright straw. Nose: medium intensity, fresh fruit, dried herbs, fine lees, floral. Palate: fresh, fruity, flavourful, good acidity.

Maria Rigol Ordi Rosat 2012 BN Reserva
trepat, monastrell

86

MARQUÉS DE LA CONCORDIA FAMILY OF WINES

Monistrol D'Anoia, s/n
08770 Sant Sadurní D'Anoia
(Barcelona)
☎: +34 913 878 612
www.haciendas-espana.com

Marqués de la Concordia Reserva de la Familia Brut Nature Millesime 2008 BN Reserva
30% chardonnay, 25% macabeo, 20% xarel.lo, 25% parellada

88

Colour: bright yellow. Nose: ripe fruit, fine lees, balanced, dried herbs, dried flowers. Palate: good acidity, flavourful, ripe fruit, long.

Marqués de la Concordia Selección Especial 2013 BR
40% macabeo, 30% xarel.lo, 30% parellada

84

Marqués de la Concordia Selección Especial Rosé 2013 BR
30% pinot noir, 70% monastrell

85

MM Reserva de la Familia Brut Millesime Rosé 2009 BR
70% pinot noir, 30% monastrell

88

Colour: coppery red. Nose: red berry notes, ripe fruit, fragrant herbs, expressive, floral. Palate: powerful, balanced, flavourful.

MARQUÉS DE MONISTROL

Monistrol d'Anoia s/n
08770 Sant Sadurní D'Anoia
(Barcelona)
☎: +34 914 365 924
www.haciendas-espana.com

Clos de Monistrol 2012 BN
25% chardonnay, 20% macabeo, 35% xarel.lo, 20% parellada

86

Monistrol Premium Cuvée 2009 BN
25% chardonnay, 30% macabeo, 15% xarel.lo, 30% parellada

85

Monistrol Premium Cuvée Rosé 2010 BR
70% pinot noir, 30% monastrell

86

Monistrol Selección Especial BR
30% macabeo, 15% xarel.lo, 30% parellada, 25% chardonnay

85

Monistrol Selección Especial Rosé BR
70% pinot noir, 30% monastrell

84

Monistrol Winemakers Select 2012 BN
25% chardonnay, 30% macabeo, 15% xarel.lo, 30% parellada

86

MARTÍ SERDÀ

Camí Mas del Pont s/n
08792 Santa Fe del Penedès
(Barcelona)
☎: +34 938 974 411
Fax: +34 938 974 405
info@martiserda.com
www.martiserda.com

Martí Serdà BN Reserva
35% macabeo, 40% xarel.lo, 25% parellada

87

Colour: bright straw. Nose: fine lees, floral, fragrant herbs. Palate: powerful, flavourful, good acidity, fine bead, balanced.

Martí Serdà BR Reserva
35% macabeo, 30% xarel.lo, 35% parellada

88

Colour: bright straw. Nose: medium intensity, fresh fruit, dried herbs, fine lees, floral. Palate: fresh, fruity, flavourful, good acidity.

Martí Serdà Brut Rosé
30% trepat, 35% pinot noir, 35% garnacha

87

Colour: rose. Nose: floral, jasmine, fragrant herbs, ripe fruit. Palate: fresh, fruity, easy to drink.

Martí Serdà SS
20% macabeo, 35% xarel.lo, 45% parellada

85

Martí Serdà 2007 BN Gran Reserva
15% macabeo, 30% xarel.lo, 25% chardonnay, 30% vino reserva

90

Colour: bright yellow. Nose: ripe fruit, fine lees, balanced, dried herbs. Palate: good acidity, flavourful, ripe fruit, long.

Martí Serdà Chardonnay BR
100% chardonnay

87

Colour: bright straw. Nose: fine lees, floral, fragrant herbs. Palate: flavourful, good acidity, fine bead.

Martí Serdà Cuvée Real 2006 BN Gran Reserva
50% macabeo, 25% xarel.lo, 25% vino reserva

90

Colour: bright golden. Nose: fine lees, dry nuts, fragrant herbs, complex. Palate: powerful, flavourful, good acidity, fine bead, fine bitter notes.

Masía D'Or BN
30% macabeo, 25% parellada, 45% xarel.lo

87

Colour: bright straw. Nose: medium intensity, fresh fruit, dried herbs, fine lees, floral. Palate: fresh, fruity, flavourful, good acidity.

Masía D'Or BR
macabeo, parellada, xarel.lo

84

MAS CODINA

Barri El Gorner, s/n - Mas Codina
08797 Puigdalber (Barcelona)
☎: +34 938 988 166
Fax: +34 938 988 166
info@mascodina.com
www.mascodina.com

Mas Codina 2010 BN Gran Reserva
chardonnay, macabeo, xarel.lo, pinot noir

88

Colour: bright golden. Nose: fine lees, fragrant herbs, ripe fruit, dry nuts. Palate: powerful, flavourful, good acidity, fine bitter notes.

Mas Codina 2011 BN Reserva
chardonnay, macabeo, xarel.lo, pinot noir

86

Mas Codina 2011 BR Reserva
chardonnay, macabeo, xarel.lo, pinot noir

82

Mas Codina Rosé 2012 BR
pinot noir

84

MAS GOMÀ 1724

08794 Les Cabanyes (Barcelona)
☎: +34 660 881 185
jmvendrell@masgoma1724.com
www.masgoma1724.com

Vendrell Olivella Organic 2011 BN
xarel.lo, macabeo, parellada

90

Colour: bright golden. Nose: fine lees, dry nuts, fragrant herbs, toasty. Palate: powerful, flavourful, good acidity, fine bitter notes.

Vendrell Olivella Organic 2011 BR
xarel.lo, macabeo, parellada

90

Colour: bright yellow. Nose: ripe fruit, fine lees, balanced, dried herbs. Palate: good acidity, flavourful, ripe fruit, long.

Vendrell Olivella Original 2011 BN
xarel.lo, macabeo, parellada

88

Colour: bright straw. Nose: medium intensity, dried herbs, fine lees. Palate: fresh, fruity, flavourful, good acidity.

Vendrell Olivella Original 2012 BR
xarel.lo, macabeo, parellada

87

Colour: bright yellow. Nose: ripe fruit, fine lees, balanced, dried herbs. Palate: good acidity, flavourful, ripe fruit, long.

MASCARÓ

Casal, 9
08720 Vilafranca del Penedès
(Barcelona)
☎: +34 938 901 628
Fax: +34 938 901 358
mascaro@mascaro.es
www.mascaro.es

Mascaró "Ambrosia" SS Reserva
parellada, macabeo, xarel.lo

85

Mascaro Cuvée Antonio Mascaró 2010 BN Gran Reserva
parellada, macabeo, chardonnay

90

Colour: bright yellow. Nose: fine lees, dry nuts, fragrant herbs, complex. Palate: powerful, flavourful, good acidity, fine bead, fine bitter notes.

Mascaró Nigrum 2011 BR Reserva
parellada, macabeo, xarel.lo

86

Mascaró Pure 2011 BN Reserva
parellada, macabeo

89

Colour: bright straw. Nose: fine lees, balanced, dried herbs, citrus fruit. Palate: good acidity, flavourful, long, balanced.

Mascaró Rosé "Rubor Aurorae" 2013 BR
garnacha

89

Colour: raspberry rose. Nose: fragrant herbs, candied fruit, floral. Palate: fresh, fruity, flavourful, balanced.

MASET DEL LLEÓ

Ctra. Vilafranca-Igualada C-15 (Km.19)
08792 La Granada (Barcelona)
☎: +34 902 200 250
Fax: +34 938 921 333
info@maset.com
www.maset.com

Maset del Lleó BR
macabeo, xarel.lo, parellada

83

Maset del Lleó BR Reserva

87

Colour: bright straw. Nose: fine lees, floral, fragrant herbs. Palate: powerful, flavourful, good acidity, fine bead, balanced.

Maset del Lleó Colección Privada 1917 BN Reserva

90

Colour: bright straw. Nose: medium intensity, fresh fruit, dried herbs, fine lees, floral. Palate: fresh, fruity, flavourful, good acidity.

Maset del Lleó L'Avi Pau BN Reserva

89

Colour: bright straw. Nose: fine lees, floral, fragrant herbs, expressive. Palate: powerful, flavourful, good acidity, fine bead, balanced.

Maset del Lleó Vintage BN Reserva

85

Nu Brut de Maset del Lleó BR Reserva

88

Colour: bright straw. Nose: fine lees, floral, fragrant herbs, dry nuts. Palate: flavourful, good acidity, fine bead.

Nu Maset Rosé
garnacha, trepat

87

Colour: coppery red, bright. Nose: medium intensity, fresh, red berry notes, floral, elegant. Palate: correct, good finish, fruity.

MASIA VALLFORMOSA

La Sala, 45
08735 Vilobi del Penedès (Barcelona)
☎: +34 938 978 286
Fax: +34 938 978 355
vallformosa@vallformosa.com
www.vallformosagroup.com

Vallformosa Clàssic 2013 BN
macabeo, xarel.lo, parellada

86

Vallformosa Clàssic 2013 BR
macabeo, xarel.lo, parellada

86

Vallformosa Clàssic 2013 SS
macabeo, xarel.lo, parellada

85

Vallformosa Clàssic Rosat 2013 BR
garnacha, monastrell

85

Vallformosa Col.lecció 2012 BN Reserva
macabeo, xarel.lo, parellada, chardonnay

88

Colour: bright yellow. Nose: ripe fruit, fine lees, balanced, dried herbs. Palate: good acidity, flavourful, ripe fruit, long.

Vallformosa Col.lecció 2012 BR Reserva
macabeo, xarel.lo, parellada, chardonnay

89

Colour: bright straw. Nose: medium intensity, fresh fruit, dried herbs, fine lees, floral. Palate: fresh, fruity, flavourful, good acidity.

Vallformosa Col.lecció Pinot Noir Rosado 2012 BR
pinot noir

89

Colour: raspberry rose. Nose: floral, jasmine, fragrant herbs, candied fruit. Palate: fresh, fruity, flavourful, correct, balanced.

Vallformosa Origen 2012 BN
macabeo, xarel.lo, parellada

89

Colour: bright straw. Nose: fine lees, floral, fragrant herbs, expressive. Palate: powerful, flavourful, good acidity, fine bead, balanced.

Vallformosa Origen 2012 BR
macabeo, xarel.lo, parellada

88

Colour: bright straw. Nose: fine lees, floral, fragrant herbs, expressive. Palate: powerful, flavourful, good acidity, fine bead.

Vallformosa Origen 2012 SS
macabeo, xarel.lo, parellada

87

Colour: bright straw. Nose: floral, fragrant herbs, candied fruit. Palate: fresh, fruity, flavourful, sweet.

Vallformosa Origen Rosado 2013 BR
garnacha, monastrell

87

Colour: coppery red. Nose: floral, jasmine, fragrant herbs, candied fruit. Palate: fresh, fruity, flavourful, correct.

MATA I COLOMA
Montserrat, 73
08770 Sant Sadurní D'Anoia
(Barcelona)
info@matacoloma.com
www.matacoloma.com

Pere Mata 2011 BR Reserva
macabeo, xarel.lo, parellada

87

Colour: bright straw. Nose: fresh fruit, dried herbs, fine lees, floral. Palate: fresh, fruity, flavourful, good acidity.

Pere Mata Cupada Nº 12 2011 BN Reserva
macabeo, xarel.lo, parellada

88

Colour: bright straw. Nose: fine lees, floral, fragrant herbs, expressive. Palate: powerful, flavourful, good acidity, fine bead, balanced.

Pere Mata Cupada Rosat 2013 BR Reserva
trepat

90

Colour: salmon. Nose: floral, red berry notes, ripe fruit, fragrant herbs, expressive. Palate: powerful, balanced, flavourful.

Pere Mata Cuvée Barcelona 2009 BR Gran Reserva
macabeo, xarel.lo, parellada

90

Colour: bright yellow. Nose: fine lees, fragrant herbs, characterful, ripe fruit, dry nuts. Palate: powerful, flavourful, good acidity, fine bead, fine bitter notes.

Pere Mata Gran Coloma 2009 BR Gran Reserva
macabeo, xarel.lo, parellada

89

Colour: yellow. Nose: medium intensity, fresh fruit, dried herbs, fine lees, floral. Palate: fresh, fruity, good acidity.

Pere Mata L'Ensamblatge 2008 BN Gran Reserva
macabeo, xarel.lo, parellada

91

Colour: bright golden. Nose: fine lees, dry nuts, fragrant herbs, complex. Palate: powerful, flavourful, good acidity, fine bead, fine bitter notes.

Pere Mata L'Origen 2009 BR Gran Reserva
macabeo, xarel.lo

89

Nose: fine lees, fragrant herbs, characterful, ripe fruit, spicy. Palate: powerful, flavourful, good acidity, fine bead, fine bitter notes.

Pere Mata Reserva Familia 2009 BN Gran Reserva
macabeo, xarel.lo, parellada

89

Colour: bright straw. Nose: fine lees, floral, fragrant herbs, expressive. Palate: powerful, flavourful, good acidity, fine bead, balanced.

MIQUEL PONS
Baix Llobregat, 5
08792 La Granada (Barcelona)
☎: +34 938 974 541
Fax: +34 938 974 710
miquelpons@cavamiquelpons.com
www.cavamiquelpons.com

Eulàlia de Pons Rosé 2012 BN
trepat

86

Miquel Pons 2008 BN Gran Reserva
55% xarel.lo, 40% macabeo, 5% parellada

90

Colour: bright yellow. Nose: characterful, ripe fruit, dry nuts, lees reduction notes. Palate: powerful, flavourful, good acidity, fine bead, fine bitter notes.

Miquel Pons 2012 BR Reserva
50% xarel.lo, 40% macabeo, 10% parellada

87

Colour: bright straw. Nose: medium intensity, fresh fruit, dried herbs, fine lees, floral. Palate: fresh, fruity, flavourful, good acidity.

Miquel Pons Montargull 2008 Brut Extra Gran Reserva
40% xarel.lo, 20% xarel.lo pasado por barrica, 35% macabeo, 5% parellada

87

Colour: bright golden. Nose: fragrant herbs, ripe fruit, dry nuts, creamy oak. Palate: flavourful, fine bead, fine bitter notes.

MONT MARÇAL

Finca Manlleu, s/n
08732 Castellví de la Marca (Barcelona)
☎: +34 938 918 281
Fax: +34 938 919 045
export@mont-marcal.com
www.mont-marcal.com

Aureum de Mont Marçal 2009 BN Gran Reserva

50% xarel.lo, 30% chardonnay, 10% pinot noir, 10% parellada

91

Colour: bright golden. Nose: fine lees, dry nuts, fragrant herbs, complex. Palate: powerful, flavourful, good acidity, fine bead, fine bitter notes, elegant.

Cava Palau BR

40% macabeo, 30% xarel.lo, 30% parellada

86

Extremarium de Mont Marçal BR Reserva

35% xarel.lo, 25% macabeo, 20% parellada, 20% chardonnay

88

Colour: bright straw. Nose: fine lees, floral, fragrant herbs, expressive. Palate: powerful, flavourful, good acidity, fine bead, balanced.

Extremarium de Mont Marçal Rosado BN

100% trepat

88

Colour: rose. Nose: floral, red berry notes, ripe fruit, fragrant herbs, expressive. Palate: powerful, balanced, flavourful.

Gran Cuvée de Mont Marçal BR Reserva

40% xarel.lo, 25% macabeo, 15% parellada, 20% chardonnay

89

Colour: bright yellow. Nose: ripe fruit, fine lees, balanced, dried herbs, dried flowers. Palate: good acidity, flavourful, ripe fruit, long.

Gran Cuvée de Mont Marçal Rosado BR

100% pinot noir

86

Mont Marçal BR Reserva

40% xarel.lo, 30% macabeo, 20% parellada, 10% chardonnay

87

Colour: bright straw. Nose: fine lees, fragrant herbs, medium intensity. Palate: good acidity, fine bead, light-bodied.

Mont Marçal Rosado BR

100% trepat

85

Portaceli BR

50% macabeo, 30% xarel.lo, 20% parellada

85

MONT-FERRANT

Camí de Can Garra, s/n
08391 Tiana (Barcelona)
☎: +34 935 153 100
Fax: +34 933 739 571
sac@montferrant.com
www.montferrant.com

Agustí Vilaret Extra Brut
macabeo, xarel.lo, parellada, chardonnay

90

Colour: bright yellow. Nose: fine lees, floral, fragrant herbs, expressive. Palate: powerful, flavourful, good acidity, fine bead, balanced.

Berta Bouzy Extra Brut
macabeo, xarel.lo, parellada, chardonnay

90

Colour: bright straw. Nose: fine lees, balanced, dried herbs. Palate: good acidity, flavourful, ripe fruit, long, fine bead.

Blanes Nature Extra Brut
macabeo, xarel.lo, parellada, chardonnay

87

Colour: bright straw. Nose: fine lees, floral, fragrant herbs. Palate: flavourful, good acidity, fine bead.

L´Americano BR Reserva
macabeo, xarel.lo, parellada, chardonnay

89

Colour: bright straw. Nose: fine lees, floral, fragrant herbs, balanced. Palate: flavourful, good acidity, fine bead, fine bitter notes.

Mont Ferrant Tradició BR
macabeo, xarel.lo, parellada, chardonnay

88

Colour: bright straw. Nose: medium intensity, fresh fruit, dried herbs, fine lees. Palate: fresh, fruity, good acidity.

Mont-Ferrant Gran Cuvée 2008 BR Gran Reserva
macabeo, xarel.lo, parellada, chardonnay

92

Colour: bright yellow. Nose: ripe fruit, fine lees, balanced, dried herbs. Palate: good acidity, flavourful, ripe fruit, long, balanced.

Mont-Ferrant Rosé BR
garnacha, monastrell

86

MUNGUST S.L.

San Josep, 10-12
(Sant Jaume Sesoliveres)
08784 Sant Jaume Sesoliveres (Piera)
(Barcelona)
☎: +34 937 763 016
info@cavesmungust.com
www.cavesmungust.com

Mungust 2007 BN Reserva
xarel.lo, macabeo, parellada

86

Mungust 2008 BR Reserva
xarel.lo, macabeo, parellada

85

Pere Munné Durán 2011 BN
xarel.lo, macabeo, parellada

85

Pere Munné Durán 2011 BR

85

Pere Munné Durán Et. Blanca 2013 BN
xarel.lo, macabeo, parellada

88

Colour: bright yellow. Nose: ripe fruit, fine lees, balanced, dried herbs. Palate: good acidity, flavourful, ripe fruit, long.

Pere Munné Durán Et. Negra 2008 BN Reserva
xarel.lo, macabeo, parellada

82

NADAL

Finca Nadal de la Boadella, s/n
08775 Torrelavit (Barcelona)
☎: +34 938 988 011
Fax: +34 938 988 443
comunicacio@nadal.com
www.nadal.com

Nadal 2008 BN Gran Reserva
58% parellada, 32% macabeo, 10% xarel.lo

89

Colour: bright golden. Nose: fine lees, dry nuts, fragrant herbs, rancio notes. Palate: powerful, flavourful, good acidity, fine bead, fine bitter notes.

RNG 2008 BR Gran Reserva
68% xarel.lo, 32% parellada

88

Colour: bright yellow. Nose: lees reduction notes, sweet spices, dried herbs. Palate: powerful, flavourful, spicy.

Salvatge 2011 BR Gran Reserva
62% macabeo, 13% xarel.lo, 15% parellada

89

Colour: bright yellow. Nose: dry nuts, dried herbs, complex, spicy. Palate: powerful, flavourful, good acidity, fine bitter notes.

Salvatge Rosé 2011 BR Reserva
100% pinot noir

87

Colour: coppery red. Nose: floral, jasmine, fragrant herbs, candied fruit. Palate: fresh, fruity, flavourful, correct.

ORIOL ROSSELL

Masia Cassanyes
08729 Sant Marçal (Barcelona)
☎: +34 977 671 061
Fax: +34 977 671 050
oriolrossell@oriolrossell.com
www.oriolrossell.com

Oriol Rossell 2011 BN Gran Reserva
macabeo, xarel.lo

88

Colour: bright straw. Nose: fresh fruit, dried herbs, fine lees, floral. Palate: fresh, fruity, flavourful, good acidity.

Oriol Rossell 2012 BN Reserva
macabeo, xarel.lo, parellada

88

Colour: bright straw. Nose: fresh fruit, dried herbs, fine lees, floral. Palate: fresh, fruity, flavourful, good acidity.

Oriol Rossell Cuvée Especial 2013 BR
macabeo, xarel.lo, parellada

87

Colour: bright straw. Nose: fine lees, floral, fragrant herbs. Palate: flavourful, good acidity, fine bead.

Oriol Rossell Reserva de la Propietat 2009 BN Gran Reserva
macabeo, xarel.lo, parellada

90

Colour: bright golden. Nose: fine lees, dry nuts, complex, toasty. Palate: powerful, flavourful, good acidity, fine bead, fine bitter notes.

Oriol Rossell Rosat 2012 BR
trepat

89

Colour: rose. Nose: floral, red berry notes, ripe fruit, fragrant herbs, expressive. Palate: powerful, flavourful.

OSBORNE CAVA

Salvatierra, 6
28034 Madrid (Madrid)
☎: +34 917 283 880
Fax: +34 917 283 888
www.osborne.es

Abadia de Montserrat BR Reserva
30% macabeo, 20% xarel.lo, 50% parellada

88

Colour: bright straw. Nose: fine lees, floral, fragrant herbs. Palate: flavourful, good acidity, fine bead.

PAGÉS ENTRENA

Ctra. de Piera-Sant Sadurní D'Anoia, Km. 10,3
08784 Sant Jaume Sesoliveres (Barcelona)
☎: +34 938 183 827
cava@pagesentrena.com
www.pagesentrena.com

L'Avi Pages 2008 BN Gran Reserva
macabeo, xarel.lo, parellada

88

Colour: bright yellow. Nose: fine lees, dry nuts, toasty. Palate: powerful, flavourful, good acidity, fine bitter notes.

Pagés Entrena 2010 BN Gran Reserva
macabeo, xarel.lo, parellada

88

Colour: bright yellow. Nose: fine lees, floral, fragrant herbs, expressive. Palate: powerful, flavourful, good acidity, fine bead, balanced.

Pagès Entrena Jove BR Reserva
macabeo, xarel.lo, parellada

86

PAGO DE THARSYS

Ctra. Nacional III, km. 274
46340 Requena (Valencia)
☎: +34 962 303 354
Fax: +34 962 329 000
pagodetharsys@pagodetharsys.com
www.pagodetharsys.com

Pago de Tharsys 2011 BN Reserva
macabeo, chardonnay

88

Colour: bright yellow. Nose: ripe fruit, fine lees, balanced, dried herbs. Palate: good acidity, flavourful, ripe fruit, long.

Pago de Tharsys Millésime Chardonnay 2011 BN
chardonnay

89

Colour: bright straw. Nose: ripe fruit, fine lees, balanced, dried herbs. Palate: good acidity, flavourful, ripe fruit, long.

Pago de Tharsys Millésime Rosé Reserva 2011 BR
garnacha

87

Colour: raspberry rose. Nose: floral, jasmine, fragrant herbs, candied fruit. Palate: fresh, fruity, flavourful, correct.

PARATÓ
Can Respall de Renardes
08733 El Pla del Penedès (Barcelona)
☎: +34 938 988 182
Fax: +34 938 988 510
info@parato.es
www.parato.es

Ática 2010 Extra Brut Gran Reserva
macabeo, xarel.lo, parellada

88

Colour: bright straw. Nose: medium intensity, fresh fruit, dried herbs, fine lees, floral. Palate: fresh, fruity, flavourful, good acidity.

Ática Rosado 2011 BR Reserva
pinot noir

87

Colour: rose. Nose: floral, red berry notes, ripe fruit, fragrant herbs, expressive. Palate: powerful, balanced, flavourful.

Elias i Terns 2005 BN Gran Reserva
xarel.lo, macabeo, parellada, chardonnay

87

Colour: bright golden. Nose: dry nuts, fragrant herbs, lees reduction notes, toasty. Palate: powerful, flavourful, good acidity, fine bead, fine bitter notes.

Parató 2012 BN Reserva
macabeo, xarel.lo, parellada, chardonnay

84

Parató 2012 BR Reserva
macabeo, xarel.lo, parellada, chardonnay

82

PARÉS BALTÀ
Masía Can Baltá, s/n
08796 Pacs del Penedès (Barcelona)
☎: +34 938 901 399
paresbalta@paresbalta.com
www.paresbalta.com

Blanca Cusiné 2010 BR Gran Reserva
60% xarel.lo, 20% chardonnay, 20% pinot noir

93 ♣

Colour: bright golden. Nose: fine lees, dry nuts, fragrant herbs, complex, toasty. Palate: powerful, flavourful, good acidity, fine bead, fine bitter notes.

Cuvée de Carol 2009 BN Gran Reserva
macabeo, chardonnay

93 ♣

Colour: bright golden. Nose: fine lees, dry nuts, fragrant herbs, complex. Palate: powerful, flavourful, good acidity, fine bead, fine bitter notes.

Parés Baltà 2012 BN
macabeo, xarel.lo, parellada

88 ♣

Colour: bright straw. Nose: medium intensity, fresh fruit, dried herbs, fine lees, floral. Palate: fresh, fruity, flavourful, good acidity.

Parés Baltà Selectio 2009 BR Gran Reserva
macabeo, xarel.lo, parellada, chardonnay

90 ♣

Colour: bright yellow. Nose: ripe fruit, fine lees, balanced, dried herbs. Palate: good acidity, flavourful, ripe fruit, long.

Rosa Cusine Rosado 2011 BR Gran Reserva
garnacha

90 ♣

Colour: coppery red. Nose: jasmine, fragrant herbs, candied fruit, elegant. Palate: fresh, fruity, flavourful, correct.

PARXET
Camí de Can Garra, s/n
08391 Tiana (Barcelona)
☎: +34 933 950 811
info@parxet.es
www.parxet.es

Parxet Aniversari 92 BN
chardonnay, pinot noir

93

Colour: bright golden. Nose: fine lees, dry nuts, fragrant herbs, complex, toasty. Palate: powerful, flavourful, good acidity, fine bead, fine bitter notes.

Parxet BR
pansa blanca, macabeo, parellada

87

Colour: bright straw. Nose: fresh fruit, dried herbs, fine lees. Palate: fresh, fruity, good acidity.

Parxet SS
pansa blanca, macabeo, parellada

88

Colour: bright straw. Nose: floral, fragrant herbs, candied fruit. Palate: fresh, fruity, flavourful, sweet.

Parxet 2011 BN
pansa blanca, macabeo, parellada

88

Colour: bright straw. Nose: medium intensity, fresh fruit, dried herbs, fine lees, floral. Palate: fresh, fruity, flavourful, good acidity.

Parxet 2012 BR Reserva
pansa blanca, macabeo, parellada

88

Colour: bright straw. Nose: fine lees, floral, fragrant herbs. Palate: flavourful, good acidity, fine bead.

Parxet Cuvée 21 Ecológic BR
pansa blanca, macabeo, parellada

90

Colour: bright yellow. Nose: ripe fruit, fine lees, balanced, dried herbs. Palate: good acidity, flavourful, ripe fruit, long.

Parxet Cuvée Dessert 375 ml. RD
pinot noir

86

Parxet María Cabané 2010 Extra Brut Gran Reserva
pansa blanca, macabeo, parellada

92

Colour: bright yellow. Nose: fine lees, dried herbs, white flowers. Palate: good acidity, flavourful, ripe fruit, long.

Parxet Rosé BR
pinot noir

89

Colour: rose. Nose: floral, red berry notes, ripe fruit, fragrant herbs, expressive. Palate: powerful, flavourful.

PERE VENTURA

Ctra Vilafranca Km 0,4 (C-243a)
08770 Sant Sadurní D'Anoia
(Barcelona)
☎: +34 938 183 371
Fax: +34 938 912 679
info@pereventura.com
www.pereventura.com

Pere Ventura Cupatge D'Honor 2011 BR Reserva
60% xarel.lo, 40% chardonnay

91

Colour: bright straw. Nose: fine lees, floral, fragrant herbs, expressive. Palate: flavourful, good acidity, fine bead.

Pere Ventura María del Mar 2011 Gran Reserva
30% macabeo, 40% xarel.lo, 15% parellada, 15% chardonnay

89

Colour: bright yellow. Nose: toasty, spicy, ripe fruit. Palate: full, long, good acidity, fine bitter notes.

Pere Ventura Tresor BN Reserva
40% macabeo, 40% xarel.lo, 20% parellada

90

Colour: bright straw, greenish rim. Nose: fresh fruit, citrus fruit, spicy, fine lees. Palate: spicy, long, good acidity, fine bead.

Pere Ventura Tresor Rosé BR
100% trepat

89

Colour: light cherry, bright. Nose: medium intensity, fresh fruit, dried herbs, fine lees, floral. Palate: fresh, fruity, flavourful, good acidity.

RAIMAT

Ctra. Lleida, s/n
25111 Raimat (Lleida)
☎: +34 973 724 000
info@raimat.es
www.raimat.com

Castell de Raimat Chardonnay Pinot Noir BN
chardonnay, pinot noir

90

Colour: bright yellow. Nose: fresh fruit, dried herbs, fine lees, floral. Palate: fresh, fruity, flavourful, good acidity, balanced.

Castell de Raimat Chardonnay Xarel.lo BN
chardonnay, xarel.lo

85

Raimat Brut BR
60% chardonnay, 40% pinot noir

89

Colour: bright straw. Nose: medium intensity, fresh fruit, dried herbs, fine lees, floral. Palate: fresh, fruity, flavourful, good acidity.

Raimat Chardonnay BR
100% chardonnay

91

Colour: bright yellow. Nose: ripe fruit, fine lees, balanced, dried herbs. Palate: good acidity, flavourful, ripe fruit, long, elegant.

RECAREDO
Tamarit, 10 Apartado 15
08770 Sant Sadurní D'Anoia
(Barcelona)
☎: +34 938 910 214
Fax: +34 938 911 697
info@recaredo.com
www.recaredo.com

Recaredo Brut de Brut Finca Serral del Vell 2006 BN Gran Reserva
53% xarel.lo, 47% macabeo

93

Colour: bright golden. Nose: fine lees, fragrant herbs, ripe fruit, dry nuts. Palate: flavourful, good acidity, fine bead, fine bitter notes, balanced.

PODIUM

Recaredo Reserva Particular 2004 BN Gran Reserva
67% macabeo, 33% xarel.lo

96

Colour: bright golden. Nose: fragrant herbs, complex, dry nuts, sweet spices. Palate: powerful, flavourful, good acidity, fine bead, fine bitter notes.

Recaredo Subtil 2007 BN Gran Reserva
62% xarel.lo, 8% macabeo, 30% chardonnay

91

Colour: bright yellow. Nose: ripe fruit, fine lees, balanced, dried herbs. Palate: good acidity, flavourful, ripe fruit, long.

PODIUM

Recaredo Terrers 2008 BN Gran Reserva
46% xarel.lo, 40% macabeo, 14% parellada

95

Colour: bright golden. Nose: fine lees, dry nuts, fragrant herbs, complex, toasty. Palate: powerful, flavourful, good acidity, fine bead, fine bitter notes.

Recaredo Terrers 2009 BN Gran Reserva
52% xarel.lo, 32% macabeo, 16% parellada

94

Colour: bright golden. Nose: fine lees, dry nuts, fragrant herbs, complex, toasty. Palate: powerful, flavourful, good acidity, fine bead, fine bitter notes.

PODIUM

Turo d'en Mota 2003 BN
100% xarel.lo

96

Colour: bright golden. Nose: dry nuts, fragrant herbs, complex, fine lees, macerated fruit, sweet spices, expressive. Palate: powerful, flavourful, good acidity, fine bitter notes, elegant.

REXACH BAQUES
Santa María, 12
08736 Guardiola de Font-Rubí
(Barcelona)
☎: +34 938 979 170
info@rexachbaques.com
www.rexachbaques.com

Rexach Baques 2010 BN Gran Reserva
xarel.lo, macabeo, parellada

87

Colour: bright yellow. Nose: ripe fruit, fine lees, balanced, dried herbs. Palate: good acidity, flavourful, ripe fruit, long.

Rexach Baques Brut Imperial 2011 BR Reserva
xarel.lo, macabeo, parellada

88

Colour: bright straw. Nose: fresh fruit, dried herbs, fine lees, floral. Palate: fresh, fruity, flavourful, good acidity.

Rexach Baques Gran Carta 2012 BR Reserva
macabeo, parellada

86

Rexach Rosado 2012 BR Reserva
pinot noir

85

RIMARTS

Avda. Cal Mir, 44
08770 Sant Sadurní D'Anoia
(Barcelona)
☎: +34 938 912 775
Fax: +34 938 912 775
rimarts@rimarts.net
www.rimarts.net

Martínez Rosé 2013 BN

garnacha, pinot noir

91

Colour: coppery red, rose, salmon. Nose: floral, jasmine, fragrant herbs, candied fruit. Palate: fresh, fruity, flavourful, correct.

Rimarts 2013 BR Reserva

xarel.lo, macabeo, parellada

92

Colour: bright straw. Nose: fine lees, floral, fragrant herbs, expressive. Palate: powerful, flavourful, good acidity, fine bead, balanced.

Rimarts 24 2012 BN Reserva

xarel.lo, macabeo, parellada

92

Colour: bright yellow. Nose: ripe fruit, fine lees, balanced, dried herbs. Palate: good acidity, flavourful, ripe fruit, long.

Rimarts 40 2011 BN Gran Reserva

xarel.lo, macabeo, parellada, chardonnay

94

Colour: bright golden. Nose: fine lees, dry nuts, fragrant herbs, complex, toasty. Palate: powerful, flavourful, good acidity, fine bead, fine bitter notes.

Rimarts Chardonnay 2010 BN Gran Reserva

chardonnay

93

Colour: bright golden. Nose: fine lees, dry nuts, fragrant herbs, complex. Palate: powerful, flavourful, good acidity, fine bead, fine bitter notes.

Rimarts Magnum 2011 BN Gran Reserva

xarel.lo, macabeo, parellada, chardonnay

93

Colour: bright yellow. Nose: fine lees, fragrant herbs, characterful, ripe fruit, dry nuts. Palate: balanced, balsamic, good acidity, fine bitter notes.

Rimarts Uvae 2007 BN Reserva

xarel.lo, chardonnay

87

Colour: bright yellow. Nose: ripe fruit, fruit liqueur notes, lees reduction notes, dried herbs. Palate: correct, slightly evolved.

ROCAMAR

Major, 80
08755 Castellbisbal (Barcelona)
☎: +34 937 720 900
Fax: +34 937 721 495
info@rocamar.net
www.rocamar.net

Castell de Ribes BN

85

ROGER GOULART

Major, 6
08635 Sant Esteve Sesrovires
(Barcelona)
☎: +34 934 191 000
Fax: +34 931 148 209
sac@rogergoulart.com
www.rogergoulart.com

Roger Goulart 2010 BN Reserva

45% xarel.lo, 25% macabeo, 25% parellada, 5% chardonnay

89

Colour: bright yellow. Nose: ripe fruit, fine lees, balanced, dried herbs. Palate: good acidity, flavourful, ripe fruit, long.

Roger Goulart 2011 BR Reserva

40% xarel.lo, 30% macabeo, 30% parellada

88

Colour: bright yellow. Nose: fresh fruit, dried flowers, balanced. Palate: fruity, fresh, easy to drink, good finish.

Roger Goulart Gran Cuvée 2008 Extra Brut Gran Reserva

35% xarel.lo, 30% chardonnay, 20% macabeo, 15% parellada

90

Colour: bright yellow. Nose: fine lees, dry nuts, fragrant herbs, pattiserie. Palate: powerful, flavourful, good acidity, fine bead, fine bitter notes.

Roger Goulart Rosé 2011 BR

60% garnacha, 35% monastrell, 5% pinot noir

86

ROSELL & FORMOSA

Rambla de la Generalitat, 14
08770 Sant Sadurní D'Anoia
(Barcelona)
☎: +34 938 911 013
Fax: +34 938 911 967
rformosa@roselliformosa.com
www.roselliformosa.com

Rosell & Formosa BR Reserva

40% xarel.lo, 35% macabeo, 25% riesling

89

Colour: yellow. Nose: fine lees, fragrant herbs, expressive, smoky. Palate: powerful, flavourful, good acidity, fine bead, balanced.

Rosell & Formosa 2010 BN Gran Reserva

40% xarel.lo, 30% macabeo, 30% parellada

89

Colour: bright straw. Nose: fine lees, floral, fragrant herbs, spicy. Palate: flavourful, good acidity, fine bead.

Rosell & Formosa Daurat "Brut de Bruts" 2009 BN Gran Reserva

40% xarel.lo, 35% macabeo, 25% parellada

89

Colour: bright straw. Nose: fine lees, floral, fragrant herbs, expressive. Palate: powerful, flavourful, good acidity, fine bead, balanced.

Rosell & Formosa Rosat BR Reserva

50% garnacha, 50% monastrell

84

ROSELL MIR

Bario El Rebato s/n
08739 Subirats (Barcelona)
☎: +34 938 911 354
infoceller@rosellmir.com
www.rosellmir.com

Can Guineu 2011 BN

macabeo, chardonnay

87

Colour: bright yellow. Nose: ripe fruit, fine lees, balanced, dried herbs. Palate: good acidity, flavourful, ripe fruit, long.

El Serralet 2012 BN

macabeo

82

Marc Mir 2011

pinot noir, chardonnay

83

Marc Mir 2011 BN

pinot noir, chardonnay

85

ROVELLATS

Finca Rovellats - Bº La Bleda
08731 Sant Marti Sarroca (Barcelona)
☎: +34 934 880 575
Fax: +34 934 880 819
rovellats@cavasrovellats.com
www.rovellats.com

Rovellats 2013 BR

macabeo, xarel.lo, parellada

84

Rovellats Col.lecció 2009 Extra Brut

macabeo, xarel.lo, parellada

91

Colour: bright yellow. Nose: ripe fruit, fine lees, balanced, dried herbs, pattiserie. Palate: good acidity, flavourful, ripe fruit, long.

Rovellats Gran Reserva 2009 BN Gran Reserva

macabeo, xarel.lo, parellada

89

Colour: bright yellow. Nose: ripe fruit, fine lees, balanced, dried herbs. Palate: good acidity, flavourful, ripe fruit, long.

Rovellats Imperial 2012 BR Reserva

macabeo, xarel.lo, parellada

87

Colour: bright straw. Nose: fine lees, floral, fragrant herbs, expressive. Palate: powerful, flavourful, good acidity, fine bead, balanced.

Rovellats Imperial 37,5 cl. 2012 BR Reserva

macabeo, xarel.lo, parellada

82

Rovellats Imperial Rosé BR Reserva

garnacha

85

Rovellats Magnum 2012 BN

macabeo, xarel.lo, parellada

90

Colour: bright straw. Nose: medium intensity, fresh fruit, dried herbs, floral. Palate: fresh, fruity, flavourful, good acidity.

Rovellats Masia S. XV 2007 BN Gran Reserva
macabeo, xarel.lo, parellada, chardonnay

90

Colour: bright golden. Nose: fine lees, fragrant herbs, characterful, ripe fruit, dry nuts. Palate: powerful, flavourful, good acidity, fine bead, fine bitter notes, elegant.

Rovellats Premier 2013 BN Reserva
macabeo, parellada

88

Colour: bright straw. Nose: fine lees, floral, fragrant herbs. Palate: flavourful, good acidity, fine bead.

Rovellats Premier Brut 2013 BR Reserva
macabeo, parellada

86

SIGNAT

Camí de Can Garra, s/n
08391 Tiana (Barcelona)
☎: +34 935 153 100
Fax: +34 933 739 571
info@signat.es

Signat BN
xarel.lo, macabeo

87

Colour: bright yellow. Nose: ripe fruit, fine lees, balanced, dried herbs. Palate: good acidity, flavourful, ripe fruit, long.

Signat BR
xarel.lo, macabeo

88

Colour: bright straw. Nose: medium intensity, fresh fruit, dried herbs, fine lees, floral. Palate: fresh, fruity, flavourful, good acidity.

Signat 2011 BR Reserva
xarel.lo, macabeo

88

Colour: bright yellow. Nose: fresh fruit, dried herbs, fine lees, floral. Palate: fresh, fruity, flavourful, good acidity.

Signat Magenta Rosé BR
pinot noir

87

Colour: rose. Nose: floral, red berry notes, ripe fruit, fragrant herbs, expressive. Palate: powerful, balanced, flavourful.

SURIOL

Can Suriol del Castell
08736 Grabuac - Font-Rubí (Barcelona)
☎: +34 938 978 426
Fax: +34 938 978 426
cansuriol@suriol.com
www.suriol.com

Azimut 2013 BN
macabeo, xarel.lo, parellada

87

Colour: bright straw. Nose: medium intensity, spicy. Palate: flavourful, good acidity.

Castell de Grabuac 2001 BN Gran Reserva
macabeo, xarel.lo, parellada

89

Colour: bright golden. Nose: dry nuts, sweet spices, lees reduction notes, dried herbs. Palate: flavourful, fine bead, fine bitter notes.

Castell de Grabuac Collita 2009 BN Gran Reserva
macabeo, xarel.lo, parellada

84

Castell de Grabuac Parellada 2013 BN Reserva
parellada

88

Colour: bright straw. Nose: fresh fruit, dried herbs, fine lees, floral. Palate: fresh, fruity, flavourful, good acidity.

Castell de Grabuac Xarel.lo 2012 BN Reserva
xarel.lo

88

Colour: bright yellow. Nose: ripe fruit, fine lees, balanced, dried herbs. Palate: good acidity, flavourful, ripe fruit, long.

Suriol 2012 BN Reserva
macabeo, xarel.lo, parellada

86

Suriol 2013 BN Reserva

83

Suriol Rosat 2010 BN Gran Reserva
pinot noir, garnacha

87

Colour: coppery red. Nose: floral, jasmine, candied fruit, dried herbs. Palate: fresh, fruity, flavourful, correct.

Suriol Rosat 2012 BN Reserva
garnacha, monastrell

85

THE GRAND WINES

Ramón y Cajal 7, 1ºA
01007 Vitoria-Gasteiz (Alava)
☎: +34 945 150 589
araex@araex.com
www.araex.com

Villa Conchi BR Reserva

40% xarel.lo, 20% parellada, 10% chardonnay, 30% macabeo

88

Colour: bright straw. Nose: fine lees, floral, fragrant herbs. Palate: flavourful, good acidity, fine bead.

Villa Conchi Brut Selección BR

30% xarel.lo, 30% parellada, 30% macabeo, 10% chardonnay

88

Colour: bright straw. Nose: medium intensity, fresh fruit, dried herbs, fine lees, floral. Palate: fresh, fruity, flavourful, good acidity.

Villa Conchi Imperial Extra Brut

40% xarel.lo, 20% parellada, 30% macabeo, 10% chardonnay

90

Colour: bright straw. Nose: fine lees, floral, fragrant herbs, expressive. Palate: powerful, flavourful, good acidity, fine bead, balanced.

Villa Conchi Rosé BR

100% trepat

86

TITIANA

Camí de Can Garra, s/n
08391 Tiana (Barcelona)
☎: +34 933 950 811
info@parxet.es
www.parxet.es

Titiana 2011 BR

pansa blanca

90

Colour: bright straw. Nose: fresh fruit, dried herbs, fine lees, floral. Palate: fresh, fruity, flavourful, good acidity, good finish.

Titiana Pinot Noir Rosé 2011 BR

pinot noir

87

Colour: coppery red. Nose: floral, jasmine, fragrant herbs, candied fruit. Palate: fresh, fruity, flavourful, correct.

Titiana Vintage 2010 BN

chardonnay

90

Colour: bright straw. Nose: fine lees, floral, fragrant herbs, expressive. Palate: powerful, flavourful, good acidity, fine bead, balanced.

TORELLÓ

Can Martí de Baix (Apartado Correos nº8)
08770 Sant Sadurní D'Anoia
(Barcelona)
☎: +34 938 910 793
Fax: +34 938 910 877
torello@torello.es
www.torello.com

Gran Torelló 2009 BN Gran Reserva

macabeo, xarel.lo, parellada

93

Colour: bright yellow. Nose: fine lees, dried herbs, dry nuts, ripe fruit. Palate: good acidity, flavourful, ripe fruit, long.

Gran Torelló Gran Añada 2007 BN Gran Reserva

macabeo, xarel.lo, parellada

92

Colour: bright golden. Nose: fine lees, dry nuts, fragrant herbs, complex. Palate: powerful, flavourful, good acidity, fine bead, fine bitter notes.

Gran Torelló Gran Añada 2008 BN Gran Reserva
macabeo, xarel.lo, parellada

94

Colour: bright golden. Nose: fine lees, dry nuts, fragrant herbs, complex, toasty. Palate: powerful, flavourful, good acidity, fine bead, fine bitter notes.

Gran Torelló Magnum 2008 BN Gran Reserva
macabeo, xarel.lo, parellada

92

Colour: bright yellow. Nose: ripe fruit, fine lees, balanced, dried herbs. Palate: good acidity, flavourful, ripe fruit, long.

Jeroboam Torelló 2010 BN Gran Reserva
macabeo, xarel.lo, parellada

94

Colour: bright golden. Nose: fine lees, dry nuts, fragrant herbs, complex, toasty. Palate: powerful, flavourful, good acidity, fine bead, fine bitter notes.

Torelló 2010 BN Gran Reserva
macabeo, xarel.lo, parellada

90

Colour: bright yellow. Nose: ripe fruit, fine lees, balanced, dried herbs. Palate: good acidity, flavourful, long, fine bitter notes.

Torelló 225 2009 BN Gran Reserva
macabeo, xarel.lo, parellada

94

Colour: bright golden. Nose: dry nuts, fragrant herbs, lees reduction notes. Palate: powerful, flavourful, good acidity, fine bead, fine bitter notes.

Torelló 225 2010 BN Gran Reserva
macabeo, xarel.lo, parellada

93

Colour: bright golden. Nose: fine lees, dry nuts, fragrant herbs, complex, toasty. Palate: powerful, flavourful, good acidity, fine bead, fine bitter notes.

Torelló 225 Magnum 2010 BN Gran Reserva
macabeo, xarel.lo, parellada

94

Colour: bright golden. Nose: fine lees, dry nuts, fragrant herbs, complex, toasty. Palate: powerful, flavourful, good acidity, fine bead, fine bitter notes.

Torelló by Custo 3D 2009 BR Gran Reserva
macabeo, xarel.lo, parellada

91

Colour: bright yellow. Nose: fine lees, fragrant herbs, characterful, ripe fruit. Palate: powerful, flavourful, good acidity, fine bead, fine bitter notes.

Torelló by Etsuro Sotto 2010 BR Gran Reserva
macabeo, xarel.lo, parellada, chardonnay

91

Colour: bright golden. Nose: dry nuts, fragrant herbs, complex, fine lees, macerated fruit, sweet spices. Palate: powerful, flavourful, good acidity, fine bead, fine bitter notes, elegant.

Torelló Magnum 2009 BN Gran Reserva
macabeo, xarel.lo, parellada

92

Colour: bright golden. Nose: dry nuts, fragrant herbs, toasty. Palate: powerful, flavourful, good acidity, fine bead, fine bitter notes.

Torelló Pal-lid Rosado 2013 BN
macabeo, pinot noir

88

Colour: coppery red. Nose: floral, jasmine, fragrant herbs, candied fruit. Palate: fresh, fruity, flavourful, correct.

Torelló Reserva Especial Edition 2010 BR Reserva
macabeo, xarel.lo, parellada

90

Colour: bright yellow. Nose: fine lees, dried herbs, ripe fruit. Palate: good acidity, flavourful, ripe fruit, long.

TORRE ORIA

Ctra. Pontón - Utiel, Km. 3
46390 Derramador - Requena
(Valencia)
☎: +34 962 320 289
Fax: +34 962 320 311
info.torreoria@torreoria.es
www.torreoria.es

Torre Oria BR
100% macabeo

86

Torre Oria Chardonnay 100% BN
100% chardonnay

88

Colour: bright yellow. Nose: spicy, toasty, faded flowers, patisserie. Palate: long, spicy, flavourful, fine bitter notes.

Torre Oria Vintage BN
80% macabeo, 20% chardonnay

84

TORREBLANCA

Masia Torreblanca, s/n
08734 Olérdola (Barcelona)
☎: +34 938 915 066
Fax: +34 938 900 102
torreblanca@cavatorreblanca.com
www.vinatorreblanca.com

Torreblanca 2009 BN Gran Reserva
macabeo, xarel.lo, parellada, pinot noir

91

Colour: bright golden. Nose: fine lees, fragrant herbs, characterful, ripe fruit, dry nuts. Palate: powerful, flavourful, good acidity, fine bead, fine bitter notes.

Torreblanca 2012 BN Reserva
macabeo, xarel.lo, parellada, chardonnay

89

Colour: bright yellow. Nose: ripe fruit, fine lees, balanced, dried herbs. Palate: good acidity, flavourful, ripe fruit, long.

Torreblanca 2013 BN
macabeo, xarel.lo, parellada

87

Colour: bright straw. Nose: fine lees, floral, fragrant herbs, expressive. Palate: powerful, flavourful, good acidity, fine bead, balanced.

Torreblanca 2013 BR
macabeo, xarel.lo, parellada

88

Colour: bright straw. Nose: fine lees, floral, fragrant herbs. Palate: flavourful, good acidity, fine bead.

Torreblanca Rosat 2013 BR
pinot noir, garnacha

88

Colour: rose. Nose: floral, red berry notes, ripe fruit, fragrant herbs, expressive. Palate: powerful, balanced, flavourful.

TRIAS BATLLE

Pere El Gran, 24
08720 Vilafranca del Penedès
(Barcelona)
☎: +34 677 497 892
peptrias@jtrias.com
www.triasbatlle.com

Trias Batlle 2012 BN Reserva
macabeo, xarel.lo, parellada

87

Colour: bright straw. Nose: wild herbs, fresh, fine lees. Palate: easy to drink, correct, fine bitter notes.

Trias Batlle 2012 BR Reserva
macabeo, xarel.lo, parellada

88

Colour: bright straw. Nose: fine lees, floral, fragrant herbs. Palate: flavourful, good acidity, fine bead.

Trias Batlle Blaué 2008 BN Gran Reserva
xarel.lo, macabeo, parellada, chardonnay

89

Colour: yellow. Nose: fine lees, dry nuts, fragrant herbs, complex. Palate: powerful, flavourful, good acidity, fine bead, fine bitter notes.

Trias Batlle Rosé 2011 BR
trepat

87

Colour: raspberry rose. Nose: floral, jasmine, fragrant herbs, candied fruit. Palate: fresh, fruity, flavourful, correct, easy to drink.

UNIÓN VINÍCOLA DEL ESTE

Pl. Ind. El Romeral- Construcción, 74
46340 Requena (Valencia)
☎: +34 962 323 343
Fax: +34 962 349 413
calidad@uveste.es
www.uveste.es

Nasol de Rechenna BN
90% macabeo, 10% chardonnay

86

Vega Medien BN
80% macabeo, 20% chardonnay

85

Vega Medien Ecológico BR
50% macabeo, 50% chardonnay

87 ♣

Colour: bright straw. Nose: fine lees, floral, fragrant herbs, dried flowers. Palate: powerful, flavourful, good acidity, fine bead, balanced.

Vega Medien Rosé BR
100% garnacha

85

VALLDOLINA
Plaça de la Creu, 1
08795 Olesa de Bonesvalls (Barcelona)
☎: +34 938 984 181
Fax: +34 938 984 181
info@valldolina.com
www.valldolina.com

Tutusaus ECO 2011 BN Gran Reserva
xarel.lo, macabeo, parellada, chardonnay

87 ♣

Colour: yellow. Nose: fine lees, floral, fragrant herbs. Palate: flavourful, good acidity, fine bead, correct, fine bitter notes.

VallDolina Eco 2009 BR Gran Reserva
xarel.lo, macabeo, parellada, chardonnay

89 ♣

Colour: bright straw. Nose: fresh fruit, dried herbs, fine lees, white flowers. Palate: fresh, fruity, good acidity.

VallDolina Eco 2012 BN Reserva
macabeo, parellada, chardonnay

87 ♣

Colour: bright straw. Nose: fine lees, floral, fragrant herbs. Palate: powerful, flavourful, good acidity, fine bead, balanced.

VILARNAU
Ctra. d'Espiells, Km. 1,4 Finca "Can Petit"
08770 Sant Sadurní D'Anoia
(Barcelona)
☎: +34 938 912 361
Fax: +34 938 912 913
vilarnau@vilarnau.es
www.vilarnau.es

Albert de Vilarnau Chardonnay Pinot Noir 2010 BN
50% chardonnay, 50% pinot noir

91

Colour: bright golden. Nose: fine lees, dry nuts, fragrant herbs, complex, toasty. Palate: powerful, flavourful, good acidity, fine bead, fine bitter notes.

Albert de Vilarnau Fermentado en Barrica 2010 BN Gran Reserva
40% chardonnay, 20% macabeo, 20% parellada, 20% chardonnay

92

Colour: bright yellow. Nose: ripe fruit, fine lees, balanced, dried herbs, sweet spices. Palate: good acidity, flavourful, ripe fruit, long.

Vilarnau BR Reserva

87

Colour: bright yellow. Nose: fine lees, floral, fragrant herbs. Palate: powerful, flavourful, good acidity, fine bead, balanced.

Vilarnau 2011 BN Reserva
50% macabeo, 35% parellada, 15% chardonnay

90

Colour: bright straw. Nose: fine lees, floral, fragrant herbs, expressive. Palate: powerful, flavourful, good acidity, fine bead, balanced.

Vilarnau Brut Rosé 2012 BR Reserva
85% trepat, 15% pinot noir

88

Colour: coppery red. Nose: floral, jasmine, fragrant herbs, candied fruit. Palate: fresh, fruity, flavourful, correct.

Vilarnau Vintage 2010 BN Gran Reserva
35% macabeo, 30% parellada, 30% chardonnay, 5% pinot noir

89

Colour: bright yellow. Nose: ripe fruit, fine lees, balanced, dried herbs. Palate: good acidity, flavourful, ripe fruit, long.

VINÍCOLA DE SARRAL Í SELECCIÓ DE CREDIT
Avinguda de la Conca, 33
43424 Sarral (Tarragona)
☎: +34 977 890 031
Fax: +34 977 890 136
cavaportell@gmail.com
www.cava-portell.com

Portell 2012 BN
macabeo, parellada

86

Portell 2013 SS
macabeo, parellada

85

Portell Centenari 2012 BR Reserva
macabeo, parellada

86

Portell Petrignano 2009 BN Gran Reserva
macabeo, parellada

89

Colour: bright golden. Nose: fine lees, fragrant herbs, characterful, ripe fruit, dry nuts. Palate: powerful, flavourful, good acidity, fine bead, fine bitter notes.

Portell Rosat 2013 BR
trepat

85

Portell Vintage 2010 BN
macabeo, parellada

88

Colour: bright straw. Nose: fine lees, floral, fragrant herbs, expressive. Palate: powerful, flavourful, good acidity, fine bead, balanced.

VINS EL CEP

Can Llopart de Les Alzines, Ctra. Espiells
08770 Sant Sadurní D'Anoia
(Barcelona)
☎: +34 938 912 353
Fax: +34 938 183 956
info@vinselcep.com
www.vinselcep.com

Claror 2010 BN Gran Reserva
xarel.lo, macabeo, parellada

89

Colour: bright straw. Nose: fine lees, floral, fragrant herbs, spicy. Palate: powerful, flavourful, good acidity, fine bead, balanced.

GR 5 Senders Vi de Terrer 2013 T
tempranillo, cabernet sauvignon, syrah

90

Colour: cherry, garnet rim. Nose: ripe fruit, wild herbs, earthy notes, spicy, balsamic herbs. Palate: balanced, flavourful, long, balsamic.

GR 5 Senders Xarel.lo 2014 B
xarel.lo

88 ✿

Colour: bright straw. Nose: white flowers, fresh fruit, fragrant herbs. Palate: flavourful, fruity, good acidity, balanced.

L'Alzinar 2012 BN Reserva
macabeo, xarel.lo, parellada

87

Colour: bright straw. Nose: fresh fruit, dried herbs, fine lees, floral. Palate: fresh, fruity, flavourful, good acidity.

L'Alzinar 2012 BR Reserva
macabeo, xarel.lo, parellada

88

Colour: bright straw. Nose: fine lees, floral, fragrant herbs. Palate: flavourful, good acidity, fine bead.

Marqués de Gelida 4 Heretats 2010 BN Gran Reserva
macabeo, xarel.lo, parellada, chardonnay

87

Colour: bright yellow. Nose: ripe fruit, fine lees, balanced, dried herbs. Palate: good acidity, flavourful, ripe fruit, long.

Marqués de Gelida Exclusive 2011 BR Reserva
macabeo, xarel.lo, parellada, chardonnay

89

Colour: bright straw. Nose: fine lees, floral, fragrant herbs, expressive. Palate: powerful, flavourful, good acidity, fine bead, balanced.

Marqués de Gelida Gran Selecció 2009 BN Gran Reserva
xarel.lo, macabeo, parellada, chardonnay, pinot noir

91

Colour: bright golden. Nose: fine lees, fragrant herbs, characterful, ripe fruit, dry nuts. Palate: powerful, flavourful, good acidity, fine bead, fine bitter notes.

Marqués de Gelida Pinot Noir Rosado 2012 BR Reserva
pinot noir

88

Colour: coppery red. Nose: floral, jasmine, fragrant herbs, medium intensity. Palate: fresh, fruity, flavourful, correct, good acidity.

Mim Brut Ecològic 2011 BR Reserva
macabeo, xarel.lo, parellada, chardonnay

89 ✿

Colour: bright straw. Nose: fine lees, floral, fragrant herbs. Palate: flavourful, good acidity, fine bead, balanced.

Mim Brut Nature Ecològic BN Reserva
macabeo, xarel.lo, parellada

90 ✿

Colour: bright straw. Nose: medium intensity, fresh fruit, dried herbs, fine lees, floral. Palate: fresh, fruity, flavourful, good acidity, balanced.

VINYA NATURA

Partida Clotas 10
12118 Les Useres (Castellón)
☎: +34 670 056 497
info@vinyanatura.com
www.vinyanatura.com

Babel de Vinya Natura 2013 BR

macabeo

87

Colour: bright straw. Nose: fine lees, floral, fragrant herbs. Palate: flavourful, good acidity, fine bead.

VIÑEDOS Y BODEGAS MAYO GARCÍA

La Font 116
12192 Vilafamés (Castellón)
☎: +34 964 329 312
mail@mayogarcia.com
www.mayogarcia.com

Magnanimvs 2012 BR Reserva

chardonnay, macabeo

86

Colour: bright straw. Nose: fine lees, floral, fragrant herbs. Palate: flavourful, good acidity, fine bead.

VIÑEDOS Y BODEGAS VEGALFARO

Ctra. Pontón - Utiel, Km. 3
46340 Requena (Valencia)
☎: +34 962 320 680
Fax: +34 962 321 126
info@vegalfaro.com
www.vegalfaro.com

Vegalfaro 2011 BN Reserva

chardonnay, macabeo

90

Colour: yellow. Nose: medium intensity, fresh fruit, fine lees, floral, pattiserie. Palate: fresh, fruity, flavourful, good acidity.

VIVES AMBRÒS

Mayor, 39
43812 Montferri (Tarragona)
☎: +34 639 521 652
Fax: +34 977 606 579
mail@vivesambros.com
www.vivesambros.com

Vives Ambròs 2009 BN Gran Reserva

40% xarel.lo, 35% macabeo, 25% chardonnay

90

Colour: bright yellow. Nose: ripe fruit, fine lees, balanced, dried herbs. Palate: good acidity, flavourful, ripe fruit, long, balanced.

Vives Ambròs 2011 BR Reserva

40% xarel.lo, 35% macabeo, 25% parellada

89

Colour: bright straw. Nose: fine lees, floral, fragrant herbs. Palate: flavourful, good acidity, fine bead.

Vives Ambròs Jujol 2009 BN Gran Reserva

100% xarel.lo

92

Colour: bright yellow. Nose: expressive, varietal, dried herbs, fresh fruit, balanced, fine lees. Palate: fresh, fine bitter notes, good acidity, long.

Vives Ambròs Magnum Tradició 2008 BN Gran Reserva

60% xarel.lo, 40% macabeo

90

Colour: bright yellow. Nose: fine lees, floral, fragrant herbs, expressive. Palate: powerful, flavourful, good acidity, fine bead, balanced.

Vives Ambròs Rosado 2013 BR

40% garnacha, 40% monastrell, 20% pinot noir

89

Colour: raspberry rose. Nose: floral, jasmine, fragrant herbs, candied fruit. Palate: fresh, fruity, flavourful, correct, balanced.

Vives Ambròs Tradició 2007 BN Gran Reserva

60% xarel.lo, 40% macabeo

92

Colour: bright golden. Nose: fine lees, dry nuts, fragrant herbs, complex. Palate: powerful, flavourful, good acidity, fine bead, fine bitter notes, elegant.

DO. CIGALES

CONSEJO REGULADOR

Corro Vaca, 5
47270 Cigales (Valladolid)
:+34 983 580 074 - Fax: +34 983 586 590
@: consejo@do-cigales.es
www.do-cigales.es

LOCATION:

The region stretches to the north of the Duero depression and on both sides of the Pisuerga, bordered by the Cérvalos and the Torozos hills. The vineyards are situated at an altitude of 750 m; the DO extends from part of the municipal area of Valladolid (the wine estate known as 'El Berrocal') to the municipality of Dueñas in Palencia, also including Cabezón de Pisuerga, Cigales, Corcos del Valle, Cubillas de Santa Marte, Fuensaldaña, Mucientes, Quintanilla de Trigueros, San Martín de Valvení, Santovenia de Pisuerga, Trigueros del Valle and Valoria la Buena.

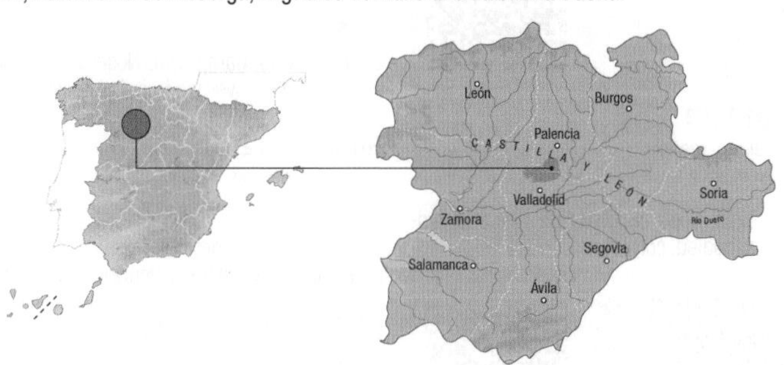

GRAPE VARIETIES:

WHITE: Verdejo, Albillo, Sauvignon Blanc and Viura.
RED: Tinta del País (Tempranillo), Garnacha Tinta, Garnacha Gris, Merlot, Syrah and Cabernet Sauvignon.

TYPES OF WINE:

Rosés: Cigales Nuevo. Produced with at least 60% of the Tinta del País variety and at least 20% of white varieties. The vintage must be displayed on the label. Cigales. Produced with at least 60% of the Tinta del País variety and at least 20% of white varieties. Marketed from 31st December of the following year. reds: Produced with at least 85% of the Tinta del País and the Garnacha Tinta varieties.

FIGURES:

Vineyard surface: 2,100 – **Wine-Growers:** 437 – **Wineries:** 34 – **2014 Harvest rating:** Excellent – **Production 14:** 5,740,000 litres – **Market percentages:** 78% National - 22% International.

SOIL:

The soil is sandy and limy with clay loam which is settled on clay and marl. It has an extremely variable limestone content which, depending on the different regions, ranges between 1% and 35%.

CLIMATE:

The climate is continental with Atlantic influences, and is marked by great contrasts in temperature, both yearly and day/night. The summers are extremely dry; the winters are harsh and prolonged, with frequent frost and fog; rainfall is irregular.

VINTAGE RATING

PEÑÍNGUIDE

2010	2011	2012	2013	2014
EXCELLENT	EXCELLENT	VERY GOOD	GOOD	GOOD

AURELIO PINACHO CENTENO

Ronda Las Huertas, 17
47194 Mucientes (Valladolid)
☎: +34 625 337 344
Fax: +34 983 586 954
lpigo@hotmail.com

Pinacho 2014 RD

80% tempranillo, 20% verdejo, viura, albillo

86

AVELINO VEGAS

Calvo Sotelo, 8
40460 Santiuste (Segovia)
☎: +34 921 596 002
Fax: +34 921 596 035
ana@avelinovegas.com
www.avelinovegas.com

Los Zarzales 2014 RD

tempranillo, garnacha, albillo, verdejo

87

Colour: coppery red, bright. Nose: candied fruit, ripe fruit, faded flowers. Palate: light-bodied, correct.

BODEGA CÉSAR PRÍNCIPE

Ctra. Fuensaldaña-Mucientes, s/n
47194 Fuensaldaña (Valladolid)
☎: +34 983 663 123
cesarprincipe@cesarprincipe.es
www.cesarprincipe.es

César Príncipe 2012 TC

100% tempranillo

93

Colour: cherry, garnet rim. Nose: mineral, expressive, spicy. Palate: flavourful, ripe fruit, long, good acidity, balanced.

BODEGA COOPERATIVA DE CIGALES

Las Bodegas, s/n
47270 Cigales (Valladolid)
☎: +34 983 580 135
Fax: +34 983 580 682
bcc@bodegacooperativacigales.com
www.bodegacooperativacigales.com

Torondos Cigales 2014 RD

84

BODEGA HIRIART

Avda. Los Cortijos, 38
47270 Cigales (Valladolid)
☎: +34 983 580 094
Fax: +34 983 100 701
info@bodegahiriart.es
www.bodegahiriart.es

Hiriart 2010 TC

100% tinta del país

90

Colour: bright cherry. Nose: ripe fruit, sweet spices, creamy oak. Palate: flavourful, fruity, toasty, round tannins.

Hiriart 2011 TC

100% tinta del país

89

Colour: cherry, garnet rim. Nose: fine reductive notes, aged wood nuances, overripe fruit. Palate: spicy, long, toasty.

Hiriart 2012 TC

100% tinta del país

87

Colour: cherry, garnet rim. Nose: smoky, spicy, fruit preserve, dark chocolate. Palate: flavourful, smoky aftertaste, ripe fruit.

Hiriart 2013 T Roble

100% tinta del país

86

Hiriart 2014 RD

tinta del país, garnacha, verdejo

88

Colour: rose, purple rim. Nose: red berry notes, floral. Palate: powerful, fruity, fresh.

BODEGA MUSEUM

Ctra. Cigales - Corcos, Km. 3
47270 Cigales (Valladolid)
☎: +34 983 581 029
Fax: +34 983 581 030
info@bodegasmuseum.com
www.bodegasmuseum.com

Museum 2010 TR

100% tempranillo

92

Colour: cherry, garnet rim. Nose: expressive, spicy, ripe fruit, creamy oak. Palate: flavourful, ripe fruit, long, good acidity.

Vinea 2011 TC

100% tempranillo

91

Colour: cherry, garnet rim. Nose: creamy oak, red berry notes, fresh fruit, balanced. Palate: flavourful, spicy, elegant.

Vinea 2014 RD
100% tempranillo

90

Colour: salmon. Nose: elegant, red berry notes, floral, fragrant herbs. Palate: light-bodied, flavourful, good acidity, long, spicy.

BODEGA VALDELOSFRAILES

Camino de Cubillas, s/n
47290 Cubillas de Santa Marta
(Valladolid)
☎: +34 983 485 028
Fax: +34 983 485 024
valdelosfrailes@matarromera.es
www.valdelosfrailes.es

Valdelosfrailes 2010 TC
100% tempranillo

90

Colour: bright cherry. Nose: ripe fruit, sweet spices, creamy oak, expressive. Palate: flavourful, fruity, toasty, round tannins.

Valdelosfrailes 2013 T Roble
100% tempranillo

89

Colour: cherry, purple rim. Nose: ripe fruit, woody, roasted coffee. Palate: flavourful, spicy, powerful.

Valdelosfrailes 2014 RD
80% tempranillo, 20% verdejo

89

Colour: rose, purple rim. Nose: red berry notes, floral, expressive. Palate: powerful, fruity, fresh, sweetness.

Valdelosfrailes Prestigio 2006 TR
100% tempranillo

92

Colour: cherry, garnet rim. Nose: complex, ripe fruit, spicy, fine reductive notes. Palate: good structure, flavourful, round tannins.

BODEGAS C.H. VINOS DE CUBILLAS

Paseo Fuente la Teja, 31
47290 Cubillas de Santa Marta
(Valladolid)
☎: +34 983 585 203
Fax: +34 983 585 203
info@bodegaschvinosdecubillas.com
www.bodegaschvinosdecubillas.com

Selección Viñedos Viejos Valdecabado 2006 TR
100% tempranillo

88

Colour: cherry, garnet rim. Nose: old leather, tobacco, fruit liqueur notes. Palate: correct, flavourful, spicy.

Valcabado 2012 T Barrica
tempranillo

84

Valdecabado 2014 RD
tempranillo, viura, garnacha, verdejo

83

BODEGAS FERNÁNDEZ CAMARERO

Don Alvaro de Bazán, 1 - 4ºB
28003 Madrid (Madrid)
☎: +34 677 682 426
javier.fernandez@balvinar.com
www.balvinar.com

Balvinar Pagos Seleccionados 2009 T

88

Colour: cherry, garnet rim. Nose: fine reductive notes, wet leather, aged wood nuances. Palate: spicy, long, toasty.

BODEGAS HIJOS DE FÉLIX SALAS

Corrales, s/n
47280 Corcos del Valle (Valladolid)
☎: +34 685 783 213
Fax: +34 983 580 262
bodega@bodegasfelixsalas.com
www.bodegasfelixsalas.com

Viña Picota 2014 RD
tempranillo, albillo, verdejo, garnacha

83

BODEGAS OVIDIO GARCÍA

Malpique, s/n
47270 Cigales (Valladolid)
☎: +34 628 509 475
info@ovidiogarcia.com
www.ovidiogarcia.com

Ovidio García 2008 TR

100% tempranillo

89

Colour: cherry, garnet rim. Nose: roasted coffee, smoky, spicy, ripe fruit. Palate: flavourful, smoky aftertaste, ripe fruit.

Ovidio García Esencia 2011 TC

100% tempranillo

90

Colour: cherry, garnet rim. Nose: smoky, spicy, ripe fruit, mineral. Palate: flavourful, smoky aftertaste, ripe fruit.

BODEGAS REMIGIO DE SALAS JALÓN

Carril de Vinateras
34210 Dueñas (Palencia)
☎: +34 979 780 056
amadasalasortega@gmail.com
www.remigiodesalasjalon.com

Las Luceras 2009 TC

100% tempranillo

87

Colour: cherry, garnet rim. Nose: smoky, spicy, ripe fruit, varnish, aromatic coffee. Palate: flavourful, smoky aftertaste.

Las Luceras 2012 T Roble

80% tempranillo, 20% garnacha

90

Colour: bright cherry. Nose: ripe fruit, sweet spices, creamy oak, expressive. Palate: flavourful, fruity, toasty, round tannins.

Las Luceras 2014 RD

70% tempranillo, 10% verdejo, 10% garnacha, 10% albillo

87

Colour: rose, purple rim. Nose: red berry notes, floral, expressive. Palate: powerful, fruity, fresh.

BODEGAS SANTA RUFINA

Pago Fuente La Teja. Pol. Ind. 3 - Parcela 102
47290 Cubillas de Santa Marta
(Valladolid)
☎: +34 983 585 202
Fax: +34 983 585 202
info@bodegassantarufina.com
www.bodegassantarufina.com

Viña Rufina 2011 TC

100% tempranillo

86

BODEGAS SINFORIANO

Ctra. Mucientes - Villalba, Km. 1 Dcha.
47194 Mucientes (Valladolid)
☎: +34 983 663 008
Fax: +34 983 660 465
sinfo@sinforianobodegas.com
www.sinforianobodegas.com

50 Vendimias de Sinforiano 2009 T

100% tempranillo

93

Colour: cherry, garnet rim. Nose: mineral, expressive, spicy, ripe fruit, powerfull. Palate: flavourful, ripe fruit, long, good acidity, balanced.

50 Vendimias de Sinforiano 2014 RD

80% tempranillo, 10% verdejo, 10% albillo

88

Colour: rose, purple rim. Nose: red berry notes, floral, expressive. Palate: powerful, fruity, fresh.

Sinfo 2013 T Roble

100% tempranillo

87

Colour: bright cherry. Nose: ripe fruit, sweet spices, creamy oak, expressive. Palate: flavourful, fruity, toasty, round tannins.

Sinforiano 2009 TR

100% tempranillo

91

Colour: light cherry. Nose: aged wood nuances, toasty, ripe fruit, fine reductive notes. Palate: spicy, toasty, flavourful.

Sinforiano 2011 TC

100% tempranillo

89

Colour: cherry, garnet rim. Nose: roasted coffee, smoky, spicy, ripe fruit. Palate: flavourful, smoky aftertaste, ripe fruit.

BODEGAS Y VIÑEDOS ALFREDO SANTAMARÍA

Poniente, 18
47290 Cubillas de Santa Marta
(Valladolid)
☎: +34 983 585 006
Fax: +34 983 440 770
info@bodega-santamaria.com
www.bodega-santamaria.com

Alfredo Santamaría 2011 TC
tempranillo

88

Colour: cherry, garnet rim. Nose: fine reductive notes, wet leather, aged wood nuances. Palate: spicy, long, toasty.

Pago el Cordonero 2013 T
tempranillo

85

Trascasas 2010 TR
tempranillo

88

Colour: cherry, garnet rim. Nose: ripe fruit, old leather, tobacco. Palate: correct, flavourful, spicy.

Valvinoso 2014 RD
tempranillo, albillo, verdejo

87

Colour: rose, purple rim. Nose: red berry notes, floral, expressive. Palate: powerful, fruity, fresh.

BODEGAS Y VIÑEDOS ROSAN

Santa María, 6
47270 Cigales (Valladolid)
☎: +34 983 580 006
Fax: +34 983 580 006
rodriguezsanz@telefonica.net

Albéitar 2012 T

90

Colour: bright cherry. Nose: sweet spices, creamy oak, characterful. Palate: flavourful, fruity, toasty, round tannins.

Rosan 2014 RD
tinta del país, garnacha, verdejo

86

COMPAÑÍA DE VINOS MIGUEL MARTÍN

Ctra. Burgos - Portugal, Km. 101
47290 Cubillas de Santa María
(Valladolid)
☎: +34 983 250 319
Fax: +34 983 250 929
comercial@ciadevinos.com
www.ciadevinos.com

Casa Castilla 2014 RD
100% tempranillo

85

Viña Goy 2014 RD
100% tempranillo

87

Colour: rose, purple rim. Nose: floral, red berry notes, ripe fruit. Palate: fruity, fresh.

CONCEJO BODEGAS

Ctra. Valoria, Km. 3.6
47200 Valoria La Buena (Valladolid)
☎: +34 983 502 263
Fax: +34 983 502 253
info@concejobodegas.com
www.concejobodegas.com

Carredueñas 2014 RD
tempranillo

87

Colour: brilliant rose. Nose: red berry notes, floral, fragrant herbs. Palate: light-bodied, flavourful, good acidity, long, spicy.

Carredueñas 2014 RD Fermentado en Barrica
tempranillo

89

Colour: light cherry. Nose: ripe fruit, spicy, red berry notes, sweet spices. Palate: flavourful, sweetness, spicy.

Carredueñas 2014 T Roble
tempranillo

88

Colour: cherry, purple rim. Nose: ripe fruit, woody, roasted coffee. Palate: flavourful, spicy, powerful.

Concejo 2011 T
tempranillo

92

Colour: cherry, garnet rim. Nose: mineral, expressive, spicy. Palate: flavourful, ripe fruit, long, good acidity, balanced.

FRUTOS VILLAR

Camino Los Barreros, s/n
47270 Cigales (Valladolid)
☎: +34 983 586 868
Fax: +34 983 580 180
bodegasfrutosvillar@bodegasfrutosvillar.com
www.bodegasfrutosvillar.com

Calderona 2009 TR

85

Calderona 2010 TC

90

Colour: bright cherry. Nose: ripe fruit, sweet spices, creamy oak, toasty. Palate: flavourful, fruity, toasty, round tannins.

Conde Ansúrez 2014 RD

100% tempranillo

86

Viña Calderona 2014 RD

100% tempranillo

87

Colour: rose, purple rim. Nose: powerfull, fruit preserve, warm. Palate: powerful, flavourful, round.

GONZÁLEZ LARA S.A.

Ctra. Fuensaldaña s/n
47194 Mucientes (Valladolid)
☎: +34 983 587 881
Fax: +34 983 587 881
gonzalezlara@bodegasgonzalezlara.com
www.bodegasgonzalezlara.com

Deo Gracias 2009 T

tempranillo

89

Colour: cherry, garnet rim. Nose: roasted coffee, smoky, spicy, ripe fruit. Palate: flavourful, smoky aftertaste, ripe fruit.

HIJOS DE MARCOS GÓMEZ S.L.

Cuarto San Pedro s/n
47194 Mucientes (Valladolid)
☎: +34 625 115 619
Fax: +34 983 587 764
bodegas@salvueros.com
www.salvueros.com

Salvueros 2014 RD

90

Colour: rose, purple rim. Nose: floral, wild herbs, fruit expression, expressive. Palate: flavourful, complex, balanced, elegant.

HIJOS DE RUFINO IGLESIAS

La Canoniga, 25
47194 Mucientes (Valladolid)
☎: +34 983 587 778
Fax: +34 983 587 778
bodega@hijosderufinoiglesias.com
www.hijosderufinoiglesias.com

Carratraviesa 2014 RD

80% tempranillo, 10% garnacha, 10% otras

87

Colour: rose, purple rim. Nose: powerfull, fruit preserve, warm. Palate: powerful, flavourful, round.

LA LEGUA

Ctra. de Cigales km 1
(salida 117 de la A-62)
47194 Fuensaldaña (Valladolid)
☎: +34 983 583 244
lalegua@lalegua.com
www.lalegua.com

7L Rosado de una Noche 2014 RD

tempranillo, garnacha, cabernet sauvignon

88

Colour: rose, purple rim. Nose: red berry notes, floral, expressive. Palate: powerful, fruity, fresh.

La Legua 2011 TR

tempranillo

88

Colour: light cherry. Nose: spicy, cocoa bean, fruit liqueur notes, wet leather. Palate: spicy, ripe fruit.

La Legua 2012 TC

tempranillo

88

Colour: cherry, purple rim. Nose: ripe fruit, woody, toasty. Palate: flavourful, spicy, powerful.

La Legua 2013 T Roble

88

Colour: bright cherry. Nose: ripe fruit, sweet spices, creamy oak, expressive. Palate: flavourful, fruity, round tannins.

La Legua 2014 T

garnacha

85

La Legua Capricho 2009 TR

tempranillo

90

Colour: cherry, garnet rim. Nose: fine reductive notes, wet leather, aged wood nuances, fruit liqueur notes. Palate: spicy, long, toasty.

La Legua Garnacha 2014 T

garnacha

89

Colour: cherry, purple rim. Nose: expressive, fresh fruit, red berry notes, floral. Palate: flavourful, fruity, good acidity.

TRASLANZAS

Barrio de las Bodegas, s/n
47194 Mucientes (Valladolid)
☎: +34 639 641 123
traslanzas@traslanzas.com
www.traslanzas.com

Traslanzas 2011 TC

100% tempranillo

90

Colour: very deep cherry, garnet rim. Nose: complex, mineral, balsamic herbs, balanced. Palate: full, flavourful, round tannins.

DO. CONCA DE BARBERÀ

CONSEJO REGULADOR
Torre del Portal de Sant Antoni De la Volta, 2
43400 Montblanc
☎ :+34 977 926 905 - Fax: +34 977 926 906
@: cr@doconcadebarbera.com
www.doconcadebarbera.com

LOCATION:

In the north of the province of Tarragona with a production area covering 14 municipalities, to which two new ones have recently been added: Savallà del Comtat and Vilanova de Prades.

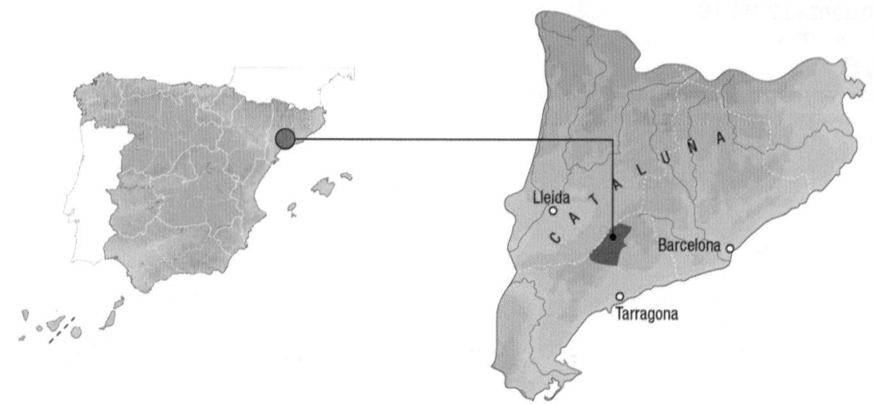

GRAPE VARIETIES:

WHITE: Macabeo, Parellada (majority 3,300 Ha) Chardonnay, Sauvignon Blanc and Viognier.
RED: Trepat, Ull de Llebre (Tempranillo), Garnatxa, Cabernet Sauvignon, Merlot, Syrah and Pinot Noir.

FIGURES:

Vineyard surface: 4,000 – **Wine-Growers:** 960 – **Wineries:** 21 – **2014 Harvest rating:** Good – **Production 14:** 1,482,770 litres – **Market percentages:** 75.4% National - 24.6% International.

SOIL:

The soil is mainly brownish-grey and limy. The vines are cultivated on slopes protected by woodland. An important aspect is the altitude which gives the wines a fresh, light character.

CLIMATE:

Mediterranean and continental influences, as the vineyards occupy a river valley surrounded by mountain ranges without direct contact with the sea.

VINTAGE RATING

PEÑÍNGUIDE

2010	2011	2012	2013	2014
GOOD	GOOD	VERY GOOD	GOOD	GOOD

BODEGAS TORRES

Miguel Torres i Carbó, 6
08720 Vilafranca del Penedès
(Barcelona)
☎: +34 938 177 400
Fax: +34 938 177 444
mailadmin@torres.es
www.torres.com

Grans Muralles 2009 TR
garnacha, cariñena, mazuelo, monastrell, garró, querol

93

Colour: very deep cherry, garnet rim. Nose: closed, scrubland, spicy, elegant, tobacco. Palate: good structure, full, flavourful, long.

Milmanda 2012 B
chardonnay

91

Colour: bright yellow. Nose: expressive, dried herbs, ripe fruit, spicy, dried flowers. Palate: flavourful, fruity, good acidity, balanced, toasty.

CARA NORD

Plaça Sant Sebastià, 13
25457 El Vilosell (Lleida)
☎: +34 973 176 029
Fax: +34 973 175 945
hola@caranordceller.com
www.caranordceller.com

Cara Nord 2014 B
macabeo, chardonnay

89

Colour: bright straw. Nose: white flowers, fresh, medium intensity. Palate: balanced, easy to drink.

Cara Nord Negre 2014 T
42% garnacha, 38% syrah, 20% garrut

92

Colour: bright cherry. Nose: ripe fruit, sweet spices, creamy oak, red berry notes. Palate: flavourful, fruity, round tannins.

CASTELL D'OR

Mare Rafols, 3- 1ºD
08720 Vilafranca del Penedès
(Barcelona)
☎: +34 938 905 385
Fax: +34 938 905 446
castelldor@castelldor.com
www.castelldor.com

Castell de la Comanda 2009 TR
cabernet sauvignon

86

Castell de la Comanda 2013 T
tempranillo, cabernet sauvignon

84

Francoli 2009 TR
tempranillo, cabernet sauvignon

86

Francoli 2011 TC
cabernet sauvignon, cabernet franc

84

Francoli 2013 T
tempranillo, cabernet sauvignon

85

Francoli 2014 B
macabeo

84

Francoli 2014 RD
trepat

83

CELLER CARLES ANDREU

Sant Sebastià, 19
43423 Pira (Tarragona)
☎: +34 977 887 404
Fax: +34 977 860 279
celler@cavandreu.com
www.cavandreu.com

Carles Andreu Parellada 2014 B Maceración Carbónica
100% parellada

88

Colour: bright yellow. Nose: dried herbs, ripe fruit, spicy. Palate: flavourful, fruity, good acidity.

Carles Andreu Vino Tinto Trepat 2013 T
100% trepat

89

Colour: cherry, garnet rim. Nose: medium intensity, red berry notes, wild herbs. Palate: balanced, good finish, spicy.

CELLER MAS FORASTER

Camí de L'Ermita de Sant Josep, s/n
43400 Montblanc (Tarragona)
☎: +34 977 860 229
Fax: +34 977 875 037
info@josepforaster.com
www.josepforaster.com

Josep Foraster 2012 TC
40% cabernet sauvignon, 25% syrah, 25% ull de llebre, 10% trepat

87

Colour: very deep cherry, garnet rim. Nose: expressive, balsamic herbs, balanced, earthy notes. Palate: full, flavourful, round tannins.

Josep Foraster Blanc del Coster 2014 B
90% macabeo, 10% garnacha blanca

84

Josep Foraster Blanc Selecció 2013 B
50% garnacha blanca, 40% macabeo, 10% chardonnay

87

Colour: yellow, pale. Nose: ripe fruit, faded flowers, wild herbs. Palate: fruity, correct, fine bitter notes, good acidity.

Josep Foraster Collita 2014 T
90% ull de llebre, 10% cabernet sauvignon

86

Josep Foraster Les Gallinetes 2014 T
garnacha, syrah, ull de llebre, cabernet sauvignon

85

Josep Foraster Macabeu 2014 B
100% macabeo

88

Colour: bright straw. Nose: fresh fruit, fragrant herbs, varietal, wild herbs. Palate: flavourful, fruity, good acidity, balanced.

Josep Foraster Rosat Trepat 2014 RD
100% trepat

86

Josep Foraster Selecció 2011 TR
50% garnacha, 50% cabernet sauvignon

90

Colour: cherry, garnet rim. Nose: wild herbs, spicy, balsamic herbs, ripe fruit. Palate: balanced, flavourful, long, balsamic.

Josep Foraster Trepat 2013 T
100% trepat

87

Colour: light cherry, garnet rim. Nose: spicy, grassy, wild herbs, fresh. Palate: easy to drink, good acidity, correct.

CELLER TINTORÉ DE VIMBODÍ I POBLET

Copèrnic, 44 Baixos
08021 (Barcelona)
☎: +34 932 096 101
info@tinto-re.com
www.tinto-re.com

Re 2012 TC
garnacha, cariñena, cabernet sauvignon

89

Colour: bright cherry, garnet rim. Nose: spicy, dried herbs, balanced. Palate: ripe fruit, round tannins.

CELLER VIDBERTUS

Anselm Clavé, 13
43440 L'Espluga de Francolí
(Tarragona)
☎: +34 626 330 511
info@vidbertus.com
www.vidbertus.com

996 2011 T
merlot, monastrell

88

Colour: dark-red cherry, garnet rim. Nose: characterful, ripe fruit, fruit preserve, scrubland, waxy notes. Palate: good structure, flavourful.

Cup3 2013 T
garnacha, trepat

86

Negre Nit 2011 T
garnacha, merlot, monastrell, trepat

88

Colour: cherry, garnet rim. Nose: ripe fruit, wild herbs, earthy notes, spicy, balsamic herbs. Palate: balanced, flavourful, long, balsamic.

T de Trepat 2013 RD
100% trepat

80

Ud2 2013 B
parellada

84

CLOS MONTBLANC

Ctra. Montblanc-Barbera, s/n
43422 Barberà de la Conca (Tarragona)
☎: +34 977 887 030
Fax: +34 977 887 032
club@closmontblanc.com
www.closmontblanc.com

Clos Montblanc Masía Les Comes 2008 TR
cabernet sauvignon, merlot

87

Colour: cherry, garnet rim. Nose: wet leather, aged wood nuances, dried herbs. Palate: spicy, long, toasty, ripe fruit.

Clos Montblanc Merlot 2011 TC
100% merlot

86

Clos Montblanc Pinot Noir 2013 TC
100% pinot noir

87

Colour: cherry, purple rim. Nose: red berry notes, balsamic herbs, faded flowers. Palate: fresh, fruity, good finish.

Clos Montblanc Sauvignon Blanc 2014 B
100% sauvignon blanc

85

Clos Montblanc Syrah 2011 T
100% syrah

84

Clos Montblanc Trepat 2012 T
100% trepat

88

Colour: cherry, garnet rim. Nose: spicy, ripe fruit, dried herbs, balanced. Palate: flavourful, balsamic, good acidity.

Xipella Rosat 2014 RD
trepat, tempranillo, merlot, syrah

85

GATZARA VINS

Comerç, 2
43422 Barberà de la Conca (Tarragona)
☎: +34 977 861 175
Fax: +34 977 861 175
info@gatzaravins.com
viverdecelleristes.concadebarbera.cat

Gatzara 2013 T
100% trepat

92

Colour: light cherry, garnet rim. Nose: wild herbs, ripe fruit, earthy notes. Palate: ripe fruit, easy to drink, balanced.

Gatzara 2013 T Barrica
100% trepat

91

Colour: bright cherry, light cherry. Nose: red berry notes, ripe fruit, expressive, fresh, balanced. Palate: spicy, good acidity.

Gatzara Blanc 2013 B
72% macabeo, 17% chardonnay, 11% trepat

90

Colour: yellow, pale. Nose: smoky, powerfull, spicy, characterful. Palate: correct, fine bitter notes, spicy, ripe fruit, good acidity.

Gatzara Blanc de Noirs 2014 B
100% trepat

88

Colour: coppery red. Nose: wild herbs, spicy, characterful. Palate: balanced, fine bitter notes, long. Personality.

Una Mica de Gatzara 2014 T
75% trepat, 25% ull de llebre

90

Colour: light cherry, garnet rim. Nose: balanced, medium intensity, ripe fruit, red berry notes. Palate: fruity, easy to drink, fine tannins.

RENDÉ MASDÉU

Avda. Catalunya, 44
43440 L'Espluga de Francolí
(Tarragona)
☎: +34 977 871 361
celler@rendemasdeu.cat
www.rendemasdeu.cat

Arnau Syrah de Rendé Masdeu 2011 T
syrah

90

Colour: cherry, garnet rim. Nose: creamy oak, balanced, ripe fruit, toasty. Palate: flavourful, spicy, round tannins.

inQuiet de Rendé Masdeu 2014 T
cabernet sauvignon

87

Colour: cherry, purple rim. Nose: expressive, fresh fruit, red berry notes, floral. Palate: flavourful, fruity, good acidity.

Manuela Ventosa de Rendé Masdéu 2011 T Fermentado en Barrica
70% cabernet sauvignon, 30% syrah

91

Colour: cherry, garnet rim. Nose: red berry notes, ripe fruit, fragrant herbs, spicy, toasty, creamy oak, mineral. Palate: powerful, flavourful, balsamic, balanced.

Peu del Bosc de Rendé Masdeu 2010 TC
90% cabernet sauvignon, 10% syrah

88

Colour: cherry, garnet rim. Nose: ripe fruit, wild herbs, earthy notes, spicy, balsamic herbs. Palate: balanced, balsamic.

Rendé Masdeu Rosat Syrah 2014 RD
syrah

87

Colour: rose. Nose: red berry notes, white flowers, balanced, ripe fruit. Palate: correct, fruity, easy to drink, good finish.

Trepat del Jordiet de Rendé Masdeu 2013 T
trepat

88

Colour: cherry, purple rim. Nose: red berry notes, expressive, wild herbs, characterful. Palate: powerful, fresh, fruity, balanced, easy to drink.

ROSA MARÍA TORRES

Avda. Anguera, 2
43424 Sarral (Tarragona)
☎: +34 977 890 013
info@rosamariatorres.com
www.rosamariatorres.com

Saüc 2011 TC
100% cabernet franc

89

Colour: bright cherry. Nose: ripe fruit, sweet spices, creamy oak, expressive, wild herbs. Palate: flavourful, fruity, toasty, round tannins.

Susel 2014 RD
100% pinot noir

88

Colour: rose, purple rim. Nose: red berry notes, floral, expressive, powerfull. Palate: powerful, fruity, fresh.

Susela Dulce Natural
cabernet sauvignon

85

Viognier 2012 BFB
100% viognier

87

Colour: bright yellow. Nose: ripe fruit, powerfull, toasty, sweet spices. Palate: flavourful, fruity, spicy, toasty, long.

SUCCÉS VINÍCOLA

Comerç, 2
43422 Barberà de la Conca (Tarragona)
☎: +34 677 144 629
succesvinicola@gmail.com
www.succesvinicola.com

Feedback de Succés Vinícola 2011 T
tempranillo, cabernet sauvignon, merlot

90

Colour: cherry, garnet rim. Nose: ripe fruit, wild herbs, earthy notes, spicy, balsamic herbs. Palate: balanced, flavourful, long, balsamic.

Succés El Mentider 2013 T
100% trepat

90

Colour: bright cherry, garnet rim. Nose: balanced, expressive, fresh, scrubland, dry stone. Palate: balanced, good acidity, round tannins.

Succés Experiència Parellada 2014 B
parellada

86

Succés La Cuca de LLum 2014 T
trepat

88

Colour: light cherry. Nose: fruit liqueur notes, fragrant herbs, spicy, fine reductive notes. Palate: balanced, elegant, spicy.

VEGA AIXALÁ

De la Font, 11
43439 Vilanova de Prades (Barcelona)
☎: +34 636 519 821
info@vegaaixala.com
www.vegaaixala.com

Barrau 2012 T
tempranillo, garnacha, syrah

87

Colour: bright cherry. Nose: fruit expression, toasty, spicy. Palate: flavourful, fruity, round tannins, easy to drink.

Caliu 2011 T
cariñena, syrah

90

Colour: cherry, garnet rim. Nose: red berry notes, ripe fruit, spicy, creamy oak, complex. Palate: flavourful, toasty, round tannins.

La Bauma 2013 B
garnacha blanca, chardonnay

88

Colour: bright straw. Nose: expressive, balanced, faded flowers, ripe fruit, dried herbs. Palate: correct, ripe fruit.

Viern 2009 TC
garnacha, cariñena, cabernet sauvignon, syrah

87 ♣

Colour: dark-red cherry, garnet rim. Nose: powerfull, old leather, tobacco, dried herbs. Palate: correct, balanced, round tannins.

VINÍCOLA DE SARRAL Í SELECCIÓ DE CREDIT

Avinguda de la Conca, 33
43424 Sarral (Tarragona)
☎: +34 977 890 031
Fax: +34 977 890 136
cavaportell@gmail.com
www.cava-portell.com

Portell 2012 TC
cabernet sauvignon, ull de llebre, merlot

86

Portell 2014 B
macabeo, parellada

84

Portell Agulla Blanc 2014 Blanco de Aguja
macabeo, parellada

82

Portell Agulla Rosat 2014 Rosado de aguja
trepat

82

Portell Merlot 2013 T
merlot

84

Portell Rosat Trepat 2014 RD
trepat

84

VINS DE PEDRA

Sant Josep, 13
43400 Montblanc (Tarragona)
☎: +34 630 405 118
celler@vinsdepedra.es
www.vinsdepedra.es

El Trempat 2013 T
trepat

86

L'Orni 2014 B
chardonnay

89

Colour: bright yellow. Nose: white flowers, fresh fruit, fragrant herbs, expressive. Palate: flavourful, fruity, good acidity, balanced.

La Musa 2012 T
cabernet sauvignon, merlot

89

Colour: cherry, garnet rim. Nose: ripe fruit, wild herbs, earthy notes, spicy, balsamic herbs. Palate: balanced, flavourful, long, balsamic.

DO. CONDADO DE HUELVA / VINO NARANJA DEL CONDADO DE HUELVA

CONSEJO REGULADOR
Plaza Ildefonso Pinto, s/n.
21710 Bollullos Par del Condado (Huelva)
☎:+34 959 410 322 - Fax: +34 959 413 859
@: cr@condadodehuelva.es
www.condadodehuelva.es

LOCATION:

In the south east of Huelva. It occupies the plain of Bajo Guadalquivir. The production area covers the municipal areas of Almonte, Beas, Bollullos Par del Condado, Bonares, Chucena, Gibraleón, Hinojos, La Palma del Condado, Lucena del Puerto, Manzanilla, Moguer, Niebla, Palos de la Frontera, Rociana del Condado, San Juan del Puerto, Villalba del Alcor, Villarrasa and Trigueros.

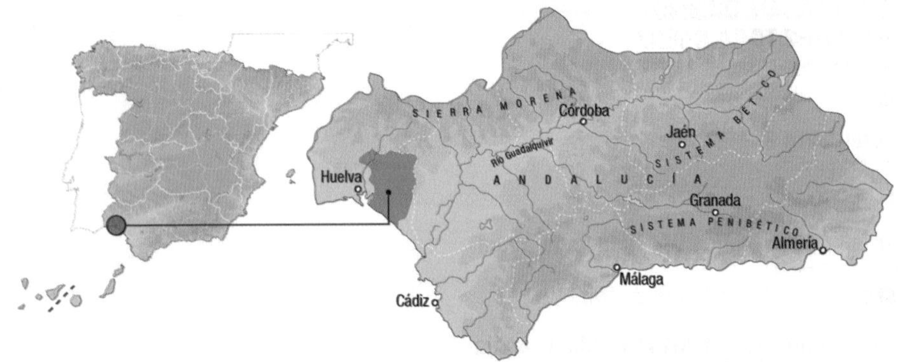

GRAPE VARIETIES:

WHITE: Zalema (majority with 86% of vineyards), Palomino, Listán de Huelva, Garrido Fino, Moscatel de Alejandría and Pedro Ximénez.
RED: Merlot, Syrah, Tempranillo, Cabernet Sauvignon and Cabernet Franc.

FIGURES:

Vineyard surface: 2,500 – **Wine-Growers:** 1,500 – **Wineries:** 27 – **2014 Harvest rating:** Good – **Production 14:** 9,359,451 litres – **Market percentages:** 95% National - 5% International.

SOIL:

In general, flat and slightly rolling terrain, with fairly neutral soils of medium fertility. The soil is mainly reddish, brownish-grey with alluvium areas in the proximity of the Guadalquivir.

CLIMATE:

Mediterranean in nature, with certain Atlantic influences. The winters and springs are fairly mild, with long hot summers. The average annual temperature is 18 °C, and the average rainfall per year is around 550 mm, with a relative humidity of between 60% and 80%.

VINTAGE RATING

PEÑÍNGUIDE

2010	2011	2012	2013	2014
GOOD	GOOD	VERY GOOD	AVERAGE	AVERAGE

BODEGAS ANDRADE

Avda. Coronación, 35
21710 Bollullos del Condado (Huelva)
☎: +34 959 410 106
Fax: +34 959 410 305
informacion@bodegasandrade.es
www.bodegasandrade.es

Andrade Vino Naranja GE

86

Castillo de Andrade 2014 B

100% zalema

83

BODEGAS DE DIEZMO NUEVO BODEGA SAENZ

Sor Ángela de la Cruz, 56
21800 Moguer (Huelva)
☎: +34 959 370 004
Fax: +34 959 371 840
info@bodegadiezmonuevo.com
www.bodegadiezmonuevo.com

El Patriarca S/C B

79

Melquiades Saenz "Vino de Naranja" B

85

BODEGAS IGLESIAS

Teniente Merchante, 2
21710 Bollullos del Condado (Huelva)
☎: +34 959 410 439
Fax: +34 959 410 463
bodegasiglesias@bodegasiglesias.com
www.bodegasiglesias.com

% UZ Cien x Cien Uva Zalema S/C B Joven

100% zalema

87

Colour: straw. Nose: medium intensity, floral, fresh fruit. Palate: correct, easy to drink, fine bitter notes, good acidity.

Letrado Solera 1992 GE Solera

100% zalema

87

Colour: light mahogany. Nose: expressive, dry nuts, spicy, aged wood nuances. Palate: full, flavourful, long, fine solera notes.

Par Vino Naranja Vino de licor

85% zalema, 15% pedro ximénez

88

Colour: light mahogany. Nose: fresh, citrus fruit, fruit liqueur notes. Palate: balanced, unctuous, fruity, flavourful.

Ricahembra Solera 1980 GE

85% zalema, 15% pedro ximénez

87

Colour: mahogany. Nose: varnish, fruit liqueur notes, caramel, aged wood nuances, dry nuts. Palate: correct, unctuous, good acidity.

UZT Tardía S/C B

100% zalema

84

BODEGAS OLIVEROS

Rábida, 12
21710 Bollullos Par del Condado (Huelva)
☎: +34 959 410 057
Fax: +34 959 410 057
info@bodegasoliveros.com
www.bodegasoliveros.com

Juan Jaime 2014 B

zalema

86

Oliveros 2012 TC

75% tempranillo, 25% syrah

86

Oliveros Pedro Ximénez PX

pedro ximénez

89

Colour: light mahogany. Nose: fruit liqueur notes, dried fruit, pattiserie, toasty. Palate: sweet, rich, unctuous.

Oliveros Vino Naranja B

pedro ximénez, zalema

86

BODEGAS PRIVILEGIO DEL CONDADO S.L.

San José, 2
21710 Bollullos del Condado (Huelva)
☎: +34 959 410 261
Fax: +34 959 410 171
comercial@vinicoladelcondado.com
www.vinicoladelcondado.com

Lantero Roble Syrah 2013 T Roble

syrah

83

Mioro 2014 B

100% zalema

84

Mioro Gran Selección 2014 B
zalema, moscatel de alejandría

86

Misterio Dulce
zalema

86

VDM Orange Dulce
moscatel, zalema

87

Colour: old gold. Nose: candied fruit, fruit liqueur notes, citrus fruit, spicy. Palate: rich, good structure, ripe fruit.

BODEGAS SAUCI

Doctor Fleming, 1
21710 Bollullos del Condado (Huelva)
☎: +34 959 410 524
Fax: +34 959 410 331
sauci@bodegassauci.es
www.bodegassauci.es

Espinapura Condádo Pálido
100% palomino

88

Colour: bright straw. Nose: balanced, fresh, saline, expressive, pungent. Palate: flavourful, fine bitter notes, long.

Riodiel Solera 1980 Condádo Viejo
100% palomino

86

S' Naranja Vino de licor
80% pedro ximénez, 20% palomino

89

Colour: light mahogany. Nose: fresh, citrus fruit, floral, balanced. Palate: full, flavourful, long, spicy, good acidity.

S' Px Dulce Natural PX
100% pedro ximénez

89

Colour: mahogany. Nose: complex, fruit liqueur notes, dried fruit, pattiserie, aged wood nuances, toasty. Palate: sweet, rich, unctuous.

S' Px Solera 1989 PX
100% pedro ximénez

91

Colour: dark mahogany. Nose: powerfull, expressive, aromatic coffee, spicy, acetaldehyde, dry nuts. Palate: balanced, elegant, fine solera notes, toasty, long.

S' Vino Dulce Vino de licor
palomino, pedro ximénez

85

Sauci Cream Solera 1980 CR
75% palomino, 25% pedro ximénez

85

CONVENTO DE MORAÑINA

Avda. de la Paz, 43
21710 Bollullos Par del Condado (Huelva)
☎: +34 959 412 250
bodega@bodegasconvento.com
www.bodegasconvento.com

Amaranto Generoso de Licor Dulce
85

Convento PX Reserva
90

Colour: mahogany. Nose: complex, fruit liqueur notes, dried fruit, pattiserie, varnish. Palate: sweet, rich, unctuous, flavourful.

Convento Naranja Dulce Semidulce
88

Colour: mahogany. Nose: ripe fruit, citrus fruit, sweet spices, faded flowers. Palate: ripe fruit, balanced, unctuous.

Convento Sureño Viejo Condado Viejo Oloroso
85

Secreto del Convento 1960 CR
91

Colour: iodine, amber rim. Nose: powerfull, complex, dry nuts, creamy oak, varnish. Palate: rich, long, spicy.

COOPERATIVA NTRA. SRA. DEL SOCORRO S.C.A.

Carril de los Moriscos, 72
21720 Rociana del Condado (Huelva)
☎: +34 959 416 069
jl63@bodegasdelsocorro.com
www.bodegasdelsocorro.com

Don Frede 2011 TC
70% tempranillo, 30% syrah

85

Don Frede 2014 RD
70% tempranillo, 30% syrah

79

Don Frede 2014 T
70% tempranillo, 30% syrah

84

El Gamo 2014 B
100% zalema

84

Viñagamo Seco 2014 B
100% zalema

84

Viñagamo Semidulce 2014 B
100% zalema

82

MARQUÉS DE VILLALÚA

Ctra. A-472, Km. 25,2
21860 Villalba del Alcor (Huelva)
☎: +34 959 420 905
Fax: +34 959 421 141
bodega@marquesdevillalua.com
www.marquesdevillalua.com

Aguadulce de Villalúa Semidulce 2014 B
zalema, moscatel

83

Marqués de Villalúa 2014 B
zalema, moscatel

87

Colour: straw. Nose: medium intensity, floral, fresh fruit, dry nuts, dried flowers. Palate: correct, easy to drink, good finish.

Marqués de Villalúa Colección 1000 2013 B
sauvignon blanc, zalema, moscatel

88

Colour: bright straw. Nose: dried herbs, fresh fruit, balanced, expressive. Palate: fine bitter notes, fruity, easy to drink, good acidity.

Santa Agueda Vino Naranja
zalema, moscatel

86

DO. COSTERS DEL SEGRE

CONSEJO REGULADOR

Complex de la Caparrella, 97
25192 Lleida
☎:+34 973 264 583 - Fax: +34 973 264 583
@: secretari@costersdelsegre.es
www.costersdelsegre.es

LOCATION:

In the southern regions of Lleida, and a few municipal areas of Tarragona. It covers the sub-regions of: Artesa de Segre, Garrigues, Pallars Jussà, Raimat, Segrià and Valls del Riu Corb.

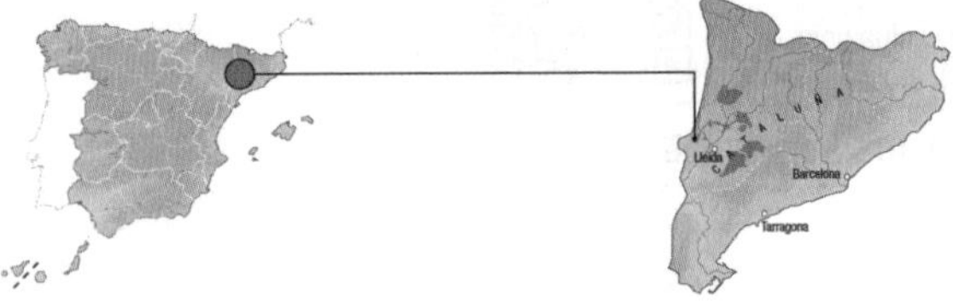

SUB-REGIONS:

Artesa de Segre: Located on the foothills of the Sierra de Montsec, just north of the Noguera region, it has mainly limestone soils. Urgell: Located in the central part of the province of Lleida, at an average altitude of 350 meters, its climate is a mix of mediterranean and continental features. **Garrigues:** To the southeast of the province of Lleida, it is a region with a complex topography and marl soils. Its higher altitude is near 700 meters. **Pallars Jussà:** Located in the Pyrinees, it is the northernmost sub-zone. Soils are predominantly limestone and its type of climate mediterranean with strong continental influence. **Raimat:** Located in the province of Lleida and with predominantly limestone soils, it has a mediterranean climate with continental features, with predominantly cold winters and very hot summers. **Segrià:** Is the central sub-zone of the DO, with limestone soils. **Valls del Riu Corb:** Located in the southeast of the DO, its climate is primarily mediterranean-continental softened by both the beneficial effect of the sea breezes (called marinada in the region) and "el Seré", a dry sea-bound inland wind.

GRAPE VARIETIES:

WHITE: PREFERRED: Macabeo, Xarel·lo, Parellada, Chardonnay, Garnacha Blanca, Moscatel de Grano Menudo, Malvasía, Gewürztraminer, Albariño, Riesling and Sauvignon Blanc.
RED: PREFERRED: Garnacha Negra, Ull de Llebre (Tempranillo), Cabernet Sauvignon, Merlot, Monastrell, Trepat, Samsó, Pinot Noir and Syrah.

FIGURES:

Vineyard surface: 4,197 – **Wine-Growers:** 593 – **Wineries:** 45 – **2014 Harvest rating:** Very Good – **Production 14:** 10,252,500 litres – **Market percentages:** 60% National - 40% International.

SOIL:

The soil is mainly calcareous and granitic in nature. Most of the vineyards are situated on soils with a poor organic matter content, brownish-grey limestone, with a high percentage of limestone and very little clay.

CLIMATE:

Rather dry continental climate in all the sub-regions, with minimum temperatures often dropping below zero in winter, summers with maximum temperatures in excess of 35° on occasions, and fairly low rainfall figures: 385 mm/year in Lleida and 450 mm/year in the remaining regions.

VINTAGE RATING

PEÑÍNGUIDE

2010	2011	2012	2013	2014
GOOD	VERY GOOD	VERY GOOD	VERY GOOD	GOOD

BODEGAS TORRES

Miguel Torres i Carbó, 6
08720 Vilafranca del Penedès
(Barcelona)
☎: +34 938 177 400
Fax: +34 938 177 444
mailadmin@torres.es
www.torres.com

Purgatori 2012 T

cariñena, garnacha, syrah

91

Colour: dark-red cherry, garnet rim. Nose: wild herbs, warm, balanced, spicy. Palate: balanced, spicy, long.

BODEGAS VILA CORONA

Camí els Nerets, s/n
25654 Vilamitjana (Lérida)
☎: +34 973 652 638
Fax: +34 973 652 638
vila-corona@avired.com
www.vilacorona.cat

Llabustes Cabernet Sauvignon 2012 TC

cabernet sauvignon

86

Llabustes Chardonnay 2013 B

chardonnay

85

Llabustes Merlot s/c T

merlot

87

Colour: bright cherry. Nose: balanced, medium intensity, dried herbs, ripe fruit. Palate: flavourful, balanced, round tannins.

Llabustes Riesling 2014 B

riesling

84

Llabustes Ull de Llebre 2011 TC

ull de llebre

85

Tu Rai 2012 T

monastrell, garnacha, ull de llebre

86

BREGOLAT

Crta L - 512 Km 13,75 Les Pletes
25738 Montmagastre (Lérida)
☎: +34 973 989 163
administracio@bregolat.com
www.bregolat.com

Bregolat 2011 T

cabernet sauvignon, garnacha, merlot

89

Colour: cherry, garnet rim. Nose: creamy oak, red berry notes, balanced, ripe fruit. Palate: flavourful, spicy, elegant.

Bregolat 2013 BFB

macabeo

88

Colour: bright straw. Nose: ripe fruit, toasty, sweet spices. Palate: flavourful, fruity, spicy, toasty, long, good acidity.

Petit Bregolat 2012 T

merlot, garnacha, cabernet sauvignon

86

Petit Bregolat 2013 B

macabeo, sauvignon blanc, gewürztraminer

84

Petit Bregolat 2013 RD

garnacha

87

Colour: onion pink. Nose: elegant, red berry notes, floral, fragrant herbs. Palate: light-bodied, flavourful, good acidity, long, spicy.

CAL CABO CELLER

Castell, 30
25344 Sant Martí de Malda (Lérida)
☎: +34 639 887 836
celler@calcaboceller.cat
www.calcaboceller.cat

Curvus 2012 T

syrah, merlot, cabernet sauvignon, ull de llebre

86

Un Onzé 2013 T

ull de llebre, cabernet sauvignon, syrah, merlot

87

Colour: cherry, garnet rim. Nose: scrubland, wild herbs, ripe fruit. Palate: flavourful, spicy, easy to drink, good acidity.

CASTELL D'ENCUS

Ctra. Tremp a Santa Engracia, Km. 5
25630 Talarn (Lleida)
☎: +34 973 252 974
ipinedo@castelldencus.com
www.castelldencus.com

Acusp 2013 T
100% pinot noir

94

Colour: light cherry, garnet rim. Nose: ripe fruit, smoky, spicy, dried herbs, expressive. Palate: balanced, good acidity, round tannins.

Ekam 2013 B
85% riesling, 15% albariño

90

Colour: straw. Nose: fresh fruit, fragrant herbs, expressive, floral. Palate: fruity, balanced, fine bitter notes, long.

Ekam 2014 B
85% riesling, 15% albariño

89

Colour: bright straw. Nose: white flowers, fresh fruit, fragrant herbs. Palate: flavourful, fruity, good acidity, slightly acidic.

Ekam Essència Semidulce 2010 B
100% riesling

93

Colour: bright straw. Nose: faded flowers, white flowers, medium intensity, balanced, dry nuts. Palate: full, flavourful, long.

Quest 2012 T
cabernet sauvignon, cabernet franc, merlot, petit verdot

93

Colour: cherry, garnet rim. Nose: ripe fruit, scrubland, dried herbs, spicy, creamy oak. Palate: fruity, flavourful, round tannins.

Quest 2013 T
cabernet sauvignon, cabernet franc, merlot, petit verdot

93

Colour: deep cherry, garnet rim. Nose: wild herbs, balanced, ripe fruit. Palate: good structure, spicy, good acidity.

Taïka 2011 ESP
pinot noir, semillón, riesling

90

Colour: bright straw. Nose: fresh fruit, dried herbs, fine lees, floral, faded flowers. Palate: fresh, fruity, flavourful, good acidity.

tALEIA 2013 B
85% sauvignon blanc, 15% semillón

91

Colour: bright straw. Nose: fresh fruit, fragrant herbs. Palate: flavourful, fruity, balanced, fine bitter notes, good acidity.

ThALARN 2013 T
100% syrah

93

Colour: cherry, purple rim. Nose: expressive, medium intensity, red berry notes, ripe fruit. Palate: good structure, balanced, good acidity.

CASTELL DEL REMEI

Castell del Remei s/n
25333 Pebelles (Lérida)
☎: +34 973 580 200
Fax: +34 973 718 312
info@castelldelremei.com
www.castelldelremei.com

Castell del Remei 1780 2009 T
cabernet sauvignon, tempranillo, garnacha, merlot, syrah

89

Colour: cherry, garnet rim. Nose: ripe fruit, wild herbs, earthy notes, spicy, balsamic herbs. Palate: balanced, flavourful, long, balsamic.

Castell del Remei Gotim Blanc 2014 B
sauvignon blanc, macabeo

88

Colour: bright straw. Nose: white flowers, fresh fruit, fragrant herbs. Palate: flavourful, fruity, good acidity.

Castell del Remei Gotim Bru 2012 T

91

Colour: bright cherry. Nose: ripe fruit, sweet spices, creamy oak. Palate: flavourful, fruity, toasty, round tannins.

Castell del Remei Oda 2012 TC
merlot, cabernet sauvignon, tempranillo, garnacha

90

Colour: cherry, garnet rim. Nose: ripe fruit, spicy, creamy oak, complex. Palate: flavourful, toasty.

Castell del Remei Oda Blanc 2014 BFB
macabeo, chardonnay

89

Colour: bright yellow. Nose: ripe fruit, powerfull, toasty, aged wood nuances, pattiserie. Palate: flavourful, fruity, spicy, toasty, long.

CELLER ANALEC

Ctra. a Nalec, s/n
25341 Nalec (Lleida)
☎: +34 973 303 190
elcelleranalec@gmail.com
www.analec.net

La Creu Blanc 2013 B
100% macabeo

87

Colour: bright straw. Nose: medium intensity, varietal, fresh fruit, dried herbs. Palate: fresh, fruity, spicy, fine bitter notes.

La Creu Negre 2012 T
tempranillo, cabernet sauvignon, syrah

87

Colour: cherry, garnet rim. Nose: balanced, spicy, dried herbs, ripe fruit, fruit preserve. Palate: good structure, round tannins.

La Romiguera 2011 TC
tempranillo, syrah, cabernet sauvignon

88

Colour: cherry, garnet rim. Nose: medium intensity, ripe fruit, dried flowers, dried herbs. Palate: correct, spicy, easy to drink.

Sort Abril 2009 ESP Reserva
macabeo, parellada

86

CELLER CASA PATAU

Costa del Senyor, s/n
25139 Menarguens (Lérida)
☎: +34 973 180 367
info@casapatau.com
www.casapatau.com

Casa Patau 2012 TC
merlot, cabernet sauvignon, garnacha

85

L'Eral de Casa Patau 2014 B
garnacha, moscatel de alejandría, macabeo

84

L'Eral de Casa Patau 2014 RD
merlot, cabernet sauvignon

86

CELLER CERCAVINS

Ctra. LV-2101, km. 0,500
25340 Verdú (Lleida)
☎: +34 646 558 515
Fax: +34 973 347 197
info@cellercercavins.com
www.cellercercavins.com

Bru de Verdú 14 2010 T
cabernet sauvignon, syrah, tempranillo, merlot

89

Colour: cherry, garnet rim. Nose: fine reductive notes, ripe fruit, expressive, wild herbs. Palate: spicy, long, toasty.

Bru de Verdú 2012 T
tempranillo, syrah, merlot

86

Guilla 2013 BFB
macabeo

86

Guillamina 2014 B
sauvignon blanc, gewürztraminer, garnacha blanca, albariño, chardonnay

84

Lo Virol 2013 T
tempranillo, merlot

85

Lo Virol 2014 B
garnacha blanca, macabeo, sauvignon blanc, gewürztraminer, albariño, chardonnay

86

Lo Virol 2014 RD
syrah

86

CELLER MAS GARCÍA MURET

Ctra. Els Masos de Llimiana, s/n
25639 Els Masos de Llimiana (Lérida)
☎: +34 973 651 748
Fax: +34 973 651 748
info@masgarciamuret.com
www.masgarciamuret.com

Colomina 2013 RD
tempranillo, pinot noir

89

Colour: coppery red. Nose: floral, wild herbs, fruit expression, expressive. Palate: fresh, fine bitter notes, easy to drink, long, good acidity.

Colomina 2014 RD
tempranillo, pinot noir, syrah

89

Colour: raspberry rose. Nose: elegant, red berry notes, floral, fragrant herbs. Palate: light-bodied, flavourful, good acidity, long.

Juna 2014 B
garnacha blanca, sauvignon blanc, chardonnay

86

Mas García Muret 2012 T
cabernet sauvignon, tempranillo

88

Colour: very deep cherry, garnet rim. Nose: expressive, balsamic herbs, balanced, smoky. Palate: flavourful, round tannins, spicy.

Muriac 2011 T
syrah

91

Colour: cherry, garnet rim. Nose: spicy, ripe fruit, creamy oak, sweet spices. Palate: flavourful, smoky aftertaste, ripe fruit.

Muriac 2012 T
syrah

90

Colour: bright cherry. Nose: ripe fruit, sweet spices, creamy oak, expressive. Palate: flavourful, fruity, round tannins.

Unua 2011 T
tempranillo

89

Colour: cherry, garnet rim. Nose: ripe fruit, wild herbs, earthy notes, spicy, balsamic herbs. Palate: balanced, flavourful, long, balsamic.

Unua 2013 T
tempranillo

89

Colour: very deep cherry, garnet rim. Nose: expressive, complex, balsamic herbs, balanced. Palate: full, flavourful, round tannins.

CELLER MATALLONGA

Raval, 8
25411 Fulleda (Lleida)
☎: +34 660 840 791
matallonga60@gmail.com
cellermatallonga.blogspot.com

Escorça 2013 B
macabeo, chardonnay

86

Matallonga Selecció 2012 T
ull de llebre, syrah

86

Vi del Banya 2013 T
ull de llebre, merlot, cabernet sauvignon

87

Colour: very deep cherry, garnet rim. Nose: expressive, balsamic herbs, balanced. Palate: flavourful, round tannins, easy to drink.

CÉRVOLES CELLER

Avda. Les Garrigues
25471 La Pobla de Cèrvoles (Lleida)
☎: +34 973 580 200
Fax: +34 973 718 312
info@cervoles.com
www.cervoles.com

Cérvoles 2014 BFB
macabeo, chardonnay

89

Colour: bright straw. Nose: ripe fruit, powerfull, toasty, pattiserie. Palate: flavourful, fruity, spicy, toasty, long.

Cérvoles Colors 2013 T
tempranillo, garnacha, cabernet sauvignon, merlot, syrah

87

Colour: bright cherry. Nose: ripe fruit, creamy oak, fine reductive notes. Palate: flavourful, fruity, toasty.

Cérvoles Colors Blanc 2014 B
macabeo, chardonnay

87

Colour: bright straw. Nose: balanced, medium intensity, wild herbs. Palate: fruity, balanced, fine bitter notes.

Cérvoles Estrats 2009 T
cabernet sauvignon, tempranillo, merlot, garnacha

93

Colour: cherry, garnet rim. Nose: mineral, spicy, toasty, fruit liqueur notes. Palate: flavourful, ripe fruit, long, good acidity, balanced.

Cérvoles Negre 2009 T
cabernet sauvignon, tempranillo, merlot, garnacha

90

Colour: bright cherry. Nose: sweet spices, creamy oak, overripe fruit. Palate: flavourful, fruity, toasty, round tannins.

CLOS PONS

Ctra. LV-7011, km. 4,5
25155 L'Albagés (Lérida)
☎: +34 973 070 737
Fax: +34 973 070 738
clospons@grup-pons.com
www.clospons.com

Clos Pons 811 2011 TR
100% marcelan

92 ♣

Colour: deep cherry, garnet rim. Nose: balsamic herbs, scrubland, ripe fruit, cocoa bean. Palate: flavourful, complex, round tannins. Personality.

Clos Pons Alges 2011 TC
garnacha, syrah, tempranillo

88

Colour: cherry, garnet rim. Nose: creamy oak, red berry notes, balanced, ripe fruit, scrubland. Palate: flavourful, spicy, round tannins.

Clos Pons Jan Petit 2013 T
garnacha, syrah

86

Clos Pons Roc de Foc 2012 B
100% macabeo

90

Colour: bright yellow. Nose: expressive, dried herbs, ripe fruit, spicy. Palate: flavourful, fruity, good acidity, balanced.

Clos Pons Roc Nu 2010 TR
garnacha, cabernet sauvignon, tempranillo

92 ♣

Colour: bright cherry, garnet rim. Nose: expressive, balanced, scrubland, spicy, ripe fruit. Palate: fruity, good structure.

Clos Pons Sisquella 2013 B
garnacha blanca, albariño

90

Colour: bright straw. Nose: white flowers, fine lees, dried herbs, ripe fruit, citrus fruit. Palate: flavourful, fruity, good acidity, elegant.

COSTERS DEL SIÓ

Ctra. de Agramunt, Km. 4,2
25600 Balaguer (Lérida)
☎: +34 973 424 062
Fax: +34 973 424 112
administracio@costersio.com
www.costersio.com

Alto Siós 2011 T
60% syrah, 30% tempranillo, 10% garnacha

92

Colour: deep cherry, garnet rim. Nose: ripe fruit, fruit preserve, scrubland, spicy, complex. Palate: good structure, round tannins.

Siós Blanc de Noirs 2012 BR Reserva
pinot noir

90

Colour: bright yellow. Nose: dried flowers, dried herbs, dry nuts. Palate: balanced, fine bitter notes, long.

Siós Cau del Gat 2013 T
85% syrah, 15% garnacha

90

Colour: cherry, garnet rim. Nose: creamy oak, red berry notes, fresh fruit, balanced. Palate: flavourful, spicy, smoky aftertaste.

Siós Rosé 2012 BR Reserva
pinot noir

91

Colour: coppery red, bright. Nose: floral, expressive, balanced, fine lees. Palate: fresh, fruity, balanced, fine bitter notes.

L'OLIVERA

La Plana, s/n
25268 Vallbona de les Monges (Lleida)
☎: +34 973 330 276
Fax: +34 973 330 276
olivera@olivera.org
www.olivera.org

Agaliu 2013 BFB
macabeo

88 ♣

Colour: bright straw. Nose: creamy oak, pattiserie, sweet spices, ripe fruit. Palate: correct, toasty, easy to drink.

Blanc de Marges 2012 BFB
parellada, xarel.lo, malvasía

88 ♣

Colour: yellow. Nose: fragrant herbs, dried flowers, ripe fruit. Palate: flavourful, fruity, good acidity, balanced.

Blanc de Roure 2013 B
macabeo, parellada, chardonnay

86 ♣

Blanc de Serè 2014 B
macabeo, parellada, chardonnay

85

Eixaders 2013 BFB
chardonnay

89

Colour: bright yellow. Nose: expressive, dried herbs, ripe fruit, spicy. Palate: flavourful, fruity, good acidity, balanced.

Missenyora 2013 BFB
macabeo

88

Colour: yellow. Nose: ripe fruit, toasty, sweet spices, medium intensity. Palate: fruity, spicy, toasty, good finish.

Naltres 2013 T
garnacha, cabernet sauvignon, monastrell, trepat

90

Colour: cherry, garnet rim. Nose: ripe fruit, wild herbs, earthy notes, spicy, balsamic herbs. Palate: balanced, flavourful, long, balsamic.

Rasim Vi Pansit Naturalmente Dulce 2013 B
malvasía, garnacha blanca, xarel.lo

90

Colour: bright yellow. Nose: balsamic herbs, honeyed notes, floral, expressive. Palate: rich, fruity, powerful, flavourful, good acidity.

Rasim Vimadur Dulce 2012 T Barrica
garnacha, touriga nacional

90

Colour: cherry, garnet rim. Nose: fruit preserve, spicy, warm, fruit liqueur notes, expressive. Palate: powerful, flavourful, sweet, rich, balsamic.

Vallisbona 89 2011 BFB
chardonnay

93

Colour: bright yellow. Nose: white flowers, dried herbs, ripe fruit, candied fruit, citrus fruit, creamy oak, sweet spices. Palate: flavourful, fruity, good acidity, elegant.

LAGRAVERA

Ctra. de Tamarite, 9
25120 Alfarrás (Lérida)
☎: +34 973 761 374
Fax: +34 973 760 218
info@lagravera.com
www.lagravera.com

La Pell Puresa Blanc 2013 B
60% garnacha blanca, 40% xarel.lo

91

Colour: bright straw. Nose: balanced, expressive, ripe fruit. Palate: balanced, good acidity, fine bitter notes, complex.

La Pell Puresa Negre 2013 T
60% monastrell, 25% picapoll, 15% otras

91

Colour: light cherry. Nose: powerfull, ripe fruit, mineral, spicy, faded flowers, varnish, violets. Palate: long, round tannins, balsamic.

La Pell Saviesa Blanc 2013 BFB
60% macabeo, 35% grumet, 5% otras

90

Colour: bright straw. Nose: expressive, faded flowers, balanced, fine lees. Palate: flavourful, full, long, spicy, balsamic.

La Pell Saviesa Negre 2013 T
100% garnacha

93

Colour: light cherry. Nose: fresh, expressive, red berry notes, ripe fruit, scrubland. Palate: balanced, long, round tannins.

Laltre 2014 T
85% monastrell, 15% garnacha

84

Ònra Blanc 2014 B
60% garnacha blanca, 25% chenin blanc, 15% sauvignon blanc

87

Colour: bright straw. Nose: faded flowers, dry nuts, balanced. Palate: correct, fine bitter notes, balsamic, good acidity.

Ónra Molta Honra Blanc 2013 BFB
80% garnacha blanca, 20% sauvignon blanc

93

Colour: yellow. Nose: ripe fruit, powerfull, toasty, smoky, sweet spices. Palate: flavourful, fruity, spicy, toasty, long.

Ónra Molta Honra Negre 2012 T
75% garnacha, 25% cabernet sauvignon

90

Colour: cherry, garnet rim. Nose: dark chocolate, fruit preserve, sweet spices, pattiserie. Palate: fruity, flavourful, round tannins.

Ònra Negre 2012 T
75% garnacha, 15% merlot, 10% cabernet sauvignon

86

Ònra Vi de Pedra B
garnacha blanca

93

Colour: bright yellow. Nose: powerfull, candied fruit, sweet spices, creamy oak, pattiserie. Palate: flavourful, sweet, fruity, good acidity, long, balsamic.

MAS BLANCH I JOVÉ

Paratge Llinars. Pol. Ind. 9- Parc. 129
25471 La Pobla de Cérvoles (Lleida)
☎: +34 973 050 018
Fax: +34 973 391 151
sara@masblanchijove.com
www.masblanchijove.com

Petit Blanc Saó 2014 B
garnacha, macabeo

86

Petit Saó 2012 T
tempranillo, garnacha, cabernet sauvignon

88

Colour: cherry, garnet rim. Nose: creamy oak, balanced, ripe fruit, dried herbs. Palate: flavourful, spicy, round tannins, balsamic.

Saó Abrivat 2010 TC
tempranillo, garnacha, cabernet sauvignon

89

Colour: cherry, garnet rim. Nose: ripe fruit, wild herbs, earthy notes, spicy, balsamic herbs. Palate: balanced, flavourful, long, balsamic.

Saó Blanc 2013 B
garnacha, macabeo

88

Colour: bright straw. Nose: white flowers, dried herbs, mineral. Palate: flavourful, fruity, good acidity, round.

Saó Expressiu 2009 T
garnacha, cabernet sauvignon, tempranillo

91

Colour: cherry, garnet rim. Nose: ripe fruit, wild herbs, earthy notes, spicy, balsamic herbs. Palate: balanced, flavourful, long, balsamic.

Saó Rosat 2014 RD
garnacha, syrah

85

RAIMAT

Ctra. Lleida, s/n
25111 Raimat (Lleida)
☎: +34 973 724 000
info@raimat.es
www.raimat.com

Ánima de Raimat 2012 T
cabernet sauvignon, tempranillo, syrah

87

Colour: cherry, garnet rim. Nose: toasty, smoky, ripe fruit. Palate: correct, spicy, round tannins.

Ánima de Raimat 2014 B
chardonnay, xarel.lo, albariño

87

Colour: bright straw. Nose: white flowers, fresh fruit, fragrant herbs, expressive. Palate: flavourful, fruity, good acidity, balanced.

Castell de Raimat Chardonnay 2014 B
100% chardonnay

88

Colour: straw. Nose: medium intensity, ripe fruit, floral. Palate: correct, easy to drink, good acidity, fine bitter notes.

Castell de Raimat Xarel.lo Chardonnay 2013 B
50% chardonnay, 50% xarel.lo

90

Colour: bright yellow. Nose: white flowers, ripe fruit. Palate: rich, flavourful, correct, balanced, fine bitter notes.

Clamor 2013 T
cabernet sauvignon, tempranillo, merlot, syrah

86

Raimat 100 2013 B
52% chardonnay, 48% xarel.lo

92

Colour: bright yellow. Nose: white flowers, fragrant herbs, expressive, sweet spices, creamy oak. Palate: flavourful, fruity, good acidity, balanced.

Raimat Abadía 2012 TC
cabernet sauvignon, tempranillo

86

Raimat Abadía 2014 RD
tempranillo, cabernet sauvignon

88

Colour: onion pink. Nose: elegant, red berry notes, floral, fragrant herbs. Palate: light-bodied, flavourful, good acidity.

Raimat Terra Chardonnay 2014 B
chardonnay

89 

Colour: bright yellow. Nose: expressive, dried herbs, ripe fruit, spicy. Palate: flavourful, fruity, good acidity, balanced.

RUBIÓ DE SÓLS
Partida de Rubió de Baix
25737 Foradada (Lérida)
☎: +34 690 872 356
juditsogas@gmail.com

Xarel 15 2013 B
100% xarel.lo

88

Colour: bright straw, greenish rim. Nose: white flowers, dried flowers, fresh fruit, smoky. Palate: easy to drink, smoky aftertaste, toasty.

TERRER DE PALLARS
Del Vent 28
25655 Figuerola d'Orcau (Lleida)
☎: +34 616 701 080
nuria@terrerdepallars.com
www.terrerdepallars.com

Conca de Tremp 2013 T
55% merlot, 45% cabernet sauvignon

90

Colour: bright cherry. Nose: powerfull, balanced, ripe fruit, fragrant herbs, spicy. Palate: balanced, round tannins, balsamic.

TOMÁS CUSINÉ
Plaça Sant Sebastià, 13
25457 El Vilosell (Lleida)
☎: +34 973 176 029
Fax: +34 973 175 945
info@tomascusine.com
www.tomascusine.com

Auzells 2014 B
macabeo, sauvignon blanc, riesling, chardonnay, albariño, müller thurgau

92

Colour: bright yellow. Nose: expressive, dried herbs, ripe fruit, spicy. Palate: flavourful, fruity, good acidity, balanced.

Finca Comabarra 2011 TGR
cabernet sauvignon, garnacha, syrah

93

Colour: cherry, garnet rim. Nose: red berry notes, ripe fruit, fragrant herbs, spicy, toasty, creamy oak, mineral. Palate: powerful, flavourful, balsamic, balanced.

Geol 2012 TR
merlot, cabernet sauvignon, garnacha, samsó

93

Colour: cherry, garnet rim. Nose: mineral, expressive, spicy. Palate: flavourful, ripe fruit, long, good acidity.

Llebre 2013 T
tempranillo, garnacha, merlot, samsó

89

Colour: cherry, purple rim. Nose: powerfull, ripe fruit, spicy. Palate: powerful, fruity, unctuous.

Vilosell 2013 T
tempranillo, syrah, merlot, cabernet sauvignon, garnacha, samsó

90

Colour: bright cherry. Nose: ripe fruit, sweet spices, creamy oak, expressive. Palate: flavourful, fruity, toasty.

VALL DE BALDOMAR
Ctra. de Alós de Balaguer, s/n
25737 Baldomar (Lleida)
☎: +34 973 402 205
info@valldebaldomar.com
www.valldebaldomar.com

Baldomà Selecció 2013 T
merlot, cabernet sauvignon, tempranillo

86

Cristiari 2014 B
muller, thurgau, incroxio

87

Colour: bright straw. Nose: white flowers, fresh fruit, balanced. Palate: easy to drink, correct, balanced, fine bitter notes.

Cristiari 2014 RD
merlot, cabernet sauvignon

87

Colour: rose, purple rim. Nose: red berry notes, floral, expressive. Palate: powerful, fruity, fresh.

Cristiari d'Alòs Merlot 2013 T Roble
merlot

85

Petit Baldoma 2014 B
macabeo, riesling, gewürztraminer

85

VINYA ELS VILARS

Camí de Puiggrós, s/n
25140 Arbeca (Lleida)
☎: +34 973 149 144
Fax: +34 973 160 719
vinyaelsvilars@vinyaelsvilars.com
www.vinyaelsvilars.com

Gerar 2011 T
merlot

87

Colour: deep cherry, purple rim. Nose: creamy oak, toasty, ripe fruit, balsamic herbs. Palate: balanced, spicy, long.

Leix 2011 T
syrah

86

Nena 2014 RD
syrah

86

Quim 2014 B
macabeo

86

Tallat de Lluna 2011 T
syrah

89

Colour: cherry, garnet rim. Nose: ripe fruit, spicy, creamy oak, complex. Palate: flavourful, toasty, round tannins.

Vilars 2010 TC
syrah, merlot

86

Vilars 2012 T Roble
syrah, merlot

85

DO. EL HIERRO

CONSEJO REGULADOR

Calle el Hoyo, 1
38911 Municipio de La Frontera (El Hierro)
☎: +34 922 559 622 - Fax: +34 922 559 622
@: doelhierro@hotmail.com
www.doelhierro.es

LOCATION:

On the island of El Hierro, part of the Canary Islands. The production area covers the whole island, although the main growing regions are Valle del Golfo, Sabinosa, El Pinar and Echedo.

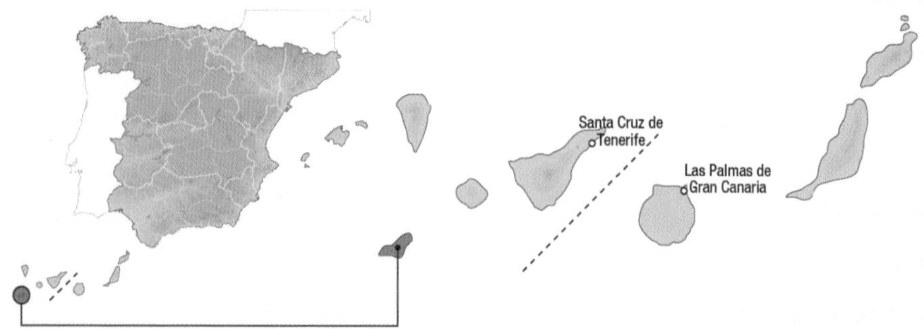

GRAPE VARIETIES:

WHITE: Verijadiego (majority with 50% of all white varieties), Listán Blanca, Bremajuelo, Uval (Gual), Pedro Ximénez, Baboso and Moscatel.
RED: Listán Negro, Negramoll, Baboso Negro and Verijadiego Negro.

FIGURES:

Vineyard surface: 120 – **Wine-Growers:** 209 – **Wineries:** 9 – **2012 Harvest rating:** Very Good – **Production 13:** 206,778 litres – **Market percentages:** 100% National.

SOIL:

Volcanic in origin, with a good water retention and storage capacity. Although the vineyards were traditionally cultivated in the higher regions, at present most of them are found at low altitudes, resulting in an early ripening of the grapes.

CLIMATE:

Fairly mild in general, although higher levels of humidity are recorded in high mountainous regions. Rainfall is relatively low.

VINTAGE RATING

PEÑÍNGUIDE

2010	2011	2012	2013	2014
VERY GOOD	N/A	N/A	N/A	N/A

SDAD. COOPERATIVA DEL CAMPO "FRONTERA" VINÍCOLA INSULAR

El Matorral, s/n
38911 Frontera - El Hierro (Tenerife)
☎: +34 922 556 016
Fax: +34 922 556 042
coopfrontera@cooperativafrontera.com
www.cooperativafrontera.com

Gran Salmor Dulce 2008 B Reserva
verijadiego blanco, bremajuelo

93

Colour: light mahogany. Nose: acetaldehyde, pungent, varnish, aged wood nuances, creamy oak. Palate: powerful, flavourful, spicy, long, balanced.

Viña Frontera 2014 B
verijadiego blanco, listán blanco

86

Viña Frontera Afrutado 2014 B
verijadiego blanco, listán blanco, vidueño

84

Viña Frontera Afrutado Selección 2014 B
verijadiego blanco, listán blanco

88

Colour: bright yellow. Nose: powerfull, candied fruit, dried herbs. Palate: flavourful, sweet, ripe fruit, good acidity.

Viña Frontera Baboso 2013 T
baboso negro

88

Colour: very deep cherry, garnet rim. Nose: expressive, complex, mineral, balsamic herbs, balanced, fruit preserve. Palate: full, flavourful.

Viña Frontera Dulce 2005 T
baboso negro, verijadiego

91

Colour: bright cherry, garnet rim. Nose: acetaldehyde, varnish, candied fruit. Palate: fruity, flavourful, sweet.

Viña Frontera Dulce 2012 T
verijadiego

87

Colour: light cherry. Nose: fruit liqueur notes, fragrant herbs, spicy. Palate: spicy, long, toasty.

Viña Frontera Tradicional 2013 T
listán negro, verijadiego, baboso negro

85

DO. EMPORDÀ

CONSEJO REGULADOR

Avda. Marignane, 2
17600 Figueres (Girona)
☎:+34 972 507 513 - Fax: +34 972 510 058
@: info@doemporda.cat
www.doemporda.cat

LOCATION:

In the far north west of Catalonia, in the province of Girona. The production area covers 40 municipal areas and is situated the slopes of the Rodes and Alberes mountain ranges forming an arch which leads from Cape Creus to what is known as the Garrotxa d'Empordà.

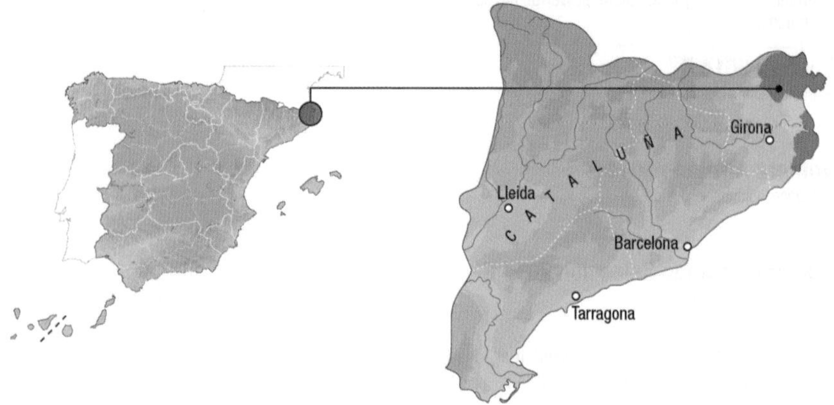

GRAPE VARIETIES:

WHITE:Preferred: Garnacha Blanca, Macabeo (Viura) and Moscatel de Alejandría.
Authorized: Xarel.lo, Chardonnay, Gewürztraminer, Malvasía, Moscatel de Gra Petit, Picapoll Blanc and Sauvignon Blanc.
RED:Preferred: Cariñena and Garnacha Tinta.
Authorized: Cabernet Sauvignon, Cabernet Franc, Merlot, Monastrell, Tempranillo, Syrah, Garnacha Roja (lledoner roig) and Garnacha Peluda.

FIGURES:

Vineyard surface: 1,795 – **Wine-Growers:** 315 – **Wineries:** 50 – **2014 Harvest rating:** Good – **Production 14:** 5,664,200 litres – **Market percentages:** 83% National - 17% International.

SOIL:

The soil is in general poor, of a granitic nature in the mountainous areas, alluvial in the plains and slaty on the coastal belt.

CLIMATE:

The climatology is conditioned by the 'Tramontana', a strong north wind which affects the vineyards. Furthermore, the winters are mild, with hardly any frost, and the summers hot, although somewhat tempered by the sea breezes. The average rainfall is around 600 mm.

VINTAGE RATING

PEÑÍNGUIDE

2010	2011	2012	2013	2014
VERY GOOD	VERY GOOD	GOOD	GOOD	GOOD

AGRÍCOLA DE GARRIGUELLA

Ctra. de Roses, s/n
17780 Garriguella (Gerona)
☎: +34 972 530 002
Fax: +34 972 531 747
info@cooperativagarriguella.com
www.cooperativagarriguella.com

Dinarells Blanc 2014 B
macabeo, moscatel, garnacha blanca

82

Dinarells Negre 2014 T
garnacha, cabernet sauvignon, merlot

84

Dinarells Rosat 2014 RD
merlot, garnacha, syrah

86

Dolç de Gerisena 2005 Vino de licor
garnacha, cariñena

91

Colour: mahogany. Nose: fruit liqueur notes, acetaldehyde, varnish, dark chocolate, creamy oak. Palate: powerful, flavourful, long.

Essencia de Gerisena Dulce 2013 B
moscatel, moscatel de alejandría

89

Colour: bright yellow. Nose: powerfull, candied fruit, dried herbs. Palate: flavourful, sweet, ripe fruit, good acidity.

Garriguella Garnatxa D'Empordá Ambré Dulce 2008 Vino del licor
garnacha rosada

85

Garriguella Garnatxa D'Empordá Robí Dulce Natural 2009 T
garnacha

86

Garriguella Moscatel D'Empordá Dulce 2013 B
moscatel

84

Gerisena Blanc 2014 B
garnacha blanca

88

Colour: bright straw. Nose: white flowers, dried herbs, candied fruit, citrus fruit, sweet spices. Palate: flavourful, fruity, good acidity.

Gerisena Rosat 2014 RD
garnacha rosada

88

Colour: onion pink. Nose: elegant, red berry notes, floral, fragrant herbs. Palate: light-bodied, flavourful, good acidity, long, spicy.

Gerisena Sel.lecció 2013 T
cabernet sauvignon, merlot, garnacha

90

Colour: deep cherry, purple rim. Nose: creamy oak, toasty, ripe fruit, balsamic herbs. Palate: balanced, spicy, long.

Puntils 2012 T
cabernet sauvignon, garnacha, merlot

86

Puntils Blanc 2014 B
garnacha blanca, moscatel

84

Puntils Negre 2014 T
cabernet sauvignon, garnacha, merlot

86

Puntils Rosat 2014 RD
garnacha, syrah

85

Tramuntanart Blanc 2014 B
garnacha blanca, moscatel

84

Tramuntanart Negre 2014 T
cabernet sauvignon, garnacha, merlot

85

Tramuntanart Rosat 2014 RD
garnacha, syrah

87

Colour: rose, purple rim. Nose: red berry notes, floral, expressive. Palate: powerful, fruity, fresh.

AV BODEGUERS

Sant Baldiri, 23
17781 Vilamaniscle (Girona)
☎: +34 872 004 229
info@avbodeguers.com
www.avbodeguers.com

Nereus 2010 T
merlot, syrah, garnacha

86

Petit Suneus 2013 T
merlot, garnacha

87

Colour: light cherry. Nose: fruit expression, fruit liqueur notes, fragrant herbs. Palate: spicy, toasty, balsamic.

Suneus 2013 T
garnacha, syrah

89

Colour: deep cherry, purple rim. Nose: ripe fruit, balsamic herbs, mineral. Palate: balanced, spicy, long.

Suneus 2014 B
garnacha blanca

87

Colour: bright straw. Nose: white flowers, fresh fruit, fragrant herbs. Palate: flavourful, fruity, good acidity.

Suneus 2014 RD
merlot

83

BODEGAS GELAMÀ

Estació, 6
17493 Vilajuiga (Girona)
☎: +34 666 763 540
info@gelama.cat
www.gelama.cat

Gelama 2013 ESP
100% macabeo

86

Gelama Macabeu 2014 B
100% macabeo

89

Colour: bright straw. Nose: white flowers, fresh fruit, fragrant herbs, expressive. Palate: flavourful, fruity, good acidity, balanced.

Gelama Xirivilla 2014 T
cariñena, merlot

82

BODEGAS MAS VIDA

Afores, 24
17741 Cistella (Gerona)
☎: +34 659 548 512
info@bodegasmasvida.com
www.bodegasmasvida.com

Mas Vida 117 2013 B Barrica
chardonnay

85

Mas Vida 23 2012 T
cabernet sauvignon, merlot, tempranillo

84

Mas Vida 32 2010 T Roble
merlot

84

BODEGAS TROBAT

Castelló, 10
17780 Garriguella (Girona)
☎: +34 972 530 092
Fax: +34 972 552 530
bodegas.trobat@bmark.es
www.bodegastrobat.com

Amat Blanc 2014 B
xarel.lo

83

Amat Merlot 2014 RD
merlot

88

Colour: raspberry rose. Nose: red berry notes, floral, fragrant herbs. Palate: light-bodied, flavourful, good acidity, long, spicy.

Amat Negre Coupage 2012 TC
merlot, garnacha, syrah

84

Amat Sauvignon Blanc 2014 B
sauvignon blanc

85

Noble Chardonnay 2014 B
chardonnay

84

Noble Negre 2011 T
cabernet sauvignon, syrah, samsó

88

Colour: cherry, garnet rim. Nose: ripe fruit, spicy, creamy oak. Palate: flavourful, toasty.

CASTILLO DE CAPMANY

Plaza del Fort, 5
17750 Capmany (Girona)
☎: +34 972 549 043
joseluismolldealba@gmail.com
www.castillodecapmany.com

Castillo Olivares 2005 TR
cabernet sauvignon, merlot, garnacha, syrah

80

Moll de Alba 2003 TR
cabernet sauvignon, merlot, garnacha, syrah

85

CASTILLO PERELADA

Pl. del Carmen, 1
17491 Perelada (Girona)
☎: +34 972 538 011
Fax: +34 972 538 277
perelada@castilloperelada.com
www.castilloperelada.com

Aires de Garbet 2012 T
100% garnacha

92

Colour: cherry, garnet rim. Nose: ripe fruit, wild herbs, earthy notes, spicy, balsamic herbs. Palate: balanced, flavourful, long, balsamic, elegant.

Aires de Garbet 2013 T
100% garnacha

93

Colour: cherry, garnet rim. Nose: red berry notes, ripe fruit, fragrant herbs, spicy, creamy oak, mineral. Palate: powerful, flavourful, balsamic, balanced.

Castillo de Perelada 3 Fincas 2012 TC
46% garnacha, 27% merlot, 13% samsó, 7% syrah, 4% ull de llebre, 3% cabernet sauvignon

85

Castillo de Perelada 5 Fincas 2011 TR
40% cabernet sauvignon, 17% samsó, 17% garnacha, 13% syrah, 12% merlot, 1% monastrell

90

Colour: cherry, garnet rim. Nose: spicy, ripe fruit, creamy oak. Palate: flavourful, ripe fruit, long, good acidity, balanced, fine tannins.

Castillo de Perelada 5 Fincas 2012 TR
31% cabernet sauvignon, 27% syrah, 14% merlot, 12% garnacha, 9% samsó, 7% monastrell, tempranillo

89

Colour: cherry, garnet rim. Nose: red berry notes, ripe fruit, spicy, creamy oak, complex. Palate: flavourful, toasty, balanced.

Castillo de Perelada Ex Ex 11 2013 T
30% cariñena, 30% garnacha, 20% macabeo, 20% garnacha blanca

93

Colour: light cherry. Nose: fruit liqueur notes, fragrant herbs, spicy, creamy oak, earthy notes. Palate: balanced, spicy, long, elegant.

Castillo Perelada Collection Blanc 2014 B
67% chardonnay, 33% sauvignon blanc

91

Colour: bright yellow. Nose: floral, ripe fruit, honeyed notes, fragrant herbs. Palate: flavourful, rich, long, balanced, elegant.

Castillo Perelada Collection Rosé 2014 RD
75% cabernet sauvignon, 19% syrah, 6% garnacha roja

89

Colour: onion pink. Nose: elegant, red berry notes, floral, fragrant herbs. Palate: light-bodied, flavourful, good acidity, long, spicy.

Castillo Perelada Finca Espolla 2011 T
75% syrah, 20% cabernet sauvignon, 5% garnacha

91

Colour: cherry, garnet rim. Nose: ripe fruit, wild herbs, spicy, balanced, expressive. Palate: flavourful, complex, elegant, fine tannins.

Castillo Perelada Finca Garbet 2007 T
100% syrah

94

Colour: pale ruby, brick rim edge. Nose: elegant, spicy, fine reductive notes, tobacco, ripe fruit. Palate: spicy, fine tannins, elegant, long.

Castillo Perelada Finca Garbet 2009 T
60% syrah, 40% cabernet sauvignon

93

Colour: cherry, garnet rim. Nose: ripe fruit, spicy, creamy oak, complex. Palate: flavourful, toasty, round tannins, balanced, elegant.

Castillo Perelada Finca Malaveïna 2011 T
80% merlot, 15% cabernet sauvignon, 5% cabernet franc

92

Colour: cherry, garnet rim. Nose: balanced, complex, ripe fruit, spicy, mineral. Palate: good structure, flavourful, round tannins, balanced.

Castillo Perelada Finca Malaveïna 2012 T
40% cabernet sauvignon, 23% merlot, 17% cabernet franc, 13% syrah, 7% garnacha

91

Colour: very deep cherry, garnet rim. Nose: expressive, complex, mineral, balsamic herbs, dry stone. Palate: full, flavourful, complex, elegant.

Castillo Perelada Garnatxa de l'Empordà Dulce Natural
80% garnacha roja, 20% garnacha blanca

92

Colour: iodine, amber rim. Nose: elegant, sweet spices, acetaldehyde, dry nuts. Palate: full, dry, spicy, long, fine bitter notes, complex.

Castillo Perelada Gran Claustro 2010 T
30% cabernet sauvignon, 29% merlot, 19% tempranillo, 13% syrah, 9% garnacha

93

Colour: cherry, garnet rim. Nose: balanced, complex, ripe fruit, spicy, fine reductive notes, balsamic herbs. Palate: good structure, flavourful, round tannins, balanced.

Castillo Perelada La Garriga 2011 T
100% samsó

91

Colour: cherry, garnet rim. Nose: creamy oak, toasty, ripe fruit, balsamic herbs, earthy notes. Palate: balanced, spicy, long.

Perelada Cigonyes 2013 T
61% garnacha, 32% syrah, 5% cabernet sauvignon, 2% merlot

87

Colour: bright cherry. Nose: ripe fruit, sweet spices, creamy oak. Palate: flavourful, fruity.

Perelada Cigonyes Blanc 2014 B
91% macabeo, 9% sauvignon blanc

87

Colour: bright straw. Nose: citrus fruit, candied fruit, dried herbs. Palate: fresh, fruity, flavourful.

Perelada Cigonyes Rosé 2014 RD
64% garnacha, 28% cabernet sauvignon, 8% samsó

87

Colour: raspberry rose. Nose: red berry notes, floral, expressive. Palate: powerful, fruity, fresh.

Perelada Garnatxa Blanca Dulce Natural 2014 B
100% garnacha blanca

88

Colour: bright yellow. Nose: fragrant herbs, floral, citrus fruit, fresh fruit. Palate: fresh, fruity, flavourful.

Perelada Jardins Blanc 2014 B
66% macabeo, 20% sauvignon blanc, 12% garnacha blanca, 2% chardonnay

86

Perelada Jardins Negre 2014 T
73% garnacha, 27% cabernet sauvignon

87

Colour: cherry, purple rim. Nose: expressive, fresh fruit, red berry notes, floral. Palate: flavourful, fruity, good acidity.

Perelada Jardins Rosé 2014 RD
42% syrah, 30% merlot, 28% garnacha

85

Perelada La Garriga 2013 B
55% chardonnay, 30% cariñena blanca, 15% sauvignon blanc

91

Colour: bright yellow. Nose: ripe fruit, powerfull, toasty, aged wood nuances, pattiserie. Palate: flavourful, fruity, spicy, toasty, long.

Perelada Rosé 2014 RD
41% cabernet sauvignon, 28% merlot, 28% ull de llebre, 3% garnacha

86

CELLER ARCHÉ PAGÈS
Sant Climent, 31
17750 Capmany (Girona)
☎: +34 626 647 251
bonfill@capmany.com
www.cellerarchepages.com

Bonfill 2009 T
garnacha, cariñena

88

Colour: very deep cherry, garnet rim. Nose: mineral, balsamic herbs, balanced. Palate: full, flavourful, harsh oak tannins.

Cartesius Blanc 2013 B
garnacha blanca

87

Colour: bright yellow. Nose: ripe fruit, powerfull, toasty, aged wood nuances. Palate: flavourful, fruity, spicy, toasty, long.

Cartesius Negre 2011 T
garnacha, merlot, cabernet sauvignon

88

Colour: cherry, garnet rim. Nose: ripe fruit, wild herbs, earthy notes. Palate: balanced, flavourful, long.

Notenom 2014 T
garnacha

88

Colour: light cherry. Nose: red berry notes, floral, balsamic herbs. Palate: powerful, fresh, fruity.

Sàtirs Blanc 2014 B
macabeo

87

Colour: straw. Nose: medium intensity, ripe fruit, floral, fragrant herbs. Palate: correct, easy to drink.

Sàtirs Negre 2010 T
garnacha, cariñena, cabernet sauvignon

85

Sàtirs Rosat 2014 RD
80% garnacha, 20% cabernet sauvignon

85

Ull de Serp La Closa Carinyena 2011 T
cariñena

91

Colour: cherry, garnet rim. Nose: fruit liqueur notes, earthy notes, spicy. Palate: powerful, flavourful, balsamic, spicy, balanced.

Ull de Serp La Closa Macabeu 2013 B
macabeo

90

Colour: bright yellow. Nose: fragrant herbs, candied fruit, spicy, floral, dry stone. Palate: fresh, fruity, flavourful, balanced.

Ull de Serp La Cumella 2011 T
garnacha

90

Colour: ruby red. Nose: ripe fruit, wild herbs, earthy notes, spicy, balsamic herbs. Palate: balanced, flavourful, long, balsamic.

CELLER BELL-LLOC
Camino de Bell-Lloc, s/n
17230 Palamós (Girona)
☎: +34 972 316 203
info@fincabell-lloc.com
www.fincabell-lloc.com

Bell-Lloc 2010 TC
23% garnacha, 10% cariñena, 40% cabernet sauvignon, 17% cabernet franc, 10% monastrell

88

Colour: pale ruby, brick rim edge. Nose: ripe fruit, wild herbs, earthy notes, spicy, balsamic herbs. Palate: balanced, flavourful, long.

Celler Bell-Lloc Blanc 2013 B
85% subirat parent, 15% xarel.lo

88

Colour: bright yellow. Nose: ripe fruit, candied fruit, citrus fruit, faded flowers, dried herbs, aged wood nuances. Palate: powerful, flavourful, ripe fruit.

CELLER CAN SAIS
Raval de Dalt, 10
17253 Vall-Llobrega (Girona)
☎: +34 647 443 873
correu@cellercansais.com
www.cellercansais.com

CanSais Expressió 2011 T
garnacha

84

CanSais Mestral 2013 B
malvasía, xarel.lo, garnacha blanca

82

CanSais Migjorn 2013 T
ull de llebre, merlot, samsó, cabernet franc, garnacha

84

CanSais Privilegi Dulce 2010 T
garnacha

87

Colour: cherry, garnet rim. Nose: fruit preserve, spicy, fruit liqueur notes. Palate: powerful, flavourful, sweet, rich.

CanSais Selecció 2011 T
garnacha, merlot

85

CanSais Sonmi Rosado 2012 ESP
garnacha

85

CELLER COOPERATIU D'ESPOLLA

Ctra. Roses, s/n
17753 Espolla (Gerona)
☎: +34 972 563 178
Fax: +34 972 563 178
info@cellerespolla.com
www.cellerespolla.com

Clos de les Dòmines 2011 TR
merlot, cabernet sauvignon, cariñena

87

Colour: cherry, garnet rim. Nose: ripe fruit, wild herbs, spicy. Palate: flavourful, long, balsamic.

Clos de les Dòmines 2013 BFB
lladoner blanco, lladoner, cariñena blanca, moscatel de alejandría

88

Colour: bright yellow. Nose: ripe fruit, powerfull, aged wood nuances. Palate: flavourful, fruity, spicy.

Garnatxa D'Empordà Espolla Dulce Natural
lladoner blanco, lledoner roig

88

Colour: iodine, amber rim. Nose: complex, fruit liqueur notes, dried fruit, pattiserie, toasty. Palate: sweet, rich, unctuous.

Moscatell D'Empordà Espolla Dulce Natural 2014 B
lladoner blanco, lledoner roig

85

Panissars 2014 B
lladoner blanco, lladoner roig, sauvignon blanc

85

Panissars Negre 2013 T
lladoner, cariñena, merlot

86

Panissars Rosat 2014 RD
lladoner blanco, lladoner roig, merlot

87

Colour: rose, purple rim. Nose: red berry notes, floral, expressive. Palate: powerful, fruity, fresh.

Solera Garnatxa d'Empordà Vino Dulce Natural AM
lladoner blanco, lledoner roig

91

Colour: iodine, amber rim. Nose: powerfull, complex, dry nuts, creamy oak, varnish. Palate: rich, long, spicy.

SoliSerena Garnatxa d'Empordà Dulce Natural
lladoner blanco, lladoner roig

90

Colour: iodine, amber rim. Nose: acetaldehyde, fruit liqueur notes, dry nuts, sweet spices, creamy oak. Palate: powerful, flavourful, complex.

CELLER HUGAS DE BATLLE

Francesc Rivera, 28-30
17469 Colera (Gerona)
☎: +34 972 389 149
info@hugasdebatlle.com
www.cellerhugasdebatlle.com

30.70 2014 B
garnacha blanca, moscatel

88

Colour: bright straw. Nose: white flowers, fresh fruit, fragrant herbs, expressive. Palate: flavourful, fruity, good acidity, balanced.

Coma de Vaixell 2013 T
cabernet sauvignon, merlot, garnacha

89

Colour: deep cherry, purple rim. Nose: creamy oak, ripe fruit, wild herbs. Palate: balanced, spicy, long.

Coma Fredosa 2011 T
garnacha, cabernet sauvignon

88

Colour: cherry, garnet rim. Nose: red berry notes, ripe fruit, spicy, creamy oak, complex. Palate: flavourful, toasty.

Falguera 2009 TC
cariñena, garnacha

90

Colour: cherry, garnet rim. Nose: ripe fruit, wild herbs, earthy notes, spicy, balsamic herbs. Palate: balanced, flavourful, long.

CELLER LA VINYETA

Ctra. de Mollet de Peralada
a Masarac, s/n
17752 Mollet de Peralada (Girona)
☎: +34 630 405 118
celler@lavinyeta.es
www.lavinyeta.es

Heus Blanc 2014 B
macabeo, xarel.lo, moscatel, malvasía, garnacha blanca

86

Heus Negre 2014 T
samsó, merlot, syrah, garnacha

88

Colour: cherry, purple rim. Nose: floral, balsamic herbs, ripe fruit. Palate: powerful, fruity, flavourful.

Heus Rosat 2014 RD
samsó, merlot, syrah, garnacha

85

Llavors 2013 TC
cabernet sauvignon, cabernet franc, merlot, samsó, syrah

87

Colour: deep cherry. Nose: creamy oak, toasty, ripe fruit, balsamic herbs. Palate: balanced, spicy, long.

Llavors Blanc 2014 B
xarel.lo, macabeo

90

Colour: bright straw. Nose: white flowers, fine lees, dried herbs, ripe fruit, creamy oak. Palate: flavourful, fruity, good acidity, elegant.

Microvins Negre 2012 T
samsó

92

Colour: cherry, garnet rim. Nose: ripe fruit, wild herbs, earthy notes, spicy, balsamic herbs. Palate: balanced, flavourful, long.

Puntiapart 2013 T
cabernet sauvignon, samsó

88

Colour: cherry, garnet rim. Nose: ripe fruit, fruit preserve, balsamic herbs. Palate: powerful, flavourful, spicy.

Sols Dulce
garnacha blanca, garnacha roja

86

CELLER MARIÀ PAGÈS

Pujada, 6
17750 Capmany (Girona)
☎: +34 972 549 160
Fax: +34 972 549 160
info@cellermpages.com
www.cellermpages.com

Celler Marià Pagès Moscat d'Empordà Dulce 2013 B
moscatel de alejandría

90

Colour: golden. Nose: powerfull, honeyed notes, candied fruit, fragrant herbs, acetaldehyde. Palate: flavourful, sweet, fresh, fruity, good acidity, long.

Celler Marià Pagès ROSA-T 2014 RD
merlot, garnacha

85

Celler Marià Pagès Vinya de L'Hort 2014 B
garnacha blanca, moscatel

83

Marià Pagès Garnatxa d'Empordà Dulce 2013 B
garnacha, garnacha blanca

89

Colour: iodine, amber rim. Nose: honeyed notes, dried herbs, spicy. Palate: powerful, flavourful, spicy.

Marià Pagès Garnatxa d'Empordà Dulce Natural AM Reserva
garnacha, garnacha blanca

89

Colour: iodine, amber rim. Nose: powerfull, complex, dry nuts, creamy oak, varnish. Palate: rich, long, spicy.

Serrasagué 2007 TC
garnacha, merlot, cabernet sauvignon

83

Serrasagué 2014 B
garnacha blanca, moscatel

84

Serrasagué 2014 RD
garnacha, merlot, tempranillo

84

Serrasagué 2014 T
garnacha, merlot, cabernet sauvignon

86

Serrasagué Taca Negra 2011 T
garnacha, merlot, cabernet franc

87

Colour: cherry, garnet rim. Nose: ripe fruit, wild herbs, earthy notes, spicy, balsamic herbs. Palate: balanced, flavourful, long.

CELLER MARTÍ FABRA

Barrio Vic, 26
17751 Sant Climent Sescebes (Gerona)
☎: +34 972 563 011
Fax: +34 972 563 011
info@cellermartifabra.com

Flor D'Albera 2012 B
100% moscatel

88

Colour: bright yellow. Nose: expressive, dried herbs, ripe fruit, spicy. Palate: flavourful, fruity, good acidity.

L'Oratori 2013 T
garnacha, cariñena, cabernet sauvignon, syrah, merlot, tempranillo

87

Colour: deep cherry, garnet rim. Nose: dried herbs, characterful, ripe fruit, spicy, warm. Palate: correct, round tannins.

Lladoner 2014 RD
100% garnacha

87

Colour: brilliant rose. Nose: red berry notes, floral, fragrant herbs. Palate: powerful, fruity, fresh.

Martí Fabra Selecció Vinyes Velles 2013 T Roble
52% garnacha, 48% cariñena

90

Colour: deep cherry, garnet rim. Nose: scrubland, ripe fruit, cocoa bean. Palate: fruity, correct, balsamic.

Masía Carreras Blanc 2012 BFB
40% cariñena blanca, 30% cariñena rosada, 10% garnacha blanca, 10% garnacha rosada, 10% picapoll

91

Colour: bright straw. Nose: white flowers, fine lees, dried herbs, ripe fruit, candied fruit, citrus fruit. Palate: flavourful, fruity, good acidity, elegant.

Masía Carreras Negre 2013 T
100% cariñena

90

Colour: cherry, garnet rim. Nose: expressive, spicy, ripe fruit, fruit preserve. Palate: flavourful, long, balanced.

Masía Pairal Can Carreras Moscat Dulce Natural 2011 B
100% moscatel

91

Colour: bright yellow. Nose: balsamic herbs, honeyed notes, floral, sweet spices, expressive. Palate: rich, fruity, powerful, flavourful, elegant.

Verd Albera 2014 B
50% garnacha blanca, 20% moscatel, 10% garnacha rosada, 10% macabeo, 10% chardonnay

88

Colour: bright straw. Nose: white flowers, fresh fruit, fragrant herbs. Palate: flavourful, fruity, good acidity.

CELLER MARTÍN FAIXÓ

Ctra. de Cadaqués s/n
17488 Cadaqués (Girona)
☎: +34 682 107 142
tastos@cellermartinfaixo.com
www.saperafita.com

Cadac 2007 TR
cabernet sauvignon, garnacha

88

Colour: pale ruby, brick rim edge. Nose: ripe fruit, wild herbs, earthy notes. Palate: correct, spicy, long.

Perafita 2010 TC
cabernet sauvignon, garnacha, merlot

87

Colour: pale ruby, brick rim edge. Nose: spicy, fine reductive notes, wet leather, aged wood nuances, fruit liqueur notes. Palate: spicy, balanced.

Perafita Picapoll 2014 B
picapoll, moscatel

86 ♣

Perafita Rosat 2014 RD
garnacha, merlot

87 ♣

Colour: onion pink. Nose: elegant, red berry notes, floral, fragrant herbs. Palate: light-bodied, flavourful, good acidity, spicy.

CELLER MAS ROMEU

Gregal, 1
17495 Palau-Saverdera (Gerona)
☎: +34 687 744 056
info@cellermasromeu.cat
www.cellermasromeu.cat

Malesa 2014 B

89

Colour: bright straw. Nose: white flowers, fresh fruit, fragrant herbs, expressive. Palate: flavourful, fruity, good acidity, balanced.

Malesa Rosat 2014 RD

garnacha

87

Colour: raspberry rose. Nose: jasmine, fragrant herbs, candied fruit, expressive. Palate: fresh, fruity, flavourful, balsamic.

Puig de Guàrdies 2013 T

92

Colour: cherry, garnet rim. Nose: ripe fruit, fragrant herbs, spicy, mineral. Palate: powerful, flavourful, balsamic, balanced.

Senglar 2013 T

88

Colour: cherry, purple rim. Nose: floral, balsamic herbs, fragrant herbs, ripe fruit. Palate: powerful, fresh, fruity.

CELLERS D'EN GUILLA

Camí de Perelada s/n
17754 Delfià Rabós d'Empordà (Gerona)
☎: +34 660 001 622
info@cellersdenguilla.com
www.cellersdenguilla.com

Bruel de l'Estany 2013 T

cariñena, garnacha

87

Colour: deep cherry, purple rim. Nose: creamy oak, toasty, ripe fruit, balsamic herbs. Palate: balanced, spicy, long.

Edith 2013 BC

garnacha

88

Colour: bright yellow. Nose: ripe fruit, dried herbs, spicy. Palate: powerful, flavourful, spicy.

Garnacha dels Cellers D'en Guilla AM

garnacha

88

Colour: iodine, amber rim. Nose: elegant, sweet spices, acetaldehyde, dry nuts. Palate: full, dry, spicy, long, fine bitter notes, complex.

Magenc 2014 B

garnacha blanca, garnacha roja, macabeo, moscatel

89

Colour: bright straw. Nose: white flowers, dried herbs, ripe fruit, citrus fruit. Palate: flavourful, fruity, good acidity, elegant.

Rec de Brau 2013 T

cariñena, garnacha

86

Sol i Serena de Damigiana

garnacha roja

90

Colour: golden. Nose: powerfull, honeyed notes, candied fruit, fragrant herbs, acetaldehyde. Palate: flavourful, sweet, fresh, fruity, good acidity, long.

Vinya del Metge 2014 RD

garnacha roja, garnacha

87

Colour: onion pink. Nose: elegant, red berry notes, floral, wild herbs. Palate: flavourful, good acidity, spicy.

CELLERS SANTAMARÍA

Plaça Major, 6
17750 Capmany (Girona)
☎: +34 972 549 033
Fax: +34 972 549 022
info@granrecosind.com
www.granrecosind.com

Gran Recosind 2004 TR

merlot, cabernet sauvignon

83

Gran Recosind 2008 TC

garnacha, tempranillo, cabernet sauvignon, merlot

81

Gran Recosind 2008 TR

syrah, merlot

85

Gran Recosind 2013 BC

chardonnay, macabeo

84

CLOS D'AGON

Afores, s/n
17251 Calonge (Girona)
☎: +34 972 661 486
Fax: +34 972 661 486
info@closdagon.com
www.closdagon.com

Amic de Clos D'Agon 2014 B

51% garnacha blanca, 41% macabeo, 3% viognier, 2% marsanne, 3% roussanne

90

Colour: bright straw. Nose: white flowers, fragrant herbs, ripe fruit. Palate: flavourful, fruity, good acidity, balanced.

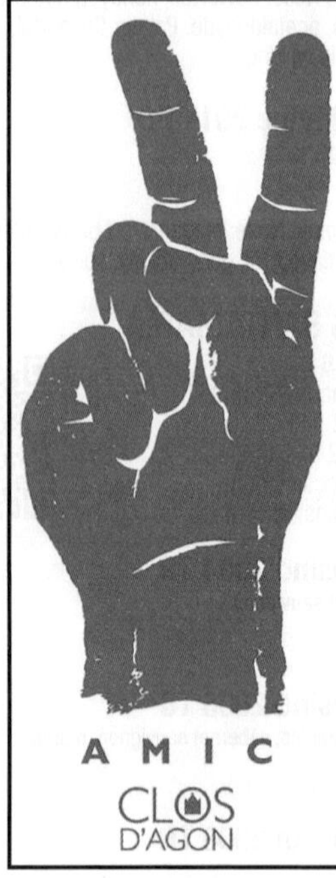

Amic de Clos D'Agon 2014 RD

88% garnacha, 8% merlot, cabernet franc

90

Colour: coppery red. Nose: elegant, red berry notes, floral, fragrant herbs. Palate: light-bodied, flavourful, good acidity, long, spicy.

COCA I FITÓ & ROIG PARALS

Garriguella, 8
17752 Mollet de Peralada (Girona)
☎: +34 636 223 919
Fax: +34 935 457 092
info@cocaifito.cat
www.cocaifito.cat

Tocat de l'Ala 2013 TC

55% cariñena, 35% garnacha, 10% syrah

91

Colour: cherry, garnet rim. Nose: ripe fruit, wild herbs, earthy notes, spicy, balsamic herbs. Palate: balanced, flavourful, long, balsamic.

Tocat i Posat 2012 TC

50% garnacha, 50% cariñena

90

Colour: cherry, garnet rim. Nose: mineral, expressive, spicy, ripe fruit. Palate: flavourful, long, balanced.

COMERCIAL VINÍCOLA DEL NORDEST

Empolla, 9
17752 Mollet de Peralada (Gerona)
☎: +34 972 563 150
Fax: +34 972 545 134
vinicola@vinicoladelnordest.com
www.vinicoladelnordest.com

Covest 2014 RD

garnacha, cariñena

86

Covest Blanc 2014 B

macabeo, garnacha, chardonnay

84

Covest Chardonnay 2014 B

chardonnay

85

Covest Garnatxa de L'Emporda Dulce Natural B Reserva

garnacha

88

Colour: light mahogany. Nose: acetaldehyde, dried fruit, dry nuts, toasty. Palate: powerful, flavourful, good finish.

Covest Moscatel de L'Emporda Dulce Natural B

moscatel

89

Colour: golden. Nose: powerfull, honeyed notes, candied fruit, fragrant herbs, acetaldehyde. Palate: flavourful, sweet, fresh, fruity, good acidity, long.

Covest Negre 2014 T
garnacha, cariñena

84

Garrigal 2011 TC

82

Colour: pale ruby, brick rim edge. Nose: spicy, slightly evolved. Palate: spicy, toasty.

Vinya Farriol Semidulce s/c B
coupage

80

DIGUEM NO S.L.U.

Ctra. de Llança, s/n
17489 El Port de la Selva (Girona)
☎: +34 630 875 649
genis@elportdelaselva.cat

Fons de Mar 2014 T

85

Llum de Mar 2014 B
50% macabeo, 30% lladoner blanco, 20% lledoner pelut

84

Vinya de L'Aví Genís 2012 T
100% cabernet sauvignon

89

Colour: cherry, garnet rim. Nose: ripe fruit, wild herbs, earthy notes, spicy. Palate: flavourful, balsamic, spicy.

Vinya de L'Aví Genís 2013 T
100% cabernet sauvignon

90

Colour: light cherry. Nose: fruit liqueur notes, fragrant herbs, spicy, creamy oak. Palate: balanced, elegant, spicy, long, toasty.

EMPORDÀLIA

Ctra. de Roses, s/n
17494 Pau (Girona)
☎: +34 972 530 140
aesteve@empordalia.com
www.empordalia.com

Antima 2013 T
cariñena, garnacha

89

Colour: deep cherry. Nose: creamy oak, toasty, ripe fruit, balsamic herbs. Palate: balanced, spicy, long.

Balmeta 2012 T
garnacha

85

Coromina 2011 T
cariñena, garnacha

86

Sinols Blanc 2014 B
macabeo, garnacha blanca

84

Sinols Negre 2014 T
garnacha, cariñena, syrah, merlot

85

Sinols Rosat 2014 RD
garnacha, mazuelo

84

ESPELT VITICULTORS

Mas Espelt s/n
17493 Vilajuiga (Gerona)
☎: +34 972 531 727
administracio@espeltviticultors.com
www.espeltviticultors.com

Espelt ComaBruna 2011 T
100% cariñena

93

Colour: cherry, garnet rim. Nose: ripe fruit, wild herbs, spicy, balsamic herbs. Palate: balanced, flavourful, long.

Espelt Corali Semidulce 2014 RD
100% garnacha

88

Colour: onion pink. Nose: elegant, floral, fragrant herbs, citrus fruit. Palate: light-bodied, flavourful, good acidity, long, spicy.

Espelt Garnatxa de l'Empordà
80% garnacha, 20% garnacha gris

87

Colour: coppery red. Nose: fruit liqueur notes, dry nuts, varnish, creamy oak. Palate: powerful, flavourful, spirituous.

Espelt Lledoner Roig 2013 B
100% garnacha gris

92

Colour: bright straw. Nose: white flowers, dried herbs, ripe fruit, spicy. Palate: flavourful, fruity, good acidity, elegant.

Espelt Quinze Roures 2014 BFB
50% garnacha gris, 50% garnacha blanca

90

Colour: bright yellow. Nose: ripe fruit, aged wood nuances, pattiserie, balsamic herbs. Palate: flavourful, fruity, spicy, long.

Espelt Sauló 2014 T
50% garnacha, 50% cariñena

86

Espelt Terres Negres 2013 T
86% cariñena, 14% garnacha

90

Colour: dark-red cherry. Nose: complex, mineral, balsamic herbs, balanced. Palate: full, flavourful, round tannins.

Espelt Vidiví 2013 T
70% garnacha, 25% merlot, 5% cabernet sauvignon

86

JOAN SARDÀ

Ctra. Vilafranca a St. Jaume dels Domenys, Km. 8,1
08732 Castellvi de la Marca (Barcelona)
☎: +34 937 720 900
Fax: +34 937 721 495
joansarda@joansarda.com
www.joansarda.com

Cap de Creus Corall 2013 T
lladoner, samsó

84

Cap de Creus Nacre 2014 B
lladoner roig, lladoner blanco

81

MAS LLUNES

Ctra. de Vilajuiga, s/n
17780 Garriguella (Gerona)
☎: +34 972 552 684
Fax: +34 972 530 112
info@masllunes.es
www.masllunes.es

Auria 2014 B
moscatel grano menudo

86

Cercium 2013 T
garnacha, samsó, syrah, cabernet sauvignon

89

Colour: cherry, garnet rim. Nose: red berry notes, ripe fruit, spicy, creamy oak, complex. Palate: flavourful, toasty, round tannins.

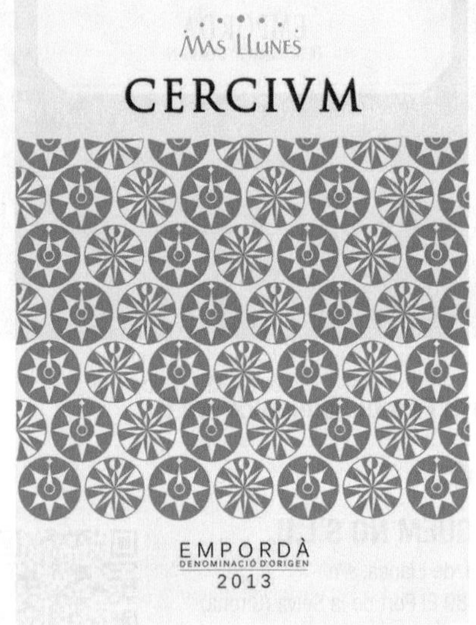

Empórion 2008 T
cabernet sauvignon, garnacha

87

Colour: pale ruby, brick rim edge. Nose: spicy, fine reductive notes, wet leather, aged wood nuances, fruit liqueur notes. Palate: spicy, balsamic.

Maragda 2013 T
garnacha, syrah, merlot

87

Nose: creamy oak, toasty, ripe fruit, balsamic herbs. Palate: balanced, spicy, long.

Maragda 2014 B
garnacha blanca, macabeo, garnacha roja

85

Maragda Rosa 2014 RD
garnacha, syrah

87

Colour: rose, purple rim. Nose: red berry notes, floral, expressive. Palate: powerful, fruity, fresh.

Mas Llunes Dolç Moscat 2013 B
moscatel grano menudo

87

Colour: bright yellow. Nose: balsamic herbs, honeyed notes, floral, sweet spices. Palate: rich, fruity, powerful, flavourful, elegant.

Mas llunes Garnatxa D'Emporda Ambre AM Solera
garnacha roja

90

Colour: iodine, amber rim. Nose: sweet spices, acetaldehyde, dry nuts, pungent. Palate: full, dry, spicy, long, fine bitter notes, complex.

Mas llunes Garnatxa D'Emporda Solera AM Solera
garnacha roja

92

Colour: iodine, amber rim. Nose: elegant, sweet spices, acetaldehyde, dry nuts. Palate: full, dry, spicy, long, fine bitter notes, complex.

Nivia 2013 BFB
garnacha blanca, garnacha roja, macabeo, samsó

90

Colour: bright yellow. Nose: ripe fruit, toasty, aged wood nuances, wild herbs. Palate: flavourful, fruity, spicy.

Rhodes 2010 T
samsó, syrah, garnacha, cabernet sauvignon

90

Colour: cherry, garnet rim. Nose: ripe fruit, wild herbs, earthy notes, spicy, balsamic herbs. Palate: balanced, flavourful, long, balsamic.

Rhodes 2011 T
samsó, syrah, garnacha, cabernet sauvignon

87

Colour: cherry, garnet rim. Nose: ripe fruit, spicy, creamy oak. Palate: flavourful, toasty, round tannins.

MAS OLLER

Ctra. GI-652, Km. 0,23
17123 Torrent de Empordà (Gerona)
☎: +34 972 300 001
info@masoller.es
www.masoller.es

Mas Oller Mar 2014 B
picapoll, malvasía

90

Colour: bright yellow. Nose: expressive, dried herbs, ripe fruit, spicy, mineral. Palate: flavourful, fruity, good acidity, balanced.

Mas Oller Plus 2013 T
syrah, garnacha

91

Colour: cherry, garnet rim. Nose: creamy oak, toasty, ripe fruit, balsamic herbs. Palate: balanced, spicy, long.

Mas Oller Pur 2013 T
syrah, garnacha, cabernet sauvignon

91

Colour: deep cherry, purple rim. Nose: scrubland, ripe fruit, spicy. Palate: balanced, round tannins, balsamic.

MASIA SERRA

Dels Solés, 20
17708 Cantallops (Girona)
☎: +34 689 703 687
masiaserra@masiaserra.com
www.masiaserra.com

Aroa 2011 T
80% garnacha, 20% marselan

90

Colour: cherry, garnet rim. Nose: balanced, complex, ripe fruit, spicy, balsamic herbs. Palate: good structure, flavourful, round tannins, balanced.

Ctònia 2014 BFB
100% garnacha blanca

91

Colour: bright straw. Nose: fine lees, dried herbs, mineral, candied fruit. Palate: flavourful, fruity, good acidity.

Gneis 2010 T
90% cabernet sauvignon, 10% garnacha

87

Colour: pale ruby, brick rim edge. Nose: spicy, fine reductive notes, wet leather, aged wood nuances, fruit liqueur notes. Palate: spicy, fine tannins, balanced.

INO Garnatxa de L'Empordà Vino dulce natural
100% garnacha roja

94

Colour: coppery red. Nose: acetaldehyde, dried fruit, dry nuts, sweet spices, creamy oak, expressive. Palate: powerful, flavourful, spicy, long.

IO Masia Serra 2012 T
70% merlot, 30% cabernet franc

90

Colour: cherry, garnet rim. Nose: ripe fruit, wild herbs, earthy notes, spicy. Palate: balanced, flavourful, long, balsamic.

Mosst 2014 B
80% garnacha blanca, 10% garnacha roja, 5% moscatel

88

Colour: bright straw. Nose: white flowers, fresh fruit, fragrant herbs, expressive. Palate: flavourful, fruity, good acidity, balanced.

OLIVEDA S.A.

La Roca, 3
17750 Capmany (Girona)
☎: +34 972 549 012
Fax: +34 972 549 106
comercial@grupoliveda.com
www.grupoliveda.com

Furot 2008 TR
garnacha, cabernet sauvignon, merlot

90

Colour: cherry, garnet rim. Nose: ripe fruit, wild herbs, earthy notes, spicy, balsamic herbs. Palate: balanced, flavourful, long, balsamic.

Furot Sauvignon Blanc 2014 B
100% sauvignon blanc

87

Colour: bright straw. Nose: white flowers, fresh fruit, fragrant herbs, balanced. Palate: flavourful, fruity, good acidity, balanced.

Rigau Ros 2011 TC
cabernet sauvignon, garnacha, merlot

86

OLIVER CONTI

Puignau, s/n
17750 Capmany (Gerona)
☎: +34 600 991 603
ocvi@oliverconti.com
www.oliverconti.com

Oliver Conti Ara 2011 TR
cabernet sauvignon, garnacha

88

Colour: cherry, garnet rim. Nose: ripe fruit, wild herbs, spicy. Palate: flavourful, spicy, long.

Oliver Conti Carlota 2011 TR
cabernet franc

89

Colour: deep cherry, purple rim. Nose: creamy oak, toasty, ripe fruit, balsamic herbs. Palate: balanced, spicy.

Oliver Conti Etiqueta Negra 2010 B Reserva
gewürztraminer, macabeo, moscatel grano menudo

90

Colour: bright yellow. Nose: ripe fruit, citrus fruit, spicy, floral. Palate: powerful, flavourful, spicy, long.

Oliver Conti Etiqueta Negra 2011 TR
cabernet sauvignon, merlot, cabernet franc

90

Colour: ruby red. Nose: ripe fruit, spicy, creamy oak, balsamic herbs, mineral. Palate: balanced, flavourful, spicy.

Oliver Conti Treyu 2013 B
macabeo, gewürztraminer

89

Colour: bright straw. Nose: white flowers, fresh fruit, fragrant herbs. Palate: flavourful, fruity, balanced.

Turó Negre d'Oliver Conti 2011 T
garnacha, cabernet sauvignon, merlot, cabernet franc

90

Colour: cherry, garnet rim. Nose: ripe fruit, wild herbs, earthy notes, spicy, balsamic herbs. Palate: balanced, flavourful, long.

Turó Negre d'Oliver Conti 2013 T
garnacha, cabernet sauvignon, merlot, cabernet franc

88

Colour: cherry, garnet rim. Nose: grassy, ripe fruit, mineral. Palate: correct, easy to drink, fresh, good acidity.

PERE GUARDIOLA

Ctra. GI-602, Km. 2,9
17750 Capmany (Gerona)
☎: +34 972 549 096
Fax: +34 972 549 097
marta@pereguardiola.com
www.pereguardiola.com

Anhel d'Empordà 2014 B
garnacha blanca, moscatel de alejandría

86

Floresta 2005 TR
merlot, garnacha, syrah, cabernet sauvignon

86

Floresta 2011 TC
cabernet sauvignon, merlot, garnacha, mazuelo, syrah

87

Colour: cherry, garnet rim. Nose: ripe fruit, balsamic herbs, sweet spices. Palate: ripe fruit, easy to drink.

Floresta 2014 B
macabeo, chardonnay, xarel.lo, moscatel, sauvignon blanc

84

Floresta 2014 RD
garnacha, merlot, mazuelo, syrah

86

Floresta 2014 T
garnacha, merlot, syrah

86

Floresta 3B8 2011 TR
mazuelo, garnacha, syrah, merlot

88

Colour: cherry, garnet rim. Nose: ripe fruit, wild herbs, spicy, balsamic herbs. Palate: balanced, flavourful.

Joncària Moscatel 2012 BFB
moscatel de alejandría

89

Colour: bright yellow. Nose: ripe fruit, citrus fruit, jasmine, floral, creamy oak. Palate: flavourful, fruity, spicy.

Torre de Capmany Garnatxa d'Empordà AM Reserva
garnacha blanca

89

Colour: iodine. Nose: acetaldehyde, pungent, varnish, aged wood nuances, creamy oak. Palate: powerful, flavourful, spicy, long.

Torre de Capmany Garnatxa d'Empordà B Gran Reserva
garnacha blanca

90

Colour: iodine, amber rim. Nose: elegant, sweet spices, acetaldehyde, dry nuts. Palate: full, dry, spicy, long, fine bitter notes, complex.

Torre de Capmany Moscatel B
moscatel de alejandría

85

ROIG PARALS

Garriguella, 8
17256 Mollet de Peralada (Girona)
☎: +34 972 634 320
info@roigparals.cat
www.roigparals.cat

Camí de Cormes 2010 T
samsó

92

Colour: cherry, garnet rim. Nose: ripe fruit, wild herbs, earthy notes, spicy, balsamic herbs. Palate: balanced, flavourful, long.

Finca Pla del Molí 2008 T
cabernet sauvignon, merlot

89

Colour: cherry, garnet rim. Nose: ripe fruit, wild herbs, earthy notes, spicy, balsamic herbs. Palate: balanced, flavourful, long, balsamic.

La Botera 2011 TC
samsó, garnacha

86

Mallolet 2014 B
macabeo, garnacha blanca

86

Mallolet 2014 T
samsó, garnacha

89

Colour: light cherry. Nose: fruit expression, fruit liqueur notes, fragrant herbs, spicy, earthy notes. Palate: long, flavourful, complex.

SOTA ELS ÀNGELS

Veinat de Rabiosas
17116 Cruïlles (Girona)
☎: +34 872 006 976
info@sotaelsangels.com
www.sotaelsangels.com

Desea 2009 TC
carménère, carignan, cabernet sauvignon, merlot, syrah

87

Colour: pale ruby, brick rim edge. Nose: spicy, fine reductive notes, wet leather, aged wood nuances, fruit liqueur notes. Palate: spicy, fine tannins, balanced.

Sota els Àngels 2008 TC
carignan, carménère, cabernet sauvignon

91

Colour: cherry, garnet rim. Nose: balanced, complex, ripe fruit, spicy, fine reductive notes. Palate: good structure, flavourful, round tannins.

Sota els Àngels 2013 BC
picapoll, viognier

91

Colour: bright yellow. Nose: ripe fruit, powerfull, aged wood nuances, pattiserie. Palate: flavourful, fruity, spicy, toasty, long.

VINOS JOC - JORDI OLIVER CONTI

Mas Marti
17467 Sant Mori (Girona)
☎: +34 607 222 002
info@vinojoc.com
www.vinojoc.com

JOC Blanc Empordà 2013 B
garnacha, macabeo

89

Colour: bright straw. Nose: dry nuts, dried herbs, ripe fruit, sweet spices. Palate: correct, fine bitter notes, spicy. Personality.

JOC Negre Empordà 2013 T
garnacha, cabernet sauvignon, merlot, cabernet franc

88

Colour: cherry, garnet rim. Nose: creamy oak, red berry notes, wild herbs. Palate: flavourful, spicy.

Sogre Gendre 2013 T
garnacha

86

VINYES D'OLIVARDOTS

Paratge Olivadots, s/n
17750 Capmany (Girona)
☎: +34 650 395 627
vdo@olivardots.com
www.olivardots.com

Blanc de Gresa 2013 B
garnacha blanca, garnacha gris, cariñena blanca

91

Colour: bright yellow. Nose: ripe fruit, citrus fruit, wild herbs, mineral, spicy. Palate: rich, powerful, flavourful, complex.

Finca Olivardots Groc D'Anfora 2013 B
garnacha gris, garnacha blanca, macabeo

90

Colour: bright yellow. Nose: ripe fruit, dried flowers, spicy, dry stone. Palate: powerful, flavourful, long. Personality.

Finca Olivardots Vermell 2012 T
syrah, garnacha, cariñena, cabernet sauvignon

90

Colour: cherry, garnet rim. Nose: creamy oak, red berry notes, balanced. Palate: flavourful, spicy, elegant.

Gresa 2009 T
40% cariñena, 30% garnacha, 20% syrah, 10% cabernet sauvignon

93

Colour: cherry, garnet rim. Nose: ripe fruit, wild herbs, earthy notes, spicy, balsamic herbs. Palate: balanced, flavourful, long, balsamic, elegant.

Vd'O 1.10 2010 T
100% cariñena

93

Colour: ruby red. Nose: elegant, spicy, fine reductive notes, dry stone. Palate: spicy, fine tannins, elegant, long.

Vd'O 5.10 2010 T
100% garnacha

91

Colour: light cherry. Nose: ripe fruit, wild herbs, earthy notes, spicy, balsamic herbs. Palate: balanced, flavourful, long.

Vd'O 7.13 2013 B
100% garnacha gris

93

Colour: bright straw. Nose: white flowers, fine lees, dried herbs, ripe fruit, earthy notes, spicy. Palate: flavourful, fruity, good acidity, elegant. Personality.

VINYES DELS ASPRES

Requesens, 7
17708 Cantallops (Girona)
☎: +34 619 741 442
Fax: +34 972 420 662
dmolas@vinyesdelsaspres.cat
www.vinyesdelsaspres.cat

Bac de les Ginesteres Vino dulce Natural 2004 AM
100% garnacha gris

92

Colour: iodine, amber rim. Nose: powerfull, complex, dry nuts, creamy oak, varnish. Palate: rich, long, spicy.

Blanc dels Aspres 2013 BFB
70% garnacha blanca, 30% garnacha gris

88

Colour: bright yellow. Nose: ripe fruit, powerfull, toasty, aged wood nuances, pattiserie. Palate: flavourful, fruity, spicy, toasty, long.

Negre dels Aspres 2011 TC
23% cariñena, 16% garnacha, 39% cabernet sauvignon, 16% merlot, 6% syrah

90

Colour: ruby red. Nose: ripe fruit, wild herbs, earthy notes. Palate: long, spicy, balsamic, balanced.

Oriol 2014 T
44% garnacha, 24% cariñena, 32% merlot

88

Colour: cherry, purple rim. Nose: red berry notes, floral, balsamic herbs. Palate: powerful, fresh, fruity.

Oriol Blanc 2014 B
garnacha gris

84

S'Alou 2011 TC
54% garnacha, 13% cariñena, 20% cabernet sauvignon, 13% syrah

92

Colour: cherry, garnet rim. Nose: ripe fruit, wild herbs, earthy notes, spicy, balsamic herbs. Palate: balanced, flavourful, long, balsamic, elegant.

Vi de Panses dels Aspres Dulce Natural B
garnacha gris

87

Colour: iodine, amber rim. Nose: complex, fruit liqueur notes, dried fruit, pattiserie, toasty, honeyed notes. Palate: sweet, rich, unctuous.

Xot 2012 TC
70% cariñena, 30% garnacha

87

Colour: cherry, garnet rim. Nose: ripe fruit, spicy, creamy oak. Palate: flavourful, toasty.

DO. GETARIAKO TXAKOLINA

CONSEJO REGULADOR

Parque Aldamar, 4 bajo
20808 Getaria (Gipuzkoa)
☎ :+34 943 140 383 - Fax: +34 943 896 030
@: info@getariakotxakolina.com
www.getariakotxakolina.com

LOCATION:

Mainly on the coastal belt of the province of Guipuzcoa, covering the vineyards situated in the municipal areas of Aia, Getaria and Zarauz, at a distance of about 25 km from San Sebastián.

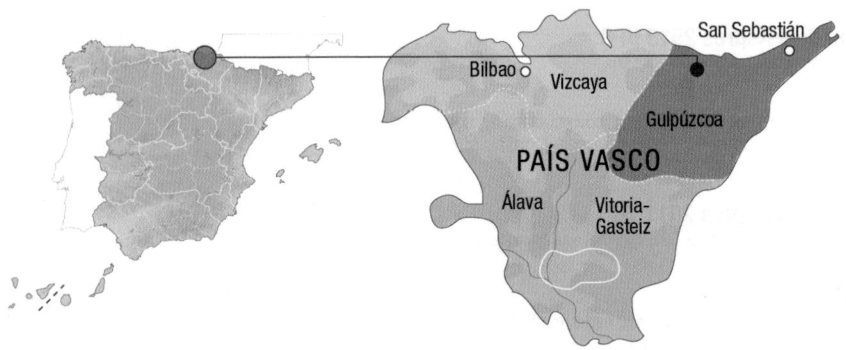

GRAPE VARIETIES:

WHITE: hondarrabi zuri, gros manseng, riesling, chardonnay y petit courbu.
RED: Hondarrabi Beltza.

FIGURES:

Vineyard surface: 402 – **Wine-Growers:** 96 – **Wineries:** 29 – **2014 Harvest rating:** Very Good – **Production 14:** 2,433,000 litres – **Market percentages:** 92% National - 8% International.

SOIL:

The vineyards are situated in small valleys and gradual hillsides at altitudes of up to 200 m. They are found on humid brownish-grey limy soil, which are rich in organic matter.

CLIMATE:

Fairly mild, thanks to the influence of the Bay of Biscay. The average annual temperature is 13°C, and the rainfall is plentiful with an average of 1,600 mm per year.

VINTAGE RATING

PEÑÍNGUIDE

2010	2011	2012	2013	2014
VERY GOOD	VERY GOOD	EXCELLENT	GOOD	GOOD

5 MAHATSONDO, S.A.

Apdo. Correos 258
20800 Zarautz (Gipuzkoa)
☎: +34 943 240 005
bodega@txakolina-k5.com
www.txakolina-k5.com

K5 2013 B
100% hondarrabi zuri

92

Colour: bright straw. Nose: fresh fruit, fragrant herbs, expressive, faded flowers. Palate: flavourful, fruity, good acidity, balanced.

Uhin Berdea 2014 B
100% hondarrabi zuri

87

Colour: bright yellow, greenish rim. Nose: white flowers, faded flowers, ripe fruit, citrus fruit, fine lees. Palate: flavourful, fruity.

ADUR

Ferrerias, 3 8ºF
20013 Donostia (Gipuzkoa)
☎: +34 617 216 617
info@adurtxakolina.com
www.adurtxakolina.com

Adur 2014 B
100% hondarrabi zuri

89

Colour: bright straw. Nose: fresh, grassy, wild herbs, mineral. Palate: correct, fine bitter notes, fresh.

AGERRE

Agerre Baserria - Bº Askizu
20808 Getaria (Gipuzkoa)
☎: +34 943 140 446
Fax: +34 943 140 446
agerre@agerretxakolina.com
www.agerretxakolina.com

Agerre 2014 B
hondarrabi zuri

86

AIZPURUA

Ctra. de Meagas
20808 Getaria (Gipuzkoa)
☎: +34 943 140 696
Fax: +34 943 140 696
aialleaizpurua@gmx.es
www.txakoliaizpurua.com

Aizpurua. B 2014 B

87

Colour: bright straw. Nose: white flowers, fresh fruit, grassy. Palate: flavourful, fruity, good acidity, balanced.

AKARREGI TXIKI

Akarregi Txiki Baserria
20808 Getaria (Gipuzkoa)
☎: +34 629 044 974
oscar.baile@tripleagourmet.com
www.akarregitxiki.com

Akarregi Txiki 2014 B
hondarrabi zuri

88

Colour: straw. Nose: medium intensity, ripe fruit, floral, wild herbs. Palate: correct, easy to drink.

Olatu 2014 B
hondarrabi zuri

89

Colour: bright straw. Nose: white flowers, fine lees, dried herbs, citrus fruit, fresh fruit. Palate: flavourful, fruity, good acidity, elegant.

AMEZTOI

Barrio Eitzaga, 10
20808 Getaria (Gipuzkoa)
☎: +34 943 140 918
Fax: +34 943 140 169
ameztoi@txakoliameztoi.com
www.txakoliameztoi.com

Primus Ameztoi 2014 B
hondarrabi zuri

90

Colour: bright straw. Nose: white flowers, fine lees, dried herbs, ripe fruit, citrus fruit. Palate: flavourful, fruity, good acidity, elegant.

Rubentis Ameztoi 2014 RD
hondarrabi zuri, hondarrabi beltza

87

Colour: brilliant rose. Nose: elegant, red berry notes, floral, fragrant herbs. Palate: light-bodied, flavourful, good acidity, good finish.

Txakoli Ameztoi 2014 B
hondarrabi zuri

88

Colour: bright yellow. Nose: ripe fruit, floral, wild herbs, fresh. Palate: flavourful, carbonic notes.

BASA LORE TXAKOLINDEGIA

Santa Bárbara Auzoa, 1
20800 Zarautz (Gipuzkoa)
☎: +34 689 921 183
Fax: +34 943 834 747
basaloretxakolindegia@gmail.com
www.basa-lore.com

Basa Lore 2014 B
hondarrabi zuri

82

Basa Lore Gorria 2014 RD
hondarrabi zuri, hondarrabi beltza

80

Igartzeta 2013 B
hondarrabi zuri

81

BODEGA KATXIÑA

Ortzaika Auzoa, 20
20810 Orio (Guipuzcoa)
☎: +34 617 909 474
info@bodegakatxina.com
www.bodegakatxina.com

Katxina 2014 B
hondarrabi zuri

87

Colour: bright straw. Nose: medium intensity, white flowers, citrus fruit. Palate: fresh, easy to drink, good finish.

BODEGA REZABAL

Itsas Begi Etxea, 628
20800 Zarautz (Gipuzkoa)
☎: +34 943 580 899
info@txakolirezabal.com
www.txakolirezabal.com

Txakoli Rezabal 2014 B
100% hondarrabi zuri

90

Colour: bright straw. Nose: white flowers, expressive, ripe fruit, dried herbs, wild herbs. Palate: balanced, easy to drink.

Txakoli Rezabal Rosé 2014 RD
100% hondarrabi beltza

87

Colour: coppery red, bright. Nose: expressive, dried flowers, wild herbs. Palate: fruity, fresh, balanced.

BODEGAS JUAN CELAYA LETAMENDI

Upaingoa-Zañartuko
20560 Oñati (Gipuzkoa)
☎: +34 670 288 086
Fax: +34 948 401 182
administracion@naparralde.com
www.upain.es

Upaingoa 2010 B

84

Upaingoa 2011 B

84

Upaingoa 2012 B

84

Upaingoa 2013 B

86

Upaingoa 2014 B

86

GOROSTI

Elorriaga Auzoa, 35
20820 Deba (Gipuzkoa)
☎: +34 670 408 439
gorostibodega@hotmail.com
www.flyschtxakolina.com

Flysch Txakolina 2014 B
hondarrabi zuri

88

Colour: bright yellow. Nose: white flowers, fragrant herbs, fresh fruit. Palate: flavourful, fruity, good acidity, balanced.

HIRUZTA

Barrio Jaizubia, 266
20280 Hondarribia (Gipuzkoa)
☎: +34 943 646 689
Fax: +34 943 260 801
info@hiruzta.com
www.hiruzta.com

Hiruzta Txakolin Berezia 2014 B
100% hondarrabi zuri

90

Colour: bright straw. Nose: white flowers, dried herbs, ripe fruit, candied fruit, citrus fruit. Palate: flavourful, fruity, good acidity, elegant.

Hiruzta Txakolina 2014 B
95% hondarrabi zuri, 5% gros manseng

87

Colour: bright straw. Nose: fresh fruit, fragrant herbs, expressive. Palate: flavourful, fruity, easy to drink.

INAZIO URRUZOLA

Garaikoetxea baserria, Arana bailara 13
20494 20494 (Gipuzkoa)
☎: +34 658 734 471
inaziourruzola@gmail.com
www.inaziourruzola.com

Inazio Urruzola 2014 B

88

Colour: bright straw. Nose: fresh fruit, grassy, expressive, neat.

MOKOROA

Urteta Auzoa Kortaburu Baserria
20800 Zarautz (Gipuzkoa)
☎: +34 630 222 653
Fax: +34 943 833 925
bodega@txakolimokoroa.com

Mokoroa B

87

Colour: bright straw. Nose: fresh fruit, balanced, expressive, medium intensity. Palate: fresh, fine bitter notes.

SAGARMIÑA

Sagarmiña Baserria
20830 Mitriku (Gipuzcoa)
☎: +34 943 603 225
txakolisagarmina@gmail.com
www.txakolisagarmina.com

Sagarmiña 2014 B

hondarrabi zuri

88

Colour: bright straw. Nose: white flowers, fresh fruit, fragrant herbs, expressive. Palate: flavourful, fruity, good acidity, balanced, carbonic notes.

TXAKOLI ARREGI

Talaimendi, 727- Bajo
20800 Zarautz (Gipuzkoa)
☎: +34 943 580 835
info@txakoliarregi.com
www.txakoliarregi.com

Arregi 2014 B

hondarrabi zuri

86

TXAKOLI ELKANO

Eitzaga Auzoa, 24
20808 Getaria (Gipuzkoa)
☎: +34 600 800 259
txakolielkano@hotmail.com
www.txakolielkano.com

Txakoli Elkano 2014 B

hondarrabi zuri

88

Colour: bright yellow, greenish rim. Nose: citrus fruit, balsamic herbs. Palate: full, flavourful, long.

TXAKOLI GAINTZA S.L.

Barrio San Prudentzio 26
20808 Getaria (Gipuzkoa)
☎: +34 943 140 032
info@gaintza.com
www.gaintza.com

Aitako 2013 B

hondarrabi zuri, hondarrabi beltza, chardonnay

86

Gaintza 2014 B

hondarrabi zuri, hondarrabi beltza, gros manseng

87

Colour: bright yellow, greenish rim. Nose: ripe fruit, white flowers, wild herbs. Palate: fine bitter notes, correct.

TXAKOLI TALAI BERRI

Barrio Talaimendi, 728
20800 Zarautz (Gipuzkoa)
☎: +34 943 132 750
Fax: +34 943 132 750
info@talaiberri.com
www.talaiberri.com

Finca Jakue 2014 B

100% hondarrabi zuri

86

Talai Berri 2014 B

90% hondarrabi zuri, 10% hondarrabi beltza

87

Colour: bright straw. Nose: white flowers, fresh fruit, fragrant herbs. Palate: flavourful, fruity, good acidity, balanced.

Talai Berri 2014 T

100% hondarrabi beltza

85

TXAKOLI ULACIA

Ctra. Meagas s/n
20808 Getaria (Gipuzkoa)
☎: +34 943 140 893
Fax: +34 943 140 893
nicolasulacia@euskalnet.net
www.txakoliulacia.com

Izaro 2014 B

hondarrabi zuri

87

Colour: bright yellow, greenish rim. Nose: wild herbs, fresh fruit, floral, citrus fruit. Palate: balanced, fine bitter notes.

Txakoli Ulacia 2014 B

hondarrabi zuri, hondarrabi beltza

86

TXAKOLI ZUDUGARAI

Ctra. Zarautz - Aia Bº Laurgain
20809 Aia (Guipuzcoa)
☎: +34 943 830 386
Fax: +34 943 835 952
txakolizudugarai@euskalnet.net
www.txakolizudugarai.com

Amats 2014 B

100% hondarrabi zuri

87

Colour: bright straw. Nose: grassy, floral, ripe fruit. Palate: fresh, balanced, good acidity.

Antxiola 2014 B

hondarrabi zuri

86

Zudugarai 2014 B

100% hondarrabi zuri

86

TXOMIN ETXANIZ

Txomin Etxaniz Barrio Eitzaiga, 21
20808 Getaria (Gipuzkoa)
☎: +34 943 140 702
txakoli@txominetxaniz.com
www.txominetxaniz.com

Eugenia Txomín Etxaníz Blanco ESP

100% hondarrabi zuri

86

Eugenia Txomín Etxaníz Rosado ESP

87

Colour: raspberry rose, bright. Nose: faded flowers, medium intensity, fresh, citrus fruit. Palate: correct, fresh, easy to drink.

Txomín Etxaníz 2014 B

hondarrabi zuri

89

Colour: bright straw. Nose: white flowers, fresh fruit, fragrant herbs, expressive. Palate: flavourful, fruity, good acidity, balanced.

Txomín Etxaníz 2014 RD

hondarrabi zuri, hondarrabi beltza

86

Colour: brilliant rose, bright. Nose: medium intensity, fragrant herbs, fresh fruit. Palate: correct, easy to drink.

Txomín Etxaníz Berezia 2014 B

90% hondarrabi zuri, 10% hondarrabi beltza

90

Colour: bright straw. Nose: white flowers, fine lees, dried herbs, ripe fruit, candied fruit, citrus fruit. Palate: flavourful, fruity, good acidity, elegant.

Txomín Etxaníz White 2014 B

80% hondarrabi zuri, 20% chardonnay

87

Colour: bright straw, greenish rim. Nose: fresh fruit, wild herbs, faded flowers. Palate: correct, fine bitter notes, good finish.

Uydi Naturalmente Dulce 2012 B

100% hondarrabi zuri

88

Colour: bright yellow. Nose: powerfull, dried herbs, faded flowers. Palate: flavourful, sweet, ripe fruit, good acidity.

DO. GRAN CANARIA

CONSEJO REGULADOR
Calvo Sotelo, 26
35300 Santa Brígida (Las Palmas)
☎ :+34 928 640 462 - Fax: +34 928 640 982
@: crdogc@yahoo.es
www.vinosdegrancanaria.es

LOCATION:

The production region covers 99% of the island of Gran Canaria, as the climate and the conditions of the terrain allow for the cultivation of grapes at altitudes close to sea level up to the highest mountain tops. The DO incorporates all the municipal areas of the island, except for the Tafira Protected Landscape which falls under an independent DO, Monte de Lentiscal, also fully covered in this Guide.

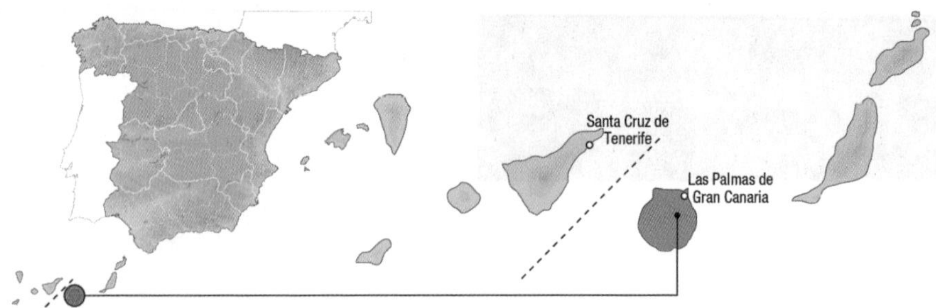

GRAPE VARIETIES:

WHITE: Preferred: Malvasía, Güal, Marmajuelo (Bermejuela), Vijariego, Albillo and Moscatel.
AUTHORIZED: Listán Blanco, Burrablanca, Torrontés, Pedro Ximénez, Brebal and Bastardo Blanco.
RED: Preferred: Listán Negro, Negramoll, Tintilla, Malvasía Rosada.
AUTHORIZED: Moscatel Negra, Bastardo Negro, Listán Prieto, Vijariego Negro, Bastardo Negro, Listón Prieto und Vijariego Negro.

FIGURES:

Vineyard surface: 242 – **Wine-Growers:** 357 – **Wineries:** 71 – **2014 Harvest rating:** N/A – **Production 14:** 341,000 litres – **Market percentages:** 95% National - 5% International.

SOIL:

The vineyards are found both in coastal areas and on higher grounds at altitudes of up to 1500 m, resulting in a varied range of soils.

CLIMATE:

As with the other islands of the archipelago, the differences in altitude give rise to several microclimates which create specific characteristics for the cultivation of the vine. Nevertheless, the climate is conditioned by the influence of the trade winds which blow from the east and whose effect is more evident in the higher-lying areas.

VINTAGE RATING

PEÑÍNGUIDE

2010	2011	2012	2013	2014
VERY GOOD	VERY GOOD	VERY GOOD	GOOD	AVERAGE

BENTAYGA

El Alberconcillo, s/n
35360 Tejeda (Las Palmas)
☎: +34 928 426 047
info@bodegasbentayga.com
www.bodegasbentayga.com

Agala 2012 TC
tintilla, vijariego negro

89

Colour: cherry, garnet rim. Nose: smoky, spicy, overripe fruit. Palate: flavourful, smoky aftertaste, ripe fruit.

Agala Altitud 1175 2014 T
baboso negro, vijariego negro, tintilla

88

Colour: bright cherry. Nose: ripe fruit, sweet spices, creamy oak. Palate: flavourful, fruity, round tannins.

Agala Altitud 1318 Semi 2014 B
vijariego blanco, albillo

87

Colour: bright straw. Nose: white flowers, fresh fruit, fragrant herbs, expressive. Palate: flavourful, fruity, good acidity, balanced.

BODEGA LOS BERRAZALES

Valle de Agaete
35480 Agaete (Las Palmas)
☎: +34 628 922 588
Fax: +34 928 898 154
lugojorge3@hotmail.com
www.bodegalosberrazales.com

Los Berrazales 2014 T
tintilla

85

Los Berrazales 2013 T Roble
tintilla, listán negro

88

Colour: deep cherry. Nose: creamy oak, toasty, ripe fruit, balsamic herbs. Palate: balanced, spicy, long.

Los Berrazales 2014 RD
listán negro

83

Los Berrazales Dulce Natural 2014 B
moscatel, malvasía

87

Colour: bright yellow. Nose: dried herbs, ripe fruit, spicy. Palate: flavourful, fruity, good acidity.

Los Berrazales Seco 2013 B
malvasía, moscatel

87

Colour: bright straw. Nose: white flowers, fresh fruit, fragrant herbs. Palate: flavourful, fruity, good acidity, balanced.

Los Berrazales Semiseco 2014 B
moscatel, malvasía

88

Colour: bright yellow. Nose: balsamic herbs, honeyed notes, floral, sweet spices. Palate: rich, fruity, powerful, flavourful, elegant.

BODEGAS LAS TIRAJANAS

Las Lagunas s/n
35290 San Bartolomé de Tirajana
(Las Palmas de Gran Canaria)
☎: +34 928 155 978
info@bodegaslastirajanas.com
www.bodegaslastirajanas.com

Blanco Las Tirajanas 2014 B
albillo, verdello, listán blanco, marmajuelo, malvasía

85

Dulce Las Tirajanas 2014 B
malvasía, pedro ximénez, moscatel

83

Las Tirajanas 2013 BFB
malvasía

83

Las Tirajanas 2013 T Barrica
tintilla, listán negro, castellana, vijariego negro

85

Las Tirajanas 2014 RD
listán negro

83

Malvasía Volcánica Las Tirajanas Seco 2014 B
malvasía

84

Malvasía Volcánica Las Tirajanas Semidulce 2014 B
malvasía

84

Tinto Las Tirajanas 2014 T
listán negro, vijariego negro, castellana

84

Verijadiego Las Tirajanas 2014 B
verijadiego

83

FRONTÓN DE ORO

35329 Vega de San Mateo
(Las Palmas de Gran Canaria)
☎: +34 670 634 863
frontondeoro@hotmail.com
www.frontondeoro.com

Frontón de Oro 2014 RD
listán negro

83

Frontón de Oro Albillo 2014 B
albillo

84

Frontón de Oro Malpais 2013 T
70% listán prieto, 15% listán negro, 15% tintilla

87

Colour: bright cherry. Nose: ripe fruit, sweet spices, creamy oak. Palate: flavourful, fruity.

Frontón de Oro Semiseco 2014 B
listán blanco, albillo, malvasía

84

Frontón de Oro Tintilla 2013 T
100% tintilla

75

Frontón de Oro Tradicional Listán Negro 2013 T
listán negro

84

LA HIGUERA MAYOR

Ctra. de Telde a Santa
Brígida, GC 80,P.K., 7,5
35200 El Palmital de Telde (Las Palmas)
☎: +34 630 285 454
Fax: +34 928 275 281
lahigueramayor@gmail.com
www.lahigueramayor.com

La Higuera Mayor 2012 T
80

La Higuera Mayor 2014 T
84

PLAZA PERDIDA - VIÑA LA VICA

Ctra. a Los Hoyos, 140 y 271
35017 Las Palmas de Gran Canaria
(Las Palmas)
☎: +34 669 680 910
Fax: +34 928 371 538
vidlavica@hotmail.com

Plaza Perdida 2014 B
listán blanco, moscatel

82

Plaza Perdida 2014 T
listán negro

85

Viña La Vica 2013 T
listán negro, tintilla

86

Viña La Vica 2014 B
malvasía

84

VEGA DE GÁLDAR

La Longuera s/n
35460 Gáldar (Las Palmas)
☎: +34 605 043 047
lamenora1960@yahoo.es
www.vegadegaldar.com

El Convento de la Vega 2013 T Roble
listán negro, castellana

80

Nubia 2014 B
listán blanco, malvasía

83

Vega de Gáldar 2014 T
listán negro, castellana

75

Viña Amable 2013 T Roble
listán negro, castellana

83

DO. JEREZ-XÈRÉS-SHERRY- MANZANILLA DE SANLÚCAR DE BARRAMEDA

CONSEJO REGULADOR

Avda. Álvaro Domecq, 2
11405 Jerez de la Frontera (Cádiz)
☎:+34 956 332 050 - Fax: +34 956 338 908
@: vinjerez@sherry.org
www.sherry.org

LOCATION:

In the province of Cádiz. The production area covers the municipal districts of Jerez de la Frontera, El Puerto de Santa María, Chipiona, Trebujena, Rota, Puerto Real, Chiclana de la Frontera and some estates in Lebrija.

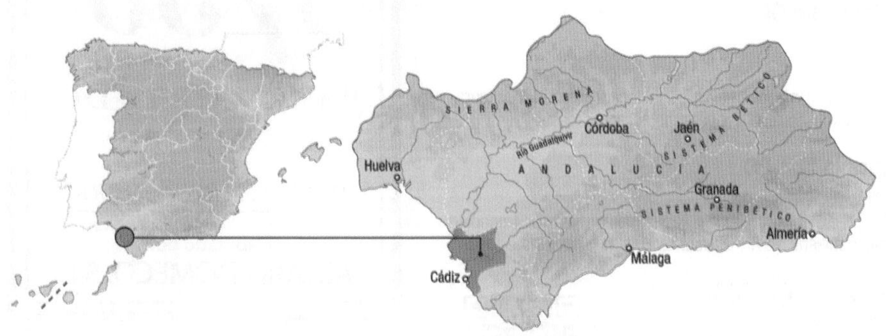

GRAPE VARIETIES:

WHITE: Palomino (90%), Pedro Ximénez, Moscatel, Palomino Fino and Palomino de Jerez.

FIGURES:

Vineyard surface: 6,838.52 – **Wine-Growers:** 1,711 – **Wineries:** 77 – **2014 Harvest rating:** N/A – **Production 14:** 52,654,090 litres – **Market percentages:** 31.35% National - 68.65% International.

SOIL:

The so-called 'Albariza' soil is a key factor regarding quality. This type of soil is practically white and is rich in calcium carbonate, clay and silica. It is excellent for retaining humidity and storing winter rainfall for the dry summer months. Moreover, this soil determines the so-called 'Jerez superior'. It is found in Jerez de la Frontera, Puerto de Santa María, Sanlúcar de Barrameda and certain areas of Trebujena. The remaining soil, known as 'Zona', is muddy and sandy.arenas.

CLIMATE:

Warm with Atlantic influences. The west winds play an important role, as they provide humidity and help to temper the conditions. The average annual temperature is 17.5°C, with an average rainfall of 600 mm per year.

VINTAGE RATING — PEÑÍNGUIDE

This denomination of origin, due to the wine-making process, does not make available single-year wines indicated by vintage, so the following evaluation refers to the overall quality of the wines that were tasted this year.

AECOVI-JEREZ

Urb. Pie de Rey, bloque 3, local izq.
11407 Jerez de la Frontera (Cádiz)
☎: +34 956 180 873
administracion@aecovi-jerez.com
www.aecovi-jerez.com

Alexandro MZ
palomino

90

Colour: yellow, pale. Nose: candied fruit, saline, rancio notes. Palate: flavourful, fine solera notes, long.

Alexandro OL
palomino

87

Colour: light mahogany. Nose: balanced, candied fruit, caramel. Palate: correct, fine bitter notes, spicy, toasty.

Mira la Mar PC

90

Colour: old gold, amber rim. Nose: medium intensity, candied fruit, pattiserie. Palate: flavourful, long, fine bitter notes.

ALVARO DOMECQ

Alamos, 23
11401 Jerez de la Frontera (Cádiz)
☎: +34 956 339 634
alvarodomecqsl@alvarodomecq.com
www.alvarodomecq.com

1730 VORS AM
100% palomino

94

Colour: iodine, amber rim. Nose: powerfull, complex, dry nuts, toasty, iodine notes. Palate: rich, fine bitter notes, fine solera notes, long, spicy.

1730 VORS OL
100% palomino

94

Colour: light mahogany. Nose: powerfull, complex, dry nuts, toasty, acetaldehyde. Palate: rich, long, fine solera notes, spicy, round.

1730 VORS PC
100% palomino

94

Colour: light mahogany. Nose: saline, iodine notes, dry nuts, varnish, acetaldehyde, powerfull. Palate: fine bitter notes, spirituous, long, powerful.

Alburejo OL
100% palomino

91

Colour: iodine, amber rim. Nose: powerfull, dry nuts, creamy oak, varnish. Palate: rich, long, spicy.

Aranda Cream CR
100% palomino

87

Colour: light mahogany. Nose: candied fruit, aged wood nuances, toasty, caramel. Palate: flavourful, sweetness, correct.

La Jaca MZ
100% palomino

88

Colour: yellow, pale. Nose: medium intensity, candied fruit, saline. Palate: flavourful, easy to drink.

La Janda FI
100% palomino

92

Colour: bright yellow. Nose: complex, expressive, pungent, saline. Palate: rich, powerful, fresh, fine bitter notes.

BEAM SUNTORY

San Ildefonso, 3
11403 Jerez de la Frontera (Cádiz)
☎: +34 956 151 500
Fax: +34 956 338 674
bodegasdejerez@beamsuntory.com
www.bodegasharveys.com

Harveys FI
100% palomino

92

Colour: bright yellow. Nose: expressive, pungent, saline. Palate: rich, powerful, fresh, fine bitter notes, long.

Harveys Blend AM
92% palomino, 8% pedro ximénez

88

Colour: iodine, amber rim. Nose: powerfull, dry nuts, creamy oak, varnish. Palate: rich, spicy, sweet.

Harveys Bristol Cream CR
80% palomino, 20% pedro ximénez

87

Colour: iodine, amber rim. Nose: dry nuts, cocoa bean, fruit liqueur notes, fruit liqueur notes. Palate: sweetness, correct.

Harveys Fine Old VORS AM
100% palomino

93

Colour: iodine, amber rim. Nose: powerfull, elegant, dry nuts, toasty, sweet spices. Palate: rich, fine bitter notes, fine solera notes, long, spicy.

Harveys Medium VORS OL
90% palomino, 10% pedro ximénez

92

Colour: iodine, amber rim. Nose: powerfull, complex, dry nuts, creamy oak, varnish. Palate: rich, long, spicy.

Harveys Medium VORS PC
98% palomino, 2% pedro ximénez

93

Colour: iodine, amber rim. Nose: powerfull, elegant, dry nuts, toasty, characterful. Palate: rich, fine solera notes, long, spicy.

Harveys Signature 12 años Rare Cream Sherry CR
80% palomino, 20% pedro ximénez

92

Colour: light mahogany. Nose: acetaldehyde, pungent, varnish, aged wood nuances, creamy oak. Palate: powerful, flavourful, spicy, long, sweet.

Harveys VORS PX
100% pedro ximénez

92

Colour: dark mahogany. Nose: powerfull, expressive, spicy, acetaldehyde, dry nuts, dark chocolate. Palate: balanced, elegant, fine solera notes, toasty, unctuous.

Terry Amontillado AM
100% palomino

92

Colour: iodine, amber rim. Nose: powerfull, complex, dry nuts, toasty, saline. Palate: rich, fine bitter notes, fine solera notes, long, spicy.

Terry Fino FI
100% palomino

91

Colour: bright yellow. Nose: complex, expressive, pungent, saline. Palate: rich, powerful, fresh, fine bitter notes.

Terry Oloroso OL
100% palomino

91

Colour: iodine, amber rim. Nose: powerfull, dry nuts, creamy oak, varnish. Palate: rich, long, spicy.

Terry Pedro Ximénez PX
100% pedro ximénez

91

Colour: mahogany. Nose: complex, fruit liqueur notes, dried fruit, pattiserie, toasty, acetaldehyde. Palate: sweet, rich, unctuous.

BODEGA CÉSAR FLORIDO

Padre Lerchundi, 35-37
11550 Chipiona (Cádiz)
☎: +34 956 371 285
Fax: +34 956 370 222
florido@bodegasflorido.com
www.bodegasflorido.com

César Florido Moscatel Dorado Moscatel
moscatel de alejandría

90

Colour: iodine, amber rim. Nose: powerfull, complex, dry nuts, creamy oak, varnish, honeyed notes, floral. Palate: spicy, round, powerful.

César Florido Moscatel Especial Moscatel
100% moscatel de alejandría

91

Colour: mahogany. Nose: overripe fruit, cocoa bean, aromatic coffee, honeyed notes, sweet spices. Palate: sweetness, spirituous, complex.

César Florido Moscatel Pasas Moscatel
moscatel

89

Colour: mahogany. Nose: complex, fruit liqueur notes, pattiserie, toasty, candied fruit, dry nuts. Palate: sweet, rich, unctuous.

Cruz del Mar CR
75% palomino, 25% moscatel de alejandría

86

Cruz del Mar OL
100% palomino

87

Colour: light mahogany. Nose: varnish, aged wood nuances, candied fruit. Palate: flavourful, correct.

Fino César Florido FI
100% palomino

89

Colour: yellow, pale. Nose: pungent, saline, toasty, rancio notes. Palate: flavourful, good finish, fine bitter notes.

BODEGAS BARBADILLO

Luis de Eguilaz, 11
11540 Sanlúcar de Barrameda (Cádiz)
☎: +34 956 385 500
Fax: +34 956 385 501
barbadillo@barbadillo.com
www.barbadillo.com

PODIUM

Barbadillo Amontillado VORS AM
palomino

96

Colour: iodine, amber rim. Nose: powerfull, complex, elegant, dry nuts, toasty, acetaldehyde, iodine notes. Palate: fine bitter notes, fine solera notes, long, spicy.

Barbadillo Cuco Oloroso Seco OL
palomino

90

Colour: light mahogany. Nose: spicy, candied fruit, roasted almonds, dry nuts. Palate: fine bitter notes, balanced.

Barbadillo Eva Cream CR
pedro ximénez, palomino

89

Colour: light mahogany. Nose: cocoa bean, sweet spices, candied fruit. Palate: correct, spicy, flavourful, sweetness.

Barbadillo La Cilla PX
pedro ximénez

88

Colour: mahogany. Nose: complex, fruit liqueur notes, dried fruit, pattiserie, toasty. Palate: sweet, rich, unctuous.

Barbadillo Laura Moscatel
moscatel

88

Colour: mahogany. Nose: caramel, overripe fruit, cocoa bean, aromatic coffee. Palate: sweetness, spirituous.

Barbadillo Medium Oloroso Dulce VORS OL
palomino, pedro ximénez

89

Colour: light mahogany. Nose: aromatic coffee, caramel, dried fruit, candied fruit, waxy notes. Palate: sweetness, toasty, fine bitter notes.

Barbadillo Obispo Gascón PC
palomino

94

Colour: old gold, amber rim. Nose: spicy, complex, iodine notes, acetaldehyde. Palate: fine solera notes, complex, long, fine bitter notes.

Barbadillo Oloroso Seco VORS OL
palomino

94

Colour: light mahogany. Nose: powerfull, complex, dry nuts, toasty, acetaldehyde. Palate: rich, long, fine solera notes, spicy, round.

Barbadillo Palo Cortado VORS PC
palomino

94

Colour: light mahogany. Nose: saline, iodine notes, dry nuts, varnish, acetaldehyde, sweet spices, characterful. Palate: fine bitter notes, spirituous, long, powerful, fine solera notes.

Barbadillo San Rafael Dulce OL
pedro ximénez, palomino

88

Colour: mahogany. Nose: complex, fruit liqueur notes, dried fruit, pattiserie, toasty. Palate: sweet, rich.

Príncipe de Barbadillo AM
palomino

91

Colour: old gold. Nose: toasty, sweet spices, pattiserie, balanced, powerfull. Palate: flavourful, full, fine bitter notes.

Solear MZ
palomino

93

Colour: bright yellow. Nose: complex, expressive, pungent, saline. Palate: rich, powerful, fresh, fine bitter notes.

🏆 PODIUM

Solear en Rama MZ
palomino

96

Colour: bright yellow. Nose: pungent, dry nuts, toasty, complex, expressive. Palate: long, powerful, fine bitter notes.

BODEGAS DIEZ-MÉRITO

Ctra. Jerez Lebrija (Morabita, Km. 2)
11407 Jerez de la Frontera (Cádiz)
☎: +34 956 186 112
Fax: +34 956 303 500
info@diezmerito.com
www.diezmerito.com

Bertola CR
palomino, pedro ximénez

88

Colour: mahogany. Nose: complex, fruit liqueur notes, dried fruit, pattiserie, toasty. Palate: sweet, rich, unctuous.

Bertola FI
100% palomino

88

Colour: bright yellow. Nose: medium intensity, dry nuts, saline. Palate: long, flavourful, balanced.

Bertola 12 años AM
100% palomino

90

Colour: old gold, amber rim. Nose: balanced, saline, expressive, varietal. Palate: long, flavourful, fine bitter notes, fine solera notes.

Bertola 12 años OL
100% palomino

90

Colour: light mahogany. Nose: roasted almonds, dry nuts. Palate: flavourful, dry, correct, balanced, long.

Bertola 12 años PX
100% pedro ximénez

89

Colour: mahogany. Nose: complex, fruit liqueur notes, dried fruit, pattiserie, toasty. Palate: sweet, rich, unctuous.

Fino Imperial 30 años VORS AM
100% palomino

92

Colour: old gold, amber rim. Nose: balanced, characterful, smoky, roasted almonds. Palate: flavourful, long.

Victoria Regina VORS OL
100% palomino

94

Colour: light mahogany. Nose: acetaldehyde, pungent, varnish, aged wood nuances, creamy oak. Palate: powerful, flavourful, spicy, long, balanced.

Vieja Solera 30 años PX
100% pedro ximénez

92

Colour: mahogany. Nose: powerfull, expressive, aromatic coffee, spicy, dark chocolate. Palate: balanced, elegant, fine solera notes, toasty, long.

BODEGAS DIOS BACO

Tecnología, A-14
11405 Jerez de la Frontera (Cádiz)
☎: +34 956 333 337
Fax: +34 956 333 825
comercial@bodegasdiosbaco.com
www.bodegasdiosbaco.com

Baco Imperial VORS PC
palomino

93

Colour: light mahogany. Nose: iodine notes, dry nuts, varnish, acetaldehyde, powerfull, sweet spices. Palate: fine bitter notes, spirituous, long, powerful.

Dios Baco AM
palomino

90

Colour: light mahogany. Nose: toasty, sweet spices, varnish. Palate: rich, flavourful, long, powerful, fine bitter notes.

Dios Baco OL
palomino

92

Colour: old gold, amber rim. Nose: pattiserie, sweet spices, dry nuts, varnish. Palate: balanced, fine bitter notes.

Esnobista Moscatel Pasa Moscatel
moscatel

88

Colour: mahogany. Nose: caramel, overripe fruit, cocoa bean, aromatic coffee. Palate: sweetness, spirituous, complex.

Oloroso Baco de Élite Medium Dry OL
palomino, pedro ximénez

90

Colour: iodine, amber rim. Nose: complex, dry nuts, toasty. Palate: rich, fine solera notes, spicy.

Oxford 1970 PX
pedro ximénez

91

Colour: mahogany. Nose: complex, fruit liqueur notes, dried fruit, pattiserie, toasty. Palate: sweet, rich, unctuous.

BODEGAS HIDALGO-LA GITANA

Banda de la Playa, 42
11540 Sanlúcar de Barrameda (Cádiz)
☎: +34 956 385 304
Fax: +34 956 363 844
bodegashidalgo@lagitana.es
www.lagitana.es

Alameda CR
75% palomino, 25% pedro ximénez

87

Colour: old gold. Nose: sweet spices, pattiserie, candied fruit. Palate: flavourful, sweetness, easy to drink.

Faraón OL
100% palomino

88

Colour: mahogany. Nose: caramel, overripe fruit, cocoa bean, aromatic coffee. Palate: sweetness, spirituous, complex.

Faraón 30 años VORS 50 cl. OL
100% palomino

93

Colour: light mahogany. Nose: acetaldehyde, pungent, varnish, aged wood nuances, creamy oak, characterful. Palate: powerful, flavourful, spicy, long.

Heredad de Hidalgo AM

88

Colour: coppery red. Nose: sweet spices, acetaldehyde, dry nuts. Palate: dry, spicy, fine bitter notes.

La Gitana MZ
100% palomino

93

Colour: bright yellow. Nose: complex, expressive, pungent, saline, elegant. Palate: rich, powerful, fresh, fine bitter notes, full.

La Gitana en Rama (Saca de Invierno) MZ
100% palomino

93

Colour: bright golden. Nose: powerfull, characterful, pungent, acetaldehyde. Palate: powerful, complex, fine bitter notes.

Napoleón AM
100% palomino

90

Colour: old gold, amber rim. Nose: medium intensity, balanced, candied fruit, roasted almonds. Palate: balanced, fine bitter notes.

Napoleón 30 años VORS 50 cl. AM
100% palomino

93

Colour: iodine, amber rim. Nose: powerfull, complex, elegant, dry nuts, toasty. Palate: rich, fine bitter notes, fine solera notes, long, spicy.

Pastrana Manzanilla Pasada MZ
100% palomino

94

Colour: yellow, pale. Nose: expressive, complex, elegant, toasty, saline, pungent. Palate: balanced, fine bitter notes, full.

Triana PX
100% pedro ximénez

90

Colour: mahogany. Nose: complex, fruit liqueur notes, dried fruit, pattiserie, toasty. Palate: sweet, rich, unctuous.

Triana 30 años VORS PX
100% pedro ximénez

92

Colour: mahogany. Nose: complex, fruit liqueur notes, dried fruit, pattiserie, toasty, cocoa bean. Palate: sweet, rich, unctuous.

Wellington 30 años VORS PC
100% palomino

93

Colour: iodine, amber rim. Nose: powerfull, complex, elegant, dry nuts, toasty. Palate: rich, fine bitter notes, fine solera notes, long, spicy.

Wellington Jerez Cortado 20 años VOS 50 cl. PC
100% palomino

91

Colour: light mahogany. Nose: acetaldehyde, pungent, varnish, aged wood nuances, creamy oak. Palate: powerful, flavourful, spicy, long, balanced.

BODEGAS LA CIGARRERA

Pza. Madre de Dios, s/n
11540 Sanlúcar de Barrameda (Cádiz)
☎: +34 956 381 285
Fax: +34 956 383 824
lacigarrera@bodegaslacigarrera.com
www.bodegaslacigarrera.com

La Cigarrera AM
palomino, listán blanco

89

Colour: bright golden. Nose: candied fruit, pattiserie, dry nuts. Palate: rich, flavourful.

La Cigarrera Moscatel
moscatel

91

Colour: mahogany. Nose: complex, fruit liqueur notes, pattiserie, toasty, honeyed notes. Palate: sweet, rich, unctuous.

La Cigarrera MZ
palomino

89

Colour: bright yellow. Nose: expressive, pungent, saline. Palate: rich, fresh, fine bitter notes.

La Cigarrera OL
palomino

88

Colour: iodine, amber rim. Nose: powerfull, complex, dry nuts, creamy oak, varnish. Palate: rich, long, spicy.

La Cigarrera PX
pedro ximénez

90

Colour: dark mahogany. Nose: aromatic coffee, spicy, acetaldehyde, dry nuts, warm. Palate: balanced, elegant, toasty.

BODEGAS OSBORNE

Fernán Caballero, 7
11500 El Puerto de Santa María (Cádiz)
☎: +34 956 869 000
carolina.cerrato@osborne.es
www.osborne.es

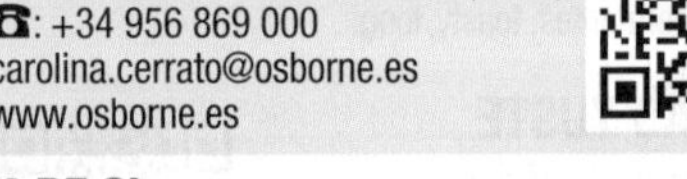

10 RF OL
palomino, pedro ximénez

88

Colour: iodine, amber rim. Nose: powerfull, dry nuts, creamy oak, varnish. Palate: rich, sweet.

PODIUM

Amontillado 51-1ª VORS AM
100% palomino

95

Colour: iodine, amber rim. Nose: candied fruit, fruit liqueur notes, spicy, varnish, acetaldehyde, iodine notes. Palate: fine solera notes, fine bitter notes, spirituous.

Bailén OL
100% palomino

88

Colour: old gold, amber rim. Nose: toasty, candied fruit, honeyed notes. Palate: flavourful, spicy, easy to drink.

Capuchino VORS PC
100% palomino

94

Colour: light mahogany. Nose: acetaldehyde, pungent, varnish, creamy oak, dried fruit, pattiserie. Palate: powerful, flavourful, spicy, long, balanced.

Coquinero FI
100% palomino

92

Colour: bright yellow. Nose: expressive, pungent, saline. Palate: rich, powerful, fresh, fine bitter notes.

Fino Quinta FI
100% palomino

92

Colour: bright yellow. Nose: pungent, saline, characterful. Palate: rich, powerful, fresh, fine bitter notes.

Osborne Pedro Ximénez 1827 PX
pedro ximénez

90

Colour: mahogany. Nose: complex, fruit liqueur notes, dried fruit, pattiserie, toasty. Palate: sweet, rich, unctuous.

PODIUM

Osborne Pedro Ximénez Viejo VORS PX
pedro ximénez

95

Colour: dark mahogany. Nose: powerfull, expressive, aromatic coffee, spicy, acetaldehyde, dry nuts. Palate: balanced, elegant, toasty, unctuous.

PODIUM

Osborne Solera AOS AM
palomino

96

Colour: dark mahogany. Nose: candied fruit, fruit liqueur notes, spicy, varnish, acetaldehyde, saline. Palate: fine solera notes, fine bitter notes, spirituous.

PODIUM

Osborne Solera BC 200 OL
pedro ximénez, palomino

97

Colour: light mahogany. Nose: powerfull, complex, dry nuts, toasty, acetaldehyde, expressive, characterful. Palate: rich, long, fine solera notes, spicy, round.

PODIUM

Osborne Solera India OL
pedro ximénez, palomino

95

Colour: light mahogany. Nose: powerfull, complex, dry nuts, toasty, acetaldehyde. Palate: rich, long, fine solera notes, spicy, round.

PODIUM

Osborne Solera PAP PC
pedro ximénez, palomino

96

Colour: light mahogany. Nose: acetaldehyde, pungent, varnish, aged wood nuances, creamy oak, saline. Palate: powerful, flavourful, spicy, balanced, fine solera notes.

Santa María Cream CR
pedro ximénez, palomino

87

Colour: iodine, amber rim. Nose: complex, fruit liqueur notes, dried fruit, pattiserie, toasty. Palate: sweet, rich, unctuous.

PODIUM

Sibarita VORS OL
98% palomino, 2% pedro ximénez

95

Colour: light mahogany. Nose: powerfull, complex, dry nuts, toasty, acetaldehyde. Palate: rich, long, fine solera notes, spicy, round.

PODIUM

Venerable VORS PX
100% pedro ximénez

97

Colour: dark mahogany. Nose: powerfull, expressive, aromatic coffee, spicy, acetaldehyde, dry nuts. Palate: balanced, elegant, fine solera notes, toasty, long.

BODEGAS TRADICIÓN
Cordobeses, 3-5
11408 Jerez de la Frontera (Cádiz)
☎: +34 956 168 628
Fax: +34 956 331 963
visitas@bodegastradicion.com
www.bodegastradicion.com

Amontillado Tradición VORS AM
palomino

93

Colour: old gold, amber rim. Nose: powerfull, complex, dry nuts, toasty. Palate: rich, fine bitter notes, fine solera notes, long, spicy.

Fino Tradición FI
palomino

93

Colour: bright golden. Nose: powerfull, dry nuts, acetaldehyde, saline. Palate: round, fine bitter notes, powerful.

PODIUM

Oloroso Tradición VORS OL
palomino

96

Colour: iodine, amber rim. Nose: powerfull, complex, dry nuts, toasty, acetaldehyde. Palate: rich, long, fine solera notes, spicy, round.

Palo Cortado Tradición VORS PC
palomino

94

Colour: iodine, amber rim. Nose: elegant, dry nuts, toasty, acetaldehyde. Palate: rich, fine bitter notes, fine solera notes, long, spicy.

Pedro Ximénez Tradición VOS PX
pedro ximénez

94

Colour: dark mahogany. Nose: powerfull, expressive, aromatic coffee, spicy, acetaldehyde, dry nuts. Palate: balanced, elegant, fine solera notes, toasty, long.

BODEGAS YUSTE
Ctra. Sanlúcar - Chipiona, 93
11540 Sanlúcar de Barrameda (Cádiz)
☎: +34 956 385 200
info@bodegasyuste.com
www.yuste.com

La Kika MZ
palomino

93

Colour: bright golden. Nose: complex, expressive, pungent, saline. Palate: rich, powerful, fresh, fine bitter notes.

La Monteria MZ
100% palomino

86

DELGADO ZULETA

Avda. Rocío Jurado, s/n
11540 Sanlúcar de Barrameda (Cádiz)
☎: +34 956 361 107
Fax: +34 956 360 780
jfcarvajal@delgadozuleta.com
www.delgadozuleta.com

Barbiana Magnum MZ
palomino

91

Colour: bright yellow. Nose: complex, expressive, pungent, saline. Palate: rich, powerful, fresh, fine bitter notes.

Goya XL MZ
palomino

94

Colour: bright golden. Nose: expressive, pungent, saline, complex. Palate: rich, powerful, fresh, fine bitter notes.

La Goya MZ
palomino

91

Colour: bright yellow. Nose: complex, expressive, saline. Palate: powerful, fresh, fine bitter notes.

EQUIPO NAVAZOS

11403 Jerez de la Frontera (Cádiz)
equipo@navazos.com
www.equiponavazos.com

PODIUM

Fino en Rama Navazos, Saca Mayo 2015 FI

95

Colour: bright yellow. Nose: flor yeasts, lees reduction notes, pungent. Palate: good acidity, fine bitter notes, spicy, long.

PODIUM

La Bota de Amontillado nº 61 "Bota NO" AM

97

Colour: dark mahogany. Nose: candied fruit, fruit liqueur notes, spicy, varnish, caramel, powerfull, complex. Palate: fine solera notes, fine bitter notes, spirituous.

PODIUM

La Bota de Amontillado nº 58 Navazos AM

95

Colour: iodine, amber rim. Nose: sweet spices, acetaldehyde, dry nuts. Palate: full, dry, spicy, long, fine bitter notes, complex.

PODIUM

La Bota de Manzanilla nª 55 MZ

95

Colour: bright yellow. Nose: saline, iodine notes, dry nuts, varnish, acetaldehyde, powerfull. Palate: fine bitter notes, spirituous, long, powerful.

PODIUM

La Bota de Manzanilla Pasada Nº59 "Capataz Rivas" MZ
palomino

98

Colour: bright yellow. Nose: saline, dry nuts, varnish, acetaldehyde, powerfull, iodine notes, dried herbs. Palate: fine bitter notes, spirituous, long, powerful.

PODIUM

La Bota de Manzanilla Pasada Nº60 "Bota Punta" MZ

97

Colour: bright yellow. Nose: iodine notes, dry nuts, varnish, acetaldehyde, saline, elegant. Palate: fine bitter notes, spirituous, long, powerful.

PODIUM

La Bota de Pedro Ximenez nº56 Bota NO PX

98

Colour: dark mahogany. Nose: powerfull, aromatic coffee, spicy, acetaldehyde, dry nuts, expressive. Palate: balanced, elegant, fine solera notes, toasty, long.

Manzanilla en Rama I Think. Saca Julio 2015 MZ

94

Colour: bright yellow. Nose: saline, iodine notes, dry nuts, varnish, powerfull. Palate: fine bitter notes, spirituous, long, powerful.

FAUSTINO GONZÁLEZ

Barja, 1
11402 Jerez de la Frontera (Cádiz)
☎: +34 626 990 482
info@bodegasfaustinogonzalez.com
www.bodegasfaustinogonzalez.com

Cruz Vieja AM
palomino

89

Colour: iodine, amber rim. Nose: powerfull, dry nuts, toasty. Palate: rich, fine bitter notes, fine solera notes, spicy.

Cruz Vieja FI
palomino

91

Colour: bright golden. Nose: pungent, saline. Palate: rich, powerful, fresh, fine bitter notes.

Cruz Vieja OL
palomino

90

Colour: iodine, amber rim. Nose: powerfull, complex, dry nuts, creamy oak, varnish. Palate: rich, long, spicy.

Cruz Vieja PC
palomino

88

Colour: iodine, amber rim. Nose: candied fruit, sweet spices, varnish, caramel. Palate: rich, correct, easy to drink.

FERNANDO DE CASTILLA

Jardinillo, 7-11
11407 Jerez de la Frontera (Cádiz)
☎: +34 956 182 454
Fax: +34 956 182 222
bodegas@fernandodecastilla.com
www.fernandodecastilla.com

Fernando de Castilla "Amontillado Antique" AM
100% palomino

94

Colour: iodine, amber rim. Nose: powerfull, dry nuts, toasty, acetaldehyde, pungent. Palate: rich, fine bitter notes, fine solera notes, long, spicy.

Fernando de Castilla "Fino Antique" FI
100% palomino

94

Colour: bright golden. Nose: expressive, pungent, saline, powerfull, characterful. Palate: rich, powerful, fine bitter notes, round.

Fernando de Castilla "Oloroso Antique" OL
100% palomino

92

Colour: iodine, amber rim. Nose: elegant, sweet spices, acetaldehyde, dry nuts. Palate: full, dry, spicy, long, fine bitter notes, complex.

PODIUM

Fernando de Castilla "P.X. Antique" PX
100% pedro ximénez

95

Colour: dark mahogany. Nose: powerfull, expressive, aromatic coffee, spicy, acetaldehyde, dry nuts. Palate: balanced, elegant, fine solera notes, toasty, long.

PODIUM

Fernando de Castilla "Palo Cortado Antique" PC
100% palomino

95

Colour: light mahogany. Nose: roasted almonds, toasty, balanced, iodine notes, expressive. Palate: complex, fine solera notes, long, elegant.

Fernando de Castilla Amontillado Classic AM
100% palomino

85

Fernando de Castilla Cream Classic CR
90% palomino, 10% pedro ximénez

87

Colour: light mahogany. Nose: candied fruit, dried fruit, tobacco, spicy. Palate: balanced, fine bitter notes, sweetness.

Fernando de Castilla Fino Classic FI
100% palomino

91

Colour: bright yellow. Nose: expressive, saline, flor yeasts, characterful. Palate: rich, powerful, fresh, fine bitter notes.

Fernando de Castilla Fino en Rama FI
100% palomino

93

Colour: bright golden. Nose: complex, expressive, pungent, saline. Palate: rich, powerful, fresh, fine bitter notes.

Fernando de Castilla Manzanilla Classic MZ
100% palomino

90

Colour: bright straw. Nose: fresh, medium intensity, flor yeasts. Palate: flavourful, long.

Fernando de Castilla Oloroso Classic OL
100% palomino

90

Colour: light mahogany. Nose: fruit liqueur notes, sweet spices, aromatic coffee, caramel. Palate: flavourful, spicy.

Fernando de Castilla PX Classic PX
100% pedro ximénez

90

Colour: mahogany. Nose: complex, fruit liqueur notes, dried fruit, pattiserie, toasty. Palate: sweet, rich, unctuous.

GARVEY

Ctra. Circunvalación, s/n
(Complejo Bellavista)
11407 Jerez de la Frontera (Cádiz)
☎: +34 956 319 650
Fax: +34 956 319 824
info@grupogarvey.com
www.grupogarvey.com

Asalto Amoroso CR
90% palomino, 10% pedro ximénez

90

Colour: iodine, amber rim. Nose: powerfull, creamy oak, varnish, dried fruit. Palate: rich, long, spicy, sweetness.

Don José María AM
100% palomino

91

Colour: iodine, amber rim. Nose: powerfull, dry nuts, toasty, warm. Palate: rich, fine bitter notes, fine solera notes, spicy.

Don José María CR
75% palomino, 25% pedro ximénez

88

Colour: iodine, amber rim. Nose: pattiserie, cocoa bean, candied fruit. Palate: correct, sweet, easy to drink.

Don José María FI
100% palomino

91

Colour: bright yellow. Nose: expressive, pungent, saline. Palate: rich, powerful, fresh, fine bitter notes.

Don José María OL
100% palomino

92

Colour: light mahogany. Nose: acetaldehyde, varnish, aged wood nuances, creamy oak. Palate: powerful, flavourful, spicy, long, balanced.

Flor de Jerez CR
75% palomino, 25% pedro ximénez

88

Colour: light mahogany. Nose: aged wood nuances, cigar, caramel, aromatic coffee. Palate: correct, unctuous.

Flor del Museo CR
75% palomino, 25% pedro ximénez

91

Colour: iodine, amber rim. Nose: roasted almonds, toasty, earthy notes, cocoa bean, candied fruit. Palate: long, balanced, fine bitter notes.

Garvey PX
100% pedro ximénez

91

Colour: mahogany. Nose: complex, fruit liqueur notes, dried fruit, pattiserie, toasty, dark chocolate, aromatic coffee. Palate: sweet, rich, unctuous.

Garvey VORS OL
100% palomino

94

Colour: light mahogany. Nose: complex, dry nuts, toasty, acetaldehyde. Palate: rich, long, fine solera notes, spicy, round.

🏆 PODIUM

Garvey VORS PX
100% pedro ximénez

95

Colour: dark mahogany. Nose: powerfull, expressive, spicy, acetaldehyde, dry nuts, dark chocolate. Palate: balanced, elegant, fine solera notes, toasty, long.

Garvey VOS OL
100% palomino

91

Colour: iodine, amber rim. Nose: powerfull, complex, dry nuts, creamy oak, varnish. Palate: rich, long, spicy.

Garvey VOS PX
100% pedro ximénez

93

Colour: dark mahogany. Nose: aromatic coffee, spicy, acetaldehyde, dry nuts. Palate: balanced, fine solera notes, toasty, long.

Gran Orden PX
100% pedro ximénez

94

Colour: mahogany. Nose: complex, fruit liqueur notes, dried fruit, pattiserie, toasty, dark chocolate, sweet spices. Palate: sweet, rich, unctuous.

🏆 PODIUM

Jauna PC
100% palomino

95

Colour: light mahogany. Nose: saline, iodine notes, dry nuts, varnish, acetaldehyde, powerfull, sweet spices. Palate: fine bitter notes, spirituous, long, powerful.

Juncal MZ
100% palomino

88

Colour: bright yellow. Nose: flor yeasts, lees reduction notes, saline. Palate: flavourful, powerful.

Ochavico OL
100% palomino

87

Colour: iodine, amber rim. Nose: powerfull, dry nuts, creamy oak, varnish. Palate: rich, long, spicy.

Oñana AM
100% palomino

93

Colour: old gold, amber rim. Nose: powerfull, complex, elegant, dry nuts, toasty, varnish. Palate: rich, fine bitter notes, fine solera notes, long, spicy.

Puerta Real OL
100% palomino

93

Colour: light mahogany. Nose: powerfull, complex, dry nuts, toasty, acetaldehyde. Palate: rich, long, fine solera notes, spicy, round.

San Patricio FI
100% palomino

92

Colour: bright yellow. Nose: complex, expressive, balanced, pungent, saline. Palate: full, flavourful, long, fine bitter notes.

Tio Guillermo AM
100% palomino

86

GONZÁLEZ BYASS JEREZ
Manuel María González, 12
11403 Jerez de la Frontera (Cádiz)
☎: +34 956 357 000
Fax: +34 956 357 043
elrincondegb@gonzalezbyass.es
www.gonzalezbyass.es

Alfonso OL
100% palomino

89

Colour: iodine, amber rim. Nose: balanced, sweet spices, caramel, smoky. Palate: fine bitter notes, flavourful.

Amontillado del Duque VORS AM
100% palomino

94

Colour: iodine, amber rim. Nose: powerfull, dry nuts, toasty, iodine notes. Palate: rich, fine bitter notes, fine solera notes, long, spicy.

🏆 PODIUM

Añada Millennium OL
100% palomino

95

Colour: light mahogany. Nose: acetaldehyde, iodine notes, fruit liqueur notes, spicy, aromatic coffee, smoky. Palate: powerful, sweet, long, toasty.

Apóstoles VORS PC
87% palomino, 13% pedro ximénez

92

Colour: iodine, amber rim. Nose: powerfull, complex, elegant, dry nuts, toasty. Palate: rich, fine solera notes, sweet, round.

🏆 PODIUM

Fino Cuatro Palmas FI
100% palomino

96

Colour: light mahogany. Nose: fruit liqueur notes, acetaldehyde, iodine notes, powerfull, toasty, smoky. Palate: flavourful, powerful, spicy, long, fine bitter notes.

🏆 PODIUM

Fino Dos Palmas FI
100% palomino

95

Colour: bright golden. Nose: dry nuts, toasty, saline, pungent, expressive, elegant. Palate: full, flavourful, dry, complex.

🏆 PODIUM

Fino Tres Palmas FI
100% palomino

95

Colour: bright golden. Nose: powerfull, complex, elegant, dry nuts, toasty. Palate: rich, fine bitter notes, fine solera notes.

Fino Una Palmas FI
100% palomino

93

Colour: bright yellow. Nose: flor yeasts, saline, fragrant herbs. Palate: flavourful, long, fine bitter notes.

Leonor PC
100% palomino

94

Colour: light mahogany. Nose: saline, iodine notes, dry nuts, varnish, acetaldehyde, powerfull. Palate: fine bitter notes, spirituous, long, powerful.

Matusalem VORS OL
75% palomino, 25% pedro ximénez

94

Colour: light mahogany. Nose: powerfull, complex, dry nuts, toasty, acetaldehyde, aromatic coffee, dark chocolate. Palate: rich, long, fine solera notes, spicy, round, sweet.

Néctar PX
100% pedro ximénez

91

Colour: mahogany. Nose: complex, fruit liqueur notes, dried fruit, pattiserie, toasty, dark chocolate. Palate: sweet, rich, unctuous.

PODIUM

Noé VORS PX
100% pedro ximénez

95

Colour: dark mahogany. Nose: aromatic coffee, spicy, acetaldehyde, dry nuts. Palate: balanced, elegant, fine solera notes, toasty.

Solera 1847 Dulce CR
palomino, pedro ximénez

88

Colour: light mahogany. Nose: fruit liqueur notes, sweet spices, dried fruit. Palate: correct, fine bitter notes, sweetness.

Tío Pepe FI
100% palomino

94

Colour: bright yellow. Nose: complex, pungent, saline, powerfull. Palate: rich, powerful, fresh, fine bitter notes.

PODIUM

Tío Pepe en Rama FI
100% palomino

95

Colour: bright yellow. Nose: flor yeasts, pungent, fine lees, saline. Palate: good acidity, fine bitter notes, spicy, long, elegant.

Viña AB AM
100% palomino

91

Colour: iodine, amber rim. Nose: powerfull, dry nuts, toasty. Palate: rich, fine bitter notes, fine solera notes, long, spicy.

GUTIÉRREZ-COLOSÍA

Avda. Bajamar, 40
11500 El Puerto de Santa María (Cádiz)
☎: +34 956 852 852
Fax: +34 956 542 936
info@gutierrezcolosia.com
www.gutierrezcolosia.com

Gutiérrez Colosía AM
palomino

90

Colour: old gold, amber rim. Nose: powerfull, sweet spices, roasted almonds, toasty. Palate: balanced, fine bitter notes, rich.

Gutiérrez Colosía CR
palomino, pedro ximénez

88

Colour: mahogany. Nose: complex, fruit liqueur notes, dried fruit, pattiserie, toasty. Palate: sweet, rich, unctuous.

Gutiérrez Colosía FI
palomino

93

Colour: bright yellow. Nose: complex, expressive, pungent, saline. Palate: rich, powerful, fresh, fine bitter notes.

Gutiérrez Colosía MZ
palomino

91

Colour: bright yellow. Nose: complex, pungent, saline, elegant. Palate: rich, powerful, fresh, fine bitter notes, balanced.

Gutiérrez Colosía OL
palomino

90

Colour: iodine, amber rim. Nose: powerfull, complex, dry nuts, creamy oak, varnish. Palate: rich, long, spicy.

Gutiérrez Colosía PX
pedro ximénez

88

Colour: mahogany. Nose: fruit liqueur notes, dried fruit, pattiserie, toasty. Palate: sweet, rich, unctuous.

Gutiérrez Colosía Fino en Rama 3 años FI
palomino

88

Colour: golden, pale. Nose: dry nuts, honeyed notes, medium intensity. Palate: powerful, flavourful, spicy.

Gutiérrez Colosía Fino en Rama 5 años FI
palomino

91

Colour: bright yellow. Nose: expressive, pungent, saline. Palate: rich, powerful, fresh, fine bitter notes, long.

Gutiérrez Colosía Moscatel Moscatel
moscatel

89

Colour: mahogany. Nose: caramel, overripe fruit, cocoa bean, fruit preserve. Palate: sweetness, spirituous, complex.

Sangre y Trabajadero OL
palomino

90

Colour: old gold, amber rim. Nose: candied fruit, sweet spices, caramel. Palate: correct, balanced.

Solera Familiar Gutiérrez Colosía OL
palomino

93

Colour: light mahogany. Nose: expressive, spicy, complex. Palate: flavourful, balanced, fine bitter notes, fine solera notes.

Solera Familiar Gutiérrez Colosía PC
palomino

93

Colour: light mahogany. Nose: expressive, acetaldehyde, dry nuts, roasted almonds. Palate: full, complex, good structure, fine solera notes.

Solera Familiar Gutiérrez Colosía PX
pedro ximénez

93

Colour: dark mahogany. Nose: powerfull, expressive, aromatic coffee, spicy, acetaldehyde, dry nuts. Palate: balanced, elegant, toasty.

Solera Familiar Gutiérrez Colosía AM
palomino

93

Colour: iodine, amber rim. Nose: powerfull, dry nuts, toasty, acetaldehyde, saline. Palate: rich, fine bitter notes, fine solera notes, long, spicy.

HIDALGO

Clavel, 29
11402 Jerez de la Frontera (Cádiz)
☎: +34 956 341 078
Fax: +34 956 320 922
info@hidalgo.com
www.hidalgo.com

PODIUM

El Tresillo 1874 Amontillado Viejo AM

95

Colour: iodine, amber rim. Nose: powerfull, complex, elegant, dry nuts, toasty, acetaldehyde. Palate: rich, fine bitter notes, fine solera notes, long, spicy.

El Tresillo Amontillado Fino AM

91

Colour: bright golden. Nose: candied fruit, sweet spices, balanced. Palate: spicy, easy to drink, fine bitter notes.

PODIUM

La Panesa Especial Fino FI

95

Colour: bright golden. Nose: acetaldehyde, pungent, iodine notes. Palate: fine bitter notes, round, long.

Marqués de Rodil PC

94

Colour: light mahogany. Nose: acetaldehyde, pungent, varnish, aged wood nuances, creamy oak. Palate: powerful, flavourful, spicy, long, balanced.

Villapanés OL

94

Colour: light mahogany. Nose: powerfull, complex, dry nuts, toasty, acetaldehyde. Palate: rich, long, fine solera notes, spicy, round.

HIJOS DE RAINERA PÉREZ MARÍN

Ctra. Nacional IV, Km. 640
11404 Jerez de la Frontera (Cádiz)
☎: +34 956 321 004
Fax: +34 956 340 216
info@grupoestevez.com
www.laguita.com

La Guita MZ
100% palomino

93

Colour: bright yellow. Nose: complex, expressive, pungent, saline. Palate: rich, powerful, fresh, fine bitter notes.

LUIS CABALLERO

San Francisco, 32
11500 El Puerto de Santa María (Cádiz)
☎: +34 956 851 751
Fax: +34 956 859 204
marketing@caballero.es
www.caballero.es

Macarena MZ
palomino

90

Colour: bright yellow. Nose: complex, expressive, saline. Palate: rich, powerful, fresh, fine bitter notes.

Pavón FI
palomino

94

Colour: bright yellow. Nose: pungent, dry nuts, complex, expressive. Palate: rich, long, spicy, fine bitter notes.

LUSTAU

Arcos, 53
11402 Jerez de la Frontera (Cádiz)
☎: +34 956 341 597
Fax: +34 956 859 204
lustau@lustau.es
www.lustau.es

Amontillado de Sanlúcar Almacenista Cuevas Jurado AM
palomino

91

Colour: old gold, amber rim. Nose: powerfull, roasted almonds, sweet spices, smoky, candied fruit. Palate: complex, rich.

Botaina AM
palomino

90

Colour: iodine, amber rim. Nose: powerfull, dry nuts, toasty. Palate: rich, fine bitter notes, fine solera notes, long, spicy.

East India CR
palomino, pedro ximénez

92

Colour: mahogany. Nose: complex, fruit liqueur notes, dried fruit, toasty, acetaldehyde, aged wood nuances. Palate: sweet, rich, unctuous.

Emilín Moscatel
moscatel

92

Colour: iodine, amber rim. Nose: powerfull, complex, dry nuts, creamy oak, varnish, floral, candied fruit, honeyed notes. Palate: rich, long, spicy.

Escuadrilla AM
palomino

90

Colour: old gold, amber rim. Nose: characterful, balanced, roasted almonds, spicy, smoky, candied fruit. Palate: flavourful, full.

Jarana FI
palomino

93

Colour: bright yellow. Nose: complex, pungent, saline. Palate: powerful, fresh, fine bitter notes.

🏆 PODIUM

La Ina FI
palomino

95

Colour: bright yellow. Nose: expressive, pungent, iodine notes, characterful. Palate: rich, powerful, fresh, fine bitter notes.

Oloroso del Puerto Almacenista González Obregón OL
palomino

94

Colour: iodine, amber rim. Nose: powerfull, complex, elegant, dry nuts, toasty. Palate: rich, long, fine solera notes, spicy.

Papirusa MZ
palomino

94

Colour: bright yellow. Nose: complex, expressive, pungent, saline. Palate: rich, powerful, fresh, fine bitter notes.

Penísula PC
palomino

92

Colour: light mahogany. Nose: candied fruit, balanced, roasted almonds. Palate: spicy, fine solera notes, flavourful.

Puerto Fino FI
palomino

94

Colour: bright yellow. Nose: complex, expressive, pungent, saline. Palate: rich, powerful, fresh, fine bitter notes.

Río Viejo OL
palomino

91

Colour: iodine, amber rim. Nose: powerfull, complex, dry nuts, creamy oak, varnish. Palate: rich, long, spicy.

San Emilio PX
pedro ximénez

92

Colour: mahogany. Nose: complex, fruit liqueur notes, dried fruit, pattiserie, toasty. Palate: sweet, rich, unctuous.

MARQUÉS DEL REAL TESORO

Ctra. Nacional IV, Km. 640
11404 Jerez de la Frontera (Cádiz)
☎: +34 956 321 004
Fax: +34 956 340 216
info@grupoestevez.com
www.grupoestevez.com

Del Príncipe AM
100% palomino

91

Colour: iodine, amber rim. Nose: powerfull, elegant, dry nuts, toasty. Palate: rich, fine bitter notes, spicy.

Tío Mateo FI
100% palomino

93

Colour: bright yellow. Nose: complex, expressive, pungent, saline. Palate: rich, powerful, fresh, fine bitter notes.

MIGUEL SÁNCHEZ AYALA

Banda Playa, 76
11540 Sanlúcar de Barrameda (Cádiz)
☎: +34 954 931 045
Fax: +34 954 931 085
jose@cebasa.com

Gabriela MZ
100% palomino

90

Colour: bright yellow. Nose: saline, pungent, spicy, dry nuts. Palate: fresh, flavourful, easy to drink.

Gabriela Oro MZ
100% palomino

94

Colour: bright golden. Nose: pungent, flor yeasts, faded flowers. Palate: powerful, flavourful, fine bitter notes, long.

PORTALES PÉREZ

Avda. San Francisco, 23
11540 Sanlúcar de Barrameda (Cádiz)
☎: +34 956 360 131
bodegaloscaireles@gmail.com

Los Caireles CR

89

Colour: iodine, amber rim. Nose: powerfull, complex, dry nuts, creamy oak, varnish. Palate: rich, long, sweetness.

Los Caireles MZ

88

Colour: bright straw. Nose: complex, pungent, saline. Palate: rich, powerful, fresh, fine bitter notes.

Los Caireles OL

88

Colour: iodine, amber rim. Nose: powerfull, elegant, dry nuts, toasty. Palate: rich, long, spicy.

ROMATE

Lealas, 26
11404 Jerez de la Frontera (Cádiz)
☎: +34 956 182 212
Fax: +34 956 185 276
comercial@romate.com
www.romate.com

Cardenal Cisneros PX
100% pedro ximénez

91

Colour: mahogany. Nose: complex, fruit liqueur notes, dried fruit, pattiserie, toasty. Palate: sweet, rich, unctuous.

Don José OL
100% palomino

92

Colour: iodine, amber rim. Nose: powerfull, complex, elegant, dry nuts, toasty. Palate: rich, long, fine solera notes, spicy.

Duquesa PX
100% pedro ximénez

90

Colour: mahogany. Nose: complex, fruit liqueur notes, dried fruit, pattiserie, toasty, acetaldehyde, dark chocolate. Palate: sweet, rich, unctuous.

Fino Perdido FI
100% palomino

93

Colour: bright golden. Nose: complex, pungent, saline, dry nuts. Palate: rich, powerful, fresh, fine bitter notes.

Iberia CR
70% palomino, 30% pedro ximénez

89

Colour: old gold, amber rim. Nose: fruit liqueur notes, fruit liqueur notes, caramel. Palate: fruity, flavourful, long.

Marismeño FI
100% palomino

91

Colour: bright yellow. Nose: candied fruit, iodine notes, saline, dried herbs. Palate: flavourful, correct, fine bitter notes.

NPU AM
100% palomino

93

Colour: iodine, amber rim. Nose: powerfull, complex, elegant, dry nuts, toasty, saline. Palate: rich, fine bitter notes, fine solera notes, long, spicy.

Old & Plus Amontillado VORS AM
100% palomino

93

Colour: iodine, amber rim. Nose: powerfull, complex, elegant, dry nuts, toasty. Palate: rich, fine bitter notes, fine solera notes, long, spicy.

Old & Plus Oloroso OL
100% palomino

94

Colour: light mahogany. Nose: powerfull, dry nuts, toasty, acetaldehyde, characterful. Palate: rich, long, fine solera notes, spicy.

Old & Plus P.X. PX
100% pedro ximénez

93

Colour: mahogany. Nose: complex, fruit liqueur notes, dried fruit, pattiserie, toasty, aromatic coffee. Palate: sweet, rich, unctuous, flavourful.

Regente PC
100% palomino

92

Colour: light mahogany. Nose: saline, iodine notes, dry nuts, varnish, acetaldehyde, complex, characterful. Palate: fine bitter notes, spirituous, long, powerful.

SANDEMAN JEREZ

Porvera, 3 of. 8 y 11
11403 Jerez de la Frontera (Cádiz)
☎: +34 956 151 700
Fax: +34 956 300 007
jose.moreno@sogrape.pt
www.sandeman.eu

Sandeman Armada Premium CR
palomino, pedro ximénez

90

Colour: light mahogany. Nose: candied fruit, cocoa bean, pattiserie, dry nuts. Palate: rich, flavourful, long.

Sandeman Character Premium AM
palomino, pedro ximénez

91

Colour: iodine, amber rim. Nose: powerfull, complex, dry nuts, creamy oak, varnish. Palate: long, spicy, sweet.

Sandeman Classic FI
palomino

87

Colour: bright yellow. Nose: lees reduction notes, iodine notes, toasty. Palate: fine bitter notes, spicy.

Sandeman Classic Medium Dry CR
palomino, pedro ximénez

88

Colour: iodine, amber rim. Nose: powerfull, complex, dry nuts, creamy oak, varnish. Palate: long, spicy, sweet.

Sandeman Don Fino Premium FI
palomino

91

Colour: bright yellow. Nose: complex, expressive, pungent, saline. Palate: rich, powerful, fresh, fine bitter notes.

Sandeman Medium Sweet CR
palomino, pedro ximénez

89

Colour: iodine, amber rim. Nose: powerfull, complex, dry nuts, creamy oak, varnish. Palate: rich, sweetness.

Sandeman Royal Ambrosante VOS PX
pedro ximénez

93

Colour: mahogany. Nose: complex, fruit liqueur notes, dried fruit, pattiserie, toasty, aromatic coffee, dark chocolate. Palate: sweet, rich, unctuous.

VALDESPINO

Ctra. Nacional IV, Km. 640
11404 Jerez de la Frontera (Cádiz)
☎: +34 956 321 004
Fax: +34 956 340 216
info@grupoestevez.com
www.grupoestevez.com

PODIUM

Don Gonzalo VOS OL
100% palomino

96

Colour: light mahogany. Nose: powerfull, complex, dry nuts, toasty, acetaldehyde. Palate: rich, long, fine solera notes, spicy, round.

El Candado PX
100% palomino

91

Colour: mahogany. Nose: complex, fruit liqueur notes, dried fruit, pattiserie, toasty, dark chocolate. Palate: sweet, rich, unctuous.

Promesa Moscatel
moscatel

93

Colour: iodine, amber rim. Nose: powerfull, complex, dry nuts, creamy oak, varnish, candied fruit, honeyed notes. Palate: rich, long, spicy.

Solera 1842 VOS OL
100% palomino

94

Colour: dark mahogany. Nose: candied fruit, fruit liqueur notes, spicy, varnish, acetaldehyde, aromatic coffee. Palate: fine solera notes, fine bitter notes, spirituous.

PODIUM

Solera de su Majestad VORS 37,5 cl. OL
100% palomino
96
Colour: light mahogany. Nose: powerfull, complex, dry nuts, toasty, acetaldehyde, aromatic coffee, fruit liqueur notes. Palate: rich, long, fine solera notes, spicy, round.

Tío Diego AM
100% palomino
91
Colour: iodine, amber rim. Nose: powerfull, dry nuts, toasty. Palate: fine bitter notes, fine solera notes, long, spicy.

Ynocente FI
100% palomino
93
Colour: bright yellow. Nose: complex, expressive, pungent, saline. Palate: rich, powerful, fresh, fine bitter notes.

VINOS DE SACRISTÍA
Sevilla, 2 1º Izq.
11540 Sanlúcar de Barrameda (Cádiz)
☎: +34 607 920 337
sacristiaab@sacristiaab.com
www.sacristiaab.com

PODIUM

Sacristía AB AM
palomino
96
Colour: iodine, amber rim. Nose: powerfull, complex, elegant, dry nuts, toasty. Palate: rich, fine bitter notes, fine solera notes, long, spicy.

PODIUM

Sacristía AB MZ
palomino
95
Colour: bright golden. Nose: expressive, powerfull, pungent, acetaldehyde, dry nuts. Palate: powerful, fine bitter notes, long.

WILLIAMS & HUMBERT S.A.
Ctra. N-IV, Km. 641,75
11408 Jerez de la Frontera (Cádiz)
☎: +34 956 353 401
Fax: +34 956 353 412
www.williams-humbert.es

Alegría MZ
90
Colour: bright yellow. Nose: pungent, saline, dry nuts. Palate: rich, powerful, fresh, fine bitter notes.

Canasta CR
86% palomino, 14% pedro ximénez
87
Colour: iodine, amber rim. Nose: cocoa bean, caramel, candied fruit, toasty. Palate: sweetness, flavourful, fruity.

Don Guido Solera Especial 20 años VOS PX
100% pedro ximénez
93
Colour: mahogany. Nose: powerfull, expressive, aromatic coffee, spicy, dry nuts, dried fruit. Palate: balanced, fine solera notes, toasty, long.

Dos Cortados VOS PC
100% palomino
93
Colour: iodine, amber rim. Nose: powerfull, dry nuts, toasty, sweet spices. Palate: rich, fine bitter notes, fine solera notes, long, spicy.

Dry Sack Medium Dry CR
89
Colour: mahogany. Nose: complex, fruit liqueur notes, dried fruit, pattiserie, toasty, aged wood nuances. Palate: sweet, rich, unctuous, fine solera notes.

Fino Pando FI
100% palomino
91
Colour: bright yellow. Nose: expressive, pungent, flor yeasts. Palate: rich, powerful, fresh, fine bitter notes.

Jalifa VORS "30 years" AM
100% palomino
94
Colour: iodine, amber rim. Nose: powerfull, dry nuts, toasty, smoky, acetaldehyde. Palate: rich, fine bitter notes, fine solera notes, long, spicy.

W & H Collection Don Zoilo AM
92
Colour: iodine, amber rim. Nose: powerfull, complex, elegant, dry nuts, toasty. Palate: rich, fine bitter notes, fine solera notes, long, spicy.

W & H Collection Don Zoilo CR
89
Colour: light mahogany. Nose: powerfull, dry nuts, toasty. Palate: rich, long, fine solera notes, spicy, round.

W & H Collection Don Zoilo FI
100% palomino
91
Colour: bright yellow. Nose: complex, expressive, pungent, saline, dry nuts. Palate: rich, powerful, fresh, fine bitter notes.

W & H Collection Don Zoilo 12 años OL
100% palomino

88

Colour: light mahogany. Nose: balanced, candied fruit, spicy. Palate: flavourful, balanced, good finish.

W & H Collection Don Zoilo PX 12 Años PX
pedro ximénez

93

Colour: dark mahogany. Nose: powerfull, expressive, aromatic coffee, spicy, acetaldehyde, dry nuts. Palate: balanced, elegant, fine solera notes, toasty, long.

DO. JUMILLA

CONSEJO REGULADOR
San Roque, 15
30520 Jumilla (Murcia)
☎:+34 968 781 761 - Fax: +34 968 781 900
@: info@vinosdejumilla.org
www.vinosdejumilla.org

LOCATION:

Midway between the provinces of Murcia and Albacete, this DO spreads over a large region in the southeast of Spain and covers the municipal areas of Jumilla (Murcia) and Fuente Álamo, Albatana, Ontur, Hellín, Tobarra and Montealegre del Castillo (Albacete).

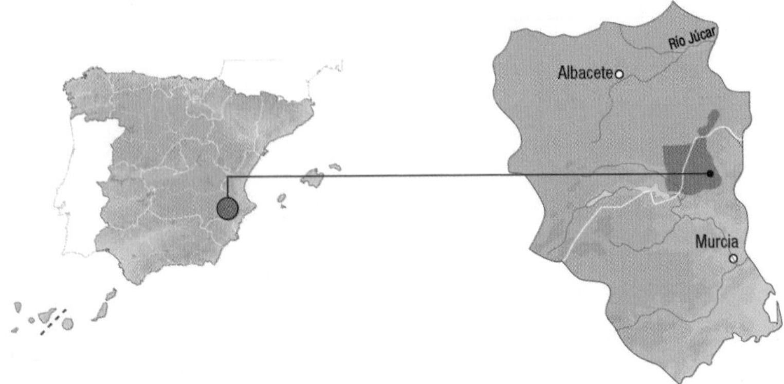

GRAPE VARIETIES:

RED: Monastrell (main 35,373 Ha), Garnacha Tinta, Garnacha Tintorera, Cencibel (Tempranillo), Cabernet Sauvignon, Merlot, Petit Verdot and Syrah.
WHITE: Airén (3,751 Ha), Macabeo, Malvasía, Pedro Ximénez, Chardonnay, Sauvignon Blanc and Moscatel de Grano Menudo.

FIGURES:

Vineyard surface: 22,000 – **Wine-Growers:** 1,980 – **Wineries:** 43 – **2014 Harvest rating:** Very Good – **Production 14:** 54,752,000 litres – **Market percentages:** 42% National - 58% International.

SOIL:

The soil is mainly brownish-grey, brownish-grey limestone and limy. In general, it is poor in organic matter, with great water retention capacity and medium permeability.

CLIMATE:

Continental in nature with Mediterranean influences. It is characterized by its aridity and low rainfall (270 mm) which is mainly concentrated in spring and autumn. The winters are cold and the summers dry and quite hot.

VINTAGE RATING

PEÑÍNGUIDE

2010	2011	2012	2013	2014
VERY GOOD	VERY GOOD	VERY GOOD	GOOD	GOOD

AROMAS EN MI COPA

Pza. Médico Luis Martínez Pérez, 2
30520 Jumilla (Murcia)
☎: +34 676 492 477
elisa@aromasenmicopa.com
www.aromasenmicopa.com

Evol 2012 T
100% monastrell

91

Colour: very deep cherry, garnet rim. Nose: expressive, balsamic herbs, balanced, earthy notes, toasty. Palate: full, flavourful, round tannins.

BODEGA ARTESANAL VIÑA CAMPANERO

Camino de Murcia, s/n- Apdo. 346
30520 Jumilla (Murcia)
☎: +34 968 780 754
Fax: +34 968 780 754
bodegas@vinacampanero.com
www.vinacampanero.com

Vegardal 2014 B
moscatel, malvasía

83 ♣

Vegardal Monastrell Cepas Viejas 2014 T
monastrell

86

Vegardal Orgánic 2012 T
monastrell

84 ♣

BODEGA TORRECASTILLO

Ctra. de Bonete, s/n
02650 Montealegre del Castillo
(Albacete)
☎: +34 967 582 188
Fax: +34 967 582 339
bodega@torrecastillo.com
www.torrecastillo.com

Antonio 2012 T
monastrell

88

Colour: very deep cherry, garnet rim. Nose: balsamic herbs, powerfull, creamy oak, fruit preserve. Palate: full, flavourful, round tannins.

TorreCastillo 2014 B
sauvignon blanc

85

TorreCastillo 2014 RD
monastrell

85

TorreCastillo 2014 T Roble
monastrell

86

TorreCastillo El Tobar 2012 TC
monastrell

86

BODEGA VIÑA ELENA S.L.

Estrecho Marín, s/n
30520 Jumilla (Murcia)
☎: +34 968 781 340
info@vinaelena.com
www.vinaelena.com

Familia Pacheco 2014 B
macabeo, airén

85

Familia Pacheco Orgánico 2013 T
monastrell, syrah

87 ♣

Colour: deep cherry, purple rim. Nose: ripe fruit, balsamic herbs, spicy. Palate: balanced, spicy, long, good finish.

BODEGAS 1890

30520 Jumilla (Murcia)
☎: +34 914 355 556
atcliente@jgc.es
www.vinosdefamilia.com

Castillo San Simón 2008 TGR
100% monastrell

84

Castillo San Simón 2010 TR
85% monastrell, 15% tempranillo

79

Mayoral 2014 T
70% monastrell, 15% syrah, 15% cabernet sauvignon

85

Colour: bright cherry, purple rim. Nose: medium intensity, red berry notes, ripe fruit. Palate: correct, easy to drink.

BODEGAS ALCEÑO

Duque, 34
30520 Jumilla (Murcia)
☎: +34 968 780 142
Fax: +34 968 716 256
info@alceno.com
www.alceno.com

Alceño 2014 RD
monastrell

87

Colour: rose, purple rim. Nose: red berry notes, floral, ripe fruit. Palate: powerful, fruity, fresh, ripe fruit, long, flavourful.

Alceño 12 meses 2012 T
85% monastrell, 7,5% syrah, 7,5% garnacha

91

Colour: cherry, garnet rim. Nose: red berry notes, ripe fruit, fragrant herbs, spicy, toasty, creamy oak, mineral, dried herbs. Palate: powerful, flavourful, balsamic, balanced.

Alceño 2014 T
70% monastrell, 20% syrah, 10% tempranillo

89

Colour: cherry, purple rim. Nose: powerfull, ripe fruit, spicy. Palate: powerful, fruity, unctuous.

Alceño 2014 T Roble
85% monastrell, 15% syrah

88

Colour: very deep cherry. Nose: ripe fruit, sweet spices, creamy oak, expressive. Palate: flavourful, fruity, toasty, round tannins.

Alceño 50 2013 T
85% syrah, 15% garnacha

91

Colour: cherry, garnet rim. Nose: red berry notes, ripe fruit, fragrant herbs, spicy, toasty, creamy oak. Palate: powerful, flavourful, balsamic, balanced.

Alceño Dulce 2012 T
100% monastrell

89

Colour: very deep cherry. Nose: fruit preserve, spicy, toasty. Palate: powerful, flavourful, sweet, rich, easy to drink.

Alceño Organic 2014 T
85% monastrell, 10% syrah, 5% garnacha

89

Colour: cherry, purple rim. Nose: powerfull, ripe fruit, candied fruit. Palate: powerful, fruity, rich, good structure.

Alceño Selección 2012 T
75% monastrell, 15% syrah, 10% tempranillo

87

Colour: deep cherry. Nose: sweet spices, creamy oak, toasty. Palate: flavourful, fruity, toasty, round tannins.

BODEGAS ARLOREN

Ctra. del Puerto. Cañada del Trigo
30520 Jumilla (Murcia)
☎: +34 968 821 096
bodegas.arloren@arloren.com
www.arloren.es

Miriar Rubí 2009 T
monastrell

86

Vegacañada 2011 T
monastrell

82

BODEGAS BLEDA

Ctra. Jumilla - Ontur, Km. 2.
30520 Jumilla (Murcia)
☎: +34 968 780 012
Fax: +34 968 782 699
vinos@bodegasbleda.com
www.bodegasbleda.com

Castillo de Jumilla 2009 TR
90% monastrell, 10% tempranillo

85

Castillo de Jumilla 2012 TC
90% monastrell, 10% tempranillo

85

Castillo de Jumilla 2014 B
sauvignon blanc, airén

85

Castillo de Jumilla 2014 RD
monastrell

86

Castillo de Jumilla Monastrell - Tempranillo 2014 T
monastrell

88

Colour: bright cherry, purple rim. Nose: ripe fruit, sweet spices. Palate: good structure, balanced, ripe fruit, long.

Castillo de Jumilla Monastrell 2014 T
monastrell

88

Colour: bright cherry, purple rim. Nose: scrubland, red berry notes, ripe fruit, balanced. Palate: balanced, ripe fruit, long.

Divus 2012 T
monastrell

90

Colour: cherry, garnet rim. Nose: expressive, spicy, earthy notes. Palate: flavourful, ripe fruit, long, good acidity, balanced, roasted-coffee aftertaste.

Pinodoncel Cinco Meses 2013 T
monastrell, syrah, petit verdot

87

Colour: cherry, purple rim. Nose: ripe fruit, woody, sweet spices. Palate: flavourful, spicy, powerful.

Pinodoncel Sauvignon Blanc 2014 B
100% sauvignon blanc

84

BODEGAS CARCHELO

Casas de la Hoya, s/n
30520 Jumilla (Murcia)
☎: +34 968 435 137
Fax: +34 968 435 200
administracion@carchelo.com
www.carchelo.com

Altico Syrah 2012 T
100% syrah

88

Colour: bright cherry, garnet rim. Nose: ripe fruit, sweet spices, lactic notes. Palate: flavourful, correct, good finish.

Canalizo 2009 TR
40% monastrell, 40% syrah, 20% tempranillo

91

Colour: cherry, garnet rim. Nose: balanced, complex, ripe fruit, cocoa bean. Palate: good structure, flavourful, round tannins, balanced.

Carchelo 2013 T
monastrell, tempranillo, syrah, cabernet sauvignon

89

Colour: cherry, garnet rim. Nose: red berry notes, ripe fruit, spicy, creamy oak, complex, dried herbs. Palate: flavourful, toasty, round tannins.

Sierva 2011 T
monastrell, tempranillo, syrah, cabernet sauvignon

91

Colour: cherry, garnet rim. Nose: ripe fruit, wild herbs, earthy notes, spicy, balsamic herbs. Palate: balanced, flavourful, long, balsamic.

Vedré 2011 T
monastrell, syrah, tempranillo

89

Colour: deep cherry, purple rim. Nose: creamy oak, toasty, ripe fruit, balsamic herbs. Palate: balanced, spicy, long.

BODEGAS CASA DE LA ERMITA

Ctra. El Carche, Km. 11,5
30520 Jumilla (Murcia)
☎: +34 968 783 035
Fax: +34 968 716 030
bodega@casadelaermita.com
www.casadelaermita.com

Altos del Cuco 2014 T
monastrell, syrah, tempranillo

86

Caracol Serrano 2014 T
monastrell, cabernet sauvignon, syrah

86

Casa de la Ermita 2011 TC
monastrell, tempranillo, cabernet sauvignon

88

Colour: deep cherry, purple rim. Nose: creamy oak, toasty, ripe fruit, balsamic herbs. Palate: balanced, spicy, long.

Casa de la Ermita 2014 B

87

Colour: bright straw. Nose: white flowers, expressive, jasmine. Palate: flavourful, fruity, good acidity, balanced.

Casa de la Ermita 2014 T
monastrell, syrah

87

Colour: cherry, purple rim. Nose: red berry notes, floral, balsamic herbs, violets. Palate: powerful, fresh, fruity.

Casa de la Ermita 2014 T Roble
monastrell, petit verdot

89

Colour: bright cherry. Nose: ripe fruit, sweet spices, creamy oak, scrubland. Palate: flavourful, fruity, toasty, round tannins.

Casa de la Ermita Crianza Ecológico 2011 TC
monastrell

89

Colour: cherry, garnet rim. Nose: ripe fruit, wild herbs, earthy notes, spicy, balsamic herbs. Palate: balanced, flavourful, long, balsamic.

Casa de la Ermita Dulce 2014 B

84

Casa de la Ermita Dulce Monastrell 2013 T
monastrell

85

Casa de la Ermita Ecológico Monastrell 2014 T
monastrell

87

Colour: cherry, purple rim. Nose: balsamic herbs, ripe fruit, candied fruit. Palate: powerful, fruity.

Casa de la Ermita Idílico 2011 TC
petit verdot, monastrell

88

Colour: cherry, garnet rim. Nose: ripe fruit, wild herbs, earthy notes, spicy, grassy. Palate: balanced, flavourful, long, balsamic.

Casa de la Ermita Petit Verdot 2011 T
petit verdot

87

Colour: black cherry. Nose: expressive, complex, balsamic herbs, balanced, ripe fruit, fruit preserve, dark chocolate. Palate: full, flavourful, round tannins.

Lunático 2012 T
monastrell

87

Colour: dark-red cherry, garnet rim. Nose: fruit preserve, fragrant herbs, spicy, tobacco. Palate: flavourful, round tannins.

Monasterio de Santa Ana Monastrell 2013 T
monastrell

79

BODEGAS CRAPULA @LANENA

Paraje La Graja
30520 Jumilla (Murcia)
☎: +34 682 172 052
gmartinez@vinocrapula.com
www.crapulawines.com

Cármine 2012 T
monastrell

89

Colour: cherry, garnet rim. Nose: red berry notes, ripe fruit, fragrant herbs, spicy, toasty, creamy oak. Palate: powerful, flavourful, balsamic, balanced.

Cármine 2013 T Barrica
100% monastrell

90

Colour: very deep cherry, purple rim. Nose: fruit expression, ripe fruit, creamy oak, spicy. Palate: balanced, ripe fruit, round tannins.

Crápula 2012 T
80% monastrell, 15% syrah, 5% cabernet sauvignon

89

Colour: black cherry, garnet rim. Nose: ripe fruit, fruit preserve, aromatic coffee, spicy. Palate: flavourful, sweet tannins.

Crápula 2012 TC
85% monastrell, 10% syrah, 5% cabernet sauvignon

89

Colour: cherry, garnet rim. Nose: ripe fruit, fruit preserve, aromatic coffee, sweet spices, dried herbs. Palate: correct, spicy, long.

Crápula Gold 2014 T
50% syrah, 50% monastrell

89

Colour: very deep cherry. Nose: powerfull, smoky, dark chocolate, red berry notes. Palate: flavourful, round tannins, spicy.

Crápula Petit Verdot 2012 T
85% petit verdot, 15% syrah

91

Colour: cherry, garnet rim. Nose: ripe fruit, wild herbs, earthy notes, spicy, balsamic herbs, dark chocolate. Palate: balanced, flavourful, long, balsamic.

Crápula Soul Edición Limitada 2012 T
50% monastrell, 30% syrah, 15% petit verdot, 5% cabernet sauvignon

92

Colour: deep cherry, garnet rim. Nose: expressive, powerfull, scrubland, ripe fruit. Palate: good structure, spicy, long, round tannins.

Dulce Crápula 2012 T
monastrell

88

Colour: very deep cherry. Nose: fruit preserve, spicy, warm, fruit liqueur notes. Palate: powerful, flavourful, sweet, rich.

BODEGAS EL INICIO

San Vicente, 22
47300 Peñafiel (Valladolid)
☎: +34 947 515 884
Fax: +34 947 515 886
info@bodegaselinicio.com
www.bodegaselinicio.com

Casper 2013 T Roble
100% monastrell

88

Colour: bright cherry. Nose: ripe fruit, sweet spices, creamy oak. Palate: flavourful, fruity, round tannins.

BODEGAS EL NIDO

Ctra. de Fuentealamo -
Paraje de la Aragona
30520 Jumilla (Murcia)
☎: +34 968 435 022
Fax: +34 968 435 653
info@bodegaselnido.com
www.orowines.com

Clío 2011 T
70% monastrell, 30% cabernet sauvignon

93

Colour: deep cherry, garnet rim. Nose: complex, expressive, powerfull, ripe fruit, sweet spices. Palate: balanced, full, round tannins, long.

Corteo 2011 T
100% syrah

93

Colour: very deep cherry, purple rim. Nose: ripe fruit, candied fruit, cocoa bean, creamy oak, violets. Palate: good structure, full, flavourful.

PODIUM

El Nido 2012 T
30% monastrell, 70% cabernet sauvignon

95

Colour: cherry, garnet rim. Nose: balanced, complex, ripe fruit, spicy, dark chocolate, aromatic coffee. Palate: good structure, flavourful, round tannins, balanced.

BODEGAS FERNÁNDEZ

Avda. Murcia s/n
30520 Jumilla (Murcia)
☎: +34 968 780 559
Fax: +34 968 782 400
export@bodegafernandez.es
www.bodegafernandez.es

Campolargo 2014 T
monastrell

78

Escudo de Plata 2009 TGR
monastrell

83

Escudo de Plata 2010 TR
monastrell

85

Perla Real 2013 T
monastrell

86

Perla Real Syrah 2012 T
syrah

84

Vega Jimena 2012 T
monastrell

85

BODEGAS HACIENDA DEL CARCHE

Ctra. del Carche, Km. 8,3
30520 Jumilla (Murcia)
☎: +34 968 975 942
info@haciendadelcarche.com
www.haciendadelcarche.com

Hacienda del Carche Cepas Viejas 2010 T
monastrell, cabernet sauvignon

88

Colour: cherry, garnet rim. Nose: fine reductive notes, spicy. Palate: spicy, long, toasty, balanced, fruity, round tannins.

Hacienda del Carche Cepas Viejas 2011 TC
70% monastrell, 30% cabernet sauvignon

89

Colour: deep cherry. Nose: creamy oak, balanced, ripe fruit. Palate: flavourful, spicy, long, round tannins, balsamic.

Infiltrado 2014 T
50% syrah, 40% monastrell, 10% garnacha

90

Colour: cherry, purple rim. Nose: expressive, fresh fruit, red berry notes, violets. Palate: flavourful, fruity, good acidity, good finish.

Taus 2014 B
50% sauvignon blanc, 50% macabeo

86

Taus 2014 T
70% monastrell, 20% syrah, 10% garnacha

90

Colour: cherry, purple rim. Nose: expressive, red berry notes, floral, fragrant herbs. Palate: flavourful, fruity, good acidity.

Taus Fusion 2013 T
100% syrah

90

Colour: bright cherry. Nose: ripe fruit, sweet spices, creamy oak, violet drops. Palate: flavourful, fruity, toasty, round tannins.

Taus Selección 2013 T
50% monastrell, 25% cabernet sauvignon, 25% syrah

90

Colour: cherry, garnet rim. Nose: red berry notes, balanced, ripe fruit, fresh, sweet spices. Palate: flavourful, spicy, easy to drink.

BODEGAS JUAN GIL

Ctra. Fuentealamo -
Paraje de la Aragona
30520 Jumilla (Murcia)
☎: +34 968 435 022
Fax: +34 968 716 051
info@juangil.es
www.juangil.es

Honoro Vera Organic 2013 T
100% monastrell

90

Colour: deep cherry, purple rim. Nose: toasty, ripe fruit, balsamic herbs. Palate: balanced, spicy, long.

Honoro Vera Organic 2014 T
100% monastrell

88

Colour: cherry, purple rim. Nose: overripe fruit, warm, powerfull. Palate: flavourful, ripe fruit, correct.

Juan Gil 12 meses 2013 T
100% monastrell

92

Colour: cherry, garnet rim. Nose: smoky, spicy, fruit preserve, ripe fruit. Palate: flavourful, ripe fruit.

Juan Gil 18 meses 2013 T
60% monastrell, 30% cabernet sauvignon, 10% syrah

93

Colour: deep cherry, garnet rim. Nose: cocoa bean, sweet spices, creamy oak, ripe fruit, dried herbs. Palate: good structure, rich, flavourful, sweet tannins.

Juan Gil 4 meses 2014 T
100% monastrell

88

Colour: cherry, purple rim. Nose: ripe fruit, toasty. Palate: flavourful, spicy, powerful.

Juan Gil Moscatel 2014 B
100% moscatel

91

Colour: bright straw. Nose: white flowers, fine lees, ripe fruit, citrus fruit, varietal. Palate: flavourful, fruity, good acidity, fine bitter notes, long.

BODEGAS LUZÓN

Ctra. Jumilla-Calasparra, Km. 3,1
30520 Jumilla (Murcia)
☎: +34 968 784 135
Fax: +34 968 781 911
info@bodegasluzon.com
www.bodegasluzon.com

Alma de Luzon 2009 T
monastrell, cabernet sauvignon, syrah

93

Colour: very deep cherry, garnet rim. Nose: expressive, complex, balsamic herbs, balanced. Palate: full, flavourful, round tannins.

Altos de Luzón 2010 T
monastrell, tempranillo, cabernet sauvignon

91

Colour: cherry, garnet rim. Nose: creamy oak, red berry notes, balanced, scrubland. Palate: flavourful, spicy, elegant, fruity.

Altos de Luzón 2011 T
monastrell, tempranillo, cabernet sauvignon

88

Colour: bright cherry. Nose: ripe fruit, sweet spices, creamy oak, expressive. Palate: flavourful, fruity, round tannins.

Finca Luzón 2014 T
monastrell, syrah

90

Colour: deep cherry, purple rim. Nose: balanced, ripe fruit, wild herbs. Palate: flavourful, spicy.

Luzón 2013 T Roble
monastrell

86

Luzón 2014 B
airén, macabeo

87

Colour: bright straw. Nose: fresh fruit, fragrant herbs. Palate: flavourful, good acidity, balanced, fine bitter notes.

Luzón Crianza Selección 12 2012 TC
monastrell, cabernet sauvignon

90

Colour: cherry, garnet rim. Nose: creamy oak, balanced, ripe fruit, scrubland. Palate: flavourful, spicy, balsamic.

Luzón Verde Organic 2014 T
monastrell

89

Colour: cherry, purple rim. Nose: red berry notes, floral, balsamic herbs. Palate: powerful, fresh, fruity.

Portú 2009 T
monastrell, cabernet sauvignon

92

Colour: cherry, garnet rim. Nose: expressive, spicy, scrubland. Palate: flavourful, ripe fruit, long, good acidity, balanced.

BODEGAS MADROÑO

Nueva, 74
02652 Ontur (Albacete)
☎: +34 610 776 281
Fax: +34 967 324 338
vbmadrono@gmail.com

Alle 2014 B
100% chardonnay

85

Madroño Petit Verdot 2012 T
100% petit verdot

89

Colour: very deep cherry. Nose: ripe fruit, wild herbs, earthy notes, spicy, balsamic herbs. Palate: balanced, flavourful, long, balsamic.

Madroño Syrah 2013 T Roble
100% syrah

89

Colour: cherry, garnet rim. Nose: red berry notes, ripe fruit, spicy, creamy oak. Palate: flavourful, toasty, round tannins.

Viña Marcelino 2013 T
100% monastrell

88

Colour: very deep cherry, garnet rim. Nose: balsamic herbs, balanced, toasty. Palate: full, flavourful, round tannins, smoky aftertaste.

BODEGAS MONTEREBRO

Barrio Iglesias, 55
30520 Jumilla (Murcia)
☎: +34 968 157 286
info@monterebro.com
www.monterebro.com

Monterebro 2012 TC
85% monastrell, 15% syrah

88

Colour: cherry, garnet rim. Nose: roasted coffee, smoky, spicy, ripe fruit. Palate: flavourful, smoky aftertaste, ripe fruit.

Monterebro 2013 T Barrica
85% monastrell, 15% syrah

86

Monterebro 2014 B
100% sauvignon blanc

85

Monterebro 2014 RD
60% monastrell, 40% syrah

86

Monterebro 2014 T
85% monastrell, 15% syrah

86

Monterebro Selección 2013 T
85% syrah, 15% monastrell

89

Colour: very deep cherry, garnet rim. Nose: expressive, complex, balsamic herbs, balanced. Palate: full, flavourful, round tannins.

BODEGAS OLIVARES

Vereda Real, s/n
30520 Jumilla (Murcia)
☎: +34 968 780 180
Fax: +34 968 756 474
correo@bodegasolivares.com
www.bodegasolivares.com

Olivares 2014 RD
70% garnacha, 30% monastrell

85

Olivares Dulce Monastrell 2011 T
100% monastrell

92

Colour: cherry, garnet rim. Nose: fruit preserve, spicy, warm, varnish, aromatic coffee. Palate: powerful, flavourful, sweet, rich.

BODEGAS PÍO DEL RAMO

Ctra. Almanza, s/n
02652 Ontur (Albacete)
☎: +34 967 323 230
info@piodelramo.com
www.piodelramo.com

Pío del Ramo 2011 TC
60% monastrell, 15% petit verdot, 15% syrah, 10% cabernet sauvignon

91

Colour: cherry, garnet rim. Nose: ripe fruit, wild herbs, earthy notes, spicy, balsamic herbs. Palate: balanced, flavourful, long, balsamic.

Pío del Ramo 2012 T Roble
60% monastrell, 25% syrah, 15% cabernet sauvignon

90

Colour: deep cherry. Nose: creamy oak, toasty, ripe fruit, balsamic herbs. Palate: balanced, spicy, long, round tannins.

Pío Ecológico 2013 T
100% monastrell

87

Colour: bright cherry. Nose: ripe fruit, sweet spices, creamy oak, expressive, scrubland. Palate: flavourful, fruity, round tannins.

Viña Betola 2013 T
70% monastrell, 15% syrah, 15% cabernet sauvignon

86

Viña Betola 2014 B
chardonnay, moscatel grano menudo

86

BODEGAS SAN DIONISIO, S. COOP.

Ctra. de la Higuera, s/n
02651 Fuenteálamo (Albacete)
☎: +34 967 543 032
Fax: +34 967 543 136
anselmocuesta@bodegassandionisio.es
www.bodegassandinisio.es

Mainetes Selección 2012 TC
34% monastrell, 33% syrah, 33% merlot

87

Colour: very deep cherry, garnet rim. Nose: balsamic herbs, powerfull, fruit preserve. Palate: full, flavourful, round tannins.

Señorío de Fuenteálamo Macabeo 2014 B
100% macabeo

83

Señorío de Fuenteálamo Merlot 2014 T
100% merlot

86

Señorío de Fuenteálamo Monastrell 2014 T
100% monastrell

84

Señorío de Fuenteálamo Monastrell Syrah 2012 TC
60% monastrell, 40% syrah

87

Colour: very deep cherry, garnet rim. Nose: expressive, balsamic herbs, balanced. Palate: full, flavourful, round tannins, easy to drink.

Señorío de Fuenteálamo Sauvignon Blanc 2014 B
100% sauvignon blanc

83

Señorío de Fuenteálamo Syrah 2014 RD
100% syrah

87

Colour: rose, purple rim. Nose: red berry notes, floral, ripe fruit, lactic notes. Palate: powerful, fruity, fresh.

Señorío de Fuenteálamo Syrah 2014 T
100% syrah

85

BODEGAS SAN JOSÉ

Camino de Hellín, s/n
02652 Ontur (Albacete)
☎: +34 967 324 212
Fax: +34 967 324 186
comercial@bodegasanjose.com
www.bodegasanjose.com

Dominio de Ontur Merlot 2013 T
100% merlot

85

Dominio de Ontur Monastrell 2013 T
100% monastrell

84

Dominio de Ontur Syrah 2013 T
100% syrah

84

Dominio de Ontur Syrah Monastrell 2013 T
50% syrah, 50% monastrell

86

Dominio de Ontur Verdejo 2014 B
100% verdejo

83

Villa de Ontur Syrah 2014 RD
100% syrah

84

BODEGAS SILVANO GARCÍA

Avda. de Murcia, 29
30520 Jumilla (Murcia)
☎: +34 968 780 767
Fax: +34 968 716 125
bodegas@silvanogarcia.es
www.silvanogarcia.es

Silvano García Dulce Monastrell 2011 T
100% monastrell

90

Colour: dark mahogany. Nose: pattiserie, aromatic coffee, candied fruit, dark chocolate. Palate: unctuous, balanced, spicy.

Silvano García Dulce Moscatel 2013 B
100% moscatel

89

Colour: bright golden. Nose: powerfull, candied fruit, white flowers, jasmine, citrus fruit. Palate: flavourful, sweet, ripe fruit, good acidity.

Viñahonda 2012 TC
50% monastrell, 20% tempranillo, 30% cabernet sauvignon

85

Viñahonda 2014 B
100% macabeo

85

Viñahonda 2014 RD
100% monastrell

85

Viñahonda Organic 2012 T
100% monastrell

83

BODEGAS SIMÓN

Madrid, 15
02653 Albatana (Albacete)
☎: +34 967 323 340
info@bodegassimon.com
www.bodegassimon.com

Galán del Siglo Petit Verdot 2011 T
petit verdot

83

Galán Selección 2012 T
tempranillo, monastrell, petit verdot

82

Galanito 2014 T
tempranillo, monastrell, petit verdot

83

BODEGAS VOLVER

Ctra de Pinoso a Fortuna
03650 Pinoso (Alicante)
☎: +34 965 978 603
export@bodegasvolver.com
www.bodegasvolver.com

Wrongo Dongo 2014 T
monastrell

90

Colour: cherry, purple rim. Nose: powerfull, ripe fruit, wild herbs. Palate: powerful, fruity, unctuous.

BSI BODEGAS SAN ISIDRO

Ctra. Murcia, s/n
30520 Jumilla (Murcia)
☎: +34 968 780 700
Fax: +34 968 782 351
bsi@bsi.es
www.bsi.es

Gémina Cuvée Selección 2011 T
100% monastrell

88

Colour: very deep cherry. Nose: ripe fruit, toasty, dried herbs, balanced. Palate: good structure, powerful, flavourful.

Gémina Monastrell 2011 T
100% monastrell

86

Genus 2013 T Roble
100% monastrell

85

Genus Monastrell Syrah 2012 T
80% monastrell, 20% syrah

87

Colour: deep cherry, garnet rim. Nose: powerfull, ripe fruit, fruit preserve, toasty, dried herbs. Palate: flavourful, toasty, long, round tannins.

Numun Monastrell 2014 T
100% monastrell

86

Numun Monastrell sin sulfitos 2014 T
100% monastrell

86

Numun Syrah 2014 T
100% syrah

87

Colour: cherry, purple rim. Nose: expressive, fresh fruit, red berry notes, floral. Palate: flavourful, fruity, good acidity.

Sabatacha 2010 TC
100% monastrell

87

Colour: very deep cherry, garnet rim. Nose: expressive, balsamic herbs, balanced, ripe fruit. Palate: full, flavourful, round tannins.

Sabatacha Monastrell 2014 T
100% monastrell

87

Colour: cherry, purple rim. Nose: balanced, scrubland, dried herbs. Palate: fruity, easy to drink, correct.

Sabatacha Syrah 2014 T
100% syrah

87

Colour: deep cherry, purple rim. Nose: powerfull, red berry notes, ripe fruit, violets. Palate: good structure, flavourful, long.

CAMPOS DE RISCA
Avda. Diagonal, 590, 5º 1ª
08021 (Barcelona)
☎: +34 660 445 464
vinergia@vinergia.com
www.vinergia.com

Campos de Risca 2014 T
90% monastrell, 10% syrah

88

Colour: cherry, purple rim. Nose: powerfull, ripe fruit, spicy. Palate: powerful, fruity, unctuous, long.

CASA ROJO
Sánchez Picazo, 53
30332 Balsapintada (Murcia)
☎: +34 968 151 520
Fax: +34 968 151 539
info@casarojo.com
www.casarojo.com

MMM Macho Man Monastrell 2013 T
monastrell

89

Colour: deep cherry. Nose: creamy oak, toasty, ripe fruit, balsamic herbs. Palate: balanced, spicy, long.

CRAPULA WINES
30520 Jumilla (Murcia)
☎: +34 662 380 985
gmartinez@vinocrapula.com
www.crapulawines.com

Baica 2013 T Roble
85% monastrell, 10% syrah, 5% garnacha

88

Colour: very deep cherry. Nose: scrubland, dried herbs, sweet spices, ripe fruit. Palate: flavourful, round tannins.

Barinas Roble 2010 T Roble
85% monastrell, 10% syrah, 5% garnacha

87

Colour: very deep cherry, purple rim. Nose: ripe fruit, fruit preserve, dark chocolate, sweet spices. Palate: flavourful, round tannins.

Célebre 2012 TC
85% monastrell, 15% syrah

90

Colour: very deep cherry, garnet rim. Nose: expressive, balsamic herbs, balanced. Palate: full, flavourful, round tannins, spicy.

Célebre 2013 T Roble
70% monastrell, 30% syrah

89

Colour: cherry, purple rim. Nose: ripe fruit, wild herbs, cocoa bean. Palate: powerful, fresh, fruity.

NdQ (Nacido del Quorum) 2013 T Roble
100% monastrell

87

Colour: dark-red cherry, purple rim. Nose: smoky, toasty, aromatic coffee. Palate: flavourful, round tannins, smoky aftertaste.

NdQ (Nacido del Quorum) Selección 2012 T
90% monastrell, 10% syrah

90

Colour: very deep cherry, garnet rim. Nose: powerfull, characterful, ripe fruit, fruit preserve, scrubland. Palate: good structure, full, flavourful.

EGO BODEGAS

Plaza Santa Gertrudis, 1
30001 Murcia (Murcia)
☎: +34 968 964 326
ioana.paunescu@egobodegas.com
www.egobodegas.com

Fuerza 2012 TC
monastrell, cabernet sauvignon

90

Colour: very deep cherry, garnet rim. Nose: balsamic herbs, balanced, closed. Palate: full, flavourful, round tannins.

Goru Monastrell 2012 TC
monastrell, cabernet sauvignon

90

Colour: bright cherry. Nose: sweet spices, creamy oak, expressive, ripe fruit, powerfull. Palate: flavourful, fruity, toasty, round tannins.

Infinito 2012 T
60% monastrell, 40% petit verdot

92

Colour: deep cherry, garnet rim. Nose: scrubland, dark chocolate, ripe fruit, sweet spices. Palate: balanced, long, round tannins.

FAMILIA BASTIDA S.L.

Canónigo Lozano, 11
30520 Jumilla (Murcia)
☎: +34 686 479 518
andresbastida@alceno.com

Genio Español 12 Meses 2012 T
100% monastrell

90

Colour: cherry, garnet rim. Nose: smoky, spicy, ripe fruit, creamy oak. Palate: flavourful, smoky aftertaste, ripe fruit.

Genio Español 2014 T
100% monastrell

85

Genio Español 2014 T Roble
100% monastrell

87

Colour: deep cherry. Nose: ripe fruit, sweet spices, powerfull, dried herbs. Palate: flavourful, fruity, toasty, round tannins.

HAMMEKEN CELLARS

Calle de la Muela, 16
03730 Jávea (Alicante)
☎: +34 965 791 967
Fax: +34 966 461 471
cellars@hammekencellars.com
www.hammekencellars.com

Finca Rosal White November Harvest 2013 B
70% viura, 10% chardonnay, 20% viognier

87

Colour: bright yellow. Nose: ripe fruit, sweet spices, dried herbs, faded flowers. Palate: rich, flavourful.

Gran Pasas November Harvest 2012 T
100% monastrell

89

Colour: cherry, purple rim. Nose: warm, powerfull, fruit preserve, spicy, cocoa bean, smoky. Palate: flavourful, ripe fruit, correct, balanced, rich.

Pasas November Harvest 2013 T
100% monastrell

87

Colour: dark-red cherry, garnet rim. Nose: fruit preserve, fruit liqueur notes, powerfull. Palate: flavourful, rich, fruity, sweet tannins.

NAVISER REPRESENTACIONES S.L.

30012 Los Dolores (Murcia)
☎: +34 609 253 533
Fax: +34 968 340 141
tgarcia@naviser.es
www.naviser.es

Bruto 2012 T
monastrell

92

Colour: cherry, garnet rim. Nose: ripe fruit, wild herbs, earthy notes, balsamic herbs, sweet spices, cocoa bean. Palate: flavourful, long, balsamic, sweet tannins.

ORO WINES

Ctra. de Fuentealamo -
Paraje de la Aragona
30520 Jumilla (Murcia)
☎: +34 968 435 022
Fax: +34 968 716 051
info@orowines.com
www.orowines.com

Comoloco 2013 T
100% monastrell

86

PROPIEDAD VITÍCOLA CASA CASTILLO

Ctra. Jumilla - Hellín, RM-428, Km. 8
30520 Jumilla (Murcia)
☎: +34 968 781 691
Fax: +34 968 781 691
info@casacastillo.es
www.casacastillo.es

Casa Castillo Monastrell 2014 T
100% monastrell

91

Colour: cherry, purple rim. Nose: powerfull, ripe fruit, red berry notes. Palate: powerful, fruity.

Casa Castillo Pie Franco 2011 T
100% monastrell

93

Colour: cherry, garnet rim. Nose: ripe fruit, wild herbs, earthy notes, spicy, balsamic herbs. Palate: balanced, flavourful, long, balsamic.

El Molar 2013 T Barrica
100% garnacha

92

Colour: bright cherry. Nose: ripe fruit, sweet spices, creamy oak, expressive. Palate: flavourful, fruity, toasty, round tannins.

El Molar 2014 T Barrica
100% garnacha

94

Colour: deep cherry, purple rim. Nose: creamy oak, toasty, ripe fruit, balsamic herbs. Palate: balanced, spicy, long, fresh.

Finca La Tercia 2011 T
60% monastrell, 30% syrah, 10% garnacha

93

Colour: cherry, garnet rim. Nose: mineral, expressive, spicy. Palate: flavourful, ripe fruit, long, good acidity, balanced.

Las Gravas 2012 T
70% monastrell, 15% garnacha, 15% syrah

94

Colour: very deep cherry, garnet rim. Nose: expressive, complex, mineral, balsamic herbs, balanced. Palate: full, flavourful, round tannins.

Valtosca V'13 2013 T
100% syrah

93

Colour: bright cherry. Nose: ripe fruit, sweet spices, creamy oak, expressive. Palate: flavourful, fruity, toasty, round tannins.

VIÑAS DE LA CASA DEL RICO

Poeta Andrés Bolarin, 1- 5ºB
30011 Murcia (Murcia)
☎: +34 609 197 353
Fax: +34 968 782 400
produccion@casadelrico.com
www.casadelrico.com

Gorgocil Monastrell 2011 T
monastrell

88

Colour: bright cherry. Nose: ripe fruit, sweet spices, creamy oak, expressive. Palate: flavourful, fruity, toasty, round tannins.

Gorgocil Tempranillo 2011 T
tempranillo

86

VIÑEDOS Y BODEGAS ASENSIO CARCELÉN

Ctra. RM-714, km. 8
30520 Jumilla (Murcia)
☎: +34 968 435 543
bodegascarcelen@gmail.com
www.facebook.com/AsensioCarcelen

100 x 100 Monastrell Ecológico 4 Lunas 2014 T
100% monastrell

82

Pura Sangre 2009 TGR
100% monastrell

84

VIÑEDOS Y BODEGAS XENYSEL

Valle Hoya Torres Pol. 5 Parc. 5
30520 Jumilla (Murcia)
☎: +34 911 924 002
info@xenysel.com
www.xenysel.com

Calzás 2012 TC
monastrell

88

Colour: bright cherry. Nose: ripe fruit, sweet spices, creamy oak, expressive, tobacco. Palate: flavourful, fruity, toasty, round tannins.

Xenys 2013 T
monastrell

84

Xenys 2014 B
chardonnay, moscatel

85

Xenys Autor 2012 T
monastrell

86

Xenysel 12 2012 TC
monastrell

87

Colour: deep cherry, purple rim. Nose: creamy oak, toasty, ripe fruit, balsamic herbs. Palate: balanced, spicy, long.

Xenysel Organic 2014 T
100% monastrell

86

Xenysel Pie Franco 2013 T
100% monastrell

85

DO. LA GOMERA

CONSEJO REGULADOR

Avda. Guillermo Ascanio,16
38840 Vallehermoso (La Gomera)
☎:+34 922 800 801 - Fax: +34 922 801 146
@: crdolagomera@922800801.e.telefonica.net
www.vinosdelagomera.es

LOCATION:

The majority of the vineyards are found in the north of the island, in the vicinity of the towns of Vallehermoso (some 385 Ha) and Hermigua. The remaining vineyards are spread out over Agulo, Valle Gran Rey –near the capital city of La Gomera, San Sebastián– and Alajeró, on the slopes of the Garajonay peak.

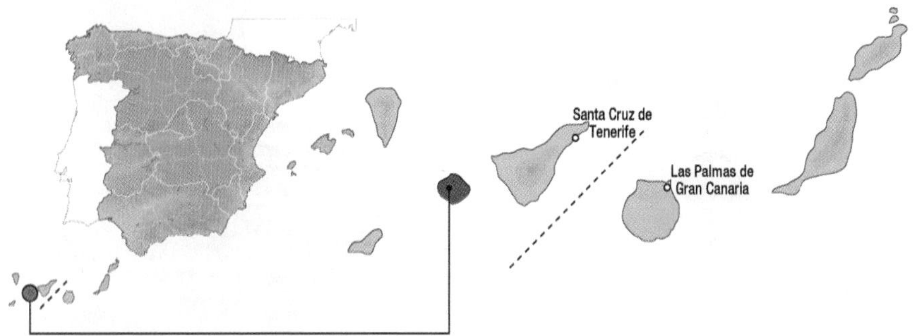

GRAPE VARIETIES:

WHITE: Forastera (90%), Gomera Blanca, Listán Blanca, Marmajuelo, Malvasía and Pedro Ximenez.
RED: Listán Negra (5%), Negramoll (2%); Experimental: Tintilla Castellana, Cabernet Sauvignon and Rubí Cabernet.

FIGURES:

Vineyard surface: 125 – **Wine-Growers:** 250 – **Wineries:** 15 – **2014 Harvest rating:** Good – **Production 14:** 90,000 litres – **Market percentages 2013:** 100% Nacional.

SOIL:

The most common soil in the higher mountain regions is deep and clayey, while, as one approaches lower altitudes towards the scrubland, the soil is more Mediterranean with a good many stones and terraces similar to those of the Priorat.

CLIMATE:

The island benefits from a subtropical climate together with, as one approaches the higher altitudes of the Garajonay peak, a phenomenon of permanent humidity known as 'mar de nubes' (sea of clouds) caused by the trade winds. This humid air from the north collides with the mountain range, thereby creating a kind of horizontal rain resulting in a specific ecosystem made up of luxuriant valleys. The average temperature is 20°C all year round.

VINTAGE RATING

PEÑÍNGUIDE

2010	2011	2012	2013	2014
N/A	N/A	N/A	N/A	N/A

DO. LA MANCHA

CONSEJO REGULADOR

Avda. de Criptana, 73
13600 Alcázar de San Juan (Ciudad Real)
☎:+34 926 541 523 - Fax: +34 926 588 040
@: consejo@lamanchawines.com
www.lamanchawines.com

LOCATION:

On the southern plateau in the provinces of Albacete, Ciudad Real, Cuenca and Toledo. It is the largest wine-growing region in Spain and in the world.

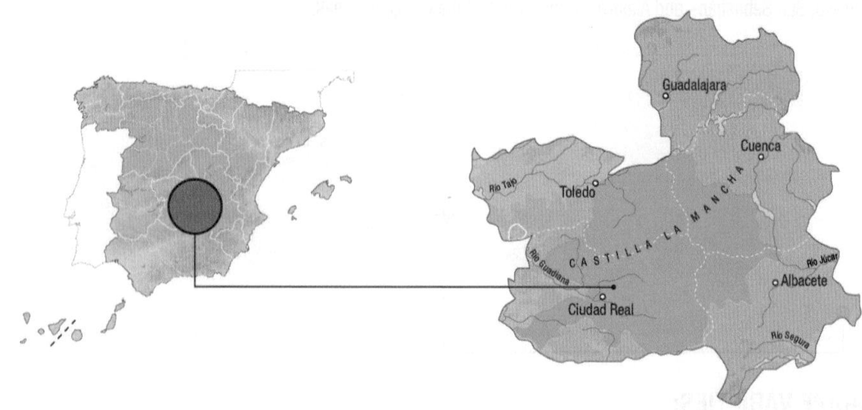

GRAPE VARIETIES:

WHITE: Airén (majority), Macabeo, Pardilla, Chardonnay, Sauvignon Blanc, Verdejo, Moscatel de Grano Menudo, Gewürztraminer, Parellada, Pero Ximénez, Riesling and Torrontés.

RED: Cencibel (majority amongst red varieties), Garnacha, Moravia, Cabernet Sauvignon, Merlot, Syrah, Cabernet Franc, Graciano, Malbec, Mencía, Monastrell, Pinot Noir, Petit Verdot and Bobal.

FIGURES:

Vineyard surface: 162,206 – **Wine-Growers:** 16,130 – **Wineries:** 263 – **2014 Harvest rating:** Excellent – **Production 14:** 152,224,575 litres – **Market percentages:** 69% National - 31% International.

SOIL:

The terrain is flat and the vineyards are situated at an altitude of about 700 m above sea level. The soil is generally sandy, limy and clayey.

CLIMATE:

Extreme continental, with temperatures ranging between 40/45°C in summer and –10/12°C in winter. Rather low rainfall, with an average of about 375 mm per year.

VINTAGE RATING

PEÑÍNGUIDE

2010	2011	2012	2013	2014
VERY GOOD	VERY GOOD	GOOD	AVERAGE	AVERAGE

¡EA! VINOS DE MANUEL MANZANEQUE SUÁREZ

Avda. Jose Prat 14, esc 3, 1o d-1
02008 Albacete (Albacete)
☎: +34 967 278 578
Fax: +34 967 278 578
info@eavinos.com
www.eavinos.com

¡Ea! 2013 T
100% cencibel

88

Colour: bright cherry. Nose: ripe fruit, sweet spices, creamy oak. Palate: flavourful, fruity, round tannins.

¡Ea! 2014 B
80% airén, 15% sauvignon blanc, 5% moscatel

89

Colour: bright straw. Nose: white flowers, fine lees, dried herbs, dry nuts, faded flowers. Palate: flavourful, fruity, good acidity, round.

Fatum 2014 T
50% tempranillo, 50% bobal

84

Mil Cepas Vino de Parcela 2014 T

92

Colour: cherry, garnet rim. Nose: mineral, expressive, spicy, red berry notes. Palate: flavourful, ripe fruit, long, good acidity.

ALENUR

Paseo de la Libertad 6 1º Izq.
02001 Albacete (Albacete)
☎: +34 967 247 001
Fax: +34 967 242 982
info@alenur.com
www.alenur.com

Alenur Airén Sauvignon Blanc 2014 B
70% airén, 30% sauvignon blanc

85

Colour: bright straw. Nose: fresh fruit, floral, dried herbs. Palate: flavourful, fruity, easy to drink.

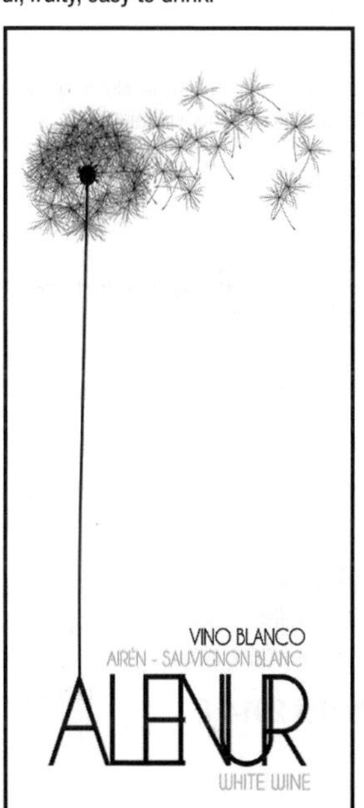

Alenur Syrah 2014 T
100% syrah

84

Alenur Tempranillo 2014 T
100% tempranillo

83

BODEGA CENTRO ESPAÑOLAS

Ctra. Alcázar, km. 1
13700 Tomelloso (Ciudad Real)
☎: +34 926 505 654
Fax: +34 926 505 652
allozo@allozo.com
www.allozo.com

Allozo 2011 TC
100% tempranillo

86

Allozo 2006 TGR
100% tempranillo

88

Colour: bright cherry, orangey edge. Nose: spicy, fine reductive notes. Palate: spicy, fine tannins, balanced.

Allozo 2009 TR
100% tempranillo

87

Colour: cherry, garnet rim. Nose: ripe fruit, spicy, creamy oak, complex. Palate: flavourful, toasty.

Allozo 927 2010 T
tempranillo, syrah, merlot

87

Colour: cherry, garnet rim. Nose: ripe fruit, spicy, creamy oak, fine reductive notes. Palate: flavourful, toasty, round tannins.

Allozo Cabernet 2014 T
100% cabernet sauvignon

85

Allozo Merlot 2014 T
100% merlot

83

Allozo Shyraz 2014 T
100% syrah

85

Allozo Tempranillo 2014 T
100% tempranillo

84

Allozo Verdejo 2014 B
100% verdejo

84

Flor de Allozo 2012 T
tempranillo, garnacha

87

Colour: bright cherry. Nose: ripe fruit, sweet spices, creamy oak. Palate: flavourful, fruity, toasty, round tannins.

BODEGA FAMILIA MATEOS DE LA HIGUERA. VEGA DEMARA

Ctra. La Solana - Villanueva de los Infantes, km. 7,1
13240 La Solana (Ciudad Real)
☎: +34 926 633 313
Fax: +34 926 633 826
info@vegamara.es
www.vegamara.es

Vega Demara 2011 TC
tempranillo

87

Colour: cherry, garnet rim. Nose: red berry notes, fresh fruit, balanced. Palate: flavourful, spicy, correct, fruity aftestaste.

Vega Demara 2013 T Roble
tempranillo

85

Vega Demara Tempranillo 2014 T
tempranillo

85

BODEGA LA TERCIA-ORGANIC WINES

Pl. Santa Quiteria, 12
13600 Alcázar de San Juan
(Ciudad Real)
☎: +34 926 550 104
Fax: +34 926 550 104
administracion@bodegalatercia.com
www.bodegalatercia.com

Yemanueva Airén Ecológico 2014 B
100% airén

84 ♣

Yemanueva Rose Ecológico 2014 RD
100% tempranillo

86 ♣

Yemanueva Tempranillo Ecológico 2013 T
100% tempranillo

84 ♣

Yemaserena Tempranillo Selección Limitada 2009 T
100% tempranillo

85 ♣

BODEGA SOLEDAD

Ctra. Tarancón, s/n
16411 Fuente de Pedro Naharro
(Cuenca)
☎: +34 969 125 039
Fax: +34 969 125 907
asv@bodegasoledad.com
www.bodegasoledad.com

Solmayor Airén 2013 B
airén

84

BODEGA Y VIÑAS ALDOBA S.A.

Ctra. Alcázar, km. 1
13700 Tomelloso (Ciudad Real)
☎: +34 926 505 653
Fax: +34 926 505 652
aldoba@allozo.com
www.allozo.com

Aldoba 2011 TC
100% tempranillo

84

Aldoba 2014 B
verdejo

84

Aldoba 2009 TR
100% tempranillo

85

Aldoba 2014 T
100% tempranillo

83

BODEGAS ALCARDET

Mayor, 130
45810 Villanueva de Alcardete (Toledo)
☎: +34 925 166 375
Fax: +34 925 166 611
alcardet@alcardet.com
www.alcardet.com

Alcardet Natura Brut 2013 ESP
chardonnay, airén

85 ♣

Alcardet Natura Red 2013 T
tempranillo, petit verdot

86 ♣

Alcardet Natura White 2014 B
chardonnay, airén

85 ♣

Alcardet Sommelier 2010 TC
petit verdot, tempranillo

88

Colour: cherry, garnet rim. Nose: red berry notes, ripe fruit, spicy, creamy oak, scrubland. Palate: flavourful, toasty, round tannins.

Alcardet Sommelier 2014 B
sauvignon blanc, airén, verdejo

85

Alcardet Sommelier 2014 RD
tempranillo, syrah, garnacha

84

Alcardet Sommelier 2014 T
tempranillo, merlot, cabernet sauvignon

85

BODEGAS ALTOVELA

Ctra. Madrid - Alicante km 100
45880 Corral de Almaguer (Toledo)
☎: +34 925 190 269
Fax: +34 925 190 268
enologo@altovela.com
www.altovela.com

Altovela Airén 2014 B
airén

85

Altovela Macabeo 2014 B
macabeo

85

Altovela Sauvignon Blanc 2014 B
100% sauvignon blanc

87

Colour: bright straw. Nose: ripe fruit, tropical fruit, dried herbs. Palate: fresh, flavourful, fine bitter notes.

Altovela Tempranillo 2014 T
tempranillo

87

Colour: cherry, purple rim. Nose: expressive, fresh fruit, red berry notes, floral. Palate: flavourful, fruity, good acidity.

Altovela Verdejo 2014 B
verdejo

84

Campo Amable 2008 TC
tempranillo

86

BODEGAS AYUSO

Miguel Caro, 6
02600 Villarrobledo (Albacete)
☎: +34 967 140 458
Fax: +34 967 144 925
comercial@bodegasayuso.es
www.bodegasayuso.es

Armiño Semidulce 2014 B
100% airén

78

Castillo de Benizar Cabernet Sauvignon 2014 RD
100% cabernet sauvignon

82

Castillo de Benizar Macabeo 2014 B
100% macabeo

84

Castillo de Benizar Tempranillo 2014 T
100% tempranillo

84

Estola 2004 TGR
65% tempranillo, 35% cabernet sauvignon

86

Estola 2010 TR
75% tempranillo, 25% cabernet sauvignon

85

Estola 2011 TC
100% tempranillo

85

Estola Verdejo 2014 B
100% verdejo

85

Finca Los Azares Cabernet Merlot 2007 T
50% cabernet sauvignon, 50% merlot

85

Finca Los Azares Petit Verdot 2009 T
100% petit verdot

88

Colour: pale ruby, brick rim edge. Nose: spicy, fine reductive notes, aged wood nuances, wild herbs. Palate: spicy, fine tannins.

Finca Los Azares Sauvignon Blanc 2014 B
100% sauvignon blanc

86

BODEGAS CAMPOS REALES

Castilla La Mancha, 4
16670 El Provencio (Cuenca)
☎: +34 967 166 066
Fax: +34 967 165 030
info@bodegascamposreales.com
www.bodegascamposreales.com

Campos Reales 2014 B
50% airén, 50% sauvignon blanc

85

Campos Reales 2014 RD
100% garnacha

83

Campos Reales 2014 T
100% tempranillo

85

Campos Reales Cabernet Sauvignon 2013 T
100% cabernet sauvignon

86

Campos Reales Selección 2013 T
100% tempranillo

85

Colour: bright cherry. Nose: ripe fruit, sweet spices, expressive, woody. Palate: flavourful, fruity, toasty, round tannins.

Campos Reales Syrah 2013 T
100% syrah

85

Cánfora 2010 TR
100% tempranillo

87

Colour: cherry, garnet rim. Nose: spicy, fine reductive notes, fruit preserve, warm, overripe fruit. Palate: good structure, flavourful, round tannins.

Canforrales 2011 TR
100% tempranillo

88

Colour: cherry, garnet rim. Nose: balanced, ripe fruit, spicy, fine reductive notes. Palate: good structure, flavourful.

Canforrales 2012 TC
100% cabernet sauvignon

87

Colour: deep cherry, purple rim. Nose: creamy oak, toasty, ripe fruit, balsamic herbs. Palate: balanced, spicy.

Canforrales Alma Verdejo 2014 B
100% verdejo

84

Canforrales Chardonnay 2014 B
100% chardonnay

88

Colour: bright straw. Nose: white flowers, dried herbs, ripe fruit, candied fruit, citrus fruit. Palate: flavourful, fruity, good acidity, elegant.

Canforrales Clásico Tempranillo 2014 T
100% tempranillo

86

Canforrales Garnacha 2014 RD
100% garnacha

84

Canforrales Lucía 2014 B
100% airén

84

Canforrales Selección 2013 T
100% tempranillo

85

Canforrales Tempranillo Syrah 2014 T
70% tempranillo, 30% syrah

86

Canforrales Viognier Sauvignon Blanc 2014 B
50% viognier, 50% sauvignon blanc

84

Gladium Viñas Viejas 2011 TC
100% tempranillo

90

Colour: cherry, garnet rim. Nose: red berry notes, ripe fruit, spicy, creamy oak, complex. Palate: flavourful, toasty, round tannins.

BODEGAS CRISTO DE LA VEGA

General Goded, 8
13630 Socuéllamos (Ciudad Real)
☎: +34 926 530 054
comercial@bodegascrisve.com
www.bodegascrisve.com

Marqués de Castilla 2014 B
80% sauvignon blanc, 20% chardonnay

82

Marqués de Castilla 2009 TR
70% tempranillo, 30% cabernet sauvignon

87

Colour: bright cherry. Nose: ripe fruit, sweet spices, creamy oak. Palate: flavourful, fruity, balanced.

Marqués de Castilla 2010 TC
100% tempranillo

84

Marqués de Castilla 2011 T Barrica
80% merlot, 20% cabernet sauvignon

86

Marqués de Castilla 2014 RD
80% garnacha, 20% tempranillo

85

Marqués de Castilla Airén 2014 B
100% airén

84

Marqués de Castilla Tempranillo Syrah Merlot 2014 T
70% tempranillo, 15% syrah, 15% merlot

84

Yugo BR
90% airén, 10% chardonnay

83

Yugo 2009 TR
100% tempranillo

88

Colour: cherry, garnet rim. Nose: ripe fruit, spicy, creamy oak, complex. Palate: flavourful, toasty, round tannins.

Yugo 2010 TC
100% tempranillo

86

Yugo 2014 T
70% tempranillo, 15% syrah, 15% merlot

86

Yugo Airén 2014 B
100% airén

86

Yugo Garnacha Tempranillo 2014 RD
80% garnacha, 20% tempranillo

88

Colour: rose, purple rim. Nose: red berry notes, floral, expressive. Palate: powerful, fruity, fresh, flavourful, balanced, fine bitter notes.

Yugo Verdejo 2014 B
verdejo

84

BODEGAS DE ALORT - DE ALORT PREMIUM WINES

Ctra. de Herencia km 2,5
13600 Alcázar de San Juan
(Ciudad Real)
☎: +34 696 254 624
contacta@dealortwines.com
www.dealortwines.com

Pétrola 2012 TC
cabernet franc, cabernet sauvignon

89

Colour: cherry, garnet rim. Nose: creamy oak, red berry notes, balanced. Palate: flavourful, spicy, elegant.

Pétrola Tempranillo 2013 T Roble
tempranillo

88

Colour: bright cherry. Nose: ripe fruit, sweet spices, creamy oak, expressive. Palate: flavourful, fruity, round tannins.

BODEGAS HERMANOS RUBIO

Ctra. de Villamuelas, s/n
45740 Villasequilla (Toledo)
☎: +34 925 310 268
Fax: +34 925 325 133
info@bhrubio.com
www.bhrubio.com

Señorío de Zocodover 2009 TR
tempranillo

86

Señorío de Zocodover 2010 TC
tempranillo

84

Zocodover Selección 2005 TR
tempranillo, cabernet sauvignon

86

Zocodover Selección 2007 TC
tempranillo, cabernet sauvignon

84

Zocodover Selección Sauvignon Blanc 2014 B
sauvignon blanc

85

BODEGAS ISIDRO MILAGRO
Pol. Ind. 2ª Fase Cº P18
13200 Manzanares (Ciudad Real)
☎: +34 926 647 005
Fax: +34 926 610 620
matias@bodegasisidromilagro.com
www.bodegasisidromilagro.com

Torre de Rejas 2009 TR
tempranillo

85

Torre de Rejas 2011 TC
tempranillo

84

Torre de Rejas 2014 B
verdejo, viura

85

Torre de Rejas 2014 RD
tempranillo, syrah

85

Torre de Rejas Tempranillo 2014 T
tempranillo

84

BODEGAS LA REMEDIADORA
Alfredo Atieza, 149
02630 La Roda (Albacete)
☎: +34 967 440 600
Fax: +34 967 441 465
export@laremediadora.com
www.laremediadora.com

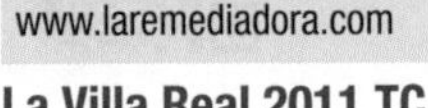

La Villa Real 2011 TC
50% cabernet sauvignon, 50% tempranillo

87

Colour: very deep cherry, garnet rim. Nose: expressive, balsamic herbs, balanced. Palate: flavourful, round tannins, correct.

La Villa Real 2014 RD
100% tempranillo

87

Colour: rose, bright. Nose: red berry notes, floral, dried flowers. Palate: fruity, fresh, easy to drink, good finish.

La Villa Real Macabeo 2014 B
100% macabeo

84

La Villa Real Vendimia Seleccionada 2013 T
tempranillo, syrah

84

Topico Moscatel Dulce 2014 B
100% moscatel grano menudo

87

Colour: pale. Nose: powerfull, candied fruit, fragrant herbs, white flowers. Palate: flavourful, sweet, ripe fruit, thin.

BODEGAS LAHOZ
Ctra. N-310 Tomelloso-Villarrobledo
Km. 108,5
13630 Socuéllamos (Ciudad Real)
☎: +34 926 699 083
Fax: +34 926 514 929
info@bodegaslahoz.com
www.bodegaslahoz.com

Vega Córcoles 2014 RD
100% tempranillo

86

Vega Córcoles Airén 2014 B
100% airén

85

Vega Córcoles Sauvignon Blanc 2014 B
100% sauvignon blanc

85

Vega Córcoles Tempranillo 2012 T Roble
100% tempranillo

88

Colour: bright cherry. Nose: ripe fruit, sweet spices, smoky, toasty. Palate: flavourful, fruity, round tannins.

Vega Córcoles Tempranillo 2014 T
100% tempranillo

85

BODEGAS LATÚE

Camino Esperilla, s/n
45810 Villanueva de Alcardete (Toledo)
☎: +34 925 166 350
Fax: +34 925 166 673
bodegaslatue@latue.com
www.latue.com

Latúe 2014 RD
tempranillo

87

Colour: rose, purple rim. Nose: rose petals, candied fruit. Palate: powerful, fruity, fresh, easy to drink.

Pingorote 2010 T
tempranillo

88

Colour: ruby red, brick rim edge. Nose: red berry notes, ripe fruit, spicy, creamy oak, complex. Palate: flavourful, toasty, round tannins.

Pingorote 2010 T Roble
tempranillo

87

Colour: cherry, garnet rim. Nose: red berry notes, ripe fruit, spicy, creamy oak. Palate: flavourful, toasty, round tannins.

Pingorote 2013 T
tempranillo

85

Pingorote Sauvignon Blanc 2014 B
sauvignon blanc

87

Colour: bright straw. Nose: white flowers, citrus fruit, tropical fruit. Palate: flavourful, fruity, good acidity, easy to drink.

BODEGAS LOZANO

Avda. Reyes Católicos, 156
02600 Villarrobledo (Albacete)
☎: +34 967 141 907
Fax: +34 967 145 843
secretaria1@bodegas-lozano.com
www.bodegas-lozano.com

Añoranza 2014 RD
tempranillo

87

Colour: rose, purple rim. Nose: red berry notes, floral, expressive. Palate: powerful, fruity, fresh, thin.

Añoranza Cabernet Shiraz 2014 T
cabernet sauvignon, syrah

85

Añoranza Sauvignon Blanc 2014 B
sauvignon blanc

85

Añoranza Tempranillo 2012 TC
tempranillo

83

Gran Oristán 2009 TGR
tempranillo, cabernet sauvignon

88

Colour: light cherry. Nose: fine reductive notes, aged wood nuances, toasty, ripe fruit. Palate: spicy, toasty, flavourful.

Marqués de Toledo 2009 TGR
tempranillo, cabernet sauvignon

87

Colour: pale ruby, brick rim edge. Nose: spicy, fine reductive notes, wet leather, aged wood nuances. Palate: spicy, fine tannins.

Marqués de Toledo 2011 TR
tempranillo, cabernet sauvignon

84

Marqués de Toledo Verdejo 2014 B
verdejo

85

Oristán 2012 TC
tempranillo, cabernet sauvignon, syrah

90

Colour: cherry, garnet rim. Nose: balanced, complex, ripe fruit, spicy, fine reductive notes. Palate: good structure, flavourful, round tannins, balanced.

BODEGAS NARANJO

Felipe II, 5
13150 Carrión de Calatrava
(Ciudad Real)
☎: +34 926 814 155
Fax: +34 926 815 335
info@bodegasnaranjo.com
www.bodegasnaranjo.com

Casa de la Dehesa 2010 TC
tempranillo

88

Colour: cherry, garnet rim. Nose: fine reductive notes, ripe fruit, creamy oak. Palate: spicy, long, toasty.

Viña Cuerva 2009 TR
tempranillo

87

Colour: cherry, garnet rim. Nose: ripe fruit, wild herbs, earthy notes, spicy, balsamic herbs. Palate: balanced, flavourful, long, balsamic.

Viña Cuerva 2012 T Roble
tempranillo, syrah
86

Viña Cuerva 2012 TC
tempranillo
86

Viña Cuerva Airén 2014 B
airén
84

BODEGAS ROMERO DE ÁVILA SALCEDO

Avda. Constitución, 4
13240 La Solana (Ciudad Real)
☎: +34 926 631 426
wine@bodegasromerodeavila.com
www.bodegasromerodeavila.com

Portento 2008 TC
85% tempranillo, 15% cabernet sauvignon
79

Portento Sauvignon Blanc 2013 B
sauvignon blanc
84

Portento Tempranillo 2013 T
tempranillo
84

Portento Tempranillo 2013 T Roble
100% tempranillo
85

BODEGAS SAN ANTONIO ABAD

Afueras, 17
45860 Villacañas (Toledo)
☎: +34 925 160 414
Fax: +34 925 162 015
export@sanantonioabad.es
www.sanantonioabad.es

Albardiales 2014 B
airén
84

Albardiales 2014 T
tempranillo
86

Espanillo 2014 B
50% sauvignon blanc, 50% verdejo
84

Espanillo 2014 T
tempranillo
84

Espanillo Semi Dulce 2014 RD
tempranillo
84

Villa Abad 2010 TC
tempranillo
84

Villa Abad 2014 B
macabeo
83

Villa Abad 2014 T
50% syrah, 50% tempranillo
87
Colour: cherry, purple rim. Nose: expressive, fresh fruit, red berry notes, floral, balanced. Palate: flavourful, fruity, good acidity.

Villa Abad Tempranillo 2014 T Roble
tempranillo
86

Villa Abad Tempranillo Semiseco 2014 T
tempranillo
86

BODEGAS SAN ISIDRO DE PEDRO MUÑOZ

13620 Pedro Muñoz (Ciudad Real)
☎: +34 926 586 057
Fax: +34 926 568 380
administracin@viacotos.com
www.viacotos.com

Gran Amigo Sancho 2012 TC
tempranillo
85

La Hijuela Airén 2014 B
airén
76

La Hijuela Tempranillo 2013 T
tempranillo
78

BODEGAS SIMBOLO

Concepción, 135
13610 Campo de Criptana
(Ciudad Real)
☎: +34 926 589 036
Fax: +34 926 589 041
produccion@bodegassimbolo.com
www.bodegassimbolo.com

Símbolo Airén 2014 B
100% airén

85

Símbolo Petit Verdot 2014 T
100% petit verdot

85

Símbolo Syrah 2014 T
100% syrah

86

Símbolo Tempranillo 2012 T Roble
100% tempranillo

85

Símbolo Tempranillo 2014 T
100% tempranillo

85

Símbolo Verdejo 2014 B
100% verdejo

84

BODEGAS VERDÚGUEZ

Los Hinojosos, 1
45810 Villanueva de Alcardete (Toledo)
☎: +34 925 167 493
Fax: +34 925 166 148
export3@bodegasverduguez.com
www.bodegasverduguez.com

Hidalgo Castilla 2010 TR
tempranillo

88

Colour: very deep cherry, garnet rim. Nose: expressive, balsamic herbs, balanced, spicy, dried herbs. Palate: full, flavourful, round tannins.

Old Vine Selection Imperial Toledo 2011 T
tempranillo

90

Colour: cherry, garnet rim. Nose: spicy, red berry notes, ripe fruit, expressive. Palate: flavourful, ripe fruit, long, good acidity, balanced.

Vereda Mayor Tempranillo 2014 T
tempranillo

82

BODEGAS VERUM

Ctra. Argamasilla de Alba, km. 0,800
13700 Tomelloso (Ciudad Real)
☎: +34 926 511 404
Fax: +34 926 515 047
administracion@bodegasverum.com
www.bodegasverum.com

Verum Gran Cueva 2007 ESP
100% chardonnay

87

Colour: bright yellow. Nose: dry nuts, spicy, faded flowers, toasty. Palate: powerful, flavourful, good acidity, fine bead, fine bitter notes.

BODEGAS VIDAL DEL SAZ S.L.U.

Maestro Manzanares, 57
13610 Campo de Criptana
(Ciudad Real)
☎: +34 926 562 424
Fax: +34 926 562 659
bodegasdelsaz@bodegasdelsaz.com
www.bodegasdelsaz.com

Vidal del Saz Selección Rosé 2014 RD
50% merlot, 50% syrah

87

Colour: brilliant rose. Nose: red berry notes, floral, fragrant herbs. Palate: powerful, fruity, fresh, correct.

Vidal del Saz Selección White 2014 B
50% macabeo, 50% chardonnay

86

Vidal del Saz Tempranillo 2008 TGR
100% tempranillo

86

Vidal del Saz Tempranillo 2011 TC
100% tempranillo

85

Vidal del Saz Tempranillo 2013 T Roble
100% tempranillo

85

BODEGAS VOLVER

Ctra de Pinoso a Fortuna
03650 Pinoso (Alicante)
☎: +34 965 978 603
export@bodegasvolver.com
www.bodegasvolver.com

Volver 2013 T

tempranillo

90

Colour: cherry, garnet rim. Nose: spicy, creamy oak, fruit preserve. Palate: flavourful, toasty, balanced.

BODEGAS Y VIÑEDOS BRO VALERO

Ctra. Las Mesas, Km. 11
02600 Villarrobledo (Albacete)
☎: +34 649 985 103
Fax: +34 914 454 675
bodegas@brovalero.es
www.brovalero.es

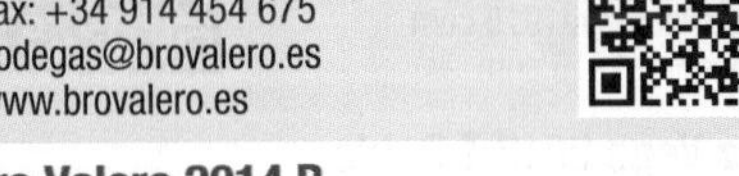

Bro Valero 2014 B

chardonnay

84

Bro Valero Cabernet Sauvignon 2012 TC

cabernet sauvignon

87

Colour: cherry, purple rim. Nose: ripe fruit, woody, scrubland. Palate: flavourful, spicy, powerful, round tannins.

Bro Valero Syrah 2011 T

syrah

86

BODEGAS Y VIÑEDOS DE CINCO CASAS

Virgen de las Nieves, 2
13720 Cinco Casas (Ciudad Real)
☎: +34 926 529 010
Fax: +34 926 526 070
bodega@bodegascasadelavina.com
www.bodegascasadelavina.com

Santa Elena 2010 TR

tempranillo

85

Colour: bright cherry. Nose: ripe fruit, sweet spices, creamy oak. Palate: flavourful, fruity, round tannins.

Santa Elena 2012 TC

tempranillo

85

Santa Elena Airén 2014 B

airén

84

Santa Elena Tempranillo 2014 T

tempranillo

86

BODEGAS Y VIÑEDOS LADERO S.L.

Ctra. Alcázar, km. 1
13700 Tomelloso (Ciudad Real)
☎: +34 926 505 653
Fax: +34 926 505 652
ladero@allozo.com
www.allozo.com

Ladero 2009 TR
100% tempranillo
85

Ladero 2011 TC
100% tempranillo
85

Ladero 2014 B
airén, verdejo
85

Ladero 2014 T
100% tempranillo
84

BODEGAS YUNTERO

Pol. Ind., Ctra. Alcázar de San Juan s/n
13200 Manzanares (Ciudad Real)
☎: +34 926 610 309
Fax: +34 926 610 516
yuntero@yuntero.com
www.yuntero.com

Epílogo 2012 TC
tempranillo, merlot
86

Epílogo 2014 B
sauvignon blanc, moscatel
87
Colour: bright straw. Nose: white flowers, fresh fruit, fragrant herbs. Palate: flavourful, fruity, good acidity.

Mundo de Yuntero 2014 T
tempranillo, merlot, syrah
86 ♣

Mundo de Yuntero 2014 B
verdejo, sauvignon blanc
85 ♣

Yuntero 2008 TR
tempranillo
84

Yuntero 2010 TC
tempranillo, petit verdot
86

Yuntero 2014 RD
tempranillo
84

Yuntero 2014 B
macabeo, sauvignon blanc
84

Yuntero 2014 T
tempranillo, syrah
85

BOGARVE 1915

Reyes Católicos, 10
45710 Madridejos (Toledo)
☎: +34 925 460 820
Fax: +34 925 467 006
bogarve@bogarve1915.com
www.bogarve1915.com

Lacruz Vega 2013 T Roble
tempranillo, syrah, merlot
83

Lacruz Vega Centenario 2012 TR
tempranillo, cabernet sauvignon, syrah
84

Lacruz Vega Sauvignon Blanc 2014 B
100% sauvignon blanc
85

Lacruz Vega Syrah 2013 T
100% syrah
84

Lacruz Vega Tempranillo 2013 T
100% tempranillo
85

Lacruz Vega Terroir 2012 T Roble
tempranillo, syrah, cabernet sauvignon
87
Colour: cherry, garnet rim. Nose: smoky, spicy, ripe fruit. Palate: flavourful, smoky aftertaste, ripe fruit, correct.

CAMPOS DE VIENTO

Avda. Diagonal, 590 - 5º 1ª
08021 (Barcelona)
☎: +34 660 445 464
vinergia@vinergia.com
www.vinergia.com

Campos de Viento 2014 T

100% tempranillo

87

Colour: cherry, purple rim. Nose: expressive, fresh fruit, red berry notes, floral. Palate: flavourful, fruity, good acidity, easy to drink.

CORDIS TERRA HISPANIA

Gamonal, 16 2ºC
28031 Madrid (Madrid)
☎: +34 911 610 024
Fax: +34 913 316 047
info@cordisterra.com
www.cordisterra.com

Cordis Terra 2014 B

macabeo

85

Cordis Terra 2014 T

tempranillo

83

Cordis Terra Semidulce 2014 RD

tempranillo

85

DOMINIO DE PUNCTUM ORGANIC & BIODYNAMIC WINES

Ctra. N-301 km 162
16660 Las Pedroñeras (Cuenca)
☎: +34 912 959 998
Fax: +34 912 959 997
export@dominiodepunctum.com
www.dominiodepunctum.com

Nortesur Chardonnay 2014 B

100% chardonnay

87 ♣

Colour: bright straw. Nose: white flowers, fresh fruit, fragrant herbs, expressive. Palate: flavourful, fruity, good acidity.

Nortesur Tempranillo Cabernet Sauvignon 2014 T

70% tempranillo, 30% cabernet sauvignon

87 ♣

Colour: cherry, purple rim. Nose: powerfull, ripe fruit, spicy. Palate: powerful, fruity, unctuous.

Uno de Mil Tempranillo Petit Verdot 2011 T Barrica

50% tempranillo, 50% petit verdot

88 ♣

Colour: cherry, garnet rim. Nose: creamy oak, toasty, ripe fruit, balsamic herbs. Palate: balanced, spicy, long.

Uno de Mil Viognier 2011 B

100% viognier

89 ♣

Colour: bright yellow. Nose: ripe fruit, floral, sweet spices, creamy oak, toasty. Palate: powerful, flavourful, spicy, long.

Viento Aliseo 2014 RD

100% garnacha

87

Colour: onion pink. Nose: candied fruit, wild herbs, floral. Palate: fresh, fruity, easy to drink.

Viento Aliseo Graciano Cabernet Sauvignon 2012 TC

50% graciano, 50% cabernet sauvignon

87 ♣

Colour: bright cherry. Nose: ripe fruit, sweet spices, creamy oak. Palate: flavourful, fruity, toasty.

Viento Aliseo Tempranillo Petit Verdot 2014 T

70% tempranillo, 30% petit verdot

88 ♣

Colour: cherry, garnet rim. Nose: ripe fruit, scrubland, spicy. Palate: powerful, flavourful, spicy.

Viento Aliseo Viognier 2014 B

100% viognier

88 ♣

Colour: bright straw. Nose: ripe fruit, tropical fruit, fragrant herbs, floral. Palate: fresh, fruity, flavourful, balanced.

EL PROGRESO SOC. COOPERATIVA DE CASTILLA LA MANCHA

Avda. de la Virgen, 89
13670 Villarubia de los Ojos
(Ciudad Real)
☎: +34 926 896 135
Fax: +34 926 896 135
administracion@bodegaselprogreso.com
www.bodegaselprogreso.com

Jijones 2010 TR

100% tempranillo

87

Colour: cherry, garnet rim. Nose: red berry notes, ripe fruit, spicy. Palate: flavourful, toasty, round tannins, fruity aftestaste.

Jijones 2011 TC
100% tempranillo

87

Colour: cherry, garnet rim. Nose: ripe fruit, spicy, fruit preserve. Palate: flavourful, toasty, round tannins.

Jijones Blend 2014 B
airén, verdejo, chardonnay

84

Jijones Selección 2012 T
syrah, merlot, cabernet sauvignon

87

Colour: very deep cherry, garnet rim. Nose: balsamic herbs, balanced, ripe fruit. Palate: full, flavourful, round tannins.

Jijones Syrah 2013 T Roble
syrah

86

Jijones Tempranillo 2014 T
100% tempranillo

85

Ojos del Guadiana 2005 TGR
100% tempranillo

87

Colour: bright cherry, garnet rim. Nose: tobacco, spicy, ripe fruit, dried herbs. Palate: flavourful, round tannins.

Ojos del Guadiana 2009 TR
100% tempranillo

87

Colour: cherry, garnet rim. Nose: red berry notes, balanced. Palate: flavourful, spicy, good acidity, round tannins.

Ojos del Guadiana 2011 TC
100% tempranillo

87

Colour: cherry, garnet rim. Nose: creamy oak, ripe fruit, spicy. Palate: flavourful, spicy, correct.

Ojos del Guadiana 2014 BR
100% chardonnay

84

Ojos del Guadiana Airén 2014 B
100% airén

84

Ojos del Guadiana Selección 2014 T
cabernet sauvignon, merlot, syrah

86

Ojos del Guadiana Syrah 2014 T Roble
100% syrah

88

Colour: bright cherry. Nose: sweet spices, creamy oak, expressive, red berry notes, ripe fruit, floral. Palate: flavourful, fruity, round tannins.

Ojos del Guadiana Tempranillo 2014 T
100% tempranillo

87

Colour: cherry, purple rim. Nose: expressive, fresh fruit, red berry notes, floral. Palate: flavourful, fruity, good acidity.

Ojos del Guadiana Verdejo 2014 B
100% verdejo

85

ELVIWINES
Ctra T-300 Falset-Marça, km 1
43775 Marça (Tarragona)
☎: +34 618 792 973
Fax: +34 936 750 316
victor@elviwines.com
www.elviwines.com

Volcanus Petit Verdot 2010 T
100% petit verdot

85

FÉLIX SOLÍS S.L.
Otumba, 2
45840 La Puebla de Almoradiel (Toledo)
☎: +34 925 178 626
Fax: +34 925 178 626
lamancha@felixsolis.com
www.felixsolis.com

Caliza 2014 B
chardonnay, verdejo, viura

85

Caliza 2014 RD
tempranillo

87

Colour: rose, purple rim. Nose: red berry notes, floral, expressive. Palate: fruity, fresh, flavourful, good acidity, fine bitter notes.

Caliza 2014 T
merlot, syrah, tempranillo

87

Colour: cherry, purple rim. Nose: expressive, red berry notes, floral, dried herbs. Palate: flavourful, fruity, good acidity, balanced.

Caliza Gran Selección 2014 T
tempranillo

88

Colour: deep cherry, purple rim. Nose: creamy oak, toasty, ripe fruit, balsamic herbs, dry stone. Palate: balanced, spicy, long.

Viña San Juan 2014 B
chardonnay, verdejo, viura

85

Viña San Juan 2014 RD
tempranillo

87

Colour: rose, purple rim. Nose: floral, wild herbs, fresh fruit. Palate: flavourful, balanced, fruity, easy to drink.

Viña San Juan 2014 T
merlot, syrah, tempranillo

87

Colour: cherry, purple rim. Nose: powerfull, ripe fruit, spicy. Palate: powerful, fruity, unctuous, fruity aftestaste.

Viña San Juan Gran Selección I 2014 T
tempranillo

89

Colour: very deep cherry, purple rim. Nose: mineral, balsamic herbs, red berry notes, ripe fruit. Palate: full, flavourful, balanced.

FINCA ANTIGUA

Ctra. Quintanar - Los Hinojosos, Km. 11,5
16417 Los Hinojosos (Cuenca)
☎: +34 969 129 700
Fax: +34 969 129 496
info@fincaantigua.com
www.familiamartinezbujanda.com

Ciclos de Finca Antigua 2005 TR
50% merlot, 25% cabernet sauvignon, 25% syrah

90

Colour: pale ruby, brick rim edge. Nose: spicy, fine reductive notes, wet leather, aged wood nuances. Palate: spicy, fine tannins, balanced.

Clavis 2006 TR

92

Colour: pale ruby, brick rim edge. Nose: elegant, spicy, fine reductive notes, tobacco, ripe fruit. Palate: spicy, fine tannins, elegant, long, balanced.

Finca Antigua 2011 TC

89

Colour: light cherry. Nose: fine reductive notes, toasty, ripe fruit. Palate: spicy, toasty, flavourful, balanced.

Finca Antigua Cabernet Sauvignon 2012 T Roble
100% cabernet sauvignon

87

Colour: deep cherry, purple rim. Nose: creamy oak, toasty, ripe fruit, balsamic herbs. Palate: balanced, spicy, long.

Finca Antigua Garnacha 2012 T
100% garnacha

87

Colour: cherry, garnet rim. Nose: balanced, grassy, wild herbs, ripe fruit. Palate: correct, round tannins.

Finca Antigua Merlot 2012 T Roble
100% merlot

88

Colour: very deep cherry, garnet rim. Nose: expressive, balsamic herbs, balanced, scrubland. Palate: full, flavourful, round tannins.

Finca Antigua Moscatel Naturalmente Dulce 2013 B
moscatel

90

Colour: bright yellow. Nose: honeyed notes, expressive, jasmine, candied fruit. Palate: rich, fruity, flavourful.

Finca Antigua Petit Verdot 2012 T
100% petit verdot

86

Finca Antigua Syrah 2012 T
100% syrah

89

Colour: cherry, garnet rim. Nose: creamy oak, red berry notes, violets. Palate: flavourful, spicy, balanced.

Finca Antigua Tempranillo 2012 T
100% tempranillo

88

Colour: cherry, garnet rim. Nose: red berry notes, ripe fruit, spicy, creamy oak, complex. Palate: flavourful, toasty, round tannins.

Finca Antigua Viura 2014 B
viura

86

FINCA LA BLANCA

Princesa, 84
45840 Puebla de Almoradiel (Toledo)
☎: +34 669 995 315
Fax: +34 968 897 675
export@fincalablanca.es
www.fincalablanca.es

Ribera de los Molinos B

83

Ribera de los Molinos 2013 T

cabernet sauvignon

80

Ribera de los Molinos 2014 T

tempranillo

82

HAMMEKEN CELLARS

Calle de la Muela, 16
03730 Jávea (Alicante)
☎: +34 965 791 967
Fax: +34 966 461 471
cellars@hammekencellars.com
www.hammekencellars.com

El Paso 2013 T

tempranillo, syrah

84

J. GARCÍA CARRIÓN

13250 Daimiel (Ciudad Real)
☎: +34 914 355 556
atcliente@jgc.es
www.vinosdefamilia.com

Don Luciano 2014 T

100% tempranillo

84

Opera Prima Chardonnay 2014 B

100% chardonnay

83

Opera Prima Shiraz 2014 T

100% syrah

85

Colour: cherry, purple rim. Nose: fresh fruit, red berry notes, floral. Palate: flavourful, fruity, correct.

Opera Prima Tempranillo 2014 T

100% tempranillo

84

NUESTRA SEÑORA DE LA PIEDAD, S. COOP. DE C. L-M

Ctra. Circunvalación, s/n
45800 Quintanar de la Orden (Toledo)
☎: +34 925 180 237
Fax: +34 925 560 092
comercial@bodegasentremontes.com

Clavelito Airén 2014 B

100% airén

82

Clavelito Macabeo 2014 B

100% macabeo

80

Clavelito Sauvignon Blanc 2014 B

100% sauvignon blanc

80

Clavelito Verdejo 2014 B

100% verdejo

79

Entremontes BN

40% verdejo, 60% macabeo

84

Entremontes SS

100% airén

82

Entremontes 2002 TGR
100% tempranillo

85

Entremontes 2003 TR
100% tempranillo

85

Entremontes 2005 TC
100% tempranillo

80

Entremontes 2009 T Roble
100% tempranillo

84

Entremontes Cabernet Sauvignon 2013 T
100% cabernet sauvignon

80

Entremontes Garnacha 2013 T
100% garnacha

83

Entremontes Merlot 2013 T
100% merlot

78

Entremontes Syrah 2013 T
100% syrah

84

Entremontes Tempranillo 2013 T
100% tempranillo

82

PAGO DE LA JARABA

Ctra. Nacional 310, Km. 142,7
02600 Villarrobledo (Albacete)
☎: +34 967 138 250
Fax: +34 967 138 252
info@lajaraba.com
www.lajaraba.com

Pago de la Jaraba Chardonnay 2014 B
100% chardonnay

84

Pago de la Jaraba Sauvignon Blanc 2014 B
100% sauvignon blanc

87

Colour: bright straw. Nose: white flowers, fresh fruit, fragrant herbs, expressive. Palate: flavourful, fruity, good acidity, balanced.

SAN ISIDRO LABRADOR SOC. COOP. CLM

Ramón y Cajal, 42
16640 Belmonte (Cuenca)
☎: +34 967 170 289
Fax: +34 967 170 289
isbelmonte@ucaman.es
www.castibell.es

Castibell 2008 TC

72

Castibell 2013 T

84

Castibell Airén 2013 B

82

SANTA CATALINA

Cooperativa, 2
13240 La Solana (Ciudad Real)
☎: +34 926 632 194
Fax: +34 926 631 085
central@santacatalina.es
www.santacatalina.es

Los Galanes 2010 TR
100% tempranillo

86

Los Galanes 2014 T
100% tempranillo

86

Los Galanes Airén 2014 B
100% airén

86

Los Galanes Macabeo 2014 B
100% macabeo

86

Los Galanes Selección 2014 T
100% tempranillo

88

Colour: bright cherry. Nose: ripe fruit, sweet spices. Palate: fruity, correct, balanced.

VINÍCOLA DE CASTILLA

Pol. Ind. Calle I, s/n
13200 Manzanares (Ciudad Real)
☎: +34 926 647 800
Fax: +34 926 610 466
nacional@vinicoladecastilla.com
www.vinicoladecastilla.com

Finca Vieja 2014 B
airén
83

Finca Vieja Tempranillo 2014 T
100% tempranillo
83

Señorío de Guadianeja 2004 TGR
100% cabernet sauvignon
86

Señorío de Guadianeja 2009 TR
100% tempranillo
84

Señorío de Guadianeja 2010 TC
100% tempranillo
86

Señorío de Guadianeja Chardonnay 2014 B
100% chardonnay
86

Señorío de Guadianeja Macabeo 2014 B
100% macabeo
84

Señorío de Guadianeja Sauvignon Blanc 2014 B
100% sauvignon blanc
84

Señorío de Guadianeja Syrah 2014 T
100% syrah
85

Señorío de Guadianeja Tempranillo 2014 T
100% tempranillo
84

Señorío de Guadianeja Verdejo 2014 B
verdejo
85

VINÍCOLA DE TOMELLOSO

Ctra. Toledo - Albacete, Km. 130,8
13700 Tomelloso (Ciudad Real)
☎: +34 926 513 004
Fax: +34 926 538 001
vinicola@vinicolatomelloso.com
www.vinicolatomelloso.com

Añil 2014 B
50% macabeo, 50% chardonnay
87
Colour: bright straw. Nose: white flowers, fresh fruit, fragrant herbs. Palate: flavourful, fruity, good acidity.

Dulce Tentatione 2013 T
100% tempranillo
85

Finca Cerrada 2007 TC
60% tempranillo, 35% cabernet sauvignon, 5% syrah
84

Finca Cerrada 2007 TR
50% tempranillo, 50% cabernet sauvignon
83

Finca Cerrada 2014 RD
100% tempranillo
84

Finca Cerrada Tempranillo 2014 T
100% tempranillo
84

Finca Cerrada Viura 2014 B
100% viura
84

Mantolán 2014 ESP
100% macabeo
85

Torre de Gazate 2004 TGR
100% cabernet sauvignon
84

Torre de Gazate 2007 TR
50% tempranillo, 50% cabernet sauvignon

85

Torre de Gazate 2011 TC
60% tempranillo, 40% cabernet sauvignon

86

Colour: cherry, garnet rim. Nose: fine reductive notes, aged wood nuances, ripe fruit, dried herbs. Palate: spicy, long, toasty.

Torre de Gazate 2013 T Roble
100% tempranillo

86

Torre de Gazate Airén 2014 B
100% airén

83

Torre de Gazate Cabernet Sauvignon 2014 RD
100% cabernet sauvignon

82

Torre de Gazate Syrah Merlot Cabernet Sauvignon 2014 T
40% syrah, 30% merlot, 30% cabernet sauvignon

84

Torre de Gazate Tempranillo 2014 T
100% tempranillo

85

Torre de Gazate Verdejo Sauvignon Blanc 2014 B
50% verdejo, 50% sauvignon blanc

83

VINOS COLOMAN S.A.T.

Goya, 17
13620 Pedro Muñoz (Ciudad Real)
☎: +34 926 586 410
Fax: +34 926 586 656
coloman@satcoloman.com
www.satcoloman.com

Besana Real 2009 TC
tempranillo

86

Besana Real 2014 RD
tempranillo

84

Besana Real Cabernet Sauvignon 2011 T Roble
cabernet sauvignon

83

Besana Real Macabeo 2014 B
macabeo

84

Besana Real Tempranillo 2014 T
tempranillo

83

Besana Real Verdejo 2014 B
verdejo

84

VIÑEDOS Y BODEGAS MUÑOZ

Ctra. Villarrubia, 11
45350 Noblejas (Toledo)
☎: +34 925 140 070
Fax: +34 925 141 334
info@bodegasmunoz.com
www.bodegasmunoz.com

Artero 2012 TC
tempranillo, merlot, syrah

87

Colour: cherry, garnet rim. Nose: fruit preserve, wild herbs, spicy, creamy oak. Palate: powerful, flavourful, toasty.

Artero 2012 TR
merlot

88

Colour: cherry, garnet rim. Nose: ripe fruit, wild herbs, spicy, balsamic herbs. Palate: balanced, flavourful, long, balsamic.

Artero 2014 RD
tempranillo
86

Artero Macabeo Verdejo 2014 B
macabeo, verdejo
85

Artero Tempranillo 2014 T
tempranillo
83

Blas Muñoz Chardonnay 2014 BFB
chardonnay
89
Colour: bright yellow. Nose: ripe fruit, dried herbs, sweet spices, creamy oak. Palate: rich, fruity, spicy, long, balanced.

VIRGEN DE LAS VIÑAS BODEGA Y ALMAZARA

Ctra. Argamasilla de Alba, 1
13700 Tomelloso (Ciudad Real)
☎: +34 926 510 865
Fax: +34 926 512 130
atencion.cliente@vinostomillar.com
www.vinostomillar.com

Tomillar 2010 TR
80% cabernet sauvignon, 20% tempranillo
86

Tomillar Chardonnay 2014 B
100% chardonnay
85

Tomillar Tempranillo 2014 T
100% tempranillo
84

DO. LA PALMA

CONSEJO REGULADOR
Esteban Acosta Gómez, 7
38740 Fuencaliente (La Palma)
☎:+34 922 444 404
Fax: +34 922 444 432
@: vinoslapalma@vinoslapalma.com
www.vinoslapalma.com

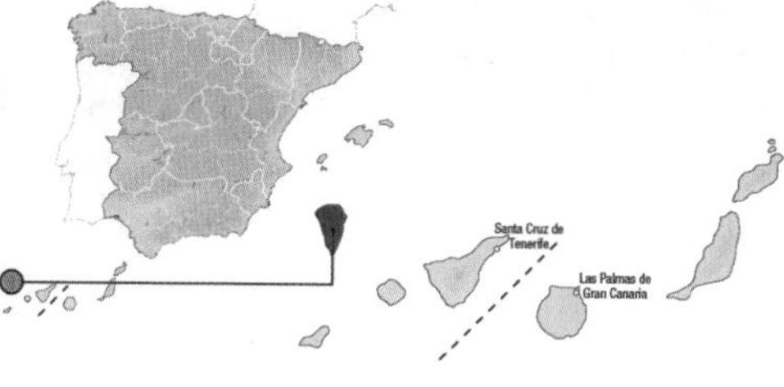

LOCATION:

The production area covers the whole island of San Miguel de La Palma, and is divided into three distinct sub-regions: Hoyo de Mazo, Fuencaliente and Northern La Palma.

SUB-REGIONS:

Hoyo de Mazo: It comprises the municipal districts of Villa de Mazo, Breña Baja, Breña Alta and Santa Cruz de La Palma, at altitudes of between 200 m and 700 m. The vines grow over the terrain on hillsides covered with volcanic stone ('Empedrados') or with volcanic gravel ('Picón Granado'). White and mainly red varieties are grown.

Fuencaliente: It comprises the municipal districts of Fuencaliente, El Paso, Los Llanos de Aridane and Tazacorte. The vines grow over terrains of volcanic ash at altitudes of between 200 m and 1900 m. The white varieties and the sweet Malvasia stand out.

Northern La Palma: Situated at an altitude of between 100 m and 200 m, It comprises the municipal areas of Puntallana, San Andrés and Sauces, Barlovento, Garafía, Puntagorda and Tijarafe. The region is richer in vegetation and the vines grow on trellises and using the goblet system. The traditional 'Tea' wines are produced here.

GRAPE VARIETIES:

WHITE: Malvasía, Güal and Verdello (main); Albillo, Bastardo Blanco, Bermejuela, Bujariego, Burra Blanca, Forastera Blanca, Listán Blanco, Moscatel, Pedro Ximénez, Sabro and Torrontés.

RED: Negramol (main), Listán Negro (Almuñeco), Bastardo Negro, Malvasía Rosada, Moscatel Negro, Tintilla, Castellana, Listán Prieto and Vijariego Negro.

FIGURES:

Vineyard surface: 610 – **Wine-Growers:** 1,132 – **Wineries:** 20 – **2014 Harvest rating:** N/A – **Production 14:** 997,923 litres – **Market percentages:** 99% National - 1% International.

SOIL:

The vineyards are situated at altitudes of between 200 m and 1,400 m above sea level in a coastal belt ranging in width which surrounds the whole island. Due to the ragged topography, the vineyards occupy the steep hillsides in the form of small terraces. The soil is mainly of volcanic origin.

CLIMATE:

This is the most north-westerly island of the archipelago of the Canary Islands. Its complex orography with altitudes which reach 2,400 metres above sea level make it a micro-continent with a wide variety of climates. The influence of the anti-cyclone of the Azores and the trade winds condition the thermal variables and the rainfall registered throughout the year. The greatest amount of rainfall is registered in the more easterly and northern parts of the island due to the entry of the trade winds.

Throughout the north-east, from Mazo to Barlovento, the climate is milder and fresher, while the western part of the island has drier and warmer weather. The average rainfall increases from the coast as the terrain ascends. The greatest amount of rainfall is in the north and east of the island.

VINTAGE RATING

PEÑÍNGUIDE

2010	2011	2012	2013	2014
GOOD	VERY GOOD	VERY GOOD	N/A	GOOD

BODEGA CASTRO Y MOGAN

Cº Bellido Alto La Montaña, s/n
38780 Tijarafe (Santa Cruz de Tenerife)
☎: +34 626 485 811
Fax: +34 922 490 066
contacto@vinostendal.com
www.vinostendal.com

Tendal 2014 B
84

Tendal Ecológico 2014 T
85

Tendal Selección 2014 T
86

BODEGA JOSÉ DAVID RODRÍGUEZ PÉREZ

Barranquito hondo Nº 4
El Pinar - Puntagorda
☎: +34 636 918 839
vinarda@hotmail.com

Viñarda RD
82

Viñarda 2014 T
83

BODEGA MATÍAS TORRES

Los Canarios s/n
38740 Fuentecaliente de la Palma
(Santa Cruz de Tenerife)
☎: +34 617 967 499
bodega@matiasitorres.com
www.matiastorres.com

Folky 2014 B
albillo, malvasía, listán blanco
90
Colour: bright straw. Nose: white flowers, fine lees, dried herbs, ripe fruit, candied fruit, dry stone. Palate: flavourful, fruity, good acidity, elegant.

Matías i Torres Albillo 2013 B
100% albillo
90
Colour: bright straw. Nose: white flowers, dried herbs, ripe fruit, citrus fruit. Palate: flavourful, fruity, good acidity, elegant.

Matías i Torres Albillo 2014 B
albillo
91
Colour: bright straw. Nose: white flowers, fine lees, dried herbs, ripe fruit, citrus fruit. Palate: flavourful, fruity, good acidity, elegant.

Matias i Torres Diego 2014 B
100% diego
91
Colour: bright yellow. Nose: expressive, dried herbs, ripe fruit, spicy. Palate: flavourful, fruity, good acidity, balanced, balsamic, rich.

PODIUM

Matias i Torres Malvasía Aromática Naturalmente Dulce 2011 B
malvasía
95
Colour: golden. Nose: honeyed notes, candied fruit, fragrant herbs, acetaldehyde. Palate: flavourful, sweet, fresh, fruity, good acidity, long.

Matías i Torres Negramoll Dulce 2013 T
100% negramoll
89
Colour: cherry, garnet rim. Nose: fruit preserve, spicy, creamy oak. Palate: powerful, flavourful, sweet, rich.

PODIUM

Vid Sur Dulce 2008 B
100% malvasía
95
Colour: light mahogany. Nose: candied fruit, fruit liqueur notes, spicy, varnish, acetaldehyde, dry nuts. Palate: spirituous, balanced, elegant, round, unctuous.

BODEGA MIL7OCHENTAYNUEVE

Dr. Esteban Acosta, 24
Los Canarios - Fuencaliente
mil7ochentaynueve@gmail.com

Blanco Marina 2014 B
83

Tinto Esperanza 2014 T
negramoll
84

BODEGA PERDOMO S.A.T.

Joaquina, 12 (Las Tricias)
38738 Garafia (La Palma)
☎: +34 922 400 089
Fax: +34 922 400 689

Piedra Jurada 2014 B
87
Colour: bright straw. Nose: white flowers, fresh fruit, fragrant herbs. Palate: flavourful, fruity, easy to drink.

Piedra Jurada 2014 T
85

Piedra Jurada Albillo 2014 B
86

Piedra Jurada Albillo Afrutado 2014 B
85

BODEGAS CARBALLO

Ctra. a Las Indias, 74
38740 Fuencaliente de La Palma
(Santa Cruz de Tenerife)
☎: +34 922 444 140
Fax: +34 922 211 744
info@bodegascarballo.com
www.bodegascarballo.com

Carballo 2014 T
80% negramoll, 15% listán negro, 5% vidueño
86

Carballo Malvasia Dulce 2012 B
malvasía
93

Colour: mahogany. Nose: complex, fruit liqueur notes, dried fruit, pattiserie, toasty. Palate: sweet, rich, unctuous, balanced, elegant.

BODEGAS NOROESTE DE LA PALMA

Camino de Bellido, s/n
38780 Tijarafe (Santa Cruz de Tenerife)
☎: +34 922 491 075
Fax: +34 922 491 075
administracion@vinosveganorte.com
www.vinosveganorte.com

Vega Norte 2013 BFB
87

Colour: bright yellow. Nose: ripe fruit, powerfull, toasty, aged wood nuances. Palate: flavourful, fruity, spicy, toasty, long.

Vega Norte 2014 T
85

Vega Norte RD
87

Colour: rose, purple rim. Nose: red berry notes, floral, expressive. Palate: powerful, fruity, fresh, easy to drink.

Vega Norte "Vino de Tea" 2014 T
89

Colour: ruby red. Nose: ripe fruit, wild herbs, scrubland, spicy. Palate: flavourful, fresh, fruity, balsamic.

Vega Norte 2014 B
87

Colour: bright yellow. Nose: expressive, dried herbs, ripe fruit. Palate: flavourful, fruity, good acidity, balanced.

Vega Norte Albillo 2014 B
87

Colour: bright yellow. Nose: expressive, ripe fruit, spicy. Palate: flavourful, fruity, good acidity, balanced, long.

Vega Norte Listán Prieto 2014 T
86

Vega Norte Vendimia Seleccionada X Aniversario 2013 T
90

Colour: light cherry. Nose: fruit expression, fruit liqueur notes, fragrant herbs, spicy, creamy oak. Palate: balanced, elegant, spicy, long, toasty.

BODEGAS TAMANCA S.L.

Las Manchas - San Nicolás
38750 El Paso (Santa Cruz de Tenerife)
☎: +34 922 494 155
Fax: +34 922 494 296
bodegas_tamanca@hotmail.com

Tamanca 2014 RD
negramoll
84

Tamanca 2014 T Roble
negramoll, almuñeco, vijariego negro, baboso negro, castellana
85

Tamanca Listán Blanco 2014 B
listán blanco
85

Tamanca Malvasía Dulce 2005 B Barrica
malvasía
94

Colour: golden. Nose: powerfull, honeyed notes, candied fruit, acetaldehyde, aged wood nuances, toasty. Palate: flavourful, sweet, fresh, fruity, good acidity, long, balanced.

Tamanca Negramoll 2014 T
negramoll
83

Tamanca Roble 2014 B
vijariego blanco, albillo, malvasía
84

Tamanca Sabro Dulce 2009/2010 B
sabro
87

Colour: golden. Nose: powerfull, honeyed notes, candied fruit, fragrant herbs, acetaldehyde. Palate: flavourful, sweet, fresh, fruity, good acidity, long.

Tamanca Selección 2014 B
albillo, vijariego blanco, marmajuelo, malvasía, sabro

87

Colour: bright straw. Nose: white flowers, fresh fruit, fragrant herbs. Palate: flavourful, fruity.

BODEGAS TENEGUÍA

Los Canarios, s/n
38740 Fuencaliente de La Palma
(Santa Cruz de Tenerife)
☎: +34 922 444 078
Fax: +34 922 444 394
enologia@vinosteneguia.com
www.bodegasteneguia.com

Teneguía 2014 B
listán blanco, vijariego blanco, gual, sabro

84

Teneguía 2014 T
negramoll, castellana, vijariego negro, almuñeco

85

Teneguía La Gota 2014 B
vijariego blanco, albillo, listán blanco, negramoll

85

Teneguía Malvasía Aromática Naturalmente Dulce 2013 B
malvasía

90

Colour: bright yellow. Nose: powerfull, candied fruit, dried herbs, citrus fruit, honeyed notes. Palate: flavourful, sweet, ripe fruit, good acidity.

Teneguía Malvasía Aromática Seco 2012 BFB
malvasía

87

Colour: bright yellow. Nose: expressive, dried herbs, ripe fruit, spicy, aged wood nuances. Palate: flavourful, fruity, good acidity, balanced.

PODIUM

Teneguía Malvasía Dulce Estelar Naturalmente Dulce 1996 B Gran Reserva
malvasía

96

Colour: light mahogany. Nose: powerfull, complex, dry nuts, toasty, acetaldehyde, creamy oak, sweet spices. Palate: rich, long, fine solera notes, spicy, round.

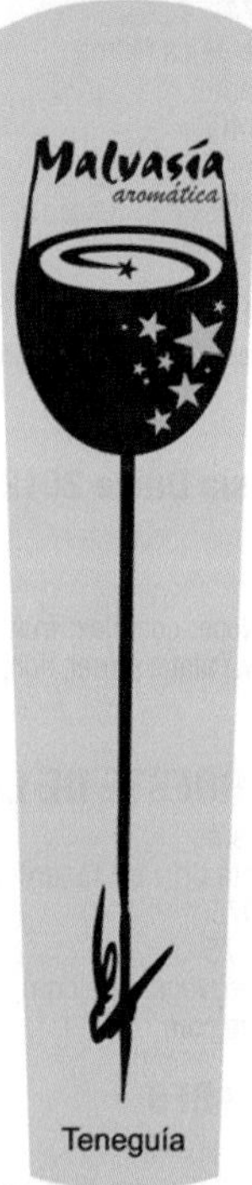

Teneguía Sabro/Gual Dulce 2012 B
sabro, gual

90

Colour: bright yellow. Nose: balsamic herbs, honeyed notes, floral, sweet spices, expressive. Palate: rich, fruity, powerful, flavourful, elegant.

Teneguía Zeus Negramoll 2012 T
negramoll

89

Colour: bright cherry, garnet rim. Nose: acetaldehyde, varnish, candied fruit. Palate: fruity, flavourful, sweet.

COOPERATIVA AGRÍCOLA VÍRGEN DEL PINO

Camino de la Cooperativa, 6 - El Pinar
38738 Puntagorda (La Palma)
☎: +34 922 493 211
Fax: +34 922 493 211
bodegastraviesa@gmail.com

Viña Traviesa 2014 B

85

LLANOS NEGROS

Los Canarios s/n
38740 Fuencaliente de La Palma
(Santa Cruz de Tenerife)
☎: +34 922 444 078
Fax: +34 922 444 394
enologa@vinosteneguia.com

Llanos Negros La Batista 2014 B

malvasía

88

Colour: bright straw. Nose: fine lees, dried herbs, ripe fruit, candied fruit, citrus fruit. Palate: flavourful, fruity, good acidity, elegant.

Llanos Negros La Tablada 2014 B

sabro, gual

85

Llanos Negros La Time 2000 B

listán blanco

90

Colour: bright straw. Nose: dried herbs, faded flowers, ripe fruit, earthy notes, complex, waxy notes, fine reductive notes. Palate: ripe fruit, spicy, long.

Llanos Negros Los Grillos 2014 T

negramoll

86

Llanos Negros Los Tabaqueros 2006 B

listán blanco, vijariego blanco, sabro, gual, malvasía

89

Colour: golden. Nose: powerfull, candied fruit, fragrant herbs. Palate: flavourful, sweet, fresh, fruity, good acidity, long.

Llanos Negros Malvasía Aromática Naturalmente Dulce 2014 B

malvasía

92

Colour: bright yellow. Nose: balsamic herbs, honeyed notes, floral, sweet spices, citrus fruit. Palate: rich, fruity, powerful, flavourful, elegant.

LUIS BRITO SOCIEDAD COOPERATIVA

Camino Los Pulidos, 13
38760 Los Llanos de Ariadne
(La Palma)
☎: +34 922 463 205

Aceró 2014 T Barrica

25% vijariego negro, 25% castellana, 50% baboso negro

83

Aceró 2014 T Roble

33% vijariego negro, 33% castellana, 33% baboso negro

84

ONÉSIMA PÉREZ RODRÍGUEZ

Las Tricias
38738 Garafia (La Palma)
☎: +34 922 463 481
Fax: +34 922 463 481
vinosvitega@terra.es

Vitega 2014 B

84

Vitega 2014 RD

83

Vitega 2014 T

85

Vitega Albillo 2014 B

82

Vitega Tea 2014 T

85

VINOS EL NÍSPERO

Briesta, 3
38787 Villa de Garafia
(Santa Cruz de Tenerife)
☎: +34 639 080 712
Fax: +34 922 400 447
adali_12@msn.com

El Níspero 2013 BFB
86

El Níspero 2014 B
88

Colour: bright straw. Nose: white flowers, fresh fruit, fragrant herbs, expressive. Palate: flavourful, fruity, good acidity, balanced.

Esencia el Níspero 2011 T
88

Colour: cherry, garnet rim. Nose: ripe fruit, spicy, creamy oak, complex. Palate: flavourful, toasty, round tannins.

DO. LANZAROTE

CONSEJO REGULADOR

Arrecife, 9
35550 San Bartolomé (Lanzarote)
☎:+34 928 521 313 - Fax: +34 928 521 049
@: info@dolanzarote.com
www.dolanzarote.com

LOCATION:

On the island of Lanzarote. The production area covers the municipal areas of Tinajo, Yaiza, San Bartolomé, Haría and Teguise.

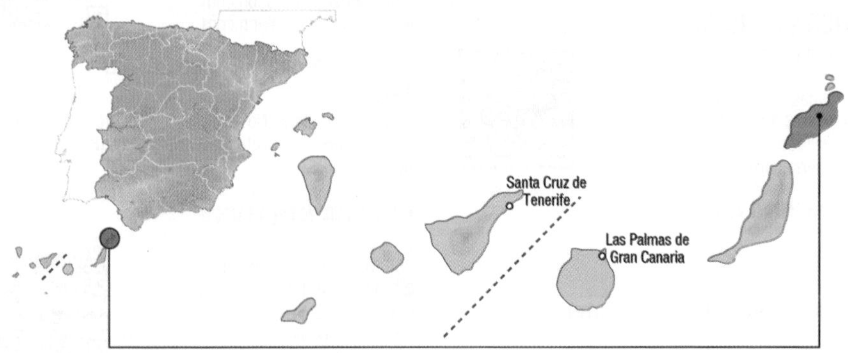

GRAPE VARIETIES:

WHITE: Malvasía (majority 75%), Pedro Ximénez, Diego, Listán Blanco, Moscatel, Burrablanca, Breval.
RED: Listán Negra (15%) and Negramoll.

FIGURES:

Vineyard surface: 1,835 – **Wine-Growers:** 1,762 – **Wineries:** 13 – **2014 Harvest rating:** Excellent – **Production 14:** 1,308,987 litres – **Market percentages:** 97% National - 3% International.

SOIL:

Volcanic in nature (locally known as 'Picón'). In fact, the cultivation of vines is made possible thanks to the ability of the volcanic sand to perfectly retain the water from dew and the scant rainfall. The island is relatively flat (the maximum altitude is 670 m) and the most characteristic form of cultivation is in 'hollows' surrounded by semicircular walls which protect the plants from the wind. This singular trainig system brings about an extremaly low density.

CLIMATE:

Dry subtropical in nature, with low rainfall (about 200 mm per year) which is spread out irregularly throughout the year. On occasions, the Levante wind (easterly), characterised by its low humidity and which carries sand particles from the African continent, causes a considerable increase in the temperatures.

VINTAGE RATING

PEÑÍNGUIDE

2010	2011	2012	2013	2014
EXCELLENT	VERY GOOD	VERY GOOD	VERY GOOD	GOOD

BODEGA LA FLORIDA

Calle de la Florida, 89
35559 San Bartolomé de Lanzarote
(Las Palmas)
☎: +34 928 593 001
bodegaslaflorida@bodegaslaflorida.com

La Florida 2013 T

85

La Florida Malvasía Volcánica 2014 B

85

BODEGA LA GERIA

Ctra. de la Geria, Km. 19
35570 Yaiza
(Las Palmas de Gran Canaria)
☎: +34 928 173 178
bodega@lageria.com
www.lageria.com

La Geria 2014 RD

listán negro

86

La Geria Antigua 1996 Moscatel

moscatel de alejandría

92

Colour: iodine, amber rim. Nose: elegant, sweet spices, acetaldehyde, dry nuts. Palate: full, spicy, long, fine bitter notes, complex.

La Geria Antigua Malvasía Dulce 2005

malvasía

90

Colour: mahogany. Nose: complex, fruit liqueur notes, dried fruit, pattiserie, toasty, dry nuts. Palate: sweet, rich, unctuous.

La Geria Malvasía 2014 Dulce

malvasía

87

Colour: bright yellow. Nose: candied fruit, citrus fruit, white flowers. Palate: rich, fruity, flavourful, balsamic.

Manto 2014 T

syrah, merlot, tintilla, listán negro

86

Manto Seco 2014 B

malvasía

89

Colour: bright straw. Nose: white flowers, candied fruit, citrus fruit. Palate: flavourful, fruity, good acidity, round.

Manto Semidulce 2014 B

malvasía

88

Colour: bright yellow. Nose: powerfull, candied fruit, dried herbs. Palate: flavourful, sweet, ripe fruit, good acidity, easy to drink.

BODEGA MARTINON

Camino del Mentidero, 2
35572 Masdache Tías (Las Palmas)
☎: +34 928 834 160
Fax: +34 928 834 160
info@bodegasmartinon.com
www.bodegasmartinon.com

Martinón Malvasía Seco 2014 B

88

Colour: bright straw. Nose: white flowers, fresh fruit, fragrant herbs, expressive. Palate: flavourful, fruity, good acidity, balanced.

BODEGA STRATVS

Ctra. La Geria, Km. 18
35570 Yaiza (Las Palmas)
☎: +34 928 809 977
Fax: +34 928 524 651
bodega@stratvs.com
www.stratvs.com

Stratvs Colección Privé 2014 T

89

Colour: cherry, purple rim. Nose: floral, balsamic herbs, fragrant herbs, fruit preserve. Palate: powerful, fresh, fruity.

Stratvs El Pícaro 2014 B

90

Colour: bright straw. Nose: white flowers, candied fruit, citrus fruit. Palate: flavourful, fruity, good acidity.

Stratvs Malvasía Seco 2014 B

89

Colour: bright straw. Nose: floral, fragrant herbs, candied fruit, citrus fruit. Palate: fresh, fruity, flavourful, long.

BODEGAS GUIGUAN

35560 Tinajo - Lanzarote (Las Palmas)
☎: +34 659 971 555
Fax: +34 928 840 715
info@bodegasguiguan.com
www.bodegasguiguan.com

Guiguan Malvasía Crianza sobre Lías 2014 B

malvasía

85

Guiguan Malvasía Seco 2014 B
malvasía
84

Guiguan Malvasia Semidulce 2014 B
malvasía, moscatel de alejandría
84

Guiguan Moscatel Dulce 2014 B
moscatel de alejandría
87
Colour: bright yellow. Nose: balsamic herbs, floral, sweet spices, candied fruit. Palate: fruity, powerful, flavourful.

BODEGAS LOS BERMEJOS

Camino a Los Bermejos, 7
35550 San Bartolomé de Lanzarote
(Las Palmas)
☎: +34 928 522 463
Fax: +34 928 522 641
bodega@losbermejos.com
www.losbermejos.com

Bermejo Diego 2014 B
diego
88
Colour: bright straw. Nose: white flowers, dried herbs, ripe fruit. Palate: flavourful, fruity, round.

Bermejo Diego Ecológico Seco 2014 B
diego
87
Colour: bright straw. Nose: dried flowers, fragrant herbs, ripe fruit. Palate: powerful, flavourful, balsamic.

Bermejo Listán 2014 RD
listán negro
85

Bermejo Listán Eco 2014 RD
listán negro
84

Bermejo Listán Negro 2013 T Barrica
listán negro
88
Colour: bright cherry. Nose: ripe fruit, sweet spices, creamy oak, expressive. Palate: flavourful, fruity, round tannins.

Bermejo Listán Negro 2014 T Maceración Carbónica
listán negro
90
Colour: cherry, purple rim. Nose: expressive, fresh fruit, red berry notes, floral. Palate: flavourful, fruity, good acidity. Personality.

Bermejo Listán Negro Rosado 2013 BN
listán negro
89
Colour: coppery red. Nose: floral, jasmine, fragrant herbs, candied fruit. Palate: fresh, fruity, flavourful, correct, balanced.

Bermejo Malvasia 2013 BN
malvasía
88
Colour: bright yellow. Nose: ripe fruit, fine lees, balanced, dried herbs. Palate: good acidity, flavourful, ripe fruit, long.

Bermejo Malvasia Naturalmente Dulce B
malvasía
93
Colour: golden. Nose: powerfull, candied fruit, fragrant herbs, acetaldehyde, aged wood nuances. Palate: flavourful, sweet, fresh, fruity, good acidity, long.

Bermejo Malvasía Seco 2014 B
malvasía
85

Bermejo Malvasía Seco 2014 BFB
malvasía
87
Colour: bright straw. Nose: ripe fruit, toasty, pattiserie. Palate: flavourful, fruity, spicy, toasty.

Bermejo Malvasía Seco Eco 2014 B
malvasía
84

Bermejo Malvasía Semidulce 2014 B
90% malvasía, 10% moscatel
85

Bermejo Moscatel Naturalmente Dulce 2012 B
moscatel
87
Colour: bright yellow. Nose: balsamic herbs, floral, sweet spices, expressive. Palate: rich, fruity.

BODEGAS MALPAÍS DE MAGUEZ

Cueva de los Verdes, 5
35542 Punta Mujeres - Haria
(Las Palmas)
☎: +34 616 908 484
Fax: +34 928 848 110
bodegamalpais@gmail.com

La Grieta Malvasía Seco 2014 B
85

BODEGAS REYMAR

Pza. Virgen de Los Dolores,
19 Mancha Blanca
35560 Tinajo (Las Palmas)
☎: +34 649 993 096
Fax: +34 928 840 737
reymarmalvasia@terra.com
www.bodegasreymar.com

Los Perdomos Crianza sobre lías 2013 B
90

Colour: bright straw. Nose: white flowers, fine lees, dried herbs, mineral, expressive. Palate: flavourful, fruity, good acidity, round, long.

Los Perdomos Diego 2014 B
88

Colour: bright straw. Nose: dried herbs, ripe fruit, citrus fruit, mineral. Palate: flavourful, fruity, good acidity.

Los Perdomos Listán Negro 2014 T
85

Los Perdomos Listán Negro Dulce 2013 T
86

Los Perdomos Malvasia Dulce B
89

Colour: bright yellow. Nose: powerfull, candied fruit, dried herbs, medium intensity. Palate: flavourful, sweet, ripe fruit, good acidity.

Los Perdomos Malvasía Moscatel Semiseco 2014 B
84

Los Perdomos Malvasía Seco 2014 B
86

Los Perdomos Moscatel Diego 2014 B
85

Los Perdomos Moscatel Dulce B
90

Colour: bright yellow. Nose: honeyed notes, floral, pattiserie, creamy oak. Palate: rich, fruity, powerful, flavourful.

BODEGAS RUBICÓN

Ctra. Teguise - Yaiza, 2 La Geria
35570 Yaiza (Las Palmas)
☎: +34 928 173 708
marketing@bodegasrubicon.com
www.bodegasrubicon.com

Amalia 2013 T
listán negro

88

Colour: bright cherry. Nose: creamy oak, fruit preserve, balsamic herbs. Palate: flavourful, fruity, toasty.

Amalia Autor 2014 T
listán negro

87

Colour: ruby red. Nose: fruit preserve, fragrant herbs, dry stone. Palate: powerful, flavourful, fruity.

Amalia Malvasía Seco 2014 B
malvasía

89

Colour: bright straw. Nose: white flowers, dried herbs, ripe fruit, candied fruit, citrus fruit. Palate: flavourful, fruity, good acidity, elegant.

Rubicón Malvasía Seco 2014 B
malvasía

88

Colour: bright straw. Nose: white flowers, fresh fruit, fragrant herbs, expressive. Palate: flavourful, fruity, good acidity, balanced.

Rubicón Malvasía Semidulce 2014 B
95% malvasía, 5% moscatel de alejandría

87

Colour: bright yellow. Nose: powerfull, candied fruit, dried herbs, white flowers. Palate: flavourful, sweet, ripe fruit.

Rubicón Moscatel Dulce 2014 B
moscatel de alejandría

89

Colour: bright yellow. Nose: balsamic herbs, honeyed notes, floral, sweet spices. Palate: rich, fruity, powerful, flavourful, elegant.

Rubicón Rosado 2014 RD
listán negro

84

EL GRIFO

Lugar de El Grifo, s/n Apdo. Correos, 6
35500 San Bartolomé
(Las Palmas de Gran Canaria)
☎: +34 928 524 036
Fax: +34 928 832 634
malvasa@elgrifo.com
www.elgrifo.com

Ariana 2013 T
70% listán negro, 30% syrah

91

Colour: cherry, purple rim. Nose: violet drops, red berry notes, ripe fruit, fragrant herbs, mineral. Palate: fresh, fruity, flavourful, easy to drink.

🏆 PODIUM

El Grifo Canari Dulce de Licor
malvasía

95

Colour: light mahogany. Nose: powerfull, complex, dry nuts, toasty, acetaldehyde. Palate: rich, long, spicy, round, balanced, elegant. Personality.

El Grifo El Afrutado Semidulce 2014 B
moscatel de alejandría, diego, listán blanco

88

Colour: bright yellow. Nose: balsamic herbs, honeyed notes, floral, sweet spices. Palate: rich, fruity, powerful, flavourful.

El Grifo Listán Negro 2014 T
listán negro

88

Colour: cherry, purple rim. Nose: red berry notes, floral, balsamic herbs. Palate: powerful, fresh, fruity, easy to drink.

El Grifo Malvasía 2014 BFB
malvasía

90

Colour: bright yellow. Nose: ripe fruit, powerfull, toasty, aged wood nuances. Palate: flavourful, fruity, spicy, toasty, long.

El Grifo Malvasía Seco Colección 2014 B
malvasía

89

Colour: bright straw. Nose: floral, dried herbs, candied fruit. Palate: fresh, fruity, flavourful.

El Grifo Malvasía Semidulce Colección 2014 B
malvasía

87

Colour: bright yellow. Nose: candied fruit, dried herbs, citrus fruit. Palate: flavourful, sweet, ripe fruit, good acidity.

El Grifo Moscatel de Ana B
moscatel de alejandría

90

Colour: bright yellow. Nose: powerfull, candied fruit, dried herbs, sweet spices. Palate: flavourful, sweet, ripe fruit.

VULCANO DE LANZAROTE

Victor Fernández, 5
35572 Tias de Lanzarote
(Las Palmas de Gran Canaria)
☎: +34 928 524 469
info@bodegavulcano.es
www.bodegavulcano.es

Vulcano de Lanzarote 2014 RD
50% listán negro, 50% negramoll

87

Colour: brilliant rose. Nose: red berry notes, ripe fruit, lactic notes, fragrant herbs. Palate: powerful, flavourful, ripe fruit.

Vulcano de Lanzarote 2014 T
50% listán negro, 50% negramoll

88

Colour: bright cherry. Nose: ripe fruit, sweet spices, creamy oak, expressive. Palate: flavourful, fruity, toasty.

Vulcano de Lanzarote Malvasía Volcánica Seco 2014 B
100% malvasía

89

Colour: bright yellow. Nose: dried herbs, ripe fruit, dry stone. Palate: flavourful, fruity, good acidity, fine bitter notes.

Vulcano de Lanzarote Malvasía Volcánica Semidulce 2014 B
malvasía

86

Vulcano Moscatel Dolce 2014 B
100% moscatel de alejandría

91

Colour: golden. Nose: powerfull, honeyed notes, candied fruit, fragrant herbs, fruit liqueur notes. Palate: flavourful, sweet, fresh, fruity, good acidity, long.

DO. MÁLAGA Y SIERRAS DE MÁLAGA

CONSEJO REGULADOR
Plaza de los Viñeros,1
29008 Málaga
☎:+34 952 227 990 - Fax: +34 952 227 990
@: info@vinomalaga.com
www.vinomalaga.com

LOCATION:

In the province of Málaga. It covers 54 municipal areas along the coast (in the vicinity of Málaga and Estepona) and inland (along the banks of the river Genil), together with the new sub-region of Serranía de Ronda, a region to which the two new municipal districts of Cuevas del Becerro and Cortes de la Frontera have been added.

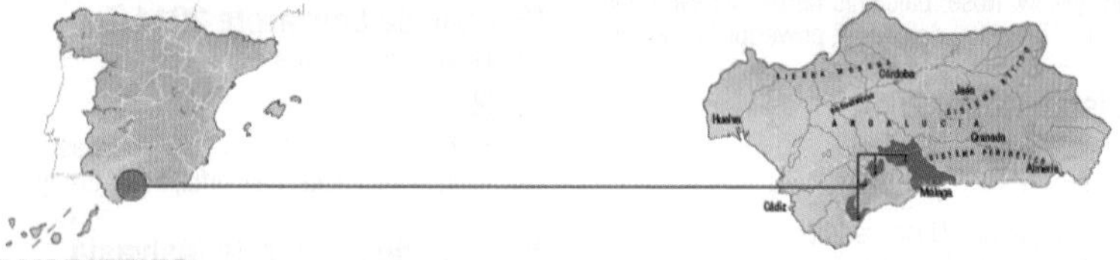

GRAPE VARIETIES:

WHITE: **DO Málaga**: Pedro Ximénez and Moscatel; **DO Sierras de Málaga**: Chardonnay, Moscatel, Pedro Ximénez, Macabeo, Sauvignon Blanc and Colombard.

RED: **only DO Sierras de Málaga**: Romé, Cabernet Sauvignon, Merlot, Syrah, Tempranillo, Petit Verdot.

TYPOLOGY OF CLASSIC WINES:

a) LIQUEUR WINES: from 15 to 22% vol.

b) NATURAL SWEET WINES: from 15 to 22 % vol. obtained from the Moscatel or Pedro Ximénez varieties, from musts with a minimum sugar content of 244 grams/litre.

c) NATURALLY SWEET WINES (with the same varieties, over 13% vol. and from musts with 300 grams of sugar/litre) and still wines (from 10 to 15% vol.).

Depending on their ageing:

- **MÁLAGA JOVEN:** Unaged still wines. - **MÁLAGA PÁLIDO:** Unaged non-still wines.
- **MÁLAGA:** Wines aged for between 6 and 24 months. - **MÁLAGA NOBLE:** Wines aged for between 2 and 3 years.
- **MÁLAGA AÑEJO:** Wines aged for between 3 and 5 years. - **MÁLAGA TRASAÑEJO:** Wines aged for over 5 years.

FIGURES:

Vineyard surface: 950 – **Wine-Growers:** 461 – **Wineries:** 45 – **2014 Harvest rating:** N/A – **Production 14:** 3,784,581 litres – **Market percentages:** 66% National - 34% International.

SOIL:

It varies from red Mediterranean soil with limestone components in the northern region to decomposing slate on steep slopes of the Axarquía.

CLIMATE:

Varies depending on the production area. In the northern region, the summers are short with high temperatures, and the average rainfall is in the range of 500 mm; in the region of Axarquía, protected from the northerly winds by the mountain ranges and facing south, the climate is somewhat milder due to the influence of the Mediterranean; whilst in the west, the climate can be defined as dry subhumid.

VINTAGE RATING

PEÑÍNGUIDE

2010	2011	2012	2013	2014
GOOD	VERY GOOD	VERY GOOD	VERY GOOD	VERY GOOD

BODEGA CUESTA LA VIÑA

Ctra. A-2300, km. 21,6. Montecorto
29400 Ronda (Málaga)
☎: +34 629 589 336
bodegacuestalavina@gmail.com

Jorge Bonet TSMC 2011 T
tempranillo, syrah, merlot, cabernet sauvignon

89

Colour: very deep cherry, garnet rim. Nose: ripe fruit, spicy, balanced, characterful. Palate: balanced, long, balsamic.

Kataviña T
tempranillo, syrah, graciano

86

BODEGA DOÑA FELISA

Cordel del Puerto s/n
29400 Ronda (Málaga)
☎: +34 951 166 033
ahernando@chinchillawine.com
www.chinchillawine.com

Chinchilla 2014 RD
petit verdot

84

Chinchilla 2014 T Roble
tempranillo, merlot

87

Colour: deep cherry, purple rim. Nose: ripe fruit, spicy, dried herbs. Palate: fruity, flavourful, good finish.

Chinchilla Doble Doce 2009 T
cabernet sauvignon, merlot

86

Chinchilla Seis + Seis 2011 T Roble
tempranillo, syrah

88

Colour: dark-red cherry, garnet rim. Nose: spicy, scrubland, dried herbs. Palate: correct, balanced, spicy.

Encaste 2009 T
cabernet sauvignon

87

Colour: black cherry, orangey edge. Nose: varietal, grassy, spicy, ripe fruit, warm. Palate: balanced, powerful, full.

BODEGA GONZALO BELTRÁN

Finca La Nogalera, Hoya de los Molinos
29400 Ronda (Málaga)
☎: +34 629 455 558
info@bodegagonzalobeltran.com
www.bodegagonzalobeltran.com

Perezoso 2012 T
100% syrah

89

Colour: bright cherry. Nose: ripe fruit, creamy oak. Palate: flavourful, fruity, spicy, long.

BODEGA JOAQUÍN FERNÁNDEZ

Partido Los Frontones
Finca Los Frutales s/n
29400 Ronda (Málaga)
☎: +34 951 166 043
Fax: +34 951 166 043
info@bodegajf.es
www.bodegajf.com

Hacienda de la Vizcondesa 2013 TC
merlot

88 🌱

Colour: cherry, garnet rim. Nose: ripe fruit, sweet spices, creamy oak. Palate: flavourful, smoky aftertaste, ripe fruit.

Los Frutales 2013 RD Roble
merlot

86 🌱

Los Frutales Cabernet Sauvignon 2012 T
cabernet sauvignon

89 🌱

Colour: cherry, garnet rim. Nose: ripe fruit, earthy notes, spicy, balsamic herbs. Palate: balanced, flavourful, long, balsamic.

Los Frutales Garnacha 2012 T
garnacha

90 🌱

Colour: cherry, garnet rim. Nose: ripe fruit, wild herbs, spicy, balsamic herbs. Palate: balanced, flavourful, long.

Los Frutales Igualado 2010 T
cabernet sauvignon, garnacha, merlot, syrah

86 🌱

Los Frutales Merlot Syrah 2009 TC
merlot, syrah

84 🌱

BODEGA KIENINGER

Los Frontones, 67
29400 Ronda (Málaga)
☎: +34 952 879 554
martin@bodegakieninger.com
www.bodegakieninger.com

Maxx 2012 T
garnacha, tintilla de rota

92

Colour: cherry, garnet rim. Nose: mineral, expressive, spicy, scrubland. Palate: flavourful, ripe fruit, long, good acidity, balanced.

Maxx 2013 T
garnacha, tintilla de rota

89

Colour: dark-red cherry, garnet rim. Nose: smoky, dried herbs, ripe fruit, toasty. Palate: flavourful, good structure, smoky aftertaste.

Vinana Cuvé 2013 T
cabernet sauvignon, cabernet franc, merlot

90

Colour: very deep cherry, garnet rim. Nose: expressive, complex, mineral, balsamic herbs, balanced. Palate: full, flavourful, round tannins.

Vinana Pinot Noir 2013 T
100% pinot noir

91

Colour: cherry, garnet rim. Nose: balanced, toasty, elegant, fragrant herbs, ripe fruit. Palate: flavourful, spicy, elegant.

BODEGA VETAS

Con Nador Finca El Baco
29350 Arriate (Málaga)
☎: +34 647 177 620
info@bodegavetas.com
www.bodegavetas.com

Vetas Junior 2013 T
cabernet sauvignon, cabernet franc, petit verdot

85

Vetas Petit Verdot 2008 T
100% petit verdot

93

Colour: very deep cherry, garnet rim. Nose: expressive, complex, mineral, balsamic herbs, balanced. Palate: full, flavourful, round tannins.

Vetas Selección 2008 T
cabernet sauvignon, cabernet franc, petit verdot

90

Colour: very deep cherry, garnet rim. Nose: spicy, dark chocolate, ripe fruit, fruit preserve. Palate: powerful, flavourful, good structure.

BODEGA Y VIÑEDOS DE LA CAPUCHINA

Cortijo La Capuchina, Ctra.
Alameda-Mollina, km. 4
29532 Mollina (Málaga)
☎: +34 952 111 565
info@bodegalacapuchina.es
www.bodegalacapuchina.es

Capuchina Vieja 2010 T
40% syrah, 30% cabernet franc, 30% cabernet sauvignon, merlot

89

Colour: cherry, garnet rim. Nose: ripe fruit, wild herbs, earthy notes, spicy, balsamic herbs. Palate: balanced, flavourful, long, balsamic.

Capuchina Vieja Moscatel Seco 2014 B
moscatel

87

Colour: bright yellow. Nose: balsamic herbs, honeyed notes, floral, expressive. Palate: rich, fruity, powerful, flavourful.

Capuchina Vieja Sol 2014 Blanco dulce

91

Colour: bright yellow. Nose: balanced, expressive, ripe fruit, candied fruit. Palate: rich, flavourful, balanced.

BODEGAS ANTAKIRA

Alcalde Bernardo Meléndez, 15
29328 Málaga (Málaga)
☎: +34 952 038 652
info@bodegasantakira.com
www.bodegasantakira.com

Antakira Dulce Dulce de licor 2013 B
100% moscatel de alejandría

91

Colour: golden. Nose: powerfull, honeyed notes, candied fruit, fragrant herbs, acetaldehyde. Palate: flavourful, sweet, fresh, fruity, good acidity, long.

Antakira Dulce Natural 2013 B
100% moscatel de alejandría

90

Colour: bright yellow. Nose: balsamic herbs, honeyed notes, floral, sweet spices, expressive. Palate: rich, fruity, powerful, flavourful, elegant.

Rebalaje 2014 B
moscatel grano menudo, pedro ximénez, doradilla, airén

85

Rebalaje 2014 T
100% syrah

84

BODEGAS CONRAD

Ctra. El Burgo, Km. 4,0
29400 Ronda (Málaga)
☎: +34 951 166 035
Fax: +34 951 166 035
conrad@vinosconrad.com
www.vinosconrad.com

Cristina 2010 T
malbec, petit verdot

88

Colour: bright cherry, garnet rim. Nose: ripe fruit, dried herbs, balanced. Palate: fruity, easy to drink, good acidity, good finish.

El Niño León 2011 TR
cabernet sauvignon, tempranillo

87

Colour: black cherry, orangey edge. Nose: balsamic herbs, tobacco, ripe fruit, spicy. Palate: flavourful, good structure, round tannins.

El Pinsapo 2013 T
cabernet franc, tempranillo

87

Colour: dark-red cherry. Nose: scrubland, ripe fruit, spicy. Palate: balanced, ripe fruit, good finish, fruity aftestaste.

León Sabio 2009 T
cabernet franc

86

Leona Hermosa 2013 B
moscatel grano menudo, viognier, sauvignon blanc

87

Colour: bright straw. Nose: white flowers, fresh fruit, fragrant herbs, expressive. Palate: flavourful, fruity, good acidity, balanced.

Soleón 2010 T
cabernet franc, merlot, cabernet sauvignon

87

Colour: deep cherry, garnet rim. Nose: spicy, smoky, dried herbs. Palate: correct, good acidity, spicy, easy to drink.

BODEGAS DIMOBE

San Bartolomé, s/n
29738 Moclinejo (Málaga)
☎: +34 952 400 594
Fax: +34 952 400 743
ignacio@dimobe.es
www.dimobe.es

Arcos de Moclinejo Dulce Trasañejo
pedro ximénez

92

Colour: light mahogany. Nose: roasted almonds, acetaldehyde, sweet spices, aged wood nuances. Palate: full, flavourful, long, complex.

Arcos de Moclinejo Seco Trasañejo
pedro ximénez

93

Colour: old gold, amber rim. Nose: candied fruit, fruit liqueur notes, spicy, varnish. Palate: fine solera notes, fine bitter notes, spirituous, full.

El Lagar de Cabrera 2010 TC
syrah

85

El Lagar de Cabrera Moscatel 2014 B
moscatel de alejandría

85

El Lagar de Cabrera Syrah 2013 T
syrah

87

Colour: deep cherry, garnet rim. Nose: ripe fruit, faded flowers. Palate: flavourful, round tannins, easy to drink.

Finca La Indiana 2010 TC
petit verdot

87

Colour: deep cherry, purple rim. Nose: creamy oak, toasty, ripe fruit, balsamic herbs, powerfull. Palate: balanced, spicy, long.

Lagar de Cabrera 2014 RD
syrah, romé

85

Piamater Dulce Natural 2013 B
moscatel de alejandría

88

Colour: bright yellow. Nose: powerfull, candied fruit, dried herbs, varietal. Palate: flavourful, sweet, ripe fruit, good acidity.

Rujaq Andalusi Dulce Natural Trasañejo
moscatel de alejandría

88

Colour: light mahogany. Nose: caramel, overripe fruit, cocoa bean, aromatic coffee. Palate: sweetness, spirituous, complex.

Señorío de Broches Dulce Natural Moscatel
moscatel de alejandría

86

Viña Axarkia Vino de Licor 2014 B
moscatel de alejandría

85

Zumbral 2010 Moscatel
moscatel de alejandría

86

Zumbral Conarte 2009 B
moscatel de alejandría

87

Colour: light mahogany. Nose: dried fruit, fruit liqueur notes, faded flowers, pattiserie. Palate: balanced, long.

BODEGAS EXCELENCIA
Almendra, 40-42
29004 Ronda (Málaga)
☎: +34 952 870 960
Fax: +34 952 877 002
info@bodegasexcelencia.com
www.bodegasexcelencia.com

Los Frontones 2009 TC
cabernet franc, cabernet sauvignon, tempranillo, syrah

86

Tagus 2013 T
cabernet franc

87

Colour: cherry, garnet rim. Nose: ripe fruit, wild herbs, earthy notes, spicy, balsamic herbs. Palate: balanced, flavourful, long, balsamic.

Viña Daron 2013 RD
cabernet franc

83

BODEGAS GARCÍA HIDALGO
Partido Rural Los Morales -
LLano de la Cruz
29400 Ronda (Málaga)
☎: +34 600 487 284
info@bodegasgarciahidalgo.es
www.bodegasgarciahidalgo.es

Alcobazín 2013 RD
syrah, merlot

82

Alcobazín 2013 T Roble
syrah, merlot, cabernet sauvignon

86

Zabel de Alcobazín 2011 TC
syrah, merlot

87

Colour: deep cherry, garnet rim. Nose: scrubland, spicy, characterful, powerfull. Palate: ripe fruit, long, toasty, balsamic.

Zabel de Alcobazín 2012 TC
merlot, syrah, cabernet sauvignon

87

Colour: deep cherry, garnet rim. Nose: characterful, powerfull, dried herbs, ripe fruit, spicy. Palate: flavourful, round tannins.

BODEGAS JOSÉ MOLINA
Fresca, 4
29170 Colmenar (Málaga)
☎: +34 952 730 956
info@bodegasjosemolina.es
www.bodegasjosemolina.es

Primera Intención s/c T
85

Primera Intención "Mountain" Naturalmente Dulce B
86

Primera Intención Seco B
85

Primera Intención Tempranillo de Montaña 2011 T
85

BODEGAS LUNARES DE RONDA

Ctra. Ronda-El Burgo, km 1
29400 Ronda (Málaga)
☎: +34 649 690 847
vinos@bodegaslunares.com
www.bodegaslunares.com

Altocielo 2011 T
syrah, graciano, cabernet sauvignon
87
Colour: deep cherry. Nose: creamy oak, toasty, ripe fruit, balsamic herbs. Palate: balanced, spicy, long.

Lunares 2013 B
chardonnay, sauvignon blanc
85

Lunares 2013 RD
merlot, garnacha
85

Lunares 2013 T
syrah, garnacha
88
Colour: very deep cherry, garnet rim. Nose: expressive, balsamic herbs, balanced, spicy. Palate: flavourful, round tannins, spicy.

BODEGAS MÁLAGA VIRGEN

Autovía A-92, Km. 132
29520 Fuente de Piedra (Málaga)
☎: +34 952 319 454
Fax: +34 952 359 819
bodegas@bodegasmalagavirgen.com
www.bodegasmalagavirgen.com

Barón de Rivero 2014 RD
86

Barón de Rivero Chardonnay 2014 B
84

Barón de Rivero Verdejo 2014 B
verdejo
85

Cartojal Naturalmente Dulce Pálido
83

Chorrera Cream Añejo
86

Don Juan Trasañejo
93
Colour: mahogany. Nose: aromatic coffee, spicy, dry nuts, powerfull. Palate: balanced, elegant, fine solera notes, toasty, long.

Don Salvador Moscatel 30 años Dulce Moscatel
93
Colour: dark mahogany. Nose: powerfull, expressive, aromatic coffee, spicy, acetaldehyde, dry nuts. Palate: balanced, elegant, toasty, long.

Málaga Virgen PX
86

Moscatel Iberia Etiqueta azul Moscatel
84

Moscatel Iberia Etiqueta Roja Dulce Malaga
85

Moscatel Reserva de Familia Moscatel
90
Colour: amber. Nose: caramel, cocoa bean, honeyed notes, fruit liqueur notes. Palate: spirituous, complex, unctuous, flavourful.

Pedro Ximénez Reserva de Familia PX
91
Colour: mahogany. Nose: complex, fruit liqueur notes, dried fruit, pattiserie, toasty. Palate: sweet, rich, unctuous, balanced.

Pernales Syrah 2012 T
syrah
86

Seco Trasañejo Dulce B
92
Colour: old gold, amber rim. Nose: candied fruit, sweet spices, caramel. Palate: full, flavourful, toasty, fine solera notes.

Sol de Málaga Vino de Licor
87
Colour: light mahogany. Nose: candied fruit, fruit liqueur notes, cocoa bean, aged wood nuances. Palate: flavourful, easy to drink, rich.

Trajinero Añejo
89
Colour: bright golden. Nose: aged wood nuances, sweet spices, pattiserie, candied fruit. Palate: balanced, fine bitter notes.

Tres Leones Naturalmente Dulce B
moscatel de alejandría
86

BODEGAS QUITAPENAS

Ctra. de Guadalmar, 12
29004 Málaga (Málaga)
☎: +34 952 247 595
Fax: +34 952 105 138
ventas@quitapenas.es
www.quitapenas.es

Málaga PX 2011 Noble
100% pedro ximénez

88

Colour: light mahogany. Nose: candied fruit, aged wood nuances, toasty, roasted almonds, aromatic coffee. Palate: balanced, full, long.

Montes de Málaga Pajarete 2011 Noble
80% pedro ximénez, 20% moscatel

87

Colour: bright golden. Nose: caramel, cocoa bean. Palate: flavourful, spicy, toasty.

Moscatel Dorado Quitapenas
100% moscatel

85

Vegasol 2014 B
100% moscatel

79

BODEGAS SÁNCHEZ ROSADO

Polígono 14 Parcela 47
29570 Cártama (Málaga)
☎: +34 600 504 302
Fax: +34 952 213 644
info@bodegassanchezrosado.com
www.bodegassanchezrosado.com

Cartima Siglo XXI 2013 T

86

Cartima Siglo XXI 2014 B
moscatel de alejandría

85

COMPAÑÍA DE VINOS TELMO RODRÍGUEZ

El Monte
01308 Lanciego (Álava)
☎: +34 945 628 315
Fax: +34 945 628 314
contact@telmorodriguez.com
www.telmorodriguez.com

PODIUM

Molino Real 2012 B
moscatel de alejandría

97

Colour: bright yellow. Nose: honeyed notes, floral, expressive, toasty, dried herbs. Palate: rich, fruity, powerful, flavourful, elegant.

Mountain 2013 B
moscatel

93

Colour: bright straw. Nose: floral, fragrant herbs, fruit expression, varietal. Palate: fruity, powerful, flavourful, elegant.

PODIUM

MR Dulce 2012 B
moscatel de alejandría

96

Colour: bright yellow. Nose: balsamic herbs, honeyed notes, floral, sweet spices. Palate: rich, fruity, powerful, flavourful, elegant.

CORTIJO LA FUENTE

Avda. La Fuente, 10
29532 Mollina (Málaga)
☎: +34 663 045 906
cortijolafuente@terra.com
www.bodegacortijolafuente.es

Cortijo La Fuente 2012 TC
cabernet sauvignon, syrah

85

Cortijo La Fuente 2013 Blanco Afrutado
moscatel grano menudo, pedro ximénez

84

Cortijo La Fuente 2013 T Roble
cabernet sauvignon, syrah

87

Colour: light cherry. Nose: creamy oak, toasty, ripe fruit, balsamic herbs, violets. Palate: balanced, spicy, long, easy to drink.

Cortijo La Fuente Blanco Pedro Ximénez PX
pedro ximénez

85

Cortijo La Fuente Dulce Delicia Nº 12 2013 Dulce
moscatel de alejandría

88

Colour: old gold, amber rim. Nose: balanced, expressive, varietal, floral. Palate: rich, long, good acidity.

Cortijo La Fuente Gran Solera 2002 Trasañejo
moscatel de alejandría

88

Colour: mahogany. Nose: aromatic coffee, caramel, pattiserie. Palate: full, long, unctuous.

Cortijo La Fuente Pedro Ximénez Solera Dulce
pedro ximénez

85

CORTIJO LOS AGUILARES

Ctra. Ronda a Campillos
29400 Ronda (Málaga)
☎: +34 952 874 457
Fax: +34 951 166 000
bodega@cortijolosaguilares.com
www.cortijolosaguilares.com

Cortijo Los Aguilares CLA 2014 RD
tempranillo, syrah

89

Colour: light cherry. Nose: elegant, red berry notes, floral, fragrant herbs. Palate: light-bodied, flavourful, good acidity, long, spicy.

Cortijo Los Aguilares CLA 2014 T
tempranillo, syrah, merlot

89

Colour: cherry, purple rim. Nose: powerfull, ripe fruit, spicy. Palate: powerful, fruity, unctuous.

Cortijo Los Aguilares Pago El Espino 2012 T
petit verdot, tempranillo, merlot

92

Colour: bright cherry. Nose: ripe fruit, sweet spices, creamy oak, expressive. Palate: flavourful, fruity, toasty, round tannins.

Cortijo Los Aguilares Pinot Noir 2014 T
100% pinot noir

93

Colour: bright cherry. Nose: creamy oak, toasty, ripe fruit, balsamic herbs, floral. Palate: balanced, spicy, long.

PODIUM

Cortijo Los Aguilares Tadeo 2012 T
100% petit verdot

95

Colour: cherry, garnet rim. Nose: balanced, complex, ripe fruit, spicy, fine reductive notes, earthy notes. Palate: good structure, flavourful, round tannins, balanced.

FINCA LA MELONERA

Paraje Los Frontones,
Camino Ronda-Setenil s/n
29400 Ronda (Málaga)
☎: +34 951 194 018
info@lamelonera.com
www.lamelonera.com

Encina del Inglés 2013 T
tempranillo, garnacha, syrah, cabernet sauvignon

87

Colour: deep cherry, purple rim. Nose: ripe fruit, fruit preserve, sweet spices, wild herbs. Palate: flavourful, fruity, round tannins.

MHV 2013 T
romé, tintilla de rota

94

Colour: deep cherry. Nose: creamy oak, toasty, ripe fruit, balsamic herbs. Palate: balanced, spicy, long.

Payoya Negra 2013 T
garnacha, syrah, tintilla de rota

92 ♣

Colour: cherry, garnet rim. Nose: ripe fruit, wild herbs, spicy, balsamic herbs, undergrowth. Palate: balanced, flavourful, long, balsamic.

GOMARA

Diseminado Maqueda Alto, 59
29590 Campanillas (Málaga)
☎: +34 952 434 195
Fax: +34 952 626 312
bodegas@gomara.com
www.gomara.com

Gran Gomara Vino de Licor
70% pedro ximénez, moscatel

91

Colour: iodine, amber rim. Nose: toasty, dark chocolate, varnish, roasted almonds, complex. Palate: full, balanced, good acidity.

Seco Añejo Gomara OL
pedro ximénez

85

Trasañejo Gomara Dulce Vino de Licor
100% pedro ximénez

90

Colour: mahogany. Nose: aromatic coffee, spicy, fruit liqueur notes, caramel. Palate: balanced, toasty, flavourful.

JORGE ORDÓÑEZ & CO

Bartolome Esteban Murillo, 11
29700 Velez-Málaga (Málaga)
☎: +34 952 504 706
Fax: +34 951 284 796
info@jorgeordonez.es
www.grupojorgeordonez.com

Botani 2014 B
100% moscatel de alejandría

92

Colour: bright straw. Nose: white flowers, fresh fruit, fragrant herbs. Palate: flavourful, fruity, good acidity, balanced.

Botani Garnacha 2014 T
100% garnacha

88

Colour: cherry, purple rim. Nose: ripe fruit, woody, roasted coffee. Palate: flavourful, spicy, powerful.

Jorge Ordóñez & Co Botani Ecológico 2014 B
moscatel

92

Colour: bright straw. Nose: white flowers, fresh fruit, fragrant herbs. Palate: flavourful, good acidity, balanced.

Jorge Ordóñez & Co Nº 1 Selección Especial Dulce 2014 B
100% moscatel de alejandría

94

Colour: bright yellow. Nose: balsamic herbs, honeyed notes, floral, sweet spices. Palate: rich, fruity, powerful, flavourful, elegant.

PODIUM

Jorge Ordóñez & Co Nº 2 Victoria Naturalmente Dulce 2014 B
100% moscatel de alejandría

95

Colour: bright yellow. Nose: faded flowers, candied fruit, fruit expression. Palate: powerful, concentrated, complex, good acidity.

PODIUM

Jorge Ordóñez & Co. Nº3 Viñas Viejas Naturalmente Dulce 2011 B
100% moscatel de alejandría

96

Colour: golden. Nose: powerfull, honeyed notes, candied fruit, fragrant herbs, acetaldehyde. Palate: flavourful, sweet, fresh, fruity, good acidity, long.

NIÑO DE LA SALINA

Corredera s/n
29330 Almargen (Málaga)
☎: +34 952 182 608
Fax: +34 952 182 609
info@fontalbacapote.es
www.fontalbacapote.es

Andresito 2013 PX
pedro ximénez

88

Colour: old gold, amber rim. Nose: candied fruit, pattiserie, fruit liqueur notes. Palate: unctuous, flavourful, long.

Andresito 2013 T
cabernet sauvignon, merlot

86

Andresito Dulce Natural 2013 B
moscatel grano menudo

87

Colour: bright yellow. Nose: candied fruit, honeyed notes, white flowers, varietal, balanced. Palate: correct, easy to drink.

SAMSARA WINES

Los Molinos del Tajo
29400 Ronda (Málaga)
☎: +34 697 911 440
info@samsarawines.com
www.samsarawines.com

Samsara 2011 TC
100% petit verdot

93

Colour: cherry, garnet rim. Nose: balanced, complex, ripe fruit, spicy, balsamic herbs. Palate: good structure, flavourful, round tannins, balanced.

SEDELLA VINOS

29715 Sedella (Málaga)
☎: +34 687 463 082
Fax: +34 967 140 723
info@sedellavinos.com
www.sedellavinos.com

Laderas de Sedella 2013 T
romé, garnacha, moscatel

89 ✿

Colour: deep cherry, purple rim. Nose: floral, violets, macerated fruit, fragrant herbs. Palate: fruity, easy to drink, good finish.

Sedella 2013 T
romé, garnacha, moscatel

92 ✿

Colour: cherry, garnet rim. Nose: expressive, spicy, balsamic herbs, fruit expression. Palate: flavourful, ripe fruit, long, good acidity, balanced.

TIERRAS DE MOLLINA

Avda. de las Américas, s/n
(Cortijo Colarte)
29532 Mollina (Málaga)
☎: +34 952 841 451
Fax: +34 952 842 555
administracion@tierrasdemollina.net
www.tierrasdemollina.net

Carpe Diem Málaga Añejo
pedro ximénez

88

Colour: mahogany. Nose: toasty, caramel, varnish. Palate: full, flavourful, balanced.

Carpe Diem Dulce Natural B
moscatel

87

Colour: bright yellow. Nose: candied fruit, white flowers, varietal. Palate: rich, balanced, easy to drink.

Carpe Diem Málaga Trasañejo Málaga Gran Reserva
pedro ximénez

89

Colour: dark mahogany. Nose: candied fruit, dark chocolate, caramel, pattiserie. Palate: flavourful, balanced, long.

Montespejo 2013 B
lairén, moscatel, doradilla

84

Montespejo 2013 T
syrah

83

Montespejo 2013 T Roble
syrah, merlot

85

DO. MANCHUELA

CONSEJO REGULADOR

Avda. San Agustín, 9
02270 Villamalea (Albacete)
☎:+34 967 090 694 - Fax: +34 967 090 696
@: domanchuela@lamanchuela.es
www.do-manchuela.com

LOCATION:

The production area covers the territory situated in the southeast of the province of Cuenca and the northeast of Albacete, between the rivers Júcar and Cabriel. It comprises 70 municipal districts, 26 of which are in Albacete and the rest in Cuenca.

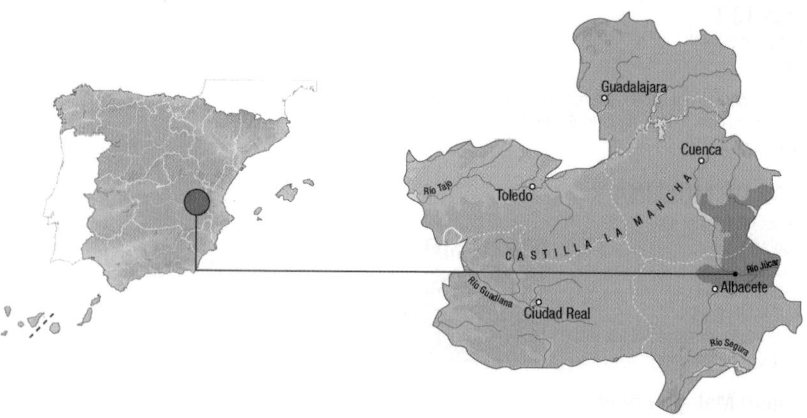

GRAPE VARIETIES:

WHITE: Albillo, Chardonnay, Macabeo, Sauvignon Blanc, Verdejo, Pardillo, Viognier and Moscatel de Grano Menudo.
RED: Bobal, Cabernet Sauvignon, Cencibel (Tempranillo), Garnacha, Merlot, Monastrell, Moravia Dulce, Syrah, Garnacha Tintorera, Malbec, Moravia agria, Mazuelo, Graciano, Rojal, Frasco (Tinto Velasco), Petit Verdot, Cabernet Franc and Pinot Noir.

FIGURES:

Vineyard surface: 5,800 – **Wine-Growers:** 850 – **Wineries:** 32 – **2014 Harvest rating:** Very Good – **Production 14:** 5,000,000 litres – **Market percentages:** 15% National - 85% International.

SOIL:

The vineyards are situated at an altitude ranging between 600 and 700 m above sea level. The terrain is mainly flat, except for the ravines outlined by the rivers. Regarding the composition of the terrain, below a clayey surface of gravel or sand, the soil is limy, which is an important quality factor for the region.

CLIMATE:

The climate is continental in nature, with cold winters and hot summers, although the cool and humid winds from the Mediterranean during the summer help to lower the temperatures at night, so creating favourable day-night temperature contrasts for a slow ripening of the grapes.

VINTAGE RATING

PEÑÍNGUIDE

2010	2011	2012	2013	2014
VERY GOOD	VERY GOOD	VERY GOOD	GOOD	GOOD

ALTOLANDÓN

Ctra. N-330, km. 242
16330 Landete (Cuenca)
☎: +34 962 300 662
Fax: +34 962 300 662
altolandon@altolandon.com
www.altolandon.com

Altolandón 2010 T
50% syrah, 50% garnacha, cabernet sauvignon

92

Colour: cherry, garnet rim. Nose: mineral, expressive, spicy. Palate: flavourful, ripe fruit, long, good acidity, balanced.

Altolandón White 2014 BFB
50% chardonnay, petit manseng

89

Colour: bright yellow. Nose: ripe fruit, powerfull, toasty, dried flowers. Palate: flavourful, fruity, spicy, toasty, long.

CF de Altolandón 2011 T
100% cabernet franc

93

Colour: cherry, garnet rim. Nose: mineral, expressive, spicy, wild herbs. Palate: flavourful, ripe fruit, long, good acidity, balanced, balsamic.

Doña Leo Altolandón 2014 B
100% moscatel grano menudo

88

Colour: bright yellow. Nose: balsamic herbs, honeyed notes, floral, sweet spices, varietal. Palate: rich, fruity, powerful, flavourful.

Irrepetible 2014 T
50% syrah, 50% malbec

91

Colour: deep cherry, purple rim. Nose: creamy oak, toasty, ripe fruit, balsamic herbs. Palate: spicy, long, unctuous, flavourful.

L´Ame Malbec 2010 T
100% malbec

89

Colour: cherry, garnet rim. Nose: ripe fruit, wild herbs, earthy notes, spicy, balsamic herbs. Palate: balanced, flavourful, long, balsamic.

Rayuelo 2012 T
100% bobal

90

Colour: very deep cherry, garnet rim. Nose: powerfull, toasty, expressive, ripe fruit, fruit preserve. Palate: full, flavourful, long, balsamic.

BODEGA INIESTA

Ctra. Fuentealbilla Villamalea, km. 1,5
02260 Fuentealbilla (Albacete)
☎: +34 967 090 650
Fax: +34 967 090 651
info@bodegainiesta.com
www.bodegainiesta.es

Corazón Loco 2014 B
sauvignon blanc, verdejo

84

Corazón Loco 2014 RD
bobal

87

Colour: raspberry rose, bright. Nose: red berry notes, fresh fruit, balanced, fresh. Palate: balanced, fine bitter notes, good acidity.

Corazón Loco 2014 T
tempranillo, syrah

87

Colour: cherry, purple rim. Nose: expressive, fresh fruit, red berry notes, floral. Palate: flavourful, fruity, good acidity.

Corazón Loco Nature 2013 T
syrah, tempranillo

84

Corazón Loco Nature 2014 B
chardonnay, sauvignon blanc

85

Corazón Loco Selección 2011 T
tempranillo, syrah, cabernet sauvignon, petit verdot

89

Colour: cherry, garnet rim. Nose: ripe fruit, wild herbs, earthy notes, spicy, balsamic herbs, toasty. Palate: flavourful, long, balsamic.

Dulce Corazón 2014 B
moscatel

89

Colour: bright yellow. Nose: powerfull, candied fruit, dried herbs, white flowers. Palate: flavourful, sweet, ripe fruit, good acidity.

Dulce Corazón 2014 RD
bobal

86

Finca El Carril 2012 T Roble
tempranillo, syrah, petit verdot

89

Colour: deep cherry. Nose: creamy oak, toasty, ripe fruit, balsamic herbs. Palate: balanced, spicy, long.

Finca El Carril 2014 B
macabeo

87

Colour: bright straw. Nose: white flowers, fresh fruit, fragrant herbs, expressive. Palate: flavourful, fruity, good acidity, balanced.

Finca El Carril Hechicero 2011 TC
syrah, cabernet sauvignon, petit verdot, tempranillo

90

Colour: cherry, garnet rim. Nose: red berry notes, ripe fruit, spicy, creamy oak, complex. Palate: flavourful, toasty, round tannins.

Finca El Carril Valeria 2013 BFB
chardonnay

88

Colour: yellow. Nose: faded flowers, expressive, candied fruit, spicy, sweet spices. Palate: flavourful, correct, fine bitter notes.

BODEGA PARDO TOLOSA

Villatoya, 26
02215 Alborea (Albacete)
☎: +34 963 517 067
Fax: +34 963 517 091
export@bodegapardotolosa.com
www.bodegapardotolosa.com

La Sima 2013 T
tempranillo, bobal

84

Mizaran Bobal 2014 RD
bobal

81

Mizaran Tempranillo 2012 T
tempranillo

83

Senda de las Rochas 2008 TC
tempranillo

87

Colour: cherry, garnet rim. Nose: roasted coffee, smoky, spicy, ripe fruit. Palate: flavourful, smoky aftertaste, ripe fruit.

Senda de las Rochas Bobal 2013 T
bobal

85

BODEGAS RECIAL

Libertad, 1
02154 Pozo Lorente (Albacete)
☎: +34 630 418 264
Fax: +34 967 572 063
gerencia@bodegasrecial.com
www.bodegasrecial.com

Divina Putea 2009 TR
garnacha tintorera

88

Colour: cherry, garnet rim. Nose: fine reductive notes, wet leather, ripe fruit, varietal. Palate: spicy, long, toasty.

Púrpura 2009 TC
garnacha tintorera

87

Colour: cherry, garnet rim. Nose: fine reductive notes, wet leather, aged wood nuances, fruit preserve. Palate: spicy, long, toasty, correct.

BODEGAS SAN ANTONIO ABAD COOPERATIVA

Valencia, 41
02270 Villamalea (Albacete)
☎: +34 967 483 023
Fax: +34 967 483 536
ann@bodegas-saac.com
www.bodegas-saac.com

Altos del Cabriel 2014 B
100% macabeo

82

Altos del Cabriel 2014 RD
bobal

84

Altos del Cabriel 2014 T
tempranillo

86

Gredas Viejas 2009 TR
syrah

86

Viñamalea 2009 TC
tempranillo, syrah

85

BODEGAS VILLAVID

Niño Jesús, 25
16280 Villarta (Cuenca)
☎: +34 962 189 006
Fax: +34 962 189 125
export@villavid.com
www.villavid.com

Villavid Bobal 2014 RD
100% bobal
85

Villavid Macabeo Verdejo 2014 B
macabeo, verdejo
84

Villavid Syrah 2011 TC
100% syrah
85

Villavid Tempranillo 2014 T
100% tempranillo
86

BODEGAS VITIVINOS

Camino de Cabezuelas, s/n
02270 Villamalea (Albacete)
☎: +34 967 483 114
Fax: +34 967 483 964
comercial@vitivinos.com
www.vitivinos.com

Azua 2008 TR
100% bobal
86

Azua 2009 TC
100% bobal
85

Azua Bobal 2012 T Roble
100% bobal
87
Colour: bright cherry. Nose: ripe fruit, sweet spices, creamy oak. Palate: flavourful, fruity, toasty.

Azua Bobal 2014 RD
100% bobal
84

Azua Macabeo 2014 B
100% macabeo
84

Azua Verdejo 2014 B
100% verdejo
84

Llanos del Marqués Tempranillo 2013 T
100% tempranillo
82

BODEGAS Y VIÑEDOS PONCE

Ctra. N-310
16230 Villanueva de la Jara (Cuenca)
☎: +34 677 434 523
bodegasponce@gmail.com

Buena Pinta 2014 T
moravia agria, garnacha
92
Colour: light cherry. Nose: fruit expression, fruit liqueur notes, fragrant herbs, spicy, creamy oak. Palate: balanced, elegant, spicy, long, toasty.

Estrecha 2013 T
100% bobal
93
Colour: deep cherry, purple rim. Nose: creamy oak, toasty, ripe fruit, balsamic herbs, mineral. Palate: balanced, spicy, long.

P.F. 2013 T
100% bobal
92
Colour: dark-red cherry, garnet rim. Nose: balanced, ripe fruit, spicy, wild herbs. Palate: balanced, round tannins, long.

Pino 2013 T
100% bobal
94
Colour: cherry, garnet rim. Nose: mineral, expressive, spicy. Palate: flavourful, ripe fruit, long, good acidity, balanced.

Reto 2014 BFB
100% albilla
92
Colour: bright straw. Nose: white flowers, fine lees, dried herbs, ripe fruit, citrus fruit, dry stone. Palate: flavourful, fruity, good acidity, elegant. Personality.

CIEN Y PICO

02240 Mahora (Albacete)
caterina@cienypico.com
www.cienypico.com

Cien y Pico Doble Pasta 2010 T
garnacha tintorera
88
Colour: very deep cherry, garnet rim. Nose: complex, mineral, balsamic herbs, fruit preserve. Palate: full, flavourful.

En Vaso 2012 T
bobal

88

Colour: cherry, garnet rim. Nose: ripe fruit, wild herbs, spicy, creamy oak. Palate: flavourful, spicy, balsamic.

Knights Errant 2009 T
garnacha tintorera

90

Colour: very deep cherry, garnet rim. Nose: characterful, ripe fruit, cocoa bean, sweet spices, smoky. Palate: good structure, flavourful.

Viña La Ceya 2012 T
bobal, garnacha tintorera

88

Colour: cherry, garnet rim. Nose: red berry notes, ripe fruit, spicy, creamy oak. Palate: flavourful, toasty, round tannins.

Winemaker's Gallant 2012 T
bobal

89

Colour: bright cherry. Nose: ripe fruit, sweet spices, creamy oak, expressive. Palate: flavourful, fruity, round tannins.

COOP. DEL CAMPO SAN ISIDRO

Extramuros, s/n
02215 Alborea (Albacete)
☎: +34 967 477 096
Fax: +34 967 477 096
coopalborea@telefonica.net
www.vinosalborea.com

Alterón 2010 TC
cencibel

83

Alterón 2014 B
macabeo

89

Colour: bright yellow. Nose: ripe fruit, toasty, aged wood nuances, pattiserie. Palate: flavourful, fruity, spicy, toasty.

Alterón s/c BFB
macabeo

85

COOP. DEL CAMPO VIRGEN DE LAS NIEVES SOC. COOP. DE CLM

Paseo Virgen de las Nieves, 1
02247 Cenizate (Albacete)
☎: +34 967 482 006
Fax: +34 967 482 805
cooperativa@virgendelasnieves.com
www.virgendelasnieves.com

Artesones de Cenizate 2014 B
100% macabeo

84

Artesones de Cenizate 2014 RD
100% bobal

86

Artesones de Cenizate Semidulce 2014 B
100% macaboo

84

Artesones de Cenizate Semidulce 2014 RD
100% bobal

86

Artesones de Cenizate Syrah 2013 T
100% syrah

83

Artesones de Cenizate Tempranillo 2014 T
100% tempranillo

86

COOP. NUESTRA SEÑORA DE LA ESTRELLA

Elías Fernández, 10
16290 El Herrumbar (Cuenca)
☎: +34 962 313 029
Fax: +34 962 313 232
info@antaresvinos.es

Antares 2012 TC
syrah

88

Colour: cherry, garnet rim. Nose: roasted coffee, smoky, ripe fruit. Palate: flavourful, smoky aftertaste, ripe fruit.

Antares 2014 RD
bobal

87

Colour: rose, purple rim. Nose: red berry notes, floral, expressive. Palate: powerful, fruity, fresh.

Antares Sauvignon Blanc 2014 B
sauvignon blanc

85

Antares Sauvignon Blanc 2014 BFB
sauvignon blanc

87

Colour: bright yellow. Nose: ripe fruit, creamy oak, sweet spices. Palate: powerful, flavourful, toasty.

COOPERATIVA SAN ISIDRO

Ctra. Valencia, 6
02240 Mahora (Albacete)
☎: +34 967 494 058
info@vinosmahora.com
www.vinosmahora.com

Mahora 2010 TC
tempranillo

87

Colour: cherry, garnet rim. Nose: smoky, spicy, ripe fruit, sweet spices. Palate: flavourful, smoky aftertaste, ripe fruit.

FINCA EL MOLAR DE RUS

Finca El Molar de Rus
02360 Fuentealbilla (Albacete)
☎: +34 647 075 371
info@elmolarderus.com
www.elmolarderus.com

Finca El Molar 2013 T
merlot, cabernet sauvignon, syrah

86

Quantum Selección 2012 TC
merlot, cabernet sauvignon, syrah

87

Colour: cherry, garnet rim. Nose: ripe fruit, wild herbs, spicy, aged wood nuances. Palate: balanced, flavourful, long.

FINCA SANDOVAL

Ctra. CM-3222, Km. 26,800
16237 Ledaña (Cuenca)
☎: +34 696 910 769
fincasandoval@gmail.com
www.fincasandoval.com

Finca Sandoval 2010 T
syrah, monastrell, bobal

93

Colour: cherry, garnet rim. Nose: ripe fruit, wild herbs, earthy notes, spicy, balsamic herbs, fine reductive notes. Palate: balanced, flavourful, long, balsamic, elegant.

Finca Sandoval Cuvée Cecilia 2013 Dulce
syrah, moscatel de alejandría

91

Colour: cherry, garnet rim. Nose: fruit preserve, spicy, warm, fruit liqueur notes. Palate: powerful, flavourful, sweet, rich.

Finca Sandoval Cuvee TNS 2009 T
touriga nacional, syrah

94

Colour: cherry, garnet rim. Nose: balanced, complex, ripe fruit, spicy, mineral, wild herbs, expressive. Palate: good structure, flavourful, round tannins, balanced.

Finca Sandoval Signo Bobal 2012 T
bobal, syrah, moravia agria

91

Colour: dark-red cherry, garnet rim. Nose: ripe fruit, balsamic herbs, spicy, balanced, toasty. Palate: good structure, flavourful, balanced, round tannins.

Finca Sandoval Signo Garnacha 2011 T
garnacha tintorera, garnacha

92

Colour: light cherry. Nose: fruit expression, fruit liqueur notes, fragrant herbs, spicy, creamy oak. Palate: balanced, spicy, long, toasty.

Salia 2011 T
syrah, garnacha tintorera, garnacha, moravia agria

91

Colour: dark-red cherry, garnet rim. Nose: spicy, ripe fruit, characterful, expressive, dried herbs. Palate: fruity, flavourful.

MONTEAGUDO RUIZ

Plaza San Pedro, 17
16234 Casas de Santa Cruz (Cuenca)
☎: +34 967 493 828
Fax: +34 967 493 841
reservas@monterruiz.com
www.señoriodemonterruiz.es

Señorio de Monterruiz 2014 T
bobal, tempranillo

84

NTRA. SRA. DE LA CABEZA DE CASAS IBÁÑEZ SOC. COOP. DE CLM

Avda. del Vino, 10
02200 Casas Ibáñez (Albacete)
☎: +34 967 460 266
Fax: +34 967 460 105
info@coop-cabeza.com
www.coop-cabeza.com

Viaril 2007 TR
70% syrah, 30% cabernet sauvignon

85

Viaril Bobal 2012 T
100% bobal

85

Viaril Bobal 2014 RD
100% bobal

85

Viaril Cabernet Sauvignon 2013 T
100% cabernet sauvignon

85

Viaril Macabeo 2014 BFB
100% macabeo

88
Colour: bright yellow. Nose: ripe fruit, powerfull, toasty, aged wood nuances, pattiserie. Palate: flavourful, fruity, spicy, toasty, long.

Viaril Selección 2013 T
100% syrah

85

SAN ANTONIO DE PADUA, SDAD. COOP. DE CLM

San Antonio, 21
16270 Villalpardo (Cuenca)
☎: +34 962 311 002
Fax: +34 962 311 002
santopadua@yahoo.es

Hoya Montés 2014 RD
bobal

85

Hoya Montés 2014 T
tempranillo

85

SOC. COOP. SAN ISIDRO

Ctra. de Albacete, s/n
16220 Quintanar del Rey (Cuenca)
☎: +34 967 495 052
Fax: +34 967 496 750
gerencia@bodegasanisidro.es
www.bodegasanisidro.es

Monte de las Mozas 2014 B
macabeo

83

Monte de las Mozas 2014 RD
bobal

84

Quinta Regia 2014 T
bobal

87
Colour: dark-red cherry, purple rim. Nose: balanced, ripe fruit, scrubland. Palate: flavourful, fruity, good finish.

Zaíno 2012 T Roble
tempranillo

85

UNION CAMPESINA INIESTENSE

San Idefonso, 1
16235 Iniesta (Cuenca)
☎: +34 967 490 120
Fax: +34 967 490 777
aurora@cooperativauci.com
www.cooperativauci.com

Realce Bobal 2007 TR
bobal

84

Realce Bobal 2014 RD
bobal

85

Realce Macabeo 2014 B
macabeo

84

Realce Tempranillo 2012 TC
tempranillo

84

Realce Tempranillo 2014 T
tempranillo

85

VEGA TOLOSA

Pol. Ind. Calle B, 11
02200 Casas Ibáñez (Albacete)
☎: +34 967 461 331
Fax: +34 967 461 331
info@vegatolosa.com
www.vegatolosa.com

11 Pinos Bobal Old Vines 2013 T Roble
bobal

89 ♣
Colour: bright cherry. Nose: sweet spices, creamy oak, fruit preserve. Palate: flavourful, fruity, toasty.

Bobal Icon 2013 T Roble
bobal

87 ♣
Colour: cherry, purple rim. Nose: floral, ripe fruit, wild herbs. Palate: powerful, fresh, fruity.

Capricho di Vino Syrah 2014 RD
syrah

85 ♣

Finca Los Halcones Cepas Viejas 2013 T
bobal

88 ♣

Colour: deep cherry, garnet rim. Nose: violets, ripe fruit, powerfull, dried herbs. Palate: flavourful, balanced, balsamic.

Finca Los Halcones Viognier 2014 B
viognier

89

Colour: bright yellow. Nose: ripe fruit, powerfull, toasty, aged wood nuances, pattiserie. Palate: flavourful, fruity, spicy, toasty, long.

Vega Tolosa Nature 2014 T
syrah, merlot, cabernet sauvignon

83 ♣

Vega Tolosa Selección 2014 B
macabeo, sauvignon blanc, chardonnay

85 ♣

DO. MÉNTRIDA

CONSEJO REGULADOR

Avda. Cristo del Amparo, 16. Piso 1 Of. 1-2.
45510 Fuensalida (Toledo)
☎:+34 925 785 185 - Fax: +34 925 784 154
@: administracion@domentrida.es
www.domentrida.es

LOCATION:

In the north of the province of Toledo. It borders with the provinces of Ávila and Madrid to the north, with the Tajo to the south, and with the Sierra de San Vicente to the west. It is made up of 51 municipal areas of the province of Toledo.

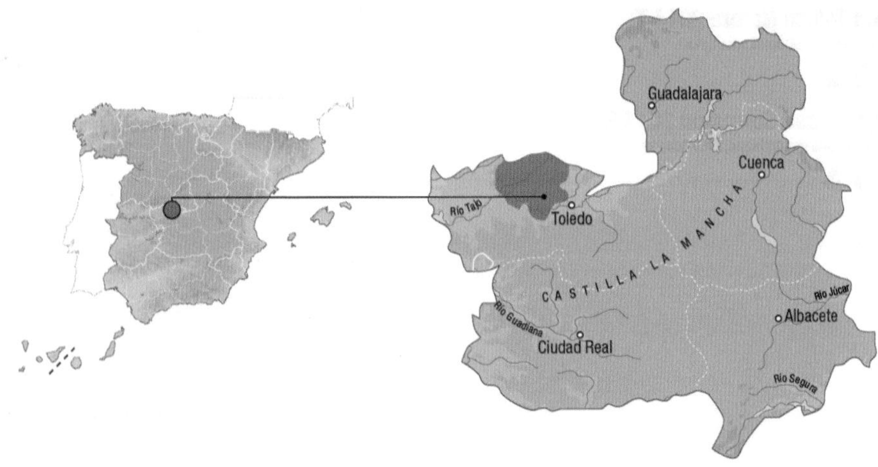

GRAPE VARIETIES:

WHITE: Albillo, Macabeo, Sauvignon Blanc, Chardonnay and Moscatel de Grano Menudo.
RED: Garnacha (majority 85% of total), Cencibel (Tempranillo), Cabernet Sauvignon, Merlot, Syrah, Petit Verdot, Cabernet Franc and Graciano.

FIGURES:

Vineyard surface: 5,693.21 – **Wine-Growers:** 1,243 – **Wineries:** 28 – **2014 Harvest rating:** Good – **Production 14:** 229,893 litres – **Market percentages:** 20% National - 80% International.

SOIL:

The vineyards are at an altitude of between 400 m and 600 m, although some municipal districts of the Sierra de San Vicente reach an altitude of 800 m. The soil is mainly sandy-clayey, with a medium to loose texture.

CLIMATE:

Continental, dry and extreme, with long, cold winters and hot summers. Late frosts in spring are quite common. The average rainfall is between 300 mm and 500 mm, and is irregularly distributed throughout the year.

VINTAGE RATING

PEÑÍNGUIDE

2010	2011	2012	2013	2014
VERY GOOD	GOOD	GOOD	GOOD	GOOD

ALONSO CUESTA

Pza. de la Constitución, 4
45920 La Torre de Esteban Hambrán (Toledo)
☎: +34 925 795 742
Fax: +34 925 795 742
administracion@alonsocuesta.com
www.alonsocuesta.com

Alonso Cuesta 2012 T
garnacha, cabernet sauvignon, tempranillo

92

Colour: bright cherry, garnet rim. Nose: ripe fruit, mineral, expressive, scrubland. Palate: good structure, flavourful.

Alonso Cuesta 2014 B
verdejo

86

Camarus 2014 T
garnacha

87

Colour: light cherry, purple rim. Nose: medium intensity, ripe fruit, wild herbs. Palate: correct, easy to drink, fruity.

Camarus 2014 T Roble
garnacha

86

Hacienda Valprimero 2013 T
garnacha, syrah

86

BODEGA LÓPEZ CAMPOS

Camino del Alamo 26C
45940 Valmojado (Toledo)
☎: +34 677 315 470
info@almavid.com
www.almavid.com

Almavid 2012 T
75% garnacha, 15% syrah, 10% tempranillo

90

Colour: cherry, garnet rim. Nose: ripe fruit, wild herbs, earthy notes, spicy, balsamic herbs. Palate: balanced, flavourful, long.

BODEGA SANTO DOMINGO DE GUZMÁN

Alameda del Fresno, 14
28054 Valmojado (Toledo)
☎: +34 918 170 904
info@santodomingodeguzman.es
www.santodomingodeguzman.es

Valdejuana Syrah 2012 TC
syrah

87

Colour: bright cherry, garnet rim. Nose: spicy, smoky, ripe fruit. Palate: flavourful, fruity, spicy, easy to drink.

Valdejuana Syrah 2014 T
syrah

86

BODEGAS ABANICO

Pol. Ind Ca l'Avellanet - Susany, 6
08553 Seva (Barcelona)
☎: +34 938 125 676
Fax: +34 938 123 213
info@exportiberia.com
www.bodegasabanico.com

Tierra Fuerte 2013 T
graciano

89

Colour: cherry, garnet rim. Nose: smoky, spicy, ripe fruit. Palate: flavourful, smoky aftertaste, ripe fruit.

BODEGAS ARRAYÁN

Gallarza, 9
28002 Madrid (Madrid)
☎: +34 916 633 131
Fax: +34 916 632 796
comercial@arrayan.es
www.arrayan.es

Arrayán 2014 RD
merlot, syrah

88

Colour: rose, bright. Nose: red berry notes, floral, fragrant herbs. Palate: easy to drink, fruity, good acidity, fine bitter notes.

Arrayán Albillo Real 2014 B
albillo

90

Colour: bright yellow. Nose: expressive, dried herbs, ripe fruit, spicy. Palate: flavourful, fruity, good acidity, balanced, fine bitter notes.

Arrayán Petit Verdot 2011 T
petit verdot

91

Colour: bright cherry. Nose: ripe fruit, wild herbs, earthy notes, spicy, balsamic herbs. Palate: balanced, flavourful, long, balsamic.

Arrayán Premium 2011 T
syrah, merlot, cabernet sauvignon, petit verdot

91

Colour: cherry, garnet rim. Nose: expressive, spicy, balsamic herbs. Palate: flavourful, ripe fruit, long, good acidity, balanced.

Arrayán Selección 2011 T
syrah, merlot, cabernet sauvignon, petit verdot

87

Colour: cherry, garnet rim. Nose: grassy, wild herbs, ripe fruit. Palate: balsamic, correct.

Arrayán Syrah 2011 T
syrah

88

Colour: cherry, garnet rim. Nose: red berry notes, ripe fruit, spicy, creamy oak. Palate: flavourful, toasty, round tannins.

Estela de Arrayán 2011 T
syrah, merlot, cabernet sauvignon, petit verdot

93

Colour: very deep cherry, bright cherry. Nose: ripe fruit, complex, spicy, scrubland. Palate: full, flavourful, good structure, balsamic, round tannins.

La Suerte de Arrayán 2013 T
garnacha

88

Colour: deep cherry, purple rim. Nose: ripe fruit, balsamic herbs, spicy, varietal. Palate: balanced, spicy.

BODEGAS CANOPY

Ctra. Toledo-Valmojado, km. 23
45180 Camarena (Toledo)
☎: +34 619 244 878
Fax: +34 925 283 680
achacon@bodegascanopy.com
www.bodegascanopy.com

Castillo de Belarfonso 2014 T
garnacha

91

Colour: cherry, purple rim. Nose: red berry notes, floral, spicy, ripe fruit. Palate: flavourful, fruity, good acidity.

La Viña Escondida 2011 TR
garnacha

93

Colour: very deep cherry, garnet rim. Nose: complex, mineral, balsamic herbs, balanced, dried herbs. Palate: full, flavourful, warm.

Loco 2013 B
garnacha blanca

93

Colour: bright straw. Nose: white flowers, fresh fruit, fragrant herbs, mineral. Palate: flavourful, fruity, good acidity, balanced.

Malpaso 2014 T
syrah

92

Colour: cherry, purple rim. Nose: fruit preserve, sweet spices, dark chocolate. Palate: flavourful, spicy, powerful.

Tres Patas 2013 T
garnacha

93

Colour: deep cherry, purple rim. Nose: creamy oak, toasty, ripe fruit, balsamic herbs, scrubland. Palate: balanced, spicy, long.

BODEGAS GONZALO VALVERDE

Río Tajo, 19
45523 Alcabón (Toledo)
☎: +34 659 452 512
info@bodegasgonzalovalverde.es
www.bodegasgonzalovalverde.es

Mensagallo Cabernet Sauvignon 2013 T
cabernet sauvignon

87

Colour: cherry, garnet rim. Nose: grassy, scrubland, spicy. Palate: ripe fruit, balsamic.

Mensagallo Garnacha 2013 T
garnacha

89

Colour: cherry, garnet rim. Nose: smoky, spicy, ripe fruit. Palate: flavourful, smoky aftertaste, ripe fruit.

Vallelobo 2013 T
syrah, cabernet sauvignon, tempranillo

85

BODEGAS JIMÉNEZ LANDI

Avda. Solana, 39
45930 Méntrida (Toledo)
☎: +34 918 178 213
Fax: +34 918 178 213
info@jimenezlandi.com
www.jimenezlandi.com

Jiménez-Landi Ataulfos 2013 T
100% garnacha

93

Colour: light cherry. Nose: mineral, expressive, spicy. Palate: flavourful, ripe fruit, long, good acidity, balanced.

Jiménez-Landi Bajondillo 2014 T
80% garnacha, 10% syrah, 10% cabernet sauvignon

89 ♣

Colour: cherry, purple rim. Nose: expressive, fresh fruit, red berry notes, floral, scrubland. Palate: flavourful, fruity, good acidity.

Jiménez-Landi Piélago 2013 T
100% garnacha

94

Colour: cherry, garnet rim. Nose: ripe fruit, wild herbs, earthy notes, spicy, balsamic herbs, mineral. Palate: balanced, flavourful, long, balsamic.

Jiménez-Landi Sotorrondero 2013 T
60% garnacha, 40% syrah

91

Colour: cherry, garnet rim. Nose: red berry notes, ripe fruit, dried flowers, wild herbs. Palate: spicy, ripe fruit, long.

BODEGAS LA CERCA

Lepanto, 15
45950 Casarrubios del Monte (Toledo)
☎: +34 918 172 456
bodegaslacerca@yahoo.es

Molino Viejo Tempranillo 2011 T Roble
tempranillo

79

BODEGAS TORRESTEBAN

Ctra. Méntrida, s/n
45920 La Torre de Esteban Hambrán (Toledo)
☎: +34 925 795 114
coopcristo@gmail.com

Remuri 2012 T Roble

84

Remuri Syrah 2012 T Fermentado en Barrica

86

BODEGAS Y VIÑEDOS TAVERA S.L.

45182 Arcicóllar (Toledo)
☎: +34 666 294 012
consuelo@bodegastavera.com
www.bodegastavera.com

Tavera 2014 T Maceración Carbónica
55% syrah, 45% tempranillo

86

Tavera Antiguos Viñedos 2013 T
100% garnacha

85

Tavera Edicción Syrah 2011 T Fermentado en Barrica
100% syrah

87

Colour: cherry, garnet rim. Nose: spicy, creamy oak, ripe fruit. Palate: flavourful, round tannins.

Tavera Rosado Antiguos Viñedos 2014 RD
100% garnacha

86

Tavera Syrah Tempranillo 2013 T
50% syrah, 50% tempranillo

84

Tavera Vendimia Seleccionada 2012 T
45% syrah, 45% tempranillo, 10% garnacha

87

Colour: cherry, garnet rim. Nose: red berry notes, ripe fruit, scrubland. Palate: flavourful, spicy, correct.

COOPERATIVA CONDES DE FUENSALIDA

Avda. San Crispín, 129
45510 Fuensalida (Toledo)
☎: +34 925 784 823
Fax: +34 925 784 823
condesdefuensalida@hotmail.com
www.condesdefuensalida.iespana.es

Condes de Fuensalida S/C T
tempranillo, garnacha

82

Condes de Fuensalida 2014 RD

84

Condes de Fuensalida Fruit Rose Semidulce 2014 RD

84

COOPERATIVA NUESTRA SEÑORA DE LA NATIVIDAD

San Roque, 1
45930 Méntrida (Toledo)
☎: +34 918 177 004
Fax: +34 918 177 004
coopnatividad@gmail.com
www.cooperativamentrida.es

El Espinillo Vino de Parcela 2014 T
garnacha

90

Colour: cherry, purple rim. Nose: floral, balsamic herbs, red berry notes, fruit liqueur notes, spicy. Palate: powerful, fresh, fruity, balanced.

Pedromoro Vino de Paraje 2014 T
garnacha

87

Colour: cherry, purple rim. Nose: powerfull, ripe fruit, spicy, wild herbs. Palate: powerful, fruity, unctuous.

Vega Berciana 2014 RD
garnacha

85

Vega Berciana 2014 T
garnacha

85

COOPERATIVA NUESTRA SEÑORA DE LINARES

Inmaculada, 95
45920 Torre de Esteban Hambrán (Toledo)
☎: +34 925 795 452
Fax: +34 925 795 452
cooplina@futurnet.es

Fortitudo 2013 T
garnacha

84

DANILANDI

Constitución, 23
28640 Cadalso de los Vidrios (Madrid)
☎: +34 918 640 602
info@danilandi.com
www.danilandi.com

PODIUM

Cantos del Diablo 2013 T
garnacha

95

Colour: bright cherry. Nose: red berry notes, floral, spicy, earthy notes, scrubland, balsamic herbs. Palate: flavourful, spicy, long, fine tannins.

Las Uvas de la Ira. Vino de Pueblo 2013 T
garnacha

92

Colour: deep cherry, purple rim. Nose: toasty, ripe fruit, balsamic herbs, red berry notes. Palate: balanced, spicy, long.

HACIENDA VILLARTA

Ctra. Nacional 403, km. 48
45910 Escalona (Toledo)
☎: +34 925 740 027
agrovillarta@gmail.com
www.haciendavillarta.com

Besanas 2009 TR
tempranillo, syrah, cabernet sauvignon, petit verdot

86

Besanas 2011 TC
tempranillo, syrah, cabernet sauvignon, petit verdot

86

Besanas 2014 B
chardonnay, sauvignon blanc

84

YX 2014 B
chardonnay, sauvignon blanc

85

HIBÉU BODEGAS

Camino Las Ventas, Pol 10 Parc. 90
45920 Torre de Esteban Hambrán
(Toledo)
☎: +34 915 043 056
info@bodegashibeu.es
www.bodegashibeu.es

Hibeu 2013 T
84

VIÑEDOS Y BODEGAS GONZÁLEZ

Real, 86
45180 Camarena (Toledo)
☎: +34 918 174 063
Fax: +34 918 174 063
bodegasgonzalez@yahoo.es
www.vinobispo.com

Viña Bispo 2013 T
84

DO. MONTERREI

CONSEJO REGULADOR

Avenida Luis Espada, 73 bajo
32600 Verín (Ourense)
☎:+34 988 410 634 - Fax: +34 988 410 634
@: info@domonterrei.com
www.domonterrei.com

LOCATION:

In the east of the province of Orense, on the border with Portugal. The vineyards occupy the valley of Monterrei, and it is made up of the municipal districts of Verín, Monterrei, Oimbra and Castrelo do Vall.

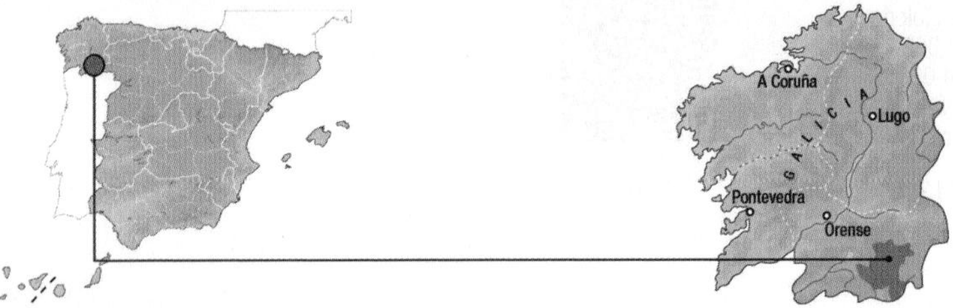

SUB-REGIONS:

Val de Monterrei. Comprising the vineyards situated in the valley region (therefore, more level terrains) and covering the parishes and municipal districts belonging to the following city councils: Castrelo do Val (Castrelo do Val, Pepín and Nocedo); Monterrei (Albarellos, Infesta, Monterrei and Vilaza); Oimbra (Oimbra, Rabal, O Rosal and San Cibrao); Verín (Abedes, Cabreiroa, Feces da Baixo, Feces de Cima, Mandín, Mourazos, Pazos, Queizás, A Rasela, Tamagos, Tamaguelos, Tintores, Verín, Vilela and Vilamaior do Val).
Ladeira de Monterrei. These vineyards occupy the hills. The parishes and municipal districts that make up this sub-region are: Castrelo do Val (Gondulfes and Servoi), Oimbra (As Chas and A Granxa), Monterrey (Flariz, Medeiros, Mixós, Estevesiños and Vences) and Verín (Queirugas).

GRAPE VARIETIES:

WHITE: Dona Blanca, Verdello (Godello) and Treixadura (Verdello Louro), Albariño, Caiño Blanco, Loureira and Blanca de Monterrei.
RED: Aranxa (Tempranillo), Caiño Tinto, Mencía, Bastardo (or María Ardoña) and Sousón.

FIGURES:

Vineyard surface: 467 – **Wine-Growers:** 384 – **Wineries:** 24 – **2014 Harvest rating:** Very Good – **Production 14:** 1,926,270 litres – **Market percentages:** 17% National - 83% International.

SOIL:

The vineyard extends over the sides of the hills and valleys irrigated by the River Támega and its tributaries. There are three types of soils in the area: slate and shale, granite and sandy, from the degradation of the granite rocks, and sediment type soils.

CLIMATE:

Midway between the Atlantic and Continental influences. Drier than in the rest of Galicia, with maximum temperatures of 35°C in summer and minimum of –5°C in winter.

VINTAGE RATING

PEÑÍNGUIDE

2010	2011	2012	2013	2014
VERY GOOD	VERY GOOD	VERY GOOD	VERY GOOD	GOOD

ADEGA ABELEDOS

Avda. Portugal, 110 2ºA
32600 Verín (Ourense)
☎: +34 988 414 075
Fax: +34 988 414 075
adegaabeledos@gmail.com

Abeledos 2014 B

godello, treixadura

85

Abeledos 2014 T

84

ADEGA PAZO DAS TAPIAS

Ctra. Ourense-Castrelo Km. 12,5
32940 Toen (Ourense)
☎: +34 988 261 256
Fax: +34 988 261 264
info@pazodomar.com
www.pazodomar.com

Alma de Blanco Godello 2014 B

godello

87

Colour: bright straw. Nose: fresh fruit, tropical fruit, white flowers. Palate: correct, fresh, good finish.

Alma de Tinto Mencía 2014 T

mencía

88

Colour: cherry, purple rim. Nose: ripe fruit, fruit preserve, mineral, scrubland. Palate: fruity, balanced.

ADEGA VALDERELLO

Rua Máximo 1 Albarellos de Monterrey
32618 Monterrei (Ourense)
☎: +34 988 411 199
valderello@yahoo.es

Valderello 2014 B

godello

86

Valderello 2014 T

88

Colour: cherry, purple rim. Nose: fresh fruit, red berry notes, floral, wild herbs. Palate: flavourful, fruity, good acidity.

ADEGAS TRIAY

Rua Ladairo, 36
32613 O'Rosal Oimbra (Ourense)
☎: +34 988 422 776
Fax: +34 988 422 776
triayadegas@gmail.com
www.bodegastriay.com

Triay 2014 B

godello

87

Colour: yellow. Nose: medium intensity, ripe fruit, dried flowers. Palate: flavourful, easy to drink, fine bitter notes.

Triay 2014 T

mencía

89

Colour: bright cherry, purple rim. Nose: balanced, expressive, varietal. Palate: balanced, balsamic, easy to drink.

ADEGAS VALMIÑOR

A Portela, s/n – San Juan de Tabagón
36760 O'Rosal (Pontevedra)
☎: +34 986 609 060
Fax: +34 986 609 313
valminor@valminorebano.com
www.adegasvalminor.com

Minius 2014 B

100% godello

88

Colour: bright yellow. Nose: ripe fruit, citrus fruit, floral, expressive. Palate: flavourful, fruity, balanced.

ALMA ATLÁNTICA

Burgáns, 91
36633 Vilariño - Cambados
(Pontevedra)
☎: +34 986 526 040
Fax: +34 986 526 901
comercial@martincodax.com
www.martincodax.com

Mara Martin Godello 2014 B

100% godello

87

Colour: bright straw. Nose: ripe fruit, dried flowers, dried herbs. Palate: correct, fine bitter notes, good finish.

BODEGA FRANCO BASALO

Lugar Fondougas s/n
32625 Castrelo do Val (Ourense)
☎: +34 988 305 576
bodega.franco.basalo@gmail.com

Estela do Val 2014 B
godello

88

Colour: bright straw. Nose: white flowers, fresh fruit, fragrant herbs. Palate: fruity, good acidity, balanced.

Estela do Val 2014 T
mencía

88

Colour: cherry, purple rim. Nose: varietal, ripe fruit, scrubland. Palate: ripe fruit, balsamic, correct, balanced.

BODEGA TABÚ

Plaza A Carreira, 6 O Rosal
32613 Oimbra (Ourense)
☎: +34 665 644 500
bodegatabu@gmail.com
www.bodegatabu.com

Stibadía Godello Barrica sobre Lías 2012 B
godello

88

Colour: bright golden. Nose: pattiserie, sweet spices, dried flowers, ripe fruit. Palate: spicy, long, balsamic.

Stibadía Godello Treixadura 2014 B
godello, treixadura

86

Stibadía Mencía Tempranillo 2011 T Barrica
mencía, tempranillo

89

Colour: very deep cherry, garnet rim. Nose: balsamic herbs, balanced, cocoa bean, sweet spices. Palate: flavourful, round tannins.

Stibadía Mencía Tempranillo 2014 T
mencía, tempranillo

87

Colour: bright cherry, purple rim. Nose: red berry notes, ripe fruit, dried herbs. Palate: correct, easy to drink, good finish.

BODEGAS GARGALO

Rua Do Castelo, 59
32619 Verín (Ourense)
☎: +34 988 590 203
Fax: +34 988 590 295
gargalo@verino.es
www.gargalo.es

Gargalo Albariño & Treixadura 2014 B
treixadura, albariño

87

Colour: bright yellow. Nose: powerfull, expressive, fruit expression, floral. Palate: correct, fine bitter notes.

Gargalo Godello 2014 B
godello

89

Colour: bright yellow. Nose: expressive, dried herbs, ripe fruit. Palate: flavourful, fruity, good acidity, balanced.

Gargalo Mencía & Arauxa 2013 T
mencía, arauxa

89

Colour: cherry, purple rim. Nose: ripe fruit, wild herbs, balanced. Palate: easy to drink, ripe fruit, balsamic.

Terra do Gargalo Carballo 2012 TC
mencía

90

Colour: very deep cherry, garnet rim. Nose: expressive, mineral, balsamic herbs, balanced. Palate: full, flavourful, round tannins.

Terra do Gargalo sobre Lías 2012 B
godello, treixadura

92

Colour: bright straw. Nose: fine lees, dried herbs, mineral, dried flowers, expressive. Palate: flavourful, fruity, good acidity, round.

Terra Rubia Godello-Treixadura 2014 B
godello, treixadura

85

Viña Verino 2012 BFB
godello

92

Colour: bright yellow. Nose: fine lees, dried herbs, ripe fruit, candied fruit, citrus fruit, dried flowers, spicy. Palate: flavourful, fruity, good acidity, rich.

BODEGAS LADAIRO

Ctra. Ladairo, 42
32613 O'Rosal (Oimbra) (Ourense)
☎: +34 988 422 757
Fax: +34 988 422 757
info@bodegasladairo.com
www.ladairo.com

Ladairo 2013 T Barrica

90

Colour: deep cherry, purple rim. Nose: creamy oak, toasty, balsamic herbs, red berry notes, ripe fruit. Palate: balanced, spicy, long.

Ladairo 2014 B

89

Colour: bright straw. Nose: balanced, expressive, ripe fruit, white flowers, varietal. Palate: balanced, fine bitter notes, flavourful.

Ladairo 2014 T

mencía, arauxa

89

Colour: cherry, purple rim. Nose: expressive, fresh fruit, red berry notes, floral, mineral. Palate: flavourful, fruity, good acidity, balanced.

CASTRO DE LOBARZÁN

Ctra. de Requeixo, 51 - Villaza
32618 Monterrei (Ourense)
☎: +34 988 418 163
lobarzan@gmail.com

Castro de Lobarzán 2014 B

godello, treixadura

86

Castro de Lobarzán 2014 T

mencía, arauxa, bastardo negro

87

Colour: deep cherry, purple rim. Nose: ripe fruit, macerated fruit, dried herbs. Palate: correct, fruity.

Lobarzán IS 2012 T

mencía, arauxa, bastardo negro

90

Colour: cherry, garnet rim. Nose: smoky, spicy, ripe fruit. Palate: flavourful, smoky aftertaste, ripe fruit, sweet tannins.

Lobarzán IS 2013 B

godello

91

Colour: bright yellow. Nose: citrus fruit, dried herbs, dried flowers, faded flowers. Palate: balanced, spicy, fine bitter notes.

Lobarzán IS 2013 T

mencía, arauxa, bastardo negro

91

Colour: very deep cherry, purple rim. Nose: ripe fruit, spicy, toasty. Palate: long, spicy, ripe fruit, fine tannins.

CREGO E MONAGUILLO

Rua Nova s/n
32618 Salgueira (Ourense)
☎: +34 988 418 164
Fax: +34 988 418 164
tito@cregoemonaguillo.com
www.cregoemonaguillo.com

Crego e Monaguillo 2014 B

85,19% godello, 11,54% treixadura, 3,27% dona blanca

88

Colour: bright straw. Nose: white flowers, fresh fruit, fragrant herbs. Palate: fruity, good acidity, balanced.

Crego e Monaguillo 2014 T

90,2% mencía, 9,8% arauxa

87

Colour: deep cherry, purple rim. Nose: red berry notes, floral, scrubland. Palate: fruity, balsamic, easy to drink.

Crego e Monaguillo Ed. Especial 2014 T

sousón, caiño, mencía

89

Colour: deep cherry, purple rim. Nose: ripe fruit, balsamic herbs. Palate: balanced, spicy, long, fruity aftestaste.

Father 1943 2013 T

mencía, arauxa, bastardo negro

89

Colour: very deep cherry. Nose: smoky, toasty, spicy. Palate: fruity, flavourful, round tannins.

Marova 2013 B

treixadura, dona blanca, godello

87

Colour: bright yellow. Nose: ripe fruit, powerfull, toasty, aged wood nuances. Palate: flavourful, fruity, spicy, toasty, long.

FRAGAS DO LECER

Touza, 22
32618 Villaza (Ourense)
☎: +34 616 670 249
Fax: +34 988 425 950
bodegaboorivero@yahoo.es
www.bodegaboorivero.es

Fragas do Lecer 2014 B

godello, treixadura

85

MANUEL GUERRA JUSTO

Ctra. Albarellos, 61
32618 Villaza (Monterrei) (Ourense)
☎: +34 687 409 618
viaarxentea@viaarxentea.com

Vía Arxéntea 2014 B
godello, treixadura

88

Colour: bright yellow. Nose: white flowers, fresh fruit, fragrant herbs. Palate: fruity, balanced, fine bitter notes.

PAZO BLANCO NÚÑEZ, S.L. (ADEGAS TAPIAS-MARIÑÁN)

Estrada Xeral 525, Km. 170,4
32619 Pazos - Verín (Ourense)
☎: +34 988 411 693
Fax: +34 988 411 693
info@tapiasmarinhan.com
www.tapiasmarinhan.com

Colleita Propia 2014 B
godello, albariño

85

Colleita Propia 2014 T
mencía

85

Pazo de Mariñan 2014 B
godello, treixadura, albariño

86

Pazo de Mariñan 2014 T
mencía, arauxa

86

Quintas das Tapias 2014 T
mencía

87

Colour: cherry, purple rim. Nose: medium intensity, balanced, varietal. Palate: fruity, easy to drink.

Quintas das Tapias Godello 2014 B
godello

86

Quintas das Tapias Treixadura 2014 B
treixadura

89

Colour: bright yellow. Nose: citrus fruit, white flowers, balanced. Palate: easy to drink, fine bitter notes, fruity.

PAZO DE VALDECONDE

Mourazos
Verín (Ourense)
☎: +34 988 422 773
Fax: +34 988 422 773
info@bodegapazodevaldeconde.com
www.bodegapazodevaldeconde.com

Souto do Rei 2014 B

87

Colour: bright straw. Nose: fragrant herbs, citrus fruit, floral. Palate: flavourful, correct, fine bitter notes.

Souto do Rei 2014 T
mencía, tempranillo

85

PAZOS DEL REY

Carrero Blanco, 33
32618 Albarellos de Monterrei (Ourense)
☎: +34 988 425 959
info@pazosdelrey.com
www.pazosdelrey.com

Pazo de Monterrey 2014 B
100% godello

88

Colour: bright straw. Nose: medium intensity, ripe fruit, floral, citrus fruit. Palate: correct, easy to drink.

QUINTA DO BUBLE

Ladeira A Machada s/n
Casas dos Montes
32613 Oimbra (Ourense)
☎: +34 988 422 960
info@quintadobuble.com
www.quintadobuble.com

Quinta do Buble 2014 B
100% godello

89

Colour: bright yellow. Nose: dried flowers, faded flowers, ripe fruit, varietal. Palate: balanced, fine bitter notes, rich.

TERRAS DO CIGARRÓN

Ctra. de Albarellos, km. 525
32618 Albarellos de Monterrei (Ourense)
☎: +34 988 418 703
bodega@terrasdocigarron.com
www.terrasdocigarron.com

Terras do Cigarrón 2014 B
100% godello

88

Colour: bright straw, greenish rim. Nose: ripe fruit, dried flowers, varietal. Palate: flavourful, balanced, fine bitter notes.

VINIGALICIA

Ctra. Antigua Santiago, km. 3
27500 Chantada (Lugo)
☎: +34 982 454 005
Fax: +34 982 454 094
vinigalicia@vinigalicia.es
www.vinigalicia.es

Lagar de Deuses Godello 2012 B

70% godello, 30% treixadura

88

Colour: bright yellow. Nose: ripe fruit, powerfull, sweet spices. Palate: flavourful, fruity, spicy, long, rich.

Lagar de Deuses Mencía 2012 T

70% mencía, 30% tempranillo

87

Colour: dark-red cherry, garnet rim. Nose: ripe fruit, balanced, dried herbs. Palate: flavourful, spicy, fruity aftestaste.

DO. MONDÉJAR

CONSEJO REGULADOR

Pza. Mayor, 10
19110 Mondéjar (Guadalajara)
☎ :+34 949 385 284 - Fax: +34 949 385 284
@: crdom@crdomondejar.com
www.crdomondejar.com

LOCATION:

In the southwest of the province of Guadalajara. It is made up of the municipal districts of Albalate de Zorita, Albares, Almoguera, Almonacid de Zorita, Driebes, Escariche, Escopete, Fuenteovilla, Illana, Loranca de Tajuña, Mazuecos, Mondéjar, Pastrana, Pioz, Pozo de Almoguera, Sacedón, Sayatón, Valdeconcha, Yebra and Zorita de los Canes.

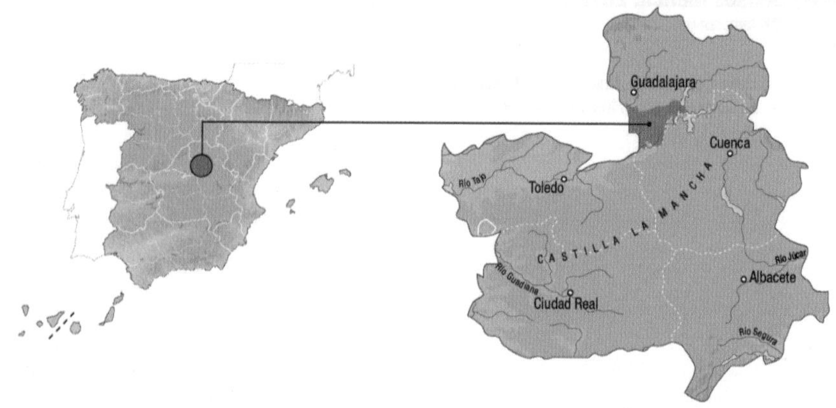

GRAPE VARIETIES:

WHITE (40%): Malvar (majority 80% of white varieties), Macabeo and Torrontés.
RED (60%): Cencibel (Tempranillo – represents 95% of red varieties), Cabernet Sauvignon (5%) and Syrah.

FIGURES:

Vineyard surface 2011: 3,000 – **Wine-Growers 2011:** 300 – **Wineries 2011:** 2 – **2011 Harvest rating:** N/A – **Production 2011:** 421,130 litres – **Market percentages 2011:** 100% National.

SOIL:

The south of the Denomination is characterized by red soil on lime-clayey sediments, and the north (the municipal districts of Anguix, Mondéjar, Sacedón, etc.) has brown limestone soil on lean sandstone and conglomerates.

CLIMATE:

Temperate Mediterranean. The average annual temperature is around 18°C and the average rainfall is 500 mm per year.

VINTAGE RATING

PEÑÍNGUIDE

2010	2011	2012	2013	2014
N/A	N/A	N/A	N/A	N/A

DO. MONTILLA - MORILES

CONSEJO REGULADOR

José Padillo Delgado, sn

14550 Montilla (Córdoba)

☎: +34 957 652 110 - Fax: +34 957652 407

@: consejo@montillamoriles.es

www.montilla-moriles.org

LOCATION:

To the south of Córdoba. It covers all the vineyards of the municipal districts of Montilla, Moriles, Montalbán, Puente Genil, Montruque, Nueva Carteya and Doña Mencía, and part of the municipal districts of Montemayor, Fernán-Núñez, La Rambla, Santaella, Aguilar de la Frontera, Lucena, Cabra, Baena, Castro del Río and Espejo.

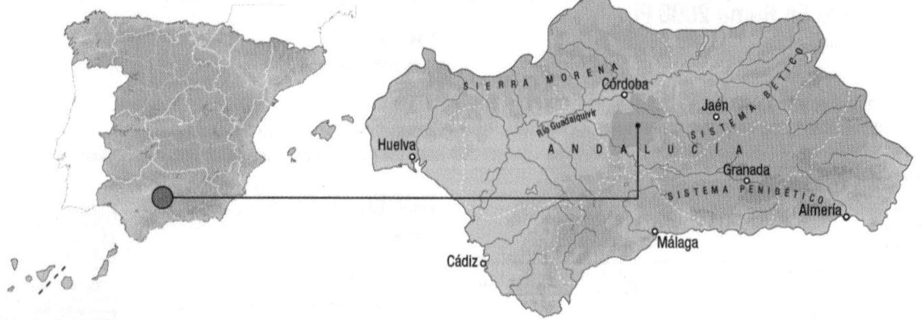

SUB-REGIONS:

We have to differentiate between the vineyards in the flatlands and those in higher areas –such as Sierra de Montilla and Moriles Alto–, prominently limestone soils of higher quality and hardly 2000 hectares planted.

GRAPE VARIETIES:

WHITE: Pedro Ximénez (main variety), Airén, Baladí, Moscatel, Torrontés and Verdejo.
RED: Tempranillo, Syrah and Cabernet Sauvignon.

FIGURES:

Vineyard surface: 5,194 – **Wine-Growers:** 2,316 – **Wineries:** 59 – **2014 Harvest rating:** N/A – **Production 14:** 32,985,700 litres – **Market percentages:** 90% National - 10% International.

SOIL:

The vineyards are situated at an altitude of between 125 m and 640 m. The soils are franc, franc-sandy and, in the higher regions, calcareous ('Albarizas'), which are precisely those of best quality, and which predominate in what is known as the Upper Sub-Region, which includes the municipal districts of Montilla, Moriles, Castro del Río, Cabra and Aguilar de la Frontera.

CLIMATE:

Semi-continental Mediterranean, with long, hot, dry summers and short winters. The average annual temperature is 16.8°C and the average rainfall is between 500 mm and 1,000 mm per year.

VINTAGE RATING

PEÑÍNGUIDE

2010	2011	2012	2013	2014
GOOD	N/A	N/A	N/A	N/A

ALVEAR

María Auxiliadora, 1
14550 Montilla (Córdoba)
☎: +34 957 650 100
Fax: +34 957 650 135
info@alvear.es
www.alvear.es

Alvear Dulce Viejo 2000 PX Reserva
100% pedro ximénez

94

Colour: dark mahogany. Nose: complex, expressive, varietal, aromatic coffee, spicy, characterful, toasty. Palate: creamy, long, good acidity.

Alvear Fino En Rama 2008 FI
100% pedro ximénez

91

Colour: bright yellow. Nose: flor yeasts, pungent, dry nuts. Palate: good acidity, spicy, long, fine bitter notes, flavourful.

Alvear PX 1927 PX
100% pedro ximénez

93

Colour: dark mahogany. Nose: powerfull, expressive, aromatic coffee, spicy, acetaldehyde, dry nuts. Palate: balanced, elegant, toasty, long.

Alvear PX de Añada 2013
100% pedro ximénez

92

Colour: old gold, amber rim. Nose: candied fruit, fruit liqueur notes, varietal, faded flowers, sweet spices. Palate: fruity, flavourful, unctuous.

PODIUM

Alvear Solera 1830 PX Reserva
100% pedro ximénez

97

Colour: dark mahogany. Nose: powerfull, aromatic coffee, spicy, acetaldehyde, dry nuts. Palate: balanced, elegant, fine solera notes, toasty, long, creamy.

Alvear Solera Fundación AM
100% pedro ximénez

94

Colour: iodine, amber rim. Nose: elegant, sweet spices, acetaldehyde, dry nuts, cocoa bean, creamy oak. Palate: full, dry, spicy, long, fine bitter notes, complex.

PODIUM

Alvear Solera Fundación PC
100% pedro ximénez

95

Colour: light mahogany. Nose: acetaldehyde, pungent, varnish, aged wood nuances, creamy oak. Palate: powerful, flavourful, spicy, long, balanced.

Asunción OL
100% pedro ximénez

90

Colour: iodine, amber rim. Nose: powerfull, complex, dry nuts, varnish, caramel. Palate: rich, long, spicy.

C.B. FI
100% pedro ximénez

90

Colour: bright yellow. Nose: balanced, fresh, saline, expressive, pungent. Palate: flavourful, fine bitter notes, long.

BODEGAS CRUZ CONDE

14550 Montilla (Córdoba)
☎: +34 957 651 250
Fax: +34 957 653 619
info@bodegascruzconde.es
www.bodegascruzconde.es

Cream Cruz Conde 1902 CR
100% pedro ximénez

84

Cruz Conde PC
100% pedro ximénez

84

Cruz Conde Solera Fundación 1902 PX
100% pedro ximénez

92

Colour: dark mahogany. Nose: powerfull, expressive, spicy, dry nuts, dark chocolate. Palate: fine solera notes, toasty, long, good acidity.

Fino Cruz Conde 1902 FI
100% pedro ximénez

86

Mercedes Cruz Conde OL
100% pedro ximénez

85

Pedro Ximénez Cruz Conde 1902 PX
pedro ximénez

90

Colour: mahogany. Nose: fruit liqueur notes, dried fruit, pattiserie, toasty, varietal. Palate: sweet, rich, unctuous, long, spicy.

BODEGAS DELGADO

Cosano, 2
14500 Puente Genil (Córdoba)
☎: +34 957 600 085
Fax: +34 957 604 571
fino@bodegasdelgado.com
www.bodegasdelgado.com

Abuelamaría OL
pedro ximénez

85

Delgado AM
pedro ximénez

91

Colour: iodine, amber rim. Nose: elegant, sweet spices, acetaldehyde, dry nuts. Palate: full, dry, spicy, long, fine bitter notes, complex.

Delgado 1874 AM
pedro ximénez

91

Colour: old gold. Nose: toasty, sweet spices, varnish, dry nuts, candied fruit. Palate: flavourful, full, balanced, fine bitter notes.

Delgado 1874 PX
pedro ximénez

91

Colour: dark mahogany. Nose: toasty, smoky, dark chocolate, dried fruit, fruit liqueur notes. Palate: flavourful, balanced, unctuous.

Segunda Bota FI
pedro ximénez

89

Colour: bright yellow. Nose: balanced, fresh, saline, expressive. Palate: flavourful, fine bitter notes, long.

BODEGAS LAGAR BLANCO

Ctra. de Cuesta Blanca
14550 Montilla (Córdoba)
☎: +34 628 319 977
Fax: +34 957 651 145
lagarblanco@lagarblanco.es
www.lagarblanco.es

Lagar Blanco PC
100% pedro ximénez

89

Colour: light mahogany. Nose: acetaldehyde, pungent, varnish, aged wood nuances, creamy oak. Palate: powerful, flavourful, spicy, long, balanced.

BODEGAS MÁLAGA VIRGEN

Autovía A-92, Km. 132
29520 Fuente de Piedra (Málaga)
☎: +34 952 319 454
Fax: +34 952 359 819
bodegas@bodegasmalagavirgen.com
www.bodegasmalagavirgen.com

Lagar de Benavides FI
88

Colour: bright yellow. Nose: flor yeasts, pungent. Palate: good acidity, fine bitter notes, spicy, long, flavourful.

BODEGAS SILLERO

Ctra. de La Redonda, s/n
14540 La Rambla (Córdoba)
☎: +34 957 684 464
sillero@bodegassillero.com
www.bodegassillero.com

Las Cármenes FI
86

Sillero PX
pedro ximénez

86

Sillero Dulce
85

Viejo Rondalla OL
87

Colour: old gold, amber rim. Nose: sweet spices, pattiserie, candied fruit, varnish. Palate: long, flavourful, good acidity.

CÍA. VINÍCOLA DEL SUR - TOMÁS GARCÍA

Avda. Luis de Góngora y Argote, s/n
14550 Montilla (Córdoba)
☎: +34 957 650 204
Fax: +34 957 652 335
info@vinicoladelsur.com
www.vinicoladelsur.com

Monte Cristo FI
100% pedro ximénez

89

Colour: bright straw. Nose: elegant, expressive, faded flowers, dry nuts, spicy. Palate: balanced, fine bitter notes, long.

Monte Cristo PX
100% pedro ximénez

90

Colour: mahogany. Nose: fruit liqueur notes, dried fruit, pattiserie, toasty. Palate: sweet, rich, unctuous, long, fruity aftestaste, fine solera notes.

Monte Cristo AM
100% pedro ximénez

89

Colour: light mahogany. Nose: cocoa bean, sweet spices, caramel, candied fruit. Palate: flavourful, balanced, fine bitter notes.

Monte Cristo OL
100% pedro ximénez

92

Colour: old gold, amber rim. Nose: powerfull, complex, dry nuts, toasty, acetaldehyde. Palate: rich, long, fine solera notes, spicy, round.

Pedro Ximénez Viejo Tomás García PX
100% pedro ximénez

89

Colour: mahogany. Nose: complex, fruit liqueur notes, dried fruit, pattiserie, toasty, varietal. Palate: sweet, rich, unctuous, long.

Verbenera FI
100% pedro ximénez

88

Colour: bright yellow. Nose: saline, dry nuts, faded flowers. Palate: balanced, fine bitter notes, flavourful, dry.

EQUIPO NAVAZOS

11403 Jerez de la Frontera (Cádiz)
equipo@navazos.com
www.equiponavazos.com

Casa del Inca 2013 PX

94

Colour: mahogany. Nose: complex, fruit liqueur notes, dried fruit, pattiserie, toasty. Palate: sweet, rich, unctuous.

GRACIA HNOS., S.A.U.

Avda. Luis de Góngora y Argote, s/n
14550 Montilla (Córdoba)
☎: +34 957 650 162
Fax: +34 957 652 335
info@bodegasgracia.com
www.bodegasgracia.com

Dulce Viejo Pedro Ximénez Gracia PX
100% pedro ximénez

89

Colour: mahogany. Nose: complex, fruit liqueur notes, dried fruit, pattiserie, toasty, cocoa bean. Palate: sweet, rich, unctuous.

Fino Corredera FI

87

Colour: yellow, pale. Nose: dry nuts, dried flowers. Palate: fine bitter notes, correct, good acidity, good finish.

Solera Fina María del Valle FI
100% pedro ximénez

88

Colour: bright yellow. Nose: balanced, fresh, saline, expressive, pungent. Palate: flavourful, fine bitter notes, long.

Solera Fina Tauromaquia FI
100% pedro ximénez

89

Colour: bright yellow. Nose: balanced, fresh, saline, expressive, pungent, dry nuts. Palate: fine bitter notes, long.

Tauromaquia OL
100% pedro ximénez

88

Colour: iodine, amber rim. Nose: dry nuts, varnish, caramel. Palate: rich, long, spicy.

Tauromaquia PX
pedro ximénez

91

Colour: dark mahogany. Nose: dried fruit, powerfull, varnish, pattiserie, complex. Palate: flavourful, full, sweet, long, creamy.

Tauromaquia Amontillado Viejo AM
100% pedro ximénez

90

Colour: light mahogany. Nose: candied fruit, varnish, caramel. Palate: flavourful, fine bitter notes, long.

Viñaverde 2014 B
pedro ximénez, moscatel, verdejo, torrontés

84

HEREDEROS TORRES BURGOS S.L.

Ronda San Francisco, 1
14900 Lucena (Córdoba)
☎: +34 957 501 062
manolog.enologo@torresburgos.es
www.torresburgos.com

Moriles 1890 CR
100% pedro ximénez

88

Colour: light mahogany. Nose: acetaldehyde, pungent, varnish, aged wood nuances, creamy oak. Palate: powerful, flavourful, spicy, long, balanced, sweetness.

TB Etiqueta Negra FI
100% pedro ximénez

88

Colour: bright yellow. Nose: balanced, dry nuts, faded flowers, flor yeasts. Palate: flavourful, fine bitter notes, balanced.

TB Pedro Ximénez PX
100% pedro ximénez

89

Colour: mahogany. Nose: complex, fruit liqueur notes, dried fruit, pattiserie, toasty. Palate: sweet, rich, unctuous.

NAVISA INDUSTRIAL VINÍCOLA ESPAÑOLA S.A.

Avda. José Padillo Delgado, s/n
14550 Montilla (Córdoba)
☎: +34 957 650 554
Fax: +34 957 651 747
abaena@navisa.es
www.navisa.es

Cobos FI
pedro ximénez

85

Dos Pasas PX
pedro ximénez

86

Montulia OL

86

Tres Pasas PX

87

Colour: mahogany. Nose: complex, fruit liqueur notes, dried fruit, pattiserie, toasty, characterful. Palate: sweet, rich, unctuous.

Vega María 2014 B
chardonnay

80

PÉREZ BARQUERO S.A.

Avda. Andalucía, 27
14550 Montilla (Córdoba)
☎: +34 957 650 500
Fax: +34 957 650 208
info@perezbarquero.com
www.perezbarquero.com

Fino Los Amigos FI
100% pedro ximénez

87

Colour: yellow, pale. Nose: fresh, saline, balanced. Palate: flavourful, spicy, long, fine bitter notes.

Gran Barquero AM
100% pedro ximénez

89

Colour: iodine, amber rim. Nose: balanced, medium intensity, dry nuts, cocoa bean. Palate: full, flavourful, long, fine bitter notes.

Gran Barquero FI
100% pedro ximénez

91

Colour: yellow. Nose: balanced, fresh, saline, expressive, pungent, dry nuts. Palate: flavourful, fine bitter notes, long, dry.

Gran Barquero OL
100% pedro ximénez

90

Colour: iodine, amber rim. Nose: powerfull, complex, dry nuts, creamy oak, varnish. Palate: rich, long, spicy.

Gran Barquero PX
100% pedro ximénez

91

Colour: dark mahogany. Nose: fruit liqueur notes, dried fruit, pattiserie, toasty, powerfull. Palate: sweet, rich, long, creamy.

PODIUM

La Cañada PX
100% pedro ximénez

96

Colour: dark mahogany. Nose: powerfull, expressive, aromatic coffee, spicy, acetaldehyde, dry nuts. Palate: balanced, elegant, fine solera notes, toasty, long, creamy.

Pérez Barquero Pedro Ximénez de Cosecha 2014 PX

100% pedro ximénez

89

Colour: old gold, amber rim. Nose: dried fruit, pattiserie, caramel. Palate: unctuous, flavourful, sweet.

Verdejo Finca La Cañada 2014 B

verdejo

85

Viña Amalia 2014 B

pedro ximénez, moscatel, verdejo, torrontés

84

TORO ALBALÁ

Avda. Antonio Sánchez, 1
14920 Aguilar de la Frontera (Córdoba)
☎: +34 957 660 046
Fax: +34 957 661 494
info@toroalbala.com
www.toroalbala.com

Don P.X. 1986 PX Gran Reserva

100% pedro ximénez

94

Colour: dark mahogany. Nose: expressive, complex, jasmine, dried fruit, aromatic coffee, smoky. Palate: balanced, unctuous, round, good acidity.

Don P.X. 2012 PX

100% pedro ximénez

90

Colour: mahogany. Nose: complex, fruit liqueur notes, dried fruit, pattiserie, toasty. Palate: sweet, rich, unctuous.

PODIUM

Don P.X. Convento Selección 1955 PX

100% pedro ximénez

96

Colour: dark mahogany. Nose: expressive, complex, spicy, candied fruit, dried flowers, aromatic coffee. Palate: elegant, round, good acidity, balanced.

PODIUM

Don P.X. Selección 1946 PX

100% pedro ximénez

97

Colour: dark mahogany. Nose: aromatic coffee, spicy, acetaldehyde, dry nuts, powerfull. Palate: balanced, elegant, fine solera notes, toasty, long.

PODIUM

Don P.X. Selección 1965 PX

100% pedro ximénez

97

Colour: dark mahogany. Nose: citrus fruit, dried fruit, elegant, spicy, cocoa bean, acetaldehyde. Palate: long, elegant, round, good acidity, creamy.

Eléctrico en Rama Solera

100% pedro ximénez

88

Colour: bright yellow. Nose: flor yeasts, lees reduction notes, pungent. Palate: good acidity, fine bitter notes, spicy, long.

DO. MONTSANT

CONSEJO REGULADOR

Plaça de la Quartera, 6
43730 Falset (Tarragona)
☎:+34 977 831 742 - Fax: +34 977 830 676
@: info@domontsant.com
www.domontsant.com

LOCATION:

In the region of Priorat (Tarragona). It is made up of Baix Priorat, part of Alt Priorat and various municipal districts of Ribera d'Ebre that were already integrated into the Falset sub-region. In total, 16 municipal districts: La Bisbal de Falset, Cabaces, Capçanes, Cornudella de Montsant, La Figuera, Els Guiamets, Marçá, Margalef, El Masroig, Pradell, La Torre de Fontaubella, Ulldemolins, Falset, El Molar, Darmós and La Serra d'Almos. The vineyards are located at widely variable altitudes, ranging between 200 m to 700 m above sea level.

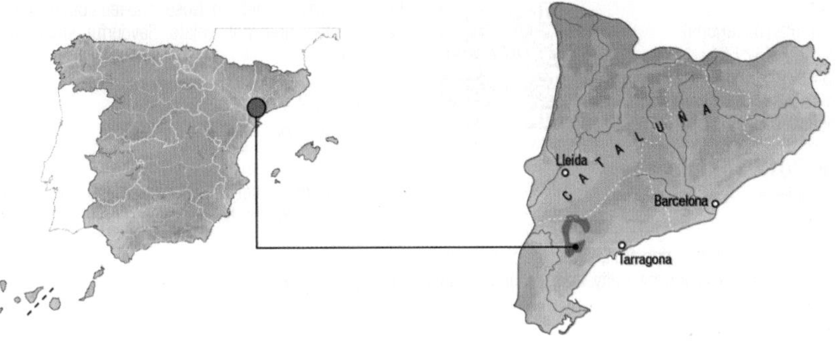

GRAPE VARIETIES:

WHITE: Chardonnay, Garnacha Blanca, Macabeo, Moscatel, Pansal, Parellada.
RED: Cabernet Sauvignon, Cariñena, Garnacha Tinta, Garnacha Peluda, Merlot, Monastrell, Picapoll, Syrah, Tempranillo and Mazuela.

FIGURES:

Vineyard surface: 1,840 – **Wine-Growers:** 730 – **Wineries:** 65 – **2014 Harvest rating:** Very Good – **Production 14:** 5,914,695 litres – **Market percentages:** 50% National - 50% International.

SOIL:

There are mainly three types of soil: compact calcareous soils with pebbles on the borders of the DO; granite sands in Falset; and siliceous slate (the same stony slaty soil as Priorat) in certain areas of Falset and Cornudella.

CLIMATE:

Although the vineyards are located in a Mediterranean region, the mountains that surround the region isolate it from the sea to a certain extent, resulting in a somewhat more Continental climate. Due to this, it benefits from the contrasts in day/night temperatures, which is an important factor in the ripening of the grapes. However, it also receives the sea winds, laden with humidity, which help to compensate for the lack of rainfall in the summer. The average rainfall is between 500 and 600 mm per year.

VINTAGE RATING

PEÑÍNGUIDE

2010	2011	2012	2013	2014
VERY GOOD	VERY GOOD	GOOD	VERY GOOD	VERY GOOD

7 MAGNIFICS

Miquel Torres i Carbó, 6
08720 Vilafranca del Penedès
(Barcelona)
☎: +34 938 177 400
Fax: +34 938 177 444
7magnifics@7magnifics.com
www.7magnifics.com

El Senat de Montsant 2013 T

samsó, garnacha, syrah

90

Colour: cherry, garnet rim. Nose: ripe fruit, scrubland, spicy. Palate: good structure, long, ripe fruit, round tannins.

ACÚSTIC CELLER

Progrés s/n
43775 Marça (Tarragona)
☎: +34 672 432 691
Fax: +34 977 660 867
acustic@acusticceller.com
www.acusticceller.com

Acústic 2012 T Roble

garnacha, cariñena

92

Colour: bright cherry. Nose: ripe fruit, sweet spices, creamy oak, expressive. Palate: flavourful, fruity, toasty, round tannins.

Acústic 2013 T Roble

garnacha, cariñena

90

Colour: cherry, purple rim. Nose: ripe fruit, woody, roasted coffee. Palate: flavourful, spicy, powerful.

Acústic 2014 RD

garnacha, garnacha roja, cariñena

88

Colour: rose, purple rim. Nose: red berry notes, floral. Palate: powerful, fruity, fresh.

Acústic Blanc 2012 BFB

garnacha blanca, macabeo, garnacha roja, pansal

92

Colour: bright yellow. Nose: expressive, dried herbs, ripe fruit. Palate: flavourful, fruity, good acidity.

Acústic Blanc 2013 BFB

garnacha blanca, macabeo, garnacha roja, pansal

91

Colour: bright yellow. Nose: toasty, aged wood nuances, pattiserie, candied fruit, citrus fruit. Palate: flavourful, fruity, spicy, toasty, long.

Acústic Blanc 2014 BFB

garnacha blanca, macabeo, garnacha roja, pansal

90

Colour: bright straw. Nose: white flowers, fine lees, dried herbs, mineral. Palate: flavourful, fruity, good acidity.

Auditori 2011 T

garnacha

91

Colour: pale ruby, brick rim edge. Nose: spicy, ripe fruit, wild herbs, sweet spices. Palate: spicy, toasty, balanced.

Auditori 2013 T

garnacha

92

Colour: cherry, garnet rim. Nose: roasted coffee, smoky, spicy, earthy notes, ripe fruit. Palate: flavourful, smoky aftertaste, ripe fruit.

Braó 2012 T

garnacha, cariñena

91

Colour: cherry, garnet rim. Nose: mineral, expressive, spicy, fruit preserve. Palate: flavourful, ripe fruit, long, good acidity, balanced.

Braó 2013 T

garnacha, cariñena

93

Colour: cherry, garnet rim. Nose: mineral, expressive, spicy. Palate: flavourful, ripe fruit, long, good acidity, balanced.

AGRÍCOLA D'ULLDEMOLINS SANT JAUME

Av. Verge de Montserrat, s/n
43363 Ulldemolins (Tarragona)
☎: +34 977 561 640
Fax: +34 977 561 613
info@coopulldemolins.com
www.coopulldemolins.com

Les Pedrenyeres 2013 T

garnacha

84

Les Pedrenyeres 2014 B

garnacha blanca, macabeo

86

Sssssshhhhh Ulldemolins 2014 T

garnacha

85

AGRÍCOLA I SC DE LA SERRA D'ALMOS

Avda. de la Cooperativa, s/n
43746 La Serra D'Almos (Tarragona)
☎: +34 977 418 125
Fax: +34 977 418 399
coopserra@telefonica.net
www.serradalmos.com

L'OM 2012 TC
cariñena, syrah, cabernet sauvignon

88

Colour: bright cherry. Nose: ripe fruit, sweet spices, creamy oak. Palate: flavourful, fruity, toasty.

L'OM 2014 T
cariñena, garnacha, merlot

87

Colour: cherry, purple rim. Nose: powerfull, ripe fruit, spicy, balsamic herbs. Palate: powerful, fruity, easy to drink.

Mussefres Blanc 2014 B
macabeo, garnacha blanca

82

Mussefres Negre 2014 T
cariñena

86

Mussefres Rosat 2014 RD
garnacha, merlot

82

Mussefres Selecció 2012 T
cariñena, syrah, cabernet sauvignon

86

ALFREDO ARRIBAS

Sort dels Capellans, 23
43730 Falset (Tarragona)
☎: +34 932 531 760
Fax: +34 934 173 591
info@portaldelpriorat.com
www.portaldelpriorat.com

Gotes del Montsant 2013 T
cariñena, garnacha

91

Colour: bright cherry. Nose: ripe fruit, sweet spices, creamy oak. Palate: flavourful, fruity, round tannins.

Trossos Sants 2013 B
garnacha blanca

93

Colour: bright straw. Nose: white flowers, fine lees, dried herbs, mineral. Palate: flavourful, fruity, good acidity, round.

Trossos Sants 2014 B
garnacha blanca

91

Colour: bright yellow. Nose: expressive, dried herbs, ripe fruit, spicy. Palate: flavourful, fruity, long, balsamic, rich, spicy.

PODIUM

Trossos Tros Blanc 2013 B
garnacha blanca

95

Colour: bright straw. Nose: white flowers, dried herbs, ripe fruit, candied fruit, earthy notes, sweet spices. Palate: flavourful, fruity, good acidity.

PODIUM

Trossos Tros Blanc Magnum 2007 B
garnacha blanca

95

Colour: bright golden. Nose: balsamic herbs, petrol notes, faded flowers, spicy, cocoa bean, expressive. Palate: rich, full, long, spicy, good acidity, balanced. Personality.

Trossos Tros Blanc Magnum 2012 B
garnacha blanca

94

Colour: bright yellow. Nose: ripe fruit, spicy, creamy oak, petrol notes, faded flowers, mineral. Palate: rich, concentrated, flavourful, balanced.

Trossos Tros Negre 2013 T
garnacha

94

Colour: very deep cherry, garnet rim. Nose: expressive, complex, mineral, balsamic herbs. Palate: full, flavourful, round tannins.

Trossos Tros Negre Magnum 2010 T
garnacha

94

Colour: ruby red. Nose: ripe fruit, spicy, scrubland, expressive. Palate: flavourful, toasty, round tannins, long, balanced, elegant.

Trossos Tros Negre Magnum 2011 T
garnacha

93

Colour: cherry, garnet rim. Nose: dried herbs, ripe fruit, spicy, earthy notes, complex. Palate: powerful, flavourful, long, spicy.

Trossos Vells 2012 T
cariñena

92

Colour: cherry, garnet rim. Nose: ripe fruit, wild herbs, earthy notes, spicy, balsamic herbs. Palate: balanced, flavourful, long.

Trossos Vells 2013 T
cariñena

91

Colour: deep cherry, garnet rim. Nose: ripe fruit, scrubland, spicy, creamy oak. Palate: rich, spicy, long, balsamic.

ANGUERA DOMENECH
Sant Pere, 2
43743 Darmós (Tarragona)
☎: +34 977 405 857
angueradomenech@gmail.com
www.vianguera.com

Reclot 2014 T
garnacha, tempranillo

86

Vinya Gasó 2013 TC
cariñena, garnacha, tempranillo

88

Colour: cherry, purple rim. Nose: woody, roasted coffee, ripe fruit. Palate: flavourful, spicy, powerful.

BODEGAS ORDÓÑEZ
Julio Romero de Torres, 12
29700 Vélez- Málaga (Málaga)
☎: +34 952 504 706
Fax: +34 951 284 796
info@jorgeordonez.es
www.grupojorgeordonez.com

Zerrán 2012 T
50% garnacha, 40% mazuelo, 10% syrah

91

Colour: bright cherry. Nose: ripe fruit, sweet spices, creamy oak, scrubland. Palate: flavourful, fruity, toasty.

Zerrán Garnatxa Blanca 2014 B
100% garnacha blanca

88

Colour: straw. Nose: ripe fruit, floral. Palate: correct, easy to drink, good acidity.

BUIL & GINÉ
Ctra. de Gratallops - Vilella
Baixa, Km. 11,5
43737 Gratallops (Tarragona)
☎: +34 977 839 810
Fax: +34 977 839 811
info@builgine.com
www.builgine.com

Baboix 2013 B
garnacha blanca, macabeo, chardonnay

90

Colour: bright straw. Nose: white flowers, fine lees, dried herbs, ripe fruit, candied fruit, citrus fruit. Palate: flavourful, fruity, good acidity, elegant.

CASTELL D'OR
Mare Rafols, 3- 1ºD
08720 Vilafranca del Penedès
(Barcelona)
☎: +34 938 905 385
Fax: +34 938 905 446
castelldor@castelldor.com
www.castelldor.com

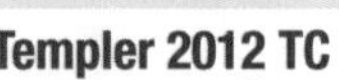

Templer 2012 TC
garnacha, tempranillo

83

CELLER CEDÓ ANGUERA
Ctra. La Serra d'Almos-Darmós, Km. 0,2
43746 La Serra d'Almos (Tarragona)
☎: +34 699 694 728
Fax: +34 977 417 369
celler@cedoanguera.com
www.cedoanguera.com

Anexe 2014 T
45% cariñena, 45% garnacha, 10% syrah

85

Anexe Syrah 2014 T
100% syrah

88

Colour: bright cherry. Nose: ripe fruit, sweet spices, creamy oak. Palate: flavourful, fruity, round tannins.

Anexe Vinyes Velles de Carinyena 2014 T
100% cariñena

90

Colour: cherry, purple rim. Nose: red berry notes, floral, balsamic herbs, dry stone. Palate: powerful, fresh, fruity, balanced.

Clònic 2010 TR
60% cariñena, 25% syrah, 15% cabernet sauvignon

88

Colour: cherry, garnet rim. Nose: roasted coffee, smoky, spicy, fruit liqueur notes. Palate: flavourful, smoky aftertaste.

Clònic Carinyena Vinyas Viejas 2013 T
100% cariñena

91

Colour: cherry, garnet rim. Nose: mineral, expressive, spicy, fruit expression. Palate: flavourful, ripe fruit, long, good acidity, balanced.

CELLER CORNUDELLA

Comte de Rius, 2
43360 Cornudella de Montsant
(Tarragona)
☎: +34 977 821 329
Fax: +34 977 821 329
info@cellercornudella.cat
www.cellercornudella.cat

Castell de Siurana Garnatxa del Montsant Dulce 2012 B
100% garnacha roja

90

Colour: coppery red. Nose: balsamic herbs, honeyed notes, floral, sweet spices. Palate: rich, fruity, powerful, flavourful, elegant.

Castell de Siurana Selecció de Costers 2011 T
70% garnacha, 30% cariñena

88

Colour: light cherry. Nose: fine reductive notes, aged wood nuances, toasty, fruit liqueur notes. Palate: spicy, toasty, flavourful.

Castella de Siurana Mistela 2012 B
100% garnacha

90

Colour: pale ruby, brick rim edge. Nose: powerfull, honeyed notes, candied fruit, acetaldehyde. Palate: flavourful, sweet, fruity, long.

El Codolar 2012 T
50% garnacha, 50% cariñena

88

Colour: cherry, purple rim. Nose: woody, roasted coffee, overripe fruit. Palate: flavourful, spicy, powerful.

Les Troies Blanc 2014 B
macabeo, garnacha roja

85

Les Troies Negre 2014 T
50% garnacha, 50% cariñena

88

Colour: cherry, purple rim. Nose: red berry notes, floral, balsamic herbs. Palate: powerful, fresh, fruity, easy to drink.

Les Troies Rosat 2014 RD
garnacha, cariñena

87

Colour: rose, purple rim. Nose: red berry notes, floral, expressive. Palate: powerful, fruity, fresh.

CELLER DE CAPÇANES

Llebaria, 4
43776 Capçanes (Tarragona)
☎: +34 977 178 319
cellercapcanes@cellercapcanes.com
www.cellercapcanes.com

2 Pájaros 2013 T
100% cariñena

93

Colour: cherry, garnet rim. Nose: mineral, expressive, spicy, ripe fruit, balanced. Palate: flavourful, ripe fruit, long, good acidity, balanced.

Cabrida 2012 T
100% garnacha

93

Colour: cherry, garnet rim. Nose: mineral, spicy. Palate: flavourful, ripe fruit, long, good acidity, balanced.

Costers del Gravet 2013 TC
cabernet sauvignon, garnacha, cariñena

89

Colour: deep cherry. Nose: creamy oak, toasty, ripe fruit, balsamic herbs. Palate: balanced, spicy, long.

Lasendal 2014 T Barrica
garnacha, syrah, merlot, tempranillo

88

Colour: bright cherry. Nose: ripe fruit, sweet spices, creamy oak. Palate: flavourful, fruity, round tannins.

Mas Collet 2014 T
cariñena, cabernet sauvignon, garnacha

86

Mas Donís 2014 T
garnacha, syrah, merlot, tempranillo

84

Mas Picosa 2014 T
garnacha, cabernet sauvignon, syrah

88 ♣

Colour: bright cherry. Nose: ripe fruit, sweet spices, creamy oak. Palate: flavourful, fruity, round tannins.

Mas Tortó 2013 T
70% garnacha, 10% syrah, 10% cabernet sauvignon, 10% merlot

88

Colour: deep cherry. Nose: creamy oak, toasty, ripe fruit, scrubland. Palate: balanced, spicy, long.

Pansal Dulce 2012 T
garnacha, cariñena

90

Colour: cherry, garnet rim. Nose: fruit preserve, spicy, warm, fruit liqueur notes. Palate: powerful, flavourful, sweet, rich.

Peraj Ha'Abib 2013 T
33% garnacha, 33% cariñena, 33% cabernet sauvignon

92

Colour: cherry, purple rim. Nose: ripe fruit, woody, roasted coffee. Palate: flavourful, spicy, powerful.

Vall del Calàs 2013 T
merlot, garnacha, tempranillo

88

Colour: cherry, garnet rim. Nose: ripe fruit, spicy, creamy oak, complex. Palate: flavourful, toasty.

CELLER DE L'ERA

Mas de las Moreras s/n
43360 Cornudella de Montsant
(Tarragona)
☎: +34 977 262 031
info@cellerdelera.com
www.cellerdelera.com

Bri del Celler de L'Era 2011 T
garnacha, cariñena, cabernet sauvignon

91

Colour: cherry, garnet rim. Nose: roasted coffee, smoky, spicy, ripe fruit. Palate: flavourful, smoky aftertaste.

Bri Rosat del Celler de L'Era 2014 RD
syrah, garnacha

86

MM 2010 T
garnacha, cariñena

89

Colour: very deep cherry, garnet rim. Nose: balsamic herbs, ripe fruit. Palate: full, flavourful, round tannins.

CELLER EL MASROIG

Passeig de L'Arbre, 3
43736 El Masroig (Tarragona)
☎: +34 977 825 026
Fax: +34 977 825 489
visites@cellermasroig.com
www.cellermasroig.com

Finca Cucó 2014 T
60% garnacha, 40% cariñena

89

Colour: bright cherry. Nose: ripe fruit, sweet spices, creamy oak. Palate: flavourful, fruity, toasty, round tannins.

Finca Cucó Blanc 2014 B
75% macabeo, 25% garnacha blanca

88

Colour: bright yellow. Nose: dried herbs, ripe fruit, spicy. Palate: flavourful, fruity, good acidity, balanced.

Finca Cucó Selecció 2013 T
70% cariñena, 30% garnacha

87

Colour: cherry, purple rim. Nose: ripe fruit, woody, roasted coffee. Palate: flavourful, spicy, powerful.

Les Sorts 2014 BFB
100% garnacha blanca

90

Colour: bright yellow. Nose: ripe fruit, powerfull, toasty, aged wood nuances, pattiserie. Palate: flavourful, fruity, spicy, toasty, long.

Les Sorts 2014 T Maceración Carbónica
garnacha, cariñena, syrah

89

Colour: cherry, purple rim. Nose: expressive, fresh fruit, red berry notes, floral. Palate: flavourful, fruity, good acidity.

Les Sorts Rosat 2014 RD
90% garnacha, 10% cariñena

89

Colour: coppery red. Nose: red berry notes, floral, fragrant herbs. Palate: flavourful, good acidity, long, spicy.

Les Sorts Sycar 2012 T
60% cariñena, 40% syrah

92

Colour: bright cherry. Nose: sweet spices, creamy oak, overripe fruit. Palate: flavourful, fruity, toasty, round tannins.

Les Sorts Vinyes Velles 2011 TC
85% cariñena, 15% garnacha

92

Colour: cherry, garnet rim. Nose: smoky, spicy, ripe fruit. Palate: flavourful, smoky aftertaste, ripe fruit.

Pinyeres Blanc 2014 B
100% garnacha blanca

88

Colour: bright straw. Nose: dried herbs, faded flowers, ripe fruit. Palate: ripe fruit, fine bitter notes.

Pinyeres Negre 2012 T
50% garnacha, 40% cariñena, 10% cabernet sauvignon

88

Colour: bright cherry. Nose: ripe fruit, sweet spices, creamy oak. Palate: flavourful, fruity, toasty, round tannins.

Solà Fred 2014 B
75% macabeo, 25% garnacha blanca

85

Solà Fred 2014 T
100% cariñena

88

Colour: cherry, purple rim. Nose: red berry notes, floral, ripe fruit. Palate: flavourful, fruity, good acidity.

Sola Fred Rosat 2014 RD
90% garnacha, 10% syrah

85

CELLER LAURONA
Ctra. Bellmunt s/n Sort
dels Capellans, 21
43730 Falset (Tarragona)
☎: +34 977 831 712
Fax: +34 977 831 797
laurona@cellerlaurona.com
www.cellerlaurona.com

Blanc de Laurona Blanc de Noir 2014 B
garnacha, macabeo

88

Colour: bright yellow. Nose: dried herbs, ripe fruit, spicy. Palate: flavourful, fruity, good acidity.

Laurona 2010 T
garnacha, cariñena, merlot, syrah, cabernet sauvignon

92

Colour: cherry, garnet rim. Nose: complex, spicy, fine reductive notes, overripe fruit. Palate: good structure, flavourful, round tannins.

CELLER LOS TROVADORES
Calle Amparo 11, bajo A
28224 Pozuelo de Alarcón (Madrid)
☎: +34 652 363 974
info@lostrovadores.com
www.lostrovadores.com

Karma de Drac 2013 T
garnacha, cariñena

88

Colour: light cherry. Nose: fruit liqueur notes, fragrant herbs, spicy, creamy oak. Palate: balanced, spicy, long, toasty.

CELLER MALONDRO
Miranda, 27
43360 Cornudella del Montsant
(Tarragona)
☎: +34 932 743 872
comercial@malondro.es
www.malondro.es

Besllum 2012 TC
50% garnacha, 40% cariñena, 10% syrah

86

Latria 2012 T
50% garnacha, 50% cariñena

88

Colour: bright cherry. Nose: ripe fruit, sweet spices, creamy oak, expressive. Palate: flavourful, fruity, toasty.

Malondro Blanc 2014 B
70% macabeo, 30% garnacha roja

90

Colour: bright straw. Nose: white flowers, fresh fruit, fragrant herbs, mineral. Palate: flavourful, fruity, good acidity, balanced.

Xabec 2012 TC
50% garnacha, 45% cariñena, 5% syrah

87

Colour: bright cherry. Nose: sweet spices, creamy oak, fruit preserve. Palate: flavourful, fruity, easy to drink.

CELLER MAS DE LES VINYES
Mas de les Vinyes, s/n
43373 Cabacés (Tarragona)
☎: +34 652 568 848
Fax: +34 977 719 690
josep@masdelesvinyes.com
www.masdelesvinyes.com

Mas de les Vinyes Blanc 2014 B
100% macabeo

84

CELLER PASCONA
Camí dels Fontals, s/n
43730 Falset (Tarragona)
☎: +34 609 291 770
info@pascona.com
www.pascona.com

La Mare de Pascona 2013 T
100% garnacha

91

Colour: cherry, garnet rim. Nose: mineral, expressive, spicy, wild herbs. Palate: flavourful, ripe fruit, long, good acidity, balanced.

Lo Pare de Pascona 2013 T
garnacha, cabernet sauvignon

93

Colour: deep cherry, purple rim. Nose: creamy oak, toasty, ripe fruit, balsamic herbs, earthy notes. Palate: spicy, long, balanced.

Lo Petitó de Pascona 2014 T
syrah, merlot

89

Colour: bright cherry. Nose: ripe fruit, sweet spices, expressive. Palate: flavourful, fruity, round tannins.

Maria Ganxa 2014 T
cariñena, garnacha

89

Colour: cherry, purple rim. Nose: fresh fruit, red berry notes, floral. Palate: flavourful, fruity, good acidity.

Trencaclosques de Pascona 2014 RD
syrah

87

Colour: coppery red. Nose: elegant, red berry notes, floral, fragrant herbs. Palate: light-bodied, flavourful, good acidity, long, spicy.

CELLER RONADELLES

Finca La Plana, s/n
43360 Cornudella del Montsant (Tarragona)
☎: +34 686 175 478
Fax: +34 977 274 913
eva.prim@ronadelles.com
www.ronadelles.com

Cap de Ruc 2010 TC
garnacha, cariñena

87

Colour: cherry, garnet rim. Nose: ripe fruit, spicy, creamy oak, complex. Palate: flavourful, toasty.

Cap de Ruc Blanc B

90

Colour: light mahogany. Nose: honeyed notes, candied fruit, fragrant herbs, acetaldehyde. Palate: flavourful, sweet, good acidity, long.

Cap de Ruc Garnacha 2014 T
garnacha

85

Giral Vinyes Velles 2007 TC
garnacha, cariñena

88

Colour: cherry, garnet rim. Nose: ripe fruit, spicy, creamy oak. Palate: flavourful, toasty, round tannins.

Jaume Giral Vinyes Velles 2007 T
garnacha, cariñena

90

Colour: light cherry. Nose: aged wood nuances, toasty, fine reductive notes, fruit liqueur notes. Palate: spicy, toasty, flavourful.

Petit Blanc 2011 B

88

Colour: bright yellow. Nose: expressive, dried herbs, ripe fruit, spicy. Palate: flavourful, good acidity.

CELLER SERRA MAJOR

Alfons El Cast, s/n
43363 Ulldemolins (Tarragona)
☎: +34 647 986 960
santi@sarroges.com

Sarroges 2011 T
garnacha, cabernet sauvignon, syrah, merlot

87

Colour: cherry, garnet rim. Nose: overripe fruit, fruit preserve, grassy. Palate: powerful, flavourful, concentrated.

Teix 2011 T
garnacha, cabernet sauvignon, syrah, merlot

84

Teix 2012 T
garnacha, cabernet sauvignon, syrah, merlot

84

CELLER VENDRELL RIVED

Bassa, 10
43775 Marçà (Tarragona)
☎: +34 637 537 383
celler@vendrellrived.com
www.vendrellrived.com

L'Alleu 2013 TC
garnacha, cariñena

90 ♣

Colour: cherry, garnet rim. Nose: creamy oak, red berry notes, fresh fruit. Palate: flavourful, spicy, elegant.

Miloca Cariñena 2014 T
cariñena

88 ♣

Colour: cherry, purple rim. Nose: red berry notes, floral, balsamic herbs. Palate: powerful, fresh, fruity.

Miloca Garnacha 2014 T
garnacha

89 ♣

Colour: cherry, purple rim. Nose: expressive, fresh fruit, red berry notes, floral. Palate: flavourful, fruity, good acidity.

Serè 2014 T
garnacha, cariñena

88

Colour: cherry, purple rim. Nose: ripe fruit, spicy, warm. Palate: powerful, fruity.

CELLER VERMUNVER

De Dalt, 29
43775 Marçà (Tarragona)
☎: +34 977 178 288
Fax: +34 977 178 288
info@genesi.cat
www.genesi.cat

Gènesi Varietal Vinyes Velles de Carinyena 2012 T
100% cariñena

92

Colour: very deep cherry. Nose: overripe fruit, warm, powerfull, toasty. Palate: flavourful, powerful.

Gènesi Varietal Vinyes Velles de Garnatxa 2012 T
100% garnacha

90

Colour: cherry, garnet rim. Nose: roasted coffee, smoky, spicy, ripe fruit. Palate: flavourful, smoky aftertaste, ripe fruit.

CELLERS BARONÍA DEL MONTSANT S.L.

Comte de Rius, 1
43360 Cornudella de Montsant (Tarragona)
☎: +34 977 821 483
englora@baronia-m.com
www.baronia-m.com

Cims del Montsant 2012 T
26% garnacha, 74% cariñena

89

Colour: bright cherry. Nose: ripe fruit, sweet spices, creamy oak. Palate: flavourful, fruity, toasty, round tannins.

Clos D'Englora AV 14 2010 T
37% garnacha, 7% garnacha peluda, 28% cariñena, merlot, 12% cabernet sauvignon, 5% syrah

92

Colour: light cherry. Nose: fine reductive notes, aged wood nuances, toasty. Palate: spicy, toasty, flavourful.

Com Gat i Gos 2012 TC
50% garnacha, 20% garnacha peluda, 30% cariñena

88

Colour: bright cherry. Nose: ripe fruit, sweet spices, creamy oak. Palate: flavourful, fruity, toasty.

Englora 2011 TC
51% garnacha, 21% cariñena, 7% syrah, 12% merlot, 9% cabernet sauvignon

92

Colour: bright cherry. Nose: ripe fruit, sweet spices, creamy oak. Palate: flavourful, fruity, round tannins.

Englora Rosé 2014 RD
100% merlot

85

Flor D'Englora Garnatxa 2014 T
100% garnacha

89

Colour: cherry, purple rim. Nose: red berry notes, floral, balsamic herbs. Palate: powerful, fresh, fruity.

Flor D'Englora Roure 2012 T
58% garnacha, 37% cariñena, 5% garnacha peluda

89

Colour: cherry, garnet rim. Nose: creamy oak, ripe fruit. Palate: flavourful, spicy, elegant.

CELLERS CAN BLAU

Ctra. Bellmunt, s/n
43730 Falset (Tarragona)
☎: +34 629 261 379
Fax: +34 968 716 051
info@orowines.com
www.orowines.com

Blau 2013 T
50% cariñena, 25% syrah, 25% garnacha

89

Colour: cherry, garnet rim. Nose: ripe fruit, toasty. Palate: powerful, toasty.

Can Blau 2013 T
40% mazuelo, syrah, 20% garnacha

93

Colour: bright cherry. Nose: ripe fruit, sweet spices, creamy oak, earthy notes. Palate: flavourful, fruity, toasty, round tannins.

Mas de Can Blau 2011 T
35% mazuelo, 35% syrah, 30% garnacha

92

Colour: cherry, garnet rim. Nose: roasted coffee, smoky, spicy, overripe fruit. Palate: flavourful, smoky aftertaste, ripe fruit.

Mas de Can Blau 2012 T
35% mazuelo, 35% syrah, 30% garnacha

93

Colour: cherry, garnet rim. Nose: roasted coffee, smoky, spicy, ripe fruit. Palate: flavourful, smoky aftertaste, ripe fruit.

CELLERS CAPAFONS OSSÓ

Finca Masía Esplanes s/n
43730 Falset (Tarragona)
☎: +34 977 831 201
cellers@capafons-osso.com
www.capafons-osso.cat

Masia Esplanes 2006 T

cabernet sauvignon, merlot, syrah, garnacha, cariñena

88

Colour: light cherry. Nose: fine reductive notes, aged wood nuances, toasty, fruit liqueur notes. Palate: spicy, toasty, flavourful.

Pedris Magnum 2007 T

cariñena, syrah

90

Colour: ruby red. Nose: spicy, fine reductive notes, wet leather, aged wood nuances, fruit liqueur notes. Palate: spicy, fine tannins, balanced.

Roigenc 2013 RD Fermentado en Barrica

syrah, cabernet sauvignon

80

Vessants 2009 T

cabernet sauvignon, merlot

80

CELLERS SANT RAFEL

Ctra. La Torre, Km. 1,7
43774 Pradell de la Teixeta (Tarragona)
☎: +34 689 792 305
xavi@cellerssantrafel.com
www.cellerssantrafel.com

Joana 2014 T

70% garnacha, 30% merlot

89

Colour: cherry, purple rim. Nose: powerfull, ripe fruit, spicy, balsamic herbs. Palate: powerful, fruity, unctuous.

Joana Seleccio 2010 T

80% garnacha, 10% merlot, 10% cabernet sauvignon

88

Colour: light cherry. Nose: fine reductive notes, aged wood nuances, toasty, fruit liqueur notes. Palate: spicy, toasty, flavourful.

Solpost 2008 TC

50% garnacha, 35% cariñena, 15% cabernet sauvignon

88

Colour: light cherry. Nose: spicy, fine reductive notes, tobacco, fruit liqueur notes. Palate: spicy, elegant, long.

Solpost 2014 B

garnacha blanca

91

Colour: bright yellow. Nose: expressive, dried herbs, ripe fruit, honeyed notes. Palate: flavourful, fruity, good acidity.

Solpost Fresc 2010 TC

80% garnacha, 10% merlot, 10% cabernet sauvignon

88

Colour: bright cherry. Nose: ripe fruit, sweet spices, creamy oak. Palate: flavourful, toasty, round tannins.

Solpost Negre 2014 T

70% garnacha, 30% merlot

90

Colour: deep cherry. Nose: creamy oak, toasty, ripe fruit, balsamic herbs. Palate: balanced, spicy, long.

CELLERS TERRA I VINS

Av. Falset, 17 Bajos
43206 Reus (Tarragona)
☎: +34 633 289 267
cterraivins@gmail.com

Clos del Gos 2013 T

45% garnacha, 45% samsó, 10% syrah

87

Colour: cherry, purple rim. Nose: woody, roasted coffee. Palate: flavourful, spicy, powerful.

CELLERS UNIÓ

43206 Reus (Tarragona)
☎: +34 977 330 055
Fax: +34 977 330 070
info@cellersunio.com
www.cellersunio.com

Cor del País 2014 T

garnacha, mazuelo, tempranillo

84

Dairo 2012 TC

garnacha, mazuelo, syrah

87

Colour: cherry, garnet rim. Nose: ripe fruit, spicy, creamy oak. Palate: flavourful, toasty, round tannins.

Mas dels Mets 2014 T

merlot, garnacha, tempranillo, mazuelo

88

Colour: cherry, purple rim. Nose: powerfull, ripe fruit, spicy. Palate: powerful, fruity, unctuous.

Perlat 2013 T
garnacha, mazuelo, syrah

87

Colour: cherry, garnet rim. Nose: ripe fruit, toasty, short. Palate: powerful, toasty.

Perlat Garnatxa 2013 T
garnacha

87

Colour: cherry, garnet rim. Nose: smoky, spicy, ripe fruit. Palate: flavourful, smoky aftertaste, ripe fruit.

Roca Blanca 2012 TC
garnacha, mazuelo, syrah

88

Colour: cherry, garnet rim. Nose: ripe fruit, spicy, creamy oak, fine reductive notes. Palate: flavourful, toasty.

Roca Blanca 2014 T
merlot, garnacha, mazuelo

86

CHARMIANWINES

M. Barceló
43730 Falset (Tarragona)
☎: +34 977 661 862
j.murillo@cataloniacava.net
www.cataloniacava.net

Charmian 2013 T
40% garnacha, 30% cariñena, 10% syrah, 10% merlot, 10% tempranillo

88

Colour: cherry, purple rim. Nose: woody, roasted coffee. Palate: flavourful, spicy, powerful.

Charmian Garnachas Viñas Viejas 2008 T
85% garnacha, 15% cabernet sauvignon

88

Colour: pale ruby, brick rim edge. Nose: spicy, fine reductive notes, wet leather, aged wood nuances. Palate: spicy, fine tannins, balanced.

Charmian Garnatxa Blanca 2012 B
garnacha blanca

90

Colour: bright yellow. Nose: ripe fruit, powerfull, toasty, petrol notes, dry stone. Palate: flavourful, fruity, spicy, toasty, long.

Charmian Negre 2011 TC
60% garnacha, 30% cariñena, 10% syrah

86

CINGLES BLAUS

Mas de les Moreres – Afores Cornudella
43360 Cornudella de Montsant (Tarragona)
☎: +34 977 310 882
Fax: +34 977 323 928
info@cinglesblaus.com
www.cinglesblaus.com

Cingles Blaus Mas de les Moreres 2010 T
garnacha, cariñena, cabernet sauvignon, merlot

87

Colour: cherry, garnet rim. Nose: ripe fruit, earthy notes, spicy, fine reductive notes. Palate: flavourful, balsamic, spicy.

Cingles Blaus Octubre 2013 T
garnacha, cariñena

90

Colour: cherry, garnet rim. Nose: creamy oak, red berry notes, ripe fruit, floral. Palate: flavourful, spicy.

Cingles Blaus Octubre 2014 B
garnacha blanca, macabeo, chardonnay

90

Colour: bright straw. Nose: white flowers, fine lees, dried herbs, mineral. Palate: flavourful, fruity, good acidity, round.

Cingles Blaus Octubre 2014 RD
garnacha

88

Colour: rose, purple rim. Nose: red berry notes, floral, expressive. Palate: powerful, fruity, fresh, easy to drink.

Cingles Blaus Selecció 2009 T
garnacha, cariñena

91

Colour: pale ruby, brick rim edge. Nose: elegant, spicy, fine reductive notes, tobacco, ripe fruit. Palate: spicy, fine tannins, elegant, long.

CLOS MESORAH

Finca "Clos Mesorah" Ctra. T-300
Falset Marça, Km. 0,97
43775 Marça (Tarragona)
☎: +34 935 343 026
victor@elviwines.com
www.elviwines.com

Clos Mesorah 2013 TR
40% cariñena, 40% garnacha, 20% syrah

91

Colour: deep cherry, garnet rim. Nose: balanced, powerfull, ripe fruit, cocoa bean, sweet spices. Palate: flavourful, round tannins, fruity, good structure.

COCA I FITÓ

Avda. Onze de Setembre s/n
43736 El Masroig (Tarragona)
☎: +34 619 776 948
Fax: +34 935 457 092
info@cocaifito.cat
www.cocaifito.cat

Coca i Fitó Dolç Dulce Natural T
50% garnacha, 50% cariñena

91

Colour: bright cherry, garnet rim. Nose: acetaldehyde, varnish, candied fruit, fruit preserve. Palate: fruity, flavourful, sweet.

Coca i Fitó Negre 2010 T
50% syrah, 30% garnacha, 20% cariñena

90

Colour: light cherry. Nose: fine reductive notes, aged wood nuances, toasty, fruit liqueur notes. Palate: spicy, toasty, flavourful.

Jaspi Maragda 2011 T
55% garnacha, 25% cariñena, 20% syrah

90

Colour: very deep cherry, garnet rim. Nose: expressive, complex, mineral, balsamic herbs, balanced. Palate: full, flavourful, round tannins.

Jaspi Negre 2012 T
45% garnacha, 25% cariñena, 15% cabernet sauvignon, 15% syrah

89

Colour: bright cherry. Nose: ripe fruit, sweet spices, creamy oak, earthy notes. Palate: flavourful, fruity, toasty, round tannins.

COFAMA VINS I CAVES

Casanovas i Bosch 57
08202 Sabadell (Barcelona)
☎: +34 937 220 338
Fax: +34 937 252 385
roger.manyosa@cofamaexport.com
www.cofamaexport.com

Clos de Nit 2012 T
40% garnacha, 40% cariñena, 20% syrah

85

Clos de Nit 2014 T
40% garnacha, 25% cariñena, 20% merlot, 10% tempranillo, 5% cabernet sauvignon

85

COOPERATIVA FALSET MARÇA

Miquel Barceló, 31
43730 Falset (Tarragona)
☎: +34 977 830 105
info@etim.cat
www.la-cooperativa.cat

Ètim 2014 B
garnacha blanca

86

Ètim Negre 2013 T
garnacha, cariñena, syrah

89

Colour: deep cherry, purple rim. Nose: creamy oak, toasty, ripe fruit, balsamic herbs. Palate: balanced, spicy, long.

Ètim Old Vines Grenache 2010 T
garnacha

90

Colour: cherry, garnet rim. Nose: red berry notes, ripe fruit, spicy, creamy oak, complex. Palate: flavourful, toasty, round tannins.

Ètim Rosat 2014 RD
garnacha, syrah

84

Ètim Verema Tardana Blanc Dulce 2014 B
garnacha blanca

88

Colour: bright straw. Nose: balsamic herbs, honeyed notes, floral, sweet spices. Palate: rich, fruity, powerful, flavourful, easy to drink.

Ètim Verema Tardana Negre Dulce 2013 T
garnacha

90

Colour: cherry, garnet rim. Nose: fruit preserve, spicy, warm, fruit liqueur notes. Palate: powerful, flavourful, sweet, rich.

La Dama de Blanc 2013 BFB
garnacha blanca

89

Colour: bright yellow. Nose: ripe fruit, powerfull, toasty, aged wood nuances, pattiserie. Palate: flavourful, fruity, spicy, toasty, long.

Lo Foc del Castell 2011 T
garnacha, cariñena, syrah, cabernet sauvignon

90

Colour: cherry, garnet rim. Nose: roasted coffee, smoky, spicy, overripe fruit. Palate: flavourful, smoky aftertaste.

Lo Senyor del Castell 2013 T
garnacha, cariñena, syrah

90

Colour: cherry, garnet rim. Nose: red berry notes, ripe fruit, spicy, creamy oak, complex. Palate: flavourful, toasty, round tannins.

DIT CELLER

Avda. 11 de Setembre, s/n
43736 El Masroig (Tarragona)
☎: +34 636 406 939
dani@azulygaranza.com
www.ditceller.com

Cabirol 2013 T
garnacha, syrah

88 ♣

Colour: bright cherry. Nose: ripe fruit, sweet spices, creamy oak. Palate: flavourful, fruity, toasty, round tannins.

Selenita 2011 T
garnacha, syrah

87 ♣

Colour: cherry, garnet rim. Nose: roasted coffee, smoky, spicy. Palate: flavourful, smoky aftertaste.

Selenita 2014 RD
garnacha, syrah

87 ♣

Colour: coppery red. Nose: red berry notes, floral, expressive. Palate: powerful, fruity, fresh.

Selenita Nit 2010 T
garnacha, samsó

90 ♣

Colour: cherry, garnet rim. Nose: mineral, expressive, spicy. Palate: flavourful, ripe fruit, long, good acidity, balanced.

EDICIONES I-LIMITADAS

43730 Falset (Tarragona)
☎: +34 932 531 760
Fax: +34 934 173 591
info@edicionesi-limitadas.com
www.edicionesi-limitadas.com

Faunus 2013 T
syrah, tempranillo, cariñena

90

Colour: very deep cherry, purple rim. Nose: balsamic herbs, ripe fruit, dry stone, complex. Palate: fruity, spicy, long.

Luno 2013 T
garnacha, cariñena, syrah, cabernet sauvignon

90

Colour: cherry, purple rim. Nose: ripe fruit, spicy, dried herbs. Palate: fruity, unctuous, balanced, easy to drink.

Núvol Blanc 2014 B
garnacha blanca, macabeo

90

Colour: bright straw. Nose: white flowers, fragrant herbs, ripe fruit. Palate: flavourful, fruity, good acidity, balanced.

Terrícola 2013 T
garnacha, cariñena, syrah

91

Colour: deep cherry. Nose: creamy oak, toasty, ripe fruit, balsamic herbs. Palate: balanced, spicy, long.

ESPECTACLE VINS

Crat. Bellmunt – sort dels Capellans
43730 Falset (Tarragona)
☎: +34 977 839 171
Fax: +34 977 839 326
closmogador@closmogador.com
www.espectaclevins.com

Espectacle 2012 TR
100% garnacha

94

Colour: deep cherry, purple rim. Nose: creamy oak, toasty, balsamic herbs, ripe fruit, earthy notes, mineral. Palate: balanced, spicy, long.

ESTONES VINS

Pl. Sort dels Capellans, Nau Bahaus
43730 Falset (Tarragona)
☎: +34 666 415 735
vins@massersal.com
www.estones.cat

Estones 2012 T
garnacha, samsó

88

Colour: bright cherry. Nose: sweet spices, creamy oak. Palate: flavourful, fruity, toasty, round tannins.

Estones de Mishima "Set Tota la Vida" 2013 T
garnacha, syrah, samsó

90

Colour: cherry, garnet rim. Nose: creamy oak, red berry notes, balanced. Palate: flavourful, spicy, elegant.

Petites Estones Negre 2013 T
garnacha, samsó

87

Colour: cherry, purple rim. Nose: woody, roasted coffee. Palate: flavourful, spicy, powerful.

FRANCK MASSARD

Rambla Arnau de Vilanova, 6
08800 Vilanova i La Geltrú (Barcelona)
☎: +34 938 956 541
Fax: +34 938 956 541
info@epicure-wines.com
www.epicure-wines.com

El Brindis 2013 T
70% cariñena, 30% garnacha

89

Colour: deep cherry. Nose: powerfull, earthy notes, toasty, fruit liqueur notes. Palate: powerful, warm.

Romero 2012 T
100% cariñena

90

Colour: deep cherry, purple rim. Nose: creamy oak, toasty, ripe fruit, balsamic herbs. Palate: balanced, spicy, long.

JOSEP GRAU VITICULTOR

Polígono 7 Parcela 27
43775 Marça (Tarragona)
☎: +34 977 054 071
celler@josepgrauviticultor.com
www.josepgrauviticultor.com

Dosterras 2013 T
100% garnacha, garnacha peluda

92

Colour: cherry, garnet rim. Nose: red berry notes, ripe fruit, fragrant herbs, spicy, toasty, creamy oak, mineral. Palate: powerful, flavourful, balsamic, balanced.

L'Efecte Volador 2014 T
50% syrah, 30% garnacha, 20% samsó

88

Colour: cherry, purple rim. Nose: powerfull, ripe fruit, spicy. Palate: powerful, fruity, unctuous.

Regina 2014 RD
90% garnacha, 10% garnacha blanca

90

Colour: rose, purple rim. Nose: floral, wild herbs, fruit expression, creamy oak. Palate: flavourful, complex, balanced.

Vespres 2014 T
90% garnacha, 10% samsó

90

Colour: deep cherry, purple rim. Nose: creamy oak, toasty, balsamic herbs. Palate: balanced, spicy, long.

Vespres Blanc 2014 B
90% garnacha blanca, 10% otras

88

Colour: bright straw. Nose: white flowers, fragrant herbs. Palate: flavourful, fruity, good acidity, balanced.

MALELLA, S.C.P.

Carrasclet, 8
43776 Capçanes (Tarragona)
☎: +34 678 416 812
malellaceller@gmail.com
www.malella.cat

Malella 2013 T
85% garnacha, 15% syrah

90

Colour: deep cherry, purple rim. Nose: creamy oak, toasty, ripe fruit, balsamic herbs. Palate: balanced, spicy, long.

MAS DE L'ABUNDÀNCIA VITICULTORS

Camí de Gratallops, s/n
43736 El Masroig (Tarragona)
☎: +34 627 471 444
info@masdelabundancia.com
www.masdelabundancia.com

Flvminis 2014 T

85

Hema 2013 T

85

NOGUERALS

Tou, 5
43360 Cornudella de Montsant (Tarragona)
☎: +34 650 033 546
cellernoguerals@gmail.com
www.noguerals.com

Corbatera 2011 T
garnacha, cabernet sauvignon, macabeo

90

Colour: deep cherry. Nose: creamy oak, toasty, ripe fruit, balsamic herbs. Palate: balanced, spicy, long.

ORIGAMI WINES

El Masroig
El Masroig (Tarragona)
☎: +34 902 800 229
Fax: +34 931 980 182
info@origamiwines.com
www.origamiwines.com

Mysti Garnatxa 2014 T
garnacha

85

Mysti Syrah 2013 T Roble
syrah

87

Colour: bright cherry. Nose: ripe fruit, sweet spices, creamy oak. Palate: flavourful, fruity, toasty, round tannins.

ORTO VINS

Les Afores, s/n
43736 El Molar (Tarragona)
☎: +34 629 171 246
info@ortovins.com

Blanc D'Orto 2014 B
100% garnacha blanca

89

Colour: bright yellow. Nose: dried herbs, spicy, candied fruit. Palate: flavourful, fruity, good acidity.

Blanc D'Orto Brisat 2013 B
100% garnacha blanca

92

Colour: bright yellow. Nose: expressive, dried herbs, spicy, candied fruit. Palate: flavourful, fruity, good acidity.

Dolç D'Orto 2014 B
80% garnacha, 20% otras

92

Colour: golden. Nose: powerfull, honeyed notes, candied fruit, fragrant herbs, acetaldehyde. Palate: flavourful, sweet, fresh, fruity, good acidity, long.

La Carrerada 2013 T
100% samsó

92

Colour: cherry, garnet rim. Nose: balanced, complex, ripe fruit, spicy, balsamic herbs, mineral. Palate: good structure, flavourful, balanced.

Les Argiles D'Orto Vins 2013 B
93% macabeo, 7% garnacha blanca

90

Colour: bright golden. Nose: white flowers, dried herbs, ripe fruit, spicy, complex. Palate: flavourful, fruity, good acidity.

Les Comes D'Orto 2013 T
50% garnacha, 45% samsó, 5% ull de llebre

91

Colour: deep cherry, purple rim. Nose: creamy oak, toasty, ripe fruit, balsamic herbs. Palate: balanced, spicy.

Les Pujoles 2013 T
100% ull de llebre

90

Colour: cherry, garnet rim. Nose: overripe fruit, fruit preserve, scrubland. Palate: powerful, flavourful, concentrated.

Les Tallades de Cal Nicolau 2013 TC
picapoll negro

93

Colour: cherry, garnet rim. Nose: mineral, expressive, spicy. Palate: flavourful, ripe fruit, long, good acidity.

Orto 2013 T
55% samsó, 29% garnacha, 10% ull de llebre, 6% cabernet sauvignon

90

Colour: cherry, purple rim. Nose: powerfull, ripe fruit, spicy, mineral. Palate: powerful, fruity, unctuous, easy to drink.

Palell 2013 TC
100% garnacha peluda

93

Colour: cherry, garnet rim. Nose: expressive, spicy, mineral. Palate: flavourful, ripe fruit, long, good acidity, balanced.

PORTAL DEL MONTSANT

Carrer de Dalt, 74
43775 Marça (Tarragona)
☎: +34 933 950 811
Fax: +34 933 955 500
tsoler@parxet.es
www.portaldelmontsant.com

Bruberry 2013 T
cariñena, garnacha

88

Colour: bright cherry. Nose: ripe fruit, sweet spices, creamy oak. Palate: flavourful, fruity, toasty.

Bruberry 2014 B
garnacha blanca, macabeo

90

Colour: bright straw. Nose: white flowers, fresh fruit, fragrant herbs. Palate: flavourful, fruity, good acidity.

Brunus 2012 T
cariñena, garnacha

92

Colour: cherry, garnet rim. Nose: creamy oak, balanced, ripe fruit. Palate: flavourful, spicy.

Brunus Rosé 2014 RD
100% garnacha

88

Colour: rose, purple rim. Nose: red berry notes, floral, expressive. Palate: powerful, fruity, fresh.

Santbru 2010 TC
cariñena, garnacha

92

Colour: cherry, garnet rim. Nose: smoky, spicy, ripe fruit. Palate: flavourful, smoky aftertaste, ripe fruit.

Santbru Blanc 2012 B
garnacha blanca, garnacha gris

92

Colour: bright yellow. Nose: ripe fruit, powerfull, toasty, balsamic herbs, petrol notes. Palate: flavourful, fruity, spicy, toasty, long.

SERRA & BARCELÓ
Sant Lluis, 12
43777 Els Guiamets (Tarragona)
☎: +34 649 670 430
josep@serra-barcelo.com
www.serra-barcelo.com

Octonia 2010 T
50% garnacha, 35% garnacha peluda, 15% mazuelo

93

Colour: cherry, garnet rim. Nose: ripe fruit, spicy, creamy oak, complex. Palate: flavourful, toasty.

SILEO
La Sort dels Capellans, 15
43730 Falset (Tarragona)
☎: +34 935 165 043
info@atroca.eu
www.atroca.eu

Sileo 2014 T
80% garnacha, 20% cariñena

88

Colour: cherry, purple rim. Nose: ripe fruit, woody, roasted coffee. Palate: flavourful, spicy, powerful.

TERRA PERSONAS
Apartado 96
43730 Falset (Tarragona)
☎: +34 662 214 291
ruud@terrapersonas.com
www.terrapersonas.com

Terra Blanca 2014 B
88

Colour: bright yellow. Nose: expressive, dried herbs, ripe fruit. Palate: flavourful, fruity, good acidity, balanced.

Terra Negra 2010 T
88

Colour: deep cherry. Nose: powerfull, fruit liqueur notes, aromatic coffee. Palate: flavourful, powerful, spicy.

Terra Vermella 2013 T
88

Colour: bright cherry. Nose: sweet spices, creamy oak. Palate: flavourful, fruity, toasty, round tannins.

VENUS LA UNIVERSAL
Ctra. Porrera, s/n
43730 Falset (Tarragona)
☎: +34 699 435 154
info@venuslauniversal.com
www.venuslauniversal.com

Dido 2013 T
garnacha, syrah, cabernet sauvignon, merlot

93

Colour: bright cherry. Nose: ripe fruit, sweet spices, creamy oak, balsamic herbs. Palate: flavourful, fruity, round tannins.

Dido Blanc 2013 B
macabeo, garnacha blanca, xarel.lo

92

Colour: bright yellow. Nose: expressive, dried herbs, ripe fruit, earthy notes. Palate: flavourful, good acidity, balanced.

Dido Rosat 2013 RD
garnacha, syrah, macabeo

88

Colour: onion pink. Nose: elegant, red berry notes, floral, fragrant herbs, mineral. Palate: light-bodied, flavourful, good acidity, long, spicy.

Venus 2009 T
cariñena, syrah, garnacha

93

Colour: cherry, garnet rim. Nose: balanced, complex, ripe fruit, spicy, earthy notes. Palate: good structure, flavourful, round tannins, balanced.

VINS NUS
43730 Falset (Tarragona)
☎: +34 932 531 760
Fax: +34 934 173 591
info@vinsnus.com
www.vinsnus.com

Siuralta Antic 2012 T
cariñena

93

Colour: cherry, garnet rim. Nose: ripe fruit, wild herbs, earthy notes, spicy, balsamic herbs. Palate: balanced, flavourful, long, balsamic.

Siuralta Antic 2013 T
cariñena

92

Colour: deep cherry, purple rim. Nose: ripe fruit, balsamic herbs, red berry notes, grassy. Palate: balanced, spicy, long.

Siuralta Gris 2013 B
garnacha gris

90 ♣

Colour: bright straw. Nose: white flowers, fresh fruit, fragrant herbs, citrus fruit. Palate: flavourful, fruity, good acidity.

Siuralta Rouge 2014 T
garnacha

89 ♣

Colour: light cherry. Nose: fruit expression, scrubland, dry stone, expressive. Palate: fresh, balsamic, good acidity, fine bitter notes.

VINYES DOMÈNECH

Camí del Collet, km. 3,8
43776 Capçanes (Tarragona)
☎: +34 670 297 395
jidomenech@vinyesdomenech.com
www.vinyesdomenech.com

Bancal del Bosc 2013 T
60% garnacha, 20% cariñena, 20% syrah

89

Colour: bright cherry. Nose: ripe fruit, sweet spices, creamy oak. Palate: flavourful, fruity, round tannins.

Bancal del Bosc Blanc 2014 B
100% garnacha blanca

90

Colour: bright yellow. Nose: dried herbs, ripe fruit, spicy. Palate: flavourful, fruity, good acidity.

Furvus 2011 T
90% garnacha, 10% merlot

93

Colour: cherry, garnet rim. Nose: mineral, expressive, spicy, balsamic herbs, ripe fruit. Palate: flavourful, ripe fruit, long, good acidity, balanced.

Furvus 2012 T
90% garnacha, 10% merlot

92

Colour: deep cherry. Nose: creamy oak, toasty, ripe fruit, balsamic herbs. Palate: balanced, spicy, long.

Rita 2014 B
100% garnacha blanca

90

Colour: bright yellow. Nose: powerfull, toasty, aged wood nuances, pattiserie. Palate: flavourful, fruity, spicy, toasty, long.

Teixar 2011 T
100% garnacha peluda

94

Colour: cherry, garnet rim. Nose: mineral, expressive, spicy, ripe fruit, overripe fruit. Palate: flavourful, ripe fruit, long, good acidity, balanced.

Teixar 2012 T
100% garnacha peluda

93

Colour: cherry, garnet rim. Nose: balanced, complex, ripe fruit, spicy, mineral. Palate: good structure, flavourful, round tannins, balanced.

VIÑAS DEL MONTSANT

Partida Coll de Mora , s/n
43775 Marça (Tarragona)
☎: +34 977 831 309
Fax: +34 977 831 356
mariajose.bajon@morlanda.com
www.fraguerau.com

Garbó 2014 T
tempranillo, merlot

87

Colour: bright cherry. Nose: ripe fruit, sweet spices, creamy oak. Palate: flavourful, toasty, round tannins.

VIÑEDOS SINGULARES

Cuzco, 26 - 28, Nave 8 - 9
08030 Barcelona (Barcelona)
☎: +34 934 807 041
Fax: +34 934 807 076
info@vinedossingulares.com
www.vinedossingulares.com

El Veïnat 2013 T
garnacha

89

Colour: bright cherry. Nose: scrubland, ripe fruit, spicy. Palate: balanced, good acidity, round tannins.

VIRÀMIDUS

Navas de Tolosa 255
08026 Barcelona (Barcelona)
☎: +34 678 734 526
viramidus.eph@gmail.com
www.viramidus.es

Viràmidus 2006 TR
garnacha, cariñena, cabernet sauvignon

86

Viràmidus Garnatxa 2008 T
garnacha, cabernet sauvignon

82

Viràmidus Gran Selecció 2006 T
garnacha, cariñena, syrah, cabernet sauvignon

88

Colour: pale ruby, brick rim edge. Nose: spicy, fine reductive notes, wet leather, aged wood nuances, fruit liqueur notes. Palate: spicy, fine tannins, balanced.

Viràmidus La Rosa de Sant Jordi 2014 T
garnacha, cariñena, merlot, cabernet sauvignon

85

Viràmidus Negre 2010 TC
garnacha, cariñena, syrah

87

Colour: cherry, garnet rim. Nose: ripe fruit, spicy, creamy oak. Palate: flavourful, toasty.

Viràmidus Syrah 2006 T
syrah

87

Colour: pale ruby, brick rim edge. Nose: spicy, fine reductive notes, tobacco. Palate: spicy, fine tannins, long.

XIROI VINS

Plaça Europa 3 5è 3a
43205 Reus (Tarragona)
☎: +34 669 486 712
teretr@yahoo.com
www.xiroi-vins.com

Xiroi 2014 T Barrica
garnacha, cariñena, cabernet sauvignon, syrah

88

Colour: bright cherry. Nose: ripe fruit, sweet spices, creamy oak. Palate: flavourful, fruity, toasty.

DO. NAVARRA

CONSEJO REGULADOR

Rúa Romana, s/n
31390 Olite (Navarra)
☎:+34 948 741 812 - Fax: +34 948 741 776
@: consejoregulador@vinonavarra.com
@: info@navarrawine.com
www.navarrawine.com

LOCATION:

In the province of Navarra. It draws together areas of different climates and soils, which produce wines with diverse characteristics.

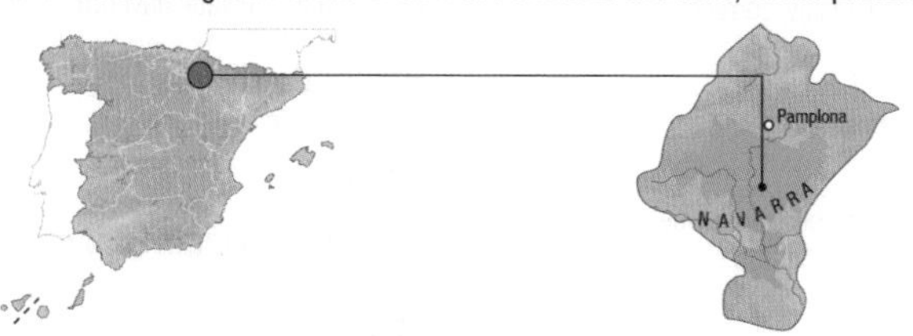

SUB-REGIONS:

Baja Montaña. Situated northeast of Navarra, it comprises 22 municipal districts with around 2,500 Ha under cultivation.
Tierra Estella. In western central Navarra, it stretches along the Camino de Santiago. It has 1,800 Ha of vineyards in 38 municipal districts.
Valdizarbe. In central Navarra. It is the key centre of the Camino de Santiago. It comprises 25 municipal districts and has 1,100 Ha of vineyards.
Ribera Alta. In the area around Olite, it takes in part of central Navarra and the start of the southern region. There are 26 municipal districts and 3,300 Ha of vineyards.
Ribera Baja. In the south of the province, it is the most important in terms of size (4,600 Ha). It comprises 14 municipal districts.

GRAPE VARIETIES:

WHITE: Chardonnay (2%), Garnacha Blanca, Malvasía, Moscatel de Grano Menudo, Viura (6% of total) and Sauvignon Blanc.
RED: Cabernet Sauvignon (9%), Garnacha Tinta (majority 42% of total), Graciano, Mazuelo, Merlot, Tempranillo (29%), Syrah and Pinot Noir.

FIGURES:

Vineyard surface: 11,300 – **Wine-Growers:** 2,451 – **Wineries:** 100 – **2014 Harvest rating:** Very Good – **Production 14:** 50,288,942 litres – **Market percentages:** 67% National - 33% International.

SOIL:

The diversity of the different regions is also reflected in the soil. Reddish or yellowish and stony in the Baja Montaña, brownish-grey limestone and limestone in Valdizarbe and Tierra Estella, limestone and alluvium marl in the Ribera Alta, and brown and grey semi-desert soil, brownish-grey limestone and alluvium in the Ribera Baja.

CLIMATE:

Typical of dry, sub-humid regions in the northern fringe, with average rainfall of between 593 mm and 683 mm per year. The climate in the central region is transitional and changes to drier conditions in southern regions, where the average annual rainfall is a mere 448 mm.

VINTAGE RATING

PEÑÍNGUIDE

2010	2011	2012	2013	2014
VERY GOOD	VERY GOOD	VERY GOOD	GOOD	GOOD

ALIAGA

Camino del Villar. N-161, Km. 3
31591 Corella (Navarra)
☎: +34 948 401 321
Fax: +34 948 781 414
sales@vinaaliaga.com
www.vinaaliaga.com

Aliaga Colección Privada 2012 TC
80% tempranillo, 20% cabernet sauvignon

87

Colour: cherry, garnet rim. Nose: ripe fruit, spicy, creamy oak, complex. Palate: flavourful, toasty, correct.

Aliaga Cuvée 2013 T
85% tempranillo, 15% cabernet sauvignon

88

Colour: bright cherry. Nose: ripe fruit, sweet spices, creamy oak, expressive. Palate: flavourful, fruity, round tannins, easy to drink.

Aliaga Doscarlos Sauvignon Blanc 2014 B
100% sauvignon blanc

87

Colour: bright straw. Nose: white flowers, fresh fruit, fragrant herbs. Palate: flavourful, fruity, good acidity.

Aliaga Garnacha Vieja 2010 T
100% garnacha

87

Colour: cherry, garnet rim. Nose: ripe fruit, spicy, creamy oak, complex. Palate: flavourful, toasty, round tannins.

Aliaga Lágrima de Garnacha 2014 RD
100% garnacha

87

Colour: light cherry. Nose: red berry notes, floral, fragrant herbs. Palate: light-bodied, flavourful, good acidity, long, spicy.

Aliaga Moscatel Vendimia Tardía 2012 B
100% moscatel grano menudo

90

Colour: bright yellow. Nose: balsamic herbs, honeyed notes, floral, sweet spices, expressive. Palate: rich, fruity, powerful, flavourful, elegant.

Aliaga Reserva de la Familia 2008 TR
75% tempranillo, 25% cabernet sauvignon

86

Aliaga Syrha 2010 T
100% syrah

88

Colour: cherry, garnet rim. Nose: ripe fruit, spicy, creamy oak, complex. Palate: flavourful, toasty, round tannins.

ANECOOP BODEGAS NAVARRA

Paraje Valijo s/n
31495 San Martín de Unx (Navarra)
☎: +34 963 938 509
Fax: +34 963 390 809
info@anecoop.com

Hacienda Uvanis 2008 TR
tempranillo, garnacha

87

Colour: cherry, garnet rim. Nose: ripe fruit, wild herbs, fine reductive notes. Palate: flavourful, long, balsamic.

Hacienda Uvanis 2012 TC
tempranillo, garnacha, merlot

85

Hacienda Uvanis Blanco Garnacha 2014 B
garnacha blanca

80

Hacienda Uvanis Garnacha 2014 RD
garnacha

85

Hacienda Uvanis Garnacha 2014 T
garnacha

84

Hacienda Uvanis Tempranillo 2014 T
tempranillo

83

AROA BODEGAS

Apalaz, 13
31292 Zurukuain (Navarra)
☎: +34 948 921 867
info@aroawines.com
www.aroawines.com

Aroa Garnatxas 2012 T
garnacha

87 ♣

Colour: ruby red. Nose: creamy oak, toasty, ripe fruit, balsamic herbs. Palate: balanced, spicy, long.

Aroa Jauna 2010 TC
cabernet sauvignon, merlot, tempranillo, garnacha

88 ♣

Colour: cherry, garnet rim. Nose: ripe fruit, spicy, balsamic herbs. Palate: flavourful, toasty, round tannins.

Aroa Laia 2014 B
garnacha blanca

88 🌱

Colour: bright straw. Nose: white flowers, fresh fruit, fragrant herbs, expressive. Palate: flavourful, fruity, good acidity.

Aroa Larrosa 2014 RD
garnacha, tempranillo

88 🌱

Colour: rose, purple rim. Nose: floral, wild herbs, fruit expression, expressive. Palate: flavourful, complex, balanced.

Aroa Mutiko 2014 T
tempranillo

86 🌱

Le Naturel 2014 T
garnacha, tempranillo

86

Le Naturel Reposado Tradicional 2013 T
garnacha

87

Colour: cherry, purple rim. Nose: expressive, fresh fruit, red berry notes, floral. Palate: fruity, good acidity, easy to drink, light-bodied.

Monastir SX 2012 T
cabernet sauvignon, merlot

87

Colour: bright cherry. Nose: sweet spices, creamy oak, fruit preserve. Palate: flavourful, fruity, toasty, round tannins.

ASENSIO VIÑEDOS Y BODEGAS

31293 Sesma (Navarra)
☎: +34 948 698 078
Fax: +34 948 698 097
info@bodegasasensio.com
www.bodegasasensio.com

Javier Asensio 2011 TC
syrah, merlot

84

Javier Asensio 2013 T Roble
tempranillo, garnacha, cabernet sauvignon

85

Javier Asensio 2014 B
sauvignon blanc, chardonnay

86

AZUL Y GARANZA BODEGAS

San Juan, 19
31310 Carcastillo (Navarra)
☎: +34 659 857 979
Fax: +34 949 115 185
fernando@azulygaranza.com
www.azulygaranza.com

Desierto de Azul y Garanza 2010 T

89

Colour: cherry, garnet rim. Nose: complex, spicy, fruit liqueur notes, ripe fruit, earthy notes. Palate: good structure, flavourful, powerful, ripe fruit.

Garciano de Azul y Garanza 2013 T Barrica
graciano

90 🌱

Colour: cherry, garnet rim. Nose: creamy oak, toasty, ripe fruit, balsamic herbs. Palate: balanced, spicy, long.

Seis de Azul y Garanza 2013 T

88 🌱

Colour: bright cherry. Nose: ripe fruit, sweet spices, creamy oak. Palate: flavourful, fruity, toasty.

BODEGA CASTILLO DE ENERIZ

Ctra. Campanas-Puente la Reina, Km. 7,4
31153 Eneriz (Navarra)
☎: +34 948 692 500
Fax: +34 948 692 700
info@manzanosenterprises.com
www.manzanoswines.com

Castillo de Eneriz 2006 TR
tempranillo, cabernet sauvignon, merlot, garnacha

84

Castillo de Eneriz 2011 TC
tempranillo, cabernet sauvignon, merlot, garnacha

85

Castillo de Enériz 2013 T
tempranillo, syrah

85

Miscelanea 2006 TR
tempranillo, cabernet sauvignon, garnacha

86

Miscelanea 2011 TC
tempranillo, cabernet sauvignon, garnacha

85

MZ 2006 TR
tempranillo, cabernet sauvignon, garnacha

88

Colour: cherry, garnet rim. Nose: ripe fruit, wild herbs, earthy notes, spicy, balsamic herbs, closed. Palate: balanced, flavourful, long, balsamic.

MZ 2011 TC
tempranillo, cabernet sauvignon, garnacha

88

Colour: cherry, garnet rim. Nose: creamy oak, red berry notes, balanced. Palate: flavourful, spicy, elegant.

MZ Chardonnay 2014 B
chardonnay

85

MZ Graciano Garnacha 2012 T
graciano, garnacha

87

Colour: light cherry. Nose: ripe fruit, spicy, creamy oak, complex. Palate: flavourful, toasty, round tannins.

MZ Rosado 2014 RD
tempranillo, garnacha, syrah

85

BODEGA COSECHEROS REUNIDOS, S.COOP

Pza. San Antón, 1
31390 Olite (Navarra)
☎: +34 948 740 067
Fax: +34 948 740 067
info@bodegacosecheros.com
www.bodegacosecheros.com

Gratianvs 2011 T
graciano

88

Colour: deep cherry, purple rim. Nose: creamy oak, toasty, ripe fruit, balsamic herbs, floral. Palate: balanced, spicy, long.

Viña Juguera 2014 B
viura

84

Viña Juguera 2014 RD
garnacha

85

Viña Juguera Tempranillo 2014 T
tempranillo

84

BODEGA DE SADA

Arrabal, 2
31491 Sada (Navarra)
☎: +34 948 877 013
Fax: +34 948 877 433
bodega@bodegadesada.com
www.bodegadesada.com

Palacio de Sada 2011 TC
garnacha

88

Colour: cherry, garnet rim. Nose: creamy oak, red berry notes, balanced, ripe fruit. Palate: flavourful, spicy, elegant.

Palacio de Sada 2014 RD
garnacha

89

Colour: rose, purple rim. Nose: red berry notes, floral, expressive. Palate: powerful, fruity, fresh.

Palacio de Sada Garnacha 2014 T

87

Colour: cherry, purple rim. Nose: red berry notes, floral, balsamic herbs. Palate: powerful, fresh, fruity.

BODEGA DE SARRÍA

Finca Señorío de Sarría, s/n
31100 Puente La Reina (Navarra)
☎: +34 948 202 200
Fax: +34 948 202 202
info@taninia.com
www.bodegadesarria.com

Señorío de Sarría 2009 TR
merlot, cabernet sauvignon

87

Colour: cherry, garnet rim. Nose: ripe fruit, spicy, creamy oak, fine reductive notes. Palate: flavourful, toasty.

Señorío de Sarría 2012 TC
cabernet sauvignon, tempranillo, garnacha, graciano

90

Colour: cherry, garnet rim. Nose: ripe fruit, spicy, creamy oak, balanced. Palate: flavourful, toasty.

Señorío de Sarría 2014 RD
garnacha

87

Colour: rose, purple rim. Nose: floral, wild herbs, fruit expression. Palate: flavourful, complex.

Señorío de Sarría Chardonnay 2014 B
chardonnay

84

Señorío de Sarría Moscatel Dulce 2013 B
moscatel grano menudo

88

Colour: bright yellow. Nose: balsamic herbs, honeyed notes, floral, sweet spices, expressive. Palate: rich, fruity, powerful, flavourful, elegant.

Señorío de Sarría Viñedo Nº 5 2014 RD
garnacha

88

Colour: rose, purple rim. Nose: red berry notes, floral, expressive. Palate: powerful, fruity, fresh.

Señorío de Sarría Viñedo Sotés 2012 TC
cabernet sauvignon, garnacha, graciano, mazuelo, tempranillo

88

Colour: bright cherry. Nose: ripe fruit, sweet spices, creamy oak. Palate: flavourful, fruity, toasty.

BODEGA INURRIETA

Ctra. Falces-Miranda de Arga, km. 30
31370 Falces (Navarra)
☎: +34 948 737 309
Fax: +34 948 737 310
info@bodegainurrieta.com
www.bodegainurrieta.com

Altos de Inurrieta 2011 TR
syrah, graciano, garnacha

90

Colour: cherry, garnet rim. Nose: roasted coffee, smoky, spicy, ripe fruit. Palate: flavourful, smoky aftertaste, ripe fruit, balanced.

Inurrieta Cuatrocientos 2012 TC
cabernet sauvignon, graciano, garnacha, merlot

87

Colour: cherry, garnet rim. Nose: ripe fruit, spicy, creamy oak. Palate: flavourful, toasty.

Inurrieta Mediodía 2014 RD
garnacha, syrah, cabernet sauvignon, merlot, graciano

90

Colour: rose, purple rim. Nose: floral, wild herbs, fruit expression. Palate: flavourful, complex.

Inurrieta Norte 2013 T Roble
cabernet sauvignon, merlot, graciano

88

Colour: cherry, purple rim. Nose: ripe fruit, toasty, creamy oak. Palate: flavourful, spicy, long.

Inurrieta Orchídea 2014 B
sauvignon blanc

88

Colour: bright straw. Nose: white flowers, fresh fruit, fragrant herbs. Palate: flavourful, fruity, good acidity.

Inurrieta Orchídea Cuvée 2013 B
sauvignon blanc

91

Colour: bright yellow. Nose: ripe fruit, powerfull, toasty, patisserie. Palate: flavourful, fruity, spicy, toasty, long.

Inurrieta Puro Vicio 2011 T
syrah

90

Colour: cherry, garnet rim. Nose: expressive, spicy, fruit expression. Palate: flavourful, ripe fruit, long, good acidity, balanced.

Inurrieta Sur 2013 T Roble
garnacha, syrah

88

Colour: deep cherry, purple rim. Nose: toasty, ripe fruit, balsamic herbs. Palate: balanced, spicy, long.

Laderas de Inurrieta 2012 T
graciano

92

Colour: cherry, garnet rim. Nose: mineral, expressive, spicy, balsamic herbs. Palate: flavourful, ripe fruit, long, good acidity, balanced.

BODEGA MARQUÉS DE MONTECIERZO

San José, 62
31590 Castejón (Navarra)
☎: +34 948 814 414
info@marquesdemontecierzo.com
www.marquesdemontecierzo.com

Emergente 2010 TR
tempranillo, merlot, cabernet sauvignon

87

Colour: cherry, garnet rim. Nose: ripe fruit, wild herbs, earthy notes, spicy, balsamic herbs. Palate: balanced, long, balsamic.

Emergente 2012 T Roble
tempranillo, garnacha, merlot, cabernet sauvignon

85

Emergente 2012 TC
tempranillo, garnacha, merlot, cabernet sauvignon

85

Emergente 2013 T
tempranillo, garnacha, merlot, cabernet sauvignon
84

Emergente 2014 RD
70% garnacha, 30% cabernet sauvignon
84

Emergente Flor 2014 RD
100% garnacha
83

Emergente Garnacha 2012 T Roble
100% garnacha
86

Emergente Garnacha 2013 T Roble
100% garnacha
84

Emergente Moscatel Semidulce 2014 B
100% moscatel grano menudo
84

Marques de Montecierzo Merlot Selección 2008 TC
100% merlot
88

Colour: deep cherry, purple rim. Nose: creamy oak, toasty, balsamic herbs, varietal. Palate: balanced, spicy, long.

BODEGA MÁXIMO ABETE
Ctra. Estella-Sangüesa, Km. 43,5
31495 San Martín de Unx (Navarra)
☎: +34 948 738 120
info@bodegasmaximoabete.com
www.bodegasmaximoabete.com

Guerinda Casa lasierra 2014 RD
100% garnacha
88

Colour: rose, purple rim. Nose: red berry notes, floral, expressive. Palate: fruity, fresh, balanced.

Guerinda El Máximo 2011 TC
garnacha, merlot, cabernet sauvignon
89

Colour: cherry, garnet rim. Nose: creamy oak, red berry notes, balanced, fragrant herbs. Palate: flavourful, spicy, elegant.

Guerinda La Blanca Chardonnay 2014 B
100% chardonnay
88

Colour: bright straw. Nose: white flowers, fresh fruit, fragrant herbs, expressive. Palate: flavourful, fruity, good acidity, balanced.

Guerinda La Cruzica 2010 T
100% tempranillo
89

Colour: cherry, garnet rim. Nose: ripe fruit, spicy, creamy oak, complex. Palate: flavourful, toasty, round tannins, balanced.

Guerinda Navasentero 3+1 2011 T
100% graciano
90

Colour: cherry, garnet rim. Nose: ripe fruit, wild herbs, earthy notes, spicy, balsamic herbs. Palate: balanced, flavourful, long, balsamic.

Guerinda Tres Partes 2013 T
100% garnacha
85

BODEGA NUESTRA SEÑORA DEL ROMERO
Ctra. de Tarazona, 33
31520 Cascante (Navarra)
☎: +34 948 851 411
Fax: +34 948 844 504
tienda@malondeechaide.com
www.malondeechaide.com

Malón de Echaide 2010 TC
100% tempranillo
85

Malón de Echaide 2014 RD
100% garnacha
84

Malón de Echaide Chardonnay 2014 B
100% chardonnay
85

Malón de Echaide Tempranillo 2014 T
100% tempranillo
84

Torrecilla 2014 RD
100% garnacha
85

Viña Parot 2007 TR
85% cabernet sauvignon, 15% tempranillo
85

BODEGA OTAZU

Señorío de Otazu, s/n
31174 Etxauri (Navarra)
☎: +34 948 329 200
Fax: +34 948 329 353
otazu@otazu.com
www.otazu.com

Otazu Chardonnay 2014 B

100% chardonnay

90

Colour: bright yellow. Nose: white flowers, fine lees, dried herbs, ripe fruit, citrus fruit. Palate: flavourful, fruity, good acidity, elegant.

Otazu Merlot 2014 RD

100% merlot

86

Otazu Premium Cuvée 2011 T

55% cabernet sauvignon, 30% tempranillo, 15% merlot

90

Colour: cherry, garnet rim. Nose: creamy oak, red berry notes, ripe fruit, sweet spices. Palate: flavourful, spicy, elegant.

Palacio de Otazu Altar 2007 T

95% cabernet sauvignon, 5% merlot

93

Colour: cherry, garnet rim. Nose: ripe fruit, spicy, creamy oak, complex, wild herbs, expressive. Palate: flavourful, toasty, round tannins, balanced.

Vitral 2007 TC

100% cabernet sauvignon

93

Colour: cherry, garnet rim. Nose: balanced, complex, ripe fruit, spicy, elegant, balsamic herbs. Palate: good structure, flavourful, round tannins, balanced.

BODEGA PAGO DE CIRSUS

Ctra. de Ablitas a Ribafora, Km. 5
31523 Ablitas (Navarra)
☎: +34 948 386 427
info@pagodecirsus.com
www.pagodecirsus.com

Pago de Cirsus Chardonnay 2014 B

chardonnay

90

Colour: bright straw. Nose: white flowers, fine lees, ripe fruit, citrus fruit, floral. Palate: flavourful, fruity, good acidity, fine bitter notes.

Pago de Cirsus Moscatel Vendimia Tardía 2008 BFB

moscatel grano menudo

92

Colour: golden. Nose: powerfull, honeyed notes, candied fruit, acetaldehyde. Palate: flavourful, sweet, fresh, fruity, good acidity, long, balanced, elegant.

Pago de Cirsus Opus 11 2009 T

tempranillo, syrah

91

Colour: cherry, garnet rim. Nose: smoky, spicy, fruit preserve. Palate: flavourful, smoky aftertaste, ripe fruit, elegant.

BODEGA SAN MARTÍN S. COOP.

Ctra. de Sangüesa, s/n
31495 San Martín de Unx (Navarra)
☎: +34 948 738 294
Fax: +34 948 738 297
admon@bodegasanmartin.com
www.bodegasanmartin.com

Alma de Unx 2010 T

garnacha

91

Colour: light cherry. Nose: expressive, complex, mineral, balsamic herbs, balanced. Palate: full, flavourful, round tannins.

Alma de Unx 2012 B Barrica

garnacha blanca

87

Colour: bright yellow. Nose: ripe fruit, powerfull, toasty. Palate: flavourful, spicy, toasty, long, smoky aftertaste.

Ilagares 2014 B

viura

84

Ilagares 2014 RD

100% garnacha

87

Colour: rose, purple rim. Nose: red berry notes, floral, balanced. Palate: powerful, fruity, fresh, easy to drink.

Ilagares 2014 T

tempranillo, garnacha

84

La Matacalva Garnacha de Montaña 2013 T

garnacha

89

Colour: ruby red. Nose: creamy oak, ripe fruit, balsamic herbs, mineral. Palate: balanced, spicy, long.

Señorío de Unx 2008 TR
tempranillo, garnacha

87

Colour: cherry, garnet rim. Nose: ripe fruit, spicy, creamy oak. Palate: flavourful, toasty, round tannins.

Señorío de Unx 2012 TC
tempranillo, garnacha

86

Señorío de Unx Garnacha 2014 T
100% garnacha

85

Señorío de Unx Garnacha Blanca 2014 B
100% garnacha blanca

85

BODEGA TÁNDEM

Ctra. Pamplona - Logroño Km. 35,9
31292 Lácar (Navarra)
☎: +34 948 536 031
Fax: +34 948 536 068
bodega@tandem.es
www.tandem.es

Ars In Vitro 2012 T
tempranillo, merlot

84

Ars Nova 2010 T
tempranillo, cabernet sauvignon, merlot

88

Colour: dark-red cherry, orangey edge. Nose: wild herbs, balanced, ripe fruit. Palate: correct, balanced, good acidity, spicy, easy to drink.

Inmácula 2013 B
viura, chardonnay

89

Colour: straw. Nose: ripe fruit, floral. Palate: easy to drink, fine bitter notes.

Mácula 2006 T
merlot, cabernet sauvignon

89

Colour: pale ruby, brick rim edge. Nose: elegant, spicy, fine reductive notes, tobacco. Palate: spicy, fine tannins, long.

Mácula 2010 T
merlot, cabernet sauvignon

88

Colour: cherry, garnet rim. Nose: roasted coffee, smoky, spicy, ripe fruit. Palate: flavourful, smoky aftertaste, ripe fruit.

BODEGA Y VIÑAS VALDELARES

Ctra. Eje del Ebro, km. 60
31579 Carcar (Navarra)
☎: +34 656 849 602
valdelares@valdelares.com
www.valdelares.com

Valdelares 2012 TC
cabernet sauvignon, merlot, tempranillo

88

Colour: cherry, garnet rim. Nose: creamy oak, red berry notes, fresh fruit, balanced. Palate: flavourful, spicy, elegant, easy to drink.

Valdelares 2014 RD
merlot

89

Colour: rose, purple rim. Nose: floral, wild herbs, fruit expression, expressive. Palate: flavourful, complex, balanced, elegant.

Valdelares Alta Expresión 2012 TC
cabernet sauvignon, merlot

89

Colour: bright cherry, garnet rim. Nose: expressive, balsamic herbs, balanced. Palate: flavourful, round tannins.

Valdelares Chardonnay 2014 B
100% chardonnay

86

Valdelares Moscatel 2014 B
100% moscatel grano menudo

86

BODEGAS AZPEA

Camino Itúrbero, s/n
31440 Lumbier (Navarra)
☎: +34 948 880 433
Fax: +34 948 880 433
info@bodegasazpea.com
www.bodegasazpea.com

Azpea 2010 T
garnacha, cabernet sauvignon, merlot

83

Azpea 2013 T
garnacha, cabernet sauvignon, tempranillo, merlot

85

Azpea Garnacha 2009 T
garnacha

84

Azpea Vino Dulce de Moscatel 2012 B

moscatel grano menudo

88

Colour: golden. Nose: powerfull, honeyed notes, candied fruit, fragrant herbs. Palate: flavourful, sweet, fresh, fruity, good acidity, long.

Azpea Viura 2013 B

viura

75

BODEGAS BERAMENDI

Ctra. Tafalla, s/n
31495 San Martín de Unx (Navarra)
☎: +34 948 738 262
Fax: +34 948 738 080
info@bodegasberamendi.com
www.bodegasberamendi.com

Beramendi 2014 B

chardonnay, viura, moscatel

85

Beramendi 2014 RD

100% garnacha

85

Beramendi 3F 2014 B

moscatel, chardonnay

84

Beramendi 3F 2014 RD

100% garnacha

86

Beramendi Etiqueta Negra 2011 TC

cabernet sauvignon, merlot

86

BODEGAS CAMILO CASTILLA

Santa Bárbara, 40
31591 Corella (Navarra)
☎: +34 948 780 006
Fax: +34 948 780 515
info@camilocastilla.com
www.bodegasab.com

Blank 2014 B

100% viura

85

Capricho de Goya Dulce B

moscatel grano menudo

93

Colour: dark mahogany. Nose: powerfull, expressive, aromatic coffee, spicy, acetaldehyde, dry nuts. Palate: balanced, elegant, fine solera notes, toasty, long.

Montecristo Dulce 2014 B

moscatel grano menudo

87

Colour: bright straw. Nose: candied fruit, fruit liqueur notes, floral, citrus fruit. Palate: balanced, flavourful.

Pink 2014 RD

100% garnacha

87

Colour: light cherry, bright. Nose: red berry notes, floral, expressive. Palate: fruity, fresh, easy to drink, balanced.

BODEGAS CASTILLO DE MONJARDÍN

Viña Rellanada, s/n
31242 Villamayor de Monjardín
(Navarra)
☎: +34 948 537 412
Fax: +34 948 537 436
patricia@monjardin.es
www.monjardin.es

Castillo de Monjardín 2012 TC

cabernet sauvignon, merlot, tempranillo

88

Colour: cherry, garnet rim. Nose: ripe fruit, spicy, creamy oak, complex. Palate: flavourful, toasty, easy to drink.

Castillo de Monjardín Chardonnay 2013 BFB

chardonnay

93

Colour: bright yellow. Nose: ripe fruit, powerfull, toasty, aged wood nuances, pattiserie. Palate: flavourful, fruity, spicy, toasty, long.

Castillo de Monjardín Chardonnay 2014 B

chardonnay

86

Castillo de Monjardín Deyo 2011 TC
merlot

91

Colour: cherry, garnet rim. Nose: mineral, expressive, spicy, elegant. Palate: flavourful, ripe fruit, long, good acidity, balanced.

Castillo de Monjardín Garnacha 2013 T
garnacha

88

Colour: cherry, garnet rim. Nose: fine reductive notes, wet leather, aged wood nuances, ripe fruit. Palate: spicy, long, toasty.

Castillo de Monjardín Pinot Noir 2012 T
pinot noir

86

Castillo de Monjardín Rosado de Lágrima 2014 RD
cabernet sauvignon

88

Colour: rose, purple rim. Nose: red berry notes, floral, expressive. Palate: powerful, fruity, fresh.

BODEGAS CORELLANAS

Santa Bárbara, 29
31591 Corella (Navarra)
☎: +34 948 780 029
Fax: +34 948 781 542
jdaniel@bodegascorellanas.com
www.bodegascorellanas.com

Moscatel Sarasate Expresión Dulce Natural 2014 B
100% moscatel

84

Viña Rubicán 2010 TC
cabernet sauvignon, merlot

84

Viña Rubicán 2014 B
100% moscatel

86

BODEGAS DE LA CASA DE LÚCULO

Ctra. Larraga, s/n
31150 Mendigorría (Navarra)
☎: +34 948 343 148
bodega@luculo.es
www.luculo.es

Jardín de Lúculo 2013 T
100% garnacha

90

Colour: cherry, garnet rim. Nose: red berry notes, ripe fruit, fragrant herbs, spicy, toasty, creamy oak, mineral. Palate: powerful, flavourful, balsamic, balanced.

Jardín de Lúculo Los Bohemios 2012 T
100% garnacha

90

Colour: bright cherry. Nose: ripe fruit, sweet spices, expressive, red berry notes. Palate: flavourful, fruity, round tannins.

Jardín de Lúculo Los Bohemios 2014 RD
100% garnacha

87

Colour: coppery red, bright. Nose: elegant, red berry notes, floral, fragrant herbs. Palate: light-bodied, good acidity, long, ripe fruit.

BODEGAS FERNÁNDEZ DE ARCAYA

La Serna, 31
31210 Los Arcos (Navarra)
☎: +34 948 640 811
info@fernandezdearcaya.com
www.fernandezdearcaya.com

Fernández de Arcaya Selección Privada 2010 TR
100% cabernet sauvignon

87

Colour: light cherry. Nose: toasty, smoky, dried herbs. Palate: spicy, toasty, flavourful.

Viña Perguita 2011 TC
80% tempranillo, 15% cabernet sauvignon, 5% merlot

87

Colour: cherry, garnet rim. Nose: fine reductive notes, spicy. Palate: spicy, long, toasty.

Viña Perguita 2013 T Roble
85% tempranillo, 10% cabernet sauvignon, 5% merlot

80

BODEGAS GRAN FEUDO

Ribera, 34
31592 Cintruénigo (Navarra)
☎: +34 948 811 000
Fax: +34 948 811 407
info@granfeudo.com
www.granfeudo.com

Gran Feudo 2009 TR
tempranillo, cabernet sauvignon, merlot

88

Colour: light cherry, garnet rim. Nose: balanced, expressive, ripe fruit, wild herbs, spicy. Palate: correct, balanced.

Gran Feudo 2011 TC
tempranillo, garnacha, cabernet sauvignon, merlot

87

Colour: cherry, garnet rim. Nose: creamy oak, wild herbs, ripe fruit. Palate: flavourful, spicy, easy to drink.

Gran Feudo 2013 T Roble
tempranillo

85

Gran Feudo 2014 RD
garnacha

87

Colour: rose, bright. Nose: red berry notes, expressive, dried flowers, dried herbs. Palate: fruity, fresh, correct.

Gran Feudo Chardonnay 2014 B
chardonnay

90

Colour: bright straw. Nose: white flowers, fresh fruit, fragrant herbs, expressive. Palate: flavourful, fruity, good acidity, balanced.

Gran Feudo Edición 2011 TC
tempranillo, merlot, cabernet sauvignon

89

Colour: cherry, garnet rim. Nose: ripe fruit, wild herbs, spicy, balsamic herbs. Palate: balanced, flavourful, long, balsamic.

Gran Feudo Edición Chardonnay 2014 B
chardonnay

92

Colour: bright yellow. Nose: expressive, dried herbs, ripe fruit, spicy. Palate: flavourful, fruity, good acidity, balanced, elegant.

Gran Feudo Edición Rosado sobre Lías 2014 RD
garnacha, tempranillo, merlot

88

Colour: onion pink. Nose: elegant, red berry notes, floral, fragrant herbs. Palate: flavourful, good acidity, long, fruity.

Gran Feudo Viñas Viejas 2009 TR
tempranillo, garnacha

88

Colour: cherry, garnet rim. Nose: ripe fruit, wild herbs, earthy notes, balsamic herbs, fine reductive notes. Palate: balanced, flavourful, long, balsamic.

Gran Feudo Viñas Viejas 2010 TR
tempranillo, garnacha

87

Colour: cherry, garnet rim. Nose: ripe fruit, spicy, creamy oak. Palate: flavourful, toasty, round tannins.

BODEGAS IRACHE

Monasterio de Irache, 1
31240 Ayegui (Navarra)
☎: +34 948 551 932
Fax: +34 948 554 954
irache@irache.com
www.irache.com

Castillo Irache 2011 TC
cabernet sauvignon, merlot

85

Castillo Irache 2014 B
chardonnay

82

Castillo Irache 2014 RD
garnacha

83

Castillo Irache Tempranillo 2014 T
tempranillo

83

Gran Irache 2010 TC
tempranillo, cabernet sauvignon, merlot

84

Irache 2007 TR
tempranillo, cabernet sauvignon, merlot

84

Real Irache 1996 TGR
tempranillo, garnacha, graciano

86

BODEGAS ITURBIDE

Término la Torre, s/n
Ctra. NA-128, km. 6,5
31350 Peralta (Navarra)
☎: +34 948 750 537
bodegasiturbide@bodegasiturbide.com
www.bodegasiturbide.com

Novem 2014 RD
garnacha, cabernet sauvignon
86

Novem 2014 T
tempranillo, garnacha, cabernet sauvignon
85

BODEGAS LA CRUZ DE MAÑERU

Autovía del Camino s/n
31130 Mañeru (Navarra)
☎: +34 948 341 001
vinobelardi@vinobelardi.com
www.vinobelardi.com

Belardi 2014 RD
100% garnacha
83

Mañeru Nature 2012 TC
garnacha
86

Mañeru Nature 2013 T
garnacha
87
Colour: light cherry, garnet rim. Nose: red berry notes, floral, balanced. Palate: fruity, correct, fine bitter notes, balanced.

BODEGAS LEZAUN

Egiarte, s/n
31292 Lakar (Navarra)
☎: +34 948 541 339
info@lezaun.com
www.lezaun.com

Egiarte 2010 TC
tempranillo, cabernet sauvignon, merlot
87
Colour: deep cherry, purple rim. Nose: creamy oak, toasty, ripe fruit, balsamic herbs. Palate: balanced, spicy, long.

Egiarte 2010 TR
tempranillo, cabernet sauvignon
88
Colour: cherry, garnet rim. Nose: ripe fruit, spicy, creamy oak. Palate: flavourful, toasty, round tannins.

Egiarte 2014 T
tempranillo, garnacha, cabernet sauvignon
84

Egiarte Rosado 2014 RD
garnacha, tempranillo
87
Colour: light cherry. Nose: red berry notes, floral, fragrant herbs. Palate: light-bodied, flavourful, good acidity.

Lezaun 0,0 Sulfitos 2014 T
tempranillo
87
Colour: cherry, purple rim. Nose: spicy, red berry notes, wild herbs. Palate: powerful, fruity.

Lezaun 2009 TR
tempranillo, cabernet sauvignon, graciano, garnacha
90
Colour: cherry, garnet rim. Nose: ripe fruit, spicy, creamy oak, complex, balsamic herbs, fine reductive notes. Palate: flavourful, toasty, elegant.

Lezaun 2010 TC
tempranillo, cabernet sauvignon, garnacha
89
Colour: cherry, garnet rim. Nose: red berry notes, ripe fruit, spicy, creamy oak, complex. Palate: flavourful, toasty, round tannins.

Lezaun Gazaga 2012 T Roble
tempranillo, cabernet sauvignon
87
Colour: cherry, garnet rim. Nose: ripe fruit, spicy, creamy oak. Palate: flavourful, toasty.

Lezaun Tempranillo 2014 T
tempranillo
88
Colour: cherry, purple rim. Nose: expressive, fresh fruit, red berry notes, floral. Palate: flavourful, fruity, good acidity.

Lezaun Txuria 2013 B
garnacha blanca
85

BODEGAS LOGOS

Avda. de los Fueros, 18
31522 Monteagudo (Navarra)
☎: +34 941 398 008
Fax: +34 941 398 070
info@familiaescudero.com
www.familiaescudero.com

Logos I 2004 T
40% garnacha, 30% cabernet sauvignon, 30% tempranillo

89

Colour: pale ruby, brick rim edge. Nose: elegant, spicy, fine reductive notes, ripe fruit. Palate: spicy, fine tannins, elegant, long.

Logos II 2009 T
40% cabernet sauvignon, 40% garnacha, 20% tempranillo

86

Pedro de Ivar 2010 TC
70% tempranillo, 20% garnacha, 10% mazuelo

86

Pedro de Ivar Prestigio 2004 TR
60% garnacha, 40% tempranillo

88

Colour: cherry, garnet rim. Nose: ripe fruit, wild herbs, spicy, balsamic herbs. Palate: balanced, flavourful, long, balsamic.

BODEGAS LUIS GURPEGUI MUGA

Avda. Celso Muerza, 8
31560 San Adrián (Navarra)
☎: +34 948 670 050
Fax: +34 948 670 259
bodegas@gurpegui.es
www.gurpegui.es

Monte Ory 2011 TC
60% tempranillo, 30% cabernet sauvignon, 10% garnacha

86

Monte Ory 2014 RD
garnacha

84

Monte Ory Tempranillo Cabernet Sauvignon 2014 T
60% tempranillo, 40% cabernet sauvignon

85

BODEGAS MACAYA

Ctra. Berbinzana, 74
31251 Larraga (Navarra)
☎: +34 948 711 549
Fax: +34 948 711 788
info@bodegasmacaya.com
www.bodegasmacaya.com

Almara Cabernet Sauvignon Vendimia Seleccionada 2009 TR
cabernet sauvignon

88

Colour: very deep cherry, garnet rim. Nose: expressive, complex, mineral, balsamic herbs. Palate: full, flavourful, round tannins.

Condado de Almara Crianza 2011 TC
tempranillo, cabernet sauvignon

87

Colour: deep cherry, purple rim. Nose: creamy oak, toasty, ripe fruit, balsamic herbs. Palate: balanced, spicy, long.

Condado de Almara Reserva 2010 TR

88

Colour: cherry, garnet rim. Nose: ripe fruit, spicy, creamy oak. Palate: flavourful, toasty, round tannins.

Condado de Almara Selección 2010 T
tempranillo

89

Colour: ruby red. Nose: red berry notes, ripe fruit, spicy, creamy oak. Palate: flavourful, toasty, round tannins.

Finca Linte 2013 T
tempranillo

85

BODEGAS MARCO REAL

31390 Olite (Navarra)
☎: +34 948 712 193
Fax: +34 948 712 343
info@familiabelasco.com
www.grupolanavarra.com

Homenaje 2011 TC
tempranillo, merlot

87

Colour: cherry, garnet rim. Nose: ripe fruit, spicy, creamy oak. Palate: flavourful, toasty.

Homenaje 2013 T
tempranillo, cabernet sauvignon, merlot, syrah

83

Homenaje 2014 B
viura, chardonnay, moscatel

86

Homenaje 2014 RD
garnacha
86

Marco Real Colección Privada 2011 TC
tempranillo, cabernet sauvignon, merlot, graciano
89
Colour: very deep cherry, garnet rim. Nose: complex, mineral, ripe fruit. Palate: full, flavourful, round tannins.

Marco Real Pequeñas Producciones Garnacha 2012 T Roble
garnacha
90
Colour: cherry, garnet rim. Nose: red berry notes, ripe fruit, fragrant herbs, spicy, toasty, creamy oak, mineral. Palate: powerful, flavourful, balanced.

Marco Real Pequeñas Producciones Syrah 2012 T Roble
syrah
89
Colour: cherry, garnet rim. Nose: creamy oak, red berry notes, balanced, ripe fruit. Palate: flavourful, spicy, elegant.

Marco Real Pequeñas Producciones Tempranillo 2012 T Roble
tempranillo
88
Colour: cherry, garnet rim. Nose: ripe fruit, spicy, creamy oak, complex. Palate: flavourful, toasty, round tannins.

Marco Real Reserva de Familia 2009 TR
tempranillo, cabernet sauvignon, merlot, graciano
91
Colour: cherry, garnet rim. Nose: mineral, expressive, spicy, ripe fruit. Palate: flavourful, ripe fruit, long, good acidity.

BODEGAS NAPARRALDE

Crtra. de Madrid s/n
31591 Corella (Navarra)
☎: +34 948 782 255
Fax: +34 948 401 182
administracion@naparralde.com
www.upain.es

Upain 2014 RD
garnacha, tempranillo, cabernet sauvignon
85

Upain 2014 T
garnacha, tempranillo, cabernet sauvignon
83

Upain Selección Privada 2009 T
garnacha
85

Upain Syrah 2010 T
100% syrah
85

Upain Tempranillo Cabernet Sauvignon 2007 TC
70% tempranillo, 30% cabernet sauvignon
84

Upain Tempranillo Merlot Cabernet Sauvignon 2007 TR
60% tempranillo, 25% cabernet sauvignon, 15% merlot
85

Upain Tres Variedades Selección Privada 2008 T
33% garnacha, 33% tempranillo, 34% cabernet sauvignon
87
Colour: cherry, garnet rim. Nose: ripe fruit, wild herbs, spicy, balsamic herbs. Palate: flavourful, long, balsamic.

BODEGAS OCHOA

M. de Arga, 35
31390 Olite (Navarra)
☎: +34 948 740 006
Fax: +34 948 740 048
info@bodegasochoa.com
www.bodegasochoa.com

Ochoa 2008 TR
tempranillo, merlot, cabernet sauvignon
87
Colour: cherry, garnet rim. Nose: ripe fruit, wild herbs, green pepper. Palate: flavourful, long, balsamic.

Ochoa Calendas 2013 T Roble
garnacha, tempranillo
86

Ochoa Calendas 2014 B
viura, chardonnay, moscatel grano menudo
83

Ochoa Moscatel Vendimia Tardía 2013 Blanco dulce
moscatel grano menudo
87
Colour: bright straw. Nose: candied fruit, honeyed notes, sweet spices, balsamic herbs. Palate: powerful, flavourful, correct.

Ochoa Rosado de Lágrima 2014 RD
garnacha, cabernet sauvignon, merlot

85

Ochoa Serie 8A Mil Gracias 2012 TC
graciano

86

Ochoa Serie 8A Origen 2011 T
tempranillo, merlot, cabernet sauvignon

88

Colour: deep cherry, purple rim. Nose: creamy oak, ripe fruit, balsamic herbs. Palate: balanced, spicy, long.

BODEGAS OLIMPIA

Avda. Río Aragón, 1
31490 Cáseda (Navarra)
☎: +34 948 186 262
Fax: +34 948 186 565
info@bodegasolimpia.com
www.bodegasolimpia.com

F. Olimpia 15 de Abril 2014 RD
100% garnacha

85

F. Olimpia Garnacha Blanca 2014 B
100% garnacha blanca

82

F. Olimpia Legado de Familia 2012 T
100% garnacha

88

Colour: cherry, garnet rim. Nose: ripe fruit, wild herbs, spicy, balsamic herbs. Palate: flavourful, balsamic.

F. Olimpia Reserva 1917 2010 T
100% garnacha

87

Colour: cherry, garnet rim. Nose: ripe fruit, spicy, creamy oak. Palate: flavourful, toasty, round tannins.

BODEGAS ORVALAIZ

Ctra. Pamplona-Logroño, s/n
31151 Óbanos (Navarra)
☎: +34 948 344 437
Fax: +34 948 344 401
bodega@orvalaiz.es
www.orvalaiz.es

8:00 AM 2011 TC
tempranillo, merlot, cabernet sauvignon

84

8:00 AM 2014 RD
merlot

86

8:00 AM Chardonnay 2014 B
chardonnay

82

8:00 AM Devoción 2011 T
merlot, cabernet sauvignon

85

Orvalaiz 2011 TC
tempranillo, merlot, cabernet sauvignon

84

Orvalaiz Rosado de Lágrima 2014 RD
cabernet sauvignon

87

Colour: rose, purple rim. Nose: red berry notes, floral. Palate: powerful, fruity, fresh, easy to drink.

Septentrión 2011 TC
merlot, cabernet sauvignon, graciano

87

Colour: cherry, garnet rim. Nose: spicy, ripe fruit, sweet spices, powerfull. Palate: flavourful, ripe fruit, round tannins.

BODEGAS PAGOS DE ARÁIZ

Camino de Araiz, s/n
31390 Olite (Navarra)
☎: +34 948 399 182
info@bodegaspagosdearaiz.com
www.bodegaspagosdearaiz.com

Blaneo by Pagos de Aráiz 2013 T
syrah

87

Colour: bright cherry. Nose: ripe fruit, sweet spices, creamy oak, expressive. Palate: flavourful, fruity, round tannins.

Pagos de Aráiz 2012 TC
50% merlot, 30% tempranillo, 20% syrah

89

Colour: cherry, garnet rim. Nose: creamy oak, red berry notes, balanced. Palate: flavourful, spicy.

Pagos de Aráiz 2013 T Roble
50% tempranillo, 40% cabernet sauvignon, 10% graciano

85

Pagos de Aráiz 2014 RD
100% garnacha

87

Colour: rose, purple rim. Nose: red berry notes, floral. Palate: powerful, fruity, fresh, ripe fruit.

BODEGAS PIEDEMONTE

Rua Romana, s/n
31390 Olite (Navarra)
☎: +34 948 712 406
Fax: +34 948 740 090
bodega@piedemonte.com
www.piedemonte.com

Piedemonte +dQuince 2011 T
100% merlot

90

Colour: dark-red cherry, orangey edge. Nose: scrubland, fine reductive notes, spicy. Palate: elegant, balanced, round tannins.

Piedemonte 2010 TC
merlot, tempranillo, cabernet sauvignon

87

Colour: deep cherry, purple rim. Nose: creamy oak, toasty, ripe fruit, balsamic herbs. Palate: balanced, spicy, long.

Piedemonte 2010 TR
merlot, tempranillo, cabernet sauvignon

85

Piedemonte 2014 RD
100% garnacha

85

Piedemonte Cabernet Sauvignon 2010 TC
cabernet sauvignon

86

Piedemonte Chardonnay 2014 B
chardonnay

87

Colour: bright yellow. Nose: expressive, dried herbs, ripe fruit, spicy. Palate: flavourful, fruity, good acidity, balanced.

Piedemonte Gamma 2013 T
merlot, tempranillo, cabernet sauvignon

84

Piedemonte Gamma 2014 B
viura, chardonnay, moscatel

85

Piedemonte Granito de Arena 2010 TC
tempranillo

88

Colour: cherry, garnet rim. Nose: red berry notes, ripe fruit, spicy, creamy oak. Palate: flavourful, toasty, round tannins.

Piedemonte Merlot 2011 TC
merlot

84

Piedemonte Moscatel Dulce 2013 B
moscatel grano menudo

87

Colour: bright yellow. Nose: balsamic herbs, honeyed notes, floral, sweet spices. Palate: rich, fruity, powerful, flavourful.

BODEGAS PRÍNCIPE DE VIANA

31521 Murchante (Navarra)
☎: +34 948 838 640
Fax: +34 948 818 574
info@principedeviana.com
www.principedeviana.com

Príncipe de Viana 2010 TR
65% tempranillo, 20% merlot, 15% cabernet sauvignon

89

Colour: cherry, garnet rim. Nose: ripe fruit, spicy, creamy oak, complex. Palate: flavourful, toasty, round tannins, balanced.

Príncipe de Viana 1423 2010 TR
75% tempranillo, 10% merlot, 10% cabernet sauvignon, 5% garnacha

88

Colour: cherry, garnet rim. Nose: spicy, creamy oak, wild herbs, fruit preserve. Palate: flavourful, toasty, round tannins.

Príncipe de Viana 2012 TC
40% tempranillo, 30% cabernet sauvignon, 30% merlot

86

Príncipe de Viana Chardonnay 2014 BFB
chardonnay

86

Príncipe de Viana Edición Limitada 2011 TC
50% merlot, 25% tempranillo, 25% cabernet sauvignon

91

Colour: cherry, garnet rim. Nose: mineral, expressive, spicy, ripe fruit. Palate: flavourful, long, good acidity, balanced.

Príncipe de Viana Edición Rosa 2014 RD
100% garnacha

88

Colour: rose, purple rim. Nose: red berry notes, floral. Palate: powerful, fruity, fresh.

Príncipe de Viana Garnacha 2014 RD
100% garnacha

87

Colour: light cherry. Nose: red berry notes, floral, fragrant herbs. Palate: powerful, fruity, fresh, easy to drink.

Príncipe de Viana Garnacha 2014 T
100% garnacha

87

Colour: cherry, purple rim. Nose: powerfull, ripe fruit, spicy, creamy oak. Palate: powerful, fruity, unctuous.

Príncipe de Viana Tempranillo 2014 T Roble
100% tempranillo

89

Colour: bright cherry. Nose: ripe fruit, sweet spices, creamy oak, expressive. Palate: flavourful, fruity, round tannins.

Príncipe de Viana Vendimia Tardía de Chardonnay Dulce 2013 B
100% chardonnay

89

Colour: bright yellow. Nose: faded flowers, sweet spices, candied fruit, honeyed notes, characterful. Palate: rich, fruity. Personality.

BODEGAS URABAIN

Ctra. Estella, 21
31262 Allo (Navarra)
☎: +34 619 110 610
vinos@bodegasurabain.com
www.bodegasurabain.com

Prado de Chica 2010 TC
merlot

88

Colour: cherry, garnet rim. Nose: ripe fruit, wild herbs, earthy notes, spicy, balsamic herbs. Palate: balanced, flavourful, long, balsamic.

Un Paso Más 2009 TC
tempranillo, cabernet sauvignon, merlot

90

Colour: cherry, garnet rim. Nose: spicy, scrubland, toasty. Palate: flavourful, ripe fruit, long, good acidity, balanced.

Urabain Rosado de Lágrima 2014 RD
merlot

86

BODEGAS VALCARLOS

Ctra. Circunvalación, s/n
31210 Los Arcos (Navarra)
☎: +34 948 640 806
Fax: +34 948 640 866
info@bodegasvalcarlos.com
www.bodegasvalcarlos.com

Élite de Fortius 2009 TR

88

Colour: cherry, garnet rim. Nose: fine reductive notes, ripe fruit, spicy. Palate: spicy, long, toasty.

Fortius 2004 TGR

88

Colour: bright cherry, orangey edge. Nose: old leather, toasty. Palate: balanced, classic aged character, flavourful.

Fortius 2014 RD

87

Colour: rose, purple rim. Nose: red berry notes, floral, expressive. Palate: powerful, fruity, fresh.

Fortius Chardonnay 2014 B

85

Fortius Chardonnay Viura 2014 B
chardonnay, viura

84

Fortius Tempranillo 2008 TR

86

Fortius Tempranillo 2010 TC
tempranillo

86

Fortius Tempranillo 2013 T Roble
84

Marqués de Valcarlos 2010 TC
86

Marqués de Valcarlos 2014 B
viura, chardonnay

86

Marqués de Valcarlos 2014 RD
86

Marqués de Valcarlos Chardonnay 2014 B
85

Marqués de Valcarlos Tempranillo 2013 T Roble
84

BODEGAS VEGA DEL CASTILLO

Rua Romana, 7
31390 Olite (Navarra)
☎: +34 948 740 012
Fax: +34 948 741 074
info@vegadelcastillo.com
www.vegadelcastillo.com

Capa Roja 2013 T Roble
tempranillo

87

Colour: deep cherry, purple rim. Nose: creamy oak, toasty, ripe fruit, balsamic herbs. Palate: balanced, spicy, long.

Merak 2009 T
merlot, cabernet sauvignon, tempranillo

88

Colour: very deep cherry, garnet rim. Nose: expressive, balsamic herbs, balanced. Palate: full, flavourful, round tannins.

Vega del Castillo 2012 TC
tempranillo, merlot, cabernet sauvignon

86

BODEGAS VINÍCOLA NAVARRA

Avda. Pamplona, 25
31398 Tiebas (Navarra)
☎: +34 948 360 131
Fax: +34 948 360 544
vinicolanavarra@pernod-ricard.com
www.bodegasvinicolanavarra.com

Las Campanas 1864 2014 B
100% chardonnay

86

Las Campanas 1864 2014 RD
100% garnacha

88

Colour: raspberry rose. Nose: elegant, red berry notes, floral, fragrant herbs. Palate: light-bodied, flavourful, good acidity, spicy.

Las Campanas 2014 RD
garnacha

87

Colour: rose, purple rim. Nose: red berry notes, rose petals, fragrant herbs. Palate: fruity, fresh.

BODEGAS Y VIÑEDOS ALZANIA

Cardiel, 1
31210 Los Arcos (Navarra)
☎: +34 607 214 279
Fax: +34 948 378 924
alzania@knet.es

Alzania 2009 TR
40% tempranillo, 30% merlot, 30% cabernet sauvignon

89

Colour: cherry, garnet rim. Nose: ripe fruit, wild herbs, earthy notes, spicy, balsamic herbs. Palate: balanced, flavourful, long, balsamic.

Alzania 21 del 10 2012 T
100% syrah

84

Alzania El Retorno 2013 T Roble
100% garnacha

87

Colour: deep cherry, purple rim. Nose: creamy oak, toasty, balsamic herbs, floral. Palate: spicy, long, balanced.

Alzania Finca la Moneda 2010 T
60% merlot, 25% syrah, 15% garnacha

88

Colour: very deep cherry, garnet rim. Nose: complex, balsamic herbs, balanced, ripe fruit. Palate: full, flavourful, round tannins.

BODEGAS Y VIÑEDOS QUADERNA VIA

Ctra. Estella - Logroño, Km. 4
31241 Iguzquiza (Navarra)
☎: +34 948 554 083
Fax: +34 948 556 540
comercial@quadernavia.com
www.quadernavia.com

Initium 2014 T
84

Quaderna Via 2010 TR
85

Quaderna Via 2011 TC
83

Quaderna Via 2014 T Maceración Carbónica
tempranillo

86

Quaderna Via Especial 2013 T
90% tempranillo, 10% cabernet sauvignon

82

QV 2010 T
88

Colour: cherry, garnet rim. Nose: spicy, creamy oak, overripe fruit. Palate: flavourful, toasty.

CRIANZAS Y VIÑEDOS R. REVERTE

Lejalde, 43
31593 Fitero (Navarra)
☎: +34 948 780 617
Fax: +34 948 401 894
odipus@rafaelreverte.es
www.rafaelreverte.es

Cistum 2012 T
85

Odipus 1899 2013 T
garnacha

88

Colour: bright cherry. Nose: ripe fruit, sweet spices, creamy oak, expressive. Palate: fruity, round tannins, balanced.

DOMAINES LUPIER

31495 San Martín de Unx (Navarra)
☎: +34 639 622 111
info@domaineslupier.com
www.domaineslupier.com

Domaines Lupier El Terroir 2012 T
100% garnacha

94

Colour: deep cherry, purple rim. Nose: creamy oak, toasty, ripe fruit, balsamic herbs. Palate: balanced, spicy, long.

PODIUM

Domaines Lupier La Dama 2012 T
100% garnacha

95

Colour: cherry, garnet rim. Nose: creamy oak, red berry notes, fresh fruit, balanced, earthy notes. Palate: flavourful, spicy, fine bitter notes, fine tannins.

EMILIO VALERIO - LADERAS DE MONTEJURRA

31263 Dicastillo (Navarra)
info@laderasdemontejurra.com
www.laderasdemontejurra.com

Emilio Valerio Laderas de Montejurra 2013 T
garnacha, tempranillo, merlot, cabernet sauvignon

92

Colour: light cherry. Nose: expressive, complex, mineral, balsamic herbs, balanced. Palate: full, flavourful, round tannins.

La Merced 2013 B
malvasía

90

Colour: bright yellow. Nose: white flowers, fine lees, ripe fruit, candied fruit, citrus fruit, sweet spices, expressive. Palate: flavourful, fruity, good acidity, elegant.

Usuaran 2011 T
garnacha, tempranillo, graciano

92

Colour: cherry, garnet rim. Nose: ripe fruit, wild herbs, earthy notes, spicy, balsamic herbs. Palate: balanced, flavourful, long, balsamic.

Viña de San Martín 2012 T
garnacha

93

Colour: cherry, garnet rim. Nose: mineral, expressive, spicy, red berry notes, balsamic herbs, elegant. Palate: flavourful, ripe fruit, long, good acidity, balanced.

Viñas de Amburza 2011 T
cabernet sauvignon

90

Colour: bright cherry. Nose: ripe fruit, wild herbs, earthy notes, spicy, balsamic herbs, old leather. Palate: balanced, flavourful, long, balsamic.

FINCA ALBRET

Ctra. Cadreita-Villafranca, s/n
31515 Cadreita (Navarra)
☎: +34 948 406 806
Fax: +34 948 406 699
info@fincaalbret.com
www.fincaalbret.com

Albret 2010 TR
85% tempranillo, 10% cabernet sauvignon, 5% merlot

90

Colour: cherry, garnet rim. Nose: balanced, complex, ripe fruit, spicy, scrubland. Palate: good structure, flavourful, round tannins, balanced.

Albret 2014 RD
100% garnacha

89

Colour: rose, bright. Nose: red berry notes, floral, expressive. Palate: fruity, balanced, ripe fruit, spicy.

Albret Chardonnay 2014 BFB
100% chardonnay

89

Colour: bright yellow. Nose: expressive, ripe fruit, spicy, tropical fruit. Palate: flavourful, fruity, good acidity, balanced.

Albret Garnacha 2013 T Roble
100% garnacha

87

Colour: cherry, garnet rim. Nose: red berry notes, ripe fruit, spicy, creamy oak, complex. Palate: flavourful, toasty, round tannins.

Albret Garnacha 2014 T Roble
100% garnacha

91

Colour: bright cherry, purple rim. Nose: wild herbs, ripe fruit, red berry notes. Palate: correct, balanced, easy to drink, fresh.

Albret La Viña de mi Madre 2010 TR
95% cabernet sauvignon, 5% merlot

93

Colour: cherry, garnet rim. Nose: mineral, expressive, spicy, elegant. Palate: flavourful, ripe fruit, long, good acidity, balanced.

Albret Tempranillo 2014 T Roble
100% tempranillo

88

Colour: bright cherry. Nose: ripe fruit, spicy, varietal. Palate: flavourful, fruity, round tannins.

Juan de Albret 2012 TC
60% tempranillo, 20% merlot, 20% cabernet sauvignon

87

Colour: bright cherry, garnet rim. Nose: fruit preserve, grassy. Palate: spicy, balanced, round tannins.

GARCÍA BURGOS

Finca La Cantera de Santa Ana, s/n
31521 Murchante (Navarra)
☎: +34 948 847 734
Fax: +34 948 847 734
info@bodegasgarciaburgos.com
www.bodegasgarciaburgos.com

Finca La Cantera de Santa Ana 2010 TR
cabernet sauvignon

90

Colour: cherry, garnet rim. Nose: ripe fruit, wild herbs, spicy, fine reductive notes. Palate: balanced, flavourful, long, balsamic.

García Burgos Sh 2011 T
syrah

89

Colour: very deep cherry, garnet rim. Nose: complex, mineral, balsamic herbs, fruit preserve. Palate: full, flavourful, round tannins.

García Burgos Vendimia Seleccionada 2011 T
cabernet sauvignon, merlot, syrah

89

Colour: cherry, garnet rim. Nose: ripe fruit, wild herbs, spicy, balsamic herbs, fine reductive notes. Palate: flavourful, long, balsamic, fine tannins.

Lola García 2010 TR
merlot

88

Colour: pale ruby, brick rim edge. Nose: spicy, fine reductive notes, wet leather, ripe fruit. Palate: spicy, long, balsamic.

GONZALO CELAYETA WINES

Barrandón, 6
31390 Olite (Navarra)
☎: +34 620 208 817
info@gonzalocelayetawines.com
www.gonzalocelayetawines.com

Hacienda El Caserío 2013 B
garnacha blanca

89

Colour: bright straw. Nose: white flowers, fresh fruit, fragrant herbs, expressive. Palate: flavourful, fruity, good acidity, balanced.

La Huella de Aitana 2014 RD
garnacha

90

Colour: light cherry. Nose: rose petals, fragrant herbs, fresh fruit, candied fruit, sweet spices. Palate: fresh, fruity, flavourful.

J. CHIVITE FAMILY ESTATE

Ctra. NA-132, Km. 3
31264 Aberin (Navarra)
☎: +34 948 811 000
Fax: +34 948 811 407
info@grupochivite.com
www.chivite.com

Chivite Colección 125 2011 TR
100% tempranillo, cabernet sauvignon

94

Colour: light cherry. Nose: fine reductive notes, aged wood nuances, toasty. Palate: spicy, toasty, flavourful, fine bitter notes, good acidity.

PODIUM

Chivite Colección 125 2012 BFB
chardonnay

95

Colour: bright straw. Nose: white flowers, fine lees, dried herbs, ripe fruit, citrus fruit. Palate: flavourful, fruity, good acidity, elegant.

Chivite Colección 125 2013 RD Fermentado en Barrica
tempranillo, garnacha

93

Colour: onion pink. Nose: elegant, red berry notes, floral, fragrant herbs. Palate: light-bodied, flavourful, good acidity, long, spicy.

Chivite Finca de Villatuerta Chardonnay sobre Lías 2013 B
chardonnay

93

Colour: bright straw. Nose: white flowers, fresh fruit, fragrant herbs. Palate: flavourful, fruity, good acidity, balanced.

Chivite Finca de Villatuerta Selección Especial 2010 T
tempranillo, merlot

92

Colour: cherry, garnet rim. Nose: ripe fruit, spicy, creamy oak. Palate: flavourful, toasty, round tannins, balanced.

Chivite Finca de Villatuerta Syrah Garnacha 2012 T
syrah, garnacha

93

Colour: deep cherry, purple rim. Nose: creamy oak, toasty, ripe fruit, balsamic herbs. Palate: balanced, spicy, long.

NEKEAS

Las Huertas, s/n
31154 Añorbe (Navarra)
☎: +34 948 350 296
Fax: +34 948 350 300
nekeas@nekeas.com
www.nekeas.com

El Chaparral de Vega Sindoa Old Vine Garnacha 2013 T
100% garnacha

87

Colour: cherry, purple rim. Nose: ripe fruit, woody, roasted coffee. Palate: flavourful, spicy, powerful.

Nekeas 2012 TC
cabernet sauvignon, tempranillo

89

Colour: bright cherry. Nose: toasty, ripe fruit, balsamic herbs. Palate: balanced, long, spicy, fruity.

Nekeas 2014 RD
merlot, garnacha, tempranillo

86

Nekeas Cabernet Sauvignon Merlot 2010 TR
cabernet sauvignon, merlot

87

Colour: cherry, garnet rim. Nose: fine reductive notes, spicy, ripe fruit. Palate: spicy, long, toasty, round tannins.

Nekeas Chardonnay 2014 B
100% chardonnay

88

Colour: bright straw. Nose: white flowers, dried herbs, ripe fruit, citrus fruit. Palate: flavourful, fruity, good acidity, elegant.

Vega Sindoa 2014 RD
garnacha

87

Colour: raspberry rose. Nose: red berry notes, floral, fragrant herbs. Palate: light-bodied, flavourful, easy to drink.

Vega Sindoa Cabernet 2013 T
100% cabernet sauvignon

85

Vega Sindoa Chardonnay Barrel Fermented 2014 BFB
100% chardonnay

87

Colour: bright yellow. Nose: ripe fruit, powerfull, toasty, aged wood nuances, pattiserie. Palate: flavourful, fruity, spicy, toasty, long.

NUEVOS VINOS CB, S.L.

San Juan Bosco 32
03804 Alcoy (Alicante)
☎: +34 965 549 172
Fax: +34 965 549 173
josecanto@nuevosvinos.es
www.nuevosvinos.es

Terraplen Rosado Garnacha 2014 RD
100% garnacha

87

Colour: light cherry. Nose: floral, wild herbs, fruit expression, expressive. Palate: flavourful, complex.

Terraplen Tinto Garnacha 2014 T
100% garnacha

86

Terraplen Viura 2014 B
100% viura

86

PAGO DE LARRÁINZAR

Camino de la Corona, s/n
31240 Ayegui (Navarra)
☎: +34 948 550 421
Fax: +34 948 556 120
info@pagodelarrainzar.com
www.pagodelarrainzar.com

Angel de Larrainzar 2014 T
40% tempranillo, 30% merlot, 20% cabernet sauvignon, 10% garnacha

87

Colour: deep cherry, purple rim. Nose: ripe fruit, balsamic herbs, aged wood nuances. Palate: balanced, spicy, long.

Pago de Larrainzar 2009 TR
50% merlot, 35% cabernet sauvignon, 10% tempranillo, 5% garnacha

91

Colour: cherry, garnet rim. Nose: balanced, complex, ripe fruit, spicy, fine reductive notes. Palate: good structure, flavourful, round tannins, balanced.

Raso de Larrainzar 2010 T
40% tempranillo, 30% cabernet sauvignon, 25% merlot, 5% garnacha

92

Colour: cherry, garnet rim. Nose: ripe fruit, wild herbs, earthy notes, spicy, balsamic herbs, elegant. Palate: balanced, flavourful, long, balsamic.

PROYECTO ZORZAL

Ctra. del Villar, s/n
31591 Corella (Navarra)
☎: +34 948 780 617
Fax: +34 948 401 894
xabi@vinazorzal.com
www.vinazorzal.com

Corral de los Altos 2013 T

91

Colour: deep cherry. Nose: creamy oak, toasty, ripe fruit, balsamic herbs, earthy notes. Palate: balanced, spicy, long.

Viña Zorzal Garnacha 2014 T
100% garnacha

89

Colour: bright cherry, purple rim. Nose: balanced, red berry notes, ripe fruit. Palate: balanced, good acidity.

Viña Zorzal Graciano 2013 T
100% graciano

91

Colour: bright cherry. Nose: ripe fruit, sweet spices, creamy oak, varietal. Palate: flavourful, fruity, round tannins.

Viña Zorzal La Señora de las Alturas 2012 T
garnacha, graciano

92

Colour: bright cherry. Nose: ripe fruit, sweet spices, creamy oak. Palate: flavourful, fruity, toasty, round tannins.

Viña Zorzal Tempranillo 2014 T
100% tempranillo

89

Colour: cherry, purple rim. Nose: red berry notes, floral, balsamic herbs, earthy notes. Palate: powerful, fresh, fruity, full.

Viñas Zorzal Malayeto 2013 T
100% garnacha

91

Colour: cherry, garnet rim. Nose: ripe fruit, fragrant herbs, spicy, creamy oak, mineral. Palate: flavourful, balsamic, balanced.

SEÑORÍO DE ANDIÓN

Ctra. Pamplona-Zaragoza, Km. 38
31390 Olite (Navarra)
☎: +34 948 712 193
Fax: +34 948 712 343
info@familiabelasco.com
www.grupolanavarra.com

Señorío de Andión 2010 T
tempranillo, cabernet sauvignon, merlot, graciano

91

Colour: cherry, garnet rim. Nose: expressive, spicy, scrubland. Palate: flavourful, ripe fruit, long, good acidity, balanced.

Señorío de Andión Moscatel Dulce 2007 B
moscatel grano menudo

94

Colour: old gold, amber rim. Nose: powerfull, honeyed notes, candied fruit, sweet spices. Palate: flavourful, sweet, fresh, fruity, good acidity, long. Personality.

SIETE PASOS THE WINE COMPANY

Calahorra, 12
26006 Logroño (La Rioja)
☎: +34 941 439 388
info@sietepasos.com
www.sietepasos.com

La Lianta 2014 B
chardonnay

85

VINOS Y VIÑEDOS DOMINIO LASIERPE

Ribera, s/n
31592 Cintruénigo (Navarra)
☎: +34 948 811 033
Fax: +34 948 815 160
comercial@dominiolasierpe.com
www.dominiolasierpe.com

Dominio Lasierpe 2012 TC
garnacha, graciano, tempranillo

85

Finca Lasierpe Blanco de Viura 2014 B
100% viura

84

Finca Lasierpe Chardonnay 2014 B
100% chardonnay

87

Colour: bright straw. Nose: white flowers, fresh fruit, fragrant herbs. Palate: flavourful, fruity, good acidity, balanced.

Finca Lasierpe Garnacha 2014 RD
100% garnacha

85

Finca Lasierpe Garnacha 2014 T
garnacha

86

VIÑA VALDORBA

Ctra. de la Estación, s7n
31395 Garinoain (Navarra)
☎: +34 948 720 505
Fax: +34 948 720 505
bodegasvaldorba@bodegasvaldorba.com
www.bodegasvaldorba.com

Cauro 2002 TR
graciano, cabernet sauvignon

89

Colour: dark-red cherry, orangey edge. Nose: toasty, fine reductive notes, scrubland, dried herbs. Palate: balanced, flavourful, ripe fruit.

Eolo 2012 TC
cabernet sauvignon, tempranillo, merlot, garnacha

86

Eolo Chardonnay 2014 B
100% chardonnay

88

Colour: bright straw. Nose: white flowers, fresh fruit, fragrant herbs, expressive. Palate: flavourful, fruity, good acidity, balanced.

Eolo Moscatel Dulce 2013 B
moscatel

87

Colour: bright straw. Nose: white flowers, fresh fruit, medium intensity. Palate: flavourful, fruity, good acidity, balanced.

Eolo Rosado Sangrado 2014 RD
70% garnacha, 30% tempranillo

87

Colour: light cherry, bright. Nose: medium intensity. Palate: easy to drink, correct, ripe fruit, good finish, fresh.

Eolo Syrah 2011 T
syrah

88

Colour: bright cherry. Nose: ripe fruit, sweet spices, creamy oak, expressive. Palate: flavourful, fruity, round tannins.

Gran Eolo 2010 TR
cabernet sauvignon, merlot

82

VIÑEDOS DE CALIDAD

Ctra. Tudela, s/n
31591 Corella (Navarra)
☎: +34 948 782 014
Fax: +34 948 782 164
javier@vinosalex.com
www.vinosalex.com

Alex 2009 TR
tempranillo, merlot

89

Colour: cherry, garnet rim. Nose: ripe fruit, wild herbs, earthy notes, spicy, balsamic herbs. Palate: balanced, flavourful, long, balsamic.

Alex 2011 TC
tempranillo, merlot, graciano

87

Colour: cherry, garnet rim. Nose: ripe fruit, spicy, creamy oak, complex. Palate: flavourful, toasty.

Alex Garnacha 2014 RD
garnacha

87

Colour: light cherry, bright. Nose: medium intensity, fresh fruit, red berry notes. Palate: fruity, easy to drink.

Alex Tempranillo 2014 T
tempranillo

87

Colour: cherry, purple rim. Nose: red berry notes, wild herbs, floral. Palate: fresh, fruity, flavourful.

Alex Viura 2014 B
viura

85

Ontinar 2010 T
tempranillo, merlot

87

Colour: ruby red. Nose: spicy, fine reductive notes, ripe fruit, balsamic herbs. Palate: spicy, elegant, long.

VIÑEDOS Y BODEGAS ALCONDE

Ctra. de Calahorra, s/n
31260 Lerín (Navarra)
☎: +34 948 530 058
Fax: +34 948 530 589
ventas@bodegasalconde.com
www.bodegasalconde.com

Bodegas Alconde 2007 TR
merlot, cabernet sauvignon, tempranillo, garnacha

89

Colour: dark-red cherry, orangey edge. Nose: ripe fruit, expressive, balanced, spicy, balsamic herbs, tobacco, fruit preserve. Palate: good structure, round tannins.

Bodegas Alconde Sauvignon Blanc Selección 2014 B
sauvignon blanc

86

Bodegas Alconde Selección "Tinto Roble" 2013 T Roble
merlot, garnacha

85

Bodegas Alconde Selección 2008 TR
tempranillo, cabernet sauvignon, merlot

90

Colour: pale ruby, brick rim edge. Nose: elegant, spicy, fine reductive notes, tobacco, balsamic herbs. Palate: spicy, fine tannins, elegant, long.

Bodegas Alconde Selección 2009 TC
tempranillo, garnacha, cabernet sauvignon

88

Colour: cherry, garnet rim. Nose: ripe fruit, spicy, creamy oak. Palate: flavourful, toasty, round tannins.

Bodegas Alconde Selección Garnacha 2008 TR
garnacha, cabernet sauvignon, merlot

89

Colour: pale ruby, brick rim edge. Nose: spicy, fine reductive notes, aged wood nuances, fruit liqueur notes. Palate: spicy, fine tannins, balanced.

Viña Sardasol 2011 TC
tempranillo

86

Viña Sardasol 2014 B
chardonnay

84

Viña Sardasol Rosado de Lágrima 2014 RD
garnacha

85

DO. PENEDÈS

CONSEJO REGULADOR

Plaça Àgora. s/n. Pol. Ind. Domenys, II
08720 Vilafranca del Penedès (Barcelona)
☎:+34 938 904 811 - Fax: +34 938 904 754
@: dopenedes@dopenedes.cat
www.dopenedes.es

LOCATION:

In the province of Barcelona, between the pre-coastal Catalonian mountain range and the plains that lead to the Mediterranean coast. There are three different areas: Penedès Superior, Penedès Central or Medio and Bajo Penedès.

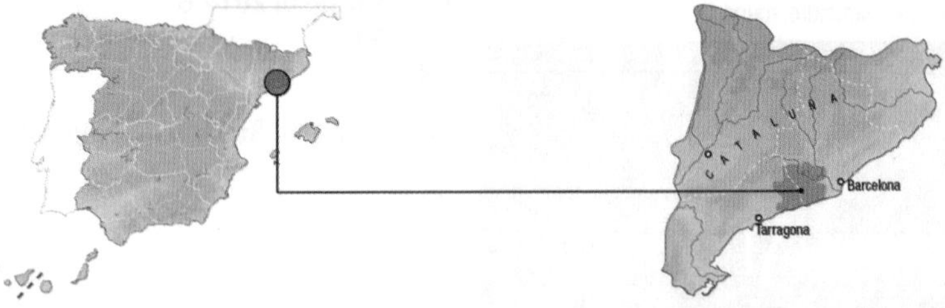

SUB-REGIONS:

Penedès Superior. The vineyards reach an altitude of 800 m; the traditional, characteristic variety is the Parellada, which is better suited to the cooler regions.

Penedès Central or Medio. Cava makes up a large part of the production in this region; the most abundant traditional varieties are Macabeo and Xarel-lo.

Bajo Penedès. This is the closest region to the sea, with a lower altitude and wines with a markedly Mediterranean character.

GRAPE VARIETIES:

WHITE: Macabeo, Xarel·lo, Parellada, Chardonnay, Riesling, Gewürztraminer, Chenin Blanc, Moscatel de Alejandría, Garnacha Blanca and Vioquier.

RED: Garnacha, Merlot, Cariñena, Ull de Llebre (Tempranillo), Pinot Noir, Monastrell, Cabernet Sauvignon, Petit Verdot, Syrah and Sumoll.

FIGURES:

Vineyard surface: 17,000 – **Wine-Growers:** 2,500 – **Wineries:** 170 – **2014 Harvest rating:** Very Good – **Production 14:** 13,844,000 litres – **Market percentages:** 75% National - 25% International.

SOIL:

There is deep soil, not too sandy or too clayey, permeable, which retains the rainwater well. The soil is poor in organic matter and not very fertile.

CLIMATE:

Mediterranean, in general warm and mild; warmer in the Bajo Penedès region due to the influence of the Mediterranean Sea, with slightly lower temperatures in Medio Penedès and Penedès Superior, where the climate is typically pre-coastal (greater contrasts between maximum and minimum temperatures, more frequent frosts and annual rainfall which at some places can reach 990 litres per square metre).

VINTAGE RATING

PEÑÍNGUIDE

2010	2011	2012	2013	2014
VERY GOOD	VERY GOOD	GOOD	VERY GOOD	GOOD

1 + 1 = 3

Masía Navinés
08736 Font-Rubí (Barcelona)
☎: +34 938 974 069
teresa@umesufan3.com
www.umesufan3.com

1+1=3 Xarel.lo 2014 B
xarel.lo

89

Colour: bright straw. Nose: white flowers, fresh fruit, fragrant herbs, expressive. Palate: flavourful, fruity, good acidity.

Dahlia 1 + 1 = 3 2013 B
viognier, xarel.lo

90

Colour: bright straw. Nose: white flowers, fresh fruit, fragrant herbs, expressive. Palate: flavourful, fruity, good acidity, balanced.

Dahlia 1 + 1 = 3 2014 RD
garnacha

90

Colour: pale. Nose: elegant, red berry notes, floral, fragrant herbs. Palate: light-bodied, flavourful, good acidity, long, spicy. Personality.

AGUSTÍ TORELLÓ MATA

La Serra, s/n
08770 Sant Sadurní D'Anoia (Barcelona)
☎: +34 938 911 173
Fax: +34 938 912 616
visites@agustitorellomata.com
www.agustitorellomata.com

Agustí Torelló Subirat Parent 2013 B
subirat parent

87

Colour: bright yellow. Nose: dried herbs, ripe fruit, spicy. Palate: flavourful, fruity, good acidity.

Aptià d'Agustí Torelló Mata 2012 BFB
100% macabeo

93

Colour: bright straw. Nose: white flowers, fine lees, dried herbs, citrus fruit, dry stone. Palate: flavourful, fruity, good acidity.

Xarel.lo d'Agustí Torelló Mata XIC 2014 B
xarel.lo

86

ALBET I NOYA

Can Vendrell de la Codina, s/n
08739 Sant Pau D'Ordal (Barcelona)
☎: +34 938 994 812
Fax: +34 938 994 930
info@albetinoya.cat
www.albetinoya.cat

Albet i Noya 2011 BR Reserva
macabeo, xarel.lo, parellada, chardonnay

87

Colour: bright straw, greenish rim. Nose: wild herbs, expressive, fresh. Palate: correct, fine bitter notes, easy to drink.

Albet i Noya 3 Macabeus 2014 B
macabeo

87

Colour: bright straw. Nose: fresh, medium intensity, wild herbs. Palate: correct, fine bitter notes, good acidity.

Albet i Noya Brut 21 2012 BR
parellada, chardonnay

90

Colour: bright golden. Nose: fine lees, dry nuts, fragrant herbs, complex, toasty. Palate: powerful, flavourful, good acidity, fine bead, fine bitter notes.

Albet i Noya Brut 21 Barrica 2007 BR Gran Reserva
pinot noir, chardonnay

92

Colour: bright golden. Nose: dry nuts, fragrant herbs, complex, fine lees, sweet spices, expressive. Palate: powerful, flavourful, good acidity, fine bead, fine bitter notes, elegant.

Albet i Noya Col.lecció Chardonnay 2014 B
chardonnay

91

Colour: bright yellow. Nose: expressive, dried herbs, ripe fruit, spicy. Palate: flavourful, fruity, balanced, rich.

Albet i Noya Col.lecció Syrah 2011 T
syrah

91

Colour: cherry, garnet rim. Nose: ripe fruit, floral, scrubland, creamy oak. Palate: good structure, flavourful, round tannins.

Albet i Noya Dolç Adrià 2007 TR
syrah, merlot

91

Colour: bright cherry, garnet rim. Nose: acetaldehyde, varnish, overripe fruit. Palate: fruity, flavourful, sweet.

Albet i Noya El Blanc XXV "ecológico" 2013 B
viognier, vidal, marina rion

92

Colour: bright straw. Nose: white flowers, fine lees, dried herbs, ripe fruit, citrus fruit. Palate: flavourful, fruity, good acidity, elegant.

Albet i Noya EL Fanio 2013 B
xarel.lo

91

Colour: bright straw. Nose: fresh fruit, fragrant herbs, expressive. Palate: flavourful, good acidity, balanced.

Albet i Noya Lignum 2012 T
tempranillo, garnacha, cabernet sauvignon, syrah, merlot

88

Colour: deep cherry. Nose: creamy oak, toasty, ripe fruit, balsamic herbs. Palate: balanced, spicy.

Albet i Noya Lignum 2013 B
xarel.lo, chardonnay, sauvignon blanc

91

Colour: bright straw. Nose: expressive, sweet spices, balanced. Palate: flavourful, ripe fruit, fine bitter notes, long.

Albet i Noya Nosodos + Xarel.lo 2014 BN
xarel.lo

87

Colour: bright yellow. Nose: ripe fruit, fine lees, balanced, dried herbs. Palate: good acidity, easy to drink.

Albet i Noya Petit Albet 2013 BR
macabeo, xarel.lo, parellada

87

Colour: bright straw. Nose: fresh fruit, dried herbs, fine lees, floral. Palate: fresh, fruity, flavourful, good acidity.

Albet i Noya Pinot Noir Brut Rosat 2011 BR
pinot noir

87

Colour: rose. Nose: floral, red berry notes, ripe fruit. Palate: powerful, balanced, flavourful.

Albet i Noya Pinot Noir Merlot Clàssic 2014 RD
pinot noir, merlot

89

Colour: raspberry rose. Nose: red berry notes, floral, fragrant herbs. Palate: light-bodied, flavourful, spicy.

Albet i Noya Reserva 3 2010 BN
macabeo, xarel.lo, parellada, chardonnay

88

Colour: bright straw. Nose: ripe fruit, fine lees, balanced, dried herbs. Palate: good acidity, flavourful, ripe fruit, long.

Albet i Noya Reserva Martí 2008 TR
tempranillo, cabernet sauvignon, syrah, merlot

93

Colour: cherry, garnet rim. Nose: ripe fruit, wild herbs, earthy notes, spicy, balsamic herbs. Palate: balanced, flavourful, long, balsamic, elegant.

Albet i Noya Tempranillo Clàssic 2013 T
tempranillo

88

Colour: dark-red cherry, garnet rim. Nose: ripe fruit, balanced, warm, spicy. Palate: flavourful, correct.

Albet i Noya Xarel.lo 2014 B
xarel.lo

87

Colour: bright straw. Nose: dried flowers, fragrant herbs. Palate: correct, fine bitter notes, easy to drink, good finish.

Albet i Noya Xarel.lo Nosodos + 2014 B
xarel.lo

85

Belat 2009 T
belat

93

Colour: cherry, garnet rim. Nose: balanced, complex, spicy, floral, fruit preserve. Palate: good structure, flavourful, round tannins, balanced. Personality.

La Milana 2012 T
caladoc, tempranillo, cabernet sauvignon, merlot

92

Colour: cherry, garnet rim. Nose: ripe fruit, wild herbs, earthy notes, spicy, balsamic herbs. Palate: balanced, flavourful, long, balsamic.

Marina Rion "ecológico" 2014 B
marina rión

88

Colour: bright straw. Nose: white flowers, fresh fruit, expressive. Palate: fruity, good acidity, balanced.

Ocell de Foc 2013 T
caladoc, marcelan, arinarnoa

90

Colour: cherry, garnet rim. Nose: red berry notes, ripe fruit, fragrant herbs, spicy, toasty, creamy oak. Palate: powerful, flavourful, balsamic, balanced.

ALEMANY I CORRIO

Melió, 78
08720 Vilafranca del Penedès
(Barcelona)
☎: +34 938 180 949
sotlefriec@sotlefriec.com
www.alemany-corrio.com

Pas Curtei 2012 T

91 ♣

Colour: bright cherry. Nose: ripe fruit, sweet spices, creamy oak. Palate: flavourful, fruity, toasty, round tannins.

Principia Mathematica 2014 B

xarel.lo

88 ♣

Colour: bright straw. Nose: dried herbs, faded flowers, ripe fruit, slightly evolved. Palate: ripe fruit, thin.

Sot Lefriec 2012 T

93

Colour: cherry, garnet rim. Nose: mineral, expressive, spicy. Palate: flavourful, ripe fruit, long, good acidity.

ALSINA & SARDÁ

Barrio Les Tarumbas, s/n
08733 Pla del Penedès (Barcelona)
☎: +34 938 988 671
Fax: +34 938 988 671
gestio@alsinasarda.com
www.alsinasarda.com

Alsina & Sardá Blanc de Blancs 2014 B

macabeo, xarel.lo, parellada

85

Alsina & Sardá Chardonnay Xarel.lo 2014 B

50% chardonnay, 50% xarel.lo

85

Alsina & Sardá Eclosió 2014 B

50% xarel.lo, 50% subirat parent

86

Alsina & Sardá Finca Cal Janes 2012 T

merlot

85

Alsina & Sardá Finca La Boltana 2014 B

xarel.lo

88

Colour: bright yellow. Nose: dried herbs, ripe fruit, spicy, floral. Palate: flavourful, fruity, good acidity.

Alsina & Sardá Finca Olérdola 2011 TR

cabernet sauvignon

89

Colour: bright cherry. Nose: balsamic herbs, balanced, ripe fruit, sweet spices. Palate: full, flavourful, spicy.

Alsina & Sardá Merlot Llàgrima 2014 RD

merlot

84

Alsina & Sardá Muscat Llàgrima 2014 B

moscatel

87

Colour: bright straw. Nose: balsamic herbs, floral, expressive. Palate: fruity, flavourful, easy to drink.

Arnau Merlot 2014 T

merlot

84

ARBOLEDA MEDITERRÁNEA

Ctra Sant Sadurni - Piera
08784 La Fortesa (Piera) (Barcelona)
☎: +34 937 279 831
Fax: +34 937 478 891
export@arboledamediterranea.com
www.arboledamediterranean.com

Amantium Cuvée Blanc 2014 B

83

Amantium Cuvée Rosé 2014 RD

ull de llebre, merlot

84

AT ROCA

La Vinya, 15
08770 Sant Sadurní D'Anoia
(Barcelona)
☎: +34 935 165 043
info@atroca.es
www.cellersatroca.com

At Roca 2013 BR Reserva

macabeo, xarel.lo, parellada

89 ♣

Colour: bright straw. Nose: fine lees, floral, fragrant herbs, expressive. Palate: powerful, flavourful, good acidity, fine bead, balanced.

At Roca Rosat 2013 ESP Reserva

macabeo, monastrell

88

Colour: raspberry rose. Nose: fine lees, floral, fragrant herbs, red berry notes. Palate: flavourful, good acidity, fine bead.

Floral D'At Roca 2014 B
macabeo, malvasía

87

Colour: bright straw. Nose: white flowers, fresh fruit, fragrant herbs. Palate: flavourful, fruity, good acidity.

Xarel.lo D'At Roca 2014 B
xarel.lo

89

Colour: bright straw. Nose: dry stone, balanced, expressive. Palate: flavourful, good acidity, full, spicy.

BLANCHER CAPDEVILA PUJOL

Plaça Pont Romà, Edificio Blancher
08770 Sant Sadurní D'Anoia
(Barcelona)
☎: +34 938 183 286
Fax: +34 938 911 961
blancher@blancher.es
www.blancher.es

Blancher Clos 7/12 2009 T
merlot, cabernet sauvignon

84

BODEGA J. MIQUEL JANÉ

Masia Cal Costas, s/n
08736 Guardiola de Font-Rubí
(Barcelona)
☎: +34 934 140 948
Fax: +34 934 140 948
info@jmigueljane.com
www.jmiqueljane.com

J. Miquel Jané Blanc Baltana 2014 B
50% macabeo, 35% parellada, 15% sauvignon blanc

86

J. Miquel Jané Cabernet Sauvignon 2014 RD
85% cabernet sauvignon, 15% garnacha

86

J. Miquel Jané Sauvignon Blanc 2014 B
100% sauvignon blanc

89

Colour: bright straw. Nose: wild herbs, fresh, citrus fruit, varietal. Palate: correct, balanced, fine bitter notes, easy to drink.

Miquel Jané Baltana Negre 2013 T
50% cabernet sauvignon, 30% garnacha, 20% syrah

85

Miquel Jané Baltana Selecció 2011 T
60% cabernet sauvignon, 40% merlot

88

Colour: cherry, garnet rim. Nose: ripe fruit, cocoa bean. Palate: flavourful, round tannins, balsamic.

BODEGA JAUME SERRA S.L. (J. GARCÍA CARRIÓN)

Ctra. de Vilanova a Vilafranca, Km. 2,5
08800 Vilanova i la Geltru (Barcelona)
☎: +34 938 936 404
Fax: +34 938 147 482
jaumeserra@jgc.es
www.garciacarrion.es

Jaume Serra 2012 TC
40% cabernet sauvignon, 40% merlot, 20% tempranillo

78

Jaume Serra 2013 T
40% merlot, 40% cabernet sauvignon, 20% tempranillo

79

Jaume Serra 2014 B
60% macabeo, 40% xarel.lo

81

Jaume Serra Merlot 2014 RD
100% merlot

82

Jaume Serra Semidulce 2014 B
60% macabeo, 40% xarel.lo

81

Pata Negra Chardonnay 2014 B
100% chardonnay

84

Colour: bright yellow. Nose: ripe fruit, sweet spices, smoky. Palate: good acidity, good finish, toasty.

BODEGAS CAPITÀ VIDAL

Ctra. Villafranca-Igualada, Km. 21
08733 Pla del Penedès (Barcelona)
☎: +34 938 988 630
Fax: +34 938 988 625
capitavidal@capitavidal.com
www.capitavidal.com

Clos Vidal Blanc de Blancs 2014 B
70% macabeo, 10% xarel.lo, 10% parellada, moscatel de frontignan

87

Colour: bright straw. Nose: fresh, fresh fruit, white flowers. Palate: fruity, fresh, balanced, easy to drink.

Clos Vidal Cabernet Sauvignon 2011 T Roble
85% cabernet sauvignon, 15% syrah

86

Clos Vidal Merlot 2011 TC
85% merlot, 15% tempranillo

88

Colour: bright cherry. Nose: ripe fruit, sweet spices, creamy oak. Palate: flavourful, fruity, toasty, easy to drink.

Clos Vidal Rosé Cuvée 2014 RD
45% syrah, 30% merlot, 25% garnacha

87

Colour: raspberry rose. Nose: fresh fruit, balanced, fragrant herbs, dried flowers. Palate: correct, balanced, good acidity.

BODEGAS PINORD

Doctor Pasteur, 6
08776 Vilafranca del Penedès (Barcelona)
☎: +34 938 903 066
pinord@pinord.com
www.pinord.com

+ Nature Xarel.lo 2014 B
xarel.lo

85

Clos de Torribas 2009 TR
tempranillo

84

Clos de Torribas 2011 TC
tempranillo

75

Diorama Chardonnay 2014 B
chardonnay

87

Colour: bright yellow. Nose: dried herbs, ripe fruit, spicy. Palate: flavourful, fruity, good acidity.

Diorama Merlot 2013 T
merlot

87

Colour: ruby red. Nose: creamy oak, toasty, ripe fruit, balsamic herbs. Palate: balanced, spicy, long.

Diorama Pinot Noir 2014 RD
pinot noir

86

Lluna Plena 2013 B
chardonnay

88

Colour: bright yellow. Nose: ripe fruit, powerfull, toasty, pattiserie. Palate: flavourful, fruity, spicy, toasty, long.

Pinord Chateldon 2008 TR
cabernet sauvignon, merlot

82

Pinord Mireia 2014 B
gewürztraminer, moscatel

86

BODEGAS TORRE DEL VEGUER

Urb. Torre de Veguer, s/n
08810 Sant Pere de Ribes (Barcelona)
☎: +34 938 963 190
Fax: +34 938 962 967
torredelveguer@torredelveguer.com
www.torredelveguer.com

Torre del Veguer Dulce Vendimia Tardía 2014 B
100% moscatel de frontignan

91

Colour: golden. Nose: powerfull, honeyed notes, candied fruit, fragrant herbs. Palate: flavourful, sweet, fresh, fruity, good acidity, long.

Torre del Veguer Eclèctic 2010 T
70% cabernet sauvignon, 25% petite syrah, 5% merlot

90

Colour: bright cherry. Nose: ripe fruit, sweet spices, creamy oak, balsamic herbs. Palate: flavourful, fruity, toasty.

Torre del Veguer Galán 2014 B
50% xarel.lo, 50% moscatel de frontignan

85

Torre del Veguer Marta Clàssic 2013 ESP
100% moscatel de frontignan

87

Colour: bright yellow. Nose: white flowers, expressive, varietal. Palate: fruity, flavourful, fine bitter notes.

Torre del Veguer Muscat 2014 B
moscatel de frontignan

86

Torre del Veguer Raïms de la Inmortalitat 2008 TR
85% cabernet sauvignon, 10% petite syrah, 5% merlot

88

Colour: pale ruby, brick rim edge. Nose: spicy, fine reductive notes, wet leather, aged wood nuances, fruit liqueur notes. Palate: spicy, fine tannins, balanced.

Torre del Veguer Xarel.lo 2014 B
100% xarel.lo vermell

87

Colour: yellow, pale. Nose: dried flowers, faded flowers, dry nuts. Palate: correct, fine bitter notes.

BODEGAS TORRES

Miguel Torres i Carbó, 6
08720 Vilafranca del Penedès
(Barcelona)
☎: +34 938 177 400
Fax: +34 938 177 444
mailadmin@torres.es
www.torres.com

Atrium Chardonnay 2013 B
chardonnay

90

Colour: bright straw. Nose: white flowers, fine lees, dried herbs, ripe fruit, citrus fruit. Palate: flavourful, fruity, good acidity, elegant.

Atrium Merlot 2013 T
merlot

88

Colour: deep cherry. Nose: creamy oak, toasty, ripe fruit, balsamic herbs. Palate: balanced, spicy, long.

Fransola 2013 B
sauvignon blanc, parellada

90

Colour: bright yellow. Nose: powerfull, candied fruit, dried herbs. Palate: flavourful, sweet, ripe fruit, good acidity.

Gran Coronas 2011 TR
cabernet sauvignon, tempranillo

89

Colour: bright cherry. Nose: ripe fruit, sweet spices, creamy oak, smoky. Palate: flavourful, fruity, toasty.

Mas La Plana Cabernet Sauvignon 2010 TGR
cabernet sauvignon

93

Colour: cherry, garnet rim. Nose: balanced, complex, ripe fruit, spicy, fine reductive notes, balsamic herbs. Palate: good structure, flavourful, round tannins, balanced.

PODIUM

Reserva Real 2010 TR
cabernet sauvignon, merlot, cabernet franc

95

Colour: bright cherry. Nose: elegant, spicy, fine reductive notes, tobacco, balsamic herbs, expressive. Palate: spicy, fine tannins, elegant, long. Personality.

Waltraud 2013 B
riesling

92

Colour: bright straw. Nose: white flowers, dried herbs, ripe fruit, citrus fruit, petrol notes. Palate: flavourful, fruity, good acidity, elegant.

BODEGUES AMETLLER CIVILL

Caspe, 139 Entr 1ª
08013 Barcelona (Barcelona)
☎: +34 933 208 439
Fax: +34 933 208 437
ametller@ametller.com
www.ametller.com

Ametller Blanc de Blancs 2014 B
80% xarel.lo, 20% chardonnay

84

Ametller Blanc Floral 2014 B
50% moscatel, 50% sauvignon blanc

89

Colour: bright straw. Nose: fresh fruit, white flowers, medium intensity. Palate: easy to drink, balanced, fine bitter notes.

BODEGUES CA N'ESTELLA

Masia Ca N'Estella, s/n
08635 Sant Esteve Sesrovires
(Barcelona)
☎: +34 934 161 387
Fax: +34 934 161 620
a.vidal@fincacanestella.com
www.fincacanestella.com

Clot dels Oms 2011 T
50% ull de llebre, 35% samsó, 15% merlot

87

Colour: bright cherry. Nose: ripe fruit, sweet spices, creamy oak, wild herbs. Palate: flavourful, fruity, toasty.

Clot dels Oms 2014 B
80% chardonnay, 20% malvasía

88

Colour: bright straw. Nose: white flowers, fresh fruit, fragrant herbs, expressive. Palate: flavourful, fruity, good acidity, balanced.

Clot dels Oms Rosat 2014 RD
100% merlot

87

Colour: rose, purple rim. Nose: red berry notes, floral. Palate: powerful, fruity, fresh, easy to drink.

Gran Clot dels Oms Negre 2011 T
100% merlot

89

Colour: cherry, garnet rim. Nose: ripe fruit, wild herbs, spicy, balsamic herbs. Palate: balanced, flavourful, long, balsamic.

Gran Clot dels Oms Rosat Dolç de Fred 2012 RD
100% merlot

84

Gran Clot dels Oms Xarel.lo 2013 B
100% xarel.lo

92

Colour: bright straw. Nose: white flowers, fine lees, dried herbs, ripe fruit, citrus fruit. Palate: flavourful, fruity, good acidity, elegant.

Petit Clot Blanc 2014 B
40% macabeo, 40% xarel.lo, 17% chardonnay, 3% moscatel

87

Colour: straw. Nose: medium intensity, ripe fruit, dried flowers. Palate: correct, easy to drink, balanced, long, good acidity.

Petit Clot Negre 2013 T
80% merlot, 20% cabernet sauvignon

86

Petit Clot Rosat 2014 RD
100% cabernet sauvignon

85

BODEGUES SUMARROCA

El Rebato, s/n
08739 Subirats (Barcelona)
☎: +34 934 750 125
Fax: +34 934 743 100
amestres@selfoods.es
www.sumarroca.es

Bòria 2011 T
syrah, cabernet sauvignon, merlot

91

Colour: deep cherry, purple rim. Nose: creamy oak, toasty, ripe fruit, balsamic herbs. Palate: balanced, spicy, long.

Santa Creu 2011 T
garnacha, syrah, cabernet franc, cabernet sauvignon

89

Colour: cherry, garnet rim. Nose: ripe fruit, wild herbs, earthy notes, spicy. Palate: balanced, flavourful, long.

Sumarroca Blanc de Blancs 2014 B
xarel.lo, macabeo, moscatel

86

Sumarroca Chardonnay 2014 B
chardonnay

89

Colour: bright straw. Nose: fruit expression, ripe fruit, floral, fragrant herbs. Palate: powerful, flavourful, good finish.

Sumarroca Gewürztraminer 2014 B
gewürztraminer

87

Colour: bright yellow. Nose: dried herbs, ripe fruit, white flowers. Palate: flavourful, fruity, good acidity.

Sumarroca HUMM Dolç de Fred B

86

Sumarroca Muscat 2014 B
moscatel

87

Colour: bright straw. Nose: balsamic herbs, honeyed notes, floral. Palate: rich, fruity, flavourful.

Sumarroca Negre 2014 T
merlot, tempranillo, cabernet sauvignon

86

Sumarroca Posidonia Rosat 2014 RD
tempranillo, merlot

86

Sumarroca Riesling 2013 B
riesling

90

Colour: bright straw. Nose: white flowers, fine lees, dried herbs, citrus fruit. Palate: flavourful, fruity, good acidity, elegant.

Sumarroca Rosat 2014 RD
merlot, tempranillo, syrah

86

Sumarroca Temps de Flors 2014 B
xarel.lo, moscatel, gewürztraminer

87

Colour: bright yellow. Nose: white flowers, jasmine, ripe fruit, powerfull. Palate: flavourful, fruity, good acidity, easy to drink.

Sumarroca Temps de Fruits 2014 T
carménère, cot, pinot noir, pinot gris

86

Sumarroca Viognier 2013 B
viognier

86

Sumarroca Xarel.lo 2013 B
xarel.lo

89

Colour: bright straw. Nose: white flowers, fresh fruit, fragrant herbs. Palate: flavourful, fruity, good acidity, balanced.

Terral 2012 T
cabernet franc, syrah, merlot, cabernet sauvignon

90

Colour: bright cherry. Nose: expressive, mineral, balsamic herbs, balanced, ripe fruit. Palate: full, flavourful, round.

BOLET – AGRICULTURA ECOLÓGICA

08732 Castellvi de la Marca (Barcelona)
☎: +34 938 918 153
Fax: +34 938 918 153
cavasbolet@cavasbolet.com
www.cavasbolet.com

Bolet 2013 T
tempranillo, ull de llebre

86 ♣

Bolet 2014 B
moscatel, gewürztraminer

86 ♣

Bolet 2014 RD
pinot noir

82 ♣

Bolet Cabernet Sauvignon 2005 T

84 ♣

Bolet Sàpiens Merlot 2005 TC

84 ♣

Bolet Xarel.lo 2014 B
xarel.lo

82 ♣

BONANS

Mas Bonans Ctra. B-224 km 6,5
08784 Piera (Barcelona)
☎: +34 679 701 982
bonans@bonans.cat
www.bonans.cat

Bonans 2012 T
ull de llebre

85 ♣

Bonans Xarel.lo 2013 B
xarel.lo

84

Bonans Xarel.lo 2014 B
xarel.lo

86 ♣

Mas Bonans 2012 BN Espumoso
xarel.lo, macabeo, parellada

85

CAN CASALS

Ignasi Mas, s/n
08635 St. Esteve Sesnovires (Barcelona)
☎: +34 600 771 625
wine.cancasals@gmail.com
www.cellercancasals.com

Can Casals Serafi 2014 B
chardonnay

79

CAN RÀFOLS DELS CAUS

Finca Can Rafols del Caus s/n
08792 Avinyonet del Penedès (Barcelona)
☎: +34 938 970 013
info@causgrup.com
www.canrafolsdelscaus.com

Ad Fines 2008 T
100% pinot noir

91

Colour: light cherry, orangey edge. Nose: ripe fruit, violets, faded flowers. Palate: flavourful, fruity, good acidity.

Can Rafols Sumoll 2011 T
100% sumoll

89

Colour: light cherry. Nose: fruit liqueur notes, fragrant herbs, spicy. Palate: balanced, spicy, toasty.

Caus Lubis 2003 T
100% merlot

91

Colour: dark-red cherry, orangey edge. Nose: balanced, ripe fruit, spicy, fine reductive notes. Palate: good structure, flavourful, round tannins, balanced.

El Rocallís 2012 BFB
100% incrocio manzoni

94

Colour: bright yellow. Nose: ripe fruit, citrus fruit, wild herbs, spicy, expressive. Palate: powerful, flavourful, spicy, balanced, elegant.

Gran Caus 2005 TR
cabernet franc, merlot, cabernet sauvignon

93

Colour: pale ruby, brick rim edge. Nose: elegant, spicy, fine reductive notes, tobacco, balsamic herbs. Palate: spicy, fine tannins, elegant, long.

Gran Caus 2012 B
xarel.lo, chenin blanc, chardonnay

91

Colour: bright straw. Nose: white flowers, dried herbs, ripe fruit, candied fruit, citrus fruit. Palate: flavourful, good acidity, elegant.

Gran Caus 2014 RD
100% merlot

89

Colour: light cherry, bright. Nose: red berry notes, floral, expressive, ripe fruit. Palate: powerful, fruity, good structure.

La Calma 2012 BFB
100% chenin blanc

92

Colour: bright yellow. Nose: floral, balsamic herbs, ripe fruit, spicy, dry stone. Palate: rich, flavourful, balsamic, balanced.

Petit Caus 2014 B
xarel.lo, macabeo, chardonnay, chenin blanc

86

Petit Caus 2014 RD
merlot, tempranillo, syrah, cabernet sauvignon

87

Colour: raspberry rose. Nose: red berry notes, ripe fruit, rose petals. Palate: fresh, fruity, flavourful.

Petit Caus 2014 T
merlot, syrah, cabernet franc, pinot noir

87

Colour: light cherry. Nose: ripe fruit, wild herbs, mineral. Palate: fresh, fruity, easy to drink.

Terraprima 2012 T
cabernet franc, garnacha, syrah

90

Colour: light cherry, garnet rim. Nose: expressive, spicy. Palate: flavourful, ripe fruit, long, good acidity, balanced.

Terraprima 2014 B
xarel.lo, riesling

89

Colour: bright yellow. Nose: expressive, dried herbs, ripe fruit, spicy, dried flowers. Palate: fruity, good acidity, balanced.

Xarel.lo Pairal 2011 BFB
100% xarel.lo

92

Colour: bright golden. Nose: ripe fruit, balsamic herbs, dried herbs, creamy oak. Palate: long, spicy, toasty, balanced.

CAN VICH

Dels Pins, 22
08773 Sant Joan de Mediona
(Barcelona)
☎: +34 646 379 850
lluisvich@hotmail.com
www.canvich.cat

Can Vich Chardonay Fermentat en Bóta 2014 B
chardonnay

87

Colour: bright yellow. Nose: ripe fruit, powerfull, toasty, aged wood nuances. Palate: flavourful, fruity, spicy, toasty, long.

Can Vich Negre 2013 T
cabernet sauvignon

87

Colour: very deep cherry. Nose: mineral, balsamic herbs, ripe fruit, grassy. Palate: full, flavourful.

Can Vich Parellada Fermentat en Bóta 2014 B
parellada

88

Colour: bright yellow. Nose: ripe fruit, powerfull, toasty, aged wood nuances, pattiserie. Palate: flavourful, fruity, spicy, toasty, long.

Can Vich Parellada, Chardonay, Riesling 2014 B
parellada, chardonnay, riesling

86

CANALS & MUNNÉ

Ctra. Sant Sadurní a Vilafranca, km 0,5
08770 Sant Sadurní D'Anoia
(Barcelona)
☎: +34 938 910 318
Fax: +34 938 911 945
info@canalsimunne.com
www.canalsimunne.com

Blanc Prínceps Ecologic 2014 B
85% xarel.lo, 15% chardonnay

86

Blanc Prínceps Muscat 2014 B
100% moscatel

88

Colour: bright straw. Nose: balsamic herbs, honeyed notes, floral, expressive. Palate: fruity, flavourful, elegant.

Gran Blanc Prínceps 2014 BFB
100% xarel.lo

89

Colour: bright yellow. Nose: ripe fruit, powerfull, toasty. Palate: flavourful, fruity, spicy, toasty.

Gran Prínceps 2011 TR
cabernet sauvignon, tempranillo, merlot

87

Colour: cherry, garnet rim. Nose: ripe fruit, spicy, creamy oak, complex. Palate: flavourful, toasty, round tannins, easy to drink.

Noir Prínceps 2012 TC
cabernet sauvignon, tempranillo, merlot

87

Colour: cherry, garnet rim. Nose: ripe fruit, spicy, creamy oak, wild herbs. Palate: flavourful, toasty.

Rose Prínceps Merlot 2014 RD
100% merlot

84

CANALS NADAL

Ponent, 2
08733 El Pla del Penedès (Barcelona)
☎: +34 938 988 081
Fax: +34 938 989 050
cava@canalsnadal.com
www.canalsnadal.com

Canals Nadal Xarel.lo 2014 B
100% xarel.lo

87

Colour: bright straw. Nose: medium intensity, wild herbs, varietal, fresh fruit. Palate: correct, fresh, good acidity.

CASA RAVELLA

Casa Ravella, 1
08739 Ordal - Subirats (Barcelona)
☎: +34 938 179 173
Fax: +34 938 179 245
bodega@casaravella.com
www.casaravella.com

Casa Ravella 2014 B
100% xarel.lo

85

Casa Ravella 2014 RD
100% merlot

87

Colour: coppery red, bright. Nose: faded flowers, dried herbs. Palate: fruity, correct, fine bitter notes.

Casa Ravella 2014 T
100% merlot

85

CASTELL D'OR

Mare Rafols, 3- 1ºD
08720 Vilafranca del Penedès
(Barcelona)
☎: +34 938 905 385
Fax: +34 938 905 446
castelldor@castelldor.com
www.castelldor.com

Cossetània 2009 TR
cabernet sauvignon

89

Colour: ruby red. Nose: spicy, fine reductive notes, wet leather, aged wood nuances, ripe fruit. Palate: spicy, balanced.

Cossetània 2010 TC
merlot, cabernet sauvignon

87

Colour: bright cherry. Nose: ripe fruit, sweet spices, creamy oak. Palate: flavourful, fruity, toasty.

Cossetània 2012 T
cabernet sauvignon, merlot

86

Cossetània 2014 B
xarel.lo

85

Cossetània 2014 RD
merlot

87

Colour: rose, purple rim. Nose: red berry notes, floral, fragrant herbs. Palate: powerful, fruity, fresh.

Cossetània Chardonnay 2014 B
chardonnay

88

Colour: bright yellow. Nose: dried herbs, ripe fruit, spicy. Palate: flavourful, fruity, good acidity.

CASTELLROIG - FINCA SABATÉ I COCA

Ctra. Sant Sadurní a Vilafranca
(c-243a), km. 1
08739 Subirats (Barcelona)
☎: +34 938 911 927
Fax: +34 938 914 055
info@castellroig.com
www.castellroig.com

Castellroig Negre Selecció 2010 T
cabernet sauvignon

88

Colour: cherry, garnet rim. Nose: cocoa bean, spicy, wild herbs, ripe fruit. Palate: balanced, round tannins.

Castellroig So Sere 2012 B
xarel.lo

90

Colour: bright yellow. Nose: expressive, dried herbs, ripe fruit, spicy, faded flowers. Palate: flavourful, fruity, good acidity, balanced.

Castellroig So Xarel.lo 2014 B
xarel.lo

89

Colour: bright straw. Nose: white flowers, fresh fruit, fragrant herbs, expressive. Palate: flavourful, fruity, good acidity, balanced, long.

Castellroig So Xarel.lo Finca Sabaté i Coca 2012 B
xarel.lo

90

Colour: bright straw. Nose: white flowers, fine lees, dried herbs, ripe fruit, citrus fruit, balanced. Palate: flavourful, fruity, good acidity, elegant.

Terroja de Sabaté i Coca 2013 B
xarel.lo

91

Colour: bright yellow. Nose: ripe fruit, powerfull, toasty, aged wood nuances, pattiserie. Palate: flavourful, fruity, spicy, toasty, long.

CASTELO DE PEDREGOSA

Holanda, 16
08770 Sant Sadurní D'Anoia
(Barcelona)
☎: +34 938 184 176
info@castelodepedregosa.com
www.castelodepedregosa.com

Pedregosa Alysumm Blanc 2014 B
moscatel, xarel.lo, gewürztraminer

85

Pedregosa Cenisia Rosé 2014 RD
garnacha, macabeo

87

Colour: raspberry rose. Nose: dried flowers, dried herbs, balanced. Palate: fruity, long, good acidity.

CAVA & HOTEL MASTINELL

Ctra. de Vilafranca a St. Martí Sarroca, Km. 0,5
08720 Vilafranca del Penedès
(Barcelona)
☎: +34 938 170 586
Fax: +34 938 170 500
info@mastinell.com
www.mastinell.com

Mas Tinell Arte 2009 TR

87

Colour: cherry, garnet rim. Nose: creamy oak, balanced, ripe fruit. Palate: flavourful, spicy, round tannins, easy to drink.

Mas Tinell Chardonnay 2014 B
100% chardonnay

86

Mas Tinell Clos Sant Pau Dulce 2014 B
moscatel

86

Mas Tinell Gisele 2014 B

86

Mas Tinell L' Alba Blanc de Lluna 2014 B

86

CAVA JOSEP M. FERRET GUASCH

Barri L'Alzinar, 68
08736 Font-Rubí (Barcelona)
☎: +34 938 979 037
Fax: +34 938 979 414
ferretguasch@ferretguasch.com
www.ferretguasch.com

Josep M. Ferret Guasch Gebre 2014 RD

85

Josep M. Ferret Guasch Xarel.lo 2014 B

86

CAVAS HILL

Bonavista, 2
08734 Moja-Olérdola (Barcelona)
☎: +34 938 900 588
Fax: +34 938 170 246
cavashill@cavashill.com
www.cavashill.com

Blanc Bruc 2014 B
chardonnay, xarel.lo

88

Colour: bright straw. Nose: floral, fragrant herbs, fruit expression, spicy. Palate: flavourful, fruity, balsamic.

Gran Civet Hill 2011 TC
cabernet sauvignon, merlot

86

Gran Toc 2011 TR
merlot, cabernet sauvignon

89

Colour: bright cherry. Nose: ripe fruit, sweet spices, creamy oak. Palate: flavourful, fruity, toasty.

Oro Penedès 2014 B
moscatel, xarel.lo

86

CAVES NAVERÁN

Masia Can Parellada -
Sant Martí Sadavesa
08775 Torrelavit (Barcelona)
☎: +34 938 988 400
Fax: +34 938 989 027
sadeve@naveran.com
www.naveran.com

Clos dels Angels 2014 T
syrah, merlot

90

Colour: deep cherry. Nose: creamy oak, toasty, ripe fruit, balsamic herbs. Palate: balanced, spicy, long.

Manuela de Naverán 2014 B
chardonnay

87

Colour: bright yellow. Nose: expressive, ripe fruit, creamy oak. Palate: flavourful, good acidity, balanced, smoky aftertaste.

Naverán Don Pablo 2013 T
cabernet sauvignon, merlot, syrah

89

Colour: very deep cherry, garnet rim. Nose: ripe fruit, wild herbs, spicy. Palate: flavourful, long, classic aged character.

CELLER CREDO

Tamarit, 10
08770 Sant Sadurní D'Anoia
(Barcelona)
☎: +34 938 910 214
Fax: +34 938 911 697
vins@cellercredo.cat
www.cellercredo.cat

Aloers 2014 B
100% xarel.lo

90

Colour: bright straw. Nose: ripe fruit, dried herbs, dried flowers, waxy notes. Palate: powerful, flavourful, spicy.

Can Credo 2012 B
xarel.lo

93

Colour: bright yellow. Nose: white flowers, fine lees, dried herbs, candied fruit. Palate: flavourful, fruity, balanced.

Can Credo 2013 B
100% xarel.lo

92

Colour: bright yellow. Nose: dry nuts, dried flowers, complex, dried herbs, saline. Palate: flavourful, long, fine bitter notes, good acidity.

Cap Ficat 2013 B
100% xarel.lo

93

Colour: bright yellow. Nose: dried herbs, faded flowers, dry nuts, spicy. Palate: balanced, flavourful, good acidity.

Estrany 2013 B
100% xarel.lo

88

Colour: bright yellow. Nose: ripe fruit, damp earth, spicy, dried herbs, animal reductive notes. Palate: powerful, flavourful, spicy.

Miranius 2013 B
84% xarel.lo, 16% macabeo

90

Colour: bright straw. Nose: fresh, dried flowers, medium intensity, mineral. Palate: elegant, fine bitter notes, good acidity.

Ratpenat 2013 B
100% macabeo

91

Colour: bright straw. Nose: white flowers, fine lees, dried herbs, ripe fruit, spicy. Palate: flavourful, fruity, good acidity, elegant.

CELLER ESTEVE I GIBERT VITICULTORS

Masia Cal Panxa s/n – Els Casots
08739 Subirats (Barcelona)
☎: +34 600 343 125
albert@esteveigibert.com
www.esteveigibert.com

L'Antana 2010 T
merlot

81

Les Vistes 2013 B
xarel.lo

90

Colour: bright straw. Nose: white flowers, fine lees, dried herbs, ripe fruit, candied fruit, citrus fruit. Palate: flavourful, fruity, good acidity, elegant.

Origen 2013 B
xarel.lo

88

Colour: bright yellow. Nose: scrubland, dried herbs, balanced. Palate: flavourful, fine bitter notes.

CELLERS AVGVSTVS FORVM

Ctra. Sant Vicenç, s/n
Apartado Correos 289
43700 El Vendrell (Tarragona)
☎: +34 977 666 910
Fax: +34 977 666 590
avgvstvs@avgvstvsforvm.com
www.avgvstvsforvm.com

Avgvstvs Cabernet Franc 2011 T
100% cabernet franc

89

Colour: deep cherry. Nose: smoky, fine reductive notes, spicy, scrubland. Palate: good structure, flavourful, round tannins.

Avgvstvs Cabernet Franc 2012 T Roble
100% cabernet franc

90

Colour: deep cherry, garnet rim. Nose: spicy, wild herbs, dried herbs, characterful, warm. Palate: flavourful, good structure.

Avgvstvs Cabernet Sauvignon-Merlot 2012 T Roble
51% cabernet sauvignon, 49% merlot

88

Colour: cherry, garnet rim. Nose: ripe fruit, dried herbs, spicy. Palate: correct, spicy.

Avgvstvs Chardonnay 2014 BFB
100% chardonnay

89

Colour: bright yellow. Nose: ripe fruit, powerfull, pattiserie, roasted coffee. Palate: flavourful, spicy, toasty, long.

Avgvstvs Chardonnay Magnum 2013 B
100% chardonnay

93

Colour: bright straw. Nose: white flowers, dried herbs, ripe fruit, candied fruit, citrus fruit, sweet spices. Palate: flavourful, fruity, good acidity, elegant.

Avgvstvs Merlot Syrah 2013 T
merlot, syrah

86

Avgvstvs Microvinificacions Garnatxa 2013 T
100% garnacha

90

Colour: deep cherry, purple rim. Nose: creamy oak, toasty, ripe fruit, balsamic herbs, mineral. Palate: balanced, spicy, correct.

Avgvstvs Microvinificacions Xarel.lo 2013 BFB
100% xarel.lo

89

Colour: bright yellow. Nose: floral, ripe fruit, fragrant herbs, creamy oak, toasty. Palate: powerful, flavourful, complex.

Avgvstvs Microvinificacions Xarel.lo 2014 B
100% xarel.lo

92

Colour: bright straw. Nose: fine lees, dried herbs, mineral, faded flowers. Palate: flavourful, fruity, good acidity, round.

Avgvstvs Microvinificacions Xarel.lo Vermell 2014 B
100% Xarel.lo Vermell

90

Colour: bright yellow. Nose: expressive, dried herbs, ripe fruit, spicy. Palate: flavourful, fruity, good acidity, balanced.

Avgvstvs Trajanvs 2010 TR
33% cabernet sauvignon, 33% merlot, 17% cabernet franc, 17% garnacha

90

Colour: cherry, garnet rim. Nose: ripe fruit, wild herbs, earthy notes, spicy, fine reductive notes. Palate: balanced, flavourful, long, balsamic.

Avgvstvs VI Varietales Magnum 2011 TC
syrah, cabernet franc, cabernet sauvignon, merlot, garnacha, ull de llebre

91

Colour: cherry, garnet rim. Nose: ripe fruit, spicy, creamy oak, complex. Palate: flavourful, toasty, round tannins.

Avgvstvs Xarel.lo Microvinificaciones 2011 BFB
100% xarel.lo

89

Colour: bright yellow. Nose: dried herbs, faded flowers, ripe fruit, smoky. Palate: ripe fruit, spicy, long.

Look 2014 B
xarel.lo, moscatel de alejandría, sauvignon blanc, garnacha blanca

86

CELLERS PLANAS ALBAREDA

Ctra. Guardiola, Km. 3
08735 Vilobí del Penedès (Barcelona)
☎: +34 938 922 143
Fax: +34 938 922 143
planasalbareda@yahoo.es
www.planasalbareda.com

Planas Albareda Desclòs 2011 T

88

Colour: dark-red cherry, orangey edge. Nose: balsamic herbs, spicy, ripe fruit. Palate: flavourful, spicy, easy to drink.

Planas Albareda L'Avenc 2014 B

82

Planas Albareda Rosat 2014 RD

84

CLOS LENTISCUS

Masía Can Ramón del Montgros, s/n
08810 Sant Pere de Ribes (Barcelona)
☎: +34 667 517 659
manel@closlentiscus.com
www.closlentiscus.com

Clos Lentiscus Sumoll Reserva Familia Blanc de noirs 2009 BN
sumoll

91

Colour: coppery red. Nose: floral, jasmine, fragrant herbs, candied fruit. Palate: fresh, fruity, flavourful, correct.

Clos Lentiscus 41ºN Rosé 2010 BN Gran Reserva

90

Colour: light cherry. Nose: ripe fruit, wild herbs, floral, spicy. Palate: fresh, spicy, long, balsamic.

Clos Lentiscus Blanc de Blancs 2012 BN
malvasía de Sitges

87

Colour: bright yellow. Nose: ripe fruit, faded flowers, dried herbs, fine lees. Palate: fresh, flavourful, balsamic.

Clos Lentiscus Colection CRV Rosé 2008 BN

85

Clos Lentiscus Perril 2014 B
xarel.lo

90

Colour: bright straw. Nose: white flowers, fresh fruit, fragrant herbs, expressive. Palate: flavourful, fruity, good acidity, balanced.

Clos Lentiscus Perril Noir 2007 T

86

CODORNÍU

Avda. Jaume Codorníu, s/n
08770 Sant Sadurní D'Anoia (Barcelona)
☎: +34 938 183 232
codinfo@codorniu.com
www.codorniu.com

Viñas de Anna 2014 B
chardonnay, moscatel

87

Colour: bright straw. Nose: white flowers, fresh fruit, expressive. Palate: flavourful, fruity, good acidity, balanced.

COLET

Camino del Salinar, s/n
08796 Pacs del Penedès (Barcelona)
☎: +34 938 170 809
Fax: +34 938 170 809
info@colet.cat
www.colet.cat

A Posteriori Rosat 2011 BR Espumoso
merlot

86

A Priori 2013 BR Espumoso
macabeo, chardonnay, riesling, moscatel, gewürztraminer

88

Colour: bright yellow. Nose: ripe fruit, fine lees, balanced, dried herbs. Palate: good acidity, flavourful, ripe fruit, long.

Colet Assemblage 2012 ESP
pinot noir, chardonnay

91

Colour: bright golden. Nose: faded flowers, ripe fruit, complex. Palate: balanced, fine bitter notes, good acidity.

Colet Grand Cuveé 2012 Extra Brut
chardonnay, macabeo, xarel.lo

91

Colour: bright straw. Nose: fresh fruit, dried herbs, fine lees, floral, spicy, fragrant herbs. Palate: fresh, fruity, flavourful, good acidity, balanced.

Colet Navazos 2010 Extra Brut Reserva

91

Colour: bright yellow. Nose: ripe fruit, lees reduction notes, spicy, toasty. Palate: flavourful, long, fine bitter notes, sweetness.

Colet Navazos 2011 Extra Brut
xarel.lo

93

Colour: bright golden. Nose: fine lees, dry nuts, fragrant herbs, complex, toasty. Palate: powerful, flavourful, good acidity, fine bead, fine bitter notes.

Colet Tradicional 2013 Extra Brut
xarel.lo, macabeo, xarel.lo, parellada

90

Colour: yellow, greenish rim. Nose: faded flowers, wild herbs, expressive. Palate: balanced, good acidity. Personality.

Vatua ! 2013 ESP
moscatel, parellada, gewürztraminer

89

Colour: bright straw. Nose: fresh fruit, dried herbs, fine lees, floral. Palate: fresh, fruity, flavourful, good acidity, fine bitter notes.

COMA ROMÀ

Can Guilera, s/n
08739 Sant Pau D'Ordal (Barcelona)
☎: +34 938 993 094
Fax: +34 938 993 094
canguilera@comaroma.net
www.comaroma.net

Coma Romà Merlot 2013 T
100% merlot

86

Coma Romà Ull Llebre 2014 RD
100% ull de llebre

86

Coma Romà Xarel.lo 2014 B
100% xarel.lo

84

Coma Romà Xarel.lo Macerat 2013 B
100% xarel.lo

89

Colour: bright straw. Nose: white flowers, fine lees, dried herbs, ripe fruit, candied fruit, citrus fruit. Palate: flavourful, fruity, good acidity, elegant.

COVIDES VIÑEDOS BODEGAS

Rambla Nostra Senyora, 45 - 1º
08720 Vilafranca del Penedès
(Barcelona)
☎: +34 938 172 552
covides@covides.com
www.covides.com

Duc de Foix Cabernet Sauvignon 2014 RD
100% cabernet sauvignon

84

Duc de Foix Merlot 2011 T Barrica
100% merlot

86

Duc de Foix Xarel.lo 2013 B
100% xarel.lo

85

CUSCÓ BERGA

Esplugues, 7
08793 Avinyonet del Penedès
(Barcelona)
☎: +34 938 970 164
cuscoberga@cuscoberga.com
www.cuscoberga.com

Cuscó Berga Cabernet Sauvignon 2009 TC
80% cabernet sauvignon, 20% merlot

84

Cuscó Berga Merlot Selecció 2014 RD
100% merlot

85

Cuscó Berga Muscat D'Alejandría 2014 B
100% moscatel de alejandría

84

Cuscó Berga Vi Negre Selecció 2013 T
80% tempranillo, 20% merlot

85

Cuscó Berga Xarel.lo Selecció 2014 B
100% xarel.lo

83

EMENDIS

Barrio de Sant Marçal, 67
08732 Castellet i La Gornal (Barcelona)
☎: +34 938 919 790
Fax: +34 938 918 169
info@emendis.es
www.emendis.es

Emendis Duet Varietal 2012 T
80% syrah, 20% tempranillo

87

Colour: light cherry. Nose: ripe fruit, spicy, scrubland, fine reductive notes. Palate: flavourful, long, balsamic.

Emendis Nox 2014 RD
50% syrah, 50% pinot noir

82

Emendis Trío Varietal 2013 B
55% macabeo, 25% moscatel, 35% chardonnay

88

Colour: bright straw. Nose: white flowers, fragrant herbs, tropical fruit. Palate: flavourful, fruity, good acidity.

ENRIC SOLER

Masia Cal Raspallet
08736 Sabanell / Font-rubí (Barcelona)
☎: +34 607 262 779
info@enricsoler.cat
www.enricsoler.cat

Espenyalluchs 2013 B
100% xarel.lo

93

Colour: bright straw. Nose: white flowers, fine lees, dried herbs, mineral. Palate: flavourful, fruity, good acidity, round.

Improvisació 2013 B
xarel.lo

92

Colour: bright straw. Nose: white flowers, fresh fruit, fragrant herbs, expressive, mineral. Palate: flavourful, fruity, good acidity, balanced.

Nun Vinya dels Taus 2013 B
xarel.lo

93

Colour: bright straw. Nose: expressive, dried herbs, ripe fruit, spicy, smoky. Palate: flavourful, fruity, good acidity, balanced.

ESTEL D'ARGENT

Font Rubí, 2 Esc. A 4º 1ª
08720 Vilafranca del Penedès
(Barcelona)
☎: +34 677 182 347
cava@esteldargent.com
www.esteldargent.com

Estel D'Argent 2012 T
merlot, tempranillo

84

Estel D'Argent 2014 B
xarel.lo, chardonnay, moscatel

82

Estel D'Argent 2014 RD
merlot, cabernet sauvignon

84

SusQuvat 2014 B Barrica
xarel.lo

88

Colour: bright yellow. Nose: ripe fruit, powerfull, toasty, aged wood nuances, pattiserie. Palate: flavourful, fruity, spicy, toasty, long.

FERRE I CATASUS

Masía Gustems s/n
08792 La Granada del Penedès
(Barcelona)
☎: +34 938 974 558
Fax: +34 938 974 708
eduard@ferreicatasus.com
www.ferreicatasus.com

Cap de Trons 2014 T
syrah, cabernet sauvignon, merlot

88

Colour: cherry, garnet rim. Nose: ripe fruit, dried herbs, spicy. Palate: flavourful, fruity, balanced.

Soc un Rosat de Ferre i Catasus 2014 RD
merlot

86

Somiatruites 2014 B
chenin blanc, sauvignon blanc, xarel.lo, chardonnay

88

Colour: bright yellow. Nose: medium intensity, floral, citrus fruit. Palate: fresh, flavourful, easy to drink, fine bitter notes.

Sonat de l'ala 2012 T
syrah, garnacha, merlot

87

Colour: very deep cherry, garnet rim. Nose: powerfull, scrubland, dried herbs, characterful. Palate: ripe fruit, correct.

FINCA VILADELLOPS

Finca Viladellops
08734 Olérdola (Barcelona)
☎: +34 938 188 371
info@viladellops.com
www.viladellops.com

Finca Viladellops Xarel.lo 2014 B
100% xarel.lo

87

Colour: bright straw. Nose: white flowers, fresh fruit, fragrant herbs. Palate: flavourful, fruity, good acidity.

Finca Viladellops 2012 TC
60% garnacha, 40% syrah

86

Finca Viladellops Xarel.lo 2013 BFB
100% xarel.lo

91

Colour: bright straw. Nose: white flowers, fine lees, dried herbs, ripe fruit, candied fruit, citrus fruit. Palate: flavourful, fruity, good acidity, elegant.

Turó de les Abelles 2011 T
50% garnacha, 50% syrah

92

Colour: very deep cherry, garnet rim. Nose: expressive, complex, mineral, balsamic herbs, ripe fruit. Palate: full, flavourful, spicy, long.

Viladellops Garnatxa 2014 T
100% garnacha

87

Colour: cherry, purple rim. Nose: floral, red berry notes, ripe fruit. Palate: fruity, balsamic, good finish.

GIRÓ DEL GORNER

Finca Giró del Gorner
08797 Puigdálber (Barcelona)
☎: +34 938 988 032
gorner@girodelgorner.com
www.girodelgorner.com

Blanc Giró del Gorner 2014 B
xarel.lo, macabeo, parellada, chardonnay

87

Colour: bright straw. Nose: fresh fruit, fragrant herbs, floral. Palate: flavourful, fruity, good acidity, balanced.

Rosat Giró del Gorner 2014 RD
100% merlot

87

Colour: light cherry, bright. Nose: red berry notes, floral, expressive. Palate: powerful, fruity, fresh.

GIRÓ RIBOT, S.L.

Finca El Pont, s/n
08792 Santa Fe del Penedès
(Barcelona)
☎: +34 938 974 050
Fax: +34 938 974 311
giroribot@giroribot.es
www.giroribot.es

Giró2 2013 BFB
100% giró

92

Colour: bright straw. Nose: white flowers, fine lees, dried herbs, ripe fruit, candied fruit, citrus fruit. Palate: flavourful, fruity, good acidity, elegant.

Mimat 2012 TR
50% marselan, 30% petit verdot, 20% cabernet franc

89

Colour: bright cherry. Nose: ripe fruit, sweet spices, creamy oak. Palate: flavourful, fruity, toasty.

GRAMONA

Industria, 36
08770 Sant Sadurní D'Anoia
(Barcelona)
☎: +34 938 910 113
Fax: +34 938 183 284
cava@gramona.com
www.gramona.com

Gramona Gessamí 2014 B
40% moscatel de frontignan, 40% sauvignon blanc, 20% gewürztraminer

90

Colour: bright straw. Nose: white flowers, expressive, jasmine. Palate: flavourful, fruity, good acidity, balanced.

Gramona Sauvignon Blanc 2014 BFB
100% sauvignon blanc

89

Colour: bright straw. Nose: ripe fruit, tropical fruit, spicy. Palate: fruity, correct, balanced.

Gramona Xarel.lo Font Jui 2014 B
100% xarel.lo

91

Colour: bright straw. Nose: faded flowers, varietal, fragrant herbs, complex, spicy. Palate: flavourful, full.

Gramona Xarel.lo Ovum 2014 B
100% xarel.lo

93

Colour: bright straw. Nose: expressive, complex, ripe fruit, faded flowers. Palate: balanced, fine bitter notes, long, good acidity.

Gramona Xarel.lo Roent 2014 B
100% Xarel.lo Vermell

92

Colour: onion pink. Nose: elegant, red berry notes, floral, fragrant herbs, creamy oak. Palate: light-bodied, flavourful, good acidity, long, spicy, balanced.

PODIUM

Vi de Glass Gewürztraminer 0,75 2008 BC
100% gewürztraminer

95

Colour: bright yellow. Nose: floral, ripe fruit, candied fruit, expressive, complex, citrus fruit. Palate: full, flavourful, complex, rich.

Vi de Glass Riesling Dulce 2011 B
100% riesling

94

Colour: bright yellow. Nose: balsamic herbs, honeyed notes, floral, sweet spices, expressive, petrol notes. Palate: rich, fruity, powerful, flavourful, elegant.

GRIMAU

Masía Torreblanca s/n
08734 Olerdola (Barcelona)
☎: +34 938 918 031
grimau@grimau.com
www.grimau.com

Grimau Blanc de Blancs 2014 B
macabeo, xarel.lo, parellada, chardonnay

84

Grimau Cabernet Sauvignon 2010 TR
cabernet sauvignon

88

Colour: cherry, garnet rim. Nose: red berry notes, ripe fruit, spicy, creamy oak, complex. Palate: flavourful, toasty.

Grimau Merlot 2014 RD
merlot

85

Grimau Rubicundus 2010 T
cabernet sauvignon, tempranillo, merlot, syrah

88

Colour: cherry, garnet rim. Nose: creamy oak, ripe fruit. Palate: flavourful, spicy, elegant.

HEREDAD SEGURA VIUDAS

Ctra. Sant Sadurní a St. Pere
de Riudebitlles, Km. 5
08775 Torrelavit (Barcelona)
☎: +34 938 917 070
Fax: +34 938 996 006
seguraviudas@seguraviudas.es
www.seguraviudas.com

Creu de Lavit 2014 BFB
xarel.lo

87

Colour: bright straw. Nose: medium intensity, floral, ripe fruit. Palate: balanced, flavourful, good finish, spicy.

Segura Viudas Xarel.lo 2014 B
xarel.lo

87

Colour: bright straw. Nose: white flowers, fresh fruit, fragrant herbs, expressive. Palate: flavourful, fruity, good acidity.

HERETAT MONT-RUBÍ

L'Avellà, 1
08736 Font- Rubí (Barcelona)
☎: +34 938 979 066
Fax: +34 938 979 066
hmr@montrubi.com
www.montrubi.com

PODIUM

Advent Samsó Dulce Natural 2010 B
100% samsó

95

Colour: coppery red. Nose: acetaldehyde, fruit preserve, dried fruit, wild herbs, spicy, toasty, varnish. Palate: powerful, flavourful, complex, spicy, long, balsamic, balanced.

Advent Sumoll Dulce Natural 2010 T
100% sumoll

94

Colour: coppery red. Nose: acetaldehyde, varnish, candied fruit, pattiserie, creamy oak, expressive. Palate: fruity, flavourful, sweet, round, unctuous, elegant.

Advent Xarel.lo Dulce Natural 2010 B
100% xarel.lo

93

Colour: golden. Nose: powerfull, honeyed notes, candied fruit, fragrant herbs. Palate: flavourful, sweet, fresh, fruity, good acidity, long.

Black Hmr 2014 T
100% garnacha

89

Colour: cherry, purple rim. Nose: powerfull, ripe fruit, spicy, wild herbs. Palate: powerful, fruity, unctuous.

Durona 2009 T
sumoll, garnacha, samsó

90

Colour: cherry, garnet rim. Nose: expressive, spicy, creamy oak. Palate: flavourful, ripe fruit, long, good acidity, balanced.

Finca Durona 2014 B
100% parellada

89

Colour: bright straw. Nose: white flowers, fine lees, dried herbs, candied fruit. Palate: flavourful, fruity, good acidity, elegant.

Gaintus 2011 T
100% sumoll

92

Colour: light cherry. Nose: ripe fruit, wild herbs, earthy notes, spicy, balsamic herbs. Palate: balanced, flavourful, long, balsamic. Personality.

Gaintus 500+ 2013 T
100% sumoll

90

Colour: cherry, garnet rim. Nose: mineral, ripe fruit, fragrant herbs. Palate: fresh, fruity, flavourful, spicy, long.

Gaintus Radical 2014 T
100% sumoll

91

Colour: bright cherry, purple rim. Nose: expressive, wild herbs, red berry notes, ripe fruit. Palate: fruity, varietal.

White Hmr 2014 B
100% xarel.lo

87

Colour: bright yellow. Nose: white flowers, fresh, powerfull. Palate: correct, easy to drink.

HERETAT SABARTÉS

Ctra Santa Oliva, s/n
43711 Banyeres del Penedès
(Tarragona)
☎: +34 934 750 125
amestres@selfoods.es
www.heretatsabartes.com

Heretat Sabartés 2014 B
sauvignon blanc, chardonnay, macabeo

86

Heretat Sabartés 2014 RD
tempranillo

88

Colour: onion pink. Nose: elegant, red berry notes, floral, fragrant herbs. Palate: light-bodied, flavourful, good acidity, long.

Heretat Sabartés Negre 2012 T
pinot noir

89

Colour: light cherry. Nose: ripe fruit, wild herbs, spicy, fine reductive notes. Palate: correct, powerful, flavourful.

JANÉ VENTURA

Ctra. Calafell, 2
43700 El Vendrell (Tarragona)
☎: +34 977 660 118
janeventura@janeventura.com
www.janeventura.com

Jané Ventura "Finca Els Camps" Macabeu 2012 B

92

Colour: bright yellow. Nose: ripe fruit, sweet spices, creamy oak, mineral. Palate: powerful, flavourful, toasty, balanced.

Jané Ventura "Finca Els Camps" Macabeu 2013 BFB

90

Colour: bright yellow. Nose: ripe fruit, powerfull, toasty, aged wood nuances, pattiserie. Palate: flavourful, fruity, spicy, toasty, long.

Jané Ventura "Mas Vilella" Costers del Rotllan 2011 T

90

Colour: cherry, garnet rim. Nose: ripe fruit, wild herbs, earthy notes, spicy, balsamic herbs. Palate: balanced, flavourful, long, balsamic.

Jané Ventura "Mas Vilella" Costers del Rotllan 2013 T

90

Colour: cherry, purple rim. Nose: ripe fruit, woody, roasted coffee. Palate: flavourful, spicy, powerful.

Jané Ventura Blanc Selecció 2014 B
xarel.lo, macabeo, malvasía, garnacha blanca

88

Colour: bright straw. Nose: white flowers, fresh fruit, fragrant herbs, expressive. Palate: flavourful, fruity, good acidity, balanced.

Jané Ventura Finca Els Camps Ull de Llebre 2013 T

93

Colour: cherry, garnet rim. Nose: ripe fruit, wild herbs, spicy, balsamic herbs, dry stone. Palate: balanced, flavourful, long, balsamic.

Jané Ventura Malvasía de Sitges 2014 B Barrica

92

Colour: bright yellow. Nose: expressive, ripe fruit, spicy, white flowers, varietal. Palate: flavourful, fruity, good acidity, balanced.

Jané Ventura Negre Selecció 2013 T

90

Colour: deep cherry, purple rim. Nose: creamy oak, ripe fruit, balsamic herbs, roasted coffee. Palate: spicy, long, roasted-coffee aftertaste.

Jané Ventura Rosat Selecció 2014 RD

88

Colour: rose. Nose: floral, wild herbs, fruit expression. Palate: flavourful, complex, balanced, elegant.

Jané Ventura Sumoll 2013 T

sumoll

93

Colour: ruby red. Nose: expressive, complex, mineral, balsamic herbs, spicy. Palate: full, flavourful, round tannins.

JAUME GIRÓ I GIRÓ

Montaner i Oller, 5
08770 Sant Sadurní D'Anoia (Barcelona)
☎: +34 938 910 165
Fax: +34 938 911 271
cavagiro@cavagiro.com
www.cavagiro.com

Tarambana 2014 B

87

Colour: bright straw. Nose: ripe fruit, dried herbs, faded flowers. Palate: flavourful, easy to drink.

Tarambana 2014 RD

60% merlot, 40% pinot noir

86

JAUME LLOPART GUELL

Cl. Font Rubí, 9
08736 Font-Rubí (Barcelona)
☎: +34 938 979 133
Fax: +34 938 979 133
info@jaumellopartalemany.com
www.jaumellopartalemany.com

Jaume Llopart Alemany 2014 B

100% xarel.lo

86

Jaume Llopart Alemany Cabernet Sauvignon 2014 RD

100% cabernet sauvignon

85

Jaume Llopart Alemany Merlot 2013 T

100% merlot

86

Vinya d'en Lluc Sauvignon Blanc 2014 B

100% sauvignon blanc

89

Colour: bright straw. Nose: floral, jasmine, candied fruit, wild herbs. Palate: fresh, fruity, spicy, balsamic.

JEAN LEON

Pago Jean León, s/n
08775 Torrelavit (Barcelona)
☎: +34 938 995 512
Fax: +34 938 995 517
jeanleon@jeanleon.com
www.jeanleon.com

Jean León 3055 2014 RD

100% pinot noir

89

Colour: onion pink. Nose: elegant, red berry notes, floral, fragrant herbs. Palate: flavourful, good acidity, long, elegant.

Jean León 3055 Chardonnay 2014 B

chardonnay

91 ♣

Colour: bright yellow. Nose: expressive, dried herbs, ripe fruit, spicy. Palate: flavourful, fruity, good acidity, balanced.

Jean León 3055 Merlot Petit Verdot 2014 T

merlot, petit verdot

90 ♣

Colour: deep cherry, purple rim. Nose: ripe fruit, wild herbs, spicy. Palate: flavourful, fruity, ripe fruit.

Jean León Vinya La Scala Cabernet Sauvignon 2003 TGR

100% cabernet sauvignon

93

Colour: pale ruby, brick rim edge. Nose: spicy, fine reductive notes, wet leather, aged wood nuances, fruit liqueur notes. Palate: spicy, fine tannins, balanced.

Jean León Vinya Le Havre 2007 TR

cabernet sauvignon, cabernet franc

90

Colour: dark-red cherry, orangey edge. Nose: creamy oak, sweet spices, ripe fruit. Palate: spicy, balsamic, round tannins.

Jean León Vinya Palau Merlot 2011 TC

100% merlot

90

Colour: cherry, garnet rim. Nose: ripe fruit, wild herbs, earthy notes, spicy, balsamic herbs. Palate: balanced, flavourful, long, balsamic.

Jean León Viña Gigi Chardonnay 2013 BC
100% chardonnay

91

Colour: bright yellow. Nose: expressive, dried herbs, ripe fruit, spicy. Palate: flavourful, fruity, good acidity, balanced.

JOAN SARDÀ

Ctra. Vilafranca a St. Jaume dels Domenys, Km. 8,1
08732 Castellvi de la Marca (Barcelona)
☎: +34 937 720 900
Fax: +34 937 721 495
joansarda@joansarda.com
www.joansarda.com

Blanc Mariner 2014 B
xarel.lo, chardonnay

87

Colour: bright yellow. Nose: ripe fruit, white flowers, balanced. Palate: fruity, fine bitter notes, easy to drink.

Joan Sardà 2009 TR
cabernet sauvignon, tempranillo, merlot

88

Colour: dark-red cherry, orangey edge. Nose: spicy, dried herbs, old leather. Palate: correct, ripe fruit, flavourful.

Joan Sardà 2011 TC
merlot, syrah

85

Joan Sardà Cabernet Sauvignon 2012 TC
cabernet sauvignon

88

Colour: cherry, garnet rim. Nose: characterful, scrubland, dried herbs, spicy. Palate: flavourful, ripe fruit, balsamic.

Joan Sardà Cabernet Sauvignon 2014 RD
cabernet sauvignon

86

Joan Sardà Chardonnay 2014 B
chardonnay

87

Colour: bright yellow. Nose: expressive, ripe fruit, spicy, floral. Palate: flavourful, fruity, good acidity.

Vinya Sardà 2013 T
merlot, tempranillo

84

Vinya Sardà 2014 B
xarel.lo

84

Vinya Sardà 2014 RD
merlot

83

JUVÉ & CAMPS

Sant Venat, 1
08770 Sant Sadurní D'Anoia (Barcelona)
☎: +34 938 911 000
Fax: +34 938 912 100
juveycamps@juveycamps.com
www.juveycamps.com

Aurora D'Espiells Rosé 2014 RD
45% pinot noir, 45% xarel.lo, 10% syrah

88

Colour: onion pink. Nose: elegant, red berry notes, floral, fragrant herbs. Palate: light-bodied, flavourful, good acidity, spicy.

Casa Vella D'Espiells 2009 T
80% cabernet sauvignon, 20% merlot

91

Colour: cherry, garnet rim. Nose: balanced, complex, ripe fruit, spicy, fine reductive notes. Palate: good structure, flavourful, round tannins, balanced.

Casa Vella D'Espiells Magnum 2011 T
80% cabernet sauvignon, 20% merlot

92

Colour: ruby red. Nose: elegant, spicy, fine reductive notes, ripe fruit, balsamic herbs, expressive. Palate: spicy, fine tannins, elegant, long.

Ermita D'Espiells 2014 B
32% macabeo, 56% xarel.lo, 12% parellada

87

Colour: straw. Nose: medium intensity, floral, fruit expression, wild herbs. Palate: correct, easy to drink.

Ermita D'Espiells Rosé 2014 RD
85% pinot noir, 15% syrah

87

Colour: coppery red. Nose: red berry notes, ripe fruit, fragrant herbs, floral. Palate: fresh, fruity, flavourful.

Flor D'Espiells 2013 BFB
100% chardonnay

88

Colour: bright yellow. Nose: spicy, smoky, dried flowers. Palate: fruity, flavourful, fine bitter notes, correct, spicy.

Gregal D'Espiells 2014 B
79% moscatel, 14% gewürztraminer, 7% malvasía

88

Colour: bright straw. Nose: balsamic herbs, honeyed notes, floral. Palate: fruity, flavourful, easy to drink.

Iohannes 2008 T
45% cabernet sauvignon, 55% merlot

93

Colour: very deep cherry, garnet rim. Nose: cigar, ripe fruit, spicy. Palate: good structure, full, flavourful, round.

Miranda D'Espiells 2014 B
100% chardonnay

89 ♣

Colour: bright straw. Nose: white flowers, fresh fruit, fragrant herbs. Palate: flavourful, fruity, good acidity.

Viña Escarlata 2010 T
100% merlot

90

Colour: bright cherry, orangey edge. Nose: cocoa bean, ripe fruit, sweet spices. Palate: flavourful, balsamic, balanced.

LLOPART CAVA

Ctra. de Sant Sadurni - Ordal, Km. 4 Els Casots
08739 Els Casots (Subirats) (Barcelona)
☎: +34 938 993 125
Fax: +34 938 993 038
llopart@llopart.com
www.llopart.com

Llopart Castell de Subirats 2011 TC
40% merlot, 30% tempranillo, 30% cabernet sauvignon

90

Colour: cherry, garnet rim. Nose: ripe fruit, wild herbs, earthy notes, spicy, balsamic herbs, fine reductive notes. Palate: balanced, flavourful, long, balsamic.

Llopart Clos dels Fòssils 2014 B
65% xarel.lo, 35% chardonnay

89

Colour: bright straw. Nose: white flowers, fresh fruit, fragrant herbs, expressive. Palate: flavourful, fruity, good acidity, balanced.

Llopart Vitis 2014 B
60% xarel.lo, 30% subirat parent, 10% moscatel

85

LOXAREL

Can Mayol, s/n
08735 Vilobí del Penedès (Barcelona)
☎: +34 938 978 001
loxarel@loxarel.com
www.loxarel.com

790 Loxarel 2008 T
cabernet sauvignon

89 ♣

Colour: pale ruby, brick rim edge. Nose: spicy, fine reductive notes, wet leather, aged wood nuances, fruit liqueur notes. Palate: spicy, fine tannins, balanced.

Amaltea de Loxarel BN
xarel.lo, macabeo, parellada

88

Colour: bright yellow. Nose: ripe fruit, fine lees, balanced, dried herbs. Palate: good acidity, flavourful.

Cora de Loxarel 2014 B

87

Colour: bright straw. Nose: white flowers, fresh fruit, fragrant herbs. Palate: flavourful, fruity, easy to drink.

Garnatxa Blanca de Loxarel 2012 BN

90

Colour: bright straw. Nose: fresh fruit, dried herbs, fine lees, floral. Palate: fresh, fruity, flavourful, good acidity, balanced.

Garnatxa Blanca de Loxarel 2014 B
garnacha blanca

90 ♣

Colour: bright straw. Nose: citrus fruit, ripe fruit, dried herbs, sweet spices. Palate: powerful, flavourful, long, spicy.

Gran Elisenda de Loxarel 2011 ESP
xarel.lo, macabeo, chardonnay

92

Colour: bright golden. Nose: fine lees, fragrant herbs, complex. Palate: powerful, flavourful, good acidity, fine bead, fine bitter notes.

Loxarel Xarel.lo 2014 B

90 ♣

Colour: bright straw. Nose: expressive, balanced, varietal, dried flowers, fragrant herbs. Palate: flavourful, balanced, long.

LXV de Loxarel Xarel.lo Vermell 2013 B
XAREL.LO VERMELL

89

Colour: bright yellow. Nose: faded flowers, ripe fruit, honeyed notes. Palate: ripe fruit, long.

MM de Loxarel 2010 ESP Reserva
89
Colour: coppery red. Nose: fine lees, floral, fragrant herbs. Palate: flavourful, good acidity, fine bead, balanced.

Ops Loxarel 2013 T
88
Colour: deep cherry, purple rim. Nose: balanced, ripe fruit, red berry notes, wild herbs. Palate: spicy, long.

Petit Arnau de Loxarel 2014 RD
86

Refugi de Loxarel 2010 ESP Reserva
90% xarel.lo, 10% chardonnay
88
Colour: bright straw. Nose: dried herbs, fine lees, floral, wild herbs. Palate: fresh, fruity, flavourful, good acidity.

MAS BERTRAN
Ctra. BP-2121 Km.7,7
08731 St. Martí Sarroca (Barcelona)
☎: +34 938 990 859
info@masbertran.com
www.masbertran.com

Argila 2010 BN Reserva
100% xarel.lo
89
Colour: bright golden. Nose: dry nuts, fragrant herbs, sweet spices, lees reduction notes. Palate: powerful, flavourful, good acidity, fine bead.

Argila Rosé 2012 BN Reserva
100% sumoll
90
Colour: coppery red. Nose: floral, jasmine, fragrant herbs, candied fruit. Palate: fresh, fruity, flavourful, correct, balanced.

Balma 2012 BN Reserva
xarel.lo, macabeo, parellada
87
Colour: bright yellow. Nose: ripe fruit, fine lees, balanced. Palate: good acidity, ripe fruit, easy to drink.

Balma 2012 BR Reserva
xarel.lo, macabeo, parellada
87
Colour: bright straw. Nose: fine lees, floral, fragrant herbs. Palate: flavourful, good acidity, fine bead, easy to drink.

Nutt 2013 B
xarel.lo
89
Colour: bright yellow. Nose: balanced, fresh fruit, fragrant herbs, dried flowers. Palate: correct, balanced, fine bitter notes, good acidity.

Nutt 2014 B
sumoll, xarel.lo
86

Nutt Rosé 2014 RD
sumoll, xarel.lo
87
Colour: raspberry rose. Nose: red berry notes, floral, fragrant herbs. Palate: flavourful, long, spicy.

MAS CANDÍ
Ctra. de Les Gunyoles, s/n
08793 Les Gunyoles d'Avinyonet
del Penedès (Barcelona)
☎: +34 680 765 275
info@mascandi.com
www.mascandi.com

Mas Candi Cova de L'Ometlló Dulce 2011 T
cabernet sauvignon
87
Colour: cherry, garnet rim. Nose: fruit preserve, spicy, warm, fruit liqueur notes. Palate: powerful, flavourful, sweet, rich.

Mas Candi Desig 2014 B
xarel.lo
89
Colour: bright straw. Nose: dried flowers, fragrant herbs, fresh fruit, balanced, fine lees. Palate: flavourful, balanced, fine bitter notes.

Mas Candí Les Forques 2010 T
cabernet sauvignon
90
Colour: dark-red cherry, garnet rim. Nose: fragrant herbs, varietal, ripe fruit. Palate: good structure, flavourful, full, complex.

Mas Candi Pecat Noble 2013 BFB
malvasía
90
Colour: bright yellow. Nose: balsamic herbs, honeyed notes, floral, sweet spices, expressive. Palate: rich, fruity, powerful, flavourful, elegant.

Mas Candí QX 2013 BFB
xarel.lo
90
Colour: yellow, greenish rim. Nose: smoky, ripe fruit, spicy. Palate: fruity, flavourful, ripe fruit, long.

Mas Candí QX Magnum 2012 BFB
xarel.lo
89
Colour: bright yellow. Nose: ripe fruit, powerfull, roasted coffee. Palate: flavourful, spicy, toasty, long.

MAS CODINA

Barri El Gorner, s/n - Mas Codina
08797 Puigdalber (Barcelona)
☎: +34 938 988 166
Fax: +34 938 988 166
info@mascodina.com
www.mascodina.com

Mas Codina 2010 T
cabernet sauvignon, merlot, syrah

87

Colour: cherry, garnet rim. Nose: fine reductive notes, spicy, creamy oak. Palate: spicy, long, toasty.

Mas Codina 2014 B
macabeo, xarel.lo, chardonnay, moscatel

87

Colour: bright straw. Nose: white flowers, fresh fruit, fragrant herbs. Palate: flavourful, fruity, good acidity.

Mas Codina 2014 RD
cabernet sauvignon, merlot, syrah

85

Mas Codina Vinya Ferrer 2009 TR
cabernet sauvignon

87

Colour: deep cherry. Nose: creamy oak, toasty, ripe fruit, balsamic herbs. Palate: balanced, spicy, long.

Mas Codina Vinya Miquel 2010 TC
syrah

86

MAS COMTAL

Mas Comtal, 1
08793 Avinyonet del Penedès (Barcelona)
☎: +34 938 970 052
Fax: +34 938 970 591
mascomtal@mascomtal.com
www.mascomtal.com

Antistiana Merlot 2013 T
merlot

90

Colour: very deep cherry, garnet rim. Nose: spicy, ripe fruit, dried herbs. Palate: flavourful, round tannins, spicy.

Antistiana Xarel.lo 2013 B
xarel.lo

91

Colour: bright straw. Nose: fine lees, dried herbs, ripe fruit, citrus fruit. Palate: flavourful, fruity, good acidity.

Mas Comtal 20 Aniversari Rosado 2012 ESP Reserva
merlot

86

Mas Comtal 2012 BR Reserva
xarel.lo, chardonnay

87

Colour: bright yellow. Nose: fresh fruit, dried flowers, medium intensity. Palate: fruity, spicy, easy to drink.

Mas Comtal Joan Milà 2011 BN Reserva
chardonnay, xarel.lo

90

Colour: bright yellow. Nose: toasty, dry nuts, fine lees, balanced. Palate: flavourful, fine bitter notes, creamy, long.

Mas Comtal Negre D'Anyada 2013 T
merlot, cabernet franc

86

Mas Comtal Pomell de Blancs 2014 B
xarel.lo, chardonnay

89

Colour: bright straw. Nose: white flowers, fine lees, dried herbs, citrus fruit. Palate: flavourful, fruity, good acidity, elegant.

Mas Comtal Rosat de Llàgrima 2014 RD
merlot

85

Pétrea Chardonnay 2009 BFB
chardonnay

87

Colour: bright yellow. Nose: powerfull, toasty, roasted coffee, smoky. Palate: flavourful, fruity, spicy, toasty, long.

Pétrea Merlot 2011 T
merlot

87

Nose: ripe fruit, grassy, spicy, creamy oak. Palate: balsamic, spicy, ripe fruit.

MAS DELS CLAVERS FINCA CAN GALLEGO

Finca Can Gallego
08718 Cabrera d'Anoia (Barcelona)
☎: +34 667 536 467
info@fincacangallego.com
www.fincacangallego.com

Mas dels Clavers Cabernet Sauvignon Vinyes de Can Codony 2013 T
cabernet sauvignon

89

Colour: cherry, garnet rim. Nose: ripe fruit, wild herbs, earthy notes, spicy, balsamic herbs. Palate: flavourful, long, balsamic.

Mas dels Clavers Selecció Xarel.lo 2013 B
xarel.lo

90

Colour: bright yellow. Nose: ripe fruit, powerfull, toasty, aged wood nuances, pattiserie. Palate: flavourful, fruity, spicy, toasty, long.

Mas dels Clavers Selecció Xarel.lo 2014 B
xarel.lo

89

Colour: bright yellow. Nose: balanced, expressive, ripe fruit, sweet spices, dried flowers. Palate: rich, flavourful.

Mas dels Clavers Selección Merlot Cabernet Sauvignon 2014 T
merlot, cabernet sauvignon

85

MAS RODÓ VITIVINÍCOLA

Km. 2 Ctra. Sant Pere Sacarrera
a Sant Joan de Mediona
08773 Mediona (Barcelona)
☎: +34 932 385 780
Fax: +34 932 174 356
info@masrodo.com
www.masrodo.com

Mas Rodó Cabernet Sauvignon 2011 T
100% cabernet sauvignon

90

Colour: cherry, garnet rim. Nose: ripe fruit, wild herbs, earthy notes, spicy, balsamic herbs. Palate: balanced, flavourful, long, balsamic.

Mas Rodó Incògnit 2014 RD
tempranillo, merlot, cabernet sauvignon

87

Colour: coppery red, bright. Nose: ripe fruit, dried flowers. Palate: fruity, long, fine bitter notes, good acidity.

Mas Rodó Macabeo 2013 B
100% macabeo

89

Colour: bright yellow. Nose: powerfull, candied fruit, dried herbs, sweet spices. Palate: flavourful, sweet, ripe fruit, good acidity.

Mas Rodó Merlot 2011 TR
100% merlot

86

Mas Rodó Montonega 2013 B
100% montonega

92

Colour: bright straw. Nose: white flowers, dried herbs, ripe fruit, spicy, balanced. Palate: flavourful, fruity, good acidity, elegant.

Mas Rodó Riesling 2014 B
100% riesling

88

Colour: bright yellow. Nose: spicy, ripe fruit, toasty. Palate: flavourful, fruity, correct, balanced.

MASET DEL LLEÓ

Ctra. Vilafranca-Igualada C-15 (Km.19)
08792 La Granada (Barcelona)
☎: +34 902 200 250
Fax: +34 938 921 333
info@maset.com
www.maset.com

Maset del Lleó Cabernet Sauvignon 2011 TR
cabernet sauvignon

87

Colour: cherry, garnet rim. Nose: dried herbs, old leather, toasty. Palate: balanced, balsamic, easy to drink.

Maset del Lleó Chardonnay Flor de Mar 2014 B
chardonnay

88

Colour: bright straw. Nose: white flowers, dried herbs, candied fruit, citrus fruit. Palate: flavourful, fruity, good acidity.

Maset del Lleó Merlot 2014 RD
merlot

86

Maset del Lleó Merlot Foc 2011 TC
merlot

89

Colour: very deep cherry, garnet rim. Nose: expressive, balsamic herbs, balanced, toasty. Palate: flavourful, round tannins.

Maset del Lleó Selección 2013 T
tempranillo

89

Colour: bright cherry. Nose: ripe fruit, sweet spices, expressive. Palate: flavourful, fruity, toasty, round tannins.

Maset del Lleó Xarel.lo Blanc de Blancs 2014 B
xarel.lo

88

Colour: bright yellow. Nose: expressive, dried herbs, ripe fruit, spicy. Palate: flavourful, fruity, good acidity, balanced.

MASIA VALLFORMOSA

La Sala, 45
08735 Vilobi del Penedès (Barcelona)
☎: +34 938 978 286
Fax: +34 938 978 355
vallformosa@vallformosa.com
www.vallformosagroup.com

Domènech.Vidal – La.Sala 2014 B
xarel.lo, macabeo, chardonnay

85

Domènech.Vidal – La.Sala 2014 RD
merlot, sumoll, tempranillo

88

Colour: raspberry rose. Nose: red berry notes, floral, expressive. Palate: powerful, fruity, fresh.

La.Sala Tempranillo Cabernet Sauvignon Garnacha 2014 T
tempranillo, cabernet sauvignon, garnacha

89

Colour: cherry, purple rim. Nose: expressive, fresh fruit, red berry notes, floral. Palate: flavourful, fruity, good acidity.

Mas La.Roca 2014 B
xarel.lo, macabeo, chardonnay

86

Mas La.Roca 2014 RD
merlot, sumoll, tempranillo

86

Mas La.Roca 2014 T
tempranillo, cabernet sauvignon, garnacha

89

Colour: cherry, purple rim. Nose: expressive, fresh fruit, red berry notes, floral, violets. Palate: flavourful, fruity, good acidity.

Masia Freyè Cabernet Sauvignon Merlot 2013 T
cabernet sauvignon, merlot

86

Masia Freyè Parellada Muscat 2014 B
parellada, moscatel

87

Colour: bright yellow. Nose: white flowers, jasmine, ripe fruit, balanced. Palate: flavourful, fruity.

Masia Freyè Syrah Sumoll 2014 RD
syrah, sumoll

88

Colour: onion pink. Nose: elegant, fragrant herbs, red berry notes, citrus fruit, floral. Palate: light-bodied, flavourful, good acidity.

Masia Freyè Syrah Tempranillo 2013 T
syrah, tempranillo

88

Colour: very deep cherry, garnet rim. Nose: expressive, complex, mineral, balsamic herbs, balanced. Palate: flavourful, round tannins.

Masia Freyè Xarel.lo Chardonnay 2014 B
xarel.lo, chardonnay

86

MIQUEL PONS

Baix Llobregat, 5
08792 La Granada (Barcelona)
☎: +34 938 974 541
Fax: +34 938 974 710
miquelpons@cavamiquelpons.com
www.cavamiquelpons.com

Miquel Pons Arrelium 2014 RD
merlot

83

Miquel Pons Montargull Xarel.lo Barrica 2014 B
xarel.lo

88

Colour: bright yellow. Nose: ripe fruit, toasty, pattiserie. Palate: flavourful, fruity, spicy, toasty.

Miquel Pons Nuria 2014 B
85% moscatel, 15% chardonnay

86

NADAL

Finca Nadal de la Boadella, s/n
08775 Torrelavit (Barcelona)
☎: +34 938 988 011
Fax: +34 938 988 443
comunicacio@nadal.com
www.nadal.com

Nadal 1510 Botrytis Noble Dulce 2001 B Roble
100% macabeo

87

Colour: bright golden. Nose: candied fruit, fruit liqueur notes, pattiserie. Palate: flavourful, rich.

Nadal 1510 Verema Tardana Dulce B
100% macabeo

90

Colour: bright yellow. Nose: balsamic herbs, honeyed notes, floral, sweet spices, expressive. Palate: rich, fruity, powerful, flavourful, elegant.

X Nadal Vermell 2014 B
100% xarel.lo vermell

82

X Nadal Xarel.lo 2014 B
100% xarel.lo

83

ORIOL ROSSELL

Masia Cassanyes
08729 Sant Marçal (Barcelona)
☎: +34 977 671 061
Fax: +34 977 671 050
oriolrossell@oriolrossell.com
www.oriolrossell.com

Oriol Rossell Les Cerveres Xarel.lo 2013 B
100% xarel.lo

88

Colour: bright yellow. Nose: ripe fruit, powerfull, toasty, aged wood nuances. Palate: flavourful, spicy, long, fruity aftestaste.

Oriol Rossell Rocaplana 2013 TC
100% syrah

87

Colour: very deep cherry, garnet rim. Nose: ripe fruit, sweet spices. Palate: flavourful, easy to drink.

Oriol Rossell Virolet Xarel.lo 2014 B
100% xarel.lo

89

Colour: bright yellow. Nose: dried herbs, ripe fruit, spicy, lees reduction notes. Palate: flavourful, fruity, spicy.

PARATÓ

Can Respall de Renardes
08733 El Pla del Penedès (Barcelona)
☎: +34 938 988 182
Fax: +34 938 988 510
info@parato.es
www.parato.es

Ática Pinot Noir 2007 T
pinot noir

86

Finca Renardes 2013 T
tempranillo, samsó, cabernet sauvignon

90

Colour: deep cherry. Nose: creamy oak, toasty, ripe fruit, balsamic herbs, earthy notes. Palate: balanced, spicy, long.

Parató Ática Tres x Tres 2013 B

85

Parató Passió 2006 T
tempranillo, cabernet sauvignon

88

Colour: pale ruby, brick rim edge. Nose: ripe fruit, spicy, creamy oak, fine reductive notes. Palate: flavourful, toasty, round tannins.

Parató Pinot Noir 2014 RD
pinot noir

86 ♣

Parató Samsó 2011 TR
samsó

90

Colour: cherry, garnet rim. Nose: ripe fruit, wild herbs, earthy notes, spicy. Palate: balanced, long, balsamic.

Parató Xarel.lo 2014 B
xarel.lo

84 ♣

PARDAS

Finca Can Comas, s/n
08775 Torrelavit (Barcelona)
☎: +34 938 995 005
pardas@cancomas.com
www.cellerpardas.com

Pardas Aspriu 2012 T

94

Colour: cherry, garnet rim. Nose: mineral, expressive, spicy. Palate: flavourful, ripe fruit, long, good acidity, balanced.

Pardas Collita Roja 2012 T

89

Colour: light cherry. Nose: fruit expression, fruit liqueur notes, fragrant herbs, spicy, creamy oak. Palate: spicy, long, toasty.

Pardas Negre Franc 2011 T
91
Colour: deep cherry, purple rim. Nose: creamy oak, ripe fruit, balsamic herbs. Palate: balanced, spicy, long.

Pardas Rupestris 2014 B
88
Colour: bright straw. Nose: white flowers, fresh fruit, dried herbs. Palate: flavourful, fruity, good acidity, balanced.

Pardas Xarel.lo 2011 B
xarel.lo

92
Colour: bright yellow. Nose: expressive, dried herbs, ripe fruit, toasty. Palate: flavourful, fruity, good acidity, balanced.

Pardas Xarel.lo Aspriu 2011 B
94
Colour: bright straw. Nose: expressive, complex, elegant, ripe fruit, balanced. Palate: full, flavourful, complex, long.

PARÉS BALTÀ
Masía Can Baltá, s/n
08796 Pacs del Penedès (Barcelona)
☎: +34 938 901 399
paresbalta@paresbalta.com
www.paresbalta.com

Absis 2011 T
60% tempranillo, 13% merlot, 19% cabernet sauvignon, 8% syrah

92
Colour: cherry, garnet rim. Nose: balanced, complex, ripe fruit, spicy, fine reductive notes, mineral. Palate: good structure, flavourful, round tannins, balanced. Personality.

Blanc de Pacs 2014 B
parellada, macabeo, xarel.lo

86

Calcari Xarel.lo 2014 B
xarel.lo

90
Colour: bright yellow. Nose: dried herbs, floral, citrus fruit, earthy notes. Palate: powerful, flavourful, fresh, mineral.

Cosmic Parés Baltà 2014 B
xarel.lo, sauvignon blanc

89
Colour: bright straw. Nose: fresh fruit, fragrant herbs, citrus fruit. Palate: fruity, good acidity, balanced, easy to drink.

Electio Xarel.lo 2013 B
xarel.lo

90
Colour: bright yellow. Nose: ripe fruit, spicy, floral. Palate: flavourful, fruity, good acidity, balanced, rich, long.

Hisenda Miret Garnatxa 2012 T
garnacha

89
Colour: cherry, garnet rim. Nose: ripe fruit, wild herbs, earthy notes, spicy, balsamic herbs. Palate: balanced, flavourful, long, balsamic.

Indígena 2013 T
garnacha

88
Colour: cherry, purple rim. Nose: red berry notes, floral, balsamic herbs, spicy. Palate: powerful, fresh, fruity.

Indígena 2014 B
garnacha blanca

91
Colour: bright yellow. Nose: balanced, ripe fruit, wild herbs. Palate: fruity, easy to drink, fine bitter notes.

Indígena 2014 RD
garnacha

89
Colour: onion pink. Nose: elegant, fragrant herbs, dried flowers. Palate: flavourful, good acidity, long. Personality.

Marta de Baltà 2012 T
syrah

91
Colour: cherry, garnet rim. Nose: ripe fruit, wild herbs, earthy notes, spicy, balsamic herbs. Palate: balanced, flavourful, long, balsamic.

Mas Elena 2012 T
merlot, cabernet sauvignon, cabernet franc

90
Colour: very deep cherry, garnet rim. Nose: expressive, balsamic herbs, balanced, earthy notes. Palate: full, flavourful, round tannins.

Mas Irene 2012 T
merlot, cabernet franc

90
Colour: cherry, garnet rim. Nose: mineral, expressive, spicy, fruit preserve. Palate: flavourful, ripe fruit, long, good acidity, balanced.

Parés Baltà Mas Petit 2013 T
cabernet sauvignon, garnacha

90
Colour: deep cherry. Nose: expressive, complex, mineral, balsamic herbs, ripe fruit, balanced. Palate: full, flavourful.

RAVENTÓS I BLANC

Plaça del Roure, s/n
08770 Sant Sadurní D'Anoia
(Barcelona)
☎: +34 938 183 262
Fax: +34 938 912 500
raventos@raventos.com
www.raventos.com

11 de Isabel Negra 2007 T
monastrell, cabernet sauvignon

91

Colour: cherry, garnet rim. Nose: balanced, ripe fruit, spicy, fine reductive notes. Palate: good structure, flavourful, round tannins, balanced.

11 de Isabel Negra 2008 T
monastrell

91

Colour: ruby red. Nose: elegant, spicy, fine reductive notes, tobacco, ripe fruit. Palate: spicy, fine tannins, elegant, long.

Extrem 2014 B
xarel.lo

91

Colour: bright straw. Nose: expressive, varietal, fragrant herbs, complex. Palate: flavourful, long, good acidity, fine bitter notes.

Isabel Negra 2011 T
cabernet sauvignon, syrah, monastrell

90

Colour: cherry, garnet rim. Nose: ripe fruit, spicy, creamy oak, complex. Palate: flavourful, toasty, round tannins.

Silencis 2014 B
xarel.lo

90

Colour: bright straw. Nose: fruit expression, saline, fragrant herbs, mineral, balanced. Palate: fresh, fruity, flavourful, elegant.

ROCAMAR

Major, 80
08755 Castellbisbal (Barcelona)
☎: +34 937 720 900
Fax: +34 937 721 495
info@rocamar.net
www.rocamar.net

Rocamar Tempranillo 2013 T
tempranillo

84

ROS MARINA VITICULTORS

Camino Casas nuevas, 14
08736 Guardiola de Font-Rubí
(Barcelona)
☎: +34 938 988 185
Fax: +34 938 988 185
rosmarina@rosmarina.es
www.rosmarina.es

Mas Uberni Negre Selecció 2013 T
tempranillo, cabernet sauvignon

87

Colour: bright cherry. Nose: ripe fruit, sweet spices, creamy oak. Palate: flavourful, fruity, toasty.

Mas Uberni Rosat Selecció 2014 RD
cabernet sauvignon, merlot

87

Colour: light cherry, bright. Nose: red berry notes, ripe fruit, rose petals, faded flowers. Palate: flavourful, fine bitter notes.

Ros Marina Cabernet Merlot 2012 T Roble
cabernet sauvignon, merlot

87 ♣

Colour: bright cherry. Nose: ripe fruit, sweet spices, creamy oak. Palate: flavourful, fruity, toasty.

Ros Marina Merlot 2010 T
100% merlot

85 ♣

Ros Marina Vinyes de Coster 2011 T Roble
tempranillo, cabernet sauvignon, merlot

86 ♣

Ros Marina Xarel.lo 2013 BFB
100% xarel.lo

89 ♣

Colour: bright yellow. Nose: powerfull, candied fruit, dried herbs, sweet spices. Palate: flavourful, sweet, ripe fruit, good acidity.

ROVELLATS

Finca Rovellats - Bº La Bleda
08731 Sant Marti Sarroca (Barcelona)
☎: +34 934 880 575
Fax: +34 934 880 819
rovellats@cavasrovellats.com
www.rovellats.com

Rovellats Blanc Primavera 2014 B
chardonnay, macabeo, xarel.lo

87

Colour: bright straw. Nose: white flowers, fresh fruit, fragrant herbs. Palate: flavourful, fruity, good acidity.

Rovellats Brut de Tardor 2011 T
merlot, cabernet sauvignon

86

Rovellats Merlot 2014 RD
merlot

87
Colour: onion pink. Nose: elegant, red berry notes, floral, fragrant herbs. Palate: light-bodied, flavourful, good acidity, long, spicy.

SURIOL

Can Suriol del Castell
08736 Grabuac - Font-Rubí (Barcelona)
☎: +34 938 978 426
Fax: +34 938 978 426
cansuriol@suriol.com
www.suriol.com

Els Bancals 2012 B
xarel.lo

85

Suriol 2013 T
ull de llebre, garnacha, samsó, monastrell, merlot

85

Suriol 2014 B
macabeo, xarel.lo, garnacha, malvasía

83

Suriol Els Lledoners 2014 RD
garnacha

79

Suriol Sang de Drac 2012 T
ull de llebre

84

TON RIMBAU FERRER

Casa Rimbau, s/n
08735 Vilobí del Penedès (Barcelona)
☎: +34 609 312 822
tonrimbau@tonrimbau.com
www.porcellanic.com

Porcellanic Espurnejant 2011 ESP
80% xarel.lo, 20% macabeo

89
Colour: straw. Nose: candied fruit, citrus fruit, spicy. Palate: fresh, fine bead, fine bitter notes, spicy.

Porcellànic Vi Dolç Natural 2012 B
100% macabeo

92
Colour: light mahogany. Nose: candied fruit, honeyed notes, dried fruit, aromatic coffee. Palate: sweet, fine bitter notes, long.

Porcellànic Vi Xarel.lo Orangebi 2012
100% xarel.lo

75

Porcellànic Xarel.lo Sur Lie 2011 B
100% xarel.lo

90
Colour: coppery red. Nose: candied fruit, citrus fruit, earthy notes, mineral. Palate: long, flavourful, fine bitter notes.

Porcellànic Xarel.lo Verema Tardana 2011 B
xarel.lo

85

TORELLÓ

Can Martí de Baix (Apartado Correos nº8)
08770 Sant Sadurní D'Anoia
(Barcelona)
☎: +34 938 910 793
Fax: +34 938 910 877
torello@torello.es
www.torello.com

Gran Crisalys 2013 B
xarel.lo, chardonnay

91
Colour: bright yellow. Nose: powerfull, toasty. Palate: flavourful, fruity, spicy, toasty, long, balanced, fine bitter notes, good acidity.

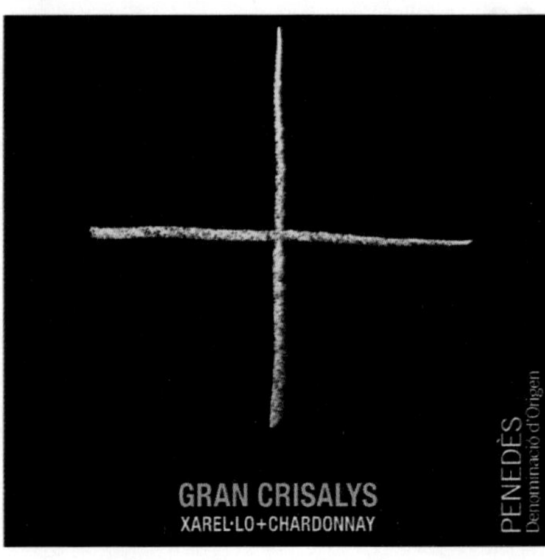

Petjades 2014 RD
merlot

87

Colour: rose, bright. Nose: wild herbs, ripe fruit. Palate: correct, fine bitter notes, easy to drink.

Raimonda 2010 TR
cabernet sauvignon, merlot

90

Colour: cherry, garnet rim. Nose: ripe fruit, wild herbs, earthy notes, spicy, fine reductive notes. Palate: balanced, flavourful, long.

Torelló Malvarel.lo 2014 B
malvasía, xarel.lo

86 ♣

Vittios Merlot Vendimia Tardía 2012 T
merlot

87

Colour: bright cherry, garnet rim. Nose: acetaldehyde, varnish, fruit preserve. Palate: fruity, flavourful, sweet.

TORREBLANCA
Masia Torreblanca, s/n
08734 Olérdola (Barcelona)
☎: +34 938 915 066
Fax: +34 938 900 102
torreblanca@cavatorreblanca.com
www.vinatorreblanca.com

Torreblanca Collita 2014 T
tempranillo, merlot, syrah

85

Torreblanca Les Atzavares 2014 B
macabeo, xarel.lo, parellada, moscatel

87

Colour: bright straw. Nose: white flowers, fresh fruit, fragrant herbs, expressive. Palate: flavourful, fruity, good acidity, balanced.

Torreblanca Merlot 2014 RD
merlot

89

Colour: rose, purple rim. Nose: red berry notes, floral, expressive. Palate: powerful, fruity, fresh.

TRIAS BATLLE
Pere El Gran, 24
08720 Vilafranca del Penedès
(Barcelona)
☎: +34 677 497 892
peptrias@jtrias.com
www.triasbatlle.com

Trias Batlle 2013 T
tempranillo, merlot

86

Trias Batlle 2014 RD
merlot, cabernet sauvignon, syrah

86

Trias Batlle 2014 B
macabeo, xarel.lo, parellada, moscatel

86

Trias Batlle Cabernet Sauvignon 2010 TC
cabernet sauvignon

88

Colour: ruby red. Nose: complex, mineral, balsamic herbs, ripe fruit, sweet spices. Palate: full, flavourful, correct.

Trias Batlle Xarel.lo 2013 B Barrica
xarel.lo

91

Colour: bright yellow. Nose: ripe fruit, powerfull, toasty, pattiserie. Palate: flavourful, fruity, spicy, toasty, long.

VALLDOLINA
Plaça de la Creu, 1
08795 Olesa de Bonesvalls (Barcelona)
☎: +34 938 984 181
Fax: +34 938 984 181
info@valldolina.com
www.valldolina.com

Bones Valls Cabernet Sauvignon 2011 T
cabernet sauvignon

89

Colour: deep cherry. Nose: creamy oak, toasty, ripe fruit, balsamic herbs. Palate: balanced, spicy, long.

Vall Dolina Xarel.lo "Ecológico" 2014 B
xarel.lo

87 ♣

Colour: bright yellow. Nose: balanced, ripe fruit, floral, citrus fruit. Palate: correct, flavourful, rich.

VallDolina Merlot 2012 TR
merlot

86 ♣

VENTURA SOLER

Cinturó Circunval.lació, km. 0,5
08770 Sant Sadurní D'Anoia
(Barcelona)
☎: +34 938 183 003
Fax: +34 938 183 376
caves@venturasoler.com
www.venturasoler.com

Ventura Soler 2014 B

moscatel, chardonnay, parellada

84

Ventura Soler 2014 RD

garnacha, merlot

84

Ventura Soler 2014 T

100% merlot

87

Colour: deep cherry, purple rim. Nose: ripe fruit, balsamic herbs, spicy. Palate: balanced, long.

VILARNAU

Ctra. d'Espiells, Km. 1,4 Finca "Can Petit"
08770 Sant Sadurní D'Anoia
(Barcelona)
☎: +34 938 912 361
Fax: +34 938 912 913
vilarnau@vilarnau.es
www.vilarnau.es

Vilarnau Xarel.lo 2014 B

xarel.lo

86

VINS EL CEP

Can Llopart de Les Alzines, Ctra. Espiells
08770 Sant Sadurní D'Anoia
(Barcelona)
☎: +34 938 912 353
Fax: +34 938 183 956
info@vinselcep.com
www.vinselcep.com

Clot del Roure 2013 B

xarel.lo

90

Colour: bright yellow. Nose: ripe fruit, powerfull, toasty, aged wood nuances. Palate: flavourful, fruity, spicy, toasty, long.

Marqués de Gélida Blanc de Blancs 2014 B

xarel.lo, chardonnay

86

Marqués de Gelida Negre Selecció 2013 T

tempranillo, syrah, cabernet sauvignon

89

Colour: dark-red cherry, garnet rim. Nose: ripe fruit, fruit preserve, violets, sweet spices, characterful. Palate: full, flavourful, round tannins.

DO. PLA DE BAGES

CONSEJO REGULADOR

Casa de La Culla - La Culla, s/n
08240 Manresa (Barcelona)
☎ :+34 938 748 236 - Fax: +34 938 748 094
@: info@dopladebages.com
www.dopladebages.com

LOCATION:

Covering one of the eastern extremes of the Central Catalonian Depression; it covers the natural region of Bages, of which the city of Manresa is the urban centre. To the south the region is bordered by the Montserrat mountain range, the dividing line which separates it from Penedés. It comprises the municipal areas of Fonollosa, Monistrol de Caldres, Sant Joan de Vilatorrada, Artés, Avinyó, Balsareny, Calders, Callús, Cardona, Castellgalí, Castellfollit del Boix, Castellnou de Bages, Manresa, Mura, Navarcles, Navàs, El Pont de Vilomara, Rajadell, Sallent, Sant Fruitós de Bages, Sant Mateu de Bages, Sant Salvador de Guardiola, Santpedor, Santa María d'Oló, Súria and Talamanca.

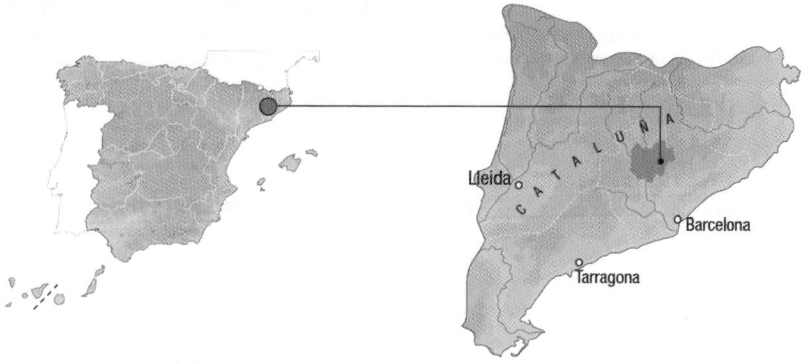

GRAPE VARIETIES:

WHITE: Chardonnay, Gewürztraminer, Macabeo, Picapoll, Parellada, Sauvignon Blanc.
RED: Sumoll, Ull de Llebre (Tempranillo), Merlot, Cabernet Franc, Cabernet Sauvignon, Syrah and Garnacha.

FIGURES:

Vineyard surface: 500 – **Wine-Growers:** 85 – **Wineries:** 12 – **2014 Harvest rating:** Good – **Production 14:** 925,450 litres – **Market percentages:** 70% National - 30% International.

SOIL:

The vineyards are situated at an altitude of about 400 m. The soil is franc-clayey, franc-sandy and franc-clayey-sandy.

CLIMATE:

Mid-mountain Mediterranean, with little rainfall (500 mm to 600 mm average annual rainfall) and greater temperature contrasts than in the Penedès.

VINTAGE RATING

PEÑÍNGUIDE

2010	2011	2012	2013	2014
GOOD	VERY GOOD	GOOD	VERY GOOD	GOOD

ABADAL

Santa María d'Horta d'Avinyó s/n
08279 Santa María D'Horta D'Avinyó (Barcelona)
☎: +34 938 743 511
Fax: +34 938 737 204
info@abadal.net
www.abadal.net

Abadal 2011 TC
50% cabernet sauvignon, 50% merlot

88

Colour: very deep cherry. Nose: grassy, wild herbs, ripe fruit, characterful. Palate: good structure, long, spicy.

Abadal 3.9 2010 TR
85% cabernet sauvignon, 15% syrah

91

Colour: very deep cherry, garnet rim. Nose: expressive, scrubland, aged wood nuances, varietal. Palate: good structure, full.

Abadal 5 Merlot 2012 TR
100% merlot

91

Colour: cherry, garnet rim. Nose: ripe fruit, wild herbs, earthy notes, spicy, balsamic herbs. Palate: balanced, flavourful, long, balsamic.

Abadal Blanc 2014 B
40% chardonnay, 30% sauvignon blanc, 15% picapoll, 15% macabeo

88

Colour: bright straw. Nose: white flowers, fresh fruit, fragrant herbs, expressive. Palate: flavourful, fruity, good acidity, balanced.

Abadal Franc 2014 T
50% cabernet franc, 40% tempranillo, 10% sumoll

89

Colour: cherry, garnet rim. Nose: red berry notes, floral, balsamic herbs. Palate: powerful, fresh, fruity.

Abadal Nuat 2012 B
80% picapoll, 20% macabeo

92

Colour: bright yellow. Nose: white flowers, fine lees, dried herbs, ripe fruit, candied fruit, citrus fruit. Palate: flavourful, fruity, good acidity, rich, long, elegant.

Abadal Picapoll 2014 B
100% picapoll

90

Colour: bright straw. Nose: fresh fruit, fragrant herbs, white flowers. Palate: flavourful, fruity, good acidity, balanced.

Abadal Rosat 2014 RD
70% cabernet sauvignon, 30% sumoll

87

Colour: brilliant rose. Nose: red berry notes, ripe fruit, balsamic herbs, floral. Palate: powerful, flavourful, long.

Abadal Selecció 2009 TR
40% cabernet sauvignon, 30% cabernet franc, 15% syrah, 10% mando, 5% sumoll

93

Colour: cherry, garnet rim. Nose: smoky, spicy, ripe fruit, earthy notes. Palate: flavourful, smoky aftertaste, ripe fruit.

CELLER MÉS QUE PARAULES

Finca Jaumandreu
08259 Fonollosa (Barcelona)
☎: +34 934 283 984
celler@mesqueparaules.cat
www.mesqueparaules.cat

Més Que Paraules 2012 T
cabernet sauvignon, merlot, syrah, sumoll

85

Més Que Paraules 2014 B
picapoll, sauvignon blanc, chardonnay

87

Colour: straw. Nose: medium intensity, ripe fruit, floral, wild herbs. Palate: correct, easy to drink, fine bitter notes.

Més Que Paraules 2014 RD
merlot, sumoll

86

Molt Més Que Paraules 2011 T
cabernet sauvignon

92

Colour: cherry, garnet rim. Nose: ripe fruit, wild herbs, earthy notes, spicy, balsamic herbs. Palate: balanced, flavourful, long, balsamic.

CELLER SOLERGIBERT

Barquera, 40
08271 Artés (Barcelona)
☎: +34 938 305 084
Fax: +34 938 305 763
josep@cellersolergibert.com
www.cellersolergibert.com

Conxita Serra Gran Selecció 2002 T
merlot

90

Colour: deep cherry, orangey edge. Nose: waxy notes, tobacco, ripe fruit, spicy, aged wood nuances. Palate: fine bitter notes, elegant, flavourful, fine tannins.

Enric Solergibert Gran Selecció 2002 T
cabernet sauvignon, cabernet franc

90

Colour: pale ruby, brick rim edge. Nose: elegant, spicy, fine reductive notes, tobacco. Palate: spicy, fine tannins, elegant, long.

Pd'A de Solergilabert 2014 B
picapoll

88

Colour: bright yellow. Nose: wild herbs, dried herbs, ripe fruit, dried flowers. Palate: correct, good finish.

Pic Solergibert 2014 B
picapoll

90

Colour: bright straw. Nose: medium intensity, ripe fruit, wild herbs, balanced. Palate: balanced, fine bitter notes, spicy.

SDM Solergibert de Matacans 2012 T
50% cabernet sauvignon, 50% cabernet franc

90

Colour: deep cherry. Nose: creamy oak, toasty, ripe fruit, balsamic herbs, earthy notes. Palate: balanced, spicy, long, balsamic.

Solergibert Cabernet 2009 TR
cabernet sauvignon, cabernet franc, merlot

90

Colour: cherry, garnet rim. Nose: ripe fruit, spicy, creamy oak, wild herbs, fine reductive notes. Palate: flavourful, toasty, round tannins.

Solergibert Merlot 2007 TR
merlot

89

Colour: cherry, garnet rim. Nose: ripe fruit, wild herbs, earthy notes, spicy, balsamic herbs. Palate: balanced, flavourful, long, balsamic.

Solergibert Sumoll 2014 T
sumoll

91

Colour: light cherry. Nose: floral, balsamic herbs, earthy notes, red berry notes, fruit liqueur notes. Palate: powerful, fresh, fruity, balanced.

Toc de Solergibert 2014 T
merlot, cabernet sauvignon, cabernet franc

87

Colour: deep cherry. Nose: creamy oak, toasty, balsamic herbs, fruit liqueur notes. Palate: balanced, spicy, long.

COLLBAIX - CELLER EL MOLI

Cami de Rajadell, km. 3
08241 Manresa (Barcelona)
☎: +34 931 021 965
collbaix@cellerelmoli.com
www.cellerelmoli.com

Collbaix Cupatge 2010 T
cabernet sauvignon, merlot, tempranillo, cabernet franc

89

Colour: bright cherry. Nose: ripe fruit, sweet spices, creamy oak, fine reductive notes. Palate: flavourful, fruity, toasty.

Collbaix La Llobeta 2010 T
cabernet sauvignon, merlot, cabernet franc

88

Colour: cherry, garnet rim. Nose: fine reductive notes, aged wood nuances, ripe fruit. Palate: spicy, long, toasty.

Collbaix Merlot 2014 RD
merlot, sumoll

88

Colour: rose, purple rim. Nose: red berry notes, floral, expressive. Palate: powerful, fruity, fresh.

Collbaix Picapoll Macabeo 2014 B
picapoll, macabeo

88

Colour: bright yellow. Nose: expressive, dried herbs, ripe fruit, spicy. Palate: flavourful, fruity, good acidity, balanced.

Collbaix Singular 2011 T
cabernet sauvignon

92

Colour: cherry, garnet rim. Nose: ripe fruit, fruit preserve, earthy notes, balsamic herbs, creamy oak. Palate: flavourful, spicy, long.

Collbaix Singular 2012 B Barrica
macabeo

93

Colour: bright straw. Nose: white flowers, fine lees, dried herbs, ripe fruit, candied fruit, citrus fruit, sweet spices. Palate: flavourful, fruity, good acidity, elegant.

El Sagal 2014 T
merlot, tempranillo

87

Colour: cherry, purple rim. Nose: balsamic herbs, ripe fruit, wild herbs, spicy. Palate: powerful, flavourful.

HERETAT OLLER DEL MAS

Ctra. de Igualada (C-37), km. 91
08241 Manresa (Barcelona)
☎: +34 938 768 315
info@ollerdelmas.com
www.ollerdelmas.com

Arnau Oller 2011 T
merlot

91 ♣

Colour: cherry, garnet rim. Nose: ripe fruit, wild herbs, earthy notes, spicy, balsamic herbs, fine reductive notes. Palate: balanced, flavourful, long, balsamic.

Bernat Oller 2012 T
merlot, picapoll negro

89 ♣

Colour: very deep cherry, garnet rim. Nose: expressive, complex, balsamic herbs, balanced. Palatc: full, flavourful, round tannins.

Bernat Oller Blanc de Picapolls 2014 B
picapoll, picapoll negro

84 ♣

Bernat Oller Rosat 2014 RD
merlot, picapoll negro

85 ♣

Oller del Mas Especial Picapoll Negre 2013 T
picapoll negro

90 ♣

Colour: light cherry. Nose: fruit expression, fruit liqueur notes, fragrant herbs, spicy, creamy oak, balsamic herbs. Palate: balanced, elegant, spicy, long.

Petit Bernat 2014 T
syrah, cabernet franc, merlot, cabernet sauvignon, picapoll negro

84 ♣

Petit Bernat Blanc 2014 B
picapoll, macabeo

88 ♣

Colour: bright straw. Nose: white flowers, fresh fruit, fragrant herbs, expressive. Palate: flavourful, fruity, good acidity, balanced.

VINS GRAU

Ctra. C-37, Km. 75,5
D'Igualada a Manresa
08255 Maians-Castellfollit del Boix
(Barcelona)
☎: +34 938 356 002
info@vinsgrau.com
www.vinsgrau.com

Jaume Grau i Grau "Gratvs" 2011 TC
tempranillo, merlot

87

Colour: cherry, garnet rim. Nose: ripe fruit, wild herbs, spicy. Palate: flavourful, long, balsamic.

Jaume Grau i Grau Avrvm 2014 B
sauvignon blanc, chardonnay, macabeo

85

Jaume Grau i Grau Merlot 2014 RD
merlot

87

Colour: rose. Nose: powerfull, ripe fruit, wild herbs. Palate: powerful, flavourful.

Jaume Grau i Grau Picapoll Cent - Kat 2014 B
picapoll

87

Colour: bright yellow. Nose: expressive, dried herbs, ripe fruit, spicy. Palate: flavourful, fruity, good acidity, sweetness.

Jaume Grau i Grau Selección Especial "Tapas" 2012 T
tempranillo, merlot, cabernet franc, syrah

87

Colour: cherry, garnet rim. Nose: smoky, spicy, ripe fruit. Palate: flavourful, ripe fruit, roasted-coffee aftertaste.

Jaume Grau i Grau Sensvs 2012 TC
cabernet franc, syrah

90

Colour: bright cherry. Nose: ripe fruit, sweet spices, creamy oak, expressive. Palate: flavourful, fruity, toasty, round tannins.

DO. PLA I LLEVANT

CONSEJO REGULADOR

Molí de N'Amengual. Dusai, 3
07260 Porreres (Illes Balears)
☎:+34 971 168 569 - Fax: +34 971 184 49 34
@: doplaillevant@gmail.com
www.doplaillevant.com

LOCATION:

The production region covers the eastern part of Majorca and consists of 18 municipal districts: Algaida, Ariany, Artá, Campos, Capdepera, Felanitx, Lluchamajor, Manacor, Mª de la Salud, Montuiri, Muro, Petra, Porreres, Sant Joan, Sant Llorens des Cardasar, Santa Margarita, Sineu and Vilafranca de Bonany.

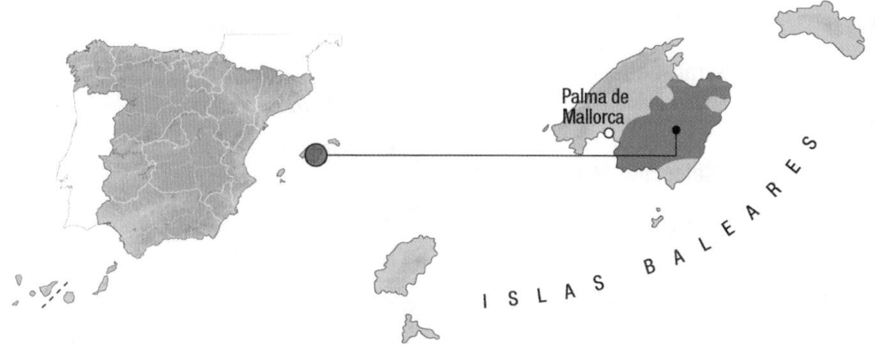

GRAPE VARIETIES:

WHITE: Prensal Blanc, Macabeo, Parellada, Moscatel and Chardonnay.
RED: Callet (majority), Manto Negro, Fogoneu, Tempranillo, Monastrell, Cabernet Sauvignon, Merlot and Syrah.

FIGURES:

Vineyard surface: 402 – **Wine-Growers:** 63 – **Wineries:** 12 – **2014 Harvest rating:** N/A – **Production 14:** 1,223,400 litres – **Market percentages:** 90% National - 10% International.

SOIL:

The soil is made up of limestone rocks, which give limy-clayey soils. The reddish Colour: of the terrain is due to the presence of iron oxide. The clays and calcium and magnesium carbonates, in turn, provide the whitish Colour: which can also be seen in the vineyards.

CLIMATE:

Mediterranean, with an average temperature of 16°C and with slightly cool winters and dry, hot summers. The constant sea breeze during the summer has a notable effect on these terrains close to the coast. The wet season is in autumn and the average annual rainfall is between 450 mm and 500 mm.

VINTAGE RATING

PEÑÍNGUIDE

2010	2011	2012	2013	2014
VERY GOOD	VERY GOOD	VERY GOOD	GOOD	GOOD

ARMERO I ADROVER

Camada Real s/n
07200 Mallorca (Illes Ballears)
☎: +34 971 827 103
Fax: +34 971 580 305
luisarmero@armeroiadrover.com
www.armeroiadrover.com

Armero Adrover 2013 T

87

Colour: cherry, garnet rim. Nose: toasty, ripe fruit, balsamic herbs. Palate: balanced, spicy.

Armero Adrover 2014 B

prensal, chardonnay

86

Armero Adrover Syrah-Callet Rosat 2014 RD

callet, syrah, merlot

86

Armero i Adrover Seleccion Familiar 2010 T

87

Colour: cherry, garnet rim. Nose: tobacco, wild herbs, dried herbs, ripe fruit. Palate: spicy, long, toasty.

BODEGA JAUME MESQUIDA

Vileta, 7
07260 Porreres (Illes Ballears)
☎: +34 971 168 646
vinsdemallorca@jaumemesquida.org
www.jaumemesquida.com

Viña del Albaricoque 2012 T

90

Colour: cherry, purple rim. Nose: creamy oak, toasty, ripe fruit, balsamic herbs. Palate: balanced, spicy, long.

BODEGA MESQUIDA MORA

Camí Pas des Frare, s/n
(Antigua Ctra. PorreresSant Joan)
07260 Porreres (Illes Balears)
☎: +34 971 647 106
Fax: +34 971 168 205
info@mesquidamora.com
www.mesquidamora.com

Trispol 2013 T

cabernet sauvignon, syrah, merlot, callet

90

Colour: deep cherry, purple rim. Nose: ripe fruit, balsamic herbs, spicy. Palate: balanced, spicy, long.

BODEGAS BORDOY

Cami Muntanya, s/n
07609 Llucmajor (Illes Ballears)
☎: +34 646 619 776
Fax: +34 971 771 246
sarota@bodegasbordoy.com
www.bodegasbordoy.es

Sa Rota 2010 TC

cabernet sauvignon, syrah, callet, merlot

89

Colour: cherry, garnet rim. Nose: spicy, balanced. Palate: flavourful, ripe fruit, long, good acidity, spicy, balsamic.

Sa Rota 2010 TR

syrah, merlot, cabernet sauvignon, callet

88

Colour: bright cherry, garnet rim. Nose: ripe fruit, cocoa bean, tobacco. Palate: correct, fruity, long.

Sa Rota 2013 T

cabernet sauvignon, syrah, callet, merlot

85

Sa Rota Blanc 2014 B

chardonnay, prensal, giró

87

Colour: bright yellow. Nose: medium intensity, ripe fruit, floral. Palate: correct, easy to drink, fine bitter notes.

Sa Rota Blanc Chardonnay 2013 BFB

chardonnay

86

Sa Rota Dulce 2014 T

merlot

86

Sa Rota Merlot 2009 T

merlot

84

Sa Rota Rosat 2014 RD

cabernet sauvignon, merlot, callet

86

Terra de Marés 2012 T

cabernet sauvignon, syrah

92

Colour: cherry, garnet rim. Nose: spicy, elegant, complex, varietal, earthy notes, balsamic herbs. Palate: flavourful, ripe fruit, long, good acidity, balanced.

BODEGAS PERE SEDA

Cid Campeador, 22
07500 Manacor (Illes Ballears)
☎: +34 971 550 219
Fax: +34 971 844 934
lucasreus@telefonica.net
www.pereseda.com

Chardonnay Pere Seda 2014 B
100% chardonnay

86

Gvivm Merlot-Callet 2011 T
80% cabernet sauvignon, 20% callet

91

Colour: cherry, garnet rim. Nose: ripe fruit, wild herbs, earthy notes, spicy, balsamic herbs. Palate: balanced, flavourful, long, balsamic, good acidity.

L'Arxiduc Pere Seda Blanc 2014 B
40% moscatel, 40% chardonnay, 20% parellada

85

Mossèn Negre 2011 T
85% cabernet sauvignon, 15% callet

90

Colour: bright cherry. Nose: balanced, expressive, ripe fruit, spicy. Palate: balanced, ripe fruit, balsamic.

Pere Seda 2009 TR
36% merlot, 33% cabernet sauvignon, 18% syrah, 13% callet

85

Pere Seda 2013 BN
95% parellada, 5% chardonnay

84

Pere Seda 2011 TC
53% merlot, 27% cabernet sauvignon, 14% syrah, 6% callet

88

Colour: cherry, garnet rim. Nose: smoky, spicy, ripe fruit. Palate: flavourful, smoky aftertaste, ripe fruit.

MIQUEL OLIVER VINYES I BODEGUES

Ctra. Petra-Sta. Margarita km. 1,8
07520 Petra-Mallorca (Illes Ballears)
☎: +34 971 561 117
Fax: +34 971 561 117
bodega@miqueloliver.com
www.miqueloliver.com

1912 Miquel Oliver 2010 T
cabernet sauvignon, merlot

92

Colour: cherry, garnet rim. Nose: ripe fruit, wild herbs, earthy notes, spicy, balsamic herbs. Palate: balanced, flavourful, long.

Aia 2011 T
merlot

91

Colour: very deep cherry, garnet rim. Nose: expressive, complex, balsamic herbs, balanced. Palate: full, flavourful, round tannins.

Original Muscat Miquel Oliver 2014 B
moscatel

89

Colour: bright straw, greenish rim. Nose: white flowers, fresh fruit, varietal. Palate: fruity, good acidity, balanced.

Ses Ferritges 2011 TR
callet, cabernet sauvignon, syrah, merlot

90

Colour: dark-red cherry. Nose: characterful, earthy notes, ripe fruit, dried herbs. Palate: balanced, flavourful, fruity, long.

Syrah Negre Miquel Oliver 2012 T
syrah

88

Colour: deep cherry, purple rim. Nose: creamy oak, toasty, ripe fruit, balsamic herbs. Palate: balanced, spicy, easy to drink.

Xperiment 2012 T
callet

91

Colour: cherry, garnet rim. Nose: ripe fruit, wild herbs, earthy notes, spicy, balsamic herbs. Palate: balanced, flavourful, long, balsamic.

VINS MIQUEL GELABERT

Salas, 50
07500 Manacor (Illes Balears)
☎: +34 971 821 444
info@vinsmiquelgelabert.com
www.vinsmiquelgelabert.com

Chardonnay Roure 2013 BFB
100% chardonnay

90

Colour: bright yellow. Nose: ripe fruit, powerfull, toasty, sweet spices. Palate: flavourful, fruity, spicy, toasty, long, rich.

Chardonnay Roure Selección Especial 2012 B
100% chardonnay

87

Colour: bright golden. Nose: powerfull, aged wood nuances, roasted coffee. Palate: flavourful, fruity, spicy, toasty, long, rich.

Golós Blanc 2013 B
riesling, moscatel, giró, viognier

87

Colour: bright yellow. Nose: wild herbs, faded flowers, ripe fruit, characterful. Palate: flavourful, fine bitter notes, good finish.

Golós Negre 2012 T
callet, manto negro, fogoneu

92

Colour: cherry, garnet rim. Nose: ripe fruit, wild herbs, spicy, balsamic herbs, dry stone. Palate: balanced, flavourful, long, balsamic.

Golós Rosat 2013 RD
pinot noir

86

Gran Vinya Son Caules 2009 T
callet

92

Colour: cherry, garnet rim. Nose: ripe fruit, wild herbs, earthy notes, spicy, balsamic herbs. Palate: balanced, flavourful, long, balsamic. Personality.

Sa Vall Selecció Privada 2011 BFB
giró, viognier

90

Colour: bright yellow. Nose: expressive, ripe fruit, spicy, faded flowers. Palate: flavourful, fruity, good acidity, balanced, fine bitter notes.

Torrent Negre 2009 T
cabernet sauvignon, merlot, syrah

88

Colour: cherry, garnet rim. Nose: dried herbs, ripe fruit, characterful, warm. Palate: flavourful, slightly dry, soft tannins.

Torrent Negre Selecció Privada Cabernet 2007 T
cabernet sauvignon

92

Colour: cherry, garnet rim. Nose: balanced, complex, ripe fruit, spicy, fine reductive notes. Palate: good structure, flavourful, round tannins, balanced.

Vinya des Moré 2009 T
pinot noir

89

Colour: light cherry. Nose: characterful, varietal, warm, spicy, faded flowers. Palate: spicy, easy to drink, fruity.

VINS TONI GELABERT

Camí dels Horts de Llodrá Km. 1,3
07500 Manacor (Illes Balears)
☎: +34 971 552 409
info@vinstonigelabert.com
www.vinstonigelabert.com

Negre de Sa Colonia 2013 T
callet

87

Colour: garnet rim, bright cherry. Nose: expressive, balsamic herbs, balanced, ripe fruit. Palate: round tannins, easy to drink.

Ses Hereves 2007 TR
cabernet sauvignon, merlot, syrah

90

Colour: cherry, garnet rim. Nose: ripe fruit, wild herbs, earthy notes, spicy, balsamic herbs. Palate: balanced, flavourful, long.

Toni Gelabert Cabernet 2007 T
cabernet sauvignon

88

Colour: cherry, garnet rim. Nose: ripe fruit, old leather, tobacco. Palate: correct, flavourful, spicy.

Toni Gelabert Chardonnay 2013 BFB
chardonnay

88

Colour: bright yellow. Nose: ripe fruit, toasty. Palate: flavourful, fruity, spicy, long.

Vinya Son Fangos Blanc 2014 B
prensal, moscatel

87

Colour: straw. Nose: medium intensity, ripe fruit, floral, dried herbs. Palate: correct, easy to drink, fresh.

Vinya Son Fangos Negre 2011 T
callet, cabernet sauvignon, merlot, syrah

89

Colour: deep cherry, purple rim. Nose: creamy oak, toasty, ripe fruit, balsamic herbs. Palate: balanced, spicy, long.

DO. Ca. PRIORAT

CONSEJO REGULADOR

Major, 2
43737 Torroja del Priorat (Tarragona)
☎ :+34 977 839 495 - Fax. +34 977 839 472
@: info@doqpriorat.org
www.doqpriorat.org

LOCATION:

In the province of Tarragona. It is made up of the municipal districts of La Morera de Montsant, Scala Dei, La Vilella, Gratallops, Bellmunt, Porrera, Poboleda, Torroja, Lloá, Falset and Mola.

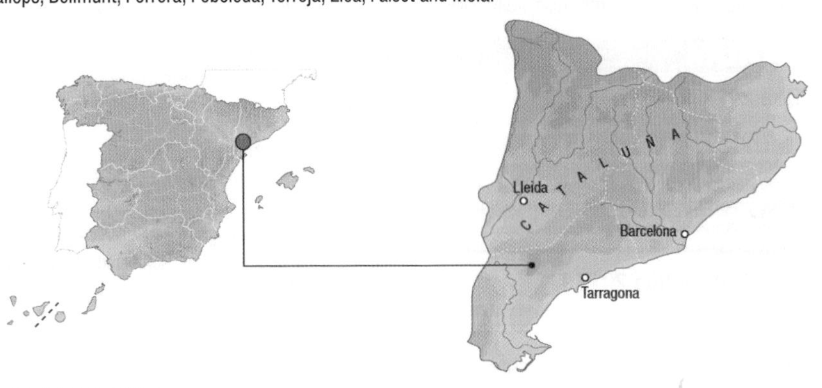

GRAPE VARIETIES:

WHITE: Chenin Blanc, Macabeo, Garnacha Blanca, Pedro Ximénez.
RED: Cariñena, Garnacha, Garnacha Peluda, Cabernet Sauvignon, Merlot, Syrah.

FIGURES:

Vineyard surface: 1,917 – **Wine-Growers:** 600 – **Wineries:** 102 – **2014 Harvest rating:** N/A – **Production 14:** 3,489,279 litres – **Market percentages:** 48% National - 52% International.

SOIL:

This is probably the most distinctive characteristic of the region and precisely what has catapulted it to the top positions in terms of quality, not only in Spain, but around the world. The soil, thin and volcanic, is composed of small pieces of slate (llicorella), which give the wines a markedly mineral character. The vineyards are located on terraces and very steep slopes.

CLIMATE:

Although with Mediterranean influences, it is temperate and dry. One of the most important characteristics is the practical absence of rain during the summer, which ensures very healthy grapes. The average rainfall is between 500 and 600 mm per year.

VINTAGE RATING

PEÑÍNGUIDE

2010	2011	2012	2013	2014
GOOD	VERY GOOD	VERY GOOD	VERY GOOD	VERY GOOD

ALVARO PALACIOS

Afores, s/n
43737 Gratallops (Tarragona)
☎: +34 977 839 195
Fax: +34 977 839 197
info@alvaropalacios.com

Camins del Priorat 2014 T

50% garnacha, 15% samsó, 20% cabernet sauvignon, 10% syrah, 5% merlot

91

Colour: cherry, purple rim. Nose: red berry notes, floral, balsamic herbs, mineral. Palate: powerful, fresh, fruity, balanced.

PODIUM

Finca Dofí 2013 TC

95% garnacha, 5% samsó

97

Colour: bright cherry, purple rim. Nose: complex, expressive, fresh, red berry notes, fragrant herbs. Palate: long, elegant, round, fine tannins.

Gratallops Vi de la Vila 2013 T

85% garnacha, 15% samsó

94

Colour: deep cherry, garnet rim. Nose: expressive, complex, scrubland, ripe fruit. Palate: flavourful, round tannins, spicy, long.

PODIUM

L'Ermita 2013 TC

90% garnacha, 8% samsó, 2% blancas

98

Colour: cherry, garnet rim. Nose: expressive, spicy, ripe fruit, earthy notes, mineral. Palate: flavourful, ripe fruit, long, good acidity, balanced.

PODIUM

Les Terrasses Velles Vinyes 2013 T

55% garnacha, 45% samsó

95

Colour: deep cherry, purple rim. Nose: elegant, expressive, balanced, red berry notes, mineral. Palate: good structure, full, fine tannins.

BODEGAS BORDALÁS GARCÍA (BG)

Ctra. T-710, Km. 9,5
43737 Gratallops (Tarragona)
☎: +34 977 839 434
Fax: +34 977 839 434
bodegasbg@yahoo.es
www.bodegasbg.es

Fra Fort 2010 T

cariñena, garnacha

87

Colour: cherry, garnet rim. Nose: fine reductive notes, wet leather, aged wood nuances. Palate: spicy, long, toasty.

Gueta Lupia 2008 T

garnacha, cariñena, merlot, cabernet sauvignon

84

Gueta Lupia 2009 T

garnacha, cariñena, merlot, cabernet sauvignon

88

Colour: cherry, garnet rim. Nose: fine reductive notes, wet leather, aged wood nuances, scrubland. Palate: spicy, long, reductive nuances.

Gueta Lupia 2010 T

garnacha, cariñena, merlot, cabernet sauvignon

89

Colour: cherry, garnet rim. Nose: ripe fruit, spicy, creamy oak, complex, fine reductive notes. Palate: flavourful, toasty.

Pamatura Vi de Familia 2011 T

garnacha, cariñena, merlot

83

BODEGAS MAS ALTA

Ctra. T-702, Km. 16,8
43375 La Vilella Alta (Tarragona)
☎: +34 977 054 151
Fax: +34 977 817 194
info@bodegasmasalta.com
www.bodegasmasalta.com

Artigas 2012 T

93

Colour: cherry, garnet rim. Nose: creamy oak, red berry notes, ripe fruit. Palate: flavourful, spicy, good acidity, fine bitter notes.

Artigas 2014 B

93

Colour: bright yellow. Nose: expressive, dried herbs, ripe fruit, spicy. Palate: flavourful, fruity, good acidity, balanced.

Cirerets 2012 T

94

Colour: cherry, garnet rim. Nose: mineral, expressive, spicy, ripe fruit. Palate: flavourful, ripe fruit, long, good acidity, balanced.

Els Pics 2013 T
93
Colour: bright cherry, garnet rim. Nose: ripe fruit, mineral, balanced, expressive. Palate: fruity, flavourful, good acidity.

La Basseta 2012 T
93
Colour: very deep cherry, garnet rim. Nose: expressive, complex, mineral, balsamic herbs, ripe fruit. Palate: full, flavourful, balanced.

PODIUM

La Creu Alta 2012 T
95
Colour: cherry, garnet rim. Nose: mineral, expressive, spicy. Palate: flavourful, ripe fruit, long, good acidity, balanced.

BODEGAS VICENTE GANDÍA
Ctra. Cheste a Godelleta, s/n
46370 Chiva (Valencia)
☎: +34 962 524 242
Fax: +34 962 524 243
info@vicentegandia.com
www.vicentegandia.es

Xibrana 2011 T
85

Xibrana 2012 T
syrah, mazuelo, garnacha
85

BUIL & GINÉ
Ctra. de Gratallops -
Vilella Baixa, Km. 11,5
43737 Gratallops (Tarragona)
☎: +34 977 839 810
Fax: +34 977 839 811
info@builgine.com
www.builgine.com

Giné Giné 2013 T
garnacha, cariñena
91
Colour: very deep cherry, garnet rim. Nose: expressive, complex, mineral, balsamic herbs, ripe fruit. Palate: full, flavourful, round.

Giné Rosat 2014 RD
garnacha, merlot
87
Colour: rose. Nose: red berry notes, floral, wild herbs. Palate: powerful, fruity, fresh.

Joan Giné 2011 T
garnacha, cariñena, cabernet sauvignon
88
Colour: very deep cherry, garnet rim. Nose: complex, balsamic herbs, balanced, dried herbs. Palate: flavourful, round tannins.

Joan Giné 2014 B
garnacha blanca, macabeo, pedro ximénez
88
Colour: bright yellow. Nose: dried herbs, ripe fruit, spicy. Palate: flavourful, fruity, balanced.

Pleret 2007 T
garnacha, cariñena, cabernet sauvignon, merlot, syrah
90
Colour: deep cherry. Nose: elegant, spicy, fine reductive notes, tobacco, balsamic herbs. Palate: spicy, fine tannins, elegant, long.

Pleret Negre Dolç 2013 T
garnacha, cariñena, cabernet sauvignon
91
Colour: cherry, garnet rim. Nose: fruit preserve, spicy, warm, fruit liqueur notes. Palate: powerful, flavourful, sweet, rich, concentrated.

CAL BATLLET - CELLERS RIPOLL SANS
Baixada de Consolació, 4
43737 Gratallops (Tarragona)
☎: +34 687 638 951
mripoll@calbatllet.cat
www.closabatllet.com

D'latra 2011 T
cariñena, garnacha, cabernet sauvignon, merlot, syrah
91
Colour: very deep cherry, garnet rim. Nose: expressive, mineral, balsamic herbs, balanced. Palate: flavourful, round tannins.

D'latra 2012 T
cariñena, garnacha, cabernet sauvignon, merlot, syrah
92
Colour: deep cherry. Nose: creamy oak, toasty, ripe fruit, balsamic herbs, earthy notes. Palate: spicy, long.

Gratallops 5 Partides 2010 T
cariñena
93
Colour: very deep cherry, garnet rim. Nose: expressive, wild herbs, waxy notes, ripe fruit, spicy. Palate: flavourful, good acidity, round tannins.

Gratallops 5 Partides 2011 T
cariñena

92

Colour: black cherry. Nose: neat, mineral, complex, expressive, spicy. Palate: balanced, good structure, round tannins, balsamic.

Gratallops Escanya-Vella 2013 B
escanyavella

94

Nose: white flowers, fine lees, dried herbs, ripe fruit, citrus fruit. Palate: flavourful, fruity, good acidity, elegant. Personality.

Torroja Ronçavall 2011 T
cariñena

92

Colour: very deep cherry. Nose: dried herbs, scrubland, ripe fruit. Palate: balanced, ripe fruit, round tannins, balsamic.

CASA GRAN DEL SIURANA

Mayor, 3
43738 Bellmunt del Priorat (Tarragona)
☎: +34 932 233 022
Fax: +34 932 231 370
perelada@castilloperelada.com
www.castilloperelada.com

Cruor 2011 T
garnacha, syrah, cabernet sauvignon, cariñena

91

Colour: cherry, garnet rim. Nose: ripe fruit, wild herbs, earthy notes, spicy, balsamic herbs. Palate: balanced, flavourful, long, balsamic.

GR-174 2014 T
garnacha, cariñena, cabernet sauvignon, syrah, merlot, cabernet franc

90

Colour: deep cherry, garnet rim. Nose: ripe fruit, fruit preserve, scrubland. Palate: balanced, flavourful, long.

Gran Cruor 2010 T
15% cariñena, 70% syrah, 15% garnacha

93

Colour: cherry, garnet rim. Nose: spicy, creamy oak, balsamic herbs, fruit preserve, dry stone. Palate: flavourful, toasty, round tannins, balanced.

Gran Cruor Caranyena Selecció 2011 T
100% samsó

92

Colour: cherry, garnet rim. Nose: ripe fruit, wild herbs, earthy notes, spicy, balsamic herbs. Palate: balanced, flavourful, long, balsamic.

CASA ROJO

Sánchez Picazo, 53
30332 Balsapintada (Murcia)
☎: +34 968 151 520
Fax: +34 968 151 539
info@casarojo.com
www.casarojo.com

Maquinon 2014 T
garnacha

88

Colour: cherry, purple rim. Nose: ripe fruit, woody, roasted coffee. Palate: flavourful, spicy, powerful.

CASTELL D'OR

Mare Rafols, 3- 1ºD
08720 Vilafranca del Penedès (Barcelona)
☎: +34 938 905 385
Fax: +34 938 905 446
castelldor@castelldor.com
www.castelldor.com

Abadía Mediterrània 2013 TC
garnacha, cariñena

89

Colour: deep cherry, purple rim. Nose: creamy oak, toasty, ripe fruit, balsamic herbs. Palate: balanced, spicy, long.

Esplugen 2014 T
garnacha, cariñena

88

Colour: bright cherry. Nose: sweet spices, creamy oak, fruit preserve. Palate: flavourful, fruity, toasty, round tannins.

Gran Abadía Mediterrània 2013 TR

88

Colour: deep cherry, purple rim. Nose: creamy oak, toasty, ripe fruit. Palate: balanced, spicy, long.

CELLER AIXALÀ I ALCAIT

Balandra, 8
43737 Torroja del Priorat (Tarragona)
☎: +34 629 507 807
pardelasses@gmail.com
www.pardelasses.blogspot.com

Destrankis 2013 T
80% garnacha, 20% cariñena

88 ♣

Colour: cherry, garnet rim. Nose: ripe fruit, fruit preserve, wild herbs, spicy, creamy oak. Palate: powerful, flavourful, spicy, toasty.

El Coster de L'Alzina 2012 TC
cariñena

88

Colour: cherry, garnet rim. Nose: spicy, creamy oak, scrubland, overripe fruit. Palate: flavourful, toasty, long.

Les Clivelles de Torroja 2013 T
cariñena

90

Colour: black cherry, purple rim. Nose: fruit preserve, sweet spices, cocoa bean, dried herbs. Palate: flavourful, good structure, round tannins.

Pardelasses 2012 T
50% garnacha, 50% cariñena

91

Colour: cherry, garnet rim. Nose: ripe fruit, wild herbs, spicy, balsamic herbs, mineral. Palate: balanced, flavourful, long, balsamic.

CELLER BALAGUER I CABRÉ

De La Font, 8
43737 Gratallops (Tarragona)
☎: +34 626 175 077
vins.jaume@yahoo.com
www.cellerbalaguercabre.blogspot.com

La Guinardera 2011 T
garnacha

87

Colour: dark-red cherry, garnet rim. Nose: fruit preserve, balsamic herbs, sweet spices, overripe fruit. Palate: long, spicy.

Lluna Vella 2012 T
garnacha

89

Colour: bright cherry. Nose: sweet spices, creamy oak, fruit preserve, wild herbs. Palate: flavourful, fruity, toasty.

CELLER BARTOLOMÉ

Major, 23
43738 Bellmunt del Priorat (Tarragona)
☎: +34 977 320 448
cellerbartolome@hotmail.com
www.cellerbartolome.com

Clos Bartolome 2013 T
45% garnacha, 45% cariñena, 10% cabernet sauvignon

89

Colour: bright cherry. Nose: sweet spices, creamy oak, fine reductive notes, fruit preserve. Palate: flavourful, fruity, toasty.

Primitiu de Bellmunt 2011 T
50% garnacha, 50% cariñena

91

Colour: very deep cherry, garnet rim. Nose: expressive, complex, mineral, balsamic herbs, balanced. Palate: full, flavourful, round tannins.

CELLER BURGOS PORTA

Mas Sinén, s/n
43376 Poboleda (Tarragona)
☎: +34 696 094 509
burgosporta@massinen.com
www.massinen.com

Mas Sinén Negre 2009 T
garnacha, cariñena, cabernet sauvignon, syrah

93

Colour: cherry, garnet rim. Nose: ripe fruit, wild herbs, earthy notes, spicy, balsamic herbs, fine reductive notes. Palate: balanced, flavourful, long, balsamic.

CELLER CECILIO

Piró, 28
43737 Gratallops (Tarragona)
☎: +34 977 839 507
Fax: +34 977 839 507
celler@cellercecilio.com
www.cellercecilio.com

Celler Cecilio Negre 2013 T
garnacha, cariñena, cabernet sauvignon, syrah

87

Colour: deep cherry, purple rim. Nose: creamy oak, toasty, ripe fruit, balsamic herbs. Palate: balanced, spicy, easy to drink.

L'Espill 2010 TC
garnacha, cariñena, cabernet sauvignon

88

Colour: cherry, garnet rim. Nose: ripe fruit, spicy, balsamic herbs, fine reductive notes. Palate: balanced, flavourful, long, balsamic.

L'Udol 2014 B
garnacha

86

CELLER DE L'ABADÍA

Font, 38
43737 Gratallops (Tarragona)
☎: +34 627 032 134
jeroni@cellerabadia.com
www.cellerabadia.com

Alice 2013 TR
40% garnacha, 40% cariñena, 10% cabernet sauvignon, 10% syrah

91

Colour: cherry, garnet rim. Nose: mineral, expressive, spicy. Palate: flavourful, ripe fruit, long, good acidity, balanced.

Sant Jeroni "Garnatxa de L'Hort 2012 T
70% garnacha, 30% syrah

88

Colour: cherry, garnet rim. Nose: toasty, scrubland, fruit preserve. Palate: powerful, toasty, correct.

Sant Jeroni "Garnatxa de L'Hort 2014 T
70% garnacha, 30% syrah

87

Colour: deep cherry, purple rim. Nose: creamy oak, ripe fruit, grassy, wild herbs. Palate: balanced, spicy, long.

Sant Jeroni Cariñena del Forn 2011 T
80% cariñena, 20% cabernet sauvignon

90

Colour: ruby red. Nose: spicy, fine reductive notes, aged wood nuances, fruit preserve, mineral. Palate: spicy, fine tannins, balanced, elegant.

Sant Jeroni Dolç de L'Abadia 2012 TGR
50% cariñena, 50% cabernet sauvignon

88

Colour: cherry, garnet rim. Nose: fruit preserve, spicy, warm, fruit liqueur notes. Palate: powerful, flavourful, sweet, rich.

CELLER DE L'ENCASTELL

Castell, 7
43739 Porrera (Tarragona)
☎: +34 630 941 959
roquers@roquers.com
www.roquers.com

Marge 2013 T
50% garnacha, 25% merlot, 10% cabernet sauvignon, 10% cariñena, 5% syrah

91

Colour: black cherry, garnet rim. Nose: scrubland, balanced, expressive. Palate: ripe fruit, balsamic, round tannins.

Roquers de Porrera 2012 TR
40% garnacha, 40% cariñena, 20% merlot, syrah

91

Colour: cherry, garnet rim. Nose: mineral, expressive, spicy, ripe fruit. Palate: flavourful, ripe fruit, long, good acidity, balanced.

CELLER DEVINSSI

De les Valls, 14
43737 Gratallops (Tarragona)
☎: +34 977 839 523
devinssi@il-lia.com
www.devinssi.com

Cupatge Devinssi 2014 T
garnacha, cariñena, cabernet sauvignon, merlot, syrah

89

Colour: deep cherry, purple rim. Nose: ripe fruit, balsamic herbs. Palate: balanced, spicy, long.

Il.lia Vi de Vila 2012 T
garnacha, cariñena, cabernet sauvignon

91

Colour: cherry, garnet rim. Nose: balanced, complex, ripe fruit, spicy, earthy notes. Palate: good structure, flavourful, round tannins, balanced.

Mas de les Valls - Vi de Vila 2013 B
pedro ximénez, garnacha blanca

89

Colour: bright straw. Nose: white flowers, fine lees, dried herbs, ripe fruit, citrus fruit. Palate: flavourful, fruity, good acidity.

Mas de les Valls 2013 TC
garnacha, cariñena, cabernet sauvignon

89

Colour: very deep cherry, garnet rim. Nose: expressive, complex, mineral, balsamic herbs, balanced, fruit preserve. Palate: full, flavourful, round tannins.

Rocapoll 2012 TC
100% cariñena

92

Colour: deep cherry, purple rim. Nose: creamy oak, wild herbs, fruit preserve. Palate: spicy, long, balanced, flavourful, elegant

CELLER ESCODA PALLEJÀ

La Font, 16
43737 Torroja del Priorat (Tarragona)
☎: +34 977 839 200
rescoda@hotmail.com
www.cellerescodapalleja.blogspot.com

Palet 2013 T

cariñena, cabernet sauvignon, syrah

88

Colour: dark-red cherry, garnet rim. Nose: fruit preserve, cocoa bean, balsamic herbs. Palate: flavourful, fruity, sweet tannins.

Palet Most de Flor 2013 T

garnacha, cariñena, cabernet sauvignon, syrah

90

Colour: very deep cherry, garnet rim. Nose: expressive, complex, mineral, balsamic herbs, balanced. Palate: full, flavourful, round tannins.

CELLER HIDALGO ALBERT

Poligono 14, Parcela 102
43376 Poboleda (Tarragona)
☎: +34 977 842 064
Fax: +34 977 842 064
hialmi@yahoo.es
www.cellerhidalgoalbert.es

1270 a Vuit 2008 T

garnacha, syrah, cabernet sauvignon, merlot, cariñena

93

Colour: deep cherry. Nose: creamy oak, toasty, ripe fruit, balsamic herbs. Palate: balanced, spicy, long, elegant.

1270 a Vuit 2009 T

garnacha, syrah, cabernet sauvignon, merlot, cariñena

92

Colour: cherry, garnet rim. Nose: balanced, complex, ripe fruit, spicy, fine reductive notes. Palate: good structure, flavourful, round tannins, balanced.

1270 a Vuit 2013 B

garnacha blanca

90

Colour: bright straw. Nose: white flowers, dried herbs, ripe fruit, dry stone. Palate: flavourful, fruity, good acidity, elegant.

Fina 2011 T

garnacha, syrah, merlot, cabernet sauvignon, cabernet franc

90 ♣

Colour: cherry, garnet rim. Nose: red berry notes, ripe fruit, spicy, creamy oak, scrubland. Palate: flavourful, toasty, round tannins.

CELLER JOAN SIMÓ

11 de Setembre, 5-7
43739 Porrera (Tarragona)
☎: +34 977 830 993
Fax: +34 977 830 993
leseres@cellerjoansimo.com
www.cellerjoansimo.com

Les Eres 2011 T

70% cariñena, 20% garnacha peluda, 10% cabernet sauvignon

93

Colour: cherry, garnet rim. Nose: ripe fruit, wild herbs, earthy notes, spicy, balsamic herbs. Palate: balanced, flavourful, long, balsamic.

Les Eres Especial dels Carners 2011 T

garnacha, cariñena

92

Colour: cherry, garnet rim. Nose: ripe fruit, wild herbs, earthy notes, spicy, balsamic herbs. Palate: balanced, flavourful, long, balsamic.

Les Sentius 2011 T

garnacha, cabernet sauvignon, syrah

90

Colour: deep cherry. Nose: creamy oak, toasty, ripe fruit, balsamic herbs. Palate: balanced, spicy, long.

CELLER JORDI DOMENECH

Sant Jaume, 4
43376 Poboleda (Tarragona)
☎: +34 646 169 210
jordidomenech@live.com
www.cellerjordidomenech.com

Petit Clos Penat 2012 T

garnacha, syrah

86

CELLER LO

Catalunya, 25
43374 La Vilella Baixa (Tarragona)
☎: +34 605 938 473
info@celler-lo.com
www.celler-lo.com

Lo Jove 2013 T

garnacha, cariñena, syrah

87

Colour: cherry, purple rim. Nose: powerfull, ripe fruit, spicy. Palate: powerful, fruity, unctuous.

Lo Magic 2013 T

garnacha, cariñena, cabernet sauvignon, syrah

88

Colour: cherry, garnet rim. Nose: smoky, spicy, ripe fruit. Palate: flavourful, ripe fruit, long.

Lo Temps 2013 T
garnacha, cabernet sauvignon, cariñena

88

Colour: cherry, garnet rim. Nose: creamy oak, ripe fruit, wild herbs. Palate: toasty, lacks balance.

CELLER MAS BASTE

Font, 38
43737 Gratallops (Tarragona)
☎: +34 629 300 291
info@cellermasbaste.com
www.cellermasbaste.com

Clos Peites 2009 TGR
80% cariñena, 10% syrah, 10% cabernet sauvignon

90

Colour: ruby red. Nose: spicy, fine reductive notes, wet leather, aged wood nuances, fruit liqueur notes. Palate: spicy, fine tannins, balanced.

Peites 2009 T
75% garnacha, 25% syrah

84

Peites 2011 TC
80% cariñena, 10% cabernet sauvignon, 10% syrah

89

Colour: cherry, garnet rim. Nose: ripe fruit, wild herbs, spicy, balsamic herbs. Palate: balanced, flavourful, long, balsamic.

Peites 2013 T
75% garnacha, 25% syrah

90

Colour: bright cherry. Nose: ripe fruit, sweet spices, creamy oak. Palate: flavourful, fruity, toasty, round tannins.

Peites Blanc 2012 B
70% pedro ximénez, 30% garnacha blanca

86

CELLER MAS DE LES PERERES

Mas de Les Pereres, s/n
43376 Poboleda (Tarragona)
☎: +34 977 827 257
Fax: +34 977 827 257
dirk@nunci.com
www.nunci.com

Nunci Abocat 2012 B
macabeo, pedro ximénez, moscatel de alejandría, moscatel grano menudo, garnacha blanca, viognier

88

Colour: bright yellow. Nose: dried herbs, ripe fruit, spicy. Palate: flavourful, fruity, good acidity.

Nunci Blanc 2012 BFB
garnacha, macabeo, viognier, pedro ximénez

91

Colour: bright straw. Nose: white flowers, fine lees, dried herbs, ripe fruit, candied fruit, citrus fruit. Palate: flavourful, fruity, good acidity, elegant.

Nunci Costero 2007 T
mazuelo, garnacha, merlot

90

Colour: dark-red cherry. Nose: spicy, fine reductive notes, tobacco, wild herbs. Palate: spicy, fine tannins, elegant, long.

Nunci Negre 2008 T
syrah, grenache, cabernet franc, mazuelo

90

Colour: cherry, garnet rim. Nose: ripe fruit, wild herbs, earthy notes, balsamic herbs, fine reductive notes. Palate: balanced, flavourful, long, balsamic.

Nuncito 2010 T Barrica
syrah, grenache, mazuelo, cabernet franc, merlot

90

Colour: cherry, garnet rim. Nose: ripe fruit, spicy, creamy oak, complex. Palate: flavourful, toasty.

Nunsweet Dulce 2011 T
merlot, grenache, syrah

90

Colour: bright cherry, garnet rim. Nose: acetaldehyde, varnish, candied fruit, fruit preserve. Palate: fruity, flavourful, sweet.

CELLER MAS DOIX

Carme, 115
43376 Poboleda (Tarragona)
☎: +34 639 356 172
info@masdoix.com
www.masdoix.com

PODIUM

1902 Cariñena Centenaria 2010 T
100% cariñena

96

Colour: cherry, garnet rim. Nose: mineral, expressive, spicy, fruit preserve. Palate: flavourful, ripe fruit, long, good acidity, round, powerful.

Doix 2012 TC
55% cariñena, 45% garnacha

94

Colour: deep cherry, purple rim. Nose: powerfull, ripe fruit, characterful, wild herbs. Palate: good structure, flavourful, good acidity, fine bitter notes.

Les Crestes 2013 T
80% garnacha, 10% cariñena, 10% syrah

92

Colour: bright cherry. Nose: ripe fruit, sweet spices, creamy oak. Palate: flavourful, fruity, round tannins.

Salanques 2012 T
65% garnacha, 25% cariñena, 10% syrah

92

Colour: bright cherry, garnet rim. Nose: characterful, expressive, scrubland, spicy. Palate: good acidity, ripe fruit, long.

CELLER SABATÉ
Nou, 6
43374 La Vilella Baixa (Tarragona)
☎: +34 977 839 209
cellersabate@cellersabate.com
www.cellersabate.com

Mas d'en Bernat 2014 T
garnacha

90

Colour: cherry, purple rim. Nose: powerfull, ripe fruit, spicy, balsamic herbs, violets. Palate: powerful, fruity, unctuous, ripe fruit, fruity aftestaste.

Mas Plantadeta 2012 T Roble
garnacha

87

Colour: bright cherry. Nose: ripe fruit, sweet spices, creamy oak. Palate: flavourful, fruity, toasty, round tannins.

Mas Plantadeta 2014 BFB
garnacha blanca, moscatel

87

Colour: bright yellow. Nose: ripe fruit, spicy, white flowers. Palate: flavourful, fruity, good acidity, balanced.

Pètals de Garnatxa 2014 RD
garnacha

88

Colour: raspberry rose. Nose: elegant, red berry notes, floral, fragrant herbs. Palate: light-bodied, flavourful, good acidity.

CELLER VALL-LLACH
Pont, 9
43739 Porrera (Tarragona)
☎: +34 977 828 244
Fax: +34 977 828 325
celler@vallllach.com
www.vallllach.com

Aigua de Llum 2013 B
80% viognier, 15% garnacha blanca, 5% macabeo

92

Colour: bright golden. Nose: ripe fruit, floral, wild herbs, spicy. Palate: powerful, flavourful, long, balsamic, balanced.

Embruix de Vall-Llach 2013 T
26% garnacha, 16% cariñena, 17% syrah, 24% merlot, 17% cabernet sauvignon

92

Colour: deep cherry. Nose: toasty, ripe fruit, balsamic herbs, scrubland. Palate: balanced, spicy, long, round tannins.

Idus de Vall-Llach 2012 T
76% cariñena, 12% merlot, 9% cabernet sauvignon, 3% garnacha

90

Colour: black cherry, garnet rim. Nose: characterful, powerfull, balsamic herbs. Palate: good structure, round tannins, ripe fruit.

Porrera Vi de Vila de Vall Llach 2013 TC
72% cariñena, 28% garnacha

94

Colour: very deep cherry. Nose: varietal, balanced, expressive, complex. Palate: full, spicy, long, complex.

Vall Llach vi de Finca Qualificada Mas de la Rosa 2013 TC
93% cariñena, 2% cabernet sauvignon, 5% garnacha

94

Colour: cherry, garnet rim. Nose: wild herbs, earthy notes, spicy, balsamic herbs, fruit preserve. Palate: flavourful, long, balsamic, balanced.

CELLERS CAPAFONS OSSÓ
Finca Masía Esplanes s/n
43730 Falset (Tarragona)
☎: +34 977 831 201
cellers@capafons-osso.com
www.capafons-osso.cat

Auseta 2014 B
garnacha blanca

83

Edènic Magnum 2007 T
garnacha, syrah

90

Colour: light cherry. Nose: aged wood nuances, toasty, tobacco, fruit liqueur notes. Palate: spicy, toasty, flavourful.

CELLERS DE SCALA DEI
Rambla de la Cartoixa, s/n
43379 Scala Dei (Tarragona)
☎: +34 977 827 027
Fax: +34 977 827 044
codinfo@codorniu.es
www.grupocodorniu.com

Masdeu de Scala Dei 2012 T

92

Colour: very deep cherry. Nose: wild herbs, ripe fruit, spicy, expressive. Palate: balsamic, ripe fruit, long. Personality.

Massipa 2013 B

94

Colour: bright straw. Nose: white flowers, fine lees, dried herbs, ripe fruit, candied fruit, citrus fruit, spicy. Palate: flavourful, fruity, good acidity, elegant.

Scala Dei Cartoixa 2009 TR

70% garnacha, 25% cariñena, 5% cabernet sauvignon

90

Colour: cherry, garnet rim. Nose: ripe fruit, old leather, wild herbs, earthy notes. Palate: correct, flavourful, spicy, long.

Scala Dei Garnatxa 2014 T

100% garnacha

89

Colour: cherry, purple rim. Nose: varietal, ripe fruit, wild herbs, mineral. Palate: balanced, fruity aftestaste.

Scala Dei Pla dels Ángels 2014 RD

100% garnacha

91

Colour: onion pink. Nose: elegant, red berry notes, floral, fragrant herbs, balanced. Palate: light-bodied, flavourful, good acidity, long, spicy, elegant.

Scala Dei Prior 2013 TC

55% garnacha, 15% cabernet sauvignon, 15% cariñena, 15% syrah

91

Colour: very deep cherry, garnet rim. Nose: complex, mineral, balsamic herbs, balanced. Palate: full, flavourful, round tannins.

PODIUM

St. Antoni de Scala Dei 2012 T

95

Colour: cherry, garnet rim. Nose: balanced, complex, ripe fruit, spicy, balsamic herbs. Palate: good structure, flavourful, round tannins, balanced, elegant.

CELLERS UNIÓ

43206 Reus (Tarragona)
☎: +34 977 330 055
Fax: +34 977 330 070
info@cellersunio.com
www.cellersunio.com

Convey 2012 T

garnacha, mazuelo

88

Colour: very deep cherry. Nose: ripe fruit, scrubland, dried herbs, spicy. Palate: flavourful, good structure.

Llicorella Vitis 60 2009 T

garnacha, mazuelo, cabernet sauvignon, syrah

90

Colour: cherry, garnet rim. Nose: ripe fruit, spicy, creamy oak, complex. Palate: flavourful, toasty, round tannins.

Tendral Selección 2013 T

garnacha, mazuelo

88

Colour: cherry, garnet rim. Nose: red berry notes, ripe fruit, spicy, creamy oak, aged wood nuances. Palate: flavourful, toasty, harsh oak tannins.

CLOS 93

Nou, 26
43737 El Lloar (Tarragona)
☎: +34 620 215 770
clos93@clos93.com
www.clos93.com

L'Exclamacio 2013 T

100% syrah

89

Colour: bright cherry. Nose: ripe fruit, sweet spices, creamy oak, toasty. Palate: flavourful, fruity, toasty.

L'Interrogant 2013 T

garnacha, cariñena, cabernet sauvignon

92

Colour: deep cherry. Nose: creamy oak, toasty, balsamic herbs, mineral, red berry notes, ripe fruit. Palate: balanced, spicy, long, elegant.

CLOS DE L'OBAC

Camí Manyetes, s/n
43737 Gratallops (Tarragona)
☎: +34 977 839 276
info@obac.es
www.obac.es

Clos de L'Obac 2011 TC

garnacha, cariñena, cabernet sauvignon, merlot, syrah

94

Colour: cherry, garnet rim. Nose: balanced, complex, ripe fruit, spicy, mineral. Palate: good structure, flavourful, round tannins, balanced.

Kyrie 2013 BC

garnacha blanca, macabeo, xarel.lo, moscatel de alejandría

91

Colour: bright golden. Nose: sweet spices, ripe fruit, candied fruit, creamy oak, citrus fruit. Palate: flavourful, long, fine bitter notes, spicy.

Miserere 2011 TC
garnacha, cariñena, tempranillo, merlot, cabernet sauvignon

94

Colour: cherry, garnet rim. Nose: ripe fruit, spicy, creamy oak, complex, mineral, scrubland. Palate: flavourful, toasty, round tannins.

CLOS DEL PORTAL
Pista de Bellmunt al Lloar s/n.
Les Solanes del Lloar
43736 Vila del Lloar (Tarragona)
☎: +34 932 531 760
Fax: +34 934 173 591
info@portaldelpriorat.com
www.portaldelpriorat.com

Gotes Blanques 2014 B
garnacha blanca

90

Colour: bright straw. Nose: white flowers, fresh fruit, grassy. Palate: flavourful, fruity, good acidity.

Gotes del Priorat 2014 T
garnacha, cariñena

90

Colour: cherry, purple rim. Nose: red berry notes, floral, balsamic herbs. Palate: powerful, fresh, fruity.

Gotes del Priorat Magnum 2013 T
garnacha, cariñena

91

Colour: deep cherry, purple rim. Nose: closed, wild herbs, mineral, ripe fruit. Palate: complex, fruity, long, spicy, good acidity.

Negre de Negres 2013 T
garnacha, cariñena, syrah

93

Colour: cherry, garnet rim. Nose: mineral, expressive, earthy notes, ripe fruit, complex. Palate: flavourful, ripe fruit, long, good acidity, balanced.

Negre de Negres Magnum 2012 T
garnacha, cariñena, syrah

92

Colour: bright cherry. Nose: ripe fruit, creamy oak, wild herbs. Palate: flavourful, fruity, toasty, round tannins.

Somni 2013 T
cariñena, syrah

93

Colour: deep cherry, garnet rim. Nose: ripe fruit, dry stone, fragrant herbs, spicy, expressive. Palate: powerful, flavourful, long, fruity aftestaste.

PODIUM

Somni Magnum 2012 T
cariñena, syrah

95

Colour: deep cherry, garnet rim. Nose: expressive, balsamic herbs, spicy, mineral. Palate: full, complex, elegant, round tannins, spicy, long.

Tros de Clos 2013 T
cariñena

94

Colour: very deep cherry. Nose: powerfull, varietal, characterful, fruit expression, toasty, balsamic herbs, balanced, elegant. Palate: flavourful, powerful, concentrated, round tannins.

Tros de Clos Magnum 2012 T
cariñena

94

Colour: cherry, garnet rim. Nose: mineral, expressive, spicy, ripe fruit, fragrant herbs. Palate: flavourful, ripe fruit, long, good acidity, balanced. Personality.

CLOS GALENA
Camino de la Solana, s/n
43736 El Molar (Tarragona)
☎: +34 619 790 956
info@closgalena.com
www.closgalena.com

Clos Galena 2010 TC
92

Colour: cherry, garnet rim. Nose: ripe fruit, spicy, creamy oak, complex. Palate: flavourful, toasty, balanced.

Crossos 2012 T
89

Colour: cherry, garnet rim. Nose: ripe fruit, spicy, creamy oak, complex. Palate: flavourful, toasty, round tannins.

Formiga de Vellut 2012 T
91

Colour: very deep cherry, garnet rim. Nose: expressive, complex, mineral, balsamic herbs, balanced. Palate: full, flavourful, round tannins.

Galena 2012 T
91

Colour: very deep cherry, garnet rim. Nose: expressive, complex, mineral, balsamic herbs, balanced. Palate: full, flavourful, round tannins.

CLOS I TERRASSES

La Font, 1
43737 Gratallops (Tarragona)
☎: +34 977 839 022
Fax: +34 977 839 179
info@closerasmus.com

🏆 PODIUM

Clos Erasmus 2013 T Barrica

97

Colour: cherry, garnet rim. Nose: mineral, expressive, spicy, earthy notes. Palate: flavourful, ripe fruit, long, good acidity, balanced.

Laurel 2013 T

93

Colour: bright cherry, purple rim. Nose: elegant, ripe fruit, complex, scrubland. Palate: balanced, fruity aftestaste.

CLOS MOGADOR

Camí Manyetes, s/n
43737 Gratallops (Tarragona)
☎: +34 977 839 171
Fax: +34 977 839 426
closmogador@closmogador.com

🏆 PODIUM

Clos Mogador 2011 T

49% garnacha, 25% cariñena, 10% cabernet sauvignon, 16% syrah

96

Colour: cherry, garnet rim. Nose: ripe fruit, wild herbs, earthy notes, spicy, balsamic herbs, powerfull. Palate: balanced, flavourful, long, balsamic, elegant.

Manyetes 2011 T

100% cariñena

94

Colour: cherry, garnet rim. Nose: mineral, expressive, spicy, scrubland. Palate: flavourful, ripe fruit, long, good acidity, balanced.

Nelin 2013 B

garnacha blanca

93

Colour: bright straw. Nose: dried herbs, faded flowers, ripe fruit, dry stone, spicy. Palate: ripe fruit, long, balsamic, elegant.

COSTERS DEL PRIORAT

Finca Sant Martí
43738 Bellmunt del Priorat (Tarragona)
☎: +34 618 203 473
info@costersdelpriorat.com
www.costersdelpriorat.com

Blanc de Pissarres 2014 B

55% garnacha blanca, 30% macabeo, 15% pedro ximénez

89

Colour: bright yellow. Nose: expressive, dried herbs, ripe fruit, spicy. Palate: flavourful, fruity, good acidity, balanced.

Clos Cypres 2013 T

100% cariñena

93

Colour: cherry, garnet rim. Nose: mineral, expressive, spicy. Palate: flavourful, ripe fruit, long, good acidity, balanced.

Elios 2013 T

50% garnacha, 15% syrah, cabernet sauvignon

91

Colour: deep cherry, garnet rim. Nose: red berry notes, ripe fruit, characterful, dried flowers, dried herbs. Palate: good structure, flavourful, full.

Pissarres 2013 T

65% cariñena, 35% garnacha

91

Colour: black cherry, purple rim. Nose: mineral, ripe fruit, fruit preserve, balsamic herbs. Palate: round, long, balanced.

DE MULLER

Camí Pedra Estela, 34
43205 Reus (Tarragona)
☎: +34 977 757 473
Fax: +34 977 771 129
lab@demuller.es
www.demuller.es

🏆 PODIUM

Dom Joan Fort 1865 Rancio

moscatel de alejandría, garnacha, garnacha blanca

95

Colour: dark mahogany. Nose: candied fruit, fruit liqueur notes, spicy, varnish, acetaldehyde, dry nuts. Palate: fine solera notes, fine bitter notes, spirituous, balanced, elegant.

Les Pusses De Muller 2012 TC

merlot, syrah

88

Colour: cherry, garnet rim. Nose: roasted coffee, smoky, spicy, ripe fruit. Palate: flavourful, ripe fruit.

Lo Cabaló 2011 TR
merlot, syrah

87

Colour: dark-red cherry, ruby red. Nose: old leather, spicy, animal reductive notes. Palate: correct, spicy.

Priorat Legitim 2013 TC
garnacha, merlot, syrah

87

Colour: deep cherry, purple rim. Nose: creamy oak, toasty, ripe fruit, balsamic herbs. Palate: balanced, spicy, long.

EDICIONES I-LIMITADAS

43730 Falset (Tarragona)
☎: +34 932 531 760
Fax: +34 934 173 591
info@edicionesi-limitadas.com
www.edicionesi-limitadas.com

Flors 2013 T
garnacha, cariñena, syrah

91

Colour: bright cherry. Nose: ripe fruit, sweet spices, fragrant herbs, expressive. Palate: flavourful, fruity, round tannins, fruity aftestaste.

EL SOLÀ D'ARES

Vista Alegre, 9
25794 Organyà (Lérida)
☎: +34 973 383 422
info@soladares.es
www.soladares.es

Bessons 2012 T
garnacha

91

Colour: cherry, garnet rim. Nose: ripe fruit, wild herbs, earthy notes, spicy, balsamic herbs, dry stone. Palate: balanced, flavourful, long, balsamic, elegant.

FERRER BOBET

Ctra. Falset a Porrera, Km. 6,5
43730 Falset (Tarragona)
☎: +34 609 945 532
Fax: +34 935 044 265
eguerre@ferrerbobet.com
www.ferrerbobet.com

Ferrer Bobet 2013 T
48% cariñena, 23% syrah, 22% garnacha, 7% cabernet sauvignon

94

Colour: bright cherry. Nose: ripe fruit, sweet spices, creamy oak, balsamic herbs, mineral. Palate: flavourful, fruity, round tannins, balanced, elegant.

Ferrer Bobet Selecció Especial Vinyes Velles 2012 T
100% cariñena

92

Colour: very deep cherry, garnet rim. Nose: expressive, complex, mineral, balsamic herbs, balanced, toasty. Palate: full, flavourful, round tannins, smoky aftertaste.

Ferrer Bobet Vinyes Velles 2013 T
70% cariñena, 30% garnacha

94

Colour: deep cherry, purple rim. Nose: fruit expression, balanced, mineral, expressive. Palate: balsamic, balanced, good acidity, complex.

FRANCK MASSARD

Rambla Arnau de Vilanova, 6
08800 Vilanova i La Geltrú (Barcelona)
☎: +34 938 956 541
Fax: +34 938 956 541
info@epicure-wines.com
www.epicure-wines.com

Eda 2012 T

90

Colour: cherry, garnet rim. Nose: balanced, ripe fruit, spicy, dried herbs. Palate: flavourful, spicy, balsamic, round tannins.

Huellas 2012 TR
60% cariñena, 40% garnacha

88

Colour: cherry, garnet rim. Nose: red berry notes, ripe fruit, spicy, creamy oak, complex. Palate: flavourful, toasty, round tannins.

Humilitat 2012 TC
60% garnacha, 40% cariñena

84

GENIUM CELLER

Nou, 92 - Bajos
43376 Poboleda (Tarragona)
☎: +34 977 827 146
Fax: +34 977 827 146
genium@geniumceller.com
www.geniumceller.com

Genium Celler 2010 TC
60% garnacha, 10% merlot, 5% cariñena, syrah, 5% cabernet sauvignon

88

Colour: cherry, garnet rim. Nose: fine reductive notes, spicy, wild herbs. Palate: spicy, long, toasty.

Genium Costers Vinyes Velles 2010 T
50% cariñena, 25% garnacha, 15% merlot, 10% syrah

88

Colour: bright cherry. Nose: ripe fruit, sweet spices, creamy oak, scrubland, earthy notes. Palate: flavourful, fruity, toasty.

Genium Ecològic 2010 TC
50% garnacha, 20% merlot, 20% syrah, 10% cariñena

89 ♣

Colour: very deep cherry, garnet rim. Nose: mineral, balsamic herbs, fruit preserve. Palate: full, flavourful, round tannins.

Genium Ximenis 2013 BFB
90% pedro ximénez, 10% garnacha blanca

86

Poboleda Vi de Vila 2010 TR
70% garnacha, 30% cariñena

90

Colour: cherry, garnet rim. Nose: ripe fruit, wild herbs, earthy notes, spicy, balsamic herbs. Palate: balanced, flavourful, long, balsamic.

GRAN CLOS

Montsant, 2
43738 Bellmunt del Priorat (Tarragona)
☎: +34 977 830 675
info@granclos.com
www.granclos.com

Cartus 2006 T
garnacha, cariñena

93

Colour: pale ruby, brick rim edge. Nose: spicy, fine reductive notes, wet leather, aged wood nuances, fruit liqueur notes, earthy notes. Palate: spicy, fine tannins, balanced, long.

Finca El Puig 2011 T
garnacha, syrah, cabernet sauvignon

89

Colour: cherry, garnet rim. Nose: ripe fruit, wild herbs, earthy notes, spicy, balsamic herbs. Palate: balanced, flavourful, long, balsamic.

Gran Clos 2008 T
garnacha, cariñena, cabernet sauvignon

93

Colour: cherry, garnet rim. Nose: ripe fruit, wild herbs, earthy notes, spicy, balsamic herbs. Palate: balanced, flavourful, long, balsamic.

Gran Clos 2012 BFB
garnacha blanca, macabeo

90

Colour: bright yellow. Nose: ripe fruit, powerfull, toasty, aged wood nuances. Palate: flavourful, fruity, spicy, toasty, long.

Les Mines 2012 T
garnacha, cariñena, merlot

88

Colour: cherry, garnet rim. Nose: wild herbs, ripe fruit. Palate: spicy, long, toasty.

Solluna 2012 T
garnacha, cariñena, merlot

88

Colour: bright cherry. Nose: ripe fruit, sweet spices, creamy oak. Palate: flavourful, fruity, toasty.

GRATAVINUM

Mas d'en Serres s/n
43737 Gratallops (Tarragona)
☎: +34 938 901 399
gratavinum@gratavinum.com
www.gratavinum.com

Gratavinum 2πr 2011 T
55% garnacha, 30% cariñena, 10% syrah, 5% cabernet sauvignon

90 ♣

Colour: cherry, garnet rim. Nose: spicy, ripe fruit, dark chocolate. Palate: flavourful, smoky aftertaste, ripe fruit.

Gratavinum Coster 2012 T
100% cariñena

90 ♣

Colour: cherry, garnet rim. Nose: wild herbs, earthy notes, spicy, balsamic herbs, fruit preserve. Palate: balanced, flavourful, long, balsamic, concentrated.

Gratavinum GV5 2011 T
60% cariñena, 30% garnacha, 10% cabernet sauvignon

91 ♣

Colour: very deep cherry, garnet rim. Nose: scrubland, cocoa bean, spicy, dried herbs. Palate: good structure, toasty.

Gratavinum Silvestris 2013 T
100% cariñena

89 ♣

Colour: very deep cherry, garnet rim. Nose: expressive, complex, mineral, balsamic herbs, fruit preserve. Palate: full, flavourful, spicy, long.

HAMMEKEN CELLARS

Calle de la Muela, 16
03730 Jávea (Alicante)
☎: +34 965 791 967
Fax: +34 966 461 471
cellars@hammekencellars.com
www.hammekencellars.com

Tosalet Vinyes Velles – Old Vines 2013 T
garnacha, carignan, cabernet sauvignon

90

Colour: very deep cherry, garnet rim. Nose: mineral, balsamic herbs, balanced. Palate: full, flavourful, round tannins.

I TANT VINS

Passeig del Ferrocarril, 337 Baixos
08860 Castelldefels (Barcelona)
☎: +34 936 628 253
Fax: +34 934 517 628
albert@aribau.es
www.aribau.es

Que Si 2013 T
50% garnacha, 50% samsó

89

Colour: bright cherry. Nose: ripe fruit, sweet spices, creamy oak, expressive. Palate: flavourful, fruity, toasty, round tannins.

JOAN AMETLLER

Ctra. La Morera de Monsant - Cornudella, km. 3,2
43361 La Morera de Monsant (Tarragona)
☎: +34 933 208 439
Fax: +34 933 208 437
info@ametller.com
www.ametller.com

Clos Corriol 2012 T
garnacha, merlot, cabernet sauvignon, syrah

85

Clos Corriol 2014 B
garnacha blanca

87

Colour: bright yellow. Nose: ripe fruit, floral. Palate: easy to drink, balanced, correct, fine bitter notes.

Clos Corriol 2014 RD
cabernet sauvignon, garnacha

87

Colour: rose, purple rim. Nose: red berry notes, floral, expressive. Palate: powerful, fruity, fresh.

Clos Mustardó 2009 TC
garnacha, cabernet sauvignon, merlot

89

Colour: cherry, garnet rim. Nose: fine reductive notes, wet leather, aged wood nuances. Palate: spicy, long, toasty.

Clos Mustardó 2011 BFB
garnacha blanca

89

Colour: bright yellow. Nose: ripe fruit, creamy oak, pattiserie, sweet spices. Palate: flavourful, rich.

Clos Mustardó 2012 BFB
garnacha blanca

88

Colour: bright yellow. Nose: ripe fruit, powerfull, toasty, aged wood nuances. Palate: flavourful, fruity, spicy, toasty.

Clos Socarrat 2012 T
garnacha, merlot, cabernet sauvignon, syrah

86

Els Igols 2005 TR
garnacha, cabernet sauvignon, merlot

90

Colour: deep cherry. Nose: ripe fruit, spicy, creamy oak, complex. Palate: flavourful, toasty, round tannins.

L'INFERNAL - COMBIER FISCHER GERIN

Polígon 8, Parcel·la 148
43737 Torroja del Priorat (Tarragona)
☎: +34 600 753 840
Fax: +34 977 828 380
contact@linfernal.es
www.linfernal.es

Aguilera 2008 T
100% cariñena

93

Colour: ruby red. Nose: elegant, spicy, fine reductive notes, tobacco, balsamic herbs. Palate: spicy, fine tannins, elegant, long.

L'Infernal El Casot 2013 T
100% garnacha

90

Colour: cherry, garnet rim. Nose: ripe fruit, wild herbs, earthy notes, spicy, balsamic herbs. Palate: balanced, flavourful, long, balsamic.

L'Infernal Face Nord 2013 T
100% syrah

93

Colour: cherry, garnet rim. Nose: red berry notes, ripe fruit, fragrant herbs, spicy, toasty, creamy oak, mineral. Palate: powerful, flavourful, balsamic, balanced.

L'Infernal Fons Clar 2013 T
100% cariñena

91

Colour: deep cherry, purple rim. Nose: varietal, wild herbs, ripe fruit, spicy, waxy notes. Palate: good structure, flavourful, round tannins.

Riu by Trío Infernal 2011 T
garnacha, syrah, cariñena

92

Colour: cherry, garnet rim. Nose: ripe fruit, old leather, tobacco. Palate: correct, flavourful, spicy.

Riu by Trío Infernal 2012 B
garnacha blanca, macabeo

90

Colour: bright golden. Nose: fine lees, dried herbs, ripe fruit, faded flowers. Palate: flavourful, fruity, good acidity.

LA CONRERIA D'SCALA DEI

Carrer Mitja Galta, 30
43379 Scala Dei (Tarragona)
☎: +34 977 827 055
Fax: +34 977 827 055
laconreria@vinslaconreria.com
www.vinslaconreria.com

Iugiter 2011 T
garnacha, syrah, cabernet sauvignon, cariñena

87

Colour: cherry, garnet rim. Nose: ripe fruit, old leather, tobacco. Palate: correct, flavourful, spicy.

Iugiter Selecció Vinyes Velles 2009 TC
garnacha, cariñena

91

Colour: very deep cherry. Nose: expressive, complex, mineral, balsamic herbs, balanced, fine reductive notes. Palate: full, flavourful, round tannins.

La Conreria 2013 T Roble
garnacha, syrah, merlot, cabernet sauvignon

91

Colour: deep cherry, garnet rim. Nose: balanced, scrubland, ripe fruit. Palate: good structure, full, flavourful.

Les Brugueres 2014 B
garnacha blanca

89

Colour: bright straw. Nose: ripe fruit, fragrant herbs, balanced. Palate: flavourful, ripe fruit, long.

MAIUS VITICULTORS

Pol. II Parcela 16
43361 La Morera de Montsant
(Tarragona)
☎: +34 696 998 575
Fax: +34 936 752 897
jgomez@maiusviticultors.com
www.maiusviticultors.com

Maius Assemblage 2012 T
cariñena, cabernet sauvignon, garnacha

90

Colour: deep cherry, purple rim. Nose: creamy oak, toasty, ripe fruit, balsamic herbs. Palate: spicy, long, fine bitter notes.

Maius Barranc de la Bruixa 2013 T
cabernet sauvignon, garnacha, cariñena

91

Colour: deep cherry, purple rim. Nose: balanced, elegant, ripe fruit, creamy oak, toasty. Palate: balanced, spicy, harsh oak tannins.

MARCO ABELLA

Ctra. de Porrera a Cornudella
de Montsant, Km. 1,2
43739 Porrera (Tarragona)
☎: +34 933 712 407
info@marcoabella.com
www.marcoabella.com

Clos Abella 2010 T
cariñena

93 ♣

Colour: cherry, garnet rim. Nose: ripe fruit, wild herbs, earthy notes, spicy, balsamic herbs. Palate: balanced, flavourful, long, balsamic.

Loidana 2012 T
44% garnacha, 38% cariñena, 18% cabernet sauvignon

91

Colour: very deep cherry, garnet rim. Nose: expressive, complex, mineral, balsamic herbs, balanced. Palate: flavourful, round tannins, easy to drink.

Mas Mallola 2011 TR
42% garnacha, 31% cariñena, 27% cabernet sauvignon

90 ♣

Colour: cherry, garnet rim. Nose: ripe fruit, spicy, creamy oak, waxy notes, complex. Palate: flavourful, toasty, balanced.

Olbia 2014 B
49% garnacha blanca, 49% viognier, 2% pedro ximénez

90

Colour: bright straw. Nose: white flowers, fragrant herbs, expressive. Palate: flavourful, fruity, good acidity, balanced.

MAS D'EN BLEI

Mas d'en Blei s/n
43363 La Morera de Montsant
(Tarragona)
☎: +34 977 262 031
info@masdenblei.com
www.masdenblei.com

Blei 2011 T
garnacha, cariñena, cabernet franc

90

Colour: cherry, garnet rim. Nose: ripe fruit, wild herbs, earthy notes, spicy, balsamic herbs. Palate: balanced, flavourful, long, balsamic.

Liber 2011 T
garnacha, cariñena

92

Colour: cherry, garnet rim. Nose: fine reductive notes, spicy, ripe fruit, expressive. Palate: long, toasty, balanced, complex, fine tannins.

MAS D'EN GIL

Finca Mas d'en Gil s/n
43738 Bellmunt del Priorat (Tarragona)
☎: +34 977 830 192
Fax: +34 977 830 152
mail@masdengil.com
www.masdengil.com

Clos Fontà 2010 TR
40% garnacha peluda, 30% garnacha, 30% cariñena

92

Colour: cherry, garnet rim. Nose: ripe fruit, wild herbs, earthy notes, spicy, balsamic herbs, fine reductive notes. Palate: balanced, flavourful, long, balsamic.

Coma Vella 2011 T
50% garnacha peluda, 20% garnacha, 20% cariñena, 10% syrah

93

Colour: cherry, garnet rim. Nose: red berry notes, ripe fruit, spicy, complex, scrubland. Palate: flavourful, toasty, round tannins.

MAS IGNEUS

Ctra. de Falset a Vilella Baixa, Km 11,1
43737 Gratallops (Tarragona)
☎: +34 977 262 259
Fax: +34 977 054 027
celler@masigneus.com
www.masigneus.com

Barranc Blanc 2014 B
90% garnacha blanca, 10% pedro ximénez

91

Colour: bright yellow. Nose: expressive, balanced, dried flowers, dried herbs, mineral, faded flowers. Palate: rich, fine bitter notes, spicy, full. Personality.

Barranc Negre 2013 T
85% garnacha, 15% otras

90

Colour: bright cherry. Nose: ripe fruit, sweet spices, expressive, fruit expression. Palate: flavourful, fruity, round tannins.

Coster de La Carinyena 2013 T
100% cariñena

92

Colour: cherry, garnet rim. Nose: ripe fruit, fragrant herbs, spicy, toasty, creamy oak, mineral. Palate: powerful, flavourful, balsamic, balanced.

Costers de L'Ermita 2012 T
100% garnacha

93

Colour: cherry, garnet rim. Nose: mineral, expressive, spicy, fruit expression. Palate: flavourful, ripe fruit, long, good acidity, balanced.

FA 104 Blanc 2013 B
100% garnacha blanca

94

Colour: bright straw. Nose: white flowers, fragrant herbs, expressive, spicy, citrus fruit. Palate: flavourful, fruity, good acidity, balanced.

FA 112 2011 T
80% garnacha, 20% cariñena

93

Colour: black cherry, garnet rim. Nose: powerfull, ripe fruit, balsamic herbs, toasty, spicy. Palate: mineral, balanced, long.

FA 206 Negre 2012 T
80% garnacha, 20% cariñena

90

Colour: bright cherry, garnet rim. Nose: ripe fruit, dried herbs, wild herbs. Palate: spicy, long.

MAS LA MOLA

Mayor, 6
43376 Poboleda (Tarragona)
☎: +34 651 034 221
info@maslamola.com
www.maslamola.com

L'Expressió del Priorat 2014 T
garnacha, cariñena, cabernet sauvignon

88

Colour: very deep cherry, garnet rim. Nose: ripe fruit, balsamic herbs, powerfull. Palate: ripe fruit, balanced, round tannins.

Mas la Mola 2012 B
60% macabeo, 40% garnacha blanca

89

Colour: bright straw. Nose: dry nuts, pattiserie, spicy, fine lees. Palate: long, balanced, fine bitter notes.

Mas la Mola Negre 2010 T
garnacha, garnacha peluda

89

Colour: ruby red. Nose: fruit preserve, spicy, creamy oak, scrubland, fine reductive notes. Palate: powerful, flavourful, long.

Mas la Mola Negre 2011 T
garnacha, garnacha peluda

89

Colour: cherry, garnet rim. Nose: fine reductive notes, aged wood nuances, ripe fruit, balsamic herbs. Palate: spicy, long, toasty.

MASET DEL LLEÓ

Ctra. Vilafranca-Igualada C-15 (Km.19)
08792 La Granada (Barcelona)
☎: +34 902 200 250
Fax: +34 938 921 333
info@maset.com
www.maset.com

Clos Viló 2013 T

90

Colour: deep cherry, garnet rim. Nose: scrubland, dried flowers, expressive. Palate: flavourful, round tannins.

Mas Viló 2014 T

89

Colour: bright cherry, purple rim. Nose: ripe fruit, scrubland, balanced. Palate: fruity, flavourful, fruity aftestaste, spicy.

MERITXELL PALLEJÀ

Carrer Piró, 10
43737 Gratallops (Tarragona)
☎: +34 670 960 735
info@nita.cat
www.nita.cat

Nita 2013 T
45% garnacha, 35% cariñena, 15% cabernet sauvignon, 5% syrah

90

Colour: very deep cherry, garnet rim. Nose: expressive, mineral, balsamic herbs, balanced. Palate: flavourful, round tannins, easy to drink.

MISTIK

Rambla Prim, 248 Bajos (Local)
08020 Barcelona (Barcelona)
☎: +34 933 134 347
administracion@rotllantorra.com

Mistik 2009 TR
45% garnacha, 45% cariñena, 10% cabernet sauvignon

89

Colour: black cherry. Nose: old leather, toasty, fruit preserve. Palate: balanced, classic aged character, flavourful.

Mistik 2010 TC
45% garnacha, 45% cariñena, 10% cabernet sauvignon

88

Colour: very deep cherry. Nose: fruit preserve, creamy oak, wild herbs. Palate: fruity, easy to drink.

NOGUERALS

Tou, 5
43360 Cornudella de Montsant
(Tarragona)
☎: +34 650 033 546
cellernoguerals@gmail.com
www.noguerals.com

Abellars - Finca Mas de L'Abella 2010 T
garnacha, cariñena, cabernet sauvignon, syrah

89

Colour: cherry, garnet rim. Nose: ripe fruit, spicy, creamy oak. Palate: flavourful, toasty, round tannins.

Tití 2010 TC
garnacha, cabernet sauvignon, syrah

87

Colour: cherry, garnet rim. Nose: smoky, spicy, ripe fruit. Palate: flavourful, smoky aftertaste, ripe fruit.

RITME CELLER

Camí Sindicat s/n
43375 La Vilella Alta (Tarragona)
☎: +34 672 432 691
Fax: +34 977 660 867
ritme@ritmeceller.com
www.acusticceller.com

+ Ritme Blanc 2011 B
garnacha blanca, macabeo

93 ♣

Colour: bright golden. Nose: expressive, complex, candied fruit, spicy, ripe fruit, faded flowers. Palate: balanced, long.

+ Ritme Blanc 2012 B
garnacha blanca, macabeo

92 ♣

Colour: bright yellow. Nose: ripe fruit, powerfull, toasty, balanced. Palate: flavourful, fruity, spicy, toasty, long.

Etern 2011 T
garnacha, cariñena

93 ♣

Colour: deep cherry, purple rim. Nose: creamy oak, toasty, ripe fruit, balsamic herbs. Palate: balanced, spicy, long, round tannins.

Etern 2013 T
garnacha, cariñena

93

Colour: bright cherry, garnet rim. Nose: ripe fruit, sweet spices, creamy oak, expressive, elegant. Palate: flavourful, fruity, toasty, round tannins, balanced.

Plaer 2012 T
garnacha, cariñena

93 ♣

Colour: cherry, garnet rim. Nose: spicy, creamy oak, fruit preserve, wild herbs, complex. Palate: flavourful, toasty.

Plaer 2013 T
garnacha, cariñena

92 ♣

Colour: deep cherry, garnet rim. Nose: smoky, toasty, characterful, earthy notes. Palate: flavourful, ripe fruit, balsamic, round tannins.

Ritme Negre 2013 T
garnacha, cariñena

92 ♣

Colour: cherry, garnet rim. Nose: creamy oak, red berry notes, wild herbs, expressive. Palate: flavourful, spicy, elegant.

RODRÍGUEZ SANZO

Manuel Azaña, 11
47014 (Valladolid)
☎: +34 983 150 150
Fax: +34 983 150 151
comunicacion@valsanzo.com
www.rodriguezsanzo.com

Nassos 2012 T
garnacha

93

Colour: cherry, garnet rim. Nose: mineral, spicy. Palate: flavourful, ripe fruit, long, good acidity, balanced.

ROTLLAN TORRA

Balandra, 6
43737 Torroja del Priorat (Tarragona)
☎: +34 933 134 347
administracion@rotllantorra.com
www.rotllantorra.com

Autor 2009 TR
40% garnacha, 40% cariñena, 20% cabernet sauvignon

88

Colour: ruby red. Nose: overripe fruit, warm, powerfull, spicy. Palate: flavourful, ripe fruit, correct.

Autor 2011 TC
40% garnacha, 40% cariñena, 20% cabernet sauvignon

85

SANGENÍS I VAQUÉ

Pl. Catalunya, 3
43739 Porrera (Tarragona)
☎: +34 977 828 252
celler@sangenisivaque.com
www.sangenisivaque.com

Garbinada 2010 T
45% garnacha, 45% cariñena, 10% syrah

85

Lo Coster Blanc 2014 B
garnacha blanca, macabeo

89

Colour: bright yellow. Nose: ripe fruit, dried flowers, dried herbs. Palate: flavourful, balanced, spicy.

SOLÀ CLÀSSIC

Clos, 1
43738 Bellmunt del Priorat (Tarragona)
☎: +34 686 115 104
info@solaclassic.com
www.solaclassic.com

Solà 1777 Blau 2012 T
garnacha, cariñena

87 ♣

Colour: bright cherry. Nose: creamy oak, expressive, ripe fruit, fruit preserve. Palate: flavourful, fruity.

Solà Classic 2011 T
garnacha, cariñena

86

Solà2 Classic 2013 T
garnacha, cariñena

89 ♣

Colour: deep cherry, purple rim. Nose: creamy oak, toasty, ripe fruit, scrubland. Palate: balanced, spicy, long.

Vinyes Josep 2008 TR
garnacha, cariñena

90

Colour: cherry, garnet rim. Nose: red berry notes, ripe fruit, spicy, creamy oak, fine reductive notes. Palate: flavourful, toasty, balanced.

TERROIR AL LIMIT
Baixa Font, 10
43737 Torroja del Priorat (Tarragona)
☎: +34 699 732 707
Fax: +34 977 839 391
dominik@terroir-al-limit.com
www.terroir-al-limit.com

PODIUM

Arbossar 2012 T
100% cariñena

95

Colour: cherry, garnet rim. Nose: expressive, complex, balsamic herbs, fragrant herbs. Palate: flavourful, balanced, fine tannins.

Dits del Terra 2012 T
100% cariñena

94

Colour: cherry, garnet rim. Nose: red berry notes, ripe fruit, spicy, creamy oak, balsamic herbs, complex. Palate: flavourful, toasty, balanced.

PODIUM

Les Manyes 2012 T
100% garnacha

97

Colour: light cherry. Nose: fruit expression, fruit liqueur notes, fragrant herbs, spicy, creamy oak, dry stone, elegant. Palate: balanced, elegant, spicy, long, toasty.

Les Tosses 2012 T
100% cariñena

93

Colour: bright cherry, purple rim. Nose: characterful, powerfull, wild herbs. Palate: spicy, good structure, flavourful.

Pedra de Guix 2012 B
33% pedro ximénez, 33% macabeo, 33% garnacha

92

Colour: bright yellow. Nose: expressive, wild herbs, dried herbs, complex, characterful. Palate: balanced, fine bitter notes.

Terra de Cuques 2013 B
90% pedro ximénez, 10% moscatel

91

Colour: golden. Nose: faded flowers, expressive, characterful. Palate: flavourful, complex, long, fine bitter notes. Personality.

PODIUM

Torroja Vi de la Vila 2013 T
50% garnacha, 50% cariñena

95

Colour: cherry, garnet rim. Nose: elegant, ripe fruit, wild herbs, expressive, earthy notes. Palate: round, long, good acidity.

TORRES PRIORAT
Finca La Soleta, s/n
43737 El Lloar (Tarragona)
☎: +34 938 177 400
Fax: +34 938 177 444
admin@torres.es
www.torres.es

Perpetual 2012 TC
cariñena, garnacha

91

Colour: cherry, garnet rim. Nose: ripe fruit, wild herbs, spicy, balsamic herbs, mineral. Palate: balanced, flavourful, long, balsamic.

Salmos 2012 TC
cariñena, garnacha, syrah

89

Colour: deep cherry, garnet rim. Nose: characterful, ripe fruit, sweet spices. Palate: ripe fruit, correct.

Secret del Priorat Dulce 2011 T
cariñena, garnacha

92

Colour: black cherry. Nose: acetaldehyde, varnish, candied fruit, fruit preserve. Palate: fruity, flavourful, sweet, balanced, elegant.

TROSSOS DEL PRIORAT
Ctra. Gratallops a La Vilella
Baixa, Km. 10,65
43737 Gratallops (Tarragona)
☎: +34 670 590 788
celler@trossosdelpriorat.com
www.trossosdelpriorat.com

Abracadabra 2013 B
garnacha blanca, macabeo

92

Colour: bright yellow. Nose: mineral, expressive, spicy, dried herbs. Palate: balanced, spicy, long, complex.

Lo Món 2010 T
garnacha, cariñena, syrah, cabernet sauvignon

91 ♣
Colour: cherry, garnet rim. Nose: ripe fruit, wild herbs, earthy notes, spicy, balsamic herbs. Palate: balanced, flavourful, long, balsamic, elegant.

Lo Petit de la Casa 2011 TC
garnacha, cabernet sauvignon

90 ♣
Colour: very deep cherry, garnet rim. Nose: mineral, balsamic herbs, balanced. Palate: flavourful, round tannins.

Pam de Nas 2010 T
garnacha, cariñena

92 ♣
Colour: cherry, garnet rim. Nose: balanced, fragrant herbs, spicy, ripe fruit. Palate: good structure, fruity, balsamic.

VINÍCOLA DEL PRIORAT
Piró, s/n
43737 Gratallops (Tarragona)
☎: +34 977 839 167
Fax: +34 977 839 201
info@vinicoladelpriorat.com
www.vinicoladelpriorat.com

Clos Gebrat 2011 TC
garnacha, mazuelo, cabernet sauvignon

87
Colour: bright cherry. Nose: sweet spices, creamy oak, fruit preserve. Palate: flavourful, fruity, toasty.

Clos Gebrat 2014 T
garnacha, mazuelo, cabernet sauvignon, merlot, syrah

88
Colour: cherry, purple rim. Nose: powerfull, ripe fruit, spicy. Palate: powerful, fruity, round.

L'Obaga 2014 T
garnacha, syrah, mazuelo

89
Colour: cherry, purple rim. Nose: floral, balsamic herbs, ripe fruit. Palate: powerful, fresh, fruity.

Nadiu 2012 TC
mazuelo, garnacha, cabernet sauvignon, merlot, syrah

86

Nadiu 2014 T
mazuelo, garnacha, cabernet sauvignon, merlot, syrah

88
Colour: cherry, purple rim. Nose: red berry notes, floral, balsamic herbs, balanced, fresh, scrubland. Palate: powerful, fresh, fruity.

Ònix Clàssic 2014 B
viura, garnacha blanca, pedro ximénez

88
Colour: bright straw. Nose: white flowers, ripe fruit, spicy. Palate: correct, ripe fruit.

Ònix Clàssic 2014 T
garnacha, mazuelo

88
Colour: cherry, purple rim. Nose: powerfull, ripe fruit, spicy, balsamic herbs. Palate: powerful, fruity, unctuous.

Ònix Evolució 2011 TC
mazuelo, garnacha, cabernet sauvignon

89
Colour: cherry, garnet rim. Nose: smoky, spicy, ripe fruit. Palate: flavourful, smoky aftertaste, ripe fruit.

Ònix Fusió 2013 T
garnacha, syrah

90
Colour: deep cherry, garnet rim. Nose: ripe fruit, creamy oak, smoky. Palate: balsamic, good structure, fruity.

Ónix Selecció Vi de Vila 2012 TC
100% mazuelo

90
Colour: cherry, garnet rim. Nose: ripe fruit, earthy notes, spicy, balsamic herbs, smoky. Palate: balanced, flavourful, long, balsamic.

VITICULTORS DEL PRIORAT
Partida Palells, s/n - Mas Subirat
43738 Bellmunt del Priorat (Tarragona)
☎: +34 977 262 268
Fax: +34 977 831 356
mariajose.bajon@morlanda.com
www.morlanda.com

Morlanda 2009 T
garnacha, cariñena

90
Colour: cherry, garnet rim. Nose: ripe fruit, old leather, tobacco. Palate: correct, flavourful, spicy, balanced.

Morlanda 2014 B
garnacha blanca, macabeo

87
Colour: bright yellow. Nose: expressive, dried herbs, ripe fruit, spicy. Palate: fruity, balanced, easy to drink.

DO. RÍAS BAIXAS

CONSEJO REGULADOR

Edif. Pazo de Mugartegui
36002 Pontevedra
☎:+34 986 854 850 / +34 864 530 - Fax: +34 986 864 546
@: consejo@doriasbaixas.com
www.doriasbaixas.com

LOCATION:

In the southwest of the province of Pontevedra, covering five distinct sub-regions: Val do Salnés, O Rosal, Condado do Tea, Soutomaior and Ribeira do Ulla.

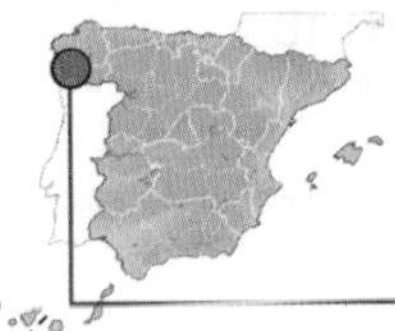

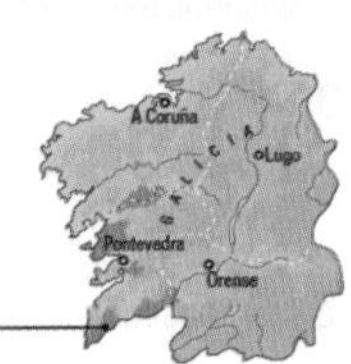

SUB-REGIONS:

Val do Salnés. This is the historic sub-region of the Albariño (in fact, here, almost all the white wines are produced as single-variety wines from this variety) and is centred around the municipal district of Cambados. It has the flattest relief of the four sub-regions.

Condado do Tea. The furthest inland, it is situated in the south of the province on the northern bank of the Miño. It is characterized by its mountainous terrain. The wines must contain a minimum of 70% of Albariño and Treixadura.

O Rosal. In the extreme southwest of the province, on the right bank of the Miño river mouth. The warmest sub-region, where river terraces abound. The wines must contain a minimum of 70% of Albariño and Loureira.

Soutomaior. Situated on the banks of the Verdugo River, about 10 km from Pontevedra, it consists only of the municipal district of Soutomaior. It produces only single-varietals of Albariño.

Ribeira do Ulla. A new sub-region along the Ulla River, which forms the landscape of elevated valleys further inland. It comprises the municipal districts of Vedra and part of Padrón, Deo, Boquixon, Touro, Estrada, Silleda and Vila de Cruce. Red wines predominate.

GRAPE VARIETIES:

WHITE: Albariño (majority), Loureira Blanca or Marqués, Treixadura and Caíño Blanco (preferred); Torrontés and Godello (authorized). **RED**: Caíño Tinto, Espadeiro, Loureira Tinta and Sousón (preferred); Tempranillo, Mouratón, Garnacha Tintorera, Mencía and Brancellao (authorized).

FIGURES:

Vineyard surface: 4,027 – **Wine-Growers:** 6,677 – **Wineries:** 179 – **2014 Harvest rating:** Good – **Production 14:** 16,187,622 litres – **Market percentages:** 50% National - 50% International.

SOIL:

Sandy, shallow and slightly acidic, which makes fine soil for producing quality wines. The predominant type of rock is granite, and only in the Concellos of Sanxenxo, Rosal and Tomillo is it possible to find a narrow band of metamorphous rock. Quaternary deposits are very common in all the sub-regions.

CLIMATE:

Atlantic, with moderate, mild temperatures due to the influence of the sea, high relative humidity and abundant rainfall (the annual average is around 1600 mm). There is less rainfall further downstream of the Miño (Condado de Tea), and as a consequence the grapes ripen earlier.

VINTAGE RATING

PEÑÍNGUIDE

2010	2011	2012	2013	2014
GOOD	VERY GOOD	VERY GOOD	VERY GOOD	VERY GOOD

A. PAZOS DE LUSCO

Grixó - Alxén
36458 Salvaterra do Miño (Pontevedra)
☎: +34 987 514 550
Fax: +34 987 514 570
info@lusco.es
www.lusco.es

Lusco 2014 B

albariño

91

Colour: bright straw. Nose: white flowers, dried herbs, ripe fruit. Palate: flavourful, fruity, good acidity, elegant.

Zios de Lusco 2013 B

albariño

92

Colour: bright straw. Nose: white flowers, fine lees, dried herbs, mineral. Palate: flavourful, fruity, good acidity, round.

Zios de Lusco 2014 B

albariño

86

ADEGA CONDES DE ALBAREI

Lugar a Bouza, 1 Castrelo
36639 Cambados (Pontevedra)
☎: +34 986 543 535
Fax: +34 986 524 251
inf@condesdealbarei.com
www.condesdealbarei.com

Albariño Condes de Albarei 2014 B

100% albariño

87

Colour: bright yellow. Nose: dried herbs, ripe fruit, spicy. Palate: flavourful, fruity, good acidity.

Albariño Condes de Albarei En Rama 2010 B

100% albariño

93

Colour: bright yellow. Nose: ripe fruit, powerfull, toasty, aged wood nuances, pattiserie, slightly evolved. Palate: flavourful, fruity, spicy, toasty, long.

Albariño Condes de Albarei Enxebre 2014 B Maceración Carbónica

100% albariño

86

ADEGA E VIÑEDOS PACO & LOLA

Valdamor, 18 - XII
36968 Meaño (Pontevedra)
☎: +34 986 747 779
Fax: +34 986 748 940
comercial@pacolola.com
www.pacolola.com

iWine 2014 B

100% albariño

88

Colour: bright yellow. Nose: expressive, dried herbs, ripe fruit, spicy. Palate: flavourful, fruity, good acidity.

Lolo 2014 B

100% albariño

86

Paco & Lola 2014 B

100% albariño

90

Colour: bright straw, greenish rim. Nose: ripe fruit, citrus fruit, floral. Palate: correct, easy to drink.

Paco & Lola Prime 2013 B

100% albariño

92

Colour: bright straw. Nose: fine lees, dried herbs, ripe fruit, citrus fruit. Palate: flavourful, fruity, good acidity, elegant.

ADEGA EIDOS

Padriñán, 65
36960 Sanxenxo (Pontevedra)
☎: +34 986 690 009
Fax: +34 986 720 307
info@adegaeidos.com
www.adegaeidos.com

Contraaparede 2010 B

100% albariño

94

Colour: bright straw. Nose: white flowers, fine lees, dried herbs, ripe fruit, sweet spices. Palate: flavourful, fruity, good acidity, elegant.

Eidos de Padriñán 2014 B

100% albariño

91

Colour: bright straw. Nose: white flowers, fine lees, dried herbs, mineral. Palate: flavourful, fruity, good acidity, round.

Veigas de Padriñán 2013 B

100% albariño

92

Colour: bright straw. Nose: dried herbs, ripe fruit, dry stone, floral, balanced. Palate: flavourful, fruity, good acidity, round, elegant.

ADEGAS AROUSA

Tirabao, 15 - Baión
36614 Vilanova de Arousa (Pontevedra)
☎: +34 986 506 113
info@adegasarousa.com
www.adegasarousa.com

Pazo da Bouciña 2014 B
albariño

89

Colour: bright straw. Nose: floral, citrus fruit, fruit expression, dried herbs. Palate: powerful, flavourful, slightly acidic.

Pazo da Bouciña Expresión 2013 B
albariño

90

Colour: bright straw. Nose: white flowers, fresh fruit, fragrant herbs, expressive. Palate: flavourful, fruity, good acidity, balanced.

Valdemonxes 2014 B
albariño

89

Colour: bright straw. Nose: fresh fruit, fragrant herbs. Palate: flavourful, fruity, good acidity, balanced.

ADEGAS CASTROBREY

Camanzo, s/n
36587 Vila de Cruces (Pontevedra)
☎: +34 986 583 643
Fax: +34 986 411 612
bodegas@castrobrey.com
www.castrobrey.com

Castro Valdés 2014 B
100% albariño

89

Colour: bright straw. Nose: white flowers, fresh fruit, expressive. Palate: flavourful, fruity, good acidity, balanced.

Nice to Meet You Castrobrey 2013 B
albariño, treixadura, godello

88

Colour: bright straw. Nose: fresh fruit, citrus fruit, floral. Palate: easy to drink, correct, fine bitter notes.

Señorío de Cruces 2014 B
100% albariño

86

Sin Palabras Castro Valdés 2014 B
100% albariño

90

Colour: bright straw. Nose: ripe fruit, dried flowers, balanced. Palate: balanced, fine bitter notes, good acidity.

ADEGAS GALEGAS

Lugar de Meder, s/n
36457 Salvaterra de Miño (Pontevedra)
☎: +34 986 657 143
Fax: +34 986 526 901
comercial@adegasgalegas.es
www.adegasgalegas.es

Bago Amarelo 2014 B
100% albariño

86

Danza Escumoso ESP
100% albariño

84

Dionisos 2014 B
100% albariño

87

Colour: bright straw. Nose: medium intensity, ripe fruit, floral, balanced. Palate: correct, easy to drink.

Don Pedro Soutomaior 2014 B
100% albariño

87

Nose: dried herbs, ripe fruit, spicy. Palate: flavourful, fruity, good acidity, easy to drink.

Don Pedro Soutomaior Macerado en Neve Carbónica 2014 B Maceración Carbónica
albariño

88

Colour: bright straw. Nose: medium intensity, white flowers, citrus fruit, ripe fruit. Palate: correct, fine bitter notes.

ADEGAS GRAN VINUM

Viñagrande 84B – San Miguel de Deiro
36620 Vilagarcía de Arousa
(Pontevedra)
☎: +34 986 555 742
Fax: +34 986 555 742
info@adegasgranvinum.com
www.granvinum.com

Esencia Diviña 2014 B
100% albariño

89

Colour: bright straw. Nose: white flowers, fragrant herbs, expressive, citrus fruit. Palate: good acidity, balanced.

Gran Vinum 2014 B
100% albariño

90

Colour: bright straw. Nose: white flowers, ripe fruit, citrus fruit. Palate: flavourful, fruity, good acidity, fine bitter notes.

ADEGAS MORGADÍO

Albeos, s/n
36429 Creciente (Pontevedra)
☎: +34 988 261 212
Fax: +34 988 261 213
info@morgadio.com
www.gruporeboredamorgadio.com

Morgadío 2014 B

albariño

88

Colour: bright yellow. Nose: fruit expression, wild herbs, balsamic herbs. Palate: fresh, fruity, good finish.

Puerta Santa 2014 B

albariño

88

Colour: bright straw. Nose: white flowers, fine lees, dried herbs, ripe fruit, citrus fruit. Palate: flavourful, fruity, good acidity, elegant.

ADEGAS TOLLODOURO

Ctra. Tui-A Guardia km. 45
36760 As Eiras, O Rosal (Pontevedra)
info@hgabodegas.com
www.adegastollod.com

Pontellón Albariño 2013 B

albariño

90

Colour: bright yellow. Nose: ripe fruit, dried herbs, floral, petrol notes. Palate: powerful, rich, flavourful, balanced.

Tollodouro Rosal 2013 B

albariño, loureiro, treixadura

90

Colour: bright yellow. Nose: fine lees, dried herbs, ripe fruit, floral. Palate: flavourful, fruity, good acidity, elegant.

ADEGAS VALMIÑOR

A Portela, s/n – San Juan de Tabagón
36760 O'Rosal (Pontevedra)
☎: +34 986 609 060
Fax: +34 986 609 313
valminor@valminorebano.com
www.adegasvalminor.com

Davila 2014 B

albariño, loureiro, treixadura

90

Colour: bright straw. Nose: ripe fruit, floral, dried herbs, mineral. Palate: flavourful, fresh, fruity.

Davila C-100 2013 T

100% castañal

88

Colour: deep cherry. Nose: creamy oak, toasty, ripe fruit, balsamic herbs. Palate: balanced, spicy, long.

Davila M-100 2011 B

loureiro, caiño blanco, albariño

93

Colour: bright straw. Nose: white flowers, fine lees, dried herbs. Palate: flavourful, fruity, good acidity, round, long, rich.

Serra da Estrela 2014 B

100% albariño

85

Torroxal 2014 B

100% albariño

86

Valmiñor 2014 B

100% albariño

89

Colour: bright yellow. Nose: ripe fruit, floral, dried herbs, earthy notes. Palate: powerful, flavourful, round.

ADEGAS VALTEA

Lg. Portela, 14
36429 Crecente (Pontevedra)
☎: +34 986 666 344
Fax: +34 986 644 914
vilarvin@vilarvin.com
www.vilarvin.com

C de V 2013 B

albariño, treixadura, loureiro

88

Colour: bright straw. Nose: faded flowers, ripe fruit. Palate: correct, good finish.

Finca Garabato 2013 B

100% albariño

92

Colour: bright straw. Nose: white flowers, fine lees, dried herbs, mineral. Palate: flavourful, fruity, good acidity, round.

Marexías 2013 B

albariño, treixadura, loureiro

88

Colour: bright yellow. Nose: faded flowers, dried herbs, ripe fruit. Palate: long, good acidity, fine bitter notes.

Valtea 2013 B
100% albariño

91

Colour: bright yellow. Nose: expressive, dried herbs, ripe fruit, spicy. Palate: flavourful, fruity, good acidity, balanced.

Valtea 2014 B
100% albariño

90

Colour: bright yellow. Nose: medium intensity, dried flowers, ripe fruit. Palate: balanced, fine bitter notes.

AGRO DE BAZÁN

Lg. Tremoedo, 46
36628 Vilanova de Arousa (Pontevedra)
☎: +34 986 555 562
Fax: +34 986 555 799
agrodebazan@agrodebazan.com
www.agrodebazan.com

Contrapunto 2014 B
100% albariño

85

Granbazán Ámbar 2014 B
100% albariño

89

Colour: bright straw. Nose: ripe fruit, white flowers, varietal. Palate: correct, fine bitter notes.

Granbazán Etiqueta Verde 2014 B
100% albariño

88

Colour: bright straw. Nose: white flowers, fresh fruit, fragrant herbs. Palate: flavourful, fruity.

Granbazán Limousin 2013 B
100% albariño

91

Colour: bright yellow. Nose: ripe fruit, powerfull, toasty, sweet spices. Palate: fruity, spicy, toasty, long, rich.

ALDEA DE ABAIXO

Novas, s/n
36770 O'Rosal (Pontevedra)
☎: +34 986 626 121
Fax: +34 986 626 121
senoriodatorre@grannovas.com
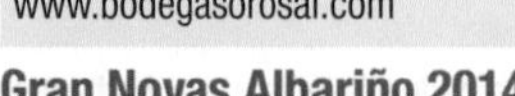
www.bodegasorosal.com

Gran Novas Albariño 2014 B
100% albariño

87

Colour: bright yellow. Nose: fragrant herbs, floral, ripe fruit. Palate: fresh, fruity, flavourful, easy to drink.

Señorío da Torre Rosal 2014 B
75% albariño, 20% loureiro, 5% caiño

86

Señorío da Torre sobre Lías 2013 B
85% albariño, 10% loureiro, 5% caiño

90

Colour: bright yellow. Nose: expressive, dried herbs, ripe fruit, spicy. Palate: flavourful, fruity, balanced.

ALMA ATLÁNTICA

Burgáns, 91
36633 Vilariño - Cambados (Pontevedra)
☎: +34 986 526 040
Fax: +34 986 526 901
comercial@martincodax.com
www.martincodax.com

Alba Martín 2013 ESP
100% albariño

87

Colour: bright straw. Nose: fresh fruit, dried herbs, fine lees, floral. Palate: fresh, fruity, flavourful, good acidity.

Anxo Martín 2014 B
albariño, caiño, loureiro

90

Colour: bright straw. Nose: ripe fruit, floral, wild herbs. Palate: powerful, rich, flavourful.

ARBOLEDA MEDITERRÁNEA

Couto de Abaixo, s/n
36639 Cambados (Pontevedra)
☎: +34 902 996 361
export@arboledamediterranea.com
www.arboledamediterranea.com

Spyro Premium Añada Seleccionada 2014 B
100% albariño

86

Spyro Premium Viñas Viejas 2014 B
100% albariño

88

Colour: bright straw. Nose: fragrant herbs, fruit expression, wild herbs. Palate: flavourful, fruity, good acidity.

ATTIS BODEGAS Y VIÑEDOS

Lg. Morouzos, 16D - Dena
36967 Meaño (Pontevedra)
☎: +34 986 744 790
administracion@attisbyv.com
www.attisbyv.com

Attis Embaixador 2012 B

albariño

91

Colour: bright golden. Nose: white flowers, fine lees, dried herbs, ripe fruit, candied fruit, citrus fruit. Palate: flavourful, fruity, good acidity, elegant. Personality.

Attis Espadeiro 2013 T

88

Colour: cherry, purple rim. Nose: wild herbs, ripe fruit, grassy. Palate: slightly acidic, fresh, balsamic.

Attis Lías Finas 2014 B

92

Colour: bright straw. Nose: white flowers, fine lees, dried herbs, mineral. Palate: flavourful, fruity, good acidity, round.

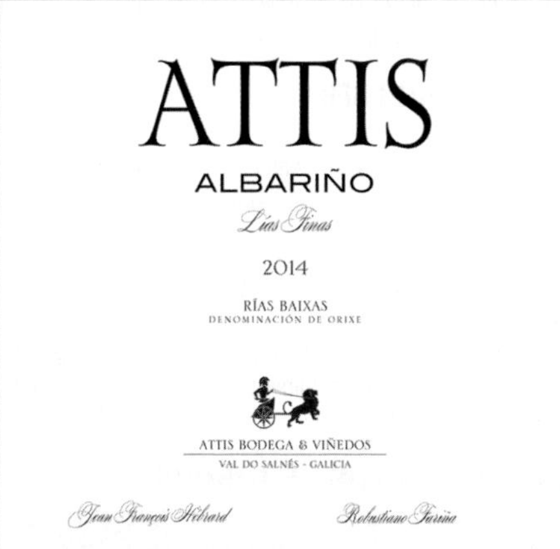

Attis Pedral 2013 T

90

Colour: cherry, garnet rim. Nose: scrubland, grassy, ripe fruit, spicy, balanced. Palate: balanced, good acidity, balsamic.

Attis Sousón 2013 T

89

Colour: bright cherry, purple rim. Nose: expressive, spicy, balsamic herbs. Palate: fresh, slightly acidic.

Nana 2012 BFB

91

Colour: bright yellow. Nose: ripe fruit, powerfull, toasty, aged wood nuances, citrus fruit. Palate: flavourful, fruity, spicy, toasty, long.

Xión 2014 B

88

Colour: bright yellow. Nose: citrus fruit, white flowers, ripe fruit, balsamic herbs. Palate: flavourful, fresh, fruity.

Xión Cuvée 2014 T

88

Colour: very deep cherry, purple rim. Nose: red berry notes, fresh, wild herbs, ripe fruit. Palate: balsamic, balanced.

BENJAMÍN MIGUEZ NOVAL

Porto de Abaixo, 10 - Porto
36458 Salvaterra de Miño (Pontevedra)
☎: +34 986 122 705
enoturismo@mariabargiela.com
www.mariabargiela.com

María Bargiela 2013 B

90% albariño, 8% treixadura, 2% loureiro

89

Colour: bright straw. Nose: fine lees, dried herbs, mineral, faded flowers. Palate: flavourful, fruity, good acidity, round.

BODEGA PAZO QUINTEIRO DA CRUZ

A Cruz 12, Lois
36635 Ribadumia (Pontevedra)
☎: +34 635 592 215
pedropinheirolago@yahoo.es
www.pazoquinteirodacruz.es

Quinteiro Da Cruz 2014 B

86

BODEGA Y VIÑEDOS VEIGA DA PRINCESA

Ctra. Ourense-Castrelo Km. 12,5
32940 Toen (Ourense)
☎: +34 988 261 256
Fax: +34 988 261 264
info@pazodomar.com
www.pazodomar.com

Coral do Mar 2014 B

albariño

87

Colour: bright straw, greenish rim. Nose: medium intensity, ripe fruit, floral. Palate: correct, easy to drink.

Veiga da Princesa 2014 B
albariño

89

Colour: bright straw, greenish rim. Nose: fragrant herbs, white flowers, balanced. Palate: easy to drink, ripe fruit.

BODEGAS AGRUPADAS PONTE

Eduardo Pondal, 3
36001 (Pontevedra)
☎: +34 986 840 064
Fax: +34 986 851 667
info@bodegasagrupadasponte.com
www.bodegasagrupadasponte.com

La Recomendación de Eva 2014 B
100% albariño

87

Colour: straw. Nose: medium intensity, ripe fruit, floral. Palate: correct, easy to drink, good finish.

BODEGAS AGUIUNCHO

Las Pedreiras, 1º Villalonga
36990 Sanxenxo (Pontevedra)
☎: +34 986 720 980
Fax: +34 986 727 063
info@aguiuncho.com
www.aguiuncho.com

Aguiuncho 2011 B Barrica
100% albariño

88

Colour: bright yellow. Nose: ripe fruit, powerfull, toasty, aged wood nuances. Palate: flavourful, fruity, spicy, toasty, long.

Aguiuncho Selección 2011 B
100% albariño

90

Colour: bright straw. Nose: expressive, ripe fruit, spicy, faded flowers. Palate: flavourful, fruity, good acidity, balanced.

Mar de Ons 2014 B
100% albariño

87

Colour: bright straw. Nose: white flowers, fresh fruit, fragrant herbs. Palate: flavourful, fruity, good acidity.

BODEGAS ALBAMAR

O Adro, 11 - Castrelo
36639 Cambados (Pontevedra)
☎: +34 660 292 750
Fax: +34 986 520 048
info@bodegasalbamar.com

Albamar 2014 B

88

Colour: straw. Nose: medium intensity, floral, grassy, citrus fruit, fresh fruit. Palate: correct, easy to drink.

Albamar Edición Especial 2013 B

91

Colour: bright yellow. Nose: expressive, dried herbs, ripe fruit, spicy. Palate: flavourful, fruity, good acidity, balanced.

Albamar Edición Especial 2014 B

90

Colour: bright straw. Nose: white flowers, fresh fruit, fragrant herbs, mineral. Palate: flavourful, fruity, good acidity, balanced.

Albamar Finca O Pereiro 2014 B

89

Colour: bright straw. Nose: white flowers, fine lees, dried herbs, mineral, ripe fruit. Palate: flavourful, fruity, good acidity, round.

Albamar O Esteiro 2013 T

91

Colour: cherry, purple rim. Nose: red berry notes, floral, balsamic herbs. Palate: powerful, fresh, fruity, balsamic.

Alma de Mar sobre Lías 2013 B

91

Colour: bright straw. Nose: white flowers, fine lees, dried herbs, mineral. Palate: flavourful, fruity, good acidity, round.

Pepe Luis 2013 BFB

92

Colour: bright straw. Nose: white flowers, dried herbs, ripe fruit, citrus fruit, spicy. Palate: flavourful, fruity, good acidity, elegant.

Sesenta e Nove Arrobas 2013 B

94

Colour: bright straw. Nose: fine lees, dried herbs, ripe fruit, candied fruit, citrus fruit, mineral. Palate: flavourful, fruity, good acidity, elegant.

BODEGAS ALTOS DE TORONA

Ctra. de Tui a la Guardia, 45
36760 As Eiras, O Rosal (Pontevedra)
☎: +34 986 288 212
Fax: +34 986 401 185
info@hgabodegas.com
www.altosdetorona.com

Albanta 2014 B
albariño

85 ♣

Altos de Torona 2013 B Barrica
albariño

88

Colour: bright yellow. Nose: ripe fruit, toasty, aged wood nuances, pattiserie. Palate: flavourful, spicy, toasty, long.

Altos de Torona Lías 2014 B
albariño

90

Colour: bright yellow. Nose: powerfull, fragrant herbs, ripe fruit. Palate: flavourful, green, correct.

Altos de Torona Rosal 2014 B
albariño, loureiro, caiño

88

Colour: bright yellow. Nose: dried herbs, ripe fruit, wild herbs. Palate: flavourful, ripe fruit, correct.

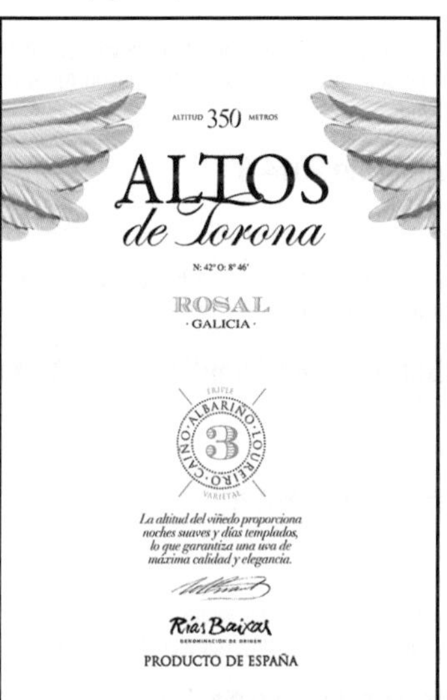

Torres de Ermelo 2014 B
albariño

86

BODEGAS AQUITANIA

Bouza, 17 Castrelo
36639 Cambados (Pontevedra)
☎: +34 986 520 895
Fax: +34 986 520 895
info@bodegasaquitania.com
www.bodegasaquitania.es

Aquitania 2013 T
mencía

74

Aquitania 2014 B
albariño

87

Colour: bright straw. Nose: fine lees, dried flowers, balanced. Palate: fine bitter notes, slightly acidic.

Bernon 2014 B
albariño

86

Raiolas D'Outono Afrutado 2014 B
albariño

84

BODEGAS AS LAXAS

As Laxas, 16
36430 Arbo (Pontevedra)
☎: +34 986 665 444
Fax: +34 986 665 554
info@bodegasaslaxas.com
www.bodegasaslaxas.com

Bágoa do Miño 2014 B
100% albariño

89

Colour: bright straw. Nose: white flowers, fragrant herbs, tropical fruit. Palate: flavourful, fruity, good acidity.

Condado Laxas 2014 B
65% albariño, 30% treixadura, 5% loureiro

89

Colour: bright straw. Nose: white flowers, fresh fruit, fragrant herbs, expressive. Palate: flavourful, fruity, good acidity.

Laxas 2014 B
100% albariño

87

Colour: bright straw. Nose: medium intensity, floral, citrus fruit. Palate: correct, easy to drink, good finish.

Sensum Laxas ESP
100% albariño

86

Val Do Sosego 2014 B
100% albariño

89

Colour: bright straw. Nose: white flowers, dried herbs, mineral, ripe fruit. Palate: flavourful, fruity, good acidity.

BODEGAS CASTRO MARTÍN

Puxafeita, 3
36636 Ribadumia (Pontevedra)
☎: +34 986 710 202
Fax: +34 986 710 607
info@castromartin.com
www.castromartin.com

Bodega Castro Martín Albariño 2014 B
albariño

86

BODEGAS DEL PALACIO DE FEFIÑANES

Pza. de Fefiñanes, s/n
36630 Cambados (Pontevedra)
☎: +34 986 542 204
Fax: +34 986 524 512
fefinanes@fefinanes.com
www.fefinanes.com

1583 Albariño de Fefiñanes 2014 B
100% albariño

91

Colour: bright straw. Nose: white flowers, fresh fruit, fragrant herbs, expressive. Palate: flavourful, fruity, good acidity, balanced.

Albariño de Fefiñanes 2014 B
100% albariño

91

Colour: bright straw. Nose: white flowers, fine lees, dried herbs, ripe fruit, citrus fruit. Palate: flavourful, fruity, fine bitter notes.

PODIUM

Albariño de Fefiñanes III año 2012 B
100% albariño

97

Colour: bright yellow. Nose: ripe fruit, spicy, complex, expressive. Palate: flavourful, fruity, good acidity, balanced.

BODEGAS EIDOSELA

Eidos de Abaixo, s/n - Sela
36494 Arbo (Pontevedra)
☎: +34 986 665 550
Fax: +34 986 665 299
info@bodegaseidosela.com
www.bodegaseidosela.com

Arbastrum 2014 B
70% albariño, 20% treixadura, 10% loureiro

89

Colour: straw. Nose: medium intensity, ripe fruit, floral, fragrant herbs. Palate: correct, easy to drink.

Eidosela 2014 B
100% albariño

88

Colour: bright straw. Nose: white flowers, fresh fruit, fragrant herbs. Palate: flavourful, fruity, good acidity.

Eidosela Burbujas del Atlántico BN
100% albariño

88

Colour: bright golden. Nose: fine lees, dry nuts, fragrant herbs, complex. Palate: powerful, flavourful, good acidity, fine bead, fine bitter notes.

Eidosela Burbujas del Atlántico Brut ESP

81

Eidosela Burbujas del Atlántico Extra Brut ESP
100% albariño

86

Eidosela Selección de Barrica 2013 B Barrica
100% albariño

90

Colour: bright yellow. Nose: ripe fruit, powerfull, toasty, aged wood nuances, sweet spices. Palate: flavourful, fruity, spicy, toasty, long.

Etra Albariño 2014 B
100% albariño

87

Colour: bright straw. Nose: white flowers, fresh fruit, fragrant herbs. Palate: flavourful, fruity, correct.

Etra Burbujas del Atlántico Extra Brut BR
100% albariño

85

Etra Condado 2014 B
70% albariño, 20% treixadura, 10% loureiro

89

Colour: bright straw. Nose: white flowers, dried herbs, ripe fruit. Palate: flavourful, fruity, good acidity, elegant.

BODEGAS FILLABOA

Lugar de Fillaboa, s/n
36459 Salvaterra do Miño (Pontevedra)
☎: +34 986 658 132
info@bodegasfillaboa.com
www.bodegasfillaboa.com

Fillaboa 2014 B
100% albariño

90

Colour: bright yellow. Nose: expressive, dried herbs, ripe fruit, spicy. Palate: flavourful, fruity, good acidity, balanced.

Fillaboa Selección Finca Montealto 2013 B
100% albariño

93

Colour: bright straw. Nose: white flowers, fine lees, dried herbs, ripe fruit, citrus fruit, balanced. Palate: flavourful, fruity, good acidity, elegant.

BODEGAS GERARDO MÉNDEZ

Galiñanes, 10 - Lores
36968 Meaño (Pontevedra)
☎: +34 986 747 046
Fax: +34 986 748 915
info@bodegasgerardomendez.com
www.bodegasgerardomendez.com

Albariño Do Ferreiro 2014 B
albariño

90

Colour: bright straw. Nose: white flowers, fine lees, dried herbs, ripe fruit, citrus fruit. Palate: flavourful, fruity, good acidity.

BODEGAS LA CANA

Camiño Novo, 36
36600 Villagarcía de Arousa
(Pontevedra)
☎: +34 952 504 706
Fax: +34 951 284 796
lacana@jorgeordonez.es
www.grupojorgeordonez.com

La Caña 2014 B
100% albariño

89

Colour: bright straw. Nose: white flowers, fresh fruit, fragrant herbs, varietal. Palate: flavourful, fruity, good acidity.

La Caña Navia 2012 B
100% albariño

93

Colour: bright yellow. Nose: ripe fruit, toasty, aged wood nuances, pattiserie. Palate: flavourful, fruity, toasty, long.

BODEGAS LA VAL

Lugar Muguiña, s/n - Arantei
36458 Salvaterra de Miño (Pontevedra)
☎: +34 986 610 728
Fax: +34 986 611 635
laval@bodegaslaval.com
www.bodegaslaval.com

Finca Arantei 2014 B
100% albariño

89

Colour: bright straw. Nose: white flowers, fresh fruit, citrus fruit. Palate: good acidity, balanced.

La Val Albariño 2011 BFB
100% albariño

93

Colour: bright yellow. Nose: ripe fruit, powerfull, toasty, candied fruit. Palate: flavourful, fruity, spicy, toasty, long.

La Val Albariño 2014 B
100% albariño

90

Colour: bright yellow. Nose: citrus fruit, ripe fruit, dried herbs, floral, mineral. Palate: flavourful, long, balanced.

PODIUM

La Val Crianza sobre Lías 2007 BC
100% albariño

95

Colour: yellow, greenish rim. Nose: fine lees, dried herbs, ripe fruit, faded flowers. Palate: flavourful, fruity, elegant, complex.

Mas que Dos 2014 B
70% albariño, 15% treixadura, 15% loureiro

87

Colour: straw. Nose: medium intensity, ripe fruit, floral. Palate: correct, easy to drink.

Orballo 2014 B
100% albariño

89

Colour: bright straw, greenish rim. Nose: balanced, varietal, ripe fruit. Palate: correct, fine bitter notes, easy to drink.

Viña Ludy 2014 B
100% albariño

89

Colour: bright straw. Nose: white flowers, dried herbs, ripe fruit. Palate: flavourful, fruity, easy to drink.

BODEGAS MAR DE FRADES

Lg. Arosa, 16 - Finca Valiñas
36637 Meis (Pontevedra)
☎: +34 986 680 911
Fax: +34 986 680 926
info@mardefrades.es
www.mardefrades.es

Finca Valiñas "crianza sobre lías" 2013 B
albariño

91

Colour: bright straw. Nose: white flowers, dried herbs, ripe fruit, fine lees. Palate: flavourful, fruity.

Mar de Frades 2014 B
albariño

88

Colour: bright yellow. Nose: ripe fruit, wild herbs, floral. Palate: flavourful, balsamic, correct.

Mar de Frades s/c BN
albariño

86

BODEGAS MARQUÉS DE VIZHOJA

Finca La Moreira s/n
36438 Cequeliños - Arbo (Pontevedra)
☎: +34 986 665 825
Fax: +34 986 665 960
marquesdevizhoja@marquesdevizhoja.com
www.marquesdevizhoja.com

Señor da Folla Verde 2014 B
70% albariño, 15% loureiro, 15% treixadura

88

Colour: bright straw. Nose: white flowers, fresh fruit, fragrant herbs, expressive. Palate: flavourful, fruity, good acidity, balanced.

Torre La Moreira 2014 B
100% albariño

89

Colour: bright straw. Nose: white flowers, fresh fruit, fragrant herbs. Palate: flavourful, fruity, good acidity, balanced.

BODEGAS MARTÍN CÓDAX

Burgáns, 91
36633 Vilariño-Cambados (Pontevedra)
☎: +34 986 526 040
Fax: +34 986 526 901
comercial@martincodax.com
www.martincodax.com

Burgáns 2014 B
100% albariño

89

Colour: bright yellow. Nose: expressive, dried herbs, ripe fruit, spicy. Palate: flavourful, fruity, good acidity, balanced.

Marieta Semidulce 2014 B
100% albariño

86

Martín Códax 2014 B
100% albariño

88

Colour: bright yellow. Nose: dried herbs, ripe fruit, spicy. Palate: flavourful, fruity, balanced.

Martín Códax Gallaecia 2011 B
100% albariño

92

Colour: yellow. Nose: expressive, complex, candied fruit, faded flowers, scrubland. Palate: rich, full, ripe fruit, long, spicy.

Martin Codax Lías 2012 B
100% albariño

91

Colour: bright straw, greenish rim. Nose: fresh fruit, citrus fruit, floral, balanced, fine lees. Palate: flavourful, rich, long.

Martín Códax Vindel 2012 B
100% albariño

93

Colour: bright straw. Nose: white flowers, fine lees, dried herbs, ripe fruit, candied fruit, citrus fruit. Palate: flavourful, fruity, good acidity, elegant.

Organistrum 2012 B
100% albariño

91

Colour: bright straw. Nose: white flowers, fine lees, dried herbs. Palate: flavourful, fruity, good acidity, round, long.

BODEGAS PABLO PADÍN

Ameiro, 24 - Dena
36967 Meaño (Pontevedra)
☎: +34 986 743 231
Fax: +34 986 745 791
info@pablopadin.com
www.pablopadin.com

Albariño Segrel 2014 B
albariño

88

Colour: bright straw. Nose: white flowers, balanced, medium intensity. Palate: light-bodied, easy to drink, good finish.

Feitizo da Noite ESP
albariño

88

Colour: bright straw. Nose: fresh, floral, fragrant herbs. Palate: correct, fine bitter notes, good acidity.

Segrel Ámbar 2013 B
100% albariño

89

Colour: bright straw, greenish rim. Nose: ripe fruit, balanced, expressive, varietal. Palate: correct, easy to drink.

BODEGAS SANTIAGO ROMA

36636 Ribadumia (Pontevedra)
☎: +34 679 469 218
bodega@santiagoroma.com
www.santiagoroma.com

Colleita de Martis Albariño 2014 B
100% albariño

90

Colour: bright straw. Nose: white flowers, fresh fruit, fragrant herbs. Palate: flavourful, fruity, good acidity, balanced, elegant.

Santiago Roma Albariño 2014 B
100% albariño

89

Colour: bright yellow. Nose: dried herbs, ripe fruit, spicy. Palate: flavourful, fruity, good finish.

Santiago Roma Albariño Selección 2014 B
100% albariño

90

Colour: bright straw. Nose: white flowers, dried herbs, ripe fruit, citrus fruit. Palate: flavourful, fruity, good acidity, elegant.

BODEGAS SEÑORÍO DE VALEI

La Granja, 65
36494 Arbo (Pontevedra)
☎: +34 698 146 950
Fax: +34 986 665 390
info@senoriodevalei.com
www.senoriodevalei.com

Estela 2014 B
100% albariño

88

Colour: bright straw. Nose: white flowers, fine lees, dried herbs. Palate: flavourful, fruity, good acidity.

Frailes do Mar 2014 B
100% albariño

89

Colour: bright straw. Nose: white flowers, fresh fruit, fragrant herbs. Palate: flavourful, fruity, good acidity.

Gran Muiño 2013 B
100% albariño

85

Oro Valei 2014 B
100% albariño

86

Pazo de Valei 2014 B
100% albariño

90

Colour: bright straw. Nose: fresh fruit, citrus fruit, floral, balanced, varietal. Palate: correct, fine bitter notes, long.

Señorío de Valei 2014 B
100% albariño

90

Colour: bright straw. Nose: varietal, expressive, medium intensity, floral. Palate: easy to drink, fruity, good acidity, balanced.

BODEGAS TERRAS GAUDA

Ctra. Tui - A Guarda, Km. 55
36760 O´Rosal (Pontevedra)
☎: +34 986 621 001
Fax: +34 986 621 084
terrasgauda@terrasgauda.com
www.terrasgauda.com

Abadía de San Campio 2014 B
100% albariño

86

La Mar 2013 B
85% caiño blanco, 8% albariño, 7% loureiro

92

Colour: bright yellow. Nose: ripe fruit, dried herbs, dry stone, floral, expressive. Palate: powerful, flavourful, long, balsamic, balanced.

Terras Gauda 2014 B
70% albariño, 18% loureiro, 12% caiño

91

Colour: bright straw. Nose: white flowers, dried herbs, ripe fruit, citrus fruit. Palate: flavourful, fruity, good acidity.

Terras Gauda Etiqueta Negra 2013 BFB
70% albariño, 18% caiño, 12% loureiro

92

Colour: bright yellow. Nose: expressive, dried herbs, ripe fruit, spicy. Palate: flavourful, fruity, good acidity, balanced.

BODEGAS TORRES

Miguel Torres i Carbó, 6
08720 Vilafranca del Penedès
(Barcelona)
☎: +34 938 177 400
Fax: +34 938 177 444
mailadmin@torres.es
www.torres.com

Pazo das Bruxas 2014 B
albariño

88

Colour: bright straw. Nose: floral, varietal, balanced. Palate: correct, good finish, slightly acidic.

BODEGAS VICENTE GANDÍA

Ctra. Cheste a Godelleta, s/n
46370 Chiva (Valencia)
☎: +34 962 524 242
Fax: +34 962 524 243
info@vicentegandia.com
www.vicentegandia.es

Con un Par Albariño 2014 B
100% albariño

88

Colour: bright straw. Nose: white flowers, fresh fruit, fragrant herbs. Palate: flavourful, fruity, slightly acidic.

Galizues 2014 B
100% albariño

86

BODEGAS VIONTA S.L.

Lugar de Axis s/n - Simes
36968 Meaño (Pontevedra)
☎: +34 986 747 566
Fax: +34 986 747 621
vionta@vionta.com
www.freixenet.es

Agnusdei Albariño 2014 B
100% albariño

87

Colour: bright straw. Nose: white flowers, ripe fruit. Palate: good acidity, easy to drink.

Vionta 2014 B
100% albariño

88

Colour: bright yellow. Nose: ripe fruit, varietal. Palate: flavourful, easy to drink, correct.

You & Me 2014 B
100% albariño

87

Colour: bright straw, greenish rim. Nose: medium intensity, ripe fruit, floral. Palate: correct, easy to drink, good finish.

BODEGAS Y VIÑEDOS DON OLEGARIO

Lg. Refoxos, s/n - Corvillón
36634 Cambados (Pontevedra)
☎: +34 986 520 886
info@donolegario.com
www.donolegario.com

Don Olegario Albariño 2014 B
100% albariño

90

Colour: bright straw. Nose: fresh fruit, white flowers, citrus fruit. Palate: flavourful, fruity, good acidity, balanced, fine bitter notes.

Mi Mamá me Mima 2014 B
100% albariño

85

BOUZA DE CARRIL

Avda. Caponiñas, 14 - Barrantes
36636 Ribadumia (Pontevedra)
☎: +34 600 020 627
Fax: +34 986 710 471
bodega@bouzacarril.com
www.bouzadecarril.com

Bouza de Carril Albariño 2014 B
albariño

85

BOUZA DO REI

Lugar de Puxafeita, s/n
36636 Ribadumia (Pontevedra)
☎: +34 986 710 257
Fax: +34 986 718 393
bouzadorei@bouzadorei.com
www.bouzadorei.com

Albariño Bouza Do Rei 2014 B

100% albariño

88

Colour: bright straw. Nose: floral, ripe fruit, dried herbs. Palate: powerful, flavourful, easy to drink.

Albariño Bouza do Rei Gran Selección 2014 B

100% albariño

90

Colour: bright yellow. Nose: expressive, balanced, floral, ripe fruit. Palate: balanced, fine bitter notes, fruity.

Albariño Castel de Bouza 2014 B

100% albariño

89

Colour: bright straw. Nose: fresh fruit, expressive, floral. Palate: flavourful, fruity, good acidity, balanced.

Albariño Gran Lagar de Bouza 2014 B

100% albariño

87

Colour: bright straw. Nose: white flowers, fresh fruit, fragrant herbs. Palate: flavourful, fruity, balanced, easy to drink.

Albariño Pazo da Torre 2014 B

100% albariño

86

CARMEN ALVAREZ OUBIÑA

Cristimil 5 Padrenda
36968 Meaño (Pontevedra)
☎: +34 616 643 559
altosdecristimil@gmail.com
www.altosdecristimil.com

Altos de Cristimil 2014 B

100% albariño

86

Dominio de Gar 2014 B

100% albariño

86

CASA DO SOL

Laraño, 8 San Julián de Sales
15885 Vedra (La Coruña)
☎: +34 981 511 634
comercial@casadosol.es
www.casadosol.es

Casa Do Sol 2013 B

albariño

90

Colour: bright yellow. Nose: dried herbs, ripe fruit. Palate: flavourful, fruity, good acidity.

CASA ROJO

Sánchez Picazo, 53
30332 Balsapintada (Murcia)
☎: +34 968 151 520
Fax: +34 968 151 539
info@casarojo.com
www.casarojo.com

La Marimorena 2014 B

albariño

88

Colour: bright straw. Nose: scrubland, ripe fruit, powerfull. Palate: flavourful, ripe fruit.

CHAN DE ROSAS

Pza. Clemencio Fernández
Pulido, Portal 2 2ºF
36630 Cambados (Pontevedra)
☎: +34 633 538 802
info@chanderosas.com
www.chanderosas.com

Chan de Rosas Clásico 2014 B

albariño

89

Colour: bright straw. Nose: white flowers, fresh fruit, fragrant herbs, expressive. Palate: flavourful, fruity, good acidity, balanced.

Chan de Rosas Cuvée Especial 2014 B

albariño

91

Colour: bright straw. Nose: white flowers, dried herbs, ripe fruit, citrus fruit. Palate: flavourful, fruity, good acidity, elegant, long.

EL ESCOCÉS VOLANTE

Barrio La Rosa Bajo, 16
50300 Calatayud (Zaragoza)
☎: +34 637 511 133
info@escocesvolante.es
www.escocesvolante.es

The Cup and Rings Albariño sobre Lías 2012 B

100% albariño

91

Colour: bright straw. Nose: fine lees, dried herbs, mineral. Palate: flavourful, fruity, good acidity, round.

ELADIO PIÑEIRO - FRORE DE CARME

Sobrán, 38
36611 Vilagarcía de Arousa
(Pontevedra)
☎: +34 986 501 218
Fax: +34 986 501 218
eladiopineiro@froredecarme.es
www.eladiopineiro.es

Envidiacochina 2013 B

100% albariño

89

Colour: bright yellow. Nose: dried herbs, mineral, ripe fruit, faded flowers. Palate: flavourful, fruity, round.

Frore de Carme 2010 B

100% albariño

92

Colour: bright straw. Nose: dried herbs, faded flowers, ripe fruit. Palate: ripe fruit, long, flavourful, complex, rich, balanced.

EULOGIO GONDAR GALIÑANES

Pereira, 6 B
36968 Meaño (Pontevedra)
☎: +34 986 747 241
Fax: +34 986 747 742
albarino@lagardecandes.com
www.lagardecandes.com

Lagar de Candes Albariño 2014 B

100% albariño

87

Colour: bright yellow. Nose: dried herbs, ripe fruit, spicy. Palate: flavourful, fruity, thin.

Quinta Vide 2014 B

100% albariño

86

FRANCK MASSARD

Rambla Arnau de Vilanova, 6
08800 Vilanova i La Geltrú (Barcelona)
☎: +34 938 956 541
Fax: +34 938 956 541
info@epicure-wines.com
www.epicure-wines.com

Alma 2013 B

100% albariño

89

Colour: bright straw. Nose: white flowers, fine lees, dried herbs. Palate: flavourful, fruity, good acidity, round.

GONZALO CELAYETA WINES

Barrandón, 6
31390 Olite (Navarra)
☎: +34 620 208 817
info@gonzalocelayetawines.com
www.gonzalocelayetawines.com

Saida 1 2012 B

albariño

86

GRUPO GALLEGO VALEI

La Granja, 65
36494 Arbo (Pontevedra)
☎: +34 698 146 950
Fax: +34 986 665 390
info@grupovalei.com
www.grupovalei.com

Camino de Cabras 2014 B

100% albariño

87

Colour: bright yellow. Nose: medium intensity, ripe fruit, dried flowers. Palate: correct, easy to drink, good acidity.

KATAME

Berlin, 5 1ºC
28850 Torrejón de Ardoz (Madrid)
☎: +34 916 749 427
katame@katamesl.com

Pekado Mortal 2013 B

90

Colour: bright yellow. Nose: dried herbs, ripe fruit, citrus fruit. Palate: flavourful, fruity, good acidity.

LA MALETA HAND MADE FINE WINES

Plaza de Eladio Rodríguez, 19
32420 San Clodio (Ourense)
☎: +34 988 614 234
hola@lamaletawines.com
lamaletawines.com

El Príncipe y el Birrete 2014 B
albariño

87

Colour: bright yellow. Nose: dried herbs, ripe fruit, spicy. Palate: flavourful, fruity, fine bitter notes.

El Rubio Infante 2014 B
albariño

86

LAGAR DA CONDESA

Lugar de Maran s/n Arcos da Condesa
36650 Caldas de Reis (Pontevedra)
☎: +34 968 435 022
Fax: +34 968 716 051
info@orowines.com
www.orowines.com

Lagar da Condesa 2014 B
100% albariño

90

Colour: bright straw. Nose: white flowers, fresh fruit, fragrant herbs. Palate: flavourful, fruity, good acidity, balanced.

LAGAR DE BESADA

Pazo, 11 Xil
36968 Meaño (Pontevedra)
☎: +34 986 747 473
Fax: +34 986 747 826
info@lagardebesada.com
www.lagardebesada.com

Baladiña 2013 B
100% albariño

88

Colour: bright yellow. Nose: dried flowers, citrus fruit, dried herbs. Palate: balanced, easy to drink, good finish.

Lagar de Besada 2014 B
100% albariño

85

LAGAR DE CERVERA

Estrada de Loureza, 86
36770 O Rosal (Pontevedra)
☎: +34 986 625 875
Fax: +34 986 625 011
lagar@riojalta.com
www.lagardecervera.com

Lagar de Cervera 2014 B
albariño

90

Colour: bright straw. Nose: white flowers, citrus fruit, ripe fruit, mineral. Palate: flavourful, fruity, good acidity, balanced.

LAGAR DE COSTA

Sartaxes, 8 - Castrelo
36639 Cambados (Pontevedra)
☎: +34 986 543 526
Fax: +34 669 086 569
contacto@lagardecosta.com
www.lagardecosta.com

Lagar de Costa 2014 B
100% albariño

86

LUAR DE MINARELLOS

Plaza de Matute 12
28012 (Madrid)
☎: +34 609 079 980
info@miravinos.es
www.miravinos.es

Contante 2014 B
albariño

88

Colour: bright straw. Nose: white flowers, fresh fruit, fragrant herbs. Palate: flavourful, fruity, good acidity.

M. CONSTANTINA SOTELO

Castriño Castrelo
36639 Cambados (Pontevedra)
☎: +34 639 835 073
adegasotelo@yahoo.es

Rosalía 2014 B
albariño

90

Colour: bright straw. Nose: white flowers, fresh fruit, fragrant herbs, expressive. Palate: flavourful, fruity, balanced.

Rosalía de Castro 2014 B
albariño

89

Colour: bright straw. Nose: white flowers, fresh fruit, fragrant herbs. Palate: flavourful, fruity, slightly acidic.

MAIOR DE MENDOZA

Rúa de Xiabre, 58
36600 Villagarcía de Arosa (Pontevedra)
☎: +34 986 508 896
Fax: +34 986 507 924
maiordemendoza@hotmail.es
www.maiordemendoza.com

Fulget 2014 B
100% albariño

85

Maior de Mendoza 3 Crianzas 2012 B
100% albariño

91

Colour: bright straw. Nose: white flowers, fine lees, dried herbs, ripe fruit. Palate: flavourful, fruity, good acidity, elegant.

Maior de Mendoza Maceración Carbónica 2014 B
100% albariño

85

Maior de Mendoza sobre Lías 2014 B
100% albariño

89

Colour: bright straw. Nose: white flowers, fresh fruit, fragrant herbs. Palate: good acidity, balanced.

MAR DE ENVERO

Lugar de Iglesia 1, Tremoedo
36620 Vilanova de Arousa (Pontevedra)
☎: +34 981 566 329
Fax: +34 981 569 552
bodega@mardeenvero.es
www.mardeenvero.es

Mar de Envero 2013 B
albariño

90

Colour: bright yellow. Nose: dried herbs, ripe fruit, spicy. Palate: flavourful, fruity, good acidity, balanced, fine bitter notes.

Troupe 2014 B
albariño

90

Colour: bright yellow. Nose: white flowers, dried herbs, ripe fruit, citrus fruit. Palate: flavourful, fruity, good acidity, elegant.

MARÍA VICTORIA DOVALO MÉNDEZ

Villarreis, 21 - Dena
36967 Meaño (Pontevedra)
☎: +34 941 454 050
Fax: +34 941 454 529
bodega@bodegasriojanas.com
www.bodegasriojanas.com

Veiga Naúm 2014 B
100% albariño

85

NOTAS FRUTALES DE ALBARIÑO

Villar, Garabelos, s/n
36429 Crecente (Pontevedra)
☎: +34 609 065 858
notasfrutales@gmail.com
www.fincagarabelos.es

Finca Garabelos 2013 B
100% albariño

88

Colour: bright straw, greenish rim. Nose: balanced, fresh fruit, varietal. Palate: fresh, easy to drink, good acidity.

La Trucha 2013 B
100% albariño

88

Colour: bright straw. Nose: ripe fruit, candied fruit, dried herbs, faded flowers. Palate: powerful, flavourful, ripe fruit.

PAGOS DEL REY

Autovía del Sur, KM 199
13300 Valdepeñas (Ciudad Real)
☎: +34 926 322 400
Fax: +34 926 322 417
nfernandez@felixsolisavantis.com
www.felixsolisavantis.com

Centola 2014 B
albariño

86

Pulpo 2014 B
albariño

89

Colour: bright yellow, greenish rim. Nose: ripe fruit, fine lees, balanced. Palate: correct, balanced, fine bitter notes.

PALACIOS VINOTECA – VINOS ORIGINALES

Ctra. de Nalda a Viguera, 46
26190 Nalda (La Rioja)
☎: +34 941 447 207
info@palaciosvinoteca.com
www.palaciosvinoteca.com

A Calma 2014 B
100% albariño

90

Colour: bright straw. Nose: white flowers, fresh fruit, fragrant herbs, expressive. Palate: flavourful, fruity, spicy.

Sete Bois 2014 B
100% albariño

89

Colour: bright straw. Nose: white flowers, fresh fruit, fragrant herbs. Palate: flavourful, fruity, good acidity.

PAZO AS BARREIRAS

El Casal, 2
36459 Salvaterra do Miño (Pontevedra)
☎: +34 986 252 411
Fax: +34 986 252 788
info@bodegasvillanueva.com
www.bodegasvillanueva.com

Villanueva 2014 B
albariño

87

Colour: bright straw. Nose: fresh fruit, medium intensity, dried flowers, citrus fruit. Palate: flavourful, easy to drink.

PAZO BAIÓN

Abelleira 4, 5, 6 - Baión
36614 Vilanova de Arousa (Pontevedra)
☎: +34 986 543 535
Fax: +34 986 524 251
inf@pazobaion.com
www.pazobaion.com

Pazo Baión 2013 B
100% albariño

92

Colour: bright straw. Nose: white flowers, fine lees, dried herbs, elegant. Palate: flavourful, fruity, good acidity, round.

PAZO DE BARRANTES

Finca Pazo de Barrantes
36636 Barrantes - Ribadumia
(Pontevedra)
☎: +34 986 718 211
Fax: +34 986 710 424
bodega@pazodebarrantes.com
www.pazodebarrantes.com

La Comtesse 2012 BFB
100% albariño

94

Colour: bright straw. Nose: fine lees, dried herbs, mineral, candied fruit. Palate: flavourful, fruity, good acidity, round.

Pazo de Barrantes Albariño 2014 B
100% albariño

91

Colour: bright straw. Nose: white flowers, fresh fruit, fragrant herbs. Palate: flavourful, fruity, good acidity.

PAZO DE SAN MAURO

Pombal, 3 - Lugar de Porto
36458 Salvaterra de Miño (Pontevedra)
☎: +34 986 658 285
Fax: +34 986 664 208
info@pazosanmauro.com
www.pazosanmauro.com

Pazo San Mauro 2014 B
albariño

89

Colour: bright straw. Nose: ripe fruit, wild herbs, floral. Palate: balanced, good finish.

Sanamaro 2012 B
albariño, loureiro

89

Colour: bright yellow. Nose: dried herbs, ripe fruit, spicy. Palate: flavourful, fruity, unctuous.

PAZO DE SEÑORANS

Vilanoviña, s/n
36616 Meis (Pontevedra)
☎: +34 986 715 373
Fax: +34 986 715 569
info@pazodesenorans.com
www.pazodesenorans.com

Pazo Señorans 2014 B
100% albariño

91

Colour: bright straw, greenish rim. Nose: white flowers, fresh fruit, expressive. Palate: flavourful, fruity, good acidity, balanced.

Pazo Señorans Colección 2011 B
100% albariño

94

Colour: bright straw. Nose: white flowers, fine lees, dried herbs, mineral, varietal. Palate: flavourful, fruity, good acidity, round.

PODIUM

Pazo Señorans Selección de Añada 2007 B
100% albariño

96

Colour: bright yellow. Nose: complex, expressive, faded flowers, ripe fruit. Palate: rich, flavourful, fine bitter notes, long, balanced.

PAZO DE VILLAREI

Ctra. de Tui a la Guardia, 45
36760 Localidad: As Eiras, O Rosal
Provincia: Pontevedra (Pontevedra)
☎: +34 986 710 827
Fax: +34 986 710 827
info@hgabodegas.com
www.pazodevillarei.com

Abadía do Seixo 2014 B

albariño

88

Colour: bright yellow. Nose: ripe fruit, faded flowers, wild herbs. Palate: powerful, flavourful.

Pazo de Villarei 2014 B

albariño

89

Colour: bright yellow. Nose: dried herbs, ripe fruit, floral. Palate: flavourful, fruity, fine bitter notes.

Villarei 2014 B

albariño

92

Colour: bright straw. Nose: white flowers, fine lees, dried herbs, ripe fruit, citrus fruit. Palate: flavourful, fruity, good acidity, elegant.

PAZO PEGULLAL

Pegullal, s/n
36470 Salceda de Caselas (Pontevedra)
☎: +34 986 246 227
Fax: +34 986 240 268
info@pazopegullal.com
www.pazopegullal.com

Pazo Pegullal 2013 B

100% albariño

90

Colour: bright yellow. Nose: white flowers, fresh fruit, fragrant herbs, complex. Palate: flavourful, fruity, long.

Pazo Pegullal 2014 B

100% albariño

88

Colour: bright yellow. Nose: expressive, ripe fruit, fine lees. Palate: fruity, good acidity, balanced, good finish.

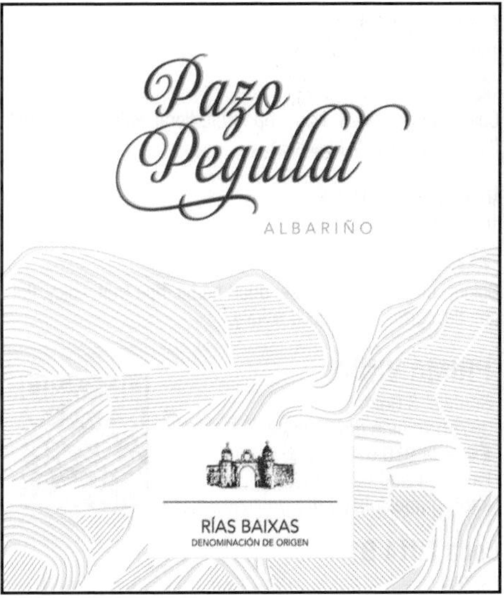

PAZO PONDAL

Coto, s/n - Cabeiras
36436 Arbo (Pontevedra)
☎: +34 986 665 551
Fax: +34 986 665 949
mktg@pazopondal.com
www.pazopondal.com

Leira Pondal 2014 B

albariño

88

Colour: bright straw. Nose: citrus fruit, white flowers. Palate: correct, fine bitter notes, easy to drink.

Pazo Pondal Albariño 2014 B

100% albariño

88

Colour: straw. Nose: medium intensity, ripe fruit, floral, fragrant herbs. Palate: correct, easy to drink, fine bitter notes.

PONTECABALEIROS

As Laxas, 16
36430 Arbo (Pontevedra)
☎: +34 986 665 444
Fax: +34 986 665 554
info@pontecabaleiros.com
www.pontecabaleiros.com

Alvinte 2014 B

100% albariño

87

Colour: bright straw. Nose: white flowers, medium intensity, citrus fruit. Palate: fruity, easy to drink.

Ferrum 2014 B

100% albariño

87

Colour: bright straw. Nose: ripe fruit, floral. Palate: flavourful, fruity, good acidity, balanced.

Valdocea 2014 B

100% albariño

88

Colour: bright yellow. Nose: dried herbs, ripe fruit, spicy. Palate: flavourful, fruity, good acidity.

PRIMA VINIA

Soutelo, 3 Goián
36750 Tomiño (Pontevedra)
☎: +34 986 620 137
Fax: +34 986 620 071
info@primavinia.com

coda 2014 B

albariño

88

Colour: bright straw. Nose: white flowers, fresh fruit, floral. Palate: flavourful, fruity, good acidity, balanced.

Gaudila 2011 B

100% albariño

92

Colour: bright yellow. Nose: white flowers, fine lees, balanced. Palate: flavourful, fruity, good acidity, round, rich.

Leira Vella 2014 B

albariño

89

Colour: bright straw. Nose: balanced, medium intensity, ripe fruit, floral. Palate: flavourful, correct, fine bitter notes.

QUINTA COUSELO

Barrio de Couselo, 13
36770 O'Rosal (Pontevedra)
☎: +34 986 625 051
Fax: +34 986 626 267
quintacouselo@quintacouselo.com
www.quintacouselo.com

Quinta de Couselo 2014 B

90% albariño, 5% caiño blanco, 5% loureiro

91 ♣

Colour: bright straw. Nose: white flowers, dried herbs, candied fruit, citrus fruit. Palate: flavourful, fruity, good acidity, elegant.

Quinta de Couselo Selección 2011 B

100% albariño

93

Colour: bright straw. Nose: white flowers, fine lees, dried herbs, mineral, ripe fruit. Palate: flavourful, fruity, good acidity, round.

Turonia 2014 B

100% albariño

90

Colour: bright yellow. Nose: expressive, dried herbs, ripe fruit, spicy, citrus fruit. Palate: flavourful, fruity, balanced.

QUINTA DE LA ERRE

Lugar de Eiras s/n
36778 Eiras O'Rosal (Pontevedra)
☎: +34 986 620 292
Fax: +34 986 620 292
labodega@quintadelaerre.com
www.quintadelaerre.com

Quinta de la Erre 2014 B

albariño

88

Colour: bright yellow. Nose: dried herbs, ripe fruit, spicy. Palate: flavourful, fruity.

Quinta de la Erre Rosal Selección 2013 B Barrica

albariño, loureiro, caiño

91

Colour: bright yellow. Nose: dried herbs, ripe fruit, spicy. Palate: flavourful, fruity, good acidity, balanced, rich.

RECTORAL DO UMIA

Rúa do Pan 9, Polig. Ind. de Ribadumia
36636 Ribadumia (Pontevedra)
☎: +34 988 384 200
Fax: +34 988 384 068
vinos@bodegasgallegas.com
www.bodegasgallegas.com

Abellio 2014 B
albariño

84

Miudiño 2014 B
albariño

87

Colour: straw, greenish rim. Nose: medium intensity, ripe fruit, floral. Palate: correct, easy to drink.

Rectoral do Umia 2014 B
albariño

87

Colour: bright yellow. Nose: expressive, dried herbs, ripe fruit. Palate: flavourful, fruity, good acidity.

RODRÍGUEZ SANZO

Manuel Azaña, 11
47014 (Valladolid)
☎: +34 983 150 150
Fax: +34 983 150 151
comunicacion@valsanzo.com
www.rodriguezsanzo.com

María Sanzo 2014 B
100% albariño

89

Colour: bright straw. Nose: white flowers, expressive, mineral, fresh fruit. Palate: flavourful, fruity, good acidity.

SANTIAGO RUIZ

Rua do Vinicultor Santiago Ruiz
36760 San Miguel de Tabagón -
O Rosal (Pontevedra)
☎: +34 986 614 083
Fax: +34 986 614 142
info@bodegasantiagoruiz.com
www.bodegasantiagoruiz.com

Rosa Ruiz 2014 B
100% albariño

90

Colour: bright straw. Nose: white flowers, fresh fruit, fragrant herbs, expressive. Palate: flavourful, fruity, good acidity, balanced.

Santiago Ruiz 2014 B
76% albariño, 10% loureiro, 6% godello, 4% caiño blanco, 4% treixadura

89

Colour: bright straw. Nose: fresh, medium intensity, floral. Palate: correct, fine bitter notes, good finish.

SEÑORÍO DE RUBIÓS

Bouza do Rato, s/n - Rubiós
36449 As Neves (Pontevedra)
☎: +34 986 667 212
Fax: +34 986 648 279
info@srubios.com
www.srubios.com

Liñar de Vides Albariño 2014 B
100% albariño

89

Colour: pale. Nose: dried herbs, ripe fruit, floral. Palate: fresh, fruity, easy to drink.

Manuel D'Amaro Pedral 2011 T
100% pedral

89

Colour: very deep cherry, garnet rim. Nose: complex, mineral, balsamic herbs, ripe fruit. Palate: full, flavourful, correct.

Manuel D'Amaro Sousón 2013 T
100% sousón

88

Colour: cherry, garnet rim. Nose: ripe fruit, wild herbs, earthy notes, spicy, balsamic herbs. Palate: balanced, flavourful, long, balsamic.

Señorío de Rubiós Albariño 2014 B
100% albariño

90

Colour: bright straw. Nose: white flowers, fresh fruit, fragrant herbs, expressive. Palate: flavourful, fruity, good acidity, balanced.

Señorío de Rubiós Condado Blanco BN
treixadura, albariño, loureiro, godello, torrontés

90

Colour: bright golden. Nose: fine lees, fragrant herbs, complex, toasty. Palate: powerful, flavourful, good acidity, fine bead, fine bitter notes.

Señorío de Rubiós Condado Blanco BR
treixadura, albariño, loureiro, godello, torrontés

89

Colour: bright straw. Nose: fresh fruit, dried herbs, fine lees, floral. Palate: fresh, fruity, flavourful, good acidity.

Señorío de Rubiós Condado do Tea Blanco 2014 B
treixadura, albariño, loureiro, godello, torrontés

89

Colour: bright straw. Nose: white flowers, fine lees, dried herbs, ripe fruit, citrus fruit. Palate: flavourful, fruity, good acidity.

Señorío de Rubiós Condado do Tea Blanco Barrica 2010 B Roble
treixadura, albariño, loureiro, godello, torrontés

92

Colour: bright yellow. Nose: balanced, complex, characterful, spicy, dried flowers. Palate: spicy, ripe fruit, long.

Señorío de Rubiós Condado Tinto 2013 T
sousón, espadeiro, caiño, mencía, pedral, loureiro tinto

81

Señorío de Rubiós Mencía 2013 T
100% mencía

84

Señorío de Rubiós Sousón 2013 T
100% sousón

87

Colour: cherry, purple rim. Nose: floral, balsamic herbs, grassy, ripe fruit. Palate: powerful, fresh, fruity.

SEÑORÍO DE SOBRAL

Lg. Porto - Finca Sobral
36458 Salvaterra do Miño (Pontevedra)
☎: +34 986 415 144
Fax: +34 986 421 744
info@ssobral.net
www.ssobral.net

Señorío de Sobral 2014 B

85

SPANISH STORY

Espronceda, 27 1ºD
28003 Madrid (Madrid)
☎: +34 915 356 184
Fax: +34 915 363 796
info@spanish-story.com
www.spanish-story.com

Spanish Story Albariño Black Pulpo 2014 B
100% albariño

87

Colour: bright yellow. Nose: dried herbs, ripe fruit, spicy. Palate: flavourful, fruity, good acidity.

SUCESORES DE BENITO SANTOS

Currás, 46 Caleiro
36629 Vilanova de Arousa (Pontevedra)
☎: +34 986 554 435
bodega@benitosantos.com
www.benitosantos.com

Benito Santos Igrexario de Saiar 2014 B
100% albariño

89

Colour: bright straw. Nose: dried herbs, floral, mineral, ripe fruit. Palate: correct, fresh, fruity.

Terra de Cálago 2014 B
100% albariño

87

Colour: straw. Nose: medium intensity, ripe fruit, floral. Palate: correct, easy to drink.

Viñedo de Bemil 2010 B
100% albariño

87

Colour: bright straw, greenish rim. Nose: medium intensity, dried flowers. Palate: flavourful, ripe fruit, long.

TERRA DE ASOREI

36630 Cambados (Pontevedra)
☎: +34 608 117 451
info@terradeasorei.com
www.terradeasorei.com

Nai e Señora 2014 B

100% albariño

87

Colour: bright straw. Nose: floral, varietal, medium intensity. Palate: correct, easy to drink, good finish.

Pazo Torrado 2014 B

100% albariño

86

Terra de Asorei sobre Lías 2014 B

100% albariño

88

Colour: bright yellow. Nose: dried herbs, ripe fruit, spicy. Palate: flavourful, fruity, fine bitter notes.

TOMADA DE CASTRO

Travesía do Freixo, 3
36636 Ribadumia (Pontevedra)
☎: +34 986 710 550
info@tomadadecastro.com
www.tomadadecastro.com

Flor de Verano 2014 B

100% albariño

85

Gran Ribad 2014 B

100% albariño

87

Colour: bright straw. Nose: expressive, dried herbs, ripe fruit, spicy. Palate: flavourful, fruity, good acidity.

Ría de Arosa 2014 B

100% albariño

85

Tomada de Castro 2014 B

100% albariño

88

Colour: bright straw. Nose: white flowers, dried herbs, ripe fruit. Palate: flavourful, fruity, good acidity.

UVAS FELICES

Agullers, 7
08003 Barcelona (Barcelona)
☎: +34 902 327 777
www.vilaviniteca.es

El Jardín de Lucia 2014 B

89

Colour: bright straw, greenish rim. Nose: ripe fruit, floral, fine lees. Palate: correct, fine bitter notes, easy to drink, good finish.

VALDAMOR

Valdamor, 8
36967 Xil - Meaño (Pontevedra)
☎: +34 986 747 111
clientes@valdamor.es
www.valdamor.es

Namorío 2014 B

100% albariño

86

Valdamor 2014 B

100% albariño

90

Colour: bright straw. Nose: white flowers, fine lees, dried herbs. Palate: flavourful, fruity, good acidity, fine bitter notes.

Valdamor Barrica 2013 B

100% albariño

88

Colour: bright yellow. Nose: ripe fruit, powerfull, sweet spices. Palate: flavourful, spicy, long, rich, fine bitter notes.

VINIGALICIA

Ctra. Antigua Santiago, km. 3
27500 Chantada (Lugo)
☎: +34 982 454 005
Fax: +34 982 454 094
vinigalicia@vinigalicia.es
www.vinigalicia.es

Terramundi 2014 B

albariño

86

VIÑA ALMIRANTE

Peroxa, 5
36658 Portas (Pontevedra)
☎: +34 986 541 471
Fax: +34 986 541 471
info@vinaalmirante.com
www.vinaalmirante.com

Pionero Maccerato 2014 B
100% albariño

88

Colour: bright straw. Nose: citrus fruit, ripe fruit, floral. Palate: balanced, fine bitter notes.

Pionero Mundi 2014 B
100% albariño

89

Colour: straw. Nose: medium intensity, ripe fruit, floral, fragrant herbs. Palate: easy to drink, correct.

Vanidade 2014 B
100% albariño

89

Colour: bright straw. Nose: floral, ripe fruit, fragrant herbs. Palate: powerful, flavourful, good acidity.

Vicius 2014 B
100% albariño

88

Colour: yellow. Nose: ripe fruit, creamy oak, spicy. Palate: correct, long, spicy, toasty.

VIÑA CARTIN

Baceiro, 1 - Lantaño
36657 Portas (Pontevedra)
☎: +34 615 646 442
bodegas@montino.es
www.terrasdelantano.com

Terras de Lantaño 2014 B

91

Colour: bright straw. Nose: white flowers, dried herbs, citrus fruit, fruit expression. Palate: flavourful, fruity, elegant, balanced.

Viña Cartin 2014 B

88

Colour: bright yellow. Nose: dried herbs, ripe fruit, spicy. Palate: flavourful, fruity, good acidity.

VIÑA NORA

Bruñeiras, 7
36440 As Neves (Pontevedra)
☎: +34 986 667 210
sperez@avanteselecta.com
www.vinanora.com

Carqueixal Albariño 2014 B
100% albariño

85

Nora 2014 B
100% albariño

90

Colour: bright yellow. Nose: ripe fruit, white flowers, tropical fruit. Palate: flavourful, balanced, fine bitter notes.

Nora da Neve 2012 BFB
100% albariño

93

Colour: bright yellow. Nose: ripe fruit, creamy oak, spicy, dried flowers. Palate: balanced, spicy, long, good acidity, fine bitter notes.

Val de Nora 2014 B
100% albariño

88

Colour: bright yellow. Nose: ripe fruit, dried herbs, powerfull. Palate: rich, correct, ripe fruit.

VIÑEDOS SINGULARES

Cuzco, 26 - 28, Nave 8 - 9
08030 Barcelona (Barcelona)
☎: +34 934 807 041
Fax: +34 934 807 076
info@vinedossingulares.com
www.vinedossingulares.com

Luna Creciente 2014 B
albariño

89

Colour: bright yellow. Nose: balanced, ripe fruit, floral. Palate: correct, flavourful, fruity.

ZÁRATE

Bouza, 23
36638 Padrenda - Meaño (Pontevedra)
☎: +34 986 718 503
Fax: +34 986 718 549
info@zarate.es
www.albarino-zarate.com

Zárate 2014 B

90

Colour: bright straw, greenish rim. Nose: ripe fruit, balanced, expressive, floral. Palate: fruity, fine bitter notes.

Zárate El Balado 2013 B

93

Colour: bright yellow. Nose: fruit expression, citrus fruit, floral, wild herbs, expressive. Palate: round, elegant, spicy, balsamic.

Zárate El Palomar 2013 BFB

93

Colour: bright straw. Nose: white flowers, fine lees, ripe fruit, candied fruit. Palate: flavourful, fruity, good acidity, elegant.

Zárate Espadeiro Tinto 2013 T

91

Colour: deep cherry. Nose: ripe fruit, grassy, balsamic herbs. Palate: light-bodied, flavourful, balsamic.

Zárate Loureiro Tinto 2013 T

90

Colour: bright cherry. Nose: sweet spices, creamy oak, balsamic herbs, scrubland. Palate: flavourful, fruity, round tannins.

Zárate Tras da Viña 2012 B

94

Colour: bright yellow. Nose: expressive, dried herbs, ripe fruit, spicy. Palate: flavourful, fruity, good acidity, long.

DO. RIBEIRA SACRA

CONSEJO REGULADOR
Rúa do Comercio, 6-8
27400 Monforte de Lemos (Lugo)
☎ :+34 982 410 968 - Fax: +34 982 411 265
@: info@ribeirasacra.org
www.ribeirasacra.org

LOCATION:

The region extends along the banks of the rivers Miño and Sil in the south of the province of Lugo and the northern region of the province of Orense; it is made up of 17 municipal districts in this region.

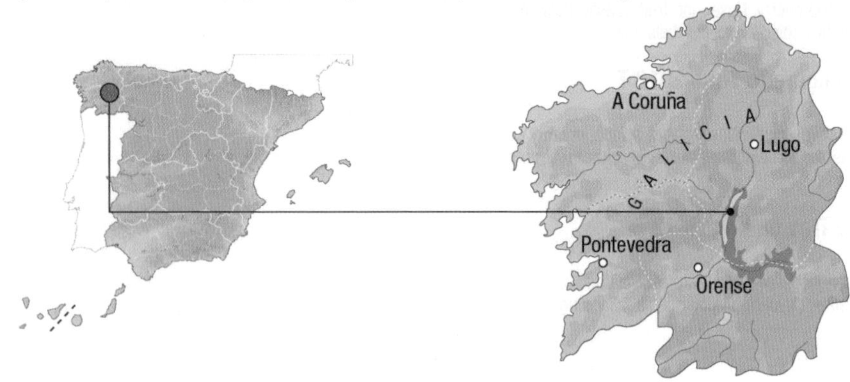

SUB-REGIONS:

Amandi, Chantada, Quiroga-Bibei, Ribeiras do Miño (in the province of Lugo) and Ribeiras do Sil.

GRAPE VARIETIES:

WHITE: Albariño, Loureira, Treixadura, Godello, Dona Blanca and Torrontés.
RED: Main: Mencía, Brancellao Merenzao, Garnacha Tintorera, Tempranillo, Sausón, Caiño Tinto and Mouratón.

FIGURES:

Vineyard surface: 1,258 – **Wine-Growers:** 2,674 – **Wineries:** 89 – **2014 Harvest rating:** Very Good – **Production 14:** 3,148,387 litres – **Market percentages:** 89% National - 11% International.

SOIL:

In general, the soil is highly acidic, although the composition varies greatly from one area to another. The vineyards are located on steep terraces and are no higher than 400 m to 500 m above sea level.

CLIMATE:

Quite variable depending on the specific area. Less rain and slightly cooler climate and greater Continental influence in the Sil valley, and greater Atlantic character in the Miño valley. Altitude, on the other hand, also has an effect, with the vineyards closer to the rivers and with a more favourable orientation (south-southeast) being slightly warmer.

VINTAGE RATING

PEÑÍNGUIDE

2010	2011	2012	2013	2014
VERY GOOD	VERY GOOD	EXCELLENT	VERY GOOD	VERY GOOD

ADEGA CRUCEIRO

Vilachá de Doade, 140
27424 (Lugo)
☎: +34 982 152 285
adegacruceiro@hotmail.com
www.adegacruceiro.es

Cruceiro 2014 T
mencía, merenzao

89

Colour: cherry, purple rim. Nose: expressive, fresh fruit, red berry notes, floral. Palate: flavourful, fruity, good acidity.

Cruceiro Rexio 2011 T
mencía, caiño, albarello

89

Colour: very deep cherry. Nose: ripe fruit, fruit preserve, cocoa bean. Palate: flavourful, balanced, balsamic.

ADEGA DO MOLLÓN

Casanova-Mollón, Viñoás
32448 Nogueira de Ramuín (Ourense)
☎: +34 988 222 272
pombares@mundo-r.com
www.pombares.com

Pombares Gloria 2014 B
godello, albariño, treixadura

86

Pombares Selección 2013 T
mencía, garnacha, tempranillo

87

Colour: bright cherry. Nose: ripe fruit, sweet spices, balsamic herbs. Palate: flavourful, fruity, toasty.

ADEGA MALCAVADA

Rosende, 67
27466 Sober (Lugo)
☎: +34 699 073 420
info@malcavada.com
www.malcavada.com

Malcavada 2014 T
88% mencía, 9% tempranillo, 3% garnacha

90

Colour: bright cherry, purple rim. Nose: fresh fruit, mineral, balanced. Palate: fruity, flavourful, balsamic, long.

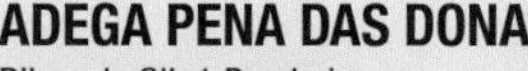

ADEGA PENA DAS DONAS

Ribas de Sil, 1 Pombeiro
27470 Pantón (Lugo)
☎: +34 988 200 045
Fax: +34 988 200 045
adega@penadasdonas.com
www.penadasdonas.com

Almalarga 2014 B
godello, treixadura

89

Colour: bright straw. Nose: white flowers, fresh fruit, fragrant herbs. Palate: flavourful, fruity, good acidity.

Almalarga 2014 B Barrica
godello, treixadura

90

Colour: bright yellow. Nose: ripe fruit, powerfull, aged wood nuances, pattiserie. Palate: flavourful, fruity, spicy, toasty, long.

Verdes Matas Mencía 2014 T
mencía

85

Verdes Matas Mencía 2014 T Barrica
mencía

87

Colour: bright cherry. Nose: ripe fruit, sweet spices, creamy oak. Palate: flavourful, fruity, toasty.

ADEGAS E VIÑEDOS VÍA ROMANA

A Ermida - Belesar
27500 Chantada (Lugo)
☎: +34 982 454 005
Fax: +34 982 454 094
info@viaromana.es
www.viaromana.es

Vía Romana Godello 2014 B
godello

87

Colour: pale. Nose: ripe fruit, citrus fruit, wild herbs. Palate: fresh, fruity, flavourful.

Vía Romana Mencía 2011 T Barrica
mencía

89

Colour: cherry, garnet rim. Nose: ripe fruit, spicy, creamy oak, complex. Palate: flavourful, toasty.

Vía Romana Mencía 2013 T
mencía

86

ADEGAS MOURE

Avda. Buenos Aires, 12
27540 Escairón (Lugo)
☎: +34 982 452 031
Fax: +34 982 452 700
abadiadacova@adegasmoure.com
www.adegasmoure.com

A Fuga 2014 T
mencía

87

Colour: bright cherry, purple rim. Nose: wild herbs, ripe fruit. Palate: fruity, easy to drink.

Abadía Da Cova 2013 T Barrica
mencía

92

Colour: bright cherry. Nose: ripe fruit, balsamic herbs. Palate: balanced, spicy, long, good structure, balsamic.

Abadía Da Cova 2014 B
85% albariño, 15% godello

89

Colour: bright straw. Nose: white flowers, fine lees, dried herbs, mineral. Palate: flavourful, fruity, good acidity.

Abadía Da Cova 2014 T Barrica
mencía

90

Colour: deep cherry, purple rim. Nose: toasty, ripe fruit, balsamic herbs. Palate: balanced, spicy, long, fine tannins.

Abadía da Cova de Autor 2013 T
mencía

94

Colour: very deep cherry, garnet rim. Nose: expressive, balsamic herbs, balanced. Palate: full, flavourful, round tannins.

Abadía da Cova de Autor 2014 T
mencía

93

Colour: bright cherry, purple rim. Nose: wild herbs, scrubland, ripe fruit, spicy, balsamic herbs. Palate: ripe fruit, long.

Abadía Da Cova Godello-Albariño 2014 B
50% albariño, 50% godello

89

Colour: bright straw. Nose: expressive, balanced, ripe fruit, dried flowers. Palate: flavourful, fruity, fine bitter notes, long.

Abadía Da Cova Mencía 2014 T
mencía

88

Colour: bright cherry, purple rim. Nose: scrubland, ripe fruit, medium intensity. Palate: correct, balsamic, easy to drink.

Cepa Vella 2014 T
mencía

86

ALGUEIRA

Francos - Doade, s/n
27460 Sober (Lugo)
☎: +34 982 410 299
Fax: +34 982 410 299
info@algueira.com
www.algueira.com

Algueira Brancellao 2013 T Roble
brancellao

93

Colour: cherry, garnet rim. Nose: mineral, expressive, spicy. Palate: flavourful, ripe fruit, long, good acidity, balanced.

Algueira Brandán Godello 2014 B
godello

87

Colour: bright yellow. Nose: dried herbs, ripe fruit, spicy. Palate: flavourful, fruity, good acidity.

Algueira Cortezada 2014 B
godello, albariño, treixadura

89

Colour: straw. Nose: medium intensity, ripe fruit, floral, fragrant herbs. Palate: correct, balsamic, easy to drink.

Algueira Escalada 2012 BFB
godello

93

Colour: bright straw. Nose: white flowers, fine lees, dried herbs, ripe fruit. Palate: flavourful, fruity, good acidity.

Algueira Fincas 2011 T Roble
50% caiño, 50% sousón

92

Colour: very deep cherry, garnet rim. Nose: expressive, complex, mineral, balsamic herbs, balanced. Palate: full, flavourful, round tannins.

Algueira Mencía 2014 T
mencía

90

Colour: cherry, purple rim. Nose: red berry notes, ripe fruit, fragrant herbs, dry stone. Palate: fresh, fruity, flavourful, balanced.

Algueira Merenzao 2013 T Roble
merenzao

93

Colour: light cherry. Nose: expressive, wild herbs, mineral. Palate: balanced, flavourful, complex. Personality.

Algueira Pizarra 2012 TC
mencía

92

Colour: cherry, garnet rim. Nose: ripe fruit, sweet spices, scrubland, varietal, mineral. Palate: balanced, round tannins.

BODEGA RIBADA

San Fiz, Paraje A Ribada
27516 Chantada (Lugo)
☎: +34 629 830 893
adegaribada@gmail.com
www.bodegaribada.com

Ribada Seleccion 2012 T
mencía

87

Colour: deep cherry, garnet rim. Nose: old leather, waxy notes, ripe fruit. Palate: flavourful, balsamic.

BODEGA VICTORINO ÁLVAREZ

Lugar Os Vazquez, s/n
32765 A Teixeira (Ourense)
☎: +34 988 207 418
adegasollio@yahoo.es

Sollio Godello 2014 B

87

Colour: bright straw. Nose: white flowers, fresh fruit, fragrant herbs. Palate: flavourful, fruity, good acidity, balanced.

Sollío Mencía 2014 T

87

Colour: deep cherry, purple rim. Nose: dried herbs, ripe fruit, spicy. Palate: fruity, flavourful.

BODEGAS ALBAMAR

O Adro, 11 - Castrelo
36639 Cambados (Pontevedra)
☎: +34 660 292 750
Fax: +34 986 520 048
info@bodegasalbamar.com

Fusco 2014 T
mencía

89

Colour: deep cherry, purple rim. Nose: creamy oak, toasty, ripe fruit, balsamic herbs. Palate: spicy, long.

Fusco Edición Especial 2013 T

90

Colour: cherry, garnet rim. Nose: candied fruit, red berry notes, scrubland. Palate: fresh, good acidity, fine bitter notes.

BODEGAS RECTORAL DE AMANDI

Amandi
32990 Sober (Lugo)
☎: +34 988 384 200
Fax: +34 988 384 068
vinos@bodegasgallegas.com
www.bodegasgallegas.com

Rectoral de Amandi 2014 T
mencía

88

Colour: cherry, purple rim. Nose: powerfull, ripe fruit, spicy. Palate: powerful, fruity, unctuous.

CASA MOREIRAS

San Martín de Siós, s/n
27430 Pantón (Lugo)
☎: +34 982 456 129
Fax: +34 982 456 129
bodega@casamoreiras.com
www.casamoreiras.com

Casa Moreiras 2014 T
85% mencía, 10% tempranillo, 5% sousón

89

Colour: cherry, purple rim. Nose: ripe fruit, balsamic herbs, wild herbs. Palate: powerful, flavourful, balsamic, good finish.

DOMINIO DE SANXIAO

Ramón del Valle Inclán, 153
27400 Monforte de Lemos (Lugo)
☎: +34 982 401 872
dominiodesanxiao@mundo-r.com

Dominio de Sanxiao 2014 T
mencía

85

DOMINIO DO BIBEI

Langullo, s/n
32781 Manzaneda (Ourense)
☎: +34 670 704 028
info@dominiodobibei.com
www.dominiodobibei.com

PODIUM

Dominio do Bibei 2011 T

95

Colour: cherry, garnet rim. Nose: red berry notes, fragrant herbs, spicy, toasty, creamy oak, mineral. Palate: powerful, flavourful, balsamic, balanced.

PODIUM

Lacima 2012 T

mencía

95

Colour: very deep cherry, garnet rim. Nose: mineral, balsamic herbs, balanced, characterful, earthy notes. Palate: full, flavourful, round tannins.

Lalama 2012 T

mencía, brancellao, mouratón, garnacha

93

Colour: bright cherry. Nose: sweet spices, creamy oak, expressive, red berry notes. Palate: flavourful, fruity, round tannins.

Lapena 2012 B

godello

94

Colour: bright straw. Nose: fine lees, dried herbs, mineral, floral. Palate: flavourful, fruity, good acidity, round.

Lapola 2013 B

godello, albariño, dona blanca

92

Colour: bright straw. Nose: white flowers, fragrant herbs. Palate: flavourful, fruity, good acidity, balanced.

DON BERNARDINO

Santa Cruz de Brosmos, 9
27460 Sober (Lugo)
☎: +34 670 882 449
info@donbernardino.com
www.donbernardino.com

Don Bernardino 2014 T

mencía

88

Colour: cherry, purple rim. Nose: powerfull, ripe fruit, spicy. Palate: powerful, fruity, unctuous.

ENVINATE

Gran Vía, 2 1ºC
27600 Sarría (Lugo)
☎: +34 682 207 160
asesoria@envinate.es
www.envinate.com

Lousas Parcela Camiño Novo 2014 T

90% mencía, 10% otras

93

Colour: ruby red. Nose: ripe fruit, wild herbs, earthy notes, spicy, balsamic herbs. Palate: balanced, flavourful, long, balsamic.

Lousas Parcela Seoane 2014 T

95% mencía, 5% otras

91

Colour: bright cherry. Nose: ripe fruit, balsamic herbs, scrubland. Palate: spicy, long, fine bitter notes, grainy tannins.

Lousas Viño de Aldeas 2014 T

95% mencía, 5% otras

93

Colour: very deep cherry, garnet rim. Nose: expressive, complex, mineral, balsamic herbs, red berry notes, balanced. Palate: full, flavourful, round tannins, balanced, elegant.

ERNESTO RODRÍGUEZ PÉREZ

Barrio Figueiroá, 13
27465 Sober (Lugo)
☎: +34 988 472 304
ernestoribadent@yahoo.es
www.adegaocancelino.tk

Viña Peón 2014 T

85% mencía, 10% garnacha tintorera, 5% tempranillo, brancellao

84

JAVIER FERNÁNDEZ GONZÁLEZ

Espasantes
27450 Pantón (Lugo)
☎: +34 670 739 470
Fax: +34 982 456 228
javier.fdez@hotmail.com
www.sainas.com

Javier Fernández 2014 T

mencía

87

Colour: deep cherry, purple rim. Nose: wild herbs, ripe fruit. Palate: correct, long.

Saiñas 2014 T

mencía

88

Colour: cherry, purple rim. Nose: red berry notes, floral, balsamic herbs. Palate: fresh, fruity.

JORGE FEIJÓO GONZÁLEZ

Eirexa, 14
32614 Abeleda - A Teixeira (Ourense)
☎: +34 606 807 897
adegavella@terra.es
www.adegavella.com

Adega Vella Godello 2014 B

88

Colour: bright straw. Nose: fresh fruit, varietal, floral, balanced. Palate: fruity, flavourful, fine bitter notes, good acidity.

Adega Vella Mencía 2014 T

88

Colour: deep cherry, purple rim. Nose: ripe fruit, balsamic herbs, wild herbs. Palate: balanced, spicy, long.

JOSÉ MANUEL RODRÍGUEZ GONZÁLEZ

Vilachá - Doade
27424 Sober (Lugo)
☎: +34 982 460 613

Décima 2011 T

84

Décima 2014 T

84

LAR DE RICOBAO

Parque Empresarial de
Quiroga, Parcela B-2
27320 Quiroga (Lugo)
☎: +34 982 060 980
Fax: +34 902 930 563
info@larderícobao.com
www.larderícobao.com

Lar de Ricobao Godello 2013 B Barrica

godello, treixadura, dona blanca

86

Lar de Ricobao Godello 2014 B

godello, treixadura, dona blanca

89

Colour: bright straw. Nose: white flowers, dried herbs, ripe fruit, citrus fruit. Palate: flavourful, fruity, good acidity.

Lar de Ricobao Selección do Val 2013 T

mencía, garnacha, brancellao, merenzao, mouratón, tempranillo

89

Colour: cherry, garnet rim. Nose: ripe fruit, wild herbs, spicy, balsamic herbs. Palate: balanced, flavourful, long, balsamic.

MANUELA VALDÉS PÉREZ

Figueiroá, 22
27460 Sober (Lugo)
☎: +34 982 460 545
tearnilovila@gmail.com

Tear 2014 T

mencía, garnacha, tempranillo

85

MARÍA JESÚS LÓPEZ CRISTÓBAL

Outeiro 20 - Bolmente
27425 Sober (Lugo)
☎: +34 982 152 981

Cividade 2014 T

mencía, brancellao

89

Colour: bright cherry, purple rim. Nose: ripe fruit, scrubland, balanced. Palate: correct, good structure, balsamic.

MOURE VIÑOS ARTESANS

Serreira, 8
27540 Escairon (Lugo)
☎: +34 686 928 809
Fax: +34 982 452 700
moure@vinosartesans.com

A Rosa Do Viño 2013 T

85% garnacha, 10% mencía, 5% tempranillo

93

Colour: deep cherry. Nose: creamy oak, toasty, ripe fruit, balsamic herbs, dry stone. Palate: balanced, spicy, long, elegant.

Moure Tradición 2013 T Barrica

mencía, garnacha, tempranillo, brancellao

92

Colour: cherry, purple rim. Nose: ripe fruit, woody, aromatic coffee. Palate: flavourful, spicy, powerful.

Moure Tradición 2014 B

60% albariño, 40% godello

92

Colour: bright straw. Nose: fine lees, dried herbs, mineral, dried flowers. Palate: flavourful, fruity, good acidity, round.

Moure Tradición 2014 T

mencía, garnacha, tempranillo, brancellao

93

Colour: bright cherry. Nose: ripe fruit, sweet spices, expressive, scrubland. Palate: flavourful, fruity, round tannins.

NOVA TOURAL

Santo Estevo de Ribas de Miño
27594 O Saviñao (Lugo)
☎: +34 620 825 362
info@novatoural.es
www.novatoural.es

Sombrero Mencía 2014 T
mencía, tempranillo, garnacha tintorera

87

Colour: bright cherry, purple rim. Nose: grassy, ripe fruit. Palate: correct, fine bitter notes, good finish.

PONTE DA BOGA

Lugar do Couto - Sampaio
32764 Castro Caldelas (Ourense)
☎: +34 988 203 306
Fax: +34 988 203 299
info@pontedaboga.es
www.pontedaboga.es

A Ponte Da Boga Albariño 2014 B
albariño

86

Bancales Olvidados Mencía 2012 T
mencía

91

Colour: deep cherry, purple rim. Nose: creamy oak, toasty, ripe fruit, balsamic herbs. Palate: balanced, spicy, long.

Capricho DE Merenzao 2012 T
merenzao

92

Colour: light cherry. Nose: fruit expression, fruit liqueur notes, fragrant herbs, spicy, creamy oak. Palate: spicy, long, toasty.

G Ponte Da Boga Godello 2014 B
86% godello, 14% albariño

89

Colour: bright yellow. Nose: balanced, ripe fruit, floral, varietal. Palate: rich, flavourful, fine bitter notes, good acidity.

P Ponte Da Boga Mencía 2014 T
mencía

88

Colour: bright cherry, purple rim. Nose: red berry notes, ripe fruit, scrubland. Palate: balanced, balsamic, easy to drink.

Ponte Da Boga E. Románica 2012 T
mencía, sousón, merenzao, brancellao

91

Colour: cherry, garnet rim. Nose: red berry notes, ripe fruit, spicy, creamy oak, complex. Palate: flavourful, toasty, correct.

Ponte Da Boga Expresión Gótica 2013 T
sausón, brancellao, merenzao

91

Colour: very deep cherry, garnet rim. Nose: expressive, complex, mineral, balsamic herbs, balanced. Palate: full, flavourful, round tannins.

Porto de Lobos 2012 T
brancellao

92

Colour: bright cherry, purple rim. Nose: wild herbs, red berry notes, ripe fruit, expressive. Palate: balanced, good acidity.

REGINA VIARUM

Doade, s/n
27424 Sober (Lugo)
☎: +34 982 096 031
info@reginaviarum.cs
www.reginaviarum.es

Regina Expresión 2011 T Barrica
mencía

88

Colour: bright cherry. Nose: ripe fruit, sweet spices, creamy oak. Palate: flavourful, fruity, toasty, round tannins.

Regina Viarum Finca la Capitana 2012 T
tempranillo

90

Colour: cherry, garnet rim. Nose: ripe fruit, spicy, creamy oak, complex, fine reductive notes. Palate: flavourful, toasty, round tannins.

Regina Viarum Godello 2014 B
godello

90

Colour: bright yellow. Nose: expressive, dried herbs, ripe fruit, fine lees. Palate: flavourful, fruity, good acidity, balanced.

Regina Viarum Mencía 2014 T
mencía

89

Colour: cherry, purple rim. Nose: red berry notes, floral, balsamic herbs, expressive. Palate: fresh, fruity.

Regina Viarum Mencía Ecológico en Barrica 2012 T
mencía

87

Colour: cherry, purple rim. Nose: ripe fruit, woody, roasted coffee. Palate: flavourful, spicy, powerful.

RONSEL DO SIL

Sacardebois
32740 Parada de Sil (Ourense)
☎: +34 988 984 923
info@ronseldosil.com
www.ronseldosil.com

Alpendre 2012 T
100% merenzao

93

Colour: light cherry. Nose: fruit liqueur notes, fragrant herbs, spicy, dry stone. Palate: balanced, elegant, spicy, long, balsamic.

Arpegio Mencía 2013 T
100% mencía

90

Colour: cherry, purple rim. Nose: ripe fruit, wild herbs, earthy notes, spicy, balsamic herbs. Palate: balanced, flavourful, long.

Ourive Dona Branca 2013 B
100% dona blanca

92

Colour: bright straw. Nose: white flowers, fine lees, candied fruit, wild herbs. Palate: flavourful, fruity, good acidity.

Ourive Godello 2013 B
100% godello

91

Colour: bright yellow. Nose: floral, wild herbs, ripe fruit, spicy. Palate: powerful, rich, complex, flavourful, elegant.

Vel'Uveyra Godello 2013 B
83% godello, 10% treixadura, 7% dona blanca

90

Colour: bright straw. Nose: white flowers, fine lees, dried herbs, mineral. Palate: flavourful, fruity, good acidity, round.

Vel'Uveyra Mencía 2013 T
90% mencía, 10% garnacha

92

Colour: cherry, garnet rim. Nose: fruit liqueur notes, wild herbs, spicy, mineral. Palate: fresh, fruity, spicy, balsamic, elegant.

RUBÉN MOURE FERNÁNDEZ

Santa Mariña de Eire, s/n
27439 Pantón (Lugo)
☎: +34 638 380 222
info@priordepanton.com
www.priordepanton.com

Finca Cuarta Godello 2014 B
godello

87

Colour: bright yellow. Nose: medium intensity, ripe fruit, spicy, balanced. Palate: easy to drink, good finish.

Finca Cuarta Mencía 2013 T Barrica
mencía

92

Colour: cherry, garnet rim. Nose: red berry notes, ripe fruit, fragrant herbs, spicy, toasty, creamy oak, mineral. Palate: powerful, flavourful, balsamic.

Finca Cuarta Mencía 2014 T
mencía

90

Colour: deep cherry, purple rim. Nose: ripe fruit, balsamic herbs, mineral, sweet spices. Palate: balanced, spicy, long.

SAT VIRXEN DOS REMEDIOS

Diomondi, 56
27548 O Saviñao (Lugo)
☎: +34 982 171 720
Fax: +34 982 171 720
info@virxendosremedios.es
www.virxendosremedios.es

Bail Mencía 2013 T
mencía

84

Viña Vella 2014 B
60% godello, 20% albariño, 20% treixadura

88

Colour: bright straw. Nose: white flowers, fresh fruit, fragrant herbs, expressive. Palate: flavourful, fruity, good acidity, balanced.

Viña Vella Mencía 2014 T
mencía

87

Colour: bright cherry, purple rim. Nose: wild herbs, grassy, varietal. Palate: flavourful, easy to drink.

VÍCTOR MANUEL RODRÍGUEZ LÓPEZ

Amandi, 22
27423 Sober (Lugo)
☎: +34 982 460 504
info@valdalenda.com
www.valdalenda.com

Val Da Lenda 2014 T
mencía

89

Colour: very deep cherry, purple rim. Nose: neat, expressive, scrubland. Palate: flavourful, easy to drink.

VIÑA D'MATEO

Eixon
27334 Puebla de Brollon (Lugo)
vina.d.mateo@outlook.es
www.dmateo.com

Massimo 2014 T
85% mencía, 10% tempranillo, 5% sousón

90

Colour: cherry, purple rim. Nose: red berry notes, floral, balsamic herbs, dry stone. Palate: powerful, fresh, fruity, balanced.

DO. RIBEIRO

CONSEJO REGULADOR
Salgado Moscoso, 9
32400 Ribadavia (Ourense)
☎ :+34 988 477 200 - Fax: +34 988 477 201
@: info@ribeiro.es
www.ribeiro.es

LOCATION:

In the west of the province of Ourense. The region comprises 13 municipal districts marked by the Miño and its tributaries.

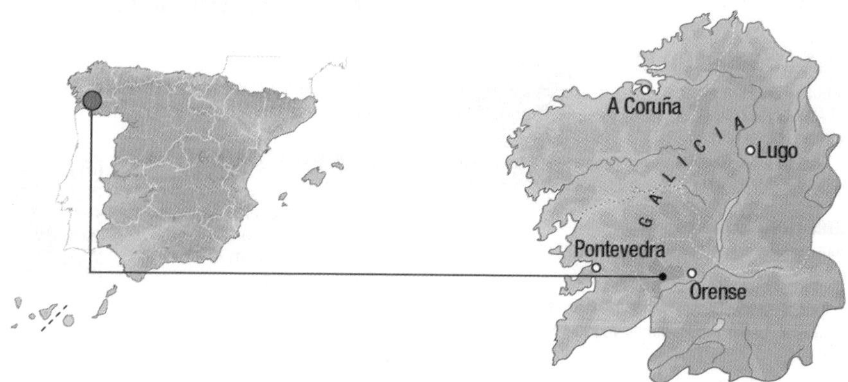

GRAPE VARIETIES:

WHITE: PREFERRED: Treixadura, Torrontés, Palomino, Godello, Macabeo, Loureira and Albariño. **Authorized**: Albilla, Macabeo, Jerez. Experimental: Lado.
RED: PREFERRED: Caíño, Alicante, Sousón, Ferrón, Mencía, Tempranillo, Brancellao.
AUTHORIZED: Tempranillo, Garnacha.

FIGURES:

Vineyard surface: 2,646 – **Wine-Growers:** 5,812 – **Wineries:** 108 – **2014 Harvest rating:** Excellent – **Production 14:** 8,206,900 litres – **Market percentages:** 93% National - 7% International.

SOIL:

Predominantly granite, deep and rich in organic matter, although in some areas clayey soils predominate. The vineyards are on the slopes of the mountains (where higher quality wines are produced) and on the plains.

CLIMATE:

Atlantic, with low temperatures in winter, a certain risk of spring frosts, and high temperatures in the summer months. The average annual rainfall varies between 800 mm and 1,000 mm.

VINTAGE RATING

PEÑÍNGUIDE

2010	2011	2012	2013	2014
VERY GOOD	VERY GOOD	VERY GOOD	VERY GOOD	GOOD

ADEGA DONA ELISA

Santo André, 110
32415 Ribadavia (Ourense)
☎: +34 609 281 616
adega.donaelisa@gmail.com
www.adegadonaelisa.com

Canción de Elisa 2014 B

treixadura, albariño, godello

89

Colour: bright yellow. Nose: white flowers, fresh fruit, fragrant herbs, expressive. Palate: flavourful, fruity, good acidity, balanced.

ADEGA MANUEL ROJO

Lugar dos Chaos s/n
32417 Arnoia (Ourense)
☎: +34 670 309 688
info@adegamanuelrojo.es
www.adegamanuelrojo.es

Manuel Rojo 2013 B

treixadura, godello, lado

92

Colour: bright straw. Nose: white flowers, fine lees, dried herbs, mineral, balanced. Palate: flavourful, fruity, good acidity, round.

Manuel Rojo 2013 T

brancellao, sousón, ferrón

90

Colour: ruby red. Nose: creamy oak, toasty, ripe fruit, balsamic herbs. Palate: balanced, spicy, long.

Manuel Rojo 2014 B

treixadura, godello, lado

91

Colour: bright straw. Nose: white flowers, fine lees, mineral, grassy. Palate: flavourful, fruity, good acidity.

ADEGA MARÍA DO PILAR

Casardeita, 14 Macendo
32430 Castrelo de Miño (Ourense)
☎: +34 988 475 236
Fax: +34 988 475 236
adega@adegamariadopilar.com
www.adegamariadopilar.com

Porta da Raiña 2014 B

treixadura

88

Colour: bright yellow. Nose: citrus fruit, ripe fruit, wild herbs. Palate: fresh, fruity, easy to drink.

Rechamante 2014 T

mencía

82

ADEGA PAZO DO MAR

Ctra. Ourense-Castrelo, Km. 12,5
32940 Toén (Ourense)
☎: +34 988 261 256
Fax: +34 988 261 264
info@pazodomar.com
www.pazodomar.com

Pazo do Mar 2014 B

treixadura, torrontés, godello

85

Pazo do Mar Expresión 2014 B

treixadura

87

Colour: bright straw. Nose: medium intensity, ripe fruit, floral, citrus fruit. Palate: correct, easy to drink.

ADEGA POUSADOIRO

A Capela, 3, Barral
32430 Castrelo de Miño (Ourense)
☎: +34 667 568 029
pousadoiro@gmail.com
www.pousadoiro.com

Pousadoiro 2014 B

83

ADEGA RAMÓN DO CASAR

Ctra. Prado, 85
32430 Castrelo de MIño (Orense)
☎: +34 988 036 097
adega@ramondocasar.es
www.ramondocasar.es

Ramón Do Casar 2014 B

90% treixadura, 5% albariño, 5% godello

90

Colour: bright straw. Nose: ripe fruit, tropical fruit, powerfull. Palate: flavourful, fruity, fine bitter notes.

Ramón Do Casar Treixadura 2014 B

100% treixadura

90

Colour: bright straw. Nose: white flowers, fresh fruit, fragrant herbs. Palate: flavourful, fruity, good acidity, balanced.

ADEGA SAMEIRÁS

San Andrés, 98
32415 Ribadavia (Ourense)
☎: +34 678 894 963
info@adegasameiras.com
www.adegasameiras.com

1040 Sameirás 2013 B
treixadura, albariño, godello, lado

92

Colour: bright golden. Nose: candied fruit, honeyed notes, white flowers, faded flowers. Palate: rich, spicy.

Sameirás 2014 B
treixadura, albariño, godello, lado, loureiro, torrontés

90

Colour: bright straw. Nose: fragrant herbs, fresh. Palate: flavourful, fruity, good acidity.

Sameirás 2014 T
sousón, caiño, brancellao

90

Colour: deep cherry. Nose: creamy oak, toasty, ripe fruit, balsamic herbs. Palate: balanced, spicy, long.

Viña Do Avó 2014 B
treixadura, albariño, godello, lado, torrontés

86

Viña Do Avó 2014 T
sousón, brancellao, caiño, mencía, garnacha

85

ADEGAS VALDAVIA

Cuñas, s/n
32454 Cenlle (Ourense)
☎: +34 669 892 681
comercial@adegasvaldavia.com
www.adegasvaldavia.com

Cuñas Davia 2013 BFB
treixadura, albariño

89

Colour: bright yellow. Nose: ripe fruit, powerfull, toasty, aged wood nuances. Palate: flavourful, fruity, spicy, long.

Cuñas Davia 2014 B
treixadura, albariño, godello, lado

87

Colour: bright yellow. Nose: fragrant herbs, medium intensity, fresh. Palate: fruity, easy to drink, correct.

AILALA-AILALELO

Gabino Bugallal, 66-2ºA
32420 Leiro (Ourense)
☎: +34 695 220 256
Fax: +34 988 488 741
export@ailalawine.com
www.ailalawine.com

Ailalá 2014 B
100% treixadura

89

Colour: bright yellow, greenish rim. Nose: ripe fruit, dried herbs, balanced. Palate: flavourful, fine bitter notes.

Ailalá 2014 T
sousón, brancellao, ferrol

88

Colour: cherry, purple rim. Nose: red berry notes, floral, balsamic herbs, dry stone. Palate: powerful, fresh, fruity.

ANTONIO MONTERO

Santa María, 7
32430 Castrelo do Miño (Ourense)
☎: +34 607 856 002
antoniomontero@antoniomontero.com
www.antoniomontero.com

Alejandrvs 2013 B
100% treixadura

90

Colour: bright yellow. Nose: spicy, ripe fruit, faded flowers. Palate: rich, flavourful, balanced.

Antonio Montero "Autor" 2014 B
80% treixadura, 10% torrontés, 5% loureiro, 5% albariño

89

Colour: yellow. Nose: ripe fruit, white flowers, dried herbs. Palate: correct, balanced, fine bitter notes.

ARCO DA VELLA A ADEGA DE ELADIO

Pza. de España, 1
32431 Beade (Ourense)
☎: +34 607 487 060
Fax: +34 986 376 800
bodega@bodegaeladio.com
www.bodegaeladio.com

Tarabelo 2012 TC

87

Colour: cherry, garnet rim. Nose: ripe fruit, wild herbs, earthy notes. Palate: flavourful, long, balsamic.

Torques do Castro 2014 B

87

Colour: bright yellow. Nose: dried herbs, ripe fruit, spicy. Palate: flavourful, fruity, good acidity.

BODEGA ALANÍS

Ctra. De Cenlle – Barbantes Estación
32450 Ourense (Ourense)
☎: +34 988 384 200
Fax: +34 988 384 068
vinos@bodegasgallegas.com
www.bodegasgallegas.com

Gran Alanís 2014 B
85% treixadura, 15% godello

87

Colour: bright yellow. Nose: medium intensity, wild herbs, dried flowers. Palate: correct, easy to drink, good finish.

San Trocado 2014 B
treixadura

85

BODEGA Y VIÑEDOS PAZO CASANOVA

Camiño Souto do Río, 1
Santa Cruz de Arrabaldo
32990 (Ourense)
☎: +34 988 384 186
Fax: +34 988 384 196
casanova@pazocasanova.com
www.pazocasanova.com

Pazo Casanova 2014 B
treixadura, godello, albariño, loureiro

88

Colour: bright yellow. Nose: expressive, dried herbs, ripe fruit, spicy. Palate: flavourful, fruity, good acidity, balanced.

BODEGAS AGRUPADAS PONTE

Eduardo Pondal, 3
36001 (Pontevedra)
☎: +34 986 840 064
Fax: +34 986 851 667
info@bodegasagrupadasponte.com
www.bodegasagrupadasponte.com

La Invitación de Pepa 2014 T
100% mencía

87

Colour: light cherry. Nose: fruit liqueur notes, fragrant herbs, spicy. Palate: long, slightly acidic.

La Propuesta de María 2014 B
100% godello

86

La Sugerencia de Manola 2014 B
70% treixadura, 30% torrontés

88

Colour: bright yellow. Nose: expressive, dried herbs, ripe fruit, spicy. Palate: flavourful, fruity, good acidity, balanced.

BODEGAS CAMPANTE

Finca Reboreda, s/n
32941 Puga (Ourense)
☎: +34 988 261 212
Fax: +34 988 261 213
info@campante.com
www.gruporeboredamorgadio.com

3Ura 2013 B
treixadura, godello, loureiro

91

Colour: bright straw. Nose: white flowers, fine lees, dried herbs, ripe fruit, candied fruit, citrus fruit. Palate: flavourful, fruity, good acidity, elegant.

A Telleira 2014 B
godello

88

Colour: bright straw. Nose: white flowers, fresh fruit, fragrant herbs, varietal. Palate: flavourful, fruity.

Adeus 2014 B
treixadura, torrontés, godello

89

Colour: bright yellow. Nose: expressive, dried herbs, ripe fruit. Palate: flavourful, fruity, good acidity, balanced.

BODEGAS DOCAMPO

San Paio s/n
32400 Ribadavia (Ourense)
☎: +34 988 470 258
Fax: +34 988 470 421
admin@bodegasdocampo.com
www.bodegasdocampo.com

Señorío da Vila 2014 B
100% treixadura

90

Colour: bright yellow. Nose: expressive, dried herbs, ripe fruit, spicy. Palate: flavourful, fruity, good acidity, balanced.

Viña Do Campo 2014 B
70% treixadura, 30% torrontés

89

Colour: bright yellow. Nose: expressive, dried herbs, ripe fruit, spicy. Palate: flavourful, fruity, good acidity, balanced.

Viña Do Campo Mencía 2014 T
100% mencía

87

Colour: cherry, purple rim. Nose: powerfull, ripe fruit, spicy, balsamic herbs. Palate: powerful, fruity, unctuous.

BODEGAS EL PARAGUAS

Lugar de Esmelle, 111
15594 Ferrol (A Coruña)
☎: +34 636 161 479
info@bodegaselparaguas.com
www.bodegaselparaguas.com

El Paraguas Atlántico 2013 B
86% treixadura, 9% godello, 5% albariño

92

Colour: bright straw. Nose: fresh, expressive, floral, balanced. Palate: fruity, long, fine bitter notes, good acidity.

Fai un Sol de Carallo 2013 B
85% treixadura, 10% godello, 5% albariño

94

Colour: bright straw. Nose: complex, fine lees, ripe fruit, floral, fragrant herbs, fresh, elegant. Palate: full, flavourful, long.

BODEGAS O'VENTOSELA

Ctra. Ribadavia - Carballiño, km. 8,8
San Clodio
32420 Leiro (Ourense)
☎: +34 981 635 829
Fax: +34 981 635 870
bodegasydestilerias@oventosela.com
www.oventosela.com

Gran Leiriña 2014 B
treixadura, albariño, godello, torrontés

87

Colour: bright yellow. Nose: ripe fruit, white flowers, balanced. Palate: correct, fine bitter notes.

O Ventosela 2014 B
palomino, torrontés

86

Viña Leiriña 2014 B
treixadura, torrontés

87

Colour: bright straw. Nose: balanced, dried flowers, ripe fruit, dried herbs. Palate: correct, fine bitter notes, good finish.

BODEGAS VALDEPUGA

Ctra. Ourense a Cortegada, km 14 Puga
32940 Toén (Ourense)
☎: +34 619 018 833
Fax: +34 988 235 817
info@valdepuga.com
www.valdepuga.com

Terraboa 2014 B

83

Valdepuga 2013 B
treixadura, albariño, godello, loureiro

89

Colour: bright straw. Nose: white flowers, dried herbs, mineral. Palate: flavourful, fruity, good acidity, round, rich.

BODEGAS VILLANUEVA SENRA

Avda. Alejandro Ferrer, 11
32430 Barral (Ourense)
☎: +34 986 252 411
Fax: +34 986 252 488
info@bodegasvillanueva.com
www.bodegasvillanueva.com

Carlos Villanueva 2014 B
godello, treixadura

89

Colour: bright yellow. Nose: ripe fruit, faded flowers. Palate: flavourful, ripe fruit, fine bitter notes.

CASAL DE ARMÁN

O Cotiño – San Andrés
de Camporedondo
32400 Ribadavia (Ourense)
☎: +34 988 491 809
Fax: +34 988 491 809
administracion@casaldearman.net
www.casaldearman.net

7 Cupos 2013 T
sousón, caiño, brancellao

86

7 Cupos 2014 B
treixadura

88

Colour: bright yellow. Nose: dried herbs, ripe fruit, spicy. Palate: flavourful, fruity.

Casal de Armán 2014 B
90% treixadura, 5% albariño, 5% godello

89

Colour: bright straw. Nose: white flowers, fresh fruit, fragrant herbs. Palate: flavourful, fruity, fine bitter notes.

Finca Misenhora 2013 B
treixadura, albariño, godello

93

Colour: bright straw. Nose: white flowers, dried herbs, ripe fruit, citrus fruit. Palate: flavourful, fruity, good acidity, elegant.

Finca Os Loureiros 2013 B
treixadura

94

Colour: bright yellow. Nose: white flowers, wild herbs, dry stone, spicy. Palate: rich, fruity, flavourful, balanced.

COTO DE GOMARIZ

Barro de Gomariz s/n
32429 Leiro (Ourense)
☎: +34 988 488 741
Fax: +34 988 488 174
mmontoto@cotodegomariz.com
www.cotodegomariz.com

Abadía de Gomariz 2011 T

sousón, brancellao, ferrol, mencía

91

Colour: dark-red cherry, garnet rim. Nose: expressive, spicy, smoky, balsamic herbs, mineral. Palate: good structure, round tannins, spicy.

Coto de Gomariz 2013 B

70% treixadura, godello, albariño, loureiro

93

Colour: bright straw. Nose: white flowers, fine lees, dried herbs, ripe fruit. Palate: flavourful, fruity, good acidity, elegant.

Coto de Gomariz Colleita Seleccionada 2012 B

70% treixadura, godello, albariño, lado, loureiro, otras

94

Colour: bright straw. Nose: white flowers, fine lees, dried herbs, ripe fruit, candied fruit, citrus fruit, creamy oak. Palate: flavourful, fruity, good acidity, elegant.

Gomariz X 2014 B

95% albariño, 5% treixadura

89

Colour: bright straw. Nose: white flowers, dried herbs, ripe fruit, spicy. Palate: flavourful, fruity, good acidity, elegant, balanced.

Hush 2010 T

ferrol, sousón, caiño, bastardo negro, otras

92

Colour: cherry, garnet rim. Nose: ripe fruit, wild herbs, earthy notes, spicy, balsamic herbs. Palate: flavourful, long, balsamic, balanced, elegant.

Salvaxe 2012 B

lado, treixadura, godello, albariño, caiño blanco, silveiriña

91

Colour: bright straw. Nose: dried herbs, mineral, fine lees, floral, ripe fruit. Palate: flavourful, fruity, good acidity, round.

Super Héroe 2011 T

ferrol, sousón, caiño, bastardo negro, otras

89

Colour: very deep cherry, garnet rim. Nose: complex, mineral, balsamic herbs, ripe fruit. Palate: full, flavourful, spicy.

The FLower and The Bee Sousón 2013 T

sousón

87

Colour: bright cherry, purple rim. Nose: ripe fruit, scrubland, spicy. Palate: correct, easy to drink, balsamic.

The FLower and The Bee Sousón 2014 T

sousón

89

Colour: cherry, garnet rim. Nose: floral, balsamic herbs, spicy, ripe fruit. Palate: powerful, fresh, fruity.

The FLower and The Bee Treixadura 2014 B

treixadura

90

Colour: bright straw. Nose: white flowers, fresh fruit, fragrant herbs. Palate: flavourful, fruity, good acidity, balanced.

CUNQUEIRO

Ctra., 4
32430 Prado de Miño (Ourense)
☎: +34 988 489 023
Fax: +34 988 489 084
info@bodegascunqueiro.es
www.bodegascunqueiro.es

Anciño 2014 B

palomino, torrontés

82

Cunqueiro III Milenium 2014 B

treixadura, godello, albariño, loureiro

88

Colour: bright yellow. Nose: dried flowers, ripe fruit. Palate: correct, balanced, ripe fruit, long.

Cuqueira 2014 B

treixadura, torrontés, otras

86

Mais de Cunqueiro 2013 B

100% torrontés

89

Colour: bright yellow. Nose: balsamic herbs, ripe fruit, dried flowers. Palate: good acidity, balanced, fine bitter notes.

EDUARDO PEÑA

Barral s/n
32430 Castelo de Miño (Ourense)
☎: +34 629 872 130
Fax: +34 988 239 704
bodega@bodegaeduardopenha.es
www.bodegaeduardopenha.es

Eduardo Peña 2014 B

90

Colour: bright yellow. Nose: expressive, dried herbs, ripe fruit, citrus fruit, floral. Palate: flavourful, fruity, good acidity, balanced.

ELISA COLLARTE BERNÁRDEZ

Santo Andrés, 78
32415 Ribadavia (Ourense)
☎: +34 670 473 266
elisacollarte@gmail.com

Elisa Collarte 2014 T Barrica

mencía, caiño, sousón, brancellao

85

Elisa Collarte en sus propias Lías 2013 B

treixadura, godello, albariño

84

Santo André 2014 B

treixadura, godello, albariño, loureiro

86

EMILIO DOCAMPO DIÉGUEZ

San Andrés, 57
32415 Ribadavia (Ourense)
☎: +34 639 332 790
Fax: +34 988 275 318
edocampodieguez@hotmail.com

Casal de Paula 2014 B

treixadura, torrontés, albariño, godello

88

Colour: bright straw. Nose: white flowers, fresh fruit, fragrant herbs. Palate: flavourful, fruity.

Casal de Paula 2014 T

sousón, ferrón, brancellao, mencía

88

Colour: cherry, purple rim. Nose: powerfull, ripe fruit, spicy, fragrant herbs. Palate: powerful, fruity, unctuous.

Casal de Paula D.H. 2013 B

100% treixadura

89

Colour: bright yellow. Nose: ripe fruit, spicy, dried flowers. Palate: rich, flavourful, toasty.

EMILIO ROJO

Lugar de Remoiño, s/n
32233 Arnoia (Ourense)
☎: +34 988 488 050
vinoemiliorojo@hotmail.com

Emilio Rojo 2013 B

93

Colour: bright straw. Nose: white flowers, fine lees, dried herbs, mineral. Palate: flavourful, fruity, good acidity.

FINCA VIÑOA

Banga
32516 O Carballiño (Ourense)
☎: +34 988 384 186
info@fincavinoa.com
www.fincavinoa.com

Finca Viñoa 2014 B

93% treixadura, 2% godello, 4% albariño, loureiro

91

Colour: bright straw. Nose: white flowers, fine lees, dried herbs, ripe fruit, citrus fruit. Palate: flavourful, fruity, good acidity, elegant.

FRANCISCO FERNÁNDEZ SOUSA

Prado, 14
32430 Castrelo do Miño (Ourense)
☎: +34 678 530 898
info@terraminei.com
www.terraminei.com

Lagar de Brais 2014 B

palomino, treixadura, torrontés

84

Terra Minei 2014 B

treixadura

87

Colour: bright straw. Nose: balanced, ripe fruit, floral, dried herbs. Palate: balanced, fine bitter notes.

JOSÉ ESTÉVEZ FERNÁNDEZ

A Ponte, 21
32417 Arnoia (Ourense)
☎: +34 696 402 970
joseestevezarnoia@gmail.com

Mauro Estevez 2014 B

treixadura, albariño, lado, loureiro

93

Colour: bright straw. Nose: white flowers, fine lees, dried herbs, candied fruit, citrus fruit. Palate: flavourful, fruity, good acidity.

Uxía da Ponte 2014 B
100% lado

91

Colour: bright straw. Nose: white flowers, fresh fruit, fragrant herbs, expressive. Palate: flavourful, fruity, balanced.

JOSÉ GONZÁLEZ ÁLVAREZ

Pazo Lalón s/n
32429 Gomariz, Leiro (Ourense)
☎: +34 653 131 487
eduardogonzalezbravo@gmail.com
www.eduardobravo.es

Eduardo Bravo 2014 B
treixadura, albariño, loureiro

87

Colour: bright yellow. Nose: medium intensity, ripe fruit, fresh. Palate: balanced, fine bitter notes, good acidity.

Pazo Lalón 2013 B
treixadura

85

LA MALETA HAND MADE FINE WINES

Plaza de Eladio Rodríguez, 19
32420 San Clodio (Ourense)
☎: +34 988 614 234
hola@lamaletawines.com
lamaletawines.com

Desde la Ladera 2014 B
treixadura, albariño, godello

88

Colour: bright straw. Nose: dried herbs, white flowers, ripe fruit, citrus fruit. Palate: correct, balanced, fine bitter notes.

NAIROA

A Ponte, 2
32417 Arnoia (Ourense)
☎: +34 988 492 867
info@bodegasnairoa.com
www.bodegasnairoa.com

Alberte 2014 B
90% treixadura, 5% albariño, 5% lado

86

Nairoa 2014 B
treixadura, torrontés, palomino

86

Val de Nairoa 2013 B
80% treixadura, 10% albariño, 5% loureiro, 5% lado

89

Colour: bright straw. Nose: white flowers, fresh fruit, fragrant herbs, medium intensity. Palate: fruity, good acidity, balanced.

Val do Couso 2014 B
treixadura, torrontés, otras

86

PAZO DE VIEITE

Ctra. Ribadavia – Carballiño,
km.6 - Vieite
32419 Leiro (Ourense)
☎: +34 988 488 229
Fax: +34 988 488 229
info@pazodevieite.es
www.pazodevieite.es

1932 de Pazo Vieite 2013 B
100% treixadura

89

Colour: bright golden. Nose: ripe fruit, faded flowers, tropical fruit. Palate: balanced, fine bitter notes, ripe fruit, long.

Viña Farnadas 2014 B
85% treixadura, 15% godello, albariño

85

PAZO TIZÓN

Rua do Bon Casares, 20
32514 Boboras (Orense)
admon@pazotizon.com
www.pazotizon.com

Extramundi 2013 B
albariño, treixadura

90

Colour: bright yellow. Nose: expressive, dried herbs, ripe fruit, spicy. Palate: flavourful, fruity, good acidity, balanced.

SANCLODIO

Cubilledo-Gomariz
32429 Leiro (Ourense)
☎: +34 686 961 681
sanclodiovino@gmail.com
www.vinosanclodio.com

Sanclodio 2013 B
treixadura, godello, loureiro, torrontés, albariño

91

Colour: bright yellow, greenish rim. Nose: dry nuts, wild herbs, fresh fruit, floral. Palate: balanced, fine bitter notes, long.

SEÑORÍO DE BEADE

Piñeiros, s/n
32431 Beade (Ourense)
☎: +34 988 480 050
Fax: +34 988 480 050
beade@beadeprimacia.com
www.beadeprimacia.com

Beade 25 Autor 2014 B
100% loureiro

91

Colour: bright straw. Nose: white flowers, dried herbs, candied fruit, citrus fruit. Palate: flavourful, fruity, good acidity, elegant.

Beade Primacía 2014 B
98% treixadura, 2% albariño, loureiro

89

Colour: bright straw. Nose: white flowers, fragrant herbs, ripe fruit, tropical fruit. Palate: flavourful, fruity, good acidity, balanced.

Señorío de Beade 2014 B
treixadura, torrontés, godello

85

Señorío de Beade 2014 T
98% mencía, 2% caiño

88

Colour: cherry, purple rim. Nose: expressive, fresh fruit, red berry notes, floral. Palate: flavourful, fruity, good acidity.

TERRA DO CASTELO

Ctra. Ribadavia - Carballiño, Km. 4
32431 Beade (Ourense)
☎: +34 988 471 522
Fax: +34 988 471 502
adegas@terradocastelo.com
www.terradocastelo.com

Terra do Castelo Treixadura 2013 B
100% treixadura

86

Terra do Castelo Treixadura Selección S/C B
100% treixadura

87

Colour: bright yellow, greenish rim. Nose: ripe fruit, balanced, floral. Palate: correct, fine bitter notes.

VAL DE SOUTO

Souto, 34
32430 Castrelo de Miño (Ourense)
☎: +34 636 024 205
info@valdesouto.com
www.valdesouto.com

Val de Souto 2014 B
treixadura, godello, loureiro

87

Colour: bright straw, greenish rim. Nose: ripe fruit, floral. Palate: correct, slightly acidic, fine bitter notes.

Val de Souto 2014 T
mencía, brancellao, caiño

84

Val de Souto Orixes 2014 B
treixadura, godello, loureiro

86

VIÑA COSTEIRA

Valdepereira, s/n
32415 Ribadavia (Ourense)
☎: +34 988 477 210
Fax: +34 988 470 330
info@costeira.es
www.vinoribeiro.com

Colección 68 Albariño 2014 B
albariño, treixadura, loureiro

87

Colour: bright straw, greenish rim. Nose: medium intensity, ripe fruit, floral. Palate: correct, easy to drink, good finish.

Colección 68 Costeira Treixadura 2014 B
treixadura, albariño, godello

89

Colour: bright straw. Nose: white flowers, fresh fruit, fragrant herbs. Palate: flavourful, fruity, good acidity.

Pazo 2014 B
palomino, torrontés

84

Colour: bright straw. Nose: medium intensity, ripe fruit, floral. Palate: correct, easy to drink.

Viña Costeira 2014 B
treixadura, torrontés, albariño, godello, loureiro

86

Colour: bright straw, greenish rim. Nose: medium intensity, floral, short. Palate: correct, easy to drink.

VIÑA DA CAL

Lg. Razamonde
32454 Razamonde (Cenlle) (Ourense)
☎: +34 636 968 880
susana@alter-vino.es
www.alter-vino.es

Alter 2013 T
60% brancellao, 40% sousón

87

Colour: light cherry. Nose: ripe fruit, balsamic herbs, spicy. Palate: balanced, long.

Alter 2014 B
80% treixadura, 20% godello

89

Colour: bright straw. Nose: white flowers, fragrant herbs, medium intensity. Palate: fine bitter notes, balanced, fruity.

VIÑA MEIN S.L.

Mein, s/n
32420 Leiro (Ourense)
☎: +34 915 768 898
Fax: +34 915 761 019
info.bodega@vinamein.com
www.vinamein.com

Tega do Sal 2014 B
50% treixadura, 45% albariño, 5% loureiro

91

Colour: bright straw. Nose: white flowers, fine lees, dried herbs, ripe fruit, candied fruit, citrus fruit. Palate: flavourful, fruity, good acidity, elegant.

Viña Mein 2014 B
treixadura, godello, albariño, loureiro, lado, albillo

90

Colour: bright straw. Nose: fragrant herbs, white flowers, mineral, dry stone. Palate: flavourful, fruity, good acidity, balanced.

Viña Mein 2014 BFB
treixadura, godello

91

Colour: bright yellow. Nose: ripe fruit, powerfull, toasty, aged wood nuances, pattiserie. Palate: flavourful, fruity, spicy, toasty, long.

DO. RIBERA DEL DUERO

CONSEJO REGULADOR
Hospital, 6
09300 Roa (Burgos)
☎:+34 947 541 221 - Fax: +34 947 541 116
@: info@riberadelduero.es
www.riberadelduero.es

LOCATION:

Between the provinces of Burgos, Valladolid, Segovia and Soria. This region comprises 19 municipal districts in the east of Valladolid, 5 in the north west of Segovia, 59 in the south of Burgos (most of the vineyards are concentrated in this province with 10,000 Ha) and 6 in the west of Soria.en la parte occidental de Soria.

GRAPE VARIETIES:

WHITE: Albillo.
RED: Tinta del País (Tempranillo – majority with 81% of all vineyards), Garnacha Tinta, Cabernet Sauvignon, Malbec and Merlot.

FIGURES:

Vineyard surface: 21,993 – **Wine-Growers:** 8,422 – **Wineries:** 282 – **2014 Harvest rating:** Very Good – **Production 14:** 122,000,000 Kg. – **Market percentages:** 71% National - 29% International.

SOIL:

In general, the soils are loose, not very fertile and with a rather high limestone content. Most of the sediment is composed of layers of sandy limestone or clay. The vineyards are located on the interfluvial hills and in the valleys at an altitude of between 700 and 850 m.

CLIMATE:

Continental in nature, with slight Atlantic influences. The winters are rather cold and the summers hot, although mention must be made of the significant difference in day-night temperatures contributing to the slow ripening of the grapes, enabling excellent acidity indexes to be achieved. The greatest risk factor in the region is the spring frosts, which are on many occasions responsible for sharp drops in production. The average annual rainfall is between 450 mm and 500 mm.

VINTAGE RATING

PEÑÍNGUIDE

2010	2011	2012	2013	2014
EXCELLENT	VERY GOOD	VERY GOOD	GOOD	GOOD

3 ASES

Camino de Pesquera, s/n
47360 Quintanilla de Arriba (Valladolid)
☎: +34 983 036 214
info@3asesvino.com
www.3asesvino.com

3 Ases 2012 TC

tempranillo

89

Colour: very deep cherry, garnet rim. Nose: cocoa bean, dried herbs, ripe fruit. Palate: flavourful, powerful, full, round tannins.

3 Ases 2013 T Roble

tempranillo

87

Colour: bright cherry. Nose: ripe fruit, sweet spices, creamy oak, dark chocolate. Palate: flavourful, fruity, toasty, round tannins.

3ELEMENTOS

Camino Cogeces s/n
47350 Quintanilla de Onésimo
(Valladolid)
☎: +34 647 252 693
info@3elementos.es
www.3elementos.es

3Elementos 2013 T

tempranillo

88

Colour: bright cherry. Nose: ripe fruit, sweet spices, creamy oak. Palate: flavourful, fruity, toasty.

AALTO BODEGAS Y VIÑEDOS

Paraje Vallejo de Carril, s/n
47360 Quintanilla de Arriba (Valladolid)
☎: +34 983 036 949
aalto@aalto.es
www.aalto.es

Aalto 2012 T

100% tempranillo

92

Colour: very deep cherry. Nose: roasted coffee, smoky. Palate: concentrated, full, round tannins, spicy.

PODIUM

Aalto PS 2012 T

100% tempranillo

95

Colour: cherry, garnet rim. Nose: mineral, expressive, spicy. Palate: flavourful, ripe fruit, long, good acidity, balanced.

ABADÍA DE ACÓN

Ctra. Hontangas, Km. 0,400
09400 Castrillo de la Vega (Burgos)
☎: +34 947 509 292
Fax: +34 947 508 586
carloscarrasco@abadiadeacon.com
www.abadiadeacon.com

Acón 2009 TR

tempranillo, cabernet sauvignon

90

Colour: cherry, garnet rim. Nose: red berry notes, ripe fruit, spicy, creamy oak, complex. Palate: flavourful, toasty, round tannins.

Acón 2010 TC

tempranillo

90

Colour: cherry, garnet rim. Nose: red berry notes, ripe fruit, spicy, creamy oak. Palate: flavourful, toasty.

Acón 2013 T Roble

tempranillo

87

Colour: bright cherry. Nose: ripe fruit, sweet spices, creamy oak, expressive. Palate: flavourful, fruity, toasty.

ALTOS DE ONTAÑÓN

Ctra. Roa s/n
09315 Fuentecén (Burgos)
☎: +34 947 532 797
Fax: +34 947 532 797
enologoduero@ontanon.es
www.ontanon.es

Teón del Condado 2011 TC

tempranillo

88

Colour: cherry, garnet rim. Nose: smoky, spicy, ripe fruit. Palate: flavourful, ripe fruit, balsamic.

Teón del Condado 2012 T Roble

tempranillo

88

Colour: bright cherry. Nose: sweet spices, creamy oak, fruit preserve. Palate: flavourful, fruity, toasty, round tannins.

ALTOS DEL ENEBRO

Regino Sainz de la Maza 13º C
05004 (Burgos)
☎: +34 619 409 097
comercial@altosdelenebro.es
www.altosdelenebro.es

Altos del Enebro 2012 T
100% tinto fino

93

Colour: cherry, garnet rim. Nose: balanced, complex, ripe fruit, spicy, fine reductive notes. Palate: good structure, flavourful, round tannins.

Tomás González 2012 T
tinto fino

91

Colour: cherry, garnet rim. Nose: smoky, spicy, ripe fruit. Palate: flavourful, smoky aftertaste, ripe fruit.

ALTOS DEL TERRAL

Barrionuevo, 11
09400 Aranda de Duero (Burgos)
☎: +34 616 953 451
bodega@altosdelterral.com
www.altosdelterral.com

Altos del Terral 2012 TC
100% tempranillo

91

Colour: cherry, garnet rim. Nose: ripe fruit, spicy, creamy oak, fine reductive notes. Palate: flavourful, toasty, round tannins.

Altos del Terral T1 2011 T
100% tempranillo

90

Colour: cherry, garnet rim. Nose: red berry notes, ripe fruit, spicy, creamy oak, complex. Palate: flavourful, toasty, round tannins.

Cuvée Julia Altos del Terral 2011 T
100% tempranillo

92

Colour: cherry, garnet rim. Nose: expressive, spicy, cocoa bean. Palate: flavourful, ripe fruit, long, good acidity, balanced, good structure.

ARBOLEDA MEDITERRÁNEA

Paraje el Salegar s/n
09443 Quintana del Pidio (Burgos)
☎: +34 902 996 361
export@arboledamediterranea.com
www.arboledamediterranea.com

Peningles Viñas Viejas 2012 T Roble
100% tinto fino

85

Peningles Viñas Viejas 2012 TC
100% tinto fino

86

ASTRALES

Ctra. Olmedillo, Km. 7
09313 Anguix (Burgos)
☎: +34 947 554 222
administracion@astrales.es
www.astrales.es

Astrales 2012 T
tempranillo

92

Colour: cherry, garnet rim. Nose: creamy oak, balanced, ripe fruit. Palate: flavourful, spicy, elegant, fruity aftestaste.

Astrales Christina 2012 T
tempranillo

90

Colour: cherry, garnet rim. Nose: roasted coffee, smoky, spicy, ripe fruit. Palate: flavourful, smoky aftertaste, ripe fruit, good structure.

ATALAYAS DE GOLBÁN

Ctra. a Morcuera, s/n
42345 Atauta (Soria)
☎: +34 975 351 349
isanz@avanteselecta.com
www.avanteselectagrupo.com

Torre de Golban 2011 TR
100% tinto fino

91

Colour: cherry, garnet rim. Nose: mineral, spicy. Palate: flavourful, ripe fruit, long, good acidity, balanced.

Torre de Golban 2012 TC
100% tinto fino

90

Colour: bright cherry. Nose: ripe fruit, sweet spices, creamy oak. Palate: flavourful, fruity, toasty, round tannins.

AVELINO VEGAS-BODEGAS FUENTESPINA

Camino Cascajo, s/n
40460 Fuentespina (Burgos)
☎: +34 921 596 002
Fax: +34 921 596 035
ana@avelinovegas.com
www.avelinovegas.com

Corona de Castilla Prestigio 2011 TC
tempranillo

90

Colour: cherry, garnet rim. Nose: smoky, spicy, ripe fruit. Palate: flavourful, smoky aftertaste, ripe fruit.

Fuentespina 2012 TC
tempranillo

86

Fuentespina 7 2013 T Roble
tempranillo

85

Fuentespina Granate 2013 T
tempranillo

87

Colour: deep cherry, purple rim. Nose: creamy oak, toasty, ripe fruit, balsamic herbs, varietal. Palate: balanced, spicy, long.

Fuentespina Selección 2011 T
tempranillo

92

Colour: cherry, garnet rim. Nose: smoky, spicy, ripe fruit. Palate: flavourful, smoky aftertaste, ripe fruit.

AXIAL
Castillo de Capua Nº 10 nave 7
50197 Zaragoza (Zaragoza)
☎: +34 976 780 136
Fax: +34 976 303 035
info@axialvinos.com
www.axialvinos.com

Zumaya Tempranillo 2014 T
100% tempranillo

86

BADEN NUMEN
Carreterilla, s/n
47359 San Bernardo (Valladolid)
☎: +34 615 995 552
bodega@badennumen.es
www.badennumen.es

Baden Numen "B" 2013 T
100% tinto fino

89

Colour: bright cherry. Nose: ripe fruit, sweet spices, creamy oak, expressive. Palate: flavourful, fruity, toasty.

Baden Numen "B" 2014 T
100% tinto fino

84

Baden Numen "N" 2012 TC
100% tinto fino

87

Colour: cherry, garnet rim. Nose: fine reductive notes, wet leather, aged wood nuances, fruit preserve. Palate: spicy, long, toasty.

Baden Numen Oro "AU" 2011 T

90

Colour: deep cherry. Nose: fruit preserve, aged wood nuances, toasty. Palate: powerful, concentrated.

BODEGA CONVENTO SAN FRANCISCO
Calvario, 22
47300 Peñafiel (Valladolid)
☎: +34 983 878 052
Fax: +34 983 873 052
bodega@bodegaconvento.com
www.bodegaconvento.com

Convento San Francisco 2011 T
100% tempranillo

90

Colour: cherry, garnet rim. Nose: fine reductive notes, wet leather, aged wood nuances, ripe fruit. Palate: spicy, long, toasty.

BODEGA COOP. SANTA ANA
Ctra. Aranda - Salas, km. 18,5
09410 Peñaranda de Duero (Burgos)
☎: +34 947 552 011
Fax: +34 947 552 011
bodega@bodegasantaana.es
www.bodegasantaana.es

Castillo de Peñaranda 2011 TC
tempranillo

87

Colour: cherry, garnet rim. Nose: medium intensity, smoky, toasty, spicy. Palate: correct, easy to drink.

Castillo de Peñaranda 2014 T Roble
tempranillo

84

Cruz Sagra 2012 T
tempranillo

89

Colour: cherry, garnet rim. Nose: roasted coffee, smoky, spicy. Palate: flavourful, smoky aftertaste, ripe fruit.

Valdepisón 2014 RD
tempranillo

84

BODEGA COOPERATIVA VIRGEN DE LA ASUNCIÓN

Las Afueras, s/n
09311 La Horra (Burgos)
☎: +34 947 542 057
Fax: +34 947 542 057
info@virgendelaasuncion.com
www.virgendelaasuncion.com

Canto del Angel 2012 T Roble
100% tempranillo

89

Colour: cherry, garnet rim. Nose: fine reductive notes, ripe fruit, dried herbs. Palate: spicy, toasty, long, balsamic, round tannins.

Corazón de la Tierra 2012 T Roble
100% tempranillo

89

Colour: cherry, garnet rim. Nose: ripe fruit, spicy, creamy oak. Palate: flavourful, toasty.

Secreto de María 2012 T Roble
100% tempranillo

90

Colour: cherry, garnet rim. Nose: characterful, balanced, ripe fruit, dried herbs, spicy. Palate: good structure, flavourful, slightly dry, soft tannins.

Viña Valera 2011 TC
100% tempranillo

87

Colour: cherry, garnet rim. Nose: dried herbs, ripe fruit. Palate: correct, spicy, round tannins.

Viña Valera 2014 T Joven
100% tempranillo

85

Viña Valera Joven 2014 RD
100% tempranillo

85

Viña Valera Reserva 2008 TR
100% tempranillo

88

Nose: ripe fruit, old leather, tobacco. Palate: correct, flavourful, spicy.

Viña Valera Selección 2012 T
100% tempranillo

88

Colour: bright cherry. Nose: sweet spices, creamy oak, overripe fruit. Palate: flavourful, fruity, toasty, round tannins.

Viña Valera Selección 2013 T Roble
100% tempranillo

85

Viña Valera Viñas Viejas 2011 T
100% tinta del país

90

Colour: bright cherry. Nose: ripe fruit, sweet spices, creamy oak, expressive. Palate: flavourful, fruity, toasty, round tannins.

Viña Valera Viñas Viejas 2012 T Roble
100% tempranillo

85

Zarzuela 2014 RD
100% tempranillo

84

Zarzuela 2014 T
100% tempranillo

85

Zarzuela Crianza 2011 TC
100% tempranillo

86

Zarzuela Reserva 2008 TR
100% tempranillo

88

Colour: dark-red cherry, orangey edge. Nose: ripe fruit, old leather, tobacco. Palate: correct, flavourful, spicy.

Zarzuela Selección 2012 T Roble
100% tempranillo

88

Colour: black cherry. Nose: ripe fruit, fruit preserve, spicy, creamy oak. Palate: powerful, flavourful, toasty.

Zarzuela Tinto 2013 T Roble
100% tempranillo

81

Zarzuela Viñas Viejas 2011 T
100% tempranillo

90

Colour: very deep cherry, garnet rim. Nose: toasty, ripe fruit, sweet spices. Palate: powerful, flavourful, good structure, round tannins.

Zarzuela Viñas Viejas 2012 T Roble
100% tempranillo

89

Colour: cherry, garnet rim. Nose: ripe fruit, spicy, creamy oak, complex. Palate: flavourful, toasty.

BODEGA CRAYON

Plaza de la Hispanidad 1, 5ºD
09400 Aranda de Duero (Burgos)
☎: +34 661 325 455
info@bodegacrayon.es
www.bodegacrayon.es

Talaia Crayon 2011 TC
100% tempranillo

88

Colour: bright cherry, garnet rim. Nose: powerfull, dried herbs, ripe fruit, spicy. Palate: spicy, ripe fruit, balsamic.

Talaia Crayon 2013 T Roble
100% tempranillo

87

Colour: deep cherry. Nose: grassy, herbaceous. Palate: fine bitter notes, easy to drink.

Talaia Crayon 2014 RD
100% tempranillo

86

BODEGA DÍAZ BAYO

Camino de los Anarinos, s/n
09471 Fuentelcésped (Burgos)
☎: +34 947 561 020
Fax: +34 947 561 204
info@bodegadiazbayo.com
www.bodegadiazbayo.com

FDB 2007 T Barrica
tempranillo

91 ♣

Colour: black cherry, orangey edge. Nose: old leather, animal reductive notes, toasty. Palate: balanced, classic aged character, flavourful.

Majuelo de la Hombría 2011 T
95% tempranillo, 5% albillo

92 ♣

Colour: black cherry, garnet rim. Nose: closed, characterful, ripe fruit. Palate: elegant, ripe fruit, long, balsamic, round tannins.

Nuestro 12 meses 2012 T Barrica
tempranillo

88 ♣

Colour: cherry, garnet rim. Nose: creamy oak, red berry notes, ripe fruit, balanced. Palate: flavourful, spicy, easy to drink.

Nuestro 20 meses 2010 T Barrica
tempranillo

92 ♣

Colour: very deep cherry, garnet rim. Nose: expressive, spicy, balsamic herbs. Palate: flavourful, ripe fruit, long, good acidity, balanced.

Nuestro Crianza 2010 TC
tempranillo

91 ♣

Colour: cherry, garnet rim. Nose: ripe fruit, spicy, creamy oak, complex. Palate: flavourful, toasty, round tannins.

BODEGA EMINA

Ctra. San Bernardo, s/n
47359 Valbuena de Duero (Valladolid)
☎: +34 983 683 315
Fax: +34 902 430 189
emina@emina.es
www.emina.es

Emina 2010 TR
100% tempranillo

88

Colour: very deep cherry, garnet rim. Nose: dark chocolate, ripe fruit, spicy. Palate: long, creamy, toasty.

Emina 2012 TC
100% tempranillo

88

Colour: bright cherry, garnet rim. Nose: creamy oak, toasty, ripe fruit, balsamic herbs. Palate: balanced, spicy, long.

Emina Atio 2010 TR
100% tempranillo

90

Colour: cherry, garnet rim. Nose: ripe fruit, spicy, creamy oak, complex. Palate: flavourful, toasty.

Emina Pasión 2014 T Roble
100% tempranillo

85

Emina Prestigio 2010 TR
tempranillo

89

Colour: cherry, garnet rim. Nose: ripe fruit, spicy, creamy oak, complex. Palate: flavourful, toasty.

BODEGA HEMAR

09315 Fuentecén (Burgos)
☎: +34 947 532 718
Fax: +34 947 532 768
info@bodegahemar.com
www.bodegahemar.com

Hemar 12 meses 2012 T
tempranillo

88

Colour: cherry, garnet rim. Nose: roasted coffee, smoky, spicy, fruit preserve. Palate: flavourful, smoky aftertaste, ripe fruit.

Hemar 7 meses 2013 T
tempranillo

85

Llanum Vendimia Seleccionada 2012 T
tempranillo

89

Colour: bright cherry, garnet rim. Nose: characterful, fruit preserve, sweet spices. Palate: flavourful, round tannins.

BODEGA HERMANOS DEL VILLAR

Zarcillo, s/n
47490 Rueda (Valladolid)
☎: +34 983 868 904
Fax: +34 983 868 905
pablo@orodecastilla.com
www.orodecastilla.com

Gaudeamus 2013 T Roble
100% tempranillo

86

BODEGA LOS MATUCOS

Ctra. BU-131, km. 4.800
09317 San Martín de Rubiales (Burgos)
☎: +34 947 613 922
Fax: +34 947 613 922
bodegalosmatucos@gmail.com
www.bodegalosmatucos.com

Matucos 2011 T
100% tempranillo

87

Colour: cherry, garnet rim. Nose: ripe fruit, spicy, creamy oak, complex. Palate: flavourful, toasty, round tannins.

Matucos 2014 T Roble
100% tempranillo

87

Colour: bright cherry. Nose: ripe fruit, sweet spices, creamy oak. Palate: flavourful, fruity, round tannins.

BODEGA MATARROMERA

Ctra. Renedo-Pesquera, Km. 30
47359 Valbuena de Duero (Valladolid)
☎: +34 983 683 315
Fax: +34 902 430 189
matarromera@matarromera.es
www.bodegamatarromera.es

Matarromera 2005 TGR
100% tempranillo

92

Colour: pale ruby, brick rim edge. Nose: spicy, fine reductive notes, wet leather, aged wood nuances, fruit liqueur notes. Palate: spicy, fine tannins, balanced.

Matarromera 2011 TR
100% tempranillo

91

Colour: cherry, garnet rim. Nose: red berry notes, ripe fruit, spicy, creamy oak, complex. Palate: flavourful, toasty.

Matarromera 2012 TC
100% tempranillo

90

Colour: cherry, garnet rim. Nose: fine reductive notes, wet leather, aged wood nuances, ripe fruit. Palate: spicy, long, toasty.

Matarromera Prestigio 2011 TGR
100% tempranillo

90

Colour: deep cherry. Nose: elegant, spicy, fine reductive notes, tobacco. Palate: spicy, elegant, long.

Melior 2014 T Roble
100% tempranillo

85

BODEGA NEXUS

Ctra. Pesquera de Duero a Renedo, s/n
47315 Pesquera de Duero (Valladolid)
☎: +34 983 880 488
Fax: +34 983 870 065
info@bodegasnexus.com
www.bodegasnexus.com

Nexus + 2009 T
100% tempranillo

93

Colour: cherry, garnet rim. Nose: complex, expressive, ripe fruit, scrubland, spicy. Palate: long, spicy, ripe fruit, round tannins.

Nexus 2009 TC
100% tempranillo

92

Colour: cherry, garnet rim. Nose: mineral, expressive, spicy. Palate: flavourful, ripe fruit, long, good acidity, balanced.

Nexus One 2013 T
100% tempranillo

88

Colour: very deep cherry, garnet rim. Nose: balanced, spicy, creamy oak, ripe fruit. Palate: full, flavourful, harsh oak tannins.

BODEGA RENACIMIENTO

Santa María, 36
47359 Olivares de Duero (Valladolid)
☎: +34 983 683 315
matarromera@matarromera.es
www.bodegamatarromera.es

Rento 2011 T
100% tempranillo

90

Colour: very deep cherry, garnet rim. Nose: characterful, spicy, ripe fruit, dried herbs. Palate: balanced, spicy.

BODEGA S. ARROYO

Avda. del Cid, 99
09441 Sotillo de la Ribera (Burgos)
☎: +34 947 532 444
Fax: +34 947 532 444
info@tintoarroyo.com
www.tintoarroyo.com

Tinto Arroyo 2007 TGR

88

Colour: dark-red cherry. Nose: spicy, fine reductive notes, ripe fruit, fruit preserve. Palate: spicy, fine tannins, balanced.

Tinto Arroyo 2010 TR
100% tempranillo

88

Colour: cherry, garnet rim. Nose: woody, creamy oak, sweet spices. Palate: flavourful, spicy.

Tinto Arroyo 2012 TC
100% tempranillo

88

Colour: cherry, garnet rim. Nose: characterful, ripe fruit, sweet spices. Palate: good structure, flavourful, round tannins.

Tinto Arroyo 2013 T Roble
100% tempranillo

88

Colour: deep cherry. Nose: creamy oak, toasty, ripe fruit, balsamic herbs. Palate: balanced, spicy, long.

Tinto Arroyo 2014 T
100% tempranillo

87

Colour: cherry, purple rim. Nose: fresh fruit, red berry notes, floral, wild herbs. Palate: flavourful, fruity, good acidity.

Tinto Arroyo Vendimia Seleccionada 2011 T
100% tempranillo

92

Colour: very deep cherry. Nose: expressive, balanced, ripe fruit, cocoa bean. Palate: good structure, flavourful, complex, round tannins.

Viñarroyo 2014 RD
100% tempranillo

87

Colour: rose, purple rim. Nose: balanced, red berry notes, ripe fruit, citrus fruit. Palate: fruity, easy to drink, good acidity.

BODEGA SAN MAMÉS, S. COOP.

Ctra. Valladolid, s/n
09315 Fuentecén (Burgos)
☎: +34 947 532 693
Fax: +34 947 532 653
info@bodegasanmames.com
www.bodegasanmames.com

Doble R 2011 TC
100% tempranillo

88

Colour: cherry, garnet rim. Nose: ripe fruit, fruit preserve, sweet spices, toasty. Palate: powerful, flavourful.

Doble R 2013 T
tempranillo

86

Doble R 2013 T Roble
100% tempranillo

85

Doble R 2014 RD
100% tempranillo

86

Doble R Vendimia Seleccionada 2010 T
100% tempranillo

91

Colour: cherry, garnet rim. Nose: ripe fruit, spicy, creamy oak, complex. Palate: flavourful, toasty, round tannins.

BODEGA SAN PEDRO REGALADO

Ctra. de Aranda, s/n
09370 La Aguilera (Burgos)
☎: +34 947 545 017
Fax: +34 947 545 017
bspregalado@terra.com
www.bodegaspregalado.com

Embocadero 2013 T
tempranillo

87

Colour: bright cherry. Nose: ripe fruit, sweet spices, creamy oak. Palate: flavourful, fruity, toasty.

Embocadero Viña El Águila 2011 T
tempranillo

89

Colour: cherry, garnet rim. Nose: creamy oak, balanced, ripe fruit. Palate: flavourful, spicy, easy to drink.

BODEGA SEVERINO SANZ

Del Rio, s/n
40542 Montejo De La Vega
De La Serrezuela (Segovia)
☎: +34 944 659 659
Fax: +34 944 531 442
erika@bodegaseverinosanz.es
www.bodegaseverinosanz.es

Alma de Severino 2014 RD
100% tempranillo

86

Herencia de Llanomingomez 2010 T
100% tempranillo

91

Colour: cherry, garnet rim. Nose: ripe fruit, wild herbs, earthy notes, spicy, balsamic herbs. Palate: balanced, flavourful, balsamic, long.

Muron 2013 T Roble
100% tempranillo

89

Colour: bright cherry. Nose: ripe fruit, sweet spices, creamy oak. Palate: flavourful, fruity, toasty.

Muron Autor 2013 T
100% tempranillo

87

Colour: cherry, garnet rim. Nose: ripe fruit, spicy, creamy oak. Palate: flavourful, toasty.

Muron Edición Limitada 2011 T
100% tempranillo

90

Colour: cherry, garnet rim. Nose: red berry notes, ripe fruit, spicy, creamy oak, complex. Palate: flavourful, toasty.

Pico del Llano 2014 T
100% tempranillo

85

BODEGA TOMÁS POSTIGO

Estación, 12
47300 Peñafiel (Valladolid)
☎: +34 983 873 019
Fax: +34 983 880 258
administracion@tomaspostigo.es
www.tomaspostigo.es

Tomás Postigo 2012 TC
80% tinto fino, 10% merlot, 8% cabernet sauvignon, 2% malbec

93

Colour: cherry, garnet rim. Nose: ripe fruit, wild herbs, earthy notes, spicy, balsamic herbs. Palate: balanced, flavourful, long, balsamic.

BODEGA VALDRINAL

Francisco Suárez, 18
28036 Madrid (Madrid)
☎: +34 914 113 522
general@valdrinal.com
www.valdrinal.com

Valdrinal 2010 TR
tempranillo

93

Colour: cherry, garnet rim. Nose: mineral, expressive, spicy. Palate: flavourful, ripe fruit, long, good acidity, balanced.

Valdrinal 2012 TC
tempranillo

87

Colour: bright cherry. Nose: sweet spices, creamy oak, fruit preserve, candied fruit. Palate: flavourful, fruity, toasty, round tannins.

Valdrinal 2013 T
tempranillo

85

Valdrinal Entrega 2013 T
tempranillo

88

Colour: cherry, garnet rim. Nose: red berry notes, ripe fruit, spicy, creamy oak. Palate: flavourful, toasty, round tannins.

Valdrinal SQR 2009 T
tempranillo

92

Colour: cherry, garnet rim. Nose: balanced, complex, ripe fruit, spicy, fine reductive notes. Palate: good structure, flavourful, round tannins, balanced.

Valdrinal Tradición 2012 TC
tempranillo

91

Colour: cherry, garnet rim. Nose: red berry notes, ripe fruit, spicy, creamy oak, complex. Palate: flavourful, toasty, round tannins.

BODEGA Y VIÑEDOS MILÉNICO

Avda. de la Paz, 6 Bis
09317 San Martín de Rubiales (Burgos)
☎: +34 695 382 848
milenico@milenico.com
www.milenico.com

Milénico 2012 T
tempranillo

92

Colour: deep cherry, garnet rim. Nose: characterful, powerfull, ripe fruit, spicy, creamy oak. Palate: good structure, long, spicy.

Valdepila 2012 T
tempranillo

88

Colour: deep cherry, garnet rim. Nose: cocoa bean, ripe fruit, fruit preserve, scrubland. Palate: flavourful, round tannins, smoky aftertaste.

BODEGAS ABADÍA LA ARROYADA

La Tejera, s/n
09442 Terradillos de Esgueva (Burgos)
☎: +34 947 545 309
bodegas@abadialaarroyada.es
www.abadialaarroyada.es

Abadía la Arroyada 2010 TC
100% tempranillo

88

Colour: deep cherry, garnet rim. Nose: powerfull, ripe fruit, fruit preserve, cocoa bean. Palate: correct, round tannins.

Abadía la Arroyada 2013 T
100% tempranillo

86

Abbatia Vendimia Seleccionada 2009 T
100% tempranillo

88

Colour: bright cherry. Nose: ripe fruit, sweet spices, creamy oak, dark chocolate. Palate: flavourful, fruity, toasty, round tannins.

BODEGAS ALTOGRANDE

Crta. Peñafiel Pesquera, Km 6
47316 Curiel de Duero (Valladolid)
☎: +34 983 880 489
Fax: +34 983 880 489
bodega@altogrande.es
www.altogrande.es

Altogrande 2011 TC
tempranillo

89

Colour: deep cherry, purple rim. Nose: creamy oak, toasty, ripe fruit, balsamic herbs. Palate: balanced, spicy, long.

Altogrande 2011 TR
tempranillo

89

Colour: bright cherry, garnet rim. Nose: powerfull, ripe fruit, fruit preserve, tobacco, sweet spices. Palate: flavourful, long.

Altogrande Vendimia Seleccionada 2011 T
tempranillo

90

Colour: cherry, garnet rim. Nose: fine reductive notes, wet leather, aged wood nuances, ripe fruit. Palate: spicy, long, toasty.

Valdecuriel 2014 T Roble
tempranillo

84

BODEGAS ANTÍDOTO

Elias Alvarez nº31 1ºB
42330 San Esteban de Gormaz (Soria)
☎: +34 676 536 390
bebervino@hotmail.com
www.bodegasantidoto.com

Antídoto 2013 T
100% tinto fino

90

Colour: cherry, garnet rim. Nose: creamy oak, red berry notes, mineral, expressive. Palate: flavourful, spicy, elegant.

La Hormiga de Antídoto 2013 T
tinto fino

91

Colour: cherry, garnet rim. Nose: creamy oak, red berry notes, fresh fruit, balanced. Palate: flavourful, spicy, elegant.

Le Rosé de Antídoto 2014 RD
tinto fino, albillo

92

Colour: coppery red. Nose: floral, wild herbs, fruit expression, expressive, sweet spices, pattiserie. Palate: flavourful, complex, balanced.

Roselito 2014 RD
tinto fino, albillo

88

Colour: coppery red. Nose: elegant, red berry notes, floral, fragrant herbs. Palate: light-bodied, flavourful, good acidity, long, spicy.

BODEGAS ARROCAL

Eras de Santa María, s/n
09443 Gumiel de Mercado (Burgos)
☎: +34 947 561 290
Fax: +34 947 561 290
rodrigo@arrocal.com
www.arrocal.com

Arrocal Angel 2011 T

92

Colour: cherry, garnet rim. Nose: ripe fruit, spicy, creamy oak, complex. Palate: flavourful, toasty, balsamic, elegant.

Arrocal Máximo 2009 T
tempranillo

93

Colour: cherry, garnet rim. Nose: ripe fruit, wild herbs, earthy notes, spicy, balsamic herbs. Palate: balanced, flavourful, long, balsamic, elegant.

Arrocal Passión 2012 T
tempranillo

89

Colour: bright cherry. Nose: ripe fruit, sweet spices, creamy oak. Palate: flavourful, fruity, toasty.

Arrocal Selección 2012 T
tempranillo

90

Colour: cherry, garnet rim. Nose: ripe fruit, wild herbs, spicy, creamy oak. Palate: powerful, flavourful, concentrated, balanced.

BODEGAS ARZUAGA NAVARRO

Ctra. N-122, Km. 325
47350 Quintanilla de Onésimo
(Valladolid)
☎: +34 983 681 146
Fax: +34 983 681 147
bodeg@arzuaganavarro.com
www.arzuaganavarro.com

Amaya Arzuaga Colección Autor 2011 T
95% tempranillo, 5% albillo

93

Colour: light cherry. Nose: fine reductive notes, aged wood nuances, toasty, ripe fruit. Palate: spicy, toasty, flavourful.

Arzuaga 2013 TC
90% tempranillo, 7% cabernet sauvignon, 3% merlot

88

Colour: cherry, garnet rim. Nose: roasted coffee, smoky, spicy, ripe fruit. Palate: flavourful, smoky aftertaste, ripe fruit.

Arzuaga 2011 TR
95% tempranillo, 5% merlot, albillo

91

Colour: cherry, garnet rim. Nose: smoky, spicy, roasted coffee. Palate: flavourful, smoky aftertaste, ripe fruit.

Arzuaga Ecológico 2011 TC
100% tempranillo

91 ✿

Colour: cherry, garnet rim. Nose: creamy oak, red berry notes, fresh fruit, balanced. Palate: flavourful, spicy, elegant.

Arzuaga Reserva Especial 2011 TR
95% tinto fino, 5% albillo

93

Colour: cherry, garnet rim. Nose: roasted coffee, smoky, spicy. Palate: flavourful, smoky aftertaste, ripe fruit.

Gran Arzuaga 2011 T
75% tempranillo, 20% cabernet sauvignon, 5% albillo

92

Colour: light cherry. Nose: fine reductive notes, aged wood nuances, toasty, overripe fruit. Palate: spicy, toasty, flavourful.

Rosae Arzuaga 2014 RD
100% tempranillo

90

Colour: salmon, bright. Nose: elegant, red berry notes, floral, fragrant herbs. Palate: light-bodied, flavourful, long, good acidity.

Viñedos y Bodegas La Planta 2014 T Roble
100% tempranillo

88

Colour: cherry, purple rim. Nose: ripe fruit, woody, roasted coffee. Palate: flavourful, spicy, powerful.

BODEGAS ASENJO & MANSO

Ctra. Palencia, km. 58,200
09311 La Horra (Burgos)
☎: +34 636 972 524
info@asenjo-manso.com
www.asenjo-manso.com

A&M Autor 2009 T
100% tempranillo

90

Colour: cherry, garnet rim. Nose: red berry notes, ripe fruit, spicy, creamy oak, complex. Palate: flavourful, toasty, round tannins.

Asenjo & Manso 2014 T
100% tempranillo

89

Colour: cherry, purple rim. Nose: expressive, fresh fruit, red berry notes, floral. Palate: flavourful, fruity, good acidity.

Ceres 2011 TC
100% tempranillo

88 ✿

Colour: very deep cherry. Nose: characterful, powerfull, ripe fruit. Palate: flavourful, round tannins, easy to drink.

Silvanus 2011 TC
100% tempranillo

88 ✿

Colour: cherry, garnet rim. Nose: roasted coffee, spicy, ripe fruit. Palate: flavourful, ripe fruit, toasty.

Silvanus Edición Limitada 2010 T
100% tempranillo

90

Colour: cherry, garnet rim. Nose: ripe fruit, spicy, creamy oak, complex. Palate: flavourful, toasty, round tannins.

BODEGAS BALBÁS

La Majada, s/n
09311 La Horra (Burgos)
☎: +34 947 542 111
Fax: +34 947 542 112
bodegas@balbas.es
www.balbas.es

Alitus 2006 TR
75% tempranillo, 20% cabernet sauvignon, 5% merlot

91

Colour: light cherry. Nose: fine reductive notes, aged wood nuances, toasty, smoky. Palate: spicy, toasty, flavourful, ripe fruit.

Ardal 2009 TR
80% tempranillo, 20% cabernet sauvignon

90

Colour: cherry, garnet rim. Nose: ripe fruit, wild herbs, earthy notes, spicy, balsamic herbs. Palate: balanced, flavourful, long, balsamic.

Ardal 2012 TC
80% tempranillo, 20% cabernet sauvignon

87

Colour: cherry, garnet rim. Nose: ripe fruit, sweet spices, creamy oak. Palate: powerful, flavourful, toasty.

Balbás 2012 TC
90% tempranillo, 10% cabernet sauvignon

90

Colour: cherry, garnet rim. Nose: ripe fruit, spicy, creamy oak, complex. Palate: flavourful, toasty, round tannins.

Ritus 2011 T
75% tempranillo, 25% merlot

91

Colour: cherry, garnet rim. Nose: ripe fruit, wild herbs, earthy notes, spicy, balsamic herbs. Palate: balanced, flavourful, long, balsamic.

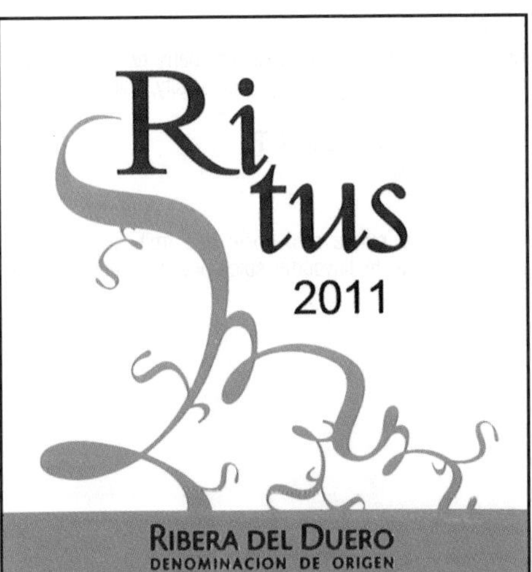

BODEGAS BOHÓRQUEZ

Ctra. Peñafiel a Pesquera de Duero, km. 4
47315 Pesquera de Duero (Valladolid)
☎: +34 915 643 751
Fax: +34 915 618 602
info@bodegasbohorquez.com
www.bodegasbohorquez.com

Bohórquez 2006 TR
tempranillo, merlot, cabernet sauvignon

88

Colour: bright cherry, orangey edge. Nose: wild herbs, ripe fruit, tobacco. Palate: balanced, spicy, long.

Cardela 2011 TC
tempranillo, merlot, cabernet sauvignon

88

Colour: cherry, garnet rim. Nose: red berry notes, ripe fruit, spicy, creamy oak, complex. Palate: flavourful, toasty.

BODEGAS BRIEGO

Ctra. Cuellar, s/n
47311 Fompedraza (Valladolid)
☎: +34 983 892 156
Fax: +34 983 892 156
info@bodegasbriego.com
www.bodegasbriego.com

Ankal 2012 TC
100% tempranillo

90

Colour: black cherry, garnet rim. Nose: characterful, powerfull, smoky, creamy oak, toasty, ripe fruit, fruit preserve. Palate: flavourful, round tannins.

Ankal 2013 T Roble
100% tempranillo

88

Colour: deep cherry, garnet rim. Nose: creamy oak, toasty, ripe fruit, balsamic herbs. Palate: balanced, spicy, long.

Ankal Edición Limitada 2009 TR
100% tempranillo

89

Colour: cherry, garnet rim. Nose: ripe fruit, spicy, creamy oak, smoky. Palate: flavourful, toasty.

Briego Fiel Edición Limitada 2009 T
100% tempranillo

89

Colour: cherry, garnet rim. Nose: ripe fruit, spicy, creamy oak. Palate: flavourful, toasty, round tannins.

Briego Infiel 2011 T

90

Colour: cherry, garnet rim. Nose: expressive, spicy. Palate: flavourful, ripe fruit, long, good acidity, balanced, slightly dry, soft tannins.

Briego Oyada 2011 T

100% tempranillo

92

Colour: very deep cherry, garnet rim. Nose: complex, ripe fruit, spicy, varietal. Palate: full, flavourful, good structure, fruity.

Briego Tiempo 2012 TC

100% tempranillo

89

Colour: dark-red cherry. Nose: ripe fruit, sweet spices, creamy oak. Palate: flavourful, fruity, toasty.

Briego Vendimia Seleccionada 2013 T Roble

100% tempranillo

88

Colour: deep cherry. Nose: creamy oak, toasty, ripe fruit, balsamic herbs. Palate: balanced, spicy, long.

Supernova 2012 TC

100% tempranillo

91

Colour: cherry, garnet rim. Nose: mineral, expressive, spicy. Palate: flavourful, ripe fruit, long, good acidity, balanced.

Supernova Edición Limitada 2009 T

100% tempranillo

90

Colour: deep cherry, garnet rim. Nose: toasty, smoky, spicy. Palate: balanced, fruity, spicy, correct, good structure.

Supernova Roble 2013 T Roble

100% tempranillo

90

Colour: cherry, garnet rim. Nose: ripe fruit, fragrant herbs, spicy, toasty, creamy oak. Palate: powerful, flavourful, balsamic, balanced.

BODEGAS BRIONES ABAD

Isabel la Católica, 42
09300 Roa de Duero (Burgos)
☎: +34 947 540 613
Fax: +34 947 540 613
brionesabad@cantamuda.com
www.cantamuda.com

Canta Muda 2013 T Roble

100% tempranillo

87

Colour: cherry, garnet rim. Nose: ripe fruit, spicy, aged wood nuances. Palate: powerful, flavourful, toasty.

Canta Muda Finca la Cebolla 2012 T

100% tempranillo

91

Colour: cherry, garnet rim. Nose: red berry notes, ripe fruit, spicy, creamy oak, complex. Palate: flavourful, toasty, round tannins.

Canta Muda Parcela 64 2012 T

100% tempranillo

90

Colour: bright cherry. Nose: ripe fruit, sweet spices, creamy oak, expressive. Palate: flavourful, fruity, toasty.

BODEGAS BRIONES BANIANDRÉS

Camino Valdeguzmán, s/n
09314 Quintanamanvirgo (Burgos)
☎: +34 625 579 347
Fax: +34 947 561 386
bodegas@apricus.es
www.apricus.es

Apricus 2011 TC

100% tempranillo

88

Colour: cherry, garnet rim. Nose: ripe fruit, spicy, creamy oak, complex. Palate: flavourful, toasty.

Apricus 2013 T Roble

100% tempranillo

88

Colour: deep cherry. Nose: creamy oak, toasty, ripe fruit, balsamic herbs. Palate: balanced, spicy, long.

Apricus 2014 T Joven

100% tempranillo

88

Colour: cherry, purple rim. Nose: red berry notes, floral, balanced. Palate: flavourful, fruity, good acidity, fruity aftestaste.

Apricus Sensus 2011 T

100% tempranillo

90

Colour: cherry, purple rim. Nose: ripe fruit, sweet spices, creamy oak. Palate: flavourful, spicy, powerful, round tannins.

BODEGAS CASAJÚS

Cercados s/n
09370 Quintana del Pidío (Burgos)
☎: +34 947 545 626
Fax: +34 947 545 626
info@bodegascasajus.com
www.bodegascasajus.com

Casajús 2011 TC
100% tempranillo

92

Colour: deep cherry, garnet rim. Nose: powerfull, balanced, expressive, dried herbs, ripe fruit. Palate: good structure, flavourful, ripe fruit.

Casajús 6 meses de barrica 2013 T Barrica
tempranillo

87

Colour: cherry, purple rim. Nose: floral, balsamic herbs, spicy, red berry notes, ripe fruit, dried herbs. Palate: powerful, fresh, fruity.

BODEGAS CEPA 21

Ctra. N-122, Km. 297
47315 Castrillo de Duero (Valladolid)
☎: +34 983 484 083
Fax: +34 983 480 017
comunicacion@cepa21.com
www.cepa21.com

Cepa 21 2011 T
100% tinto fino

91

Colour: cherry, garnet rim. Nose: balanced, complex, ripe fruit, sweet spices. Palate: good structure, flavourful, round tannins, balanced.

Hito 2014 RD
100% tinto fino

86

Hito 2014 T
100% tinto fino

89

Colour: bright cherry. Nose: ripe fruit, sweet spices, creamy oak, expressive. Palate: flavourful, fruity, toasty.

Malabrigo 2011 T
100% tinto fino

93

Colour: cherry, garnet rim. Nose: smoky, spicy, ripe fruit, mineral. Palate: flavourful, ripe fruit, long, balanced.

BODEGAS COPABOCA

Autovía A-62, Salida 148
47100 Tordesillas (Valladolid)
☎: +34 983 486 010
club@copaboca.com
www.copaboca.com

Finca Feroes 2013 T Roble
100% tempranillo

86

Gorgorito 2013 T
100% tempranillo

87

Colour: bright cherry. Nose: ripe fruit, wild herbs, spicy. Palate: flavourful, fruity, easy to drink.

BODEGAS CRUZ DE ALBA

Síndico, 4 y 5
47350 Quintanilla de Onésimo
(Valladolid)
☎: +34 941 310 295
info@bodegasramonbilbao.es
www.cruzdealba.es

Cruz de Alba 2013 TC
100% tempranillo

88

Colour: deep cherry. Nose: creamy oak, toasty, ripe fruit, balsamic herbs. Palate: balanced, spicy, long.

Lucero de Alba 2014 T Roble
100% tempranillo

87

Colour: cherry, garnet rim. Nose: powerfull, ripe fruit, spicy. Palate: powerful, fruity, unctuous.

BODEGAS CUEVAS JIMÉNEZ - FERRATUS

Ctra. Madrid-Irún, A-I km. 165
09370 Gumiel de Izán (Burgos)
☎: +34 947 679 999
Fax: +34 947 613 873
bodega@ferratus.es
www.ferratus.es

Ferratus 2009 T
100% tempranillo

93

Colour: cherry, garnet rim. Nose: ripe fruit, wild herbs, earthy notes, spicy, balsamic herbs. Palate: balanced, flavourful, long, round.

Ferratus A0 2014 T Roble
100% tempranillo

89

Colour: bright cherry. Nose: ripe fruit, sweet spices, creamy oak, expressive. Palate: flavourful, fruity, spicy.

Ferratus Sensaciones 2008 T
100% tempranillo

92

Colour: light cherry. Nose: fine reductive notes, aged wood nuances, toasty. Palate: spicy, toasty, flavourful.

PODIUM

Ferratus Sensaciones Décimo 2003 T

96

Colour: cherry, garnet rim. Nose: balanced, complex, ripe fruit, spicy, fine reductive notes. Palate: good structure, flavourful, round tannins, balanced.

BODEGAS DE LOS RÍOS PRIETO

Ctra. Pesquera - Renedo, s/n
47315 Pesquera de Duero (Valladolid)
☎: +34 983 880 383
Fax: +34 983 878 032
administracion@bodegasdelosriosprieto.com
www.bodegasdelosriosprieto.com

Prios Maximus 2012 TC
100% tempranillo

87

Colour: bright cherry. Nose: ripe fruit, sweet spices, creamy oak, toasty. Palate: flavourful, fruity, toasty.

Prios Maximus 2012 TR
100% tempranillo

88

Colour: cherry, garnet rim. Nose: smoky, spicy, ripe fruit. Palate: flavourful, smoky aftertaste.

Prios Maximus 2014 T Roble
100% tempranillo

86

BODEGAS DEL CAMPO

Camino Fuentenavares, s/n
09370 Quintana del Pidío (Burgos)
☎: +34 947 561 034
bodegas@pagosdequintana.com
www.pagosdequintana.com

Pagos de Quintana 2010 TC
100% tinto fino

89

Colour: bright cherry. Nose: ripe fruit, sweet spices, creamy oak. Palate: flavourful, fruity, toasty.

Pagos de Quintana Roble 2013 T
100% tinto fino

85

Pagos de Quintana Vendimia Seleccionada 2011 T
100% tinto fino

89

Colour: deep cherry. Nose: fruit preserve, spicy, creamy oak. Palate: powerful, flavourful, toasty.

BODEGAS DÍEZ LLORENTE

Ctra. Circunvalación, s/n
09300 Roa (Burgos)
☎: +34 615 293 031
Fax: +34 947 540 341
bodegas@diezllorente.com
www.diezllorente.com

Díez Llorente 2012 TC
tempranillo

89

Colour: cherry, garnet rim. Nose: roasted coffee, smoky, spicy, fruit preserve. Palate: flavourful, smoky aftertaste, ripe fruit.

Díez Llorente 2014 T Roble
tempranillo

87

Colour: cherry, purple rim. Nose: powerfull, ripe fruit, spicy. Palate: powerful, fruity, unctuous.

Señorío de Brenda 2012 TC
tempranillo

87

Colour: very deep cherry, garnet rim. Nose: balsamic herbs, balanced, fruit preserve. Palate: full, flavourful.

Señorío de Brenda 2014 T Roble
tempranillo

87

Colour: bright cherry. Nose: ripe fruit, sweet spices, creamy oak. Palate: flavourful, fruity, toasty.

BODEGAS DOMINIO DE CAIR

Ctra. Aranda a la Aguilera. km. 9
09370 La Aguilera (Burgos)
☎: +34 947 545 276
Fax: +34 947 545 383
bodegas@dominiodecair.com
www.dominiodecair.com

Cair 2011 TC
100% tempranillo

93

Colour: cherry, garnet rim. Nose: creamy oak, red berry notes, balanced. Palate: flavourful, spicy, elegant.

Cair Cuvée 2012 T
85% tempranillo, 15% merlot

92

Colour: cherry, garnet rim. Nose: creamy oak, red berry notes, fresh fruit, balanced. Palate: flavourful, spicy.

Tierras de Cair 2010 TR
100% tempranillo

93

Colour: cherry, garnet rim. Nose: smoky, spicy, ripe fruit, earthy notes. Palate: flavourful, smoky aftertaste, ripe fruit.

BODEGAS EL INICIO

San Vicente, 22
47300 Peñafiel (Valladolid)
☎: +34 947 515 884
Fax: +34 947 515 886
info@bodegaselinicio.com
www.bodegaselinicio.com

Admiración Selección Especial 2011 T
100% tempranillo

89

Colour: cherry, garnet rim. Nose: red berry notes, ripe fruit, spicy, creamy oak, complex. Palate: flavourful, toasty.

Rivendel 2012 TC
100% tempranillo

88

Colour: cherry, garnet rim. Nose: roasted coffee, smoky, spicy, fruit preserve. Palate: flavourful, smoky aftertaste, ripe fruit.

Rivendel 2014 T Roble
100% tempranillo

87

Colour: bright cherry. Nose: ripe fruit, sweet spices, creamy oak, expressive. Palate: flavourful, fruity.

BODEGAS EMILIO MORO

Ctra. Peñafiel - Valoria, s/n
47315 Pesquera de Duero (Valladolid)
☎: +34 983 878 400
Fax: +34 983 870 195
comunicacion@emiliomoro.com
www.emiliomoro.com

Emilio Moro 2013 T
100% tinto fino

90

Colour: cherry, garnet rim. Nose: ripe fruit, fragrant herbs, spicy, toasty, creamy oak. Palate: powerful, flavourful, balsamic, balanced.

Finca Resalso 2014 T
100% tinto fino

90

Colour: cherry, garnet rim. Nose: red berry notes, ripe fruit, fragrant herbs, spicy, toasty, mineral. Palate: powerful, flavourful, balsamic, balanced.

Malleolus 2011 T
100% tinto fino

93

Colour: cherry, garnet rim. Nose: mineral, expressive, spicy. Palate: flavourful, ripe fruit, long, good acidity, balanced.

Malleolus de SanchoMartín 2010 T
100% tinto fino

93

Colour: cherry, garnet rim. Nose: smoky, spicy, ripe fruit, dark chocolate. Palate: flavourful, smoky aftertaste, ripe fruit.

Malleolus de Valderramiro 2010 T
100% tinto fino

92

Colour: light cherry. Nose: fine reductive notes, aged wood nuances, toasty, dark chocolate, ripe fruit. Palate: spicy, toasty, flavourful.

BODEGAS EPIFANIO RIVERA

Onésimo Redondo, 1
47315 Pesquera de Duero (Valladolid)
☎: +34 983 870 109
Fax: +34 983 870 109
info@epifaniorivera.com
www.epifaniorivera.com

Erial 2013 T
100% tinto fino

90

Colour: bright cherry, purple rim. Nose: expressive, balanced, ripe fruit. Palate: flavourful, fruity, spicy.

Erial TF 2012 T
100% tinto fino

90

Colour: very deep cherry, garnet rim. Nose: smoky, spicy, ripe fruit, toasty. Palate: good structure, flavourful, fruity.

BODEGAS FÉLIX CALLEJO

Avda. del Cid, km. 16
09441 Sotillo de la Ribera (Burgos)
☎: +34 947 532 312
Fax: +34 947 532 304
callejo@bodegasfelixcallejo.com
www.bodegasfelixcallejo.com

Callejo 2012 TC
100% tempranillo

90

Colour: cherry, garnet rim. Nose: red berry notes, ripe fruit, spicy, creamy oak, complex. Palate: flavourful, toasty.

Félix Callejo 2012 T
100% tempranillo

91

Colour: cherry, garnet rim. Nose: ripe fruit, wild herbs, earthy notes, spicy, balsamic herbs, warm. Palate: balanced, flavourful, long, balsamic.

Flores de Callejo 2013 T
100% tempranillo

89

Colour: deep cherry, purple rim. Nose: creamy oak, toasty, ripe fruit, balsamic herbs. Palate: balanced, spicy, long.

Gran Callejo 2009 T
100% tempranillo

89

Colour: deep cherry, garnet rim. Nose: wild herbs, ripe fruit. Palate: flavourful, fruity, ripe fruit, spicy.

Viña Pilar 2014 RD
100% tempranillo

86

BODEGAS FUENTENARRO

Constitución, 32
09311 La Horra (Burgos)
☎: +34 947 542 092
Fax: +34 947 542 083
bodegas@fuentenarro.com
www.fuentenarro.com

Viña Fuentenarro 2009 TR
tempranillo

90

Colour: cherry, garnet rim. Nose: ripe fruit, tobacco, balsamic herbs. Palate: correct, flavourful, spicy.

Viña Fuentenarro 2012 TC
tempranillo

89

Colour: cherry, garnet rim. Nose: ripe fruit, spicy, creamy oak. Palate: flavourful, toasty.

Viña Fuentenarro Cuatro Meses Barrica 2013 T Barrica
tempranillo

87

Colour: deep cherry, purple rim. Nose: toasty, ripe fruit, balsamic herbs, grassy. Palate: balanced, spicy, long.

Viña Fuentenarro Vendimia Seleccionada 2013 T
tempranillo

87

Colour: very deep cherry, garnet rim. Nose: balsamic herbs, balanced. Palate: full, flavourful, round tannins.

BODEGAS FUSIÓN

Isilla 1
09400 Aranda de Duero (Burgos)
☎: +34 947 510 914
info@bodegasfusion.com
www.bodegasfusion.com

Lara O Hispania 2009 T
100% tempranillo

90

Colour: cherry, garnet rim. Nose: ripe fruit, spicy, creamy oak, fine reductive notes. Palate: flavourful, toasty, round tannins.

Lara O Pro 2010 T
100% tempranillo

92

Colour: cherry, garnet rim. Nose: expressive, spicy, complex. Palate: flavourful, ripe fruit, long, good acidity, balanced.

BODEGAS GARCÍA DE ARANDA

Ctra. de Soria, s/n
09400 Aranda de Duero (Burgos)
☎: +34 947 501 817
Fax: +34 947 506 355
bodega@bodegasgarcia.com
www.bodegasgarcia.com

Edades de Baldíos 2012 T Roble
tempranillo

87

Colour: cherry, purple rim. Nose: woody, roasted coffee. Palate: flavourful, spicy, powerful.

PG Pedro García 2011 TC
tempranillo

90

Colour: very deep cherry, garnet rim. Nose: mineral, balsamic herbs, balanced. Palate: full, flavourful, round tannins.

Señorío de los Baldíos 2008 TR
tempranillo

86

Señorío de los Baldíos 2012 TC
tempranillo

87

Colour: cherry, garnet rim. Nose: roasted coffee, smoky, spicy, ripe fruit. Palate: flavourful, smoky aftertaste, ripe fruit.

Señorío de los Baldíos 2013 T Roble
tempranillo

84

Señorío de los Baldíos 2014 T
tempranillo

85

Señorío de los Baldíos Don Anastasio 2014 RD
tempranillo

84

BODEGAS GRUPO YLLERA

Autovía A-6, Km. 173,5
47490 Rueda (Valladolid)
☎: +34 983 868 097
Fax: +34 983 868 177
grupoyllera@grupoyllera.com
www.grupoyllera.com

Boada Pepe Yllera 2013 T Roble
tempranillo

88

Colour: cherry, garnet rim. Nose: ripe fruit, spicy, complex. Palate: flavourful, toasty, good acidity.

Bracamonte 2011 TC
tempranillo

90

Colour: cherry, garnet rim. Nose: balanced, complex, ripe fruit, spicy, fine reductive notes. Palate: good structure, flavourful, balanced.

Bracamonte 2011 TR
tempranillo

89

Colour: cherry, garnet rim. Nose: roasted coffee, smoky, spicy, ripe fruit. Palate: flavourful, smoky aftertaste, ripe fruit.

Bracamonte 2013 T Roble
tempranillo

88

Colour: bright cherry. Nose: ripe fruit, sweet spices. Palate: flavourful, fruity, spicy, correct.

Viña del Val 2014 T
tempranillo

87

Colour: cherry, purple rim. Nose: red berry notes, floral, balsamic herbs. Palate: powerful, fresh, fruity.

BODEGAS HACIENDA MONASTERIO

Ctra. Pesquera - Valbuena, s/n
47315 Pesquera de Duero (Valladolid)
☎: +34 983 484 002
bmonasterio@haciendamonasterio.com
www.haciendamonasterio.com

PODIUM

Hacienda Monasterio 2010 TR
80% tinto fino, 20% cabernet sauvignon

95

Colour: cherry, garnet rim. Nose: balanced, complex, ripe fruit, spicy. Palate: good structure, flavourful, round tannins, balanced.

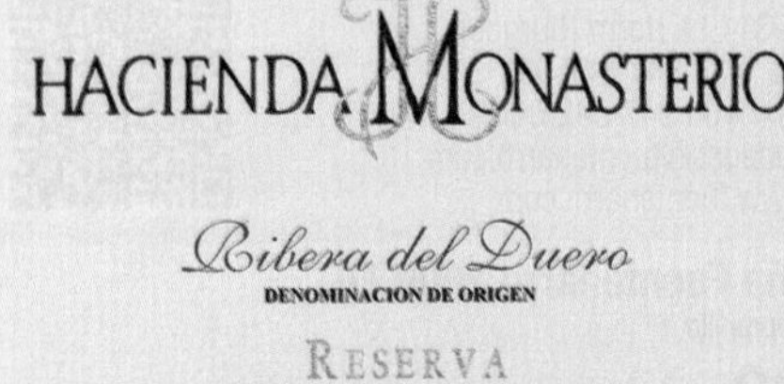

Hacienda Monasterio 2012 T
80% tinto fino, 10% cabernet sauvignon, 10% merlot

92

Colour: light cherry. Nose: fine reductive notes, aged wood nuances, toasty, earthy notes. Palate: spicy, toasty, flavourful.

Hacienda Monasterio Reserva Especial 2011 TR
75% tinto fino, 25% cabernet sauvignon

94

Colour: bright cherry. Nose: balanced, complex, ripe fruit, spicy. Palate: good structure, flavourful, round tannins, balanced, elegant.

BODEGAS HERMANOS SASTRE

San Pedro, s/n
09311 La Horra (Burgos)
☎: +34 947 542 108
Fax: +34 947 542 108
sastre@vinasastre.com
www.vinasastre.com

🏆 PODIUM

Regina Vides 2012 T
tinta del país

95

Colour: bright cherry. Nose: expressive, complex, ripe fruit, cocoa bean. Palate: long, fruity aftestaste, good structure, flavourful, round.

Viña Sastre 2012 TC
tinta del país

93

Colour: cherry, garnet rim. Nose: creamy oak, red berry notes, fresh fruit, balanced. Palate: flavourful, spicy, elegant.

Viña Sastre 2013 T Roble
tinta del país

92

Colour: bright cherry. Nose: ripe fruit, sweet spices, creamy oak, expressive. Palate: flavourful, fruity, round tannins.

Viña Sastre Pago de Santa Cruz 2012 T
tinta del país

94

Colour: bright cherry, garnet rim. Nose: expressive, ripe fruit, spicy, complex, varietal. Palate: good structure, full, balanced, long.

🏆 PODIUM

Viña Sastre Pesus 2012 T
80% tinta del país, 20% cabernet sauvignon

95

Colour: cherry, garnet rim. Nose: balanced, complex, ripe fruit, spicy, mineral. Palate: good structure, flavourful, round tannins, balanced, full.

BODEGAS HNOS. PÁRAMO ARROYO

Ctra. de Roa - Pedrosa, km. 4
09314 Pedrosa de Duero (Burgos)
☎: +34 947 530 041
bodega@paramoarroyo.com
www.paramoarroyo.com

Eremus 2010 TC
100% tempranillo

87 ♣

Colour: light cherry. Nose: fine reductive notes, aged wood nuances, toasty, ripe fruit. Palate: spicy, toasty, flavourful.

Eremus 2013 T
100% tempranillo

83 ♣

BODEGAS HNOS. PÉREZ PASCUAS

Ctra. Roa, s/n
09314 Pedrosa de Duero (Burgos)
☎: +34 947 530 100
Fax: +34 947 530 002
vinapedrosa@perezpascuas.com
www.perezpascuas.com

Cepa Gavilán 2013 T
100% tinta del país

89

Colour: bright cherry. Nose: ripe fruit, creamy oak, wild herbs. Palate: flavourful, fruity, toasty, balanced.

Pérez Pascuas Gran Selección 2010 TGR
90% tinta del país, 10% cabernet sauvignon

94

Colour: bright cherry, garnet rim. Nose: elegant, spicy, fine reductive notes, balsamic herbs, mineral, expressive. Palate: spicy, fine tannins, elegant, long.

Viña Pedrosa 2010 TGR
90% tinta del país, 10% cabernet sauvignon

94

Colour: cherry, garnet rim. Nose: mineral, expressive, spicy, ripe fruit, balanced. Palate: flavourful, ripe fruit, long, good acidity, elegant.

Viña Pedrosa 2012 TR
90% tinta del país, 10% cabernet sauvignon

92

Colour: cherry, garnet rim. Nose: ripe fruit, spicy, creamy oak, complex. Palate: flavourful, toasty, round tannins.

Viña Pedrosa 2013 TC
100% tinta del país

90

Colour: cherry, garnet rim. Nose: red berry notes, ripe fruit, fragrant herbs, spicy, mineral. Palate: powerful, flavourful, balsamic, balanced.

Viña Pedrosa La Navilla 2012 T
tinta del país

93

Colour: cherry, garnet rim. Nose: ripe fruit, wild herbs, earthy notes, spicy, elegant. Palate: balanced, flavourful, long, balsamic.

BODEGAS IMPERIALES

Ctra. Madrid - Irun, Km. 171
09370 Gumiel de Izán (Burgos)
☎: +34 947 544 070
Fax: +34 947 525 759
adminis@bodegasimperiales.com
www.bodegasimperiales.com

Abadía de San Quirce 2009 TR
100% tempranillo

89

Colour: cherry, garnet rim. Nose: fine reductive notes, ripe fruit, spicy. Palate: spicy, long, toasty.

Abadía de San Quirce 2012 TC
100% tempranillo

91

Colour: very deep cherry, garnet rim. Nose: expressive, complex, balsamic herbs, balanced, characterful. Palate: full, flavourful, round tannins.

Abadía de San Quirce 2013 T Roble
100% tempranillo

90

Colour: bright cherry. Nose: ripe fruit, sweet spices, creamy oak, expressive. Palate: flavourful, fruity, round tannins.

Abadía de San Quirce Finca Helena Autor 2009 T
100% tempranillo

93

Colour: very deep cherry, garnet rim. Nose: spicy, smoky, tobacco, ripe fruit, characterful, powerfull. Palate: good structure, flavourful, round tannins, spicy.

BODEGAS ISMAEL ARROYO - VALSOTILLO

Los Lagares, 71
09441 Sotillo de la Ribera (Burgos)
☎: +34 947 532 309
Fax: +34 947 532 487
bodega@valsotillo.com
www.valsotillo.com

Mesoneros de Castilla 2013 T Roble
100% tinta del país

89

Colour: bright cherry. Nose: ripe fruit, sweet spices, creamy oak, expressive. Palate: flavourful, fruity, toasty, round tannins.

ValSotillo 2004 TGR
100% tinta del país

92

Colour: dark-red cherry, orangey edge. Nose: ripe fruit, fruit liqueur notes, aged wood nuances. Palate: flavourful, fine tannins, spicy.

ValSotillo 2009 TR
100% tinta del país

89

Colour: cherry, garnet rim. Nose: tobacco, ripe fruit, smoky, spicy. Palate: balanced, correct, spicy, easy to drink.

ValSotillo 2011 TC
100% tinta del país

87

Colour: deep cherry. Nose: spicy, fine reductive notes, wet leather, aged wood nuances, ripe fruit. Palate: spicy, fine tannins, balanced.

ValSotillo 2012 T
100% tinta del país

91

Colour: cherry, garnet rim. Nose: ripe fruit, wild herbs, earthy notes, spicy. Palate: balanced, flavourful, long.

ValSotillo Finca Buenavista 2012 T
100% tinta del país

88

Colour: very deep cherry, garnet rim. Nose: ripe fruit, spicy, wild herbs. Palate: flavourful, spicy, easy to drink.

ValSotillo VS 2004 TR
100% tinta del país

92

Colour: pale ruby, brick rim edge. Nose: spicy, fine reductive notes, wet leather, aged wood nuances, fruit liqueur notes. Palate: spicy, fine tannins, balanced.

BODEGAS LA CEPA ALTA

Ctra. de Quintanilla, 28
47359 Olivares de Duero (Valladolid)
☎: +34 983 681 010
Fax: +34 983 681 010
info@lacepaalta.com
www.lacepaalta.com

Cepa Alta 2011 TC
tempranillo

87

Colour: cherry, garnet rim. Nose: ripe fruit, spicy, creamy oak. Palate: flavourful, toasty.

Cepa Alta 2013 T
tempranillo, cabernet sauvignon

86

Cepa Alta 2013 T Roble
tempranillo, cabernet sauvignon

85

Cinco Elemento 2010 TC
tempranillo

88

Colour: cherry, garnet rim. Nose: ripe fruit, spicy, creamy oak. Palate: flavourful, toasty, round tannins.

Cinco Elemento 2013 T Roble
tempranillo, cabernet sauvignon

85

Cinco Elementos 2014 T
tempranillo, cabernet sauvignon

84

Laveguilla 2009 TR
tempranillo

87

Colour: cherry, garnet rim. Nose: fine reductive notes, aged wood nuances, spicy. Palate: spicy, long, toasty, correct.

Laveguilla 2011 TC
tempranillo

90

Colour: cherry, garnet rim. Nose: red berry notes, ripe fruit, spicy, creamy oak, complex. Palate: flavourful, toasty.

Laveguilla 2013 T Roble
tempranillo

87

Colour: cherry, purple rim. Nose: ripe fruit, woody, roasted coffee. Palate: flavourful, spicy, powerful.

Laveguilla Autor 2011 T
tempranillo

88

Colour: cherry, garnet rim. Nose: ripe fruit, fruit preserve, creamy oak. Palate: powerful, flavourful.

Laveguilla Expresión Tempranillo 2013 T
tempranillo

88

Colour: bright cherry. Nose: ripe fruit, sweet spices, creamy oak. Palate: flavourful, fruity, toasty.

Laveguilla Selección 2011 T
tempranillo

87

Colour: cherry, garnet rim. Nose: ripe fruit, spicy, creamy oak, complex. Palate: flavourful, toasty.

Satiro 2009 T
tempranillo

90

Colour: cherry, garnet rim. Nose: red berry notes, ripe fruit, spicy, creamy oak, complex. Palate: flavourful, toasty, round tannins.

BODEGAS LA HORRA

Camino de Anguix, s/n
09311 La Horra (Burgos)
☎: +34 947 613 963
Fax: +34 947 613 963
rodarioja@roda.es
www.bodegaslahorra.es

Corimbo 2012 T
100% tinta del país

89

Colour: very deep cherry, garnet rim. Nose: ripe fruit, spicy, creamy oak, balanced. Palate: good structure, flavourful.

Corimbo I 2010 T
100% tinta del país

93

Colour: light cherry. Nose: fine reductive notes, aged wood nuances, toasty, ripe fruit. Palate: spicy, toasty, flavourful.

BODEGAS LAMBUENA

Ctra. Fuentecén, s/n
09300 Roa (Burgos)
☎: +34 947 540 016
Fax: +34 947 540 614
lambuena@bodegaslambuena.com
www.bodegaslambuena.com

Lagunero Selección 2013 T

86

Lambuena 2009 TR

90

Colour: cherry, garnet rim. Nose: fine reductive notes, wet leather, toasty, ripe fruit. Palate: spicy, long, toasty, round tannins.

Lambuena 2011 TC

87

Colour: cherry, garnet rim. Nose: smoky, spicy, ripe fruit. Palate: flavourful, smoky aftertaste, ripe fruit, harsh oak tannins.

Lambuena 2013 T Roble

86

Lambuena Rosado Selección 2014 RD

87

Colour: raspberry rose. Nose: elegant, red berry notes, floral, fragrant herbs. Palate: light-bodied, flavourful, good acidity, fine bitter notes.

Lambuena Viñas Viejas 2010 T

91

Colour: cherry, garnet rim. Nose: red berry notes, ripe fruit, spicy, creamy oak, complex. Palate: flavourful, toasty, round tannins.

BODEGAS LAN

Paraje del Buicio, s/n
26360 Fuenmayor (La Rioja)
☎: +34 941 450 950
Fax: +34 941 450 567
info@bodegaslan.com
www.bodegaslan.com

8000 Marqués de Burgos 2011 T
100% tinto fino

92

Colour: very deep cherry, garnet rim. Nose: expressive, complex, balsamic herbs, balanced, fragrant herbs, tobacco. Palate: full, flavourful, round tannins.

Marqués de Burgos 2011 TC
100% tempranillo

87

Colour: cherry, garnet rim. Nose: ripe fruit, spicy, creamy oak. Palate: flavourful, toasty.

Marqués de Burgos 2012 T Roble
100% tempranillo

87

Colour: bright cherry. Nose: ripe fruit, sweet spices, creamy oak. Palate: fruity, toasty, correct, easy to drink.

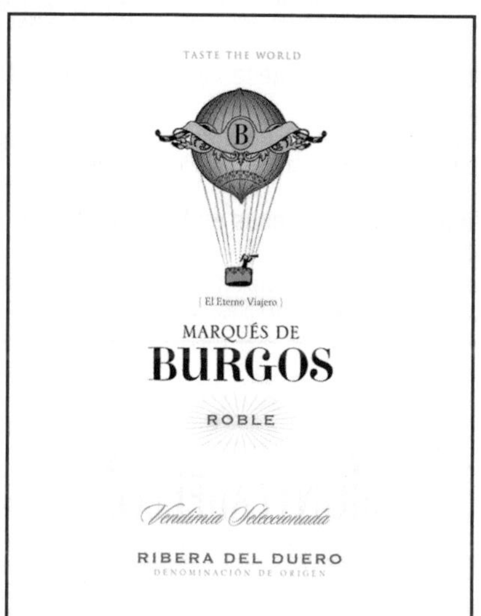

BODEGAS LIBA Y DELEITE
Turina, 11
47006 Valladolid (Valladolid)
☎: +34 629 450 436
acontia@acontia.es
www.acontia.es

Liba y Deleite & Acontia 06 2014 T
100% tempranillo

85

Liba y Deleite & Acontia 12 2012 T
100% tempranillo

88

Colour: cherry, garnet rim. Nose: wild herbs, balsamic herbs, fruit preserve. Palate: balanced, flavourful, long.

BODEGAS LÓPEZ CRISTÓBAL
Barrio Estación, s/n
09300 Roa de Duero (Burgos)
☎: +34 947 561 139
Fax: +34 947 540 606
info@lopezcristobal.com
www.lopezcristobal.com

Bagús 2012 T
100% tempranillo

90

Colour: cherry, garnet rim. Nose: ripe fruit, spicy, creamy oak, complex. Palate: flavourful, toasty.

López Cristobal 2011 TR
95% tempranillo, 5% merlot

91

Colour: cherry, garnet rim. Nose: ripe fruit, wild herbs, earthy notes, spicy, balsamic herbs. Palate: balanced, flavourful, long.

López Cristobal 2012 TC
95% tempranillo, 5% merlot

89

Colour: cherry, garnet rim. Nose: ripe fruit, wild herbs, earthy notes, spicy, balsamic herbs. Palate: flavourful, long, balsamic.

López Cristobal 2014 T Roble
95% tempranillo, 5% merlot

90

Colour: cherry, purple rim. Nose: ripe fruit, toasty, spicy. Palate: flavourful, spicy, powerful, varietal.

López Cristobal Selección 2011 T
100% tempranillo

92

Colour: cherry, garnet rim. Nose: expressive, spicy, complex. Palate: flavourful, ripe fruit, long, good acidity, balanced.

BODEGAS MARTA MATÉ

Camino de Caleruega s/n
09453 Tubilla del Lago (Burgos)
☎: +34 947 613 924
Fax: +34 947 546 666
bodega@martamate.com
www.martamate.com

Marta Maté 2012 T

tinto fino

91

Colour: cherry, garnet rim. Nose: mineral, expressive, spicy. Palate: flavourful, ripe fruit, long, good acidity, balanced.

Píxide 2013 T

tinto fino

86

Primordium 2010 T

tinto fino

88

Colour: cherry, garnet rim. Nose: ripe fruit, old leather, tobacco. Palate: correct, flavourful, spicy.

BODEGAS MONTEABELLÓN

Calvario, s/n
09318 Nava de Roa (Burgos)
☎: +34 947 550 000
Fax: +34 947 550 219
info@monteabellon.com
www.monteabellon.com

Monteabellón 14 meses en barrica 2012 T

90

Colour: cherry, garnet rim. Nose: roasted coffee, smoky, spicy, ripe fruit. Palate: flavourful, smoky aftertaste, ripe fruit.

Monteabellón 5 meses en barrica 2014 T

86

Colour: very deep cherry, purple rim. Nose: powerfull, ripe fruit, wild herbs, waxy notes, fruit preserve. Palate: flavourful.

Monteabellón Finca La Blanquera 2009 T

91

Colour: black cherry, garnet rim. Nose: ripe fruit, tobacco, candied fruit, powerfull. Palate: good structure, flavourful, toasty.

BODEGAS MUÑOZ Y MAZÓN

Avda. Doctor Ruiz Azcárraga, 1
26350 Cenicero (La Rioja)
☎: +34 941 454 050
Fax: +34 941 454 529
bodega@bodegasriojanas.com
www.bodegasriojanas.com

Azuel 2012 TC

100% tempranillo

87

Colour: bright cherry. Nose: sweet spices, creamy oak, overripe fruit. Palate: flavourful, fruity, toasty, round tannins.

Azuel Cosecha 2014 T

100% tempranillo

88

Colour: cherry, purple rim. Nose: expressive, fresh fruit, red berry notes, floral. Palate: flavourful, fruity, good acidity.

Azuel Roble 2014 T
100% tempranillo

86

BODEGAS ORDÓÑEZ

Julio Romero de Torres, 12
29700 Vélez- Málaga (Málaga)
☎: +34 952 504 706
Fax: +34 951 284 796
info@jorgeordonez.es
www.grupojorgeordonez.com

Avante 2012 T
100% tinto fino

93

Colour: cherry, garnet rim. Nose: creamy oak, red berry notes, fresh fruit, mineral. Palate: flavourful, spicy, elegant.

Tineta 2013 T
100% tinto fino

88

Colour: bright cherry. Nose: ripe fruit, sweet spices, creamy oak. Palate: flavourful, fruity, round tannins.

BODEGAS PAGOS DE MOGAR

Ctra. Pesquera, km. 0,2
47359 Valbuena de Duero (Valladolid)
☎: +34 983 683 011
comercial@bodegaspagosdemogar.com
www.bodegaspagosdemogar.com

Mogar 2013 T Roble
100% tinta del país

86

Mogar Vendimia Seleccionada 2011 TC
100% tinta del país

87

Colour: dark-red cherry. Nose: fruit preserve, sweet spices, cocoa bean. Palate: flavourful, spicy, slightly overripe.

BODEGAS PASCUAL

Ctra. de Aranda, Km. 5
09471 Fuentelcésped (Burgos)
☎: +34 947 557 351
Fax: +34 947 557 312
export@bodegaspascual.com
www.bodegaspascual.com

Buró de Peñalosa 2010 TR
100% tempranillo

89

Colour: cherry, garnet rim. Nose: red berry notes, ripe fruit, spicy, creamy oak. Palate: flavourful, toasty.

Buró de Peñalosa 2011 TC
100% tempranillo

91

Colour: cherry, garnet rim. Nose: creamy oak, fresh fruit, balanced. Palate: flavourful, spicy, elegant.

Buró Vendimia Seleccionada 2011 T
100% tempranillo

88

Colour: cherry, garnet rim. Nose: varietal, balanced, ripe fruit, spicy, smoky. Palate: flavourful, long.

Castildiego 2014 T
100% tempranillo

87

Colour: cherry, purple rim. Nose: red berry notes, floral, lactic notes. Palate: fresh, fruity, easy to drink.

Diodoro Autor 2009 T
100% tempranillo

92

Colour: cherry, garnet rim. Nose: balanced, complex, ripe fruit, spicy, fine reductive notes, mineral. Palate: good structure, flavourful, round tannins, balanced.

Heredad de Peñalosa 2014 T Roble
100% tempranillo

89

Colour: bright cherry, purple rim. Nose: ripe fruit, spicy. Palate: correct, balanced, flavourful.

BODEGAS PEÑAFIEL

Ctra. N-122, Km. 311
47300 Peñafiel (Valladolid)
☎: +34 983 881 622
Fax: +34 983 881 944
bodegaspenafiel@bodegaspenafiel.com
www.bodegaspenafiel.com

Miros 2013 T Roble
5% cabernet sauvignon, 10% merlot, 85% tempranillo

84

Miros de Ribera 2009 TC
85% tempranillo, 11% merlot, 4% cabernet sauvignon

89

Colour: cherry, garnet rim. Nose: ripe fruit, wild herbs, earthy notes, spicy, balsamic herbs. Palate: balanced, flavourful, long, balsamic.

Miros de Ribera 2009 TR
100% tempranillo

88

Colour: dark-red cherry, garnet rim. Nose: grassy, ripe fruit, spicy. Palate: flavourful, round tannins.

BODEGAS PEÑALBA HERRAIZ

Sol de las Moreras, 3 2º
09400 Aranda de Duero (Burgos)
☎: +34 617 331 609
oficina@carravid.com
www.carravid.es

Aptus 2013 T Roble
100% tempranillo

87

Colour: deep cherry, purple rim. Nose: creamy oak, toasty, ripe fruit, balsamic herbs. Palate: balanced, spicy, long.

Carravid 2011 T
100% tinta del país

89

Colour: cherry, garnet rim. Nose: ripe fruit, spicy, creamy oak, complex. Palate: flavourful, toasty.

BODEGAS PINGÓN

Ctra. N-122, Km. 311
47300 Peñafiel (Valladolid)
☎: +34 983 880 623
Fax: +34 983 985 869
carramimbre@bodegaspingon.com
www.bodegaspingon.com

Carramimbre 2011 TC
95% tempranillo, 5% cabernet sauvignon

89

Colour: cherry, garnet rim. Nose: ripe fruit, spicy, creamy oak, complex. Palate: flavourful, toasty.

Altamimbre 2011 T
100% tempranillo

90

Colour: cherry, garnet rim. Nose: ripe fruit, spicy, creamy oak. Palate: flavourful, toasty.

Carramimbre 2011 TR
95% tempranillo, 5% cabernet sauvignon

90

Colour: cherry, garnet rim. Nose: balanced, complex, ripe fruit, spicy, fine reductive notes. Palate: good structure, flavourful, balanced.

Torrepingón Selección 2011 T
100% tempranillo

90

Colour: bright cherry. Nose: ripe fruit, sweet spices, creamy oak, expressive. Palate: flavourful, fruity, toasty.

BODEGAS PORTIA

Antigua Ctra. N-I, km. 170
09370 Gumiel de Izán (Burgos)
☎: +34 947 102 700
Fax: +34 947 107 004
info@bodegasportia.com
www.bodegasportia.com

Portia 2012 TC
100% tempranillo

89

Colour: cherry, garnet rim. Nose: roasted coffee, smoky, spicy, ripe fruit, fine reductive notes. Palate: flavourful, smoky aftertaste, ripe fruit.

Portia 2014 T Roble
100% tempranillo

87

Colour: bright cherry. Nose: ripe fruit, sweet spices, creamy oak. Palate: flavourful, fruity, toasty, round tannins.

Portia Ebeia 2014 T Roble
tempranillo

86

Portia Prima 2012 T
100% tempranillo

90

Colour: deep cherry, purple rim. Nose: creamy oak, toasty, ripe fruit, balsamic herbs, wet leather. Palate: balanced, spicy, long.

Triennia 2011 T
100% tempranillo

89

Colour: very deep cherry, garnet rim. Nose: balsamic herbs, balanced, old leather. Palate: full, flavourful, round tannins.

BODEGAS PRADO DE OLMEDO

Paraje El Salegar, s/n
09370 Quintana del Pidío (Burgos)
☎: +34 947 546 960
Fax: +34 947 546 960
pradodeolmedo@pradodeolmedo.com
www.pradodeolmedo.com

Monasterio de San Miguel 2011 TR
100% tinta del país

91

Colour: cherry, garnet rim. Nose: red berry notes, ripe fruit, spicy, creamy oak, complex. Palate: flavourful, toasty, round tannins.

Monasterio de San Miguel 2012 TC
100% tempranillo

90

Colour: cherry, garnet rim. Nose: ripe fruit, spicy, creamy oak, balsamic herbs. Palate: flavourful, toasty.

Monasterio de San Miguel 2014 T Roble
100% tempranillo

90

Colour: bright cherry. Nose: ripe fruit, sweet spices, creamy oak. Palate: flavourful, fruity, toasty, round tannins.

Monasterio de San Miguel Selección 2012 T

90

Colour: cherry, garnet rim. Nose: smoky, spicy, ripe fruit. Palate: flavourful, smoky aftertaste, ripe fruit.

BODEGAS RAIZ Y PÁRAMO DE GUZMÁN

Ctra. Circunvalación R-30, s/n
09300 Roa (Burgos)
☎: +34 947 541 191
Fax: +34 947 541 192
info@raizyparamodeguzman.es
www.raizyparamodeguzman.es

Raíz de Guzmán 2011 TR
100% tempranillo

92

Colour: cherry, garnet rim. Nose: ripe fruit, spicy, fine reductive notes. Palate: good structure, flavourful, balanced.

Raíz de Guzmán 2012 TC
100% tempranillo

91

Colour: cherry, garnet rim. Nose: ripe fruit, wild herbs, earthy notes, spicy. Palate: balanced, flavourful, long, balsamic.

Raíz de Guzmán 2013 T Roble
100% tempranillo

86

Raíz de Guzmán 2014 RD
100% tempranillo

89

Colour: rose, purple rim. Nose: floral, expressive, ripe fruit. Palate: powerful, fruity.

Raiz Profunda 2010 T
100% tempranillo

94

Colour: light cherry. Nose: fine reductive notes, aged wood nuances, toasty, ripe fruit. Palate: spicy, toasty, flavourful.

BODEGAS RESALTE DE PEÑAFIEL

Ctra. N-122, Km. 312
47300 Peñafiel (Valladolid)
☎: +34 983 878 160
Fax: +34 983 880 601
info@resalte.com
www.resalte.com

Gran Resalte 2009 T
100% tempranillo

90

Colour: cherry, garnet rim. Nose: creamy oak, balanced, ripe fruit, sweet spices. Palate: flavourful, spicy, long.

Gran Resalte 2010 TGR
100% tempranillo

92

Colour: very deep cherry, garnet rim. Nose: mineral, balsamic herbs, ripe fruit, toasty. Palate: full, flavourful, correct.

Lecco 2009 TR
100% tempranillo

90

Colour: cherry, garnet rim. Nose: ripe fruit, spicy, creamy oak, complex. Palate: flavourful, toasty, round tannins.

Lecco 2011 TC
100% tempranillo

90

Colour: cherry, garnet rim. Nose: smoky, spicy, ripe fruit. Palate: flavourful, smoky aftertaste, ripe fruit.

Lecco Roble 2014 T
100% tempranillo

88

Colour: bright cherry. Nose: ripe fruit, sweet spices, creamy oak, expressive. Palate: flavourful, fruity, round tannins.

Peña Roble 2011 TC
100% tempranillo

87

Colour: cherry, garnet rim. Nose: smoky, spicy, ripe fruit. Palate: flavourful, smoky aftertaste, ripe fruit.

Peña Roble 2014 T Roble
100% tempranillo

85

Resalte 2009 TR
100% tempranillo

90

Colour: cherry, garnet rim. Nose: expressive, spicy. Palate: flavourful, ripe fruit, long, good acidity, balanced, round tannins.

Resalte 2010 TR
100% tempranillo

90

Colour: bright cherry. Nose: ripe fruit, sweet spices, creamy oak. Palate: flavourful, fruity, toasty, long.

Resalte 2011 TC
100% tempranillo

90

Colour: cherry, garnet rim. Nose: red berry notes, ripe fruit, spicy, creamy oak, complex. Palate: flavourful, toasty.

Resalte Vendimia Seleccionada 2013 T
100% tempranillo

88

Colour: bright cherry. Nose: sweet spices, creamy oak, overripe fruit. Palate: flavourful, fruity, toasty.

BODEGAS REYES

Ctra. Valladolid - Soria, Km. 54
47300 Peñafiel (Valladolid)
☎: +34 983 873 015
Fax: +34 983 873 017
info@teofiloreyes.com
www.bodegasreyes.com

Tamiz 2013 T Roble
tempranillo

86

Teófilo Reyes 2011 TC
tempranillo

90

Colour: cherry, garnet rim. Nose: red berry notes, ripe fruit, spicy, creamy oak, complex. Palate: flavourful, toasty, round tannins.

BODEGAS RODERO

Ctra. Boada, s/n
09314 Pedrosa de Duero (Burgos)
☎: +34 947 530 046
Fax: +34 947 530 097
rodero@bodegasrodero.com
www.bodegasrodero.com

Carmelo Rodero 2012 TC
90% tempranillo, 10% cabernet sauvignon

92

Colour: cherry, garnet rim. Nose: creamy oak, red berry notes, fresh fruit, balanced. Palate: flavourful, spicy, mineral.

Carmelo Rodero 2012 TR
90% tempranillo, 10% cabernet sauvignon

92

Colour: light cherry. Nose: fine reductive notes, aged wood nuances, toasty, dark chocolate. Palate: spicy, toasty, flavourful.

Carmelo Rodero 2014 T
100% tempranillo

88

Colour: very deep cherry, purple rim. Nose: ripe fruit. Palate: flavourful, fruity.

Carmelo Rodero 9 meses 2014 T
100% tempranillo

87

Colour: cherry, purple rim. Nose: ripe fruit, woody, roasted coffee. Palate: flavourful, spicy, powerful.

Carmelo Rodero TSM 2011 T
75% tempranillo, 10% cabernet sauvignon, 15% merlot

93

Colour: cherry, garnet rim. Nose: balanced, complex, ripe fruit, spicy. Palate: good structure, flavourful, round tannins, balanced.

Pago de Valtarreña 2012 T
100% tempranillo

91

Colour: bright cherry, garnet rim. Nose: toasty, characterful, ripe fruit, warm, powerfull. Palate: spicy, toasty, good structure.

BODEGAS SANTA EULALIA

Malpica, s/n
09311 La Horra (Burgos)
☎: +34 983 586 868
Fax: +34 947 580 180
bodegasfrutosvillar@bodegasfrutosvillar.com
www.bodegasfrutosvillar.com

Conde de Siruela 2009 TR
100% tinta del país

88

Colour: cherry, garnet rim. Nose: ripe fruit, wild herbs, earthy notes, spicy, balsamic herbs. Palate: balanced, flavourful, long, balsamic.

Conde de Siruela 2010 TC
100% tinta del país

90

Colour: cherry, garnet rim. Nose: ripe fruit, spicy, creamy oak. Palate: flavourful, toasty, round tannins.

Conde de Siruela 2013 T Roble
100% tinta del país

86

Conde de Siruela 2014 T
100% tinta del país

88

Colour: bright cherry. Nose: ripe fruit, sweet spices, creamy oak, expressive. Palate: flavourful, fruity, round tannins.

La Horra 2014 T
100% tinta del país

84

Riberal 2010 TC
100% tinta del país

89

Colour: bright cherry, garnet rim. Nose: balanced, red berry notes, ripe fruit, smoky, spicy. Palate: correct, easy to drink.

BODEGAS SEÑORÍO DE NAVA

Ctra Valladolid a Soria, 62
09318 Nava de Roa (Burgos)
☎: +34 947 550 003
Fax: +34 947 550 003
snava@senoriodenava.es
www.senoriodenava.es

Señorío de Nava 2010 TR
100% tempranillo

88

Colour: cherry, garnet rim. Nose: red berry notes, ripe fruit, spicy, creamy oak. Palate: flavourful, toasty.

Señorío de Nava 2011 TC
tempranillo

88

Colour: very deep cherry, garnet rim. Nose: spicy, tobacco, ripe fruit, warm. Palate: fruity, round tannins, balanced.

Señorío de Nava 2013 T Roble
85% tempranillo, 15% cabernet sauvignon

87

Colour: deep cherry. Nose: creamy oak, toasty, ripe fruit, balsamic herbs. Palate: balanced, spicy, long.

Señorío de Nava 2014 RD
100% tempranillo

86

Señorío de Nava 2014 T
100% tempranillo

87

Colour: cherry, purple rim. Nose: ripe fruit, grassy, herbaceous. Palate: fine bitter notes, easy to drink.

Señorío de Nava Finca San Cobate 2005 TR
100% tempranillo

93

Colour: pale ruby, brick rim edge. Nose: elegant, spicy, fine reductive notes, tobacco. Palate: spicy, fine tannins, elegant, long.

Vega Cubillas 2013 T
100% tempranillo

81

Vega Cubillas 2013 T Roble
100% tempranillo

84

Vega Cubillas 2014 RD
100% tempranillo

85

Vega Cubillas 2014 T
84

BODEGAS TARSUS

Ctra. de Roa - Anguix, Km. 3
09312 Anguix (Burgos)
☎: +34 947 554 218
tarsus@pernod-ricard.com
www.bodegastarsus.com

Quinta de Tarsus 2011 TC
tinta del país

92

Colour: cherry, garnet rim. Nose: creamy oak, balanced, ripe fruit. Palate: flavourful, spicy, elegant.

Tarsus 2010 TR
tinta del país, cabernet sauvignon

89

Colour: cherry, garnet rim. Nose: ripe fruit, wild herbs, spicy. Palate: flavourful, long, balsamic.

Tarsus 2014 T Roble
tinta del país

87

Colour: bright cherry. Nose: ripe fruit, sweet spices, creamy oak. Palate: flavourful, fruity, toasty.

BODEGAS THESAURUS

Ctra. Cuellar - Villafuerte, s/n
47359 Olivares de Duero (Valladolid)
☎: +34 983 250 319
Fax: +34 983 250 329
comercial@ciadevinos.com
www.bodegasthesaurus.com

Casa Castilla 2011 TC
100% tempranillo

88

Colour: cherry, garnet rim. Nose: ripe fruit, spicy, creamy oak, complex. Palate: flavourful, toasty.

Castillo de Peñafiel 2008 TR
100% tempranillo

88

Colour: cherry, garnet rim. Nose: red berry notes, ripe fruit, spicy, creamy oak. Palate: flavourful, toasty.

Castillo de Peñafiel 2012 TC
100% tempranillo

87

Colour: cherry, garnet rim. Nose: ripe fruit, spicy, creamy oak. Palate: flavourful, toasty, round tannins.

Castillo de Peñafiel 2014 T Roble
100% tempranillo

86

Flumen Dorivm 2008 TR
100% tempranillo

89

Colour: cherry, garnet rim. Nose: ripe fruit, wild herbs, spicy, balsamic herbs. Palate: balanced, flavourful, long, balsamic.

Flumen Dorivm 2012 TC
100% tempranillo

89

Colour: cherry, garnet rim. Nose: ripe fruit, spicy, creamy oak, complex. Palate: flavourful, toasty.

Flumen Dorivm 2014 T Roble
100% tempranillo

88

Colour: bright cherry. Nose: ripe fruit, sweet spices, creamy oak, expressive. Palate: flavourful, fruity, toasty.

BODEGAS TIONIO

Carretera de Valoria, Km 7
47315 Pesquera de Duero (Valladolid)
☎: +34 933 950 811
Fax: +34 933 955 500
bodega@tionio.es
www.tionio.es

Austum 2013 T
100% tinto fino

91

Colour: bright cherry. Nose: ripe fruit, sweet spices, creamy oak, expressive. Palate: flavourful, fruity, toasty, round tannins.

Tionio 2011 TR
100% tinto fino

90

Colour: cherry, garnet rim. Nose: ripe fruit, wild herbs, earthy notes, spicy, balsamic herbs. Palate: balanced, flavourful, long, balsamic.

Tionio 2012 TC
100% tinto fino

93

Colour: very deep cherry, garnet rim. Nose: characterful, powerfull, dried herbs, ripe fruit. Palate: flavourful, full, round tannins.

BODEGAS TORREDEROS

Ctra. Valladolid, Km. 289,300
09318 Fuentelisendo (Burgos)
☎: +34 947 532 627
Fax: +34 947 532 731
administracion@torrederos.com
www.torrederos.com

Torrederos 2010 TR
100% tempranillo

90

Colour: ruby red. Nose: ripe fruit, spicy, creamy oak. Palate: flavourful, toasty, round tannins.

Torrederos 2012 TC
100% tempranillo

90

Colour: bright cherry. Nose: ripe fruit, sweet spices, creamy oak, expressive. Palate: flavourful, fruity, toasty, round tannins.

Torrederos Selección 2010 T
100% tempranillo

91

Colour: deep cherry. Nose: fine reductive notes, aged wood nuances, toasty, ripe fruit. Palate: spicy, toasty, flavourful.

BODEGAS TORREMORÓN

Ctra. Boada, s/n
09314 Quintanamanvirgo (Burgos)
☎: +34 947 554 075
Fax: +34 947 554 036
torremoron@wanadoo.es
www.torremoron.es

Senderillo 2012 TC
100% tempranillo
88
Colour: cherry, garnet rim. Nose: creamy oak, balanced, ripe fruit. Palate: flavourful, spicy.

Senderillo 2014 T
tempranillo
86

Torremorón 2010 TR
tempranillo
87
Colour: cherry, garnet rim. Nose: smoky, spicy, ripe fruit, woody. Palate: flavourful, smoky aftertaste, ripe fruit.

Torremorón 2012 TC
100% tempranillo
86

Torremorón Tempranillo 2014 T
100% tempranillo
85

BODEGAS TRUS

Ctra . Pesquera de Duero-Encinas km 3
47316 Piñel de Abajo (Valladolid)
☎: +34 983 872 033
Fax: +34 983 872 041
trus@bodegastrus.com
www.bodegastrus.com

Tramuz 2014 T
tinto fino
89
Colour: bright cherry. Nose: ripe fruit, sweet spices. Palate: flavourful, fruity, round tannins.

Trus 2010 TR
tinto fino
94
Colour: cherry, garnet rim. Nose: mineral, expressive, spicy. Palate: flavourful, ripe fruit, long, good acidity, balanced.

Trus 2012 TC
tinto fino
93
Colour: cherry, garnet rim. Nose: roasted coffee, smoky, spicy, ripe fruit. Palate: flavourful, smoky aftertaste, ripe fruit.

Trus 2014 T Roble
tinto fino
90
Colour: cherry, purple rim. Nose: ripe fruit, woody, roasted coffee. Palate: flavourful, spicy, powerful.

BODEGAS VALDEMAR

Camino Viejo s/n
01320 Oyón (Álava)
☎: +34 945 622 188
Fax: +34 945 622 111
info@valdemar.es
www.valdemar.es

Fincas de Valdemacuco 2012 TC
100% tempranillo
91
Colour: cherry, garnet rim. Nose: ripe fruit, spicy, creamy oak complex. Palate: flavourful, toasty, round tannins.

Fincas de Valdemacuco 2013 T Roble
100% tempranillo
89
Colour: cherry, garnet rim. Nose: roasted coffee, smoky, spicy ripe fruit. Palate: flavourful, smoky aftertaste, ripe fruit.

Fincas Valdemar 2012 TC
100% tempranillo
90
Colour: black cherry, garnet rim. Nose: ripe fruit, fruit preserve, spicy, dried herbs, characterful. Palate: flavourful, fruity, round tannins.

BODEGAS VALDUBÓN

Antigua Ctra. N-I, Km. 151
09460 Milagros (Burgos)
☎: +34 947 546 251
Fax: +34 947 546 250
valdubon@valdubon.es
www.valdubon.es

Honoris de Valdubón 2011 T
90
Colour: cherry, garnet rim. Nose: red berry notes, ripe fruit, spicy, creamy oak, complex. Palate: flavourful, toasty, round tannins.

BODEGAS VALLE DE MONZÓN

Paraje El Salegar, s/n
09370 Quintana del Pidío (Burgos)
☎: +34 947 545 694
Fax: +34 947 545 694
bodega@vallemonzon.com
www.vallemonzon.com

Hoyo de la Vega 2010 TR
tinta del país

89

Colour: ruby red. Nose: ripe fruit, spicy, creamy oak. Palate: flavourful, toasty.

Hoyo de la Vega 2013 TC
tinta del país

88

Colour: cherry, purple rim. Nose: ripe fruit, roasted coffee. Palate: flavourful, spicy, powerful.

Hoyo de la Vega 2014 RD
albillo, tinta del país

88

Colour: rose, purple rim. Nose: red berry notes, floral, expressive. Palate: powerful, fruity, fresh.

Hoyo de la Vega 2014 T Roble
tinta del país

87

Colour: cherry, purple rim. Nose: powerfull, ripe fruit, spicy, creamy oak. Palate: powerful, fruity, unctuous.

BODEGAS VALPARAISO

Paraje los Llanillos, s/n
09370 Quintana del Pidío (Burgos)
☎: +34 947 545 286
Fax: +34 947 545 163
info@bodegasvalparaiso.com
www.bodegasvalparaiso.com

Finca El Encinal 2012 TC
100% tempranillo

88

Colour: deep cherry, purple rim. Nose: creamy oak, toasty, ripe fruit, scrubland, characterful. Palate: balanced, spicy, long.

Finca El Encinal 2014 T Roble
100% tempranillo

85

Valparaíso 2012 TC
100% tempranillo

88

Colour: bright cherry. Nose: ripe fruit, sweet spices, creamy oak. Palate: flavourful, fruity, toasty, round tannins, balsamic.

Valparaíso 2014 T Roble
100% tempranillo

88

Colour: bright cherry. Nose: ripe fruit, sweet spices, creamy oak. Palate: flavourful, fruity, toasty, round tannins.

BODEGAS VALPINCIA

Ctra. de Melida, 3,5
47300 Peñafiel (Valladolid)
☎: +34 983 878 007
comunicacion@bodegasvalpincia.com
www.bodegasvalpincia.com

Pagos de Valcerracín 2013 T Roble
tempranillo

87

Colour: bright cherry. Nose: ripe fruit, sweet spices, creamy oak. Palate: flavourful, fruity, toasty.

Pagos de Valcerracín 2014 T
tempranillo

87

Colour: bright cherry. Nose: ripe fruit, sweet spices, creamy oak. Palate: flavourful, fruity, round tannins.

Pagos de Valcerracín Vendimia Seleccionada 2011 TC
tempranillo

89

Colour: deep cherry, garnet rim. Nose: balanced, varietal, ripe fruit. Palate: good structure, flavourful.

Valpincia 2010 TR
tempranillo

84

Valpincia 2012 TC
tempranillo

86

Valpincia 2013 T Roble
tempranillo

86

Valpincia 2014 T
tempranillo

85

BODEGAS VEGA SICILIA

Ctra. N-122, Km. 323
47359 Valbuena de Duero (Valladolid)
☎: +34 983 680 147
Fax: +34 983 680 263
vegasicilia@vega-sicilia.com
www.vega-sicilia.com

PODIUM

Valbuena 5º 2011 T
92% tinto fino, 8% merlot

96

Colour: cherry, garnet rim. Nose: smoky, ripe fruit, sweet spices, cocoa bean. Palate: flavourful, ripe fruit, toasty, long.

PODIUM

Vega Sicilia Reserva Especial 96/98/02 T

97

Colour: pale ruby, brick rim edge. Nose: elegant, spicy, fine reductive notes, tobacco, ripe fruit. Palate: spicy, fine tannins, elegant, long, flavourful.

Vega Sicilia Único 2008 T
95% tinto fino, 5% cabernet sauvignon

94

Colour: cherry, garnet rim. Nose: ripe fruit, old leather, tobacco. Palate: correct, flavourful, spicy.

BODEGAS VEGARANDA

Avda. Arangón, s/n
09400 Aranda de Duero (Burgos)
☎: +34 626 996 974
comercial@bodegasvegaranda.com
www.bodegasvegaranda.com

Vegaranda 2008 TR
tempranillo

87

Colour: dark-red cherry, orangey edge. Nose: animal reductive notes, aromatic coffee. Palate: correct, spicy, reductive nuances.

Vegaranda 2012 TC
tempranillo

85

Vegaranda 2013 T Roble
tempranillo

83

Vegaranda 2014 RD
tempranillo

85

Vegaranda 2014 T
tempranillo

83

BODEGAS VICENTE GANDÍA

Ctra. Cheste a Godelleta, s/n
46370 Chiva (Valencia)
☎: +34 962 524 242
Fax: +34 962 524 243
info@vicentegandia.com
www.vicentegandia.es

Dolmo Tempranillo 2013 TC
tempranillo

86

Nebla 2013 T Roble

87

Colour: cherry, purple rim. Nose: ripe fruit, woody, roasted coffee. Palate: flavourful, spicy, powerful.

BODEGAS VIÑA VILANO

Ctra. de Anguix, 10
09314 Pedrosa de Duero (Burgos)
☎: +34 947 530 029
Fax: +34 947 530 037
info@vinavilano.com
www.vinavilano.com

Terra Incógnita 2010 T
tempranillo

90

Colour: cherry, garnet rim. Nose: red berry notes, ripe fruit, spicy, creamy oak, complex. Palate: flavourful, toasty, round tannins.

Viña Vilano 2010 TR
tempranillo

90

Colour: cherry, garnet rim. Nose: ripe fruit, spicy, creamy oak, fine reductive notes. Palate: flavourful, toasty, round tannins.

Viña Vilano 2012 TC
tempranillo

91

Colour: cherry, garnet rim. Nose: creamy oak, red berry notes, fresh fruit, balanced. Palate: flavourful, spicy, elegant.

Viña Vilano 2014 RD
tempranillo

87

Colour: rose, purple rim. Nose: red berry notes, floral, wild herbs. Palate: powerful, fruity, fresh.

Viña Vilano 2014 T Roble
tempranillo

87

Colour: cherry, purple rim. Nose: ripe fruit, woody, roasted coffee. Palate: flavourful, spicy, powerful.

Viña Vilano Roble Black 2013 T Roble
tempranillo

88

Colour: cherry, garnet rim. Nose: creamy oak, toasty, ripe fruit, balsamic herbs. Palate: balanced, spicy, long.

Viña Vilano Roble Black 2014 T
tempranillo

86

BODEGAS VITULIA

Sendín, 49
09400 Aranda de Duero (Burgos)
☎: +34 947 515 051
Fax: +34 947 515 051
vitulia@bodegasvitulia.com
www.bodegasvitulia.com

Hacienda Vitulia 2009 T
95% tinto fino, 5% merlot

91

Colour: cherry, garnet rim. Nose: ripe fruit, wild herbs, spicy, balsamic herbs. Palate: balanced, flavourful, long, balsamic.

Vitulia 11 meses barrica 2013 T Barrica
100% tinto fino

87

Colour: very deep cherry. Nose: fruit preserve, dried herbs, powerfull. Palate: flavourful, fruity.

Vitulia 2012 TC
95% tinto fino, 5% cabernet sauvignon

91

Colour: cherry, garnet rim. Nose: creamy oak, red berry notes, balanced, ripe fruit. Palate: flavourful, spicy, elegant.

Vitulia 2014 RD
tinto fino

85

BODEGAS VIYUELA

Ctra. de Quintanamanvirgo, s/n
09314 Boada de Roa (Burgos)
☎: +34 947 530 072
Fax: +34 947 530 075
viyuela@bodegasviyuela.com
www.bodegasviyuela.com

Viyuela 2011 TC
100% tempranillo

86

Viyuela 10 2011 T
100% tempranillo

86

Viyuela 2014 T Fermentado en Barrica
100% tempranillo

87

Colour: deep cherry, purple rim. Nose: creamy oak, toasty, ripe fruit, balsamic herbs. Palate: balanced, spicy, long.

Viyuela 3 + 3 2014 T
100% tempranillo

87

Colour: bright cherry. Nose: ripe fruit, sweet spices, creamy oak. Palate: flavourful, fruity.

Viyuela X Aniversario 2011 T
100% tempranillo

88

Colour: bright cherry. Nose: sweet spices, creamy oak, fruit preserve. Palate: flavourful, fruity, toasty, round tannins.

BODEGAS VIZCARRA

Finca Chirri, s/n
09317 Mambrilla de Castrejón (Burgos)
☎: +34 947 540 340
Fax: +34 947 540 340
bodegas@vizcarra.es
www.vizcarra.es

Celia Vizcarra 2011 TR
95% tinto fino, 5% garnacha

93

Colour: very deep cherry, garnet rim. Nose: expressive, complex, mineral, balsamic herbs, balanced. Palate: full, flavourful, round tannins.

Inés Vizcarra 2011 T
90% tinto fino, 10% merlot

93

Colour: cherry, garnet rim. Nose: mineral, expressive, spicy, scrubland. Palate: flavourful, ripe fruit, long, good acidity, balanced.

Vizcarra 15 meses 2013 T
100% tinto fino

90

Colour: bright cherry, purple rim. Nose: creamy oak, sweet spices, ripe fruit, cocoa bean. Palate: balanced, good structure.

Vizcarra Senda del Oro 2014 T
100% tinto fino

90

Colour: bright cherry. Nose: ripe fruit, sweet spices, creamy oak, expressive. Palate: flavourful, fruity, round tannins.

Vizcarra Torralvo 2012 T
100% tinto fino

93

Colour: very deep cherry. Nose: aromatic coffee, smoky, toasty, mineral. Palate: concentrated, good structure, round tannins, spicy.

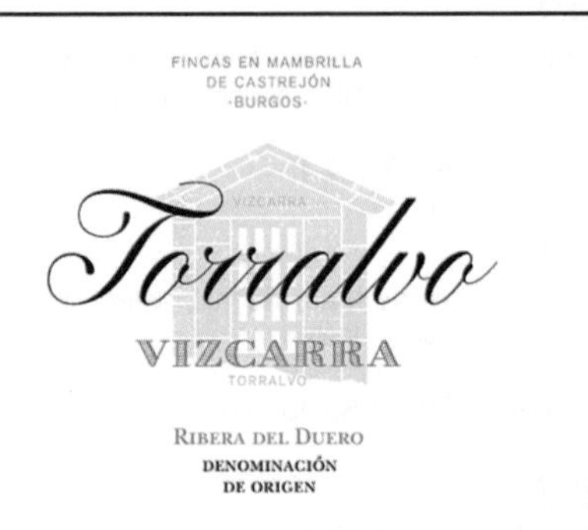

BODEGAS Y VIÑEDOS ALILIAN

Ctra. de la Aguilera km 3,5
09400 Aranda de Duero (Burgos)
☎: +34 947 506 659
info@bodegasalilian.es
www.bodegasalilian.es

Alilian Prémora 2014 T
tempranillo, aragonés

89

Colour: bright cherry, purple rim. Nose: balanced, red berry notes, ripe fruit, spicy. Palate: flavourful, ripe fruit.

BODEGAS Y VIÑEDOS ALIÓN

Ctra. N-122, Km. 312,4
Padilla de Duero
47300 Peñafiel (Valladolid)
☎: +34 983 881 236
Fax: +34 983 881 246
alion@bodegasalion.com
www.bodegasalion.com

Alión 2012 T
100% tinto fino

94

Colour: cherry, garnet rim. Nose: creamy oak, earthy notes, ripe fruit. Palate: flavourful, spicy, ripe fruit.

BODEGAS Y VIÑEDOS CONDE DE SAN CRISTÓBAL

Ctra. Valladolid a Soria, Km. 303
47300 Peñafiel (Valladolid)
☎: +34 983 878 055
Fax: +34 983 878 196
bodega@condesancristobal.com
www.marquesdevargas.com

Conde de San Cristóbal 2012 T
tinto fino, merlot, cabernet sauvignon

90

Colour: cherry, garnet rim. Nose: ripe fruit, wild herbs, earthy notes, spicy, balsamic herbs. Palate: balanced, flavourful, long, balsamic.

Conde de San Cristóbal Raíces 2010 TR
tinto fino, merlot

90

Colour: light cherry. Nose: fine reductive notes, aged wood nuances, toasty. Palate: spicy, toasty, flavourful.

BODEGAS Y VIÑEDOS ESCUDERO

Camino El Ramo, s/n
09311 Olmedillo de Roa (Burgos)
☎: +34 629 857 575
Fax: +34 947 551 070
info@costaval.com
www.costaval.com

Costaval 2009 TR
100% tempranillo

89

Colour: cherry, garnet rim. Nose: red berry notes, ripe fruit, spicy, creamy oak, complex. Palate: flavourful, toasty, round tannins.

Costaval 2011 TC
100% tempranillo

86

Costaval 2012 T Roble
100% tempranillo

88

Colour: cherry, garnet rim. Nose: ripe fruit, spicy, creamy oak. Palate: flavourful, toasty.

Eloy Escudero 2009 T
100% tempranillo

87

Colour: ruby red. Nose: fine reductive notes, wet leather, aged wood nuances. Palate: spicy, long, toasty.

BODEGAS Y VIÑEDOS GALLEGO ZAPATERO

Segunda Travesía de la Olma, 4
09313 Anguix (Burgos)
☎: +34 648 180 777
info@bodegasgallegozapatero.com
www.bodegasgallegozapatero.com

Yotuel 2013 T Roble
100% tinta del país

87

Colour: deep cherry, purple rim. Nose: sweet spices, creamy oak, ripe fruit. Palate: flavourful, spicy, easy to drink.

Yotuel Finca La Nava 2012 T
100% tinta del país

90

Colour: cherry, garnet rim. Nose: ripe fruit, spicy, creamy oak, complex. Palate: flavourful, toasty.

Yotuel Finca Valdepalacios 2008 T
100% tinta del país

90

Colour: cherry, garnet rim. Nose: ripe fruit, wild herbs, earthy notes, spicy, balsamic herbs, old leather. Palate: balanced, flavourful, long, balsamic.

Yotuel Selección 2012 T
100% tinta del país

90

Colour: bright cherry, garnet rim. Nose: varietal, ripe fruit, balanced, neat, spicy. Palate: balanced, flavourful, spicy.

BODEGAS Y VIÑEDOS JUAN MANUEL BURGOS (AVAN VINOS)

Aranda, 39
09471 Fuentelcesped (Burgos)
☎: +34 947 557 443
juanmanuelburgos@byvjuanmanuelburgos.com
www.byvjuanmanuelburgos.com

Avan Cepas Centenarias 2012 TR
100% tempranillo

94

Colour: cherry, garnet rim. Nose: balanced, complex, ripe fruit, spicy, mineral. Palate: good structure, flavourful, round tannins, balanced.

Avan Concentración 2012 T
100% tempranillo

91

Colour: cherry, garnet rim. Nose: ripe fruit, spicy, creamy oak, complex. Palate: flavourful, toasty, balanced.

Avan Nacimiento 2012 T
100% tempranillo

90

Colour: cherry, garnet rim. Nose: creamy oak, toasty, ripe fruit, balsamic herbs. Palate: balanced, spicy, long.

Avan OK 2014 T
100% tempranillo

88

Colour: bright cherry. Nose: ripe fruit, sweet spices, creamy oak. Palate: flavourful, fruity, toasty.

Avan Terruño de Valdehernando 2012 T
100% tempranillo

93

Colour: cherry, garnet rim. Nose: mineral, expressive, spicy, creamy oak, earthy notes. Palate: flavourful, ripe fruit, long, good acidity, balanced.

Avan Viñedo del Torrubio 2012 T
100% tempranillo

92

Colour: cherry, garnet rim. Nose: ripe fruit, fragrant herbs, spicy, toasty, creamy oak, mineral. Palate: powerful, flavourful, balsamic, balanced.

BODEGAS Y VIÑEDOS LLEIROSO

Ctra. Monasterio, s/n
47359 Valbuena del Duero (Valladolid)
☎: +34 983 683 300
Fax: +34 983 683 301
administracin@bodegaslleiroso.com
www.bodegaslleiroso.com

Lleiroso 2010 TR
100% tempranillo

89

Colour: cherry, garnet rim. Nose: ripe fruit, spicy, fine reductive notes. Palate: good structure, flavourful, balanced.

Lleiroso 2012 TC
100% tempranillo

88

Colour: deep cherry, garnet rim. Nose: powerfull, ripe fruit, sweet spices. Palate: balanced, round tannins.

Lvzmillar 2014 T Roble
100% tempranillo

87

Colour: bright cherry. Nose: ripe fruit, sweet spices, creamy oak. Palate: flavourful, fruity, toasty.

BODEGAS Y VIÑEDOS MARTÍN BERDUGO

Pº de la Colonia, s/n
09400 Aranda de Duero (Burgos)
☎: +34 947 506 331
Fax: +34 947 506 602
bodega@martinberdugo.com
www.martinberdugo.com

Martín Berdugo 2009 TR
tempranillo

90

Colour: cherry, garnet rim. Nose: ripe fruit, wild herbs, earthy notes, spicy, balsamic herbs. Palate: balanced, flavourful, long, balsamic.

Martín Berdugo 2012 TC
tempranillo

89

Colour: cherry, garnet rim. Nose: fruit preserve, wild herbs, spicy, creamy oak. Palate: powerful, flavourful.

Martín Berdugo 2013 T Barrica
tempranillo

88

Colour: bright cherry. Nose: ripe fruit, sweet spices, creamy oak, expressive. Palate: flavourful, fruity, round tannins.

Martín Berdugo 2014 RD
tempranillo

88

Colour: raspberry rose. Nose: elegant, red berry notes, floral, fragrant herbs. Palate: light-bodied, flavourful, good acidity.

Martín Berdugo 2014 T
tempranillo

88

Colour: cherry, purple rim. Nose: expressive, fresh fruit, red berry notes, floral. Palate: flavourful, fruity, good acidity.

Martín Berdugo MB Especial 2009 T
tempranillo

92

Colour: cherry, garnet rim. Nose: balanced, complex, ripe fruit, spicy, fine reductive notes. Palate: good structure, flavourful, round tannins, balanced.

BODEGAS Y VIÑEDOS MONTECASTRO

Ctra. VA-130, km. 12
47318 Castrillo de Duero (Valladolid)
☎: +34 983 484 013
Fax: +34 983 443 939
info@bodegasmontecastro.es

Alconte 2012 TC
tempranillo

89

Colour: cherry, garnet rim. Nose: ripe fruit, spicy, creamy oak, mineral. Palate: flavourful, toasty, round tannins.

Montecastro y Llanahermosa 2012 T
tempranillo

88

Colour: cherry, garnet rim. Nose: roasted coffee, smoky, spicy, ripe fruit. Palate: flavourful, smoky aftertaste, ripe fruit.

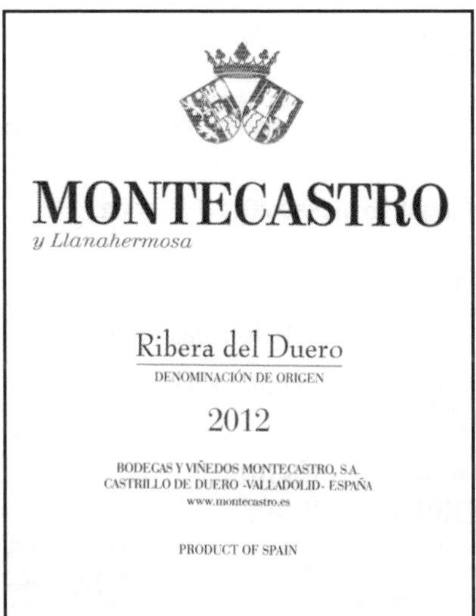

BODEGAS Y VIÑEDOS NEO

Ctra. N-122, Km. 274,5
09391 Castrillo de la Vega (Burgos)
☎: +34 947 514 393
Fax: +34 947 515 445
info@bodegasconde.com
www.bodegasneo.com

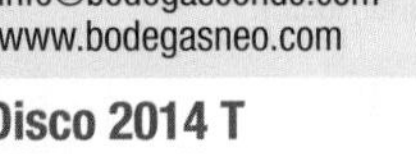

Disco 2014 T
100% tempranillo

88

Colour: bright cherry. Nose: ripe fruit, sweet spices, creamy oak, expressive. Palate: flavourful, fruity, round tannins.

El Arte de Vivir 2014 T

86

Neo 2012 T
100% tempranillo

90

Colour: cherry, garnet rim. Nose: smoky, spicy, ripe fruit. Palate: flavourful, smoky aftertaste, ripe fruit.

Neo Punta Esencia 2012 T
100% tempranillo

93

Colour: cherry, garnet rim. Nose: balanced, complex, ripe fruit, spicy. Palate: good structure, flavourful, balanced.

Sentido 2013 T
100% tempranillo

87

Colour: bright cherry. Nose: ripe fruit, sweet spices, creamy oak. Palate: flavourful, fruity, toasty.

BODEGAS Y VIÑEDOS ORTEGA FOURNIER

Finca El Pinar, s/n
09316 Berlangas de Roa (Burgos)
☎: +34 947 533 006
Fax: +34 947 533 010
ofournier-ribera@ofournier.com
www.ofournier.com

Alfa Spiga 2008 T
100% tinta del país

92

Colour: cherry, garnet rim. Nose: ripe fruit, earthy notes, spicy, balsamic herbs, dried herbs, scrubland. Palate: balanced, flavourful, long, balsamic.

O. Fournier 2008 T
100% tinta del país

93

Colour: light cherry. Nose: fine reductive notes, aged wood nuances, toasty, ripe fruit. Palate: spicy, toasty, flavourful.

Spiga 2009 T
100% tinta del país

91

Colour: cherry, garnet rim. Nose: ripe fruit, spicy, creamy oak, complex. Palate: flavourful, toasty, round tannins.

Urban Ribera 2012 T Roble
100% tinta del país

88

Colour: deep cherry, purple rim. Nose: toasty, ripe fruit, balsamic herbs. Palate: balanced, spicy, long.

BODEGAS Y VIÑEDOS RAUDA S. COOP.

Ctra. de Pedrosa, s/n
09300 Roa de Duero (Burgos)
☎: +34 947 540 224
informacion@vinosderauda.com
www.vinosderauda.com

Musai de Tinto Roa 2011 TR
100% tinta del país

88

Colour: very deep cherry. Nose: ripe fruit, fruit preserve, dark chocolate, dried herbs. Palate: flavourful, long.

Tinto Roa 2011 TC
100% tinta del país

86

Tinto Roa 2014 T
100% tinta del país

87

Colour: bright cherry. Nose: ripe fruit, sweet spices, creamy oak. Palate: flavourful, fruity, toasty, round tannins.

BODEGAS Y VIÑEDOS ROBEAL

Ctra. Anguix, s/n
09300 Roa (Burgos)
☎: +34 947 484 706
Fax: +34 947 482 817
info@bodegasrobeal.com
www.bodegasrobeal.com

Buen Miñón 2014 RD
50% albillo, 50% tempranillo

84

Buen Miñón 2014 T
tempranillo

86

La Capilla 2010 TR
90

Colour: cherry, garnet rim. Nose: grassy, ripe fruit. Palate: flavourful, good structure, fruity, spicy.

La Capilla 2011 TC
tempranillo

87

Colour: deep cherry, purple rim. Nose: toasty, ripe fruit, scrubland. Palate: balanced, spicy, long, flavourful.

La Capilla Vendimia Seleccionada 2011 T
92

Colour: cherry, garnet rim. Nose: balanced, complex, ripe fruit, spicy. Palate: good structure, flavourful, round tannins, balanced.

Valnogal 16 meses 2011 T Barrica
tempranillo

89

Colour: very deep cherry, garnet rim. Nose: balanced, ripe fruit, dark chocolate, tobacco. Palate: correct, ripe fruit, long.

Valnogal 6 meses 2013 T Roble
86

BODEGAS Y VIÑEDOS SEÑORIO DE BOCOS

Camino La Canaleja, s/n
47317 Bocos de Duero (Valladolid)
☎: +34 983 880 988
Fax: +34 983 880 988
bodegas@senoriodebocos.com
www.bocos.eu

Autor de Bocos 2012 T
tempranillo

89

Colour: cherry, garnet rim. Nose: red berry notes, ripe fruit, spicy, creamy oak. Palate: flavourful, toasty.

Señorio de Bocos 2011 TC
tempranillo

89

Colour: deep cherry, garnet rim. Nose: ripe fruit, characterful, creamy oak, cocoa bean. Palate: correct, fruity, easy to drink.

Señorio de Bocos 2013 T Roble
tempranillo

84

BODEGAS Y VIÑEDOS TÁBULA

Ctra. de Valbuena, km. 2
47359 Olivares de Duero (Valladolid)
☎: +34 608 219 019
Fax: +34 983 107 300
armando@bodegastabula.es
www.bodegastabula.es

Clave de Tábula 2012 T

100% tempranillo

94

Colour: cherry, garnet rim. Nose: mineral, expressive, spicy, ripe fruit. Palate: flavourful, ripe fruit, long, good acidity, balanced.

Damana 2012 TC

100% tempranillo

90

Colour: bright cherry. Nose: ripe fruit, sweet spices, creamy oak. Palate: flavourful, fruity, round tannins.

Damana 5 2013 T

100% tempranillo

87

Colour: deep cherry. Nose: ripe fruit, fruit preserve, spicy, creamy oak. Palate: powerful, flavourful, toasty.

Gran Tábula 2012 T

100% tempranillo

93

Colour: cherry, garnet rim. Nose: roasted coffee, smoky, spicy, ripe fruit. Palate: flavourful, smoky aftertaste, ripe fruit.

Tábula 2012 T

100% tempranillo

92

Colour: cherry, garnet rim. Nose: ripe fruit, spicy, creamy oak, complex. Palate: flavourful, toasty.

BODEGAS Y VIÑEDOS TAMARAL

Crta. N-122 Valladolid-Soria, Km.310,6
47300 Peñafiel (Valladolid)
☎: +34 983 878 017
Fax: +34 983 878 089
info@tamaral.com
www.tamaral.com

Tamaral 2010 TR

100% tempranillo

92

Colour: cherry, garnet rim. Nose: ripe fruit, spicy, creamy oak, complex. Palate: flavourful, toasty, round tannins, balanced.

Tamaral 2011 TC

100% tempranillo

91

Colour: cherry, garnet rim. Nose: smoky, spicy, ripe fruit, fruit liqueur notes. Palate: flavourful, smoky aftertaste, ripe fruit.

Tamaral 2013 T Roble

100% tempranillo

86

Tamaral 2014 RD

100% tempranillo

87

Colour: rose, purple rim. Nose: powerfull, fruit preserve, warm. Palate: powerful, flavourful, round.

Tamaral Finca la Mira 2009 T

100% tempranillo

91

Colour: cherry, garnet rim. Nose: ripe fruit, wild herbs, earthy notes, spicy, balsamic herbs. Palate: balanced, flavourful, long, balsamic.

BODEGAS Y VIÑEDOS VALDERIZ

Ctra. Pedrosa, km 1
09300 Roa de Duero (Burgos)
☎: +34 947 540 460
Fax: +34 947 541 032
bodega@valderiz.com
www.valderiz.com

Valdehermoso 2013 T Roble

100% tinta del país

87

Colour: deep cherry. Nose: creamy oak, toasty, ripe fruit, balsamic herbs. Palate: balanced, spicy, long.

Valdehermoso 2013 TC

100% tinta del país

90

Colour: bright cherry. Nose: sweet spices, creamy oak, overripe fruit. Palate: flavourful, fruity, toasty, round tannins.

Valdehermoso 2014 T

100% tinta del país

87

Colour: cherry, purple rim. Nose: powerfull, ripe fruit. Palate: powerful, fruity, unctuous.

Valderiz 2011 T
95% tinta del país, 5% albillo

91

Colour: deep cherry, garnet rim. Nose: powerfull, expressive, wild herbs, ripe fruit, balanced. Palate: flavourful, good structure, long.

Valderiz Juegabolos 2011 T
95% tinta del país, 5% albillo

93

Colour: very deep cherry. Nose: expressive, complex, varietal, spicy. Palate: good structure, round, long, fruity aftestaste, spicy, round tannins.

Valderiz Tomás Esteban 2009 T
95% tinta del país, 5% albillo

94

Colour: cherry, garnet rim. Nose: balanced, complex, ripe fruit, spicy, fine reductive notes. Palate: good structure, flavourful, round tannins, balanced.

BODEGAS Y VIÑEDOS VEGA DE YUSO S.L.

Basilón, 9
47350 Quintanilla de Onésimo
(Valladolid)
☎: +34 983 680 054
Fax: +34 983 680 294
bodega@vegadeyuso.com
www.vegadeyuso.com

Pozo de Nieve 2013 T Barrica
100% tempranillo

85

Tres Matas 2011 TR
100% tempranillo

90

Colour: cherry, garnet rim. Nose: ripe fruit, wild herbs, spicy balsamic herbs. Palate: balanced, flavourful, long, balsamic.

Tres Matas 2012 TC
100% tempranillo

92

Colour: cherry, garnet rim. Nose: creamy oak, red berry notes, balanced, ripe fruit. Palate: flavourful, spicy, elegant, long.

Tres Matas Vendimia Seleccionada 2011 T
100% tempranillo

89

Colour: cherry, garnet rim. Nose: fine reductive notes, wet leather, aged wood nuances, ripe fruit. Palate: spicy, long, toasty.

Vegantigua 10 meses 2013 T Barrica
100% tempranillo

84

BODEGAS Y VIÑEDOS VIÑA MAYOR

Ctra. Valladolid - Soria, Km. 325,6
47350 Quintanilla de Onésimo
(Valladolid)
☎: +34 983 680 461
Fax: +34 915 006 006
rrpp@vina-mayor.com
www.vina-mayor.es

Viña Mayor 2009 TGR
100% tinta del país

90

Colour: pale ruby, brick rim edge. Nose: spicy, fine reductive notes, wet leather, aged wood nuances, fruit liqueur notes. Palate: spicy, fine tannins, balanced.

Viña Mayor 2011 TR
100% tinta del país

92

Colour: cherry, garnet rim. Nose: red berry notes, ripe fruit, spicy, creamy oak, complex. Palate: flavourful, toasty.

Viña Mayor 2012 TC

88

Colour: deep cherry, garnet rim. Nose: ripe fruit, spicy, balsamic herbs. Palate: flavourful, fruity, round tannins.

Viña Mayor 2014 T Roble

89

Colour: bright cherry. Nose: ripe fruit, sweet spices. Palate: flavourful, fruity, toasty, round tannins, fruity aftestaste.

BODEGUEROS QUINTA ESENCIA

Eras, 37
47520 Castronuño (Valladolid)
☎: +34 605 887 100
Fax: +34 983 866 391
ferrin@bodeguerosquintaesencia.com
www.bodeguerosquintaesencia.com

Al-Nabiz 2012 T
100% tempranillo

87

Colour: deep cherry. Nose: ripe fruit, fruit preserve, balsamic herbs, toasty. Palate: powerful, flavourful, spicy.

BOSQUE DE MATASNOS

Ctra. Aranda s/n
09462 Moradillo de Roa (Burgos)
☎: +34 947 530 804
administracion@bosquedematasnos.es
www.bosquedematasnos.es

Bosque de Matasnos 2012 T
95% tempranillo, 5% merlot

94

Colour: cherry, garnet rim. Nose: mineral, expressive, spicy. Palate: flavourful, ripe fruit, long, good acidity, balanced.

PODIUM

Bosque de Matasnos Edición Limitada 2011 T
95% tempranillo, 5% merlot

96

Colour: cherry, garnet rim. Nose: mineral, expressive, spicy. Palate: flavourful, ripe fruit, long, good acidity, balanced.

CAMPOS GÓTICOS

Parcela 622
09313 Anguix (Burgos)
☎: +34 979 165 121
Fax: +34 979 712 644
clientedirecto@camposgoticos.es
www.camposgoticos.es

7 Lunas Vendimia Seleccionada 2005 TR
100% tempranillo

91

Colour: pale ruby, brick rim edge. Nose: spicy, fine reductive notes, wet leather, aged wood nuances, fruit liqueur notes. Palate: spicy, fine tannins, balanced.

7 Lunas Viñedos de la Joya 2004 T
100% tempranillo

92

Colour: black cherry, orangey edge. Nose: toasty, fine reductive notes, fruit liqueur notes, spicy. Palate: balanced, classic aged character, flavourful.

Campos Góticos 2004 TR
100% tempranillo

90

Colour: pale ruby, brick rim edge. Nose: elegant, spicy, fine reductive notes, tobacco. Palate: spicy, fine tannins, elegant, long.

Campos Góticos 2012 TC
100% tempranillo

85

Campos Góticos 2013 T Roble
100% tempranillo

88

Colour: bright cherry. Nose: ripe fruit, sweet spices, creamy oak, expressive. Palate: flavourful, fruity, round tannins.

Pecunia 2012 T
100% tempranillo

85

CARRASVILLA
Ctra. Pesquera VA-101, P.K. 3,700
47300 Peñafiel (Valladolid)
☎: +34 983 218 925
Fax: +34 983 218 926
comercial@carrasvilla.es
www.carrasvilla.es

Terralux 2012 T
tempranillo

89

Colour: deep cherry, purple rim. Nose: characterful, ripe fruit, powerfull, sweet spices. Palate: good structure, full.

CASA ROJO
Sánchez Picazo, 53
30332 Balsapintada (Murcia)
☎: +34 968 151 520
Fax: +34 968 151 539
info@casarojo.com
www.casarojo.com

Alexander VS The Ham Factory 2012 T
tinto fino

90

Colour: cherry, garnet rim. Nose: ripe fruit, spicy, creamy oak, complex. Palate: flavourful, toasty, round tannins.

CEPAS DE CASTILLA S.L.U.
Ctra. Aranda - Salas, km. 14
09490 San Juan del Monte (Burgos)
☎: +34 947 552 233
Fax: +34 947 552 233
castillalta@gmail.com

Enrique I 2012 TC
tempranillo

85

Enrique I 2014 T Joven
tempranillo

86

CILLAR DE SILOS
Paraje El Soto, s/n
09370 Quintana del Pidio (Burgos)
☎: +34 947 545 126
Fax: +34 947 545 605
bodega@cillardesilos.es
www.cillardesilos.es

Cillar de Silos 2012 TC
100% tempranillo

92

Colour: cherry, garnet rim. Nose: red berry notes, ripe fruit, spicy, creamy oak. Palate: flavourful, toasty, round tannins.

El Quintanal 2014 T
100% tempranillo

88

Colour: cherry, purple rim. Nose: powerfull, ripe fruit, spicy. Palate: powerful, fruity, unctuous.

Joven de Silos 2014 T
100% tempranillo

89

Colour: cherry, purple rim. Nose: expressive, fresh fruit, red berry notes, floral. Palate: flavourful, fruity, good acidity.

La Viña de Amalio 2011 T
100% tempranillo

92

Colour: deep cherry, garnet rim. Nose: ripe fruit, fruit preserve, creamy oak, sweet spices. Palate: good structure, flavourful, full.

Rosado de Silos 2014 RD
tempranillo, albillo

87

Colour: light cherry, bright. Nose: fragrant herbs, citrus fruit, balanced, red berry notes. Palate: fresh, ripe fruit, good acidity.

Torresilo 2012 TR
100% tempranillo

93

Colour: cherry, garnet rim. Nose: smoky, spicy, ripe fruit, complex. Palate: flavourful, smoky aftertaste, ripe fruit, round tannins.

CINEMA WINES

Felipe Gómez, 1
47140 Laguna de Duero (Valladolid)
☎: +34 983 544 696
Fax: +34 983 545 539
info@cinemawines.es
www.cinemawines.es

Cinema 2012 TC
100% tempranillo

89

Colour: cherry, garnet rim. Nose: smoky, spicy, ripe fruit. Palate: flavourful, smoky aftertaste, ripe fruit.

Cinema 6 meses Barrica 2013 T Barrica
100% tempranillo

86

Cinema Paraiso 2011 T Roble
100% tempranillo

91

Colour: deep cherry, purple rim. Nose: creamy oak, toasty, ripe fruit, balsamic herbs, dry stone. Palate: balanced, spicy, long.

Magnum Cinema 2010 TC
100% tempranillo

90

Colour: bright cherry, garnet rim. Nose: sweet spices, ripe fruit, spicy. Palate: balanced, long, round tannins.

COMENGE

Camino del Castillo, s/n
47316 Curiel de Duero (Valladolid)
☎: +34 983 880 363
Fax: +34 983 880 717
admin@comenge.com
www.comenge.com

Biberius 2014 T

88

Colour: bright cherry. Nose: ripe fruit, sweet spices, creamy oak. Palate: flavourful, fruity, toasty.

Comenge 2010 TR
100% tempranillo

92

Colour: cherry, garnet rim. Nose: balanced, complex, ripe fruit, spicy. Palate: balanced, spicy, elegant.

Don Miguel Comenge 2011 T
90% tempranillo, 10% cabernet sauvignon

94

Colour: bright cherry, garnet rim. Nose: fruit expression, balanced, elegant, spicy. Palate: flavourful, fruity, good structure, round tannins.

Familia Comenge Reserva 2011 T
100% tempranillo

91

Colour: cherry, garnet rim. Nose: creamy oak, red berry notes, balanced. Palate: flavourful, spicy, elegant.

COMPAÑÍA DE VINOS TELMO RODRÍGUEZ

El Monte
01308 Lanciego (Álava)
☎: +34 945 628 315
Fax: +34 945 628 314
contact@telmorodriguez.com
www.telmorodriguez.com

M2 de Matallana 2011 T
tinto fino

89

Colour: very deep cherry. Nose: powerfull, overripe fruit, aromatic coffee, dark chocolate. Palate: powerful, sweetness.

Matallana 2011 T
tinto fino

92

Colour: cherry, garnet rim. Nose: roasted coffee, smoky, spicy, ripe fruit. Palate: flavourful, smoky aftertaste, ripe fruit.

CONVENTO DE LAS CLARAS S.L.

Plaza de los Comuneros, 1
47300 Peñafiel (Valladolid)
☎: +34 608 223 346
bodega@bodegasconventodelasclaras.com
www.bodegasconventodelasclaras.com

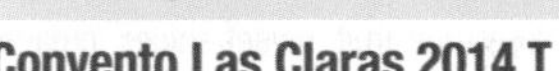

Convento Las Claras 2014 T
100% tempranillo

91

Colour: deep cherry, purple rim. Nose: expressive, ripe fruit, red berry notes, spicy. Palate: correct, balanced, spicy, long.

Heritage Convento de las Claras 2012 T
100% tempranillo

92

Colour: bright cherry. Nose: ripe fruit, sweet spices, creamy oak, expressive. Palate: flavourful, fruity, toasty, round tannins.

Paraje de San Juan Convento Las Claras 2011 T
100% tempranillo

93

Colour: cherry, garnet rim. Nose: mineral, expressive, spicy, ripe fruit. Palate: flavourful, ripe fruit, long, good acidity, balanced, elegant.

CONVENTO DE OREJA

Avda. Palencia, 1
47010 Valladolid (Valladolid)
☎: +34 685 990 596
convento@conventooreja.es
www.conventooreja.net

Convento Oreja 2011 TC

88

Colour: cherry, garnet rim. Nose: powerfull, characterful, ripe fruit, creamy oak. Palate: flavourful, long, round tannins.

Convento Oreja 2014 T Roble

100% tempranillo

88

Colour: bright cherry. Nose: ripe fruit, sweet spices, creamy oak. Palate: flavourful, fruity, toasty.

CORDIS TERRA HISPANIA

Gamonal, 16 2ºC
28031 Madrid (Madrid)
☎: +34 911 610 024
Fax: +34 913 316 047
info@cordisterra.com
www.cordisterra.com

Cuatro Runas 2012 T

tempranillo

88

Colour: cherry, garnet rim. Nose: creamy oak, ripe fruit. Palate: flavourful, spicy, elegant.

Cuatro Runas 2013 T Roble

tempranillo

87

Colour: bright cherry. Nose: ripe fruit, sweet spices, creamy oak. Palate: flavourful, fruity, round tannins.

CVNE

Barrio de la Estación, s/n
26200 Haro (La Rioja)
☎: +34 941 304 800
Fax: +34 941 304 815
marketing@cvne.com
www.cvne.com

Buenos Días Roble by Cune 2013 T

100% tempranillo

86

Cune Ribera del Duero 2013 T Roble

100% tempranillo

85

DEHESA DE LOS CANÓNIGOS S.A.

Ctra. Renedo - Pesquera, Km. 39
47315 Pesquera de Duero (Valladolid)
☎: +34 983 484 001
Fax: +34 983 484 040
comercial@dehesacanonigos.com
www.bodegadehesadeloscanonigos.com

Dehesa de los Canónigos 2012 TC

85% tempranillo, 15% cabernet sauvignon

89

Colour: very deep cherry, garnet rim. Nose: mineral, balsamic herbs, balanced, fruit preserve. Palate: full, flavourful, round tannins.

Dehesa de los Canónigos 2013 T

100% tempranillo

88

Colour: bright cherry. Nose: ripe fruit, sweet spices, creamy oak, expressive. Palate: flavourful, fruity, round tannins.

Solideo 2009 TR
85% tempranillo, 12% cabernet sauvignon, 3% albillo

90

Colour: dark-red cherry, garnet rim. Nose: complex, balanced, scrubland, spicy. Palate: full, flavourful, good structure.

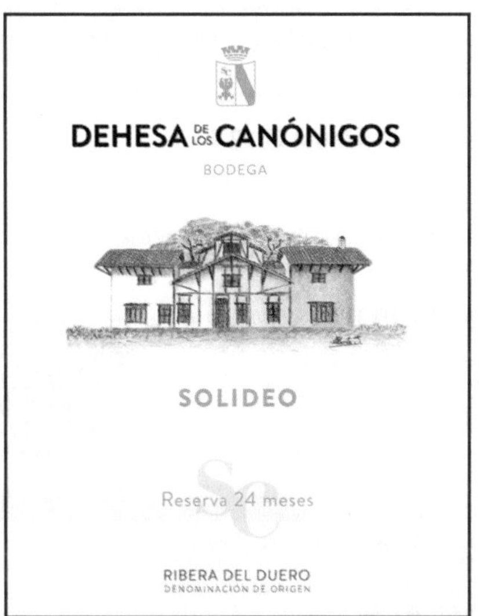

DEHESA VALDELAGUNA

Ctra. Valoria, Km. 16
47315 Pesquera de Duero (Valladolid)
☎: +34 619 460 308
montelaguna@montelaguna.es
www.montelaguna.es

Montelaguna 2011 TR
tempranillo

89

Colour: cherry, garnet rim. Nose: red berry notes, ripe fruit, spicy, creamy oak, complex. Palate: flavourful, toasty.

Montelaguna 2012 TC
tempranillo

88

Colour: bright cherry. Nose: ripe fruit, sweet spices, creamy oak, fine reductive notes. Palate: flavourful, fruity, toasty.

Montelaguna Rosé 2014 RD
tempranillo

85

Montelaguna Selección 2012 T
tempranillo

90

Colour: cherry, garnet rim. Nose: smoky, spicy, sweet spices, ripe fruit. Palate: flavourful, smoky aftertaste.

Ra s/c T
tempranillo

88

Colour: bright cherry. Nose: ripe fruit, sweet spices, creamy oak. Palate: flavourful, fruity, toasty.

Ra Vendimia Seleccionada 2009 T
tempranillo

88

Colour: cherry, garnet rim. Nose: fine reductive notes, wet leather, aged wood nuances, fruit preserve. Palate: spicy, long, toasty.

DOMINIO BASCONCILLOS

09370 Gumiel de Izán (Burgos)
☎: +34 947 473 300
Fax: +34 947 473 360
info@dominiobasconcillos.com
www.dominiobasconcillos.com

Dominio Basconcillos 12 meses 2011 TC
100% tempranillo

92

Colour: cherry, garnet rim. Nose: mineral, expressive, spicy, ripe fruit. Palate: flavourful, ripe fruit, long, good acidity, balanced.

Dominio Basconcillos Ecológico 6 meses 2013 T
100% tempranillo

89

Colour: bright cherry. Nose: ripe fruit, sweet spices, creamy oak, expressive. Palate: flavourful, fruity, round tannins.

Viña Magna 2011 TR
85% tempranillo, 10% cabernet sauvignon, 5% merlot

93

Colour: cherry, garnet rim. Nose: red berry notes, ripe fruit, spicy, creamy oak, complex. Palate: flavourful, toasty, round tannins.

Viña Magna 2011 TC
90% tempranillo, 10% cabernet sauvignon

91

Colour: cherry, garnet rim. Nose: balanced, complex, ripe fruit, spicy, fine reductive notes. Palate: good structure, flavourful, balanced.

Viña Magna 6 meses 2013 T
100% tempranillo

90

Colour: deep cherry, purple rim. Nose: creamy oak, toasty, ripe fruit, balsamic herbs. Palate: balanced, spicy, long.

DOMINIO DE ATAUTA

Ctra. a Morcuera, s/n
42345 Atauta (Soria)
☎: +34 975 351 349
info@dominiodeatauta.com
www.dominiodeatauta.com

Dominio de Atauta 2011 T

100% tinto fino

94

Colour: cherry, garnet rim. Nose: mineral, expressive, spicy. Palate: flavourful, ripe fruit, good acidity, balanced, round.

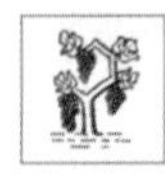

DOMINIO DE ATAUTA

RIBERA DEL DUERO
DENOMINACIÓN DE ORIGEN

Dominio de Atauta 2012 T

100% tinto fino

92

Colour: cherry, garnet rim. Nose: red berry notes, ripe fruit, spicy, creamy oak, fine reductive notes. Palate: flavourful, toasty, round tannins.

Dominio de Atauta La Mala 2010 TC

100% tinto fino

94

Colour: deep cherry, purple rim. Nose: creamy oak, toasty, ripe fruit, balsamic herbs. Palate: balanced, spicy, long.

🏆 PODIUM

Dominio de Atauta Llanos del Almendro 2010 T

100% tinto fino

96

Colour: very deep cherry, garnet rim. Nose: expressive, complex, mineral, balanced, scrubland. Palate: full, flavourful, round tannins.

🏆 PODIUM

Dominio de Atauta Valdegatiles 2010 T

100% tinto fino

95

Colour: very deep cherry, garnet rim. Nose: expressive, complex, mineral, balsamic herbs, balanced. Palate: full, flavourful, round tannins.

Parada de Atauta 2012 T

100% tinto fino

93

Colour: cherry, garnet rim. Nose: creamy oak, red berry notes, fresh fruit, balanced. Palate: flavourful, spicy, elegant.

DOMINIO DE ES

Manuel de Falla, nº 37 2ºE
26007 Logroño (La Rioja)
☎: +34 676 536 390
bebervino@hotmail.com

🏆 PODIUM

Dominio de Es La Diva 2013 T

tinto fino, albillo

95

Colour: cherry, garnet rim. Nose: mineral, ripe fruit, red berry notes, spicy, toasty. Palate: fruity, ripe fruit, spicy.

🏆 PODIUM

Dominio de Es Viñas Viejas de Soria 2013 T

tinto fino

95

Colour: very deep cherry, garnet rim. Nose: expressive, complex, mineral, balsamic herbs, balanced. Palate: full, flavourful, round tannins, balsamic.

DOMINIO DE PINGUS S.L.

Millán Alonso, 49
47350 Quintanilla de Onésimo
(Valladolid)
info@pingus.es
www.pingus.es

PODIUM

Flor de Pingus 2013 T

100% tempranillo

95

Colour: deep cherry, purple rim. Nose: creamy oak, toasty, ripe fruit, balsamic herbs. Palate: balanced, spicy, long.

PODIUM

Pingus 2013 T

100% tempranillo

95

Colour: cherry, garnet rim. Nose: red berry notes, ripe fruit, fragrant herbs, spicy, creamy oak, mineral. Palate: powerful, flavourful, balsamic, balanced.

PSI 2013 T

93% tempranillo, 7% garnacha

92

Colour: cherry, purple rim. Nose: red berry notes, floral, balsamic herbs, sweet spices. Palate: powerful, fresh, fruity.

DOMINIO DEL ÁGUILA

Los Lagares, 42
09370 La Aguilera (Burgos)
☎: +34 638 899 236
info@dominiodelaguila.com
www.dominiodelaguila.com

PODIUM

Dominio del Aguila 2011 TR

tempranillo, garnacha, bobal, blanca del pais

97

Colour: very deep cherry, garnet rim. Nose: expressive, complex, mineral, balsamic herbs, balanced. Palate: flavourful, round tannins, spicy.

Pícaro del Aguila 2013 Clarete

89

Colour: light cherry, bright. Nose: toasty, creamy oak, red berry notes, ripe fruit. Palate: flavourful, correct, fine bitter notes.

Pícaro del Aguila 2013 T

tempranillo, garnacha, bobal, blanca del pais

92

Colour: deep cherry, purple rim. Nose: creamy oak, toasty, ripe fruit, balsamic herbs. Palate: balanced, spicy, long.

DOMINIO ROMANO

Lagares, s/n
47319 Rábano (Valladolid)
☎: +34 983 871 661
Fax: +34 938 901 143
dominioromano@dominioromano.es
www.dominioromano.es

Camino Romano 2014 T

tinto fino

88

Colour: deep cherry, purple rim. Nose: toasty, ripe fruit, balsamic herbs, sulphur notes. Palate: balanced, spicy, long.

ÉBANO VIÑEDOS Y BODEGAS

Ctra. N-122 Km., 299,6
47318 Castrillo de Duero (Valladolid)
☎: +34 983 106 440
Fax: +34 986 609 313
ebano@valminorebano.com
www.ebanovinedosybodegas.com

Ébano 2011 TC

tempranillo

91

Colour: cherry, garnet rim. Nose: smoky, spicy, fruit liqueur notes. Palate: flavourful, smoky aftertaste, ripe fruit.

Ébano 6 2014 T

tempranillo

87

Colour: very deep cherry, purple rim. Nose: characterful, ripe fruit, raspberry. Palate: fruity, easy to drink.

EL LAGAR DE ISILLA

Camino Real, 1
09471 La Vid (Burgos)
☎: +34 947 530 434
Fax: +34 947 530 434
bodegas@lagarisilla.es
www.lagarisilla.es

El Lagar de Isilla 2010 TR

100% tempranillo

91

Colour: very deep cherry, garnet rim. Nose: spicy, ripe fruit, cocoa bean. Palate: good structure, full, flavourful, round tannins, long.

El Lagar de Isilla 2011 TC

96% tempranillo, 3% merlot, 3% cabernet sauvignon

89

Colour: deep cherry, garnet rim. Nose: warm, ripe fruit, scrubland. Palate: spicy, long.

El Lagar de Isilla 2013 T Roble
95% tempranillo, 5% cabernet sauvignon

88

Colour: bright cherry, garnet rim. Nose: balanced, ripe fruit, spicy, wild herbs. Palate: fruity, flavourful, easy to drink.

El Lagar de Isilla 2014 T
100% tempranillo

85

El Lagar de Isilla Gestación 9 meses 2012 T Roble
100% tempranillo

91

Colour: deep cherry, purple rim. Nose: creamy oak, toasty, ripe fruit, balsamic herbs. Palate: balanced, spicy, long.

El Lagar de Isilla Vendimia Seleccionada 2011 T
100% tempranillo

90

Colour: bright cherry, garnet rim. Nose: wild herbs, dried herbs. Palate: balanced, fruity, good structure, flavourful.

EL MOSAICO DE BACO

Avda Extremadura, 55
09400 Aranda de Duero (Burgos)
☎: +34 947 512 866
Fax: +34 947 512 866
info@elmosaicodebaco.com
www.elmosaicodebaco.com

Mosaico de Baco 2011 TC
tinto fino

88

Colour: cherry, garnet rim. Nose: ripe fruit, earthy notes, spicy, balsamic herbs. Palate: balanced, balsamic, easy to drink.

Mosaico de Baco 2014 RD
tinto fino, albillo

84

Mosaico de Baco 2014 T
tinto fino

85

Mosaico de Baco Viñas del Monte 2009 T
tinto fino

89

Colour: cherry, garnet rim. Nose: ripe fruit, wild herbs, earthy notes, spicy, balsamic herbs. Palate: balanced, flavourful, long, balsamic.

FINCA TORREMILANOS

Finca Torremilanos
09400 Aranda de Duero (Burgos)
☎: +34 947 512 852
Fax: +34 947 508 044
reservas@torremilanos.com
www.torremilanos.com

Cyclo 2013 T

91

Colour: deep cherry. Nose: creamy oak, ripe fruit, balsamic herbs. Palate: balanced, spicy, long.

Los Cantos de Torremilanos 2013 T

90

Colour: bright cherry. Nose: ripe fruit, sweet spices, creamy oak. Palate: flavourful, fruity, toasty.

Montecastrillo 2014 RD

87

Colour: raspberry rose. Nose: red berry notes, floral, expressive. Palate: powerful, fruity, fresh.

Montecastrillo 2014 T Roble

88

Colour: bright cherry, purple rim. Nose: ripe fruit, sweet spices, expressive. Palate: flavourful, fruity, toasty.

Torre Albéniz 2011 TR

90

Colour: cherry, garnet rim. Nose: ripe fruit, wild herbs, earthy notes, spicy. Palate: flavourful, long, balsamic.

Torremilanos 2011 TR

90

Colour: very deep cherry. Nose: complex, mineral, balsamic herbs, ripe fruit. Palate: full, flavourful.

Torremilanos 2012 TC

89

Colour: bright cherry. Nose: ripe fruit, sweet spices, creamy oak. Palate: flavourful, fruity, toasty.

FINCA VILLACRECES

Ctra. Soria N-122 Km 322
47350 Quintanilla de Onésimo
(Valladolid)
☎: +34 983 680 437
Fax: +34 983 683 314
villacreces@villacreces.com
www.villacreces.com

Finca Villacreces 2012 T
86% tempranillo, 10% cabernet sauvignon, 4% merlot

92

Colour: cherry, garnet rim. Nose: roasted coffee, smoky, spicy, ripe fruit. Palate: flavourful, smoky aftertaste, ripe fruit.

🏆 PODIUM

Finca Villacreces Nebro 2011 TC
100% tinto fino

96

Colour: cherry, garnet rim. Nose: mineral, expressive, spicy. Palate: flavourful, ripe fruit, long, good acidity, balanced, round tannins.

Pruno 2013 T
90% tinto fino, 10% cabernet sauvignon

89

Colour: bright cherry. Nose: sweet spices, creamy oak. Palate: flavourful, fruity, toasty, round tannins.

GRANDES BODEGAS

Ctra. de Sotillo , s/n
09311 La Horra (Burgos)
☎: +34 947 542 165
Fax: +34 947 542 165
bodega@marquesdevelilla.com
www.marquesdevelilla.com

Doncel de Mataperras 2009 TR
100% tinta del país

90

Colour: dark-red cherry, garnet rim. Nose: ripe fruit, fruit preserve, dried herbs, fine reductive notes. Palate: correct, balanced.

Finca La María 2012 T Roble
100% tinta del país

88

Colour: cherry, garnet rim. Nose: ripe fruit, spicy, creamy oak. Palate: flavourful, toasty.

Marqués de Velilla 2009 TR
tinta del país

89

Colour: cherry, garnet rim. Nose: ripe fruit, wild herbs, earthy notes, spicy, balsamic herbs, tobacco. Palate: flavourful, long.

Marqués de Velilla 2011 TC
100% tinta del país

87

Colour: deep cherry, purple rim. Nose: creamy oak, toasty, ripe fruit, balsamic herbs. Palate: balanced, spicy, long.

Marqués de Velilla 2011 TR
tinta del país

88

Colour: cherry, garnet rim. Nose: ripe fruit, spicy, creamy oak, complex. Palate: flavourful, toasty, round tannins.

Marqués de Velilla 2012 T Roble
100% tinta del país

86

Marqués de Velilla 2014 T
100% tinta del país

85

GRANDES DOMINIOS

Casanovas i Bosch, 57
08202 Sabadell (Barcelona)
☎: +34 937 220 338
Fax: +34 937 252 385
info@grandominios.com
www.grandominios.com

Dominios de Castilla 2012 T
tinto fino

85

HACIENDA URBIÓN

Ctra. Nalda, km. 9
26120 Albelda de Iregua (Rioja)
☎: +34 941 444 233
Fax: +34 941 444 427
info@vinicolareal.com
www.vinicolareal.com

El Brujo 2012 TC
100% tempranillo

84

Vega Vieja 2012 TC
tempranillo

86

Vega Vieja Cosecha 2014 T
100% tempranillo

86

HAMMEKEN CELLARS

Calle de la Muela, 16
03730 Jávea (Alicante)
☎: +34 965 791 967
Fax: +34 966 461 471
cellars@hammekencellars.com
www.hammekencellars.com

Aventino 200 Barrels 2011 T
tempranillo

89

Colour: cherry, garnet rim. Nose: spicy, ripe fruit. Palate: flavourful, smoky aftertaste, ripe fruit.

Aventino Tempranillo 2014 T
tempranillo

88

Colour: bright cherry. Nose: ripe fruit, sweet spices, creamy oak, expressive. Palate: flavourful, fruity, round tannins.

Oraculo 2009 T
tempranillo

88

Colour: cherry, garnet rim. Nose: roasted coffee, smoky, spicy, ripe fruit. Palate: flavourful, smoky aftertaste, ripe fruit.

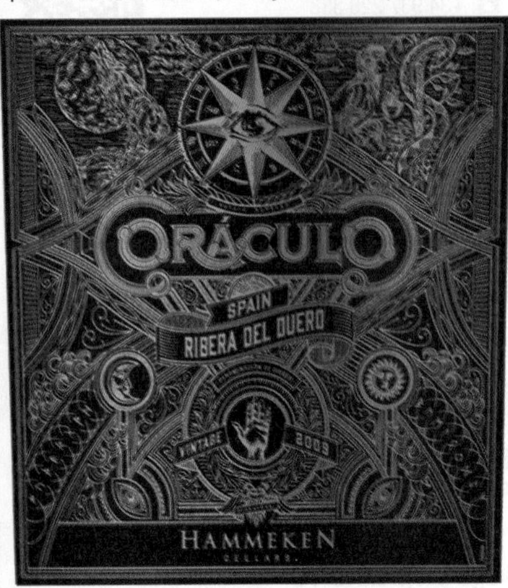

Viña Altamar Tempranillo 2014 T
tempranillo

84

HESVERA

Ctra. Peñafiel - Pesquera, Km. 5,5
47315 Pesquera de Duero (Valladolid)
☎: +34 626 060 516
Fax: +34 983 870 201
hesvera@hesvera.es
www.hesvera.es

Hesvera 2011 TC
100% tempranillo

87

Colour: deep cherry. Nose: fruit preserve, spicy, creamy oak. Palate: powerful, flavourful, spicy.

Hesvera Cosecha Limitada 2010 T
100% tempranillo

89

Colour: cherry, garnet rim. Nose: ripe fruit, old leather, tobacco. Palate: correct, flavourful, spicy.

Hesvera Seis Meses 2013 T Barrica
100% tempranillo

84

HIJOS DE ANTONIO POLO

La Olma, 5
47300 Peñafiel (Valladolid)
☎: +34 983 873 183
Fax: +34 983 881 808
info@pagopenafiel.com
www.pagopenafiel.com

Pagos de Peñafiel 2010 TC
100% tempranillo

86

Pagos de Peñafiel 2013 T Roble
100% tempranillo

85

HORNILLOS BALLESTEROS

Camino Tenerías, 9
09300 Roa de Duero (Burgos)
☎: +34 947 541 071
Fax: +34 947 541 071
hornillosballesteros@telefonica.net

MiBal 2011 TC
100% tinta del país

89

Colour: cherry, garnet rim. Nose: balanced, spicy, ripe fruit. Palate: flavourful, easy to drink, correct, balanced.

MiBal 2013 T
100% tinta del país

85

MiBal Selección 2012 T
100% tinta del país

87

Colour: bright cherry. Nose: ripe fruit, sweet spices, creamy oak. Palate: flavourful, fruity, toasty.

Perfil de MiBal 2009 T
100% tinta del país

92

Colour: cherry, garnet rim. Nose: ripe fruit, wild herbs, earthy notes, spicy, balsamic herbs. Palate: balanced, flavourful, long, balsamic.

LA MALETA HAND MADE FINE WINES

Plaza de Eladio Rodríguez, 19
32420 San Clodio (Ourense)
☎: +34 988 614 234
hola@lamaletawines.com
lamaletawines.com

Finca La Viajera 2010 TC
100% tempranillo

91

Colour: bright cherry, garnet rim. Nose: expressive, balanced, ripe fruit. Palate: flavourful, round tannins, fruity aftestaste.

Finca La Viajera 2013 T
100% tempranillo

89

Colour: bright cherry. Nose: ripe fruit, sweet spices, expressive, varietal. Palate: flavourful, fruity, round tannins.

Finca La Viajera Vendimia Seleccionada 2010 TGR

93

Colour: cherry, garnet rim. Nose: ripe fruit, spicy, creamy oak, complex. Palate: flavourful, toasty, round tannins.

LA VIÑA DEL LOCO

Plaza de Matute 12
28012 (Madrid)
☎: +34 609 079 980
info@miravinos.es
www.miravinos.es

Sonante 2013 T
100% tinto fino

87

Colour: deep cherry, purple rim. Nose: creamy oak, toasty, ripe fruit, balsamic herbs. Palate: balanced, spicy, long.

Venta El Loco 2012 TC
100% tinto fino

89

Colour: cherry, garnet rim. Nose: ripe fruit, complex, sweet spices. Palate: flavourful, toasty, complex.

LAGAR DE PROVENTUS

Pago de las Bodegas, s/n
47314 Padilla de Duero (Valladolid)
☎: +34 983 882 103
Fax: +34 983 881 514
info@lagardeproventus.es

Proventus 2011 TR
100% tempranillo

90

Colour: cherry, garnet rim. Nose: red berry notes, ripe fruit, spicy, creamy oak. Palate: flavourful, toasty.

Proventus 2012 TC
100% tempranillo

91

Colour: cherry, garnet rim. Nose: expressive, spicy. Palate: flavourful, ripe fruit, long, good acidity, balanced.

LEGARIS

Ctra. de Peñafiel - Encinas de Esgueva, km. 2,5
47316 Curiel de Duero (Valladolid)
☎: +34 983 878 088
e.izquierdo@codorniu.es
www.legaris.com

Legaris 2011 TR

89

Colour: cherry, garnet rim. Nose: ripe fruit, wild herbs, spicy, balsamic herbs. Palate: flavourful, long, balsamic.

Legaris 2012 TC
tinto fino

88

Colour: cherry, garnet rim. Nose: roasted coffee, smoky, ripe fruit. Palate: flavourful, smoky aftertaste, ripe fruit.

Legaris Calmo 2009 T

89

Colour: deep cherry, garnet rim. Nose: aromatic coffee, spicy, smoky. Palate: flavourful, fruity, round tannins.

LOESS

El Monte, 7
47195 Arroyo de la Encomienda (Valladolid)
☎: +34 983 664 898
Fax: +34 983 406 579
loess@loess.es
www.loess.es

Loess 2011 T
tempranillo

91

Colour: bright cherry, garnet rim. Nose: ripe fruit, spicy, complex, varietal, earthy notes. Palate: full, good structure, long.

Loess Collection 2011 T
tempranillo

93

Colour: cherry, garnet rim. Nose: expressive, spicy, varietal, ripe fruit, creamy oak. Palate: flavourful, ripe fruit, long, good acidity.

Loess Inspiration 2012 T
tempranillo

87

Colour: cherry, garnet rim. Nose: red berry notes, spicy, toasty, stalky. Palate: powerful, flavourful.

LONG WINES

Avda. del Puente Cultural, 8 Bloque B Bajo 7
28702 San Sebastián de los Reyes
(Madrid)
☎: +34 916 221 305
Fax: +34 916 220 029
customer.service@longwines.com
www.longwines.com

Lamatum 2011 TC
tempranillo

87

Colour: cherry, garnet rim. Nose: fine reductive notes, wet leather, aged wood nuances. Palate: spicy, long, toasty.

LYNUS VIÑEDOS Y BODEGAS

Camino de las Pozas, s/n
47350 Quintanilla de Onésimo
(Valladolid)
☎: +34 661 879 016
info@lynus.es
www.lynus.es

Lynus 2011 TC
100% tempranillo

89

Colour: deep cherry. Nose: creamy oak, toasty, ripe fruit, balsamic herbs. Palate: balanced, spicy, long.

MARÍA ASCENSIÓN REPISO BOCOS

47315 Pesquera de Duero (Valladolid)
☎: +34 983 870 178
info@veronicasalgado.es
www.veronicasalgado.es

Verónica Salgado 2013 T Roble
tinto fino

89

Colour: deep cherry. Nose: creamy oak, toasty, ripe fruit, balsamic herbs. Palate: balanced, spicy, long.

Verónica Salgado Capricho 2011 TC
tinto fino

93

Colour: very deep cherry, garnet rim. Nose: expressive, complex, mineral, balsamic herbs, balanced, red berry notes. Palate: full, flavourful, round tannins.

Verónica Salgado Capricho Viñas Viejas Vino de Autor 2011 T
tinto fino

92

Colour: cherry, garnet rim. Nose: creamy oak, red berry notes, fresh fruit, balanced, toasty. Palate: flavourful, spicy, elegant.

MARQUÉS DE LA CONCORDIA FAMILY OF WINES

Hacienda Abascal, N-122, Km. 321,5
47360 Quintanilla de Onésimo
(Valladolid)
☎: +34 913 878 612
www.the-haciendas.com

Hacienda Abascal Vineyard 2009 TR
100% tempranillo

90

Colour: cherry, garnet rim. Nose: red berry notes, ripe fruit, spicy, creamy oak, complex. Palate: flavourful, toasty, round tannins.

Hacienda Abascal Vineyard 2011 TC
100% tempranillo

88

Colour: cherry, garnet rim. Nose: ripe fruit, toasty, fine reductive notes. Palate: powerful, toasty.

Hacienda Abascal Vineyard Premium 2010 T
100% tempranillo

90

Colour: cherry, garnet rim. Nose: ripe fruit, wild herbs, earthy notes, spicy, balsamic herbs, fine reductive notes. Palate: balanced, flavourful, long, balsamic.

MARQUÉS DE REVILLA

Paraje Tiemblos, Pol 509- Parcela 5146
09441 Sotillo de la Ribera (Burgos)
☎: +34 913 739 689
guiomaro@marquesderevilla.com
www.marquesderevilla.com

Marqués de Revilla 2008 TR
tempranillo, merlot

88

Colour: dark-red cherry, orangey edge. Nose: waxy notes, ripe fruit, smoky, spicy. Palate: correct, easy to drink, balanced.

Marqués de Revilla 2009 TC
tempranillo, merlot

82

Marqués de Revilla 2012 T Roble
tempranillo, merlot

86

Marqués de Revilla 2014 T
tempranillo, merlot

86

MONTEBACO

Finca Montealto s/n
47300 Valbuena de Duero (Valladolid)
☎: +34 983 485 128
Fax: +34 983 485 033
montebaco@bodegasmontebaco.com
www.bodegasmontebaco.com

Montebaco 2013 TC

89

Colour: cherry, garnet rim. Nose: ripe fruit, spicy, creamy oak. Palate: flavourful, toasty, balsamic.

Montebaco Vendimia Seleccionada 2012 T

91

Colour: cherry, garnet rim. Nose: ripe fruit, spicy, creamy oak, complex. Palate: flavourful, toasty.

Semele 2013 TC

92

Colour: cherry, garnet rim. Nose: red berry notes, ripe fruit, spicy, creamy oak, complex. Palate: flavourful, toasty, balanced.

MONTEVANNOS

Paraje Tiemblos, Pol 509 - Parcela 5146
09411 Sotillo de la Ribera (Burgos)
☎: +34 947 534 277
Fax: +34 947 534 016
bodega@montevannos.es
www.montevannos.es

M Montevannos 2009 T

75% tempranillo, 25% merlot

84

Montevannos 2010 TC

80% tempranillo, 20% merlot

84

Montevannos 2012 T Roble

tempranillo, merlot

87

Colour: bright cherry. Nose: sweet spices, creamy oak, fruit preserve. Palate: flavourful, fruity, toasty, round tannins.

Montevannos 2014 T

90% tempranillo, 10% merlot

83

Opimius 2007 TR

100% tempranillo

88

Colour: cherry, garnet rim. Nose: ripe fruit, wild herbs, earthy notes, spicy, balsamic herbs. Palate: balanced, flavourful, long, balsamic.

OSBORNE RIBERA DEL DUERO

Crta. Fuenmayor - Navarrete, km. 2
26360 Fuenmayor (La Rioja)
☎: +34 925 860 990
Fax: +34 925 860 905
comunicaciones@osborne.es
www.osborne.es

Señorío del Cid 2013 T Roble

100% tinta del país

87

Colour: bright cherry, purple rim. Nose: smoky, toasty. Palate: ripe fruit, correct, good finish.

PAGO DE CARRAOVEJAS

Camino de Carraovejas, s/n
47300 Peñafiel (Valladolid)
☎: +34 983 878 020
info@pagodecarraovejas.com
www.pagodecarraovejas.com

PODIUM

Pago de Carraovejas "Cuesta de las Liebres" Vendimia Seleccionada 2011 TR

100% tinto fino

96

Colour: cherry, garnet rim. Nose: ripe fruit, spicy, complex, powerfull, earthy notes. Palate: good structure, flavourful, round tannins, balanced.

PODIUM

Pago de Carraovejas 2012 TR

76% tinto fino, 16% cabernet sauvignon, 8% merlot

95

Colour: cherry, garnet rim. Nose: balanced, complex, ripe fruit, spicy. Palate: good structure, flavourful, round tannins, balanced.

Pago de Carraovejas 2013 TC

83% tinto fino, 12% cabernet sauvignon, 5% merlot

92

Colour: cherry, garnet rim. Nose: creamy oak, red berry notes, fresh fruit, balanced. Palate: flavourful, spicy, elegant.

Pago de Carraovejas El Anejón 2011 T
91% tinto fino, 4% cabernet sauvignon, 5% merlot

94

Colour: cherry, garnet rim. Nose: complex, ripe fruit, spicy, fine reductive notes. Palate: good structure, flavourful, round tannins, balanced.

PAGO DE INA

Ctra. Renedo-Pesquera km. 26
47359 Olivares de Duero (Valladolid)
☎: +34 933 576 658
pagodeina@pagodeina.com
www.pagodeina.com

Pago de Ina 2011 T
100% tempranillo

90

Colour: cherry, garnet rim. Nose: creamy oak, balanced, ripe fruit, powerfull. Palate: flavourful, spicy, elegant.

PAGO DE LOS CAPELLANES

Camino de la Ampudia, s/n
09314 Pedrosa de Duero (Burgos)
☎: +34 947 530 068
Fax: +34 947 530 111
bodega@pagodeloscapellanes.com
www.pagodeloscapellanes.com

Pago de los Capellanes 2012 TC
100% tempranillo

92

Colour: cherry, garnet rim. Nose: smoky, spicy, ripe fruit, dark chocolate. Palate: flavourful, smoky aftertaste, ripe fruit.

Pago de los Capellanes 2012 TR
100% tempranillo

93

Colour: cherry, garnet rim. Nose: balanced, complex, ripe fruit, spicy. Palate: good structure, flavourful, round tannins, balanced.

Pago de los Capellanes 2014 T Roble
100% tempranillo

90

Colour: bright cherry. Nose: ripe fruit, sweet spices, creamy oak, expressive. Palate: flavourful, fruity, round tannins, easy to drink.

Pago de los Capellanes Parcela El Nogal 2011 T

93

Colour: cherry, garnet rim. Nose: mineral, expressive, spicy. Palate: flavourful, ripe fruit, long, good acidity, balanced.

Pago de los Capellanes Parcela El Picón 2010 T
100% tempranillo

94

Colour: very deep cherry. Nose: complex, ripe fruit, spicy, fine reductive notes, cocoa bean. Palate: good structure, flavourful, round tannins, balanced, long.

PAGOS DE MATANEGRA

Ctra. Santa María, 27
09311 Olmedillo de Roa (Burgos)
☎: +34 947 551 310
Fax: +34 947 551 309
info@pagosdematanegra.es
www.pagosdematanegra.es

Matanegra 14M 2010 TC
100% tempranillo

89

Colour: cherry, garnet rim. Nose: ripe fruit, spicy, creamy oak, complex. Palate: flavourful, toasty, round tannins.

Matanegra Media Crianza 7 meses 2013 T
100% tempranillo

88

Colour: deep cherry. Nose: creamy oak, toasty, ripe fruit, balsamic herbs. Palate: balanced, spicy, long.

Matanegra Vendimia Seleccionada 2010 T
100% tempranillo

91

Colour: cherry, garnet rim. Nose: mineral, expressive, spicy, ripe fruit. Palate: flavourful, ripe fruit, long, good acidity, balanced.

PAGOS DEL REY

Ctra. Palencia-Aranda, Km. 53
09311 Olmedillo de Roa (Burgos)
☎: +34 947 551 111
Fax: +34 947 551 311
pdr@pagosdelrey.com
www.felixsolisavantis.com

Altos de Tamarón 2014 T Roble
tempranillo

86

Altos de Tamarón 2007 TGR
tempranillo

86

Altos de Tamarón 2010 TR
tempranillo

88

Colour: cherry, garnet rim. Nose: smoky, spicy, ripe fruit. Palate: flavourful, smoky aftertaste, ripe fruit.

Altos de Tamarón 2012 TC
tempranillo

87

Colour: cherry, garnet rim. Nose: ripe fruit, wild herbs, spicy. Palate: balanced, flavourful, toasty.

Altos de Tamarón 2014 T
tempranillo

87

Colour: cherry, purple rim. Nose: red berry notes, floral, balsamic herbs. Palate: fruity, easy to drink, good finish.

Condado de Oriza 2010 TR
tempranillo

89

Colour: cherry, garnet rim. Nose: ripe fruit, wild herbs, spicy, balsamic herbs. Palate: balanced, flavourful, long, balsamic.

Condado de Oriza 2012 TC
tempranillo

87

Colour: cherry, garnet rim. Nose: roasted coffee, smoky, spicy, ripe fruit. Palate: flavourful, smoky aftertaste, ripe fruit.

Condado de Oriza 2014 T
tempranillo

87

Colour: cherry, purple rim. Nose: red berry notes, floral. Palate: flavourful, fruity, good acidity.

Condado de Oriza 2014 T Roble
tempranillo

85

Condado de Oriza 409 2010 T
tempranillo

90

Colour: cherry, garnet rim. Nose: ripe fruit, wild herbs, spicy, balsamic herbs. Palate: balanced, flavourful, long, balsamic.

Olmillos 2009 TR

88

Colour: cherry, garnet rim. Nose: ripe fruit, spicy, creamy oak, complex. Palate: flavourful, toasty.

Olmillos 2010 TR
tinta del país

86

PALACIO DE BORNOS

Ctra. Madrid - Coruña, km. 170,6
47490 Rueda (Valladolid)
☎: +34 983 868 116
Fax: +34 983 868 432
info@taninia.com
www.palaciodebornos.com

Dominio de Bornos 2011 TC
100% tinto fino

86

Dominio de Bornos 2013 T Roble
100% tinto fino

86

PICO CUADRO

Del Río, 22
47350 Quintanilla de Onésimo
(Valladolid)
☎: +34 620 547 057
www.picocuadro.com

Pico Cuadro 2012 T
tempranillo

89

Colour: cherry, garnet rim. Nose: spicy, balsamic herbs, varietal. Palate: balanced, flavourful, round tannins.

Pico Cuadro Original 2012 T
tempranillo

91

Colour: cherry, garnet rim. Nose: red berry notes, ripe fruit, spicy, creamy oak. Palate: flavourful, toasty.

Pico Cuadro Vendimia Seleccionada 2012 T
tempranillo

90

Colour: very deep cherry, garnet rim. Nose: spicy, ripe fruit, balanced, cocoa bean. Palate: spicy, long, fruity.

PINNA FIDELIS

Camino Llanillos, s/n
47300 Peñafiel (Valladolid)
☎: +34 983 878 034
Fax: +34 983 878 035
clientes@pinnafidelis.com
www.pinnafidelis.com

Pinna Fidelis 2011 TC
tinta del país

87

Colour: cherry, garnet rim. Nose: roasted coffee, smoky, spicy, ripe fruit. Palate: flavourful, smoky aftertaste, ripe fruit.

Pinna Fidelis 2005 TGR
tinta del país

87

Colour: black cherry, orangey edge. Nose: old leather, toasty. Palate: balanced, classic aged character, flavourful.

Pinna Fidelis 2009 TR
tinta del país

89

Colour: dark-red cherry, garnet rim. Nose: spicy, ripe fruit, balanced. Palate: correct, easy to drink.

PROTOS BODEGAS RIBERA DUERO DE PEÑAFIEL

Bodegas Protos, 24-28
47300 Peñafiel (Valladolid)
☎: +34 983 878 011
Fax: +34 983 878 012
bodega@bodegasprotos.com
www.bodegasprotos.com

Protos 2011 TR
100% tinto fino

93

Colour: cherry, garnet rim. Nose: red berry notes, ripe fruit, spicy, creamy oak, complex. Palate: flavourful, toasty, round tannins.

Protos 2012 TC
100% tinto fino

91

Colour: cherry, garnet rim. Nose: smoky, spicy, ripe fruit, mineral. Palate: flavourful, smoky aftertaste, ripe fruit.

Protos 2010 TGR
100% tinto fino

93

Colour: cherry, garnet rim. Nose: ripe fruit, spicy, complex, creamy oak, toasty. Palate: flavourful, toasty, round tannins.

Protos 2013 T Roble
100% tinto fino

88

Colour: cherry, purple rim. Nose: ripe fruit, woody, roasted coffee. Palate: flavourful, spicy, powerful.

Protos 2014 RD
tempranillo

88

Colour: rose, purple rim. Nose: red berry notes, floral, expressive. Palate: powerful, fruity, fresh, easy to drink.

Protos Selección Finca el Grajo Viejo 2012 T
100% tinto fino

93

Colour: cherry, garnet rim. Nose: cocoa bean, ripe fruit, creamy oak, characterful, powerfull. Palate: concentrated, flavourful, good structure, round tannins.

REAL SITIO DE VENTOSILLA

Ctra. CL-619 (Magaz - Aranda) Km. 66,1
09443 Gumiel del Mercado (Burgos)
☎: +34 947 546 900
Fax: +34 947 546 999
bodega@pradorey.com
www.pradorey.com

Adaro de PradoRey 2011 TC
100% tempranillo

93

Colour: cherry, garnet rim. Nose: smoky, spicy, ripe fruit. Palate: flavourful, ripe fruit, toasty, round tannins.

Adaro de PradoRey 2012 T
100% tempranillo

92

Colour: cherry, garnet rim. Nose: ripe fruit, wild herbs, earthy notes, spicy, balsamic herbs. Palate: balanced, flavourful, long, balsamic.

Élite de PradoRey 2010 T
100% tempranillo

94

Colour: cherry, garnet rim. Nose: ripe fruit, wild herbs, earthy notes, spicy, balsamic herbs. Palate: balanced, flavourful, long, balsamic, elegant.

Élite de PradoRey 2011 T
100% tempranillo

93

Colour: cherry, garnet rim. Nose: red berry notes, ripe fruit, spicy, creamy oak, complex. Palate: flavourful, toasty.

Lía de PradoRey 2014 RD
100% tempranillo

87

Colour: brilliant rose. Nose: red berry notes, floral, expressive, medium intensity. Palate: fruity, fresh, light-bodied, easy to drink.

PradoRey 2004 TGR
95% tempranillo, 3% cabernet sauvignon, 2% merlot

90

Colour: dark-red cherry, orangey edge. Nose: tobacco, spicy, wild herbs. Palate: balanced, long, spicy.

PradoRey 2009 TGR
95% tempranillo, 3% cabernet sauvignon, 2% merlot

90

Colour: pale ruby, brick rim edge. Nose: spicy, fine reductive notes, wet leather, aged wood nuances. Palate: spicy, fine tannins, balanced.

PradoRey 2014 RD
50% merlot, 50% tempranillo

89

Colour: rose, purple rim. Nose: powerfull, fruit preserve, warm, creamy oak. Palate: powerful, flavourful, round.

PradoRey 2014 T Roble
95% tempranillo, 3% cabernet sauvignon, 2% merlot

90

Colour: deep cherry, purple rim. Nose: creamy oak, ripe fruit, balsamic herbs. Palate: balanced, spicy, long.

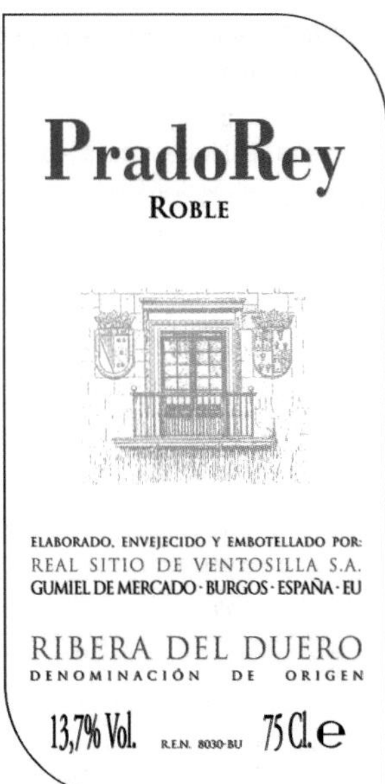

PradoRey Finca La Mina 2009 TR
95% tempranillo, 3% cabernet sauvignon, 2% merlot

92

Colour: cherry, garnet rim. Nose: expressive, spicy, scrubland. Palate: flavourful, ripe fruit, long, good acidity, balanced.

PradoRey Finca Valdelayegua 2011 TC
95% tempranillo, 3% cabernet sauvignon, 2% merlot

92

Colour: cherry, garnet rim. Nose: spicy, mineral. Palate: flavourful, ripe fruit, long, good acidity, balanced.

PradoRey Finca Valdelayegua 2013 TC
95% tempranillo, 3% cabernet sauvignon, 2% merlot

90

Colour: cherry, garnet rim. Nose: roasted coffee, smoky, spicy, ripe fruit. Palate: flavourful, smoky aftertaste, ripe fruit.

RODRÍGUEZ SANZO

Manuel Azaña, 11
47014 (Valladolid)
☎: +34 983 150 150
Fax: +34 983 150 151
comunicacion@valsanzo.com
www.rodriguezsanzo.com

Vall Sanzo 2011 TC
100% tinto fino

90

Colour: bright cherry. Nose: ripe fruit, sweet spices, creamy oak, expressive. Palate: flavourful, fruity, toasty, round tannins.

Vall Sanzo RS Selección de Familia 2011 T
95% tempranillo, 5% cabernet sauvignon

93

Colour: cherry, garnet rim. Nose: mineral, expressive, spicy. Palate: flavourful, ripe fruit, long, good acidity, balanced.

RUDELES

Rudeles
42345 Peñalba de San Esteban (Soria)
☎: +34 618 644 633
tguijarral@rudeles.com
www.rudeles.com

Rudeles "23" 2013 T
95% tempranillo, 5% garnacha

89

Colour: cherry, garnet rim. Nose: red berry notes, ripe fruit, spicy, toasty, creamy oak. Palate: powerful, flavourful, balsamic, balanced.

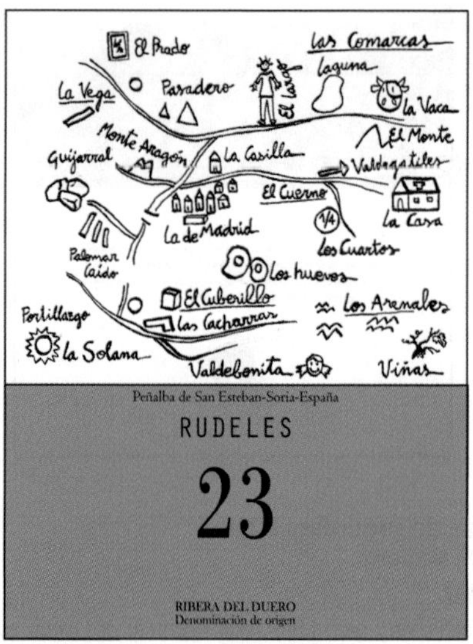

Rudeles Cerro El Cuberillo 2009 T
100% tempranillo

93

Colour: cherry, garnet rim. Nose: balanced, complex, ripe fruit, spicy, fine reductive notes, mineral. Palate: good structure, flavourful, round tannins, balanced.

Rudeles Finca La Nación 2009 T
95% tempranillo, 5% garnacha

92

Colour: ruby red. Nose: mineral, expressive, spicy, ripe fruit. Palate: flavourful, ripe fruit, long, good acidity, balanced.

SAN ROQUE DE LA ENCINA, SDAD. COOP.

San Roque, 73
09391 Castrillo de la Vega (Burgos)
☎: +34 947 536 001
Fax: +34 947 536 183
info@bodegasanroquedelaencina.com
www.bodegasanroquedelaencina.com

Monte del Conde 2011 TC
100% tinto fino

89

Colour: cherry, garnet rim. Nose: ripe fruit, wild herbs, earthy notes, spicy. Palate: balanced, flavourful, long.

Monte del Conde 2013 T Roble
100% tinto fino

86

Monte del Conde 2014 T
100% tinto fino

86

Monte Pinadillo 2012 TC
100% tinto fino

89

Colour: bright cherry. Nose: ripe fruit, sweet spices, creamy oak. Palate: flavourful, fruity, toasty, round tannins.

Monte Pinadillo 2013 T Roble
100% tinto fino

87

Colour: bright cherry. Nose: ripe fruit, sweet spices, creamy oak. Palate: flavourful, fruity, toasty, round tannins.

Monte Pinadillo 2014 T
100% tinto fino

85

SELECCIÓN DE TORRES

Del Rosario, 56
47311 Fompedraza (Valladolid)
☎: +34 938 177 400
Fax: +34 938 177 444
mailadmin@torres.es
www.torres.es

Celeste 2012 TC
tinto fino

90

Colour: cherry, garnet rim. Nose: red berry notes, ripe fruit, spicy, creamy oak, complex. Palate: flavourful, toasty, round tannins.

Celeste 2014 T Roble
tinto fino

86

SOLTERRA

Ctra. de Pedrosa, km. 1,5
09300 Roa (Burgos)
☎: +34 915 196 651
Fax: +34 914 135 907
m.antonia@cvsolterra.com
www.cvsolterra.com

Alto de los Zorros 10 meses 2012 T

100% tempranillo

87

Colour: cherry, garnet rim. Nose: ripe fruit, spicy, creamy oak. Palate: flavourful, toasty.

Alto de los Zorros 2010 TC

100% tempranillo

89

Colour: cherry, garnet rim. Nose: ripe fruit, wild herbs, earthy notes, spicy, balsamic herbs. Palate: balanced, flavourful, long.

Alto de los Zorros Autor 2010 TR

100% tempranillo

91

Colour: cherry, garnet rim. Nose: red berry notes, ripe fruit, spicy, creamy oak, complex. Palate: flavourful, toasty, round tannins.

THE GRAND WINES

Ramón y Cajal 7, 1ºA
01007 Vitoria-Gasteiz (Alava)
☎: +34 945 150 589
araex@araex.com
www.araex.com

Rolland Galarreta 2011 T

92

Colour: cherry, garnet rim. Nose: balanced, complex, ripe fruit, spicy. Palate: good structure, flavourful, round tannins, concentrated, balanced.

UNESDI DISTRIBUCIONES S.A

Aurora, 11
11500 El Puerto de Santa María (Cádiz)
☎: +34 956 541 329
marketing@unesdi.com
www.unesdi.com

Mataveras 2012 T

88% tinto fino, 8% cabernet sauvignon, 4% merlot

88

Colour: dark-red cherry, garnet rim. Nose: closed, spicy, ripe fruit. Palate: ripe fruit, round tannins.

Palomo Cazador 2013 T

100% tinto fino

87

Colour: bright cherry. Nose: ripe fruit, sweet spices, creamy oak, expressive. Palate: flavourful, fruity, round tannins.

UVAS FELICES

Agullers, 7
08003 Barcelona (Barcelona)
☎: +34 902 327 777
www.vilaviniteca.es

Venta Las Vacas 2013 T

92

Colour: deep cherry, purple rim. Nose: creamy oak, toasty, ripe fruit, balsamic herbs, red berry notes. Palate: balanced, spicy, long.

VALDEMONJAS

Antonio Machado, 14 1ºD
47008 Valladolid (Valladolid)
☎: +34 983 248 294
alejandro.moyano@valdemonjas.es
www.valdemonjas.es

El Primer Beso 2013 T

tempranillo

87

Colour: bright cherry. Nose: ripe fruit, sweet spices, creamy oak. Palate: flavourful, fruity.

Entre Palabras 2012 T

tempranillo

88

Colour: cherry, garnet rim. Nose: smoky, spicy, ripe fruit. Palate: flavourful, smoky aftertaste, ripe fruit.

Los Tres Dones 2012 T

tempranillo

93

Colour: cherry, garnet rim. Nose: expressive, spicy, mineral, ripe fruit. Palate: flavourful, ripe fruit, long, good acidity, balanced.

VALTOÑAR

Ctra. de Roa, Km. 5
09313 Anguix (Burgos)
☎: +34 617 196 323
riojalopez@valtonar.com
www.valtonar.com

Alvar Núñez 2010 TR
97% tempranillo, 3% cabernet sauvignon

88

Colour: cherry, garnet rim. Nose: smoky, spicy, ripe fruit. Palate: flavourful, smoky aftertaste, ripe fruit.

Dominio de Castellares 2010 T Barrica
100% tempranillo

87

Colour: cherry, garnet rim. Nose: fine reductive notes, wet leather, aged wood nuances. Palate: spicy, long, toasty.

Valtoñar 2010 TC
97% tempranillo, 3% cabernet sauvignon

85

Valtoñar 2014 T
90% tempranillo, 10% merlot

82

VALTRAVIESO

Finca La Revilla, s/n
47316 Piñel de Arriba (Valladolid)
☎: +34 983 484 030
valtravieso@valtravieso.com
www.valtravieso.com

Gran Valtravieso 2011 TR
100% tinto fino

90

Colour: cherry, garnet rim. Nose: balanced, complex, ripe fruit, spicy, dried herbs. Palate: good structure, flavourful, round tannins, balanced.

Valtravieso 2010 TR
90% tinto fino, 5% merlot, 5% cabernet sauvignon

90

Colour: cherry, garnet rim. Nose: scrubland, ripe fruit, spicy. Palate: balanced, round tannins, spicy.

Valtravieso 2012 TC
90% tinto fino, 5% merlot, 5% cabernet sauvignon

90

Colour: cherry, garnet rim. Nose: ripe fruit, wild herbs, earthy notes, spicy, balsamic herbs. Palate: balanced, flavourful, long, balsamic.

Valtravieso 2014 T Roble
90% tinto fino, 5% merlot, 5% cabernet sauvignon

88

Colour: bright cherry. Nose: ripe fruit, sweet spices, creamy oak. Palate: flavourful, fruity, toasty.

Valtravieso VT Tinta Fina 2010 T
100% tinto fino

91

Colour: cherry, garnet rim. Nose: red berry notes, ripe fruit, spicy, creamy oak, complex. Palate: flavourful, toasty.

Valtravieso VT Vendimia Seleccionada 2010 T
75% tinto fino, 15% cabernet sauvignon, 10% merlot

89

Colour: cherry, garnet rim. Nose: ripe fruit, wild herbs, earthy notes, spicy, balsamic herbs. Palate: balanced, flavourful, long, balsamic.

VEGA CLARA

Ctra. N-122, Km 328
47350 Quintanilla De Onesimo (Valladolid)
☎: +34 677 570 779
Fax: +34 983 361 005
vegaclara@vegaclara.com
www.vegaclara.com

10 Almendros 2013 T
tempranillo, otras

89

Colour: bright cherry. Nose: toasty, ripe fruit, balsamic herbs, varietal. Palate: balanced, spicy, long, good structure.

Mario VC 2012 T
75% tempranillo, 25% cabernet sauvignon

90

Colour: deep cherry, garnet rim. Nose: balanced, expressive, ripe fruit, scrubland, spicy. Palate: good structure, flavourful.

VEGA REAL

Ctra. N-122, Km. 298,6
47318 Castrillo de Duero (Valladolid)
☎: +34 983 881 580
Fax: +34 983 873 188
visitas@vegareal.net
www.vegareal.com

Vega Real 2014 T Roble

88

Colour: bright cherry. Nose: ripe fruit, sweet spices, creamy oak, expressive. Palate: flavourful, fruity, toasty, round tannins.

VELVETY WINES

Ctra. Peñafiel - Valoria, s/n
47315 Pesquera de Duero (Valladolid)
☎: +34 983 870 199
info@velvetywines.com
www.velvetywines.com

Velvet 2012 T
100% tempranillo

90

Colour: cherry, garnet rim. Nose: red berry notes, ripe fruit, spicy, creamy oak. Palate: flavourful, toasty.

Velvety 2014 T
100% tempranillo

85

VINOS HERCAL

Santo Domingo, 2
09300 Roa (Burgos)
☎: +34 947 541 281
ventas@somanilla.es
www.somanilla.es

Bocca 2013 T Roble

88

Colour: deep cherry, garnet rim. Nose: medium intensity, red berry notes, ripe fruit, spicy. Palate: light-bodied, easy to drink.

Bocca 2014 RD

84

Somanilla 2012 TC

90

Colour: cherry, garnet rim. Nose: ripe fruit, spicy, creamy oak, complex. Palate: flavourful, toasty.

VINOS JOC - JORDI OLIVER CONTI

Mas Marti
17467 Sant Mori (Girona)
☎: +34 607 222 002
info@vinojoc.com
www.vinojoc.com

JOC Tinto Fino 2011 T
tinto fino

89

Colour: cherry, garnet rim. Nose: ripe fruit, spicy, creamy oak. Palate: flavourful, toasty.

VINOS SANTOS ARRANZ (LÁGRIMA NEGRA)

Ctra. de Valbuena, s/n
47315 Pesquera de Duero (Valladolid)
☎: +34 983 870 008
Fax: +34 983 870 008
lagrimanegra82@hotmail.com
www.lagrima-negra.com

Lágrima Negra "La Pintada" 2012 TC
90% tempranillo, 10% cabernet sauvignon

84

Lágrima Negra 2013 T Roble
tempranillo, cabernet sauvignon

86

VINOS TERRIBLES

Avda. Menendez Pelayo 13 B
28009 Madrid (Madrid)
☎: +34 914 092 131
esther@vinosterribles.com
www.latintoreriavinoteca.com

+Terrible 2012 T

89

Colour: cherry, garnet rim. Nose: fruit preserve, spicy, creamy oak, balsamic herbs. Palate: powerful, flavourful, spicy.

Terrible 2014 T Roble
100% tempranillo

88

Colour: bright cherry. Nose: ripe fruit, sweet spices, creamy oak. Palate: flavourful, fruity, toasty.

VINOS Y VIÑEDOS TUDANCA

Ctra. Madrid Irún, km. 153
09400 Fuentespina - Aranda de Duero (Burgos)
☎: +34 947 506 011
vinos@tudanca-aranda.com
www.vinostudanca.es

Tudanca 2011 TC

90

Colour: bright cherry. Nose: ripe fruit, sweet spices, creamy oak. Palate: flavourful, fruity, toasty.

Tudanca 2012 T Roble
tempranillo

87

Colour: cherry, garnet rim. Nose: creamy oak, red berry notes, ripe fruit, balanced. Palate: flavourful, spicy, easy to drink.

Tudanca Vendimia Seleccionada 2009 T
tempranillo

89

Colour: cherry, garnet rim. Nose: ripe fruit, wild herbs, spicy, balsamic herbs. Palate: balanced, flavourful, long, balsamic.

Vicenta Mater 2010 TC
tempranillo

89

Colour: cherry, garnet rim. Nose: creamy oak, red berry notes, balanced, ripe fruit. Palate: flavourful, spicy.

VINUM VITAE

Puerta Nueva, 19
09370 Gumiel de Izán (Burgos)
☎: +34 916 703 078
www.avañate.es

Avañate 2012 T
100% tempranillo

87

Colour: bright cherry, garnet rim. Nose: ripe fruit, red berry notes, sweet spices, varietal. Palate: correct, easy to drink, good finish.

VIÑA ARNAIZ

Ctra. N-122, km. 281
09463 Haza (Burgos)
☎: +34 947 536 227
Fax: +34 947 536 216
atcliente@jgc.es
www.garciacarrion.es

Mayor de Castilla 2013 T Roble
tinta del país

83

Pata Negra 2009 TR
100% tempranillo

87

Colour: ruby red. Nose: ripe fruit, spicy, creamy oak. Palate: flavourful, toasty, round tannins.

Pata Negra 2011 TC
100% tempranillo

86

Pata Negra 2012 TC
100% tinta del tinta del país

86

Colour: bright cherry. Nose: ripe fruit, sweet spices, creamy oak. Palate: flavourful, fruity, round tannins.

Pata Negra 2013 T Roble
100% tempranillo

85

Pata Negra 2014 RD
100% tempranillo

85

Viña Arnáiz 2010 TR
85% tempranillo, 10% cabernet sauvignon, 5% merlot

88

Colour: ruby red. Nose: spicy, fine reductive notes, wet leather, aged wood nuances. Palate: spicy, balanced.

Viña Arnáiz 2011 TC
100% tempranillo

86

Viña Arnáiz 2013 T Roble
95% tempranillo, 3% cabernet sauvignon, 2% merlot

85

VIÑA MAMBRILLA
Ctra. Pedrosa s/n
09317 Mambrilla de Castrejón (Burgos)
☎: +34 947 540 234
Fax: +34 947 540 234
bodega@mambrilla.com
www.mambrilla.com

Alidis 2014 T
100% tempranillo

85

Alidis 6 meses Barrica 2013 T
100% tempranillo

86

Alidis Crianza 2011 TC
100% tempranillo

89

Colour: very deep cherry, garnet rim. Nose: powerfull, spicy, ripe fruit. Palate: good structure, fruity, round tannins.

Alidis Expresión 2011 T
100% tempranillo

88

Colour: cherry, garnet rim. Nose: ripe fruit, wild herbs, earthy notes, spicy, balsamic herbs. Palate: balanced, flavourful, long, balsamic.

VIÑA SOLORCA
Ctra. Circunvalación, s/n
09300 Roa (Burgos)
☎: +34 947 541 823
Fax: +34 947 540 035
info@bodegassolorca.com
www.bodegassolorca.com

Barón del Valle 2009 TR
100% tempranillo

89

Colour: cherry, garnet rim. Nose: red berry notes, ripe fruit, spicy, creamy oak, complex. Palate: flavourful, toasty, round tannins.

Barón del Valle 2011 TC
100% tempranillo

87

Colour: cherry, garnet rim. Nose: fine reductive notes, wet leather, aged wood nuances, fruit preserve. Palate: spicy, long, toasty.

Viña Solorca 2011 TC
100% tempranillo

89

Colour: bright cherry. Nose: ripe fruit, sweet spices, creamy oak. Palate: flavourful, fruity, toasty.

VIÑA TUELDA
Camino de las Bodegas, 23
09310 Villatuelda (Burgos)
☎: +34 947 551 145
Fax: +34 947 551 145
info@vintuelda.com
www.vintuelda.com

Viña Tvelda 2012 TC
tinto fino

88

Colour: cherry, garnet rim. Nose: red berry notes, creamy oak, sweet spices, balsamic herbs. Palate: flavourful, spicy, harsh oak tannins.

VIÑEDOS ALONSO DEL YERRO

Finca Santa Marta. Ctra.
Roa-Anguix, km. 1,8
09300 Roa (Burgos)
☎: +34 913 160 121
Fax: +34 913 160 121
mariadelyerro@vay.es
www.alonsodelyerro.es

"María" Alonso del Yerro 2010 T
tempranillo

92

Colour: cherry, garnet rim. Nose: smoky, spicy, overripe fruit. Palate: flavourful, smoky aftertaste, ripe fruit.

Alonso del Yerro 2011 T
100% tempranillo

92

Colour: cherry, garnet rim. Nose: creamy oak, balanced, overripe fruit. Palate: flavourful, spicy.

VIÑEDOS SINGULARES

Cuzco, 26 - 28, Nave 8 - 9
08030 Barcelona (Barcelona)
☎: +34 934 807 041
Fax: +34 934 807 076
info@vinedossingulares.com
www.vinedossingulares.com

Entrelobos 2014 T
tinto fino

86

VIÑEDOS Y BODEGAS ÁSTER

Finca El Caño. Ctra.
Palencia-Aranda Km. 54,9
09313 Anguix (Burgos)
☎: +34 947 522 700
Fax: +34 947 522 701
aster@riojalta.com
www.riojalta.com

Áster 2010 TC
tinta del país

91

Colour: cherry, garnet rim. Nose: creamy oak, ripe fruit, sweet spices, toasty. Palate: flavourful, spicy.

Áster Finca el Otero 2010 T
tinta del país

93

Colour: cherry, garnet rim. Nose: mineral, expressive, spicy. Palate: flavourful, ripe fruit, long, good acidity, balanced.

VIÑEDOS Y BODEGAS GARCÍA FIGUERO

Ctra. La Horra - Roa, Km. 2,2
09311 La Horra (Burgos)
☎: +34 947 542 127
Fax: +34 947 542 033
comercial@tintofiguero.com
www.tintofiguero.com

Figuero Noble 2010 T
100% tempranillo

92

Colour: light cherry. Nose: fine reductive notes, aged wood nuances, toasty, ripe fruit. Palate: spicy, toasty, flavourful.

Figuero Tinus 2011 T
100% tinta del país

94

Colour: cherry, garnet rim. Nose: roasted coffee, smoky, spicy, ripe fruit. Palate: flavourful, smoky aftertaste, ripe fruit.

PODIUM

Milagros de Figuero 2010 T
100% tempranillo

95

Colour: cherry, garnet rim. Nose: aged wood nuances, dark chocolate, earthy notes, mineral, ripe fruit. Palate: spicy, long, toasty.

Tinto Figuero 12 Meses Barrica 2012 TC
100% tempranillo

91

Colour: cherry, garnet rim. Nose: ripe fruit, spicy, creamy oak, complex. Palate: flavourful, toasty, balanced.

Tinto Figuero 15 Meses Barrica 2010 TR
100% tempranillo

93

Colour: cherry, garnet rim. Nose: smoky, spicy, ripe fruit, aromatic coffee. Palate: flavourful, smoky aftertaste, ripe fruit.

Tinto Figuero 4 2014 T
100% tempranillo

88

Colour: very deep cherry, purple rim. Nose: toasty, ripe fruit. Palate: flavourful, long, balanced, spicy, balsamic.

Tinto Figuero Viñas Viejas 2012 T
100% tempranillo

92

Colour: cherry, garnet rim. Nose: ripe fruit, wild herbs, earthy notes, spicy, balsamic herbs. Palate: balanced, flavourful, long, balsamic.

VIÑEDOS Y BODEGAS GORMAZ

Ctra. de Soria, s/n
42330 San Esteban de Gormaz (Soria)
☎: +34 975 350 404
Fax: +34 975 351 313
carlos.garcia@hispanobodegas.com
www.hispanobodegas.com

12 Linajes 2010 TR
100% tempranillo

93

Colour: light cherry. Nose: fine reductive notes, aged wood nuances, toasty, ripe fruit, fruit expression. Palate: spicy, toasty, flavourful.

12 Linajes 2012 TC
100% tempranillo

91

Colour: cherry, garnet rim. Nose: creamy oak, red berry notes, fresh fruit, balanced. Palate: flavourful, spicy, elegant.

12 Linajes 2013 T Roble
100% tempranillo

90

Colour: deep cherry. Nose: creamy oak, toasty, ripe fruit, balsamic herbs. Palate: balanced, spicy, long.

Catania 2012 TC
100% tempranillo

90

Colour: bright cherry. Nose: ripe fruit, sweet spices, creamy oak, expressive. Palate: flavourful, fruity, toasty, round tannins.

Catania 2014 T
100% tempranillo

88

Colour: cherry, purple rim. Nose: violets, ripe fruit, red berry notes, balanced. Palate: fruity, easy to drink, good acidity.

Viña Gormaz 2012 TC
100% tempranillo

91

Colour: deep cherry, garnet rim. Nose: ripe fruit, balsamic herbs, cocoa bean, balanced, varietal. Palate: flavourful, round tannins.

Viña Gormaz 2014 T
100% tempranillo

88

Colour: cherry, purple rim. Nose: powerfull, ripe fruit, spicy. Palate: powerful, fruity.

VIÑEDOS Y BODEGAS RIBÓN

Basilón, 15
47350 Quintanilla de Onésimo
(Valladolid)
☎: +34 983 680 015
Fax: +34 983 680 015
info@bodegasribon.com
www.bodegasribon.com

Tinto Ribón 2012 TC
100% tempranillo

91

Colour: cherry, garnet rim. Nose: creamy oak, red berry notes, fresh fruit, balanced. Palate: flavourful, spicy.

Tinto Ribón 2013 T Roble
100% tempranillo

87

Colour: deep cherry, purple rim. Nose: creamy oak, toasty, ripe fruit, balsamic herbs. Palate: balanced, spicy, long.

DO. RIBERA DEL GUADIANA

CONSEJO REGULADOR

Avda. Pte, Juan Carlos Rodríguez Ibarra, s/n. Apdo. 299

06200 Almendralejo (Badajoz)

☎: +34 924 671 302

Fax: +34 924 664 703

@: info@riberadelguadiana.eu

www.riberadelguadiana.eu

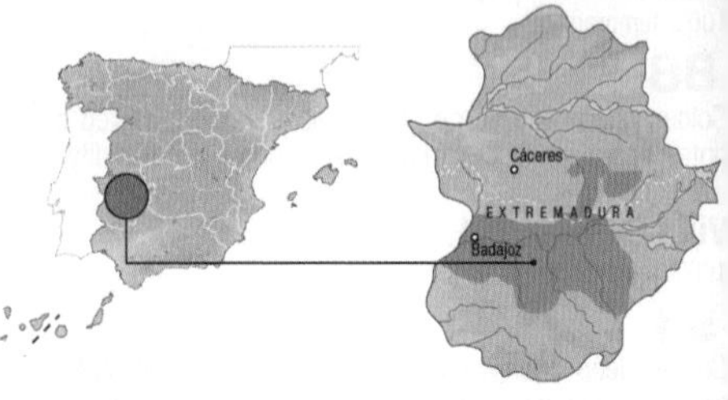

LOCATION:

Covering the 6 wine-growing regions of Extremadura, with a total surface of more than 87,000 Ha as described below.

SUB-REGIONS AND CLIMATE:

Cañamero. To the south east of the province of Cáceres, in the heart of the Sierra de Guadalupe. It comprises the municipal districts of Alia, Berzocana, Cañamero, Guadalupe and Valdecaballeros. The vineyards are located on the mountainside, at altitudes of between 600 m to 800 m. The terrain is rugged and the soil is slaty and loose. The climate is mild without great temperature contrasts, and the average annual rainfall is 750 mm to 800 mm. The main grape variety is the white Alarije. **Montánchez.** Comprising 27 municipal districts. It is characterised by its complex terrain, with numerous hills and small valleys. The vineyards are located on brown acidic soil. The climate is Continental in nature and the average annual rainfall is between 500 mm and 600 mm. The white grape variety Borba occupies two thirds of the vineyards in the region. **Ribera Alta.** This covers the Vegas del Guadiana and the plains of La Serena and Campo de Castuera and comprises 38 municipal districts. The soil is very sandy. The most common varieties are Alarije, Borba (white), Tempranillo and Garnacha (red)**. Ribera Baja.** Comprising 11 municipal districts. The vineyards are located on clayey-limy soil. The climate is Continental, with a moderate Atlantic influence and slight contrasts in temperature. The most common varieties are: Cayetana Blanca and Pardina among the whites, and Tempranillo among the reds. **Matanegra.** Rather similar to Tierra de Barros, but with a milder climate. It comprises 8 municipal districts, and the most common grape varieties are Beba, Montua (whites), Tempranillo, Garnacha and Cabernet Sauvignon (reds). **Tierra de Barros.** Situated in the centre of the province of Badajoz and the largest (4475 Ha and 37 municipal districts). It has flat plains with fertile soils which are rich in nutrients and have great water retention capacity (Rainfall is low: 350 mm to 450 mm per year). The most common varieties are the white Cayetana Blanca and Pardina, and the red Tempranillo, Garnacha and Cabernet Sauvignon.

GRAPE VARIETIES:

WHITE: Alarije, Borba, Cayetana Blanca, Pardina, Macabeo, Chardonnay, Chelva or Montua, Malvar, Parellada, Pedro Ximénez, Verdejo, Eva, Cigüente, Perruno, Moscatel de Alejandría, Moscatel de Grano Menudo, Sauvignon Blanc and Bobal Blanca.

RED: Garnacha Tinta, Tempranillo, Bobal, Cabernet Sauvignon, Garnacha Tintorera, Graciano, Mazuela, Merlot, Monastrell, Syrah, Pinot Noir and Jaén Tinto.

FIGURES:

Vineyard surface: 34,051 – **Wine-Growers:** 3,193 – **Wineries:** 16 – **2014 Harvest rating:** N/A – **Production 14:** 18,075,243 Kg. – **Market percentages:** 86% National - 14% International.

VINTAGE RATING

PEÑÍNGUIDE

2010	2011	2012	2013	2014
VERY GOOD	GOOD	GOOD	AVERAGE	GOOD

BODEGA CARABAL

Ctra. Alía - Castilblanco, Km. 10
10137 Alía (Cáceres)
☎: +34 917 346 152
Fax: +34 913 720 440
info@carabal.es
www.carabal.es

Carabal Cávea 2009 TC
syrah, tempranillo, cabernet sauvignon, graciano

90

Colour: cherry, garnet rim. Nose: ripe fruit, spicy, creamy oak, fine reductive notes. Palate: flavourful, toasty, round tannins.

Carabal Gulae 2010 TC

91

Colour: very deep cherry, garnet rim. Nose: complex, mineral, balsamic herbs, ripe fruit, expressive. Palate: full, flavourful, round tannins, balanced.

Carabal Rasgo 2010 T
syrah, tempranillo

89

Colour: deep cherry, garnet rim. Nose: ripe fruit, wild herbs, spicy, creamy oak. Palate: powerful, flavourful, spicy, long.

BODEGA SAN MARCOS

Ctra. Aceuchal, s/n
06200 Almendralejo (Badajoz)
☎: +34 924 670 410
Fax: +34 924 665 505
ventas@bodegasanmarcos.com
www.bodegasanmarcos.com

Campobarro 2005 TR

84

Campobarro 2011 TC
100% tempranillo

86

Campobarro 2014 RD
100% tempranillo

83

Campobarro Macabeo 2014 B
100% macabeo

83

Campobarro Pardina 2014 B
100% pardina

86

Campobarro Selección 2012 T
mazuelo, tempranillo

84

Heredad de Barros 2005 TR
100% tempranillo

84

Heredad de Barros 2011 TC
100% tempranillo

83

BODEGAS LUIS GURPEGUI MUGA

Avda. Celso Muerza, 8
31560 San Adrián (Navarra)
☎: +34 948 670 050
Fax: +34 948 670 259
bodegas@gurpegui.es
www.gurpegui.es

Cinco Viñas 2014 T
tempranillo, garnacha

84

Gurpegui 2014 T
tempranillo, cabernet sauvignon

85

BODEGAS MARTÍNEZ PAIVA SAT

Ctra. Gijón - Sevilla N-630,
Km. 646, Apdo. Correos 87
06200 Almendralejo (Badajoz)
☎: +34 924 671 130
Fax: +34 924 663 056
info@payva.es
www.payva.es

56 Barricas 2011 TC
tempranillo

88

Colour: cherry, garnet rim. Nose: ripe fruit, spicy, creamy oak, complex. Palate: flavourful, toasty.

Doña Francisquita 2014 T
tempranillo

84

Payva 2010 TR
tempranillo, graciano, garnacha, mazuelo

88

Colour: deep cherry, garnet rim. Nose: scrubland, dried herbs, spicy. Palate: balanced, round tannins.

Payva 2011 TC
tempranillo, cabernet sauvignon, graciano

85

Payva 2014 T
tempranillo

85

Payva Cayetana Blanca 2014 B
cayetana blanca

86

Payva Graciano 2014 T
graciano

87

Colour: cherry, purple rim. Nose: powerfull, ripe fruit, spicy. Palate: powerful, fruity, unctuous.

BODEGAS ORAN

Granados, 1
06200 Almendralejo (Badajoz)
☎: +34 662 952 801
info@bodegasoran.com
www.bodegasoran.com

Castillo de Feria 2012 T
tempranillo

84

Flor de Señorío de Orán 2013 T Roble
tempranillo

86

Señorío de Orán 2012 TC
tempranillo

86

Señorío de Orán 2014 B
pardina

84

Viña Roja Tempranillo 2014 T
tempranillo

83

BODEGAS ROMALE

Pol. Ind. Parc. 6, Manz. D
06200 Almendralejo (Badajoz)
☎: +34 924 667 255
Fax: +34 924 665 877
romale@romale.com
www.romale.com

Privilegio de Romale 2011 TC
100% tempranillo

86

Privilegio de Romale 2013 T Roble
60% tempranillo, 20% merlot, 20% cabernet sauvignon

86

Viña Romale Macabeo 2014 B
macabeo

82

BODEGAS RUIZ TORRES

Ctra. EX 116, km.33,8
10136 Cañamero (Cáceres)
☎: +34 927 369 027
Fax: +34 927 369 302
info@ruiztorres.com
www.ruiztorres.com

Attelea 2010 TC
tempranillo, cabernet sauvignon

84

Attelea 2013 T Roble
100% tempranillo

84

BODEGAS TORIBIO

Luis Chamizo, 12 y 21
06310 Puebla de Sancho Pérez
(Badajoz)
☎: +34 924 551 449
Fax: +34 924 551 449
info@bodegastoribio.com
www.bodegastoribio.com

Madre del Agua 2013 TC
garnacha tintorera, syrah, graciano, cabernet sauvignon

89

Colour: deep cherry, purple rim. Nose: balanced, expressive, sweet spices, ripe fruit, floral. Palate: fruity, flavourful, toasty.

Viña Puebla Esenzia 2012 TC
tempranillo, garnacha, syrah

88

Colour: deep cherry, garnet rim. Nose: ripe fruit, smoky, cocoa bean. Palate: balanced, long, round tannins.

Viña Puebla Macabeo 2014 BFB
100% macabeo

86

Viña Puebla Selección 2013 T Roble
cabernet sauvignon, tempranillo, garnacha, syrah

88

Colour: bright cherry, purple rim. Nose: ripe fruit, violets, sweet spices, grassy. Palate: balanced, balsamic, correct.

Viña Puebla Verdejo 2014 B
100% verdejo

84

COSECHA EXTREMEÑA

Ctra. Villafranca, 23
06360 Fuente del Maestre (Badajoz)
☎: +34 924 530 705
Fax: +34 924 530 705
admon@cosechaextremadura.com
www.cosechaextremadura.com

Señorío de Badajoz Merlot 2014 T
100% merlot

85

Señorío de Badajoz Semidulce 2014 B
100% macabeo

84

PAGO LOS BALANCINES

Paraje la Agraria, s/n
06475 Oliva de Mérida (Badajoz)
☎: +34 924 367 399
info@pagolosbalancines.com
www.pagolosbalancines.com

Alunado 2014 BFB
chardonnay

92

Colour: bright yellow. Nose: expressive, dried herbs, ripe fruit, spicy. Palate: flavourful, fruity, good acidity.

Balancines 2014 T Roble
tempranillo, syrah

89

Colour: cherry, purple rim. Nose: ripe fruit, floral, wild herbs. Palate: good acidity, easy to drink, spicy.

Balancines Blanco Sobre Lías 2014 B
100% sauvignon blanc

87

Colour: bright yellow. Nose: expressive, dried herbs, ripe fruit, spicy. Palate: flavourful, fruity, sweetness.

Haragán Magnum 2012 TR
100% tempranillo

93

Colour: very deep cherry, garnet rim. Nose: expressive, complex, mineral, balsamic herbs, ripe fruit. Palate: full, flavourful.

Los Balancines Huno 2013 T
garnacha tintorera, tempranillo, cabernet sauvignon, syrah

91

Colour: cherry, garnet rim. Nose: creamy oak, red berry notes, fresh fruit. Palate: flavourful, spicy, fine bitter notes, grainy tannins.

Los Balancines Matanegra 2012 TC
cabernet sauvignon, tempranillo, garnacha tintorera

92

Colour: cherry, garnet rim. Nose: smoky, spicy, ripe fruit. Palate: flavourful, ripe fruit, round tannins.

Vaso de Luz 2009 TR
100% cabernet sauvignon

93

Colour: light cherry. Nose: aged wood nuances, toasty, ripe fruit, varietal. Palate: spicy, toasty, flavourful.

PALACIO QUEMADO

Ctra. Almendralejo - Palomas, km 13,9
06840 Alange (Badajoz)
☎: +34 924 120 082
Fax: +34 924 120 028
palacioquemado@alvear.es
www.palacioquemado.com

Palacio Quemado 2011 TR
tempranillo, cabernet sauvignon

88

Colour: cherry, garnet rim. Nose: red berry notes, ripe fruit, spicy, creamy oak, complex. Palate: flavourful, toasty, round tannins.

Palacio Quemado 2012 TC
tempranillo

88

Colour: bright cherry. Nose: sweet spices, creamy oak, expressive, aromatic coffee, dark chocolate, overripe fruit. Palate: flavourful, toasty, round tannins.

Palacio Quemado La Zarcita 2014 T
40% tempranillo, 40% syrah, 20% cabernet sauvignon

89

Colour: bright cherry. Nose: ripe fruit, sweet spices, creamy oak. Palate: flavourful, fruity, round tannins.

Palacio Quemado Los Acilates 2011 T
tempranillo, syrah

90

Colour: bright cherry. Nose: ripe fruit, sweet spices, creamy oak, expressive. Palate: flavourful, fruity, round tannins.

Palacio Quemado Primicia 2014 T
100% tempranillo

90

Colour: bright cherry. Nose: ripe fruit, sweet spices, creamy oak, expressive. Palate: flavourful, fruity, round tannins.

SOCIEDAD COOPERATIVA SANTA Mª EGIPCIACA

Ctra. Entrín Bajo, s/n
06196 Corte de Peleas (Badajoz)
☎: +34 924 693 014
Fax: +34 924 693 270
administracion@bodegaslacorte.com
www.bodegaslacorte.com

Conde de la Corte 2012 T
tempranillo

84

ZALEO-VIÑAOLIVA

Pol. Ind., Las Plcadas II, Parcela 4-17
06200 Almendralejo (Badajoz)
☎: +34 924 677 321
Fax: +34 924 660 989
acoex@bme.es
www.zaleo.es

Zaleo 2014 RD
tempranillo

84

Zaleo Pardina 2014 B
pardina

85

Zaleo Premium 2013 T
tempranillo

85

Zaleo Selección 2013 T
tempranillo

85

Zaleo Semidulce 2014 B
pardina

84

Zaleo Tempranillo 2014 T
tempranillo

86

Zaleo Tempranillo Semidulce 2014 T
tempranillo

83

DO. RIBERA DEL JÚCAR

CONSEJO REGULADOR

Deportes, 4.
16700 Sisante (Cuenca)
☎ :+34 969 387 182 - Fax: +34 969 387 208
@: do@vinosriberadeljucar.com
www.vinosriberadeljucar.com

LOCATION:

The 7 wine producing municipal districts that make up the DO are located on the banks of the Júcar, in the south of the province of Cuenca. They are: Casas de Benítez, Casas de Guijarro, Casas de Haro, Casas de Fernando Alonso, Pozoamargo, Sisante and El Picazo. The region is at an altitude of between 650 and 750 m above sea level.

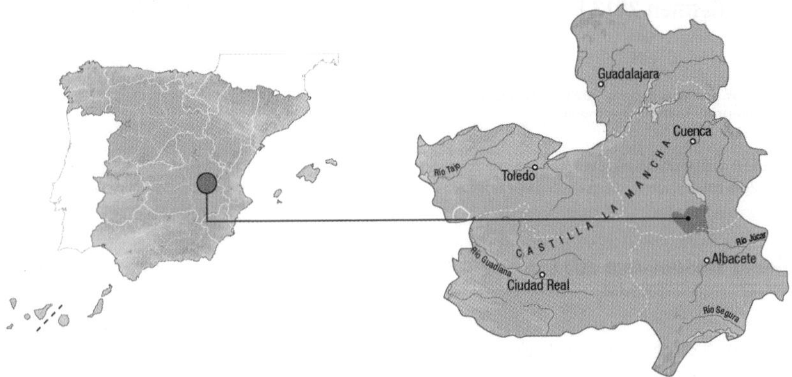

GRAPE VARIETIES:

RED: Cencibel or Tempranillo, Cabernet Sauvignon, Merlot, Syrah, Bobal, Cabernet Franc and Petit Verdot.
WHITE: Moscatel de Grano Menudo and Sauvignon Blanc.

FIGURES:

Vineyard surface: 9,100 – **Wine-Growers:** 935 – **Wineries:** 10 – **2014 Harvest rating:** Very Good – **Production 14:** 780,000 litres – **Market percentages:** 30% National - 70% International.

SOIL:

The most common type of soil consists of pebbles on the surface and a clayey subsoil, which provides good water retention capacity in the deeper levels.

CLIMATE:

Continental in nature, dry, and with very cold winters and very hot summers. The main factor contributing to the quality of the wine is the day-night temperature contrasts during the ripening season of the grapes, which causes the process to be carried out slowly.

VINTAGE RATING

PEÑÍNGUIDE

2010	2011	2012	2013	2014
VERY GOOD	VERY GOOD	VERY GOOD	VERY GOOD	GOOD

BODEGAS Y VIÑEDOS ILLANA

02630 Pozoamargo (Cuenca)
☎: +34 969 147 039
Fax: +34 969 147 057
administracin@bodegasillana.com
www.bodegasillana.com

Casa de Illana Alma 2014 B
90% sauvignon blanc, 10% airén

88

Colour: straw. Nose: medium intensity, ripe fruit, floral, tropical fruit. Palate: correct, easy to drink.

Casa de Illana Carmen 2013 BFB
100% sauvignon blanc

90

Colour: bright yellow. Nose: ripe fruit, powerfull, toasty, sweet spices. Palate: flavourful, fruity, spicy, toasty, long.

Casa de Illana Expression 2014 T
80% tempranillo, 20% bobal

86

Casa de Illana Tresdecinco 2011 TC
43% petit verdot, 32% merlot, 25% syrah

88

Colour: bright cherry. Nose: ripe fruit, sweet spices, creamy oak. Palate: flavourful, fruity, toasty.

Petit Yllana Bobal 2014 T
100% bobal

87

Colour: cherry, purple rim. Nose: fresh fruit, red berry notes, floral. Palate: flavourful, fruity, easy to drink.

Petit Yllana Petit Verdot 2014 T
100% petit verdot

85

CASA GUALDA

Tapias, 8
16708 Pozoamargo (Cuenca)
☎: +34 969 387 173

info@casagualda.com
www.casagualda.com

Casa Gualda 2012 TC
tempranillo, cabernet sauvignon

86

Casa Gualda Bobal 2013 T
bobal

85

Casa Gualda Selección 50 Aniversario 2011 T
petit verdot, syrah

86

Casa Gualda Selección C&J 2010 T
tempranillo

85

Casa Gualda Syrah 2013 T
syrah

86

Casa Gualda Tempranillo 2014 T
tempranillo

85

DO. Ca. RIOJA

CONSEJO REGULADOR

Estambrera, 52
26006 Logroño (La Rioja)
☎:+34 941 500 400 - Fax: +34 941 500 672
@: info@riojawine.com
www.riojawine.com

LOCATION:

Occupying the Ebro valley. To the north it borders with the Sierra de Cantabria and to the south with the Sierra de la Demanda, and is made up of different municipal districts of La Rioja, the Basque Country and Navarra. The most western region is Haro and the easternmost, Alfaro, with a distance of 100 km between the two. The region is 40 km wide.es de 40 kilómetros.

SUB-REGIONS:

Rioja Alta. This has Atlantic influences; it is the most extensive with some 20,500 Ha and produces wines well suited for ageing. **Rioja Alavesa.** A mixture of Atlantic and Mediterranean influences, with an area under cultivation of some 11,500 Ha; both young wines and wines suited for ageing are produced. **Rioja Baja.** With approximately 18,000 Ha, the climate is purely Mediterranean; white wines and rosés with a higher alcohol content and extract are produced.

GRAPE VARIETIES:

WHITE: Viura (7,045 Ha), Malvasía, Garnacha Blanca, Chardonnay, Sauvignon Blanc, Verdejo, Maturana Blanca, Tempranillo Blanco and Torrontés.
RED: Tempranillo (majority with 38,476 Ha), Garnacha, Graciano, Mazuelo and Maturana Tinta.

FIGURES:

Vineyard surface: 63,542.42 – **Wine-Growers:** 16,413 – **Wineries:** 802 – **2014 Harvest rating:** Good – **Production 14:** 293,520,000 litres – **Market percentages:** 62,4% National - 37,6% International.

SOIL:

Various types: the clayey calcareous soil arranged in terraces and small plots which are located especially in Rioja Alavesa, la Sonsierra and some regions of Rioja Alta; the clayey ferrous soil, scattered throughout the region, with vineyards located on reddish, strong soil with hard, deep rock; and the alluvial soil in the area close to the rivers; these are the most level vineyards with larger plots; here the soil is deeper and has pebbles.

CLIMATE:

Quite variable depending on the different sub-regions. In general, there is a combination of Atlantic and Mediterranean influences, the latter becoming more dominant as the terrain descends from west to east, becoming drier and hotter. The average annual rainfall is slightly over 400 mm.

VINTAGE RATING

PEÑÍNGUIDE

2010	2011	2012	2013	2014
EXCELLENT	EXCELLENT	VERY GOOD	GOOD	GOOD

AKELARRE

Camino del Cementerio, s/n
26338 San Vicente de la Sonsierra
(La Rioja)
☎: +34 629 578 001
ecoetica@arrakis.es
www.akelarrewine.com

Akelarre 2012 T

tempranillo, graciano, garnacha

86

Akelarre 2014 B

100% viura

88

Colour: bright straw. Nose: white flowers, fine lees, dried herbs, mineral. Palate: flavourful, fruity, good acidity, round.

ALEGRE & VALGAÑÓN

Ctra. Tirgo - Miranda, km. 4,8
26212 Sajazarra (La Rioja)
☎: +34 609 886 652
oscar@alegrevalganon.com
www.alegrevalganon.com

Alegre Valgañón 2012 T

80% tempranillo, 20% garnacha

88

Colour: cherry, purple rim. Nose: ripe fruit, woody, roasted coffee. Palate: flavourful, spicy, powerful.

La Calleja 2010 T

100% tempranillo

90

Colour: bright cherry. Nose: ripe fruit, sweet spices, creamy oak. Palate: flavourful, toasty, round tannins.

ALTOS DE RIOJA VITICULTORES Y BODEGUEROS

Solomillo, s/n
01309 Elvillar de Álava (Alava)
☎: +34 945 600 693
Fax: +34 945 600 692
altosderioja@altosderioja.com
www.altosderioja.com

Altos R 2008 TR

100% tempranillo

90

Colour: cherry, garnet rim. Nose: red berry notes, ripe fruit, spicy, complex. Palate: flavourful, toasty, round tannins.

Altos R 2010 TR

tempranillo

90

Colour: cherry, garnet rim. Nose: red berry notes, ripe fruit, spicy, creamy oak, complex. Palate: flavourful, toasty, round tannins.

Altos R 2012 TC

100% tempranillo

88

Colour: cherry, garnet rim. Nose: smoky, spicy, ripe fruit. Palate: flavourful, smoky aftertaste, ripe fruit.

Altos R 2014 B

60% viura, 40% malvasía

90

Colour: bright straw. Nose: white flowers, fresh fruit, fragrant herbs, expressive. Palate: flavourful, fruity, good acidity, balanced, round.

Altos R Pigeage 2011 T

90% tempranillo, 10% graciano

91

Colour: cherry, garnet rim. Nose: expressive, spicy, smoky, toasty. Palate: flavourful, ripe fruit, long, good acidity, balanced.

Altos R Tempranillo 2014 T

100% tempranillo

88

Colour: cherry, purple rim. Nose: red berry notes, floral, wild herbs. Palate: powerful, fresh, ripe fruit.

ALVAREZ ALFARO

Ctra. Comarcal 384, Km. 0,8
26559 Aldeanueva de Ebro (La Rioja)
☎: +34 941 144 210
info@bodegasalvarezalfaro.com
www.alvarezalfaro.com

Alvarez Alfaro 2009 TR
100% tempranillo

88

Colour: very deep cherry, garnet rim. Nose: balsamic herbs, balanced, ripe fruit, fruit preserve. Palate: full, flavourful, round tannins.

Alvarez Alfaro 2012 TC
80% tempranillo, 8% garnacha, 10% mazuelo, 2% graciano

87

Colour: cherry, garnet rim. Nose: ripe fruit, tobacco, dried herbs. Palate: correct, flavourful, spicy.

Alvarez Alfaro 2012 TC
100% tempranillo

88

Colour: cherry, garnet rim. Nose: ripe fruit, wild herbs, earthy notes, spicy, balsamic herbs. Palate: balanced, flavourful, long, balsamic.

ARBOLEDA MEDITERRÁNEA BODEGAS

Ctra. de Samaniego, 12
01307 Villabuena (Álava)
☎: +34 902 996 361
export@arboledamediterranea.com
www.arboledamediterranean.com

Pérez Basoco Blanco Selección 2014 B
100% viura

83

Pérez Basoco Tinto Selección 2014 T
100% tempranillo

85

Pérez Basoco Vendimia Seleccionada de Autor Viñas Viejas 2011 T
100% tempranillo

87

Colour: cherry, garnet rim. Nose: ripe fruit, spicy, creamy oak. Palate: flavourful, toasty.

ARBOLEDA MEDITERRÁNEA BODEGAS

C. San Ignacio, 26
26313 Uruñuela (La Rioja)
☎: +34 902 996 361
export@arboledamediterranea.com
www.arboledamediterranean.com

Entregado 2006 TGR
90% tempranillo, 10% garnacha

87

Colour: pale ruby, brick rim edge. Nose: spicy, fine reductive notes, wet leather, aged wood nuances. Palate: spicy, fine tannins.

Entregado 2012 TC
90% tempranillo, 10% garnacha

87

Colour: cherry, garnet rim. Nose: powerfull, ripe fruit, spicy. Palate: powerful, fruity, unctuous.

Entregado Colección Alta Expresión Viñas Viejas 2011 T
tempranillo

90

Colour: cherry, garnet rim. Nose: ripe fruit, fragrant herbs, spicy, creamy oak, mineral. Palate: powerful, flavourful, balsamic.

Entregado Selección 2009 TR
90% tempranillo, 10% garnacha

88

Colour: cherry, garnet rim. Nose: ripe fruit, old leather, tobacco. Palate: correct, flavourful, spicy.

ARTUKE BODEGAS Y VIÑEDOS

01307 Baños de Ebro (Álava)
☎: +34 945 623 323
Fax: +34 945 623 323
artuke@artuke.com
www.artuke.com

Artuke 2014 T Maceración Carbónica
95% tempranillo, 5% viura

90

Colour: cherry, purple rim. Nose: fresh fruit, red berry notes, floral, expressive. Palate: flavourful, fruity, good acidity, balanced.

Artuke Finca de los Locos 2013 T
80% tempranillo, 20% graciano

94

Colour: bright cherry, purple rim. Nose: creamy oak, sweet spices, red berry notes, ripe fruit. Palate: flavourful, fruity, full.

Artuke K4 2013 T
75% tempranillo, 25% graciano

94

Colour: cherry, purple rim. Nose: ripe fruit, wild herbs, earthy notes, spicy, balsamic herbs. Palate: balanced, flavourful, long, balsamic, elegant.

PODIUM

Artuke La Condenada 2013 T
80% tempranillo, 20% graciano, garnacha, palomino

96

Colour: cherry, garnet rim. Nose: creamy oak, red berry notes, fresh fruit, balanced, mineral, balsamic herbs. Palate: flavourful, spicy, elegant.

Artuke Pies Negros 2013 TC
90% tempranillo, 10% graciano

91

Colour: cherry, garnet rim. Nose: creamy oak, red berry notes, balanced. Palate: spicy, easy to drink, balsamic.

BAIGORRI

Ctra. Vitoria-Logroño, Km. 53
01300 Samaniego (Álava)
☎: +34 945 609 420
mail@bodegasbaigorri.com
www.bodegasbaigorri.com

Baigorri 2013 BFB
90% viura, 10% malvasía

88

Colour: bright yellow. Nose: ripe fruit, powerfull, toasty, smoky. Palate: flavourful, fruity, spicy, toasty, long.

Baigorri 2009 TR
100% tempranillo

90

Colour: very deep cherry, garnet rim. Nose: expressive, complex, mineral, balsamic herbs, balanced. Palate: full, flavourful, round tannins.

Baigorri 2011 TC
90% tempranillo, 10% otras

88

Colour: bright cherry. Nose: ripe fruit, sweet spices, creamy oak. Palate: flavourful, fruity, toasty.

Baigorri 2014 BFB
90% viura, 10% malvasía

88

Colour: bright straw. Nose: fresh fruit, fragrant herbs, expressive, grassy. Palate: flavourful, fruity, good acidity, balanced, spicy.

Baigorri 2014 T Maceración Carbónica
100% tempranillo

83

Baigorri B70 2010 T
100% tempranillo

91

Colour: cherry, garnet rim. Nose: mineral, expressive, spicy, ripe fruit. Palate: flavourful, ripe fruit, long, good acidity, balanced.

Baigorri Belus 2010 T
80% tempranillo, 15% mazuelo, 5% otras

90

Colour: cherry, garnet rim. Nose: ripe fruit, wild herbs, earthy notes, spicy, balsamic herbs. Palate: balanced, flavourful, long, balsamic.

Baigorri de Garage 2010 T
100% tempranillo

89

Colour: very deep cherry. Nose: balsamic herbs, fruit preserve, sweet spices, creamy oak. Palate: full, flavourful.

Baigorri Garnacha 2011 T
100% garnacha

89

Colour: cherry, garnet rim. Nose: fruit preserve, scrubland, spicy, creamy oak. Palate: powerful, flavourful, spicy, ripe fruit.

BARÓN DE LEY

Ctra. Mendavia - Lodosa, Km. 5,5
31587 Mendavia (Navarra)
☎: +34 948 694 303
Fax: +34 948 694 304
info@barondeley.com
www.barondeley.com

Barón de Ley 2009 TGR
100% tempranillo

88

Colour: pale ruby, brick rim edge. Nose: elegant, spicy, fine reductive notes, tobacco. Palate: spicy, fine tannins, long, balanced.

Barón de Ley 2011 TR
85% tempranillo, 5% maturana, 10% graciano

90

Colour: cherry, garnet rim. Nose: ripe fruit, wild herbs, earthy notes, spicy, balsamic herbs. Palate: balanced, flavourful, long.

Barón de Ley 2014 B
85% viura, 15% malvasía

88

Colour: bright straw. Nose: fruit expression, wild herbs, floral. Palate: powerful, flavourful, fresh, fruity.

Barón de Ley 2014 RD
60% tempranillo, 40% garnacha

85

Baron de Ley 3 Viñas 2010 B Reserva
70% viura, 15% malvasía, 15% garnacha blanca

90

Colour: bright yellow. Nose: roasted coffee, smoky, dry nuts. Palate: fruity, rich, smoky aftertaste.

Barón de Ley Finca Monasterio 2012 T
80% tempranillo, 20% otras

91

Colour: cherry, garnet rim. Nose: mineral, expressive, spicy, ripe fruit. Palate: flavourful, long, good acidity.

Barón de Ley Rosado de Lágrima 2014 RD
100% garnacha

87

Colour: onion pink. Nose: elegant, red berry notes, floral, fragrant herbs. Palate: light-bodied, flavourful, good acidity, spicy.

Barón de Ley Varietal Garnacha 2012 T
100% garnacha

89

Colour: cherry, garnet rim. Nose: ripe fruit, spicy, wild herbs. Palate: good structure, flavourful, balanced.

Barón de Ley Varietal Graciano 2011 T
100% graciano

90

Colour: cherry, garnet rim. Nose: ripe fruit, spicy, creamy oak. Palate: flavourful, toasty.

Barón de Ley Varietal Maturana 2012 T
100% maturana

90

Colour: cherry, garnet rim. Nose: ripe fruit, fruit preserve, scrubland, spicy. Palate: powerful, flavourful, spicy, long.

Barón de Ley Varietal Tempranillo 2011 T
100% tempranillo

90

Colour: cherry, garnet rim. Nose: red berry notes, ripe fruit, spicy, creamy oak. Palate: flavourful, toasty.

BODEGA ABEL MENDOZA

26338 San Vicente de la Sonsierra
(La Rioja)
☎: +34 941 308 010
Fax: +34 941 308 010
jarrarte.abelmendoza@gmail.com

Abel Mendoza 5V 2014 B
viura, malvasía, torrontés, garnacha blanca, tempranillo blanco

88

Colour: bright straw. Nose: dried herbs, faded flowers, ripe fruit. Palate: ripe fruit, thin, fine bitter notes.

Abel Mendoza Graciano Grano a Grano 2011 T
100% graciano

92

Colour: cherry, garnet rim. Nose: roasted coffee, smoky, spicy, ripe fruit. Palate: flavourful, smoky aftertaste, ripe fruit.

Abel Mendoza Malvasía 2014 BFB
100% malvasía

88

Colour: bright yellow. Nose: dried herbs, ripe fruit, fruit preserve, creamy oak. Palate: flavourful, fruity, good acidity, balanced.

Abel Mendoza Viura 2014 BFB
100% viura

87

Colour: bright straw. Nose: dried herbs, faded flowers, fruit preserve. Palate: ripe fruit, thin.

Jarrarte 2010 T
100% tempranillo

88

Colour: cherry, garnet rim. Nose: creamy oak, balanced, ripe fruit. Palate: flavourful, spicy, elegant.

Jarrarte 2014 T Maceración Carbónica
100% tempranillo

90

Colour: cherry, purple rim. Nose: fresh fruit, floral. Palate: flavourful, fruity, good acidity.

BODEGA BELELUIN

Ctra. La Estación, 12
26509 Alcanadre (La Rioja)
☎: +34 687 562 769
bodega@beleluin.com
www.beleluin.com

Beleluin 2014 B
100% viura

85

Beleluin 2014 T
90% tempranillo, 10% garnacha

84

Beleluin Garnacha 2014 T
100% garnacha

83

Beleluin Selección 2011 T
90% tempranillo, 10% garnacha

85

BODEGA CONTADOR

Ctra. Baños de Ebro, Km. 1
26338 San Vicente de la Sonsierra
(La Rioja)
☎: +34 941 334 228
Fax: +34 941 334 537
info@bodegacontador.com
www.bodegacontador.com

La Cueva del Contador 2013 T
tempranillo

94

Colour: cherry, garnet rim. Nose: red berry notes, fresh fruit, expressive, varietal, creamy oak. Palate: flavourful, spicy, elegant.

Predicador 2013 T

92

Colour: bright cherry. Nose: sweet spices, creamy oak, ripe fruit, red berry notes. Palate: flavourful, fruity, round tannins.

Predicador 2014 B

93

Colour: bright straw. Nose: fine lees, dried herbs, mineral. Palate: flavourful, fruity, good acidity, round.

Qué Bonito Cacareaba 2014 B
garnacha blanca, malvasía, viura

94

Colour: bright yellow. Nose: ripe fruit, powerfull, toasty, aged wood nuances, pattiserie. Palate: flavourful, fruity, spicy, toasty, long.

BODEGA IGNACIO PETRALANDA

Avda. La Estación, 44
26360 Fuenmayor (La Rioja)
☎: +34 608 893 732
info@vinoart.es
www.vinoart.es

Nonno 2007 TR
tempranillo

89 

Colour: ruby red. Nose: spicy, fine reductive notes, wet leather, aged wood nuances, fruit liqueur notes. Palate: spicy, fine tannins, balanced.

Nonno 2010 TC
tempranillo

88

Colour: bright cherry. Nose: ripe fruit, sweet spices, creamy oak, expressive. Palate: flavourful, fruity, toasty, round tannins.

Nonno Magnum 2010 T
tempranillo

90

Colour: cherry, garnet rim. Nose: ripe fruit, wild herbs, spicy. Palate: flavourful, long, balsamic.

BODEGA VIÑA EGUILUZ

Camino de San Bartolomé, 10
26339 Abalos (La Rioja)
☎: +34 941 334 064
Fax: +34 941 583 022
info@bodegaseguiluz.es
www.bodegaseguiluz.es

Eguiluz 2008 TR
100% tempranillo

87

Colour: cherry, garnet rim. Nose: wet leather, aged wood nuances, ripe fruit. Palate: spicy, long, toasty.

Eguiluz 2011 TC
100% tempranillo

84

Eguiluz 2014 T
100% tempranillo

88

Colour: cherry, purple rim. Nose: expressive, fresh fruit, red berry notes, floral. Palate: flavourful, fruity, good acidity.

BODEGAS 1808

Ctra. El Villar Polígono 7
Biribil, 33 Apdo. 26
01300 Laguardia (Alava)
☎: +34 685 752 384
Fax: +34 945 293 450
1808@rioja1808.com
www.rioja1808.com

1808 Temperamento Natural 2010 TR
tempranillo

90

Colour: cherry, garnet rim. Nose: ripe fruit, spicy, creamy oak, complex. Palate: flavourful, toasty.

1808 Temperamento Natural 2012 TC
tempranillo

88

Colour: deep cherry. Nose: creamy oak, toasty, ripe fruit, balsamic herbs. Palate: balanced, spicy, long.

1808 Temperamento Natural Viura 2013 B
viura

86

BODEGAS AGE

Barrio de la Estación, s/n
26360 Fuenmayor (La Rioja)
☎: +34 941 293 500
bodegasage@pernod-ricard.com
www.bodegasage.com

Siglo 2008 TGR
tempranillo, mazuelo, graciano

86

Siglo 2010 TR
tempranillo, mazuelo, graciano

88

Colour: cherry, garnet rim. Nose: ripe fruit, spicy, creamy oak, fine reductive notes. Palate: flavourful, toasty.

Siglo Saco 2012 TC
tempranillo, garnacha, mazuelo

85

BODEGAS ALABANZA

Avda. de Cameros, 27 Pol. Sequero
26150 Agoncillo (La Rioja)
☎: +34 941 437 051
bodegasalabanza@bodegasalabanza.com
www.bodegasalabanza.com

Alabanza 2009 TR

87

Colour: cherry, garnet rim. Nose: ripe fruit, wild herbs, balsamic herbs. Palate: balanced, flavourful, balsamic.

Alabanza 2013 T

85

Alabanza 2012 TC

87

Colour: bright cherry. Nose: ripe fruit, sweet spices, creamy oak. Palate: flavourful, fruity, toasty.

BODEGAS ALTANZA

Ctra. Nacional 232, Km. 419,5
26360 Fuenmayor (Rioja)
☎: +34 941 450 860
Fax: +34 941 450 804
altanza@bodegasaltanza.com
www.bodegasaltanza.com

Altanza Reserva Especial 2010 TR
100% tempranillo

90

Colour: light cherry. Nose: fine reductive notes, aged wood nuances, toasty, ripe fruit. Palate: spicy, toasty, flavourful.

Edulis 2012 TC
100% tempranillo

87

Colour: bright cherry. Nose: ripe fruit, sweet spices, creamy oak. Palate: flavourful, fruity, toasty, round tannins.

Hacienda Valvarés 2012 TC
100% tempranillo

88

Colour: cherry, purple rim. Nose: ripe fruit, woody, roasted coffee. Palate: flavourful, spicy, powerful.

Lealtanza 2008 TGR
tempranillo

91

Colour: pale ruby, brick rim edge. Nose: spicy, fine reductive notes, wet leather, aged wood nuances, ripe fruit. Palate: spicy, fine tannins, balanced.

Lealtanza 2010 TR
100% tempranillo

90

Colour: light cherry. Nose: fine reductive notes, aged wood nuances, toasty, ripe fruit. Palate: spicy, toasty, flavourful.

Lealtanza 2014 B
sauvignon blanc, viura

87

Colour: bright straw. Nose: white flowers, fresh fruit, dried herbs. Palate: flavourful, fruity, good acidity.

Lealtanza 2014 RD
100% tempranillo

87

Colour: rose, purple rim. Nose: powerfull, fruit preserve, dried herbs. Palate: powerful, flavourful.

Lealtanza Club 2008 TR
100% tempranillo

91

Colour: cherry, garnet rim. Nose: balanced, ripe fruit, spicy, fine reductive notes. Palate: good structure, flavourful, round tannins, balanced.

Lealtanza Colección Artistas Españoles Goya 2008 TR
100% tempranillo

91

Colour: light cherry. Nose: fine reductive notes, aged wood nuances, toasty, ripe fruit, warm. Palate: spicy, toasty, flavourful.

Lealtanza Reserva de Familia 2009 TR
100% tempranillo

89

Colour: pale ruby, brick rim edge. Nose: spicy, wet leather, tobacco. Palate: spicy, toasty.

BODEGAS ALTOS DEL MARQUÉS

Ctra. Navarrete, 1
26372 Hornos de Moncalvillo (La Rioja)
☎: +34 941 286 728
Fax: +34 941 286 729
info@altosdelmarques.com
www.altosdelmarques.com

Altos del Marqués 2011 TC
100% tempranillo

87

Colour: cherry, garnet rim. Nose: ripe fruit, spicy, creamy oak. Palate: flavourful, toasty.

Altos del Marqués 2014 T
85% tempranillo, 10% garnacha, 5% mazuelo

86

BODEGAS ALTÚN

Las Piscinas, 30
01307 Baños de Ebro (Álava)
☎: +34 945 609 317
Fax: +34 945 603 909
altun@bodegasaltun.com
www.bodegasaltun.com

Albiker 2014 T Maceración Carbónica
tempranillo, viura

88

Colour: cherry, purple rim. Nose: expressive, fresh fruit, red berry notes, floral, maceration notes. Palate: flavourful, fruity, good acidity.

Altún 2009 TR
tempranillo

91

Colour: cherry, garnet rim. Nose: red berry notes, ripe fruit, spicy, creamy oak, complex. Palate: flavourful, toasty, round tannins.

Altún 2012 TC
tempranillo

91

Colour: cherry, garnet rim. Nose: mineral, expressive, spicy, ripe fruit. Palate: flavourful, ripe fruit, long, good acidity, balanced.

Altún Rosé 2014 RD
tempranillo

85

Ana de Altún 2014 B
viura, malvasía

85

Everest 2011 T
tempranillo

94

Colour: cherry, garnet rim. Nose: balanced, complex, ripe fruit, spicy, fine reductive notes. Palate: good structure, flavourful, round tannins, balanced, long.

Secreto de Altún 2012 T
tempranillo

92

Colour: bright cherry. Nose: ripe fruit, sweet spices, creamy oak, expressive. Palate: flavourful, fruity, toasty, elegant.

BODEGAS AMADOR GARCÍA

Avda. Río Ebro, 68 - 70
01015 Vitoria (Álava)
☎: +34 945 623 322
Fax: +34 975 290 373
pbodegasamadorgarcia@gmail.com
www.bodegasamadorgarcia.com

Amador García 2011 TC
95% tempranillo, 5% garnacha, mazuelo

84

Amador García 2014 BFB

88

Colour: bright straw. Nose: white flowers, fresh fruit, fragrant herbs. Palate: flavourful, fruity, good acidity.

Peñagudo 2012 TC
95% tempranillo, 2% graciano, 3% garnacha

84

Peñagudo 2014 B
100% viura

82

Peñagudo 2014 RD
85% tempranillo, 15% viura

84

Peñagudo 2014 T
90% tempranillo, 10% viura

86

BODEGAS AMAREN

Ctra. Baños de Ebro, s/n
01307 Villabuena (Álava)
☎: +34 945 175 240
Fax: +34 945 174 566
bodegas@bodegasamaren.com

Amaren 2013 BFB

85% viura, 15% malvasía

91

Colour: bright yellow. Nose: expressive, dried herbs, ripe fruit, spicy. Palate: flavourful, fruity, good acidity, balanced.

Amaren Graciano 2010 T

100% graciano

94

Colour: cherry, garnet rim. Nose: ripe fruit, wild herbs, earthy notes, spicy, balsamic herbs. Palate: balanced, flavourful, balsamic, long.

Amaren Tempranillo 2008 TR

100% tempranillo

93

Colour: very deep cherry, garnet rim. Nose: expressive, complex, mineral, balsamic herbs, fine reductive notes, ripe fruit. Palate: full, flavourful, round tannins, elegant.

Ángeles de Amaren 2010 T

85% tempranillo, 15% graciano

93

Colour: cherry, garnet rim. Nose: mineral, expressive, spicy. Palate: flavourful, ripe fruit, long, good acidity, balanced.

BODEGAS AMÉZOLA DE LA MORA S.A.

Paraje Viña Vieja, s/n
26359 Torremontalbo (La Rioja)
☎: +34 941 454 532
Fax: +34 941 454 537
info@bodegasamezola.es
www.bodegasamezola.es

Iñigo Amézola 2011 T Fermentado en Barrica

tempranillo

86

Iñigo Amézola 2012 BFB

100% viura

88

Colour: bright yellow. Nose: ripe fruit, powerfull, toasty, patisserie. Palate: flavourful, fruity, spicy, toasty.

Señorío Amézola 2008 TR

tempranillo, mazuelo, graciano

87

Colour: pale ruby, brick rim edge. Nose: spicy, fine reductive notes, wet leather, aged wood nuances, fruit liqueur notes. Palate: spicy, balanced, balsamic.

Solar Amézola 2006 TGR

tempranillo, mazuelo, graciano

89

Colour: pale ruby, brick rim edge. Nose: elegant, spicy, fine reductive notes, tobacco. Palate: spicy, fine tannins, long.

Viña Amézola 2011 TC

tempranillo, mazuelo, graciano

88

Colour: cherry, garnet rim. Nose: ripe fruit, scrubland, spicy. Palate: balanced, round tannins.

BODEGAS ANTONIO ALCARAZ

Ctra. Vitoria-Logroño, Km. 57
01300 Laguardia (Álava)
☎: +34 658 959 745
Fax: +34 965 888 359
rioja@antonio-alcaraz.es
www.antonio-alcaraz.es

Altea de Antonio Alcaraz 2013 TC

100% tempranillo

85

Antonio Alcaraz 2010 TR
90% tempranillo, 10% graciano, mazuelo

89

Colour: cherry, garnet rim. Nose: balanced, red berry notes, ripe fruit, spicy. Palate: fruity, easy to drink, balanced.

Gloria Antonio Alcaraz 2011 TC
100% tempranillo

91

Colour: cherry, garnet rim. Nose: expressive, spicy, ripe fruit. Palate: flavourful, ripe fruit, long, good acidity, balanced.

Men to Men 2011 T
90% tempranillo, 10% graciano, mazuelo

89

Colour: bright cherry, garnet rim. Nose: ripe fruit, sweet spices, toasty, smoky. Palate: correct, spicy, round tannins.

BODEGAS ARACO

Ctra. Lapuebla, s/n
01300 Laguardia (Álava)
☎: +34 945 600 209
Fax: +34 945 600 067
araco@bodegasaraco.com
www.bodegasaraco.com

Araco 2012 TC
tempranillo

84

Araco 2014 T
tempranillo

87

Colour: cherry, purple rim. Nose: expressive, fresh fruit, red berry notes, floral. Palate: flavourful, fruity, good acidity.

BODEGAS BASAGOITI

Camí de Can Garra, s/n
08391 Tiana (Barcelona)
☎: +34 933 950 811
Fax: +34 933 955 500
info@glevaestates.es
www.basagoiti.com

Basagoiti 2012 TC
tempranillo, graciano, garnacha

88

Colour: bright cherry. Nose: ripe fruit, sweet spices, creamy oak. Palate: flavourful, fruity, toasty, round tannins.

Nabari 2014 T
tempranillo, garnacha

87

Colour: cherry, purple rim. Nose: expressive, fresh fruit, red berry notes, floral. Palate: flavourful, fruity, good acidity.

BODEGAS BENETAKOA

Ctra. Samaniego, 12
01307 Villabuena de Alava (Álava)
☎: +34 945 609 098
contacta@benetakoa.com
www.benetakoa.com

CMC Carlos Mtz de Cañas 2011 TC
tempranillo

89

Colour: cherry, garnet rim. Nose: ripe fruit, spicy, creamy oak, fine reductive notes. Palate: flavourful, toasty.

Goren 2011 T
tempranillo

89

Colour: deep cherry, purple rim. Nose: creamy oak, toasty, ripe fruit, balsamic herbs. Palate: balanced, spicy, long.

Haritz 2014 B
viura

86

Haritz 2014 T
tempranillo

85

Pretextos 2011 T
tempranillo

86

BODEGAS BENJAMÍN DE ROTHSCHILD & VEGA SICILIA S.A.

Ctra. Logroño - Vitoria, km. 61
01309 Leza (Alava)
☎: +34 983 680 147
Fax: +34 983 680 263
vegasicilia@vega-sicilia.com
www.vegasicilia.com

🏆 PODIUM

Macán 2012 T
100% tempranillo

95

Colour: cherry, garnet rim. Nose: balanced, ripe fruit, toasty, spicy, earthy notes, mineral. Palate: flavourful, spicy, round tannins, long.

Macán Clásico 2012 T
100% tempranillo

93

Colour: bright cherry. Nose: sweet spices, creamy oak, expressive, red berry notes. Palate: flavourful, fruity, round tannins.

BODEGAS BERCEO

Cuevas, 32-36
26200 Haro (La Rioja)
☎: +34 941 310 744
Fax: +34 948 670 259
bodegas@gurpegui.es
www.gurpegui.es

Berceo Selección 2013 T
tempranillo, mazuelo, graciano

90

Colour: cherry, garnet rim. Nose: ripe fruit, spicy, creamy oak. Palate: flavourful, toasty, round tannins.

Berceo "Nueva Generación" 2013 T
tempranillo, graciano, mazuelo

90

Colour: cherry, purple rim. Nose: powerfull, ripe fruit, spicy. Palate: powerful, fruity, toasty.

Gonzalo de Berceo 2006 TGR
tempranillo, graciano, mazuelo

89

Colour: pale ruby, brick rim edge. Nose: fine reductive notes, wet leather, aged wood nuances, ripe fruit. Palate: spicy, classic aged character.

Gonzalo de Berceo 2010 TR
tempranillo, graciano, mazuelo, graciano

88

Colour: cherry, garnet rim. Nose: fine reductive notes, wild herbs, spicy. Palate: spicy, long, toasty.

Los Dominios de Berceo "Reserva 36" 2010 TR
tempranillo

89

Colour: bright cherry. Nose: ripe fruit, sweet spices, creamy oak. Palate: flavourful, fruity, toasty.

Los Dominios de Berceo Prefiloxerico 2014 T
tempranillo

88

Colour: cherry, purple rim. Nose: powerfull, ripe fruit, spicy. Palate: powerful, fruity, unctuous.

Viña Berceo 2013 TC
tempranillo, garnacha, graciano

88

Colour: cherry, purple rim. Nose: ripe fruit, roasted coffee. Palate: flavourful, spicy, powerful.

BODEGAS BERONIA

Ctra. Ollauri - Nájera, Km. 1,8
26220 Ollauri (La Rioja)
☎: +34 941 338 000
Fax: +34 941 338 266
beronia@beronia.es
www.beronia.es

Beronia 2007 TGR
92% tempranillo, 6% graciano, 2% mazuelo

91

Colour: dark-red cherry, garnet rim. Nose: spicy, fine reductive notes, aged wood nuances. Palate: spicy, fine tannins, balanced, classic aged character.

Beronia 2008 TGR
90% tempranillo, 5% graciano, 5% mazuelo

90

Colour: ruby red. Nose: fine reductive notes, fruit liqueur notes, ripe fruit. Palate: spicy, balanced, long.

Beronia 2010 TR
93% tempranillo, 5% graciano, 2% mazuelo

89

Colour: light cherry. Nose: fine reductive notes, toasty, ripe fruit. Palate: spicy, toasty, flavourful.

Beronia 2011 TC
90% tempranillo, 8% garnacha, 2% mazuelo

88

Colour: bright cherry. Nose: ripe fruit, sweet spices, creamy oak, balsamic herbs. Palate: flavourful, fruity, toasty.

Beronia 2011 TR
93% tempranillo, 5% graciano, 2% mazuelo

90

Colour: cherry, garnet rim. Nose: spicy, dried herbs. Palate: correct, flavourful, spicy.

Beronia 2012 TC
88% tempranillo, 10% garnacha, 2% mazuelo

88

Colour: cherry, garnet rim. Nose: toasty, ripe fruit, scrubland. Palate: spicy, long, easy to drink.

Beronia Graciano 2011 T
graciano

89

Colour: bright cherry. Nose: ripe fruit, wild herbs, balsamic herbs, creamy oak. Palate: powerful, flavourful, complex, round.

Beronia Graciano 2012 T
graciano

89

Colour: dark-red cherry, garnet rim. Nose: creamy oak, toasty, ripe fruit, balsamic herbs. Palate: balanced, spicy, long.

Beronia Mazuelo 2010 TR
mazuelo

90

Colour: cherry, garnet rim. Nose: ripe fruit, earthy notes, spicy, old leather. Palate: balanced, flavourful, long.

Beronia Selección 198 Barricas 2008 TR
tempranillo, mazuelo, graciano

91

Colour: cherry, garnet rim. Nose: ripe fruit, old leather, tobacco. Palate: correct, flavourful, spicy, balanced, long.

Beronia Tempranillo Elaboración Especial 2012 T
tempranillo

88

Colour: cherry, garnet rim. Nose: smoky, toasty, ripe fruit, aromatic coffee. Palate: good structure, toasty.

Beronia Viñas Viejas 2011 T
tempranillo

88

Colour: cherry, garnet rim. Nose: cocoa bean, tobacco, ripe fruit. Palate: balanced, spicy, long.

Beronia Viñas Viejas 2012 T
tempranillo

89

Colour: cherry, garnet rim. Nose: smoky, spicy, ripe fruit. Palate: flavourful, smoky aftertaste, ripe fruit.

III a.C., Beronia 2011 T
tempranillo, graciano, mazuelo

93

Colour: cherry, garnet rim. Nose: smoky, spicy, ripe fruit. Palate: flavourful, ripe fruit, complex, good structure.

BODEGAS BETOLAZA S.C.

Cuesta Dulce, 12
26330 Briones (La Rioja)
☎: +34 650 862 104
Fax: +34 941 322 281
betolaza@betolaza.es
www.betolaza.es

Betolaza 2012 TC
90% tempranillo, 5% garnacha, 5% mazuelo

84

BODEGAS BILBAÍNAS

Estación, 3
26200 Haro (La Rioja)
☎: +34 941 310 147
info@bodegasbilbainas.com
www.grupocodorniu.com

La Vicalanda 2008 TGR
100% tempranillo

94

Colour: cherry, garnet rim. Nose: balanced, complex, ripe fruit, spicy, fine reductive notes. Palate: good structure, flavourful, round tannins, balanced.

La Vicalanda 2010 TR
100% tempranillo

92

Colour: light cherry. Nose: aged wood nuances, toasty, wet leather, aromatic coffee, dark chocolate. Palate: spicy, toasty, flavourful.

Vinos Singulares de Viña Pomal Garnacha 2010 T
100% garnacha

90

Colour: very deep cherry, garnet rim. Nose: expressive, complex, mineral, balsamic herbs, balanced. Palate: full, flavourful, round tannins.

Vinos Singulares de Viña Pomal Graciano 2010 T
100% graciano

93

Colour: cherry, garnet rim. Nose: smoky, spicy, ripe fruit, balsamic herbs. Palate: flavourful, smoky aftertaste, ripe fruit.

Vinos Singulares de Viña Pomal Tempranillo 2013 B
100% tempranillo blanco

90

Colour: bright straw, greenish rim. Nose: fresh fruit, expressive, characterful, dried flowers, faded flowers. Palate: easy to drink, fine bitter notes.

Viña Pomal "Alto de la Caseta" 2010 T
100% tempranillo

92

Colour: cherry, garnet rim. Nose: ripe fruit, creamy oak, balsamic herbs. Palate: spicy, toasty, flavourful.

Viña Pomal 106 Barricas 2010 T
90% tempranillo, 5% garnacha, 5% graciano

90

Colour: light cherry. Nose: aged wood nuances, toasty, ripe fruit, expressive, wet leather. Palate: spicy, toasty, flavourful.

Viña Pomal 2009 TGR
100% tempranillo

91

Colour: pale ruby, brick rim edge. Nose: spicy, fine reductive notes, wet leather, aged wood nuances, fruit liqueur notes. Palate: spicy, fine tannins, balanced.

Viña Pomal 2010 TR
100% tempranillo

89

Colour: light cherry. Nose: fine reductive notes, aged wood nuances, toasty, ripe fruit. Palate: spicy, toasty, flavourful.

Viña Pomal 2011 TC
100% tempranillo

88

Colour: ruby red. Nose: ripe fruit, wild herbs, earthy notes, spicy, fine reductive notes. Palate: balanced, flavourful, long.

Viña Pomal 2012 TC
100% tempranillo

87

Colour: bright cherry. Nose: sweet spices, creamy oak, wet leather. Palate: flavourful, fruity, toasty, round tannins.

Viña Pomal 2013 B
70% viura, 30% malvasía

85

Viña Zaco 2010 T
tempranillo

86 ♣

Viña Zaco 2012 T
100% tempranillo

87

Colour: bright cherry. Nose: ripe fruit, sweet spices, creamy oak. Palate: flavourful, toasty, round tannins.

BODEGAS BURGO VIEJO

Concordia, 8
26540 Alfaro (La Rioja)
☎: +34 941 183 405
Fax: +34 941 181 603
bodegas@burgoviejo.com
www.burgoviejo.com

Burgo Viejo 2010 TR
85% tempranillo, 10% graciano, 5% mazuelo

88

Colour: cherry, garnet rim. Nose: ripe fruit, earthy notes, balsamic herbs, creamy oak. Palate: balanced, flavourful, long, balsamic.

Burgo Viejo 2012 TC
90% tempranillo, 10% graciano
86

Burgo Viejo 2014 T
85% tempranillo, 10% garnacha, 5% mazuelo
85

Burgo Viejo Graciano 2014 T
100% graciano
82

Licenciado 2010 TR
100% tempranillo
89
Colour: cherry, garnet rim. Nose: ripe fruit, spicy, creamy oak, complex. Palate: flavourful, toasty.

Palacio de Invierno 2010 TR
100% tempranillo
88
Colour: bright cherry. Nose: ripe fruit, sweet spices, creamy oak, expressive. Palate: flavourful, fruity, toasty, round tannins.

Palacio de Invierno 2012 TC
100% tempranillo
86

BODEGAS CAMPILLO

Ctra. de Logroño, s/n
01300 Laguardia (Álava)
☎: +34 945 600 826
Fax: +34 945 600 837
info@bodegascampillo.es
www.bodegascampillo.es

Campillo 2004 TGR
93
Colour: cherry, garnet rim. Nose: balanced, complex, ripe fruit, spicy, fine reductive notes. Palate: good structure, flavourful, balanced.

Campillo 2011 TC
90
Colour: cherry, garnet rim. Nose: creamy oak, red berry notes, balanced, ripe fruit. Palate: flavourful, spicy, elegant.

Campillo 2014 BFB
90
Colour: bright yellow. Nose: ripe fruit, powerfull, toasty, aged wood nuances. Palate: spicy, toasty, long.

Campillo 2014 RD
85

Campillo Finca Cuesta Clara 2008 TR
94
Colour: cherry, garnet rim. Nose: balanced, complex, ripe fruit, spicy, fine reductive notes. Palate: good structure, flavourful, round tannins, balanced.

Campillo Reserva Especial 2008 TR
90
Colour: bright cherry, garnet rim. Nose: ripe fruit, fine reductive notes, spicy, expressive. Palate: flavourful, classic aged character.

Campillo Reserva Selecta 2008 TR
92
Colour: cherry, garnet rim. Nose: ripe fruit, wild herbs, earthy notes, spicy, balsamic herbs, tobacco. Palate: balanced, flavourful, long, balsamic.

El Niño de Campillo 2013 T
88
Colour: bright cherry. Nose: ripe fruit, sweet spices, expressive. Palate: flavourful, fruity, round tannins, easy to drink.

BODEGAS CAMPO VIEJO

Camino de la Puebla, 50
26006 Logroño (La Rioja)
☎: +34 941 279 900
campoviejo@pernod-ricard.com
www.campoviejo.com

Alcorta 2009 TR
tempranillo
88
Colour: cherry, garnet rim. Nose: ripe fruit, spicy, creamy oak, fine reductive notes. Palate: flavourful, toasty, round tannins.

Alcorta 2010 TR
tempranillo
90
Colour: cherry, garnet rim. Nose: red berry notes, ripe fruit, spicy, complex. Palate: flavourful, toasty, round tannins.

Alcorta 2012 TC
tempranillo

87

Colour: cherry, garnet rim. Nose: balanced, medium intensity, ripe fruit, spicy. Palate: correct, easy to drink.

Azpilicueta 2010 TR
tempranillo, graciano, mazuelo

91

Colour: cherry, garnet rim. Nose: red berry notes, ripe fruit, spicy, creamy oak, complex. Palate: flavourful, toasty, round tannins.

Azpilicueta 2012 TC
tempranillo, graciano, mazuelo

90

Colour: cherry, garnet rim. Nose: creamy oak, red berry notes, balanced. Palate: flavourful, spicy, fruity aftestaste.

Azpilicueta 2014 B
viura

89

Colour: bright yellow. Nose: expressive, dried herbs, ripe fruit, spicy. Palate: flavourful, fruity, good acidity, balanced.

Azpilicueta 2014 RD
tempranillo, viura

88

Colour: brilliant rose. Nose: ripe fruit, rose petals, balanced, expressive. Palate: fruity, flavourful, good acidity, fine bitter notes.

Azpilicueta Origen 2011 TC
tempranillo

92

Colour: cherry, garnet rim. Nose: ripe fruit, spicy, creamy oak, complex. Palate: powerful, flavourful, round tannins.

Campo Viejo 2009 TGR
tempranillo, graciano, mazuelo

89

Colour: cherry, garnet rim. Nose: balanced, complex, ripe fruit, spicy, fine reductive notes. Palate: good structure, flavourful, round tannins, balanced.

Campo Viejo 2012 TC
tempranillo, garnacha, mazuelo

86

Campo Viejo 2014 B
viura, verdejo, tempranillo blanco

86

Campo Viejo 2010 TR
tempranillo, graciano, mazuelo

87

Colour: ruby red. Nose: spicy, fine reductive notes, wet leather, aged wood nuances, fruit liqueur notes. Palate: spicy, balanced.

Campo Viejo 2014 RD
tempranillo

85

Campo Viejo 2014 Semidulce
viura

82

Campo Viejo Ecológico 2014 T
tempranillo, garnacha

86

Campo Viejo Vendimia Seleccionada 2012 TC
tempranillo

90

Colour: cherry, garnet rim. Nose: ripe fruit, spicy, balsamic herbs. Palate: balanced, flavourful, balsamic.

Dominio Campo Viejo 2011 T
tempranillo, graciano, mazuelo

91

Colour: cherry, garnet rim. Nose: red berry notes, ripe fruit, spicy, creamy oak, complex. Palate: flavourful, toasty, round tannins.

Félix Azpilicueta Colección Privada 2009 T
tempranillo, graciano, mazuelo

92

Colour: cherry, garnet rim. Nose: ripe fruit, wild herbs, earthy notes, spicy, balsamic herbs. Palate: balanced, flavourful, long.

Félix Azpilicueta Colección Privada 2013 BFB
viura

89

Colour: bright straw. Nose: white flowers, fine lees, dried herbs, ripe fruit, creamy oak. Palate: flavourful, fruity, good acidity, toasty.

Herencia Juan Alcorta 2009 TR
tempranillo

87

Colour: cherry, garnet rim. Nose: ripe fruit, old leather, tobacco. Palate: correct, flavourful, spicy.

Herencia Juan Alcorta 2012 TC
tempranillo

86

BODEGAS CARLOS SAN PEDRO PÉREZ DE VIÑASPRE

Páganos, 44- Bajo
01300 Laguardia (Álava)
☎: +34 945 600 146
Fax: +34 945 621 111
info@bodegascarlossampedro.com
www.bodegascarlossampedro.com

Carlos San Pedro 2008 T
tempranillo

90

Colour: ruby red. Nose: spicy, fine reductive notes, aged wood nuances, fruit liqueur notes. Palate: spicy, fine tannins, balanced.

Viñasperi 2011 TC
tempranillo

88

Colour: cherry, garnet rim. Nose: red berry notes, ripe fruit, spicy, creamy oak, complex. Palate: flavourful, toasty, round tannins.

BODEGAS CASA PRIMICIA

Camino de la Hoya, 1
01300 Laguardia (Álava)
☎: +34 945 600 296
Fax: +34 945 621 252
info@bodegascasaprimicia.com
www.bodegascasaprimicia.com

Carravalseca 2012 T
97% tempranillo, 3% graciano

90

Colour: cherry, garnet rim. Nose: smoky, spicy, ripe fruit. Palate: flavourful, smoky aftertaste, ripe fruit.

Casa Primicia GR Graciano 2012 T
100% graciano

87

Colour: cherry, garnet rim. Nose: ripe fruit, old leather, tobacco. Palate: correct, flavourful, spicy.

Casa Primicia T Tempranillo 2011 T
100% tempranillo

87

Colour: cherry, garnet rim. Nose: smoky, spicy, ripe fruit. Palate: flavourful, smoky aftertaste, ripe fruit.

Julián Madrid 2009 TR
80% tempranillo, 20% otras

88

Colour: cherry, garnet rim. Nose: roasted coffee, smoky, spicy, ripe fruit. Palate: flavourful, smoky aftertaste, ripe fruit.

BODEGAS CASTILLO DE MENDOZA, S.L.

Paraje San Juan, s/n
26338 San Vicente de la Sonsierra
(La Rioja)
☎: +34 941 334 496
Fax: +34 941 334 566
comercial@castillodemendoza.com
www.castillodemendoza.com

Castillo de Mendoza 2006 TR
100% tempranillo

87

Colour: cherry, garnet rim. Nose: ripe fruit, old leather, tobacco. Palate: correct, flavourful, spicy.

Chirimendo 2014 T Maceración Carbónica
100% tempranillo

87

Colour: cherry, purple rim. Nose: fresh fruit, red berry notes, floral. Palate: flavourful, fruity, good acidity.

Evento Castillo de Mendoza 2004 T
100% tempranillo

92

Colour: light cherry. Nose: fine reductive notes, aged wood nuances, toasty. Palate: spicy, toasty, flavourful.

Noralba Agricultura Ecológica 2012 TC
80% tempranillo, 20% graciano

87

Colour: cherry, garnet rim. Nose: ripe fruit, grassy, smoky. Palate: fine bitter notes, toasty.

Vitarán 2012 TC
100% tempranillo

88

Colour: bright cherry. Nose: ripe fruit, sweet spices, creamy oak, expressive. Palate: flavourful, fruity, round tannins.

Vitarán Cepas Viejas 2014 B
100% viura

86

BODEGAS CASTILLO DE SAJAZARRA

Del Río, s/n
26212 Sajazarra (La Rioja)
☎: +34 941 320 066
Fax: +34 941 320 251
bodega@castillodesajazarra.com
www.castillodesajazarra.com

Castillo de Sajazarra 2008 TR
97% tempranillo, 3% graciano

89

Colour: dark-red cherry, orangey edge. Nose: balanced, fine reductive notes, spicy, smoky. Palate: balanced, fine tannins.

Castillo de Sajazarra 2010 TR
95% tempranillo, 5% graciano

90

Colour: cherry, garnet rim. Nose: ripe fruit, spicy, creamy oak, complex. Palate: flavourful, toasty, round tannins.

Digma Graciano 2009 TR
95% graciano, 5% tempranillo

92

Colour: cherry, garnet rim. Nose: ripe fruit, wild herbs, earthy notes, spicy, balsamic herbs. Palate: balanced, flavourful, long, balsamic.

Digma Tempranillo 2009 TR
100% tempranillo

93

Colour: cherry, garnet rim. Nose: balanced, complex, ripe fruit, spicy. Palate: good structure, flavourful, round tannins, balanced.

Solar de Líbano 2009 TR
97% tempranillo, 3% graciano, garnacha

88

Colour: light cherry, orangey edge. Nose: ripe fruit, old leather, tobacco. Palate: correct, flavourful, spicy.

Solar de Líbano 2011 TC
93% tempranillo, 7% graciano

88

Colour: very deep cherry, garnet rim. Nose: balanced, scrubland, ripe fruit. Palate: flavourful, round tannins.

Solar de Líbano 2012 TC
93% tempranillo, 7% graciano

88

Colour: bright cherry. Nose: ripe fruit, sweet spices, creamy oak. Palate: flavourful, fruity, toasty.

BODEGAS CERROLAZA

Ctra. Burgos, Km. 5
Salida 13, La Grajera
26007 Logroño (La Rioja)
☎: +34 941 286 728
Fax: +34 941 286 729
info@altosdelmarques.com
www.altosdelmarques.com

Aticus 2008 TR
100% tempranillo

87

Colour: cherry, garnet rim. Nose: roasted coffee, smoky, spicy. Palate: flavourful, smoky aftertaste, ripe fruit.

Aticus 2012 TC
100% tempranillo

86

BODEGAS CONVERSA

Los Molinos de Ocon (La Rioja)
☎: +34 914 114 546
Fax: +34 915 642 498
clara@conversa-larioja.es
www.conversa-larioja.es

Conversa 2014 B
tempranillo blanco, sauvignon blanc, verdejo

85

BODEGAS CORRAL

Ctra. de Logroño, Km. 10
26370 Navarrete (La Rioja)
☎: +34 941 440 193
Fax: +34 941 440 195
info@donjacobo.es
www.donjacobo.es

Altos de Corral Single Estate 2005 TR
100% tempranillo

91

Colour: cherry, garnet rim. Nose: balanced, complex, ripe fruit, fine reductive notes, cocoa bean. Palate: good structure, flavourful, round tannins, balanced.

Don Jacobo 2004 TGR
85% tempranillo, 15% garnacha, graciano

90

Colour: light cherry, garnet rim. Nose: ripe fruit, old leather, tobacco. Palate: flavourful, spicy, classic aged character, fine tannins.

Don Jacobo 2009 TR
90% tempranillo, 10% garnacha, mazuelo, graciano

86

Don Jacobo 2010 TC
85% tempranillo, 10% garnacha, 5% mazuelo, graciano

87

Colour: cherry, garnet rim. Nose: old leather, tobacco, ripe fruit, fruit liqueur notes. Palate: spicy, reductive nuances.

Don Jacobo 2014 B
100% viura

84

Don Jacobo 2014 RD
50% tempranillo, 50% garnacha

80

BODEGAS COVILA

Camino del Soto, 26
01306 Lapuebla de Labarca (Álava)
☎: +34 945 627 232
Fax: +34 945 627 295
comercial@covila.es
www.covila.es

Covila 2009 TR
100% tempranillo

87

Colour: cherry, garnet rim. Nose: ripe fruit, spicy, creamy oak. Palate: flavourful, toasty, round tannins.

Covila 2013 TC
100% tempranillo

85

Covila 2014 B
100% viura

87

Colour: bright straw. Nose: white flowers, fresh fruit, fragrant herbs. Palate: flavourful, fruity, good acidity.

Pagos de Labarca AEX 2010 T
100% tempranillo

89

Colour: cherry, garnet rim. Nose: ripe fruit, spicy, creamy oak, woody. Palate: flavourful, toasty.

BODEGAS DAVID MORENO

Ctra. de Villar de Torre, s/n
26310 Badarán (La Rioja)
☎: +34 941 367 338
Fax: +34 941 418 685
davidmoreno@davidmoreno.es
www.davidmoreno.es

David Moreno 2007 TGR
90% tempranillo, 10% garnacha

90

Colour: pale ruby, brick rim edge. Nose: elegant, spicy, fine reductive notes, tobacco. Palate: spicy, fine tannins, elegant, long.

David Moreno 2008 TR
90% tempranillo, 10% garnacha

86

David Moreno 2012 TC
85% tempranillo, 15% garnacha

85

David Moreno 2014 B
100% viura

81

David Moreno 2014 RD
50% viura, 50% garnacha

84

David Moreno 2014 T
85% tempranillo, 15% garnacha

84

Dmoreno Selección de la Familia 2011 TC
90% tempranillo, 10% garnacha

87

Colour: cherry, garnet rim. Nose: fine reductive notes, wet leather, aged wood nuances. Palate: spicy, long, toasty.

BODEGAS DE CRIANZA MARQUÉS DE GRIÑÓN

Ctra. de El Ciego, s/n
26350 Cenicero (La Rioja)
☎: +34 913 878 612

Marqués de Griñón Alea 2012 TC

87

Colour: pale ruby, brick rim edge. Nose: spicy, fine reductive notes, fruit preserve, waxy notes. Palate: spicy, long, ripe fruit.

Marqués de Griñón Alea 2013 T

85

BODEGAS DE LOS HEREDEROS DEL MARQUÉS DE RISCAL S.L.

Torrea, 1
03140 Elciego (Álava)
☎: +34 945 606 000
Fax: +34 945 606 023
marquesderical@marquesderical.com
www.marquesderiscal.com

Arienzo 2012 TC

90% tempranillo, 5% graciano, 5% mazuelo

89

Colour: cherry, garnet rim. Nose: ripe fruit, spicy, creamy oak. Palate: powerful, flavourful, spicy.

Barón de Chirel 2011 TR

70% tempranillo, 30% otras

94

Colour: cherry, garnet rim. Nose: ripe fruit, wild herbs, earthy notes, spicy, balsamic herbs. Palate: balanced, flavourful, long, balsamic, elegant.

Finca Torrea 2011 T

90% tempranillo, 10% graciano

93

Colour: cherry, garnet rim. Nose: complex, ripe fruit, spicy, elegant, fine reductive notes. Palate: good structure, round tannins, balanced, full.

Marqués de Riscal 2005 TGR

90% tempranillo, 7% graciano, 3% mazuelo

93

Colour: cherry, garnet rim. Nose: balanced, ripe fruit, spicy, fine reductive notes, elegant. Palate: good structure, flavourful, balanced, fine tannins.

Marqués de Riscal 2011 TR

90% tempranillo, 7% graciano, 3% mazuelo

92

Colour: ruby red. Nose: balanced, complex, ripe fruit, spicy, fine reductive notes. Palate: good structure, flavourful, round tannins, balanced, classic aged character.

BODEGAS DEL MEDIEVO

Circunvalación San Roque, s/n
26559 Aldeanueva de Ebro (La Rioja)
☎: +34 941 116 314
Fax: +34 941 144 204
info@bodegasdelmedievo.com
www.bodegasdelmedievo.com

Cofrade 2014 T Maceración Carbónica

tempranillo

86

Medievo 2011 TR

tempranillo, garnacha, graciano, mazuelo

89

Colour: cherry, garnet rim. Nose: ripe fruit, spicy, creamy oak, complex. Palate: flavourful, toasty, round tannins.

Medievo 2012 TC

tempranillo, garnacha, mazuelo, graciano

87

Colour: bright cherry. Nose: ripe fruit, sweet spices, creamy oak, expressive. Palate: flavourful, fruity, toasty, round tannins.

Medievo 2013 T

tempranillo

83

Medievo 2014 B

viura

87

Colour: bright straw. Nose: white flowers, fine lees, dried herbs, ripe fruit, candied fruit, citrus fruit, varietal. Palate: flavourful, fruity, good acidity.

Notas del Medievo 2012 T

tempranillo

88

Colour: cherry, garnet rim. Nose: ripe fruit, wild herbs, earthy notes, spicy, balsamic herbs. Palate: balanced, flavourful, long, balsamic.

Tuercebotas 2012 TC

graciano

90

Colour: cherry, garnet rim. Nose: ripe fruit, wild herbs, earthy notes, spicy, balsamic herbs. Palate: balanced, flavourful, long, balsamic.

BODEGAS DOMECO DE JARAUTA

Camino Sendero Royal, 5
26559 Aldeanueva de Ebro (La Rioja)
☎: +34 941 163 078
Fax: +34 941 163 078
info@bodegasdomecodejarauta.com
www.bodegasdomecodejarauta.com

El Ansiado 2014 RD
100% garnacha
84

Viña Marro 2010 TR
90% tempranillo, 10% graciano
87
Colour: bright cherry, garnet rim. Nose: tobacco, dark chocolate, ripe fruit, dried herbs. Palate: correct, easy to drink.

Viña Marro 2012 TC
100% tempranillo
88
Colour: cherry, garnet rim. Nose: smoky, spicy, ripe fruit. Palate: flavourful, ripe fruit, toasty.

Viña Marro 2014 T
80% tempranillo, 20% garnacha
86

Viña Marro Ecológico 2013 T
100% tempranillo
87
Colour: cherry, garnet rim. Nose: scrubland, dried herbs, ripe fruit. Palate: fruity, easy to drink, correct.

Viña Marro Vendimia Seleccionada 2013 T
100% tempranillo
88
Colour: bright cherry, garnet rim. Nose: balanced, ripe fruit, sweet spices, toasty. Palate: correct, long.

BODEGAS EL CIDACOS

Ctra. de Carbonera, s/n
26512 Tudelilla (La Rioja)
☎: +34 941 152 058
Fax: +34 941 152 303
info@bodegaselcidacos.com
www.bodegaselcidacos.com

Conde Otiñano 2010 TR
80% tempranillo, 15% garnacha, 5% graciano
83

Conde Otiñano 2012 TC
80% tempranillo, 20% garnacha
86

Marqués de Abadía 2010 TR
80% tempranillo, 15% garnacha, 5% graciano
86

Marqués de Abadía 2011 TC
80% tempranillo, 20% garnacha
85

BODEGAS ESCUDERO

Finca La Legua, Ctra. N-232, km. 364
26510 Pradejon (La Rioja)
☎: +34 941 398 008
Fax: +34 941 398 070
info@familiaescudero.com
www.familiaescudero.com

Becquer 2011 T
70% tempranillo, 30% garnacha
87
Colour: cherry, garnet rim. Nose: wild herbs, earthy notes, spicy, old leather, fruit preserve. Palate: flavourful, long.

Becquer 2013 BFB
60% chardonnay, 40% viura
87
Colour: bright yellow. Nose: ripe fruit, faded flowers, creamy oak. Palate: spicy, ripe fruit.

Becquer Ecológico 2012 T
100% tempranillo
85

Becquer Ecológico 2012 TC
100% tempranillo
87
Colour: deep cherry, garnet rim. Nose: fruit preserve, sweet spices, cocoa bean. Palate: long, flavourful, round tannins.

Solar de Becquer 2012 TC
70% tempranillo, 20% mazuelo, 10% garnacha
86

Solar de Becquer 2014 T
40% tempranillo, 60% garnacha
86

Vinsacro 2010 T
40% vidau, 50% tempranillo, 10% mazuelo
89
Colour: cherry, garnet rim. Nose: ripe fruit, wild herbs, earthy notes, spicy, balsamic herbs. Palate: balanced, flavourful, long, balsamic.

Vinsacro Dioro 2010 T
100% vidau

90

Colour: very deep cherry, garnet rim. Nose: complex, balanced, cocoa bean, waxy notes. Palate: full, flavourful, round tannins.

BODEGAS ESTRAUNZA

Avda. La Poveda, 25
01306 Lapuebla de Labarca (Álava)
☎: +34 945 627 245
Fax: +34 945 627 293
contacto@bodegasestraunza.com
www.bodegasestraunza.com

Blas de Lezo 2012 TC
tempranillo

84

Blas de Lezo 2014 T
tempranillo

84

Solar de Estraunza 2005 TGR
tempranillo

86

Solar de Estraunza 2012 TC
tempranillo

86

Colour: cherry, garnet rim. Nose: smoky, spicy, ripe fruit. Palate: flavourful, smoky aftertaste, ripe fruit.

Solar de Estraunza 2007 TR
tempranillo

87

Colour: cherry, garnet rim. Nose: ripe fruit, wild herbs, spicy, tobacco. Palate: flavourful, long.

Solar de Estraunza 2014 B
viura

84

Solar de Estraunza 2014 RD
viura, tempranillo

85

Solar de Estraunza 2014 T
tempranillo

84

Solar de Estraunza Selección 2011 T
tempranillo

87

Colour: cherry, purple rim. Nose: ripe fruit, woody, roasted coffee. Palate: flavourful, spicy, powerful.

BODEGAS EXOPTO

Ctra. de Elvillar, 26
01300 Laguardia (Álava)
☎: +34 650 213 993
info@exopto.net
www.exopto.net

Bozeto de Exopto 2014 RD
50% garnacha, 50% tempranillo

85

Exopto Cuvée Paola 2012 T
60% graciano, 20% garnacha, 20% tempranillo

93

Colour: cherry, garnet rim. Nose: ripe fruit, wild herbs, earthy notes, spicy, balsamic herbs. Palate: balanced, flavourful, long, balsamic.

Horizonte de Exopto 2013 T
80% tempranillo, 10% graciano, 10% garnacha

89

Colour: cherry, purple rim. Nose: ripe fruit, woody, roasted coffee. Palate: flavourful, spicy, powerful, balanced.

BODEGAS FAUSTINO

Ctra. de Logroño, s/n
01320 Oyón (Álava)
☎: +34 945 622 500
Fax: +34 945 622 511
info@bodegasfaustino.es
www.bodegasfaustino.com

Faustino 2011 TC

87

Colour: cherry, garnet rim. Nose: creamy oak, spicy, ripe fruit, balanced. Palate: flavourful, spicy, correct.

Faustino de Autor Reserva Especial 2006 TR

89

Colour: cherry, garnet rim. Nose: ripe fruit, old leather, tobacco. Palate: correct, flavourful, spicy.

Faustino I 2005 TGR

90

Colour: cherry, garnet rim. Nose: spicy, fine reductive notes, aged wood nuances, ripe fruit. Palate: spicy, fine tannins, balanced.

Faustino I 75 Aniversario 2005 TGR

91

Colour: dark-red cherry. Nose: tobacco, spicy, characterful. Palate: classic aged character, long, fine tannins, ripe fruit.

Faustino V 2010 TR

88

Colour: very deep cherry, garnet rim. Nose: balsamic herbs, balanced, tobacco. Palate: full, flavourful, round tannins, spicy.

Faustino V 2014 B

86

Faustino V 2014 RD

88

Colour: rose, purple rim. Nose: red berry notes, floral. Palate: powerful, fruity, fresh.

Faustino VII S/C T

85

BODEGAS FINS DE SIGLO

Camino Arenzana de Arriba, 16
26311 Arenzana de Abajo (La Rioja)
☎: +34 932 233 022
Fax: +34 932 231 370
perelada@castilloperelada.com
www.bodegasfindesiglo.com

XIII Lunas 2012 T

55% garnacha, 45% tempranillo

87

Colour: cherry, garnet rim. Nose: creamy oak, red berry notes, balanced, ripe fruit. Palate: flavourful, spicy.

BODEGAS FLORENTINO MARTÍNEZ

Ermita, 33
26311 Cordovín (La Rioja)
☎: +34 941 418 614
Fax: +34 941 418 614
bodegas@florentinomartinez.com
www.florentinomartinez.com

Distercio 2010 T

100% tempranillo

86

Florentius 2014 B

80% viura, 20% malvasía

85

Tanka 2005 T

100% tempranillo

90

Colour: dark-red cherry, garnet rim. Nose: tobacco, fine reductive notes, balanced, ripe fruit, cocoa bean. Palate: good structure, flavourful.

BODEGAS FOS

Término de Vialba, s/n
01340 Elciego (Álava)
☎: +34 945 606 681
Fax: +34 945 606 608
fos@bodegasfos.com
www.bodegasfos.com

Fos 2009 TR

tempranillo, graciano

90

Colour: deep cherry, garnet rim. Nose: sweet spices, creamy oak, ripe fruit, expressive. Palate: good structure, round tannins.

Fos 2010 TR

85% tempranillo, 15% graciano

90

Colour: very deep cherry. Nose: ripe fruit, dried herbs, tobacco. Palate: balanced, ripe fruit, long, flavourful.

Fos 2011 TC

95% tempranillo, 5% graciano

89

Colour: bright cherry, garnet rim. Nose: balanced, ripe fruit, spicy, dried herbs. Palate: ripe fruit, round tannins, balanced.

Fos 2012 TC

95% tempranillo, 5% graciano

90

Colour: bright cherry. Nose: ripe fruit, sweet spices, creamy oak. Palate: flavourful, fruity, toasty, round tannins.

Fos 2014 B
100% viura

88

Colour: straw, greenish rim. Nose: medium intensity, ripe fruit, wild herbs. Palate: correct, easy to drink, fresh, fruity.

Fos 2014 T Maceración Carbónica
100% tempranillo

88

Colour: cherry, purple rim. Nose: expressive, red berry notes, violets, ripe fruit. Palate: flavourful, fruity, good acidity.

Fos Baranda 2011 T
100% tempranillo

93

Colour: cherry, garnet rim. Nose: mineral, expressive, spicy, ripe fruit. Palate: flavourful, ripe fruit, long, good acidity.

BODEGAS FRANCO ESPAÑOLAS

Cabo Noval, 2
26009 Logroño (La Rioja)
☎: +34 941 251 300
Fax: +34 941 262 948
info@francoespanolas.com
www.francoespanolas.com

Baron D'Anglade 2009 TR
tempranillo, mazuelo, graciano

92

Colour: light cherry. Nose: fine reductive notes, aged wood nuances, toasty. Palate: spicy, toasty, flavourful.

Excelso 2006 TGR
tempranillo, graciano, mazuelo

90

Colour: pale ruby, brick rim edge. Nose: spicy, fine reductive notes, wet leather, aged wood nuances, fruit liqueur notes. Palate: spicy, fine tannins, balanced.

Graciela 2003 B Reserva
viura, malvasía

90

Colour: bright yellow. Nose: balsamic herbs, honeyed notes, floral, sweet spices, expressive. Palate: rich, fruity, powerful, flavourful, elegant.

Rioja Bordón 2006 TGR
tempranillo, graciano, mazuelo

89

Colour: cherry, garnet rim. Nose: smoky, spicy, ripe fruit. Palate: flavourful, smoky aftertaste, ripe fruit.

Rioja Bordón 2009 TR
tempranillo, garnacha, mazuelo

87

Colour: cherry, garnet rim. Nose: ripe fruit, old leather, tobacco. Palate: correct, flavourful, spicy.

Rioja Bordón 2012 TC
tempranillo, garnacha

84

Rioja Bordón RB 2012 TC
tempranillo

88

Colour: bright cherry. Nose: ripe fruit, sweet spices, creamy oak. Palate: flavourful, fruity, toasty, round tannins.

Viña Soledad 2014 B
100% viura

84

BODEGAS FUIDIO

San Bartolome, 32
01322 Yécora (Álava)
☎: +34 679 255 045
bodegas@fuidio.com
www.fuidio.com

Fuidio 2014 B
viura

83

Fuidio 2014 T
tempranillo

84

Fuidio Iraley 2012 T
tempranillo

84

BODEGAS GARCÍA DE OLANO

Ctra. Vitoria, s/n
01309 Paganos (Álava)
☎: +34 945 621 146
info@garciadeolano.com
www.garciadeolano.com

3 de Olano 2012 TC
100% tempranillo

88

Colour: cherry, garnet rim. Nose: smoky, spicy, ripe fruit. Palate: flavourful, ripe fruit.

3 de Olano Selección 2010 T
100% tempranillo

92

Colour: cherry, garnet rim. Nose: creamy oak, red berry notes, balanced, ripe fruit. Palate: flavourful, spicy, elegant.

Heredad García de Olano 2012 TC
100% tempranillo

88

Colour: bright cherry, garnet rim. Nose: ripe fruit, spicy, varietal. Palate: fruity, balanced.

Heredad García de Olano 2013 T Barrica
100% tempranillo

87

Colour: bright cherry. Nose: ripe fruit, sweet spices, creamy oak, balsamic herbs. Palate: fruity, round tannins.

Heredad García de Olano 2014 B
90% viura, 10% verdejo

84

Heredad García de Olano 2014 T
95% tempranillo, 5% viura

84

Mauleón 2008 TR
100% tempranillo

86

Olanum Selección 2009 T Barrica
100% tempranillo

89

Colour: cherry, garnet rim. Nose: spicy, ripe fruit. Palate: flavourful, ripe fruit, long, good acidity, balanced.

BODEGAS GONZÁLEZ-PURAS

Los Carros, 34
26340 San Asensio (La Rioja)
☎: +34 687 936 272
info@bodegasgonzalezpuras.com
www.bodegasgonzalezpuras.com

González Puras 2012 TC
tempranillo

87

Colour: cherry, garnet rim. Nose: creamy oak, red berry notes, balanced. Palate: flavourful, spicy.

González Puras 2014 B
viura

84

González Puras 2014 RD
70% viura, 30% tempranillo

84

González Puras 2014 T
tempranillo

86

BODEGAS GRAN FEUDO

Ribera, 34
31592 Cintruénigo (Navarra)
☎: +34 948 811 000
Fax: +34 948 811 407
info@granfeudo.com
www.granfeudo.com

Gran Feudo Tempranillo Rioja 2014 T
tempranillo

85

BODEGAS GRUPO YLLERA

Autovía A-6, Km. 173,5
47490 Rueda (Valladolid)
☎: +34 983 868 097
Fax: +34 983 868 177
grupoyllera@grupoyllera.com
www.grupoyllera.com

Coelus 2009 TR
tempranillo

84

Coelus 2011 TC
tempranillo

86

Coelus Joven 2014 T
tempranillo

85

BODEGAS HEREDAD DE BAROJA

Cercas Altas, 6
01309 Elvillar (Álava)
☎: +34 945 604 068
Fax: +34 945 604 105
info@heredadbaroja.com
www.heredadbaroja.com

Mendizabal 2014 T

84

BODEGAS HERMANOS LAREDO VILLANUEVA C.B.

Mayor, 18
01309 Leza (Álava)
☎: +34 945 605 018
Fax: +34 945 605 178
bodegaslaredo@telefonica.net
www.bodegaslaredo.com

Laredo Anaiak 2013 T
90% tempranillo, 10% mazuelo

84

Laredo Anaiak 2014 B
80% viura, 20% malvasía

83

Laredo Anaiak 2014 RD
80% tempranillo, 20% garnacha

87

Colour: rose, purple rim. Nose: fruit preserve, warm. Palate: powerful, flavourful, round.

Señorío de Laredo 2004 TGR
80% tempranillo, 10% graciano, 10% mazuelo

89

Colour: pale ruby, brick rim edge. Nose: spicy, fine reductive notes, wet leather, aged wood nuances, fruit liqueur notes. Palate: spicy, fine tannins, balanced, elegant.

Señorío de Laredo 2005 TR
80% tempranillo, 10% graciano, 10% mazuelo

87

Colour: ruby red. Nose: fine reductive notes, wet leather, aged wood nuances. Palate: spicy, long, toasty.

Señorío de Laredo 2010 TC
80% tempranillo, 10% graciano, 10% mazuelo

85

BODEGAS HERMANOS PECIÑA

Ctra. de Vitoria, Km. 47
26338 San Vicente de la Sonsierra (La Rioja)
☎: +34 941 334 366
Fax: +34 941 334 180
info@bodegashermanospecina.com
www.bodegashermanospecina.com

Chobeo de Peciña 2009 T
100% tempranillo

89

Colour: cherry, garnet rim. Nose: ripe fruit, old leather, tobacco. Palate: correct, flavourful, spicy, fruity.

Chobeo de Peciña 2014 BFB
100% viura

88

Colour: bright yellow. Nose: ripe fruit, toasty, aged wood nuances, pattiserie. Palate: flavourful, spicy, toasty, long.

Gran Chobeo de Peciña 2008 T
100% tempranillo

91

Colour: cherry, garnet rim. Nose: balanced, complex, ripe fruit, spicy, fine reductive notes. Palate: flavourful, round tannins, balanced.

Señorío de P. Peciña 2009 TR
95% tempranillo, 5% graciano, garnacha

87

Colour: dark-red cherry, orangey edge. Nose: fruit preserve, woody, tobacco. Palate: correct, balanced, spicy, classic aged character.

Señorío de P. Peciña 2011 TC
95% tempranillo, 5% graciano, garnacha

86

Señorío de P. Peciña 2014 B
100% viura

85

Señorío de P. Peciña Vendimia Seleccionada 2006 T
95% tempranillo, 5% graciano, garnacha

88

Colour: dark-red cherry, orangey edge. Nose: animal reductive notes, old leather, spicy. Palate: reductive nuances, spicy.

BODEGAS HERMOSILLA

Avda. del Río Ebro, 36
01307 Baños de Ebro (Álava)
☎: +34 945 609 162
www.bodegashermosilla.com

Hermosilla 2010 TR
100% tempranillo

88

Colour: bright cherry, purple rim. Nose: ripe fruit, red berry notes, sweet spices, balsamic herbs. Palate: fruity, round tannins, fruity aftestaste.

Hermosilla 2012 TC
100% tempranillo

86

J. I. Hermosilla 2014 T Maceración Carbónica
tempranillo, viura

84

BODEGAS IDIAQUEZ
San Vicente, 33
01307 Baños de Ebro (Álava)
☎: +34 626 078 840
info@bodegasidiaquez.com
www.bodegasidiaquez.com

Idiaquez 2014 T
95% tempranillo, 5% viura

85

BODEGAS IZADI
Herrería Travesía II, 5
01307 Villabuena de Álava (Álava)
☎: +34 945 609 086
Fax: +34 945 609 261
izadi@izadi.com
www.izadi.com

Izadi 2012 TC
100% tempranillo

89

Colour: bright cherry. Nose: sweet spices, creamy oak, overripe fruit. Palate: flavourful, fruity, toasty, round tannins.

Izadi 2014 BFB
80% viura, 20% malvasía

91

Colour: bright straw. Nose: white flowers, fresh fruit, fragrant herbs, sweet spices, toasty. Palate: flavourful, fruity, good acidity, balanced.

Izadi El Regalo 2012 TR
100% tempranillo

93

Colour: cherry, garnet rim. Nose: mineral, spicy. Palate: flavourful, ripe fruit, long, good acidity, balanced.

Izadi Larrosa 2014 RD
85% garnacha, 15% tempranillo

88

Colour: onion pink. Nose: red berry notes, floral, fragrant herbs. Palate: light-bodied, flavourful, good acidity, long, spicy.

Izadi Selección 2011 T
80% tempranillo, 20% graciano

93

Colour: cherry, garnet rim. Nose: mineral, spicy. Palate: flavourful, ripe fruit, long, good acidity, balanced.

BODEGAS JAVIER SAN PEDRO ORTEGA
Camino de la Hoya, 5
01300 Laguardia (Alava)
☎: +34 636 082 927
info@bodegasjaviersanpedro.com
www.bodegasjaviersanpedro.com

Anahi Dulce 2014 B
malvasía, sauvignon blanc, tempranillo blanco

88

Colour: bright yellow. Nose: powerfull, candied fruit, dried herbs. Palate: flavourful, sweet, ripe fruit, good acidity.

Cueva de Lobos 2012 TC
tempranillo

88

Colour: very deep cherry, garnet rim. Nose: balsamic herbs, balanced. Palate: full, flavourful, round tannins.

Cueva de Lobos 2014 B
tempranillo blanco, viura

87

Colour: yellow. Nose: ripe fruit, faded flowers, dried flowers. Palate: easy to drink, fine bitter notes.

Cueva de Lobos 2014 T
tempranillo

88

Colour: cherry, purple rim. Nose: expressive, fruit expression, red berry notes, floral. Palate: correct, easy to drink, good finish.

Viuda Negra "Nunca Jamás" 2014 T
tempranillo, garnacha, graciano

90

Colour: deep cherry, purple rim. Nose: scrubland, ripe fruit, floral, balanced, spicy. Palate: easy to drink, ripe fruit, balsamic.

Viuda Negra 2012 TC
100% tempranillo

89

Colour: deep cherry, garnet rim. Nose: ripe fruit, dried herbs, spicy. Palate: balanced, good acidity, round tannins.

Viuda Negra La Taconera 2013 T
tempranillo

92

Colour: cherry, garnet rim. Nose: mineral, expressive, spicy. Palate: flavourful, ripe fruit, long, good acidity, balanced.

Viuda Negra Villahuercos 2014 B
tempranillo blanco

92

Colour: bright straw. Nose: ripe fruit, spicy, balanced, tropical fruit, expressive. Palate: balanced, good acidity.

BODEGAS LA CATEDRAL

Avda. de Mendavia, 30
26009 Logroño (La Rioja)
☎: +34 941 235 299
Fax: +34 941 253 703

Rivallana 2010 TR

90% tempranillo, 5% garnacha, 5% mazuelo, graciano

89

Colour: light cherry. Nose: fine reductive notes, aged wood nuances, toasty, ripe fruit. Palate: spicy, toasty, flavourful.

Rivallana 2013 TC

80% tempranillo, 10% garnacha, 10% mazuelo, graciano

84

Rivallana Segundo Año 2013 T

80% tempranillo, 10% garnacha, 10% mazuelo, graciano

83

BODEGAS LA EMPERATRIZ

Ctra. Santo Domingo - Haro, km. 31,5
26241 Baños de Rioja (La Rioja)
☎: +34 941 300 105
Fax: +34 941 300 231
correo@bodegaslaemperatriz.com
www.bodegaslaemperatriz.com

Finca La Emperatriz 2009 TR

94% tempranillo, 3% garnacha, 2% viura, 1% graciano

90

Colour: dark-red cherry, garnet rim. Nose: creamy oak, sweet spices, cocoa bean. Palate: good structure, flavourful, round tannins.

Finca La Emperatriz 2010 TR

94% tempranillo, 3% garnacha, 2% viura, 1% graciano

91

Colour: cherry, garnet rim. Nose: ripe fruit, wild herbs, earthy notes, spicy, balsamic herbs. Palate: balanced, flavourful, long, balsamic.

Finca La Emperatriz 2012 TC

95% tempranillo, 3% garnacha, 2% viura

90

Colour: cherry, garnet rim. Nose: red berry notes, ripe fruit, fragrant herbs, spicy, creamy oak. Palate: powerful, flavourful, balanced.

Finca La Emperatriz Garnacha Cepas Viejas 2013 T

100% garnacha

91

Colour: ruby red. Nose: creamy oak, toasty, ripe fruit, balsamic herbs. Palate: balanced, spicy, good finish.

Finca La Emperatriz Terruño 2011 T

100% tempranillo

93

Colour: cherry, garnet rim. Nose: ripe fruit, spicy, creamy oak, complex, fragrant herbs, expressive. Palate: flavourful, toasty, round tannins, balanced.

RIOJA
DENOMINACIÓN DE ORIGEN CALIFICADA
RIOJA ALTA

Finca La Emperatriz
terruño

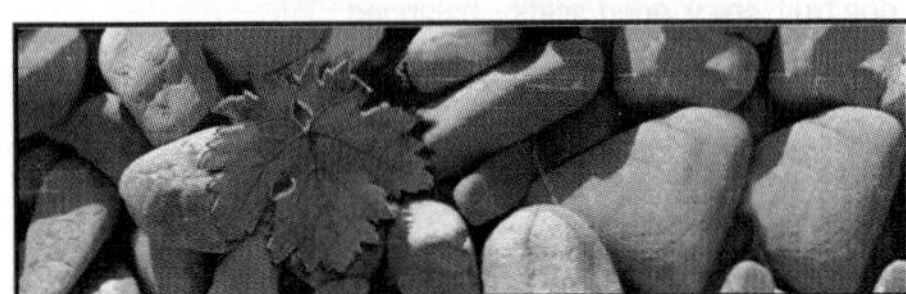

Finca La Emperatriz Parcela nº 1 2012 T
100% tempranillo

94

Colour: cherry, garnet rim. Nose: balanced, complex, ripe fruit, spicy, wild herbs, toasty. Palate: good structure, flavourful, round tannins, balanced.

Finca La Emperatriz Viura 2014 B
viura

88

Colour: bright straw, greenish rim. Nose: fresh fruit, fragrant herbs, balanced. Palate: fresh, fine bitter notes, good acidity.

Finca La Emperatriz Viura Cepas Viejas 2013 B
100% viura

91

Colour: bright yellow. Nose: balanced, ripe fruit, spicy. Palate: rich, smoky aftertaste, balanced, good acidity.

BODEGAS LACORT

Avda. Santo Domingo, 11
26200 Haro (La Rioja)
☎: +34 941 251 300
Fax: +34 941 262 948
info@bodegaslacort.com
www.bodegaslacort.com

Lacort 2012 TC
tempranillo, garnacha, mazuelo

87

Colour: deep cherry, purple rim. Nose: creamy oak, toasty, ripe fruit. Palate: balanced, spicy, long.

BODEGAS LACUS

Cervantes, 18
26559 Aldeanueva de Ebro (La Rioja)
☎: +34 649 331 799
Fax: +34 941 144 128
inedito@bodegaslacus.com
www.bodegaslacus.com

Inédito 2013 B
garnacha blanca

88

Colour: bright yellow. Nose: ripe fruit, floral. Palate: correct, ripe fruit, spicy, good acidity, balanced.

Inédito 3/3 2014 T
60% tempranillo, 20% garnacha, 20% graciano

89

Colour: cherry, purple rim. Nose: floral, balsamic herbs, ripe fruit. Palate: fruity, easy to drink, balanced.

Inédito Finca Turrax 2013 B
50% torrontés, 50% maturana blanca

92

Colour: bright straw. Nose: ripe fruit, complex, fresh fruit, fragrant herbs, mineral. Palate: balanced, long, good acidity.

Inédito S 2011 T
40% garnacha, 60% graciano

89

Colour: deep cherry, garnet rim. Nose: scrubland, dried herbs ripe fruit, balanced, spicy. Palate: flavourful, balanced.

BODEGAS LAGAR DE ZABALA

Pza. Mayor, 2
26338 San Vicente de la Sonsierra (La Rioja)
☎: +34 941 334 435
Fax: +34 941 334 435
bodegaslagardezabala@hotmail.com
www.bodegaslagardezabala.com

Lagar de Zabala 2010 TR
95% tempranillo, 5% garnacha

88

Colour: dark-red cherry, orangey edge. Nose: old leather, tobacco, spicy. Palate: flavourful, round tannins, balanced.

Lagar de Zabala 2011 TC
95% tempranillo, 5% garnacha

86

Lagar de Zabala 2014 T
100% tempranillo

87

Colour: bright cherry, purple rim. Nose: ripe fruit, expressive. Palate: flavourful, fruity, toasty, round tannins.

BODEGAS LAGUNILLA MARQUÉS DE LA CONCORDIA FAMILY OF WINES

Ctra. de Elciego, s/n
26350 Cenicero (La Rioja)
☎: +34 913 878 612
www.unitedwineries.com

Lagunilla 2011 TC
84

Lagunilla 2012 TC
84

Lagunilla Optimus 2010 T
tempranillo, syrah, merlot, cabernet sauvignon

90

Colour: cherry, garnet rim. Nose: fine reductive notes, ripe fruit, tobacco, complex. Palate: spicy, long, toasty, fine tannins.

Lagunilla The Family Collection 2007 TGR
0% tempranillo, 20% garnacha

87

Colour: pale ruby, brick rim edge. Nose: spicy, fine reductive notes, tobacco. Palate: spicy, fine tannins, long.

Lagunilla The Family Collection 2009 TR
80% tempranillo, 20% garnacha

88

Colour: cherry, garnet rim. Nose: ripe fruit, old leather, tobacco. Palate: correct, spicy.

BODEGAS LAN

Paraje del Buicio, s/n
26360 Fuenmayor (La Rioja)
☎: +34 941 450 950
Fax: +34 941 450 567
info@bodegaslan.com
www.bodegaslan.com

Culmen 2010 TR
85% tempranillo, 15% graciano

94

Colour: cherry, garnet rim. Nose: ripe fruit, wild herbs, earthy notes, spicy, balsamic herbs, balanced. Palate: balanced, flavourful, long, balsamic, elegant.

Lan 2007 TGR
90% tempranillo, 10% mazuelo

91

Colour: pale ruby, brick rim edge. Nose: elegant, spicy, fine reductive notes, tobacco. Palate: spicy, fine tannins, elegant, long.

Lan 2009 TR
92% tempranillo, 8% graciano

90

Colour: pale ruby, brick rim edge. Nose: spicy, fine reductive notes, aged wood nuances, fruit preserve. Palate: spicy, fine tannins, balanced.

Lan 2011 TC
95% tempranillo, 5% mazuelo

87

Colour: very deep cherry. Nose: expressive, complex, mineral, balsamic herbs, balanced. Palate: full, flavourful, round tannins.

Lan A Mano 2011 T
80% tempranillo, 12% graciano, 8% mazuelo

93

Colour: cherry, garnet rim. Nose: balanced, complex, ripe fruit, spicy, fine reductive notes, elegant. Palate: good structure, flavourful, round tannins, balanced.

Lan D-12 2012 T
100% tempranillo

90

Colour: cherry, garnet rim. Nose: ripe fruit, spicy, creamy oak, complex. Palate: flavourful, toasty, round tannins.

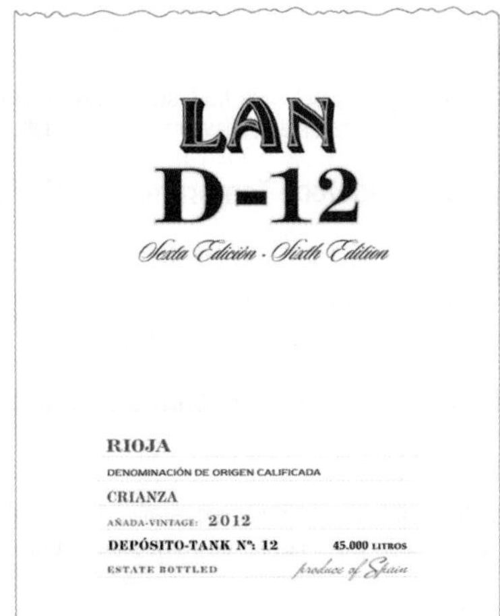

Viña Lanciano 2010 TR
85% tempranillo, 10% graciano, 5% mazuelo

90

Colour: cherry, garnet rim. Nose: ripe fruit, spicy, creamy oak, complex. Palate: flavourful, toasty, round tannins.

BODEGAS LANDALUCE
Ctra. Los Molinos, s/n
01300 Laguardia (Álava)
☎: +34 944 953 622
asier@bodegaslandaluce.es
www.bodegaslandaluce.es

Capricho de Landaluce 2009 T
100% tempranillo

92

Colour: cherry, garnet rim. Nose: ripe fruit, wild herbs, earthy notes, spicy, balsamic herbs. Palate: balanced, flavourful, long, balsamic, elegant.

Elle de Landaluce 2011 TC
90% tempranillo, 10% graciano

90

Colour: bright cherry. Nose: ripe fruit, sweet spices, creamy oak. Palate: flavourful, fruity, easy to drink.

Elle de Landaluce 2014 B
60% viura, 40% malvasía

85

Fincas de Landaluce 2010 TR
100% tempranillo

91

Colour: deep cherry. Nose: creamy oak, toasty, ripe fruit, balsamic herbs, expressive. Palate: spicy, long.

Fincas de Landaluce Graciano 2012 T
100% graciano

87

Colour: bright cherry. Nose: ripe fruit, sweet spices, creamy oak, fine reductive notes. Palate: flavourful, fruity, toasty.

Fincas de Landaluce Tempranillo 2012 TC
100% tempranillo

89

Colour: deep cherry, purple rim. Nose: creamy oak, toasty, ripe fruit, balsamic herbs. Palate: balanced, spicy, long.

Landaluce 2014 T Maceración Carbónica
95% tempranillo, 5% viura

89

Colour: cherry, purple rim. Nose: expressive, fresh fruit, red berry notes, floral. Palate: flavourful, fruity, good acidity.

BODEGAS LAR DE PAULA
Coscojal, s/n
01309 Elvillar (Álava)
☎: +34 945 604 068
Fax: +34 945 604 105
info@lardepaula.com
www.lardepaula.com

Lar de Paula 2009 TR
100% tempranillo

90

Colour: cherry, garnet rim. Nose: expressive, spicy, tobacco. Palate: flavourful, ripe fruit, long, good acidity, balanced.

Lar de Paula Madurado en Bodega 2013 T
100% tempranillo

86

Lar de Paula Merus 2011 TC
100% tempranillo

87

Colour: cherry, garnet rim. Nose: ripe fruit, tobacco, spicy. Palate: correct, good finish, good acidity.

Lar de Paula Merus 2013 BFB
60% viura, 40% malvasía

87

Colour: bright yellow. Nose: ripe fruit, toasty, aged wood nuances, pattiserie. Palate: flavourful, fruity, spicy.

Merus.4 2010 T
100% tempranillo

90

Colour: dark-red cherry. Nose: balsamic herbs, balanced, ripe fruit. Palate: full, flavourful, round tannins.

BODEGAS LARRAZ
Paraje Ribarrey. Pol. 12- Parcela 50
26350 Cenicero (La Rioja)
☎: +34 639 728 581
info@bodegaslarraz.com
www.bodegaslarraz.com

Caudum Bodegas Larraz 2008 T
100% tempranillo

89

Colour: ruby red. Nose: spicy, fine reductive notes, aged wood nuances. Palate: spicy, fine tannins, balanced.

Caudum Bodegas Larraz 2010 T
100% tempranillo

90

Colour: cherry, garnet rim. Nose: ripe fruit, wild herbs, spicy, balsamic herbs, fine reductive notes. Palate: balanced, flavourful, long, balsamic.

Caudum Bodegas Larraz 2011 T
100% tempranillo

88

Colour: cherry, garnet rim. Nose: ripe fruit, spicy, creamy oak. Palate: flavourful, toasty.

Caudum Bodegas Larraz Selección Especial 2007 T
100% tempranillo

91

Colour: cherry, garnet rim. Nose: ripe fruit, wild herbs, earthy notes, spicy, balsamic herbs. Palate: balanced, flavourful, long, balsamic.

Caudum Bodegas Larraz Selección Especial 2009 T
100% tempranillo

90

Colour: cherry, garnet rim. Nose: ripe fruit, spicy, creamy oak, complex. Palate: flavourful, toasty.

BODEGAS LAS CEPAS

Ctra Najera-Cenicero s/n
26007 Uruñuela (La Rioja)
☎: +34 615 996 878
dominiodelaertes@hotmail.com
www.lascepasriojawine.com

Costalarbol 2012 TC
60% graciano, 20% garnacha, 20% tempranillo

90

Colour: cherry, garnet rim. Nose: red berry notes, ripe fruit, spicy, creamy oak, complex. Palate: flavourful, toasty, round tannins.

Costalarbol Graciano 2012 T
100% graciano

89

Colour: cherry, garnet rim. Nose: ripe fruit, wild herbs, earthy notes, spicy, balsamic herbs. Palate: balanced, flavourful, long, balsamic.

Costalarbol Graciano 2013 T
100% graciano

88

Colour: deep cherry, purple rim. Nose: creamy oak, toasty, ripe fruit, balsamic herbs. Palate: balanced, spicy, long.

Dominio de Laertes 2012 TC
80% tempranillo, 20% graciano

87

Colour: dark-red cherry, garnet rim. Nose: fruit preserve, overripe fruit, spicy. Palate: correct, round tannins.

Dominio de Laertes Eco 2012 TC
70% tempranillo, 15% garnacha, 15% graciano

88

Colour: cherry, garnet rim. Nose: smoky, spicy, ripe fruit. Palate: flavourful, ripe fruit.

Garnacha 1921 2014 T
100% garnacha

88

Colour: very deep cherry, purple rim. Nose: expressive, floral, fruit preserve. Palate: flavourful, fruity, good acidity, balsamic.

Legado Decand 2012 T
80% graciano, 20% garnacha

90

Colour: bright cherry, garnet rim. Nose: ripe fruit, fruit preserve, spicy. Palate: good structure, flavourful.

Legado Decand 2013 T
100% graciano

89

Colour: very deep cherry, garnet rim. Nose: scrubland, varietal, ripe fruit. Palate: flavourful, round tannins, balsamic.

Serezhade 2014 B
70% verdejo, 30% viura

88

Colour: bright yellow. Nose: ripe fruit, powerfull, toasty, sweet spices. Palate: flavourful, fruity, spicy.

BODEGAS LAUNA

Ctra. Vitoria-Logroño, Km. 57
01300 Laguardia (Alava)
☎: +34 946 824 108
Fax: +34 956 824 108
info@bodegaslauna.com
www.bodegaslauna.com

Ikunus Magnum 2011 T
100% tempranillo

91

Colour: cherry, garnet rim. Nose: ripe fruit, spicy, creamy oak, complex. Palate: flavourful, toasty, round tannins.

Launa 2013 TC
90% tempranillo, 10% mazuelo

87

Colour: cherry, garnet rim. Nose: creamy oak, red berry notes, balanced. Palate: flavourful, spicy, elegant.

Launa Selección Familiar 2011 TR
90% tempranillo, 10% mazuelo, graciano

91

Colour: cherry, garnet rim. Nose: ripe fruit, spicy, creamy oak, complex, fine reductive notes. Palate: flavourful, toasty, round tannins.

Launa Selección Familiar 2013 TC
100% tempranillo

88

Colour: cherry, garnet rim. Nose: roasted coffee, smoky, spicy, ripe fruit. Palate: flavourful, smoky aftertaste, ripe fruit.

Teo's 2011 T
100% tempranillo

90

Colour: deep cherry, purple rim. Nose: creamy oak, toasty, ripe fruit, balsamic herbs, fine reductive notes. Palate: balanced, spicy, long.

BODEGAS LEZA GARCÍA

San Ignacio, 26
26313 Uruñuela (La Rioja)
☎: +34 941 371 142
Fax: +34 941 371 035
bodegasleza@bodegasleza.com
www.bodegasleza.com

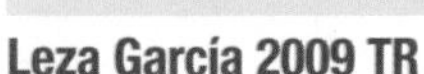

Leza García 2009 TR
90% tempranillo, 10% garnacha

87

Colour: cherry, garnet rim. Nose: ripe fruit, old leather, tobacco. Palate: correct, flavourful, spicy.

Leza García Tinto Familia 2011 T
100% tempranillo

88

Colour: cherry, purple rim. Nose: ripe fruit, woody, roasted coffee. Palate: flavourful, spicy, powerful.

LG de Leza García 2012 T
100% tempranillo

88

Colour: cherry, garnet rim. Nose: roasted coffee, smoky, spicy, ripe fruit. Palate: flavourful, smoky aftertaste, ripe fruit.

Nube de Leza García 2014 B
100% viura

85

Nube de Leza García Semidulce 2014 RD
100% garnacha

84

Valdepalacios 2012 TC
85% tempranillo, 10% garnacha, mazuelo

85

Valdepalacios 2014 B
100% viura

85

Valdepalacios Vendimia Seleccionada 2012 T
80% tempranillo, 20% garnacha

86

BODEGAS LOLI CASADO

Avda. La Poveda, 46
01306 Lapuebla de Labarca (Álava)
☎: +34 945 607 096
Fax: +34 945 607 412
loli@bodegaslolicasado.com
www.bodegaslolicasado.com

Jaun de Alzate 2009 TR
90% tempranillo, 5% graciano, 5% mazuelo

90

Colour: cherry, garnet rim. Nose: mineral, expressive, spicy. Palate: flavourful, ripe fruit, long, good acidity, balanced.

Jaun de Alzate 2011 TC
90% tempranillo, 5% graciano, 5% mazuelo

89

Colour: bright cherry. Nose: ripe fruit, sweet spices, creamy oak, expressive. Palate: flavourful, fruity, toasty, round tannins.

Jaun de Alzate 2014 T
90% tempranillo, 5% graciano, 5% mazuelo

88

Colour: cherry, purple rim. Nose: expressive, fresh fruit, red berry notes, floral, maceration notes. Palate: flavourful, fruity, good acidity.

Jaun de Alzate Vendimia Seleccionada 2013 T
90% tempranillo, 5% graciano, 5% mazuelo

87

Colour: bright cherry. Nose: toasty, balsamic herbs, fruit liqueur notes. Palate: balanced, spicy, long.

Polus 2011 TC
100% tempranillo

88

Colour: very deep cherry, garnet rim. Nose: balsamic herbs, ripe fruit, fine reductive notes. Palate: full, flavourful, round tannins.

Polus Graciano 2011 T
85% graciano, 15% tempranillo

89

Colour: cherry, garnet rim. Nose: spicy, fragrant herbs, ripe fruit. Palate: flavourful, ripe fruit, good acidity, balanced.

Polus Tempranillo 2013 T
100% tempranillo

84

Polus Vendimia Seleccionada 2012 T
100% tempranillo

87

Colour: cherry, garnet rim. Nose: ripe fruit, wild herbs, balsamic herbs. Palate: balanced, flavourful, long, balsamic.

Polus Viura 2014 B
100% viura

85

BODEGAS LÓPEZ ORIA

Ctra. Elvillar, 21
01300 Laguardia (Alava)
☎: +34 649 628 420
info@bodegaslopezoria.com
www.bodegaslopezoria.com

Pola 2008 TR
tempranillo

86

Pola 2012 TC
tempranillo

87

Colour: bright cherry. Nose: ripe fruit, sweet spices, creamy oak. Palate: flavourful, fruity, round tannins.

Pola 2014 T Maceración Carbónica
tempranillo

89

Colour: cherry, purple rim. Nose: expressive, fresh fruit, red berry notes, floral. Palate: flavourful, fruity, good acidity.

Pola Antonio López 2011 T

86

BODEGAS LUIS ALEGRE

Ctra. Navaridas, s/n
01300 Laguardia (Álava)
☎: +34 945 600 089
Fax: +34 945 600 729
luisalegre@bodegasluisalegre.com
www.luisalegre.com

Finca la Reñana 2011 TR
95% tempranillo, 5% graciano, garnacha, mazuelo

90

Colour: cherry, garnet rim. Nose: balanced, complex, ripe fruit, spicy, fine reductive notes. Palate: good structure, flavourful, round tannins, balanced.

Gran Vino Pontac 2011 T
95% tempranillo, 5% graciano

91

Colour: cherry, garnet rim. Nose: mineral, expressive, spicy, ripe fruit. Palate: flavourful, ripe fruit, long, balanced.

Gran Vino Pontac de Portiles 2011 T
90% tempranillo, 10% garnacha

92

Colour: cherry, garnet rim. Nose: ripe fruit, spicy, creamy oak, complex. Palate: flavourful, toasty, round tannins.

Koden de Luis Alegre 2014 T

90

Colour: cherry, purple rim. Nose: red berry notes, floral, balsamic herbs, balanced. Palate: powerful, fresh, fruity.

Luis Alegre 2011 TR
90% tempranillo, 10% graciano, garnacha, mazuelo

89

Colour: cherry, garnet rim. Nose: ripe fruit, sweet spices, creamy oak, expressive. Palate: powerful, flavourful, correct.

Luis Alegre 2014 RD
60% tempranillo, 40% viura

85

Luis Alegre Parcela Nº 5 La Minoría 2011 TR
100% tempranillo

89

Colour: cherry, garnet rim. Nose: ripe fruit, spicy, creamy oak, complex. Palate: flavourful, toasty, balanced.

Luis Alegre Selección Especial 2006 TR
95% tempranillo, 5% graciano, garnacha, mazuelo

90

Colour: pale ruby, brick rim edge. Nose: elegant, spicy, fine reductive notes, tobacco. Palate: spicy, fine tannins, elegant, long.

BODEGAS LUIS CAÑAS

Ctra. Samaniego, 10
01307 Villabuena (Álava)
☎: +34 945 623 373
Fax: +34 945 609 289
bodegas@luiscanas.com
www.luiscanas.com

Luis Cañas 2008 TGR

95% tempranillo, 5% graciano

91

Colour: ruby red. Nose: elegant, spicy, fine reductive notes, tobacco, ripe fruit. Palate: spicy, fine tannins, elegant, long.

Luis Cañas 2010 TR

95% tempranillo, 5% graciano

92

Colour: cherry, garnet rim. Nose: balanced, complex, ripe fruit, spicy, fine reductive notes. Palate: good structure, flavourful, round tannins, balanced.

Luis Cañas 2012 TC

95% tempranillo, 5% garnacha

89

Colour: bright cherry. Nose: ripe fruit, sweet spices, creamy oak. Palate: flavourful, fruity, toasty.

Luis Cañas 2014 BFB

85% viura, 15% malvasía

89

Colour: bright straw. Nose: expressive, dried herbs, ripe fruit, spicy. Palate: flavourful, good acidity, rich, toasty.

PODIUM

Luis Cañas Hiru 3 Racimos 2007 T

90% tempranillo, 10% graciano

95

Colour: cherry, garnet rim. Nose: balanced, complex, ripe fruit, spicy, fine reductive notes. Palate: good structure, flavourful, round tannins, balanced.

Luis Cañas Selección de Familia 2009 TR

85% tempranillo, 15% otras

93

Colour: cherry, garnet rim. Nose: ripe fruit, spicy, creamy oak, complex. Palate: flavourful, toasty, round tannins.

BODEGAS LUIS GURPEGUI MUGA

Avda. Celso Muerza, 8
31560 San Adrián (Navarra)
☎: +34 948 670 050
Fax: +34 948 670 259
bodegas@gurpegui.es
www.gurpegui.es

Primi 2014 T

tempranillo, graciano, garnacha

83

BODEGAS MARQUÉS DE CÁCERES

Ctra. Logroño, s/n
26350 Cenicero (La Rioja)
☎: +34 941 454 000
comunicacion@marquesdecaceres.com
www.marquesdecaceres.com

Gaudium Gran Vino 2009 TR

95% tempranillo, 5% graciano

94

Colour: very deep cherry. Nose: balanced, complex, ripe fruit, spicy. Palate: good structure, flavourful, round tannins, balanced.

Marqués de Cáceres 2008 TGR

85% tempranillo, 10% garnacha, 5% graciano

91

Colour: dark-red cherry, garnet rim. Nose: toasty, old leather, tobacco. Palate: balanced, classic aged character, fine tannins.

Marqués de Cáceres 2010 TR
85% tempranillo, 10% garnacha, 5% graciano

89

Colour: cherry, garnet rim. Nose: balanced, ripe fruit, spicy. Palate: correct, easy to drink, spicy.

Marqués de Cáceres 2011 TC
85% tempranillo, 10% garnacha, 5% graciano

88

Colour: bright cherry. Nose: ripe fruit, sweet spices, creamy oak, expressive. Palate: flavourful, fruity, toasty.

Marqués de Cáceres 2014 B
100% viura

86

Marqués de Cáceres 2014 RD
96% tempranillo, 4% garnacha

86

Marqués de Cáceres Antea 2013 BFB
viura, malvasía

84

Marqués de Cáceres Ecológico Bio 2014 T
88% tempranillo, 12% graciano

88

Colour: cherry, purple rim. Nose: expressive, fresh fruit, red berry notes, floral, wild herbs. Palate: flavourful, fruity, good acidity.

Marqués de Cáceres Excellens Rose 2014 RD
60% garnacha, 40% tempranillo

87

Colour: onion pink. Nose: elegant, red berry notes, floral, fragrant herbs. Palate: light-bodied, flavourful, good acidity, long, spicy.

MC Marqués de Cáceres 2012 T
100% tempranillo

91

Colour: cherry, garnet rim. Nose: creamy oak, red berry notes, balanced, ripe fruit. Palate: flavourful, spicy, round tannins.

MC Marqués de Cáceres Cepas Antiguas 2013 T
100% tempranillo

89

Colour: bright cherry. Nose: ripe fruit, sweet spices, creamy oak. Palate: flavourful, fruity, toasty, round tannins.

Satinela Semi-dulce 2014 B
95% viura, 5% malvasía

86

BODEGAS MARQUÉS DE LA CONCORDIA FAMILY OF WINES

Ctra. El Ciego, s/n
26350 Cenicero (La Rioja)
☎: +34 913 878 612
www.the-haciendas.com

Hacienda de Susar 2010 T
85% tempranillo, 5% syrah, 5% merlot, 5% cabernet sauvignon

87

Colour: cherry, garnet rim. Nose: ripe fruit, old leather, tobacco. Palate: correct, flavourful, spicy.

Marqués de la Concordia 2009 TR
100% tempranillo

88

Colour: cherry, garnet rim. Nose: fine reductive notes, aged wood nuances. Palate: spicy, long, toasty, ripe fruit.

Marqués de la Concordia 2011 TC
100% tempranillo

88

Colour: cherry, garnet rim. Nose: smoky, spicy, ripe fruit, toasty. Palate: flavourful, smoky aftertaste, ripe fruit.

Viña Alarde 2009 TR
80% tempranillo, 20% garnacha

85

BODEGAS MARQUÉS DE REINOSA

26560 Autol (La Rioja)
☎: +34 941 401 327
Fax: +34 941 390 065
bodegas@marquesdereinosa.com
www.marquesdereinosa.com

Castillo de Berisa 2014 B
verdejo

87

Colour: bright straw. Nose: white flowers, fresh fruit, fragrant herbs, citrus fruit. Palate: flavourful, fruity, good acidity.

Marqués de Reinosa 2010 TR
tempranillo

87

Colour: bright cherry. Nose: ripe fruit, sweet spices, creamy oak, smoky. Palate: flavourful, fruity, toasty, round tannins.

Marqués de Reinosa 2012 TC
tempranillo

86

Marqués de Reinosa 2014 B
viura, tempranillo blanco, verdejo

85

Marqués de Reinosa 2014 RD
garnacha, tempranillo

86

Marqués de Reinosa Edición Especial 2010 TR
tempranillo

88

Colour: cherry, garnet rim. Nose: fine reductive notes, ripe fruit. Palate: spicy, long, toasty, round tannins.

Marqués de Reinosa Tempranillo 2014 T
tempranillo

86

BODEGAS MARQUÉS DE TERÁN

Ctra. de Nájera, Km. 1
26220 Ollauri (La Rioja)
☎: +34 941 338 373
Fax: +34 941 338 374
info@marquesdeteran.com
www.marquesdeteran.com

Marqués de Terán 2009 TR
90% tempranillo, 5% mazuelo, 5% garnacha

88

Colour: ruby red. Nose: spicy, fine reductive notes, wild herbs, expressive. Palate: spicy, fine tannins, balanced.

Marqués de Terán 2010 TC
95% tempranillo, 5% mazuelo

89

Colour: cherry, garnet rim. Nose: ripe fruit, wild herbs, spicy, balsamic herbs, fine reductive notes. Palate: balanced, flavourful, long.

Marqués de Terán Edición Limitada 2009 TR
100% tempranillo

91

Colour: dark-red cherry. Nose: elegant, spicy, fine reductive notes, tobacco, balanced. Palate: spicy, fine tannins, elegant, long.

Marqués de Terán Selección Especial 2011 T
100% tempranillo

93

Colour: cherry, garnet rim. Nose: ripe fruit, spicy, creamy oak, complex, balanced. Palate: flavourful, toasty, round tannins.

Ollamendi 2009 T
100% tempranillo

89

Colour: cherry, garnet rim. Nose: ripe fruit, spicy, complex, fine reductive notes. Palate: flavourful, toasty, round tannins.

Versum 2012 T
100% tempranillo

91

Colour: bright cherry. Nose: ripe fruit, sweet spices, creamy oak. Palate: flavourful, fruity, toasty.

BODEGAS MARTÍNEZ ALESANCO

José García, 20
26310 Badarán (La Rioja)
☎: +34 941 367 075
Fax: +34 941 367 075
info@bodegasmartinezalesanco.com
www.bodegasmartinezalesanco.com

Martínez Alesanco 2005 TGR
80% tempranillo, 20% garnacha

88

Colour: pale ruby, brick rim edge. Nose: spicy, fine reductive notes, wet leather, aged wood nuances. Palate: spicy, fine tannins, balanced.

Martínez Alesanco 2010 TR
90% tempranillo, 10% garnacha

90

Colour: cherry, garnet rim. Nose: ripe fruit, spicy, creamy oak, complex. Palate: flavourful, toasty, slightly dry, soft tannins.

Martínez Alesanco 2012 TC
80% tempranillo, 20% garnacha

87

Colour: bright cherry. Nose: ripe fruit, sweet spices, creamy oak, fine reductive notes. Palate: flavourful, fruity, toasty, round tannins.

Martínez Alesanco 2014 BFB
80% viura, 20% tempranillo blanco

83

Martínez Alesanco 2014 RD Fermentado en Barrica
100% garnacha

84

Martínez Alesanco 2014 T
80% tempranillo, 20% garnacha

80

Nada que Ver 2011 TC
100% maturana

88

Colour: cherry, garnet rim. Nose: ripe fruit, earthy notes, spicy, grassy. Palate: balanced, flavourful, long, balsamic.

Pedro Martínez Alesanco Selección 2010 TR
40% maturana, 30% tempranillo, 30% garnacha

91

Colour: cherry, garnet rim. Nose: ripe fruit, wild herbs, creamy oak. Palate: balanced, flavourful, balsamic.

BODEGAS MARTÍNEZ CORTA

Ctra. Cenicero, s/n
20313 Uruñuela (La Rioja)
☎: +34 670 937 520
administracion.bodega@bodegasmartinezcorta.com
www.bodegasmartinezcorta.com

Martínez Corta Cepas Antiguas 2014 T
tempranillo

86

Martínez Corta Selección Especial 2009 T
tempranillo

87

Colour: cherry, garnet rim. Nose: fine reductive notes, wet leather, aged wood nuances. Palate: spicy, long, toasty.

Soros 2012 TC
tempranillo

87

Colour: cherry, garnet rim. Nose: spicy, toasty, ripe fruit. Palate: correct, easy to drink.

Soros Edición Limitada 2009 TR

89

Colour: cherry, garnet rim. Nose: ripe fruit, spicy, creamy oak. Palate: flavourful, toasty.

Tentación Garnacha 2012 T
garnacha

87

Colour: very deep cherry, garnet rim. Nose: complex, balsamic herbs, balanced. Palate: full, flavourful, round tannins.

Tentación Tempranillo 2014 T
tempranillo

88

Colour: cherry, purple rim. Nose: powerfull, ripe fruit, spicy. Palate: powerful, fruity, unctuous.

BODEGAS MARTÍNEZ PALACIOS

Real, 48
26220 Ollauri (Rioja)
☎: +34 941 338 023
Fax: +34 941 338 023
bodega@bodegasmartinezpalacios.com
www.bodegasmartinezpalacios.com

Itran 2013 T
tempranillo

85

Martínez Palacios 2008 TR
90% tempranillo, 10% graciano

88

Colour: cherry, garnet rim. Nose: smoky, spicy, ripe fruit. Palate: flavourful, smoky aftertaste, ripe fruit.

Martínez Palacios 2012 TC
tempranillo

88

Colour: cherry, garnet rim. Nose: scrubland, ripe fruit, spicy. Palate: spicy, correct, balanced.

Martínez Palacios 2014 T
tempranillo

87

Colour: cherry, purple rim. Nose: expressive, fresh fruit, red berry notes, floral, violets. Palate: flavourful, fruity, good acidity.

Martínez Palacios Pago Candela 2008 T
90% tempranillo, 10% graciano

91

Colour: cherry, garnet rim. Nose: ripe fruit, old leather, tobacco. Palate: flavourful, spicy, classic aged character, long.

BODEGAS MAS QUE VINOS

Camino de los Molinos, s/n
45312 Cabañas de Yepes (Toledo)
☎: +34 925 122 281
Fax: +34 925 137 033
mqv@bodegasmasquevinos.com
www.bodegasmasquevinos.com

La Buena Vid 2010 T
80% tempranillo, 20% graciano

88

Colour: cherry, garnet rim. Nose: fine reductive notes, aged wood nuances, ripe fruit. Palate: spicy, long, toasty.

BODEGAS MEDRANO IRAZU S.L.

San Pedro, 14
01309 Elvillar (Álava)
☎: +34 945 604 066
Fax: +34 945 604 126
fernando@bodegasmedranoirazu.com
www.bodegasmedranoirazu.com

Luis Medrano Tempranillo 2012 TC
100% tempranillo

92

Colour: cherry, garnet rim. Nose: spicy, creamy oak, earthy notes, fruit preserve, complex. Palate: flavourful, toasty, balanced.

Mas de Medrano Single Vineyard 2012 T
100% tempranillo

89

Colour: bright cherry. Nose: ripe fruit, sweet spices, creamy oak. Palate: flavourful, fruity, toasty.

Medrano Irazu 2012 TC
100% tempranillo

87

Colour: cherry, garnet rim. Nose: creamy oak, ripe fruit. Palate: flavourful, spicy, correct.

Medrano Irazu Reserva de Familia 2009 TR
100% tempranillo

90

Colour: cherry, garnet rim. Nose: ripe fruit, spicy, creamy oak, complex. Palate: flavourful, toasty, round tannins.

BODEGAS MITARTE

Avda. La Rioja, 5
01330 Labastida (Álava)
☎: +34 607 343 289
bodegas@mitarte.com
www.mitarte.com

De Faula 2011 TR

91

Colour: very deep cherry, garnet rim. Nose: expressive, complex, mineral, balsamic herbs, balanced. Palate: full, flavourful, round tannins.

Mitarte 2011 TR

89

Colour: cherry, garnet rim. Nose: red berry notes, ripe fruit, creamy oak, complex. Palate: flavourful, toasty, round tannins.

Mitarte 2012 TC

85

Mitarte 2014 BFB

84

Mitarte 2014 RD

85

Mitarte 2014 T Maceración Carbónica

85

Mitarte Mazuelo 2012 T

90

Colour: cherry, garnet rim. Nose: ripe fruit, wild herbs, earthy notes, spicy, balsamic herbs. Palate: balanced, flavourful, long, balsamic, fresh.

Mitarte Tercera Hoja 2014 T

84

Mitarte Vendimia Seleccionada 2012 TC

88

Colour: bright cherry. Nose: ripe fruit, sweet spices, creamy oak, expressive. Palate: flavourful, fruity, toasty, round tannins.

Mitarte Viura 2014 B

85

S y C de Mitarte 2012 T

91

Colour: cherry, garnet rim. Nose: balanced, ripe fruit, spicy, fine reductive notes. Palate: good structure, flavourful, round tannins, balanced.

Tatos Mitarte 2012 T

100% garnacha

90

Colour: cherry, garnet rim. Nose: ripe fruit, spicy, creamy oak, complex. Palate: flavourful, toasty, round tannins.

BODEGAS MONTEABELLÓN

Calvario, s/n
09318 Nava de Roa (Burgos)
☎: +34 947 550 000
Fax: +34 947 550 219
info@monteabellon.com
www.monteabellon.com

Finca Athus 2012 TC

90% tempranillo, 10% mazuelo

90

Colour: cherry, garnet rim. Nose: creamy oak, balanced, ripe fruit, warm. Palate: flavourful, spicy, round tannins.

BODEGAS MONTECILLO

Ctra. Navarrete-Fuenmayor, Km. 6
26307 Navarrete (La Rioja)
☎: +34 952 869 000
carolina.cerrato@osborne.es
www.osborne.es

Montecillo 2010 TR

100% tempranillo

89

Colour: cherry, garnet rim. Nose: ripe fruit, spicy, creamy oak, fine reductive notes. Palate: flavourful, toasty, round tannins.

Montecillo 2008 TGR

100% tempranillo

89

Colour: pale ruby, brick rim edge. Nose: spicy, fine reductive notes, wet leather, aged wood nuances, fruit liqueur notes. Palate: spicy, fine tannins, balanced.

Montecillo 2011 TC

100% tempranillo

87

Colour: cherry, garnet rim. Nose: fine reductive notes, ripe fruit, spicy. Palate: spicy, long, toasty.

Viña Cumbrero 2011 TC

85

BODEGAS MUGA

Barrio de la Estación, s/n
26200 Haro (La Rioja)
☎: +34 941 311 825
marketing@bodegasmuga.com
www.bodegasmuga.com

Muga 2011 TC

90

Colour: very deep cherry, garnet rim. Nose: expressive, complex, balsamic herbs, balanced, spicy, fine reductive notes. Palate: full, flavourful, round tannins.

Muga 2014 BFB

89

Colour: bright yellow. Nose: expressive, dried herbs, ripe fruit, spicy. Palate: flavourful, fruity, good acidity, balanced.

Muga 2014 RD

88

Colour: raspberry rose. Nose: red berry notes, floral, fragrant herbs. Palate: light-bodied, good acidity, long.

Muga Selección Especial 2010 TR
92

Colour: very deep cherry, garnet rim. Nose: mineral, balsamic herbs, balanced. Palate: full, flavourful, round tannins.

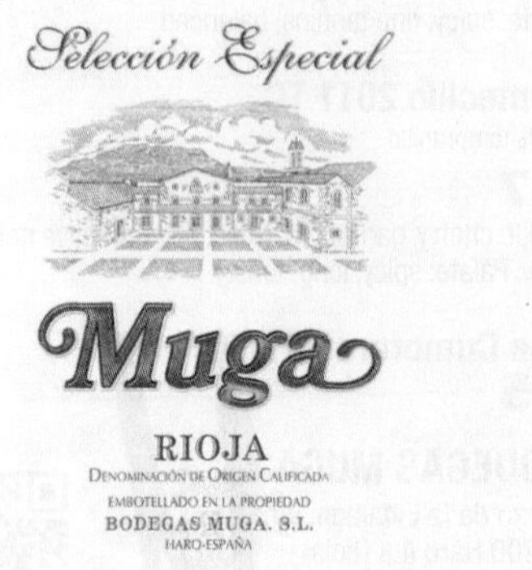

Muga Selección Especial Magnum 2009 T
93

Colour: bright cherry, garnet rim. Nose: balanced, expressive, spicy, ripe fruit, fine reductive notes. Palate: spicy, balsamic.

Prado Enea 2006 TGR
93

Colour: cherry, garnet rim. Nose: ripe fruit, spicy, creamy oak, complex, fine reductive notes. Palate: flavourful, toasty, round tannins, balanced, elegant.

Torre Muga 2011 T
tempranillo, graciano, mazuelo, otras

94

Colour: very deep cherry. Nose: smoky, creamy oak, ripe fruit. Palate: good structure, spicy, long, round tannins.

BODEGAS MURÚA
Ctra. Laguardia s/n
01340 Elciego (Álava)
☎: +34 945 606 260
info@bodegasmurua.com
www.bodegasmurua.com

M Murúa 2010 T
95% tempranillo, 5% graciano

90

Colour: cherry, garnet rim. Nose: ripe fruit, wild herbs, earthy notes, spicy, balsamic herbs. Palate: balanced, flavourful, long, balsamic.

Murúa 2007 TR
93% tempranillo, 5% graciano, 2% mazuelo

92

Colour: cherry, garnet rim. Nose: ripe fruit, spicy, creamy oak, complex, balsamic herbs. Palate: flavourful, toasty, round tannins, elegant.

Murúa 2011 BFB
70% viura, 20% malvasía, 10% garnacha

90

Colour: bright yellow. Nose: ripe fruit, powerfull, toasty, aged wood nuances. Palate: flavourful, fruity, spicy, toasty, long.

VS Murúa 2011 T
92% tempranillo, 5% graciano, 3% mazuelo

91

Colour: cherry, garnet rim. Nose: balanced, complex, ripe fruit, spicy. Palate: good structure, flavourful, round tannins, balanced.

BODEGAS NAVA-RIOJA
Ctra. Eje del Ebro, s/n
31261 Andosilla (Navarra)
☎: +34 948 690 454
Fax: +34 948 674 491
info@bodegasnavarioja.com
www.bodegasnavarioja.com

Otis Tarda 2012 TC
100% tempranillo

86 🌷

Colour: cherry, garnet rim. Nose: creamy oak, ripe fruit, slightly evolved. Palate: toasty, easy to drink.

Otis Tarda 2014 B
tempranillo blanco

84

Otis Tarda 2014 T
100% tempranillo

83 ♣

BODEGAS NAVAJAS
Camino Balgarauz, 2
26370 Navarrete (La Rioja)
☎: +34 941 440 140
Fax: +34 941 440 657
info@bodegasnavajas.com
www.bodegasnavajas.com

Navajas 2012 TC
85% tempranillo, 15% graciano

86

Navajas 2014 T
90% tempranillo, 5% mazuelo, 5% graciano

84

Navajas Graciano 2011 TC
100% graciano

88

Colour: cherry, garnet rim. Nose: roasted coffee, smoky, spicy, ripe fruit, varietal. Palate: flavourful, smoky aftertaste, ripe fruit.

BODEGAS NIVARIUS
Ctra. de Nalda a Viguera, 46
26190 Nalda (La Rioja)
☎: +34 941 447 207
info@nivarius.com
www.nivarius.com

Nivarius 2014 B
55% tempranillo blanco, 45% viura

93

Colour: bright straw. Nose: white flowers, dried herbs, ripe fruit, candied fruit, citrus fruit. Palate: flavourful, fruity, good acidity.

Nivarius Tempranillo Blanco 2014 B
55% tempranillo blanco, 45% viura

91

Colour: bright straw. Nose: white flowers, fine lees, dried herbs. Palate: flavourful, fruity, good acidity, round.

Nivei 2014 B
tempranillo blanco, viura, chardonnay, malvasía, sauvignon blanc, maturana

89

Colour: straw. Nose: medium intensity, ripe fruit, floral. Palate: correct, ripe fruit, good acidity, round.

BODEGAS OBALO
Ctra. N-232 A, Km. 26
26339 Abalos (La Rioja)
☎: +34 941 744 056
info@bodegasobalo.com
www.bodegaobalo.com

La Tarara 2012 T
100% tempranillo

89

Colour: cherry, garnet rim. Nose: smoky, spicy, ripe fruit. Palate: flavourful, smoky aftertaste, ripe fruit.

Matulán 2012 T
100% tempranillo

90

Colour: bright cherry. Nose: ripe fruit, sweet spices, creamy oak. Palate: flavourful, fruity, toasty.

Obalo 2009 TR
100% tempranillo

93

Colour: light cherry. Nose: aged wood nuances, toasty, roasted coffee, ripe fruit. Palate: spicy, toasty, flavourful.

Obalo 2011 TC
100% tempranillo

93

Colour: cherry, garnet rim. Nose: ripe fruit, spicy, creamy oak, complex. Palate: flavourful, toasty, round tannins.

Obalo 2014 T
100% tempranillo

90

Colour: deep cherry, purple rim. Nose: creamy oak, toasty, ripe fruit, balsamic herbs. Palate: balanced, spicy, long.

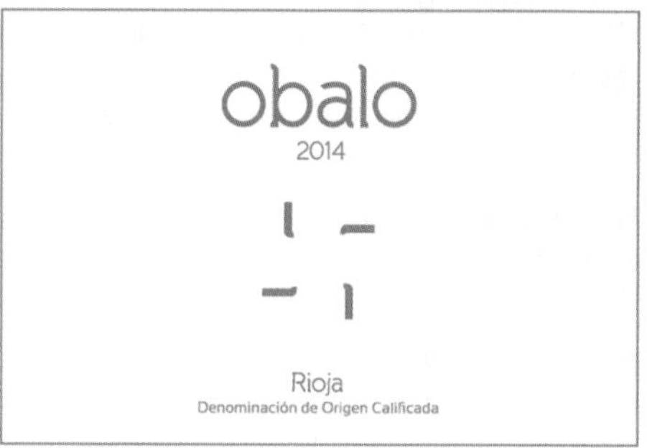

BODEGAS OLARRA

Avda. de Mendavia, 30
26009 Logroño (La Rioja)
☎: +34 941 235 299
Fax: +34 941 253 703
bodegasolarra@bodegasolarra.es
www.bodegasolarra.es

Añares 2010 TR
90% tempranillo, 5% garnacha, 5% mazuelo, graciano

88

Colour: light cherry. Nose: fine reductive notes, aged wood nuances, toasty. Palate: spicy, toasty, flavourful.

Añares 2013 TC
90% tempranillo, 5% garnacha, 5% mazuelo, graciano

84

Cerro Añón 2010 TR
80% tempranillo, 5% garnacha, 15% mazuelo, graciano

91

Colour: bright cherry. Nose: sweet spices, creamy oak, fine reductive notes. Palate: flavourful, fruity, toasty, round tannins.

Cerro Añón 2013 TC
80% tempranillo, 10% garnacha, 10% mazuelo, graciano

89

Colour: cherry, garnet rim. Nose: creamy oak, red berry notes, fresh fruit. Palate: flavourful, spicy, elegant.

Otoñal 2010 TR
75% tempranillo, 10% garnacha, 15% mazuelo, graciano

88

Colour: light cherry. Nose: fine reductive notes, aged wood nuances, toasty. Palate: spicy, toasty, flavourful.

Otoñal 2012 TC
90% tempranillo, 5% garnacha, 5% mazuelo, graciano

87

Colour: cherry, garnet rim. Nose: ripe fruit, toasty, short. Palate: powerful, toasty.

Otoñal 2014 T
100% tempranillo

83

Summa 2010 TR
85% tempranillo, 5% mazuelo, 10% graciano

91

Colour: cherry, garnet rim. Nose: ripe fruit, wild herbs, earthy notes, spicy, balsamic herbs. Palate: balanced, flavourful, long, balsamic.

BODEGAS ONDALÁN

Ctra. de Logroño, 22
01230 Oyón (Álava)
☎: +34 945 622 537
Fax: +34 945 622 538
ondalan@ondalan.es
www.ondalan.es

100 Abades Graciano Selección 2012 T
100% graciano

88

Colour: deep cherry, purple rim. Nose: toasty, ripe fruit, balsamic herbs, dark chocolate. Palate: balanced, spicy, long.

Ondalán 2010 TR
70% tempranillo, 30% graciano

89

Colour: cherry, garnet rim. Nose: ripc fruit, old leather, tobacco, spicy, smoky. Palate: correct, flavourful, spicy.

Ondalán 2012 TC
80% tempranillo, 20% graciano

86

Ondalán 2014 B
100% viura

86

Ondalán 2014 T
90% tempranillo, 10% garnacha

84

Ondalán Tempranillo Selección 2011 T
100% tempranillo

89

Colour: cherry, garnet rim. Nose: creamy oak, balanced, ripe fruit. Palate: flavourful, spicy.

BODEGAS ONDARRE

Ctra. de Aras, s/n
31230 Viana (Navarra)
☎: +34 948 645 300
Fax: +34 948 646 002
bodegasondarre@bodegasondarre.es
www.bodegasondarre.es

Mayor de Ondarre 2010 TR
88% tempranillo, 12% mazuelo

92

Colour: light cherry. Nose: fine reductive notes, aged wood nuances, toasty, ripe fruit. Palate: spicy, toasty, flavourful.

Señorío de Ondarre 2010 TR
85% tempranillo, 5% garnacha, 10% mazuelo

90

Colour: light cherry. Nose: fine reductive notes, aged wood nuances, toasty. Palate: spicy, toasty, flavourful.

BODEGAS ONECA

Ctra. Logroño-Vitoria, Km. 57
01300 Laguardia (Rioja)
☎: +34 941 499 206
info@bodegasoneca.com
www.bodegasoneca.com

El 4 de Oneca 2012 T

100% tempranillo

88

Colour: deep cherry, garnet rim. Nose: ripe fruit, fruit preserve, cocoa bean, sweet spices. Palate: powerful, spicy, round tannins.

Finca Oneca 2011 TC

80% tempranillo, 20% mazuelo

90

Colour: deep cherry, purple rim. Nose: creamy oak, toasty, ripe fruit, balsamic herbs. Palate: balanced, spicy, long.

Princesa Oneca 2013 B

80% viura, 10% malvasía, 10% chardonnay

88

Colour: bright yellow. Nose: ripe fruit, powerfull, toasty, aged wood nuances, pattiserie. Palate: flavourful, fruity, spicy, toasty, long.

The Special Oneca 2012 T

100% tempranillo

89

Colour: cherry, garnet rim. Nose: creamy oak, red berry notes, balanced, ripe fruit. Palate: flavourful, spicy, smoky aftertaste.

BODEGAS ONTAÑON

26559 Aldeanueva de Ebro (La Rioja)
☎: +34 941 142 317
Fax: +34 941 144 002
administracion1@ontanon.es
www.ontanon.es

Ontañón 2005 TR

95% tempranillo, 5% graciano

87

Colour: cherry, garnet rim. Nose: fine reductive notes, wet leather, aged wood nuances. Palate: spicy, long, toasty.

Ontañón 2012 TC

90% tempranillo, 10% garnacha

90

Colour: bright cherry. Nose: ripe fruit, sweet spices, creamy oak, expressive. Palate: flavourful, fruity, round tannins.

Ontañón Mitológica 2005 T

95% tempranillo, 5% graciano

88

Colour: cherry, garnet rim. Nose: ripe fruit, old leather, tobacco. Palate: correct, flavourful, spicy.

Vetiver Viura 2013 B

100% viura

87

Colour: bright straw. Nose: white flowers, fresh fruit, tropical fruit. Palate: flavourful, fruity, good acidity, balanced.

BODEGAS ORBEN

Ctra. Laguardia, Km. 60
01300 Laguardia (Álava)
☎: +34 945 609 086
Fax: +34 945 609 261
izadi@izadi.com
www.grupoartevino.com

Malpuesto 2013 T

100% tempranillo

94

Colour: cherry, garnet rim. Nose: balanced, complex, ripe fruit, spicy, fine reductive notes. Palate: good structure, flavourful, round tannins, balanced.

Orben 2012 T

100% tempranillo

93

Colour: cherry, garnet rim. Nose: mineral, expressive, spicy. Palate: flavourful, ripe fruit, long, good acidity, grainy tannins.

BODEGAS OSTATU

Ctra. Vitoria, 1
01307 Samaniego (Álava)
☎: +34 945 609 133
Fax: +34 945 623 338
info@ostatu.com
www.ostatu.com

Gloria de Ostatu 2007 T

tempranillo

92

Colour: light cherry. Nose: fine reductive notes, aged wood nuances, toasty, overripe fruit. Palate: spicy, toasty, flavourful.

Laderas Ostatu 2010 T

tempranillo, viura

88

Colour: cherry, garnet rim. Nose: roasted coffee, smoky, spicy, ripe fruit. Palate: flavourful, smoky aftertaste, ripe fruit.

Lore de Ostatu 2012 B

viura, malvasía

90

Colour: bright yellow. Nose: expressive, dried herbs, ripe fruit, spicy. Palate: flavourful, fruity, good acidity, balanced.

Ostatu 2012 TC

tempranillo, graciano, mazuelo, garnacha

92

Colour: cherry, garnet rim. Nose: creamy oak, red berry notes, fresh fruit, balanced. Palate: flavourful, spicy, balsamic.

Selección Ostatu 2011 T

tempranillo, graciano

90

Colour: cherry, garnet rim. Nose: roasted coffee, smoky, spicy, ripe fruit. Palate: flavourful, smoky aftertaste, ripe fruit.

BODEGAS PACO GARCÍA

Crta. de Ventas Blancas s/n
26143 Murillo de Rio Leza (La Rioja)
☎: +34 941 432 372
Fax: +34 941 432 156
info@bodegaspacogarcia.com
www.bodegaspacogarcia.com

Beautiful Things de Paco García 2010 T

90% tempranillo, 10% graciano

89

Colour: cherry, garnet rim. Nose: ripe fruit, spicy, creamy oak, complex. Palate: flavourful, toasty, round tannins.

Paco García 2012 TC

90% tempranillo, 10% garnacha

89

Colour: very deep cherry. Nose: expressive, mineral, balsamic herbs, ripe fruit. Palate: full, flavourful, round tannins.

Paco García Seis 2014 T

100% tempranillo

88

Colour: bright cherry. Nose: ripe fruit, sweet spices, creamy oak. Palate: flavourful, fruity, toasty.

BODEGAS PALACIO

San Lázaro, 1
01300 Laguardia (Álava)
☎: +34 945 600 057
Fax: +34 945 600 297
cosme@bodegaspalacio.com
www.bodegaspalacio.es

Cosme Palacio 2012 TC
100% tempranillo

92

Colour: cherry, garnet rim. Nose: creamy oak, balanced, ripe fruit. Palate: flavourful, spicy, round tannins.

🏆 PODIUM

Cosme Palacio 1894 2012 T
100% tempranillo

95

Colour: cherry, garnet rim. Nose: mineral, expressive, spicy, red berry notes. Palate: flavourful, ripe fruit, long, good acidity, balanced.

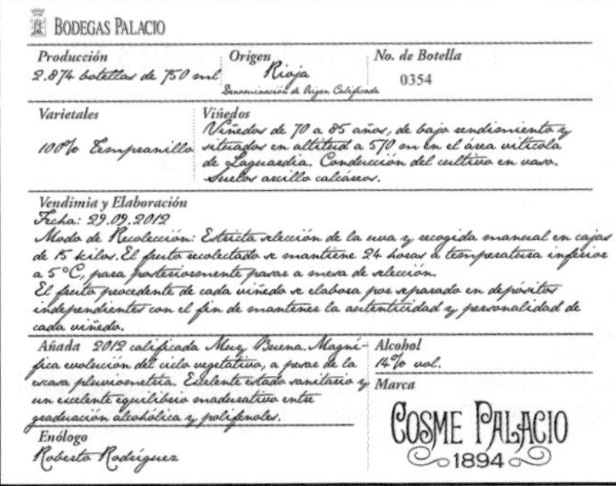

Cosme Palacio 2010 TR
100% tempranillo

92

Colour: cherry, garnet rim. Nose: red berry notes, ripe fruit, spicy, creamy oak, complex. Palate: flavourful, toasty, round tannins.

Glorioso 2007 TGR
100% tempranillo

91

Colour: pale ruby, brick rim edge. Nose: spicy, fine reductive notes, wet leather, aged wood nuances, fruit liqueur notes. Palate: spicy, fine tannins, balanced.

Glorioso 2010 TR
100% tempranillo

91

Colour: cherry, garnet rim. Nose: balanced, ripe fruit, spicy. Palate: good structure, flavourful, round tannins, balanced.

Glorioso 2012 TC
100% tempranillo

90

Colour: cherry, garnet rim. Nose: smoky, spicy, ripe fruit. Palate: flavourful, smoky aftertaste, ripe fruit.

Milflores 2014 T
88

Colour: cherry, purple rim. Nose: fresh fruit, red berry notes, floral. Palate: flavourful, fruity, good acidity.

BODEGAS PALACIOS REMONDO

Avda. Zaragoza, 8
26540 Alfaro (La Rioja)
☎: +34 941 180 207
Fax: +34 941 181 628
info@palaciosremondo.com

La Montesa 2012 TC
80% garnacha, 20% tempranillo

93

Colour: very deep cherry, garnet rim. Nose: expressive, complex, mineral, balsamic herbs, balanced. Palate: round tannins, fruity.

La Montesa 2013 TC
80% garnacha, 20% tempranillo

91

Colour: light cherry, garnet rim. Nose: ripe fruit, wild herbs, balanced, expressive. Palate: balanced, easy to drink.

La Vendimia 2014 T
88

Colour: cherry, purple rim. Nose: expressive, red berry notes, floral, spicy. Palate: flavourful, fruity, good acidity.

Plácet Valtomelloso 2012 B
100% viura

92

Colour: bright straw. Nose: sweet spices, ripe fruit, faded flowers, expressive. Palate: rich, flavourful, full.

Propiedad 2011 T
100% garnacha

94

Colour: light cherry, garnet rim. Nose: expressive, complex, mineral, balsamic herbs, balanced. Palate: full, flavourful, round tannins.

Propiedad 2012 T
100% garnacha

94

Colour: cherry, garnet rim. Nose: elegant, balanced, dried herbs, complex. Palate: full, spicy, balanced.

BODEGAS PATERNINA MARQUÉS DE LA CONCORDIA FAMILY OF WINES

Crta. Elciego, s/n
26350 Cenicero (La Rioja)
☎: +34 913 878 612

Paternina 2009 TR
tempranillo, garnacha, mazuelo

86

Paternina Banda Azul 2011 TC
80% tempranillo, 20% garnacha

84

Paternina Banda Azul 2012 TC
85

BODEGAS PATROCINIO

Ctra. Cenicero, s/n
26313 Uruñuela (La Rioja)
☎: +34 941 371 319
Fax: +34 941 371 435
info@bodegaspatrocinio.com
www.bodegaspatrocinio.com

Lágrimas de María TC
89

Colour: cherry, garnet rim. Nose: ripe fruit, spicy, creamy oak. Palate: flavourful, toasty.

Lágrimas de María 2010 TR
86

Lágrimas de María 2014 RD
tempranillo

87

Colour: coppery red, bright. Nose: red berry notes, floral, fragrant herbs. Palate: light-bodied, good acidity, long.

Lágrimas de María 2014 T
85

Lágrimas de María Madurado 2013 TC
86

Lágrimas de María Viura 2014 B
viura, tempranillo blanco

86

Zinio Garnacha 2014 T
88

Colour: cherry, purple rim. Nose: expressive, red berry notes, floral, varietal. Palate: flavourful, fruity, good acidity.

Zinio Tempranillo Graciano 2013 T
85% tempranillo, 15% graciano

87

Colour: very deep cherry, garnet rim. Nose: expressive, balsamic herbs, balanced. Palate: full, flavourful, round tannins.

Zinio Tempranillo selección de suelos 2011 T
tempranillo

87

Colour: cherry, garnet rim. Nose: smoky, spicy, ripe fruit. Palate: flavourful, smoky aftertaste, ripe fruit.

Zinio Vendimia Seleccionada 2010 TR

89

Colour: cherry, garnet rim. Nose: complex, ripe fruit, spicy, fine reductive notes. Palate: good structure, flavourful, round tannins.

Zinio Vendimia Seleccionada 2012 TC
100% tempranillo

88

Colour: bright cherry. Nose: ripe fruit, sweet spices, creamy oak. Palate: flavourful, fruity, toasty.

BODEGAS PERICA

Avda. de la Rioja, 59
26340 San Asensio (La Rioja)
☎: +34 941 457 152
Fax: +34 941 457 240
info@bodegasperica.com
www.bodegasperica.com

6 Cepas 6 2013 T
100% tempranillo

88

Colour: deep cherry, purple rim. Nose: creamy oak, toasty, ripe fruit, balsamic herbs. Palate: balanced, spicy, long.

6 Cepas 6 2014 B
60% viura, 40% verdejo

87

Colour: bright straw. Nose: white flowers, fresh fruit, fragrant herbs, expressive. Palate: flavourful, fruity, good acidity, balanced.

6 Cepas 6 2014 RD
60% garnacha, 30% tempranillo, 10% viura

86

Mi Villa 2014 T
85% tempranillo, 15% garnacha

86

Olagosa 2009 TR
90% tempranillo, 5% garnacha, 5% mazuelo

89

Colour: cherry, garnet rim. Nose: ripe fruit, wild herbs, earthy notes, spicy, balsamic herbs. Palate: balanced, flavourful, long.

Olagosa 2012 TC
90% tempranillo, 5% garnacha, 5% mazuelo

87

Colour: cherry, garnet rim. Nose: creamy oak, balanced, ripe fruit. Palate: flavourful, spicy, toasty.

Olagosa 2014 B
95% viura, 5% malvasía

86

Perica Oro 2010 TR
95% tempranillo, 5% graciano

92

Colour: cherry, garnet rim. Nose: ripe fruit, spicy, creamy oak, complex. Palate: flavourful, toasty, round tannins.

BODEGAS PROELIO

Ctra . Nalda a Viguera ,46
26190 Nalda (La Rioja)
☎: +34 941 447 207
info@bodegasproelio.com
www.bodegasproelio.com

Proelio 2012 TC
100% tempranillo

90

Colour: cherry, garnet rim. Nose: fine reductive notes, wet leather, aged wood nuances, ripe fruit, spicy. Palate: spicy, long, toasty.

Proelio 2014 RD
100% graciano

89

Colour: rose, purple rim. Nose: powerfull, fruit preserve, warm. Palate: powerful, flavourful, good acidity.

Proelio 23 2012 T

92

Colour: cherry, garnet rim. Nose: ripe fruit, spicy, creamy oak, complex. Palate: flavourful, toasty, round tannins.

BODEGAS PUELLES

Camino de los Molinos, s/n
26339 Ábalos (La Rioja)
☎: +34 941 334 415
Fax: +34 941 334 132
informacion@bodegaspuelles.com
www.bodegaspuelles.com

Molino de Puelles Ecológico 2009 T
tempranillo

86

Puelles 2012 TC
tempranillo

86

Puelles 2014 B
viura

85

Puelles Zenus 2004 T
tempranillo

86

BODEGAS RAMÍREZ DE LA PISCINA

Ctra. Vitoria Laguardia s/n
26338 San Vicente de la Sonsierra
(La Rioja)
☎: +34 941 334 505
Fax: +34 941 334 506
info@ramirezdelapiscina.com
www.ramirezdelapiscina.com

Ramírez de la Piscina 2007 TGR
100% tempranillo

89

Colour: pale ruby, brick rim edge. Nose: spicy, fine reductive notes, wet leather, aged wood nuances, fruit liqueur notes. Palate: spicy, balanced.

Ramírez de la Piscina 2008 TR
100% tempranillo

89

Colour: cherry, garnet rim. Nose: red berry notes, ripe fruit, spicy, creamy oak, fine reductive notes. Palate: flavourful, toasty, round tannins.

Ramírez de la Piscina 2012 TC
100% tempranillo

88

Colour: bright cherry. Nose: ripe fruit, sweet spices, creamy oak, expressive. Palate: flavourful, fruity, toasty.

Ramírez de la Piscina 2014 B
85% viura, 15% malvasía

84

Ramírez de la Piscina 2014 RD
50% garnacha, 50% viura

85

Ramírez de la Piscina 2014 T
100% tempranillo

86

Ramírez de la Piscina Selección 2010 TR
100% tempranillo

90

Colour: cherry, garnet rim. Nose: ripe fruit, wild herbs, earthy notes, spicy, balsamic herbs. Palate: balanced, flavourful, long, balsamic.

BODEGAS RAMÓN BILBAO

Avda. Santo Domingo, 34
26200 Haro (La Rioja)
☎: +34 941 310 295
Fax: +34 941 310 832
info@bodegasramonbilbao.es
www.bodegasramonbilbao.es

Mirto de Ramón Bilbao 2011 T
100% tempranillo

93

Colour: cherry, garnet rim. Nose: balanced, complex, ripe fruit, spicy. Palate: good structure, flavourful, balanced.

Ramón Bilbao 2008 TGR
tempranillo, mazuelo, graciano

91

Colour: cherry, garnet rim. Nose: balanced, complex, ripe fruit, spicy, fine reductive notes. Palate: good structure, flavourful, round tannins, balanced.

Ramón Bilbao 2009 TGR
90% tempranillo, 5% mazuelo, 5% graciano

91

Colour: pale ruby, brick rim edge. Nose: spicy, fine reductive notes, ripe fruit, wild herbs. Palate: spicy, fine tannins, elegant, long.

Ramón Bilbao 2011 TR
90% tempranillo, 5% graciano, 5% mazuelo

90

Colour: cherry, garnet rim. Nose: ripe fruit, spicy, creamy oak. Palate: flavourful, toasty, round tannins.

Ramón Bilbao 2013 TC
100% tempranillo

88

Colour: cherry, garnet rim. Nose: smoky, spicy, ripe fruit. Palate: flavourful, smoky aftertaste, ripe fruit.

Ramón Bilbao Edición Limitada 2013 T
100% tempranillo

89

Colour: cherry, garnet rim. Nose: ripe fruit, fragrant herbs, spicy, creamy oak. Palate: powerful, flavourful, spicy.

Ramón Bilbao Rosé 2014 RD
100% garnacha

87

Colour: onion pink. Nose: red berry notes, floral, fragrant herbs. Palate: light-bodied, flavourful, good acidity, long, spicy.

Ramón Bilbao Viñedos de Altura 2013 TC
50% tempranillo, 50% garnacha

91

Colour: cherry, garnet rim. Nose: ripe fruit, wild herbs, earthy notes, spicy, balsamic herbs. Palate: balanced, flavourful, long, balsamic.

BODEGAS REAL DIVISA

Barrio del Montalvo, s/n
26339 Abalos (La Rioja)
☎: +34 941 258 133
Fax: +34 941 258 155
realdivisa@fer.es
www.realdivisa.com

Draco 2004 TR
100% tempranillo

92

Colour: pale ruby, brick rim edge. Nose: spicy, fine reductive notes, complex. Palate: spicy, fine tannins, balanced, long, classic aged character.

Marqués de Legarda 2005 TGR
100% tempranillo

87

Colour: dark-red cherry, orangey edge. Nose: spicy, wet leather, aged wood nuances, animal reductive notes. Palate: spicy, fine tannins.

Marqués de Legarda 2009 TR
100% tempranillo

87

Colour: cherry, garnet rim. Nose: ripe fruit, spicy, creamy oak, waxy notes. Palate: flavourful, toasty, round tannins.

Marqués de Legarda 2011 TC
91% tempranillo, 7% graciano, 2% mazuelo

85

Real Divisa Vendimia Manual 2012 T
91% tempranillo, 7% graciano, 2% mazuelo

84

BODEGAS REMÍREZ DE GANUZA

Constitución, 1
01307 Samaniego (Álava)
☎: +34 945 609 022
Fax: +34 945 623 335
visitas@remirezdeganuza.com
www.remirezdeganuza.com

Erre Punto 2014 AM Maceración Carbónica
90% tempranillo, 5% graciano, 5% viura, malvasía

91

Colour: cherry, purple rim. Nose: expressive, fresh fruit, red berry notes, floral. Palate: flavourful, fruity, good acidity.

Fincas de Ganuza 2008 TR
90% tempranillo, 10% graciano

91

Colour: light cherry. Nose: fine reductive notes, aged wood nuances, toasty. Palate: spicy, toasty, flavourful.

Remírez de Ganuza 2008 TR
85% tempranillo, 10% graciano, 5% viura, malvasía

94

Colour: cherry, garnet rim. Nose: balanced, complex, ripe fruit, spicy, fine reductive notes. Palate: good structure, flavourful, round tannins.

Remírez de Ganuza 2013 B
70% viura, 30% malvasía, garnacha blanca

93

Colour: bright straw. Nose: white flowers, fine lees, dried herbs, mineral. Palate: flavourful, fruity, good acidity, round.

BODEGAS RIOJANAS

Avda. Ricardo Ruiz Azcarraga, 1
26350 Cenicero (La Rioja)
☎: +34 941 454 050
Fax: +34 941 454 529
bodega@bodegasriojanas.com
www.bodegasriojanas.com

Canchales 2014 T
100% tempranillo

85

Gran Albina 2009 TR
34% tempranillo, 33% mazuelo, 33% graciano

91

Colour: cherry, garnet rim. Nose: tobacco, fine reductive notes, complex, expressive. Palate: flavourful, spicy, classic aged character, fine tannins.

Gran Albina Vendimia 2010 T
34% tempranillo, 33% mazuelo, 33% graciano

89

Colour: dark-red cherry, orangey edge. Nose: old leather, spicy, toasty. Palate: flavourful, balanced, fine tannins, classic aged character.

Monte Real 2007 TGR
100% tempranillo

89

Colour: dark-red cherry, garnet rim. Nose: spicy, ripe fruit, old leather. Palate: correct, balanced.

Monte Real 2009 TR
100% tempranillo

89

Colour: ruby red. Nose: spicy, fine reductive notes, wet leather, aged wood nuances, fruit liqueur notes. Palate: spicy, fine tannins.

Monte Real 2012 TC
100% tempranillo

88

Colour: ruby red. Nose: red berry notes, ripe fruit, spicy, creamy oak, complex. Palate: flavourful, toasty, classic aged character.

Monte Real 2014 B
90% viura, 10% malvasía

80

Monte Real Reserva de Familia 2009 TR
100% tempranillo

90

Colour: cherry, garnet rim. Nose: ripe fruit, old leather, tobacco. Palate: correct, flavourful, spicy, balanced.

Puerta Vieja 2009 TR
80% tempranillo, 15% mazuelo, 5% graciano

87

Colour: ruby red. Nose: ripe fruit, fruit preserve, scrubland, aged wood nuances, fine reductive notes. Palate: correct, flavourful.

Puerta Vieja 2012 TC
80% tempranillo, 15% mazuelo, 5% graciano

87

Colour: deep cherry. Nose: creamy oak, toasty, ripe fruit, balsamic herbs. Palate: balanced, spicy, long.

Puerta Vieja Selección 2012 TC
100% tempranillo

89

Colour: cherry, garnet rim. Nose: fine reductive notes, aged wood nuances, ripe fruit. Palate: spicy, long, toasty, classic aged character.

Viña Albina 2014 B
100% viura

85

Viña Albina 2007 TGR
80% tempranillo, 15% mazuelo, 5% graciano

90

Colour: cherry, garnet rim. Nose: ripe fruit, spicy, balsamic herbs, fine reductive notes. Palate: balanced, flavourful, long, balsamic.

Viña Albina 2009 TR
80% tempranillo, 15% mazuelo, 5% graciano

88

Colour: dark-red cherry, garnet rim. Nose: dried herbs, spicy, fine reductive notes. Palate: balanced, spicy, reductive nuances.

Viña Albina Selección 2009 TR
80% tempranillo, 15% mazuelo, 5% graciano

90

Colour: cherry, garnet rim. Nose: ripe fruit, spicy, fine reductive notes. Palate: good structure, flavourful, round tannins, balanced.

Viña Albina Semidulce 2001 B Reserva
90% viura, 10% malvasía

92

Colour: golden. Nose: powerfull, honeyed notes, candied fruit, fragrant herbs, aged wood nuances. Palate: flavourful, sweet, fresh, fruity, good acidity, long.

Viña Albina Semidulce 2014 B
90% viura, 10% malvasía

86

BODEGAS RIOLANC

Curillos, 36
01308 Lanciego (Álava)
☎: +34 945 608 140
riolanc@riolanc.com
www.riolanc.com

Riolanc 2011 TC
100% tempranillo

87

Colour: cherry, garnet rim. Nose: creamy oak, red berry notes, fresh fruit. Palate: flavourful, spicy.

Riolanc Vendimia Seleccionada 2014 T
85% tempranillo, 15% mazuelo

87

Colour: cherry, purple rim. Nose: fresh fruit, red berry notes, floral. Palate: flavourful, fruity, good acidity.

BODEGAS RODA

Avda. de Vizcaya, 5
26200 Haro (La Rioja)
☎: +34 941 303 001
Fax: +34 941 312 703
rodarioja@roda.es
www.roda.es

Bodegas Roda Sela 2012 T
96% tempranillo, 3% graciano, 1% garnacha

90

Colour: bright cherry. Nose: ripe fruit, sweet spices, creamy oak. Palate: flavourful, fruity, round tannins.

PODIUM

Cirsion 2010 T
100% tempranillo

96

Colour: cherry, garnet rim. Nose: balanced, complex, ripe fruit, spicy, fine reductive notes. Palate: good structure, flavourful, round tannins, balanced.

Roda 2009 TR
tempranillo, graciano

93

Colour: cherry, garnet rim. Nose: ripe fruit, spicy, creamy oak, complex. Palate: flavourful, toasty, round tannins.

Roda 2010 TR
90% tempranillo, 10% graciano

92

Colour: bright cherry. Nose: ripe fruit, sweet spices, creamy oak. Palate: flavourful, fruity, toasty, round tannins.

Roda I 2007 TR
100% tempranillo

94

Colour: cherry, garnet rim. Nose: mineral, expressive, spicy, tobacco. Palate: flavourful, ripe fruit, long, good acidity, balanced.

Roda I 2008 TR
100% tempranillo

93

Colour: cherry, garnet rim. Nose: fine reductive notes, aged wood nuances, ripe fruit. Palate: spicy, long, toasty.

BODEGAS SAN PRUDENCIO

Ctra. de Viana, Km. 1
01320 Moreda (Álava)
☎: +34 945 601 034
Fax: +34 945 622 451
info@bodegasanprudencio.es
www.bodegasanprudencio.es

DePadre Garnacha 2012 T
100% garnacha

91

Colour: very deep cherry, garnet rim. Nose: expressive, complex, balsamic herbs, balanced. Palate: full, flavourful, round tannins.

BODEGAS SANTALBA

Avda. de la Rioja, s/n
26221 Gimileo (La Rioja)
☎: +34 941 304 231
Fax: +34 941 304 326
santalba@santalba.com
www.santalba.com

Abando 2009 T
tempranillo

89

Colour: cherry, garnet rim. Nose: fine reductive notes, ripe fruit, dried herbs. Palate: spicy, long, toasty.

Nabot Single Vineyard 2008 T
tempranillo

89

Colour: cherry, garnet rim. Nose: ripe fruit, sweet spices, creamy oak, dark chocolate. Palate: flavourful, fruity, toasty, round tannins.

Santalba Cotas Altas 2012 T

88

Colour: very deep cherry, garnet rim. Nose: balsamic herbs, balanced, ripe fruit. Palate: round tannins, good finish.

Santalba Ecológico Resveratrol 2013 T
tempranillo

88

Colour: light cherry. Nose: toasty, ripe fruit, smoky. Palate: correct, balanced, easy to drink.

Viña Hermosa 2009 TR
tempranillo

88

Colour: cherry, garnet rim. Nose: balanced, spicy, tobacco, ripe fruit. Palate: fruity, correct, easy to drink.

Viña Hermosa 2012 TC
tempranillo

86

BODEGAS SEÑORÍA DE YERGA

Barrio Bodegas, s/n
26142 Villamediana (La Rioja)
☎: +34 941 435 003
info@senoriodeyerga.com

Castillo de Yerga 2007 TGR
85% tempranillo, 10% graciano, 5% mazuelo

88

Colour: pale ruby, brick rim edge. Nose: spicy, fine reductive notes, wet leather, aged wood nuances, fruit liqueur notes. Palate: spicy, fine tannins, balanced.

Castillo de Yerga 2011 TC
90% tempranillo, 10% garnacha

86

Castillo Yerga 2009 TR
90% tempranillo, 10% mazuelo

85

BODEGAS SOLAR VIEJO

Camino de la Hoya, s/n
01300 Laguardia (Álava)
☎: +34 945 600 113
Fax: +34 945 600 600
solarviejo@solarviejo.com
www.solarviejo.com

Orube 2012 TC
tempranillo, garnacha, graciano

90

Colour: cherry, garnet rim. Nose: creamy oak, red berry notes, fresh fruit, balanced. Palate: flavourful, spicy.

Orube Alta Expresión 2011 T
tempranillo

92

Colour: bright cherry. Nose: ripe fruit, sweet spices, creamy oak. Palate: flavourful, fruity, toasty, round tannins.

Solar Viejo 2008 TR
tempranillo, graciano

88

Colour: cherry, garnet rim. Nose: smoky, spicy, ripe fruit. Palate: flavourful, smoky aftertaste, ripe fruit.

Solar Viejo 2012 TC
tempranillo

84

Solar Viejo Tempranillo 2014 T
tempranillo

83

BODEGAS SONSIERRA, S. COOP.

El Remedio, s/n
26338 San Vicente de la Sonsierra
(La Rioja)
☎: +34 941 334 031
Fax: +34 941 334 245
administracion@sonsierra.com
www.sonsierra.com

Avior 2010 TR
tempranillo

87

Colour: cherry, garnet rim. Nose: fine reductive notes, wet leather, aged wood nuances. Palate: spicy, long, toasty.

Avior 2011 TR
tempranillo

86

Avior 2012 TC
tempranillo

84

Avior 2014 RD
tempranillo

86

Pagos de la Sonsierra 2009 TR
tempranillo

90

Colour: cherry, garnet rim. Nose: balanced, ripe fruit, spicy, fine reductive notes. Palate: good structure, flavourful, round tannins, balanced.

Perfume de Sonsierra David Delfín 2010 T
tempranillo

91

Colour: bright cherry, garnet rim. Nose: expressive, spicy, ripe fruit. Palate: flavourful, ripe fruit, long, good acidity, balanced.

Sonsierra 2008 TGR
tempranillo

90

Colour: cherry, garnet rim. Nose: ripe fruit, wild herbs, spicy, balsamic herbs, tobacco. Palate: balanced, flavourful, long, balsamic.

Sonsierra 2010 TR
tempranillo

90

Colour: cherry, garnet rim. Nose: spicy, ripe fruit, violets. Palate: flavourful, ripe fruit, long, good acidity, balanced.

Sonsierra 2012 TC
tempranillo

87

Colour: bright cherry. Nose: ripe fruit, sweet spices, creamy oak. Palate: flavourful, fruity, toasty, round tannins.

Sonsierra 2014 BFB
viura

87

Colour: yellow. Nose: ripe fruit, toasty, aged wood nuances. Palate: flavourful, fruity, spicy, toasty, long.

Sonsierra Selección 2014 B
viura

87

Colour: bright straw. Nose: white flowers, fresh fruit, fragrant herbs. Palate: flavourful, fruity, good acidity.

Sonsierra Selección 2014 RD
tempranillo

86

Sonsierra Selección 2014 T
tempranillo

87

Colour: bright cherry, purple rim. Nose: ripe fruit, spicy, balanced. Palate: fruity, flavourful, easy to drink.

Sonsierra Vendimia Seleccionada 2010 TC
tempranillo

89

Colour: cherry, garnet rim. Nose: red berry notes, ripe fruit, fragrant herbs, spicy, toasty, creamy oak. Palate: flavourful, balsamic, balanced.

BODEGAS TARÓN

Ctra. de Miranda, s/n
26211 Tirgo (La Rioja)
☎: +34 941 301 650
Fax: +34 941 301 817
info@bodegastaron.com
www.bodegastaron.com

Tarón 2006 TR
90% tempranillo, 10% mazuelo

91

Colour: cherry, garnet rim. Nose: ripe fruit, spicy, creamy oak, complex. Palate: flavourful, toasty, round tannins.

Tarón 2011 TC
95% tempranillo, 5% mazuelo

88

Colour: bright cherry. Nose: sweet spices, creamy oak, overripe fruit. Palate: flavourful, toasty, round tannins.

Tarón 2014 B
100% viura

85

Tarón 2014 RD
50% garnacha, 50% viura

84

Tarón 4M 2012 T
100% tempranillo

90

Colour: bright cherry. Nose: ripe fruit, sweet spices, creamy oak. Palate: flavourful, fruity, round tannins.

Tarón Cepas Centenarias 2012 TR
100% tempranillo

92

Colour: light cherry. Nose: fine reductive notes, aged wood nuances, toasty, earthy notes, ripe fruit. Palate: spicy, toasty, flavourful.

TARON
CEPAS CENTENARIAS
2 0 1 2
Rioja
Denominación de Origen Calificada
Rioja Alta

Tarón Tempranillo 2014 T
100% tempranillo

87

Colour: cherry, purple rim. Nose: ripe fruit, spicy, balsamic herbs. Palate: powerful, fruity, unctuous.

BODEGAS TERMINUS

Camino de Baños, 23
01307 Villabuena de Alava (Álava)
☎: +34 626 636 997
correo@bodegasterminus.com
www.bodegasterminus.com

4D 2014 BFB
viura

88

Colour: bright yellow. Nose: ripe fruit, powerfull, toasty, aged wood nuances. Palate: flavourful, fruity, spicy, toasty, long.

4D 2014 T Fermentado en Barrica
tempranillo

88

Colour: cherry, purple rim. Nose: powerfull, ripe fruit, spicy. Palate: powerful, fruity, unctuous.

Imagina! 2013 T
tempranillo

89

Colour: cherry, garnet rim. Nose: ripe fruit, spicy, creamy oak, complex. Palate: flavourful, toasty, round tannins.

BODEGAS TOBÍA

Paraje Senda Rutia, s/n
26214 Cuzcurrita de Río Tirón (La Rioja)
☎: +34 941 301 789
Fax: +34 941 328 045
tobia@bodegastobia.com
www.bodegastobia.com

Alma de Tobía 2013 RD Fermentado en Barrica
55% tempranillo, 35% graciano, 10% otras

86

Alma de Tobía 2014 RD Fermentado en Barrica
55% tempranillo, 35% graciano, 10% otras

88

Colour: rose, purple rim. Nose: powerfull, fruit preserve, warm. Palate: powerful, flavourful, round.

Daimon 2013 T
85% garnacha, 15% tempranillo

90

Colour: bright cherry. Nose: ripe fruit, sweet spices, creamy oak. Palate: flavourful, fruity, round tannins.

Daimon 2014 B
30% viura, 25% malvasía, 15% tempranillo blanco, 30% sauvignon blanc

90

Colour: bright yellow. Nose: ripe fruit, powerfull, toasty, aged wood nuances, pattiserie. Palate: flavourful, fruity, spicy, toasty, long.

Oscar Tobía 2011 T
93% tempranillo, 7% graciano

89

Colour: cherry, garnet rim. Nose: smoky, spicy, ripe fruit. Palate: flavourful, smoky aftertaste, ripe fruit.

Oscar Tobía 2012 B
52% viura, 32% malvasía, 10% garnacha blanca, 6% tempranillo

blanco

89

Colour: bright yellow. Nose: expressive, dried herbs, ripe fruit, spicy, creamy oak. Palate: flavourful, fruity, good acidity, balanced.

Tobía 2012 TC

100% tempranillo

86

Tobía 2014 RD

100% garnacha

87

Colour: rose, purple rim. Nose: red berry notes, floral, lactic notes. Palate: powerful, fruity, fresh.

Tobía 2001 TGR

100% tempranillo

91

Colour: pale ruby, brick rim edge. Nose: spicy, fine reductive notes, wet leather, aged wood nuances, fruit liqueur notes. Palate: spicy, fine tannins, balanced.

Tobía Graciano 2013 T

100% graciano

87

Colour: cherry, garnet rim. Nose: smoky, spicy, ripe fruit. Palate: smoky aftertaste, ripe fruit.

Tobía Selección 2011 TC

74% tempranillo, 13% graciano, 13% garnacha

90

Colour: bright cherry. Nose: ripe fruit, sweet spices, creamy oak. Palate: flavourful, fruity, toasty, round tannins.

Viña Tobía 2014 B

80% viura, 20% verdejo

88

Colour: bright straw. Nose: white flowers, fresh fruit, fragrant herbs, expressive. Palate: flavourful, fruity, good acidity, balanced.

Viña Tobía 2014 T

50% garnacha, 50% tempranillo

87

Colour: cherry, purple rim. Nose: powerfull, ripe fruit, spicy. Palate: powerful, fruity, unctuous.

BODEGAS VALDELACIERVA

Ctra. Burgos, Km. 13
26370 Navarrete (La Rioja)
☎: +34 941 440 620
carlos.garcia@hispanobodegas.com
www.hispanobodegas.com

Valdelacierva 2012 TC

100% tempranillo

90

Colour: bright cherry, garnet rim. Nose: balanced, spicy, ripe fruit. Palate: good structure, fruity.

BODEGAS VALDELANA

Puente Barricuelo, 67-69
01340 Elciego (Álava)
☎: +34 945 606 055
Fax: +34 945 606 587
export@bodegasvaldelana.com
www.bodegasvaldelana.com

Agnus de Valdelana de Autor 2012 TC
95% tempranillo, 5% graciano

88

Colour: cherry, garnet rim. Nose: ripe fruit, spicy, creamy oak, complex. Palate: flavourful, toasty.

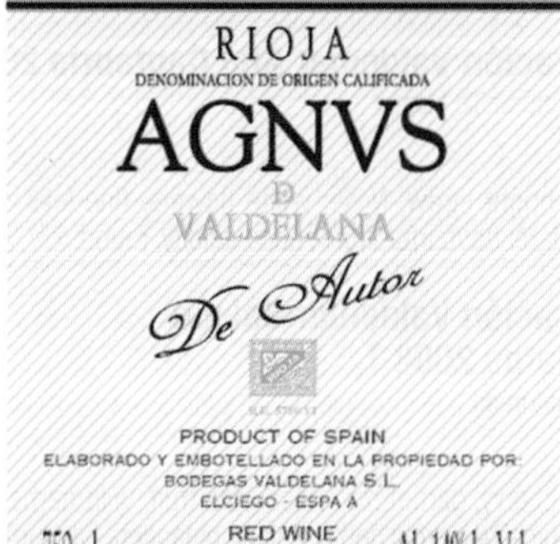

Agnus de Valdelana de Autor 2014 T
95% tempranillo, 5% graciano

90

Colour: bright cherry, purple rim. Nose: scrubland, wild herbs, ripe fruit, sweet spices. Palate: correct, fruity.

Duquesa de la Victoria 2012 TC
95% tempranillo, 5% mazuelo

88

Colour: bright cherry. Nose: ripe fruit, creamy oak. Palate: flavourful, fruity, toasty.

Forlán 2011 TR
95% tempranillo, 5% graciano

89

Colour: cherry, garnet rim. Nose: red berry notes, ripe fruit, spicy, creamy oak. Palate: flavourful, toasty, round tannins.

Forlán 2012 TC
95% tempranillo, 5% mazuelo

88

Colour: cherry, garnet rim. Nose: ripe fruit, spicy, creamy oak. Palate: flavourful, toasty, round tannins.

Ladrón de Guevara 2011 TR
95% tempranillo, 5% graciano

90

Colour: cherry, garnet rim. Nose: ripe fruit, wild herbs, spicy, balsamic herbs. Palate: balanced, flavourful, long, balsamic.

Ladrón de Guevara 2012 TC
95% tempranillo, 5% mazuelo

89

Colour: bright cherry. Nose: ripe fruit, sweet spices, creamy oak. Palate: flavourful, fruity, toasty.

Ladrón de Guevara de Autor 2012 TC
95% tempranillo, 5% graciano

90

Colour: cherry, garnet rim. Nose: ripe fruit, spicy, creamy oak, complex. Palate: flavourful, toasty.

Ladrón de Guevara de Autor 2014 T
95% tempranillo, 5% graciano

89

Colour: cherry, purple rim. Nose: powerfull, ripe fruit, spicy. Palate: powerful, fruity, unctuous.

Valdelana Selección 2011 TR
95% tempranillo, 5% graciano

90

Colour: cherry, garnet rim. Nose: red berry notes, ripe fruit, spicy, creamy oak, complex. Palate: flavourful, toasty, round tannins.

Valdelana Selección 2012 TC
95% tempranillo, 5% mazuelo

89

Colour: deep cherry, garnet rim. Nose: fruit preserve, spicy, dried herbs. Palate: balanced, round tannins.

BODEGAS VALDEMAR

Camino Viejo s/n
01320 Oyón (Álava)
☎: +34 945 622 188
Fax: +34 945 622 111
info@valdemar.es
www.valdemar.es

Conde de Valdemar 2007 TGR
85% tempranillo, 10% mazuelo, 5% graciano

89

Colour: dark-red cherry, orangey edge. Nose: spicy, fine reductive notes, wet leather, aged wood nuances. Palate: spicy, fine tannins, balanced.

Conde de Valdemar 2008 TR
90% tempranillo, 5% graciano, 5% mazuelo

88

Colour: light cherry. Nose: fine reductive notes, aged wood nuances, toasty, ripe fruit. Palate: spicy, toasty, flavourful.

Conde de Valdemar 2011 TC
90% tempranillo, 10% mazuelo

87

Colour: dark-red cherry, garnet rim. Nose: characterful, powerfull, fruit preserve, spicy. Palate: correct, spicy, ripe fruit.

Conde de Valdemar Finca Alto Cantabria 2014 BFB
100% viura

88

Colour: bright straw. Nose: white flowers, fine lees, dried herbs. Palate: flavourful, fruity, good acidity, round.

Conde de Valdemar Garnacha 2012 T
100% garnacha

88

Colour: cherry, garnet rim. Nose: ripe fruit, wild herbs, earthy notes, spicy, balsamic herbs. Palate: flavourful, long, balsamic.

Conde de Valdemar Viura Verdejo 2014 B
85% viura, 15% verdejo

85

Conde Valdemar Rosé 2014 RD
70% garnacha, 30% viura

85

Conde Valdemar Tempranillo 2014 T
100% tempranillo

88

Colour: cherry, purple rim. Nose: red berry notes, floral, ripe fruit. Palate: flavourful, fruity, good acidity.

Inspiración de Valdemar Las Canteras 2010 T
70% tempranillo, 30% graciano

90

Colour: very deep cherry, purple rim. Nose: creamy oak, toasty, smoky, ripe fruit. Palate: flavourful, powerful, round tannins.

Inspiración Valdemar Alto Cantabria 2014 B
100% tempranillo blanco

87

Colour: bright straw. Nose: white flowers, fine lees, tropical fruit. Palate: flavourful, fruity, good acidity, round.

Inspiración Valdemar Balcón de Pilatos 2008 T
100% maturana

90

Colour: cherry, garnet rim. Nose: ripe fruit, wild herbs, earthy notes, spicy, balsamic herbs. Palate: balanced, flavourful, long, balsamic.

Inspiración Valdemar Edición Limitada 2008 T
70% tempranillo, 10% graciano, 10% maturana, 10% experimental

90

Colour: cherry, garnet rim. Nose: balanced, ripe fruit, spicy, fine reductive notes. Palate: good structure, flavourful, round tannins, balanced.

Inspiración Valdemar Las Seis Alhajas 2005 T
100% graciano

90

Colour: cherry, garnet rim. Nose: balanced, complex, ripe fruit, spicy, fine reductive notes. Palate: good structure, flavourful, round tannins, balanced.

LAS SEIS ALHAJAS

Inspiración Valdemar Selección 2011 T
80% tempranillo, 10% graciano, 10% maturana

89

Colour: cherry, garnet rim. Nose: ripe fruit, spicy, creamy oak. Palate: flavourful, toasty, ripe fruit.

BODEGAS VALLEMAYOR

Ctra. Logroño-Vitoria, 38
26360 Fuenmayor (La Rioja)
☎: +34 941 450 142
Fax: +34 941 450 376
vallemayor@fer.es
www.vallemayor.com

Colección Valle Mayor Viña Cerradilla 2010 TC
88

Colour: cherry, garnet rim. Nose: red berry notes, ripe fruit, spicy, creamy oak, fine reductive notes. Palate: flavourful, toasty, round tannins.

Colección Valle Mayor Viña Encineda 2012 T
85

Vallemayor 2005 TGR
87

Colour: pale ruby, brick rim edge. Nose: spicy, fine reductive notes, tobacco. Palate: spicy, long, flavourful.

Vallemayor 2007 TR
87

Colour: pale ruby, brick rim edge. Nose: spicy, wet leather, aged wood nuances, fruit liqueur notes. Palate: spicy, balanced.

Vallemayor 2012 BFB
86

Vallemayor 2012 TC
84

Vallemayor 2014 B
83

Vallemayor 2014 T
83

BODEGAS VICENTE GANDÍA

Ctra. Cheste a Godelleta, s/n
46370 Chiva (Valencia)
☎: +34 962 524 242
Fax: +34 962 524 243
info@vicentegandia.com
www.vicentegandia.es

Altos de Raiza Tempranillo 2014 T
100% tempranillo

86

Raiza Tempranillo 2007 TGR
100% tempranillo

87

Colour: cherry, garnet rim. Nose: spicy, ripe fruit, waxy notes. Palate: correct, good finish, round tannins.

Raiza Tempranillo 2010 TR
100% tempranillo

87

Colour: light cherry. Nose: aged wood nuances, toasty, ripe fruit. Palate: spicy, toasty, flavourful.

Raiza Tempranillo 2012 TC
100% tempranillo

86

BODEGAS VINÍCOLA REAL

Ctra. Nalda, km. 9
26120 Albelda de Iregua (La Rioja)
☎: +34 941 444 233
Fax: +34 941 444 427
info@vinicolareal.com
www.vinicolareal.com

200 Monges 2008 TR
85% tempranillo, 10% graciano, 5% garnacha

89

Colour: cherry, garnet rim. Nose: complex, ripe fruit, spicy. Palate: good structure, flavourful, balanced.

200 Monges Selección Especial 2008 B Reserva
70% viura, 20% malvasía, 10% otras

93

Colour: bright yellow. Nose: expressive, dried herbs, ripe fruit, spicy, complex, faded flowers. Palate: flavourful, fruity, good acidity, balanced.

Cueva del Monge 2011 T
100% tempranillo

89

Colour: cherry, garnet rim. Nose: red berry notes, ripe fruit, spicy, creamy oak. Palate: flavourful, toasty, round tannins.

Cueva del Monge 2013 BFB
70% viura, 20% malvasía, 10% otras

91

Colour: bright yellow. Nose: ripe fruit, powerfull, toasty. Palate: flavourful, fruity, spicy, toasty, long, good acidity.

Viña Los Valles 50 & 50 2012 TC
50% garnacha, 50% graciano

88 ♣

Colour: cherry, garnet rim. Nose: ripe fruit, spicy, creamy oak. Palate: flavourful, toasty.

Viña Los Valles 70 & 30 2012 TC
70% tempranillo, 30% graciano

87 ♣

Colour: bright cherry. Nose: ripe fruit, sweet spices, creamy oak. Palate: flavourful, fruity, toasty.

Viña Los Valles 80 & 20 2012 TC
80% tempranillo, 20% mazuelo

87 ♣

Colour: dark-red cherry, garnet rim. Nose: smoky, toasty, characterful. Palate: flavourful, easy to drink, good finish.

Viña Los Valles Tempranillo 2014 T
100% tempranillo

87 ♣

Colour: cherry, purple rim. Nose: powerfull, ripe fruit, wild herbs. Palate: powerful, fruity, unctuous.

BODEGAS VIÑA BERNEDA

Ctra. Somalo, 59
26313 Uruñuela (La Rioja)
☎: +34 941 371 304
Fax: +34 941 371 304
berneda@vinaberneda.com
www.vinaberneda.com

Berneda Vendimia Seleccionada 2009 TC
100% tempranillo

87

Colour: cherry, garnet rim. Nose: ripe fruit, old leather, tobacco. Palate: correct, flavourful, spicy.

Viña Berneda 2014 BFB
100% viura

88

Colour: bright yellow. Nose: ripe fruit, powerfull, toasty, aged wood nuances. Palate: flavourful, fruity, spicy, toasty, long.

Viña Berneda 2014 T Maceración Carbónica
100% tempranillo

83

BODEGAS VIÑA HERMINIA

Camino de los Agudos, 1
26559 Aldeanueva de Ebro (La Rioja)
☎: +34 941 142 305
Fax: +34 941 142 303
vherminia@vherminia.es
www.viñaherminia.es

Viña Herminia 2010 TR
85% tempranillo, 10% garnacha, 5% graciano

89

Colour: cherry, garnet rim. Nose: scrubland, ripe fruit, toasty. Palate: balanced, ripe fruit, round tannins.

Viña Herminia 2012 TC
85% tempranillo, 15% garnacha

86

Viña Herminia Excelsus 2012 T
50% tempranillo, 50% garnacha

87

Colour: cherry, garnet rim. Nose: grassy, wild herbs, ripe fruit. Palate: spicy, round tannins.

BODEGAS VIVANCO

Ctra. Nacional 232, s/n
26330 Briones (La Rioja)
☎: +34 941 322 323
info@vivancoculturadevino.es
www.dinastiavivanco.com

Colección Vivanco 4 Varietales 2012 T
70% tempranillo, 15% garnacha, 10% graciano, 5% mazuelo

91

Colour: bright cherry, garnet rim. Nose: ripe fruit, wild herbs, spicy. Palate: balanced, good structure, flavourful.

Colección Vivanco Parcelas de Garnacha 2011 T
garnacha

91

Colour: very deep cherry, garnet rim. Nose: expressive, balsamic herbs, balanced, varietal. Palate: full, flavourful, round tannins.

Colección Vivanco Parcelas de Graciano 2009 T
graciano

91

Colour: cherry, garnet rim. Nose: mineral, expressive, spicy. Palate: flavourful, ripe fruit, long, good acidity, balanced.

Colección Vivanco Parcelas de Maturana 2012 T
maturana

92

Colour: very deep cherry, garnet rim. Nose: expressive, complex, balsamic herbs, balanced, wild herbs. Palate: full, flavourful, round tannins.

Colección Vivanco Parcelas de Mazuelo 2011 T
mazuelo

89

Colour: deep cherry, garnet rim. Nose: old leather, tobacco, ripe fruit, dried herbs. Palate: flavourful, long.

Vivanco 2010 TR
90% tempranillo, 10% graciano

91

Colour: cherry, garnet rim. Nose: balanced, complex, ripe fruit, spicy, fine reductive notes. Palate: flavourful, round tannins, balanced.

Vivanco 2011 TC
tempranillo

89

Colour: dark-red cherry, garnet rim. Nose: spicy, toasty, fine reductive notes, scrubland, ripe fruit. Palate: balanced, round tannins.

Vivanco Tempranillo Garnacha 2014 RD
85% tempranillo, 15% garnacha

87

Colour: rose, purple rim. Nose: red berry notes, floral, fragrant herbs. Palate: powerful, fruity, fresh.

Vivanco Viura Malvasía Tempranillo Blanco 2014 B
60% viura, 20% malvasía, 20% tempranillo blanco

87

Colour: bright straw. Nose: white flowers, fresh fruit, fragrant herbs, expressive. Palate: flavourful, fruity, good acidity, balanced.

BODEGAS Y VIÑAS DEL CONDE

Calle Bodegas, 18
01306 LaPuebla de Labarca (Álava)
☎: +34 673 736 155
Fax: +34 945 063 173
condedealtava@gmail.com
www.casadomorales.es

Conde de Altava 2011 TC
100% tempranillo

89

Colour: bright cherry. Nose: ripe fruit, sweet spices, creamy oak, wild herbs. Palate: flavourful, fruity, toasty.

Conde de Altava 2014 RD
85% tempranillo, 15% garnacha

87

Colour: raspberry rose. Nose: elegant, red berry notes, floral, fragrant herbs. Palate: flavourful, good acidity, long, spicy.

Marqués del Cerro 2009 TR
100% tempranillo

87

Colour: cherry, garnet rim. Nose: ripe fruit, spicy, creamy oak, fine reductive notes. Palate: flavourful, toasty, balsamic.

Marqués del Cerro Tempranillo 2014 T
100% tempranillo

88

Colour: cherry, purple rim. Nose: expressive, fresh fruit, red berry notes, floral. Palate: flavourful, fruity, good acidity.

BODEGAS Y VIÑAS SENDA GALIANA

Barrio Bodegas, s/n
26142 Villamediana (La Rioja)
☎: +34 941 435 375
Fax: +34 941 436 072
info@sendagaliana.com

Senda Galiana 2007 TGR
85% tempranillo, 10% graciano, 5% mazuelo

88

Colour: cherry, garnet rim. Nose: fine reductive notes, wet leather, aged wood nuances. Palate: spicy, long, toasty, classic aged character.

Senda Galiana 2009 TR
90% tempranillo, 10% mazuelo

84

Senda Galiana 2011 TC
90% tempranillo, 10% garnacha

82

BODEGAS Y VIÑEDOS ARRANZ-ARGOTE

Mayor Alta, 43
26370 Navarrete (La Rioja)
☎: +34 699 046 043
carlos@vinoarar.com
www.vinoarar.com

Arar 2011 TC
tempranillo, graciano, garnacha

87

Colour: cherry, garnet rim. Nose: balsamic herbs, balanced. Palate: full, flavourful, round tannins, ripe fruit.

Arar 2014 T
tempranillo, graciano

86

Arar Autor 2004 T
tempranillo, graciano, garnacha, maturana

89

Colour: pale ruby, brick rim edge. Nose: spicy, fine reductive notes, wet leather, aged wood nuances, fruit liqueur notes. Palate: spicy, fine tannins, balanced.

BODEGAS Y VIÑEDOS ARTADI

Ctra. de Logroño, s/n
31300 Laguardia (Álava)
☎: +34 945 600 119
Fax: +34 945 600 850
comunicacion@artadi.com
www.artadi.com

PODIUM

Artadi El Carretil 2013 T
100% tempranillo

96

Colour: cherry, garnet rim. Nose: roasted coffee, smoky, spicy, ripe fruit. Palate: flavourful, ripe fruit, powerful, good acidity.

PODIUM

Artadi La Poza de Ballesteros 2013 T
100% tempranillo

95

Colour: cherry, garnet rim. Nose: creamy oak, balanced, ripe fruit, red berry notes. Palate: flavourful, spicy, fine bitter notes, powerful.

PODIUM

Artadi Valdeginés 2013 T
100% tempranillo

95

Colour: cherry, garnet rim. Nose: roasted coffee, smoky, spicy, ripe fruit. Palate: flavourful, smoky aftertaste, ripe fruit.

PODIUM

Artadi Viña El Pisón 2013 T
100% tempranillo

97

Colour: cherry, garnet rim. Nose: smoky, spicy, ripe fruit, powerfull. Palate: flavourful, smoky aftertaste, ripe fruit, mineral.

Artadi Viñas de Gain 2013 T
100% tempranillo

93

Colour: bright cherry. Nose: ripe fruit, sweet spices, creamy oak. Palate: flavourful, fruity, round tannins.

BODEGAS Y VIÑEDOS CASADO MORALES, S.C.

Avda. La Póveda 12-14
01306 Lapuebla de Labarca (Alava)
☎: +34 945 607 017
Fax: +34 945 063 173
info@casadomorales.es
www.casadomorales.es

Casado Morales Selección Privada 2010 TR

95% tempranillo, 3% garnacha, 2% mazuelo

92

Colour: cherry, garnet rim. Nose: ripe fruit, wild herbs, earthy notes, spicy, balsamic herbs. Palate: balanced, flavourful, long, balsamic.

Casado Morales Tempranillo Vendimia 2011 TC

95% tempranillo, 5% graciano

90

Colour: cherry, garnet rim. Nose: red berry notes, ripe fruit, spicy, creamy oak, complex. Palate: flavourful, toasty, round tannins.

Eme de Casado Morales Graciano 2010 T

100% graciano

86

Nobleza Casado Morales 2014 T Maceración Carbónica

90% tempranillo, 10% viura

89

Colour: cherry, purple rim. Nose: expressive, fresh fruit, red berry notes, floral. Palate: flavourful, fruity, good acidity.

Nobleza Dimidium 2012 T

100% tempranillo

89

Colour: bright cherry. Nose: ripe fruit, sweet spices, creamy oak, expressive. Palate: flavourful, fruity, round tannins.

BODEGAS Y VIÑEDOS HERAS CORDÓN

Ctra. Lapuebla, Km. 2
26360 Fuenmayor (La Rioja)
☎: +34 941 451 413
Fax: +34 941 450 265
exportacion@herascordon.com
www.herascordon.com

Heras Cordón 2010 TR

tempranillo, graciano, mazuelo

88

Colour: cherry, garnet rim. Nose: balanced, ripe fruit, dried herbs, waxy notes. Palate: balanced, round tannins.

Heras Cordón Vendimia Seleccionada 2012 TC

tempranillo, graciano, mazuelo

87

Colour: deep cherry. Nose: toasty, ripe fruit, balsamic herbs. Palate: balanced, spicy, long.

Marqués del Hueco 2005 TR

tempranillo, graciano, mazuelo

87

Colour: cherry, garnet rim. Nose: ripe fruit, old leather, tobacco. Palate: correct, flavourful, spicy.

BODEGAS Y VIÑEDOS ILURCE

Ctra. Alfaro - Grávalos (LR-289), km. 23
26540 Alfaro (La Rioja)
☎: +34 941 180 829
Fax: +34 941 183 897
info@ilurce.com
www.ilurce.com

Ilurce 2014 RD

100% garnacha

88

Colour: rose, purple rim. Nose: red berry notes, floral, expressive. Palate: powerful, fruity, fresh, easy to drink.

Ilurce 2014 T

100% tempranillo

86

Ilurce Graciano 2010 TC

100% graciano

88

Colour: deep cherry, garnet rim. Nose: expressive, balanced, fruit preserve, ripe fruit, wild herbs. Palate: spicy, long.

BODEGAS Y VIÑEDOS LABASTIDA - SOLAGÜEN

Avda. Diputación, 22
01330 Labastida (Álava)
☎: +34 945 331 118
Fax: +34 945 331 118
info@bodegaslabastida.com
www.bodegaslabastida.com

Solagüen 2009 TR

100% tempranillo

89

Colour: cherry, garnet rim. Nose: ripe fruit, old leather, tobacco. Palate: correct, flavourful, spicy.

Solagüen 2012 TC

100% tempranillo

88

Colour: cherry, garnet rim. Nose: creamy oak, red berry notes. Palate: flavourful, spicy.

Solagüen Selección Aniversario 2011 TC
100% tempranillo

88

Colour: cherry, garnet rim. Nose: smoky, spicy, ripe fruit. Palate: flavourful, smoky aftertaste, ripe fruit.

BODEGAS Y VIÑEDOS MARQUÉS DE CARRIÓN

Ctra. Logroño, s/n
01330 Labastida (Álava)
☎: +34 945 331 643
Fax: +34 945 331 694
eromero@jgc.es
www.garciacarrion.es

Antaño 2011 TR
tempranillo, graciano, mazuelo, garnacha

82

Antaño 2012 TC
tempranillo, graciano, mazuelo, garnacha

84

Antaño 2014 B
viura

84

Antaño 2014 RD
tempranillo

84

Antaño 2014 T
tempranillo, garnacha, mazuelo

82

Marqués de Carrión 2010 TR
tempranillo, graciano, mazuelo

84

Marqués de Carrión 2011 TC
tempranillo, graciano, mazuelo

85

Pata Negra 2010 TR
tempranillo, graciano, mazuelo

86

Pata Negra 2012 TC
tempranillo, graciano, mazuelo

84

Pata Negra Graciano 2012 TC
graciano

87

Colour: cherry, garnet rim. Nose: ripe fruit, spicy, balsamic herbs, fragrant herbs. Palate: balanced, flavourful, balsamic.

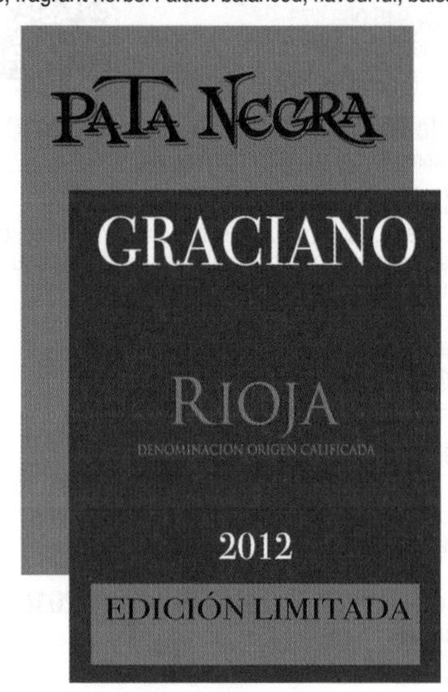

Pata Negra Gran Selección 2013 T
tempranillo

85

BODEGAS Y VIÑEDOS MARQUÉS DE VARGAS

Ctra. Zaragoza, Km. 6
26006 Logroño (La Rioja)
☎: +34 941 261 401
Fax: +34 941 238 696
bodega@marquesdevargas.com
www.marquesdevargas.com

Marqués de Vargas 2010 TR
75% tempranillo, 10% mazuelo, 5% garnacha, 10% otras

88

Colour: bright cherry. Nose: sweet spices, creamy oak, ripe fruit, wild herbs, fruit preserve. Palate: flavourful, fruity, toasty.

Marqués de Vargas Hacienda Pradolagar 2005 TR
40% tempranillo, 10% mazuelo, 10% garnacha, 40% otras

92

Colour: light cherry. Nose: fine reductive notes, aged wood nuances, toasty. Palate: spicy, toasty, flavourful.

Marqués de Vargas Reserva Privada 2009 TR
60% tempranillo, 10% mazuelo, 10% garnacha, 20% otras

92

Colour: cherry, garnet rim. Nose: mineral, expressive, spicy. Palate: flavourful, ripe fruit, long, good acidity, balanced.

BODEGAS Y VIÑEDOS PUJANZA

Ctra. Elvillar, s/n
01320 Laguardia (Álava)
☎: +34 945 600 548
Fax: +34 945 600 522
info@bodegaspujanza.com
www.bodegaspujanza.com

Pujanza Finca Valdepoleo 2012 T
100% tempranillo

92

Colour: bright cherry. Nose: sweet spices, creamy oak, ripe fruit. Palate: flavourful, fruity, toasty, round tannins.

Pujanza Norte 2012 T
100% tempranillo

93

Colour: cherry, garnet rim. Nose: smoky, ripe fruit, dark chocolate. Palate: flavourful, smoky aftertaste, ripe fruit.

BODEGAS Y VIÑEDOS TRITIUM

Avda. de la Libertad 9
26350 Cenicero (La Rioja)
☎: +34 629 152 822
bodegastritium@gmail.com
www.tritium.es

Tritium El Largo 4 Variedades 2012 T
tempranillo, garnacha, graciano, mazuelo

90

Colour: black cherry, garnet rim. Nose: toasty, sweet spices, ripe fruit, dried herbs. Palate: good structure, round tannins, long.

Tritium El Largo Graciano 2012 T
graciano

91

Colour: deep cherry, garnet rim. Nose: expressive, wild herbs, ripe fruit, spicy, varietal, warm. Palate: balanced, round tannins, balsamic.

Tritium Night 2012 TC
tempranillo

87

Colour: deep cherry. Nose: fruit preserve, cocoa bean, sweet spices. Palate: flavourful, sweet tannins.

BODEGAS Y VIÑEDOS VARAL

San Vicenta, 40
01307 Baños de Ebro (Álava)
☎: +34 945 623 321
Fax: +34 945 623 321
bodegasvaral@bodegasvaral.com
www.bodegasvaral.com

Blanco de Varal 2014 B
viura

85

Crianza de Varal 2012 T
tempranillo

88

Colour: cherry, garnet rim. Nose: ripe fruit, spicy, creamy oak. Palate: flavourful, toasty, ripe fruit.

Ecos de Varal 2014 T
90% tempranillo, 10% viura

89 ♣

Colour: cherry, purple rim. Nose: powerfull, ripe fruit, balsamic herbs, earthy notes. Palate: powerful, fruity, unctuous.

Esencias de Varal 2012 T
tempranillo

90

Colour: cherry, garnet rim. Nose: ripe fruit, spicy, creamy oak, sweet spices. Palate: flavourful, toasty, round tannins.

Joven de Varal 2014 T
tempranillo

88

Colour: cherry, purple rim. Nose: expressive, fresh fruit, red berry notes, floral, wild herbs. Palate: flavourful, fruity, good acidity.

Varal Vendimia Seleccionada 2011 T
tempranillo

89

Colour: cherry, garnet rim. Nose: ripe fruit, wild herbs, spicy, aged wood nuances. Palate: balanced, flavourful, long, balsamic, toasty.

BODEGAS Y VIÑEDOS ZUAZO GASTÓN

Las Norias, 2
01320 Oyón (Álava)
☎: +34 945 601 526
Fax: +34 945 622 917
zuazogaston@zuazogaston.com
www.zuazogaston.com

ZG Zuazo Gastón 2012 TC
95% tempranillo, 5% graciano

88

Colour: cherry, garnet rim. Nose: ripe fruit, spicy, creamy oak, complex. Palate: flavourful, toasty.

Zuazo Gastón 2010 TR
95% tempranillo, 5% graciano

90

Colour: ruby red. Nose: spicy, fine reductive notes, wet leather, aged wood nuances. Palate: spicy, fine tannins, balanced.

Zuazo Gastón 2014 B
viura

85

Zuazo Gastón 2012 TC
tempranillo

87

Colour: deep cherry. Nose: creamy oak, toasty, ripe fruit, balsamic herbs. Palate: balanced, spicy, long.

Zuazo Gastón Reserva de Familia 2009 T
80% tempranillo, 20% graciano

90

Colour: cherry, garnet rim. Nose: fine reductive notes, spicy, ripe fruit, dried herbs. Palate: spicy, long, toasty.

BODEGAS YSIOS

Camino de la Hoya, s/n
01300 Laguardia (Álava)
☎: +34 945 600 640
ysios@pernod-ricard.com
www.ysios.com

Ysios 2008 TR
tempranillo

90

Colour: cherry, garnet rim. Nose: ripe fruit, spicy, fine reductive notes. Palate: good structure, flavourful, round tannins, balanced.

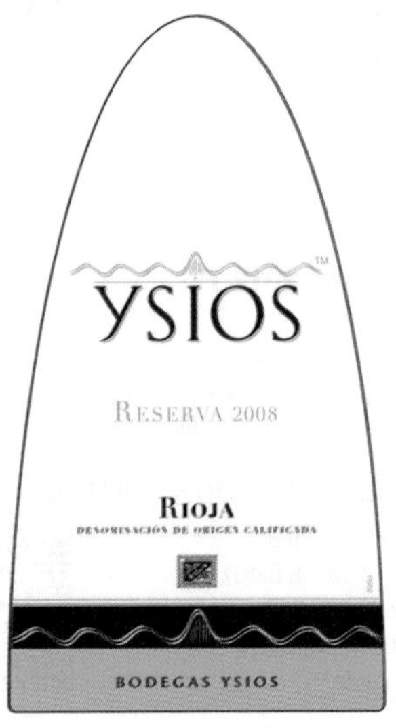

Ysios Edición Limitada 2009 TR
tempranillo

93

Colour: cherry, garnet rim. Nose: ripe fruit, wild herbs, earthy notes, spicy, balsamic herbs. Palate: balanced, flavourful, long, balsamic.

BODEGAS ZUGOBER

Tejerías, 13-15
01306 Lapuebla de Labarca (Álava)
☎: +34 945 627 228
Fax: +34 945 627 281
contacto@belezos.com
www.zugober.com

Belezos 2001 TGR
95% tempranillo, 5% graciano, mazuelo

91

Colour: pale ruby, brick rim edge. Nose: spicy, fine reductive notes, wet leather, aged wood nuances, fruit liqueur notes. Palate: spicy, fine tannins, balanced.

Belezos 2012 BFB
100% viura

89

Colour: bright yellow. Nose: powerfull, toasty, pattiserie. Palate: flavourful, fruity, spicy, toasty, long, roasted-coffee aftertaste.

Belezos 2012 TC
95% tempranillo, 5% graciano, mazuelo

87

Colour: cherry, garnet rim. Nose: fine reductive notes, wet leather, aged wood nuances. Palate: spicy, long, toasty.

Belezos 2014 T
100% tempranillo

87

Colour: cherry, purple rim. Nose: red berry notes, floral. Palate: flavourful, fruity, good acidity.

Belezos Ecológico 2011 T
100% tempranillo

90

Colour: very deep cherry, garnet rim. Nose: complex, mineral, balsamic herbs, balanced. Palate: full, flavourful, round tannins.

Belezos Único de la Familia 2009 TR
95% tempranillo, 5% graciano, mazuelo

88

Colour: cherry, garnet rim. Nose: wet leather, aged wood nuances, ripe fruit, aromatic coffee. Palate: spicy, long, toasty.

Belezos Vendimia Seleccionada 2011 T
100% tempranillo

91

Colour: cherry, garnet rim. Nose: smoky, spicy, ripe fruit. Palate: flavourful, smoky aftertaste, ripe fruit.

BOHEDAL

Crta Pancorbo. Camino de Los Lirios s/n
26240 Cuzcurrita de Río Tirón (La Rioja)
☎: +34 941 328 064
info@bohedal.com
www.bohedal.com

Bohedal 2014 B
100% viura

86

Bohedal 2014 T
100% tempranillo

85

Gran Bohedal 2009 TR
100% tempranillo

88

Colour: bright cherry. Nose: ripe fruit, sweet spices, creamy oak, fine reductive notes. Palate: flavourful, fruity, toasty, round tannins.

Gran Bohedal 2011 TC
100% tempranillo

87

Colour: cherry, garnet rim. Nose: red berry notes, ripe fruit, spicy, creamy oak. Palate: flavourful, toasty.

Gran Bohedal 2014 B
100% viura

86

Hebabe Garnacha 2012 T
100% garnacha

91

Colour: cherry, garnet rim. Nose: ripe fruit, wild herbs, earthy notes, spicy, balsamic herbs. Palate: balanced, flavourful, long, balsamic.

Hebabe Graciano 2010 T
100% graciano

88

Colour: cherry, garnet rim. Nose: fruit preserve, balsamic herbs, spicy. Palate: powerful, flavourful, ripe fruit, long.

Hebabe Tempranillo 2010 T
100% tempranillo

92

Colour: cherry, garnet rim. Nose: red berry notes, ripe fruit, spicy, creamy oak, complex. Palate: flavourful, toasty, round tannins, balanced.

CAMPOS DE HOJAS

Avda. Diagonal, 590, 5º 1ª
08021 (Barcelona)
☎: +34 660 445 464
vinergia@vinergia.com
www.vinergia.com

Campos de Hojas 2006 TR
100% tempranillo

88

Colour: cherry, garnet rim. Nose: ripe fruit, wild herbs, spicy, balsamic herbs, fine reductive notes. Palate: flavourful, long, balsamic.

Campos de Hojas 2011 TC
100% tempranillo

87

Colour: cherry, garnet rim. Nose: red berry notes, ripe fruit, spicy, creamy oak, fine reductive notes. Palate: flavourful, toasty.

Campos de Hojas 2014 T
80% tempranillo, 20% garnacha

85

CARLOS SERRES

Avda. Santo Domingo, 40
26200 Haro (La Rioja)
☎: +34 941 310 279
Fax: +34 941 310 418
info@carlosserres.com
www.carlosserres.com

Carlos Serres 2005 TGR
85% tempranillo, 10% graciano, 5% mazuelo

88

Colour: light cherry, garnet rim. Nose: fruit preserve, sweet spices, old leather, tobacco. Palate: correct, balanced.

Carlos Serres 2009 TR
90% tempranillo, 10% graciano

89

Colour: cherry, garnet rim. Nose: ripe fruit, wild herbs, earthy notes, spicy, balsamic herbs, fine reductive notes. Palate: balanced, flavourful, long.

Carlos Serres 2011 TC
85% tempranillo, 15% garnacha

87

Colour: cherry, garnet rim. Nose: creamy oak, red berry notes, balanced. Palate: flavourful, spicy.

Onomástica 2007 TR
80% tempranillo, 10% graciano, 10% mazuelo

92

Colour: pale ruby, brick rim edge. Nose: elegant, spicy, fine reductive notes, balsamic herbs, ripe fruit. Palate: spicy, fine tannins, elegant, long.

Onomástica 2011 B Reserva
viura

89

Colour: bright yellow. Nose: ripe fruit, powerfull, toasty, creamy oak. Palate: flavourful, spicy, toasty, long.

Serres Tempranillo 2014 T
tempranillo

85

Serres Tempranillo Garnacha 2014 RD
80% tempranillo, 20% garnacha

84

Serres Viura 2014 B
viura

85

CASA ROJO

Sánchez Picazo, 53
30332 Balsapintada (Murcia)
☎: +34 968 151 520
Fax: +34 968 151 539
info@casarojo.com
www.casarojo.com

The Invisible Man 2013 TC

88

Colour: bright cherry. Nose: ripe fruit, sweet spices, creamy oak. Palate: flavourful, fruity, toasty.

CASTILLO CLAVIJO

Ctra. de Clavijo, s/n
26141 Alberite (La Rioja)
☎: +34 941 436 702
Fax: +34 941 436 430
info@castilloclavijo.com
www.criadoresderioja.com

Castillo Clavijo 2007 TGR
80% tempranillo, 10% graciano, 10% mazuelo

84

Castillo Clavijo 2011 TC
90% tempranillo, 10% garnacha

86

Castillo Clavijo 2013 BFB
100% viura

85

CASTILLO DE CUZCURRITA

San Sebastián, 1
26214 Cuzcurrita del Río Tirón
(La Rioja)
☎: +34 941 328 022
Fax: +34 941 301 620
info@castillodecuzcurrita.com
www.castillodecuzcurrita.com

Cerrado del Castillo 2008 T
100% tempranillo

91

Colour: very deep cherry, garnet rim. Nose: expressive, complex, mineral, balsamic herbs, balanced, ripe fruit. Palate: full, flavourful, round tannins.

COMERCIAL GRUPO FREIXENET

Joan Sala, 2
08770 Sant Sadurní D'Anoia
(Barcelona)
☎: +34 938 917 000
Fax: +34 938 183 095
freixenet@freixenet.es
www.freixenet.es

Monólogo 2012 TC

85

COMPAÑÍA DE VINOS TELMO RODRÍGUEZ

El Monte
01308 Lanciego (Álava)
☎: +34 945 628 315
Fax: +34 945 628 314
contact@telmorodriguez.com
www.telmorodriguez.com

Altos de Lanzaga 2011 T

tempranillo, graciano, garnacha

93

Colour: cherry, garnet rim. Nose: smoky, spicy, ripe fruit. Palate: flavourful, smoky aftertaste, ripe fruit.

Corriente 2012 T

tempranillo, graciano, garnacha

91

Colour: bright cherry. Nose: sweet spices, creamy oak, ripe fruit. Palate: flavourful, fruity, round tannins.

Lanzaga 2011 T

tempranillo, graciano, garnacha

93

Colour: bright cherry. Nose: sweet spices, creamy oak, fruit expression. Palate: flavourful, fruity, toasty.

PODIUM

Las Beatas 2012 T

tempranillo, graciano, garnacha

97

Colour: very deep cherry, garnet rim. Nose: complex, mineral, balsamic herbs, balanced, characterful, earthy notes. Palate: full, flavourful, round tannins.

LZ 2014 T

tempranillo, graciano, garnacha

92

Colour: cherry, purple rim. Nose: fresh fruit, red berry notes, floral. Palate: flavourful, fruity, good acidity.

CORDIS TERRA HISPANIA

Gamonal, 16 2ºC
28031 Madrid (Madrid)
☎: +34 911 610 024
Fax: +34 913 316 047
info@cordisterra.com
www.cordisterra.com

Vega Valbosque 2009 TR

90% tempranillo, 10% garnacha

87

Colour: ruby red. Nose: wild herbs, fine reductive notes, ripe fruit. Palate: powerful, flavourful, spicy.

Vega Valbosque 2012 T

85% tempranillo, 10% garnacha, 5% mazuelo

86

CÓRDOBA MARTÍNEZ S.C.

La Poveda, 64
01306 Lapuebla de Labarca (Álava)
☎: +34 945 627 212
info@bodegascordobamartinez.com
www.bodegascordobamartinez.com

José Córdoba 2014 B

90% viura, 10% malvasía

81

José Córdoba 2014 T

100% tempranillo

84

Onardoa 2011 TC

95% tempranillo, 5% graciano, mazuelo, viura

85

CREACIONES EXEO

Costanilla del Hospital s/n
01330 Labastida (Álava)
☎: +34 945 331 230
Fax: +34 945 331 257
export@bodegasexeo.com
www.bodegasexeo.com

Cifras 2012 B Roble

100% garnacha

90

Colour: bright yellow. Nose: expressive, dried herbs, ripe fruit, spicy. Palate: flavourful, fruity, good acidity, balanced.

Letras 2012 T

tempranillo

91

Colour: cherry, garnet rim. Nose: red berry notes, ripe fruit, spicy, creamy oak, complex. Palate: flavourful, toasty, round tannins.

Letras Minúsculas 2012 T
60% tempranillo, 20% garnacha, 10% graciano

90

Colour: cherry, garnet rim. Nose: ripe fruit, wild herbs, earthy notes, spicy, balsamic herbs. Palate: balanced, flavourful, long, balsamic.

CUNA DE MARAS

Nueva, 1
01306 Lapuebla de Labarca (Álava)
☎: +34 652 721 152
Fax: +34 945 627 281
cunademaras@gmail.com

Cuna de Maras 2014 T Maceración Carbónica
100% tempranillo

86

Cuna de Maras Malvasia 2013 BFB
100% malvasía

83

El Valle de Cuna de Maras 2011 T
100% tempranillo

91

Colour: cherry, garnet rim. Nose: creamy oak, red berry notes, balanced, ripe fruit. Palate: flavourful, spicy, good structure.

CVNE

Barrio de la Estación, s/n
26200 Haro (La Rioja)
☎: +34 941 304 800
Fax: +34 941 304 815
marketing@cvne.com
www.cvne.com

Corona Semidulce 2014 B
85% viura, 15% malvasía, garnacha blanca

89

Colour: bright yellow. Nose: balsamic herbs, honeyed notes, floral, sweet spices. Palate: rich, fruity, powerful, flavourful.

Cune 18,7 cl. s/c T

88

Colour: cherry, garnet rim. Nose: medium intensity, dried herbs, ripe fruit. Palate: balanced, ripe fruit.

Cune 2010 TGR
85% tempranillo, 10% graciano, 5% mazuelo

91

Colour: cherry, garnet rim. Nose: elegant, spicy, fine reductive notes, tobacco. Palate: spicy, fine tannins, elegant, long.

Cune 2011 TR
85% tempranillo, 15% mazuelo, garnacha, graciano

89

Colour: cherry, garnet rim. Nose: ripe fruit, spicy, creamy oak Palate: flavourful, toasty, round tannins.

Cune 2013 TC
85% tempranillo, 15% garnacha, mazuelo

88

Colour: deep cherry, purple rim. Nose: creamy oak, toasty, ripe fruit. Palate: balanced, spicy, long.

Cune 2014 RD
100% tempranillo

85

Cune 50 cl 2011 TC
tempranillo

89

Colour: cherry, garnet rim. Nose: red berry notes, ripe fruit, spicy, creamy oak, complex. Palate: flavourful, toasty, round tannins.

Cune Semidulce 2014 B
85% viura, 15% malvasía, garnacha blanca

82

Cune White 2014 B
100% viura

87

Colour: bright straw. Nose: white flowers, fresh fruit, fragrant herbs. Palate: flavourful, fruity, good acidity.

Imperial 2010 TGR
85% tempranillo, 10% graciano, 5% mazuelo

92

Colour: cherry, garnet rim. Nose: red berry notes, ripe fruit, spicy, creamy oak, complex. Palate: flavourful, toasty, round tannins.

Imperial 2011 TR
85% tempranillo, 5% mazuelo, 10% graciano

92

Colour: bright cherry. Nose: ripe fruit, sweet spices, creamy oak, expressive. Palate: flavourful, fruity, toasty, round tannins.

Monopole 2014 B
100% viura

87

Colour: bright straw. Nose: white flowers, fresh fruit, fragrant herbs, expressive. Palate: flavourful, fruity, good acidity, balanced.

Real de Asúa 2010 T
100% tempranillo

93

Colour: cherry, garnet rim. Nose: fresh fruit, balanced, creamy oak, spicy. Palate: flavourful, spicy, elegant.

DIEZ-CABALLERO

Barrihuelo, 73
01340 Elciego (Álava)
☎: +34 944 807 295
Fax: +34 944 630 938
diez-caballero@diez-caballero.es
www.diez-caballero.es

Díez-Caballero 2012 TC
tempranillo

88

Colour: deep cherry, garnet rim. Nose: cocoa bean, sweet spices, ripe fruit. Palate: flavourful, fruity, spicy.

Díez-Caballero 2009 TR
tempranillo

88

Colour: cherry, garnet rim. Nose: wild herbs, ripe fruit, balanced. Palate: flavourful, easy to drink, good finish.

Díez-Caballero Vendimia Seleccionada 2010 TR
tempranillo

89

Colour: cherry, garnet rim. Nose: expressive, spicy. Palate: flavourful, ripe fruit, long, good acidity, balanced, fruity aftestaste.

Victoria Díez-Caballero 2011 T
tempranillo

89

Colour: bright cherry. Nose: expressive, balsamic herbs, balanced. Palate: full, flavourful, round tannins.

DIOSARES S.L.

Ctra. de Navaridas, s/n
01320 Laguardia (Alava)
☎: +34 945 600 678
Fax: +34 945 600 522
info@bodegasdiosares.com
www.bodegasdiosares.com

Ares 2012 TC
100% tempranillo

90

Colour: cherry, garnet rim. Nose: mineral, expressive, spicy, scrubland. Palate: flavourful, ripe fruit, long, good acidity, balanced.

DOMINIO DE BERZAL

Término Río Salado, s/n
01307 Baños de Ebro (Álava)
☎: +34 945 623 368
Fax: +34 945 609 090
info@dominioberzal.com
www.dominioberzal.com

Dominio de Berzal 2012 TC
90% tempranillo, 10% viura

89

Colour: cherry, garnet rim. Nose: balsamic herbs, ripe fruit, damp earth. Palate: full, flavourful, round tannins.

Dominio de Berzal 2014 B
90% viura, 10% malvasía

86

Dominio de Berzal 2014 T Maceración Carbónica
90% tempranillo, 10% viura

86

Dominio de Berzal Selección Privada 2012 T
tempranillo

91

Colour: cherry, garnet rim. Nose: ripe fruit, spicy, creamy oak, complex. Palate: flavourful, toasty, balanced.

DOMINIO DE NOBLEZA
Bodegas San Cristóbal, 79
26360 Fuenmayor (La Rioja)
☎: +34 941 450 507
Fax: +34 941 450 187
bodegas@dominiodenobleza.com
www.dominiodenobleza.com

Dominio de Nobleza 2009 TR
100% tempranillo

90

Colour: cherry, garnet rim. Nose: red berry notes, ripe fruit, spicy, creamy oak, complex. Palate: flavourful, toasty, round tannins.

Dominio de Nobleza 2011 TC
tempranillo

88

Colour: cherry, garnet rim. Nose: creamy oak, red berry notes, balanced. Palate: flavourful, spicy, easy to drink.

Dominio de Nobleza Vendimia Seleccionada 2008 TR
tempranillo

91

Colour: pale ruby, brick rim edge. Nose: spicy, fine reductive notes, wet leather, ripe fruit. Palate: spicy, fine tannins, balanced.

EGUREN UGARTE
Ctra. A-124, Km. 61
01309 Laguardia (Álava)
☎: +34 945 282 844
Fax: +34 945 271 319
info@egurenugarte.com
www.egurenugarte.com

Anastasio 2009 T
100% tempranillo

90

Colour: light cherry. Nose: fine reductive notes, aged wood nuances, toasty, roasted coffee. Palate: spicy, toasty, flavourful.

Martín Cendoya 2010 TR
80% tempranillo, 15% graciano, 5% mazuelo

90

Colour: cherry, garnet rim. Nose: smoky, spicy, ripe fruit. Palate: flavourful, smoky aftertaste, ripe fruit.

Martín Cendoya Malvasía 2014 B
100% malvasía

89

Colour: bright straw. Nose: white flowers, fine lees, sweet spices, creamy oak. Palate: flavourful, fruity, good acidity, round.

Ochenta Ugarte 2011 T
100% tempranillo

90

Colour: cherry, garnet rim. Nose: ripe fruit, spicy, creamy oak, complex. Palate: flavourful, toasty, round tannins.

Ugarte 2009 TGR
90% tempranillo, 10% graciano

87

Colour: cherry, garnet rim. Nose: ripe fruit, old leather, tobacco. Palate: correct, flavourful, spicy.

Ugarte 2010 TR
95% tempranillo, 5% graciano

87

Colour: light cherry. Nose: fine reductive notes, aged wood nuances, toasty. Palate: spicy, toasty, flavourful.

Ugarte 2012 TC
92% tempranillo, 8% garnacha

87

Colour: bright cherry. Nose: ripe fruit, sweet spices, creamy oak. Palate: flavourful, toasty, round tannins.

Ugarte 2014 RD
50% viura, 50% tempranillo

86

Ugarte Cincuenta 2012 T
100% tempranillo

87

Colour: light cherry. Nose: fine reductive notes, aged wood nuances, toasty. Palate: spicy, toasty, flavourful.

Ugarte Cosecha 2013 T
80% tempranillo, 20% garnacha

87

Colour: deep cherry. Nose: ripe fruit, red berry notes. Palate: flavourful, ripe fruit.

Ugarte Tempranillo 2014 T
100% tempranillo

86

Ugarte Viura 2014 B
100% viura

85

EL CONJURO DEL CIEGO

Barrihuelo, 77
01340 Elciego (Alava)
☎: +34 945 264 866
Fax: +34 945 264 866
lur@elconjurodelciego.com
www.elconjurodelciego.com

Lur Tempranillo 2010 T

tempranillo

90

Colour: cherry, garnet rim. Nose: ripe fruit, spicy, creamy oak, complex. Palate: flavourful, toasty.

EL COTO DE RIOJA

Camino Viejo de Logroño, 26
01320 Oyón (Álava)
☎: +34 945 622 216
Fax: +34 945 622 315
info@elcoto.com
www.elcoto.com

Coto de Imaz 2008 TGR

100% tempranillo

88

Colour: pale ruby, brick rim edge. Nose: spicy, fine reductive notes, wet leather, fruit liqueur notes. Palate: spicy, fine tannins.

Coto de Imaz 2010 TR

100% tempranillo

90

Colour: cherry, garnet rim. Nose: ripe fruit, wild herbs, earthy notes, spicy, balsamic herbs, fine reductive notes. Palate: balanced, flavourful, long, balsamic.

Coto de Imaz Selección Viñedos 2010 TR

100% tempranillo

91

Colour: cherry, garnet rim. Nose: balanced, complex, ripe fruit, spicy, fine reductive notes. Palate: good structure, flavourful, balanced.

Coto Mayor 2012 TC

100% tempranillo

89

Colour: cherry, garnet rim. Nose: roasted coffee, smoky, spicy, ripe fruit. Palate: flavourful, smoky aftertaste, ripe fruit.

Coto Mayor 2014 B

viura, sauvignon blanc

87

Colour: bright straw. Nose: white flowers, fresh fruit, fragrant herbs, expressive, varietal. Palate: flavourful, fruity, good acidity, balanced, easy to drink.

Coto Real 2011 T

100% tempranillo

90

Colour: cherry, garnet rim. Nose: ripe fruit, creamy oak, complex, wild herbs. Palate: flavourful, toasty, fine tannins.

El Coto 2012 TC

100% tempranillo

88

Colour: bright cherry. Nose: ripe fruit, sweet spices, creamy oak. Palate: flavourful, fruity, toasty.

El Coto 2014 B

100% viura

86

El Coto 2014 RD

100% tempranillo

87

Colour: onion pink. Nose: red berry notes, floral, fragrant herbs. Palate: light-bodied, flavourful, good acidity, spicy.

EL OTERO

El Otero, 11
01330 Labastida (Alava)
☎: +34 945 331 002
el.otero.sc@gmail.com

Aimarez 2014 T Maceración Carbónica

84

ELVIWINES

Ctra T-300 Falset-Marça, km 1
43775 Marça (Tarragona)
☎: +34 618 792 973
Fax: +34 936 750 316
victor@elviwines.com
www.elviwines.com

Herenza Kosher Elviwines 2010 TR

95% tempranillo, 5% graciano

90

Colour: cherry, garnet rim. Nose: expressive, spicy, dry stone. Palate: flavourful, ripe fruit, long, good acidity, balanced.

EMPATÍA

Pza. Fermín Gurbindo, 2
26339 Abalos (La Rioja)
☎: +34 649 841 746
Fax: +34 941 308 023
direccion@hotelvilladeabalos.com
www.hotelvilladeabalos.com

Empatía 2013 BFB

80% viura, 15% malvasía, garnacha blanca

88

Colour: bright yellow. Nose: ripe fruit, powerfull, aged wood nuances. Palate: flavourful, fruity, spicy, toasty, long.

Empatía Vendimia Seleccionada 2008 T
90% tempranillo, 10% garnacha

88

Colour: cherry, garnet rim. Nose: red berry notes, ripe fruit, spicy, creamy oak. Palate: flavourful, toasty, correct.

Empatía Vendimia Seleccionada 2010 T
90% tempranillo, 10% garnacha

87

Colour: ruby red. Nose: balsamic herbs, ripe fruit, fine reductive notes. Palate: full, flavourful, round tannins.

ENEO

Pº Virgen de la Vega, 4 1º I
26200 Haro (La Rioja)
☎: +34 941 310 494
Fax: +34 941 310 494
soto@comercialeneo.com
www.comercialeneo.com

Rey Eneo 2010 TR
tempranillo

85

Rey Eneo 2012 TC
tempranillo

84

FERNÁNDEZ EGUILUZ

Los Morales, 7 bajo
26339 Abalos (La Rioja)
☎: +34 941 334 166
Fax: +34 941 308 055
p.larosa@hotmail.es
www.penalarosa.com

Peña La Rosa 2014 B
viura, malvasía

85

Peña la Rosa 2014 T Maceración Carbónica
tempranillo

87

Colour: cherry, purple rim. Nose: fresh fruit, red berry notes, floral. Palate: flavourful, fruity, good acidity.

Peña la Rosa Vendimia Seleccionada 2010 T
tempranillo

90

Colour: cherry, garnet rim. Nose: creamy oak, red berry notes, balanced. Palate: flavourful, spicy, elegant.

FINCA ALLENDE

Pza. Ibarra, 1
26330 Briones (La Rioja)
☎: +34 941 322 301
Fax: +34 941 322 302
info@finca-allende.com
www.finca-allende.com

Allende 2010 T
100% tempranillo

93

Colour: very deep cherry, garnet rim. Nose: expressive, complex, mineral, balanced. Palate: full, flavourful, round tannins.

Allende 2011 B
95% viura, 5% malvasía

93

Colour: bright yellow. Nose: expressive, dried herbs, ripe fruit, toasty. Palate: flavourful, fruity, good acidity, balanced.

Allende 2011 T
100% tempranillo

94

Colour: bright cherry. Nose: ripe fruit, sweet spices, creamy oak. Palate: flavourful, fruity, toasty, round tannins.

Allende 2012 B
95% viura, 5% malvasía

94

Colour: bright yellow. Nose: toasty, aged wood nuances, pattiserie, fruit expression, ripe fruit. Palate: flavourful, fruity, spicy, toasty, long.

PODIUM

Allende Dulce 2011 B
100% viura

95

Colour: bright yellow. Nose: balsamic herbs, honeyed notes, floral, sweet spices, expressive, acetaldehyde. Palate: rich, fruity, powerful, flavourful, sweet, good acidity.

PODIUM

Avrvs 2010 T
85% tempranillo, 15% graciano

97

Colour: cherry, garnet rim. Nose: balanced, complex, ripe fruit, spicy, fine reductive notes. Palate: good structure, flavourful, round tannins, balanced.

🏆 PODIUM

Calvario 2011 T
90% tempranillo, 8% garnacha, 2% graciano

95

Colour: cherry, garnet rim. Nose: expressive, spicy. Palate: flavourful, ripe fruit, long, good acidity, balanced.

Calvario 2012 T
90% tempranillo, 8% garnacha, 2% graciano

94

Colour: cherry, garnet rim. Nose: expressive, spicy, earthy notes, toasty. Palate: flavourful, ripe fruit, long, good acidity, balanced.

🏆 PODIUM

Mártires 2013 B
100% viura

96

Colour: bright straw. Nose: white flowers, fine lees, dried herbs, ripe fruit, candied fruit, citrus fruit. Palate: flavourful, fruity, good acidity, elegant.

🏆 PODIUM

Mártires 2014 B
100% viura

96

Colour: bright straw. Nose: fine lees, dried herbs, ripe fruit, candied fruit, citrus fruit, faded flowers, spicy. Palate: flavourful, fruity, good acidity, powerful.

FINCA DE LA RICA

Las Cocinillas, s/n
01330 Labastida (Rioja)
☎: +34 941 509 406
info@fincadelarica.com
www.fincadelarica.com

El Buscador de Finca de la Rica 2012 TC
tempranillo, garnacha

89

Colour: bright cherry. Nose: ripe fruit, sweet spices, creamy oak, expressive. Palate: flavourful, fruity, toasty, round tannins.

El Buscador de Finca de la Rica 2013 TC
tempranillo, garnacha

88

Colour: bright cherry. Nose: ripe fruit, sweet spices, creamy oak. Palate: flavourful, fruity, toasty, thin.

El Guía de Finca de la Rica 2014 T
tempranillo, viura

89

Colour: cherry, purple rim. Nose: expressive, fresh fruit, red berry notes, floral. Palate: flavourful, fruity, good acidity.

El Nómada 2011 T
tempranillo, graciano

92

Colour: cherry, garnet rim. Nose: ripe fruit, tobacco, spicy. Palate: balanced, complex, flavourful, good structure.

El Nómada 2012 T
tempranillo, graciano

92

Colour: cherry, garnet rim. Nose: expressive, spicy, neat. Palate: flavourful, ripe fruit, long, good acidity, balanced.

FINCA DE LOS ARANDINOS

Ctra. LR 137, km. 4,6
26375 Entrena (La Rioja)
☎: +34 941 446 065
Fax: +34 941 446 423
bodega@fincadelosarandinos.com
www.fincadelosarandinos.com

Finca de los Arandinos 2013 TC
90% tempranillo, 5% garnacha, 5% mazuelo

87

Colour: bright cherry. Nose: ripe fruit, sweet spices, creamy oak. Palate: flavourful, fruity, toasty.

Malacapa 2014 T
95% tempranillo, 5% mazuelo

86

FINCA EGOMEI

26540 Alfaro (La Rioja)
☎: +34 948 780 110
Fax: +34 948 780 515
info@egomei.es
www.bodegasab.com

Carpess 2010 TC
tempranillo

92

Colour: very deep cherry, garnet rim. Nose: expressive, complex, balsamic herbs, balanced. Palate: flavourful, round tannins.

Egomei 2011 T
tempranillo, graciano

90

Colour: cherry, garnet rim. Nose: expressive, spicy. Palate: ripe fruit, long, good acidity, balanced, flavourful.

Egomei Alma 2009 T
tempranillo, graciano

92

Colour: very deep cherry, garnet rim. Nose: ripe fruit, fruit preserve, tobacco, spicy. Palate: full, complex, round tannins.

FINCA MANZANOS

Ctra. NA-134, km. 49
31560 Azagra (Navarra)
☎: +34 948 692 500
Fax: +34 948 692 700
info@manzanoswines.com
www.manzanoswines.com

Finca Manzanos 2009 TR
tempranillo, garnacha, graciano

86

Finca Manzanos 2012 TC
tempranillo, garnacha, mazuelo

84

Finca Manzanos 2014 B
viura, chardonnay

86

Finca Manzanos 2014 BFB
viura, chardonnay

87

Colour: bright yellow. Nose: expressive, dried herbs, ripe fruit. Palate: flavourful, fruity, good acidity, balanced.

Finca Manzanos 2014 T
tempranillo, garnacha

85

Finca Manzanos Garnacha 2014 T
garnacha

87

Colour: ruby red. Nose: floral, wild herbs, fruit liqueur notes, ripe fruit. Palate: powerful, flavourful.

Finca Manzanos Graciano 2014 T
graciano

86

Los Hermanos Manzanos 2012 TC
tempranillo, garnacha

86

Los Hermanos Manzanos Tempranillo 2014 T
tempranillo

85

Voché 2007 TR
tempranillo, graciano

88

Colour: light cherry. Nose: fine reductive notes, aged wood nuances, toasty. Palate: spicy, toasty, flavourful.

Voché 2011 TC
tempranillo, graciano

89

Colour: cherry, garnet rim. Nose: mineral, expressive, spicy, ripe fruit. Palate: flavourful, ripe fruit, long, good acidity.

Voché 2013 BFB
viura, chardonnay

87

Colour: straw. Nose: ripe fruit, floral, sweet spices, toasty. Palate: correct, easy to drink.

Voché Selección Graciano 2012 T
graciano

90

Colour: cherry, garnet rim. Nose: balanced, complex, ripe fruit, spicy. Palate: good structure, flavourful, round tannins, balanced.

FINCA NUEVA

Ctra. de Fuenmayor, km. 1,5
26370 Navarrete (La Rioja)
☎: +34 941 322 301
Fax: +34 941 322 302
info@fincanueva.com
www.fincanueva.com

Finca Nueva 2004 TGR
100% tempranillo

92

Colour: pale ruby, brick rim edge. Nose: spicy, fine reductive notes, wet leather, aged wood nuances, fruit liqueur notes. Palate: spicy, fine tannins, balanced.

Finca Nueva 2008 TR
100% tempranillo

92

Colour: cherry, garnet rim. Nose: fine reductive notes, wet leather, aged wood nuances, fruit liqueur notes. Palate: spicy, long, toasty.

Finca Nueva 2010 TC
100% tempranillo

89

Colour: bright cherry. Nose: sweet spices, creamy oak, overripe fruit. Palate: flavourful, fruity, toasty, round tannins.

Finca Nueva Vendimia 2014 T
100% tempranillo

88

Colour: deep cherry. Nose: ripe fruit, spicy, toasty. Palate: powerful, ripe fruit.

Finca Nueva Viura 2014 B
100% viura

89

Colour: bright straw. Nose: white flowers, fresh fruit, fragrant herbs. Palate: flavourful, fruity, good acidity, balanced.

Finca Nueva Viura 2014 BFB
100% viura

91

Colour: bright yellow. Nose: ripe fruit, toasty, aged wood nuances, pattiserie. Palate: flavourful, fruity, toasty, long.

FINCA VALPIEDRA

Término El Montecillo, s/n
26360 Fuenmayor (La Rioja)
☎: +34 941 450 876
Fax: +34 941 450 875
info@bujanda.com
www.familiamartinezbujanda.com

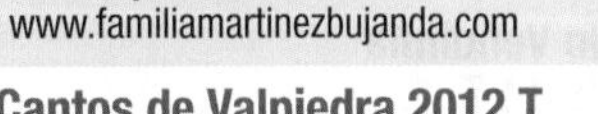

Cantos de Valpiedra 2012 T
100% tempranillo

89

Colour: bright cherry. Nose: ripe fruit, sweet spices, creamy oak, expressive. Palate: flavourful, fruity, round tannins.

Finca Valpiedra 2009 TR
92% tempranillo, 4% graciano, 4% maturana

91

Colour: cherry, garnet rim. Nose: ripe fruit, spicy, creamy oak, complex, fine reductive notes. Palate: flavourful, toasty.

FINCAS DE AZABACHE

Avda. Juan Carlos I, 100
26559 Aldeanueva de Ebro (La Rioja)
☎: +34 941 163 039
Fax: +34 941 163 585
va@aldeanueva.com
www.fincasdeazabache.com

Azabache Ecológico Vendimia Seleccionada 2012 TC
60% tempranillo, 30% garnacha, 10% graciano

88

Colour: bright cherry. Nose: ripe fruit, sweet spices, creamy oak. Palate: flavourful, fruity, toasty, round tannins.

Azabache Tempranillo 2014 T
100% tempranillo

86

Azabache Vendimia Seleccionada 2012 TC
70% tempranillo, 20% garnacha, 10% mazuelo

89

Colour: cherry, garnet rim. Nose: creamy oak, red berry notes, fresh fruit, balanced. Palate: flavourful, spicy, elegant.

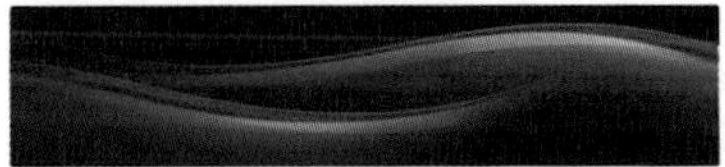

Barón de Ebro 2012 TC

87

Colour: cherry, garnet rim. Nose: ripe fruit, spicy, creamy oak. Palate: flavourful, toasty, easy to drink.

Culto 2010 T

89

Colour: pale ruby, brick rim edge. Nose: spicy, slightly evolved, fruit liqueur notes. Palate: spicy, toasty.

Fincas de Azabache Garnacha 2012 TC
100% garnacha

90

Colour: cherry, garnet rim. Nose: red berry notes, ripe fruit, spicy, creamy oak, complex. Palate: flavourful, toasty, round tannins.

Viña Amate Tempranillo 2014 T

83

GIL BERZAL

Ctra. Elvillar, 2
01300 Laguardia (Álava)
☎: +34 945 600 735
Fax: +34 945 600 735
gilberzal@gilberzal.com
www.gilberzal.com

Almapura - Colección Esencias 2011 T

85% tempranillo, 15% graciano

89

Colour: cherry, garnet rim. Nose: roasted coffee, smoky, spicy, ripe fruit. Palate: flavourful, smoky aftertaste, ripe fruit.

Recoveco Colección Privada 2009 TR

80% tempranillo, 20% graciano

89

Colour: light cherry. Nose: toasty, spicy, fruit preserve, dried herbs. Palate: spicy, toasty, flavourful.

Recoveco Racimos Enteros 2014 T Maceración Carbónica

90% tempranillo, 10% viura

89

Colour: bright cherry, purple rim. Nose: expressive, fresh fruit, red berry notes, floral, violets. Palate: fruity, good acidity.

Recoveco Selección 2014 B

90% viura, 10% malvasía

84

Recoveco Vendimia Seleccionada 2011 TC

80% tempranillo, 10% garnacha, 10% graciano

86

GÓMEZ CRUZADO

Avda. Vizcaya, 6 (Barrio de la Estación)
26200 Haro (La Rioja)
☎: +34 941 312 502
Fax: +34 941 303 567
bodega@gomezcruzado.com
www.gomezcruzado.com

Gómez Cruzado 2009 TR

tempranillo

90

Colour: cherry, garnet rim. Nose: ripe fruit, spicy, creamy oak. Palate: flavourful, toasty, round tannins.

Gómez Cruzado 2012 TC

80% tempranillo, 20% garnacha

91

Colour: cherry, garnet rim. Nose: creamy oak, red berry notes, balanced. Palate: flavourful, spicy, elegant.

Gómez Cruzado 2014 B

16% tempranillo blanco, 84% viura

88

Colour: bright yellow. Nose: dried herbs, ripe fruit, spicy. Palate: flavourful, fruity, good acidity.

Gómez Cruzado Cerro Las Cuevas 2012 T

tempranillo

88

Colour: cherry, garnet rim. Nose: roasted coffee, smoky, spicy, fruit preserve. Palate: flavourful, smoky aftertaste.

Gómez Cruzado Magnum 2007 TGR

70% tempranillo, 30% garnacha

91

Colour: cherry, garnet rim. Nose: ripe fruit, old leather, tobacco, aged wood nuances. Palate: correct, flavourful, spicy.

Gómez Cruzado Vendimia Seleccionada 2014 T

50% tempranillo, 50% garnacha

87

Colour: cherry, purple rim. Nose: ripe fruit, aromatic coffee. Palate: flavourful, spicy, powerful.

Honorable Gómez Cruzado 2011 T

tempranillo

91

Colour: cherry, garnet rim. Nose: ripe fruit, old leather, tobacco. Palate: correct, flavourful, spicy.

Pancrudo de Gómez Cruzado 2013 T

garnacha

92

Colour: very deep cherry, garnet rim. Nose: expressive, complex, mineral, balsamic herbs, balanced. Palate: full, flavourful, round tannins.

GÓMEZ DE SEGURA

El Campillar
01300 Laguardia (Álava)
☎: +34 615 929 828
Fax: +34 945 600 227
info@gomezdesegura.com
www.gomezdesegura.com

Finca Ratón 2010 T

100% tempranillo

89

Colour: cherry, garnet rim. Nose: ripe fruit, earthy notes, spicy, balsamic herbs, fine reductive notes. Palate: balanced, flavourful.

Gómez de Segura 2011 TR
100% tempranillo

88

Colour: cherry, garnet rim. Nose: ripe fruit, spicy, fine reductive notes. Palate: good structure, flavourful, round tannins.

Gómez de Segura 2012 TC
100% tempranillo

87

Colour: cherry, garnet rim. Nose: fine reductive notes, spicy, ripe fruit. Palate: spicy, long, toasty.

Gómez de Segura 2014 RD
100% tempranillo

84

Gómez de Segura 2014 B
50% viura, 50% malvasía

84

Gómez de Segura 2014 T Maceración Carbónica
100% tempranillo

86

Gómez de Segura Vendimia Seleccionada 2014 T
100% tempranillo

88

Colour: cherry, purple rim. Nose: red berry notes, floral, balsamic herbs, balanced. Palate: powerful, fresh, fruity, easy to drink.

HACIENDA GRIMÓN

Gallera, 6
26131 Ventas Blancas (La Rioja)
☎: +34 941 482 181
Fax: +34 941 482 184
info@haciendagrimon.com
www.haciendagrimon.com

Finca La Oración 2013 T
100% tempranillo

91

Colour: cherry, garnet rim. Nose: balanced, spicy, complex. Palate: correct, ripe fruit, balsamic, good acidity, long.

Hacienda Grimón 2010 TR
85% tempranillo, 15% graciano

89

Colour: deep cherry, garnet rim. Nose: characterful, powerfull, tobacco, spicy, balsamic herbs. Palate: flavourful, good structure.

Hacienda Grimón 2012 TC
100% tempranillo

89

Colour: cherry, garnet rim. Nose: characterful, powerfull, scrubland, spicy. Palate: balanced, good acidity, round tannins.

HACIENDA URBIÓN

Ctra. Nalda, km. 9
26120 Albelda de Iregua (Rioja)
☎: +34 941 444 233
Fax: +34 941 444 427
info@vinicolareal.com
www.vinicolareal.com

Palacio de Alcántara 2013 TC
100% tempranillo

84

Palacio de Alcántara 2014 T
100% tempranillo

84

Palacio de Alcántara PA 20 2014 T
100% tempranillo

86

Palacio de Alcántara PA 30 2013 T
100% tempranillo

85

Palacio de Alcántara PA 40 2011 T
100% tempranillo

88

Colour: bright cherry. Nose: ripe fruit, sweet spices, creamy oak. Palate: flavourful, fruity, toasty, round tannins.

Urbión Cuvée 2013 T
90% tempranillo, 10% garnacha

86

Urbión Vendimia 2012 TC
90% tempranillo, 10% garnacha

85

Urbión Vendimia 2013 TC
90% tempranillo, 10% garnacha

88

Colour: cherry, garnet rim. Nose: smoky, spicy, ripe fruit. Palate: flavourful, ripe fruit, long, toasty.

HACIENDA Y VIÑEDO MARQUÉS DEL ATRIO

Ctra. de Logroño NA-134, Km. 86,2
31587 Mendavia (Navarra)
☎: +34 948 379 994
Fax: +34 948 389 049
info@marquesdelatrio.com
www.marquesdelatrio.com

Bardesano 2012 TC

85

Chitón 2012 TC

85% tempranillo, 15% garnacha

84

Faustino Rivero Ulecia 2012 TC

85% tempranillo, 15% garnacha

84

Marqués del Atrio 2011 TC

85% tempranillo, 15% garnacha

86

HAMMEKEN CELLARS

Calle de la Muela, 16
03730 Jávea (Alicante)
☎: +34 965 791 967
Fax: +34 966 461 471
cellars@hammekencellars.com
www.hammekencellars.com

El Cántico 2012 TC

tempranillo

88

Colour: cherry, garnet rim. Nose: ripe fruit, spicy, creamy oak. Palate: flavourful, toasty, round tannins.

HEREDAD SAN ANDRÉS

26338 San Vicente de la Sonsierra
(La Rioja)
☎: +34 941 308 048
Fax: +34 945 121 568
sircupani@gmail.com
www.cupani.es

Cupani 2010 T

100% tempranillo

90

Colour: cherry, garnet rim. Nose: ripe fruit, spicy, creamy oak, complex, earthy notes. Palate: flavourful, toasty, round tannins, balanced.

Cupani Garnacha 2012 T

100% garnacha

92

Colour: cherry, garnet rim. Nose: ripe fruit, wild herbs, earthy notes, spicy, balsamic herbs. Palate: balanced, flavourful, long, balsamic.

Rielo 2011 BFB

100% viura

87

Colour: bright yellow. Nose: ripe fruit, powerfull, toasty, aged wood nuances. Palate: flavourful, fruity, spicy, toasty, long, fine bitter notes.

Sir Cupani 2007 T

100% tempranillo

92

Colour: ruby red. Nose: elegant, spicy, fine reductive notes, ripe fruit. Palate: spicy, fine tannins, elegant, long, balanced.

HERMANOS FRÍAS DEL VAL

Herrerías, 13
01307 Villabuena de Alava (Álava)
☎: +34 656 782 714
Fax: +34 945 609 172
info@friasdelval.com
www.friasdelval.com

Don Peduz 2014 T

100% tempranillo

88

Colour: cherry, purple rim. Nose: expressive, red berry notes, floral, ripe fruit. Palate: flavourful, fruity, good acidity.

Hermanos Frías del Val "Viña El Flako" 2012 B

60% malvasía, 40% viura

91

Colour: bright yellow. Nose: expressive, dried herbs, ripe fruit, spicy. Palate: flavourful, fruity, good acidity, balanced.

Hermanos Frías del Val 2009 TR

100% tempranillo

89

Colour: cherry, garnet rim. Nose: ripe fruit, wild herbs, earthy notes, spicy, balsamic herbs, tobacco. Palate: balanced, flavourful, long, balsamic.

Hermanos Frías del Val 2011 TC

100% tempranillo

88

Colour: cherry, garnet rim. Nose: smoky, spicy, ripe fruit. Palate: flavourful, ripe fruit.

Hermanos Frías del Val 2014 B
60% malvasía, 40% viura

85

Hermanos Frías del Val Experiencia 2010 T
100% tempranillo

91

Colour: cherry, garnet rim. Nose: mineral, expressive, spicy. Palate: flavourful, ripe fruit, long, good acidity, balanced.

Hermanos Frías del Val Selección Personal 2011 T
100% tempranillo

90

Colour: very deep cherry, garnet rim. Nose: expressive, complex, balanced. Palate: full, flavourful, round tannins, balanced.

HEVIA

Serrano, 118
28006 Madrid (Madrid)
☎: +34 649 917 608
hevia@heviamadrid.com
www.heviamadrid.com

Hevia 51 2011 TC
tempranillo

89

Colour: cherry, garnet rim. Nose: red berry notes, ripe fruit, spicy, creamy oak, complex. Palate: flavourful, toasty, round tannins.

HNOS. CASTILLO PÉREZ

Camino de la Estación, 15
26330 Briones (La Rioja)
☎: +34 667 730 651
info@bodegaszurbal.com
www.bodegaszurbal.es

Zurbal 2009 TR
tempranillo

87

Colour: cherry, garnet rim. Nose: red berry notes, ripe fruit, spicy, creamy oak. Palate: flavourful, toasty, round tannins.

Zurbal 2011 TC
tempranillo

88

Colour: cherry, garnet rim. Nose: smoky, spicy, ripe fruit. Palate: flavourful, ripe fruit.

Zurbal 2014 B
viura

87

Colour: bright straw. Nose: white flowers, fresh fruit, fragrant herbs. Palate: fruity, good acidity, balanced.

Zurbal 2014 T
tempranillo

84

Zurbal Ecológico 2014 T
tempranillo

87

Colour: cherry, purple rim. Nose: red berry notes, floral. Palate: flavourful, fruity, good acidity.

IÑIGUEZ DE MENDOZA

Avda. de La Rioja, 8
01300 Laguardia (Alava)
☎: +34 673 223 955
bodegas@bodegasidemendoza.com
www.bodegasidemendoza.com

Obssidiana 2013 T
100% tempranillo

84

JESÚS FERNANDO GÓMEZ-CRUZADO CÁRCAMO

Las Heras 9 parcela 6
26330 Briones (La Rioja)
☎: +34 645 309 357
f.gomezcruzado@kzgunea.net

Corral del Sordo 2009 T

80% tempranillo, 20% garnacha

92

Colour: very deep cherry, garnet rim. Nose: complex, mineral, balsamic herbs, balanced. Palate: full, flavourful, round tannins.

JOSÉ BASOCO BASOCO

Ctra. de Samaniego, s/n
01307 Villabuena (Álava)
☎: +34 657 794 964
info@fincabarronte.com
www.fincabarronte.com

Finca Barronte 2011 TC

tempranillo

89

Colour: cherry, garnet rim. Nose: red berry notes, ripe fruit, spicy, creamy oak, complex. Palate: flavourful, toasty, round tannins.

Finca Barronte Garnacha 2014 T

garnacha

88

Colour: cherry, purple rim. Nose: powerfull, ripe fruit, spicy. Palate: powerful, fruity, unctuous, balanced.

Finca Barronte Graciano 2011 T

graciano

90

Colour: deep cherry. Nose: creamy oak, toasty, ripe fruit, balsamic herbs. Palate: balanced, spicy, long.

Finca Barronte Tempranillo 2011 T

tempranillo

88

Colour: cherry, garnet rim. Nose: smoky, spicy, ripe fruit. Palate: flavourful, ripe fruit.

Finca Barronte Vendimia Seleccionada 2014 T

tempranillo

88

Colour: cherry, purple rim. Nose: red berry notes, floral, balsamic herbs. Palate: powerful, fresh, fruity.

JUAN CARLOS SANCHA

Cº de Las Barreras, s/n
26320 Baños de Río Tobía (La Rioja)
☎: +34 639 216 011
juancarlossancha@yahoo.es
www.juancarlossancha.com

Ad Libitum Maturana Blanca 2014 B

100% maturana blanca

89

Colour: bright yellow. Nose: ripe fruit, powerfull, toasty, aged wood nuances, pattiserie. Palate: flavourful, fruity, spicy, toasty, long.

Ad Libitum Maturana Tinta 2013 T

100% maturana

88

Colour: very deep cherry, purple rim. Nose: grassy, scrubland, spicy. Palate: ripe fruit, balanced.

Ad Libitum Tempranillo Blanco 2014 B

100% tempranillo blanco

90

Colour: bright straw. Nose: white flowers, fine lees, dried herbs, ripe fruit, citrus fruit. Palate: flavourful, fruity, good acidity, elegant.

Peña El Gato Garnacha 2014 T

100% garnacha

91

Colour: cherry, purple rim. Nose: red berry notes, floral, scrubland. Palate: fresh, fruity, balanced, fruity aftestaste.

LA MALETA HAND MADE FINE WINES

Plaza de Eladio Rodríguez, 19
32420 San Clodio (Ourense)
☎: +34 988 614 234
hola@lamaletawines.com
lamaletawines.com

Marquesado del Alto 2010 TC

100% tempranillo

88

Colour: cherry, garnet rim. Nose: fine reductive notes, ripe fruit, balsamic herbs. Palate: spicy, long, toasty.

Marquesado del Alto 2013 T

100% tempranillo

87

Colour: deep cherry, purple rim. Nose: creamy oak, toasty, ripe fruit, balsamic herbs. Palate: balanced, spicy, long.

LA RIOJA ALTA S.A.

Avda. de Vizcaya, 8
26200 Haro (La Rioja)
☎: +34 941 310 346
Fax: +34 941 312 854
info@riojalta.com
www.gruporiojalta.com

PODIUM

Gran Reserva 904 Rioja Alta 2005 TGR
tempranillo, graciano

95

Colour: pale ruby, brick rim edge. Nose: spicy, fine reductive notes, wet leather, aged wood nuances, ripe fruit. Palate: spicy, fine tannins, balanced, elegant. Personality.

PODIUM

La Rioja Alta Gran Reserva 890 Selección Especial 2001 TGR
tempranillo, graciano, mazuelo

96

Colour: pale ruby, brick rim edge. Nose: spicy, fine reductive notes, old leather. Palate: spicy, fine tannins, balanced, classic aged character.

Viña Alberdi 2009 TC
tempranillo

91

Colour: cherry, garnet rim. Nose: balanced, complex, ripe fruit, spicy, waxy notes, tobacco, wet leather. Palate: good structure, flavourful, balanced.

Viña Arana 2006 TR
tempranillo, mazuelo

93

Colour: pale ruby, brick rim edge. Nose: elegant, spicy, fine reductive notes, tobacco, ripe fruit. Palate: spicy, fine tannins, elegant, long.

Viña Ardanza 2007 TR
tempranillo, garnacha

93

Colour: cherry, garnet rim. Nose: ripe fruit, spicy, creamy oak, complex, fine reductive notes. Palate: flavourful, toasty, round tannins, balanced, elegant.

LA SORDA

Avda. Diagonal, 590, 5º 1ª
08021 Barcelona (Barcelona)
☎: +34 660 445 464
vinergia@vinergia.com
www.vinergia.com

La Sorda 2013 T
80% tempranillo, 15% graciano, 5% mazuelo

87

Colour: cherry, purple rim. Nose: red berry notes, floral, balsamic herbs. Palate: powerful, fresh, fruity.

La Sorda Graciano 2011 T
100% graciano

89

Colour: cherry, garnet rim. Nose: ripe fruit, wild herbs, spicy, balsamic herbs. Palate: balanced, flavourful, long, balsamic.

LECEA

Barrio de las Bodegas,
s/n Cerrillo Verballe
26340 San Asensio (La Rioja)
☎: +34 941 457 444
info@bodegaslecea.com
www.bodegaslecea.com

Corazón de Lago 2014 T Maceración Carbónica

87

Colour: cherry, purple rim. Nose: expressive, fresh fruit, red berry notes, floral. Palate: flavourful, fruity, good acidity.

Lecea 2009 TR
90% tempranillo, 10% mazuelo

88

Colour: light cherry. Nose: fine reductive notes, aged wood nuances, toasty, ripe fruit. Palate: spicy, toasty, flavourful.

Lecea Viura Chardonnay 2012 BC
50% viura, 50% chardonnay

86

LONG WINES

Avda. del Puente Cultural, 8 Bloque B Bajo 7
28702 San Sebastián de los Reyes
(Madrid)
☎: +34 916 221 305
Fax: +34 916 220 029
customer.service@longwines.com
www.longwines.com

Finca Amalia 2012 TC
80% tempranillo, 20% garnacha

84

Finca Amalia Tempranillo 2014 T
tempranillo

78

Finca Mónica 2012 TC
100% tempranillo

89

Colour: bright cherry. Nose: sweet spices, creamy oak, expressive, ripe fruit, fruit preserve. Palate: flavourful, fruity, toasty, round tannins.

Finca Mónica Tempranillo 2014 T
100% tempranillo

86

LUBERRI MONJE AMESTOY

Camino de Rehoyos, s/n
01340 Elciego (Álava)
☎: +34 945 606 010
Fax: +34 945 606 482
luberri@luberri.com
www.luberri.com

Biga de Luberri 2012 TC

89

Colour: cherry, garnet rim. Nose: ripe fruit, sweet spices, creamy oak. Palate: flavourful, spicy, long, round tannins.

Luberri 2014 T Maceración Carbónica

90

Colour: cherry, purple rim. Nose: expressive, fresh fruit, red berry notes, floral, lactic notes. Palate: flavourful, fruity, easy to drink.

Luberri Cepas Viejas 2009 TC

90

Colour: black cherry. Nose: wild herbs, creamy oak, cocoa bean, ripe fruit. Palate: powerful, flavourful, good structure, spicy.

Luberri Zuri 2014 B
80% viura, 20% malvasía

86

Monje Amestoy de Luberri 2008 TR
90% tempranillo

92

Colour: deep cherry, garnet rim. Nose: ripe fruit, balsamic herbs, earthy notes, spicy, complex. Palate: flavourful, balanced, elegant, long.

Seis de Luberri 2013 T

90

Colour: bright cherry. Nose: ripe fruit, sweet spices, creamy oak, expressive. Palate: flavourful, fruity, round tannins.

MARQUÉS DE MURRIETA

Ctra. N232/LO-20 Logroño-Zaragoza
(Salida 0)
26006 Logroño (La Rioja)
☎: +34 941 271 370
Fax: +34 941 251 606
bodegas@marquesdemurrieta.com
www.marquesdemurrieta.com

Capellania 2010 B
100% viura

93

Colour: bright yellow. Nose: expressive, dried herbs, ripe fruit, spicy. Palate: flavourful, fruity, good acidity, long.

Castillo Ygay 2007 TGR

86% tempranillo, 14% mazuelo

94

Colour: pale ruby, brick rim edge. Nose: spicy, fine reductive notes, wet leather, aged wood nuances, fruit liqueur notes, ripe fruit. Palate: spicy, fine tannins, balanced.

🏆 PODIUM

Dalmau 2011 TR

79% tempranillo, 15% cabernet sauvignon, 6% graciano

96

Colour: cherry, garnet rim. Nose: mineral, expressive, spicy, wet leather. Palate: flavourful, ripe fruit, long, good acidity, balanced

Marqués de Murrieta 2010 TR

93% tempranillo, 4% mazuelo, 2% graciano, 1% garnacha

92

Colour: cherry, garnet rim. Nose: balanced, complex, ripe fruit, fine reductive notes. Palate: good structure, flavourful, round tannins, balanced.

Marqués de Murrieta 2011 TR

92

Colour: light cherry. Nose: aged wood nuances, ripe fruit, tobacco. Palate: spicy, toasty, flavourful.

MARQUÉS DE TOMARES

Ctra. de Cenicero, s/n
26360 Fuenmayor (La Rioja)
☎: +34 941 451 129
Fax: +34 941 450 297
info@marquesdetomares.com
www.marquesdetomares.com

Marqués de Tomares 2011 TR

80% tempranillo, 17% graciano, 3% viura

87

Colour: cherry, garnet rim. Nose: ripe fruit, old leather, tobacco. Palate: correct, flavourful, spicy.

Marqués de Tomares 2012 TC

90% tempranillo, 10% graciano

88

Colour: ruby red. Nose: mineral, balsamic herbs, spicy, ripe fruit. Palate: full, flavourful.

Marqués de Tomares 2014 BFB

75% viura, 25% tempranillo blanco

88

Colour: bright yellow. Nose: powerfull, toasty, aged wood nuances, pattiserie. Palate: flavourful, fruity, spicy, toasty, long.

Marqués de Tomares Excellence 3F 2014 T
90% tempranillo, 10% graciano

86

Marqués de Tomares Reserva de Familia "Finca Izon" 2010 TR
88

Colour: cherry, garnet rim. Nose: ripe fruit, wild herbs, earthy notes, spicy, balsamic herbs. Palate: balanced, flavourful, long, balsamic.

Monteleiva 2012 TC
90% tempranillo, 10% graciano

87

Colour: cherry, garnet rim. Nose: ripe fruit, spicy, creamy oak. Palate: flavourful, toasty, correct.

MARQUÉS DE ULÍA

Paraje del Buicio, s/n
26360 Fuenmayor (La Rioja)
☎: +34 941 450 950
Fax: +34 941 450 567
info@marquesdeulia.com
www.marquesdeulia.com

La Vendimia Marqués de Ulía 2010 TR
91

Colour: cherry, garnet rim. Nose: ripe fruit, spicy, creamy oak, complex. Palate: flavourful, toasty, round tannins.

Marqués de Ulía 2009 TR
90

Colour: cherry, garnet rim. Nose: ripe fruit, spicy, creamy oak, complex. Palate: flavourful, toasty, round tannins.

Marqués de Ulía 2011 TC
89

Colour: cherry, garnet rim. Nose: powerfull, ripe fruit, spicy, fine reductive notes. Palate: powerful, fruity, unctuous, balanced.

MARQUÉS DE VITORIA

Camino de Santa Lucía, s/n
01320 Oyón (Álava)
☎: +34 945 622 134
Fax: +34 945 601 496
info@bodegasmarquesdevitoria.es
www.marquesdevitoria.com

Ecco de Marqués de Vitoria 2014 T
85

Marqués de Vitoria 2005 TGR
89

Colour: pale ruby, brick rim edge. Nose: spicy, fine reductive notes, wet leather, ripe fruit. Palate: spicy, fine tannins, balanced.

Marqués de Vitoria 2009 TR
89

Colour: cherry, garnet rim. Nose: ripe fruit, spicy, creamy oak. Palate: flavourful, toasty.

Marqués de Vitoria 2011 TC
89

Colour: very deep cherry. Nose: expressive, balsamic herbs, balanced, ripe fruit. Palate: full, flavourful, round tannins.

Marqués de Vitoria 2014 B
86

Marqués de Vitoria 2014 RD
85

MARQUÉS DEL PUERTO

Ctra. de Logroño s/n
26360 Fuenmayor (La Rioja)
☎: +34 941 450 001
Fax: +34 941 450 051
bmp@mbrizard.com
www.bodegamarquesdelpuerto.com

Marqués del Puerto 2007 TR
90% tempranillo, 10% mazuelo

85

Colour: cherry, garnet rim. Nose: ripe fruit, old leather, tobacco. Palate: correct, flavourful, spicy.

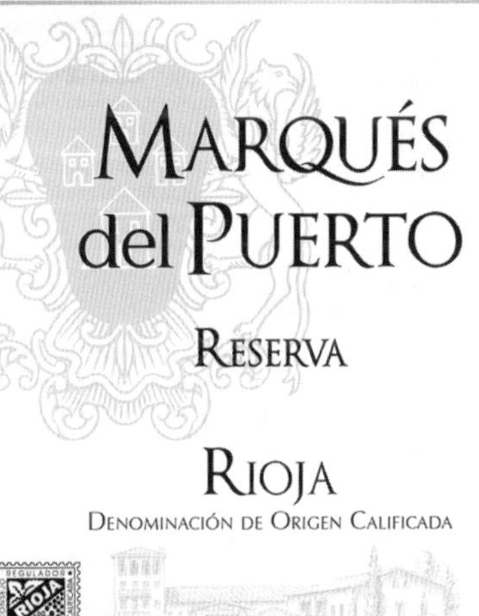

Marqués del Puerto 2011 TC
90% tempranillo, 10% mazuelo

88

Colour: bright cherry. Nose: ripe fruit, sweet spices, creamy oak. Palate: flavourful, fruity, toasty.

Marqués del Puerto 2014 B
viura

84

Marqués del Puerto 2014 RD
tempranillo, garnacha

88

Colour: rose, purple rim. Nose: red berry notes, floral, expressive. Palate: powerful, fruity, fresh.

MARTÍNEZ LACUESTA

Paraje de Ubieta, s/n
26200 Haro (La Rioja)
☎: +34 941 310 050
Fax: +34 941 303 748
bodega@martinezlacuesta.com
www.martinezlacuesta.com

Cynthia 2011 T
tempranillo

90

Colour: cherry, garnet rim. Nose: red berry notes, ripe fruit, spicy, creamy oak, complex. Palate: flavourful, toasty, round tannins.

Félix Martínez Lacuesta 2010 TR
tempranillo, garnacha, mazuelo

90

Colour: cherry, garnet rim. Nose: ripe fruit, spicy, balsamic herbs. Palate: balanced, flavourful, long, balsamic.

Martínez Lacuesta 2007 TGR
tempranillo, graciano, mazuelo

89

Colour: pale ruby, brick rim edge. Nose: spicy, fine reductive notes, wet leather, aged wood nuances. Palate: spicy, fine tannins, balanced.

Ventilla 71 2011 T
tempranillo

89

Colour: deep cherry, purple rim. Nose: creamy oak, toasty, ripe fruit, balsamic herbs. Palate: balanced, spicy, long.

MIGUEL ÁNGEL MURO

Avda. Diputación, 4
01306 Lapuebla de Labarca (Álava)
☎: +34 945 607 081
info@bodegasmuro.es
www.bodegasmuro.com

Amenital 2013 T
80% tempranillo, 20% garnacha

88

Colour: very deep cherry, purple rim. Nose: ripe fruit, floral, sweet spices. Palate: correct, spicy, balanced.

Miguel Ángel Muro 2014 T Maceración Carbónica
90% tempranillo, 10% viura

87

Colour: cherry, purple rim. Nose: expressive, fresh fruit, red berry notes, floral. Palate: flavourful, fruity, good acidity.

Muro 2006 TR
90% tempranillo, 10% graciano

89

Colour: light cherry. Nose: fine reductive notes, aged wood nuances, toasty, dried herbs. Palate: spicy, toasty, flavourful, ripe fruit.

Muro Bujanda 2011 TC
100% tempranillo

89

Colour: cherry, garnet rim. Nose: balanced, ripe fruit, spicy. Palate: balanced, ripe fruit, flavourful.

Muro Maturana 2010 T
100% maturana

90

Colour: very deep cherry, garnet rim. Nose: expressive, balsamic herbs, balanced. Palate: full, flavourful, round tannins.

Muro Viura 2014 B
viura

86

MIGUEL MERINO

Ctra. de Logroño, 16
26330 Briones (La Rioja)
☎: +34 941 322 263
info@miguelmerino.com
www.miguelmerino.com

Mazuelo de la Quinta Cruz 2012 T
100% mazuelo

87

Colour: cherry, purple rim. Nose: ripe fruit, grassy, herbaceous, spicy. Palate: fine bitter notes, easy to drink.

Unnum 2010 TC
100% tempranillo

90

Colour: cherry, garnet rim. Nose: creamy oak, fresh fruit, balanced. Palate: flavourful, spicy, elegant.

Vitola Miguel Merino 2008 TR
96% tempranillo, 4% graciano

87

Colour: cherry, garnet rim. Nose: ripe fruit, tobacco, wet leather. Palate: correct, flavourful, spicy.

MIRAVINOS RIOJA

Plaza de Matute, 12
28012 (Madrid)
☎: +34 609 079 980
info@miravinos.es
www.miravinos.es

Atuendo Colección 2014 T
85% tempranillo, 10% garnacha, 5% graciano

85

OJUEL

Mayor, 49
26376 Sojuela (La Rioja)
☎: +34 669 923 267
ojuelwine@hotmail.com
www.ojuelwine.com

Ojuel 2014 B
tempranillo blanco

84

Ojuel Especial 2013 T
maturana, garnacha, tempranillo

85

Ojuel Supurao Dulce 2013 T
garnacha, tempranillo

86

OLIVIER RIVIÈRE VINOS

Breton de los Herreros, 14 Entreplanta
26001 Logroño (La Rioja)
☎: +34 690 733 541
olivier@olivier-riviere.com
www.olivier-riviere.com

Ganko 2013 T
80% garnacha, 20% mazuelo

92

Colour: light cherry. Nose: fruit expression, fruit liqueur notes, fragrant herbs, spicy, creamy oak, earthy notes. Palate: balanced, elegant, spicy, long, toasty.

Jequitibá 2014 B
viura

92

Colour: bright yellow. Nose: expressive, dried herbs, ripe fruit, spicy. Palate: flavourful, fruity, good acidity, balanced.

Mirando al Sur Vendimia Seleccionada 2013 B
viura

92

Colour: bright golden. Nose: complex, expressive, pungent, saline, ripe fruit, dry nuts, balsamic herbs, flor yeasts. Palate: rich, powerful, fresh, fine bitter notes, balanced. Personality.

Rayos Uva 2014 T
50% tempranillo, 30% garnacha, 20% mazuelo

89

Colour: ruby red. Nose: red berry notes, floral, balsamic herbs, wild herbs, spicy. Palate: powerful, fresh, fruity, balanced.

PAGO DE LARREA

Ctra. de Cenicero, Km. 0,2
01340 Elciego (Álava)
☎: +34 945 606 063
Fax: +34 945 606 697
bodega@pagodelarrea.com
www.pagodelarrea.com

8 de Caecus 2012 T
100% tempranillo

88

Colour: cherry, garnet rim. Nose: fruit preserve, wild herbs, spicy, creamy oak. Palate: powerful, flavourful.

Caecus 2011 TR
100% tempranillo

89

Colour: bright cherry. Nose: ripe fruit, sweet spices, creamy oak, expressive. Palate: flavourful, fruity, toasty.

Caecus 2012 TC
100% tempranillo

87

Colour: cherry, garnet rim. Nose: red berry notes, ripe fruit, spicy, creamy oak. Palate: flavourful, toasty.

Caecus 2014 T
95% tempranillo, 5% garnacha

86

Caecus Verderón 2014 BFB
90% viura, 10% malvasía

85

PAGOS DE LEZA

Ctra. Vitoria - Logroño A-124
01309 Leza (Álava)
☎: +34 945 621 212
Fax: +34 945 621 222
pagosdeleza@pagosdeleza.com
www.pagosdeleza.com

Angel Santamaría 2009 TR
tempranillo

89

Colour: bright cherry. Nose: ripe fruit, sweet spices, creamy oak, fruit preserve. Palate: flavourful, fruity, toasty, round tannins.

Angel Santamaría 2011 TC
tempranillo

89

Colour: cherry, garnet rim. Nose: ripe fruit, wild herbs, earthy notes, spicy, balsamic herbs. Palate: balanced, flavourful, long, balsamic.

Editor 2012 TC
tempranillo

87

Colour: cherry, garnet rim. Nose: creamy oak, sweet spices, smoky, ripe fruit. Palate: balanced, toasty, ripe fruit.

Editor 2014 T
tempranillo

86

PAGOS DEL CAMINO

01300 Laguardia (Álava)
☎: +34 941 444 233
Fax: +34 941 444 427
info@vinicolareal.com
www.pagosdelcamino.com

Loriñón 2012 TC
85% tempranillo, 10% garnacha, 5% graciano

88

Colour: bright cherry. Nose: ripe fruit, sweet spices, creamy oak. Palate: flavourful, fruity.

PAGOS DEL REY

Ctra. N-232, PK 422,7
26360 Fuenmayor (La Rioja)
☎: +34 941 450 818
Fax: +34 941 450 818
jfernandez@pagosdelrey.com
www.pagosdelrey.com

Arnegui 2010 TR
tempranillo

88

Colour: cherry, garnet rim. Nose: ripe fruit, old leather, tobacco. Palate: correct, flavourful, spicy.

Arnegui 2012 TC
tempranillo

87

Colour: cherry, garnet rim. Nose: smoky, spicy, ripe fruit. Palate: flavourful, smoky aftertaste.

Arnegui 2014 B
viura

83

Arnegui 2014 RD
garnacha

84

Arnegui 2014 T
tempranillo

85

Castillo de Albai 2010 TR
tempranillo

86

Castillo de Albai 2012 TC
tempranillo

85

Castillo de Albai 2014 B
viura

84

Castillo de Albai 2014 RD
garnacha

84

Castillo de Albai 2014 T
tempranillo

85

PROYECTO ZORZAL
Ctra. del Villar, s/n
31591 Corella (Navarra)
☎: +34 948 780 617
Fax: +34 948 401 894
xabi@vinazorzal.com
www.vinazorzal.com

Viña Zorzal Tempranillo 2014 T
100% tempranillo

91

Colour: bright cherry. Nose: sweet spices, creamy oak, red berry notes. Palate: flavourful, fruity, round tannins.

Xanum Vinae 2012 T
95% tempranillo, 5% garnacha

88

Colour: bright cherry. Nose: ripe fruit, sweet spices, creamy oak. Palate: flavourful, fruity, toasty.

PUENTE DEL EA
Camino Aguachal, s/n
26212 Sajazarra (La Rioja)
☎: +34 941 320 405
Fax: +34 941 320 406
info@puentedelea.com
www.puentedelea.com

Eridano 2011 TC
100% tempranillo

87

Colour: cherry, garnet rim. Nose: ripe fruit, wild herbs, creamy oak. Palate: powerful, flavourful, balanced.

Eridano 2014 B
viura

84

Eridano Edición Especial 2010 TR

89

Colour: cherry, garnet rim. Nose: ripe fruit, wild herbs, earthy notes, spicy, aged wood nuances. Palate: balanced, flavourful, long, balsamic.

Eridano Vendimia Seleccionada 2012 T
90% tempranillo, 10% garnacha

87

Colour: cherry, garnet rim. Nose: creamy oak, red berry notes, ripe fruit. Palate: flavourful, spicy.

Puente del Ea 2012 BFB
viura

87

Colour: bright straw. Nose: ripe fruit, sweet spices. Palate: flavourful, fine bitter notes.

Puente del Ea 2014 RD
tempranillo, garnacha

84

Puente del Ea Vino de Autor Garnacha 2012 T
garnacha

89

Colour: cherry, garnet rim. Nose: ripe fruit, wild herbs, earthy notes, spicy, balsamic herbs. Palate: balanced, flavourful, long, balsamic.

Puente del Ea Vino de Autor Graciano 2012 T
graciano

90

Colour: cherry, garnet rim. Nose: wild herbs, earthy notes, spicy, ripe fruit. Palate: flavourful, long, balsamic.

Puente del Ea Vino de Autor Tempranillo 2012 T Barrica
tempranillo

88

Colour: deep cherry. Nose: toasty, ripe fruit, balsamic herbs. Palate: balanced, spicy, long.

Puente del Ea, Monovarietal Tempranillo 2011 T
tempranillo

88

Colour: light cherry. Nose: fine reductive notes, aged wood nuances, toasty, wild herbs. Palate: spicy, toasty, flavourful.

QUIROGA DE PABLO

Antonio Pérez, 24
26323 Azofra (La Rioja)
☎: +34 941 379 334
Fax: +34 941 379 334
info@bodegasquiroga.com
www.bodegasquiroga.com

Heredad de Judima 2008 TR
100% tempranillo

87

Colour: light cherry. Nose: fine reductive notes, aged wood nuances, toasty. Palate: spicy, toasty, flavourful.

Heredad de Judima 2012 TC
100% tempranillo

87

Colour: cherry, garnet rim. Nose: spicy, ripe fruit. Palate: flavourful, smoky aftertaste, ripe fruit.

Heredad de Judima 2014 B
95% viura, 2,5% chardonnay, 2,5% verdejo

87

Colour: bright straw. Nose: medium intensity, ripe fruit, floral, spicy. Palate: correct, easy to drink, rich.

Heredad de Judima 2014 T
85% tempranillo, 15% garnacha

85

Heredad de Judima 6 MB 2013 T
100% tempranillo

88

Colour: bright cherry. Nose: ripe fruit, sweet spices, creamy oak. Palate: flavourful, fruity, round tannins.

Heredad de Judima Clarete 2014 Clarete
60% tempranillo, 40% garnacha

84

Heredad de Judima Gold 2010 T
100% tempranillo

91

Colour: cherry, garnet rim. Nose: spicy, earthy notes, smoky. Palate: flavourful, ripe fruit, long, good acidity, balanced.

Lagar de Cayo 2008 TR
100% tempranillo

88

Colour: light cherry. Nose: fine reductive notes, aged wood nuances, toasty, smoky, dark chocolate. Palate: spicy, toasty, flavourful.

Lagar de Cayo 2012 TC
100% tempranillo

87

Colour: bright cherry. Nose: ripe fruit, sweet spices, creamy oak, smoky. Palate: flavourful, fruity, toasty, round tannins.

Lagar de Cayo 2014 B
viura, chardonnay, verdejo

87

Colour: bright straw, greenish rim. Nose: ripe fruit, tropical fruit, floral. Palate: correct, long, fine bitter notes.

Lagar de Cayo 2014 T
85% tempranillo, 15% garnacha

85

Lagar de Cayo 6 MB 2013 T
100% tempranillo

88

Colour: bright cherry. Nose: ripe fruit, sweet spices, creamy oak. Palate: flavourful, fruity, round tannins.

Lagar de Cayo Clarete 2014 RD
60% tempranillo, 40% garnacha

84

Lagar de Cayo Gold 2010 T
100% tempranillo

90

Colour: cherry, garnet rim. Nose: smoky, spicy, ripe fruit. Palate: flavourful, smoky aftertaste, ripe fruit.

Marqués de Soguilla 2008 TR
100% tempranillo

87

Colour: light cherry. Nose: fine reductive notes, aged wood nuances, toasty, smoky, aromatic coffee. Palate: spicy, toasty, flavourful.

Marqués de Soguilla 2012 TC
100% tempranillo

88

Colour: very deep cherry, garnet rim. Nose: complex, balsamic herbs, balanced. Palate: full, flavourful, round tannins.

Marqués de Soguilla 2014 B
viura, chardonnay, verdejo

85

Marqués de Soguilla 2014 T
85% tempranillo, 15% garnacha

88

Colour: cherry, purple rim. Nose: ripe fruit, spicy, grassy. Palate: fruity, unctuous.

Marqués de Soguilla 6 MB 2013 T
100% tempranillo

87

Colour: cherry, purple rim. Nose: powerfull, ripe fruit, spicy, dark chocolate. Palate: powerful, fruity.

Marqués de Soguilla Clarete 2014 T
60% tempranillo, 40% garnacha

84

Marqués de Soguilla Gold 2010 T
100% tempranillo

91

Colour: cherry, garnet rim. Nose: expressive, spicy. Palate: flavourful, ripe fruit, long, good acidity, balanced.

Quirus 2012 TC
100% tempranillo

89

Colour: very deep cherry, garnet rim. Nose: complex, balsamic herbs, balanced. Palate: full, flavourful, round tannins.

Quirus 2014 B
95% viura, chardonnay, verdejo

87

Colour: bright straw. Nose: white flowers, fresh fruit, expressive, varietal. Palate: flavourful, fruity, good acidity, balanced.

Quirus 2014 RD
60% tempranillo, 40% garnacha

85

Quirus 2014 T
85% tempranillo, 15% garnacha

85

Quirus 4MB 2013 T
100% tempranillo

88

Colour: cherry, garnet rim. Nose: creamy oak, balanced, ripe fruit. Palate: flavourful, spicy, elegant.

Quirus Selección de Familia 2010 T
100% tempranillo

89

Colour: bright cherry. Nose: ripe fruit, sweet spices, smoky. Palate: flavourful, fruity, toasty, round tannins.

RAMÓN DE AYALA LETE E HIJOS

Fuentecilla, 12
26290 Briñas (La Rioja)
☎: +34 941 310 575
Fax: +34 941 312 544
bodegas@rayalaehijos.com

Deóbriga Colección Privada 2010 T
70% tempranillo, 30% graciano

86

Deóbriga Selección Familiar 2010 T
90% tempranillo, 10% graciano

87

Colour: deep cherry. Nose: creamy oak, toasty, ripe fruit, balsamic herbs. Palate: balanced, spicy, long.

Gotas de Santurnia 2009 T
70% tempranillo, 30% graciano

88

Colour: light cherry. Nose: fine reductive notes, aged wood nuances, toasty, smoky. Palate: spicy, toasty, flavourful, long.

Viña Santurnia 2004 TGR
90% tempranillo, 5% graciano, 5% mazuelo

84

Viña Santurnia 2008 TR
90% tempranillo, 5% graciano, 5% mazuelo

86

Viña Santurnia 2010 TC
tempranillo

85

Viña Santurnia 2014 T
tempranillo

85

RAMÓN SAENZ BODEGAS Y VIÑEDOS

Mayor, 12
01307 Baños de Ebro (Álava)
☎: +34 945 609 212
bodegasrs@hotmail.com
www.bodegasramonsaenz.com

Erramun 2014 T Maceración Carbónica
95% tempranillo, 5% viura

86

Mahasti Sonie 2013 B
viura, malvasía

82

REMELLURI

Ctra. Rivas de Tereso, s/n
01330 Labastida (Álava)
☎: +34 945 331 801
Fax: +34 945 331 802
remelluri@remelluri.com
www.remelluri.com

La Granja Remelluri 2009 TGR
tempranillo, garnacha, graciano

93

Colour: deep cherry. Nose: spicy, fine reductive notes, tobacco, characterful, ripe fruit. Palate: spicy, fine tannins, elegant, long.

Lindes de Remelluri Labastida 2012 T
tempranillo, garnacha, graciano

90

Colour: cherry, garnet rim. Nose: spicy, creamy oak, fruit preserve. Palate: powerful, flavourful, spicy, long.

Lindes de Remelluri San Vicente 2012 T
tempranillo, garnacha, graciano

93

Colour: bright cherry. Nose: ripe fruit, sweet spices, creamy oak. Palate: flavourful, fruity, toasty, round tannins.

PODIUM

Remelluri 2010 TR
tempranillo, garnacha, graciano

96

Colour: cherry, garnet rim. Nose: ripe fruit, spicy, creamy oak, complex, expressive. Palate: flavourful, toasty, round tannins, balanced, elegant.

PODIUM

Remelluri 2012 B

95

Colour: bright yellow. Nose: ripe fruit, wild herbs, spicy, creamy oak. Palate: rich, spicy, balsamic, long, balanced.

RIOJA VEGA

Ctra. Logroño-Mendavia, Km. 92
31230 Viana (Navarra)
☎: +34 948 646 263
Fax: +34 948 645 612
info@riojavega.com
www.riojavega.com

Rioja Vega 130 Aniversario 2006 TR
75% tempranillo, 20% graciano, 5% mazuelo

87

Colour: cherry, garnet rim. Nose: ripe fruit, old leather, tobacco. Palate: correct, flavourful, spicy, fine tannins.

Rioja Vega 2009 TGR
75% tempranillo, 20% graciano, 5% mazuelo

88

Colour: bright cherry, orangey edge. Nose: characterful, ripe fruit, fruit liqueur notes, dried herbs, old leather. Palate: flavourful, spicy.

Rioja Vega 2010 TR
85% tempranillo, 10% graciano, 5% mazuelo

90

Colour: cherry, garnet rim. Nose: expressive, complex, balsamic herbs, balanced. Palate: full, flavourful, round tannins.

Rioja Vega 2012 TC
80% tempranillo, 5% mazuelo, 15% garnacha

88

Colour: very deep cherry, garnet rim. Nose: expressive, balsamic herbs, balanced. Palate: full, flavourful, round tannins.

Rioja Vega Edición Limitada 2012 TC
80% tempranillo, 20% graciano

90

Colour: cherry, garnet rim. Nose: mineral, expressive, spicy. Palate: flavourful, ripe fruit, long, good acidity, balanced.

Rioja Vega G y G 2014 T
50% garnacha, 50% graciano

85

Rioja Vega Rosado Pálido 2014 RD
50% tempranillo, 50% tempranillo blanco

89

Colour: onion pink. Nose: elegant, red berry notes, floral, fragrant herbs. Palate: light-bodied, flavourful, good acidity, long, spicy.

Rioja Vega Tempranillo Blanco 2014 B
100% tempranillo blanco

90

Colour: bright straw. Nose: white flowers, fine lees, dried herbs, creamy oak. Palate: flavourful, fruity, good acidity, round.

RODRÍGUEZ SANZO

Manuel Azaña, 11
47014 (Valladolid)
☎: +34 983 150 150
Fax: +34 983 150 151
comunicacion@valsanzo.com
www.rodriguezsanzo.com

La Senoba 2011 T
50% tempranillo, 50% graciano

89

Colour: cherry, garnet rim. Nose: spicy, creamy oak, toasty, ripe fruit. Palate: flavourful, ripe fruit, good acidity.

Lacrimus 2012 TC
85% tempranillo, 15% graciano

91

Colour: bright cherry. Nose: ripe fruit, sweet spices, creamy oak, expressive. Palate: flavourful, fruity, round tannins.

Lacrimus Apasionado 2014 T
75% tempranillo, 25% graciano

91

Colour: cherry, garnet rim. Nose: fruit preserve, spicy, fruit liqueur notes. Palate: powerful, flavourful, sweet, rich.

Lacrimus Garnacha 2014 T
100% garnacha

88

Colour: cherry, purple rim. Nose: powerfull, ripe fruit, spicy. Palate: powerful, fruity, round tannins.

Lacrimus Reserva Selección Familiar 2011 T
85% tempranillo, 17% graciano, 3% garnacha, 2% maturana

91

Colour: cherry, garnet rim. Nose: ripe fruit, spicy, creamy oak, complex. Palate: flavourful, toasty, round tannins.

Lacrimus Rex 2013 T
75% garnacha, 25% graciano

90

Colour: deep cherry, purple rim. Nose: creamy oak, toasty, ripe fruit, earthy notes. Palate: balanced, spicy, long.

SDAD. COOP. BODEGA SAN MIGUEL

Ctra. de Zaragoza, 7
26513 Ausejo (La Rioja)
☎: +34 941 430 005
Fax: +34 941 430 209
administracion@bodegasanmiguelsc.es
www.abradawine.com

Hebe 2011 TC
100% tempranillo

90

Colour: cherry, garnet rim. Nose: spicy. Palate: flavourful, ripe fruit, long, good acidity, balanced.

Obrada 2011 TC
80% tempranillo, 20% garnacha

88

Colour: cherry, garnet rim. Nose: smoky, spicy, ripe fruit. Palate: flavourful, smoky aftertaste, ripe fruit.

Obrada 2014 B
100% viura

87

Colour: straw. Nose: ripe fruit, floral. Palate: correct, easy to drink.

Obrada 2014 T
100% tempranillo

87

Colour: cherry, purple rim. Nose: fresh fruit, red berry notes, floral. Palate: flavourful, fruity, good acidity.

SEÑORÍO DE ARANA

La Cadena, 20
01330 Labastida (Álava)
☎: +34 945 331 150
Fax: +34 945 331 150
info@senoriodearana.com
www.senoriodearana.com

Sommelier 2007 TR
90% tempranillo, 5% mazuelo, 5% graciano

90

Colour: cherry, garnet rim. Nose: ripe fruit, wild herbs, spicy, balsamic herbs. Palate: balanced, flavourful, long, balsamic.

Sommelier 2011 TC
100% tempranillo

89

Colour: bright cherry. Nose: ripe fruit, sweet spices, creamy oak, expressive. Palate: flavourful, fruity, toasty, round tannins.

Viña del Oja 2005 TR
90% tempranillo, 5% mazuelo, 5% graciano

87

Colour: ruby red. Nose: spicy, fine reductive notes, wet leather, aged wood nuances, fruit liqueur notes. Palate: spicy, fine tannins, balsamic.

Viña del Oja 2012 TC
90% tempranillo, 10% mazuelo

86

SEÑORÍO DE LAS VIÑAS S.L.

Mayor, s/n
01321 Laserna - Laguardia (Álava)
☎: +34 945 621 110
Fax: +34 945 621 110
bodega@senoriodelasvinas.com
www.senoriodelasvinas.com

Colono 2011 TC
85% tempranillo, 15% graciano

87

Colour: dark-red cherry, garnet rim. Nose: cocoa bean, dried herbs, ripe fruit. Palate: correct, balanced, spicy, fine tannins.

Colono Expresión 2011 T
85% tempranillo, 15% graciano

89

Colour: very deep cherry, garnet rim. Nose: balsamic herbs, balanced, aged wood nuances. Palate: full, flavourful, round tannins.

Sellado 2004 TR
100% tempranillo

83

Señorío de las Viñas 2001 TGR
85% tempranillo, 15% graciano

87

Colour: dark-red cherry, orangey edge. Nose: wild herbs, waxy notes, fruit liqueur notes. Palate: spicy, easy to drink, dry wood.

Señorío de las Viñas 2004 TR
100% tempranillo

87

Colour: cherry, garnet rim. Nose: ripe fruit, wild herbs, earthy notes, spicy, balsamic herbs. Palate: balanced, flavourful, long, balsamic.

Señorío de las Viñas 2011 TC
95% tempranillo, 5% graciano

86

Señorío de las Viñas 2014 B
100% viura

83

Señorío de las Viñas 2014 T Maceración Carbónica
95% tempranillo, 5% viura

84

SEÑORÍO DE SAN VICENTE

Los Remedios, 27
26338 San Vicente de la Sonsierra (La Rioja)
☎: +34 945 600 590
Fax: +34 945 600 885
info@sierracantabria.com
www.sierracantabria.com

PODIUM

San Vicente 2011 T

95

Colour: cherry, garnet rim. Nose: complex, spicy, fine reductive notes, fruit liqueur notes. Palate: good structure, flavourful, round tannins, balanced.

PODIUM

San Vicente 2012 T

96

Colour: cherry, garnet rim. Nose: creamy oak, red berry notes, fresh fruit, balanced. Palate: flavourful, spicy, elegant.

SEÑORÍO DE SOMALO

Ctra. de Baños, 62
26321 Bobadilla (La Rioja)
☎: +34 941 202 351
Fax: +34 941 202 351
info@bodegasomalo.com
www.bodegasomalo.com

Señorío de Somalo 2003 TGR
90% tempranillo, 10% garnacha

87

Colour: deep cherry, orangey edge. Nose: waxy notes, tobacco, spicy, aged wood nuances. Palate: fine bitter notes, elegant, flavourful, fine tannins.

Señorío de Somalo 2003 TR
90% tempranillo, 10% garnacha

88

Colour: cherry, garnet rim. Nose: ripe fruit, old leather, tobacco. Palate: correct, flavourful, spicy.

Señorío de Somalo 2007 TR
85% tempranillo, 15% garnacha

84

Señorío de Somalo 2009 B Reserva
95% viura, 5% garnacha blanca, malvasía

89

Colour: bright yellow. Nose: faded flowers, sweet spices, ripe fruit, complex. Palate: balanced, fine bitter notes, spicy.

Señorío de Somalo 2011 TC
95% tempranillo, 5% garnacha

85

Señorío de Somalo 2014 B
100% viura

82

Señorío de Somalo 2014 RD
garnacha, viura

85

Señorío de Somalo 2014 T
87% tempranillo, 8% garnacha, 5% viura

85

Señorío de Somalo Magnum 2001 TGR
85% tempranillo, 15% garnacha

91

Colour: pale ruby, brick rim edge. Nose: elegant, spicy, fine reductive notes, tobacco. Palate: spicy, fine tannins, elegant, long.

SEÑORÍO DE URARTE

La Fuente, 14
01308 Lanciego (Álava)
☎: +34 678 612 038
info@senoriodeurarte.com
www.senoriodeurarte.com

Señorío de Urarte 5 Varietales 2012 TC
tempranillo, mazuelo, graciano, malvasía, viura

84

Señorío de Urarte 5 Varietales 2014 T
tempranillo, mazuelo, graciano, malvasía, viura

83

SIERRA CANTABRIA

Amorebieta, 3
26338 San Vicente de la Sonsierra
(La Rioja)
☎: +34 941 334 080
Fax: +34 941 334 371
info@sierracantabria.com
www.sierracantabria.com

Murmurón 2014 T

88

Colour: cherry, purple rim. Nose: fresh fruit, red berry notes, floral. Palate: flavourful, fruity, good acidity.

Sierra Cantabria 2005 TGR

93

Colour: pale ruby, brick rim edge. Nose: spicy, fine reductive notes, wet leather, aged wood nuances, fruit liqueur notes. Palate: spicy, fine tannins, good acidity.

Sierra Cantabria 2009 TR

93

Colour: very deep cherry, garnet rim. Nose: expressive, complex, mineral, balsamic herbs, balanced. Palate: full, flavourful, round tannins.

Sierra Cantabria 2011 TC

91

Colour: cherry, garnet rim. Nose: smoky, spicy, ripe fruit. Palate: flavourful, smoky aftertaste, ripe fruit.

Sierra Cantabria 2014 RD
tempranillo, garnacha, viura

89

Colour: coppery red. Nose: elegant, red berry notes, floral, fragrant herbs. Palate: light-bodied, flavourful, good acidity, long, spicy.

Sierra Cantabria Garnacha 2011 T

94

Colour: very deep cherry, garnet rim. Nose: complex, mineral, balsamic herbs, balanced. Palate: full, flavourful, round tannins.

Sierra Cantabria Garnacha 2012 T
93
Colour: bright cherry. Nose: ripe fruit, sweet spices, creamy oak, red berry notes. Palate: flavourful, fruity, round tannins.

Sierra Cantabria Selección 2013 T
89
Colour: bright cherry. Nose: ripe fruit, sweet spices, creamy oak. Palate: flavourful, fruity, good acidity, fine tannins.

SIETE PASOS THE WINE COMPANY

Calahorra, 12
26006 Logroño (La Rioja)
☎: +34 941 439 388
info@sietepasos.com
www.sietepasos.com

EL Figura 2014 T
tempranillo, garnacha
85

El Importante 2012 T
tempranillo
87
Colour: dark-red cherry, garnet rim. Nose: smoky, toasty, ripe fruit. Palate: correct, spicy, long.

El Prenda 2012 T
tempranillo, garnacha
86

La Fresca 2014 B
viura
84

SOC. COOP. SAN ESTEBAN P.

Ctra. Agoncillo s/n
26143 Murillo de Río Leza (La Rioja)
☎: +34 941 432 031
export@bodegassanesteban.com
www.bodegassanesteban.com

Tierras de Murillo 2012 TC
100% tempranillo
88
Colour: cherry, garnet rim. Nose: creamy oak, red berry notes, fresh fruit, balanced. Palate: flavourful, spicy, elegant.

Tierras de Murillo 2014 RD
100% tempranillo
85

Tierras de Murillo Colección Antique nº 1 2011 T
100% tempranillo
90
Colour: cherry, garnet rim. Nose: creamy oak, red berry notes, fresh fruit, balanced. Palate: flavourful, spicy.

Tierras de Murillo Colección Antique nº 1 2012 T
100% tempranillo
90
Colour: very deep cherry, garnet rim. Nose: expressive, complex, balsamic herbs, balanced. Palate: full, flavourful, round tannins.

Tierras de Murillo Tempranillo 2014 T
100% tempranillo
85

Tierras de Murillo Viura 2014 B
100% viura
86

SOLABAL

Camino San Bartolomé, 6
26339 Abalos (La Rioja)
☎: +34 941 334 492
Fax: +34 941 308 164
solabal@solabal.es
www.solabal.es

Esculle de Solabal 2010 T
tempranillo
87
Colour: cherry, garnet rim. Nose: fine reductive notes, wet leather, aged wood nuances, ripe fruit. Palate: spicy, long, toasty.

Muñarrate de Solabal 2014 B
viura
85

Muñarrate de Solabal 2014 RD
tempranillo, garnacha
83

Muñarrate de Solabal 2014 T
tempranillo
84

Solabal 2009 TR
tempranillo
89
Colour: cherry, garnet rim. Nose: ripe fruit, spicy, creamy oak, complex. Palate: flavourful, toasty.

Solabal 2012 TC
tempranillo

88

Colour: cherry, garnet rim. Nose: ripe fruit, spicy, creamy oak, tobacco, fine reductive notes. Palate: flavourful, toasty, correct.

Vala de Solabal 2010 T
tempranillo

90

Colour: cherry, garnet rim. Nose: ripe fruit, wild herbs, earthy notes, spicy, balsamic herbs, fine reductive notes. Palate: balanced, flavourful, long, balsamic.

SOTO DE TORRES

Camino Los Arenales, s/n
01330 Labastida (Álava)
☎: +34 938 177 400
Fax: +34 938 177 444
mailadmin@torres.es
www.torres.es

Altos Ibéricos 2012 TC
tempranillo

88

Colour: cherry, garnet rim. Nose: creamy oak, red berry notes, balanced. Palate: spicy, ripe fruit, easy to drink.

Altos Ibéricos Parcelas de Graciano 2011 T
graciano

89

Colour: cherry, garnet rim. Nose: ripe fruit, wild herbs, earthy notes, spicy, balsamic herbs. Palate: balanced, flavourful, long, balsamic.

SPANISH STORY

Espronceda, 27 1ºD
28003 Madrid (Madrid)
☎: +34 915 356 184
Fax: +34 915 363 796
info@spanish-story.com
www.spanish-story.com

Spanish Story Garnacha Rioja 2013 T
100% garnacha

86

Spanish Story Tempranillo 2013 T
100% tempranillo

88

Colour: cherry, garnet rim. Nose: red berry notes, ripe fruit, spicy, creamy oak, complex. Palate: flavourful, toasty.

THE GRAND WINES

Ramón y Cajal 7, 1ºA
01007 Vitoria-Gasteiz (Alava)
☎: +34 945 150 589
araex@araex.com
www.araex.com

Rolland Galarreta 2011 T

92

Colour: cherry, garnet rim. Nose: ripe fruit, spicy, creamy oak, complex. Palate: flavourful, toasty, round tannins.

TIERRA DE AGRÍCOLA LA BASTIDA

El Olmo, 16
01330 Labastida (Álava)
☎: +34 945 331 230
Fax: +34 945 331 257
info@tierrayvino.com
www.tierrayvino.com

El Belisario 2010 T
100% tempranillo

93

Colour: cherry, garnet rim. Nose: balanced, complex, ripe fruit, spicy. Palate: good structure, flavourful, round tannins.

El Primavera 2014 T

89

Colour: bright cherry. Nose: ripe fruit, sweet spices, aged wood nuances. Palate: flavourful, fruity.

Fernández Gómez 2014 T
90% tempranillo, 5% garnacha, 5% viura

86

La Hoja 2012 TC
tempranillo

88

Colour: cherry, garnet rim. Nose: roasted coffee, smoky, spicy, ripe fruit. Palate: flavourful, smoky aftertaste, ripe fruit.

Tierra 2012 T
tempranillo

88

Colour: cherry, garnet rim. Nose: roasted coffee, smoky, spicy, ripe fruit. Palate: flavourful, smoky aftertaste, ripe fruit.

Tierra 2014 BFB
60% viura, 30% malvasía, 10% garnacha

87

Colour: straw. Nose: medium intensity, ripe fruit, floral. Palate: correct, easy to drink.

Tierra de Fidel 2012 B
viura, malvasía, garnacha, moscatel, torrontés, otras

91

Colour: bright yellow. Nose: ripe fruit, powerfull, toasty, aged wood nuances, pattiserie. Palate: flavourful, fruity, spicy, toasty, long.

Tierra de Fidel 2013 B
viura, malvasía, garnacha, moscatel, torrontés, otras

88

Colour: bright straw. Nose: white flowers, fine lees, dried herbs, candied fruit. Palate: flavourful, fruity, good acidity, round.

Tierra Fidel 2010 T
50% graciano, 50% garnacha

88

Colour: cherry, garnet rim. Nose: smoky, spicy, ripe fruit. Palate: flavourful, smoky aftertaste.

TOBELOS BODEGAS Y VIÑEDOS

Ctra. N 124, Km. 45
26290 Briñas (La Rioja)
☎: +34 941 305 630
Fax: +34 941 313 028
tobelos@tobelos.com
www.tobelos.com

Tahón de Tobelos 2011 TR
100% tempranillo

91

Colour: cherry, garnet rim. Nose: mineral, expressive, spicy, ripe fruit. Palate: flavourful, ripe fruit, long, good acidity, balanced.

Tobelos 2014 BFB
80% viura, 20% garnacha blanca

88

Colour: straw. Nose: medium intensity, floral, ripe fruit, slightly evolved, toasty. Palate: correct, easy to drink.

Tobelos Garnacha 2010 T
100% garnacha

88

Colour: cherry, garnet rim. Nose: ripe fruit, wild herbs, earthy notes, spicy. Palate: balanced, flavourful, long, balsamic.

Tobelos Tempranillo 2011 TC
100% tempranillo

88

Colour: cherry, garnet rim. Nose: ripe fruit, spicy, creamy oak. Palate: flavourful, toasty, round tannins.

TORRE DE OÑA

Finca San Martín
01309 Páganos (Álava)
☎: +34 945 621 154
Fax: +34 941 312 854
info@torredeona.com
www.torredeona.com

Finca San Martín 2012 T
tempranillo

91

Colour: cherry, garnet rim. Nose: ripe fruit, wild herbs, earthy notes, spicy, balsamic herbs. Palate: balanced, flavourful, long, balsamic.

Torre de Oña 2012 TR
tempranillo, mazuelo

91

Colour: cherry, garnet rim. Nose: red berry notes, ripe fruit, spicy, creamy oak, complex. Palate: flavourful, toasty, round tannins.

UVAS FELICES

Agullers, 7
08003 Barcelona (Barcelona)
☎: +34 902 327 777
www.vilaviniteca.es

La Locomotora 2004 TGR

91

Colour: light cherry. Nose: fine reductive notes, aged wood nuances, toasty, ripe fruit. Palate: spicy, toasty, flavourful.

La Locomotora 2010 TR

90

Colour: cherry, garnet rim. Nose: red berry notes, ripe fruit, spicy, creamy oak. Palate: flavourful, toasty.

La Locomotora 2012 TC

86

Locomotora 2014 T

tempranillo

89

Colour: deep cherry, purple rim. Nose: ripe fruit, fruit preserve, sweet spices. Palate: correct, balanced.

VALLOBERA

Camino de la Hoya, s/n
01300 Laguardia (Álava)
☎: +34 945 621 204
Fax: +34 945 600 040
bsanpedro@vallobera.com
www.vallobera.com

Caudalia 2014 BFB

tempranillo blanco

89

Colour: bright yellow. Nose: ripe fruit, powerfull, toasty, aged wood nuances, pattiserie. Palate: flavourful, fruity, spicy, toasty, long.

Colección Familia San Pedro 2011 T

tempranillo

91

Colour: cherry, garnet rim. Nose: balanced, complex, ripe fruit, spicy, fine reductive notes. Palate: good structure, flavourful, round tannins, balanced.

Pago Malarina 2013 T

tempranillo

87

Colour: cherry, purple rim. Nose: powerfull, ripe fruit, spicy. Palate: powerful, fruity, unctuous, fine bitter notes.

Terran de Vallobera 2011 T

tempranillo

92

Colour: cherry, garnet rim. Nose: ripe fruit, wild herbs, earthy notes, spicy, balsamic herbs. Palate: balanced, flavourful, long balsamic.

Vallobera 2010 TR

tempranillo

90

Colour: cherry, garnet rim. Nose: ripe fruit, spicy, creamy oak Palate: flavourful, toasty, balanced.

Vallobera 2012 TC

tempranillo, garnacha

88

Colour: deep cherry. Nose: creamy oak, toasty, ripe fruit, balsamic herbs. Palate: balanced, spicy, long.

Vallobera 2014 B

viura, sauvignon blanc, tempranillo

87

Colour: bright straw. Nose: fresh fruit, fragrant herbs, expressive. Palate: flavourful, fruity, good acidity, balanced.

VALORIA

26006 Logroño (La Rioja)
☎: +34 941 204 393
Fax: +34 941 204 155
www.bvaloria.com

Finca la Pica 2012 TC

tempranillo

85

Viña Valoria 1982 T

tempranillo

92

Colour: pale ruby, brick rim edge. Nose: elegant, spicy, fine reductive notes, tobacco. Palate: spicy, fine tannins, elegant, long.

Viña Valoria 2001 TGR

tempranillo

89

Colour: pale ruby, brick rim edge. Nose: spicy, fine reductive notes, wet leather, aged wood nuances, fruit liqueur notes. Palate: spicy, fine tannins, balanced.

Viña Valoria 2010 TR

tempranillo

88

Colour: cherry, garnet rim. Nose: ripe fruit, old leather, tobacco. Palate: correct, flavourful, spicy, fine tannins, classic aged character.

Viña Valoria 2012 TC
tempranillo

87

Colour: cherry, garnet rim. Nose: fine reductive notes, aged wood nuances. Palate: spicy, toasty, classic aged character.

Viña Valoria 2014 T
tempranillo

86

VINÍCOLA RIOJANA DE ALCANADRE S.C.

San Isidro, 46
26509 Alcanadre (La Rioja)
☎: +34 941 165 036
Fax: +34 941 165 289
vinicola@riojanadealcanadre.com
www.riojanadealcanadre.com

Aradon 2012 TC
90% tempranillo, 5% garnacha, 5% mazuelo

87

Colour: bright cherry. Nose: ripe fruit, sweet spices, creamy oak. Palate: flavourful, fruity, toasty.

Aradon 2009 TR
90% tempranillo, 5% garnacha, 5% mazuelo

86

Aradon 2014 B
viura

86

Aradon 2014 RD
garnacha

83

Aradon 2014 T
90% tempranillo, 10% garnacha

84

Aradon Garnacha Selección 2012 T
garnacha

89

Colour: cherry, garnet rim. Nose: ripe fruit, wild herbs, earthy notes, spicy, balsamic herbs. Palate: flavourful, long, balsamic.

VIÑA BUJANDA

Ctra. Logroño, s/n
01320 Oyón (Alava)
☎: +34 941 450 876
Fax: +34 941 450 875
info@bujanda.com
www.familiamartinezbujanda.com

Viña Bujanda 2007 TGR
100% tempranillo

88

Colour: pale ruby, brick rim edge. Nose: spicy, fine reductive notes, wet leather, aged wood nuances, fruit liqueur notes. Palate: spicy, balanced.

Viña Bujanda 2010 TR
100% tempranillo

87

Colour: cherry, garnet rim. Nose: red berry notes, spicy, creamy oak, fine reductive notes. Palate: flavourful, toasty.

Viña Bujanda 2012 TC
100% tempranillo

85

Viña Bujanda 2014 T
100% tempranillo

83

VIÑA IJALBA

Ctra. Pamplona, Km. 1
26006 Logroño (La Rioja)
☎: +34 941 261 100
Fax: +34 941 261 128
vinaijalba@ijalba.com
www.ijalba.com

Ijalba 2011 TR
80% tempranillo, 20% graciano

90

Colour: cherry, garnet rim. Nose: ripe fruit, spicy, creamy oak, fine reductive notes. Palate: flavourful, toasty, balanced.

Ijalba 2012 TC
90% tempranillo, 10% graciano

87

Colour: bright cherry. Nose: ripe fruit, sweet spices, creamy oak. Palate: flavourful, fruity, toasty.

Ijalba Aloque 2014 RD Joven
50% tempranillo, 50% garnacha

86

Ijalba Genoli 2014 B
viura

87

Colour: straw. Nose: medium intensity, ripe fruit, floral, dried herbs. Palate: correct, long, balsamic.

Ijalba Livor 2014 T Joven
100% tempranillo

84

Ijalba Maturana Blanca 2014 B
100% maturana blanca

88

Colour: bright straw. Nose: white flowers, fresh fruit, fragrant herbs, expressive. Palate: flavourful, fruity, good acidity, balanced.

Ijalba Maturana Dionisio Ruiz Ijalba 2014 T
100% maturana

90

Colour: cherry, purple rim. Nose: powerfull, ripe fruit, spicy, creamy oak, varietal. Palate: powerful, fruity, unctuous.

Ijalba Múrice 2012 TC
85% tempranillo, 10% graciano, 5% maturana

89

Colour: cherry, garnet rim. Nose: ripe fruit, wild herbs, earthy notes, spicy, balsamic herbs. Palate: flavourful, long, balsamic.

VIÑA OLABARRI

Ctra. Haro - Anguciana, s/n
26200 Haro (La Rioja)
☎: +34 941 310 937
Fax: +34 941 311 602
info@bodegasolabarri.com
www.bodegasolabarri.com

Viña Olabarri 2008 TGR
80% tempranillo, 20% mazuelo, graciano

90

Colour: dark-red cherry, orangey edge. Nose: spicy, fine reductive notes, wet leather, aged wood nuances. Palate: spicy, fine tannins, balanced.

Viña Olabarri 2011 TR
90% tempranillo, 10% graciano

85

VIÑA REAL

Ctra. Logroño - Laguardia, Km. 4,8
01300 Laguardia (Álava)
☎: +34 945 625 255
Fax: +34 945 625 211
marketing@cvne.com
www.cvne.com

Pagos de Viña Real 2010 T
100% tempranillo

93

Colour: cherry, garnet rim. Nose: smoky, spicy, ripe fruit. Palate: flavourful, smoky aftertaste, ripe fruit.

Viña Real 2010 TGR
95% tempranillo, 5% graciano

91

Colour: cherry, garnet rim. Nose: spicy, fine reductive notes, wet leather, aged wood nuances, fruit liqueur notes. Palate: spicy, fine tannins, balanced.

Viña Real 2011 TR
90% tempranillo, 10% garnacha, mazuelo, graciano

91

Colour: cherry, garnet rim. Nose: roasted coffee, smoky, spicy, ripe fruit. Palate: flavourful, smoky aftertaste, ripe fruit.

Viña Real 2012 TC
tempranillo, garnacha, mazuelo

92

Colour: dark-red cherry, garnet rim. Nose: balanced, expressive, red berry notes, ripe fruit, sweet spices, dried herbs. Palate: balanced, round tannins.

Viña Real 2013 TC
90% tempranillo, 10% garnacha, mazuelo, graciano

91

Colour: cherry, garnet rim. Nose: creamy oak, red berry notes, balanced. Palate: flavourful, spicy, elegant.

Viña Real 2014 B
viura

89

Colour: bright straw. Nose: ripe fruit, sweet spices, creamy oak, powerfull. Palate: flavourful, spicy, ripe fruit, long.

Viña Real 2014 RD
85% viura, 15% tempranillo

88

Colour: onion pink. Nose: elegant, floral, fragrant herbs. Palate: light-bodied, good acidity, long, spicy.

VIÑA SALCEDA

Ctra. Cenicero, Km. 3
01340 Elciego (Álava)
☎: +34 945 606 125
Fax: +34 945 606 069
info@vinasalceda.com
www.vinasalceda.es

Conde de la Salceda 2010 TR
100% tempranillo

93

Colour: cherry, garnet rim. Nose: red berry notes, ripe fruit, spicy, creamy oak, complex. Palate: flavourful, toasty, round tannins.

Puente de Salceda 2012 T
100% tempranillo

90

Colour: cherry, garnet rim. Nose: red berry notes, ripe fruit, spicy, creamy oak, complex. Palate: flavourful, toasty.

Viña Salceda 2011 TR
95% tempranillo, 5% graciano

90

Colour: cherry, garnet rim. Nose: spicy, fine reductive notes, aged wood nuances. Palate: spicy, fine tannins, balanced.

Viña Salceda 2012 TC
95% tempranillo, 5% mazuelo, graciano

89

Colour: cherry, garnet rim. Nose: ripe fruit, wild herbs, aged wood nuances, fine reductive notes. Palate: powerful, flavourful.

VIÑAS LEIZAOLA

Crta Elvillar, Pol Biribil, 10
01300 Laguardia (Alava)
☎: +34 607 920 735
info@elsacramento.com
www.elsacramento.com

El Sacramento 2011 T
tempranillo, graciano

90

Colour: cherry, garnet rim. Nose: mineral, expressive, spicy. Palate: flavourful, ripe fruit, long, good acidity, balanced.

El Sacramento 2012 T
tempranillo, graciano

88

Colour: dark-red cherry, garnet rim. Nose: toasty, smoky, spicy. Palate: flavourful, fruity, easy to drink.

VIÑASPRAL

Camino Del Soto s/n
01309 Elvillar (Álava)
info@maisulan.com
www.maisulan.com

Maisulan 12 2011 TC
90% tempranillo, 10% graciano

86

Maisulan Los Lagos 2012 T
graciano

88

Colour: bright cherry. Nose: ripe fruit, sweet spices, creamy oak. Palate: flavourful, fruity, toasty, round tannins.

Maisulan Sobremoro 2012 T Barrica
tempranillo

90

Colour: cherry, garnet rim. Nose: smoky, spicy, ripe fruit. Palate: flavourful, smoky aftertaste, ripe fruit.

VIÑEDOS DE ALFARO

Camino de los Agudos s/n
26559 Aldeanueva de Ebro (La Rioja)
☎: +34 941 142 389
Fax: +34 941 142 386
info@vinedosdealfaro.com
www.vinedosdealfaro.com

Conde del Real Agrado 2005 TR
garnacha, tempranillo, mazuelo, graciano

84

Conde del Real Agrado 2007 TR
garnacha, tempranillo, mazuelo, graciano

87

Colour: cherry, garnet rim. Nose: red berry notes, ripe fruit, spicy, creamy oak. Palate: flavourful, toasty.

Conde del Real Agrado 2012 TC
garnacha, tempranillo, mazuelo, graciano

86

Real Agrado 2014 B
viura

85

Real Agrado 2014 RD
garnacha

86

Real Agrado 2014 T
garnacha, tempranillo

86

Rodiles 2005 TR
garnacha, tempranillo, mazuelo, graciano

87

Colour: ruby red. Nose: spicy, fine reductive notes, wet leather, aged wood nuances, fruit liqueur notes. Palate: spicy, harsh oak tannins.

Rodiles Vendimia Seleccionada 2005 T
graciano

88

Colour: pale ruby, brick rim edge. Nose: spicy, fine reductive notes, aged wood nuances, ripe fruit. Palate: spicy, balanced.

VIÑEDOS DE PÁGANOS

Ctra. Navaridas, s/n
01309 Páganos (Álava)
☎: +34 945 600 590
Fax: +34 945 600 885
info@sierracantabria.com
www.sierracantabria.com

El Puntido 2006 TGR

93

Colour: cherry, garnet rim. Nose: spicy, wet leather, aged wood nuances, fruit liqueur notes. Palate: spicy, fine tannins, balanced.

El Puntido 2011 T

94

Colour: cherry, garnet rim. Nose: smoky, spicy, ripe fruit, fruit liqueur notes. Palate: flavourful, smoky aftertaste, ripe fruit.

PODIUM

El Puntido 2012 T

95

Colour: very deep cherry, garnet rim. Nose: expressive, complex, mineral, balsamic herbs, balanced. Palate: full, flavourful, round tannins.

PODIUM

La Nieta 2012 T
100% tempranillo

98

Colour: cherry, garnet rim. Nose: balanced, complex, ripe fruit, spicy. Palate: good structure, flavourful, round tannins, balanced.

VIÑEDOS DEL CONTINO

Finca San Rafael, s/n
01321 Laserna (Álava)
☎: +34 945 600 201
Fax: +34 945 621 114
laserna@contino.es
www.cvne.com

Contino 2009 TGR

94

Colour: pale ruby, brick rim edge. Nose: elegant, spicy, fine reductive notes, tobacco, ripe fruit. Palate: spicy, fine tannins, elegant, long.

Contino 2009 TR

91

Colour: bright cherry, garnet rim. Nose: balanced, ripe fruit, spicy. Palate: spicy, ripe fruit, long, round tannins.

Contino Garnacha 2012 T

94

Colour: cherry, garnet rim. Nose: expressive, spicy, dried flowers. Palate: flavourful, ripe fruit, long, good acidity, balanced.

Contino Graciano 2011 T

90

Colour: cherry, garnet rim. Nose: fruit preserve, wild herbs, balsamic herbs, creamy oak. Palate: powerful, flavourful, ripe fruit.

PODIUM

Contino Viña del Olivo 2011 T

95

Colour: cherry, garnet rim. Nose: mineral, expressive, spicy, ripe fruit, fragrant herbs. Palate: flavourful, ripe fruit, long, good acidity, balanced, elegant.

VIÑEDOS DEL TERNERO

Finca El Ternero
09200 Miranda de Ebro (Burgos)
☎: +34 941 320 021
Fax: +34 941 302 719
info@elternero.com
www.elternero.com

Hacienda Ternero 2010 TR

95% tempranillo, 5% mazuelo

90

Colour: cherry, garnet rim. Nose: ripe fruit, spicy, creamy oak, complex. Palate: flavourful, toasty, round tannins.

Hacienda Ternero 2011 TC

100% tempranillo

88

Colour: very deep cherry, garnet rim. Nose: expressive, complex, mineral, balsamic herbs, balanced, ripe fruit. Palate: full, flavourful, round tannins.

Hacienda Ternero 2013 BFB

100% viura

89

Colour: yellow. Nose: faded flowers, ripe fruit, spicy, balanced. Palate: correct, easy to drink, fine bitter notes, long.

Picea 650 2009 TR

95% tempranillo, 5% mazuelo

90

Colour: cherry, garnet rim. Nose: ripe fruit, wild herbs, earthy notes, spicy, balsamic herbs. Palate: balanced, flavourful, long, balsamic.

VIÑEDOS SIERRA CANTABRIA

Calle Fuente de la Salud s/n
26338 San Vicente de la Sonsierra
(La Rioja)
☎: +34 941 334 080
Fax: +34 941 334 371
info@sierracantabria.com
www.sierracantabria.com

Amancio 2011 T

94

Colour: cherry, garnet rim. Nose: roasted coffee, smoky, spicy, overripe fruit. Palate: flavourful, smoky aftertaste.

PODIUM

Amancio 2012 T
95

Colour: cherry, garnet rim. Nose: mineral, expressive, spicy, toasty, dark chocolate. Palate: flavourful, ripe fruit, long, good acidity, balanced.

PODIUM

Finca El Bosque 2012 T
96

Colour: cherry, garnet rim. Nose: smoky, spicy, ripe fruit, fruit expression, powerfull, creamy oak. Palate: flavourful, smoky aftertaste, ripe fruit.

PODIUM

Sierra Cantabria Colección Privada 2012 T
95

Colour: cherry, garnet rim. Nose: mineral, spicy, characterful, earthy notes. Palate: flavourful, ripe fruit, long, good acidity, balanced.

Sierra Cantabria Colección Privada 2013 T
93

Colour: cherry, garnet rim. Nose: creamy oak, red berry notes, fresh fruit. Palate: flavourful, spicy, elegant.

Sierra Cantabria Cuvèe Especial 2011 T
93

Colour: cherry, garnet rim. Nose: smoky, spicy, ripe fruit. Palate: flavourful, smoky aftertaste, ripe fruit.

Sierra Cantabria Organza 2013 B
92

Colour: bright straw. Nose: white flowers, fine lees, dried herbs, ripe fruit, citrus fruit. Palate: flavourful, fruity, good acidity.

VIÑEDOS SINGULARES

Cuzco, 26 - 28, Nave 8 - 9
08030 Barcelona (Barcelona)
☎: +34 934 807 041
Fax: +34 934 807 076
info@vinedossingulares.com
www.vinedossingulares.com

Jardín Rojo 2014 T
tempranillo

87

Colour: cherry, garnet rim. Nose: spicy, ripe fruit, balsamic herbs. Palate: long, fruity aftestaste.

VIÑEDOS Y BODEGAS DE LA MARQUESA

Herrería, 76
01307 Villabuena de Álava (Álava)
☎: +34 945 609 085
Fax: +34 945 623 304
info@valserrano.com
www.valserrano.com

Valserrano 2008 TGR
90% tempranillo, 10% graciano

88

Colour: cherry, garnet rim. Nose: ripe fruit, old leather, tobacco. Palate: correct, flavourful, spicy.

Valserrano 2010 TR
90% tempranillo, 10% graciano

90

Colour: cherry, garnet rim. Nose: smoky, spicy, ripe fruit. Palate: flavourful, smoky aftertaste, ripe fruit.

Valserrano 2012 TC
90% tempranillo, 10% mazuelo

89

Colour: cherry, garnet rim. Nose: ripe fruit, spicy, creamy oak, complex. Palate: flavourful, toasty.

Valserrano 2014 BFB
95% viura, 5% malvasía

88

Colour: straw. Nose: medium intensity, ripe fruit, floral, creamy oak. Palate: correct, easy to drink.

Valserrano Finca Monteviejo 2011 T
95% tempranillo, 5% graciano, garnacha

93

Colour: light cherry. Nose: fine reductive notes, aged wood nuances, toasty, sweet spices, creamy oak. Palate: spicy, toasty, flavourful.

Valserrano Premium 2008 B Gran Reserva
95% viura, 5% malvasía

93

Colour: bright straw. Nose: white flowers, fine lees, dried herbs, ripe fruit, candied fruit, citrus fruit. Palate: flavourful, fruity, good acidity, elegant.

WOS
Cartago, 2 Escalera derecha 1ºA
28022 Madrid (Madrid)
☎: +34 911 263 478
Fax: +34 913 270 601
sdiez@woswinesofspain.com
www.woswinesofspain.com

Sensaciones 2005 TR
95% tempranillo, 5% graciano

87

Colour: cherry, garnet rim. Nose: smoky, spicy, characterful. Palate: correct, round tannins, easy to drink.

Sensaciones 2010 TC
90% tempranillo, 10% garnacha

86

Sensaciones Tempranillo Ecológico 2012 TC
100% tempranillo

86

DO. RUEDA

CONSEJO REGULADOR

Real, 8
47490 Rueda (Valladolid)
☎ :+34 983 868 248 - Fax: +34 983 868 135
@: crdo.rueda@dorueda.com
www.dorueda.com

LOCATION:

In the provinces of Valladolid (53 municipal districts), Segovia (17 municipal districts) and Ávila (2 municipal districts). The vineyards are situated on the undulating terrain of a plateau and are conditioned by the influence of the river Duero that runs through the northern part of the region.

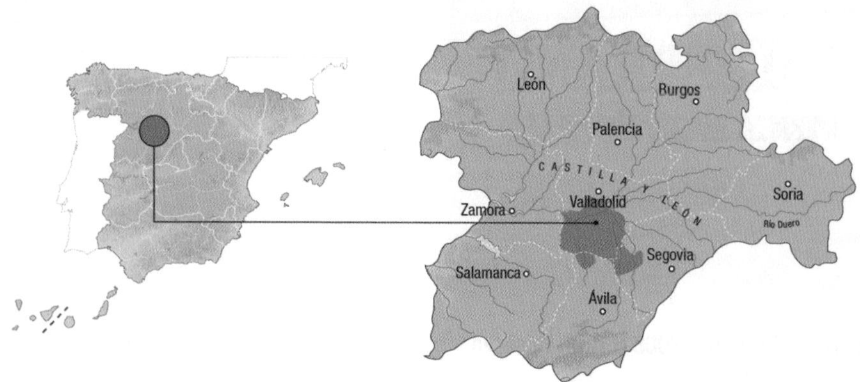

GRAPE VARIETIES:

WHITE: Verdejo (52%), Viura (22%), Sauvignon Blanc (7%) and Palomino Fino (19%).
RED: Tempranillo, Cabernet Sauvignon, Merlot and Garnacha.

FIGURES:

Vineyard surface: 13,032 – **Wine-Growers:** 4,513 – **Wineries:** 63 – **2014 Harvest rating:** N/A – **Production 14:** 68,603,212.8 litres – **Market percentages:** 84.87% National - 15.13% International.

SOIL:

Many pebbles on the surface. The terrain is stony, poor in organic matter, with good aeration and drainage. The texture of the soil is variable although, in general, sandy limestone and limestone predominate.

CLIMATE:

Continental in nature, with cold winters and short hot summers. Rainfall is concentrated in spring and autumn. The average altitude of the region is between 600 m and 700 m, and only in the province of Segovia does it exceed 800 m.

VINTAGE RATING

PEÑÍNGUIDE

2010	2011	2012	2013	2014
EXCELLENT	VERY GOOD	VERY GOOD	VERY GOOD	VERY GOOD

AGRÍCOLA CASTELLANA - BODEGA CUATRO RAYAS

Ctra. Rodilana, s/n
47491 La Seca (Valladolid)
☎: +34 983 816 320
Fax: +34 983 816 562
info@cuatrorayas.org
www.cuatrorayas.org

Azumbre Verdejo Viñedos Centenarios 2014 B

100% verdejo

90

Colour: bright straw, greenish rim. Nose: ripe fruit, citrus fruit, white flowers. Palate: balanced, correct, fine bitter notes.

Bitácora Verdejo 2014 B

verdejo

87

Colour: straw. Nose: floral, tropical fruit. Palate: correct, easy to drink.

Cuatro Rayas 2013 BFB

verdejo

89

Colour: bright yellow. Nose: ripe fruit, powerfull, toasty, aged wood nuances. Palate: flavourful, fruity, spicy, toasty, long.

Cuatro Rayas Ecológico 2013 T

tempranillo

85

Cuatro Rayas Ecológico 2014 B

verdejo

90

Colour: bright straw. Nose: fresh, dried herbs, fresh fruit. Palate: fruity, easy to drink, fine bitter notes, good acidity, long.

Cuatro Rayas Sauvignon 2014 B

sauvignon blanc

88

Colour: bright straw. Nose: citrus fruit, balanced, medium intensity. Palate: fresh, fruity, ripe fruit, fine bitter notes.

Cuatro Rayas Verdejo 2014 B

verdejo

90

Colour: bright straw. Nose: white flowers, dried herbs, candied fruit, citrus fruit. Palate: flavourful, fruity, good acidity, balanced.

Cuatro Rayas Viñedos Centenarios 2014 B

verdejo

90

Colour: bright yellow. Nose: expressive, dried herbs, ripe fruit, spicy. Palate: flavourful, fruity, good acidity, balanced.

Dama del Lago 2014 B

verdejo

86

Four Lines 2014 B
verdejo

84

Nave Sur 2014 B
verdejo

86

Colour: bright straw. Nose: tropical fruit, dried herbs, medium intensity. Palate: fruity, good acidity, thin.

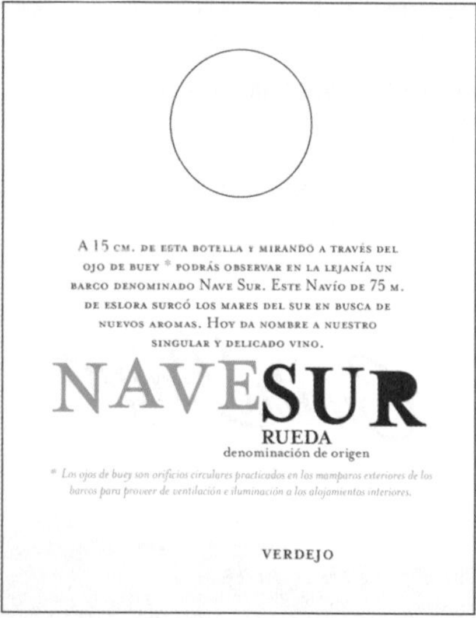

Pámpano Semidulce 2014 B
verdejo

87

Colour: bright yellow. Nose: powerfull, candied fruit, dried herbs. Palate: flavourful, sweet, ripe fruit, good acidity.

Vacceos 2011 TC
tempranillo

87

Colour: very deep cherry, garnet rim. Nose: balsamic herbs, balanced, ripe fruit, spicy, creamy oak. Palate: full, flavourful.

Vacceos Tempranillo 2013 T Roble
tempranillo

86

Veliterra 2014 B

88

Colour: bright straw. Nose: fresh fruit, fragrant herbs, floral. Palate: fruity, good acidity, easy to drink.

Visigodo Verdejo 2014 B
verdejo

89

Colour: bright straw. Nose: fragrant herbs, fruit expression, white flowers, varietal. Palate: fresh, fruity, easy to drink.

AGRÍCOLA SANZ

Santísimo Cristo, 107
47490 Rueda (Valladolid)
☎: +34 983 804 132
Fax: +34 983 804 132
info@agricolasanz.com
www.lacubaderueda.com

La Casona de los Condes 2014 B

90

Colour: bright straw. Nose: white flowers, fragrant herbs, ripe fruit. Palate: flavourful, fruity, good acidity, balanced.

ÁLVAREZ Y DÍEZ

Juan Antonio Carmona, 12
47500 Nava del Rey (Valladolid)
☎: +34 983 850 136
Fax: +34 983 850 761
bodegas@alvarezydiez.com
www.alvarezydiez.com

Gorrión 2014 B

100% sauvignon blanc

88

Colour: bright straw. Nose: white flowers, fresh fruit, fragrant herbs. Palate: flavourful, fruity, good acidity, balanced.

Mantel Blanco 2010 BFB

100% verdejo

91

Colour: bright yellow. Nose: ripe fruit, powerfull, toasty, aged wood nuances, pattiserie. Palate: flavourful, fruity, spicy, toasty, long.

Mantel Blanco Sauvignon Blanc 2014 B

100% sauvignon blanc

88

Colour: bright straw. Nose: white flowers, fresh fruit, fragrant herbs. Palate: flavourful, fruity, good acidity, correct.

Mantel Blanco Verdejo 2014 B

100% verdejo

88

Colour: bright yellow. Nose: dried herbs, ripe fruit, citrus fruit. Palate: flavourful, fruity, good acidity.

Monte Alina Rueda 2014 B

verdejo, viura

86

ÁNGEL RODRÍGUEZ VIDAL

Torcido, 1
47491 La Seca (Valladolid)
☎: +34 983 816 302
Fax: +34 983 816 302
martinsancho@martinsancho.com

Martínsancho 2014 B

100% verdejo

93

Colour: bright straw. Nose: white flowers, fine lees, dried herbs, mineral. Palate: flavourful, fruity, good acidity, round.

AVELINO VEGAS

Calvo Sotelo, 8
40460 Santiuste (Segovia)
☎: +34 921 596 002
Fax: +34 921 596 035
ana@avelinovegas.com
www.avelinovegas.com

Casa de la Vega Verdejo 2014 B

verdejo

86

Circe 2014 B

verdejo

89

Colour: bright yellow. Nose: white flowers, fresh fruit, fragrant herbs. Palate: flavourful, fruity, good acidity, balanced.

Montespina Sauvignon 2014 B

sauvignon blanc

88

Colour: bright straw. Nose: white flowers, fresh fruit, fragrant herbs. Palate: flavourful, fruity, good acidity, balanced.

Montespina Verdejo 2014 B

verdejo

88

Colour: bright yellow. Nose: dried herbs, ripe fruit, spicy. Palate: flavourful, fruity, good acidity, balanced.

AXIAL

Castillo de Capua Nº 10 nave 7
50197 Zaragoza (Zaragoza)
☎: +34 976 780 136
Fax: +34 976 303 035
info@axialvinos.com
www.axialvinos.com

Esperanza Rueda Verdejo 2014 B

100% verdejo

87

Colour: bright straw, greenish rim. Nose: medium intensity, ripe fruit, floral. Palate: correct, easy to drink.

Esperanza Verdejo Viura 2014 B

85% verdejo, 15% viura

86

BELONDRADE

Quinta San Diego -
Camino del Puerto, s/n
47491 La Seca (Valladolid)
☎: +34 983 481 001
info@belondrade.com
www.belondrade.com

Belondrade y Lurton 2013 BFB

verdejo

94

Colour: bright yellow. Nose: powerfull, toasty, aged wood nuances, pattiserie, citrus fruit, ripe fruit. Palate: flavourful, fruity, spicy, toasty, long.

BODEGA ALTAENCINA

Limonero, 41
47008 Valladolid (Valladolid)
☎: +34 639 780 716
Fax: +34 983 868 905
pablo@altaencina.com
www.altaencina.com

Quivira Verdejo 2014 B

100% verdejo

87

Colour: bright straw, greenish rim. Nose: balanced, varietal, wild herbs. Palate: balanced, fine bitter notes, good acidity.

BODEGA AYUNTAMIENTO MADRIGAL DE LAS ALTAS TORRES

05220 Madrigal de las Altas Torres
(Ávila)
☎: +34 920 320 001
Fax: +34 920 320 164
ayuntamientodemadrigal@aytomadrigal.es
www.ayuntamientodemadrigaldelasaltastorres.com

Cuna de Ysabel 2014 B

verdejo

88

Colour: bright straw. Nose: fragrant herbs, citrus fruit, ripe fruit. Palate: flavourful, fruity, good acidity, correct, balanced.

Don Vasco 2014 B

verdejo

88

Colour: bright yellow. Nose: expressive, dried herbs, ripe fruit, spicy. Palate: flavourful, fruity, good acidity, balanced.

BODEGA BURDIGALA

Calle Nueva, 12
49800 La Seca (Valladolid)
☎: +34 980 082 027
Fax: +34 983 034 040
bodega@burdigala.es
www.burdigala.es

Campo Alegre 2014 B

100% verdejo

91

Colour: bright yellow. Nose: ripe fruit, powerfull, toasty, aged wood nuances, smoky. Palate: flavourful, fruity, spicy, toasty, long.

Campo Eliseo 2013 B

100% verdejo

93

Colour: bright straw. Nose: white flowers, fine lees, dried herbs, ripe fruit, candied fruit, citrus fruit, sweet spices, creamy oak. Palate: flavourful, fruity, good acidity, elegant.

BODEGA COOPERATIVA VIRGEN DE LA ASUNCIÓN

Las Afueras, s/n
09311 La Horra (Burgos)
☎: +34 947 542 057
Fax: +34 947 542 057
info@virgendelaasuncion.com
www.virgendelaasuncion.com

Zarzuela Verdejo 2014 B

100% verdejo

87

Colour: bright straw. Nose: medium intensity, ripe fruit, fragrant herbs. Palate: correct, easy to drink, flavourful.

BODEGA DE ALBERTO

Ctra. de Valdestillas, 2
47231 Serrada (Valladolid)
☎: +34 983 559 107
Fax: +34 983 559 084
info@dealberto.com
www.dealberto.com

De Alberto Dorado Añejo
100% verdejo

94

Colour: iodine, amber rim. Nose: elegant, sweet spices, acetaldehyde, dry nuts. Palate: full, dry, spicy, long, fine bitter notes, complex.

De Alberto Verdejo 2014 B
100% verdejo

89

Colour: bright yellow. Nose: dried herbs, ripe fruit, spicy. Palate: flavourful, fruity, good acidity.

Guti Verdejo 2014 B
100% verdejo

87

Colour: straw. Nose: medium intensity, ripe fruit, floral, wild herbs. Palate: correct, easy to drink.

Monasterio de Palazuelos Rueda 2014 B
verdejo, viura

86

Monasterio de Palazuelos Sauvignon Blanc 2014 B
100% sauvignon blanc

88

Colour: bright straw. Nose: white flowers, fragrant herbs, expressive, tropical fruit. Palate: flavourful, fruity, good acidity, balanced.

Monasterio de Palazuelos Verdejo 2014 B
100% verdejo

87

Colour: straw. Nose: medium intensity, ripe fruit, floral, fragrant herbs. Palate: easy to drink, fine bitter notes, correct.

BODEGA EL ALBAR LURTON

Calle Nueva, 12
47491 La Seca (Valladolid)
☎: +34 983 034 030
Fax: +34 983 034 040
bodega@francoislurton.es
www.francoislurton.com

Hermanos Lurton Cuesta de Oro 2014 BFB
100% verdejo

91

Colour: bright yellow. Nose: powerfull, aged wood nuances, pattiserie, candied fruit, roasted coffee. Palate: flavourful, fruity, spicy, toasty, long.

Hermanos Lurton Sauvignon 2014 B
100% sauvignon blanc

90

Colour: bright straw. Nose: white flowers, fresh fruit, fragrant herbs, expressive. Palate: flavourful, fruity, good acidity, balanced.

Hermanos Lurton Verdejo 2014 B
100% verdejo

91

Colour: bright straw. Nose: white flowers, fine lees, dried herbs, ripe fruit, citrus fruit. Palate: flavourful, fruity, good acidity, elegant, long.

BODEGA EMINA RUEDA

Ctra. Medina del Campo -
Olmedo, Km. 1,5
47290 Medina del Campo (Valladolid)
☎: +34 983 803 346
Fax: +34 902 430 189
emina@emina.es
www.eminarueda.es

Emina Rueda 2014 B

90% verdejo, 10% viura

85

Emina Sauvignon 2014 B

100% sauvignon blanc

87

Colour: bright straw. Nose: fresh fruit, fragrant herbs, tropical fruit. Palate: flavourful, fruity, good acidity, balanced.

Emina Verdejo 2014 B

100% verdejo

88

Colour: straw. Nose: medium intensity, ripe fruit, floral, tropical fruit. Palate: correct, easy to drink.

BODEGA HERMANOS DEL VILLAR

Zarcillo, s/n
47490 Rueda (Valladolid)
☎: +34 983 868 904
Fax: +34 983 868 905
pablo@orodecastilla.com
www.orodecastilla.com

Oro de Castilla Sauvignon Blanc 2014 B

100% sauvignon blanc

87

Colour: straw. Nose: medium intensity, ripe fruit, floral. Palate: correct, easy to drink.

Oro de Castilla Verdejo 2014 B

100% verdejo

89

Colour: bright straw. Nose: white flowers, fragrant herbs, expressive, ripe fruit. Palate: flavourful, fruity, good acidity, balanced.

BODEGA MATARROMERA

Ctra. Renedo-Pesquera, Km. 30
47359 Valbuena de Duero (Valladolid)
☎: +34 983 683 315
Fax: +34 902 430 189
matarromera@matarromera.es
www.bodegamatarromera.es

Matarromera Verdejo Edición Limitada 25 Aniversario 2013 B

100% verdejo

89

Colour: bright yellow. Nose: powerfull, toasty, aged wood nuances, pattiserie, overripe fruit. Palate: flavourful, fruity, spicy, toasty, long.

Melior Verdejo 2013 B

100% verdejo

87

Colour: straw. Nose: ripe fruit, floral. Palate: correct, easy to drink.

BODEGA REINA DE CASTILLA

Cº de la Moya, s/n
47491 La Seca (Valladolid)
☎: +34 983 816 667
bodega@reinadecastilla.es
www.reinadecastilla.es

EL Bufón Verdejo 2014 B

100% verdejo

89

Colour: bright yellow. Nose: expressive, dried herbs, ripe fruit, spicy. Palate: flavourful, fruity, good acidity, balanced, long, ripe fruit.

Isabelino 2014 RD

100% tempranillo

87

Colour: rose, purple rim. Nose: red berry notes, floral, expressive. Palate: powerful, fruity, fresh.

Isabelino Rueda 2014 B

95% verdejo, 5% viura

86

Isabelino Verdejo 2014 B

100% verdejo

89

Colour: bright yellow. Nose: expressive, dried herbs, ripe fruit, spicy. Palate: flavourful, fruity, good acidity, balanced.

Reina de Castilla Sauvignon Blanc 2014 B
100% sauvignon blanc

88

Colour: bright straw. Nose: ripe fruit, tropical fruit. Palate: flavourful, sweetness.

Reina de Castilla Verdejo 2014 B
100% verdejo

89

Colour: bright straw. Nose: white flowers, dried herbs, ripe fruit, candied fruit, citrus fruit. Palate: flavourful, fruity, good acidity, elegant.

BODEGA SOLAR DE MUÑOSANCHO
47491 La Seca (Valladolid)
☎: +34 983 394 254
Fax: +34 983 481 038
solar@solarmsancho.com
www.solarmsancho.com

Prius de Moraña Verdejo 2014 B
100% verdejo

86

BODEGA TOMÁS POSTIGO
Estación, 12
47300 Peñafiel (Valladolid)
☎: +34 983 873 019
Fax: +34 983 880 258
administracion@tomaspostigo.es
www.tomaspostigo.es

Tomás Postigo Verdejo 2011 BFB
verdejo

91

Colour: bright golden. Nose: sweet spices, creamy oak, candied fruit. Palate: full, rich, long, creamy, balanced.

BODEGA VALDEHERMOSO
Ctra. Nava del Rey - Rueda, km. 12,6
47500 Nava del Rey (Valladolid)
☎: +34 983 090 936
valdehermoso@valdehermoso.com
www.valdehermoso.com

Lagar del Rey Sauvignon Blanc 2013 B
100% sauvignon blanc

86

Lagar del Rey Verdejo 100% Lías 2014 B
100% verdejo

88

Colour: bright yellow. Nose: expressive, dried herbs, ripe fruit, spicy. Palate: flavourful, fruity, good acidity, balanced.

Viña Perez Verdejo 2014 B
100% verdejo

88

Colour: bright straw. Nose: fine lees, dried herbs, dried flowers. Palate: flavourful, fruity, good acidity, round.

BODEGA VALDRINAL
Francisco Suárez, 18
28036 Madrid (Madrid)
☎: +34 914 113 522
general@valdrinal.com
www.valdrinal.com

Valdrinal de Santamaría 2014 B
verdejo

89

Colour: bright straw. Nose: wild herbs, fresh fruit, balanced. Palate: flavourful, fruity, good acidity, fine bitter notes.

BODEGAS ARROCAL
Eras de Santa María, s/n
09443 Gumiel de Mercado (Burgos)
☎: +34 947 561 290
Fax: +34 947 561 290
rodrigo@arrocal.com
www.arrocal.com

Arrocal Verdejo 2014 B
verdejo

89

Colour: bright yellow, greenish rim. Nose: dried herbs, ripe fruit, varietal. Palate: flavourful, fruity, good acidity, balanced.

BODEGAS AURA

Ctra. Autovía del Noroeste, Km. 175
47490 Rueda (Valladolid)
☎: +34 983 868 286
aura@pernod-ricard.com
www.bodegasaura.com

Aura Verdejo Vendimia Nocturna 2014 B

verdejo

91

Colour: bright straw. Nose: white flowers, fresh fruit, fragrant herbs, expressive. Palate: flavourful, fruity, good acidity, balanced.

AuraSelección Parcela Avutarda 2014 BFB

verdejo

93

Colour: bright straw. Nose: white flowers, fine lees, dried herbs, mineral, sweet spices, varietal. Palate: flavourful, fruity, good acidity, round.

BODEGAS BERONIA

Ctra. Ollauri - Nájera, Km. 1,8
26220 Ollauri (La Rioja)
☎: +34 941 338 000
Fax: +34 941 338 266
beronia@beronia.es
www.beronia.es

Beronia Rueda 2014 B

100% verdejo

88

Colour: bright straw. Nose: white flowers, fresh fruit, tropical fruit. Palate: flavourful, fruity, good acidity, balanced.

BODEGAS BILBAÍNAS

Estación, 3
26200 Haro (La Rioja)
☎: +34 941 310 147
info@bodegasbilbainas.com
www.grupocodorniu.com

Ederra 2014 B

verdejo

87

Colour: bright straw. Nose: citrus fruit, ripe fruit, floral, fragrant herbs. Palate: fresh, fruity, easy to drink, fine bitter notes.

BODEGAS CAÑALVA

Coto, 54
10136 Cañamero (Cáceres)
☎: +34 927 369 405
Fax: +34 927 369 405
info@bodegascanalva.com
www.bodegascanalva.com

Cañalva Verdejo 2014 B

100% verdejo

84

BODEGAS CASTELO DE MEDINA

Ctra. CL-602, Km. 48
47465 Villaverde de Medina (Valladolid)
☎: +34 983 831 932
Fax: +34 983 831 857
info@castelodemedina.com
www.castelodemedina.com

Castelo de la Dehesa 2014 B

50% verdejo, 30% viura, 20% sauvignon blanc

87

Colour: bright straw. Nose: white flowers, fresh fruit, fragrant herbs, tropical fruit. Palate: flavourful, fruity, good acidity.

Castelo de Medina Sauvignon Blanc 2014 B

100% sauvignon blanc

90

Colour: bright straw. Nose: white flowers, fresh fruit, fragrant herbs, expressive. Palate: flavourful, fruity, good acidity, balanced.

Castelo de Medina Sauvignon Blanc Vendimia Seleccionada 2014 B

100% sauvignon blanc

91

Colour: bright straw. Nose: white flowers, dried herbs, candied fruit, citrus fruit. Palate: flavourful, fruity, good acidity, elegant.

Castelo de Medina Verdejo 2014 B

100% verdejo

90

Colour: bright straw. Nose: white flowers, fine lees, dried herbs, mineral. Palate: flavourful, fruity, good acidity, round.

Castelo de Medina Verdejo Vendimia Seleccionada 2014 B
100% verdejo

92

Colour: bright straw. Nose: white flowers, dried herbs, candied fruit, citrus fruit, varietal. Palate: flavourful, fruity, good acidity, elegant.

Castelo Noble 2013 BFB
85% verdejo, 15% sauvignon blanc

90

Colour: bright yellow. Nose: ripe fruit, powerfull, toasty, aged wood nuances, pattiserie. Palate: flavourful, fruity, spicy, toasty, long.

Real Castelo 2014 B
85% verdejo, 15% sauvignon blanc

90

Colour: bright yellow. Nose: expressive, dried herbs, ripe fruit, spicy. Palate: flavourful, fruity, good acidity, balanced.

BODEGAS COPABOCA

Autovía A-62, Salida 148
47100 Tordesillas (Valladolid)
☎: +34 983 486 010
club@copaboca.com
www.copaboca.com

Copaboca 2014 B
100% verdejo

88

Colour: straw. Nose: medium intensity, ripe fruit, floral. Palate: correct, easy to drink.

Finca Feroes 2014 B
100% verdejo

88

Colour: straw. Nose: ripe fruit, floral, tropical fruit, medium intensity. Palate: correct, easy to drink.

Gorgorito Verdejo 2014 B
100% verdejo

88

Colour: bright straw. Nose: white flowers, fresh fruit, fragrant herbs. Palate: flavourful, fruity, balanced.

Juan Galindo Lías 2014 B
100% verdejo

91

Colour: bright straw. Nose: white flowers, fine lees, dried herbs, mineral. Palate: flavourful, fruity, good acidity, round.

BODEGAS DE LOS RÍOS PRIETO

Ctra. Pesquera - Renedo, s/n
47315 Pesquera de Duero (Valladolid)
☎: +34 983 880 383
Fax: +34 983 878 032
administracion@bodegasdelosriosprieto.com
www.bodegasdelosriosprieto.com

Prios Maximus Verdejo 2014 B
verdejo

88

Colour: bright straw. Nose: white flowers, fresh fruit, fragrant herbs, expressive. Palate: flavourful, fruity, good acidity, balanced.

BODEGAS EL INICIO

San Vicente, 22
47300 Peñafiel (Valladolid)
☎: +34 947 515 884
Fax: +34 947 515 886
info@bodegaselinicio.com
www.bodegaselinicio.com

Pluma Blanca 2014 B
100% verdejo

86

BODEGAS FÉLIX LORENZO CACHAZO S.L.

Ctra. Medina del Campo, Km. 9
47220 Pozáldez (Valladolid)
☎: +34 983 822 008
Fax: +34 983 822 008
administracion@cachazo.com
www.cachazo.com

Carrasviñas Espumoso 2013 BR
verdejo

86

Carrasviñas Verdejo 2014 B
verdejo

88

Colour: straw. Nose: medium intensity, ripe fruit, floral. Palate: correct, easy to drink.

Gran Cardiel Rueda Verdejo 2014 B
verdejo

87

Colour: bright straw. Nose: white flowers, fresh fruit, fragrant herbs. Palate: flavourful, fruity, good acidity.

Mania Rueda Verdejo 2014 B
verdejo

90

Colour: bright straw. Nose: white flowers, dried herbs, ripe fruit, citrus fruit, varietal. Palate: flavourful, fruity, elegant, good acidity.

Mania Sauvignon 2014 B
sauvignon blanc

88

Colour: bright straw. Nose: white flowers, fragrant herbs, powerfull, tropical fruit. Palate: flavourful, fruity, good acidity, balanced.

BODEGAS FÉLIX SANZ

Santísimo Cristo, 28
47490 Rueda (Valladolid)
☎: +34 983 868 044
Fax: +34 983 868 133
info@bodegasfelixsanz.es
www.bodegasfelixsanz.es

Viña Cimbrón 2012 BFB
100% verdejo

89

Colour: bright yellow. Nose: powerfull, toasty, aged wood nuances, pattiserie. Palate: flavourful, fruity, spicy, toasty, long.

Viña Cimbrón Sauvignon 2014 B
100% sauvignon blanc

88

Colour: bright straw. Nose: white flowers, fresh fruit, fragrant herbs. Palate: flavourful, fruity, good acidity.

Viña Cimbrón Verdejo 2014 B
100% verdejo

88

Colour: straw. Nose: medium intensity, ripe fruit, floral, citrus fruit. Palate: correct, easy to drink.

Viña Cimbrón Verdejo Edición Especial Aniversario 2013 B
100% verdejo

90

Colour: bright yellow. Nose: expressive, dried herbs, ripe fruit, spicy. Palate: flavourful, fruity, good acidity, balanced.

Viña Cimbrón Verdejo Selección 2014 B
100% verdejo

89

Colour: straw. Nose: medium intensity, ripe fruit, floral, dried herbs. Palate: correct, easy to drink, balanced.

BODEGAS FRUTOS VILLAR

Ctra. Burgos-Portugal Km. 113,7
47270 Cigales (Valladolid)
☎: +34 983 586 868
Fax: +34 983 580 180
bodegasfrutosvillar@bodegasfrutosvillar.com
www.bodegasfrutosvillar.com

María Molina Rueda 2014 B
verdejo, viura

86

María Molina Verdejo 2014 B
100% verdejo

88

Colour: bright straw. Nose: fresh fruit, fragrant herbs, expressive. Palate: flavourful, fruity, good acidity, balanced.

Muruve Verdejo 2014 B
100% verdejo

88

Colour: straw. Nose: medium intensity, ripe fruit, varietal. Palate: correct, easy to drink, fine bitter notes.

Viña Cansina Verdejo 2014 B
100% verdejo

86

Viña Morejona Rueda 2014 B
verdejo, viura

87

Colour: bright yellow. Nose: ripe fruit, floral, tropical fruit. Palate: ripe fruit, fine bitter notes, correct.

Viña Morejona Verdejo 2014 B
100% verdejo

87

Colour: bright straw, greenish rim. Nose: wild herbs, ripe fruit. Palate: correct, fine bitter notes, easy to drink.

BODEGAS GARCI GRANDE

Aradillas s/n
47490 Rueda (Valladolid)
☎: +34 983 868 561
Fax: +34 983 868 449
carlos.garcia@hispanobodegas.com
www.hispanobodegas.com

12 Linajes Verdejo 2014 B
100% verdejo

90

Colour: bright straw. Nose: white flowers, fresh fruit, fragrant herbs, expressive. Palate: flavourful, fruity, good acidity, balanced.

Anier Verdejo Vendimia Seleccionada 2014 B
100% verdejo

92

Colour: bright straw. Nose: white flowers, fine lees, dried herbs, mineral, powerfull. Palate: flavourful, fruity, good acidity, round.

Señorío de Garci Grande Verdejo 2014 B
100% verdejo

90

Colour: bright straw. Nose: fresh fruit, fragrant herbs, floral. Palate: flavourful, fruity, good acidity.

BODEGAS GARCÍA DE ARANDA

Ctra. de Soria, s/n
09400 Aranda de Duero (Burgos)
☎: +34 947 501 817
Fax: +34 947 506 355
bodega@bodegasgarcia.com
www.bodegasgarcia.com

Oro Blanco Rueda 2014 B
60% verdejo, 40% viura

85

Oro Blanco Verdejo 2014 B
100% verdejo

86

BODEGAS GARCÍAREVALO

Pza. San Juan, 4
47230 Matapozuelos (Valladolid)
☎: +34 983 832 914
garciarevalo@garciarevalo.com
www.garciarevalo.com

Tres Olmos Lías 2014 B
100% verdejo

90

Colour: bright straw. Nose: white flowers, fresh fruit, fragrant herbs, expressive. Palate: flavourful, fruity, good acidity.

Viña Adaja Verdejo 2014 B
100% verdejo

90

Colour: bright yellow. Nose: dried herbs, ripe fruit, spicy. Palate: flavourful, fruity, good acidity, balanced.

BODEGAS GRAN FEUDO

Ribera, 34
31592 Cintruénigo (Navarra)
☎: +34 948 811 000
Fax: +34 948 811 407
info@granfeudo.com
www.granfeudo.com

Gran Feudo Verdejo 2014 B
verdejo

86

BODEGAS GRUPO YLLERA

Autovía A-6, Km. 173,5
47490 Rueda (Valladolid)
☎: +34 983 868 097
Fax: +34 983 868 177
grupoyllera@grupoyllera.com
www.grupoyllera.com

Bracamonte Verdejo 2014 B
verdejo

89

Colour: bright straw. Nose: white flowers, fresh fruit, fragrant herbs, expressive. Palate: flavourful, fruity, good acidity, balanced.

Bracamonte Verdejo Viñas Viejas 2014 B
verdejo

89

Colour: straw. Nose: ripe fruit, floral, grassy, expressive. Palate: correct, easy to drink.

Cantosán 2013 BR
verdejo

86

Cantosán 2013 SS
verdejo

86

Cantosán 2013 BN
verdejo

87

Colour: bright yellow. Nose: ripe fruit, fine lees, balanced, dried herbs. Palate: good acidity, flavourful, ripe fruit, long.

Cantosán Reserva Especial ESP
verdejo

88

Colour: bright straw. Nose: medium intensity, fresh fruit, dried herbs, fine lees, floral. Palate: fresh, fruity, flavourful, good acidity.

Cantosán Verdejo Viñas Viejas 2014 B
verdejo

88

Colour: straw. Nose: medium intensity, ripe fruit, floral, citrus fruit. Palate: correct, easy to drink.

Tierra Buena 2014 B
verdejo

89

Colour: bright straw. Nose: fresh fruit, fragrant herbs, white flowers. Palate: flavourful, fruity, good acidity, balanced.

Viña 65 Verdejo 2014 B
verdejo

89

Colour: bright straw. Nose: white flowers, fresh fruit, fragran herbs. Palate: flavourful, fruity, good acidity, balanced.

Viña 65 Verdejo Sauvignon Blanc 2014 B
verdejo, sauvignon blanc

88

Colour: straw. Nose: medium intensity, ripe fruit, floral, tropica fruit. Palate: correct, easy to drink.

Viña Garedo Verdejo 2014 B
verdejo

88

Colour: straw. Nose: medium intensity, ripe fruit, floral, tropical fruit. Palate: correct, easy to drink.

Viña Garedo Verdejo Sauvignon Blanc 2014 B
verdejo, sauvignon blanc

89

Colour: bright straw. Nose: white flowers, fresh fruit. Palate: flavourful, fruity, good acidity, balanced.

Yllera Sauvignon Blanc 2014 B
sauvignon blanc

87

Colour: bright straw. Nose: white flowers, fresh fruit, fragrant herbs, tropical fruit. Palate: flavourful, fruity, good acidity.

Yllera Verdejo Vendimia Nocturna 2014 B
verdejo

90

Colour: bright straw. Nose: white flowers, fresh fruit, fragrant herbs. Palate: flavourful, fruity, good acidity, balanced.

BODEGAS IMPERIALES

Ctra. Madrid - Irun, Km. 171
09370 Gumiel de Izán (Burgos)
☎: +34 947 544 070
Fax: +34 947 525 759
adminis@bodegasimperiales.com
www.bodegasimperiales.com

Abadía de San Quirce Verdejo 2014 B
100% verdejo

89

Colour: bright yellow. Nose: expressive, dried herbs, ripe fruit, spicy. Palate: flavourful, fruity, good acidity, balanced.

BODEGAS JAVIER RUIZ PANIAGUA

Tomillo, 1
47239 Villanueva de Duero (Valladolid)
☎: +34 636 407 752
nicolas@bodegasjavierruiz.com
www.bodegasjavierruiz.com

Pagus Nova 2014 B
verdejo

86

Veyovis 2014 B
verdejo

90

Colour: bright straw. Nose: white flowers, fine lees, dried herbs, ripe fruit, candied fruit, citrus fruit. Palate: flavourful, fruity, good acidity, elegant.

BODEGAS JOSÉ PARIENTE

Ctra. de Rueda, km. 2.5
47491 La Seca (Valladolid)
☎: +34 983 816 600
Fax: +34 983 816 620
info@josepariente.com
www.josepariente.com

Apasionado de Jose Pariente 2013 B
100% sauvignon blanc

90

Colour: bright straw. Nose: expressive, dried herbs, ripe fruit, spicy. Palate: flavourful, good acidity.

José Pariente 2013 BFB
100% verdejo

93

Colour: bright straw. Nose: white flowers, fine lees, dried herbs, ripe fruit, balanced. Palate: flavourful, fruity, good acidity, elegant.

José Pariente Cuvee Especial 2013 B
100% verdejo

92

Colour: bright yellow. Nose: expressive, dried herbs, ripe fruit, spicy, toasty. Palate: flavourful, fruity, good acidity, balanced.

José Pariente Sauvignon Blanc 2014 B
100% sauvignon blanc

91

Colour: bright straw. Nose: fresh fruit, fragrant herbs, grassy. Palate: flavourful, fruity, good acidity, balanced.

José Pariente Verdejo 2014 B
100% verdejo

92

Colour: bright straw. Nose: white flowers, dried herbs, ripe fruit, candied fruit, citrus fruit. Palate: flavourful, fruity, good acidity, elegant.

BODEGAS LAN

Paraje del Buicio, s/n
26360 Fuenmayor (La Rioja)
☎: +34 941 450 950
Fax: +34 941 450 567
info@bodegaslan.com
www.bodegaslan.com

Duquesa de Valladolid 2014 B
100% verdejo

88

Colour: bright straw. Nose: fragrant herbs, citrus fruit, fruit expression. Palate: flavourful, fruity, good acidity, long.

BODEGAS MARQUÉS DE CÁCERES

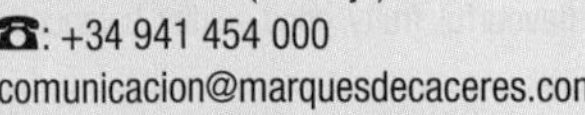

Ctra. Logroño, s/n
26350 Cenicero (La Rioja)
☎: +34 941 454 000
comunicacion@marquesdecaceres.com
www.marquesdecaceres.com

Excellens de Marqués de Cáceres Sauvignon Blanc 2014 B

100% sauvignon blanc

88

Colour: bright straw. Nose: fresh fruit, fragrant herbs, ripe fruit. Palate: flavourful, fruity, good acidity, correct.

Marqués de Cáceres Verdejo 2014 B

100% verdejo

89

Colour: bright straw. Nose: fresh fruit, fragrant herbs, expressive. Palate: flavourful, fruity, good acidity, balanced.

BODEGAS MARQUÉS DE RISCAL

Ctra. N-VI, km. 172,600
47490 Rueda (Valladolid)
☎: +34 983 868 083
Fax: +34 983 868 563
rherrero@marquesderiscal.com
www.marquesderiscal.com

Marqués de Riscal Finca Montico 2014 B

100% verdejo

92

Colour: bright straw. Nose: white flowers, fine lees, dried herbs, medium intensity. Palate: flavourful, fruity, good acidity, round.

Marqués de Riscal Limousin 2013 BFB

100% verdejo

90

Colour: bright yellow. Nose: ripe fruit, powerfull, aged wood nuances, pattiserie, roasted coffee. Palate: flavourful, fruity, spicy, toasty, long.

Marqués de Riscal Rueda Verdejo 2014 B

100% verdejo

92

Colour: bright straw. Nose: white flowers, fine lees, dried herbs, mineral. Palate: flavourful, fruity, good acidity, round.

Marqués de Riscal Sauvignon Blanc 2014 B

100% sauvignon blanc

91

Colour: bright straw. Nose: white flowers, fragrant herbs. Palate: flavourful, fruity, good acidity, balanced.

Viña Calera Rueda Verdejo 2014 B

85% verdejo, 10% sauvignon blanc, 5% viura

87

Colour: bright straw. Nose: white flowers, fresh fruit, fragrant herbs. Palate: flavourful, fruity, good acidity.

BODEGAS MOCÉN

Arribas, 7-9
47490 Rueda (Valladolid)
☎: +34 983 868 533
Fax: +34 983 868 514
info@bodegasmocen.com
www.bodegasantano.com

Alta Plata Verdejo 2014 B

verdejo

89

Colour: bright straw. Nose: white flowers, fresh fruit, fragrant herbs, expressive. Palate: flavourful, fruity, good acidity, balanced.

Leguillón Verdejo 2014 B

verdejo

90

Colour: bright straw. Nose: white flowers, fresh fruit, fragrant herbs. Palate: flavourful, fruity, good acidity.

Mocén Blanco Rueda 2014 B

verdejo

85

Mocén Sauvignon 2014 B
100% sauvignon blanc

90

Colour: bright straw. Nose: balsamic herbs, citrus fruit, fresh fruit, floral, jasmine. Palate: fresh, fruity, flavourful, balanced.

Mocén Verdejo Selección Especial 2014 B
100% verdejo

90

Colour: bright yellow. Nose: expressive, dried herbs, ripe fruit, spicy. Palate: flavourful, fruity, good acidity, balanced, long.

Mocén Verdejo 2014 BFB
verdejo

89

Colour: bright straw. Nose: white flowers, fine lees, dried herbs, mineral, creamy oak, sweet spices. Palate: flavourful, fruity, good acidity, round.

BODEGAS MONTE BLANCO

Ctra. Valladolid, Km. 24,5
47239 Serrada (Valladolid)
☎: +34 941 310 295
Fax: +34 941 310 832
info@bodegas-monteblanco.es
www.bodegas-monteblanco.es

Ramón Bilbao Verdejo "Monte Blanco" 2014 B
100% verdejo

90

Colour: bright yellow. Nose: expressive, dried herbs, fruit expression. Palate: flavourful, fruity, good acidity, balanced.

BODEGAS MONTEABELLÓN

Calvario, s/n
09318 Nava de Roa (Burgos)
☎: +34 947 550 000
Fax: +34 947 550 219
info@monteabellon.com
www.monteabellon.com

Monteabellón Verdejo 2014 B

100% verdejo

89

Colour: bright straw. Nose: fresh fruit, fragrant herbs, expressive. Palate: flavourful, fruity, good acidity, balanced.

BODEGAS NAIA

Camino San Martín, s/n
47491 La Seca (Valladolid)
☎: +34 628 434 933
info@bodegasnaia.com
www.bodegasnaia.com

K-Naia 2014 B

85% verdejo, 15% sauvignon blanc

90

Colour: bright straw. Nose: white flowers, fragrant herbs, tropical fruit. Palate: flavourful, fruity, good acidity, balanced.

Las Brisas 2014 B

50% verdejo, 40% viura, 10% sauvignon blanc

88

Colour: bright straw. Nose: white flowers, fresh fruit, fragrant herbs. Palate: flavourful, fruity, good acidity.

Naia 2014 B

100% verdejo

91

Colour: bright straw. Nose: fine lees, dried herbs, floral. Palate: flavourful, fruity, good acidity, round.

Naiades 2012 BFB

100% verdejo

94

Colour: bright straw. Nose: white flowers, fine lees, dried herbs, ripe fruit, candied fruit, citrus fruit. Palate: flavourful fruity, good acidity, elegant.

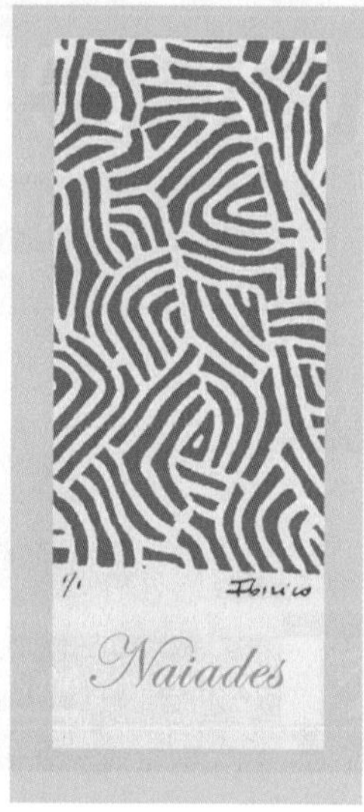

S-Naia 2014 B

100% sauvignon blanc

90

Colour: bright straw. Nose: tropical fruit, citrus fruit, grassy. Palate: flavourful, fine bitter notes.

Venta Mazarrón Verdejo 2014 B

90% verdejo, 10% sauvignon blanc

91

Colour: bright straw. Nose: fragrant herbs, dried flowers. Palate: flavourful, fruity, good acidity, balanced.

BODEGAS NIDIA

Ctra. La Seca 17
47400 Medina del Campo (Valladolid)
☎: +34 983 812 581
Fax: +34 983 837 021
info@bodegasnidia.com
www.bodegasnidia.com

Nidia 2014 B

verdejo

86

BODEGAS NILO

Federico García Lorca, 7
47490 Rueda (Valladolid)
☎: +34 690 068 682
info@bodegasnilo.com
www.bodegasnilo.com

Bianca 2014 B

verdejo

90

Colour: bright straw, greenish rim. Nose: fragrant herbs, varietal, expressive. Palate: balanced, fine bitter notes, good acidity.

BODEGAS ORDÓÑEZ

Julio Romero de Torres, 12
29700 Vélez- Málaga (Málaga)
☎: +34 952 504 706
Fax: +34 951 284 796
info@jorgeordonez.es
www.grupojorgeordonez.com

PODIO

Nisia 2014 B

100% verdejo

95

Colour: bright straw. Nose: white flowers, fine lees, dried herbs, mineral. Palate: flavourful, fruity, good acidity, round.

BODEGAS PEÑAFIEL

Ctra. N-122, Km. 311
47300 Peñafiel (Valladolid)
☎: +34 983 881 622
Fax: +34 983 881 944
bodegaspenafiel@bodegaspenafiel.com
www.bodegaspenafiel.com

Alba de Miros 2014 B

100% verdejo

89

Colour: bright straw, greenish rim. Nose: fresh fruit, fragrant herbs, varietal, balanced. Palate: correct, fine bitter notes, good acidity.

BODEGAS PRADOREY

Ctra. A-VI, Km. 172,5
47490 Rueda (Valladolid)
☎: +34 983 444 048
Fax: +34 983 868 564
bodega@pradorey.com
www.pradorey.com

Birlocho 2014 B

95% verdejo, 5% sauvignon blanc

88

Colour: bright yellow. Nose: expressive, dried herbs, ripe fruit, spicy. Palate: flavourful, fruity, good acidity.

PR 3 Barricas 2009 BFB

100% verdejo

93

Colour: bright yellow. Nose: ripe fruit, powerfull, toasty, aged wood nuances, pattiserie. Palate: flavourful, fruity, spicy, toasty, long.

PR 3 Barricas 2010 BFB

100% verdejo

94

Colour: bright golden. Nose: ripe fruit, sweet spices, creamy oak, dried herbs. Palate: powerful, flavourful, creamy, long.

PR2 2014 B

100% verdejo

91

Colour: bright straw. Nose: white flowers, fine lees, dried herbs, mineral. Palate: flavourful, fruity, good acidity, round.

Pradorey Verdejo 2014 B

100% verdejo

90

Colour: bright yellow. Nose: expressive, dried herbs, ripe fruit, dried flowers. Palate: flavourful, fruity, fine bitter notes.

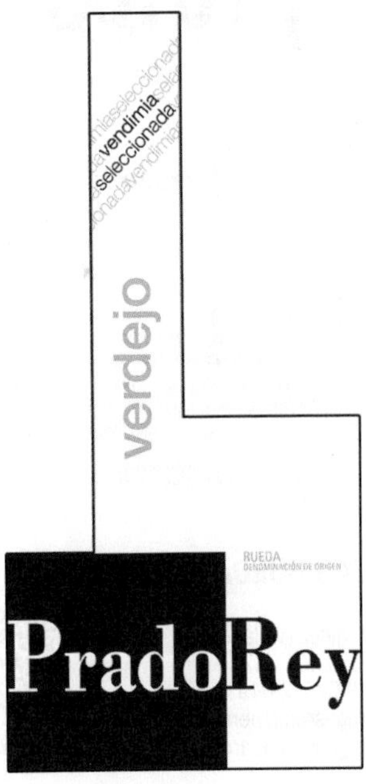

BODEGAS PROTOS

Ctra. CL 610, Km. 32,5
47491 La Seca (Valladolid)
☎: +34 983 878 011
Fax: +34 983 878 012
bodega@bodegasprotos.com
www.bodegasprotos.com

Protos Verdejo 2013 BFB
100% verdejo

91

Colour: bright yellow. Nose: ripe fruit, powerfull, toasty, aged wood nuances, pattiserie. Palate: flavourful, fruity, spicy, toasty, long.

Protos Verdejo 2014 B
100% verdejo

91

Colour: bright straw. Nose: white flowers, fresh fruit, fragrant herbs. Palate: flavourful, fruity, good acidity, balanced.

BODEGAS RUEDA PÉREZ

Boyón, 17
47220 Pozáldez (Valladolid)
☎: +34 650 454 657
Fax: +34 983 822 049
info@bodegasruedaperez.es
www.bodegasruedaperez.es

José Galo Vendimia Seleccionada 2014 B
100% verdejo

91

Colour: bright straw. Nose: white flowers, ripe fruit, candied fruit, citrus fruit, fragrant herbs. Palate: flavourful, fruity, good acidity, elegant.

Viña Burón Verdejo 2014 B
100% verdejo

90

Colour: bright straw. Nose: white flowers, fresh fruit, fragrant herbs, sweet spices. Palate: flavourful, fruity, good acidity.

Zapadorado Verdejo 2014 B
100% verdejo

89

Colour: bright straw. Nose: white flowers, fresh fruit, fragrant herbs. Palate: flavourful, fruity, good acidity.

BODEGAS SEÑORÍO DE NAVA

Tejares, 5
47500 Nava del Rey (Valladolid)
☎: +34 987 209 712
Fax: +34 987 209 800
snava@senoriodenava.es
www.senoriodenava.es

Señorío de Nava Verdejo 100% 2014 B
100% verdejo

88

Colour: straw. Nose: medium intensity, ripe fruit, floral, tropical fruit. Palate: correct, easy to drink.

Val de Lamas Rueda 2014 B
90% verdejo, 10% viura

84

Viña Marian Rueda 2014 B
90% verdejo, 10% viura

87

Colour: bright yellow. Nose: citrus fruit, tropical fruit, ripe fruit. Palate: powerful, flavourful.

Viña Marian Verdejo 100% 2014 B
100% verdejo

87

Colour: straw. Nose: medium intensity, ripe fruit, floral. Palate: correct, easy to drink.

BODEGAS TARSUS

Ctra. de Roa - Anguix, Km. 3
09312 Anguix (Burgos)
☎: +34 947 554 218
tarsus@pernod-ricard.com
www.bodegastarsus.com

Tarsus 2014 B

89

Colour: bright straw. Nose: white flowers, fresh fruit, fragrant herbs. Palate: flavourful, fruity, easy to drink.

BODEGAS TEODORO RECIO

Ctra. La Seca - Rueda s/n
47491 La Seca (Valladolid)
☎: +34 983 816 418
info@robeser.es
www.robeser.es

Robeser Verdejo 2014 B
100% verdejo

86

BODEGAS TIONIO

Carretera de Valoria, Km 7
47315 Pesquera de Duero (Valladolid)
☎: +34 933 950 811
Fax: +34 933 955 500
bodega@tionio.es
www.tionio.es

Austum Verdejo 2014 B
100% verdejo

89

Colour: bright yellow, greenish rim. Nose: wild herbs, ripe fruit, balanced. Palate: long, balsamic, balanced, fine bitter notes, good acidity.

BODEGAS TORREDEROS

Ctra. Valladolid, Km. 289,300
09318 Fuentelisendo (Burgos)
☎: +34 947 532 627
Fax: +34 947 532 731
administracion@torrederos.com
www.torrederos.com

Torrederos 2014 B
100% verdejo

88

Colour: bright straw. Nose: white flowers, fresh fruit, fragrant herbs. Palate: flavourful, fruity, good acidity.

BODEGAS VAL DE VID

Carretera de Valladolid - Peñaranda, Km. 26,300
47239 Serrada (Valladolid)
☎: +34 983 559 914
Fax: +34 983 559 914
info@valdevid.es
www.valdevid.es

Condesa Eylo 2014 B

90

Colour: bright straw. Nose: white flowers, dried herbs, ripe fruit, citrus fruit. Palate: flavourful, fruity, good acidity, elegant.

Eylo Rueda 2014 B

88

Colour: bright straw. Nose: white flowers, fresh fruit, fragrant herbs. Palate: flavourful, fruity, good acidity, balanced.

La Almendrera 2014 B

90

Colour: bright straw. Nose: white flowers, fresh fruit, fragrant herbs. Palate: flavourful, fruity, good acidity, balanced.

Musgo 2014 B

86

Val de Vid Rueda 2014 B

88

Colour: bright straw. Nose: white flowers, fresh fruit, fragrant herbs. Palate: flavourful, fruity, good acidity, balanced.

Val de Vid Verdejo 2014 B
verdejo

90

Colour: bright yellow. Nose: ripe fruit, powerfull, toasty, aged wood nuances, pattiserie. Palate: flavourful, fruity, spicy, toasty, long.

BODEGAS VALDECUEVAS

Ctra. Rueda- Nava del Rey, Km 2,5
47490 Rueda (Valladolid)
☎: +34 983 034 356
Fax: +34 983 034 356
bodega@valdecuevas.es
www.valdecuevas.es

Flor Innata Verdejo 2014 B
verdejo

87

Colour: straw. Nose: medium intensity, ripe fruit, floral. Palate: correct, easy to drink.

Valdecuevas Verdejo 2013 BFB
100% verdejo

90

Colour: bright yellow. Nose: ripe fruit, powerfull, toasty, aged wood nuances, pattiserie. Palate: flavourful, fruity, spicy, toasty, long.

Valdecuevas Verdejo 2014 B
100% verdejo

88

Colour: straw. Nose: medium intensity, floral, ripe fruit. Palate: correct, easy to drink, balanced.

BODEGAS VALPINCIA

Ctra. de Melida, 3,5
47300 Peñafiel (Valladolid)
☎: +34 983 878 007
comunicacion@bodegasvalpincia.com
www.bodegasvalpincia.com

Valpincia Rueda Verdejo Viura 2014 B
50% viura, 50% verdejo

85

Valpincia Verdejo 2014 B
100% verdejo

87

Colour: bright straw. Nose: ripe fruit, citrus fruit, dried herbs, floral. Palate: powerful, flavourful.

BODEGAS VERACRUZ S.L.
Juan Antonio Carmona, 1
47500 Nava del Rey (Valladolid)
☎: +34 983 850 136
Fax: +34 983 850 761
j.benito@bodegasveracruz.com
www.bodegasveracruz.com

Ermita Veracruz 2010 BFB
100% verdejo

91

Colour: bright yellow. Nose: expressive, dried herbs, ripe fruit, spicy. Palate: flavourful, fruity, good acidity, balanced.

Ermita Veracruz Verdejo 2014 B
100% verdejo

92

Colour: bright straw. Nose: white flowers, fine lees, dried herbs, mineral. Palate: flavourful, fruity, good acidity, round.

Ermita Veracruz Viñas Jóvenes 2014 B
100% verdejo

89

Colour: bright straw. Nose: white flowers, fresh fruit, fragrant herbs, expressive. Palate: flavourful, fruity, good acidity, balanced.

BODEGAS VERDEAL
Nueva, 8
40200 Cuéllar (Segovia)
☎: +34 921 140 125
Fax: +34 921 142 421
info@bodegasverdeal.com
www.bodegasverdeal.com

Ayre 2014 B

87

Colour: bright straw. Nose: white flowers, fresh fruit, fragrant herbs. Palate: flavourful, fruity, good acidity.

Verdeal 2014 B
100% verdejo

90

Colour: bright straw. Nose: fragrant herbs, medium intensity, varietal. Palate: good acidity, balanced, fine bitter notes.

BODEGAS VETUS
Ctra. Toro a Salamanca, Km. 9,5
49800 Toro (Zamora)
☎: +34 945 609 086
Fax: +34 980 056 012
vetus@bodegasvetus.com
www.bodegasvetus.com

Flor de Vetus Verdejo 2014 B
100% verdejo

88

Colour: straw. Nose: medium intensity, ripe fruit, floral, tropical fruit. Palate: correct, easy to drink.

BODEGAS VICENTE GANDÍA
Ctra. Cheste a Godelleta, s/n
46370 Chiva (Valencia)
☎: +34 962 524 242
Fax: +34 962 524 243
info@vicentegandia.com
www.vicentegandia.es

Nebla Verdejo 2014 B
100% verdejo

88

Colour: bright straw. Nose: white flowers, fresh fruit, fragrant herbs. Palate: flavourful, fruity, good acidity.

Simue Verdejo 2014 B
100% verdejo

90

Colour: bright straw. Nose: white flowers, dried herbs, ripe fruit, citrus fruit. Palate: flavourful, fruity, good acidity.

BODEGAS VIORE

Miguel Hernández, 31
47490 Rueda (Valladolid)
☎: +34 941 454 050
Fax: +34 941 454 529
bodega@bodegasriojanas.com
www.bodegasriojanas.com

Pregón 2014 B

100% verdejo

86

Viore Verdejo 2014 B

100% verdejo

87

Colour: bright yellow. Nose: balanced, fresh fruit, dried herbs, varietal. Palate: easy to drink, correct, balanced.

BODEGAS Y VIÑEDOS ÁNGEL LORENZO CACHAZO

Estación, 53
47220 Pozaldez (Valladolid)
☎: +34 983 822 481
Fax: +34 983 822 012
comercial@martivilli.com
www.martivilli.com

Martivillí Sauvignon Blanc 2014 B

100% sauvignon blanc

88

Colour: bright straw. Nose: jasmine, floral, wild herbs, citrus fruit, herbaceous. Palate: powerful, flavourful, good structure, balanced.

Martivillí Verdejo 2013 BFB

verdejo

90

Colour: bright yellow. Nose: powerfull, toasty, aged wood nuances, pattiserie, ripe fruit. Palate: flavourful, fruity, spicy, toasty, long.

Martivillí Verdejo 2014 B

100% verdejo

90

Colour: bright straw. Nose: white flowers, dried herbs, ripe fruit, citrus fruit. Palate: flavourful, fruity, good acidity, elegant.

BODEGAS Y VIÑEDOS DE NIEVA

Camino Real, s/n
40447 Nieva (Segovia)
☎: +34 921 504 628
Fax: +34 921 595 409
info@vinedosdenieva.com
www.vinedosdenieva.com

Blanco Nieva Pie Franco 2010 BFB

100% verdejo

89

Colour: bright yellow. Nose: ripe fruit, powerfull, aged wood nuances, pattiserie, roasted coffee. Palate: flavourful, fruity, spicy, toasty, long.

Blanco Nieva Sauvignon 2014 B

100% sauvignon blanc

89

Colour: bright straw. Nose: white flowers, fresh fruit, fragrant herbs, expressive. Palate: flavourful, fruity, good acidity, balanced.

Blanco Nieva Verdejo 2014 B

100% verdejo

90

Colour: bright straw. Nose: fresh fruit, fragrant herbs, white flowers. Palate: flavourful, fruity, good acidity, balanced.

Los Navales Verdejo 2014 B

100% verdejo

89

Colour: straw. Nose: medium intensity, ripe fruit, floral, fragrant herbs. Palate: correct, easy to drink, balanced.

BODEGAS Y VIÑEDOS MARTÍN BERDUGO

Pº de la Colonia, s/n
09400 Aranda de Duero (Burgos)
☎: +34 947 506 331
Fax: +34 947 506 602
bodega@martinberdugo.com
www.martinberdugo.com

Martín Berdugo Verdejo 2014 B
verdejo

86

BODEGAS Y VIÑEDOS MAYOR DE CASTILLA

Ctra. Comarcal 610, km. 26,7
47491 La Seca (Valladolid)
☎: +34 667 750 773
adela@hugad.es
www.garciacarrion.es

Arribeño 2014 B
verdejo

85

Castillo de Aza Verdejo 2014 B
verdejo

86

Mayor de Castilla Rueda 2014 B
verdejo, viura

84

Mayor de Castilla Verdejo 2014 B
verdejo

87

Colour: bright yellow. Nose: dried herbs, ripe fruit, spicy. Palate: flavourful, fruity, good acidity.

Pata Negra Verdejo 2014 B
verdejo

84

Colour: bright yellow. Nose: dried herbs, ripe fruit. Palate: fruity, thin.

Solar de la Vega 2014 B
verdejo, viura

84

Solar de la Vega Verdejo 2014 B
verdejo

85

BODEGAS Y VIÑEDOS NEO

Ctra. N-122, Km. 274,5
09391 Castrillo de la Vega (Burgos)
☎: +34 947 514 393
Fax: +34 947 515 445
info@bodegasconde.com
www.bodegasneo.com

Primer Motivo Verdejo 2014 B

100% verdejo

88

Colour: bright straw. Nose: white flowers, fresh fruit, fragrant herbs. Palate: flavourful, fruity, good acidity.

BODEGAS Y VIÑEDOS SHAYA

Ctra. Aldeanueva del Codonal s/n
40642 Aldeanueva del Codonal (Segovia)
☎: +34 968 435 022
Fax: +34 968 716 051
info@orowines.com
www.orowines.com

Arindo 2014 B

100% verdejo

87

Colour: bright straw. Nose: fresh fruit, fragrant herbs, tropical fruit. Palate: flavourful, fruity, good acidity, balanced.

Shaya 2014 B

100% verdejo

93

Colour: straw. Nose: medium intensity, ripe fruit, floral, scrubland. Palate: correct, flavourful, round.

Shaya Habis 2011 BFB

100% verdejo

92

Colour: bright yellow. Nose: ripe fruit, powerfull, toasty, aged wood nuances, pattiserie. Palate: flavourful, fruity, spicy, toasty, long.

Shaya Habis 2012 BFB

100% verdejo

93

Colour: bright yellow. Nose: expressive, dried herbs, ripe fruit, spicy. Palate: flavourful, fruity, good acidity, balanced.

BODEGAS Y VIÑEDOS TÁBULA

Ctra. de Valbuena, km. 2
47359 Olivares de Duero (Valladolid)
☎: +34 608 219 019
Fax: +34 983 107 300
armando@bodegastabula.es
www.bodegastabula.es

Damana Verdejo 2014 B

100% verdejo

87

Colour: straw. Nose: medium intensity, floral, fruit expression. Palate: correct, easy to drink.

BODEGAS Y VIÑEDOS TAMARAL

Crta. N-122 Valladolid-Soria, Km.310,6
47300 Peñafiel (Valladolid)
☎: +34 983 878 017
Fax: +34 983 878 089
info@tamaral.com
www.tamaral.com

Tamaral Verdejo 2014 B

100% verdejo

87

Colour: bright yellow. Nose: medium intensity, ripe fruit, dried herbs. Palate: easy to drink, correct, rich.

BODEGAS Y VIÑEDOS VERDERRUBI

Camino Sendero del Monte s/n
47494 Rubí de Bracamonte (Valladolid)
☎: +34 606 755 606
emilio.pita@verderrubi.com
www.verderrubi.com

Atipyque de Verderrubi 2013 B

100% verdejo

90

Colour: bright yellow. Nose: ripe fruit, toasty, dried herbs. Palate: flavourful, fruity, spicy, toasty, long.

Dominio de Verderrubi 2014 B

verdejo

89

Colour: bright straw. Nose: white flowers, fresh fruit, fragrant herbs, tropical fruit. Palate: flavourful, fruity, good acidity.

Pita 2013 BFB

verdejo

91

Colour: bright yellow. Nose: ripe fruit, powerfull, toasty, aged wood nuances, sweet spices. Palate: flavourful, fruity, spicy, toasty, long.

BODEGAS Y VIÑEDOS VITERRA

Pol. Ind. Ingruinsa, Avd. D.
Jerónimo Roure, Parc. 45
46520 Puerto de Sagunto (Valencia)
☎: +34 962 691 090
Fax: +34 962 690 963
export1@bodegasviterra.com
www.bodegasviterra.com

Dinastía de Helenio 2014 B

100% verdejo

87

Colour: bright straw. Nose: white flowers, fresh fruit, fragrant herbs. Palate: flavourful, fruity, good acidity.

Naxus 2014 B

100% verdejo

87

Colour: bright yellow. Nose: dried herbs, ripe fruit, sweet spices. Palate: flavourful, fruity, good acidity, fine bitter notes.

Optimus 2014 B

100% verdejo

87

Colour: bright yellow, greenish rim. Nose: faded flowers, ripe fruit, dried herbs. Palate: fruity, easy to drink, good finish, good acidity.

Theseus 2014 B

100% sauvignon blanc

87

Colour: bright yellow. Nose: dried herbs, ripe fruit, spicy. Palate: flavourful, fruity, good acidity.

BUIL & GINÉ

Ctra. de Gratallops -
Vilella Baixa, Km. 11,5
43737 Gratallops (Tarragona)
☎: +34 977 839 810
Fax: +34 977 839 811
info@builgine.com
www.builgine.com

Nosis 2014 B

87

Colour: bright straw. Nose: white flowers, fragrant herbs, ripe fruit. Palate: flavourful, fruity, good acidity, balanced.

CAMPOS DE SUEÑOS

Avda. Diagonal, 590, 5º 1ª
08021 Barcelona (Barcelona)
☎: +34 660 445 464
vinergia@vinergia.com
www.vinergia.com

Campos de Sueños 2014 B

100% verdejo

88

Colour: bright yellow. Nose: expressive, dried herbs, ripe fruit. Palate: flavourful, fruity, good acidity.

CASA ROJO

Sánchez Picazo, 53
30332 Balsapintada (Murcia)
☎: +34 968 151 520
Fax: +34 968 151 539
info@casarojo.com
www.casarojo.com

El Gordo del Circo 2014 B

89

Colour: bright yellow. Nose: dried herbs, ripe fruit, spicy. Palate: flavourful, fruity, good acidity.

COMENGE

Camino del Castillo, s/n
47316 Curiel de Duero (Valladolid)
☎: +34 983 880 363
Fax: +34 983 880 717
admin@comenge.com
www.comenge.com

Comenge Verdejo 2014 B

100% verdejo

89

Colour: bright straw. Nose: white flowers, dried herbs, ripe fruit, candied fruit, citrus fruit. Palate: flavourful, fruity, good acidity, fine bitter notes.

COMERCIAL GRUPO FREIXENET

Joan Sala, 2
08770 Sant Sadurní D'Anoia
(Barcelona)
☎: +34 938 917 000
Fax: +34 938 183 095
freixenet@freixenet.es
www.freixenet.es

Fray Germán Verdejo 2014 B

85% verdejo, 15% viura

89

Colour: bright straw. Nose: medium intensity, ripe fruit, varietal. Palate: correct, easy to drink, fruity, good acidity, fine bitter notes.

Monólogo Verdejo 2014 B
85% verdejo, 15% viura

86

Paramus Verdejo 2014 B
85% verdejo, 15% viura

85

Valdubon Verdejo 2014 B
verdejo

88

Colour: bright straw. Nose: white flowers, fresh fruit, fragrant herbs. Palate: flavourful, fruity, good acidity.

COMPAÑÍA DE VINOS MIGUEL MARTÍN

Ctra. Burgos - Portugal, Km. 101
47290 Cubillas de Santa María
(Valladolid)
☎: +34 983 250 319
Fax: +34 983 250 929
comercial@ciadevinos.com
www.ciadevinos.com

Casa Castilla 2014 B
100% verdejo

85

Castical Verdejo 2014 B
100% verdejo

84

Dòmine 2014 B
95% verdejo, 5% sauvignon blanc

84

Viña Goy Rueda 2014 B
100% verdejo

85

COMPAÑÍA DE VINOS TELMO RODRÍGUEZ

El Monte
01308 Lanciego (Álava)
☎: +34 945 628 315
Fax: +34 945 628 314
contact@telmorodriguez.com
www.telmorodriguez.com

Basa 2014 B
verdejo, viura

91

Colour: bright straw. Nose: fruit expression, floral, dried herbs. Palate: fresh, fruity, easy to drink.

El Transistor 2014 B
verdejo

94

Colour: bright straw. Nose: expressive, dried herbs, ripe fruit, spicy. Palate: flavourful, fruity, good acidity, balanced, long, fine bitter notes, round.

CONDE DE ISCAR

Ctra. N-6, km. 170
47490 Rueda (Valladolid)
☎: +34 647 723 785
bodegas@condedeiscar.com
www.fideles.es

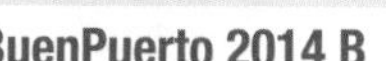

BuenPuerto 2014 B
100% verdejo

85

Colour: straw. Nose: medium intensity, ripe fruit, floral. Palate: correct, easy to drink.

Fideles Fresco 2014 B
90% verdejo, 10% viura

88

Colour: bright straw. Nose: medium intensity, ripe fruit, dried herbs, citrus fruit, expressive. Palate: correct, easy to drink, balanced.

Fideles Intenso 2014 B
100% verdejo

90

Colour: bright yellow. Nose: wild herbs, varietal, ripe fruit. Palate: flavourful, fruity, long, fine bitter notes.

CVNE

Barrio de la Estación, s/n
26200 Haro (La Rioja)
☎: +34 941 304 800
Fax: +34 941 304 815
marketing@cvne.com
www.cvne.com

Cune Rueda 2014 B
100% verdejo

86

Monopole S. XXI 2014 B
100% verdejo

88

Colour: bright straw, greenish rim. Nose: medium intensity, fragrant herbs, ripe fruit, balanced. Palate: correct, fine bitter notes.

DIEZ SIGLOS DE VERDEJO

Ctra. Valladolid Km. 24,5
47231 Serrada (Valladolid)
☎: +34 983 559 910
info@diezsiglos.es
www.diezsiglosdeverdejo.es

Canto 5 2014 B
verdejo

84

Canto Real 2014 B
verdejo

87

Colour: straw. Nose: medium intensity, ripe fruit, floral, citrus fruit. Palate: correct, easy to drink.

Diez Siglos 2012 BFB
verdejo

89

Colour: bright yellow. Nose: ripe fruit, powerfull, toasty, aged wood nuances, pattiserie. Palate: flavourful, fruity, spicy, toasty, long.

Diez Siglos 2014 B
verdejo

88

Colour: bright straw. Nose: white flowers, fresh fruit, fragrant herbs. Palate: flavourful, fruity, good acidity, balanced.

Diez Siglos Blush 2014 RD
tempranillo, viura

87

Colour: onion pink. Nose: elegant, red berry notes, floral, fragrant herbs. Palate: light-bodied, flavourful, good acidity, long, spicy.

Nekora 2014 B
verdejo

88

Colour: bright yellow. Nose: expressive, dried herbs, ripe fruit. Palate: flavourful, fruity, good acidity.

FINCA CASERÍO DE DUEÑAS

Ctra. Cl. 602, (Medina del Campo - Nava del Rey) km. 50,2
47465 Villaverde de Medina (Valladolid)
☎: +34 915 006 000
Fax: +34 915 006 006
comunicacin@habarcelo.es
www.caserioduenas.es

Viña Mayor Caseríoa de Dueñas 2013 BFB
100% verdejo

89

Colour: bright yellow. Nose: ripe fruit, powerfull, toasty, aged wood nuances, pattiserie. Palate: flavourful, fruity, spicy, toasty, long.

Viña Mayor Verdejo 2014 B
100% verdejo

89

Colour: bright yellow. Nose: expressive, dried herbs, ripe fruit. Palate: flavourful, fruity, good acidity, balanced.

FINCA MONTEPEDROSO

Término La Morejona, s/n
47490 Rueda (Valladolid)
☎: +34 983 868 977
Fax: +34 983 868 055
acabezas@bujanda.com
www.familiamartinezbujanda.com

Finca Montepedroso Verdejo 2014 B
100% verdejo

89

Colour: bright straw, greenish rim. Nose: fresh fruit, fragrant herbs, expressive. Palate: flavourful, fruity, good acidity, balanced.

FRANCK MASSARD

Rambla Arnau de Vilanova, 6
08800 Vilanova i La Geltrú (Barcelona)
☎: +34 938 956 541
Fax: +34 938 956 541
info@epicure-wines.com
www.epicure-wines.com

Herbis 2014 B
100% verdejo

87

Colour: bright straw. Nose: fresh, medium intensity, fresh fruit. Palate: easy to drink, good finish.

GRANDES DOMINIOS

Casanovas i Bosch, 57
08202 Sabadell (Barcelona)
☎: +34 937 220 338
Fax: +34 937 252 385
info@grandominios.com
www.grandominios.com

Dominio de Castilla 2014 B
verdejo

85

HAMMEKEN CELLARS

Calle de la Muela, 16
03730 Jávea (Alicante)
☎: +34 965 791 967
Fax: +34 966 461 471
cellars@hammekencellars.com
www.hammekencellars.com

Aventino Verdejo 2014 B
verdejo

85

Viña Altamar Verdejo 2014 B
verdejo

87

Colour: bright straw. Nose: white flowers, fresh fruit, fragrant herbs, citrus fruit. Palate: flavourful, fruity, good acidity, thin.

JAVIER SANZ VITICULTOR

San Judas, 2
47491 La Seca (Valladolid)
☎: +34 983 816 669
info@bodegajaviersanz.com
www.bodegajaviersanz.com

Javier Sanz Viticultor V1863 2011 B
verdejo

93

Colour: bright straw. Nose: white flowers, fine lees, dried herbs, ripe fruit, candied fruit, citrus fruit, sweet spices, creamy oak. Palate: flavourful, fruity, good acidity, elegant.

Javier Sanz Viticultor Verdejo 2014 B
verdejo

92

Colour: bright straw. Nose: white flowers, fresh fruit, fragrant herbs, expressive. Palate: flavourful, fruity, good acidity, balanced.

VMarcorta Verdejo 2014 B
verdejo

92

Colour: bright straw. Nose: white flowers, fine lees, ripe fruit, candied fruit, citrus fruit. Palate: flavourful, fruity, good acidity, elegant.

LA MALETA HAND MADE FINE WINES

Plaza de Eladio Rodríguez, 19
32420 San Clodio (Ourense)
☎: +34 988 614 234
hola@lamaletawines.com
lamaletawines.com

Finca La Viajera Rueda 2013 B
100% verdejo

90

Colour: bright yellow. Nose: ripe fruit, powerfull, toasty, aged wood nuances, pattiserie. Palate: flavourful, fruity, spicy, toasty, long, balanced.

Pizpireta 2013 B
100% verdejo

88

Colour: bright yellow. Nose: ripe fruit, dried herbs, floral, spicy. Palate: rich, flavourful, balanced.

LA SOTERRAÑA - ERESMA

Ctra. N-601, Km. 151
47410 Olmedo (Valladolid)
☎: +34 983 601 026
Fax: +34 983 602 807
info@bodegaslasoterrana.com
www.bodegaslasoterrana.com

Eresma 2013 BFB
verdejo

90

Colour: bright straw. Nose: white flowers, fine lees, dried herbs, toasty. Palate: flavourful, fruity, good acidity, round.

Eresma Sauvignon 2014 B
sauvignon blanc

89

Colour: bright straw. Nose: ripe fruit, tropical fruit, grassy. Palate: good acidity, fine bitter notes.

Eresma Verdejo 2014 B
verdejo

88

Colour: bright straw. Nose: fresh fruit, fragrant herbs, floral. Palate: flavourful, fruity, good acidity, balanced.

Siete Siete Rueda 2014 B
verdejo

85

V&R Verdejo 2014 B
verdejo

87

Colour: bright straw. Nose: white flowers, fresh fruit, fragrant herbs. Palate: flavourful, fruity, good acidity.

LEGARIS

Ctra. de Peñafiel - Encinas
de Esgueva, km. 2,5
47316 Curiel de Duero (Valladolid)
☎: +34 983 878 088
e.izquierdo@codorniu.es
www.legaris.com

Legaris Verdejo 2014 B
100% verdejo

88

Colour: bright straw. Nose: medium intensity, ripe fruit, balsamic herbs. Palate: correct, easy to drink, good acidity.

LLANOS Y AYLLÓN S.L.

Rafael Alberti, 3
47490 Rueda (Valladolid)
☎: +34 627 400 316
ventas@verdejomaroto.es
www.verdejomaroto.es

Maroto Selección Especial 2014 B

88

Colour: bright straw. Nose: white flowers, fresh fruit, fragrant herbs, expressive. Palate: flavourful, fruity, good acidity, balanced.

LOESS

El Monte, 7
47195 Arroyo de la Encomienda (Valladolid)
☎: +34 983 664 898
Fax: +34 983 406 579
loess@loess.es
www.loess.es

Loess 2014 B

verdejo

90

Colour: bright straw. Nose: white flowers, fine lees, dried herbs, mineral. Palate: flavourful, fruity, good acidity, round.

Loess Collection 2014 BFB

verdejo

93

Colour: bright straw. Nose: white flowers, fine lees, dried herbs, ripe fruit, citrus fruit. Palate: flavourful, fruity, good acidity, balanced.

LONG WINES

Avda. del Puente Cultural, 8 Bloque B Bajo 7
28702 San Sebastián de los Reyes (Madrid)
☎: +34 916 221 305
Fax: +34 916 220 029
customer.service@longwines.com
www.longwines.com

Calamar Verdejo 2014 B

100% verdejo

88

Colour: bright straw, greenish rim. Nose: fresh, medium intensity, wild herbs. Palate: correct, fine bitter notes, good acidity.

MÁQUINA & TABLA

Villalba de los Alcores, 2-3 B
47008 Valladolid (Valladolid)
☎: +34 609 885 083
hola@maquina-tabla.com
www.maquina-tabla.com

Máquina & Tabla 2014 B

verdejo

90

Colour: bright straw. Nose: candied fruit, citrus fruit, wild herbs, earthy notes. Palate: fresh, fruity, balanced.

Páramos de Nicasia 2014 B

verdejo

92

Colour: bright straw. Nose: white flowers, dried herbs, ripe fruit, citrus fruit, dry stone. Palate: flavourful, fruity, good acidity, elegant.

MARQUÉS DE IRÚN

Juan de Mena, 10
28014 Madrid (Madrid)
☎: +34 913 080 420
marketing1@caballero.es
www.marquesdeirun.com

Marqués de Irún Verdejo 2014 B

100% verdejo

88

Colour: bright straw. Nose: fresh fruit, fragrant herbs, citrus fruit. Palate: flavourful, fruity, good acidity, balanced.

MARQUÉS DE LA CONCORDIA FAMILY OF WINES

Avenida Nava del Rey, 8
47490 Rueda (Valladolid)
☎: +34 913 878 612
www.the-haciendas.com

Federico Paternina Verdejo 2014 B

100% verdejo

85

Vega de la Reina Verdejo 2014 B

100% verdejo

88

Colour: bright yellow. Nose: dried herbs, ripe fruit, spicy. Palate: flavourful, fruity, good acidity.

MENADE

Ctra. Rueda Nava del Rey, km. 1
47490 Rueda (Valladolid)
☎: +34 983 103 223
Fax: +34 983 816 561
info@menade.es
www.menade.es

Antonio Sanz Sauvignon Blanc 2014 B

sauvignon blanc

91

Colour: bright straw. Nose: fine lees, dried herbs. Palate: flavourful, fruity, good acidity, round.

Antonio Sanz Verdejo 2014 B

verdejo

90

Colour: bright straw. Nose: white flowers, fresh fruit, fragrant herbs. Palate: flavourful, fruity, good acidity, balanced.

Menade Sauvignon Blanc 2014 B

sauvignon blanc

90

Colour: bright straw. Nose: fine lees, dried herbs, grassy. Palate: flavourful, fruity, good acidity, round.

Menade Sauvignon Blanc Dulce 2014 B

sauvignon blanc

87

Colour: bright yellow. Nose: expressive, dried herbs, ripe fruit, spicy. Palate: flavourful, good acidity, sweetness.

Menade Verdejo 2014 B

verdejo

91

Colour: bright straw. Nose: white flowers, fine lees, dried herbs, ripe fruit, citrus fruit. Palate: flavourful, fruity, elegant, long.

V3 2013 BFB

verdejo

92

Colour: bright yellow. Nose: expressive, dried herbs, ripe fruit, spicy, creamy oak, toasty. Palate: flavourful, fruity, good acidity, balanced.

MIGUEL ARROYO IZQUIERDO

Calle Real, 34
47419 Puras (Valladolid)
☎: +34 983 626 095
Fax: +34 983 626 095
info@arroyo-izquierdo.com
www.arroyo-izquierdo.com

Demimo Verdejo 2014 B

verdejo

87

Colour: bright yellow. Nose: medium intensity, ripe fruit, floral. Palate: easy to drink, fine bitter notes, good finish.

MIguel Arroyo Izquierdo 2014 B

verdejo

90

Colour: bright straw. Nose: white flowers, dried herbs, ripe fruit, candied fruit, citrus fruit. Palate: flavourful, fruity, good acidity.

MIRAVINOS RUEDA

Plaza de Matute, 12
28012 (Madrid)
☎: +34 609 079 980
info@miravinos.es
www.miravinos.es

Infraganti 2014 B

100% verdejo

87

Colour: bright straw. Nose: dried herbs, faded flowers, ripe fruit. Palate: ripe fruit, thin.

MONTEBACO

Finca Montealto s/n
47300 Valbuena de Duero (Valladolid)
☎: +34 983 485 128
Fax: +34 983 485 033
montebaco@bodegasmontebaco.com
www.bodegasmontebaco.com

Montebaco Verdejo 2014 B

100% verdejo

88

Colour: bright yellow. Nose: dried herbs, ripe fruit, spicy. Palate: flavourful, fruity, good acidity.

NUEVOS VINOS CB, S.L.

San Juan Bosco 32
03804 Alcoy (Alicante)
☎: +34 965 549 172
Fax: +34 965 549 173
josecanto@nuevosvinos.es
www.nuevosvinos.es

Perla Maris Verdejo 2014 B

100% verdejo

86

Colour: bright yellow, greenish rim. Nose: medium intensity, faded flowers, ripe fruit. Palate: correct, easy to drink.

PAGO TRASLAGARES

Autovía Noroeste km 166,4
47490 Rueda (Valladolid)
☎: +34 983 034 363
info@traslagares.com
www.traslagares.com

Traslagares Verdejo 2014 B

100% verdejo

88

Colour: bright straw. Nose: fresh fruit, fragrant herbs, expressive. Palate: flavourful, fruity, good acidity.

Viña El Torreón Verdejo 2014 B

100% verdejo

85

PAGOS DEL REY

Avda. Morejona, 6
47490 Rueda (Valladolid)
☎: +34 983 868 182
Fax: +34 983 868 182
rueda@pagosdelrey.com
www.pagosdelrey.com

Analivia Rueda 2014 B

verdejo, viura

87

Colour: straw. Nose: medium intensity, ripe fruit, floral, wild herbs. Palate: easy to drink, correct, good acidity.

Analivia Sauvignon Blanc 2014 B

sauvignon blanc

87

Colour: bright yellow. Nose: expressive, dried herbs, ripe fruit, spicy. Palate: flavourful, fruity, good acidity.

Analivia Verdejo 2014 B

verdejo

87

Colour: bright straw. Nose: white flowers, fresh fruit, fragrant herbs. Palate: flavourful, fruity, fine bitter notes.

Blume Rueda 2014 B

verdejo, viura

86

Blume Sauvignon Blanc 2014 B

sauvignon blanc

88

Colour: bright straw. Nose: candied fruit, dried flowers. Palate: sweetness, fine bitter notes.

Blume Verdejo 2014 B

verdejo

86

PALACIO DE BORNOS

Ctra. Madrid - Coruña, km. 170,6
47490 Rueda (Valladolid)
☎: +34 983 868 116
Fax: +34 983 868 432
info@taninia.com
www.palaciodebornos.com

Bornos Frizzante RD

tempranillo

85

Bornos Frizzante Verdejo B

verdejo

84

Bornos Palacios de Bornos BN
verdejo

84

Bornos Palacios de Bornos SS
verdejo

85

Bornos Palacios de Bornos Rosado SS
tempranillo

85

Bornos Palacios de Bornos s/c BR
verdejo

86

Palacio de Bornos Sauvignon Blanc 2014 B
sauvignon blanc

88

Colour: straw. Nose: ripe fruit, floral, tropical fruit. Palate: correct, easy to drink.

Palacio de Bornos Semidulce 2014 B
sauvignon blanc

86

Palacio de Bornos Vendimia Seleccionada Verdejo 2011 BFB
verdejo

91

Colour: bright straw. Nose: dried herbs, faded flowers, ripe fruit. Palate: ripe fruit, thin.

Palacios de Bornos La Caprichosa 2012 B
verdejo

90

Colour: bright straw. Nose: fine lees, dried herbs, ripe fruit, candied fruit, citrus fruit. Palate: flavourful, fruity, good acidity, elegant.

Palacios de Bornos Verdejo 2013 BFB
verdejo

89

Colour: bright yellow. Nose: ripe fruit, powerfull, toasty, aged wood nuances, pattiserie, roasted coffee. Palate: flavourful, fruity, spicy, toasty, long.

Palacios de Bornos Verdejo 2014 B
100% verdejo

89

Colour: bright straw. Nose: white flowers, fresh fruit, fragrant herbs, expressive. Palate: flavourful, fruity, good acidity, balanced.

PALACIO DE VILLACHICA

Ctra. Nacional 122, Km. 433,2
49800 Toro (Zamora)
☎: +34 609 144 711
Fax: +34 983 381 356
bodegavillachica@yahoo.es
www.palaciodevillachica.com

Abside Verdejo 2014 B
100% verdejo

88

Colour: bright straw. Nose: white flowers, fresh fruit, expressive, citrus fruit. Palate: flavourful, fruity, good acidity, balanced.

Villachica Verdejo 2014 B
100% verdejo

88

Colour: bright straw. Nose: white flowers, fresh fruit, fragrant herbs. Palate: flavourful, fruity, good acidity.

PALACIOS VINOTECA – VINOS ORIGINALES

Ctra. de Nalda a Viguera, 46
26190 Nalda (La Rioja)
☎: +34 941 447 207
info@palaciosvinoteca.com
www.palaciosvinoteca.com

Trillón 2014 B
100% verdejo

87

Colour: bright straw. Nose: white flowers, fresh fruit, grassy. Palate: flavourful, fruity, good acidity.

PERSEO 7

Montero Calvo, 7
47001 Valladolid (Valladolid)
☎: +34 983 297 830
info@perseo7.com

Perseo 7 sobre Lías 2014 B
100% verdejo

90

Colour: bright yellow. Nose: expressive, dried herbs, ripe fruit, spicy. Palate: flavourful, fruity, good acidity, balanced.

RODRÍGUEZ SANZO

Manuel Azaña, 11
47014 (Valladolid)
☎: +34 983 150 150
Fax: +34 983 150 151
comunicacion@valsanzo.com
www.rodriguezsanzo.com

Viña Sanzo Verdejo Viñas Viejas 2014 B

100% verdejo

91

Colour: bright straw. Nose: fresh fruit, fragrant herbs, grassy. Palate: flavourful, fruity, good acidity, balanced.

SELECCIÓN DE TORRES RUEDA, S.L.

Camino Magarín, s/n
47529 Villafranca del Duero (Valladolid)
☎: +34 938 177 400
Fax: +34 938 177 444
mailadmin@torres.es
www.torres.es

Verdeo 2014 B

verdejo

88

Colour: bright yellow. Nose: dried herbs, ripe fruit, spicy. Palate: flavourful, fruity, good acidity, easy to drink.

SPANISH STORY

Espronceda, 27 1ºD
28003 Madrid (Madrid)
☎: +34 915 356 184
Fax: +34 915 363 796
info@spanish-story.com
www.spanish-story.com

Spanish Story Verdejo 2014 B

85% verdejo, 15% sauvignon blanc

86

THE GRAND WINES

Ramón y Cajal 7, 1ºA
01007 Vitoria-Gasteiz (Alava)
☎: +34 945 150 589
araex@araex.com
www.araex.com

Rolland Galarreta 2014 B

92

Colour: bright straw. Nose: white flowers, fine lees, dried herbs, mineral. Palate: flavourful, fruity, good acidity, round.

UNESDI DISTRIBUCIONES S.A

Aurora, 11
11500 El Puerto de Santa María (Cádiz)
☎: +34 956 541 329
marketing@unesdi.com
www.unesdi.com

Palomo Cojo 2014 B

100% verdejo

89

Colour: bright straw. Nose: fresh fruit, fragrant herbs, expressive. Palate: flavourful, fruity, good acidity, balanced.

UVAS FELICES

Agullers, 7
08003 Barcelona (Barcelona)
☎: +34 902 327 777
www.vilaviniteca.es

El Perro Verde 2014 B

verdejo

90

Colour: bright straw. Nose: white flowers, fresh fruit, fragrant herbs. Palate: flavourful, fruity, good acidity.

Fenomenal 2014 B

89

Colour: bright straw. Nose: white flowers, fresh fruit, fragrant herbs. Palate: flavourful, fruity, good acidity, easy to drink.

VALTRAVIESO

Finca La Revilla, s/n
47316 Piñel de Arriba (Valladolid)
☎: +34 983 484 030
valtravieso@valtravieso.com
www.valtravieso.com

Dominio de Nogara 2014 B

100% verdejo

88

Colour: bright yellow. Nose: dried herbs, ripe fruit, citrus fruit, floral, spicy. Palate: powerful, flavourful, long, balsamic.

VEGA DEL PAS

Ctra. CL-602, Kilómetro 48
47465 Villaverde de Medina (Valladolid)
☎: +34 983 831 884
Fax: +34 983 831 857
comunicacion@vegadelpas.com
www.vegadelpas.com

Vega del Pas Rueda 2014 B

50% verdejo, 30% viura, 20% sauvignon blanc

86

Vega del Pas Rueda Verdejo 2014 B
85% verdejo, 15% sauvignon blanc

86

Vega del Pas Sauvignon Blanc 2014 B
100% sauvignon blanc

86

Vega del Pas Verdejo 2014 B
100% verdejo

88

Colour: bright straw. Nose: white flowers, fresh fruit, fragrant herbs. Palate: flavourful, fruity, good acidity, balanced.

VEGA LACUESTA

Cobalto, 67
47012 Valladolid (Valladolid)
☎: +34 983 314 522
administracion@bellorivinos.com
www.bellorivinos.com

Bellori 2012 BFB
100% verdejo

91

Colour: bright yellow. Nose: expressive, ripe fruit, faded flowers, complex, sweet spices. Palate: rich, toasty, smoky aftertaste.

Bellori 2014 B
100% verdejo

90

Colour: yellow, greenish rim. Nose: balanced, dry nuts, wild herbs, ripe fruit. Palate: correct, balanced, fine bitter notes, good acidity.

VINOS SANZ

Ctra. Madrid - La Coruña, Km. 170,5
47490 Rueda (Valladolid)
☎: +34 983 868 100
Fax: +34 983 868 117
vinossanz@vinossanz.com
www.vinossanz.com

Finca La Colina Sauvignon Blanc 2014 B
100% sauvignon blanc

93

Colour: bright straw. Nose: white flowers, fine lees, dried herbs, ripe fruit, candied fruit, citrus fruit. Palate: flavourful, fruity, good acidity, elegant, long.

Finca La Colina Verdejo Cien x Cien 2014 B
100% verdejo

91

Colour: bright yellow. Nose: dried herbs, ripe fruit, spicy, candied fruit. Palate: flavourful, fruity, good acidity, balanced.

Fri Sanz Te Semidulce de Aguja 2014 B
100% verdejo

88

Colour: bright yellow. Nose: powerfull, candied fruit, dried herbs. Palate: flavourful, sweet, ripe fruit, good acidity, easy to drink.

Sanz Clásico 2014 B
70% verdejo, 30% viura

89

Colour: bright straw. Nose: white flowers, fresh fruit, fragrant herbs. Palate: flavourful, fruity, good acidity, balanced.

Sanz Sauvignon Blanc 2014 B
100% sauvignon blanc

89

Colour: bright straw. Nose: white flowers, fresh fruit, fragrant herbs, expressive. Palate: flavourful, fruity, good acidity, balanced.

Sanz Verdejo 2014 B
100% verdejo

90

Colour: bright straw. Nose: fresh fruit, fragrant herbs, varietal, grassy. Palate: flavourful, fruity, good acidity, balanced.

VINOS TERRIBLES

Avda. Menendez Pelayo 13 B
28009 Madrid (Madrid)
☎: +34 914 092 131
esther@vinosterribles.com
www.latintoreriavinoteca.com

Terrible 2014 B
100% verdejo

88

Colour: bright straw. Nose: white flowers, fresh fruit, fragrant herbs. Palate: flavourful, fruity, good acidity.

VINOS VEGA DEO

Ctra. CL-602, Kilómetro 48
47465 Villaverde de Medina (Valladolid)
☎: +34 983 831 884
Fax: +34 983 831 857
comunicacion@vinosvegadeo.com
www.vinosvegadeo.com

Vega Deo Rueda 2014 B
50% verdejo, 30% viura, 20% sauvignon blanc

86

Vega Deo Rueda Verdejo 2014 B
85% verdejo, 15% sauvignon blanc

88

Colour: bright straw. Nose: ripe fruit, grassy, wild herbs. Palate: flavourful, fruity, good acidity.

Vega Deo Sauvignon Blanc 2014 B
100% sauvignon blanc

87

Colour: straw. Nose: medium intensity, ripe fruit, floral. Palate: correct, easy to drink.

Vega Deo Verdejo 2014 B
100% verdejo

87

Colour: bright yellow. Nose: expressive, ripe fruit, spicy, wild herbs. Palate: flavourful, fruity, good acidity, balanced.

VIÑA Y TIA

Paraje El Soto, s/n
09370 Quintana del Pidio (Burgos)
☎: +34 947 545 126
Fax: +34 947 545 605
bodega@cillardesilos.es

El Quintanal Verdejo 2014 B
100% verdejo

86

VIÑEDOS SINGULARES

Cuzco, 26 - 28, Nave 8 - 9
08030 Barcelona (Barcelona)
☎: +34 934 807 041
Fax: +34 934 807 076
info@vinedossingulares.com
www.vinedossingulares.com

Afortunado 2014 B
verdejo

89

Colour: bright yellow. Nose: fragrant herbs, varietal, ripe fruit. Palate: correct, balanced, fine bitter notes.

WOS

Cartago, 2 Escalera derecha 1ºA
28022 Madrid (Madrid)
☎: +34 911 263 478
Fax: +34 913 270 601
sdiez@woswinesofspain.com
www.woswinesofspain.com

Xo 2014 B
100% verdejo

85

DO. SOMONTANO

CONSEJO REGULADOR

Avda. de la Merced, 64
22300 Barbastro (Huesca)
☎ :+34 974 313 031 - Fax: +34 974 315 132
@: erio@dosomontano.com
www.dosomontano.com

LOCATION:

In the province of Huesca, around the town of Barbastro. The region comprises 43 municipal districts, mainly centred round the region of Somontano and the rest of the neighbouring regions of Ribagorza and Monegros.

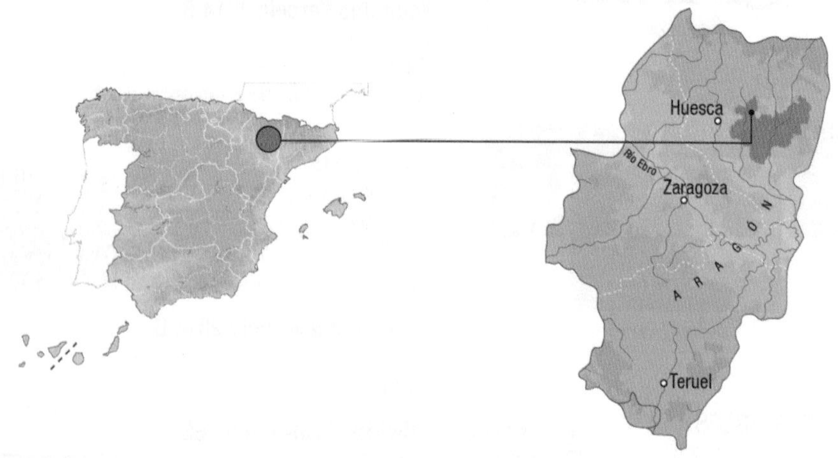

GRAPE VARIETIES:

WHITE: Macabeo, Garnacha Blanca, Alcañón, Chardonnay, Riesling, Sauvignon Blanc and Gewürztraminer.
RED: Tempranillo, Garnacha Tinta, Cabernet Sauvignon, Merlot, Moristel, Parraleta, Pinot Noir and Syrah.

FIGURES:

Vineyard surface: 4,187 – **Wine-Growers:** 424 – **Wineries:** 31 – **2014 Harvest rating:** Very Good – **Production 14:** 10,573,700 litres – **Market percentages:** 72% domestic - 28% export.

SOIL:

The soil is mainly brownish limestone, not very fertile, with a good level of limestone and good permeability.

CLIMATE:

Characterised by cold winters and hot summers, with sharp contrasts in temperature at the end of spring and autumn. The average annual rainfall is 500 mm, although the rains are scarcer in the south and east

VINTAGE RATING

PEÑÍNGUIDE

2010	2011	2012	2013	2014
VERY GOOD	VERY GOOD	VERY GOOD	VERY GOOD	GOOD

BAL D'ISABENA BODEGAS

Ctra. A-1605, Km. 11,2
22587 Laguarres (Huesca)
☎: +34 605 785 178
Fax: +34 974 310 151
info@baldisabena.com
www.baldisabena.com

Cojón de Gato 2013 T Roble
syrah, merlot, otras

88

Colour: deep cherry, purple rim. Nose: violets, ripe fruit, wild herbs. Palate: spicy, ripe fruit.

Cojón de Gato 2014 B
gewürztraminer, chardonnay

87

Colour: bright straw. Nose: fragrant herbs, fresh fruit, dried flowers. Palate: balanced, good acidity, fine bitter notes.

Garnacha de Bal d'Isabena 2014 T
garnacha

86

Ixeia 2014 RD
merlot, garnacha

87

Colour: rose, purple rim. Nose: powerfull, fruit preserve, warm. Palate: powerful, flavourful, round.

Ixeia 2014 T
cabernet sauvignon, merlot, tempranillo

84

Moristel de Bal d'Isabena 2014 T
moristel

85

Reis d'Isabena 2013 T
merlot, cabernet sauvignon

88

Colour: bright cherry, garnet rim. Nose: balanced, ripe fruit, wild herbs. Palate: toasty, balanced, long, spicy.

Reis d'Isabena 2014 B
gewürztraminer, chardonnay

85

BATAN DE SALAS DE BEROZ

Pol. Ind. Valle del Cinca, Calle B, 4
22300 Barbastro (Huesca)
☎: +34 974 316 217
Fax: +34 974 310 973
bodega@deberoz.es
www.batandesalas.com

Batán de Salas 2013 T
cabernet sauvignon, merlot, tempranillo

87

Colour: bright cherry. Nose: ripe fruit, expressive, lactic notes. Palate: flavourful, fruity, round tannins.

Batán de Salas 2014 RD
merlot, cabernet sauvignon

83

Batán de Salas Cabernet 2014 T
cabernet sauvignon

89

Colour: cherry, purple rim. Nose: red berry notes, floral, balsamic herbs, mineral. Palate: powerful, fresh, fruity, balanced.

Batán de Salas Merlot 2012 T
merlot

89

Colour: cherry, garnet rim. Nose: ripe fruit, wild herbs, earthy notes, spicy, balsamic herbs. Palate: balanced, flavourful, long, balsamic.

Batán de Salas Syrah 2013 T
syrah

88

Colour: cherry, purple rim. Nose: ripe fruit, fruit preserve, fragrant herbs. Palate: powerful, flavourful, spicy.

De Beroz Crianza Especial 2008 T
cabernet sauvignon, merlot, syrah

89

Colour: cherry, garnet rim. Nose: balanced, complex, ripe fruit, spicy, fine reductive notes. Palate: good structure, flavourful, round tannins, balanced.

De Beroz Esencia de Gewürztraminer 2014 B
gewürztraminer

86

De Beroz Nuestro Roble 2012 T
cabernet sauvignon, merlot

87

Colour: very deep cherry, garnet rim. Nose: fruit preserve, sweet spices, creamy oak. Palate: balanced, flavourful, fruity.

Lar de Beroz 2007 T
cabernet sauvignon, syrah, garnacha, parraleta

90

Colour: cherry, garnet rim. Nose: ripe fruit, wild herbs, earthy notes, spicy, balsamic herbs, fine reductive notes. Palate: balanced, flavourful, long, balsamic.

BLECUA

Ctra. de Naval, Km. 3,7
22300 Barbastro (Huesca)
☎: +34 974 302 216
Fax: +34 974 302 098
marketing@vinasdelvero.es
www.bodegablecua.com

Blecua 2009 TR
cabernet sauvignon, syrah, tempranillo

93

Colour: cherry, garnet rim. Nose: balanced, complex, ripe fruit, spicy, fine reductive notes. Palate: good structure, flavourful, round tannins, balanced.

Blecua Magnum 2007 TR
cabernet sauvignon, merlot, tempranillo, garnacha

94

Colour: cherry, garnet rim. Nose: balanced, ripe fruit, spicy, fine reductive notes, complex. Palate: good structure, flavourful, round tannins, balanced, round.

BODEGA ALDAHARA

Ctra. Barbastro, 10
22423 Estadilla (Huesca)
☎: +34 974 305 236
Fax: +34 974 430 523
bodega@aldahara.es
www.valdalferche.com

Aldahara 2011 TC
cabernet sauvignon, merlot, syrah

84

Aldahara 2013 B
100% chardonnay

85

Aldahara 2014 B
100% chardonnay

83

Aldahara 2014 RD
100% merlot

84

Aldahara 2014 T
tempranillo, merlot, syrah

86

Aldahara Rasé 2012 T Roble
100% syrah

83

Val d'Alferche Chardonnay 2014 B
100% chardonnay

86

Val d'Alferche Crianza 2011 TC
50% merlot, 40% cabernet sauvignon, 10% syrah

85

Val d'Alferche Syrah 2012 T
100% syrah

88

Colour: light cherry. Nose: fruit expression, fruit liqueur notes, fragrant herbs, spicy, creamy oak. Palate: balanced, elegant, spicy.

BODEGA OTTO BESTUÉ

Ctra. A-138, Km. 0,5
22312 Enate (Huesca)
☎: +34 974 305 157
info@bodega-ottobestue.com
www.bodega-ottobestue.com

Bestué de Otto Bestué 2014 RD
50% cabernet sauvignon, 50% merlot

85

Bestué de Otto Bestué 2014 T
100% merlot

84

Bestué de Otto Bestué Chardonnay Abuela Joaquina 2014 B
100% chardonnay

84

Bestué de Otto Bestué Finca Rableros 2012 T
50% cabernet sauvignon, 50% tempranillo

86

Bestué de Otto Bestué Finca Santa Sabina 2012 TR
80% cabernet sauvignon, 20% tempranillo

87

Colour: cherry, garnet rim. Nose: smoky, spicy, ripe fruit, balsamic herbs. Palate: flavourful, smoky aftertaste, ripe fruit.

BODEGA PIRINEOS

Ctra. Barbastro - Naval, Km. 3,5
22300 Barbastro (Huesca)
☎: +34 974 311 289
Fax: +34 974 306 688
info@bodegapirineos.com
www.bodegapirineos.com

Pirineos 2013 T
merlot, syrah

86

Pirineos 2014 B
chardonnay, gewürztraminer, sauvignon blanc

87

Colour: bright yellow. Nose: white flowers, balanced, fresh fruit. Palate: fruity, flavourful, good acidity, easy to drink.

Pirineos 2014 RD
tempranillo, cabernet sauvignon

87

Colour: onion pink. Nose: elegant, red berry notes, floral, fragrant herbs. Palate: light-bodied, flavourful, good acidity.

Pirineos Gewürztraminer 2014 B
100% gewürztraminer

89

Colour: bright straw. Nose: white flowers, fresh fruit, fragrant herbs, expressive. Palate: flavourful, fruity, good acidity, balanced.

Señorio de Lazan Reserva Especial 50 Aniversario 2006 T
tempranillo, cabernet sauvignon, merlot, moristel, parraleta

89

Colour: pale ruby, brick rim edge. Nose: elegant, spicy, fine reductive notes, tobacco. Palate: spicy, fine tannins, elegant, long.

BODEGA SOMMOS

Ctra. N-240, Km. 154,5
22300 Barbastro (Huesca)
☎: +34 974 269 900
info@bodegasommos.com
www.bodegasommos.com

Glárima de Sommos 2014 B
gewürztraminer, chardonnay

89

Colour: bright straw. Nose: white flowers, dried herbs, ripe fruit, candied fruit, citrus fruit. Palate: flavourful, fruity, good acidity, elegant.

Glárima de Sommos 2014 B Roble
gewürztraminer, chardonnay

88

Colour: bright yellow. Nose: ripe fruit, powerfull, toasty, aged wood nuances. Palate: flavourful, fruity, spicy, toasty, long.

Glárima de Sommos 2014 RD
syrah

88

Colour: rose, purple rim. Nose: red berry notes, floral, expressive. Palate: powerful, fruity, fresh.

Glárima de Sommos 2014 T
merlot, tempranillo, syrah, cabernet sauvignon

86

Colour: cherry, purple rim. Nose: fresh fruit, red berry notes, wild herbs, violets. Palate: flavourful, fruity, good acidity.

Glárima de Sommos 2014 T Roble
cabernet sauvignon, merlot, tempranillo

86

Glárima de Sommos Varietales 2012 T
tempranillo, merlot, cabernet sauvignon, syrah

87

Colour: cherry, purple rim. Nose: ripe fruit, woody, roasted coffee. Palate: flavourful, spicy, powerful.

Glárima de Sommos Varietales 2013 T
tempranillo, merlot, cabernet sauvignon, syrah

88

Colour: cherry, purple rim. Nose: ripe fruit, woody, roasted coffee. Palate: flavourful, spicy, powerful.

Glárima de Sommos Varietales 2014 B

89

Colour: bright straw. Nose: white flowers, fine lees, dried herbs, ripe fruit, candied fruit, citrus fruit. Palate: flavourful, fruity, good acidity, elegant.

Sommos Colección Gewürztraminer 2014 B

gewürztraminer

89

Colour: bright yellow. Nose: expressive, dried herbs, ripe fruit, spicy, floral. Palate: flavourful, fruity, good acidity, balanced, long.

Sommos Colección Merlot 2010 T

merlot

89

Colour: cherry, garnet rim. Nose: roasted coffee, smoky, spicy, ripe fruit. Palate: flavourful, smoky aftertaste, ripe fruit.

Sommos Premium 2009 T

tempranillo, merlot, cabernet sauvignon, syrah

90

Colour: cherry, garnet rim. Nose: roasted coffee, smoky, spicy, ripe fruit. Palate: flavourful, smoky aftertaste, ripe fruit.

BODEGAS ABINASA

Ctra. N-240, Km. 180
22124 Lascellas (Huesca)
☎: +34 974 319 156
Fax: +34 974 319 156
info@bodegasabinasa.com
www.bodegasabinasa.com

Ana 2011 TC

merlot, cabernet sauvignon

84

Ana 2014 RD

merlot, cabernet sauvignon

85

Ana 2014 T Roble

merlot

84

BODEGAS EL GRILLO Y LA LUNA

Ctra. Berbegal, Km. 2,5
22300 Barbastro (Huesca)
☎: +34 974 269 188
info@elgrillo.net
www.elgrillo.net

12 Lunas 2012 T
88
Colour: cherry, garnet rim. Nose: ripe fruit, spicy, creamy oak, complex. Palate: flavourful, toasty, round tannins.

12 Lunas 2014 B
90
Colour: bright yellow. Nose: ripe fruit, dried flowers, fine lees, mineral. Palate: fine bitter notes, powerful, flavourful, complex.

12 Lunas 2014 RD
88
Colour: rose, purple rim. Nose: powerfull, ripe fruit, red berry notes. Palate: powerful, flavourful, round.

Cri, Cri, Cri 2012 T
89
Colour: cherry, garnet rim. Nose: ripe fruit, spicy, toasty, creamy oak. Palate: powerful, flavourful, balsamic.

Cri, Cri, Cri 2014 B
90
Colour: bright yellow. Nose: ripe fruit, powerfull, toasty, aged wood nuances, pattiserie. Palate: flavourful, fruity, spicy, toasty, long.

Grillo 2009 T
90
Colour: cherry, garnet rim. Nose: red berry notes, ripe fruit, spicy, creamy oak, complex. Palate: flavourful, toasty, round tannins.

Grillo Sp 2009 T
91
Colour: cherry, garnet rim. Nose: ripe fruit, wild herbs, earthy notes, spicy, balsamic herbs. Palate: balanced, flavourful, long, balsamic.

BODEGAS ESTADA

Ctra. A-1232, Km. 6,4
22313 Castillazuelo (Huesca)
☎: +34 628 430 823
info@bodegasestada.com
www.bodegasestada.com

Estada 2014 RD
89
Colour: rose, purple rim. Nose: floral, wild herbs, fruit expression, expressive. Palate: flavourful, complex, balanced, elegant.

Estada San Carbás 2014 B
87
Colour: bright straw. Nose: white flowers, fresh fruit, fragrant herbs. Palate: flavourful, fruity, good acidity.

Estada Syrah 2013 T
syrah
88
Colour: cherry, purple rim. Nose: expressive, fresh fruit, red berry notes, floral. Palate: flavourful, fruity, good acidity.

Giménez del Tau 2008 TR
87
Colour: pale ruby, brick rim edge. Nose: spicy, fine reductive notes, wet leather, aged wood nuances, fruit liqueur notes. Palate: spicy, fine tannins, balanced.

Giménez del Tau 2012 T Roble
85

BODEGAS FÁBREGAS

Cerler, s/n
22300 Barbastro (Huesca)
☎: +34 974 310 498
info@bodegasfabregas.com
www.bodegasfabregas.com

Fábregas Puro Syrah 2009 TC
syrah
86

Mingua 2010 TC
cabernet sauvignon, syrah
85

Mingua 2013 T
garnacha, cabernet sauvignon
87
Colour: deep cherry, purple rim. Nose: ripe fruit, balsamic herbs, sweet spices. Palate: balanced, spicy, long.

Mingua 2014 B
garnacha blanca, chardonnay
87
Colour: bright straw. Nose: white flowers, fresh fruit, fragrant herbs, expressive. Palate: flavourful, fruity, good acidity, balanced.

Mingua 2014 RD
garnacha
84

Mingua Gewürztraminer 2013 B
gewürztraminer
85

Vega Ferrera 2008 TC
cabernet sauvignon, merlot, syrah

85

BODEGAS LASIERRA - BESPEN
Baja, 12
22133 Bespén (Huesca)
☎: +34 652 791 187
Fax: +34 974 260 365
info@bodegaslasierra.es
www.bodegaslasierra.es

Bespén 2012 TC
cabernet sauvignon

85

Bespén 2014 T
tempranillo, merlot

87

Colour: cherry, purple rim. Nose: powerfull, ripe fruit. Palate: powerful, fruity, unctuous, easy to drink.

Bespén Vendimia Seleccionada Merlot 2013 T
merlot

87

Colour: deep cherry, purple rim. Nose: creamy oak, ripe fruit, balsamic herbs. Palate: balanced, spicy, long.

Bespén Vendimia Seleccionada Syrah 2013 T
syrah

86

BODEGAS MELER
Ctra. N-240, km. 154,2
22300 Barbastro (Huesca)
☎: +34 679 954 988
Fax: +34 974 269 907
info@bodegasmeler.com
www.bodegasmeler.com

Andres Meler 2009 T
100% cabernet sauvignon

86

Meler 2006 T
merlot, cabernet sauvignon

85

Meler 2010 TC
cabernet sauvignon, merlot

87

Colour: cherry, garnet rim. Nose: ripe fruit, old leather, tobacco. Palate: correct, flavourful, spicy.

Meler 95 sobre Aljez Chardonnay 2010 B
100% chardonnay

90

Colour: bright yellow. Nose: ripe fruit, powerfull, honeyed notes, fine lees, balsamic herbs. Palate: flavourful, fruity, spicy, long, rich.

Meler Cabernet 2014 RD
100% cabernet sauvignon

85

Meler Chardonnay 2014 B
100% chardonnay

87

Colour: bright yellow. Nose: dried herbs, ripe fruit, spicy. Palate: flavourful, fruity, good acidity.

Meler Lumbreta 2012 TC
cabernet sauvignon, garnacha, tempranillo

87

Colour: dark-red cherry, orangey edge. Nose: ripe fruit, fruit preserve, wild herbs. Palate: reductive nuances.

Meler Syrah 2013 T
100% syrah

85

Muac de Meler 2012 T
merlot, cabernet sauvignon, syrah

85

BODEGAS MONTE ODINA
Monte Odina, s/n
22415 Ilche (Huesca)
☎: +34 974 343 480
Fax: +34 974 942 750
bodega@monteodina.com
www.monteodina.com

Monte Odina Cabernet 2010 T
100% cabernet sauvignon

88

Colour: cherry, garnet rim. Nose: ripe fruit, wild herbs, spicy, balsamic herbs. Palate: balanced, flavourful, long, balsamic.

Monte Odina Crianza 2010 TC
50% cabernet sauvignon, 50% merlot

87

Colour: very deep cherry, garnet rim. Nose: balsamic herbs, balanced, smoky. Palate: full, flavourful, round tannins.

Monte Odina Garnacha 2013 T
100% garnacha

87

Colour: cherry, garnet rim. Nose: violets, ripe fruit, spicy, wild herbs. Palate: flavourful, ripe fruit, round tannins.

Monte Odina Roble 2010 T Roble
00% cabernet sauvignon

85

Monte Odina Verso 2006 TGR
50% cabernet sauvignon, 50% merlot

86

BODEGAS OBERGO

Ctra. La Puebla, Km. 0,6
22439 Ubiergo (Huesca)
☎: +34 669 357 866
bodegasobergo@obergo.es
www.obergo.es

Lágrimas de Obergo 2014 RD
garnacha, merlot

88

Colour: rose, bright. Nose: fragrant herbs, red berry notes. Palate: balanced, good acidity, fine bitter notes, easy to drink.

Obergo "Finca la Mata" 2013 T
merlot, cabernet sauvignon, garnacha

89

Colour: deep cherry, purple rim. Nose: creamy oak, toasty, ripe fruit, balsamic herbs. Palate: balanced, spicy, long.

Obergo Expression 2014 BFB
chardonnay, sauvignon blanc

90

Colour: bright straw. Nose: white flowers, fine lees, dried herbs, ripe fruit, citrus fruit. Palate: flavourful, fruity, good acidity, elegant.

Obergo Merlot 2011 T
merlot

92

Colour: cherry, garnet rim. Nose: ripe fruit, wild herbs, earthy notes, spicy, balsamic herbs. Palate: balanced, flavourful, long, balsamic.

Obergo Syrah 2012 T
syrah

89

Colour: cherry, garnet rim. Nose: ripe fruit, spicy, creamy oak. Palate: flavourful, toasty, concentrated.

Obergo Varietales 2011 T
cabernet sauvignon

91

Colour: very deep cherry, garnet rim. Nose: expressive, complex, mineral, balsamic herbs, balanced. Palate: full, flavourful, round tannins.

Obergo Viña Antiqua 2012 T
garnacha

91

Colour: cherry, garnet rim. Nose: mineral, expressive, spicy, ripe fruit. Palate: flavourful, ripe fruit, long, good acidity, balanced.

Sueños by Obergo 2014 B
chardonnay

87

Colour: bright straw. Nose: white flowers, fresh fruit, fragrant herbs, varietal. Palate: flavourful, fruity, good acidity, balanced.

BODEGAS OSCA

La Iglesia, 1
22124 Ponzano (Huesca)
☎: +34 974 319 017
Fax: +34 974 319 175
bodega@bodegasosca.com
www.bodegasosca.com

Mascún Garnacha 2010 T
garnacha

84

Mascun Gewurztraminer 2014 B
100% gewürztraminer

85

Mascún Gran Reserva de la Familia 2006 T
merlot, cabernet sauvignon, syrah, garnacha

87

Colour: pale ruby, brick rim edge. Nose: spicy, fine reductive notes, wet leather, aged wood nuances, fruit liqueur notes. Palate: spicy, fine tannins, balanced.

Osca 2011 TC
tempranillo, merlot

87

Colour: cherry, garnet rim. Nose: ripe fruit, wild herbs, earthy notes, spicy, balsamic herbs. Palate: balanced, flavourful, long, balsamic.

Osca 2014 RD
tempranillo, cabernet sauvignon, moristel

85

Osca 2014 B
macabeo, garnacha blanca

84

Osca 2014 T
tempranillo, cabernet sauvignon

85

Osca Gran Eroles 2009 TR
cabernet sauvignon

88

Colour: cherry, garnet rim. Nose: red berry notes, ripe fruit, spicy, creamy oak, complex. Palate: flavourful, toasty, round tannins.

Osca Merlot Reserva Colección 2009 TR
merlot

87

Colour: ruby red. Nose: expressive, balsamic herbs, balanced, creamy oak. Palate: full, flavourful, round tannins.

Osca Moristel 2009 TR
100% moristel

86

Osca Moristel 2011 TC
100% moristel

85

Osca Syrah 2010 TR
100% syrah

86

BODEGAS RASO HUETE
Joaquín Costa, 23
22423 Estadilla (Huesca)
☎: +34 974 305 357
Fax: +34 974 305 357
info@bodegasrasohuete.com
www.bodegasrasohuete.com

Arnazas Cabernet-Merlot 2011 TC
84

Arnazas Merlot 2007 T Roble
84

Arnazas Selección 2008 T Roble
82

Partida Arnazas 2014 RD
82

Trashumante 2004 TR
84

Trashumante 2011 TC
84

BODEGAS SERS
Pza. Mayor, 7
22417 Cofita (Huesca)
☎: +34 652 979 718
info@bodegassers.es
www.bodegassers.es

Sèrs 2008 TGR
cabernet sauvignon, syrah, merlot

92

Colour: pale ruby, brick rim edge. Nose: elegant, spicy, fine reductive notes, tobacco. Palate: spicy, fine tannins, elegant, long.

Sèrs 2010 TR
cabernet sauvignon, merlot, syrah

90

Colour: dark-red cherry, orangey edge. Nose: scrubland, spicy, fine reductive notes, balanced. Palate: flavourful, ripe fruit, good structure.

Sèrs Blanqué 2014 BFB
chardonnay

89

Colour: bright yellow. Nose: white flowers, dried herbs, ripe fruit, citrus fruit, spicy. Palate: flavourful, fruity, good acidity, elegant.

Sèrs Primer 2013 T
syrah

88

Colour: bright cherry. Nose: ripe fruit, expressive, dried flowers. Palate: flavourful, fruity, round tannins.

Sèrs Singular 2013 T Barrica
parraleta

88

Colour: deep cherry, purple rim. Nose: creamy oak, toasty, ripe fruit, balsamic herbs, premature reduction notes. Palate: balanced, spicy, long.

Sèrs Temple 2011 TC
cabernet sauvignon, merlot

90

Colour: dark-red cherry, garnet rim. Nose: ripe fruit, wild herbs, spicy, waxy notes. Palate: balanced, flavourful, long, balsamic.

BODEGAS VALDOVINOS
Camino de la Almunia, s/n
22133 Antillón (Huesca)
☎: +34 974 260 437
Fax: +34 974 260 147
info@bodegasvaldovino.com
www.bodegasvaldovinos.com

Valdovinos 2013 TC
84

Valdovinos 2014 T

85

Valdovinos Chardonnay 2014 B

100% chardonnay

85

Viñas de Antillón 2014 B

84

Viñas de Antillón 2014 RD

84

Viñas de Antillón 2014 T

cabernet sauvignon, merlot

83

BODEGAS VILLA D'ORTA

Ctra. Alquezar s/n
22313 Huerta de Vero (Huesca)
☎: +34 695 991 967
villadorta@hotmail.com
www.villadorta.com

Villa D'Orta Bio 2013 T

cabernet sauvignon, merlot

86

Villa D'Orta Bio 2014 RD

cabernet sauvignon

85

Villa D'Orta Bio Cabernet Sauvignon 2013 T

cabernet sauvignon

85

Villa D'Orta Moristel 2013 T

moristel

84

BODEGAS Y VIÑEDOS BALLABRIGA

Ctra. de Cregenzán, Km. 3
22300 Barbastro (Huesca)
☎: +34 974 310 216
Fax: +34 974 306 163
info@bodegasballabriga.com
www.bodegasballabriga.com

Auctor Selección Finca Rosellas 2009 T

cabernet sauvignon, merlot, garnacha

88

Colour: cherry, garnet rim. Nose: ripe fruit, wild herbs, spicy, balsamic herbs, waxy notes. Palate: balanced, flavourful, long, balsamic.

Ballabriga Nunc 2009 TC

merlot, syrah, garnacha, parraleta, moristel

89

Colour: cherry, garnet rim. Nose: ripe fruit, wild herbs, spicy, balsamic herbs, old leather. Palate: balanced, flavourful, long, balsamic.

Ballabriga Parraleta 2014 T

100% parraleta

87

Colour: bright cherry. Nose: ripe fruit, expressive, wild herbs. Palate: flavourful, fruity, balanced.

Ballabriga Parraleta Emoción 2008 TC

100% parraleta

91

Colour: cherry, garnet rim. Nose: balanced, complex, ripe fruit, spicy, fine reductive notes. Palate: good structure, flavourful, round tannins, balanced.

Petret 2012 TC

cabernet sauvignon, merlot

86

Petret 2014 B

chardonnay, gewürztraminer

85

Petret 2014 RD

cabernet sauvignon, garnacha

87

Colour: rose, bright. Nose: floral, rose petals, fragrant herbs, expressive. Palate: fruity, fresh, good acidity.

Señor José 2013 T

100% syrah

87

Colour: cherry, purple rim. Nose: powerfull, ripe fruit, spicy. Palate: powerful, fruity, unctuous, easy to drink.

BODEGAS Y VIÑEDOS OLVENA

22300 Barbastro (Huesca)
☎: +34 974 308 481
calidad@bodegasolvena.com
www.bodegasolvena.com

Olvena 2014 RD

merlot

84

Olvena 2014 T

tempranillo, merlot

85

Olvena Chardonnay 2013 BFB
chardonnay

87

Colour: bright straw. Nose: ripe fruit, powerfull, toasty, smoky, faded flowers. Palate: flavourful, fruity, spicy, toasty, long.

Olvena Chardonnay 2014 B
chardonnay

88

Colour: bright straw. Nose: white flowers, expressive, ripe fruit. Palate: flavourful, fruity, good acidity, balanced.

Olvena Cuatro 4 Pago de la Libélula 2013 T
merlot, cabernet sauvignon, tempranillo, syrah

87

Colour: cherry, garnet rim. Nose: aged wood nuances, creamy oak, ripe fruit. Palate: spicy, flavourful, balsamic.

Olvena Hache 2013 T
cabernet sauvignon, syrah

86

CHESA

Autovía A-22, km. 57
22300 Barbastro (Huesca)
☎: +34 649 870 637
Fax: +34 974 313 552
bodegaschesa@hotmail.com
www.bodegaschesa.com

Chesa 2012 T Roble
merlot, cabernet sauvignon

88

Colour: deep cherry, purple rim. Nose: creamy oak, toasty, ripe fruit, balsamic herbs. Palate: balanced, spicy, long.

Chesa 2012 TC
merlot, cabernet sauvignon

89

Colour: very deep cherry, garnet rim. Nose: expressive, complex, mineral, balsamic herbs, balanced. Palate: full, flavourful, round tannins, easy to drink.

Chesa 2014 RD
cabernet sauvignon

87

Colour: rose, purple rim, purple rim. Nose: red berry notes, expressive, wild herbs. Palate: powerful, fruity, fresh.

Chesa Biológico 2013 T Roble
cabernet sauvignon, merlot

86

Chesa Garnacha 2014 T
garnacha

85

Chesa Gewürztraminer 2014 B
gewürztraminer

85

Chesa Merlot Cabernet Garnacha 2014 T
merlot, cabernet sauvignon, garnacha

84

O'Pueyé 2014 T
merlot, cabernet sauvignon

85

DALCAMP

Pedanía Monte Odina s/n
22415 Monesma de San Juan (Huesca)
☎: +34 973 760 018
Fax: +34 973 760 523
ramondalfo44@gmail.com
www.castillodemonesma.com

Castillo de Monesma 2011 TR
cabernet sauvignon

88

Colour: cherry, garnet rim. Nose: ripe fruit, spicy, creamy oak, fine reductive notes. Palate: flavourful, toasty, round tannins.

Castillo de Monesma 2012 T Roble
80% cabernet sauvignon, 20% merlot

86

Castillo de Monesma 2012 T Roble

84

Castillo de Monesma 2012 TC
90% cabernet sauvignon, 10% merlot

87

Colour: cherry, garnet rim. Nose: ripe fruit, wild herbs, earthy notes, spicy, balsamic herbs. Palate: balanced, flavourful, long, balsamic.

Castillo de Monesma 2013 T
merlot, cabernet sauvignon

83

Castillo de Monesma 2014 B
70% gewürztraminer, 21% chardonnay, 5% macabeo, 4% sauvignon blanc

86

ENATE

Avda. de las Artes, 1
22314 Salas Bajas (Huesca)
☎: +34 974 302 580
Fax: +34 974 300 046
bodega@enate.es
www.enate.es

Enate 2014 RD

cabernet sauvignon

89

Colour: rose, purple rim. Nose: red berry notes, floral, expressive. Palate: powerful, fruity, fresh, good acidity.

Enate 2008 TR

cabernet sauvignon

91

Colour: cherry, garnet rim. Nose: ripe fruit, wild herbs, earthy notes, spicy, balsamic herbs, tobacco. Palate: balanced, flavourful, long, balsamic.

Enate 2009 TC

tempranillo, cabernet sauvignon

87

Colour: bright cherry. Nose: fragrant herbs, spicy, ripe fruit. Palate: balsamic, spicy, long, easy to drink, ripe fruit.

Enate Cabernet - Cabernet 2011 T

cabernet sauvignon

91

Colour: cherry, garnet rim. Nose: expressive, scrubland. Palate: flavourful, ripe fruit, long, good acidity, balanced.

Enate Cabernet Sauvignon Merlot 2012 T

cabernet sauvignon, merlot

89

Colour: light cherry. Nose: fruit expression, fruit liqueur notes, fragrant herbs, spicy, creamy oak. Palate: balanced, spicy.

Enate Chardonnay 2013 BFB

chardonnay

91

Colour: bright yellow. Nose: ripe fruit, powerfull, toasty, aged wood nuances, pattiserie, sweet spices. Palate: flavourful, fruity, spicy, toasty, long.

Enate Chardonnay-234 2014 B

chardonnay

90

Colour: bright straw. Nose: white flowers, varietal, fresh, fragrant herbs, fruit expression. Palate: fresh, fruity, flavourful, balanced.

Enate Gewürztraminer 2014 B

gewürztraminer

90

Colour: bright straw. Nose: candied fruit, fragrant herbs, white flowers, jasmine. Palate: fresh, fruity, easy to drink, balanced.

Enate Merlot-Merlot 2010 T

merlot

93

Colour: cherry, garnet rim. Nose: balanced, complex, ripe fruit, spicy, fragrant herbs. Palate: good structure, flavourful, round tannins, balanced, elegant.

Enate Reserva Especial 2006 T

cabernet sauvignon, merlot

93

Colour: deep cherry, garnet rim. Nose: smoky, spicy, ripe fruit, scrubland. Palate: balanced, spicy, long.

ENATE
RESERVA ESPECIAL
2006
SOMONTANO
DENOMINACIÓN DE ORIGEN

Enate Syrah-Shiraz 2011 T
syrah

90

Colour: cherry, garnet rim. Nose: red berry notes, ripe fruit, spicy, creamy oak, complex. Palate: flavourful, toasty, round tannins.

Enate Tapas 2014 T
tempranillo, cabernet sauvignon, merlot

88

Colour: cherry, purple rim. Nose: expressive, fresh fruit, red berry notes, floral, fragrant herbs. Palate: flavourful, fruity, good acidity.

Enate Uno 2009 T
cabernet sauvignon, syrah

94

Colour: cherry, garnet rim. Nose: balanced, complex, ripe fruit, spicy, fine reductive notes. Palate: good structure, flavourful, round tannins, balanced, elegant.

Enate Uno Chardonnay 2011 B
chardonnay

93

Colour: golden. Nose: powerfull, honeyed notes, candied fruit, fragrant herbs, pattiserie. Palate: flavourful, fresh, fruity, good acidity, long.

Enate Varietales 2006 T
cabernet sauvignon, merlot, tempranillo, syrah

93

Colour: deep cherry, garnet rim. Nose: expressive, complex, balsamic herbs, spicy, fine reductive notes. Palate: full, flavourful, elegant.

VIÑAS DEL VERO

Ctra. de Naval, Km. 3,7
22300 Barbastro (Huesca)
☎: +34 974 302 216
Fax: +34 974 302 098
marketing@vinasdelvero.es
www.vinasdelvero.es

Viñas del Vero Cabernet Sauvignon Colección 2012 T
100% cabernet sauvignon

88

Colour: ruby red. Nose: complex, balsamic herbs, creamy oak. Palate: full, flavourful, round tannins.

Viñas del Vero Chardonnay Colección 2014 B
100% chardonnay

91

Colour: bright straw. Nose: white flowers, fresh fruit, fragrant herbs, expressive, varietal. Palate: flavourful, fruity, good acidity, balanced. Personality.

Viñas del Vero Clarión 2010 B

93

Colour: bright yellow. Nose: expressive, faded flowers, ripe fruit, petrol notes, spicy. Palate: balanced, long, complex.

Viñas del Vero Gewürztraminer Colección 2014 B
100% gewürztraminer

91

Colour: bright straw. Nose: white flowers, expressive, varietal. Palate: flavourful, fruity, good acidity, balanced, long.

Viñas del Vero Gran Vos 2009 TR

92

Colour: cherry, garnet rim. Nose: ripe fruit, tobacco, fine reductive notes. Palate: flavourful, spicy, elegant, round tannins.

Viñas del Vero Gran Vos Magnum 2006 T

93

Colour: cherry, garnet rim. Nose: balanced, complex, ripe fruit, spicy, fine reductive notes. Palate: good structure, flavourful, round tannins, balanced.

Viñas del Vero La Miranda de Secastilla 2013 T
garnacha, syrah, parraleta

90

Colour: cherry, garnet rim. Nose: creamy oak, toasty, ripe fruit, balsamic herbs, earthy notes. Palate: balanced, spicy, long.

Viñas del Vero Merlot Cabernet 2014 T

87

Colour: cherry, purple rim. Nose: powerfull, ripe fruit, spicy, scrubland. Palate: powerful, fruity, unctuous.

Viñas del Vero Merlot Colección 2012 T
100% merlot

90

Colour: very deep cherry, garnet rim. Nose: expressive, complex, mineral, balsamic herbs, balanced, varietal. Palate: full, flavourful, round tannins.

Viñas del Vero Pinot Noir Colección 2014 RD
100% pinot noir

88

Colour: onion pink. Nose: elegant, red berry notes, floral, fragrant herbs. Palate: light-bodied, flavourful, good acidity, long, spicy.

Viñas del Vero Riesling Colección 2014 B
100% riesling

87

Colour: bright straw. Nose: white flowers, citrus fruit, faded flowers. Palate: fruity, flavourful, correct.

Viñas del Vero Secastilla 2011 T
garnacha

93

Colour: cherry, garnet rim. Nose: ripe fruit, wild herbs, earthy notes, spicy, balsamic herbs, smoky. Palate: balanced, flavourful, long, full.

Viñas del Vero Syrah Colección 2012 T
100% syrah

88

Colour: bright cherry. Nose: ripe fruit, sweet spices, creamy oak, expressive, lactic notes. Palate: flavourful, fruity, toasty, round tannins.

Viñas del Vero Tempranillo Cabernet 2014 RD

84

VIÑEDOS DE HOZ

Mayor, 17
22312 Hoz de Barbastro (Huesca)
☎: +34 619 686 765
info@vinosdehoz.com
www.vinosdehoz.com

Hoz 2011 TC
tempranillo, syrah, garnacha

86

DO. TACORONTE - ACENTEJO

CONSEJO REGULADOR

Ctra. General del Norte, 97
38350 Tacoronte (Santa Cruz de Tenerife)
☎:+34 922 560 107 - Fax: +34 922 561 155
@: consejo@tacovin.com
www.tacovin.com

LOCATION:

Situated in the north of Tenerife, stretching for 23 km and is composed of 9 municipal districts: Tegueste, Tacoronte, E Sauzal, La Matanza de Acentejo, La Victoria de Acentejo, Santa Úrsula, La Laguna, Santa Cruz de Tenerife and El Rosario

SUB-REGIONS:

Anaga (covering the municipal areas of La Laguna, Santa Cruz de Tenerife and Tegueste) which falls within the limits of the Anaga Rural Park.

GRAPE VARIETIES:

WHITE: PREFERRED: Güal, Malvasía, Listán Blanco and Marmajuelo.
AUTHORIZED: Pedro Ximénez, Moscatel, Verdello, Vijariego, Forastera Blanca, Albillo, Sabro, Bastardo Blanco, Breval, Burra Blanca and Torrontés.
RED: PREFERRED: Listán Negra and Negramoll.
AUTHORIZED: Tintilla, Moscatel Negro, Castellana Negra, Cabernet Sauvignon, Merlot, Pinot Noir, Ruby Cabernet, Syrah, Tempranillo, Bastardo Negro, Listán Prieto, Vijariego Negro and Malvasía Rosada.

FIGURES:

Vineyard surface: 1,081.48 – **Wine-Growers:** 1,914 – **Wineries:** 46 – **2014 Harvest rating:** Good – **Production 14:** 1,050,000 litres – **Market percentages:** 98% National - 2% International.

SOIL:

The soil is volcanic, reddish, and is made up of organic matter and trace elements. The vines are cultivated both in the valleys next to the sea and higher up at altitudes of up to 1,000 m.

CLIMATE:

Typically Atlantic, affected by the orientation of the island and the relief which give rise to a great variety of microclimates. The temperatures are in general mild, thanks to the influence of the trade winds, which provide high levels of humidity, around 60%, although the rains are scarce.

VINTAGE RATING

PEÑÍNGUIDE

2010	2011	2012	2013	2014
GOOD	AVERAGE	VERY GOOD	GOOD	AVERAGE

BODEGA BALCÓN DE LA LAGUNA

Cno. Las Mercedes, 270
38205 La Laguna
(Santa Cruz de Tenerife)
☎: +34 637 761 205
bodegasbalcondelalaguna@gmail.com
www.bodegasbalcondelalaguna.com

Ainhoa Afrutado 2014 B
listán blanco, moscatel de alejandría

70

Ainhoa Dulce 2014 B
moscatel de alejandría, malvasía

88

Colour: bright yellow. Nose: balsamic herbs, honeyed notes, floral, sweet spices. Palate: rich, fruity, powerful, flavourful.

Ainhoa Seco 2014 B
listán blanco

78

Capote 2014 RD
listán negro

85

Capote 2014 T
listán negro, negramoll

85

HC Castellana 2014 T
castellana

85

BODEGA DOMÍNGUEZ CUARTA GENERACIÓN

Calvario, 79
38350 Tacoronte
(Santa Cruz de Tenerife)
☎: +34 922 572 435
Fax: +34 922 572 435
info@bodegadominguez.es
www.bodegadominguez.com

Domínguez 2012 T
listán negro, negramoll, listán blanco, tintilla

86

Domínguez Antología 2012 T
negramoll, castellana, baboso negro, verdello

87

Colour: cherry, garnet rim. Nose: roasted coffee, spicy, ripe fruit. Palate: flavourful, smoky aftertaste, ripe fruit.

Domínguez Blanco de Uva Tinta 2013 B
negramoll, malvasía

85

Domínguez Colección Castellana Negra 2013 T
castellana

85

Domínguez Colección Cuvée Blanc 2013 BFB
malvasía, verdello

84

Domínguez Colección Negramoll 2013 T
negramoll

86

Domínguez con Firma 2010 T
castellana, negramoll

79

Domínguez Malvasía Clásico 2012 B
malvasía, moscatel

91

Colour: golden. Nose: powerfull, honeyed notes, candied fruit, fragrant herbs. Palate: flavourful, sweet, good acidity, long.

BODEGA EL LOMO

Ctra. El Lomo, 18
38280 Tegueste
(Santa Cruz de Tenerife)
☎: +34 922 545 254
oficina@bodegaellomo.com
www.bodegaellomo.com

El Lomo 2012 TC
listán negro, tempranillo, negramoll

84

El Lomo 2014 RD
listán negro

80

El Lomo 2014 T Maceración Carbónica
listán negro

87

Colour: cherry, purple rim. Nose: fresh fruit, red berry notes, floral. Palate: flavourful, fruity, good acidity.

El Lomo Blanco de Listán Negro 2014 B
listán negro

82

BODEGA EL MOCANERO

Ctra. General, 347
38350 Tacoronte
(Santa Cruz de Tenerife)
☎: +34 922 560 762
Fax: +34 922 564 452
elmocanero@bodegaelmocanero.com
www.bodegaelmocanero.com

El Mocanero 2013 T Roble
listán negro, negramoll

88

Colour: bright cherry. Nose: ripe fruit, sweet spices, creamy oak. Palate: flavourful, fruity, round tannins.

El Mocanero 2014 T
listán negro, negramoll

84

El Mocanero 2014 T Maceración Carbónica
listán negro, negramoll

83

El Mocanero Afrutado 2014 B
listán blanco

82

El Mocanero Negramoll 2014 T
negramoll

85

BODEGA INSERCASA

Finca El Fresal - Juan Fernandez, 254
Valle Guerra
38270 San Cristóbal de La Laguna
(Santa Cruz de Tenerife)
☎: +34 680 446 868
info@vinobronce.com
www.vinobronce.com

Bronce Listán Negro 2013 T
listán negro

86

Bronce Syrah 2013 T
syrah

82

BODEGA TABAIDAL

Fray Diego, 4
38350 Tacoronte (Tenerife)
☎: +34 922 564 013
Fax: +34 922 564 013
bodega@tabaibal.es
www.tabaibal.es

Tabaibal 2014 B
listán blanco, gual, verdello

85

Tabaibal 2014 T
listán negro, negramoll

82

Tabaibal 2014 T Barrica
listán negro, negramoll

88

Colour: bright cherry. Nose: ripe fruit, sweet spices, creamy oak. Palate: flavourful, fruity, toasty, round tannins.

BODEGAS CRÁTER

San Nicolás, 122
38360 El Sauzal
(Santa Cruz de Tenerife)
☎: +34 922 573 272
crater@craterbodegas.com
www.craterbodegas.com

Cráter 2013 T Barrica
listán negro, negramoll

90

Colour: very deep cherry, garnet rim. Nose: complex, mineral, balsamic herbs, balanced. Palate: full, flavourful, round tannins.

BODEGAS INSULARES TENERIFE

Vereda del Medio, 48
38350 Tacoronte
(Santa Cruz de Tenerife)
☎: +34 922 570 617
Fax: +34 922 570 043
bitsa@bodegasinsularestenerife.es
www.bodegasinsularestenerife.es

Humboldt 2001 T
listán negro

94

Colour: bright cherry, garnet rim. Nose: acetaldehyde, varnish, candied fruit. Palate: fruity, flavourful, sweet, balanced, elegant.

Humboldt Blanco Dulce 2012 B
listán blanco

90

Colour: bright yellow. Nose: powerfull, candied fruit, dried herbs, floral. Palate: flavourful, sweet, ripe fruit, good acidity.

Humboldt Blanco Dulce Gual 2013 B
gual

90

Colour: bright yellow. Nose: powerfull, candied fruit, dried herbs. Palate: flavourful, sweet, ripe fruit, good acidity.

Humboldt Malvasía Dulce 2012 B
malvasía

92

Colour: iodine, amber rim. Nose: powerfull, honeyed notes, fragrant herbs, acetaldehyde. Palate: flavourful, sweet, fresh, fruity, good acidity, long.

Viña Norte 2012 TC
listán negro

87

Colour: bright cherry. Nose: ripe fruit, sweet spices, creamy oak. Palate: flavourful, fruity, toasty.

Viña Norte 2013 T Barrica

87

Colour: bright cherry. Nose: ripe fruit, sweet spices, creamy oak, wild herbs. Palate: flavourful, fruity.

Viña Norte 2014 T Maceración Carbónica
listán negro

88

Colour: cherry, purple rim. Nose: expressive, fresh fruit, red berry notes, floral. Palate: flavourful, fruity, good acidity, easy to drink.

Viña Norte Afrutado 2014 RD
listán negro

86

CÁNDIDO HERNÁNDEZ PÍO

Acentejo, 1
38370 La Matanza de Acentejo
(Santa Cruz de Tenerife)
☎: +34 922 513 288
Fax: +34 922 511 631
info@bodegaschp.es
www.bodegaschp.es

Balcón Canario 2014 T
listán negro, negramoll

84

Viña Riquelas 2014 T
negramoll, listán negro

88

Colour: light cherry. Nose: fruit liqueur notes, fragrant herbs, spicy, creamy oak. Palate: balanced, elegant, spicy, long, toasty.

Viña Riquelas Gual 2014 B
gual

86

HACIENDA DE ACENTEJO

Pérez Díaz, 44
38380 La Victoria de Acentejo
(Santa Cruz de Tenerife)
☎: +34 922 581 003
Fax: +34 922 581 831
almac.gutierrez@gmail.com
www.haciendadeacentejo.com

Hacienda Acentejo 2014 T Barrica
listán negro, negramoll

82

Hacienda de Acentejo 2014 T
listán negro, negramoll

87

Colour: cherry, purple rim. Nose: red berry notes, balsamic herbs, earthy notes, grassy. Palate: fresh, fruity.

MARBA

Ctra. Portezuelo - Las Toscas, 253
38280 Tegueste
(Santa Cruz de Tenerife)
☎: +34 639 065 015
Fax: +34 922 638 400
marba@bodegasmarba.es
www.bodegasmarba.es

Marba Seco 2014 B
85% listán blanco, 15% varietal

85

Marba 2013 B Barrica
85% listán blanco, 15% varietal

87

Colour: bright yellow. Nose: ripe fruit, powerfull, toasty, aged wood nuances. Palate: flavourful, fruity, spicy, toasty.

Marba 2014 B Barrica
85% listán blanco, 15% varietal

87

Colour: bright yellow. Nose: ripe fruit, toasty, aged wood nuances, pattiserie. Palate: flavourful, fruity, toasty.

Marba 2014 RD
80% listán negro, 20% varietal

85

Marba 2014 T Barrica
50% listán negro, 50% varietal

86

Marba 2014 T Maceración Carbónica
80% listán negro, 20% varietal

85

Marba Afrutado 2014 B
85% listán blanco, 15% moscatel, malvasía

86

Marba Tradicional 2014 T
80% listán negro, 20% varietal

85

PRESAS OCAMPO

Los Alamos de San Juan, 5
38350 Tacoronte
(Santa Cruz de Tenerife)
☎: +34 922 571 689
Fax: +34 922 561 700
administracion@presasocampo.com
www.presasocampo.com

Presas Ocampo 2014 T Maceración Carbónica
listán negro

85

Presas Ocampo Afrutado 2014 B
listán blanco, moscatel

85

Presas Ocampo Seco 2014 B
listán blanco, moscatel

81

Presas Ocampo Vendimia Seleccionada 2013 T
listán negro, merlot, syrah

86

Presas Ocampo Viñedos Propios 2014 T
listán negro, merlot, syrah

84

VIÑA ESTEVEZ

Pérez Díaz, 80
38380 La Victoria de Acentejo
(Santa Cruz de Tenerife)
☎: +34 608 724 671
domingo.vinaestevez@gmail.com

Viña Estévez 2013 T
60% baboso negro, 20% vijariego negro, 20% listán negro

87

Colour: deep cherry. Nose: creamy oak, toasty, ripe fruit, balsamic herbs. Palate: balanced, spicy, long.

DO. TARRAGONA

CONSEJO REGULADOR

Calle La Cort, 41
43800 Valls (Tarragona)
☎:+34 977 217 931 - Fax: +34 977 229 102
@: info@dotarragona.cat
www.dotarragona.cat

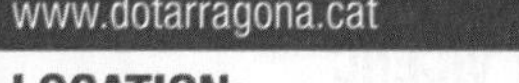

LOCATION:

The region is situated in the province of Tarragona. It comprises two different wine-growing regions: El Camp and Ribera d'Ebre, with a total of 72 municipal areas.

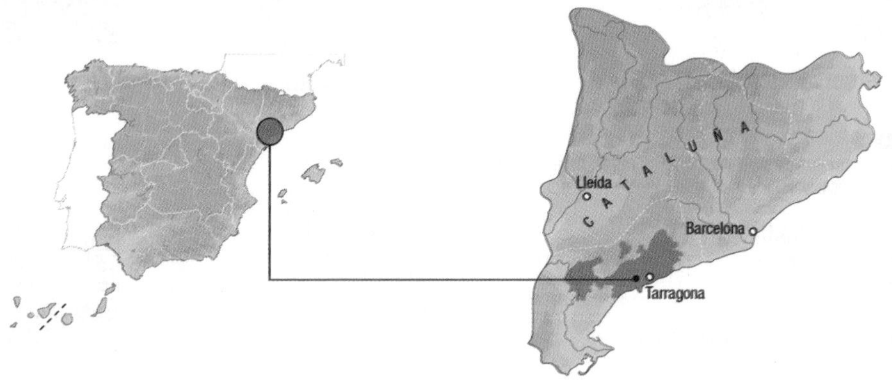

SUB-REGIONS:

El Camp and Ribera d'Ebre (See specific characteristics in previous sections).

GRAPE VARIETIES:

WHITE: Chardonnay, Macabeo, Xarel·lo, Garnacha Blanca, Parellada, Moscatel de Alejandría, Moscatel de Frontignan, Sauvignon Blanc, Malvasía.
RED: Samsó (Cariñena), Garnacha, Ull de Llebre (Tempranillo), Cabernet Sauvignon, Merlot, Monastrell, Pinot Noir, Syrah.

FIGURES:

Vineyard surface: 5,013 – **Wine-Growers:** 1,338 – **Wineries:** 33 – **2014 Harvest rating:** Very Good – **Production 14:** 2,200,000 litres – **Market percentages:** 80% National - 20% International.

SOIL:

El Camp is characterized by its calcareous, light terrain, and the Ribera has calcareous terrain and also some alluvial terrain.

CLIMATE:

Mediterranean in the region of El Camp, with an average annual rainfall of 500 mm. The region of the Ribera has a rather harsh climate with cold winters and hot summers; it also has the lowest rainfall in the region (385 mm per year).

VINTAGE RATING

PEÑÍNGUIDE

2010	2011	2012	2013	2014
GOOD	VERY GOOD	GOOD	GOOD	AVERAGE

ADERNATS VINÍCOLA DE NULLES

Raval de Sant Joan, 7
43887 Nulles (Tarragona)
☎: +34 977 602 622
botiga@vinicoladenulles.com
www.adernats.cat

Adernats Ánima 2013 T
tempranillo, merlot
84

Adernats Blanc 2014 B
macabeo, xarel.lo, parellada
84

Adernats Essència 2013 BFB
100% xarel.lo
88
Colour: bright yellow. Nose: honeyed notes, floral, sweet spices, expressive. Palate: rich, fruity, flavourful, elegant.

Adernats Instint 2014 T
tempranillo, merlot
84

Adernats Negre Jove 2014 T
tempranillo, merlot
83

Adernats Rosat 2014 RD
tempranillo, merlot
85

Adernats Seducció 2014 B
moscatel, xarel.lo, chardonnay
86

AGRÍCOLA I CAIXA AGRÀRIA I SECCIÓ DE CRÈDIT DE BRÀFIM

Agrícola de Bràfim
43812 Brafim (Tarragona)
☎: +34 977 620 061
Fax: +34 977 620 061
oficina@agricolabrafim.cat
www.agricolabrafim.cat

Puig Rodó 2014 RD
tempranillo
84

Puig Rodó Macabeu 2014 B
macabeo
82

Puig Rodó Negre 2014 T
ull de llebre, merlot
84

Puig Rodó Xarel.lo 2014 B
xarel.lo
83

AGRÍCOLA SANT VICENÇ

Sant Antoni, 29
43748 Ginestar (Ribera d'Ebre) (Tarragona)
☎: +34 977 409 039
Fax: +34 977 409 006
www.vinsiolisuner.com

Suñer 2014 RD
83

Suñer 2014 T
82

BIOPAUMERÀ

Plaça St. Joan, 3
43513 Rasquera (Tarragona)
☎: +34 647 983 004
biopaumera@biopaumera.com
www.biopaumera.com

Adrià de Paumera 2010 T Roble
70% garnacha, 30% cabernet sauvignon
88 🌱
Colour: cherry, garnet rim. Nose: balanced, floral, wild herbs. Palate: flavourful, spicy, ripe fruit.

Blanc de Noirs Biopaumerà 2014 B
garnacha
84 🌱

Esther de Paumerà 2011 TC
50% garnacha, 50% cabernet sauvignon
81 🌱

Iuvenis de Biopaumerà 2013 T
20% garnacha, 80% cabernet sauvignon
84 🌱

CASTELL D'OR

Mare Rafols, 3- 1ºD
08720 Vilafranca del Penedès
(Barcelona)
☎: +34 938 905 385
Fax: +34 938 905 446
castelldor@castelldor.com
www.castelldor.com

Flama Roja 2014 B
macabeo, xarel.lo

81

Flama Roja Negre 2014 T
cabernet sauvignon, merlot

83

Flama Roja Rosat 2014 RD
tempranillo

83

CELLER 9+

Cases Noves, 19
43763 La Nou de Gaià (Tarragona)
☎: +34 977 655 940
moisesvirgili@gmail.com
www.9mes.cat

Nuce Selecció 2012 T
83

Nuce Vinyassa 2014 B
83

CELLER LA BOELLA

Autovía Reus - Tarragona (T-11), km. 12
43110 La Canonja (Tarragona)
☎: +34 977 771 515
celler@laboella.com
www.laboella.com

Mas la Boella Guarda 2010 T
76% cabernet sauvignon, 24% merlot

90

Colour: cherry, garnet rim. Nose: ripe fruit, spicy, creamy oak, balsamic herbs. Palate: flavourful, toasty, round tannins.

Mas la Boella Guarda Selecció Magnum 2010 T
100% cabernet sauvignon

90

Colour: cherry, garnet rim. Nose: balanced, complex, ripe fruit, spicy, fine reductive notes, tobacco. Palate: good structure, flavourful, round tannins, balanced.

Ullals 2011 T
47% merlot, 42% monastrell, 11% cabernet sauvignon

84

CELLER MAS BELLA

Sant Roc, 8 - Masmolets
43813 Valls (Tarragona)
☎: +34 977 613 092
Fax: +34 977 613 092
cellermasbella@gmail.com
www.cellermasbella.com

Bella Blanc 2014 B
84

Bella Blanc Cartoixa 2014 B
83

Bella Negre 2010 TC
86

Bella Negre 2012 T
87

Colour: bright cherry. Nose: ripe fruit, sweet spices, creamy oak. Palate: flavourful, fruity, toasty.

CELLER MAS DEL BOTÓ

Bon Recer, 13
43007 Alforja (Tarragona)
☎: +34 630 982 747
Fax: +34 977 236 396
pep@masdelboto.cat
www.masdelboto.cat

Ganagot 2005 TR
garnacha, samsó, cabernet sauvignon

90

Colour: cherry, garnet rim. Nose: balanced, complex, ripe fruit, spicy, fine reductive notes. Palate: good structure, flavourful, round tannins, balanced.

Ganagot 2006 T
garnacha, samsó, cabernet sauvignon

88

Colour: dark-red cherry, garnet rim. Nose: old leather, ripe fruit, aged wood nuances, spicy. Palate: aged character, fine tannins.

Ganagot 2007 T
garnacha, cabernet sauvignon, samsó

87

Colour: cherry, garnet rim. Nose: ripe fruit, spicy, creamy oak, complex. Palate: flavourful, toasty.

Ganagot 2008 T
garnacha, samsó

87

Colour: cherry, garnet rim. Nose: ripe fruit, wild herbs, spicy, creamy oak, fine reductive notes. Palate: powerful, flavourful, spicy.

Mas del Botó 2010 T
garnacha, cabernet sauvignon, samsó

87

Colour: cherry, garnet rim. Nose: fine reductive notes, scrubland. Palate: spicy, long.

CELLER PEDROLA
Ctra T-324 Km 14
43747 Miravet (Tarragona)
☎: +34 650 093 906
pedrola97@yahoo.es

Camí de Sirga 2014 T
syrah, merlot

84

Camí de Sirga Moscatel Macabeo 2014 B
moscatel, macabeo

83

Camí de Sirga Sauvignon Blanc Macabeo 2014 B
sauvignon blanc, macabeo

83

CELLER SUÑER
Sant Antoni, 29
43748 Ginestar (Tarragona)
☎: +34 977 409 039
Fax: +34 977 409 039
suner.info@gmail.com
www.vinsiolisuner.com

Blanc Macabeu 2014 B
macabeo

84

CELLERS UNIÓ
43206 Reus (Tarragona)
☎: +34 977 330 055
Fax: +34 977 330 070
info@cellersunio.com
www.cellersunio.com

Roureda Blanc de Blancs 2014 B
macabeo, xarel.lo

85

Roureda Cabernet Sauvignon 2014 T
cabernet sauvignon

82

DE MULLER
Camí Pedra Estela, 34
43205 Reus (Tarragona)
☎: +34 977 757 473
Fax: +34 977 771 129
lab@demuller.es
www.demuller.es

De Muller Avreo Dulce vino de licor
garnacha blanca, garnacha

94

Colour: coppery red. Nose: fruit preserve, dried herbs, spicy, dry nuts, caramel. Palate: complex, round, unctuous, powerful, flavourful, toasty, elegant.

De Muller Avreo Seco AM Crianza
garnacha blanca, garnacha

92

Colour: light mahogany. Nose: candied fruit, fruit liqueur notes, spicy, varnish, acetaldehyde, dry nuts. Palate: fine solera notes, fine bitter notes, spirituous.

De Muller Cabernet Sauvignon 2012 TC
cabernet sauvignon

84

De Muller Chardonnay 2014 BFB
chardonnay

88

Colour: bright yellow. Nose: ripe fruit, powerfull, toasty, aged wood nuances, pattiserie. Palate: flavourful, fruity, spicy, toasty, long.

PODIUM

De Muller Garnacha Solera 1926 Solera
garnacha

95

Colour: light mahogany. Nose: powerfull, aromatic coffee, spicy, acetaldehyde, dry nuts. Palate: balanced, elegant, fine solera notes, toasty, long.

De Muller Merlot 2012 TC
merlot

85

De Muller Moscatel Añejo Vino de licor
moscatel de alejandría

91

Colour: old gold. Nose: candied fruit, fruit liqueur notes, white flowers. Palate: balanced, flavourful, sweet, good acidity, unctuous.

De Muller Moscatel Oro B
moscatel de alejandría

89

Colour: bright golden. Nose: honeyed notes, floral, sweet spices. Palate: rich, fruity, flavourful, sweet.

De Muller Muscat 2014 B
moscatel de alejandría

87

Colour: bright yellow. Nose: balsamic herbs, honeyed notes, floral. Palate: rich, fruity, powerful, flavourful.

De Muller Rancio Seco Vino de licor
garnacha

91

Colour: light mahogany. Nose: candied fruit, dark chocolate, sweet spices, roasted almonds. Palate: flavourful, long, fine bitter notes, complex.

De Muller Syrah 2014 T
syrah

86

Mas de Valls 2013 BN
macabeo, chardonnay, moscatel de alejandría

87

Colour: bright yellow. Nose: ripe fruit, fine lees, balanced, dried herbs. Palate: good acidity, flavourful, ripe fruit, long.

Mas de Valls 2013 BR Reserva
macabeo, chardonnay, moscatel de alejandría

85

Mas de Valls Rosat 2013 BR
merlot, cabernet sauvignon, pinot noir

84

Porpores De Muller 2010 TR
syrah, pinot noir, cabernet sauvignon

88

Colour: ruby red. Nose: spicy, fine reductive notes, tobacco, balsamic herbs, toasty. Palate: spicy, fine tannins, elegant, long.

Reina Violant 2013 ESP Gran Reserva
pinot noir, chardonnay

89

Colour: bright yellow. Nose: fresh fruit, dried herbs, fine lees, floral. Palate: fresh, fruity, flavourful, good acidity.

Solimar 2012 TC
cabernet sauvignon, merlot

85

Solimar 2014 B
macabeo, moscatel de alejandría, chardonnay

85

Solimar 2014 RD
merlot, cabernet sauvignon, pinot noir

84

Trilogía Chardonnay Reserva 2013 BN
chardonnay

87

Colour: bright yellow. Nose: ripe fruit, honeyed notes, floral. Palate: flavourful, good acidity, fine bitter notes.

Trilogía Muscat Reserva 2013 BR
moscatel de alejandría

88

Colour: yellow. Nose: fine lees, white flowers, varietal. Palate: flavourful, good acidity, fine bead.

Trilogía Pinot Noir Reserva 2013 BN
pinot noir

90

Colour: bright golden. Nose: fine lees, dry nuts, fragrant herbs, complex, toasty. Palate: powerful, flavourful, good acidity, fine bead, fine bitter notes.

Vino de Misa Dulce Superior Dulce MZ
garnacha blanca, macabeo

91

Colour: bright golden. Nose: saline, iodine notes, dry nuts, varnish, acetaldehyde, powerfull. Palate: fine bitter notes, spirituous, long, powerful, balanced.

MAS VICENÇ

Mas Vicenç, s/n
43811 Cabra de Camp (Tarragona)
☎: +34 977 630 024
masvicens@masvicens.com
www.masvicens.com

Dent de Lleó 2014 B
chardonnay

84

El Vi del Vent Dulce 2014 B
moscatel grano menudo

87

Colour: bright yellow. Nose: powerfull, candied fruit, dried herbs, honeyed notes. Palate: flavourful, sweet, ripe fruit, good acidity.

Rombes d'Arlequi 2012 TC
samsó, syrah, cabernet sauvignon

87

Colour: cherry, garnet rim. Nose: smoky, spicy, ripe fruit, cocoa bean. Palate: flavourful, smoky aftertaste, ripe fruit, sweet tannins.

MOLÍ DE RUÉ
Dels Portellets s/n
43792 Vinebre (Tarragona)
☎: +34 977 405 782
Fax: +34 977 405 782
npoquet@moliderue.com

Mims Blanc 2013 B
50% macabeo, garnacha blanca, 20% moscatel

85

Mims Negre 2014 T
70% syrah, 30% garnacha

83

Sol i Serena Vino de Licor
100% macabeo

93

Colour: old gold, amber rim. Nose: candied fruit, honeyed notes, cocoa bean, expressive, dry nuts. Palate: unctuous, long, flavourful, complex.

SERRA DE LLABERIA
Avda. Vidal i Barraquer, 12, 8º- 4ª
43005 Tarragona (Tarragona)
☎: +34 977 824 122
Fax: +34 977 824 122
info@serradellaberia.com
www.serradellaberia.com

Serra de Llaberia Elisabeth 2006 TR
60% cabernet sauvignon, 30% merlot, 10% garnacha

89

Colour: black cherry. Nose: old leather, toasty, tobacco. Palate: balanced, classic aged character, flavourful.

Serra de Llaberia Elisabeth 2007 TR
60% cabernet sauvignon, 30% merlot, 10% garnacha

87

Colour: cherry, garnet rim. Nose: fine reductive notes, wet leather, aged wood nuances, ripe fruit. Palate: spicy, long, toasty.

UNIVERSITAT ROVIRA I VIRGILI
Ctra TV 7211 km 7,2
43120 Constantí (Tarragona)
☎: +34 977 520 197
Fax: +34 977 522 156
fincafe@urv.cat
www.urv.cat/vins

Universitat Rovira i Virgili 2011 ESP
40% xarel.lo, 20% chardonnay, 30% macabeo, parellada

84

Universitat Rovira i Virgili 2012 TC
50% cabernet sauvignon, 25% merlot, 25% tempranillo

85

Universitat Rovira i Virgili 2014 B
85% moscatel, 15% macabeo

85

Universitat Rovira i Virgili 2014 T

85

VINOS PADRÓ
Avda. Catalunya, 56-58
43812 Brafim (Tarragona)
☎: +34 977 620 012
Fax: +34 977 620 486
info@vinspadro.com
www.vinspadro.com

Capitol 2011 TC
tempranillo, merlot

87

Colour: cherry, garnet rim. Nose: ripe fruit, wild herbs, spicy, balsamic herbs. Palate: flavourful, long, balsamic, toasty.

Capitol 2014 T
tempranillo

86

Capitol Blanc 2014 B
macabeo, moscatel, xarel.lo

85

Capitol Rosat 2014 RD
tempranillo, merlot

86

Ipsis 2011 TC
tempranillo, merlot

87

Colour: cherry, garnet rim. Nose: ripe fruit, fruit preserve, grassy, spicy. Palate: powerful, flavourful, spicy.

Ipsis Blanc Flor 2014 B
macabeo, xarel.lo, moscatel

85

Ipsis Chardonnay 2014 B
chardonnay

86

Ipsis Mas D'Infants 2014 B
moscatel, chardonnay, xarel.lo

84

Ipsis Tempranillo Merlot 2014 T
tempranillo, merlot

86

Ipsis Tempranillo Selecció 2011 T
tempranillo

87

Colour: cherry, garnet rim. Nose: creamy oak, balanced, ripe fruit. Palate: flavourful, spicy.

VINYA JANINE

Sant Antoni, 5
43812 Rodonyá (Tarragona)
☎: +34 977 628 305
Fax: +34 977 628 857
vjanine@tinet.org
www.vinyajanine.com

Vinya Janine 2014 B
84

Vinya Janine SYH 2013 T
82

VINYES DEL TERRER

Camí del Terrer, s/n
43480 Vila-Seca (Tarragona)
☎: +34 977 269 229
eduard@terrer.net
www.terrer.net

Blanc del Terrer 2014 B
macabeo

88

Colour: bright yellow. Nose: dried herbs, dry nuts, ripe fruit, fine lees. Palate: correct, balanced, fine bitter notes.

Nus del Terrer 2010 T
garnacha, cabernet sauvignon

93

Colour: cherry, garnet rim. Nose: ripe fruit, scrubland, fine reductive notes, expressive, balanced. Palate: good structure, flavourful, elegant, good acidity.

Terrer d'Aubert 2012 T
cabernet sauvignon, garnacha

89

Colour: very deep cherry, garnet rim. Nose: balsamic herbs, fruit preserve, earthy notes, creamy oak. Palate: full, flavourful.

DO. TERRA ALTA

CONSEJO REGULADOR

Ctra. Vilalba, 31
43780 Gandesa (Tarragona)
☎:+34 977 421 278- Fax: +34 977 421 623
@: info@terraaltawine.com
www.doterraalta.com

LOCATION:

In the southeast of Catalonia, in the province of Tarragona. It covers the municipal districts of Arnes, Batea, Bot, Caseres, Corbera d'Ebre, La Fatarella, Gandesa, Horta de Sant Joan, Pinell de Brai, La Pobla de Massaluca, Prat de Comte and Vilalba dels Arcs.

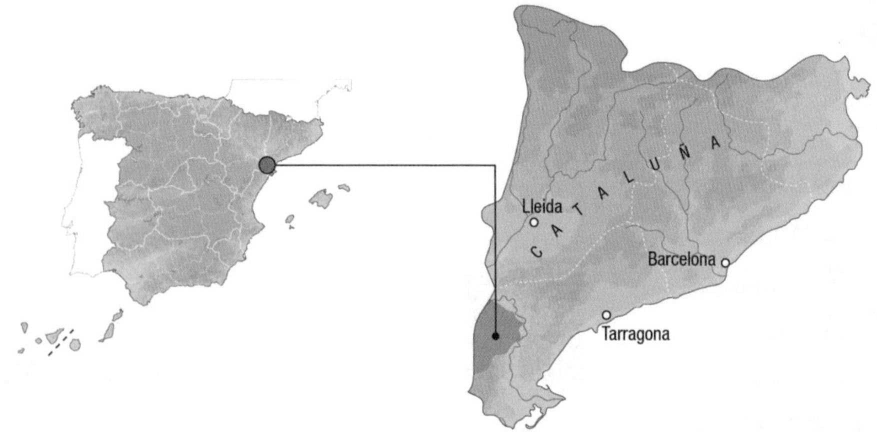

GRAPE VARIETIES:

WHITE: Chardonnay, Garnacha Blanca, Parellada, Macabeo, Moscatel, Sauvignon Blanc, Chenin, Pedro Ximénez. Experimental: Viognier.
RED: Cabernet Sauvigon, Cariñena, Garnacha Tinta, Garnacha Peluda, Syrah, Tempranillo, Merlot, Samsó, Cabernet Franc. Experimental: Petit Verdot, Marselane, Caladoc.

FIGURES:

Vineyard surface: 6,800 – **Wine-Growers:** 1,255 – **Wineries:** 49 – **2014 Harvest rating: White**: N/A – **Rest**: N/A – **Production 14:** 15,815,410 litres – **Market percentages:** 40% National - 60% International.

SOIL:

The vineyards are located on an extensive plateau at an altitude of slightly over 400 m. The soil is calcareous and the texture mainly clayey, poor in organic matter and with many pebbles.

CLIMATE:

Mediterranean, with continental influences. It is characterized by its hot, dry summers and very cold winters, especially in the higher regions in the east. The average annual rainfall is 400 mm. Another vital aspect is the wind: the 'Cierzo' and the 'Garbi' (Ábrego) winds.

VINTAGE RATING

PEÑÍNGUIDE

2010	2011	2012	2013	2014
VERY GOOD	GOOD	GOOD	GOOD	GOOD

7 MAGNIFICS

Miquel Torres i Carbó, 6
08720 Vilafranca del Penedès
(Barcelona)
☎: +34 938 177 400
Fax: +34 938 177 444
7magnifics@7magnifics.com
www.7magnifics.com

Rebels de Batea 2013 B
100% garnacha blanca
90
Colour: bright yellow. Nose: expressive, dried herbs, ripe fruit, spicy. Palate: flavourful, fruity, good acidity, balanced.

Rebels de Batea 2013 T
100% garnacha
89
Colour: cherry, purple rim. Nose: expressive, red berry notes, wild herbs, balanced. Palate: flavourful, fruity, good acidity.

AGRÍCOLA CORBERA D'EBRE

Ponent, 21
43784 Corbera d'Ebre (Tarragona)
☎: +34 977 420 432
Fax: +34 977 420 304
miro@agricolacorbera.com
www.agricolacorberadebre.com

Mirmil-ló Garnacha Blanca 2013 B
garnacha blanca
81

Mirmil-ló Garnacha Blanca 2014 B
garnacha blanca
83

Mirmil-ló Negre 2014 T
70% garnacha, 20% cariñena, 5% tempranillo, 5% syrah
82

Mirmil-ló Parellada 2014 B
parellada
82

Mirmil-ló Rosat 2014 RD
garnacha
82

Nakens Blanc 2014 B
parellada, moscatel de alejandría
78

Nakens Escumós 2013 ESP
parellada
80

Nakens Negre 2013 T
garnacha, cariñena, tempranillo, merlot
85

Poble Vell Blanco Dulce Natural 2012 B
garnacha blanca
84

Poble Vell Dulce 2012 Vino de licor Tinto
garnacha
87
Colour: ruby red. Nose: dried fruit, wild herbs, sweet spices, smoky, fruit liqueur notes. Palate: flavourful, complex, spicy.

Vall Excels 2011 TC
garnacha, tempranillo
82

Vall Excels 2013 BFB
garnacha blanca
79

AGRÍCOLA SANT JOSEP

Estació, 2
43785 Bot (Tarragona)
☎: +34 977 428 352
Fax: +34 977 428 192
info@santjosepwines.com
www.santjosepwines.com

Clot D'Encis Rancio
100% garnacha blanca
88
Colour: mahogany. Nose: complex, fruit liqueur notes, dried fruit, pattiserie, toasty. Palate: rich, unctuous, powerful, flavourful.

Clot D'Encís 2014 B
garnacha blanca
85

Clot D'Encis 2014 RD
garnacha, syrah
85

Clot D'Encís 2014 T
garnacha, syrah, samsó
84

Clot D'Encis Blanc de Negres 2014 B
100% garnacha
89
Colour: bright straw. Nose: white flowers, dried herbs, ripe fruit, candied fruit, citrus fruit. Palate: flavourful, fruity, good acidity, elegant.

La Plana d'en Fonoll 2013 T
76% cabernet sauvignon, 24% syrah

87

Colour: very deep cherry, garnet rim. Nose: expressive, balanced, wild herbs. Palate: flavourful, round tannins, balsamic.

Llàgrimes de Tardor 2008 TR
garnacha, samsó, syrah

85

Llàgrimes de Tardor 2009 TC
garnacha, samsó, syrah, cabernet sauvignon

88

Colour: cherry, garnet rim. Nose: fine reductive notes, wet leather, aged wood nuances. Palate: spicy, long, toasty.

Llàgrimes de Tardor 2013 BFB
100% garnacha blanca

89

Colour: bright yellow. Nose: ripe fruit, powerfull, toasty, aged wood nuances. Palate: flavourful, fruity, spicy, toasty, long.

Llàgrimes de Tardor Mistela Blanca Dulce 2014 B
100% garnacha blanca

89

Colour: golden. Nose: powerfull, honeyed notes, candied fruit, faded flowers, fruit liqueur notes. Palate: flavourful, sweet, fruity, good acidity.

Llàgrimes de Tardor Mistela Negra 2014 Mistela
100% garnacha

88

Colour: ruby red. Nose: dried fruit, fruit preserve, wild herbs, toasty, creamy oak. Palate: powerful, rich, sweet.

ALTAVINS VITICULTORS

Ctra. Vilalba dels Arcs s/n
43786 Batea (Tarragona)
☎: +34 977 430 596
altavins@altavins.com
www.altavins.com

Almodí 2014 T
garnacha

86

Almodí Petit 2014 B
garnacha blanca, chardonnay, viognier, chenin blanc

86

Almodí Petit 2014 T
garnacha, syrah, merlot, cariñena

85

Domus Pensi 2010 TR
cabernet sauvignon, garnacha, merlot, syrah

89

Colour: cherry, garnet rim. Nose: ripe fruit, wild herbs, earthy notes. Palate: balanced, flavourful, long, balsamic.

Ilercavonia 2014 B
garnacha blanca

87

Colour: bright straw. Nose: dried herbs, ripe fruit, candied fruit, citrus fruit. Palate: flavourful, fruity, good acidity.

Tempus 2011 TC
garnacha, syrah, cariñena, merlot

88

Colour: very deep cherry, garnet rim. Nose: fruit preserve, dark chocolate, spicy. Palate: good structure, flavourful, sweet tannins.

BERNAVÍ

Finca Mas Vernet - Camí de Berrús km.4
43782 Vilalba dels Arcs (Tarragona)
☎: +34 651 031 835
info@bernavi.com
www.bernavi.com

Bernaví 3D3 2013 T
garnacha, syrah, merlot

84

Bernaví Ca'Vernet 2012 T
cabernet franc, cabernet sauvignon

84

Bernaví Notte Bianca 2014 B
garnacha blanca, viognier

84

Bernaví Ventuno 2014 RD
garnacha

86

MMXI 2011 T Roble
samsó, garnacha, cabernet sauvignon, merlot

88

Colour: cherry, garnet rim. Nose: ripe fruit, spicy, creamy oak. Palate: flavourful, toasty, correct.

Negreita 2012 T
morenillo, otras

88

Colour: cherry, garnet rim. Nose: ripe fruit, spicy, creamy oak. Palate: flavourful, toasty.

BODEGA HORTA

Navarra, 53
43596 Horta de Sant Joan (Tarragona)
☎: +34 977 422 000
Fax: +34 977 422 001
coop.horta@tinet.cat
www.bodegahorta.cat

Raco del Convent 2011 TC
garnacha, cariñena, tempranillo

84

Raco del Convent 2014 B
garnacha blanca, macabeo

84

Raco del Convent 2014 RD
garnacha

83

Raco del Convent 2014 T
garnacha, cariñena, tempranillo

83

CELLER BÁRBARA FORÉS

Santa Anna, 28
43780 Gandesa (Tarragona)
☎: +34 977 420 160
Fax: +34 977 421 399
info@cellerbarbarafores.com
www.cellerbarbarafores.com

Bárbara Forés 2014 B
garnacha blanca

88

Colour: bright straw. Nose: fruit expression, fragrant herbs, white flowers, expressive. Palate: flavourful, fresh, fruity, balanced.

Bárbara Forés 2014 RD
74% garnacha, 14% syrah, 14% cariñena

87

Colour: light cherry. Nose: floral, wild herbs, fruit expression. Palate: flavourful, balanced, elegant.

Bárbara Forés Negre 2012 T
63% garnacha, 26% syrah, 11% cariñena

89

Colour: cherry, garnet rim. Nose: red berry notes, fresh fruit, balanced, spicy. Palate: flavourful, spicy, balsamic, easy to drink.

Coma d'En Pou Bàrbara Forés 2012 T
74% garnacha, 18% syrah, 8% cariñena

90

Colour: dark-red cherry, garnet rim. Nose: ripe fruit, spicy, dried herbs. Palate: balanced, flavourful, spicy.

Dolç Natural Bárbara Forés 2011 B
garnacha blanca

90

Colour: bright golden. Nose: ripe fruit, honeyed notes, white flowers, sweet spices. Palate: flavourful, fruity, good acidity.

El Quintà Bárbara Forés 2013 BFB
garnacha blanca

93

Colour: bright yellow. Nose: dried flowers, sweet spices, ripe fruit. Palate: balanced, ripe fruit, spicy, long.

El Templari Bárbara Forés 2013 T
70% morenillo, 30% garnacha

90

Colour: light cherry. Nose: fruit expression, fruit liqueur notes, fragrant herbs, spicy, creamy oak. Palate: balanced, elegant, spicy, long, toasty.

CELLER BATEA

Moli, 30
43786 Batea (Tarragona)
☎: +34 977 430 056
Fax: +34 977 430 589
cellerbatea@cellerbatea.com
www.cellerbatea.com

Equinox Batea Dulce 2010 B
100% moscatel

91

Colour: old gold, amber rim. Nose: jasmine, white flowers, honeyed notes, expressive. Palate: full, flavourful, complex. Personality.

Equinox Dulce 2010 T
100% garnacha

90

Colour: cherry, garnet rim. Nose: fruit preserve, spicy, fruit liqueur notes. Palate: powerful, flavourful, sweet, rich.

L'Aube "Seleccio de Vinyes Velles" 2010 TC
50% merlot, 30% garnacha, 20% cabernet sauvignon

90

Colour: cherry, garnet rim. Nose: smoky, sweet spices, ripe fruit, dried herbs. Palate: correct, balanced.

Naturalis Mer 2013 T
85% garnacha, 15% cabernet sauvignon

89

Colour: very deep cherry, garnet rim. Nose: expressive, balanced, scrubland, ripe fruit. Palate: flavourful, round tannins.

Naturalis Mer 2014 T Roble
85% garnacha, 15% cabernet sauvignon

87

Colour: very deep cherry, purple rim. Nose: characterful, fruit preserve. Palate: flavourful, spicy, round tannins.

Primicia Chardonnay 2014 B
100% chardonnay

85

Tipicitat 2010 TC
85% garnacha, 15% samsó

89

Colour: cherry, garnet rim. Nose: ripe fruit, wild herbs, earthy notes, spicy, balsamic herbs. Palate: balanced, flavourful, long, balsamic.

Vallmajor 2014 B
100% garnacha blanca

86

Vallmajor 2014 RD
90% garnacha, 10% syrah

85

Vallmajor Negre 2014 T
90% garnacha, 10% syrah

84

Vivertell 2010 TC
garnacha, tempranillo, syrah, cabernet sauvignon

89

Colour: cherry, garnet rim. Nose: ripe fruit, spicy, creamy oak. Palate: flavourful, toasty.

CELLER COOPERATIU GANDESA SCCL

Avda. Catalunya, 28
43780 Gandesa (Tarragona)
☎: +34 977 420 017
Fax: +34 977 420 403
info@coopgandesa.com
www.coopgandesa.com

Gandesa Mistela Blanca Vino de licor
garnacha blanca

86

Gandesola Red 2013 T
mazuelo, tempranillo, garnacha, cabernet sauvignon

84

Gandesola Rose 2014 RD
garnacha

86

Gandesola White 2014 B
garnacha blanca, macabeo, moscatel

84

Somdinou 2012 TC
mazuelo, garnacha, syrah, cabernet sauvignon

87

Colour: dark-red cherry, garnet rim. Nose: ripe fruit, fruit preserve, warm, dried herbs. Palate: balanced, round tannins.

Somdinou 2013 BFB
garnacha blanca, macabeo

88

Colour: bright yellow. Nose: ripe fruit, powerfull, toasty, sweet spices. Palate: flavourful, fruity, spicy, toasty.

Somdinou Blanc Jove 2014 B
garnacha blanca, macabeo

87

Colour: bright straw. Nose: white flowers, fresh fruit, fragrant herbs. Palate: flavourful, fruity, good acidity.

Somdinou Negre Jove 2013 T
mazuelo, garnacha, tempranillo, cabernet sauvignon

87

Colour: cherry, garnet rim. Nose: scrubland, ripe fruit, spicy. Palate: balanced, spicy, ripe fruit.

Vi de Licor 1919 Rancio
garnacha blanca

91

Colour: dark mahogany. Nose: candied fruit, fruit liqueur notes, spicy, varnish, acetaldehyde, dry nuts. Palate: fine solera notes, fine bitter notes, spirituous.

CELLER GERMANS BALART

Carrer Buenos Aires, 4
43780 Gandesa (Tarragona)
☎: +34 600 484 900
cellermvbalart@gmail.com

Llepolia Blanc 2014 B
70% garnacha blanca, 30% sauvignon blanc

86

Llepolia Negre 2013 T
60% cariñena, 40% garnacha

85

Set Sitis 2012 T
cariñena

88

Colour: deep cherry, garnet rim. Nose: floral, ripe fruit. Palate: balanced, sweet tannins.

Set Sitis Blanc 2014 BFB
100% garnacha blanca

86

CELLER JORDI MIRÓ

Sant Marc, 96
43784 Corbera d'Ebre (Tarragona)
☎: +34 629 602 354
jordi@ennak.com
www.ennak.com

Ennak 2014 T
garnacha, mazuelo, tempranillo, merlot

85

Ennak+ 2013 TC
cabernet sauvignon, garnacha, mazuelo, syrah, tempranillo, merlot

87

Colour: ruby red. Nose: fruit liqueur notes, creamy oak, balsamic herbs, wild herbs. Palate: spicy, long, toasty.

Jordi Miró Garnacha Tinta Syrah 2014 T
garnacha, syrah

87

Colour: cherry, purple rim. Nose: floral, balsamic herbs, fruit liqueur notes. Palate: powerful, fresh, fruity.

Jordi Miró Garnatxa Blanca 2014 B
garnacha blanca

81

CELLER JOSEP VICENS VALLESPÍ

Aragó, 20
43780 Gandesa (Tarragona)
☎: +34 686 135 921
celler@vinsjosepvicens.com
www.vinsjosepvicens.com

Mon Iaio Sisco 2012 TR
samsó

87

Colour: bright cherry. Nose: sweet spices, creamy oak, fruit preserve. Palate: flavourful, fruity, toasty, round tannins.

Vinyes del Grau 2014 RD
syrah, garnacha

85

Vinyes del Grau Blanc Coupatge 2014 B
macabeo, viognier, moscatel

86

Vinyes del Grau Negre 2014 T
garnacha, samsó

85

Vinyes del Grau Sauvignon 2014 B
sauvignon blanc

85

Vinyes del Grau Syrah 2010 TC
syrah

88

Colour: cherry, garnet rim. Nose: ripe fruit, wild herbs, spicy, balsamic herbs. Palate: flavourful, long, balsamic.

CELLER MARIOL

Rosselló, 442
08025 (Barcelona)
☎: +34 934 367 628
Fax: +34 934 500 281
celler@cellermariol.es
www.casamariol.com

Casa Mariol Cabernet Sauvignon 2011 TR
cabernet sauvignon

83

Casa Mariol Macabeo Garnacha Blanca 2014 B
macabeo, garnacha blanca

82

Casa Mariol Samsó 2011 TC
samsó

84

Casa Mariol Syrah 2009 TR
syrah

85

CELLER PIÑOL

Avda. Aragón, 9
43786 Batea (Tarragona)
☎: +34 977 430 505
Fax: +34 977 430 498
info@cellerpinol.com
www.cellerpinol.com

Finca Morenillo 2012 T
100% morenillo

92

Colour: cherry, garnet rim. Nose: balanced, complex, ripe fruit, spicy. Palate: good structure, flavourful, round tannins, balanced.

Josefina Piñol Dulce 2013 B
100% garnacha blanca

91

Colour: bright golden. Nose: honeyed notes, white flowers, faded flowers, citrus fruit. Palate: rich, flavourful, good acidity.

Josefina Piñol Vendimia Tardía 2012 Tinto Dulce
100% garnacha

92

Colour: ruby red. Nose: dried fruit, wild herbs, creamy oak, sweet spices, toasty, expressive. Palate: spirituous, round, unctuous, spicy, long.

L'Avi Arrufí 2009 T
60% cariñena, 30% garnacha, 10% syrah

92

Colour: cherry, garnet rim. Nose: balanced, complex, ripe fruit, spicy, fine reductive notes. Palate: good structure, flavourful, round tannins, balanced.

L'Avi Arrufí 2012 BFB
100% garnacha blanca

94

Colour: bright yellow. Nose: dried herbs, ripe fruit, spicy. Palate: flavourful, fruity, good acidity, balanced, complex.

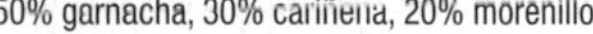

Mather Teresina Selección de Viñas Viejas 2010 T
50% garnacha, 30% cariñena, 20% morenillo

91

Colour: cherry, garnet rim. Nose: ripe fruit, wild herbs, earthy notes, spicy, balsamic herbs. Palate: balanced, flavourful, long, balsamic.

Nuestra Sra. del Portal 2014 B
85% garnacha blanca, 5% sauvignon blanc, 5% viognier, 5% macabeo

90

Colour: bright straw. Nose: white flowers, dried herbs, ripe fruit, candied fruit, citrus fruit. Palate: flavourful, fruity, good acidity, elegant.

Portal N. Sra. Portal 2012 T
60% garnacha, 15% cariñena, 15% syrah, 10% merlot

88

Colour: cherry, garnet rim. Nose: smoky, spicy, ripe fruit, wild herbs. Palate: flavourful, smoky aftertaste, ripe fruit.

Raig de Raim 2013 T
cariñena, syrah, merlot

86

Raig de Raim 2014 B
80% garnacha blanca, 20% macabeo

89

Colour: bright straw. Nose: white flowers, fresh fruit, fragrant herbs, expressive. Palate: flavourful, fruity, good acidity, balanced.

Sa Natura 2012 T
50% cariñena, 20% syrah, 10% tempranillo, 20% merlot

88

Colour: ruby red. Nose: ripe fruit, wild herbs, creamy oak. Palate: powerful, flavourful, spicy.

CELLER TERN, OBRADOR DE VI

Avinguda Terra Alta, 28
43786 Batea (Tarragona)
☎: +34 654 352 964
Fax: +34 977 430 433
ternobradordevi@gmail.com
www.ternobradordevi.com

Tern Arrel de Nou 2013 T
50% cariñena, 30% garnacha, 20% syrah

88

Colour: garnet rim, cherry, garnet rim. Nose: expressive, balsamic herbs, spicy. Palate: full, flavourful, round tannins.

Tern gb Garnatxa Blanca 2014 B
garnacha blanca

88

Colour: bright straw. Nose: sweet spices, ripe fruit, white flowers. Palate: rich, flavourful, powerful.

CELLER XAVIER CLUA

Ctra. Vilalba-Gandesa, km. 9
43782 Vilalba dels Arcs (Tarragona)
☎: +34 977 263 069
Fax: +34 977 439 003
rosa@cellerclua.com
www.cellerclua.com

Clua Mil.lennium 2012 TC
60% garnacha, 20% cabernet sauvignon, 15% syrah, 5% merlot

88

Colour: black cherry, garnet rim. Nose: ripe fruit, fruit preserve, spicy. Palate: balsamic, round tannins, long.

Il.lusió de Clua 2014 B
100% garnacha blanca

88

Colour: straw. Nose: medium intensity, ripe fruit, dried flowers. Palate: correct, easy to drink, ripe fruit, balanced, fine bitter notes.

Mas d'en Pol 2012 T Barrica
garnacha, syrah, merlot, cabernet sauvignon

85

Mas d'en Pol 2014 B
garnacha blanca, chardonnay, sauvignon blanc

84

Mas d'en Pol 2014 T
50% garnacha, 20% syrah, 15% merlot, 15% cabernet sauvignon

83

CELLERS TARRONÉ

Calvari, 22
43786 Batea (Tarragona)
☎: +34 977 430 109
Fax: +34 977 430 109
info@cellerstarrone.com
www.cellerstarrone.com

Merian 2014 B
100% garnacha blanca

89

Colour: bright straw. Nose: white flowers, fragrant herbs, ripe fruit. Palate: flavourful, fruity, good acidity, balanced.

Merian 2014 T
garnacha, syrah, merlot

86

Merian Dolç Natural 2012 T
garnacha

90

Colour: bright cherry, garnet rim. Nose: varnish, candied fruit, dried fruit, balanced. Palate: fruity, flavourful, sweet.

Punt i... 2014 T
garnacha, syrah

87

Colour: bright cherry. Nose: ripe fruit, sweet spices, creamy oak. Palate: flavourful, fruity, toasty.

Seguit 2013 T
garnacha

87

Colour: cherry, garnet rim. Nose: roasted coffee, smoky, spicy, ripe fruit. Palate: flavourful, smoky aftertaste, ripe fruit.

Sisquera 2014 B
garnacha blanca, macabeo

82

Sisquera 2014 T
garnacha, syrah

84

CELLERS UNIÓ

43206 Reus (Tarragona)
☎: +34 977 330 055
Fax: +34 977 330 070
info@cellersunio.com
www.cellersunio.com

Clos del Pinell Garnatxa 2014 T
garnacha

84

Clos del Pinell Garnatxa Blanca 2014 B
garnacha blanca

84

Gran Copos 2011 TR

79

Reina Elionor 2011 TR
garnacha, tempranillo, mazuelo

85

COCA I FITÓ

Avda. Onze de Setembre s/n
43736 El Masroig (Tarragona)
☎: +34 619 776 948
Fax: +34 935 457 092
info@cocaifito.cat
www.cocaifito.cat

Jaspi Blanc 2013 B
70% garnacha blanca, 30% macabeo

87

Colour: bright straw. Nose: white flowers, fresh fruit, fragrant herbs. Palate: flavourful, fruity, good acidity.

Jaspi D'Or 2013 B
80% garnacha blanca, 20% macabeo

85

EDETÀRIA

Finca El Mas - Ctra. Gandesa a Vilalba s/n
43780 Gandesa (Tarragona)
☎: +34 977 421 534
Fax: +34 977 421 534
info@edetaria.com
www.edetaria.com

Edetària Dolç 2009 T
70% garnacha, 30% syrah

89

Colour: bright cherry, garnet rim. Nose: acetaldehyde, varnish, candied fruit, creamy oak. Palate: fruity, flavourful, sweet.

Edetària Selecció 2007 B
85% garnacha blanca, 15% macabeo

91

Colour: golden. Nose: powerfull, honeyed notes, candied fruit, fragrant herbs. Palate: flavourful, fresh, good acidity, spirituous.

Edetària Selecció 2008 B
85% garnacha blanca, 15% macabeo

92

Colour: bright golden. Nose: powerfull, characterful, cocoa bean, dry nuts. Palate: flavourful, smoky aftertaste, toasty, complex, full.

Edetària Selecció 2011 B
85% garnacha blanca, 15% macabeo

92

Colour: bright yellow. Nose: elegant, expressive, complex. Palate: balanced, spicy, long, full. Personality.

Edetària Selecció 2011 T
60% garnacha peluda, 30% syrah, 10% samsó

92

Colour: deep cherry. Nose: complex, ripe fruit, balsamic herbs. Palate: good structure, full, long, fruity aftestaste, round tannins.

Edetària Selecció 2012 B
100% garnacha blanca

90

Colour: bright yellow. Nose: expressive, dried herbs, ripe fruit, spicy. Palate: flavourful, fruity, good acidity, balanced.

Edetària Selecció 2012 T
60% garnacha peluda, 30% syrah, 10% samsó

91

Colour: deep cherry, garnet rim. Nose: expressive, ripe fruit, spicy, dried herbs. Palate: good structure, warm.

Edetària Selecció 2013 T
60% garnacha peluda, 30% garnacha, 10% samsó

91

Colour: cherry, garnet rim. Nose: ripe fruit, fragrant herbs, spicy, toasty, creamy oak, mineral. Palate: powerful, flavourful, balsamic, balanced.

La Pedrissa de Edetària 2012 T
100% samsó

93

Colour: very deep cherry. Nose: expressive, wild herbs, dried herbs, ripe fruit, mineral. Palate: balanced, long, complex.

La Personal de Edetària 2013 T
100% garnacha peluda

93

Colour: cherry, garnet rim. Nose: expressive, spicy, mineral. Palate: flavourful, ripe fruit, long, good acidity, balanced.

Vía Edetana 2013 T
60% garnacha, 30% syrah, 10% samsó

89

Colour: very deep cherry, garnet rim. Nose: mineral, balsamic herbs, ripe fruit. Palate: full, flavourful, correct.

Vía Edetana 2014 B
70% garnacha blanca, 30% viognier

91

Colour: bright yellow. Nose: faded flowers, ripe fruit, spicy, balanced. Palate: full, flavourful, balanced.

Vía Edetana Magnum 2012 T
60% garnacha, 30% garnacha peluda, 10% samsó

89

Colour: cherry, garnet rim. Nose: spicy, creamy oak, ripe fruit, fruit preserve, earthy notes. Palate: flavourful, toasty, balanced.

Vía Edetana Magnum 2013 B Barrica
70% garnacha blanca, 30% viognier

91

Colour: bright straw. Nose: fruit expression, floral, fragrant herbs, spicy, mineral. Palate: elegant, good acidity, fresh, fruity, balsamic, balanced.

Vía Terra 2014 B
100% garnacha blanca

88

Colour: bright straw. Nose: balanced, medium intensity, ripe fruit, dried herbs. Palate: balanced, fine bitter notes, good acidity.

Vía Terra 2014 RD
100% garnacha peluda

87

Colour: onion pink. Nose: red berry notes, floral, fragrant herbs. Palate: light-bodied, flavourful, good acidity, easy to drink.

Vía Terra 2014 T
100% garnacha

88

Colour: cherry, purple rim. Nose: red berry notes, floral, balsamic herbs. Palate: fresh, fruity, fruity aftestaste.

ESCOLA AGRÀRIA DE GANDESA

Assis Garrote
43780 Gandesa (Tarragona)
☎: +34 977 420 164
Fax: +34 977 420 607
phernandeza@gencat.cat
www.gencat.cat/agricultura/eca/gandesa

Glau-k 2014 BFB
100% garnacha blanca

84

L'abella 2014 B
40% garnacha, 40% macabeo, 20% moscatel

79

La Formiga 2014 RD
tempranillo

81

Les Feixes Eixutes 2013 T
80% garnacha, 20% samsó

87

Colour: bright cherry. Nose: ripe fruit, sweet spices, creamy oak. Palate: flavourful, fruity, toasty.

ESTONES VINS

Pl. Sort dels Capellans, Nau Bahaus
43730 Falset (Tarragona)
☎: +34 666 415 735
vins@massersal.com
www.estones.cat

Estones de Mishima "Vine" 2014 B Roble
garnacha blanca, macabeo

89

Colour: bright yellow. Nose: ripe fruit, powerfull, toasty. Palate: flavourful, fruity, spicy, toasty, long.

Petites Estones Blanc 2014 B
garnacha blanca

87

Colour: bright straw. Nose: white flowers, fresh fruit, fragrant herbs, expressive. Palate: flavourful, fruity, good acidity, balanced.

HERÈNCIA ALTÉS

Tarragona, 42
43786 Batea (Tarragona)
☎: +34 977 430 681
nuria@exportiberia.com
www.herenciaaltes.com

Herencia Altés Benufet 2014 B
garnacha blanca

89

Colour: bright straw. Nose: white flowers, dried herbs, ripe fruit, candied fruit, citrus fruit. Palate: flavourful, fruity, good acidity, elegant.

Herencia Altés Garnatxa Blanca 2014 B
garnacha blanca

87

Colour: straw. Nose: medium intensity, ripe fruit, floral. Palate: correct, easy to drink, balanced, fine bitter notes.

Herencia Altés Garnatxa Negra 2014 T
garnacha

84

Herencia Altés L'Estel 2013 T
garnacha, syrah, cariñena

87

Colour: very deep cherry, garnet rim. Nose: ripe fruit, fruit preserve, aromatic coffee. Palate: flavourful, ripe fruit.

Herencia Altés La Serra 2013 T Barrica
garnacha, cariñena

91

Colour: very deep cherry, garnet rim. Nose: expressive, complex, balsamic herbs, balanced. Palate: full, flavourful, round tannins.

Herencia Altés La Serra Blanc 2013 B
garnacha blanca

91

Colour: bright yellow. Nose: expressive, dried herbs, ripe fruit, spicy. Palate: flavourful, fruity, good acidity, balanced.

I TANT VINS

Passeig del Ferrocarril, 337 Baixos
08860 Castelldefels (Barcelona)
☎: +34 936 628 253
Fax: +34 934 517 628
albert@aribau.es
www.aribau.es

I Tant Garnatxa Blanca 2014 B

100% garnacha blanca

88

Colour: bright straw. Nose: balanced, fresh, white flowers. Palate: fruity, flavourful, fine bitter notes.

LAFOU CELLER

Plaça Catalunya, 34
43786 Batea (Tarragona)
☎: +34 938 743 511
Fax: +34 938 737 204
info@lafou.net
www.lafou.net

Lafou de Batea 2010 TR

85% garnacha, 15% cariñena

93

Colour: cherry, garnet rim. Nose: red berry notes, ripe fruit, spicy, creamy oak, complex. Palate: flavourful, toasty, round tannins.

Lafou El Sender 2013 TC

65% garnacha, 25% syrah, 10% morenillo

92

Colour: very deep cherry, garnet rim. Nose: expressive, complex, mineral, balsamic herbs, balanced. Palate: full, flavourful, round tannins.

Lafou Els Amelers 2013 B

100% garnacha

92

Colour: bright straw. Nose: white flowers, fine lees, dried herbs, ripe fruit, dry stone, spicy. Palate: flavourful, fruity, good acidity, elegant.

PAGOS DE HÍBERA

Pilonet, 8
43594 Pinell de Brai (Tarragona)
☎: +34 977 426 234
Fax: +34 977 426 290
bodega@catedraldelvi.com
www.catedraldelvi.com

Gamberro Garnacha Blanca 2013 B

garnacha blanca

90

Colour: bright straw. Nose: white flowers, fine lees, dried herbs. Palate: flavourful, fruity, good acidity, elegant.

Gamberro Negre de Guarda 2011 T

syrah, samsó, cabernet sauvignon

89

Colour: cherry, garnet rim. Nose: wild herbs, earthy notes, spicy, balsamic herbs, ripe fruit. Palate: balanced, flavourful, unctuous.

L'Indià 2014 B

garnacha blanca

89

Colour: bright straw. Nose: fruit expression, dried herbs, mineral, expressive. Palate: flavourful, fresh, fruity, correct.

L'Indià Negre 2013 T

garnacha, cariñena

87

Colour: deep cherry. Nose: creamy oak, toasty, ripe fruit, balsamic herbs. Palate: balanced, spicy, long.

SERRA DE CAVALLS

Bonaire, 1
43594 El Pinell de Brai (Tarragona)
☎: +34 977 426 049
sat@serradecavalls.com
www.serradecavalls.com

Serra de Cavalls 2011 TC

garnacha, syrah, merlot, cabernet sauvignon

82

Serra de Cavalls 2014 B

garnacha blanca

86

Serra de Cavalls 2014 T

garnacha, syrah, tempranillo, merlot

81

VINS DE MESIES

La Verge, 6
43782 Vilalba dels Arcs (Tarragona)
☎: +34 977 438 196
info@ecovitres.com
www.ecovitres.com

Mesies 2010 TC

garnacha, syrah, cabernet sauvignon, merlot

87

Colour: cherry, garnet rim. Nose: fine reductive notes, wet leather, cigar, ripe fruit. Palate: spicy, long, toasty.

Mesies Garnatxa 2013 T

87

Colour: deep cherry, purple rim. Nose: creamy oak, toasty, ripe fruit, balsamic herbs. Palate: balanced, spicy, long.

VINS DEL TROS

Major, 12
43782 Vilalba dels Arcs (Tarragona)
☎: +34 605 096 447
info@vinsdeltros.com
www.vinsdeltros.com

Ay de Mí 2012 TC
garnacha peluda, cariñena

88

Colour: bright cherry. Nose: sweet spices, creamy oak, fruit preserve. Palate: flavourful, fruity, toasty.

Cent x Cent Pla de Pey 2014 B
garnacha blanca

87

Colour: bright yellow. Nose: expressive, dried herbs, ripe fruit, spicy, wild herbs. Palate: flavourful, fruity, good acidity.

Te la Dedico 2014 B
garnacha blanca, chenin blanc

86

VINS LA BOTERA

Sant Roc, 26
43786 Batea (Tarragona)
☎: +34 977 430 009
Fax: +34 977 430 801
labotera@labotera.com
www.labotera.com

Arnot Blanc 2014 B
garnacha blanca, macabeo

84

Arnot Negre 2014 T
garnacha, syrah

84

Arnot Rosat 2014 RD
syrah

84

Bruna Dolç T
garnacha, syrah

90

Colour: bright cherry, garnet rim. Nose: acetaldehyde, varnish, overripe fruit, dried fruit. Palate: fruity, flavourful, sweet, spirituous.

Mudèfer 2011 TC
garnacha, cariñena, syrah, merlot

86

Vila Closa 2014 T
garnacha

85

Vila Closa Chardonnay 2013 BFB
chardonnay

85

Vila Closa Garnatxa Blanca 2014 B
100% garnacha blanca

86

Vila Closa Rosat 2014 RD
garnacha

86

VINS PERDIGONS

Rovira y Virgili, 6
43002 Tarragona (Tarragona)
☎: +34 618 435 937
vinsperdigons@gmail.com
www.vinsperdigons.com

Perdigons Blanc 2014 B
85% macabeo, 15% viognier

87

Colour: straw. Nose: medium intensity, ripe fruit, floral. Palate: correct, easy to drink.

Perdigons Negre 2014 T
100% garnacha

86

VINYA D'IRTO

Plaça Comerç , 5
43780 Gandesa (Tarragona)
☎: +34 977 421 534
Fax: +34 977 421 534
info@edetaria.com

Vinya d'Irto 2014 B
70% garnacha blanca, 20% macabeo, 10% viognier

87

Colour: bright straw. Nose: fresh fruit, fragrant herbs, expressive. Palate: flavourful, fruity, good acidity, balanced.

Vinya d'Irto 2014 T
70% garnacha, 30% syrah

86

DO. TIERRA DE LEÓN

CONSEJO REGULADOR

Alonso Castrillo, 29.
24200 Valencia de Don Juan (León)
☎ :+34 987 751 089 - Fax: +34 987 750 012
@: directortecnico@dotierradeleon.es
www.dotierradeleon.es

LOCATION:

In the southeast of Catalonia, in the province of Tarragona. It covers the municipal districts of Arnes, Batea, Bot, Caseres, Corbera d´Ebre, La Fatarella, Gandesa, Horta de Sant Joan, Pinell de Brai, La Pobla de Massaluca, Prat de Comte and Vilalba dels Arcs.

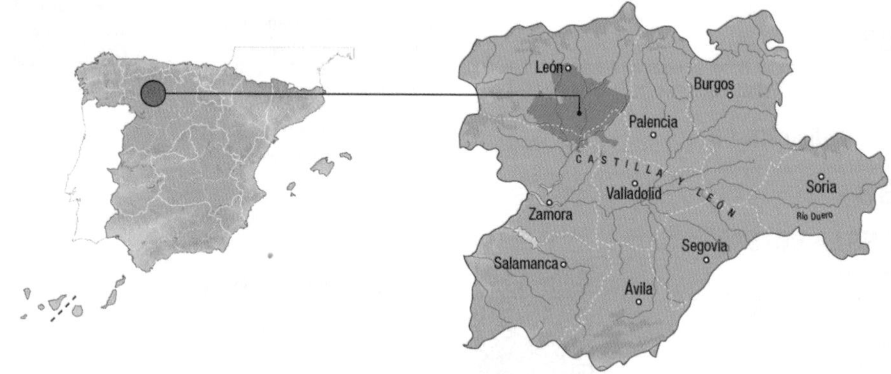

GRAPE VARIETIES:

WHITE: Chardonnay, Garnacha Blanca, Parellada, Macabeo, Moscatel, Sauvignon Blanc, Chenin, Pedro Ximénez. Experimental: Viognier.
RED: Cabernet Sauvigon, Cariñena, Garnacha Tinta, Garnacha Peluda, Syrah, Tempranillo, Merlot, Samsó, Cabernet Franc. Experimental: Petit Verdot, Marselane, Caladoc.

FIGURES:

Vineyard surface: 1,400 – **Wine-Growers:** 325 – **Wineries:** 40 – **2014 Harvest rating:** Excellent – **Production 14:** 2,700,000 litres – **Market percentages:** 98% National - 2% International.

SOIL:

The vineyards are located on an extensive plateau at an altitude of slightly over 400 m. The soil is calcareous and the texture mainly clayey, poor in organic matter and with many pebbles.

CLIMATE:

Mediterranean, with continental influences. It is characterized by its hot, dry summers and very cold winters, especially in the higher regions in the east. The average annual rainfall is 400 mm. Another vital aspect is the wind: the 'Cierzo' and the 'Garbi' (Ábrego) winds.

VINTAGE RATING

PEÑÍNGUIDE

2010	2011	2012	2013	2014
VERY GOOD	VERY GOOD	VERY GOOD	GOOD	GOOD

BODEGA 100 CEPAS

Pago de las Bodegas
24225 Corbillo de los Oteros (León)
☎: +34 687 809 531
Fax: +34 987 570 059
cesar@100cepas.es

100 Cepas 2012 T
prieto picudo

87

Colour: cherry, garnet rim. Nose: smoky, ripe fruit. Palate: flavourful, fruity, smoky aftertaste.

100 Cepas 2012 TC
prieto picudo

86

BODEGAS ÁBREGO

Manuel Cadenas, 4
24230 Valdevimbre (León)
☎: +34 987 304 133
bodegasabrego@hotmail.com

Pegalahebra 2014 B
verdejo

85

Pegalahebra 2014 RD
prieto picudo

85

Pegalahebra 2014 T
prieto picudo

88

Colour: deep cherry, garnet rim. Nose: scrubland, dry nuts, ripe fruit, earthy notes. Palate: balanced, balsamic.

BODEGAS MARCOS MIÑAMBRES

Camino de Pobladura, s/n
24234 Villamañán (León)
☎: +34 987 767 038
satvined@picos.com

Los Silvares 2009 TR

89

Colour: dark-red cherry, orangey edge. Nose: fruit preserve, fine reductive notes, wet leather. Palate: flavourful, full, rich, smoky aftertaste.

BODEGAS MARGÓN

Avda Valencia de Don Juan, s/n
24209 Pajares de los Oteros (León)
☎: +34 987 750 800
Fax: +34 987 750 481
comercial@bodegasmargon.com
www.bodegasmargon.com

Pricum 2014 RD
prieto picudo

88

Colour: ochre. Nose: red clay notes, dry stone, raspberry, red berry notes. Palate: fruity, powerful, flavourful.

Pricum Albarín 2013 B Barrica
albarín

91

Colour: bright yellow. Nose: ripe fruit, balanced, powerfull, varietal, wild herbs, faded flowers. Palate: flavourful, fruity, rich.

Pricum El Voluntario 2010 T
prieto picudo

92

Colour: dark-red cherry. Nose: fresh fruit, varietal, powerfull, expressive, fruit expression. Palate: balsamic, fruity, creamy, smoky aftertaste.

Pricum Paraje del Santo 2011 T
prieto picudo

92

Colour: dark-red cherry. Nose: spicy, earthy notes, closed, ripe fruit, fruit expression. Palate: balsamic, creamy, powerful, flavourful.

Pricum Prieto Picudo 2010 T
prieto picudo

91

Colour: cherry, garnet rim. Nose: ripe fruit, wild herbs, spicy, balsamic herbs. Palate: balanced, flavourful, long, balsamic.

Pricum Primeur 2012 T
prieto picudo

89

Colour: cherry, garnet rim. Nose: wild herbs, ripe fruit, balanced, varietal. Palate: flavourful, fine bitter notes.

Valdemuz 2010 T
prieto picudo

90

Colour: cherry, garnet rim. Nose: ripe fruit, fruit preserve, sweet spices, scrubland. Palate: flavourful, powerful, good structure.

Valdemuz 2011 T
prieto picudo

92

Colour: cherry, garnet rim. Nose: ripe fruit, wild herbs, earthy notes, spicy, balsamic herbs. Palate: balanced, flavourful, long, balsamic.

BODEGAS PELÁEZ

Calabozo, 12 - Grajal de la Ribera
24796 La Antigua (León)
☎: +34 987 202 350
Fax: +34 987 006 913
bodegaspelaez@ono.com

Airad 2014 B
verdejo

86

Senoel 2014 RD
prieto picudo

85

Senoel 2014 T
prieto picudo

85

Tres Almas "Madreado de la Aldea" 2014 RD
prieto picudo

89

Colour: light cherry, bright. Nose: red berry notes, ripe fruit, rose petals, expressive. Palate: good acidity, balanced, fine bitter notes, carbonic notes, sweetness.

Tres Almas 2012 TC
86

BODEGAS VINOS DE LEÓN

Finca Monteleon
Valdevimbre (León)
☎: +34 987 209 712
Fax: +34 987 209 800
info@bodegasvinosdeleon.es
www.bodegasvinosdeleon.es

Valjunco 2014 RD
100% prieto picudo

85

Valjunco 2014 T
87

Colour: cherry, purple rim. Nose: red berry notes, floral, wild herbs. Palate: fresh, fruity, correct, good acidity.

Valjunco Albarín 2014 B
100% albarín

86

BODEGAS VITALIS

Ctra. Villamañan-Astorga, km. 33
24234 Villamañan (León)
☎: +34 987 131 019
vitalis@bodegasvitalis.com
www.bodegasvitalis.com

Vitalis 2009 TC
prieto picudo

84

Vitalis 6 meses 2012 T Roble
84

Lágrima de Vitalis 2014 B
albarín

88

Colour: bright straw. Nose: fresh fruit, white flowers, citrus fruit, balanced. Palate: correct, balanced.

Lágrima de Vitalis 2014 RD
prieto picudo

84

BODEGAS Y VIÑEDOS CASIS

Las Bodegas, s/n
24325 Gordaliza del Pino (León)
☎: +34 987 699 618
anacasis@gmail.com
www.bodegascasis.com

Casis 2012 T
85

Casis 2014 B
82

Casis Godello 2014 B
83

Casis Mencía 2012 TC
prieto picudo, mencía, tempranillo

81

Casis Prieto Picudo 2011 TC
85

Casis Prieto Picudo 2013 T
82

Casis Prieto Picudo 2014 RD
82

BODEGAS Y VIÑEDOS LA SILVERA

Ctra. Valencia de Don Juan s/n
24209 Pajares de los Oteros (León)
☎: +34 618 174 176
pretocorreo@gmail.com

Preto 2014 RD
prieto picudo

87

Colour: brilliant rose. Nose: white flowers, neat, varietal, fruit expression. Palate: complex, fresh, powerful, flavourful, balsamic.

GORDONZELLO

Alto de Santa Marina, s/n
24294 Gordoncillo (León)
☎: +34 987 758 030
Fax: +34 987 757 201
info@gordonzello.com
www.gordonzello.com

Gurdos 2014 RD
100% prieto picudo

88

Colour: rose, purple rim. Nose: red berry notes, faded flowers. Palate: powerful, fruity, long.

Kyra Peregrino 2013 BFB
albarín

87

Colour: bright yellow. Nose: sweet spices, cedar wood, macerated fruit, fresh, varietal, smoky, woody. Palate: powerful, oaky, ripe fruit.

Peregrino 2009 TR
prieto picudo

88

Colour: cherry, garnet rim. Nose: ripe fruit, old leather, tobacco, dried herbs. Palate: correct, flavourful, spicy.

Peregrino 2011 TC
100% prieto picudo

86

Peregrino 2014 T
100% prieto picudo

85

Peregrino 14 2011 TC
prieto picudo

88

Colour: deep cherry, garnet rim. Nose: ripe fruit, scrubland, spicy. Palate: spicy, long, round tannins.

Peregrino 2013 T Roble
100% prieto picudo

84

Peregrino 2014 RD
100% prieto picudo

86

Peregrino Albarín 2014 B
100% albarín

86

Peregrino Blanco 2014 B
100% verdejo

85

Peregrino Mil 100 2011 T Roble
100% prieto picudo

91

Colour: very deep cherry, garnet rim. Nose: expressive, complex, balsamic herbs, balanced. Palate: full, flavourful, round tannins.

LEYENDA DEL PÁRAMO

Ctra. de León s/n, Paraje El Cueto
24230 Valdevimbre (León)
☎: +34 987 050 039
Fax: +34 987 050 039
info@leyendadelparamo.com
www.leyendadelparamo.com

El Aprendiz 2013 T
prieto picudo

87

Colour: bright cherry, purple rim. Nose: red berry notes, fresh fruit, wild herbs. Palate: correct, flavourful.

El Aprendiz 2014 B
albarín

89

Colour: bright straw. Nose: white flowers, dried herbs, ripe fruit, citrus fruit. Palate: flavourful, fruity, good acidity, elegant.

El Aprendiz 2014 RD
prieto picudo

88

Colour: rose. Nose: neat, medium intensity, varietal. Palate: fresh, fruity, powerful, flavourful.

El Médico 2012 T Roble
prieto picudo

91

Colour: dark-red cherry, purple rim. Nose: characterful, varietal, ripe fruit, fruit preserve. Palate: flavourful, dry, toasty.

El Músico 2011 T
prieto picudo

92

Colour: cherry, garnet rim. Nose: characterful, expressive, fruit preserve, balsamic herbs. Palate: ripe fruit, long, good acidity.

MELGARAJO
Plaza Mayor, 9
47687 Melgar de Abajo (Valladolid)
☎: +34 983 786 012
melgarajo@melgarajo.es
www.melgarajo.es

Melgus 2011 TC
prieto picudo

90

Colour: deep cherry, garnet rim. Nose: wild herbs, varietal, ripe fruit, spicy. Palate: balanced, spicy, ripe fruit, long.

Melgus 2011 TR
prieto picudo

89

Colour: deep cherry. Nose: earthy notes, ripe fruit, cedar wood. Palate: flavourful, full, powerful.

Valdeleña 2012 T Roble
prieto picudo

85

Valdeleña 2013 B
verdejo

83

Valdeleña 2013 T
prieto picudo

82

Valdeleña 2013 T Roble
prieto picudo

82

Valdeleña 2014 RD
prieto picudo

85

Valdeleña Tinto de Autor 2012 T
prieto picudo

88

Colour: deep cherry. Nose: creamy oak, toasty, ripe fruit, balsamic herbs, smoky. Palate: balanced, spicy, long.

NOELIA DE PAZ CALVO
24230 Valdevimbre (León)
☎: +34 666 217 032
depaznoelia@gmail.com

Grizzly 2011 T
prieto picudo

89

Colour: dark-red cherry, garnet rim. Nose: ripe fruit, smoky, spicy, balsamic herbs. Palate: flavourful, balanced.

SEÑORÍO DE LOS ARCOS
La Iglesia, s/n
24191 Ardoncino (León)
☎: +34 987 226 594
Fax: +34 987 226 594
admin@senoriodelosarcos.es
www.senoriodelosarcos.es

Vega Carriegos 2011 TC
prieto picudo

89

Colour: cherry, garnet rim. Nose: ripe fruit, spicy, scrubland, dried herbs. Palate: flavourful, spicy, balsamic.

Vega Carriegos 2012 T Roble
prieto picudo

87

Colour: deep cherry, purple rim. Nose: creamy oak, toasty, ripe fruit, balsamic herbs. Palate: balanced, spicy, long.

Vega Carriegos 2014 RD
86

SOC. COOP. VINÍCOLA COMARCAL DE VALDEVIMBRE
Ctra. de León, s/n
24230 Valdevimbre (León)
☎: +34 987 304 195
Fax: +34 987 304 195
valdevim@gmail.com
www.vinicoval.com

Abadía de Balderedo 2011 T
prieto picudo

84

Abadía de Balderedo 2014 RD
prieto picudo

84

Abadía de Balderedo 2014 T
prieto picudo

87

Colour: dark-red cherry. Nose: balsamic herbs, fresh fruit, red berry notes. Palate: balsamic, fresh, fruity, flavourful.

Abadía de Balderedo Verdejo 2014 B
verdejo

84

VIÑEDOS Y BODEGA JULIO CRESPO AGUILOCHE

Ctra. Sahagún-Renedo Km. 6
24326 Sahagún (León)
☎: +34 987 130 010
Fax: +34 987 130 010
info@bodegasjuliocrespo.com
www.bodegasjuliocrespo.com

Alevosía 2012 T
mencía

87

Colour: dark-red cherry, garnet rim. Nose: ripe fruit, spicy, balsamic herbs. Palate: correct, spicy, ripe fruit.

Finca Villazán 2014 B
albarín

87

Colour: bright straw. Nose: fresh fruit, fragrant herbs, expressive. Palate: flavourful, fruity, good acidity, balanced.

Finca Villazán 2014 RD
prieto picudo

86

Premeditación 2012 T
prieto picudo

88

Colour: bright cherry. Nose: expressive, balsamic herbs, balanced, varietal. Palate: flavourful, round tannins, good acidity.

VIÑEDOS Y BODEGA PARDEVALLES

Ramón y Cajal, 22
24230 Valdevimbre (León)
☎: +34 987 304 222
Fax: +34 987 304 222
info@pardevalles.es
www.pardevalles.es

Pardevalles 2014 RD
100% prieto picudo

88

Colour: rose, purple rim. Nose: red berry notes, expressive, wild herbs. Palate: powerful, fruity, fresh, fine bitter notes.

Pardevalles 2014 T
100% prieto picudo

88

Colour: dark-red cherry. Nose: fresh, balanced, fruit expression, fresh fruit. Palate: fresh, fruity, flavourful, balsamic.

Pardevalles Albarín 2014 B
100% albarín

90

Colour: bright straw. Nose: fragrant herbs, fresh fruit, varietal, powerfull, fresh, characterful. Palate: full, powerful, flavourful.

Pardevalles Carroleón 2010 T
100% prieto picudo

91

Colour: cherry, garnet rim. Nose: smoky, spicy, ripe fruit, toasty. Palate: flavourful, ripe fruit, balsamic.

Pardevalles Carroleón 2014 BFB
100% albarín

91

Colour: bright straw. Nose: expressive, complex, varietal, fresh fruit. Palate: elegant, powerful, full, flavourful.

Pardevalles Gamonal 2012 T
100% prieto picudo

91

Colour: dark-red cherry, garnet rim. Nose: scrubland, smoky, ripe fruit, varietal. Palate: flavourful, fruity, long.

DO. TIERRA DEL VINO DE ZAMORA

CONSEJO REGULADOR

Plaza Mayor, 1
49708 Villanueva de Campeán (Zamora)
☎ :+34 980 560 055 - Fax: +34 980 560 055
@: info@tierradelvino.net
www.tierradelvino.net

LOCATION:

In the southeast part of Zamora, on the Duero river banks. This region comprises 46 municipal districts in the province Zamora and 10 in neighbouring Salamanca. Average altitude is 750 meters.

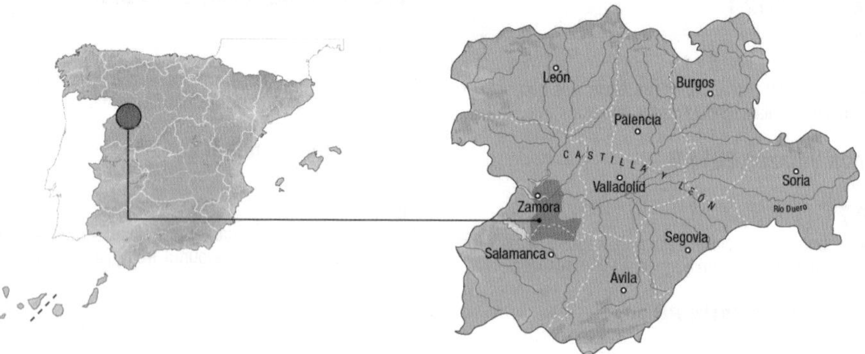

GRAPE VARIETIES:

WHITE: Malvasía, Moscatel de grano menudo and Verdejo (preferential); Albillo, Palomino and Godello (authorized).
RED: Tempranillo (main), Cabernet Sauvignon and Garnacha.

FIGURES:

Vineyard surface: 665.33 – **Wine-Growers:** 194 – **Wineries:** 10 – **2014 Harvest rating:** N/A – **Production 14:** 623,544 litres – **Market percentages:** 65.95% National - 34.05% International.

SOIL:

The character of the territory derives from the river Duero tributaries, so it is predominantly alluvial and clay in the lower strata that might not allow great drainage, though they vary a lot depending on the altitude. There are also some sandy patches on the plain land and stony ones on the hill side.

CLIMATE:

Extreme temperatures as correspond to a dry continental pattern, with very hot summers and cold winters. It does not rain much and average annual rainfall hardly reaches 400 mm.

VINTAGE RATING

PEÑÍNGUIDE

2010	2011	2012	2013	2014
N/A	N/A	VERY GOOD	VERY GOOD	GOOD

BODEGA GUILLERMO FREIRE

Cl. Pozo, 33
49150 Moraleja del Vino (Zamora)
☎: +34 980 571 188

Jarreño 2014 T Roble

84

BODEGAS EL SOTO

Ctra. de Circunvalación, s/n
49708 Villanueva de Campeán (Zamora)
☎: +34 980 560 330
Fax: +34 980 560 330
info@bodegaselsoto.com
www.bodegaselsoto.com

Proclama 2014 B

89

Colour: bright straw. Nose: white flowers, fresh fruit, fragrant herbs, expressive. Palate: flavourful, fruity, good acidity.

Proclama Tempranillo 2014 T

89

Colour: cherry, purple rim. Nose: fresh fruit, red berry notes, floral. Palate: flavourful, fruity, good acidity.

BODEGAS TESO BLANCO

Larga, 12
49709 Cabañas de Sayago (Zamora)
☎: +34 980 577 820
Fax: +34 980 560 055
tesoblanco@terra.es

Brochero 2014 B

85

Brochero Finca Monte Concejo 2008 T

89

Colour: light cherry. Nose: fine reductive notes, aged wood nuances, toasty. Palate: spicy, toasty, flavourful.

BODEGAS Y VIÑEDOS SEÑORIO DE BOCOS

Camino La Canaleja, s/n
47317 Bocos de Duero (Valladolid)
☎: +34 983 880 988
Fax: +34 983 880 988
bodegas@senoriodebocos.com
www.bocos.eu

Señorio de Bocos 2014 B

88

Colour: straw. Nose: medium intensity, ripe fruit, floral. Palate: correct, easy to drink.

Señorio de Bocos 2014 RD

89

Colour: coppery red. Nose: elegant, red berry notes, floral, fragrant herbs. Palate: light-bodied, flavourful, good acidity, long, spicy.

MALANDRÍN WINES

Miguel S. Herrador, 3
47014 Valladolid (Valladolid)
☎: +34 644 172 122
info@malandrinwines.com
www.malandrinwines.com

Malandrín Tempranillo 2010 T

tempranillo

89

Colour: cherry, garnet rim. Nose: fine reductive notes, wet leather, aged wood nuances, ripe fruit. Palate: spicy, long, toasty.

Malandrín Verdejo 2014 B

verdejo, godello, malvasía, albillo

87

Colour: straw. Nose: medium intensity, ripe fruit, floral, candied fruit. Palate: correct, easy to drink.

MICROBODEGA DEL ALUMBRO

Del Prado, 14
49719 Villamor de los Escuderos (Zamora)
☎: +34 980 609 047
info@microbodega.es
microbodegabio.blogspot.com.es

Alumbro 2013 B

godello, verdejo, albillo

91

Colour: bright straw. Nose: white flowers, fine lees, dried herbs, mineral. Palate: flavourful, fruity, good acidity, round.

Alumbro 2013 T

tempranillo, cabernet sauvignon

90

Colour: bright cherry. Nose: ripe fruit, sweet spices, creamy oak, expressive. Palate: flavourful, fruity, round tannins.

Alumbro 2014 Clarete

tempranillo, palomino

88

Colour: bright cherry. Nose: raspberry, floral, fragrant herbs. Palate: flavourful, good acidity.

TESO LA ENCINA BODEGA Y VIÑEDOS

Teso la Encina
49719 Villamor de los Escuderos
(Zamora)
☎: +34 639 824 200
bodega@tesolaencina.es
www.tesolaencina.es

Chalán 2013 T
86

Huguichu 2014 B
87

Colour: bright straw. Nose: dried herbs, faded flowers, slightly evolved. Palate: ripe fruit, thin.

Sr. Polo 2013 B
88

Colour: bright straw. Nose: white flowers, fine lees, dried herbs, mineral. Palate: flavourful, fruity, good acidity, round.

VIÑA VER

Poal, 6
49700 Corrales del Vino (Zamora)
☎: +34 923 361 345
ramiro@vinaver.es
www.vinaver.es

Viñaver 2013 T
tempranillo

87

Colour: bright cherry. Nose: ripe fruit, sweet spices, creamy oak, expressive. Palate: flavourful, fruity, toasty, round tannins.

VIÑAS DEL CÉNIT

Ctra. de Circunvalación, s/n
49708 Villanueva de Campeán
(Zamora)
☎: +34 980 569 346
aalberca@avanteselecta.com
www.vinasdelcenit.com

Cenit 2011 T
93

Colour: cherry, garnet rim. Nose: smoky, spicy, fruit liqueur notes. Palate: flavourful, smoky aftertaste, ripe fruit.

Via Cenit 2013 T
91

Colour: cherry, purple rim. Nose: ripe fruit, woody. Palate: flavourful, spicy, powerful.

DO. TORO

CONSEJO REGULADOR

De la Concepción, 3. Palacio de los Condes de Requena
49800 Toro (Zamora)
☎:+34 980 690 335 - Fax: +34 980 693 201
@: consejo@dotoro.es
www.dotoro.es

LOCATION:

Comprising 12 municipal districts of the province of Zamora (Argujillo, Boveda de Toro, Morales de Toro, El Pego, Peleagonzalo, El Piñero, San Miguel de la Ribera, Sanzoles, Toro, Valdefinjas, Venialbo and Villanueva del Puente) and three in the province of Valladolid (San Román de la Hornija, Villafranca de Duero and the vineyards of Villaester de Arriba and Villaester de Abajo in the municipal district of Pedrosa del Rey), which practically corresponds to the agricultural region of Bajo Duero. The production area is to the south of the course of the Duero, which crosses the region from east to west.

GRAPE VARIETIES:

WHITE: Malvasía and Verdejo.
RED: Tinta de Toro (majority) and Garnacha.

FIGURES:

Vineyard surface: 5,800 – **Wine-Growers:** 1,200 – **Wineries:** 57 – **2014 Harvest rating:** Very Good – **Production 14:** 8,606,250 litres – **Market percentages:** 70% National - 30% International.

SOIL:

The geography of the DO is characterised by a gently-undulating terrain. The vineyards are situated at an altitude of 620 m to 750 m and the soil is mainly brownish-grey limestone. However, the stony alluvial soil is better.

CLIMATE:

Extreme continental, with Atlantic influences and quite arid, with an average annual rainfall of between 350 mm and 400 mm. The winters are harsh (which means extremely low temperatures and long periods of frosts) and the summers short, although not excessively hot, with significant contrasts in day-night temperatures.

VINTAGE RATING

PEÑÍNGUIDE

2010	2011	2012	2013	2014
VERY GOOD	GOOD	VERY GOOD	VERY GOOD	GOOD

ALVAR DE DIOS HERNANDEZ

Zamora Nº8
47154 El Pego (Zamora)
eldelarecella@gmail.com

Aciano 2013 T
tinta de Toro

90

Colour: light cherry. Nose: fruit liqueur notes, fragrant herbs, spicy. Palate: spicy, long, toasty.

Tío Uco 2014 T
tinta de Toro

91

Colour: cherry, purple rim. Nose: powerfull, ripe fruit, spicy, balsamic herbs. Palate: powerful, fruity, unctuous.

BODEGA BURDIGALA

Calle Nueva, 12
49800 La Seca (Valladolid)
☎: +34 980 082 027
Fax: +34 983 034 040
bodega@burdigala.es
www.burdigala.es

Campesino 2013 T
100% tinta de Toro

90

Colour: deep cherry, purple rim. Nose: creamy oak, toasty, ripe fruit, balsamic herbs. Palate: balanced, spicy, long.

Campo Alegre 2012 TC
100% tinta de Toro

90

Colour: cherry, garnet rim. Nose: mineral, expressive, spicy. Palate: flavourful, ripe fruit, long, good acidity, balanced.

Campo Eliseo 2011 T
100% tinta de Toro

93

Colour: cherry, garnet rim. Nose: red berry notes, ripe fruit, spicy, creamy oak, complex. Palate: flavourful, toasty, round tannins.

BODEGA CAMPIÑA

Ctra. Toro-Veniablo, Km. 6,9
49800 Valdefinjas (Zamora)
☎: +34 980 568 125
Fax: +34 980 059 965
www.bodegapagodecubas.com

Campiña 2010 TC
100% tinta de Toro

85

Campiña 2014 T
100% tinta de Toro

85

BODEGA CUATROMIL CEPAS

Rafael Alonso nº 21
49154 El Pego (Zamora)
☎: +34 670 095 149
cuatromilcepas@gmail.com
www.discolovino.com

Cinco de Copas 2013 T Roble
tinta de Toro

88

Colour: deep cherry. Nose: creamy oak, toasty, ripe fruit, balsamic herbs. Palate: balanced, spicy, long.

Díscolo 2011 T
tinta de Toro

90

Colour: cherry, garnet rim. Nose: red berry notes, ripe fruit, spicy, creamy oak, complex. Palate: flavourful, toasty, balanced.

BODEGA CYAN

Ctra. Valdefinjas - Venialbo, Km. 9,2,
Finca La Calera
49800 Toro (Zamora)
☎: +34 980 568 029
cyan@matarromera.es
www.bodegacyan.es

Cyan 2011 TC
100% tinta de Toro

87

Colour: cherry, garnet rim. Nose: ripe fruit, spicy, creamy oak. Palate: flavourful, toasty.

Cyan 2012 T Roble
100% tinta de Toro

87

Colour: bright cherry. Nose: ripe fruit, sweet spices, creamy oak. Palate: flavourful, fruity, toasty.

Selección Personal Carlos Moro Cyan 2004 T
100% tinta de Toro

89

Colour: pale ruby, brick rim edge. Nose: elegant, spicy, fine reductive notes, tobacco. Palate: spicy, fine tannins, elegant, long.

BODEGA FLORENCIO SALGADO NARROS

Ctra. Toro - Salamanca, Km. 3,20
49800 Toro (Zamora)
☎: +34 649 761 324
bodegasalgadonarros@yahoo.com

Pico Royo 2009 T

84

BODEGA LIBERALIA ENOLÓGICA

Camino del Palo, s/n
49800 Toro (Zamora)
☎: +34 980 692 571
Fax: +34 980 692 571
liberalia@liberalia.es
www.liberalia.es

Liber 2007 TGR

92

Colour: cherry, garnet rim. Nose: balanced, complex, ripe fruit, spicy, fine reductive notes. Palate: good structure, flavourful, round tannins, balanced.

Liberalia Cabeza de Cuba 2007 TC

90

Colour: cherry, garnet rim. Nose: fine reductive notes, ripe fruit, expressive, balanced. Palate: spicy, long, toasty.

Liberalia Cero 2014 T

90

Colour: bright cherry. Nose: ripe fruit, sweet spices, creamy oak, expressive. Palate: flavourful, fruity, toasty, round tannins.

Liberalia Cinco 2007 TR

91

Colour: cherry, garnet rim. Nose: fine reductive notes, wet leather, aged wood nuances. Palate: spicy, long, toasty.

Liberalia Cuatro 2010 TC

88

Colour: cherry, garnet rim. Nose: ripe fruit, spicy, creamy oak. Palate: flavourful, toasty.

Liberalia Dos 2014 T

88

Colour: cherry, purple rim. Nose: fresh fruit, red berry notes, floral, creamy oak. Palate: flavourful, fruity, good acidity.

Liberalia Tres 2013 T Roble

88

Colour: cherry, purple rim. Nose: ripe fruit, woody, smoky, toasty. Palate: flavourful, spicy, powerful.

BODEGA MARXUACH

Autovía Tordesilla - Zamora, salida 438
Toro (Zamora)
☎: +34 923 541 050
Fax: +34 923 568 425
montelareina@yahoo.es

Marxuach 2008 TC
100% tinta de Toro

86

Marxuach 2009 TR
100% tinta de Toro

88

Colour: cherry, garnet rim. Nose: ripe fruit, wild herbs, spicy, balsamic herbs. Palate: flavourful, long, balsamic.

BODEGA NUMANTHIA

Real s/n
49882 Valdefinjas (Zamora)
☎: +34 980 699 147
mlacombe@moet-hennessy.com
www.numanthia.com

PODIUM

Numanthia 2012 T
tinta de Toro

96

Colour: cherry, garnet rim. Nose: creamy oak, red berry notes, fresh fruit, balanced. Palate: flavourful, spicy, elegant.

PODIUM

Termanthia 2012 T
tinta de Toro

97

Colour: cherry, garnet rim. Nose: mineral, expressive, spicy. Palate: flavourful, ripe fruit, long, good acidity, balanced.

BODEGA PAGO DE CUBAS

Ctra. Toro Valdefinjas, Km. 6,9
49800 Valdefinjas (Zamora)
☎: +34 980 568 125
Fax: +34 980 059 965
www.bodegapagodecubas.com

Asterisco 2013 TC
100% tinta de Toro

85

Incrédulo 2009 T
100% tinta de Toro

90

Colour: cherry, garnet rim. Nose: red berry notes, ripe fruit, spicy, creamy oak, complex. Palate: flavourful, toasty, harsh oak tannins.

Incrédulo 2010 T
100% tinta de Toro

89

Colour: cherry, garnet rim. Nose: ripe fruit, spicy, creamy oak, complex. Palate: flavourful, toasty.

BODEGA TOROENO

Judería, 25
49800 Toro (Zamora)
☎: +34 980 698 172
jpguyjpg@infonie.fr
www.toroeno.com

Eponimo 2011 TC
100% tempranillo

91

Colour: cherry, garnet rim. Nose: balanced, complex, ripe fruit, spicy, toasty. Palate: good structure, flavourful, round tannins, balanced.

Eponimo 2012 TC
100% tempranillo

93

Colour: cherry, garnet rim. Nose: mineral, expressive, spicy. Palate: flavourful, ripe fruit, long, good acidity, balanced.

BODEGA VALDIGAL

Capuchinos, 6
49800 Toro (Zamora)
☎: +34 629 113 992
valdigal@valdigal.com
www.valdigal.com

Valdigal 2011 T
100% tinta de Toro

89

Colour: very deep cherry, garnet rim. Nose: spicy, ripe fruit, balanced. Palate: long, balanced.

BODEGA VALMARTIN

Moclín, 37
49716 Argujillo (Zamora)
☎: +34 627 737 050
bypval@gmail.com

Martin Krachler 2013 T
tinta de Toro

92

Colour: cherry, purple rim. Nose: ripe fruit, woody, earthy notes. Palate: flavourful, spicy, powerful.

Theson 2012 TC
tinta de Toro

92

Colour: cherry, garnet rim. Nose: balanced, complex, ripe fruit, spicy, fine reductive notes. Palate: good structure, flavourful, round tannins, balanced.

BODEGAS COPABOCA

Autovía A-62, Salida 148
47100 Tordesillas (Valladolid)
☎: +34 983 486 010
club@copaboca.com
www.copaboca.com

Finca Feroes 2014 T
100% tinta de Toro

85

Gorgorito 2014 T
100% tinta de Toro

86

BODEGAS COVITORO

Ctra. de Tordesillas, 13
49800 Toro (Zamora)
☎: +34 980 690 347
Fax: +34 980 690 143
covitoro@covitoro.com
www.covitoro.com

Arco del Reloj 2010 T
100% tinta de Toro

92

Colour: cherry, garnet rim. Nose: red berry notes, ripe fruit, spicy, creamy oak, complex. Palate: flavourful, toasty, round tannins, elegant.

Barón de la Villa 2012 TC
100% tinta de Toro

88

Colour: cherry, purple rim. Nose: ripe fruit, woody, roasted coffee. Palate: flavourful, spicy, powerful.

Barón de la Villa 2014 T
100% tinta de Toro

85

Cañus Verus Viñas Viejas 2010 T
100% tinta de Toro

87

Colour: cherry, garnet rim. Nose: fine reductive notes, wet leather, aged wood nuances. Palate: spicy, long, toasty.

Cermeño 2014 RD
100% tinta de Toro

88

Colour: rose, purple rim. Nose: red berry notes, floral, expressive. Palate: powerful, fruity, fresh, balanced.

Cermeño Malvasia 2014 B
95% malvasía, 5% verdejo

86

Cermeño Vendimia Seleccionada 2014 T
100% tinta de Toro

86

Cien 2014 RD
100% tinta de Toro

86

Cien Malvasía 2014 B
95% malvasía, 5% verdejo

86

Cien Roble 2013 T
100% tinta de Toro

88

Colour: bright cherry. Nose: ripe fruit, sweet spices, creamy oak, expressive. Palate: flavourful, fruity, round tannins.

Gran Cermeño 2011 TC
100% tinta de Toro

90

Colour: cherry, garnet rim. Nose: ripe fruit, spicy, creamy oak. Palate: flavourful, toasty, round tannins.

Gran Cermeño 2012 TC
100% tinta de Toro

91

Colour: cherry, garnet rim. Nose: creamy oak, balanced, ripe fruit. Palate: flavourful, spicy, good acidity.

Marqués de la Villa 2014 T
100% tinta de Toro

87

Colour: deep cherry, purple rim. Nose: powerfull, ripe fruit, balanced. Palate: flavourful, fruity, balanced.

Vizconde de la Villa 2011 TC
100% tinta de Toro

87

Colour: cherry, garnet rim. Nose: smoky, spicy, ripe fruit. Palate: flavourful, smoky aftertaste, ripe fruit.

Vizconde de la Villa 2012 T Roble
100% tinta de Toro

88

Colour: bright cherry. Nose: ripe fruit, sweet spices, creamy oak, expressive. Palate: flavourful, fruity, toasty, round tannins.

BODEGAS FARIÑA

Camino del Palo, s/n
49800 Toro (Zamora)
☎: +34 980 577 673
Fax: +34 980 577 720
comercial@bodegasfarina.com
www.bodegasfarina.com

Colegiata 2014 RD
100% tinta de Toro

86

Colegiata 2014 T
100% tinta de Toro

88

Colour: cherry, purple rim. Nose: expressive, fresh fruit, red berry notes, floral. Palate: flavourful, fruity, good acidity.

Colegiata Malvasía 2014 B
100% malvasía

85

Dama de Toro 2008 TR
100% tinta de Toro

89

Colour: cherry, garnet rim. Nose: ripe fruit, wild herbs, earthy notes, spicy, balsamic herbs. Palate: balanced, flavourful, long, balsamic.

Gran Colegiata Campus 2010 TC
100% tinta de Toro

93

Colour: cherry, garnet rim. Nose: creamy oak, red berry notes, fresh fruit, balanced. Palate: flavourful, spicy, elegant.

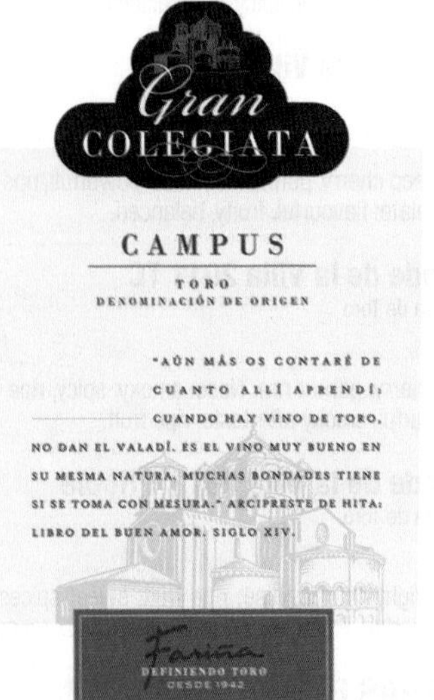

Gran Colegiata Roble Francés 2011 TC
100% tinta de Toro

90

Colour: cherry, garnet rim. Nose: ripe fruit, spicy, creamy oak. Palate: flavourful, toasty.

Gran Colegiata Vino de Lágrima 2013 T Barrica
100% tinta de Toro

90

Colour: bright cherry. Nose: ripe fruit, sweet spices, creamy oak, expressive. Palate: flavourful, fruity, toasty.

BODEGAS FRANCISCO CASAS

Avda. de Los Comuneros, 67
49810 Morales de Toro (Zamora)
☎: +34 980 698 032
Fax: +34 980 698 506
toro@bodegascasas.com
www.bodegascasas.com

Camparrón 2009 TR
tinta de Toro

89

Colour: bright cherry. Nose: ripe fruit, sweet spices, creamy oak, expressive. Palate: flavourful, fruity, toasty, round tannins.

Camparrón 2012 TC
tinta de Toro

86

Camparrón Novum 2014 T
tinta de Toro

88

Colour: bright cherry, purple rim. Nose: balanced, fruit expression, floral. Palate: ripe fruit, correct, good acidity.

Camparrón Seleccion 2012 T
tinta de Toro

87

Colour: very deep cherry, purple rim. Nose: creamy oak, smoky, ripe fruit. Palate: fruity, easy to drink.

Caray 2010 T Barrica
tinta de Toro

89

Colour: cherry, garnet rim. Nose: ripe fruit, wild herbs, spicy, balsamic herbs. Palate: balanced, flavourful, long, balsamic.

Caray 2011 T Barrica
tinta de Toro

88

Colour: bright cherry. Nose: ripe fruit, sweet spices, creamy oak, expressive. Palate: flavourful, fruity, round tannins.

Caray 2014 T Barrica
tinta de Toro

86

Los Bayones Selección D'Oro 2011 T Barrica
tinta de Toro

88

Colour: cherry, garnet rim. Nose: ripe fruit, wild herbs, spicy, balsamic herbs. Palate: balanced, flavourful, long, balsamic.

BODEGAS FRONTAURA

Ctra. Pesquera de Duero a Renedo, s/n
47315 Pesquera de Duero (Valladolid)
☎: +34 983 880 488
Fax: +34 983 870 065
info@bodegasfrontaura.com
www.bodegasfrontaura.com

Aponte 2006 T
100% tinta de Toro

93

Colour: dark-red cherry. Nose: elegant, spicy, fine reductive notes, tobacco, ripe fruit. Palate: spicy, fine tannins, elegant, long.

Dominio de Valdelacasa 2009 T Roble
100% tempranillo

91

Colour: cherry, garnet rim. Nose: expressive, spicy, scrubland. Palate: flavourful, ripe fruit, long, good acidity, balanced.

Frontaura 2006 TC
100% tinta de Toro

88

Colour: cherry, garnet rim. Nose: ripe fruit, wild herbs, earthy notes, fine reductive notes. Palate: balanced, flavourful, long.

Frontaura 2006 TR
100% tinta de Toro

92

Colour: light cherry. Nose: fine reductive notes, aged wood nuances, toasty. Palate: spicy, toasty, flavourful.

BODEGAS GIL LUNA

Ctra. Toro - Salamanca, Km. 2
49800 Toro (Zamora)
☎: +34 980 698 509
Fax: +34 980 698 294
info@giluna.es
www.giluna.es

Gil Luna 2009 T
100% tinta de Toro

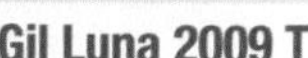

89

Colour: cherry, garnet rim. Nose: old leather, spicy, characterful, dried herbs. Palate: balanced, round tannins, good structure.

Sin Complejos 2013 T
100% tinta de Toro

89

Colour: bright cherry. Nose: ripe fruit, sweet spices, creamy oak, expressive. Palate: flavourful, fruity, toasty, round tannins.

Tres Lunas 2012 T
100% tinta de Toro

85

Tres Lunas Verdejo 2014 B
100% verdejo

86

BODEGAS ITURRIA

Avda. Torrecilla De La Abadesa 2,2E
47100 Tordesillas (Valladolid)
☎: +34 600 523 070
contact@bodegas-iturria.com
www.bodegas-iturria.com

Tinto Iturria 2010 T
90% tinta de Toro, 10% garnacha

89

Colour: dark-red cherry. Nose: fruit preserve, sweet spices, dried herbs. Palate: correct, balanced, long.

Valdosan 2010 T
tinta de Toro

88

Colour: cherry, garnet rim. Nose: roasted coffee, smoky, spicy, ripe fruit. Palate: flavourful, smoky aftertaste, ripe fruit.

BODEGAS LIBA Y DELEITE

Turina, 11
47006 Valladolid (Valladolid)
☎: +34 629 450 436
acontia@acontia.es
www.acontia.es

Acontia 12 2012 TC
85% tinta de Toro, 15% garnacha

88

Colour: bright cherry. Nose: ripe fruit, sweet spices, warm. Palate: flavourful, fruity, toasty, sweet tannins.

Acontia 6 2013 T
85% tinta de Toro, 15% garnacha

88

Colour: deep cherry, purple rim. Nose: creamy oak, toasty, ripe fruit, balsamic herbs. Palate: balanced, spicy, long.

Acontia Verdejo 100% 2014 B
100% verdejo

85

BODEGAS MATARREDONDA

Ctra. Valdefinjas km 2,5
49800 Toro (Zamora)
☎: +34 687 965 280
libranza@vinolibranza.com
www.matarredonda.es

Juan Rojo 2010 T
100% tinta de Toro

89

Colour: cherry, garnet rim. Nose: ripe fruit, wild herbs, earthy notes, spicy, balsamic herbs. Palate: flavourful, long, balsamic.

Libranza 2010 T
100% tinta de Toro

90

Colour: cherry, garnet rim. Nose: ripe fruit, wild herbs, earthy notes, spicy, balsamic herbs. Palate: balanced, flavourful, long, balsamic.

Valdefama 2013 T
100% tinta de Toro

86

BODEGAS ORDÓÑEZ

Julio Romero de Torres, 12
29700 Vélez- Málaga (Málaga)
☎: +34 952 504 706
Fax: +34 951 284 796
info@jorgeordonez.es
www.grupojorgeordonez.com

Tritón Tinta Toro 2014 T
100% tinta de Toro

91

Colour: cherry, garnet rim. Nose: smoky, spicy, ripe fruit. Palate: flavourful, smoky aftertaste, ripe fruit.

Vatan 2012 T
100% tinta de Toro

93

Colour: cherry, garnet rim. Nose: wet leather, aged wood nuances, ripe fruit, mineral. Palate: spicy, long, toasty.

BODEGAS REJADORADA S.L.

Rejadorada, 11
49800 Toro (Zamora)
☎: +34 980 693 089
Fax: +34 980 693 089
rejadorada@rejadorada.com
www.rejadorada.com

Bravo de Rejadorada 2009 T
100% tinta de Toro

92

Colour: cherry, garnet rim. Nose: balanced, complex, ripe fruit, spicy, characterful, creamy oak. Palate: good structure, flavourful, round tannins.

Novellum de Rejadorada 2011 TC
100% tinta de Toro

87

Colour: cherry, garnet rim. Nose: fine reductive notes, ripe fruit spicy. Palate: spicy, long, toasty.

Rejadorada Roble 2013 T Roble
100% tinta de Toro

87

Colour: bright cherry, purple rim. Nose: balanced, red berry notes, ripe fruit, sweet spices. Palate: ripe fruit, balanced, easy to drink.

BODEGAS SIETECERROS

Finca Villaester N-122, km. 409
47540 Villaester de Arriba -
Pedrosa del Rey (Valladolid)
☎: +34 983 784 083
Fax: +34 983 784 142
sietecerros@bodegasietecerros.com
www.bodegasietecerros.com

Quebrantarrejas 2014 T
100% tinta de Toro

85

Valdelazarza 2009 TR
100% tinta de Toro

87

Colour: cherry, garnet rim. Nose: red berry notes, ripe fruit, spicy, creamy oak, complex. Palate: flavourful, toasty.

Valdelazarza 2011 TC
100% tinta de Toro

82

Valdelazarza 2012 T Roble
100% tinta de Toro

83

BODEGAS SOBREÑO

Ctra. N-122, Km. 423
49800 Toro (Zamora)
☎: +34 980 693 417
Fax: +34 980 693 416
sobreno@sobreno.com
www.sobreno.com

Finca Sobreño 2013 T Roble
100% tempranillo

84

Finca Sobreño Crianza 2012 TC

100% tempranillo

84

Colour: cherry, garnet rim. Nose: overripe fruit, spicy, creamy oak. Palate: powerful, flavourful.

Finca Sobreño Ecológico 2013 T

100% tempranillo

83

Finca Sobreño Ildefonso 2010 T

100% tempranillo

90

Colour: cherry, garnet rim. Nose: fine reductive notes, ripe fruit, spicy. Palate: spicy, long, toasty, flavourful, round tannins.

Finca Sobreño Selección Especial 2010 TR

100% tempranillo

89

Colour: deep cherry, garnet rim. Nose: sweet spices, dried herbs, balanced. Palate: flavourful, fruity, round tannins.

Finca Sobreño Selección Especial 2011 T

100% tempranillo

90

Colour: cherry, garnet rim. Nose: ripe fruit, wild herbs, earthy notes, spicy, balsamic herbs. Palate: balanced, flavourful, long, balsamic.

BODEGAS TORREDUERO

Pol. Ind. Toro Norte s/n
49800 Toro (Zamora)
☎: +34 941 454 050
Fax: +34 941 454 529
bodega@bodegasriojanas.com
www.bodegasriojanas.com

Marqués de Peñamonte 2009 TR

100% tinta de Toro

87

Colour: cherry, garnet rim. Nose: ripe fruit, old leather, tobacco. Palate: correct, flavourful, spicy.

Marqués de Peñamonte Colección Privada 2011 T

100% tinta de Toro

90

Colour: deep cherry, garnet rim. Nose: balanced, cocoa bean, sweet spices, creamy oak, ripe fruit. Palate: good structure, flavourful, fruity, full.

Peñamonte 2012 TC

100% tinta de Toro

87

Colour: cherry, garnet rim. Nose: spicy, ripe fruit, creamy oak, tobacco. Palate: flavourful, easy to drink.

Peñamonte 2013 T Barrica

100% tinta de Toro

86

Peñamonte 2014 RD

85% tinta de Toro, 15% garnacha

84

Peñamonte 2014 T

100% tinta de Toro

83

Peñamonte Verdejo 2014 B

100% verdejo

84

BODEGAS VEGA SAUCO

Avda. Comuneros, 108
49810 Morales de Toro (Zamora)
☎: +34 980 698 294
Fax: +34 980 698 294
vegasauco@vegasauco.com
www.vegasauco.es

Adoremus 2009 TR

88

Colour: light cherry. Nose: fine reductive notes, aged wood nuances, toasty. Palate: spicy, toasty, flavourful.

Adoremus 1999 TGR

89

Colour: pale ruby, brick rim edge. Nose: spicy, fine reductive notes, wet leather, aged wood nuances, fruit liqueur notes. Palate: spicy, fine tannins, balanced.

Adoremus 2006 TGR

86

Vega Saúco El Beybi 2013 T Roble

100% tinta de Toro

86

Vega Saúco Selección 2010 T

100% tinta de Toro

84

Wences 2004 T

87

Colour: cherry, garnet rim. Nose: ripe fruit, old leather, tobacco. Palate: correct, flavourful, spicy.

BODEGAS VELASCO E HIJO

Corredera, 23
49800 Toro (Zamora)
☎: +34 980 692 455
admon@bodegasvelascoehijos.com
www.bodegasvelascoehijos.com

Garabitas Premium Vendimia Seleccionada 2009 T

tinta de Toro

86

Peña Rejas Ecológico 2014 T

tinta de Toro

89

Colour: cherry, purple rim. Nose: expressive, fresh fruit, red berry notes, floral. Palate: flavourful, fruity, good acidity.

BODEGAS VETUS

Ctra. Toro a Salamanca, Km. 9,5
49800 Toro (Zamora)
☎: +34 945 609 086
Fax: +34 980 056 012
vetus@bodegasvetus.com
www.bodegasvetus.com

PODIUM

Celsus 2013 T

100% tinta de Toro

95

Colour: cherry, garnet rim. Nose: balanced, complex, ripe fruit, spicy, fine reductive notes. Palate: good structure, flavourful, round tannins, balanced.

Flor de Vetus 2013 T

100% tinta de Toro

91

Colour: bright cherry. Nose: ripe fruit, sweet spices, creamy oak, expressive. Palate: flavourful, fruity, round tannins.

BODEGAS VIORE

Miguel Hernández, 31
47490 Rueda (Valladolid)
☎: +34 941 454 050
Fax: +34 941 454 529
bodega@bodegasriojanas.com
www.bodegasriojanas.com

Viore 2012 TC

100% tinta de Toro

90

Colour: cherry, garnet rim. Nose: creamy oak, red berry notes, fresh fruit, balanced. Palate: flavourful, spicy, elegant.

Viore 2013 T Barrica

100% tinta de Toro

87

Colour: bright cherry. Nose: ripe fruit, sweet spices, creamy oak, expressive. Palate: flavourful, fruity, toasty, round tannins.

Viore 2014 B

100% verdejo

86

Viore 2014 RD

85% tempranillo, 15% garnacha

86

Viore 2014 T

100% tinta de Toro

86

BODEGAS Y VIÑEDOS ANZIL

Ctra. Toro a Villabuena del Puente, km. 9,400
49800 Toro (Zamora)
☎: +34 915 006 000
Fax: +34 915 006 006
comunicacion@habarcelo.es
www.bodegasanzil.es

Finca Anzil 2012 T

100% tinta de Toro

90

Colour: cherry, garnet rim. Nose: red berry notes, ripe fruit, spicy, creamy oak, complex. Palate: flavourful, toasty.

Viña Mayor Vendimia Seleccionada 2013 T
100% tinta de Toro

88

Colour: bright cherry. Nose: ripe fruit, sweet spices, creamy oak, lactic notes. Palate: flavourful, fruity, round tannins.

BODEGAS Y VIÑEDOS MAURODOS

Ctra. N-122, Km. 411 - Villaester
47112 Pedrosa del Rey (Valladolid)
☎: +34 983 784 118
Fax: +34 983 784 018
comunicacion@bodegasmauro.com
www.bodegasanroman.com

Prima 2013 T
90% tinta de Toro, 10% garnacha

87

Colour: bright cherry. Nose: ripe fruit, sweet spices, creamy oak. Palate: flavourful, fruity, toasty.

San Román 2012 T
100% tinta de Toro

93

Colour: bright cherry. Nose: sweet spices, creamy oak, expressive, ripe fruit, fruit preserve. Palate: flavourful, fruity, toasty, round tannins.

BODEGAS Y VIÑEDOS MAYOR DE CASTILLA

Ctra. Comarcal 610, km. 26,7
47491 La Seca (Valladolid)
☎: +34 667 750 773
adela@hugad.es
www.garciacarrion.es

Mayor de Castilla 2012 T Roble
85

BODEGAS Y VIÑEDOS PINTIA

Ctra. de Morales, s/n
47530 San Román de Hornija (Valladolid)
☎: +34 983 680 147
Fax: +34 983 680 263
cupos@vega-sicilia.com
www.bodegaspintia.com

Pintia 2012 T
100% tinta de Toro

94

Colour: bright cherry. Nose: sweet spices, creamy oak, expressive, ripe fruit, red berry notes. Palate: flavourful, fruity, toasty, round tannins.

BODEGUEROS QUINTA ESENCIA

Eras, 37
47520 Castronuño (Valladolid)
☎: +34 605 887 100
Fax: +34 983 866 391
ferrin@bodeguerosquintaesencia.com
www.bodeguerosquintaesencia.com

Sofros 2012 T
100% tinta de Toro

92

Colour: cherry, garnet rim. Nose: ripe fruit, wild herbs, earthy notes, spicy, balsamic herbs. Palate: balanced, flavourful, long, balsamic.

BOUTIQUE WINES

Jacinto Benavente 2 – Bajo Sur
47195 Arroyo de la Encomienda (Valladolid)
☎: +34 639 250 225
Fax: +34 983 211 407
info@contaderowine.com
www.contaderowine.com

Campiña Viñas Centenarias 2009 T
100% tinta de Toro

88

Colour: very deep cherry. Nose: ripe fruit, woody, roasted coffee. Palate: flavourful, spicy, powerful.

Contadero 2014 T
100% tinta de Toro

85

Contadero Viñas Centenarias 2009 T
100% tinta de Toro

88

Colour: cherry, garnet rim. Nose: ripe fruit, spicy, creamy oak, complex. Palate: flavourful, toasty, round tannins.

CAÑADA DEL PINO

Pol. Ind. 6 - Parcela 83
49810 Morales de Toro (Zamora)
☎: +34 676 701 918
Fax: +34 980 698 318
fincayerro@gmail.com

Finca Yerro 2010 T Roble
89

Colour: cherry, garnet rim. Nose: creamy oak, red berry notes, fresh fruit, balanced. Palate: flavourful, spicy, elegant.

CARMEN RODRÍGUEZ MÉNDEZ

Ctra. Salamanca, ZA 605, Km. 1,5
49800 Toro (Zamora)
☎: +34 980 568 005
info@carodorum.com
www.carodorum.com

Carodorum 2012 TC
tinta de Toro

90

Colour: deep cherry, garnet rim. Nose: ripe fruit, varietal, expressive, spicy. Palate: good structure, full, balanced, round tannins.

Carodorum Issos 2012 TC
tinta de Toro

90

Colour: cherry, garnet rim. Nose: ripe fruit, spicy, creamy oak, complex. Palate: flavourful, toasty.

Carodorum Selección Especial 2012 TC
tinta de Toro

89

Colour: very deep cherry. Nose: fruit preserve, spicy, toasty, balsamic herbs, fine reductive notes. Palate: powerful, flavourful.

Carodorum Vendimia Seleccionada 2013 T Roble
tinta de Toro

87

Colour: deep cherry, purple rim. Nose: creamy oak, toasty, ripe fruit, balsamic herbs. Palate: balanced, spicy, long.

COMPAÑÍA DE VINOS TELMO RODRÍGUEZ

El Monte
01308 Lanciego (Álava)
☎: +34 945 628 315
Fax: +34 945 628 314
contact@telmorodriguez.com
www.telmorodriguez.com

Dehesa Gago 2014 T
tinta de Toro

90

Colour: cherry, purple rim. Nose: expressive, fresh fruit, red berry notes, floral. Palate: flavourful, fruity, good acidity.

Gago 2012 T
tinta de Toro

92

Colour: bright cherry. Nose: sweet spices, creamy oak, ripe fruit, red berry notes. Palate: flavourful, fruity, toasty, round tannins.

PODIUM

Pago La Jara 2011 T
tinta de Toro

95

Colour: cherry, garnet rim. Nose: creamy oak, red berry notes, fresh fruit, balanced. Palate: flavourful, spicy, elegant.

CORAL DUERO

Ascensión, s/n
49154 El Pego (Zamora)
☎: +34 980 606 333
Fax: +34 980 606 391
rompesedas@rompesedas.com
www.rompesedas.com

Rompesedas 2008 T Barrica
100% tinta de Toro

90

Colour: cherry, garnet rim. Nose: roasted coffee, smoky, spicy, ripe fruit. Palate: flavourful, smoky aftertaste, ripe fruit.

Rompesedas 2013 T
100% tinta de Toro

91

Colour: bright cherry. Nose: ripe fruit, sweet spices, expressive, balanced. Palate: flavourful, fruity, round tannins.

DIVINA PROPORCIÓN

Camino del Cristo s/n
49800 Toro (Zamora)
☎: +34 980 059 018
info@divinaproporcionbodegas.es
www.divinaproporcionbodegas.es

24 Mozas 2014 T
tinta de Toro

88

Colour: cherry, garnet rim. Nose: sweet spices, smoky, spicy, ripe fruit. Palate: correct, fruity, flavourful, spicy.

Abracadabra 2014 T
tinta de Toro

90

Colour: cherry, garnet rim. Nose: mineral, spicy, ripe fruit. Palate: flavourful, ripe fruit, long, good acidity.

Encomienda de la Vega 2014 T
tinta de Toro

89

Colour: bright cherry. Nose: ripe fruit, sweet spices, creamy oak, balsamic herbs. Palate: flavourful, fruity, toasty.

Madremia 2013 T
tinta de Toro

90

Colour: bright cherry. Nose: ripe fruit, sweet spices, creamy oak, cocoa bean. Palate: flavourful, fruity, toasty, round tannins.

DOMINIO DEL BENDITO

Pza. Santo Domingo, 8
49800 Toro (Zamora)
☎: +34 980 693 306
Fax: +34 980 694 991
info@bodegadominiodelbendito.es
www.bodegadominiodelbendito.es

Dominio del Bendito El Primer Paso 2013 T Roble

91

Colour: cherry, purple rim. Nose: ripe fruit, spicy, fresh, balsamic herbs. Palate: flavourful, spicy, powerful, balanced.

Dominio del Bendito Las Sabias 16 meses 2011 T

93

Colour: bright cherry. Nose: ripe fruit, sweet spices, creamy oak, expressive. Palate: flavourful, fruity, toasty, round tannins.

Dominio del Bendito Las Sabias 2012 T
tinta de Toro

92

Colour: cherry, garnet rim. Nose: ripe fruit, wild herbs, earthy notes, spicy, balsamic herbs. Palate: balanced, flavourful, long, balsamic.

El Titán del Bendito 2012 T
tinta de Toro

94

Colour: cherry, garnet rim. Nose: mineral, expressive, spicy. Palate: flavourful, ripe fruit, long, good acidity, balanced.

ELÍAS MORA

Elías Mora
47530 San Román de Hornija
(Valladolid)
☎: +34 983 784 029
info@bodegaseliasmora.com
www.bodegaseliasmora.com

Descarte 2013 T
100% tinta de Toro

89

Colour: deep cherry, purple rim. Nose: creamy oak, toasty, ripe fruit, balsamic herbs. Palate: balanced, spicy, long, toasty.

Elías Mora 2010 TR
100% tinta de Toro

93

Colour: cherry, garnet rim. Nose: balanced, complex, ripe fruit, spicy, fine reductive notes. Palate: good structure, flavourful, round tannins, balanced.

Elías Mora 2012 TC
100% tinta de Toro

91

Colour: cherry, garnet rim. Nose: ripe fruit, spicy, creamy oak, complex. Palate: flavourful, toasty, round tannins.

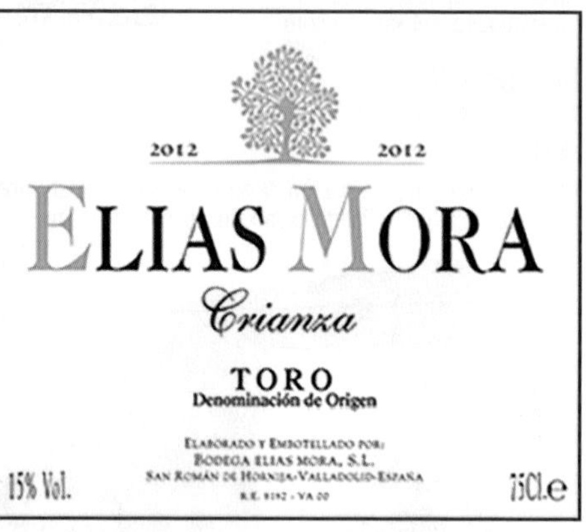

Viñas Elías Mora 2013 T Roble
100% tinta de Toro

90

Colour: bright cherry. Nose: ripe fruit, sweet spices, creamy oak, expressive. Palate: flavourful, fruity, toasty, round tannins.

ESTANCIA PIEDRA

Ctra. Toro a Salamanca km. 5
49800 Toro (Zamora)
☎: +34 980 693 900
piedra@estanciapiedra.com
www.estanciapiedra.com

La Garona 2010 T
75% tinta de Toro, 25% garnacha

91

Colour: cherry, garnet rim. Nose: ripe fruit, wild herbs, earthy notes, spicy, balsamic herbs. Palate: balanced, flavourful, long, balsamic, elegant.

Paredinas 2008 TGR
100% tinta de Toro

91

Colour: cherry, garnet rim. Nose: balanced, complex, ripe fruit, spicy, fine reductive notes. Palate: good structure, flavourful, round tannins, balanced.

Piedra 2012 T Roble
90% tinta de Toro, 10% garnacha

88

Colour: cherry, garnet rim. Nose: red berry notes, ripe fruit, spicy, creamy oak, complex. Palate: flavourful, toasty, round tannins.

Piedra Platino Selección 2009 TGR
100% tinta de Toro

93

Colour: cherry, garnet rim. Nose: ripe fruit, wild herbs, earthy notes, spicy, balsamic herbs. Palate: balanced, flavourful, long, balsamic.

Piedra Roja 2011 TC
100% tinta de Toro

91

Colour: deep cherry. Nose: creamy oak, toasty, ripe fruit, balsamic herbs. Palate: balanced, spicy, long.

Piedra Roja 2012 T
100% tinta de Toro

92

Colour: deep cherry. Nose: creamy oak, toasty, ripe fruit, balsamic herbs. Palate: balanced, spicy, long.

Piedra Viña Azul 2014 T
100% tinta de Toro

87

Colour: deep cherry. Nose: sulphur notes, ripe fruit, grassy. Palate: flavourful, good acidity.

FINCA VOLVORETA
San Esteban, s/n
49152 Sanzoles (Zamora)
☎: +34 619 149 062
info@fincavolvoreta.com
www.vinovolvoreta.com

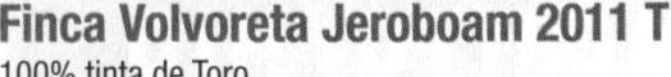

Finca Volvoreta Jeroboam 2011 T
100% tinta de Toro

93

Colour: cherry, garnet rim. Nose: scrubland, balsamic herbs, red berry notes, earthy notes. Palate: long, spicy, balsamic, good acidity.

Finca Volvoreta Magnum 2012 T
100% tinta de Toro

92

Colour: bright cherry. Nose: ripe fruit, sweet spices, creamy oak, expressive, red berry notes. Palate: flavourful, fruity, toasty, round tannins.

FRUTOS VILLAR
Eras de Santa Catalina, s/n
49800 Toro (Zamora)
☎: +34 983 586 868
Fax: +34 983 580 180
bodegasfrutosvillar@bodegasfrutosvillar.com
www.bodegasfrutosvillar.com

Muruve 2010 TR
100% tinta de Toro

89

Colour: cherry, garnet rim. Nose: ripe fruit, wild herbs, earthy notes, spicy, balsamic herbs. Palate: balanced, flavourful, long, balsamic.

Muruve 2011 TC
100% tinta de Toro

88

Colour: bright cherry. Nose: ripe fruit, sweet spices, creamy oak. Palate: flavourful, fruity, round tannins.

Muruve 2012 T Roble
100% tinta de Toro

85

Muruve Élite 2011 T
100% tinta de Toro

91

Colour: cherry, garnet rim. Nose: ripe fruit, spicy, creamy oak, complex. Palate: flavourful, toasty, round tannins.

Puerta de la Majestad 2013 T
100% tinta de Toro

87

Colour: cherry, purple rim. Nose: fresh fruit, red berry notes, floral. Palate: flavourful, fruity, good acidity.

GRANDES DOMINIOS
Casanovas i Bosch, 57
08202 Sabadell (Barcelona)
☎: +34 937 220 338
Fax: +34 937 252 385
info@grandominios.com
www.grandominios.com

DominioS de Castilla 2013 T
85% tinta de Toro, 15% garnacha

86

HAMMEKEN CELLARS

Calle de la Muela, 16
03730 Jávea (Alicante)
☎: +34 965 791 967
Fax: +34 966 461 471
cellars@hammekencellars.com
www.hammekencellars.com

Viña Altamar Barrel Select Tempranillo 2010 T

tempranillo

86

HEREDAD DE URUEÑA

Ctra. Toro a Medina de Rioseco, km 21,300
47862 Urueña (Valladolid)
☎: +34 915 610 894
Fax: +34 915 634 131
dlreccion@heredaduruena.com
www.heredaduruena.com

Moises Gran Vino 2010 T

100% tinta de Toro

91

Colour: cherry, garnet rim. Nose: ripe fruit, old leather, tobacco, dark chocolate. Palate: correct, flavourful, spicy.

Toralto 2012 T

100% tinta de Toro

89

Colour: very deep cherry, garnet rim. Nose: expressive, balsamic herbs, balanced, ripe fruit. Palate: full, flavourful, round tannins.

LA CASA MAGUILA

Ctra. El Piñero s/n Pol. 1 P. 715
49153 Venialbo (Zamora)
☎: +34 980 051 020
casamaguila@casamaguila.com
www.casamaguila.com

Angelitos Negros 2013 T

100% tinta de Toro

89

Colour: cherry, garnet rim. Nose: ripe fruit, wild herbs, earthy notes, spicy, balsamic herbs. Palate: balanced, flavourful, long.

Angelitos Negros 2014 T

100% tinta de Toro

88

Colour: cherry, purple rim. Nose: ripe fruit, woody, roasted coffee. Palate: flavourful, spicy, powerful, smoky aftertaste.

Cachito Mío 2013 T

100% tinta de Toro

88

Colour: cherry, garnet rim. Nose: roasted coffee, smoky, ripe fruit, aromatic coffee. Palate: flavourful, smoky aftertaste, ripe fruit.

Cachito Mío 2014 T

tinta de Toro

90

Colour: bright cherry. Nose: ripe fruit, sweet spices, creamy oak. Palate: flavourful, fruity, toasty, round tannins.

Quizás 2011 T

91

Colour: cherry, garnet rim. Nose: ripe fruit, wild herbs, earthy notes, spicy, balsamic herbs. Palate: balanced, flavourful, long, balsamic.

LA VIÑA DEL ABUELO

Comedias, 3
49800 Toro (Zamora)
☎: +34 980 030 631
bodega@abuelovino.com;
www.abuelovino.com

La Viña del Abuelo 2009 T

tinta de Toro

88

Colour: cherry, garnet rim. Nose: fine reductive notes, wet leather, aged wood nuances. Palate: spicy, long, toasty.

La Viña del Abuelo Selección Especial 2010 T

tinta de Toro

92

Colour: cherry, garnet rim. Nose: mineral, expressive, spicy. Palate: flavourful, ripe fruit, long, good acidity, balanced.

LEGADO DE ORNIZ

Real de Pedrosa, 20
47530 San Román de Hornija
(Valladolid)
☎: +34 669 545 976
Fax: +34 649 226 258
info@legadodeorniz.com
www.legadodeorniz.com

Epitafio 2011 T

tinta de Toro

92

Colour: cherry, garnet rim. Nose: ripe fruit, wild herbs, earthy notes, spicy, balsamic herbs, tobacco. Palate: balanced, flavourful, long, balsamic.

Epitafio 2012 T

tinta de Toro

91

Colour: cherry, garnet rim. Nose: smoky, spicy, ripe fruit. Palate: flavourful, smoky aftertaste, ripe fruit.

Triens 2012 T

tinta de Toro

88

Colour: cherry, garnet rim. Nose: roasted coffee, smoky, spicy, ripe fruit. Palate: flavourful, ripe fruit.

LONG WINES

Avda. del Puente Cultural, 8 Bloque B Bajo 7
28702 San Sebastián de los Reyes
(Madrid)
☎: +34 916 221 305
Fax: +34 916 220 029
customer.service@longwines.com
www.longwines.com

El Bos 2012 T

100% tinta de Toro

88

Colour: bright cherry, garnet rim. Nose: ripe fruit, characterful, expressive, sweet spices. Palate: good structure, flavourful, round tannins, fruity aftestaste.

MÁQUINA & TABLA

Villalba de los Alcores, 2-3 B
47008 Valladolid (Valladolid)
☎: +34 609 885 083
hola@maquina-tabla.com
www.maquina-tabla.com

Máquina & Tabla 2013 T
tinta de Toro, garnacha

90

Colour: deep cherry, garnet rim. Nose: ripe fruit, scrubland, spicy. Palate: flavourful, round tannins, balsamic.

Paramo de Nicasia 2013 T
tinta de Toro

93

Colour: deep cherry, purple rim. Nose: creamy oak, toasty, ripe fruit, balsamic herbs. Palate: balanced, spicy, long, fine tannins.

PAGOS DEL REY

Avda. de los Comuneros, 90
49810 Morales de Toro (Zamora)
☎: +34 980 698 023
toro@pagosdelrey.com
www.felixsolisavantis.com

Bajoz 2012 TC
tinta de Toro

86

Bajoz 2014 RD
tinta de Toro

86

Bajoz 2014 T Roble
tinta de Toro

86

Bajoz Malvasía 2014 B
malvasía

83

Bajoz Tempranillo 2014 T
tinta de Toro

84

Finca La Meda 2012 TC
tinta de Toro

89

Colour: cherry, garnet rim. Nose: smoky, spicy, ripe fruit. Palate: flavourful, smoky aftertaste, ripe fruit.

Finca La Meda 2014 RD
tinta de Toro

85

Finca La Meda 2014 T
tinta de Toro

86

Finca La Meda 2014 T Roble
tinta de Toro

86

Finca La Meda Alta Expresión 2011 T
tinta de Toro

91

Colour: cherry, garnet rim. Nose: ripe fruit, earthy notes, spicy, balsamic herbs. Palate: balanced, flavourful, long, balsamic.

Finca La Meda Malvasía 2014 B
malvasía

84

Gran Bajoz 2012 T
tinta de Toro

90

Colour: cherry, garnet rim. Nose: ripe fruit, spicy, creamy oak, complex. Palate: flavourful, toasty.

Ouno 2014 T
tinta de Toro

86

PALACIO DE VILLACHICA

Ctra. Nacional 122, Km. 433,2
49800 Toro (Zamora)
☎: +34 609 144 711
Fax: +34 983 381 356
bodegavillachica@yahoo.es
www.palaciodevillachica.com

Palacio de Villachica 2011 TC

100% tinta de Toro

89

Colour: cherry, garnet rim. Nose: ripe fruit, wild herbs, earthy notes, spicy, balsamic herbs. Palate: balanced, flavourful, long, balsamic.

Palacio de Villachica 2013 T Roble

100% tinta de Toro

87

Colour: bright cherry. Nose: ripe fruit, sweet spices, creamy oak. Palate: flavourful, fruity, toasty.

Villachica Viñas Viejas 2010 T

100% tinta de Toro

90

Colour: cherry, garnet rim. Nose: ripe fruit, earthy notes, spicy, toasty. Palate: balanced, flavourful, long, balsamic.

QUINOLA SUÁREZ

Paseo de Zorrilla, 11- 4 izq.
47007 Valladolid (Valladolid)
☎: +34 625 227 321
garagewine@quinola.es
www.quinola.es

Quinola Garage Wine 2012 T Roble

100% tinta de Toro

93

Colour: cherry, garnet rim. Nose: expressive, spicy, cocoa bean. Palate: flavourful, ripe fruit, long, good acidity, balanced, complex.

QUINTA DE LA QUIETUD

Camino de Bardales, s/n
49800 Toro (Zamora)
☎: +34 980 568 019
info@quintaquietud.com
www.quintaquietud.com

Corral de Campanas 2013 T

tinta de Toro

90

Colour: bright cherry. Nose: ripe fruit, sweet spices, creamy oak, expressive. Palate: flavourful, fruity, toasty, round tannins.

Quinta Quietud 2010 T

100% tinta de Toro

89

Colour: very deep cherry, garnet rim. Nose: characterful, fruit preserve, dark chocolate, sweet spices. Palate: flavourful, powerful.

RODRÍGUEZ SANZO

Manuel Azaña, 11
47014 (Valladolid)
☎: +34 983 150 150
Fax: +34 983 150 151
comunicacion@valsanzo.com
www.rodriguezsanzo.com

Damalisco 2012 TC

100% tinta de Toro

91

Colour: cherry, garnet rim. Nose: creamy oak, red berry notes, fresh fruit. Palate: flavourful, spicy.

TERRA D'URO

Campanas, 4, 1º A
47001 (Valladolid)
☎: +34 983 362 591
Fax: +34 983 357 663
administracion@terraduro.com
www.terraduro.com

Terra D'uro Finca La Rana 2012 T

100% tinta de Toro

90

Colour: very deep cherry, garnet rim. Nose: expressive, complex, mineral, balsamic herbs, ripe fruit. Palate: full, flavourful, round tannins.

Terra D'uro Selección 2011 T
100% tinta de Toro

91

Colour: cherry, garnet rim. Nose: red berry notes, ripe fruit, spicy, creamy oak, complex, mineral. Palate: flavourful, toasty, round tannins.

Uro 2011 T
100% tinta de Toro

93

Colour: cherry, garnet rim. Nose: ripe fruit, wild herbs, earthy notes, spicy, balsamic herbs. Palate: balanced, flavourful, long, balsamic.

TESO LA MONJA

Paraje Valdebuey Ctra. ZA-611, Km. 6,3
49882 Valdefinjas (Zamora)
☎: +34 980 568 143
Fax: +34 980 508 144
info@sierracantabria.com
www.tesolamonja.com

PODIUM

Alabaster 2012 T
tinta de Toro

96

Colour: cherry, garnet rim. Nose: complex, ripe fruit, spicy. Palate: good structure, flavourful, round tannins, balanced.

PODIUM

Alabaster 2013 T
tinta de Toro

98

Colour: very deep cherry. Nose: ripe fruit, fruit expression, red berry notes, creamy oak, toasty, dark chocolate. Palate: flavourful, powerful, ripe fruit, fine bitter notes.

Almirez 2013 T

94

Colour: cherry, garnet rim. Nose: creamy oak, red berry notes, fresh fruit, balanced. Palate: flavourful, spicy, fine bitter notes, ripe fruit.

Romanico 2013 T

91

Colour: bright cherry. Nose: ripe fruit, sweet spices, creamy oak. Palate: flavourful, fruity, round tannins.

PODIUM

Victorino 2012 T
tinta de Toro

97

Colour: cherry, garnet rim. Nose: mineral, expressive, spicy, creamy oak, floral. Palate: flavourful, ripe fruit, long, good acidity, balanced.

TORESANAS

Ctra. Tordesillas, s/n
49800 Toro (Zamora)
☎: +34 983 868 116
Fax: +34 983 868 432
info@taninia.com
www.toresanas.com

Orot 2011 TC
100% tinta de Toro

87

Colour: cherry, garnet rim. Nose: red berry notes, ripe fruit, spicy, toasty. Palate: flavourful, toasty.

Orot 2013 T Roble
100% tinta de Toro

85

Orot 2014 T
100% tinta de Toro

87

Colour: cherry, purple rim. Nose: powerfull, ripe fruit, spicy. Palate: powerful, fruity, unctuous.

VALBUSENDA

Ctra. Toro - Peleagonzalo s/n
49800 Toro (Zamora)
☎: +34 980 699 560
Fax: +34 980 699 566
export@valbusenda.com
www.bodegasvalbusenda.es

Valbusenda 2007 TR
100% tinta de Toro

89

Colour: very deep cherry. Nose: dried herbs, tobacco, spicy, old leather. Palate: correct, flavourful, spicy.

Valbusenda 2009 T Roble
100% tinta de Toro

87

Colour: bright cherry. Nose: ripe fruit, sweet spices, creamy oak. Palate: flavourful, fruity, toasty, round tannins.

Valbusenda Cepas Viejas 2008 T
100% tinta de Toro

89

Colour: cherry, garnet rim. Nose: smoky, spicy, ripe fruit, dark chocolate. Palate: flavourful, smoky aftertaste, ripe fruit.

VIÑAGUAREÑA

Ctra. Toro a Salamanca, Km. 12,5
49800 Toro (Zamora)
☎: +34 980 568 013
Fax: +34 980 568 013
info@vinotoro.com
www.vinotoro.com

Iduna 2010 B
100% verdejo

91

Colour: bright straw. Nose: white flowers, dried herbs, ripe fruit, candied fruit, citrus fruit. Palate: flavourful, fruity, good acidity, elegant.

Munia (14 meses en barrica) 2011 T Roble
100% tinta de Toro

89

Colour: bright cherry. Nose: ripe fruit, sweet spices, creamy oak. Palate: flavourful, fruity, toasty.

Munia (6 meses en barrica) 2012 T Roble
100% tinta de Toro

87

Colour: deep cherry, garnet rim. Nose: scrubland, ripe fruit, sweet spices. Palate: flavourful, round tannins.

Munia Especial 2010 T Roble
100% tinta de Toro

90

Colour: cherry, garnet rim. Nose: red berry notes, ripe fruit, fragrant herbs, spicy, toasty, creamy oak. Palate: powerful, flavourful, balsamic, balanced.

VIÑEDOS ALONSO DEL YERRO

Finca Santa Marta. Ctra.
Roa-Anguix, km. 1,8
09300 Roa (Burgos)
☎: +34 913 160 121
Fax: +34 913 160 121
mariadelyerro@vay.es
www.alonsodelyerro.es

Paydos 2011 T
100% tinta de Toro

92

Colour: cherry, garnet rim. Nose: ripe fruit, wild herbs, earthy notes, spicy, balsamic herbs. Palate: balanced, flavourful, long, balsamic.

VIÑEDOS DE VILLAESTER

49800 Toro (Zamora)
☎: +34 948 645 008
Fax: +34 948 645 166
info@familiabelasco.com
www.familiabelasco.com

Taurus 2011 TC
100% tinta de Toro

87

Colour: cherry, garnet rim. Nose: red berry notes, ripe fruit, spicy, creamy oak. Palate: flavourful, toasty, round tannins, easy to drink.

Taurus 2013 T Roble
100% tinta de Toro

84

Villaester 2005 T
100% tinta de Toro

88

Colour: cherry, garnet rim. Nose: ripe fruit, spicy, creamy oak, complex. Palate: flavourful, toasty, ripe fruit.

VOCARRAJE

Ctra. San Román, s/n 2º Izq.
49810 Moral de Toro (Zamora)
☎: +34 980 698 234
Fax: +34 980 698 172
info@vocarraje.es
www.vocarraje.es

Abdón Segovia 2011 TC
100% tinta de Toro

85

Abdón Segovia 2013 T Roble
100% tinta de Toro

88

Colour: cherry, garnet rim. Nose: creamy oak, red berry notes, fresh fruit, balanced. Palate: flavourful, spicy, elegant.

Abdón Segovia 2014 T

88

Colour: cherry, purple rim. Nose: powerfull, ripe fruit, spicy. Palate: powerful, fruity, unctuous.

DO. UCLÉS

CONSEJO REGULADOR

Avda. Miguel Cervantes, 93
16400 Tarancón (Cuenca)
☎ :+34 969 135 056 - Fax: +34 969 135 421
@: gerente@vinosdeucles.com
www.vinosdeucles.com

LOCATION:

Midway between Cuenca (to the west) and Toledo (to the northwest), this DO is made up of 25 towns from the first province and three from the second. However, the majority of vineyards are situated in Tarancón and the neighbouring towns of Cuenca, as far as Huete - where La Alcarria starts - the largest stretch of border in the DO.

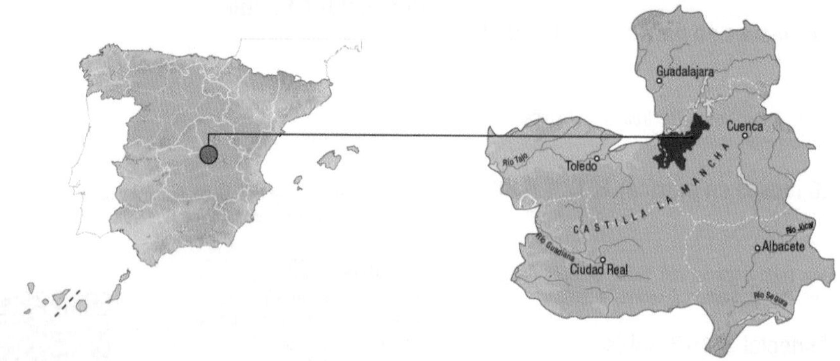

GRAPE VARIETIES:

RED: Tempranillo, Merlot, Cabernet Sauvignon, Garnacha and Syrah.
WHITE: Verdejo, Moscatel de Grano Menudo, Chardonnay, Sauvignon Blanc and Viura (macabeo).

FIGURES:

Vineyard surface: 1,700 – **Wine-Growers:** 187 – **Wineries:** 5 – **2014 Harvest rating:** Very Good – **Production 14:** 2,418,241.25 litres – **Market percentages:** 62% National - 38% International.

SOIL:

Despite spreading over two provinces with different soil components, the communal soils are deep and not very productive, of a sandy and consistent texture, becoming more clayey as you move towards the banks of the rivers Riansares and Bendija.

CLIMATE:

The Altamira sierra forms gentle undulations that rise from an average of 600 metres in La Mancha, reaching 1,200 metres. These ups and downs produce variations in the continental climate, which is less extreme, milder and has a Mediterranean touch. As such, rain is scarce, more akin to a semi-dry climate.

VINTAGE RATING

PEÑÍNGUIDE

2010	2011	2012	2013	2014
VERY GOOD	VERY GOOD	GOOD	AVERAGE	GOOD

BODEGA SOLEDAD

Ctra. Tarancón, s/n
16411 Fuente de Pedro Naharro (Cuenca)
☎: +34 969 125 039
Fax: +34 969 125 907
asv@bodegasoledad.com
www.bodegasoledad.com

Bisiesto Chardonnay 2012 BFB
chardonnay

86

Bisiesto Tempranillo 2011 TC
tempranillo

88

Colour: deep cherry, garnet rim. Nose: dried herbs, ripe fruit, spicy. Palate: balsamic, good acidity, correct.

Solmayor 2011 TC
tempranillo

86

Solmayor 2012 T Roble
tempranillo

85

Solmayor 2014 T
tempranillo

84

Solmayor Chardonnay 2014 B
chardonnay

84

Solmayor Sauvignon Blanc 2014 B
sauvignon blanc

84

BODEGAS FINCA LA ESTACADA

Ctra. N-400, Km. 103
16400 Tarancón (Cuenca)
☎: +34 969 327 099
Fax: +34 969 327 199
enologia@fincalaestacada.com
www.laestacada.com

Finca la Estacada 12 meses barrica 2013 T Barrica
tempranillo

88

Colour: cherry, garnet rim. Nose: red berry notes, ripe fruit, spicy, creamy oak. Palate: flavourful, toasty, good finish.

Finca la Estacada 6 meses barrica 2014 T Roble
tempranillo

88

Colour: bright cherry. Nose: ripe fruit, sweet spices, creamy oak. Palate: flavourful, fruity, spicy.

Finca La Estacada Chardonnay Sauvignon Blanc 2014 B
chardonnay, sauvignon blanc

83

Finca la Estacada Varietales 2010 TC
tempranillo, cabernet sauvignon, syrah, merlot

89

Colour: cherry, garnet rim. Nose: ripe fruit, spicy, creamy oak, complex. Palate: flavourful, toasty.

La Estacada Syrah Merlot 2013 T Roble
syrah, merlot

89

Colour: cherry, garnet rim. Nose: wild herbs, earthy notes, spicy, balsamic herbs, fruit preserve. Palate: balanced, flavourful, long, balsamic.

FONTANA BODEGAS & VIÑEDOS

Extramuros, s/n
16411 Fuente de Pedro Naharro (Cuenca)
☎: +34 969 125 433
Fax: +34 969 125 387
info@bodegasfontana.com
www.bodegasfontana.com

Dominio de Fontana 2012 TC
70% tempranillo, 30% cabernet sauvignon

89

Colour: cherry, garnet rim. Nose: red berry notes, ripe fruit, spicy, creamy oak, complex. Palate: flavourful, toasty.

Dominio de Fontana 2013 T Roble
80% tempranillo, 20% syrah

87

Colour: bright cherry. Nose: ripe fruit, sweet spices, creamy oak. Palate: flavourful, fruity, toasty.

Dominio de Fontana Lías Finas 2014 B
80% sauvignon blanc, 20% verdejo

86

Dominio de Fontana Vendimia Seleccionada 2012 T
90% tempranillo, 10% graciano

88

Colour: cherry, garnet rim. Nose: ripe fruit, wild herbs, earthy notes, spicy. Palate: balanced, flavourful, balsamic.

Mesta 2014 B
100% verdejo

84

Mesta 2014 RD
100% tempranillo

87

Colour: rose, purple rim. Nose: red berry notes, floral, lactic notes. Palate: powerful, fruity, fresh.

Mesta 2014 T
100% tempranillo

88

Colour: cherry, purple rim. Nose: expressive, fresh fruit, red berry notes, floral. Palate: flavourful, fruity, good acidity.

Quinta de Quercus 2012 T
100% tempranillo

90

Colour: cherry, garnet rim. Nose: ripe fruit, wild herbs, earthy notes, spicy, balsamic herbs. Palate: balanced, flavourful, balsamic, long.

DO. UTIEL - REQUENA

CONSEJO REGULADOR

Sevilla, 12. Apdo. 61
46300 Utiel (Valencia)
☎:+34 962 171 062 - Fax: +34 962 172 185
@: info@utielrequena.org
www.utielrequena.org

LOCATION:

In thewest of the province of Valencia. It comprises the municipal districts of Camporrobles, Caudete de las Fuentes, Fuenterrobles, Requena, Siete Aguas, Sinarcas, Utiel, Venta del Moro and Villagordo de Cabriel.

GRAPE VARIETIES:

RED: Bobal, Tempranillo, Garnacha, Cabernet Sauvignon, Merlot, Syrah, Pinot Noir, Garnacha Tintorera, Petit Verdot and Cabernet Franc.

WHITE: Tardana, Macabeo, Merseguera, Chardonnay, Sauvignon Blanc, Parellada,Xarel.lo, Verdejo, Moscatel de Grano Menudo, Viognier and Albariño.

FIGURES:

Vineyard surface: 34,312 – **Wine-Growers:** 5,604 – **Wineries:** 95 – **2014 Harvest rating:** Very Good – **Production 14:** 28,991,868 litres – **Market percentages:** 22% National - 78% International.

SOIL:

Mainly brownish-grey, almost red limestone, poor in organic matter andwith good permeability. The horizon of the vineyards are broken by the silhouette of the odd tree planted in the middle of the vineyards,which, bordered bywoods, offer a very attractive landscape.

CLIMATE:

Continental,with Mediterranean influences, coldwinters and slightly milder summers than in other regions of the province. Rainfall is quite scarcewith an annual average of 400 mm.

VINTAGE RATING

PEÑÍNGUIDE

2010	2011	2012	2013	2014
VERY GOOD	VERY GOOD	VERY GOOD	GOOD	GOOD

AGRO DE BAZÁN - MAS BAZÁN

Lg/ Tremoedo, 46
36628 Vilanova de Arousa (Pontevedra)
☎: +34 986 555 562
Fax: +34 986 555 799
agrodebazan@agrodebazan.com
www.agrodebazansa.es

Mas de Bazan 2014 RD
100% bobal

86

Mas de Bazán Bobal 2011 TR
100% bobal

88

Colour: cherry, garnet rim. Nose: ripe fruit, spicy, creamy oak. Palate: flavourful, toasty, round tannins, balsamic.

Mas de Bazán Bobal 2012 TC
100% bobal

87

Colour: cherry, garnet rim. Nose: ripe fruit, spicy, creamy oak, complex. Palate: flavourful, toasty.

ARANLEÓN

Ctra. Caudete, 3
46310 Los Marcos, Venta del Moro (Valencia)
☎: +34 963 631 640
Fax: +34 962 185 150
vinos@aranleon.com
www.aranleon.com

Aranleón Sólo 2011 T
bobal, tempranillo, syrah

91 ♣

Colour: cherry, garnet rim. Nose: ripe fruit, fragrant herbs, spicy, toasty, creamy oak, mineral. Palate: powerful, flavourful, balsamic, balanced.

Aranleón Sólo 2014 B
chardonnay, macabeo, sauvignon blanc

87 ♣

Colour: yellow. Nose: faded flowers, ripe fruit. Palate: rich, flavourful, spicy, long.

BODEGA SEBIRAN

Pérez Galdos, 1
46352 Campo Arcis - Requena (Valencia)
☎: +34 962 303 321
Fax: +34 962 301 560
info@sebiran.es
www.sebiran.es

Sebirán "C" 2012 TC
bobal

84

Sebirán "J" 2012 TC
bobal

86

BODEGA VERA DE ESTENAS

Junto N-III, km. 266 -
Paraje La Cabezuela
46300 Utiel (Valencia)
☎: +34 962 171 141
estenas@veradeestenas.es
www.veradeestenas.es

Casa Don Ángel Bobal 2012 T
bobal

92

Colour: very deep cherry, garnet rim. Nose: spicy, ripe fruit, scrubland, warm. Palate: balanced, good structure, spicy, long.

Estenas 2011 TC
bobal, cabernet sauvignon, merlot, tempranillo

88

Colour: cherry, garnet rim. Nose: red berry notes, ripe fruit, spicy, creamy oak, dried herbs. Palate: flavourful, toasty, round tannins.

Estenas 2014 B
macabeo, chardonnay

85

Estenas Bobal 2014 RD
bobal

87

Colour: light cherry, bright. Nose: rose petals, red berry notes, balanced, fresh. Palate: correct, fine bitter notes, good acidity.

Estenas Madurado en Barrica 2014 T
bobal, cabernet sauvignon, merlot, tempranillo

85

BODEGA Y VIÑEDOS CARRES

Francho, 1
46352 Casas de Eufema (Valencia)
☎: +34 675 515 729
torrescarpiojl@gmail.com
www.bodegacarres.com

El Olivastro 2010 T
bobal

86 ♣

Membrillera 2014 T
bobal

89 ♣

Colour: bright cherry. Nose: ripe fruit, sweet spices, creamy oak, expressive. Palate: flavourful, fruity, round tannins, balanced.

BODEGAS COVIÑAS

Avda. Rafael Duyos, s/n
46340 Requena (Valencia)
☎: +34 962 300 680
Fax: +34 962 302 651
covinas@covinas.es
www.covinas.es

Adnos Bobal Alta Expresión 2012 T
bobal
90
Colour: cherry, garnet rim. Nose: smoky, spicy, ripe fruit, aged wood nuances. Palate: flavourful, smoky aftertaste, ripe fruit.

Al Vent Bobal 2014 RD
bobal
88
Colour: light cherry, bright. Nose: violets, red berry notes, fresh. Palate: easy to drink, flavourful, balanced, fine bitter notes.

Al Vent Bobal 2014 T
bobal
89
Colour: bright cherry. Nose: ripe fruit, sweet spices, creamy oak, expressive. Palate: flavourful, fruity, round tannins.

Al Vent Sauvignon Blanc 2014 B
sauvignon blanc
88
Colour: bright straw. Nose: fresh fruit, fragrant herbs, expressive, wild herbs. Palate: flavourful, fruity, good acidity, balanced.

Aula Cabernet Sauvignon 2012 T
cabernet sauvignon
87
Colour: deep cherry. Nose: creamy oak, toasty, ripe fruit, balsamic herbs. Palate: balanced, spicy, long.

Aula Merlot 2011 TC
merlot
88
Colour: cherry, garnet rim. Nose: ripe fruit, wild herbs, balsamic herbs, smoky, sweet spices. Palate: flavourful, long, balsamic.

Aula Syrah 2011 TC
syrah
85

Enterizo 2008 TGR
garnacha
85

Enterizo 2010 TR
garnacha
85

Enterizo 2012 TC
tempranillo, bobal
85

Enterizo Bobal 2014 RD
bobal
87
Colour: rose, purple rim. Nose: red berry notes, floral, expressive. Palate: powerful, fruity, fresh.

Enterizo Macabeo 2014 B
macabeo
85

Enterizo Tempranillo Bobal 2014 T
tempranillo, bobal
85

BODEGAS EMILIO CLEMENTE

Camino de San Blas, s/n
46340 Requena (Valencia)
☎: +34 962 323 391
Fax: +34 961 937 044
bodega@eclemente.es
www.eclemente.es

Bomelot 2011 T
bobal
87
Colour: dark-red cherry, garnet rim. Nose: balanced, ripe fruit, cocoa bean. Palate: good structure, balsamic, round tannins.

El Caloret 2014 T
tempranillo, bobal
82

Emilio Clemente 2011 TC
merlot, cabernet sauvignon, bobal
85

Florante 2013 BFB
chardonnay, macabeo
85

Peñas Negras 2014 T
bobal, merlot
85

Peñas Negras Madurado 2012 T
merlot, cabernet sauvignon
82

BODEGAS HISPANO SUIZAS

Ctra. N-322, Km. 451,7
46357 El Pontón (Valencia)
☎: +34 962 349 370
Fax: +34 962 138 318
rafael.roman@bodegashispanosuizas.com
www.bodegashispanosuizas.com

Bassus Dulce Bobal-Pinot Noir 2014 RD
bobal, pinot noir

90

Colour: raspberry rose. Nose: candied fruit, acetaldehyde, faded flowers, fragrant herbs. Palate: powerful, flavourful, complex, balanced.

Bassus Finca Casilla Herrera 2011 T
bobal, petit verdot, cabernet franc, merlot, syrah

92

Colour: cherry, garnet rim. Nose: ripe fruit, spicy, creamy oak, complex. Palate: flavourful, toasty, round tannins, elegant.

Bassus Pinot Noir 2013 T
pinot noir

90

Colour: cherry, garnet rim. Nose: creamy oak, red berry notes, balanced, dried flowers. Palate: flavourful, spicy, balanced.

Bobos 2013 T
bobal

92

Colour: cherry, garnet rim. Nose: expressive, spicy, scrubland. Palate: flavourful, ripe fruit, long, good acidity, balanced.

Impromptu 2014 B
sauvignon blanc

90

Colour: bright straw. Nose: ripe fruit, citrus fruit, faded flowers. Palate: flavourful, fruity, correct, fine bitter notes, spicy, long.

Quod Superius 2011 T
bobal, cabernet franc, merlot, syrah

93

Colour: cherry, garnet rim. Nose: balanced, complex, ripe fruit, spicy, smoky, toasty. Palate: good structure, flavourful, round tannins, balanced.

BODEGAS LADRÓN DE LUNAS

Pintor Peiró, 10
46010 (Valencia)
☎: +34 961 050 553
administracion@ladrondelunas.es
www.ladrondelunas.es

Bisila 2014 T
bobal

86

Bisila Madurado en Barrica 2012 T
bobal

86

Equinocio 2008 TC

89

Colour: pale ruby, brick rim edge. Nose: elegant, spicy, fine reductive notes, expressive. Palate: spicy, fine tannins, elegant, long.

Exclusive 2011 T
100% bobal

91

Colour: very deep cherry, garnet rim. Nose: balanced, powerfull, ripe fruit, scrubland, spicy. Palate: good structure, round tannins, good acidity.

Ladrón de Lunas 2010 TC
bobal, tempranillo

88

Colour: cherry, garnet rim. Nose: spicy, creamy oak, fruit preserve. Palate: flavourful, toasty, round tannins.

Ladrón de Lunas 2011 TC
bobal, tempranillo

89

Colour: cherry, garnet rim. Nose: ripe fruit, wild herbs, earthy notes, spicy, balsamic herbs. Palate: balanced, flavourful, long, balsamic.

Ladrón de Lunas 2014 B
sauvignon blanc, macabeo

87

Colour: bright straw. Nose: white flowers, fresh fruit, fragrant herbs. Palate: flavourful, fruity, good acidity, balanced.

Ladrón de Lunas Madurado 2013 T
bobal

85

Noches de Abril 2011 T

86

BODEGAS MITOS

El Azagador
46357 Requena (Valencia)
☎: +34 962 300 703
admin@bodegasmitos.com
www.bodegasmitos.com

Mitos 2010 TR

tempranillo, cabernet sauvignon

85

Mitos 2012 TC

cabernet sauvignon, tempranillo

84

BODEGAS MURVIEDRO

Ampliación Pol. El Romeral, s/n
46340 Requena (Valencia)
☎: +34 962 329 003
Fax: +34 962 329 002
murviedro@murviedro.es
www.murviedro.es

Corolilla 2012 TC

100% bobal

88

Colour: cherry, garnet rim. Nose: powerfull, ripe fruit, cocoa bean, sweet spices. Palate: flavourful, good structure, round tannins.

Cueva de la Culpa 2012 T

60% bobal, 40% merlot

90

Colour: cherry, garnet rim. Nose: red berry notes, ripe fruit, spicy, creamy oak, complex. Palate: flavourful, toasty.

DNA Murviedro Classic Bobal 2014 T

100% bobal

87

Colour: cherry, purple rim. Nose: powerfull, ripe fruit, balsamic herbs. Palate: fruity, balanced.

Murviedro Cepas Viejas 2012 T Barrica

100% bobal

92

Colour: cherry, garnet rim. Nose: ripe fruit, fragrant herbs, spicy, toasty, creamy oak, mineral. Palate: powerful, flavourful, balsamic.

Murviedro Colección Bobal 2014 T Roble

100% bobal

88

Colour: bright cherry. Nose: ripe fruit, sweet spices, creamy oak, expressive. Palate: flavourful, fruity, round tannins.

Murviedro Colección Bobal Edición Limitada 2011 TR

100% bobal

88

Colour: cherry, garnet rim. Nose: ripe fruit, spicy, creamy oak, complex. Palate: flavourful, toasty, round tannins.

Murviedro Colección Tempranillo 2014 T

100% tempranillo

86

Vega Libre 2011 TR

tempranillo, bobal

85

Vega Libre 2014 B

100% viura

84

Vega Libre 2014 RD

100% bobal

85

Vox Populi 2012 T

100% bobal

90

Colour: cherry, garnet rim. Nose: creamy oak, balanced, ripe fruit, varietal. Palate: flavourful, spicy, balsamic.

BODEGAS NODUS, S.L

Finca El Renegado, s/n
46315 Caudete de las Fuentes (Valencia)
☎: +34 962 174 029
Fax: +34 962 171 432
gestion@bodegasnodus.com
www.bodegasdeutiel.com

Nodus Bobal 2013 T

bobal

85

Nodus Merlot 2013 T

merlot

89

Colour: light cherry. Nose: creamy oak, toasty, ripe fruit, balsamic herbs. Palate: balanced, spicy, long.

Nodus Reserva de Familia 2011 T

65% tempranillo, 20% cabernet sauvignon, 15% syrah

87

Colour: dark-red cherry, garnet rim. Nose: ripe fruit, floral, balsamic herbs, spicy. Palate: correct, round tannins.

Nodus Tinto de Autor 2012 TC
45% merlot, 15% syrah, 25% cabernet sauvignon, 15% bobal

88

Colour: dark-red cherry, garnet rim. Nose: dried herbs, spicy, ripe fruit, waxy notes. Palate: correct, balanced.

BODEGAS PALMERA

Corral Charco de Agut
46300 Utiel (Valencia)
☎: +34 626 706 394
klauslauerbach@hotmail.com

Bobal y Tempranillo 2013 T
bobal, tempranillo

85 ❦

Capricho 2012 T
cabernet sauvignon, merlot

89 ❦

Colour: cherry, garnet rim. Nose: ripe fruit, wild herbs, earthy notes, spicy, balsamic herbs. Palate: balanced, flavourful, long, balsamic.

L'Angelet 2012 TC
tempranillo, cabernet sauvignon, merlot

86 ❦

L'Angelet d'Or 2012 T
bobal, tempranillo, cabernet sauvignon, merlot

87 ❦

Colour: cherry, garnet rim. Nose: aged wood nuances, toasty, fruit preserve. Palate: spicy, toasty, flavourful.

Viña Cabriel 2012 T
tempranillo, cabernet sauvignon, merlot

86 ❦

BODEGAS PASIEGO

Avda. Virgen de Tejeda, 28
46320 Sinarcas (Valencia)
☎: +34 609 076 575
Fax: +34 962 306 175
bodega@bodegaspasiego.com
www.bodegaspasiego.com

Pasiego Aurum 2014 B
85% chardonnay, 15% sauvignon blanc

90

Colour: bright yellow. Nose: ripe fruit, powerfull. Palate: flavourful, fruity, spicy, long, rich, balanced, fine bitter notes.

Pasiego Bobal 2012 T
85% bobal, 10% syrah, 5% merlot

86

Pasiego de Autor 2009 TC
55% cabernet sauvignon, 25% bobal, 20% merlot

90

Colour: cherry, garnet rim. Nose: fine reductive notes, spicy, wild herbs, dried herbs. Palate: spicy, toasty.

Pasiego La Blasca 2008 TC
39% cabernet sauvignon, 31% tempranillo, 27% merlot, 3% bobal

87

Colour: pale ruby, brick rim edge. Nose: spicy, fine reductive notes, aged wood nuances, fruit liqueur notes. Palate: spicy, fine tannins, balanced.

Pasiego La Suertes 2014 B
macabeo, sauvignon blanc

88

Colour: bright straw. Nose: white flowers, fresh fruit, fragrant herbs, expressive. Palate: flavourful, fruity, good acidity, balanced.

BODEGAS REBOLLAR ERNESTO CÁRCEL

Bodegas, 5
46391 El Rebollar - Requena (Valencia)
☎: +34 607 436 362
bodegasrebollar@carceldecorpa.es
www.carceldecorpa.es

Carcel de Corpa 2000 TGR
100% bobal

87

Colour: cherry, garnet rim. Nose: ripe fruit, old leather, tobacco. Palate: correct, flavourful, spicy.

Carcel de Corpa 2011 TR
tempranillo, bobal, garnacha

83

Carcel de Corpa 2012 T
tempranillo, bobal, garnacha

85

BODEGAS SIERRA NORTE

Pol. Ind. El Romeral. Transporte C2
46340 Requena (Valencia)
☎: +34 962 323 099
Fax: +34 962 323 048
info@bodegasierranorte.com
www.bodegasierranorte.com

Cerro Bercial 2008 TR
bobal, cabernet sauvignon

89

Colour: cherry, garnet rim. Nose: balanced, spicy, ripe fruit, fruit preserve. Palate: good structure, flavourful, round tannins, balanced, balsamic.

Cerro Bercial 2010 TC
bobal, tempranillo

88

Colour: cherry, garnet rim. Nose: red berry notes, ripe fruit, spicy, creamy oak, complex. Palate: flavourful, toasty, round tannins.

Cerro Bercial 2011 T Barrica
tempranillo, bobal

90

Colour: cherry, garnet rim. Nose: creamy oak, balanced, dried herbs. Palate: flavourful, spicy, round tannins, smoky aftertaste.

Cerro Bercial 2014 RD
bobal

87

Colour: light cherry. Nose: red berry notes, medium intensity, rose petals. Palate: easy to drink, balanced, good acidity, fresh.

Fuenteseca 2014 B
macabeo, sauvignon blanc

86 ♣

Fuenteseca 2014 RD
bobal, cabernet sauvignon

87

Colour: rose, purple rim. Nose: red berry notes, floral, expressive. Palate: powerful, fruity, fresh.

Fuenteseca 2014 T
bobal, cabernet sauvignon

86

Pasion de Bobal 2013 T Roble
bobal

89

Colour: bright cherry. Nose: ripe fruit, sweet spices, expressive, smoky. Palate: flavourful, fruity, round tannins.

Pasion de Bobal 2014 RD
bobal

89

Colour: raspberry rose. Nose: elegant, red berry notes, floral, fragrant herbs. Palate: light-bodied, flavourful, good acidity, long, spicy.

BODEGAS UTIELANAS

Actor Rambal, 31
46300 Utiel (Valencia)
☎: +34 962 171 157
Fax: +34 962 170 801
info@bodegasutielanas.com
www.bodegasutielanas.com

Vega Infante 2011 TC
bobal, tempranillo

86

Vega Infante 2014 B
macabeo

84

Vega Infante 2014 RD
bobal

87

Colour: rose. Nose: ripe fruit, dried flowers, dried herbs. Palate: flavourful, fruity, long, balanced.

Vega Infante 2014 T
bobal

80

BODEGAS VICENTE GANDÍA

Ctra. Cheste a Godelleta, s/n
46370 Chiva (Valencia)
☎: +34 962 524 242
Fax: +34 962 524 243
info@vicentegandia.com
www.vicentegandia.es

BO - Bobal Único 2013 T
100% bobal

88

Colour: bright cherry. Nose: ripe fruit, sweet spices, creamy oak. Palate: flavourful, fruity.

Ceremonia 2010 TR
60% tempranillo, 30% cabernet sauvignon, 10% bobal

88

Colour: cherry, garnet rim. Nose: ripe fruit, wild herbs, spicy, balsamic herbs. Palate: flavourful, balsamic, spicy.

Finca del Mar Cabernet Sauvignon 2014 T
100% cabernet sauvignon

83

Finca del Mar Chardonnay 2014 B
100% chardonnay

85

Finca del Mar Merlot 2013 T
100% merlot

82

Finca del Mar Tempranillo 2013 T
100% tempranillo

85

Generación 1 2010 TR
70% bobal, 15% cabernet sauvignon, 15% syrah

90

Colour: pale ruby, brick rim edge. Nose: spicy, fine reductive notes, aged wood nuances, fruit preserve. Palate: spicy, fine tannins, balanced.

Hoya de Cadenas 2014 B
chardonnay, sauvignon blanc

84

Hoya de Cadenas 130 Aniversario 2013 T
bobal, garnacha, tempranillo, cabernet sauvignon, merlot, syrah

88

Colour: cherry, garnet rim. Nose: fine reductive notes, spicy, creamy oak. Palate: spicy, long, toasty.

Hoya de Cadenas 2014 RD
100% bobal

85

Hoya de Cadenas Cabernet Sauvignon 2014 T
100% cabernet sauvignon

85

Hoya de Cadenas Chardonnay 2014 B
100% chardonnay

86

Hoya de Cadenas Heretat 2013 T
tempranillo, merlot, cabernet sauvignon, syrah

84

Hoya de Cadenas Heretat 2014 B
viura, sauvignon blanc, chardonnay

84

Hoya de Cadenas Heretat 2014 RD
bobal, cabernet sauvignon

86

Hoya de Cadenas Merlot 2013 T
merlot

85

Hoya de Cadenas Reserva Privada 2011 TR
tempranillo, cabernet sauvignon

88

Colour: cherry, garnet rim. Nose: ripe fruit, spicy, creamy oak. Palate: flavourful, toasty.

Hoya de Cadenas Shiraz 2014 T
100% syrah

85

Hoya de Cadenas Syrah 2013 T
syrah

86

Hoya de Cadenas Tempranillo 2011 TR
100% tempranillo

86

Marqués de Chivé 2011 TC
100% tempranillo

84

Marqués del Turia 2011 TC

84

CHOZAS CARRASCAL

Vereda San Antonio
46390 San Antonio de Requena
(Valencia)
☎: +34 963 410 395
chozas@chozascarrascal.es
www.chozascarrascal.es

Las Dosces 2013 T

90 ⚘

Colour: dark-red cherry, garnet rim. Nose: fruit preserve, powerfull, sweet spices. Palate: fruity, flavourful.

Las Dosces 2014 B
macabeo, sauvignon blanc, chardonnay

90 ⚘

Colour: bright straw. Nose: white flowers, dried herbs, ripe fruit, candied fruit, citrus fruit. Palate: flavourful, fruity, good acidity.

COMERCIAL GRUPO FREIXENET

Joan Sala, 2
08770 Sant Sadurní D'Anoia
(Barcelona)
☎: +34 938 917 000
Fax: +34 938 183 095
freixenet@freixenet.es
www.freixenet.es

B7 2013 B
macabeo

81

B7 2013 T
66% bobal, 23% syrah, 11% cabernet franc

84

Beso de Rechenna 2011 TC
bobal

88

Colour: cherry, garnet rim. Nose: creamy oak, balanced, ripe fruit. Palate: flavourful, spicy, toasty, round tannins.

DOMINIO DE LA VEGA

Ctra. Madrid - Valencia, N-III Km. 270
46390 Requena (Valencia)
☎: +34 962 320 570
Fax: +34 962 320 330
dv@dominiodelavega.com
www.dominiodelavega.com

Añacal Dominio de la Vega 2014 B
macabeo, sauvignon blanc

85

Añacal Dominio de la Vega 2014 RD
bobal

86

Arte Mayor VI 2012/2013/2014 T
bobal

92

Colour: cherry, garnet rim. Nose: balanced, ripe fruit, spicy, dried herbs. Palate: good structure, flavourful, round tannins, balanced.

Bobal En Calma 2013 T
bobal

87

Colour: cherry, garnet rim. Nose: red berry notes, ripe fruit, spicy, creamy oak. Palate: flavourful, toasty.

Dominio de la Vega Dulce 2013 B
sauvignon blanc, chardonnay, macabeo

90

Colour: bright yellow. Nose: powerfull, candied fruit, dried herbs. Palate: flavourful, sweet, ripe fruit, good acidity, easy to drink.

Paraje Tornel 2012 T
bobal

89

Colour: cherry, garnet rim. Nose: ripe fruit, spicy, creamy oak, complex. Palate: flavourful, toasty, elegant.

Recuérdame 2014 B
sauvignon blanc, chardonnay, macabeo

88

Colour: bright straw. Nose: white flowers, fine lees, ripe fruit, citrus fruit. Palate: flavourful, fruity, good acidity, elegant.

FINCA SAN BLAS

Partida de San Blas, s/n
46340 Requena (Valencia)
☎: +34 963 375 617
Fax: +34 963 370 707
info@fincasanblas.com
www.fincasanblas.com

Finca San Blas 2013 B
merseguera

89

Colour: bright yellow. Nose: ripe fruit, powerfull, toasty, aged wood nuances, pattiserie. Palate: flavourful, fruity, spicy, toasty, long.

Finca San Blas Bobal 2012 T
bobal

88

Colour: cherry, garnet rim. Nose: ripe fruit, spicy, creamy oak, balsamic herbs, waxy notes. Palate: flavourful, toasty. Personality.

Finca San Blas Dulce 2013 B
merseguera, chenin blanc

88

Colour: bright yellow. Nose: balsamic herbs, honeyed notes, floral, sweet spices, expressive. Palate: rich, fruity, powerful, flavourful, sweet.

Labor del Almadeque 2010 TR
tempranillo, cabernet sauvignon

86

HAECKY IMPORT AG FINCA CASA LO ALTO

Ctra. Caudete - Los Isidros
46310 Venta del Moro (Valencia)
☎: +34 962 139 101
info@casaloalto.es
www.casa-lo-alto.es

Casa Lo Alto 2010 TR
syrah, garnacha, cabernet sauvignon

89

Colour: cherry, garnet rim. Nose: ripe fruit, wild herbs, earthy notes, spicy, balsamic herbs, characterful. Palate: balanced, flavourful, long, balsamic.

Casa Lo Alto 2011 TC
tempranillo, garnacha, cabernet sauvignon, syrah

86

Casa Lo Alto 2011 TR
syrah, garnacha, cabernet sauvignon

87

Colour: very deep cherry. Nose: ripe fruit, sweet spices. Palate: flavourful, fruity, toasty, round tannins.

Casa Lo Alto 2012 T
bobal

89

Colour: cherry, garnet rim. Nose: ripe fruit, wild herbs, earthy notes, spicy, balsamic herbs, roasted coffee. Palate: balanced, flavourful, long, balsamic.

Casa Lo Alto Chardonnay 2013 B
100% chardonnay

88

Colour: bright yellow. Nose: ripe fruit, powerfull, toasty, aged wood nuances, pattiserie, smoky. Palate: flavourful, fruity, spicy, toasty, long.

LATORRE AGROVINÍCOLA
Ctra. Requena, 2
46310 Venta del Moro (Valencia)
☎: +34 962 185 028
Fax: +34 962 185 422
vinos@latorreagrovinicola.com
www.latorreagrovinicola.com

Catamarán 2014 B
macabeo, verdejo

86

Duque de Arcas 2011 TC
bobal, tempranillo, cabernet sauvignon

84

Duque de Arcas 2013 T
tempranillo, cabernet sauvignon

83

Duque de Arcas Bobal 2012 T
bobal

87

Colour: very deep cherry, garnet rim. Nose: characterful, powerfull, dried herbs, warm, ripe fruit. Palate: spicy, balanced, round tannins.

Parreño 2014 T
tempranillo, cabernet sauvignon

85

Parreño 2014 B
viura, verdejo

82

Parreño 2014 RD
bobal

85

NOEMI WINES
Rambla, 47
46314 Fuenterrobles (Valencia)
☎: +34 672 149 357
bodega@noemiwines.com
www.noemiwines.com

Exuperio 2013 T
100% bobal

93

Colour: cherry, garnet rim. Nose: ripe fruit, wild herbs, earthy notes, spicy, balsamic herbs. Palate: balanced, flavourful, long, balsamic.

PAGO DE THARSYS
Ctra. Nacional III, km. 274
46340 Requena (Valencia)
☎: +34 962 303 354
Fax: +34 962 329 000
pagodetharsys@pagodetharsys.com
www.pagodetharsys.com

Carlota Suria 2008 TR
70% tempranillo, 30% cabernet franc

85

Dominio de Requena 2014 B
100% macabeo

84

Tharsys Único 2008 ESP Reserva
100% bobal

84

PRIMUM BOBAL
Constitución, 50 pta. 6
46340 Requena (Valencia)
☎: +34 625 464 377
vinos@primumbobal.com
www.primumbobal.com

Primum Bobal 2014 T

88

Colour: cherry, purple rim. Nose: expressive, floral, red berry notes, ripe fruit. Palate: flavourful, fruity, good acidity.

TORRE ORIA
Ctra. Pontón - Utiel, Km. 3
46390 Derramador - Requena (Valencia)
☎: +34 962 320 289
Fax: +34 962 320 311
info.torreoria@torreoria.es
www.torreoria.es

Marqués de Requena 2009 TGR
tempranillo, cabernet sauvignon

85

Marqués de Requena 2010 TR
tempranillo, cabernet sauvignon

85

Marqués de Requena 2011 TC
tempranillo, cabernet sauvignon

85

Marqués de Requena Chardonnay Macabeo 2014 B
chardonnay, macabeo

80

Marqués de Requena Tempranillo Syrah 2014 T
syrah, tempranillo

86

Torre Oria 2011 TC
tempranillo, cabernet sauvignon

85

Torre Oria Chardonnay Macabeo 2014 B
chardonnay, macabeo

81

Torre Oria Tempranillo Shiraz 2014 T
tempranillo, syrah

84

UNIÓN VINÍCOLA DEL ESTE

Pl. Ind. El Romeral- Construcción, 74
46340 Requena (Valencia)
☎: +34 962 323 343
Fax: +34 962 349 413
calidad@uveste.es
www.uveste.es

Nit del Foc 2013 T
66% bobal, 23% syrah, 11% cabernet franc

84

Vega Medien 2013 T
66% bobal, 23% syrah, 11% cabernet franc

83

VINOS BIO PEDRO OLIVARES

Avda. La Victoria
La Puerta de Segura (Jaén)
☎: +34 607 861 329
olivares.enologo@gmail.com
www.vinosbiopedroolivares.com

Bobal Serie Wild 2014 T
100% bobal

88

Colour: very deep cherry, purple rim. Nose: wild herbs, ripe fruit, varietal, spicy. Palate: correct, easy to drink, balsamic.

Eclo 2013 T

79

VINOS Y SABORES ECOLÓGICOS

La Iglesia, 6
46357 La Portera (Requena) (Valencia)
☎: +34 686 428 020
mangeles.novella@gmail.com
www.vinosysaboresecologicos.com

Aniceta 2013 T
bobal

85

VIÑEDOS Y BODEGAS VEGALFARO

Ctra. Pontón - Utiel, Km. 3
46340 Requena (Valencia)
☎: +34 962 320 680
Fax: +34 962 321 126
info@vegalfaro.com
www.vegalfaro.com

Caprasia 2014 B
chardonnay, macabeo

87

Colour: bright yellow. Nose: ripe fruit, powerfull, toasty, aged wood nuances. Palate: flavourful, fruity, spicy, toasty, long.

Caprasia 2014 T Roble
bobal, merlot

88

Colour: deep cherry, purple rim. Nose: creamy oak, toasty, ripe fruit, balsamic herbs. Palate: balanced, spicy, long.

Caprasia Bobal 2013 T
bobal

90

Colour: cherry, garnet rim. Nose: creamy oak, red berry notes, balanced, ripe fruit. Palate: flavourful, spicy, elegant.

Rebel.lia 2014 B
sauvignon blanc, chardonnay

86

Rebel.lia 2014 RD
bobal, merlot

88

Colour: onion pink. Nose: candied fruit, ripe fruit, faded flowers, herbaceous. Palate: light-bodied, correct.

Rebel.lia 2014 T Roble
bobal, garnacha tintorera, tempranillo

89

Colour: bright cherry, purple rim. Nose: ripe fruit, spicy, balsamic herbs. Palate: correct, balanced, ripe fruit.

VITICULTORES SAN JUAN BAUTISTA

Ctra. Cheste - Godelleta, Km. 1
46370 Chiva (Valencia)
☎: +34 962 510 861
Fax: +34 962 511 361
cherubino@cherubino.es
www.cherubino.es

Bobal Desanjuan 2013 T
100% bobal

88

Colour: deep cherry, purple rim. Nose: creamy oak, toasty, ripe fruit, balsamic herbs. Palate: balanced, spicy, long.

Bobal Desanjuan 2014 RD
100% bobal

87

Colour: rose, purple rim. Nose: powerfull, ripe fruit, fragrant herbs. Palate: powerful, flavourful, round.

Clos Desanjuan 2012 T
100% bobal

89

Colour: cherry, garnet rim. Nose: ripe fruit, wild herbs, spicy, balsamic herbs, smoky. Palate: balanced, flavourful, long, balsamic.

DO. VALDEORRAS

CONSEJO REGULADOR

Ctra. Nacional 120, km. 463
32340 Vilamartín de Valdeorras (Ourense)
☎:+34 988 300 295 - Fax: +34 988 300 455
@: consello@dovaldeorras.com
www.dovaldeorras.tv

LOCATION:

The DO Valdeorras is situated in the northeast of the province of Orense. It comprises the municipal areas of Larouco, Petín, O Bolo, A Rua, Vilamartín, O Barco, Rubiá and Carballeda de Valdeorras.

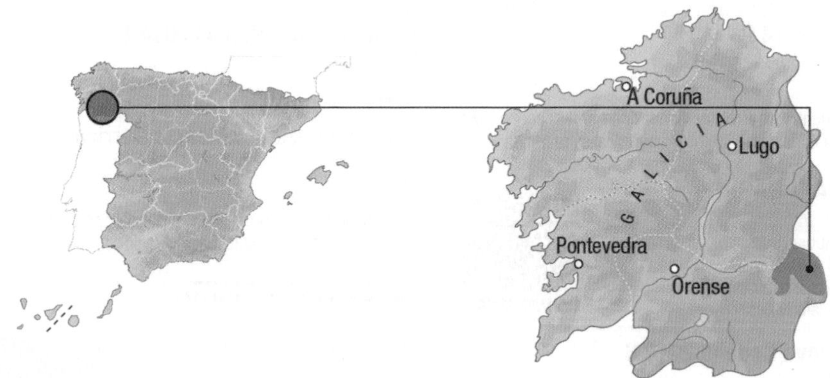

GRAPE VARIETIES:

WHITE: Godello, Dona Blanca, Palomino, Loureira, Treixadura, Dona Branca, Albariño, Torrontes, Lado and Palomino.
RED: Mencía, Merenzao, Grao Negro, Garnacha, Tempranillo (Araúxa), Brancellao, Sousón, Caíño Tinto, Espadeiro, Ferrón, Gran Negro, Garnacha Tintureira and Mouratón.

FIGURES:

Vineyard surface: 1,165 – **Wine-Growers:** 1,471 – **Wineries:** 46 – **2014 Harvest rating:** N/A – **Production 14:** 4,363,989 litres – **Market percentages:** 89% National - 11% International.

SOIL:

Quite varied. There are three types: the first type which is settled on shallow slate with many stones and a medium texture; the second type on deeper granite with a lot of sand and finally the type that lies on sediments and terraces, where there are usually a lot of pebbles.

CLIMATE:

Continental, with Atlantic influences. The average annual temperature is 11°C and the average annual rainfall ranges between 850 mm and 1,000 mm.

VINTAGE RATING

PEÑÍNGUIDE

2010	2011	2012	2013	2014
VERY GOOD	EXCELLENT	EXCELLENT	EXCELLENT	VERY GOOD

ADEGA A COROA

A Coroa, s/n
32350 A Rúa (Ourense)
☎: +34 988 310 648
Fax: +34 988 311 439
acoroa@acoroa.com
www.acoroa.com

A Coroa "Lías" 2013 B
100% godello

91

Colour: bright straw. Nose: white flowers, fine lees, dried herbs, mineral. Palate: flavourful, fruity, good acidity, round.

A Coroa 2014 B
100% godello

90

Colour: bright yellow. Nose: floral, dried herbs, earthy notes, ripe fruit. Palate: fresh, fruity, flavourful, easy to drink.

ADEGA O CASAL

Malladín, s/n
32310 Rubiá (Ourense)
☎: +34 689 675 800
casalnovo@casalnovo.es
www.casalnovo.es

Casal Novo Godello 2014 B
100% godello

91

Colour: bright straw. Nose: expressive, dried herbs, ripe fruit, spicy. Palate: flavourful, fruity, good acidity, balanced.

Casal Novo Mencía 2014 T
90% mencía, 5% garnacha, 5% merenzao

86

ADEGA O CEPADO

O Patal, 11
32310 Rubia de Valdeorras (Ourense)
☎: +34 686 611 589
info@cepado.com
www.cepado.com

Cepado Godello 2014 B
100% godello

90

Colour: bright straw. Nose: white flowers, expressive, varietal, floral. Palate: flavourful, fruity, good acidity, balanced.

Cepado Mencía 2014 T
100% mencía

86

ADEGA QUINTA DA PEZA

Ctra. Nacional 120, km. 467
32350 A Rua de Valdeorras (Ourense)
☎: +34 988 311 537
Fax: +34 981 232 642
quintadapeza@gmail.com
www.quintadapeza.es

Quinta da Peza Godello 2014 B
100% godello

88

Colour: bright straw. Nose: white flowers, fragrant herbs, varietal. Palate: flavourful, good acidity, balanced.

Quinta da Peza Mencía 2014 T
100% mencía

86

Quinta da Peza Oro Mencía Barrica 2013 TC
100% mencía

88

Colour: deep cherry, purple rim. Nose: creamy oak, toasty, ripe fruit, balsamic herbs. Palate: balanced, spicy, long.

ADEGA SANTA MARTA

Ctra. San Vicente s/n
32348 Córgomo-Vilamartin
de Valdeorras (Ourense)
☎: +34 988 324 559
Fax: +34 988 324 559
gerencia@vinaredo.com
www.vinaredo.com

Viñaredo Garnacha Centenaria 2011 T
garnacha tintorera

89

Colour: cherry, garnet rim. Nose: red berry notes, ripe fruit, spicy, creamy oak, complex. Palate: flavourful, toasty, round tannins.

Viñaredo Godello 2014 B
godello

90

Colour: bright straw. Nose: white flowers, fresh fruit, fragrant herbs, expressive. Palate: flavourful, fruity, good acidity, balanced.

Viñaredo Godello Barrica 2014 B
godello

87

Colour: bright yellow. Nose: ripe fruit, powerfull, toasty, aged wood nuances. Palate: flavourful, fruity, spicy, toasty, long.

Viñaredo Mencía 2014 T
mencía

87

Colour: cherry, purple rim. Nose: red berry notes, floral, balsamic herbs, mineral. Palate: powerful, fresh, fruity.

Viñaredo Sousón 2011 T Barrica
sousón

88

Colour: cherry, garnet rim. Nose: ripe fruit, wild herbs, earthy notes, spicy, balsamic herbs. Palate: balanced, flavourful, long, balsamic.

Viñaredo Tostado Dulce 2013 B
godello

93

Colour: golden. Nose: powerfull, honeyed notes, fragrant herbs, dry nuts, aged wood nuances. Palate: flavourful, sweet, fresh, fruity, good acidity, long.

ALAN DE VAL

San Roque, 36
32350 A Rua de Valdeorras (Ourense)
☎: +34 988 310 431
Fax: +34 988 682 640
alandeval@alandeval.com
www.alandeval.com

A Costiña 2011 T
100% brancellao

92

Colour: very deep cherry, garnet rim. Nose: expressive, complex, mineral, balsamic herbs, creamy oak. Palate: full, flavourful, round tannins.

Alan de Val Castes Nobres 2013 T
85% brancellao, 10% caiño, 5% sousón

92

Colour: deep cherry, purple rim. Nose: creamy oak, toasty, ripe fruit, balsamic herbs, mineral. Palate: balanced, spicy, long.

Alan de Val Godello 2014 B
100% godello

90

Colour: straw. Nose: ripe fruit, floral, balanced, expressive. Palate: correct, easy to drink, balanced.

Alan de Val Mencía 2014 T
mencía

88

Colour: cherry, purple rim. Nose: floral, balsamic herbs, ripe fruit, varietal. Palate: powerful, fresh, fruity.

Escada Garnacha Selección Lembranzas 2013 T
100% garnacha tintorera

89

Colour: bright cherry. Nose: sweet spices, creamy oak, fruit preserve. Palate: flavourful, fruity, toasty, concentrated.

Escada Garnacha Tintureira 2013 T
100% garnacha tintorera

88

Colour: bright cherry. Nose: ripe fruit, sweet spices, creamy oak, expressive. Palate: flavourful, fruity, concentrated.

Pedrazais Godello 2014 BFB
100% godello

90

Colour: bright straw. Nose: white flowers, dried herbs, citrus fruit, varietal. Palate: flavourful, good acidity, elegant, fine bitter notes.

Pedrazais Godello sobre Lías 2014 B
100% godello

92

Colour: bright straw. Nose: white flowers, fine lees, dried herbs, mineral. Palate: flavourful, fruity, good acidity, round.

Pedrazais Mencía 2013 T Barrica
90% mencía, 10% otras

89

Colour: cherry, garnet rim. Nose: creamy oak, red berry notes, balanced, ripe fruit. Palate: flavourful, spicy, easy to drink.

Pedrazais Mencía sobre Lías 2014 T
90% mencía, 10% otras

86

BODEGA COOPERATIVA JESÚS NAZARENO

Avda. Florencio Delgado Gurriarán, 62
32300 O Barco de Valdeorras (Ourense)
☎: +34 988 320 262
Fax: +34 988 320 242
coopbarco@infonegocio.com
www.vinosbarco.com

Aurensis 2012 BFB
godello

88

Colour: bright yellow. Nose: ripe fruit, powerfull, toasty, aged wood nuances, pattiserie. Palate: flavourful, fruity, spicy, toasty, long.

Valdouro 2013 T Barrica
mencía, garnacha

86

Viña Abad Godello 2014 B
godello

87

Colour: straw. Nose: medium intensity, ripe fruit, floral. Palate: correct, fine bitter notes, good finish.

BODEGA ELADIO SANTALLA PARADELO

Ucediños, 45
32300 Barco de Valdeorras (Ourense)
☎: +34 686 240 374
eladio@bodegaseladiosantalla.com
www.bodegaseladiosantalla.com

Hacienda Ucediños Godello 2014 B
godello

88

Colour: straw. Nose: medium intensity, ripe fruit, floral. Palate: correct, easy to drink.

Hacienda Ucediños Mencía 2012 T Barrica
mencía

87

Colour: cherry, purple rim, garnet rim. Nose: powerfull, ripe fruit, spicy, balsamic herbs. Palate: powerful, fruity, unctuous.

Hacienda Ucediños Mencía 2014 T
mencía

87

Colour: cherry, garnet rim. Nose: varietal, scrubland, ripe fruit. Palate: flavourful, balanced.

BODEGA LA TAPADA

Finca La Tapada
32310 Rubiá de Valdeorras (Ourense)
☎: +34 988 324 197
Fax: +34 988 324 197
bodega.atapada@gmail.com

Guitián Godello 2012 BFB
100% godello

92

Colour: bright yellow. Nose: ripe fruit, powerfull, toasty, mineral. Palate: flavourful, fruity, spicy, toasty, long.

Guitián Godello 2014 B
100% godello

90

Colour: bright straw. Nose: white flowers, fresh fruit, fragrant herbs. Palate: flavourful, fruity, good acidity, balanced.

Guitián Godello sobre lías 2014 B
100% godello

93

Colour: yellow. Nose: fine lees, dried herbs, floral, expressive, varietal. Palate: flavourful, fruity, good acidity, round, rich.

Guitián Godello Vendimia Tardía Dulce 2011 B
100% godello

94

Colour: bright yellow. Nose: balsamic herbs, honeyed notes, floral, sweet spices, expressive. Palate: rich, fruity, powerful, flavourful, elegant.

BODEGA ROANDI

O Lagar, 1
32336 O Barco de Valdeorras (Ourense)
Fax: +34 988 335 198
info@bodegaroandi.com
www.bodegaroandi.com

Bancales de Moral Barrica 2012 T
85% mencía, 10% sousón, 5% albarello

89

Colour: dark-red cherry, garnet rim. Nose: ripe fruit, dried herbs, spicy. Palate: flavourful, round tannins, balsamic.

Brinde de Roandi 2013 ESP
100% godello

85

Domus de Roandi 2011 TC
85% sousón, 10% albarello, 5% mencía

90

Colour: cherry, garnet rim. Nose: mineral, expressive, balsamic herbs. Palate: flavourful, ripe fruit, long, good acidity, balanced.

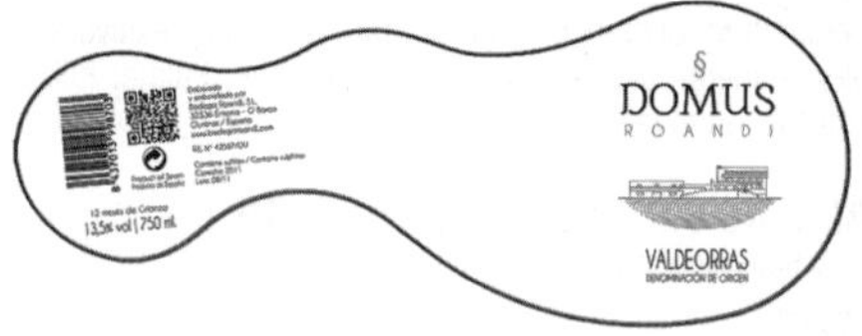

Dona Delfina 2013 B
100% godello

88

Colour: bright straw. Nose: medium intensity, balanced, varietal. Palate: easy to drink, fine bitter notes, correct.

Flavia 2013 T
85% mencía, 10% tempranillo, 5% garnacha

88

Colour: dark-red cherry, garnet rim. Nose: spicy, ripe fruit, dried herbs. Palate: flavourful, balanced.

O Gran Pendón 2014 T
100% mencía

85

BODEGA RUA

Campo Grande, 97
32350 A Rua de Valdeorras (Ourense)
☎: +34 988 310 607
Fax: +34 988 312 016
market@cooperativarua.com
www.cooperativarua.com

Marquesiño 2014 B
godello

84

Marquesiño 2014 T
mencía

88

Colour: cherry, purple rim. Nose: expressive, fresh fruit, red berry notes, floral. Palate: flavourful, fruity, good acidity.

Pingadelo 2014 B
godello

89

Colour: bright yellow. Nose: ripe fruit, dried herbs, faded flowers. Palate: powerful, flavourful, long.

Pingadelo 2014 T
mencía

91

Colour: cherry, purple rim. Nose: red berry notes, floral, balsamic herbs, mineral. Palate: powerful, fresh, fruity, easy to drink.

BODEGAS AVANCIA

Parque Empresarial a Raña, 7
32300 O Barco de Valdeorras (Ourense)
☎: +34 952 504 706
Fax: +34 951 284 796
avancia@jorgeordonez.es
www.grupojorgeordonez.com

Avancia Cuvee de O Godello 2014 B
100% godello

93

Colour: bright straw. Nose: white flowers, fresh fruit, fragrant herbs, varietal. Palate: flavourful, fruity, good acidity, balanced.

Avancia Godello 2014 B
100% godello

93

Colour: bright straw. Nose: white flowers, fine lees, dried herbs, mineral, fruit expression, creamy oak. Palate: flavourful, fruity, good acidity, round.

Avancia Mencía 2013 T
100% mencía

92

Colour: very deep cherry, garnet rim. Nose: expressive, complex, mineral, balsamic herbs, ripe fruit. Palate: full, flavourful, round tannins.

AvanciaCuvee de O Mencía 2014 T
100% mencía

90

Colour: deep cherry, purple rim. Nose: creamy oak, toasty, ripe fruit, balsamic herbs. Palate: balanced, spicy, long.

BODEGAS CARBALLAL

Ctra. de Carballal, km 2,2
32356 Petín de Valdeorras (Ourense)
☎: +34 988 311 281
Fax: +34 988 311 281
bodegascarballal@hotmail.com

Erebo Godello 2014 B
100% godello

90

Colour: bright yellow. Nose: ripe fruit, wild herbs, floral. Palate: fresh, fruity, flavourful, balanced.

Erebo Mencía 2014 T
100% mencía

88

Colour: cherry, purple rim. Nose: red berry notes, floral, balsamic herbs. Palate: powerful, fresh, fruity, easy to drink.

BODEGAS GODEVAL

Avda. de Galicia, 20
32300 El Barco de Valdeorras (Ourense)
☎: +34 988 108 282
Fax: +34 988 325 309
godeval@godeval.com
www.godeval.com

Godeval 2014 B
100% godello

90

Colour: bright straw. Nose: white flowers, fresh fruit, fragrant herbs, citrus fruit. Palate: flavourful, fruity, good acidity.

Godeval Cepas Vellas 2013 B
100% godello

93

Colour: bright yellow. Nose: expressive, dried herbs, ripe fruit, spicy, fine lees. Palate: flavourful, fruity, good acidity, balanced.

Godeval Cepas Vellas 2014 B
100% godello

93

Colour: bright straw. Nose: white flowers, fine lees, dried herbs, mineral, varietal. Palate: flavourful, fruity, good acidity, round, fine bitter notes.

Godeval Revival 2014 B
100% godello

93

Colour: bright straw. Nose: white flowers, fine lees, dried herbs, ripe fruit, citrus fruit. Palate: flavourful, fruity, good acidity, elegant.

BODEGAS SAMPAYOLO

Ctra. de Barxela, s/n
32358 Petín de Valdeorras (Ourense)
☎: +34 679 157 977
Info@sampayolo.com
www.sampayolo.com

Sampayolo Godello sobre Lías 2014 B
100% godello

90

Colour: bright straw. Nose: white flowers, fine lees, dried herbs, mineral, fruit expression. Palate: flavourful, fruity, round.

Sampayolo Mencía 2014 T
100% mencía

88

Colour: bright cherry. Nose: ripe fruit, sweet spices, creamy oak, expressive. Palate: flavourful, fruity, round tannins.

CAMPOS DA NÉBOA

Avda. Diagonal, 590, 5º 1ª
08021 Barcelona (Barcelona)
☎: +34 660 445 464
vinergia@vinergia.com
www.vinergia.com

Campos da Néboa Godello 2014 B
100% godello

89

Colour: bright straw. Nose: white flowers, fresh fruit, fragrant herbs. Palate: flavourful, fruity, good acidity, easy to drink.

Campos da Néboa Mencía 2013 T
100% mencía

86

COMPAÑÍA DE VINOS TELMO RODRÍGUEZ

El Monte
01308 Lanciego (Álava)
☎: +34 945 628 315
Fax: +34 945 628 314
contact@telmorodriguez.com
www.telmorodriguez.com

PODIUM

As Caborcas 2012 T
mencía, merenzao, sousón, garnacha, godello, brancellao

95

Colour: ruby red. Nose: expressive, complex, mineral, balsamic herbs, red berry notes, balanced. Palate: full, flavourful, round tannins, balsamic, round, elegant.

PODIUM

Branco de Santa Cruz 2012 B
godello, loureiro, dona blanca, palomino, otras

95

Colour: bright straw. Nose: white flowers, dried herbs, ripe fruit, citrus fruit, dry stone. Palate: flavourful, fruity, good acidity, elegant, balanced.

Falcoeira 2012 T

93

Colour: light cherry. Nose: fruit expression, fruit liqueur notes, fragrant herbs, spicy, mineral. Palate: balanced, elegant, spicy, long.

Gaba do Xil Godello 2014 B
godello

91

Colour: bright straw. Nose: white flowers, fruit expression, fragrant herbs, mineral. Palate: fresh, fruity, balsamic.

Gaba do Xil Mencía 2013 T
mencía

90

Colour: cherry, garnet rim. Nose: ripe fruit, balsamic herbs, wild herbs. Palate: spicy, long, balanced.

FRANCK MASSARD

Rambla Arnau de Vilanova, 6
08800 Vilanova i La Geltrú (Barcelona)
☎: +34 938 956 541
Fax: +34 938 956 541
info@epicure-wines.com
www.epicure-wines.com

Audacia 2013 B
100% godello

90

Colour: bright straw. Nose: white flowers, fine lees, dried herbs, mineral. Palate: flavourful, fruity, good acidity, round.

GUITIAN Y BLANCO S.C. (BODEGAS D'BERNA)

Córgomo
32348 Villamartín de Valdeorras (Ourense)
☎: +34 667 435 778
Fax: +34 988 324 557
info@bodegasdberna.com
www.bodegasdberna.com

D'Berna Godello 2014 B
100% godello

88

Colour: bright straw. Nose: ripe fruit, varietal, fresh. Palate: correct, fine bitter notes, easy to drink.

D'Berna Mencía Barrica 2011 T
mencía

89

Colour: deep cherry, garnet rim. Nose: spicy, wild herbs, ripe fruit. Palate: long, balsamic, good acidity.

JOAQUÍN REBOLLEDO

San Roque, 11
32350 A Rúa (Ourense)
☎: +34 988 372 307
Fax: +34 988 371 427
info@joaquinrebolledo.com
www.joaquinrebolledo.com

Joaquín Rebolledo 2013 T Barrica
mencía, tempranillo, sousón

90

Colour: dark-red cherry, purple rim. Nose: expressive, wild herbs, spicy. Palate: balanced, long.

Joaquín Rebolledo Godello 2014 B
godello

89

Colour: bright yellow. Nose: floral, dried herbs, ripe fruit. Palate: fruity, flavourful, correct.

Joaquín Rebolledo Mencía 2014 T
mencía

89

Colour: cherry, purple rim. Nose: scrubland, expressive, varietal. Palate: ripe fruit, balsamic, balanced.

LA MALETA HAND MADE FINE WINES

Plaza de Eladio Rodríguez, 19
32420 San Clodio (Ourense)
☎: +34 988 614 234
hola@lamaletawines.com
lamaletawines.com

El Precipicio Godello 2012 B
100% godello

92

Colour: bright straw. Nose: complex, expressive, ripe fruit, faded flowers. Palate: long, rich, fruity, balanced, fine bitter notes.

El Precipicio Mencía Garnacha 2013 T
mencía, garnacha

91

Colour: very deep cherry, garnet rim. Nose: expressive, complex, mineral, balsamic herbs, balanced. Palate: full, flavourful, round tannins.

MANUEL CORZO RODRÍGUEZ

Chandoiro, s/n
32372 O Bolo (Ourense)
☎: +34 689 978 094
manuelcorzorodriguez@hotmail.com

Viña Corzo Godello 2014 B

88

Colour: bright yellow. Nose: dried herbs, ripe fruit, spicy, slightly evolved. Palate: flavourful, fruity, good acidity.

Viña Corzo Mencía 2014 T

84

PALACIOS VINOTECA – VINOS ORIGINALES

Ctra. de Nalda a Viguera, 46
26190 Nalda (La Rioja)
☎: +34 941 447 207
info@palaciosvinoteca.com
www.palaciosvinoteca.com

Lóstrego 2014 B
100% godello

90

Colour: bright straw. Nose: white flowers, fresh fruit, fragrant herbs. Palate: flavourful, fruity, good acidity.

RAFAEL PALACIOS

Avda. de Somoza, 22
32350 A Rúa de Valdeorras (Ourense)
☎: +34 988 310 162
Fax: +34 988 310 643
bodega@rafaelpalacios.com
www.rafaelpalacios.com

As Sortes 2014 B

94

Colour: bright straw. Nose: white flowers, citrus fruit, wild herbs, balanced. Palate: flavourful, fruity, good acidity, elegant.

Louro Godello 2014 B

godello

92

Colour: bright straw. Nose: fine lees, dried herbs, ripe fruit, citrus fruit, spicy. Palate: flavourful, fruity, good acidity, round.

VALDESIL

Ctra. a San Vicente OU 807, km. 3
32348 Vilamartín de Valdeorras (Ourense)
☎: +34 988 337 900
Fax: +34 988 337 901
valdesil@valdesil.com
www.valdesil.com

Montenovo Godello 2014 B

100% godello

92

Colour: bright straw. Nose: white flowers, dried herbs, ripe fruit, varietal. Palate: flavourful, fruity, good acidity.

PODIUM

Pezas da Portela 2012 BFB

100% godello

95

Colour: bright straw. Nose: white flowers, fine lees, dried herbs, ripe fruit, citrus fruit. Palate: flavourful, fruity, good acidity, elegant, long, balanced.

Valderroa 2013 T

100% mencía

91

Colour: light cherry, garnet rim. Nose: medium intensity, scrubland, spicy, varietal. Palate: ripe fruit, balsamic.

Valdesil Godello sobre Lías 2013 B

100% godello

91

Colour: bright straw. Nose: elegant, varietal, fresh, ripe fruit, dried flowers. Palate: balanced, long, fine bitter notes.

Valdesil Parcela O Chao 2012 BFB

100% godello

93

Colour: yellow, pale. Nose: ripe fruit, complex, dried herbs, faded flowers, sweet spices. Palate: full, rich, fine bitter notes.

Valteiro 2012 T

100% maria ardoña

91

Colour: bright cherry. Nose: ripe fruit, sweet spices, balsamic herbs, dry stone. Palate: flavourful, fruity, balanced, elegant.

VINIGALICIA

Ctra. Antigua Santiago, km. 3
27500 Chantada (Lugo)
☎: +34 982 454 005
Fax: +34 982 454 094
vinigalicia@vinigalicia.es
www.vinigalicia.es

Verdes Castros Godello 2014 B

godello

87

Colour: straw. Nose: medium intensity, ripe fruit, floral. Palate: correct, easy to drink.

Verdes Castros Mencía 2014 T

mencía

88

Colour: cherry, purple rim. Nose: red berry notes, balsamic herbs, ripe fruit, grassy. Palate: powerful, fresh, fruity.

VINOS JOC - JORDI OLIVER CONTI

Mas Marti
17467 Sant Mori (Girona)
☎: +34 607 222 002
info@vinojoc.com
www.vinojoc.com

Necora de Jordi Oliver Conti 2014 B

godello

90

Colour: bright straw. Nose: white flowers, fresh fruit, fragrant herbs, expressive. Palate: flavourful, fruity, good acidity.

VIÑA SOMOZA

Rua do Pombar s/n
32350 A Rúa (Ourense)
☎: +34 988 310 918
bodega@vinosomoza.com

Neno Viña Somoza Godello Sobre Lias 2014 B

100% godello

90

Colour: bright straw. Nose: fragrant herbs, dry stone, fresh fruit, citrus fruit. Palate: fresh, fruity, flavourful, easy to drink.

Viña Somoza Godello Selección 2013 B Roble

100% godello

91

Colour: bright yellow. Nose: expressive, dried herbs, ripe fruit, spicy. Palate: flavourful, fruity, good acidity, balanced.

VIÑOS DE ENCOSTAS

Florentino López Cuevillas, 6 1ºA
32500 O Carballiño (Ourense)
☎: +34 988 101 733
Fax: +34 988 488 174
miguel@losvinosdemiguel.com
www.xlsebio.es

Máis Alá 2013 B

godello

92

Colour: bright straw. Nose: white flowers, fine lees, dried herbs, mineral. Palate: flavourful, fruity, good acidity, round, elegant.

VIRXE DE GALIR

Las Escuelas, s/n Estoma
32336 O Barco de Valdeorras (Ourense)
☎: +34 988 335 600
Fax: +34 988 335 592
bodega@pagosdegalir.com
www.pagosdegalir.com

Pagos del Galir Godello 2014 B

100% godello

91

Colour: bright straw. Nose: white flowers, fresh fruit, fragrant herbs, expressive. Palate: flavourful, fruity, good acidity, balanced.

Pagos del Galir Mencía 2013 T Roble

100% mencía

89

Colour: light cherry, garnet rim. Nose: balanced, wild herbs, earthy notes, expressive. Palate: balanced, balsamic, long.

Pagos del Galir Selección Rosa Rivero 2011 TC

100% mencía

91

Colour: very deep cherry, garnet rim. Nose: expressive, complex, mineral, balsamic herbs, balanced. Palate: full, flavourful, round tannins.

Vía Nova Godello 2014 B

100% godello

89

Colour: bright yellow. Nose: expressive, dried herbs, ripe fruit, varietal. Palate: flavourful, fruity, good acidity, balanced.

Vía Nova Mencía 2014 T

100% mencía

88

Colour: cherry, purple rim. Nose: medium intensity, ripe fruit, balsamic herbs. Palate: powerful, flavourful, correct.

DO. VALDEPEÑAS

CONSEJO REGULADOR

Constitución, 23
13300 Valdepeñas (Ciudad Real)
☎ :+34 926 322 788 - Fax: +34 926 321 054
@: consejo@dovaldepenas.es
www.dovaldepenas.es

LOCATION:

On the southern border of the southern plateau, in the province of Ciudad Real. It comprises the municipal districts of Alcubillas, Moral de Calatrava, San Carlos del Valle, Santa Cruz de Mudela, Torrenueva and Valdepeñas and part of Alhambra, Granátula de Calatrava, Montiel and Torre de Juan Abad.

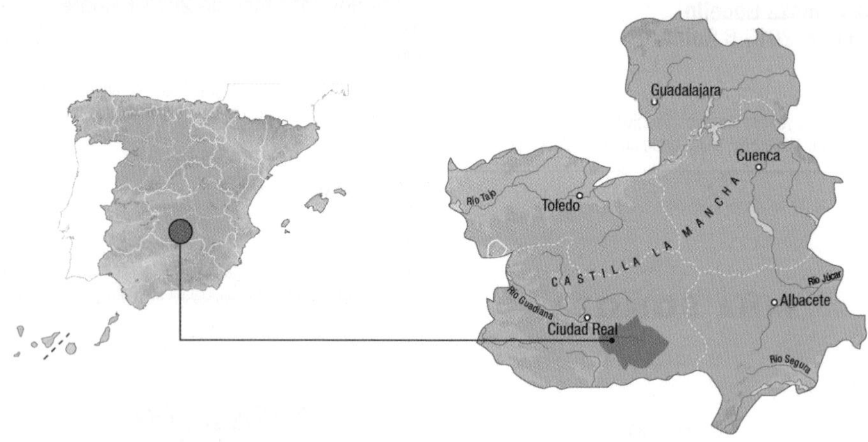

GRAPE VARIETIES:

WHITE: Airén, Macabeo, Chardonnay, Sauvignon Blanc, Moscatel de Grano Menudo and Verdejo.
RED: Cencibel (Tempranillo), Garnacha, Cabernet Sauvignon, Merlot, Syrah and Petit Verdot.

FIGURES:

Vineyard surface: 23,100 – **Wine-Growers:** 2,691 – **Wineries:** 24 – **2014 Harvest rating:** Very Good – **Production 14:** 54,809,616 litres – **Market percentages:** 61.26% National - 38.74% International.

SOIL:

Mainly brownish-red and brownish-grey limestone soil with a high lime content and quite poor in organic matter.

CLIMATE:

Continental in nature, with cold winters, very hot summers and little rainfall, which is usually around 250 and 400 mm per year.

VINTAGE RATING

PEÑÍNGUIDE

2010	2011	2012	2013	2014
GOOD	GOOD	GOOD	GOOD	GOOD

BODEGAS FERNANDO CASTRO

Paseo Castelar, 70
13730 Santa Cruz de Mudela
(Ciudad Real)
☎: +34 926 342 168
Fax: +34 926 349 029
info@bodegasfernandocastro.com
www.bodegasfernandocastro.com

Alba de los Infantes 2007 TGR
100% tempranillo

84

Alba de los Infantes 2010 TR
100% tempranillo

83

Alba de los Infantes 2011 TC
100% tempranillo

84

Castillo de Poto 2007 TGR
100% tempranillo

84

Castillo de Poto 2010 TR
100% tempranillo

82

Castillo de Poto 2011 TC
100% tempranillo

86

Montecruz 2008 TGR
100% tempranillo

84

Montecruz 2010 TR
100% tempranillo

84

Raíces 2007 TGR
100% tempranillo

85

Raíces 2010 TR
100% tempranillo

84

Raíces 2011 TC
100% tempranillo

84

Raíces VI Generación 2011 TC
100% tempranillo

82

Valdemonte 2014 T
100% tempranillo

79

Venta Real 2008 TGR
100% tempranillo

83

BODEGAS LOS LLANOS - GRUPO DE BODEGAS VINARTIS

A-4, Km. 200,5
13300 Valdepeñas (Ciudad Real)
☎: +34 926 320 300
Fax: +34 926 348 483
atcliente@jgc.es
www.vinosdefamilia.com

Armonioso s/c B
100% airén

80

Pata Negra 2006 TGR
100% tempranillo

85

Colour: cherry, garnet rim. Nose: red berry notes, ripe fruit, spicy, creamy oak. Palate: flavourful, toasty, harsh oak tannins.

Pata Negra 2007 TR
100% tempranillo

84

Pata Negra 2008 TC
100% tempranillo

83

Pata Negra 2012 T
80% tempranillo, 20% cabernet sauvignon

82

Pata Negra 2012 T Roble
100% tempranillo

83

Señorío de los Llanos 2008 TGR
100% tempranillo

83

Señorío de los Llanos 2010 TR
100% tempranillo

83

Señorío de los Llanos 2011 TC
100% tempranillo

82

Señorío de los Llanos 2012 B
100% airén

70

Señorío de los Llanos 2012 T
80% tempranillo, 20% cabernet sauvignon

81

Señorío de los Llanos s/c B
100% airén

80

Señorío de los Llanos Tempranillo s/c T
100% tempranillo

83

BODEGAS MARÍN PERONA

Castellanos, 99
13300 Valdepeñas (Ciudad Real)
☎: +34 926 313 192
Fax: +34 926 313 347
bodega@tejeruelas.com
www.tejeruelas.com

Calar Viejo 2011 TC
tempranillo

84

Marín Perona 2006 TGR
tempranillo

83

BODEGAS MEGÍA E HIJOS -CORCOVO

Magdalena, 33
13300 Valdepeñas (Ciudad Real)
☎: +34 926 347 828
Fax: +34 926 347 829
jamegia@corcovo.com
www.corcovo.com

Corcovo 2011 TR
100% tempranillo

89

Colour: cherry, garnet rim. Nose: red berry notes, ripe fruit, spicy, creamy oak, complex. Palate: flavourful, toasty, round tannins, balanced.

Corcovo 2012 TC
100% tempranillo

88

Colour: bright cherry. Nose: ripe fruit, sweet spices, creamy oak, expressive. Palate: flavourful, fruity, round tannins.

Corcovo 2014 RD
100% tempranillo

89

Colour: raspberry rose. Nose: red berry notes, floral, expressive. Palate: powerful, fruity, fresh.

Corcovo Airen 2014 B
100% airén

88

Colour: bright straw. Nose: white flowers, fresh fruit, fragrant herbs, expressive. Palate: flavourful, fruity, good acidity, balanced.

Corcovo Airen 24 Barricas 2013 B Roble
100% airén

86

Corcovo Syrah 2014 T
100% syrah

89

Colour: cherry, purple rim. Nose: expressive, fresh fruit, red berry notes, floral, ripe fruit. Palate: flavourful, fruity, good acidity.

Corcovo Syrah 24 Barricas 2013 T Roble
100% syrah

88

Colour: cherry, garnet rim. Nose: smoky, spicy, ripe fruit. Palate: flavourful, smoky aftertaste, ripe fruit, balanced.

Corcovo Tempranillo 2013 T Roble
100% tempranillo

87

Colour: bright cherry. Nose: ripe fruit, sweet spices, creamy oak, expressive. Palate: flavourful, fruity, round tannins.

Corcovo Tempranillo 2014 T
100% tempranillo

88

Colour: cherry, purple rim. Nose: expressive, fresh fruit, red berry notes, floral. Palate: flavourful, fruity, good acidity.

Corcovo Verdejo 2014 B
100% verdejo

88

Colour: bright straw. Nose: fresh fruit, fragrant herbs, expressive. Palate: flavourful, fruity, good acidity, balanced.

Corcovo Verdejo 24 Barricas 2012 B Roble
100% verdejo

86

BODEGAS MIGUEL CALATAYUD

Postas, 20
13300 Valdepeñas (Ciudad Real)
☎: +34 926 348 070
Fax: +34 926 322 150
vegaval@vegaval.com
www.vegaval.com

Vegaval Plata 2008 TGR
tempranillo

86

Vegaval Plata 2009 TR
tempranillo

84

Vegaval Plata 2010 TC
tempranillo

84

Vegaval Plata Airén 2014 B
airén

83

Vegaval Plata Cabernet Sauvignon 2013 T
cabernet sauvignon

80

Vegaval Plata Garnacha 2013 T
garnacha

84

Vegaval Plata Merlot 2013 T
merlot

83

Vegaval Plata Syrah 2013 T
syrah

84

Vegaval Plata Tempranillo 2013 T
tempranillo

82

Vegaval Plata Verdejo 2014 B
verdejo

86

BODEGAS NAVARRO LÓPEZ

Autovía Madrid - Cádiz, Km. 193
13200 Valdepeñas (Ciudad Real)
☎: +34 902 193 431
Fax: +34 902 193 432
laboratorio@navarrolopez.com
www.navarrolopez.com

Don Aurelio 2009 TGR
100% tempranillo

85

Don Aurelio 2010 TR
100% tempranillo

86

Don Aurelio 2012 TC
100% tempranillo

87

Colour: cherry, garnet rim. Nose: creamy oak, red berry notes, balanced. Palate: flavourful, spicy.

Don Aurelio 2013 T Barrica
100% tempranillo

86

Don Aurelio 2014 RD
100% tempranillo

89

Colour: salmon. Nose: elegant, red berry notes, floral, fragrant herbs. Palate: light-bodied, flavourful, good acidity, long, spicy.

Don Aurelio Garnacha 2014 T
100% garnacha

88

Colour: cherry, purple rim. Nose: expressive, fresh fruit, red berry notes, floral. Palate: flavourful, fruity, good acidity.

Don Aurelio Tempranillo Selección 2014 T
100% tempranillo

86

Don Aurelio Verdejo 2014 B
100% verdejo

85

FÉLIX SOLÍS

Autovía del Sur, Km. 199
13300 Valdepeñas (Ciudad Real)
☎: +34 926 322 400
Fax: +34 926 322 417
nfernandez@felixsolisavantis.com
www.felixsolisavantis.com

Ayrum 2009 TGR
tempranillo

86

Ayrum 2010 TR
tempranillo

87

Colour: pale ruby, brick rim edge. Nose: ripe fruit, aged wood nuances, spicy, creamy oak. Palate: powerful, flavourful, spicy.

Ayrum 2011 TC
tempranillo

87

Colour: cherry, garnet rim. Nose: smoky, spicy, ripe fruit. Palate: flavourful, smoky aftertaste, ripe fruit.

Ayrum 2014 RD
tempranillo

88

Colour: rose, purple rim. Nose: red berry notes, floral, expressive. Palate: powerful, fruity, fresh.

Ayrum Tempranillo 2014 T
tempranillo

86

Ayrum Verdejo 2014 B
verdejo

86

Casa Albali 2014 B
verdejo, sauvignon blanc

84

Casa Albali 2014 RD
garnacha

86

Casa Albali Gran Selección 2014 T
tempranillo

87

Colour: cherry, purple rim. Nose: powerfull, ripe fruit, spicy. Palate: powerful, fruity, unctuous, correct.

Casa Albali Tempranillo Shiraz 2014 T
tempranillo, syrah

85

Casa AlbaliGran Reserva de Familia 2008 T
tempranillo, cabernet sauvignon

85

Los Molinos 2009 TGR
tempranillo

85

Los Molinos 2010 TR
tempranillo

82

Los Molinos 2011 TC
tempranillo

81

Los Molinos 2014 RD
tempranillo

84

Los Molinos Tempranillo 2014 T
tempranillo

85

Los Molinos Verdejo 2014 B
verdejo

82

Viña Albali 2009 TGR
tempranillo

86

Viña Albali 2010 TR
tempranillo

85

Viña Albali 2011 TC
tempranillo

83

Viña Albali 2014 RD
tempranillo

85

Viña Albali Gran Reserva de la Familia 2008 TGR
85% tempranillo, 15% cabernet sauvignon

89

Colour: cherry, garnet rim. Nose: ripe fruit, wild herbs, earthy notes, spicy, balsamic herbs, waxy notes. Palate: balanced, flavourful, long, balsamic.

Viña Albali Gran Selección 2014 T
tempranillo

87

Colour: cherry, purple rim. Nose: powerfull, ripe fruit, spicy. Palate: powerful, fruity, unctuous, balanced.

Viña Albali Selección Privada 2009 TGR
tempranillo

88

Colour: very deep cherry, garnet rim. Nose: expressive, balsamic herbs, balanced. Palate: full, flavourful, round tannins.

Viña Albali Tempranillo 2014 T
tempranillo

85

Viña Albali Verdejo 2014 B
verdejo

84

DO. VALENCIA

CONSEJO REGULADOR

Quart, 22
46001 Valencia
☎:+34 963 910 096 - Fax: +34 963 910 029
@: info@vinovalencia.org
www.vinovalencia.org

LOCATION:

In the province of Valencia. It comprises 66 municipal districts in 4 different sub-regions: Alto Turia, Moscatel de Valencia, Valentino and Clariano.

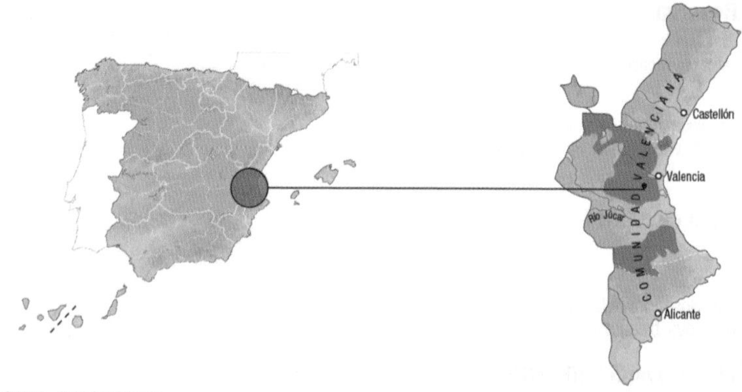

SUB-REGIONS:

There are four in total: Alto Turia, the highest sub-region (700 to 800 m above sea level) comprising 6 municipal districts; **Valentino** (23 municipal districts), in the centre of the province; the altitude varies between 250 m and 650 m; **Moscatel de Valencia** (9 municipal districts), also in the central region where the historical wine from the region is produced; and **Clariano** (33 municipal districts), to the south, at an altitude of between 400 m and 650 m.

GRAPE VARIETIES:

WHITE: Macabeo, Malvasía, Merseguera, Moscatel de Alejandría, Moscatel de Grano Menudo, Pedro Ximénez, Plantafina, Plantanova, Tortosí, Verdil, Chardonnay, Semillon Blanc, Sauvignon Blanc, Verdejo, Riesling, Viognier and Gewüztraminer.
RED: Garnacha, Monastrell, Tempranillo, Tintorera, Forcallat Tinta, Bobal, Cabernet Cauvignon, Merlot, Pinot Noir, Syrah, Graciano, Malbec, Mandó, Marselan, Mencía, Merlot, Mazuelo and Petit Verdot.

FIGURES:

Vineyard surface: 13,079 – **Wine-Growers:** 7,100 – **Wineries:** 92 – **2014 Harvest rating:** Very Good – **Production 14:** 49,615,100 litres – **Market percentages:** 26% National - 74% International.

SOIL:

Mostly brownish-grey with limestone content; there are no drainage problems.

CLIMATE:

Mediterranean, marked by strong storms and downpours in summer and autumn. The average annual temperature is 15°C and the average annual rainfall is 500 mm.

VINTAGE RATING

PEÑÍNGUIDE

2010	2011	2012	2013	2014
EXCELLENT	EXCELLENT	VERY GOOD	GOOD	GOOD

ARANLEÓN

Ctra. Caudete, 3
46310 Los Marcos, Venta del Moro (Valencia)
☎: +34 963 631 640
Fax: +34 962 185 150
vinos@aranleon.com
www.aranleon.com

Blés 2014 T Roble

bobal, tempranillo, cabernet sauvignon

86

Blés Crianza de Aranleón 2012 TC

monastrell, tempranillo, cabernet sauvignon

87

Colour: cherry, garnet rim. Nose: ripe fruit, wild herbs, earthy notes, spicy, balsamic herbs. Palate: balanced, balsamic.

El Árbol de Aranleón 2011 TR

tempranillo, monastrell, cabernet sauvignon

90

Colour: cherry, garnet rim. Nose: mineral, expressive, spicy, ripe fruit, balsamic herbs. Palate: flavourful, ripe fruit, long, good acidity, balanced.

ARTISWINE BODEGAS

46160 Lliria (Valencia)
☎: +34 605 378 213
info@artiswine.es
www.artiswine.es

Artiswine 2013 B

25% moscatel, 25% verdejo, 25% sauvignon blanc, 25% chardonnay

88

Colour: bright yellow. Nose: ripe fruit, spicy, faded flowers. Palate: rich, ripe fruit, flavourful, balsamic.

Artiswine 2013 T

50% monastrell, 50% syrah

84

BODEGA CASAS DE MOYA

Nuevo Tollo A 202
46300 Utiel (Valencia)
☎: +34 665 330 991
info@demoya.es
www.demoya.es

Justina 2012 T

bobal

88

Colour: cherry, garnet rim. Nose: balanced, ripe fruit, spicy. Palate: good structure, flavourful, round tannins.

María 2012 T

85% bobal, 6% merlot, 9% cabernet sauvignon

87

Colour: very deep cherry, garnet rim. Nose: scrubland, ripe fruit, smoky, toasty. Palate: flavourful, easy to drink.

Sofía 2012 T
85% bobal, 10% merlot, 5% cabernet sauvignon

89

Colour: bright cherry. Nose: ripe fruit, sweet spices, creamy oak, expressive. Palate: flavourful, fruity, toasty, round tannins.

BODEGA EL ANGOSTO

Finca Santa Rosa, Ctra. Fontanars
CV-660, km. 23,5
46870 Ontinyent (Valencia)
☎: +34 962 380 638
Fax: +34 962 911 349
info@bodegaelangosto.com
www.bodegaelangosto.com

Almendros 2013 T
50% syrah, 30% marselan, 20% garnacha tintorera

90

Colour: cherry, garnet rim. Nose: ripe fruit, spicy, creamy oak, complex. Palate: flavourful, toasty.

Almendros 2014 B
60% chardonnay, 40% verdejo

91

Colour: bright yellow. Nose: ripe fruit, powerfull, toasty, aged wood nuances, sweet spices. Palate: flavourful, fruity, spicy, toasty, long.

Angosto Blanco 2014 B
25% moscatel, 25% sauvignon blanc, 25% verdejo, 25% chardonnay

90

Colour: bright straw. Nose: white flowers, fresh fruit, fragrant herbs, expressive. Palate: flavourful, fruity, good acidity, balanced.

Angosto Tinto 2013 T
50% syrah, 30% garnacha, 20% cabernet franc

89

Colour: cherry, garnet rim. Nose: roasted coffee, smoky, spicy, ripe fruit. Palate: flavourful, smoky aftertaste, ripe fruit.

El Jefe de la Tribu 2012 T
50% syrah, 50% garnacha

92

Colour: cherry, garnet rim. Nose: ripe fruit, wild herbs, earthy notes, spicy, balsamic herbs. Palate: balanced, flavourful, long, balsamic.

La Tribu 2014 T
34% garnacha tintorera, 33% monastrell, 33% syrah

89

Colour: bright cherry. Nose: ripe fruit, sweet spices, creamy oak, expressive. Palate: flavourful, fruity, toasty.

BODEGA J. BELDA

Avda. Conde Salvatierra, 54
46635 Fontanars dels Alforins
(Valencia)
☎: +34 962 222 278
Fax: +34 962 222 245
info@danielbelda.com
www.danielbelda.com

Daniel Belda MC Tintorera 2013 T
garnacha tintorera

80

Daniel Belda Merlot Rosat 2014 RD
merlot

86

Daniel Belda Pinot Noir 12 + 1 2013 T Barrica
pinot noir

86

Daniel Belda Verdil 2014 B
verdil

87

Colour: bright yellow. Nose: dried herbs, ripe fruit, spicy. Palate: flavourful, fruity, good acidity.

Heretat de Belda 2009 T
pinot noir, garnacha tintorera

89

Colour: light cherry. Nose: fruit expression, fruit liqueur notes, fragrant herbs, spicy, creamy oak. Palate: balanced, elegant, spicy.

Migjorn 2007 T
cabernet sauvignon, merlot, garnacha tintorera
84

BODEGA LA VIÑA - ANECOOP BODEGAS

Portal de Valencia, 52
46630 La Font de la Figuera (Valencia)
☎: +34 962 290 078
Fax: +34 962 232 039
info@vinosdelavina.com
www.ventadelpuerto.com

Casa L'Angel Cepas Viejas 2011 T
cabernet sauvignon, tempranillo
88
Colour: cherry, garnet rim. Nose: ripe fruit, wild herbs, earthy notes, spicy, balsamic herbs. Palate: balanced, flavourful, long, balsamic.

Castillo de Alcoy 2008 TGR
tempranillo
85

Castillo de Alcoy 2011 TR
tempranillo, monastrell
84

Castillo de Alcoy 2012 TC
monastrell
85

Icono Cabernet Sauvignon 2014 T
cabernet sauvignon
85

Icono Chardonnay 2014 B
chardonnay
89
Colour: bright straw. Nose: white flowers, dried herbs, ripe fruit, candied fruit, citrus fruit. Palate: flavourful, fruity, good acidity.

Icono Selección 2012 T
garnacha tintorera, monastrell, tempranillo, cabernet sauvignon, syrah
89
Colour: cherry, garnet rim. Nose: expressive, spicy, ripe fruit. Palate: flavourful, ripe fruit, long, good acidity, balanced.

Icono Syrah 2014 T
syrah
87
Colour: bright cherry. Nose: ripe fruit, expressive, spicy. Palate: flavourful, fruity, round tannins.

Juan de Juanes Vendimia Oro 2014 BFB
chardonnay
86

Juan de Juanes Vendimia Plata Petit Verdot 2013 T
petit verdot
85

Tirant Lo Blanch Vendimia Oro 2012 T
syrah, merlot, cabernet sauvignon, cabernet franc
87
Colour: cherry, garnet rim. Nose: spicy, ripe fruit, smoky, dried herbs. Palate: flavourful, smoky aftertaste, ripe fruit.

Venta del Puerto Nº 12 2012 T
cabernet sauvignon, tempranillo, merlot, syrah
89
Colour: bright cherry. Nose: ripe fruit, sweet spices, creamy oak, smoky. Palate: flavourful, fruity, toasty, round tannins.

Venta del Puerto Nº 18 2010 T Barrica
cabernet sauvignon, tempranillo, merlot, syrah
88
Colour: cherry, garnet rim. Nose: ripe fruit, spicy, creamy oak, fine reductive notes. Palate: flavourful, toasty.

BODEGAS 40 GRADOS NORTE

Camí Estació de Dalt s/n
46630 La Font de la Figuera (Valencia)
☎: +34 615 167 272
Fax: +34 960 963 724
40gradosnorte@40gradosnorte.com
www.40gradosnorte.com

Cota 830 2011 T
bobal, tempranillo, cabernet sauvignon
87
Colour: bright cherry. Nose: sweet spices, creamy oak, red berry notes, scrubland. Palate: flavourful, fruity, toasty.

Mar de So 2011 T
syrah, malbec, monastrell, bobal
86

Mar de So Chardonnay 2014 B
chardonnay
79

So de Bobal 2014 T
bobal
87
Colour: cherry, purple rim. Nose: powerfull, raspberry, red berry notes. Palate: powerful, fruity, unctuous.

So de Syrah 2014 T
syrah

86

BODEGAS ARRAEZ
Arcediano Ros, 35
46321 La Font de la Figuera (Valencia)
☎: +34 962 290 031
info@bodegasarraez.com
www.bodegasarraez.com

Calabuig 2014 T
tempranillo, monastrell

86

Eduardo Bermejo 2013 T
tempranillo

88

Colour: bright cherry. Nose: sweet spices, creamy oak, red berry notes, ripe fruit. Palate: flavourful, fruity, round tannins.

Eduardo Bermejo 2014 B
moscatel, macabeo, merseguera

88

Colour: bright straw. Nose: white flowers, fresh fruit, fragrant herbs, expressive. Palate: flavourful, fruity, good acidity, balanced.

Lagares 2013 TC
cabernet sauvignon

87

Colour: dark-red cherry, garnet rim. Nose: powerfull, fruit preserve, spicy. Palate: flavourful, balsamic.

Mala Vida 2013 T Roble
monastrell, tempranillo, cabernet sauvignon, syrah

87

Colour: bright cherry. Nose: ripe fruit, sweet spices, dried herbs. Palate: flavourful, fruity, round tannins.

Toni Arraez Verdil 2014 B
verdil

91

Colour: bright yellow. Nose: ripe fruit, powerfull, toasty, pattiserie. Palate: flavourful, fruity, spicy, toasty, long.

BODEGAS EL VILLAR
Avda. del Agricultor, 1
46170 Villar de Arzobispo (Valencia)
☎: +34 962 720 050
Fax: +34 961 646 060
exportacion@elvillar.com
www.elvillar.com

Laderas 2014 B
merseguera, macabeo

84

Laderas Tempranillo 2014 T
tempranillo

84

Laderas Tempranillo Bobal 2014 RD
tempranillo, bobal

85

Tapias 2007 TC
merlot

82

Viña Nora 2012 TC
tempranillo, garnacha

80

Viña Villar 2012 TC
tempranillo, merlot

85

BODEGAS ENGUERA
Ctra. CV - 590, Km. 51,5
46810 Enguera (Valencia)
☎: +34 962 224 318
Fax: +34 962 224 831
exportacion@bodegasenguera.com
www.bodegasenguera.com

Angelical 2011 T
60% monastrell, 30% tempranillo, 10% syrah

86

Blanc d'Enguera 2014 B
70% verdil, 10% chardonnay, 10% viognier, 10% sauvignon blanc

87

Colour: bright yellow. Nose: ripe fruit, powerfull, toasty, aged wood nuances, pattiserie. Palate: flavourful, fruity, spicy, toasty, long.

Megala 2011 T
50% monastrell, 20% syrah, 20% marselan

90

Colour: cherry, garnet rim. Nose: expressive, spicy, floral. Palate: flavourful, ripe fruit, long, good acidity, balanced.

Verdil de Gel 2014 B
100% verdil

88

Colour: bright yellow. Nose: powerfull, candied fruit, dried herbs. Palate: flavourful, sweet, ripe fruit, good acidity.

BODEGAS HISPANO SUIZAS

Ctra. N-322, Km. 451,7
46357 El Pontón (Valencia)
☎: +34 962 349 370
Fax: +34 962 138 318
rafael.roman@bodegashispanosuizas.com
www.bodegashispanosuizas.com

Impromptu 2014 RD
pinot noir

92

Colour: salmon, bright. Nose: floral, fruit expression, expressive, varietal. Palate: flavourful, complex, balanced, elegant, good acidity.

BODEGAS LADRÓN DE LUNAS

Pintor Peiró, 10
46010 (Valencia)
☎: +34 961 050 553
administracion@ladrondelunas.es
www.ladrondelunas.es

Bisila 2011 TC
bobal

87

Colour: cherry, garnet rim. Nose: ripe fruit, spicy, creamy oak, complex. Palate: flavourful, toasty, round tannins.

Bisila 2014 B
sauvignon blanc

85

BODEGAS LOS PINOS

Casa Los Pinos, s/n
46635 Fontanars dels Alforins
(Valencia)
☎: +34 600 584 397
bodegaslospinos@bodegaslospinos.com
www.bodegaslospinos.com

Brote Blanco de Dominio Los Pinos 2014 BFB
verdil, viognier

85

Brote Tinto de Dominio Los Pinos 2012 TC
monastrell, garnacha

88

Colour: cherry, garnet rim. Nose: ripe fruit, spicy, creamy oak, complex, balsamic herbs. Palate: flavourful, toasty.

Ca'ls Pins 2014 T Barrica
monastrell, cabernet sauvignon, merlot

86

Dx de Dominio Los Pinos 2013 T Roble
monastrell, cabernet sauvignon

86

Los Pinos 0 % 2014 T
garnacha, monastrell, syrah

87

Colour: cherry, purple rim. Nose: expressive, red berry notes, floral. Palate: flavourful, fruity, good acidity.

Los Pinos 1909 2012 TC
monastrell, merlot, cabernet sauvignon

86

Los Pinos 2013 T Barrica
cabernet sauvignon, syrah, tempranillo

86

BODEGAS MITOS

El Azagador
46357 Requena (Valencia)
☎: +34 962 300 703
admin@bodegasmitos.com
www.bodegasmitos.com

Mitos 2014 B
macabeo, moscatel

84

Mitos One 2014 T
tempranillo

86

Mitos Selección 2014 T
cabernet sauvignon, merlot, syrah

86

BODEGAS MURVIEDRO

Ampliación Pol. El Romeral, s/n
46340 Requena (Valencia)
☎: +34 962 329 003
Fax: +34 962 329 002
murviedro@murviedro.es
www.murviedro.es

Cueva del Pecado 2011 T
60% tempranillo, 40% cabernet sauvignon

89

Colour: cherry, garnet rim. Nose: ripe fruit, spicy, creamy oak, complex. Palate: flavourful, toasty, round tannins.

DNA de Murviedro Fashion Alba 2014 B
60% sauvignon blanc, 40% moscatel

86

DNA de Murviedro Fashion Alma Mística 2014 B
85% moscatel, 15% viura

85

DNA de Muviedro Fashion Rosa Blush 2014 RD
tempranillo, bobal, viura, cabernet sauvignon

86

DNA Murviedro Classic Tempranillo 2014 T
100% tempranillo

86

DNA Muviedro Classic Viura 2014 B
100% viura

84

Estrella de Murviedro Frizzante B
moscatel de alejandría

85

Estrella de Murviedro Frizzante Rosé RD
35% tempranillo, 35% bobal, 30% moscatel

85

Gran Castillo Signature 2011 TR
40% tempranillo, 40% monastrell, 20% cabernet sauvignon

88

Colour: cherry, garnet rim. Nose: ripe fruit, spicy, creamy oak, complex. Palate: flavourful, toasty, round tannins.

Los Monteros 2011 TR
40% tempranillo, 40% monastrell, 20% cabernet sauvignon

87

Colour: dark-red cherry, orangey edge. Nose: waxy notes, wild herbs, ripe fruit. Palate: spicy, balsamic, easy to drink.

Los Monteros 2012 TC
60% monastrell, 40% merlot

84

Los Monteros 2014 B
50% moscatel, 50% viura

85

Los Monteros 2014 RD
100% bobal

85

Murviedro Colección 2011 TR
40% tempranillo, 40% monastrell, 20% cabernet sauvignon

89

Colour: cherry, garnet rim. Nose: earthy notes, spicy, scrubland, smoky. Palate: balanced, flavourful, long, balsamic.

Murviedro Colección 2012 TC
50% tempranillo, 30% monastrell, 20% syrah

88

Colour: cherry, garnet rim. Nose: ripe fruit, earthy notes, spicy dried herbs. Palate: balanced, flavourful, long, balsamic.

Murviedro Colección Petit Verdot 2014 T
100% petit verdot

89

Colour: cherry, purple rim. Nose: fruit preserve, fruit liqueur notes, wild herbs. Palate: powerful, flavourful, unctuous.

Murviedro Colección Sauvignon Blanc 2014 B
100% sauvignon blanc

85

Murviedro Colección Syrah 2014 T
100% syrah

86

Murviedro Expresión Solidarity Cuvée 2011 T Barrica
55% monastrell, 45% garnacha

90

Colour: cherry, garnet rim. Nose: balanced, complex, ripe fruit, spicy, fine reductive notes. Palate: good structure, flavourful, round tannins, balanced.

BODEGAS NODUS, S.L

Finca El Renegado, s/n
46315 Caudete de las Fuentes
(Valencia)
☎: +34 962 174 029
Fax: +34 962 171 432
gestion@bodegasnodus.com
www.bodegasdeutiel.com

Actum Renegado 2014 B
moscatel, macabeo

87

Colour: straw. Nose: medium intensity, ripe fruit, dried herbs. Palate: correct, easy to drink, fine bitter notes.

Actum Renegado 2014 T
bobal

89

Colour: deep cherry, purple rim. Nose: ripe fruit, balsamic herbs, spicy. Palate: balanced, spicy, long.

El Renegado 2012 T Barrica
bobal

87

Colour: deep cherry, purple rim. Nose: creamy oak, toasty, ripe fruit, balsamic herbs. Palate: balanced, spicy, long.

BODEGAS ONTINIUM

Avda. Almansa, 17-21
46870 Ontinyent (Valencia)
☎: +34 962 380 849
Fax: +34 962 384 419
info@coopontinyent.com
www.coopontinyent.com

Codolla 2014 B
airén, macabeo, merseguera, malvasía
81

Embolicaire 2014 T
100% bonicaire
86

Ontinium 2013 T Barrica
100% tempranillo
85

Ontinium 2014 B
macabeo, malvasía, chardonnay
82

Ontinium 2014 RD
100% monastrell
84

Ontinium Monastrell 2014 T
100% monastrell
84

Ontinium Syrah 2014 T
syrah
86

Ontinium Tempranillo 2014 T
100% tempranillo
86

Viña Umbria 2014 T
100% monastrell
84

BODEGAS POLO MONLEÓN

Ctra. Valencia - Ademuz, Km. 86
46178 Titaguas (Valencia)
☎: +34 961 634 148
info@hoyadelcastillo.com
www.hoyadelcastillo.com

Hoya del Castillo 2014 B
75% merseguera, 25% macabeo
89
Colour: bright straw. Nose: fragrant herbs, ripe fruit, floral. Palate: flavourful, fruity, balanced.

BODEGAS REYMOS - ANECOOP BODEGAS

La Estación, 5
46380 Cheste (Valencia)
☎: +34 962 511 671
Fax: +34 962 511 732
buzon@chesteagraria.com
www.bodegasreymos.com

Amatista 2014 B
moscatel
83

Amatista Blanco ESP
moscatel
84

Amatista Rosado Aguja ESP
moscatel, garnacha
83

Reymos S/C B
84

Reymos Selección ESP
moscatel
85

Sol de Reymos Vino de Licor
moscatel
90
Colour: bright golden. Nose: pattiserie, powerfull, caramel, sweet spices, floral. Palate: balanced, rich, complex.

Viña Tendida Moscato B
moscatel
85

Viña Tendida Moscato Rosé RD
moscatel, garnacha
84

BODEGAS SANTA BÁRBARA

Ctra. de Alpuente, 27
46178 Titaguas (Valencia)
info@vinosaltoturia.com
www.vinosaltoturia.com

Llanos de Titaguas 2014 B
100% merseguera
87
Colour: bright straw. Nose: white flowers, fresh fruit, fragrant herbs, expressive. Palate: flavourful, fruity, good acidity, balanced.

Llanos de Titaguas 2014 T
tempranillo

86

Mersé 2013 BFB
100% merseguera

90

Colour: bright yellow. Nose: floral, candied fruit, ripe fruit, fragrant herbs, spicy, elegant. Palate: balanced, round, spicy.

BODEGAS SIERRA NORTE
Pol. Ind. El Romeral. Transporte C2
46340 Requena (Valencia)
☎: +34 962 323 099
Fax: +34 962 323 048
info@bodegasierranorte.com
www.bodegasierranorte.com

Mariluna 2013 T
bobal, tempranillo, monastrell

88

Colour: bright cherry. Nose: ripe fruit, sweet spices, creamy oak, expressive. Palate: flavourful, fruity, round tannins.

Mariluna 2014 B
macabeo, chardonnay, sauvignon blanc

87

Colour: straw. Nose: medium intensity, ripe fruit, floral, citrus fruit. Palate: correct, easy to drink.

Pasión de Monastrell 2013 T
monastrell

90

Colour: bright cherry. Nose: ripe fruit, sweet spices, creamy oak, expressive. Palate: flavourful, fruity, round tannins.

Pasion de Moscatel 2014 B
moscatel

87

Colour: bright straw. Nose: white flowers, fresh fruit, expressive. Palate: flavourful, fruity, good acidity, balanced.

BODEGAS TERRA VINEAS
Colón, 2
46357 La Portera (Requena) (Valencia)
☎: +34 653 989 696
terravineas@terravineas.com
www.terravineas.com

Flor de Alejandría 2014 B
moscatel de alejandría

91

Colour: bright straw. Nose: white flowers, fresh fruit, expressive, varietal. Palate: flavourful, fruity, good acidity, balanced.

Renovatium White "El Principio de Todo" 2014 B
moscatel de alejandría

88

Colour: yellow. Nose: varietal, expressive, white flowers. Palate: balanced, fine bitter notes, ripe fruit, flavourful.

BODEGAS TORREVELLISCA
Ctra. L'Ombria, Km. 1
46635 Fontanars dels Alforins
(Valencia)
☎: +34 962 222 261
Fax: +34 962 222 257
info@bodegas-torrevellisca.es
www.bodegas-torrevellisca.es

Argentum de Zagromonte 2010 TC
50% tempranillo, 50% cabernet sauvignon

86

Aurum de Zagromonte 2012 TC
50% merlot, 50% cabernet sauvignon

86

Brundisium de Zagromonte 2011 TR
50% tempranillo, 25% cabernet sauvignon, 25% cabernet franc

84

Torrevellisca 2006 TC
100% merlot

84

Torrevellisca 2009 TR
50% tempranillo, 50% syrah

80

Torrevellisca 2014 T
50% tempranillo, 50% syrah

85

Torrevellisca 2014 T Roble
100% petit verdot

87

Colour: bright cherry. Nose: ripe fruit, sweet spices, expressive. Palate: flavourful, fruity.

BODEGAS UTIELANAS

Actor Rambal, 31
46300 Utiel (Valencia)
☎: +34 962 171 157
Fax: +34 962 170 801
info@bodegasutielanas.com
www.bodegasutielanas.com

Sueños del Mediterráneo 2014 B
macabeo

86

Sueños del Mediterráneo 2014 RD
bobal

87

Colour: rose, purple rim. Nose: floral, ripe fruit. Palate: powerful, fruity, fresh, easy to drink.

Sueños del Mediterráneo 2014 T
bobal

87

Colour: bright cherry. Nose: ripe fruit, expressive, wild herbs. Palate: flavourful, fruity, round tannins.

BODEGAS VEGAMAR

Garcesa, s/n
46175 Calles (Valencia)
☎: +34 962 109 813
info@bodegasvegamar.com
www.bodegasvegamar.com

Vegamar 2011 TR
syrah, merlot, cabernet sauvignon

87

Colour: cherry, garnet rim. Nose: ripe fruit, wild herbs, earthy notes, spicy, balsamic herbs. Palate: balanced, flavourful, long, balsamic.

Vegamar 2012 TC
merlot, syrah, tempranillo

88

Colour: cherry, garnet rim. Nose: smoky, spicy, ripe fruit. Palate: flavourful, smoky aftertaste, ripe fruit.

Vegamar 2014 B
sauvignon blanc, moscatel

87

Colour: bright straw. Nose: white flowers, fresh fruit, fragrant herbs, expressive. Palate: flavourful, fruity, good acidity, balanced.

Vegamar Dulce 2014 B
moscatel de alejandría

87

Colour: bright yellow. Nose: powerfull, candied fruit, dried herbs. Palate: flavourful, sweet, ripe fruit, good acidity.

Vegamar Selección Garnacha 2014 T
garnacha tintorera

88

Colour: deep cherry, purple rim. Nose: toasty, ripe fruit, balsamic herbs. Palate: balanced, spicy, long, flavourful.

Vegamar Selección Merlot 2014 T
merlot

86

Vegamar Selección Merseguera 2014 B
merseguera

87

Colour: bright straw. Nose: white flowers, dried herbs, citrus fruit, fruit expression. Palate: flavourful, fruity, good acidity, elegant.

Vegamar Selección Sauvignon Blanc 2014 B
sauvignon blanc

86

BODEGAS VICENTE GANDÍA

Ctra. Cheste a Godelleta, s/n
46370 Chiva (Valencia)
☎: +34 962 524 242
Fax: +34 962 524 243
info@vicentegandia.com
www.vicentegandia.es

Castillo de Liria 2010 TR
100% tempranillo
84

Castillo de Liria 2011 TC
tempranillo, syrah
82

Castillo de Liria 2013 T
60% bobal, 40% syrah
80

Castillo de Liria 2014 B
80% viura, 20% sauvignon blanc
83

Castillo de Liria 2014 RD
100% bobal
84

Castillo de Liria Premium Semi Dulce 2013 T
100% cabernet sauvignon
80

Castillo de Liria Semi Dulce 2014 B
80% viura, 20% sauvignon blanc
82

El Miracle 120 Aniversario 2012 T
tempranillo, syrah
87
Colour: cherry, garnet rim. Nose: balsamic herbs, balanced, ripe fruit, creamy oak. Palate: full, flavourful, spicy.

El Miracle 120 Aniversario 2013 T
65% tempranillo, 35% syrah
86

El Miracle 120 Aniversario 2014 B
60% chardonnay, 40% sauvignon blanc
86

El Miracle 120 Aniversario 2014 RD
50% syrah, 50% garnacha
86

El Miracle by Mariscal 2013 T
100% garnacha tintorera
89
Colour: cherry, garnet rim. Nose: ripe fruit, spicy, creamy oak, complex. Palate: flavourful, toasty, ripe fruit.

El Miracle Fusión 2014 B
chardonnay, sauvignon blanc, macabeo
85

Fusta Nova Moscatel Dulce B
moscatel de alejandría
87
Colour: bright yellow. Nose: balsamic herbs, honeyed notes, floral, sweet spices. Palate: rich, fruity, powerful, flavourful.

Hoya de Cadenas 130 Aniversario 2014 B
sauvignon blanc, verdejo
89
Colour: bright yellow. Nose: white flowers, dried herbs, citrus fruit, ripe fruit. Palate: flavourful, fruity, good acidity, balanced.

Hoya de Cadenas Night Harvest 2014 B
moscatel, viura, chardonnay, verdejo
86

Pluvium Premium Selection 2014 B
merseguera, sauvignon blanc
80

Pluvium Premium Selection 2014 RD
bobal, garnacha
83

Pluvium Premium Selection 2014 T
bobal, cabernet sauvignon
82

BODEGAS Y DESTILERÍAS VIDAL

Pol. Ind. El Mijares Valencia, 16
12550 Almazora (Castellón)
☎: +34 964 503 300
Fax: +34 964 560 604
jordan@bodegasvidal.com
www.bodegasvidal.com

Uva D'Or Moscatel de Licor B
moscatel
90
Colour: bright golden. Nose: balsamic herbs, honeyed notes, floral, sweet spices, expressive. Palate: rich, fruity, powerful, flavourful, elegant.

BODEGAS Y VIÑEDOS HAYA

Nueva, s/n
46354 Los Cojos (Requena) (Valencia)
☎: +34 678 126 449
Fax: +34 962 335 053
info@bodegashaya.com
www.bodegashaya.com

Publio Elio Adriano 2014 B
macabeo, chardonnay, sauvignon blanc

83

Publio Elio Adriano 2014 T Roble
bobal, merlot

85

BODEGUES I VINYES LA CASA DE LAS VIDES

Corral el Galtero, s/n
46890 Agullent (Valencia)
☎: +34 962 135 003
Fax: +34 962 135 494
bodega@lacasadelasvides.com
www.lacasadelasvides.com

Abc 2014 T
85

Acvlivs 2010 T
87

Colour: cherry, garnet rim. Nose: fine reductive notes, ripe fruit. Palate: spicy, long, toasty.

Cup de Cup 2011 T
40% tempranillo, 40% syrah, 20% garnacha

84

Rosa Rosae 2014 RD
84

Vallblanca 2014 B
verdil, gewürztraminer

84

CARMELITANO BODEGAS Y DESTILERÍA

Bodolz, 12
12560 Benicasim (Castellón)
☎: +34 964 300 849
Fax: +34 964 304 489
carmelitano@carmelitano.com
www.carmelitano.com

Carmelitano Moscatel 2014 Vino de licor
moscatel de alejandría

88

Colour: bright golden. Nose: fruit liqueur notes, fruit liqueur notes, floral. Palate: balanced, powerful, flavourful.

Carmelitano Vino de Misa Dulce Natural 2014
87

Colour: mahogany. Nose: caramel, overripe fruit, dried herbs. Palate: sweetness, spirituous, complex.

CASA LOS FRAILES

Casa Los Frailes, s/n
46635 Fontanares dels Alforins (Valencia)
☎: +34 962 222 220
Fax: +34 963 363 153
info@bodegaslosfrailes.com
www.casalosfrailes.es

After 3 Monastrell Dulce 2011 TC
monastrell

87

Colour: cherry, garnet rim. Nose: fruit preserve, spicy, warm, fruit liqueur notes. Palate: powerful, flavourful, sweet, rich.

Bilogía 2012 T
monastrell, syrah

85

Casa Los Frailes 1771 2012 T
monastrell

89

Colour: cherry, garnet rim. Nose: dried herbs, wild herbs, ripe fruit, characterful. Palate: balanced, spicy.

La Danza de la Moma 2011 T Barrica
monastrell, marcelan

91

Colour: cherry, garnet rim. Nose: ripe fruit, wild herbs, earthy notes, spicy, balsamic herbs. Palate: balanced, flavourful, long, balsamic.

Los Frailes Monastrell 2014 RD
monastrell

85

Los Frailes Monastrell 2014 T
monastrell

85

Los Frailes Monastrell Garnacha 2013 T Barrica
monastrell, garnacha tintorera

84

Trilogía 2011 T
monastrell, cabernet sauvignon, tempranillo

89

Colour: very deep cherry, garnet rim. Nose: expressive, complex, mineral, balsamic herbs, balanced. Palate: full, flavourful, round tannins.

CELLER DEL ROURE

Ctra. de Les Alcusses, Km. 11,1
46640 Moixent (Valencia)
☎: +34 962 295 020
info@cellerdelroure.es
www.cellerdelroure.es

Cullerot 2014 B
30% pedro ximénez, 30% verdil, 30% chardonnay, 10% malvasía

91

Colour: bright straw. Nose: white flowers, fine lees, dried herbs, mineral, ripe fruit. Palate: flavourful, fruity, good acidity, round, elegant.

Les Alcusses 2011 T
40% monastrell, 20% garnacha tintorera, 20% cabernet sauvignon, 10% syrah, 10% petit verdot

89

Colour: cherry, garnet rim. Nose: ripe fruit, wild herbs, earthy notes, spicy, balsamic herbs. Palate: balanced, flavourful, long, balsamic.

Maduresa 2009 T
35% mando, 20% garnacha tintorera, 15% syrah, 15% petit verdot, 10% cabernet sauvignon, 5% monastrell

92

Colour: cherry, garnet rim. Nose: mineral, expressive, spicy. Palate: flavourful, ripe fruit, long, good acidity, balanced.

Parotet 2012 T
75% mando, 25% monastrell

90

Nose: complex, mineral, balsamic herbs, ripe fruit. Palate: full, flavourful, round tannins.

Parotet Vermell 2012 T
40% garnacha tintorera, 40% monastrell, 20% mando

91

Colour: deep cherry. Nose: creamy oak, toasty, ripe fruit, balsamic herbs, mineral. Palate: balanced, spicy, long.

Setze Gallets 2013 T
25% garnacha tintorera, 25% monastrell, 25% merlot, 10% mando, 5% cabernet sauvignon, 5% petit verdot

87

Colour: deep cherry, purple rim. Nose: toasty, ripe fruit, balsamic herbs. Palate: balanced, spicy, long.

CLOS COR VÍ

Camino del Cementerio s/n
46006 Moixent (Valencia)
☎: +34 963 746 273
Fax: +34 963 746 842
lcorbi@ono.com
www.closcorvi.com

Clos Cor Ví Riesling + Viognier 2014 B
viognier, riesling

89

Colour: yellow, greenish rim. Nose: ripe fruit, tropical fruit, floral. Palate: fruity, long, flavourful.

Clos Cor Ví Riesling 2014 B
riesling

89

Colour: bright yellow. Nose: dried flowers, ripe fruit, citrus fruit. Palate: correct, good acidity, easy to drink.

Clos Cor Ví Viognier 2014 B
viognier

87

Colour: bright yellow. Nose: balanced, dried flowers, ripe fruit. Palate: correct, ripe fruit, easy to drink.

Versat 2014 B
verdil, moscatel, riesling, viognier

87

Colour: bright straw. Nose: white flowers, fresh fruit. Palate: flavourful, fruity, good acidity, balanced.

CLOS DE LA VALL

Pza. de la Hispanidad, 4
46640 Moixent (Valencia)
☎: +34 962 260 020
pablocortesangel@gmail.com
www.closdelavall.com

Clos de la Vall Autor 2012 T
mando

87

Colour: bright cherry. Nose: ripe fruit, sweet spices, smoky, toasty. Palate: flavourful, fruity, toasty, round tannins.

Clos de la Vall Negre 2012 T
monastrell, cabernet sauvignon

86

Clos de la Vall Premium 2013 T
monastrell, cabernet sauvignon

85

Clos de la Vall PX 2014 BFB
100% pedro ximénez

87
Colour: yellow. Nose: ripe fruit, spicy, toasty, woody. Palate: flavourful, fruity, creamy.

Clos de la Vall Único 2010 TC
monastrell, cabernet sauvignon

87
Colour: dark-red cherry, garnet rim. Nose: smoky, spicy, ripe fruit, dried herbs. Palate: flavourful, fruity, balsamic.

Moixaranga 2014 B
macabeo, merseguera

84

Moixaranga 2014 T
monastrell

85

COSTERA ALTA
Ctra. de Les Alcusses, km. 2,5
46640 Moixent (Valencia)
☎: +34 962 261 188
Fax: +34 962 261 300
info@costera-alta.com
www.costera-alta.com

Córdula 2014 T
mandó

88
Colour: light cherry. Nose: fruit expression, fruit liqueur notes, fragrant herbs, spicy, creamy oak. Palate: balanced, elegant, spicy, toasty.

Úrsula 2012 T
monastrell

88
Colour: light cherry. Nose: spicy, wild herbs, ripe fruit. Palate: balanced, elegant, spicy, long, toasty.

HERETAT DE TAVERNERS
Ctra. Fontanars - Moixent, Km. 1,87
46635 Fontanars dels Alforins (Valencia)
☎: +34 962 132 437
Fax: +34 961 140 181
info@heretatdetaverners.com
www.heretatdetaverners.com

Heretat de Taverners Argument Negre 2014 T
cabernet sauvignon, monastrell

84

Heretat de Taverners El Vern 2012 TC
35% tempranillo, 25% cabernet sauvignon, 25% monastrell, 15% merlot

87
Colour: cherry, purple rim. Nose: ripe fruit, spicy, toasty, creamy oak. Palate: flavourful, spicy, powerful.

Heretat de Taverners Graciano 2011 TC
100% graciano

91
Colour: cherry, garnet rim. Nose: red berry notes, ripe fruit, spicy, creamy oak, complex. Palate: flavourful, toasty, round tannins.

Heretat de Taverners Mallaura 2012 TC
50% tempranillo, 25% cabernet sauvignon, 15% garnacha tintorera, 10% monastrell

88
Colour: cherry, garnet rim. Nose: ripe fruit, wild herbs, earthy notes, spicy, balsamic herbs. Palate: balanced, flavourful, long, balsamic.

Heretat de Taverners Reixiu 2014 B
70% chardonnay, 30% sauvignon blanc

89
Colour: bright straw. Nose: expressive, fresh, wild herbs, dried flowers. Palate: balanced, ripe fruit, fine bitter notes.

Punt Dolç T
monastrell, garnacha tintorera

90
Colour: bright cherry, garnet rim. Nose: acetaldehyde, varnish, candied fruit. Palate: fruity, flavourful, sweet.

RAFAEL CAMBRA
Naus Artesanals, 14
46870 Fontanars dels Alforoins (Valencia)
☎: +34 626 309 327
rafael@rafaelcambra.es
www.rafaelcambra.es

El Bon Homme 2014 T
50% monastrell, 50% cabernet sauvignon

87
Colour: bright cherry. Nose: ripe fruit, sweet spices, creamy oak. Palate: flavourful, fruity, toasty.

Forcalla 2013 T
forcalla

89
Colour: cherry, purple rim. Nose: expressive, balsamic herbs, balanced, ripe fruit. Palate: flavourful, fruity, spicy.

Minimum 2011 T
monastrell

90

Colour: very deep cherry, garnet rim. Nose: expressive, complex, mineral, balsamic herbs, balanced, ripe fruit. Palate: full, flavourful, round tannins.

Rafael Cambra Dos 2013 T
cabernet sauvignon, cabernet franc, monastrell

90

Colour: cherry, garnet rim. Nose: ripe fruit, spicy, creamy oak, complex. Palate: flavourful, toasty, round tannins.

Soplo 2012 T
garnacha

88

Colour: dark-red cherry, garnet rim. Nose: toasty, ripe fruit, balsamic herbs. Palate: balanced, spicy, long, easy to drink.

RISKY GRAPES

Avd. Cortes Valencianas, 39 – 3ºC1
46015
☎: +34 960 663 914
info@riskygrapes.com
www.riskygrapes.com

La Traca 2014 T
85% bobal, 15% tempranillo

88

Colour: cherry, purple rim. Nose: fresh fruit, red berry notes, floral. Palate: flavourful, fruity, good acidity.

TORRE ORIA

Ctra. Pontón - Utiel, Km. 3
46390 Derramador - Requena
(Valencia)
☎: +34 962 320 289
Fax: +34 962 320 311
info.torreoria@torreoria.es
www.torreoria.es

Alicia en el País de las Uvas 2014 T
petit verdot, merlot, tempranillo, cabernet sauvignon

84

Caperucita Tinta 2014 T
bobal, tempranillo, petit verdot

84

Mamarracho Selección 2014 T
petit verdot, syrah, tempranillo

84

Niche de Torre Oria Bobal 2013 T
bobal

86

Torre Oria 2009 TGR
tempranillo, cabernet sauvignon

83

Torre Oria 2010 TR
tempranillo, cabernet sauvignon

83

VALSAN 1831

Ctra. Cheste - Godelleta, Km. 1
46370 Chiva (Valencia)
☎: +34 962 510 861
Fax: +34 962 511 361
cherubino@cherubino.es
www.cherubino.es

Cuva Vella 1980 Moscatel
100% moscatel

94

Colour: mahogany. Nose: caramel, cocoa bean, aromatic coffee, candied fruit. Palate: spirituous, complex, rich, spicy, good acidity.

Drassanes 2011 T
60% bobal, 25% tempranillo, 15% syrah

88

Colour: cherry, garnet rim. Nose: ripe fruit, wild herbs, earthy notes, spicy, balsamic herbs. Palate: balanced, flavourful, long, balsamic.

Drassanes 2013 B
50% chardonnay, 24% merseguera, 25% semillón, 1% moscatel

89

Colour: bright straw. Nose: white flowers, dried herbs. Palate: flavourful, fruity, good acidity, round, balanced.

El Novio Perfecto 2014 B
50% moscatel, 50% viura

87

Colour: bright straw. Nose: white flowers, fresh fruit, fragrant herbs. Palate: flavourful, fruity, good acidity, sweetness.

Vittore Moscatel de Licor B
100% moscatel

87

Colour: bright straw. Nose: fruit liqueur notes, white flowers, ripe fruit, fruit liqueur notes. Palate: rich, full.

VIÑAS DEL PORTILLO

F2 P4; Pol. Ind. El Llano
46360 Buñol (Valencia)
☎: +34 962 504 827
Fax: +34 962 500 937
alturiavalencia@gmail.com
www.alturia.es

Albufera 2012 T

cencibel, monastrell

87

Colour: cherry, garnet rim. Nose: ripe fruit, wild herbs, earthy notes, spicy, balsamic herbs. Palate: balanced, flavourful, long, balsamic.

Alturia 2014 B

malvasía, moscatel, merseguera

85

DO. VALLE DE GÜÍMAR

CONSEJO REGULADOR

Tafetana, 14
38500 Güímar (Santa Cruz de Tenerife)
☎ :+34 922 514 709 - Fax: +34 922 514 485
@: consejo@vinosvalleguimar.com
www.vinosvalleguimar.com

LOCATION:

On the island of Tenerife. It practically constitutes a prolongation of the Valle de la Orotava region to the southeast, forming a valley open to the sea, with the Las Dehesas region situated in the mountains and surrounded by pine forests where the vines grow in an almost Alpine environment. It covers the municipal districts of Arafo, Candelaria and Güímar.

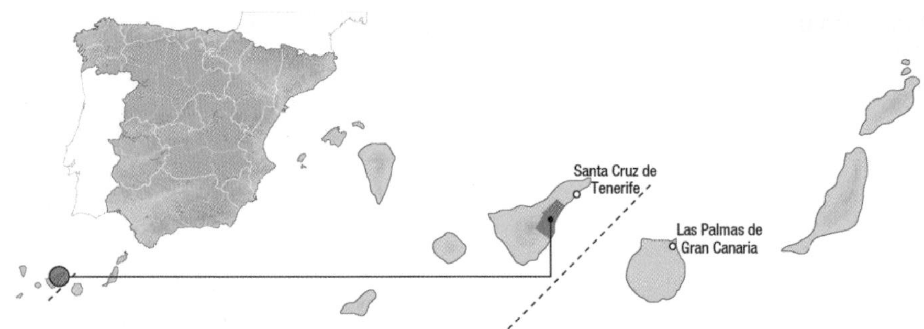

GRAPE VARIETIES:

WHITE: Gual, Listán Blanco, Malvasía, Moscatel, Verdello and Vijariego.
RED: Bastardo Negro, Listán Negro (15% of total), Malvasía Tinta, Moscatel Negro, Negramoll, Vijariego Negro, Cabernet Sauvignon, Merlot, Pinot Noir, Ruby Cabernet, Syrah and Tempranillo.

FIGURES:

Vineyard surface: 271 – **Wine-Growers:** 555 – **Wineries:** 14 – **2014 Harvest rating:** N/A – **Production 14:** 278,103 litres – **Market percentages:** 100% National.

SOIL:

Volcanic at high altitudes, there is a black tongue of lava crossing the area where the vines are cultivated on a hostile terrain with wooden frames to raise the long vine shoots.

CLIMATE:

Although the influence of the trade winds is more marked than in Abona, the significant difference in altitude in a much reduced space must be pointed out, which gives rise to different microclimates, and pronounced contrasts in day-night temperatures, which delays the harvest until 1st November.

VINTAGE RATING

PEÑÍNGUIDE

2010	2011	2012	2013	2014
VERY GOOD	GOOD	VERY GOOD	AVERAGE	AVERAGE

BODEGA COMARCAL VALLE DE GÜIMAR

Ctra. Subida a Los Loros, Km. 4,5
38550 Arafo (Santa Cruz de Tenerife)
☎: +34 922 510 437
info@bodegavalledeguimar.com
www.bodegavalledeguimar.com

Brumas de Ayosa 2013 BN
listán blanco

87

Colour: bright straw. Nose: medium intensity, fresh fruit, dried herbs, fine lees, floral. Palate: fresh, fruity, flavourful, good acidity.

Brumas de Ayosa 2014 T
listán negro, merlot

85

Brumas de Ayosa Afrutado 2013 SS
listán blanco

80

Brumas de Ayosa Afrutado 2014 Semidulce
listán blanco, moscatel de alejandría

85

Brumas de Ayosa Frizzante Mosto Parcialmente Fermentado 2014 RD
listán negro

85

Brumas de Ayosa Malvasía Dulce 2013 B
malvasía

87

Colour: bright yellow. Nose: balsamic herbs, honeyed notes, floral, sweet spices. Palate: rich, fruity, powerful, flavourful, elegant.

Brumas de Ayosa Seco 2014 B
100% listán blanco

84

Pico Cho Marcial 2014 B

83

BODEGA HERMANOS MESA

De Sosa, 2
38550 Arafo (Santa Cruz de Tenerife)
☎: +34 678 404 137
info@bodegahmesa.com
www.bodegahmesa.com

LoCartas 2014 RD
listán negro

84

LoCartas 2014 T
listán negro, tempranillo, syrah

82

LoCartas Afrutado 2014 B
listán blanco, marmajuelo, moscatel de alejandría

87

Colour: bright straw. Nose: white flowers, fresh fruit, fragrant herbs, expressive. Palate: flavourful, fruity.

LoCartas Seco 2014 B
listán blanco, moscatel de alejandría

84

CÁNDIDO HERNÁNDEZ PÍO

Acentejo, 1
38370 La Matanza de Acentejo
(Santa Cruz de Tenerife)
☎: +34 922 513 288
Fax: +34 922 511 631
info@bodegaschp.es
www.bodegaschp.es

Calius 2012 TC
vijariego negro, castellana, tempranillo, tintilla

84

Calius 2014 T
vijariego negro, castellana, tempranillo, tintilla

84

EL BORUJO

Subida Los Loros, km. 4,2
38550 Arafo (Santa Cruz de Tenerife)
☎: +34 636 824 919
jfcofarina@movistar.es
www.elborujo.com

El Borujo 2014 B
listán blanco, albillo, moscatel

86

Los Loros 2013 BFB
gual, marmajuelo, albillo

91

Colour: bright yellow. Nose: expressive, dried herbs, ripe fruit, spicy. Palate: flavourful, fruity, good acidity, balanced.

Los Loros 2013 T
tempranillo, listán negro

86

Los Loros 2014 BFB
marmajuelo, gual

91

Colour: bright straw. Nose: white flowers, fresh fruit, dried herbs. Palate: flavourful, fruity, good acidity.

EL REBUSCO BODEGAS

La Punta, 75 Araya
38530 Candelaria
(Santa Cruz de Tenerife)
☎: +34 608 014 944
elrebusco@gmail.com
www.elrebuscobodegas.es

Dis-Tinto 2014 T
100% merlot

85

La Tentación Afrutado 2014 B
listán blanco, malvasía, moscatel

86

La Tentación Seco 2014 B
listán blanco, malvasía, moscatel

84

FERRERA

Calvo Sotelo, 44
38550 Arafo (Santa Cruz de Tenerife)
☎: +34 649 487 835
Fax: +34 922 237 359
carmengloria@bodegasferrera.com
www.bodegasferrera.com

Momentos de Ferrera 2012 TC

87

Colour: bright cherry. Nose: ripe fruit, sweet spices, creamy oak. Palate: flavourful, fruity, toasty.

Momentos de Ferrera 2014 BFB

90

Colour: bright straw. Nose: white flowers, fine lees, dried herbs, mineral. Palate: flavourful, fruity, good acidity, round.

SAT VIÑA LAS CAÑAS

Barranco Badajoz
38500 Güimar (Santa Cruz de Tenerife)
☎: +34 637 592 759
vegalascanas@hotmail.com

Amor Alma & Origen 2014 B

80

Amor Alma & Origen Afrutado 2014 RD
listán negro

84

Gran Virtud 2014 B
listán blanco

79

Gran Virtud Naturalmente Dulce 2008 B
listán blanco, malvasía, moscatel

92

Colour: iodine, amber rim. Nose: sweet spices, acetaldehyde, dry nuts. Palate: full, dry, spicy, long, fine bitter notes, complex.

Vega Las Cañas 2013 T
listán negro, tempranillo, ruby cabernet, negramoll

84

Vega Las Cañas Afrutado 2014 B
listán blanco, moscatel

82

VIÑA HERZAS

38004 Santa Cruz de Tenerife (Tenerife)
☎: +34 922 511 405
Fax: +34 922 290 064
morraherzas@yahoo.es

Viñas Herzas 2014 B

88

Colour: bright straw. Nose: white flowers, dried herbs, mineral. Palate: flavourful, fruity, good acidity, round.

Viñas Herzas 2014 T

84

DO. VALLE DE LA OROTAVA

CONSEJO REGULADOR

Parque Recreativo El Bosquito, nº1. Urb. La Marzagana II - La Perdona
38315 La Orotava (Santa Cruz de Tenerife)
☎:+34 922 309 923 - Fax: +34 922 309 924
@: info@dovalleorotava.com
www.dovalleorotava.com

LOCATION:

In the north of the island of Tenerife. It borders to the west with the DO Ycoden-Daute-Isora and to the east with the DO Tacoronte-Acentejo. It extends from the sea to the foot of the Teide, and comprises the municipal districts of La Orotava, Los Realejos and El Puerto de la Cruz.

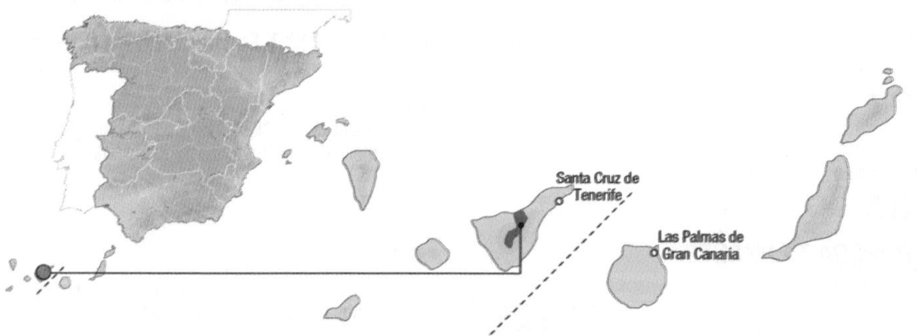

GRAPE VARIETIES:

WHITE: MAIN: Güal, Malvasía, Verdello, Vijariego, Albillo, Forastera Blanca o Doradilla, Sabro, Breval and Burrablanca. AUTHORIZED: Bastardo Blanco, Forastera Blanca (Gomera), Listán Blanco, Marmajuelo, Moscatel, Pedro Ximénez and Torrontés.

RED: MAIN: Listán Negro, Malvasía Rosada, Negramoll, Castellana Negra, Mulata, Tintilla, Cabernet Sauvignon, Listán Prieto, Merlot, Pinot Noir, Ruby Cabernet, Syrah and Tempranillo.
AUTHORIZED: Bastardo Negro, Moscatel Negra, Tintilla and Vijariego Negra.

FIGURES:

Vineyard surface: 357 – **Wine-Growers:** 637 – **Wineries:** 14 – **2014 Harvest rating:** N/A – **Production 14:** 450,000 litres – **Market percentages:** 90% National - 10% International.

SOIL:

Light, permeable, rich in mineral nutrients and with a slightly acidic pH due to the volcanic nature of the island. The vineyards are at an altitude of between 250 mm and 700 m.

CLIMATE:

As with the other regions on the islands, the weather is conditioned by the trade winds, which in this region result in wines with a moderate alcohol content and a truly Atlantic character. The influence of the Atlantic is also very important, in that it moderates the temperature of the costal areas and provides a lot of humidity. Lastly, the rainfall is rather low, but is generally more abundant on the north face and at higher altitudes.

VINTAGE RATING

PEÑÍNGUIDE

2010	2011	2012	2013	2014
GOOD	VERY GOOD	VERY GOOD	VERY GOOD	GOOD

BODEGA TAFURIASTE

Las Candias Altas, 11
38312 La Orotava
(Santa Cruz de Tenerife)
☎: +34 647 421 256
Fax: +34 922 336 027
vinos@bodegatafuriaste.com
www.bodegatafuriaste.com

Tafuriaste Afrutado Semidulce 2014 B
listán blanco

88

Colour: bright yellow. Nose: powerfull, candied fruit, dried herbs. Palate: flavourful, sweet, ripe fruit, good acidity.

Tafuriaste Afrutado Semidulce 2014 RD
listán negro

82

Tafuriaste Seco 2014 B
listán blanco

82

BODEGA TAJINASTE

El Ratiño 5, La Habanera
38315 La Orotava
(Santa Cruz de Tenerife)
☎: +34 922 308 720
Fax: +34 922 105 080
bodega@tajinaste.net
www.tajinaste.net

Can 2013 T
50% listán negro, 50% vijariego negro

91

Colour: cherry, garnet rim. Nose: red berry notes, ripe fruit, fragrant herbs, spicy, toasty, creamy oak, mineral. Palate: powerful, flavourful, balsamic, balanced.

Tajinaste 2014 RD
100% listán negro

85

Tajinaste 2014 T Maceración Carbónica

86

Tajinaste Tradicional 2014 T
100% listán negro

88

Colour: cherry, purple rim. Nose: fresh fruit, red berry notes, floral. Palate: flavourful, fruity, good acidity.

Tajinaste Vendimia Seleccionada 2013 T
100% listán negro

89

Colour: light cherry. Nose: fruit expression, fruit liqueur notes, fragrant herbs, spicy. Palate: balanced, elegant, spicy, long.

BODEGAS EL PENITENTE

Camino La Habanera, 288
38300 La Orotava
(Santa Cruz de Tenerife)
☎: +34 922 309 024
Fax: +34 922 321 264
bodegas@elpenitentesl.es
www.bodegaselpenitente.es

Arautava 2013 T
listán negro

90

Colour: bright cherry. Nose: ripe fruit, sweet spices, expressive. Palate: flavourful, fruity, round tannins.

Arautava 2013 T Fermentado en Barrica
listán negro

88

Colour: bright cherry. Nose: ripe fruit, sweet spices, creamy oak. Palate: flavourful, fruity, toasty, round tannins.

Arautava 2014 B
listán blanco

87

Colour: bright straw. Nose: white flowers, fine lees, dried herbs. Palate: flavourful, fruity, good acidity.

Arautava Finca la Habanera 2013 B
albillo

88

Colour: bright straw. Nose: white flowers, fresh fruit, fragrant herbs, expressive. Palate: flavourful, fruity, good acidity, balanced.

Arautava Kryos 2013 T Maceración Carbónica
listán negro

88

Colour: cherry, purple rim. Nose: red berry notes, floral. Palate: flavourful, fruity, good acidity.

LA HAYA

Calzadillas, s/n La Cruz Santa
38415 Los Realejos
(Santa Cruz de Tenerife)
☎: +34 629 051 413
Fax: +34 922 345 313
jaghcatire@telefonica.net

La Haya 2014 B

82

La Haya 2013 B Barrica

83

La Haya Afrutado 2014 B

80

LA SUERTITA

Real de la Cruz Santa, 35-A
38413 Los Realejos
(Santa Cruz de Tenerife)
☎: +34 669 408 761
bodegalasuertita@yahoo.es

La Suertita 2012 B Barrica

86

La Suertita 2014 B

87

Colour: bright straw. Nose: dried herbs, faded flowers, ripe fruit. Palate: ripe fruit, spicy, balsamic.

La Suertita Afrutado 2014 B

87

Colour: bright straw. Nose: white flowers, fresh fruit, fragrant herbs. Palate: flavourful, fruity, good acidity.

La Suertita Albillo 2013 B

83

SUERTES DEL MARQUÉS

Cº Las Suertes s/n, La Perdoma
38300 La Orotava
(Santa Cruz de Tenerife)
☎: +34 922 501 300
Fax: +34 922 503 462
ventas@suertesdelmarques.com
www.suertesdelmarques.com

7 Fuentes 2014 T

listán negro, tintilla

89

Colour: cherry, purple rim. Nose: floral, balsamic herbs, grassy. Palate: powerful, fresh, fruity.

7 Fuentes El Lance 2013 TC

vijariego negro, tintilla, listán negro, baboso negro, malvasía rosada

92

Colour: deep cherry, purple rim. Nose: toasty, ripe fruit, balsamic herbs. Palate: balanced, spicy, long, mineral.

Suertes del Marqués Candio 2011 T

listán negro

93

Colour: very deep cherry, garnet rim. Nose: expressive, complex, mineral, balsamic herbs, fruit liqueur notes. Palate: full, flavourful, round tannins, good acidity.

🏆 PODIUM

Suertes del Marqués Dulce 2010 B

malvasía, listán blanco

95

Colour: golden. Nose: powerfull, honeyed notes, candied fruit, fragrant herbs, acetaldehyde. Palate: flavourful, sweet, fresh, fruity, good acidity, long.

Suertes del Marqués El Ciruelo 2013 T

listán negro

93

Colour: deep cherry, purple rim. Nose: creamy oak, toasty, ripe fruit, balsamic herbs. Palate: balanced, spicy, long.

Suertes del Marqués El Esquilón 2013 T

listán negro, tintilla

92

Colour: very deep cherry, garnet rim. Nose: expressive, complex, mineral, balsamic herbs, balanced. Palate: full, flavourful, round tannins.

Suertes del Marqués La Solana 2013 T

listán negro

90

Colour: ruby red. Nose: toasty, ripe fruit, balsamic herbs, wild herbs. Palate: balanced, spicy, long.

Suertes del Marqués Los Pasitos 2013 T

baboso negro

92

Colour: bright cherry. Nose: ripe fruit, sweet spices, creamy oak, expressive, earthy notes, mineral. Palate: flavourful, fruity, round tannins.

Suertes del Marqués Trenzado 2014 B

listán blanco, pedro ximénez, gual, marmajuelo, albillo, baboso blanco

89

Colour: bright straw. Nose: white flowers, fine lees, dried herbs, ripe fruit. Palate: flavourful, fruity, good acidity.

Suertes del Marqués Vidonia 2013 B

listán blanco

92

Colour: bright yellow. Nose: expressive, dried herbs, ripe fruit, spicy, earthy notes. Palate: flavourful, fruity, good acidity.

DO. VINOS DE MADRID

CONSEJO REGULADOR

Ronda de Atocha, 7
28012 Madrid
☎ : +34 915 348 511 / Fax: +34 915 538 574
@: prensa@vinosdemadrid.es
www.vinosdemadrid.es

LOCATION:

In the south of the province of Madrid, it covers three distinct sub-regions: Arganda, Navalcarnero and San Martín de Valdeiglesias.

SUB-REGIONS:

San Martín. It comprises 9 municipal districts and has more than 3,821 Ha of vineyards, with mainly the Garnacha (red) and Albillo (white) varieties.

Navalcarnero. It comprises 19 municipal districts with a total of about 2,107 Ha. The most typical wines are reds and rosés based on the Garnacha variety.

Arganda. With 5,830 Ha and 26 municipal districts, it is the largest sub-region of the DO. The main varieties are the white Malvar and the red Tempranillo or Tinto Fino.

GRAPE VARIETIES:

WHITE: Malvar, Airén, Albillo, Parellada, Macabeo, Torrontés, Moscatel de Grano Menudo and Sauvignon Blanc.

RED: Tinto Fino (Tempranillo), Garnacha, Merlot, Cabernet Sauvignon, Syrah and Petit Verdot.

FIGURES:

Vineyard surface: 8,391 – **Wine-Growers:** 2,890 – **Wineries:** 46 – **2014 Harvest rating:** Excellent – **Production 14:** 3,855,810 litres – **Market percentages:** 70% National - 30% International.

SOIL:

Rather unfertile soil and granite subsoil in the sub-region of San Martín de Valdeiglesias; in Navalcarnero the soil is brownish-grey, poor, with a subsoil of coarse sand and clay; In the sub-region of Arganda the soil is brownish-grey, with an acidic pH and granite subsoil.

CLIMATE:

Extreme continental, with cold winters and hot summers. The average annual rainfall ranges from 461 mm in Arganda to 658 mm in San Martín.

VINTAGE RATING

PEÑÍNGUIDE

2010	2011	2012	2013	2014
VERY GOOD	VERY GOOD	GOOD	VERY GOOD	GOOD

BERNABELEVA

Ctra. Avila Toledo (N-403), Km. 81,600
28680 San Martín de Valdeiglesias (Madrid)
☎: +34 915 091 909
bodega@bernabeleva.com
www.bernabeleva.com

Bernabeleva "Arroyo de Tórtolas" 2013 T
garnacha

93

Colour: cherry, garnet rim. Nose: ripe fruit, wild herbs, earthy notes, spicy, balsamic herbs. Palate: balanced, flavourful, long, balsamic.

Bernabeleva "Carril del Rey" 2013 T
garnacha

94

Colour: light cherry. Nose: expressive, spicy, waxy notes, ripe fruit, varietal. Palate: flavourful, fruity, balanced.

Bernabeleva Viña Bonita 2013 T
garnacha

92

Colour: cherry, garnet rim. Nose: red berry notes, ripe fruit, balanced, varietal, dried herbs. Palate: ripe fruit, long, fruity aftestaste, balanced.

Cantocuerdas Albillo 2013 B
albillo

92

Colour: golden. Nose: white flowers, fine lees, mineral, spicy, floral, faded flowers. Palate: flavourful, fruity, good acidity, round.

Navaherreros Blanco de Bernabeleva 2013 B
albillo, macabeo

90

Colour: bright yellow. Nose: dried flowers, expressive, spicy. Palate: fruity, rich, flavourful, balanced, fine bitter notes.

Navaherreros Garnacha de Bernabeleva 2013 T
garnacha

93

Colour: light cherry. Nose: elegant, expressive, ripe fruit, dried herbs, wild herbs. Palate: flavourful, good acidity.

BODEGA ECOLÓGICA ANDRÉS MORATE

Camino del Horcajuelo, s/n
28390 Belmonte de Tajo (Madrid)
☎: +34 918 747 165
bodegas@andresmorate.com
www.andresmorate.com

Esther 2012 TC
tempranillo, cabernet sauvignon, syrah

84

Viña Bosquera 2013 T
100% tempranillo

84

Viña Bosquera 2014 B
60% airén, 40% moscatel grano menudo

84

BODEGA ECOLÓGICA LUIS SAAVEDRA

Ctra. de Escalona, 5
28650 Cenicientos (Madrid)
☎: +34 916 893 400
Fax: +34 914 606 053
info@bodegasaavedra.com
www.bodegasaavedra.com

Chotis 2013 T Roble
100% garnacha

87

Colour: bright cherry. Nose: ripe fruit, sweet spices, creamy oak, expressive. Palate: flavourful, fruity, toasty, round tannins.

Corucho 2012 TC
95% garnacha, 5% tinto fino

89

Colour: cherry, garnet rim. Nose: ripe fruit, candied fruit, dried herbs, spicy. Palate: balanced, correct, round tannins.

Corucho 2014 RD
100% garnacha

84

Corucho 2014 T Roble
90% garnacha, 10% tinto fino

85

Corucho Albillo Moscatel 2014 B
85% albillo, 15% moscatel grano menudo

86

Corucho Finca Peazo de la Encina 2013 T Roble
85% garnacha, 10% syrah, 5% merlot

88

Colour: cherry, purple rim. Nose: wild herbs, ripe fruit. Palate: fruity, round tannins, spicy.

Flor del Amanecer 2014 B
sauvignon blanc

86

Luis Saavedra 2011 T
90% garnacha, 10% syrah

87

Colour: very deep cherry, garnet rim. Nose: balsamic herbs, balanced. Palate: full, flavourful, slightly dry, soft tannins.

BODEGA MARAÑONES

Av. Marcial Llorente, 69 Naves B y C
28696 Pelayos de la Presa (Madrid)
☎: +34 918 647 702
Fax: +34 914 464 937
bodega@bodegamaranones.com
www.bodegamaranones.com

Labros 2013 T
100% garnacha

93

Colour: light cherry. Nose: characterful, mineral, ripe fruit. Palate: balanced, round, round tannins, ripe fruit.

Marañones 2013 T
100% garnacha

93

Colour: cherry, garnet rim. Nose: red berry notes, ripe fruit, wild herbs, varietal, expressive. Palate: fruity, flavourful, long, fruity aftestaste.

Peña Caballera 2013 T
100% garnacha

94

Colour: light cherry, garnet rim. Nose: mineral, expressive, spicy. Palate: flavourful, ripe fruit, long, good acidity, balanced.

Picarana 2014 B
100% albillo

93

Colour: yellow. Nose: expressive, dried herbs, ripe fruit, spicy. Palate: flavourful, fruity, good acidity, balanced.

Piesdescalzos 2013 B
100% albillo

92

Colour: bright yellow. Nose: faded flowers, expressive, mineral, ripe fruit. Palate: flavourful, good structure, spicy, long. Personality.

Treinta Mil Maravedíes 2014 T
90% garnacha, 10% variedad local

92

Colour: light cherry, purple rim. Nose: dry nuts, dried herbs, faded flowers. Palate: good structure, flavourful, ripe fruit. Personality.

BODEGA Y VIÑEDOS GOSÁLBEZ ORTI

Real, 14
28813 Pozuelo del Rey (Madrid)
☎: +34 607 625 806
Fax: +34 918 725 399
bodega@qubel.com
www.qubel.com

Mayrit 2012 T Barrica

89

Colour: cherry, garnet rim. Nose: ripe fruit, fragrant herbs, spicy. Palate: powerful, flavourful, balsamic.

Mayrit 2013 B

82

Qubél Nature 2006 T

87

Colour: pale ruby, brick rim edge. Nose: spicy, fine reductive notes, wet leather, aged wood nuances, fruit liqueur notes. Palate: spicy, fine tannins, balanced.

Qubél Paciencia 2005 T

75

Qubél Revelación 2013 T

88

Colour: deep cherry. Nose: ripe fruit, scrubland, earthy notes. Palate: powerful, flavourful, concentrated.

BODEGAS CASTEJÓN

Real, 118
28500 Arganda del Rey (Madrid)
☎: +34 918 710 264
Fax: +34 918 713 343
castejon@bodegascastejon.com
www.bodegascastejon.com

Viña Rey "70 Barricas" 2013 T
100% tempranillo

82

Viña Rey 2014 B
malvar, viura

84

Viña Rey Tempranillo 2014 T
100% tempranillo

83

Viñardul 2009 TR
100% tempranillo

86

Viñardul 2011 TC
100% tempranillo

86

BODEGAS NUEVA VALVERDE

Ctra. M507 Km 34
28630 Villa del Prado (Madrid)
☎: +34 915 649 495
info@bodegasnuevavalverde.com
www.bodegasnuevavalverde.com

750 2007 TR
40% merlot, 30% cabernet sauvignon, 20% syrah, 10% garnacha

90

Colour: cherry, garnet rim. Nose: balanced, complex, ripe fruit, spicy, fine reductive notes. Palate: good structure, flavourful, round tannins, balanced.

Tejoneras 2010 TC
merlot, syrah, cabernet sauvignon, garnacha

89

Colour: deep cherry, garnet rim. Nose: ripe fruit, spicy, dried herbs. Palate: balanced, flavourful, fruity.

BODEGAS ORUSCO

Alcalá, 48
28511 Valdilecha (Madrid)
☎: +34 918 738 006
Fax: +34 918 738 336
bo@bodegasorusco.com
www.bodegasorusco.com

Armonium 2010 T
70% merlot, 30% cabernet sauvignon

89

Colour: cherry, garnet rim. Nose: ripe fruit, wild herbs, earthy notes, spicy, balsamic herbs. Palate: balanced, flavourful, long, balsamic.

Maín 2012 TC
80% tempranillo, 20% cabernet sauvignon

84

Viña Maín 2014 B
malvar blanco

84

BODEGAS PABLO MORATE - MUSEO DEL VINO

Avda. Generalísimo, 34
28391 Valdelaguna (Madrid)
☎: +34 918 937 172
Fax: +34 918 937 172
bodegasmorate@bodegasmorate.com
www.bodegasmorate.com

Arate Premium Selección 2014 B
viura, malvar

82

Señorío de Morate Gran Selección Tempranillo 2006 T

86

Señorío de Morate Selección 2004 TGR
tempranillo, syrah

86

Señorío de Morate Selección 2010 TR

85

Señorío de Morate Selección 2012 TC
syrah, tempranillo

83

Señorío de Morate Selección 2014 T Roble
tempranillo, syrah

83

BODEGAS TAGONIUS

Ctra. de Tielmes a Carabaña Km 4,4
28550 Tielmes (Madrid)
☎: +34 918 737 505
Fax: +34 918 746 161
gerencia@tagonius.com
www.tagonius.com

Tagonius 2004 TR
tempranillo, syrah, merlot, cabernet sauvignon

92

Colour: cherry, garnet rim. Nose: balanced, complex, ripe fruit, spicy, fine reductive notes. Palate: good structure, flavourful, round tannins, balanced.

Tagonius 2005 TR
tempranillo, syrah, merlot, cabernet sauvignon

91

Colour: dark-red cherry. Nose: old leather, tobacco, fruit liqueur notes, spicy, dried herbs. Palate: flavourful, good structure, round tannins.

Tagonius 2006 TR
tempranillo, syrah, merlot, cabernet sauvignon

90

Colour: very deep cherry, garnet rim. Nose: warm, characterful, dried herbs, grassy, spicy. Palate: round tannins, ripe fruit.

Tagonius 2007 TC
tempranillo, syrah, merlot, cabernet sauvignon

86

Tagonius 2010 TC
tempranillo, syrah, merlot, cabernet sauvignon

89

Colour: deep cherry, garnet rim. Nose: medium intensity, red berry notes, ripe fruit, balanced. Palate: flavourful, fruity, round tannins, balsamic.

Tagonius 2012 T Roble
tempranillo, syrah, merlot, cabernet sauvignon

87

Colour: bright cherry. Nose: ripe fruit, sweet spices, creamy oak. Palate: flavourful, fruity, toasty, round tannins, easy to drink.

Tagonius 2012 TC
tempranillo, syrah, merlot, cabernet sauvignon

88

Colour: cherry, garnet rim. Nose: ripe fruit, fragrant herbs, spicy, toasty, creamy oak. Palate: powerful, flavourful, balsamic, balanced.

Tagonius Blanc 2013 B
malvar, sauvignon blanc

87

Colour: bright yellow. Nose: wild herbs, fresh fruit, dried flowers. Palate: balanced, fine bitter notes, easy to drink, spicy.

Tagonius Cosecha 2012 T
tempranillo, syrah, merlot, cabernet sauvignon

85

Tagonius Gran Vino 2004 TR
tempranillo, syrah, cabernet sauvignon

93

Colour: bright cherry, orangey edge. Nose: cocoa bean, ripe fruit, creamy oak, balsamic herbs, fine reductive notes. Palate: balanced, long, good acidity.

Tagonius Merlot 2010 T
merlot

90

Colour: deep cherry, orangey edge. Nose: scrubland, varietal, tobacco, ripe fruit, characterful. Palate: full, flavourful, round tannins.

Tagonius Syrah 2010 T
syrah

89

Colour: cherry, garnet rim. Nose: red berry notes, ripe fruit, spicy, expressive, dried flowers. Palate: correct, easy to drink, round tannins, fruity aftestaste.

BODEGAS Y VIÑEDOS VALLEYGLESIAS

Camino Fuente de los Huertos s/n
28680 San Martín de Valdeiglesias (Madrid)
☎: +34 606 842 636
bodega@valleyglesias.com
www.valleyglesias.com

Garnacha Rock 2013 T
100% garnacha

89

Colour: cherry, garnet rim. Nose: mineral, expressive, ripe fruit, balsamic herbs. Palate: spicy, toasty, balanced, round tannins.

La Pájara 2014 B
100% albillo

88

Colour: bright straw. Nose: white flowers, fragrant herbs, expressive. Palate: flavourful, fruity, good acidity, balanced, toasty, smoky aftertaste.

Septem Eremi Puro Albillo 2014 BFB
100% albillo

90

Colour: bright yellow. Nose: expressive, dried herbs, ripe fruit, spicy, creamy oak. Palate: flavourful, fruity, good acidity, balanced.

Valleyglesias Albillo Moscatel 2014 B
85% albillo, 15% moscatel grano menudo

88

Colour: bright straw. Nose: white flowers, jasmine, expressive, powerfull. Palate: balanced, good acidity, flavourful, fruity.

Valleyglesias Garnacha Centenaria 2013 T
100% garnacha

90

Colour: cherry, garnet rim. Nose: expressive, mineral, ripe fruit, characterful, warm. Palate: good structure, flavourful, fruity.

COMANDO G VITICULTORES

Avda. Constitución, 23
28640 Cadalso de los Vidrios (Madrid)
☎: +34 918 640 602
info@comandog.es
www.comandog.es

La Bruja Avería 2014 T
garnacha

92

Colour: cherry, purple rim. Nose: red berry notes, floral, balsamic herbs. Palate: powerful, fresh, fruity.

Las Umbrías 2013 T
100% garnacha

92

Colour: deep cherry. Nose: fruit liqueur notes, spicy, mineral, earthy notes. Palate: flavourful, light-bodied, good acidity, fine bitter notes, long.

Rozas 1er Cru 2013 T
100% garnacha

93

Colour: deep cherry. Nose: fruit liqueur notes, spicy, scrubland, balsamic herbs. Palate: light-bodied, flavourful, sweetness, good acidity.

COMERCIAL GRUPO FREIXENET

Joan Sala, 2
08770 Sant Sadurní D'Anoia
(Barcelona)
☎: +34 938 917 000
Fax: +34 938 183 095
freixenet@freixenet.es
www.freixenet.es

Heredad Torresano 2013 T Roble
tinto fino

85

IN THE MOOD FOR WINE

Calle Altamirano 12, 6º izq.
28008 Madrid (Madrid)
☎: +34 696 877 811
contact@inthemoodforwine.com
www.inthemoodforwine.com

Chulapa 2010 TC
tempranillo

89

Colour: deep cherry, garnet rim. Nose: spicy, ripe fruit, varietal. Palate: ripe fruit, spicy, long, round tannins.

JESÚS FIGUEROA

28380 Colmenar de Oreja (Madrid)
☎: +34 918 944 859
Fax: +34 918 944 859
bodegasjesusfigueroa@hotmail.com
www.bodegasfigueroa.es

Figueroa 2012 TC
tempranillo

87

Colour: cherry, garnet rim. Nose: creamy oak, balanced, ripe fruit. Palate: flavourful, spicy, correct, toasty, easy to drink.

Figueroa 2013 T Roble
80% tempranillo, 20% merlot

87

Colour: deep cherry, purple rim. Nose: powerfull, ripe fruit, warm, dried herbs. Palate: balanced, toasty, ripe fruit.

Figueroa 2014 B
moscatel, malvar, macabeo

86

Figueroa 2014 T

86

Figueroa Cabernet 2013 T Roble
100% cabernet sauvignon

86

Figueroa Semidulce 2014 B
moscatel, malvar

84

KRONOS SELECCIÓN

Camino San Martín de la Vega, 16
28500 Arganda del Rey (Madrid)
☎: +34 696 708 016
oscar@kronosseleccion.com
www.kronosseleccion.com

Kronos Selección 2012 T
100% tempranillo

87

Colour: cherry, garnet rim. Nose: smoky, spicy, ripe fruit, balsamic herbs. Palate: flavourful, smoky aftertaste, ripe fruit, sweet tannins.

LAS MORADAS DE SAN MARTÍN

Pago de Los Castillejos
Ctra. M-541, Km. 4,7
28680 San Martín de Valdeiglesias
(Madrid)
☎: +34 691 676 570
bodega@lasmoradasdesanmartin.es
www.lasmoradasdesanmartin.es

Las Moradas de San Martín Initio 2008 T
garnacha

89

Colour: dark-red cherry, orangey edge. Nose: balanced, fragrant herbs, old leather, spicy. Palate: flavourful, good structure, good acidity.

Las Moradas de San Martín La Sabina 2008 T
garnacha

90

Colour: very deep cherry, garnet rim. Nose: balsamic herbs, balanced, spicy, dried herbs. Palate: full, flavourful, round tannins.

Las Moradas de San Martín Senda 2012 T
garnacha

91

Colour: cherry, garnet rim. Nose: wild herbs, dried herbs, ripe fruit, varietal, expressive. Palate: full, flavourful, long.

Las Moradas de San Martín, Libro Ocho Las Luces 2008 T
garnacha

93

Colour: cherry, garnet rim. Nose: scrubland, waxy notes, ripe fruit, mineral, expressive, complex. Palate: full, flavourful, spicy, long.

MARQUÉS DE GRIÑÓN

Finca Casa de Vacas CM-4015, Km. 23
45692 Malpica de Tajo (Toledo)
☎: +34 925 597 222
service@pagosdefamilia.com
www.pagosdefamilia.com

El Rincón 2010 T
syrah, garnacha

91

Colour: very deep cherry, garnet rim. Nose: expressive, complex, mineral, balsamic herbs, ripe fruit. Palate: full, flavourful, spicy, long.

UVAS FELICES

Agullers, 7
08003 Barcelona (Barcelona)
☎: +34 902 327 777
www.vilaviniteca.es

El Hombre Bala 2013 T
100% garnacha

92

Colour: cherry, purple rim. Nose: red berry notes, floral, balsamic herbs, scrubland. Palate: powerful, fresh, fruity.

La Mujer Cañón 2013 T
100% garnacha

93

Colour: light cherry, bright cherry. Nose: ripe fruit, neat, expressive, mineral, fresh. Palate: balanced, long, balsamic, elegant, good structure.

Reina de los deseos 2013 T
100% garnacha

94

Colour: deep cherry, purple rim. Nose: toasty, ripe fruit, balsamic herbs, red berry notes. Palate: balanced, spicy, long.

VINOS JEROMÍN

San José, 8
28590 Villarejo de Salvanés (Madrid)
☎: +34 918 742 030
Fax: +34 918 744 139
comercial@vinosjeromin.com
www.vinosjeromin.com

Dos de Mayo Edición Limitada 2010 TC
tempranillo

89

Colour: cherry, garnet rim. Nose: ripe fruit, wild herbs, earthy notes, spicy, balsamic herbs. Palate: balanced, flavourful, long, balsamic.

Félix Martínez Cepas Viejas 2011 TR
90% tempranillo, 10% syrah

90

Colour: deep cherry, garnet rim. Nose: expressive, spicy. Palate: flavourful, ripe fruit, long, good acidity, balanced.

Grego 2010 TC
tempranillo, syrah, garnacha

89

Colour: bright cherry, garnet rim. Nose: wild herbs, ripe fruit, spicy, balsamic herbs. Palate: fruity, flavourful, balanced.

Grego 2013 T Roble
tempranillo, syrah

86

Grego Garnacha Centenarias 2012 T Roble
garnacha

86

Grego Moscatel Seco 2013 B
moscatel grano menudo

87

Colour: bright yellow. Nose: white flowers, ripe fruit, expressive, varietal, balsamic herbs. Palate: fruity, fine bitter notes, good acidity.

Manu Vino de Autor 2009 TC
tempranillo, syrah, garnacha, cabernet sauvignon, merlot

90

Colour: cherry, garnet rim. Nose: ripe fruit, wild herbs, earthy notes, spicy, balsamic herbs. Palate: balanced, flavourful, long, balsamic.

Puerta Cerrada 2014 B
malvar, airén

84

Puerta Cerrada 2014 RD
tempranillo, garnacha, malvar

84

Puerta Cerrada 2014 T
tempranillo, garnacha

83

Puerta de Alcalá 2011 TC
tempranillo

87

Colour: deep cherry, garnet rim. Nose: ripe fruit, spicy, balanced. Palate: flavourful, fruity, round tannins.

Puerta de Alcalá 2011 TR
tempranillo

87

Colour: cherry, garnet rim. Nose: ripe fruit, earthy notes, spicy, balsamic herbs. Palate: balanced, flavourful, long, balsamic.

Puerta de Alcalá 2014 B
malvar

84

Puerta de Alcalá 2014 RD
tempranillo, garnacha

84

Puerta de Alcalá 2014 T
tempranillo, syrah

84

Puerta de Hierro 2011 TC
tempranillo

84

Puerta del Sol Malvar Nº1 2014 B
malvar

86

Puerta del Sol Nº 4 Varietales 2010 TC
cabernet sauvignon, merlot

87

Colour: very deep cherry. Nose: varietal, ripe fruit, scrubland, wild herbs, spicy. Palate: good structure, flavourful.

Puerta del Sol Nº2 2014 T Joven
tempranillo, syrah, merlot

85

Puerta del Sol Nº3 2014 BFB
malvar

86

Puerta del Sol Nº5 Tempranillo 2010 TC
tempranillo

87

Colour: very deep cherry, garnet rim. Nose: expressive, balsamic herbs, balanced. Palate: full, flavourful, round tannins.

Purificación Garnacha 2012 T
garnacha

89

Colour: light cherry, garnet rim. Nose: balanced, varietal, red berry notes, ripe fruit, warm. Palate: flavourful, good structure, long.

Purita Dynamita Garnacha 2013 T
garnacha

88

Colour: dark-red cherry, garnet rim. Nose: ripe fruit, dried herbs, varietal, characterful. Palate: balanced, round tannins.

Vega Madroño 2014 B
malvar, airén

84

Vega Madroño 2014 RD
tempranillo, garnacha, syrah, merlot, malvar

82

Vega Madroño 2014 T
tempranillo, merlot

83

VINOS SANZ

Ctra. Madrid - La Coruña, Km. 170,5
47490 Rueda (Valladolid)
☎: +34 983 868 100
Fax: +34 983 868 117
vinossanz@vinossanz.com
www.vinossanz.com

Sanz La Capital 2014 T
100% tempranillo

87

Colour: cherry, garnet rim. Nose: powerfull, ripe fruit, wild herbs. Palate: powerful, fruity, unctuous.

VINOS Y ACEITES LAGUNA

Illescas, 5
28360 Villaconejos (Madrid)
☎: +34 918 938 196
Fax: +34 918 938 344
info@lagunamadrid.com
www.lagunamadrid.com

Alma de Valdeguerra 2012 TC
tempranillo, merlot

87

Colour: very deep cherry, garnet rim. Nose: expressive, balsamic herbs, balanced, creamy oak, cocoa bean. Palate: full, flavourful, round tannins.

Alma de Valdeguerra 2014 B
malvar

86

Alma de Valdeguerra 2014 T
tempranillo

87

Colour: cherry, purple rim. Nose: expressive, red berry notes, floral, lactic notes. Palate: flavourful, fruity, good acidity, easy to drink.

Alma de Valdeguerra Semidulce 2014 B
malvar

85

Alma de Valdeguerra Semidulce 2014 RD
tempranillo

86

Exun 2012 T
tempranillo, cabernet sauvignon, merlot

88

Colour: bright cherry, purple rim. Nose: creamy oak, sweet spices, ripe fruit. Palate: spicy, balsamic, long.

VIÑAS EL REGAJAL

Antigua Ctra. Andalucía, Km. 50,5
28300 Aranjuez (Madrid)
☎: +34 913 078 903
Fax: +34 913 576 312
reservas@elregajal.es
www.elregajal.es

El Regajal Selección Especial 2013 T
tempranillo, syrah, merlot, cabernet sauvignon, petit verdot

90

Colour: very deep cherry, purple rim. Nose: balanced, red berry notes, ripe fruit, wild herbs, sweet spices. Palate: good structure, flavourful.

Las Retamas del Regajal 2013 T
tempranillo, syrah, merlot, cabernet sauvignon

88

Colour: very deep cherry, garnet rim. Nose: ripe fruit, red berry notes, wild herbs, grassy. Palate: fruity, spicy, balsamic.

DO. YCODEN-DAUTE-ISORA

CONSEJO REGULADOR
La Palmita, 10
38440 La Guancha (Sta. Cruz de Tenerife)
☎:+34 922 130 246 - Fax: +34 922 828 159
@: ycoden@ycoden.com / promocion@ycoden.com
www.ycoden.com

LOCATION:

Occupying the northeast of the island of Tenerife and comprising the municipal districts of San Juan de La Rambla, La Guancha, Icod de los Vinos, Los Silos, El Tanque, Garachico, Buenavista del Norte, Santiago del Teide and Guía de Isora.

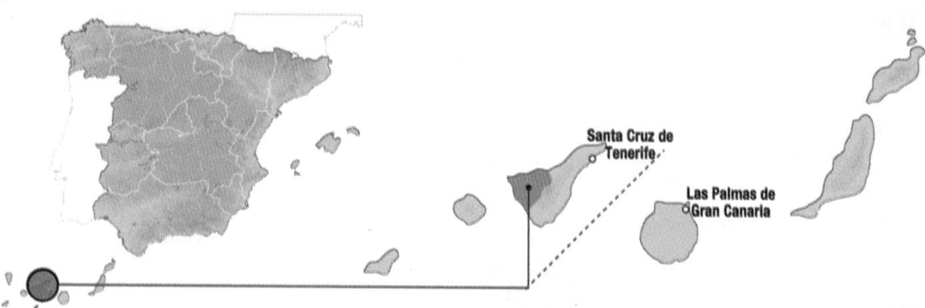

GRAPE VARIETIES:

WHITE: Bermejuela (or Marmajuelo), Güal, Malvasía, Moscatel, Pedro Ximénez, Verdello, Vijariego, Albillo, Bastardo Blanco, Forastera Blanca, Listán Blanco (majority), Sabro and Torrontés.
RED: Tintilla, Listán Negro (majority), Malvasía Rosada, Negramoll Castellana, Bastardo Negra, Moscatel Negra and Vijariego Negra.

FIGURES:

Vineyard surface: 185 – **Wine-Growers:** 480 – **Wineries:** 14 – **2014 Harvest rating:** Excellent – **Production 14:** 526,400 litres – **Market percentages:** 85% National - 15% International.

SOIL:

Volcanic ash and rock on the higher grounds, and clayey lower down. The vines are cultivated at very different heights, ranging from 50 to 1,400 m.

CLIMATE:

Mediterranean, characterised by the multitude of microclimates depending on the altitude and other geographical conditions. The trade winds provide the humidity necessary for the development of the vines. The average annual temperature is 19°C and the average annual rainfall is around 540 mm.

VINTAGE RATING

PEÑÍNGUIDE

2010	2011	2012	2013	2014
VERY GOOD	VERY GOOD	VERY GOOD	GOOD	GOOD

BODEGAS INSULARES TENERIFE S.A.

Vereda del Medio, 48
38350 Tacoronte
(Santa Cruz de Tenerife)
☎: +34 922 570 617
Fax: +34 922 570 043
bitsa@bodegasinsularestenerife.es
www.bodegasinsularestenerife.es

El Ancón 2014 T
listán negro

89

Colour: cherry, purple rim. Nose: expressive, fresh fruit, red berry notes, floral. Palate: flavourful, fruity, good acidity.

El Ancón 2014 T Barrica
listán negro, tintilla

90

Colour: bright cherry. Nose: ripe fruit, sweet spices, creamy oak, expressive. Palate: flavourful, fruity, round tannins.

Tágara 2014 B
listán blanco

87

Colour: bright straw. Nose: white flowers, fine lees, dried herbs, mineral. Palate: fruity, good acidity.

Tágara Afrutado 2014 B
listán blanco

85

Tágara Malvasía Marmajuelo 2014 B
malvasía, marmajuelo

87

Colour: bright yellow. Nose: expressive, dried herbs, ripe fruit, spicy. Palate: flavourful, fruity, good acidity, balanced.

BODEGAS VIÑÁTIGO

Cabo Verde, s/n
38440 La Guancha
(Santa Cruz de Tenerife)
☎: +34 922 828 768
Fax: +34 922 829 936
vinatigo@vinatigo.com
www.vinatigo.com

Viñátigo Gual 2014 B
100% gual

87

Colour: bright yellow. Nose: dried herbs, ripe fruit, spicy. Palate: flavourful, fruity, good acidity.

Viñátigo Malvasía Afrutado 2014 B
100% malvasía

86

Viñátigo Tintilla 2012 T Roble
100% tintilla

86

Viñátigo Vijariego Blanco 2013 BFB
100% vijariego blanco

88

Colour: bright yellow. Nose: ripe fruit, powerfull, toasty, aged wood nuances. Palate: flavourful, fruity, spicy, toasty.

BORJA PÉREZ GONZÁLEZ

Avda. Villanueva, 34
38440 La Guancha
(Santa Cruz de Tenerife)
☎: +34 630 575 464
info@borjaperezviticultor.com
www.borjaperezviticultor.com

Artificie 2014 BFB
listán blanco

89

Colour: bright yellow. Nose: ripe fruit, wild herbs, aged wood nuances, spicy. Palate: rich, fresh, toasty.

Artificie 2014 T
90% listán negro, 10% baboso negro, vijariego negro

90

Colour: light cherry. Nose: mineral, wild herbs, ripe fruit, balsamic herbs, expressive. Palate: powerful, flavourful, spicy.

Artificie Vidueños 2014 B
80% albillo, gual, 20% baboso negro, vijariego negro

90

Colour: bright yellow. Nose: expressive, dried herbs, ripe fruit, spicy, mineral. Palate: flavourful, fruity, good acidity, balanced.

Ignios Origenes Baboso Negro 2013 T
baboso negro

90

Colour: ruby red. Nose: creamy oak, toasty, ripe fruit, balsamic herbs. Palate: balanced, spicy, long.

Ignios Origenes Listán Negro Vendimia Seleccionada 2013 T
listán negro

93

Colour: very deep cherry, garnet rim. Nose: expressive, complex, mineral, balsamic herbs, balanced. Palate: full, flavourful, round tannins.

Ignios Origenes Marmajuelo 2013 B
marmajuelo

89

Colour: bright straw. Nose: white flowers, fine lees, dried herbs, ripe fruit, candied fruit, citrus fruit. Palate: flavourful, fruity, good acidity.

Ignios Origenes Vijariego Negro 2013 T
vijariego negro

94

Colour: cherry, garnet rim. Nose: mineral, expressive, earthy notes. Palate: flavourful, ripe fruit, long, good acidity, balanced.

C.B. LUIS, ANTONIO Y JAVIER LÓPEZ DE AYALA

El Majuelos, 2
38450 Garachico
(Santa Cruz de Tenerife)
☎: +34 922 133 079
Fax: +34 922 830 066
jlopezaz38@hotmail.es

Hacienda San Juan BN
76

Hacienda San Juan 2013 T
79

Hacienda San Juan 2014 B
verdello

83

Hacienda San Juan Malvasía 2014 B
72

VIÑA LA GUANCHA

El Sol, 3
38440 La Guancha
(Santa Cruz de Tenerife)
☎: +34 922 828 166
Fax: +34 922 828 166
zanata@zanata.net
www.zanata.net

Viña Zanata Afrutado 2014 B
listán blanco, moscatel, vijariego blanco

84

Viña Zanata Marmajuelo 2014 B
marmajuelo

84

Viña Zanata Tradicional 2014 B
listán blanco

84

DO YECLA

CONSEJO REGULADOR

Poeta Francisco A. Jiménez, s/n - P.I. Urbayecla II
30510 Yecla (Murcia)
☎:+34 968 792 352 - Fax: +34 968 792 352
@: info@yeclavino.com
www.yeclavino.com

LOCATION:

In the northeast of the province of Murcia, within the plateau region, and comprising a single municipal district, Yecla.

SUB-REGIONS:

Yecla Campo Arriba, with Monastrell as the most common variety and alcohol contents of up to 14°, and Yecla Campo Abajo, whose grapes produce a lower alcohol content (around 12° for reds and 11.5° for whites).

GRAPE VARIETIES:

WHITE: Merseguera, Airén, Macabeo, Malvasía, Chardonnay.
RED: Monastrell (majority 85% of total), Garnacha Tinta, Cabernet Sauvignon, Cencibel (Tempranillo), Merlot, Tintorera, Syrah.

FIGURES:

Vineyard surface: 6,314 – **Wine-Growers:** 538 – **Wineries:** 7 – **2014 Harvest rating:** Excellent – **Production 14:** 6,384,135 litres – **Market percentages:** 6% National - 94% International.

SOIL:

Fundamentally deep limestone, with good permeability. The vineyards are on undulating terrain at a height of between 400 m and 800 m above sea level.

CLIMATE:

Continental, with a slight Mediterranean influence, with hot summers and cold winters, and little rainfall, which is usually around 300 mm per annum.

VINTAGE RATING

PEÑÍNGUIDE

2010	2011	2012	2013	2014
VERY GOOD	VERY GOOD	VERY GOOD	VERY GOOD	GOOD

BODEGA TRENZA

Avda. Matías Saenz Tejada, s/n.
Edif. Fuengirola Center
29640 Fuengirola (Málaga)
☎: +34 615 343 320
Fax: +34 952 588 467
info@bodegatrenza.com
www.bodegatrenza.com

Trenza Family Collection 2010 T

50% monastrell, 19% syrah, 17% cabernet sauvignon, 8% garnacha tintorera, 6% merlot

93

Colour: cherry, garnet rim. Nose: balanced, complex, ripe fruit, spicy, scrubland. Palate: good structure, flavourful, round tannins, balanced.

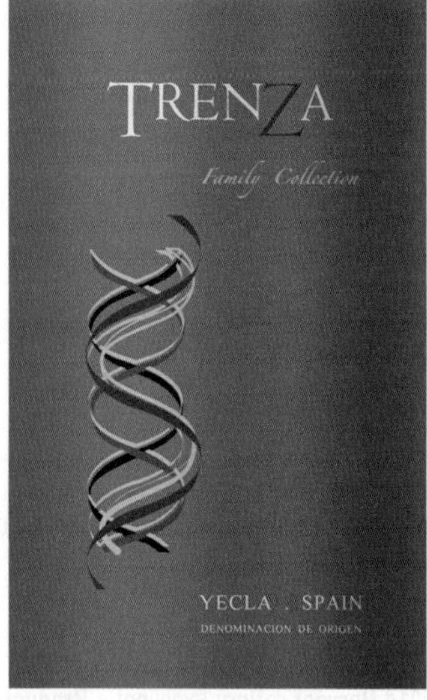

Trenza Z-Strand 2011 T

92% syrah, 8% cabernet sauvignon

92

Colour: cherry, garnet rim. Nose: red berry notes, ripe fruit, spicy, toasty, creamy oak, complex. Palate: powerful, flavourful, balsamic, balanced.

BODEGAS BARAHONDA

Ctra. de Pinoso, km. 3
30510 Yecla (Murcia)
☎: +34 968 718 696
Fax: +34 968 790 928
info@barahonda.com
www.barahonda.com

Barahonda 2012 TC

monastrell, syrah, petit verdot

88

Colour: cherry, garnet rim. Nose: ripe fruit, wild herbs, earthy notes, spicy, balsamic herbs. Palate: balanced, flavourful, long, balsamic.

Barahonda 2014 B

verdejo, macabeo

84

Barahonda 2014 RD

monastrell

86

Barahonda Barrica 2013 T

monastrell, syrah

88

Colour: very deep cherry, garnet rim. Nose: red berry notes, ripe fruit, dried herbs, spicy. Palate: flavourful, fruity.

Barahonda Monastrell 2014 T

monastrell

88

Colour: cherry, purple rim. Nose: red berry notes, ripe fruit, scrubland, varietal. Palate: powerful, fresh, fruity.

Barahonda Summum 2012 TC

monastrell

89

Colour: cherry, garnet rim. Nose: roasted coffee, smoky, spicy, ripe fruit. Palate: flavourful, smoky aftertaste, ripe fruit.

Campo Arriba 2013 T

monastrell, syrah, garnacha tintorera

88

Colour: very deep cherry, garnet rim. Nose: balanced, powerfull, ripe fruit, red berry notes, dried flowers. Palate: balanced, flavourful.

Carro 2014 T

monastrell, merlot, syrah, tempranillo

87

Colour: cherry, purple rim. Nose: expressive, red berry notes, floral, ripe fruit, wild herbs. Palate: flavourful, fruity, good acidity.

HC Monastrell 2013 T
monastrell

90

Colour: very deep cherry, garnet rim. Nose: expressive, complex, balsamic herbs, balanced, varietal. Palate: full, flavourful, round tannins, smoky aftertaste.

Tranco 2013 T
monastrell, cabernet sauvignon

86

BODEGAS CASTAÑO

Ctra. Fuenteálamo, 3
30510 Yecla (Murcia)
☎: +34 968 791 115
Fax: +34 968 791 900
info@bodegascastano.com
www.bodegascastano.com

Casa Cisca 2012 T
100% monastrell

93

Colour: cherry, garnet rim. Nose: expressive, spicy, cocoa bean. Palate: flavourful, ripe fruit, long, good acidity, balanced, full.

Casa de la Cera 2012 T
50% monastrell, 50% garnacha tintorera, cabernet sauvignon, syrah, merlot

94

Colour: cherry, garnet rim. Nose: red berry notes, ripe fruit, fragrant herbs, spicy, toasty, creamy oak, mineral. Palate: powerful, flavourful, balsamic, balanced.

Castaño Colección 2013 T
70% monastrell, 30% cabernet sauvignon

90

Colour: cherry, garnet rim. Nose: ripe fruit, wild herbs, earthy notes, spicy, balsamic herbs, smoky. Palate: balanced, flavourful, long.

Castaño GSM 2013 T
40% monastrell, 40% syrah, 20% garnacha tintorera

88

Colour: very deep cherry. Nose: medium intensity, red berry notes, ripe fruit, dried herbs. Palate: balanced, fruity, easy to drink, good acidity.

Castaño Macabeo Chardonnay 2014 B
50% macabeo, 50% chardonnay

87

Colour: bright straw. Nose: white flowers, fresh fruit, fragrant herbs, expressive. Palate: flavourful, fruity, good acidity, balanced.

Castaño Monastrell 2014 RD
100% monastrell

89

Colour: rose, purple rim. Nose: floral, wild herbs, fruit expression, expressive. Palate: flavourful, complex, balanced, elegant.

Castaño Monastrell 2014 T
100% monastrell

89

Colour: very deep cherry, garnet rim. Nose: expressive, balsamic herbs, balanced, ripe fruit, varietal. Palate: full, flavourful, round tannins.

Castaño Monastrell Dulce 2013 T
100% monastrell

86

Castaño Monastrell Ecológico 2014 T
100% monastrell

87 ♣

Colour: cherry, purple rim. Nose: expressive, red berry notes, scrubland, varietal. Palate: flavourful, fruity, good acidity.

Dominio Espinal 2014 B
100% macabeo

85

Dominio Espinal 2014 RD
100% monastrell

87

Colour: coppery red, bright. Nose: red berry notes, expressive, fresh, fragrant herbs. Palate: powerful, fruity, fresh, easy to drink, good acidity.

Dominio Espinal 2014 T
85% monastrell, 15% syrah

84

Dominio Espinal Selección 2013 T
80% monastrell, 10% cabernet sauvignon, 10% syrah

86

Hécula 2013 T
100% monastrell

88

Colour: black cherry, garnet rim. Nose: toasty, smoky, ripe fruit. Palate: flavourful, fruity, balsamic.

Solanera 2013 T
70% monastrell, 15% garnacha tintorera, 15% cabernet sauvignon

89

Colour: bright cherry. Nose: ripe fruit, sweet spices, creamy oak, expressive. Palate: flavourful, fruity, toasty, round tannins.

Viña al lado de la Casa 2011 T
monastrell, cabernet sauvignon, syrah, garnacha tintorera

88

Colour: cherry, garnet rim. Nose: scrubland, spicy, ripe fruit. Palate: correct, balsamic.

BODEGAS LA PURÍSIMA

Ctra. de Pinoso, 3
30510 Yecla (Murcia)
☎: +34 968 751 257
Fax: +34 968 795 116
info@bodegaslapurisima.com
www.bodegaslapurisima.com

Enesencia Dulce Natural 2014 T
monastrell

85

Estío 2014 RD
monastrell, syrah, merlot

84

Estío 2014 T
70% monastrell, 30% syrah

86

Estío Macabeo 2014 B
macabeo

82

Iglesia Vieja 2010 TC
monastrell, tempranillo, cabernet sauvignon

86

IV Expresión 2008 T
monastrell, syrah, garnacha

87

Colour: very deep cherry. Nose: balanced, ripe fruit, waxy notes, dried herbs. Palate: flavourful, good structure, round tannins.

La Purísima 2014 B
70% macabeo, 30% sauvignon blanc

86

La Purísima 2014 RD
monastrell, syrah

87

Colour: rose, bright. Nose: floral, wild herbs, fruit expression, expressive. Palate: flavourful, complex, balanced.

La Purísima Monastrell 2014 T
monastrell

88

Colour: black cherry, purple rim. Nose: ripe fruit, smoky, spicy, dried herbs. Palate: flavourful, spicy, powerful, round tannins.

La Purísima Old Vines Expressión 2010 T
monastrell, syrah, garnacha

92

Colour: very deep cherry. Nose: spicy, expressive, tobacco, fine reductive notes, wild herbs. Palate: flavourful, ripe fruit, long, good acidity, balanced.

La Purísima Premium 2010 T
monastrell, garnacha

93

Colour: cherry, garnet rim. Nose: mineral, expressive, spicy, complex. Palate: flavourful, ripe fruit, long, good acidity, balanced, balsamic.

La Purísima Syrah 2014 T
syrah

88

Colour: very deep cherry, purple rim. Nose: red berry notes, ripe fruit, violets, balanced, expressive, varietal. Palate: balanced, round tannins.

Trapío 2010 T
100% monastrell

89

Colour: deep cherry, purple rim. Nose: creamy oak, ripe fruit, scrubland. Palate: balanced, spicy, long.

Valcorso 2014 B
macabeo

86

Valcorso Cabernet Sauvignon 2014 T

100% cabernet sauvignon

87

Colour: very deep cherry, purple rim. Nose: powerfull, ripe fruit, characterful. Palate: flavourful, fruity, fruity aftestaste.

Valcorso Merlot 2014 T

merlot

87

Colour: cherry, purple rim. Nose: powerfull, ripe fruit, spicy. Palate: powerful, fruity, good acidity, round tannins.

Valcorso Monastrell 2013 T Barrica

100% monastrell

87

Colour: very deep cherry, purple rim. Nose: balanced, medium intensity, red berry notes, ripe fruit, spicy. Palate: fruity, flavourful, easy to drink, fruity aftestaste.

Valcorso Syrah 2014 T

100% syrah

88

Colour: cherry, purple rim. Nose: expressive, red berry notes, floral, ripe fruit. Palate: flavourful, fruity, good acidity.

DANIEL ALBA BODEGAS

Avda. Córdoba, 25
30510 Yecla (Murcia)
☎: +34 628 687 673
info@danielalbabodegas.com
www.danielalbabodegas.com

La Máquina Monastrell 2011 T

85% monastrell, 8% syrah, 7% garnacha tintorera

92

Colour: cherry, garnet rim. Nose: red berry notes, ripe fruit, fragrant herbs, spicy, toasty, creamy oak. Palate: powerful, flavourful, balsamic, balanced.

EVINE

Camino Sax, km. 7
30510 Yecla (Murcia)
☎: +34 677 692 317
info@bodegasevine.com
www.bodegasevine.com

Evine Rosé 2014 RD

monastrell

85

Kyathos 2012 T

monastrell

90 ♣

Colour: cherry, garnet rim. Nose: expressive, spicy, cocoa bean, creamy oak. Palate: flavourful, ripe fruit, long, good acidity, balanced.

Llano Quintanilla 2011 TC

monastrell

87 ♣

Colour: cherry, garnet rim. Nose: ripe fruit, spicy, dried herbs. Palate: toasty, fruity, good finish, balsamic.

HAMMEKEN CELLARS

Calle de la Muela, 16
03730 Jávea (Alicante)
☎: +34 965 791 967
Fax: +34 966 461 471
cellars@hammekencellars.com
www.hammekencellars.com

Bésame Mucho Monastell 2013 T

monastrell

85

Finca Rosal Old Vines Monastell 2012 T

monastrell

88

Colour: cherry, garnet rim. Nose: ripe fruit, wild herbs, earthy notes, spicy, balsamic herbs. Palate: balanced, flavourful, long, balsamic.

Flor del Montgó Organic Monastrell 2014 T

monastrell

88 ♣

Colour: cherry, purple rim. Nose: red berry notes, balsamic herbs, varietal. Palate: powerful, fruity, flavourful, easy to drink, long.

Montgó 2013 T

87

Colour: bright cherry. Nose: ripe fruit, sweet spices, creamy oak. Palate: flavourful, fruity, toasty.

LONG WINES

Avda. del Puente Cultural, 8 Bloque B Bajo 7
28702 San Sebastián de los Reyes
(Madrid)
☎: +34 916 221 305
Fax: +34 916 220 029
customer.service@longwines.com
www.longwines.com

Alma de Casa 2013 T

70% monastrell, 20% cabernet sauvignon, 10% syrah

85

Casa del Canto 2011 TR

80% monastrell, 20% cabernet sauvignon

91

Colour: cherry, garnet rim. Nose: ripe fruit, wild herbs, earthy notes, spicy, balsamic herbs. Palate: balanced, flavourful, long, balsamic.

Casa del Canto 2012 T Roble

65% monastrell, 25% cabernet sauvignon, 10% syrah

90

Colour: cherry, garnet rim. Nose: ripe fruit, wild herbs, earthy notes, spicy, balsamic herbs. Palate: balanced, flavourful, long, balsamic.

VINOS DE PAGO

The "Vinos de Pago" are linked to a single winery, and it is a status given to that winery on the grounds of unique micro-climatic features and proven evidence of consistent high quality over the years, with the goal to produce wines of sheer singularity. So far, only 17 "Vinos de Pago" labels have been granted for different autonomous regions (Aragón, La Mancha, Comunidad Valenciana and Navarra). The "Vinos de Pago" category has the same status as a DO. This "pago" should not be confused with the other "pago" term used in the wine realm, which refers to a plot, a smaller vineyard within a bigger property. The "Pagos de España" association was formed in 2000 when a group of small producers of single estate wines got together to defend the singularity of their wines. In 2003, the association became Grandes Pagos de España, responding to the request of many colleagues in other parts of the country who wished to make the single-growth concept better known, and to seek excellence through the direct relationship between wines and their places of origin.

PAGO DE AYLES

Situated in the municipality of Mezalocha (Zaragoza), within the limits of the Cariñena appellation. The production area is located within the Ebro basin, principally around the depression produced by the River Huerva. The soils consist of limestone, marl and composites. The climate is temperate continental with low average annual rainfall figures of 350 to 550mm. The varieties authorized for the production of red and rosé wines are: garnacha, merlot, tempranillo and cabernet sauvignon.

PAGO CALZADILLA

Located in the Mayor river valley, in the part of the Alcarria region that belongs to the province of Cuenca, it enjoys altitude levels ranging between 845 and 1005 meters. The vines are mostly planted on limestone soils with pronounced slopes (with up to a 40% incline), so terraces and slant plots have become the most common feature, following the altitude gradients. The grape varieties planted are tempranillo, cabernet-sauvignon, garnacha and syrah.

PAGO CAMPO DE LA GUARDIA

The vineyards are in the town of La Guardia, to the northeast of the province of Toledo, on a high plateau known as Mesa de Ocaña. Soils are deep and with varying degrees of loam, clay and sand. The climate follows a continental pattern, with hot and dry summers and particularly dry and cold winters. The presence of the Tajo River to the north and the Montes de Toledo to the south promote lower rainfall levels than in neighbouring areas, and thus more concentration of aromas and phenolic compounds.

PAGO CASA DEL BLANCO

Its vineyards are located at an altitude of 617 metres in Campo de Calatrava, in the town of Manzanares, right in the centre of the province of Ciudad Real, and therefore with a mediterranean/continental climate. Soils have varying degrees of loam and sand, and are abundant in lithium, surely due to the ancient volcanic character of the region.

PAGO CHOZAS CARRASCAL

In San Antonio de Requena. This is the third Estate of the Community of Valencia, with just 31 hectares. Located at 720 metres above sea level. It has a continental climatology with Mediterranean influence. Low rainfall (and average of 350-400 litres annually), its soils are loam texture tending to clay and sandy. The varieties uses are: bobal, tempranillo, garnacha, cabernet sauvignon, merlot, syrah, cabernet franc and monastrell for red wines and chardonnay, sauvignon blanc and macabeo for white wines.

PAGO DEHESA DEL CARRIZAL

Property of Marcial Gómez Sequeira, Dehesa del Carrizal is located in the town of Retuerta de Bullaque, to the north of Ciudad Real. It enjoys a continental climate and high altitude (900 metres). The winemaker, Ignacio de Miguel, uses primarily foreign (French) varieties such as cabernet sauvignon.

PAGO DOMINIO DE VALPEDUSA

Located in the town of Malpica de Tajo (Toledo), its owner, Carlos Falcó (Marqués de Griñón) pioneered the introduction in Spain of foreign grape varieties such as cabernet sauvignon.

PAGO EL TERRERAZO

El Terrerazo, property of Bodegas Mustiguilo, is the first "Vinos de Pago" label granted within the autonomous region of Valencia. It comprises 62 hectares at an altitude of 800 meters between Utiel and Sinarcas where an excellent clone of bobal –that yields small and loose berries– is grown. It enjoys a mediterranean-continental climate and the vineyard gets the influence of humid winds blowing from the sea, which is just 80 kilometres away from the property. Soils are characterized limestone and clay in nature, with abundant sand and stones.

PAGO FINCA BOLANDIN

140 hectares situated in the municipal area of Ablitas, in the southern limit of the province of Navarre, in the central area of the River Ebro Valley. This district is exposed to the influence of the Mediterranean which moves up the river valley. The vineyard is oriented to the south and has three types of soil; loam with abundant pebbles in the highest area, loam with silty clays with scarce stoniness in the upper half of the hillside and clay loam in the lower area. The authorised varieties are cabernet sauvignon, merlot, tempranillo and syrah for red wines and chardonnay, sauvignon blanc and small grain muscatel for white.

PAGO FINCA ÉLEZ

It became the first of all Vino de Pago designations of origin. Its owner is Manuel Manzaneque, and it is located at an altitude of 1000 metres in El Bonillo, in the province of Albacete. The winery became renown by its splendid chardonnay, but today also make a single-varietal syrah and some other red renderings.

PAGO FLORENTINO

Located in the municipality of Malagón (Ciudad Real), between natural lagoons to the south and the Sierra de Malagón to the north, at an altitude of some 630-670 metres. Soils are mainly siliceous with limestone and stones on the surface and a subsoil of slate and limestone. The climate is milder and dryer than that of neighbouring towns.

PAGO GUIJOSO

Finca El Guijoso is property of Bodegas Sánchez Muliterno, located in El Bonillo, between the provinces of Albacete and Ciudad Real. Surrounded by bitch and juniper woods, the vines are planted on stone (guijo in Spanish, from which it takes its name) soils at an altitude of 1000 metres. Wines are all made from French varieties, and have a clear French lean also in terms of style.

PAGO LOS BALAGUESES

The "Pago de los Balagueses" is located to the south west of the Utiel-Requena wine region, just 20 kilometres away from Requena. At approximately 700 metres over the sea level, it enjoys a continental type of climate with mediterranean influence and an average annual rainfall of around 450 mm. The vines are planted on low hills –a feature that favours water drainage– surrounded by pines, almond and olive trees, thus giving shape to a unique landscape.

PAGO PRADO DE IRACHE

Its vineyard is located in the municipality of Ayegui (Navarra) at an altitude of 450 metres. Climate is continental with strong Atlantic influence and soils are mainly of a loamy nature.

PAGO DE OTAZU

Its vineyards are located in Navarra, between two mountain ranges (Sierra del Perdón and Sierra de Echauri), and is probably the most northerly of all Spanish wine regions. It is a cool area with Atlantic climate and a high day-night temperature contrast. Soils in that part of the country, near the city of Pamplona, are limestone-based with abundant clay and stones, therefore with good drainage that allows vines to sink their roots deeper into the soil.

PAGO SEÑORIO DE ARINZANO

Sie befindet sich im Nordwesten Spaniens, genauer in Estella, Navarra. Ihr Weinstock wächst in einem Tal, das von den letzten Gebirgsausläufern der Pyrenäen gebildet wird, und das vom Fluss Ega, der die Rolle des Moderators der Temperaturen übernimmt, geteilt wird. Ihr Klima besitzt einen atlantischen Einfluss mit einem hohen thermischen Unterschied. Die Weinstöcke dieser Weinbergslagen befinden sich in einer komplexen geologischen Gegend mit unterschiedlichen Anteilen von Schlamm, Mergel, Ton und Degradierung von kalkigem Gestein.

PAGO VERA DE ESTENAS

This is located in the area of Utiel-Requena, in the province of Valencia. It has a Mediterranean climate with a continental influence. Its soils are a dark chalky with a sandy clay loam texture. The average rainfall is 420 millimetres and the varieties planted are bobal, tempranillo, cabernet sauvignon and merlot for red wines and chardonnay for white wines.

PAGO AYLÉS

BODEGA PAGO AYLÉS

Finca Aylés. Ctra. A-1101, Km. 24
50152 Mezalocha (Zaragoza)
☎: +34 976 140 473
Fax: +34 976 140 268
pagoayles@pagoayles.com
www.pagoayles.com

"A" de Aylés 2013 T
merlot, garnacha, tempranillo, cabernet sauvignon

89

Colour: cherry, purple rim. Nose: ripe fruit, woody. Palate: flavourful, spicy, powerful, toasty.

"é" de Aylés 2012 TC
tempranillo

87

Colour: cherry, garnet rim. Nose: aged wood nuances, ripe fruit, overripe fruit, wet leather. Palate: spicy, long, toasty.

"é" de Aylés 2013 T
tempranillo

89

Colour: cherry, garnet rim. Nose: smoky, spicy, ripe fruit. Palate: flavourful, smoky aftertaste, ripe fruit.

"L" de Aylés 2014 RD
garnacha, cabernet sauvignon

89

Colour: rose, purple rim. Nose: red berry notes, floral. Palate: powerful, fruity, fresh.

"s" de Aylés 2013 T
garnacha

90

Colour: deep cherry, purple rim. Nose: creamy oak, toasty, ripe fruit, balsamic herbs. Palate: balanced, spicy, long.

"Y" de Aylés 2013 T
merlot, garnacha, tempranillo, cabernet sauvignon

89

Colour: deep cherry, garnet rim. Nose: ripe fruit, old leather, characterful. Palate: spicy, round tannins.

Aylés "Tres de 3000" 2012 T
garnacha, cabernet sauvignon, merlot

91

Colour: cherry, garnet rim. Nose: spicy, ripe fruit, mineral. Palate: flavourful, smoky aftertaste, ripe fruit.

PAGO CALZADILLA

PAGO CALZADILLA

Ctra. Huete a Cuenca, Km. 3
16500 Huete (Cuenca)
☎: +34 969 143 020
Fax: +34 969 147 047
info@pagodecalzadilla.com
www.pagodecalzadilla.com

Calzadilla Allegro 2009 T
syrah, garnacha

92

Colour: cherry, garnet rim. Nose: ripe fruit, spicy, creamy oak, complex. Palate: flavourful, toasty, round tannins.

Calzadilla Classic 2009 T
tempranillo, cabernet sauvignon, garnacha, syrah

92

Colour: cherry, garnet rim. Nose: balanced, complex, ripe fruit, spicy, fine reductive notes. Palate: good structure, flavourful, round tannins, balanced.

Opta Calzadilla 2010 T
tempranillo, garnacha, syrah

91

Colour: very deep cherry, garnet rim. Nose: expressive, complex, mineral, balsamic herbs, balanced. Palate: full, flavourful, round tannins.

PAGO CAMPO DE LA GUARDIA

MARTÚE

Campo de la Guardia, s/n
45760 La Guardia (Toledo)
☎: +34 925 123 333
bodegasenlaguardia@martue.com
www.martue.com

Martúe 2011 TC
24% syrah, 21% merlot, 19% cabernet sauvignon, 18% tempranillo, 18% petit verdot

85

Martúe Chardonnay 2014 B
100% chardonnay

86

Martúe Especial 2010 TR
29% merlot, 32% cabernet sauvignon, 35% syrah, 4% malbec

87

Colour: deep cherry. Nose: ripe fruit, fruit preserve, spicy, creamy oak, fine reductive notes. Palate: powerful, flavourful, balsamic.

Martúe Syrah 2011 T
100% syrah

87

Colour: cherry, garnet rim. Nose: ripe fruit, toasty, grassy. Palate: powerful, toasty.

PAGO CASA DEL BLANCO

PAGO CASA DEL BLANCO

Ctra. Moral de Calatrava km. 23,200
13200 Manzanares (Ciudad Real)
☎: +34 917 480 606
Fax: +34 913 290 266
quixote@pagocasadelblanco.com
www.pagocasadelblanco.com

Pilas Bonas 2014 B
86

Quixote Cabernet Sauvignon Syrah 2010 T
cabernet sauvignon, syrah

86

Quixote Malbec Cabernet Franc 2010 T
malbec, cabernet franc

87

Colour: cherry, garnet rim. Nose: red berry notes, ripe fruit, spicy, creamy oak, complex. Palate: flavourful, toasty, round tannins.

Quixote Merlot Tempranillo Petit Verdot 2010 T
merlot, tempranillo, petit verdot

88

Colour: cherry, garnet rim. Nose: ripe fruit, earthy notes, balsamic herbs, fine reductive notes. Palate: flavourful, long, balsamic.

Quixote Petit Verdot 2010 T
petit verdot

89

Colour: cherry, garnet rim. Nose: ripe fruit, spicy, creamy oak, complex, expressive. Palate: flavourful, toasty, round tannins, concentrated.

VINO DE PAGO CHOZAS CARRASCAL

CHOZAS CARRASCAL

Vereda San Antonio
46390 San Antonio de Requena
(Valencia)
☎: +34 963 410 395
chozas@chozascarrascal.es
www.chozascarrascal.es

PODIUM

El Cf de Chozas Carrascal 2014 T
cabernet franc

95

Colour: very deep cherry, garnet rim. Nose: expressive, complex, mineral, balsamic herbs, balanced. Palate: full, flavourful, round tannins.

Las Ocho 2012 T
94

Colour: cherry, garnet rim. Nose: mineral, expressive, spicy. Palate: flavourful, ripe fruit, long, good acidity, balanced.

Las Tres 2014 B
93

Colour: bright yellow. Nose: ripe fruit, powerfull, toasty, creamy oak. Palate: flavourful, fruity, spicy, toasty, long.

PAGO DEHESA DEL CARRIZAL

DEHESA DEL CARRIZAL

Carretera Retuerta a Navas de Estena, Km 5
13194 Retuerta del Bullaque
(Ciudad Real)
☎: +34 925 421 773
Fax: +34 925 421 761
info@dehesadelcarrizal.com
www.dehesadelcarrizal.com

Dehesa del Carrizal Cabernet Sauvignon 2012 T
100% cabernet sauvignon

91

Colour: cherry, garnet rim. Nose: varietal, ripe fruit, spicy, scrubland. Palate: balanced, round tannins.

Dehesa del Carrizal Chardonnay 2013 B
92

Colour: bright yellow. Nose: ripe fruit, powerfull, toasty, pattiserie. Palate: flavourful, fruity, spicy, toasty, long.

Dehesa del Carrizal Colección Privada 2012 T

42% syrah, 26% petit verdot, 22% cabernet sauvignon, 10% merlot

93

Colour: very deep cherry, purple rim. Nose: complex, expressive, spicy, balsamic herbs. Palate: good structure, full, flavourful.

Dehesa del Carrizal MV 2012 T

45% tempranillo, 34,5% merlot, 13% cabernet sauvignon, 7,5% syrah

89

Colour: deep cherry, garnet rim. Nose: medium intensity, ripe fruit, sweet spices. Palate: balanced, easy to drink, spicy.

Dehesa del Carrizal Petit Verdot 2012 T

100% petit verdot

90

Colour: bright cherry, purple rim. Nose: scrubland, ripe fruit, balanced, warm. Palate: full, fruity, good structure, balsamic.

Dehesa del Carrizal Syrah 2012 T

100% syrah

90

Colour: very deep cherry, purple rim. Nose: ripe fruit, floral, spicy, warm. Palate: fruity, powerful, long.

PAGO DOMINIO DE VALDEPUSA

MARQUÉS DE GRIÑÓN

Finca Casa de Vacas CM-4015, Km. 23
45692 Malpica de Tajo (Toledo)
☎: +34 925 597 222
service@pagosdefamilia.com
www.pagosdefamilia.com

Marqués de Griñón Cabernet Sauvignon 2011 T

100% cabernet sauvignon

93

Colour: cherry, garnet rim. Nose: ripe fruit, balsamic herbs, scrubland, mineral, spicy. Palate: powerful, flavourful, spicy, balanced, balsamic.

Marqués de Griñón Caliza 2011 T

syrah, petit verdot

90

Colour: cherry, garnet rim. Nose: complex, ripe fruit, spicy, dry stone. Palate: good structure, flavourful, round tannins.

Marqués de Griñón Emeritvs 2010 TR

cabernet sauvignon, syrah, petit verdot

94

Colour: cherry, garnet rim. Nose: ripe fruit, mineral, spicy, balsamic herbs, fine reductive notes. Palate: balanced, flavourful, long, balsamic, elegant, fine tannins.

Marqués de Griñón Graciano 2010 T

100% graciano

90

Colour: cherry, garnet rim. Nose: ripe fruit, wild herbs, earthy notes, spicy, balsamic herbs. Palate: balanced, flavourful, long, balsamic.

Marqués de Griñón Petit Verdot 2011 T

100% petit verdot

92

Colour: cherry, garnet rim. Nose: ripe fruit, spicy, earthy notes, wild herbs. Palate: powerful, flavourful, concentrated, long, elegant.

Marqués de Griñón Svmma Varietalis 2010 T

45% cabernet sauvignon, 42% syrah, 13% petit verdot

91

Colour: cherry, garnet rim. Nose: ripe fruit, spicy, creamy oak, complex. Palate: flavourful, spicy, long, correct.

Marqués de Griñón Syrah 2011 T
100% syrah

90

Colour: cherry, garnet rim. Nose: fruit preserve, violets, sweet spices, creamy oak. Palate: long, toasty, powerful, flavourful.

VINO DE PAGO EL TERRERAZO

MUSTIGUILLO VIÑEDOS Y BODEGA

Ctra. N-330 km. 196
46300 Utiel (Valencia)
☎: +34 962 168 260
Fax: +34 962 168 259
info@bodegamustiguillo.com
www.bodegamustiguillo.com

Finca Terrerazo 2012 T
100% bobal

94

Colour: cherry, garnet rim. Nose: mineral, expressive, spicy. Palate: flavourful, ripe fruit, long, good acidity, balanced.

Mestizaje 2014 T
75% bobal, 25% syrah, tempranillo, merlot, garnacha

92

Colour: bright cherry. Nose: ripe fruit, sweet spices, creamy oak. Palate: flavourful, fruity, toasty, round tannins.

Mustiguillo Garnacha 2014 T
100% garnacha

90

Colour: bright cherry. Nose: ripe fruit, sweet spices, red berry notes. Palate: flavourful, fruity, round tannins.

PAGO FINCA BOLANDIN

BODEGA PAGO DE CIRSUS

Ctra. de Ablitas a Ribafora, Km. 5
31523 Ablitas (Navarra)
☎: +34 948 386 427
info@pagodecirsus.com
www.pagodecirsus.com

Pago de Cirsus Cuvée Especial 2011 T
syrah, cabernet sauvignon, merlot

91

Colour: cherry, garnet rim. Nose: ripe fruit, spicy, creamy oak, fine reductive notes. Palate: flavourful, toasty, correct.

Pago de Cirsus Selección de Familia 2011 T
syrah, cabernet sauvignon

92

Colour: cherry, garnet rim. Nose: balanced, complex, ripe fruit, spicy, fine reductive notes. Palate: good structure, flavourful, balanced.

Pago de Cirsus Vendimia Seleccionada 2012 TC
merlot, syrah, tempranillo

90

Colour: cherry, garnet rim. Nose: smoky, spicy, ripe fruit, wild herbs. Palate: flavourful, smoky aftertaste, ripe fruit.

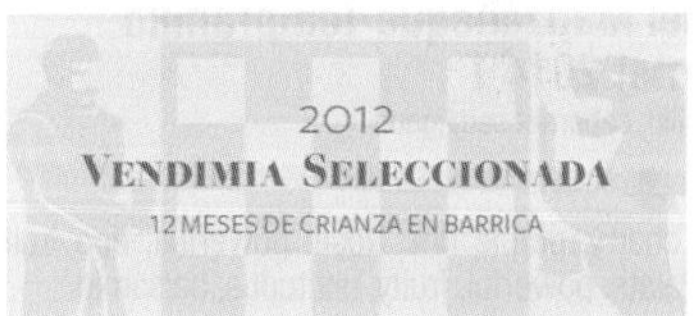

PAGO FINCA ÉLEZ

VIÑEDOS Y BODEGA MANUEL MANZANEQUE

Ctra. Ossa de Montiel a
El Bonillo, Km. 11,500
02610 El Bonillo (Albacete)
☎: +34 967 585 003
Fax: +34 967 370 649
info@manuelmanzaneque.com
www.manuelmanzaneque.com

Manuel Manzaneque Chardonnay 2013 BFB
chardonnay

88

Colour: bright yellow. Nose: ripe fruit, floral, spicy. Palate: correct, fine bitter notes, rich.

Manuel Manzaneque Chardonnay 2014 B
chardonnay

87

Colour: bright straw. Nose: white flowers, fresh fruit, dried herbs. Palate: flavourful, fruity, good acidity.

Manuel Manzaneque Finca Élez 2009 TC
tempranillo, cabernet sauvignon, merlot

89

Colour: cherry, garnet rim. Nose: old leather, spicy, ripe fruit. Palate: ripe fruit, classic aged character, round tannins.

Manuel Manzaneque Nuestra Selección 2007 T
cabernet sauvignon, merlot, tempranillo

92

Colour: cherry, garnet rim. Nose: balanced, complex, ripe fruit, spicy, fine reductive notes. Palate: good structure, flavourful, round tannins, balanced.

Manuel Manzaneque Syrah 2007 T
syrah

90

Colour: pale ruby, brick rim edge. Nose: spicy, fine reductive notes, wet leather, aged wood nuances, fruit liqueur notes. Palate: spicy, fine tannins, balanced.

Manuel Manzaneque Tempranillo Cabernet 2014 T
tempranillo, cabernet sauvignon

87

Colour: cherry, purple rim. Nose: powerfull, ripe fruit, lactic notes. Palate: powerful, fruity, unctuous, balsamic.

PAGO FLORENTINO

PAGO FLORENTINO
Ctra. Porzuna - Camino Cristo del Humilladero, km. 3
13420 Malagón (Ciudad Real)
☎: +34 983 681 146
Fax: +34 983 681 147
bodeg@arzuaganavarro.com
www.pagoflorentino.com

Pago Florentino 2012 T
100% cencibel

90

Colour: deep cherry. Nose: creamy oak, toasty, ripe fruit, balsamic herbs. Palate: spicy, long, balanced.

PAGO GUIJOSO

BODEGA FAMILIA CONESA - PAGO GUIJOSO
Crta Ossa de Montiel - El Bonillo km 11
06210 El Bonillo (Murcia)
☎: +34 618 844 583
direccion@familiaconesa.com
www.familiaconesa.com

El Beso de las Uvas 2011 B
chardonnay

86

Finca La Sabina Cabernet 2006 TGR
cabernet sauvignon

84

Finca La Sabina Merlot 2011 T
merlot

88

Colour: very deep cherry, garnet rim. Nose: complex, balsamic herbs, balanced, ripe fruit. Palate: full, flavourful, round tannins.

Finca La Sabina Syrah 2011 T
syrah

89

Colour: very deep cherry, garnet rim. Nose: ripe fruit, wild herbs, spicy, creamy oak. Palate: powerful, flavourful, round tannins.

VINO DE PAGO LOS BALAGUESES

VIÑEDOS Y BODEGAS VEGALFARO
Ctra. Pontón - Utiel, Km. 3
46340 Requena (Valencia)
☎: +34 962 320 680
Fax: +34 962 321 126
info@vegalfaro.com
www.vegalfaro.com

Pago de los Balagueses Chardonnay 2013 B

89

Colour: bright yellow. Nose: sweet spices, creamy oak, ripe fruit. Palate: spicy, good finish.

Pago de los Balagueses Syrah 2013 TC

93

Colour: very deep cherry, garnet rim. Nose: spicy, ripe fruit, varietal. Palate: balanced, spicy, ripe fruit, round tannins, smoky aftertaste.

PAGO PRADO DE IRACHE

BODEGAS IRACHE

Monasterio de Irache, 1
31240 Ayegui (Navarra)
☎: +34 948 551 932
Fax: +34 948 554 954
irache@irache.com
www.irache.com

Prado Irache 2005 TR

tempranillo, cabernet sauvignon, merlot

91

Colour: cherry, garnet rim. Nose: balanced, complex, ripe fruit, spicy, fine reductive notes. Palate: good structure, flavourful, round tannins, balanced.

VINOS DE PAGO DE OTAZU

BODEGA OTAZU

Señorío de Otazu, s/n
31174 Etxauri (Navarra)
☎: +34 948 329 200
Fax: +34 948 329 353
otazu@otazu.com
www.otazu.com

Pago de Otazu 2013 B

chardonnay

92

Colour: bright straw. Nose: white flowers, fine lees, dried herbs, mineral. Palate: flavourful, fruity, good acidity.

Señorio de Otazu 2008 T

85% cabernet sauvignon, 10% tempranillo, 5% merlot

90

Colour: bright cherry. Nose: sweet spices, creamy oak, overripe fruit. Palate: flavourful, fruity, toasty, round tannins.

PAGO SEÑORÍO DE ARINZANO

BODEGA SEÑORÍO DE ARÍNZANO

Ctra. NA-132 Km. 3,1
31264 Aberin (Navarra)
☎: +34 948 555 285
Fax: +34 948 555 415
info@arinzano.com
www.arinzano.com

PODIUM

Arínzano Gran Vino 2008 T

100% tempranillo

95

Colour: cherry, garnet rim. Nose: cocoa bean, ripe fruit, dry stone, varietal. Palate: good structure, balanced, elegant, long.

Arínzano La Casona 2010 T

100% tempranillo

94

Colour: cherry, garnet rim. Nose: ripe fruit, balanced, expressive, spicy, complex. Palate: good structure, long, good acidity.

PAGO VERA ESTENAS

BODEGA VERA DE ESTENAS

Junto N-III, km. 266 -
Paraje La Cabezuela
46300 Utiel (Valencia)
☎: +34 962 171 141
estenas@veradeestenas.es
www.veradeestenas.es

Martínez Bermell Merlot 2013 T

merlot

90

Colour: light cherry. Nose: fruit liqueur notes, fragrant herbs, spicy, creamy oak, balsamic herbs. Palate: balanced, elegant, spicy, long, toasty.

Viña Lidón 2014 BFB

chardonnay

87

Colour: bright yellow. Nose: ripe fruit, powerfull, toasty, aged wood nuances, pattiserie. Palate: flavourful, fruity, spicy, toasty, long.

VINOS DE CALIDAD

So far, there are only seven wine regions that have achieved the status "Vino de Calidad" ("Quality Wine Produced in Specified Regions"): Cangas, Lebrija, Valtiendas, Granada, Sierra de Salamanca, Valles de Benavente and Islas Canarias, regions that are allowed to label their wines with the VCPRD seal. This quality seal works as a sort of "training" session for the DO category, although it is still quite unknown for the average consumer.

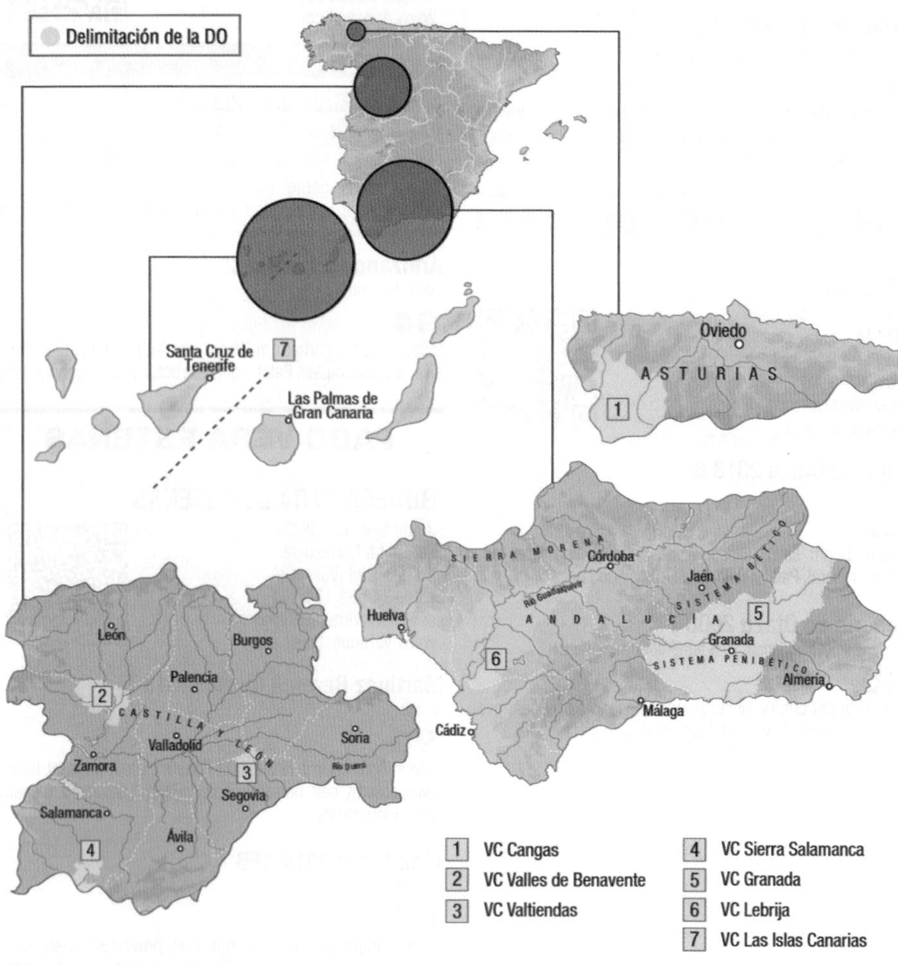

VINO DE CALIDAD / D.O.P. CANGAS

Located to the south-eastern part of the province of Asturias, bordering with León, Cangas del Narcea has unique climatic conditions, completely different to the rest of the municipalities of Asturias; therefore, its wines have sheer singularity. With lower rainfall levels and more sunshine hours than the rest the province, vines are planted on slate, siliceous and sandy soils. The main varieties are albarín blanco and albillo (white), along with garnacha tintorera, mencía and verdejo negro (red).

VINO DE CALIDAD / D.O.P. GRANADA

Wines that come from anywhere within the provincial limits of Granada, it includes nearly 20 wineries and a hundred growers. It enjoys a mediterranean climate with Atlantic influence. Characterized by a rugged topography, the vineyards occupy mostly the highest areas, with an average altitude of around 1200 meters, a feature that provides this territory with an ample day-night temperature differential. The region is promoting white grape varieties such as vijiriega, moscatel and pedro ximénez, as well as red (tempranillo, garnacha, monastrell) and even some French ones, widely planted in the province. Soil structure, although diverse, is based mainly on clay and slate.

VINO DE CALIDAD / D.O.P. LEBRIJA

Recognized by the Junta de Andalucía on March the 11th 2009. The production area includes the towns of Lebrija and El Cuervo, in the province of Sevilla.

The wines ascribed to the "Vino de Calidad de Lebrija" designation of quality will be made solely from the following grape varieties:

– White varieties: moscatel de Alejandría, palomino, palomino fino, sauvignon blanc and that traditionally known as vidueño (montúo de pilas, mollar cano, moscatel morisco, perruno).

– Red varieties: cabernet sauvignon, syrah, tempranillo, merlot and tintilla de Rota.

Types of wines: white, red, generosos (fortified) and generosos de licor, naturally sweet and mistelas.

VINO DE CALIDAD / D.O.P. SIERRA DE SALAMANCA

The "Vino de Calidad" status was ratified to Sierra de Salamanca by the Junta de Castilla y León (Castilla y León autonomous government) in June 2010, becoming the third one to be granted within the region. Sierra de Salamanca lies in the south of the province of Salamanca, and includes 26 towns, all within the same province. Vines are planted mostly on terraces at the top of the hills and on clay soils based on limestone. Authorized varieties are viura, moscatel de grano menudo and palomino (white), as well as rufete, garnacha and tempranillo (red).

VINO DE CALIDAD / D.O.P. VALLES DE BENAVENTE

Recognized by the Junta de Castilla y León in September 2000, the VCPRD comprises nowadays more than 50 municipalities and three wineries in Benavente, Santibáñez de Vidriales and San Pedro de Ceque. The production areas within the region are five (Valle Vidriales, Valle del Tera, Valle Valverde, La Vega and Tierra de Campos) around the city of Benavente, the core of the region. Four rivers (Tera, Esla, Órbigo and Valderadey, all of them tributary to the Duero river) give the region its natural borders.

VINO DE CALIDAD / D.O.P. VALTIENDAS

An area to the north of the province of Segovia relatively known thanks to the brand name Duratón, also the name of the river that crosses a region that has mainly tempranillo planted, a grape variety known there also as tinta del país. The wines are fruitier and more acidic than those from Ribera del Duero, thanks to an altitude of some 900 metres and clay soils with plenty of stones.

VINO DE CALIDAD / D.O.P. ISLAS CANARIAS

Approved in May 2011, the date of publication in the Boletín Oficial de Canarias (BOC), the constitution of its management board took place on 27 December, 2012. The production area covers the entire territory of the Canary Islands, allowing free movement of grapes in the Canary Islands. Its regulations cover broad grape varieties from the Canary Islands, as well as international ones.

VINO DE CALIDAD DE GRANADA

BODEGA LOS BARRANCOS

Ctra. Cádiar - Albuñol, km. 9,4
18449 Lobras (Granada)
☎: +34 958 343 218
info@losbarrancos.com
www.losbarrancos.es

Cerro de la Retama 2013 T
cabernet sauvignon, tempranillo, merlot

91

Colour: cherry, garnet rim. Nose: mineral, expressive, spicy, ripe fruit, powerfull. Palate: flavourful, ripe fruit, long, good acidity, balanced.

Corral de Castro 2013 T
tempranillo, cabernet sauvignon

88

Colour: deep cherry. Nose: creamy oak, toasty, ripe fruit, balsamic herbs. Palate: spicy, long, balanced.

BODEGA VERTIJANA

Paseo de Sierra Nevada, 7
18516 Policar (Granada)
☎: +34 605 074 459
vertijana@vertijana.com

Vertijana 3 2011 TC
tempranillo, merlot, cabernet sauvignon, syrah

87

Colour: deep cherry. Nose: expressive, complex, balsamic herbs, fruit preserve, damp earth. Palate: full, flavourful.

BODEGAS FONTEDEI

Doctor Horcajadas, 10
18570 Deifontes (Granada)
☎: +34 958 407 957
info@bodegasfontedei.es
www.bodegasfontedei.es

Albayda Alier 2014 B
90% sauvignon blanc, 10% chardonnay

88

Colour: bright yellow. Nose: ripe fruit, spicy, tropical fruit. Palate: flavourful, fruity, balanced.

Fontedei Lindaraja 2013 T
70% tempranillo, 30% syrah

89

Colour: deep cherry, purple rim. Nose: fruit expression, sweet spices, balanced. Palate: fruity, easy to drink, good acidity.

BODEGAS H. CALVENTE

Viñilla, 6
18699 Jete (Granada)
☎: +34 958 644 179
Fax: +34 958 644 179
ventas@bodegashcalvente.com
www.bodegashcalvente.com

Calvente Finca de la Guindalera 2010 TC
tempranillo, syrah, cabernet sauvignon, merlot

89

Colour: light cherry. Nose: fruit expression, fruit liqueur notes, fragrant herbs, spicy, creamy oak. Palate: balanced, spicy, long.

Calvente Rania 2013 BN
moscatel de alejandría

88

Colour: bright yellow. Nose: ripe fruit, fine lees, balanced, dried herbs. Palate: good acidity, flavourful, ripe fruit, long.

BODEGAS SEÑORÍO DE NEVADA

Ctra. de Cónchar, s/n
18659 Villamena (Granada)
☎: +34 958 777 092
Fax: +34 958 107 367
info@senoriodenevada.es
www.senoriodenevada.es

Señorío de Nevada Bronce 2012 T
cabernet sauvignon, merlot, syrah

86

Señorío de Nevada Oro 2012 T
syrah, cabernet sauvignon, merlot

89

Colour: deep cherry. Nose: creamy oak, toasty, ripe fruit, scrubland. Palate: balanced, spicy, long.

Señorío de Nevada Plata 2012 T
syrah, merlot, cabernet sauvignon

88

Colour: cherry, garnet rim. Nose: powerfull, ripe fruit, spicy, creamy oak. Palate: powerful, fruity, unctuous.

DOMINIO BUENAVISTA - VINOS VELETA

Ctra. de Almería, s/n
18480 Ugíjar (Granada)
☎: +34 958 767 254
Fax: +34 958 990 226
info@dominiobuenavista.com
www.vinosveleta.com

Veleta Blanco 2012 ESP
80% vijariego blanco, 20% chardonnay

86

Veleta Cabernet Sauvignon 2010 T
cabernet sauvignon

88

Colour: cherry, garnet rim. Nose: ripe fruit, wild herbs, earthy notes, spicy, balsamic herbs. Palate: balanced, flavourful, long, balsamic.

Veleta Cabernet Sauvignon 2013 T Roble
cabernet sauvignon

87

Colour: very deep cherry, garnet rim. Nose: scrubland, ripe fruit, spicy. Palate: spicy, balsamic, easy to drink.

Veleta Privilegio 2009 T
85% tempranillo, 15% graciano

90

Colour: cherry, garnet rim. Nose: ripe fruit, wild herbs, earthy notes, balsamic herbs. Palate: balanced, flavourful, long, balsamic.

Veleta Rosado 2013 ESP
tempranillo, garnacha

85

Veleta Tempranillo 2009 T
90% tempranillo, 10% cabernet sauvignon

88

Colour: deep cherry, garnet rim. Nose: spicy, creamy oak, fruit preserve, dried herbs. Palate: flavourful, correct.

Veleta Tempranillo 2013 T
tempranillo

88

Colour: cherry, purple rim. Nose: expressive, red berry notes, floral. Palate: flavourful, fruity, good acidity, easy to drink.

Veleta Tempranillo Rosé 2014 RD
tempranillo, garnacha

83

Mª AMPARO GARCÍA HINOJOSA

Isaac Albéniz 10 - 2º B
18181 Granada (Granada)
☎: +34 958 277 764
Fax: +34 958 277 764
info@anchuron.es
www.anchuron.es

Anchurón 2011 TC
cabernet sauvignon, tempranillo, syrah, merlot

88

Colour: very deep cherry, garnet rim. Nose: expressive, balsamic herbs, balanced. Palate: full, flavourful, round tannins.

Anchurón 2014 B
90% sauvignon blanc, 10% chardonnay

87

Colour: bright straw. Nose: dried flowers, dry nuts, powerfull. Palate: fruity, easy to drink, good finish.

MARQUÉS DE CASA PARDIÑAS C.B.

Finca San Torcuato
18540 Huélago (Granada)
☎: +34 630 901 094
Fax: +34 958 252 297
info@spiracp.es
www.marquesdecasapardiñas.com

Marques de Casa Pardiñas 2013 T

92

Colour: deep cherry, purple rim. Nose: creamy oak, toasty, balsamic herbs. Palate: balanced, spicy, long.

PAGO DE ALMARAES

Ctra. de Fonelas, Km. 1,5
18510 Benalúa de Guadix (Granada)
☎: +34 958 348 752
info@bodegaspagodealmaraes.es
www.bodegaspagodealmaraes.es

Memento 2010 TR
50% tempranillo, 30% cabernet sauvignon, 20% syrah

86

VINO DE CALIDAD DE LEBRIJA

BODEGAS GONZÁLEZ PALACIOS

Virgen Consolación, 60
41740 Lebrija (Sevilla)
☎: +34 955 974 084
bodegas@gonzalezpalacios.com
www.gonzalezpalacios.com

El Poeta M. Fina
palomino

90

Colour: bright straw. Nose: saline, dry nuts, varnish, acetaldehyde, powerfull. Palate: fine bitter notes, long, powerful, spicy.

Frasquito en Rama Generoso en Flor Reserva
palomino

91

Colour: bright yellow. Nose: faded flowers, pungent, dry nuts. Palate: flavourful, fine bitter notes, long.

González Palacios Lebrija Old Dulce Vino Generoso 2005
palomino, moscatel

89

Colour: iodine, amber rim. Nose: powerfull, complex, dry nuts, creamy oak, varnish, caramel. Palate: rich, long, spicy, sweetness.

González Palacios Lebrija Old Vino Generoso 1989
palomino

92

Colour: dark mahogany. Nose: candied fruit, fruit liqueur notes, spicy, varnish. Palate: fine solera notes, fine bitter notes, spirituous, long, balanced.

González Palacios M. Fina
palomino

92

Colour: bright yellow. Nose: balanced, fresh, saline, expressive, pungent, dry nuts. Palate: flavourful, fine bitter notes, long.

González Palacios Moscatel 2014
moscatel

88

Colour: bright yellow. Nose: balsamic herbs, honeyed notes, floral, sweet spices. Palate: rich, fruity, powerful, flavourful.

Overo 2013 TC
50% syrah, 50% tempranillo

87

Colour: bright cherry. Nose: ripe fruit, creamy oak, expressive. Palate: flavourful, fruity, toasty.

Solo Palomino Blanco en Flor
palomino

90

Colour: bright yellow. Nose: faded flowers, dried herbs, spicy, ripe fruit, saline. Palate: fresh, spicy, balsamic.

Viento en la Cara 2014 B
20% palomino, 80% sauvignon blanc

75

Vino de Pasas El Poeta
moscatel

91

Colour: dark mahogany. Nose: expressive, aromatic coffee, spicy, acetaldehyde, dry nuts. Palate: balanced, elegant, fine solera notes, toasty, long.

VINO DE CALIDAD DE SIERRA DE SALAMANCA

BODEGA CUATROMIL CEPAS
Rafael Alonso nº 21
49154 El Pego (Zamora)
☎: +34 670 095 149
cuatromilcepas@gmail.com
www.discolovino.com

Corneana 2012 T
rufete

90

Colour: very deep cherry, garnet rim. Nose: complex, mineral, balsamic herbs, earthy notes. Palate: full, flavourful, round tannins.

BODEGAS Y VIÑEDOS ROCHAL
Salas Pombo, 17
37670 Santibáñez de la Sierra (Salamanca)
☎: +34 923 435 260
Fax: +34 923 435 260
info@bodegasrochal.com
www.bodegasrochal.com

Zamayón 2014 T
rufete

89

Colour: cherry, purple rim. Nose: fresh fruit, red berry notes, floral. Palate: flavourful, fruity, good acidity.

Zamayón Calixto Nieto 2011 T
rufete, tempranillo

88

Colour: dark-red cherry. Nose: toasty, dark chocolate, overripe fruit, fruit liqueur notes. Palate: powerful, fine bitter notes, round tannins.

COMPAÑÍA DE VINOS LA ZORRA
San Pedro, s/n
37610 Mogarraz (Salamanca)
☎: +34 609 392 591
Fax: +34 923 418 018
estanverdes@vinoslazorra.es
www.vinoslazorra.es

La Vieja Zorra 2013 T Roble
rufete, tempranillo, garnacha

93

Colour: very deep cherry, garnet rim. Nose: expressive, mineral, balsamic herbs, earthy notes. Palate: full, flavourful, round tannins.

La Zorra 2013 T
rufete, tempranillo

92

Colour: bright cherry. Nose: sweet spices, creamy oak, earthy notes, mineral. Palate: flavourful, fruity, toasty, round tannins.

La Zorra Raro 2014 T
100% rufete

91

Colour: bright cherry. Nose: ripe fruit, sweet spices, red berry notes. Palate: flavourful, fruity, round tannins.

Laderas del Alagón 2014 T
tempranillo, rufete

88

Colour: bright cherry. Nose: ripe fruit, sweet spices, creamy oak. Palate: flavourful, fruity, round tannins.

CUARTA GENERACIÓN BODEGAS Y VIÑEDOS

Castillo, 7
37658 Sotoserrano (Salamanca)
☎: +34 618 741 461
info@bodegasantonioaparicio.com
www.bodegasantonioaparicio.com

Cuarta Generación Selección Especial 2013 T
tempranillo, rufete, garnacha

87

Colour: cherry, purple rim. Nose: ripe fruit, woody, roasted coffee. Palate: flavourful, spicy, powerful.

MANDRÁGORA VINOS

Paraje El Guijarral
37658 Villanueva del Conde
(Salamanca)
☎: +34 665 546 497
mandragoravinos@gmail.com
www.facebook.com/mandragoravinos

Tragaldabas 2013 T
rufete, aragonés

91

Colour: very deep cherry. Nose: ripe fruit, floral, scrubland, mineral. Palate: good acidity, spicy, ripe fruit, fine tannins.

VIÑAS DEL CÁMBRICO

Paraje El Guijarral s/n
37658 Villanueva del Conde
(Salamanca)
☎: +34 923 281 006
Fax: +34 923 213 605
alberto@cambrico.com
www.cambrico.com

575 Uvas de Cámbrico 2013 TR
46% tempranillo, 40% rufete, 14% garnacha

91

Colour: cherry, purple rim. Nose: ripe fruit, woody, roasted coffee, earthy notes. Palate: flavourful, spicy, powerful.

Cámbrico Rufete 2008 T
rufete

92

Colour: light cherry. Nose: fine reductive notes, aged wood nuances, toasty, ripe fruit. Palate: spicy, toasty, flavourful.

Cámbrico Tempranillo 2008 T
tempranillo

91

Colour: very deep cherry, garnet rim. Nose: expressive, complex, mineral, balsamic herbs, earthy notes. Palate: full, flavourful, round tannins, spicy.

Viñas del Cámbrico 2013 T
53% rufete, 41% tempranillo, 6% garnacha

91

Colour: cherry, garnet rim. Nose: red berry notes, spicy, ripe fruit, earthy notes. Palate: flavourful, spicy, round tannins.

Viñas del Cámbrico 2014 T
60% rufete, 40% tempranillo

93

Colour: bright cherry. Nose: ripe fruit, sweet spices, creamy oak, expressive, earthy notes. Palate: flavourful, fruity, round tannins.

VINO DE CALIDAD DE LOS VALLES DE BENAVENTE VCPRD

BODEGAS OTERO

Avda. El Ferial, 22
49600 Benavente (Zamora)
☎: +34 980 631 600
Fax: +34 980 631 722
info@bodegasotero.es
www.bodegasotero.es

Finca Valleoscuro 2014 B
verdejo

87

Colour: bright straw. Nose: white flowers, fresh fruit, fragrant herbs. Palate: flavourful, fruity, good acidity.

Finca Valleoscuro Prieto Picudo 2014 RD
prieto picudo

87

Colour: rose, purple rim. Nose: red berry notes, floral, expressive. Palate: powerful, fruity, fresh.

Finca Valleoscuro Prieto Picudo Tempranillo 2014 RD
prieto picudo, tempranillo

89

Colour: rose, purple rim. Nose: floral, wild herbs, fruit expression, expressive. Palate: flavourful, complex, balanced, elegant.

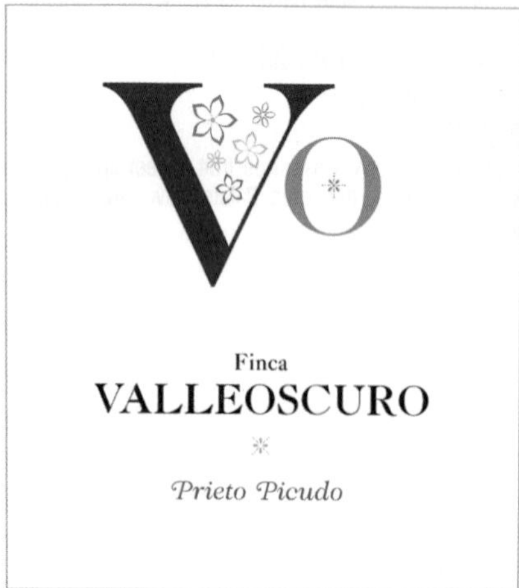

Finca Valleoscuro Prieto Picudo Tempranillo 2014 T
prieto picudo, tempranillo

88

Colour: cherry, purple rim. Nose: wild herbs, ripe fruit, balanced, medium intensity. Palate: correct, easy to drink.

Finca Valleoscuro Tempranillo 2014 RD
tempranillo

86

Otero 2008 TR
prieto picudo

89

Colour: dark-red cherry, orangey edge. Nose: ripe fruit, old leather, tobacco. Palate: correct, flavourful, spicy, balsamic.

Otero 2009 TC
prieto picudo

88

Colour: cherry, garnet rim. Nose: fine reductive notes, tobacco, balanced, characterful. Palate: spicy, balsamic, good acidity.

VINOS DE CALIDAD VALTIENDAS V.C.P.R.D.

BODEGA FINCA CÁRDABA

Coto de Cárdaba, s/n
40314 Valtiendas (Segovia)
☎: +34 921 527 470
Fax: +34 921 527 470
info@fincacardaba.com
www.fincacardaba.com

Viña Sancha 2014 RD
tinta del país

88

Colour: light cherry. Nose: red berry notes, floral, expressive, ripe fruit, powerfull. Palate: powerful, fruity.

SANZ Y NÚÑEZ S.L.

Ctra. de Valladolid - Soria, 40 H
47300 Peñafiel (Valladolid)
☎: +34 629 563 189
dominiodeperoleja@hotmail.es

Dominio de Peroleja 2011 T Roble
tempranillo

88

Colour: bright cherry. Nose: sweet spices, creamy oak, ripe fruit. Palate: flavourful, fruity, toasty, round tannins.

VINO DE CALIDAD DE LAS ISLAS CANARIAS

BODEGA COMARCAL VALLE DE GÜIMAR

Ctra. Subida a Los Loros, Km. 4,5
38550 Arafo (Santa Cruz de Tenerife)
☎: +34 922 510 437
info@bodegavalledeguimar.com
www.bodegavalledeguimar.com

Pico Cho Marcial 2013 T

83

Pico Cho Marcial Seco 2014 B

100% listán blanco

84

BODEGA TAJINASTE

El Ratiño 5, La Habanera
38315 La Orotava
(Santa Cruz de Tenerife)
☎: +34 922 308 720
Fax: +34 922 105 080
bodega@tajinaste.net
www.tajinaste.net

Paisaje de las Islas 2013 B

50% malvasía, 50% marmajuelo

90

Colour: bright straw. Nose: white flowers, fine lees, dried herbs, mineral. Palate: flavourful, fruity, good acidity, round.

Tajinaste 2013 T Roble

90% listán negro, 10% tintilla

85

Tajinaste Afrutado 2014 B

90% listán blanco, 10% moscatel

86

Tajinaste Seco 2014 B

90% listán blanco, 10% albillo

87

Colour: bright straw. Nose: white flowers, dried herbs, ripe fruit. Palate: flavourful, fruity, good acidity.

BODEGA VALLE MOLINA

Ctra. Socorro-Tegueste, 65
38292 Tegueste
(Santa Cruz de Tenerife)
☎: +34 636 789 848
alejandroalg@hotmail.com

Alejandro Gallo Malvasía Aromática y Marmajuelo 2014 B

malvasía, marmajuelo

90

Colour: bright straw. Nose: white flowers, fresh fruit, fragrant herbs, expressive. Palate: flavourful, fruity, good acidity, balanced.

Alejandro Gallo Malvasía Dulce 2014 B

malvasía

88

Colour: bright yellow. Nose: balsamic herbs, honeyed notes, floral, sweet spices. Palate: rich, fruity, powerful, flavourful.

Alejandro Gallo Vijariego Negro y Tintilla 2013 T

vijariego negro, tintilla

88

Colour: cherry, garnet rim. Nose: smoky, spicy, ripe fruit. Palate: flavourful, ripe fruit.

Valle Molina Afrutado Semidulce 2014 B

listán blanco, marmajuelo, albillo, moscatel

85

Valle Molina Traicional 2014 T

listán negro, tintilla

85

BODEGAS EL PENITENTE

Camino La Habanera, 288
38300 La Orotava
(Santa Cruz de Tenerife)
☎: +34 922 309 024
Fax: +34 922 321 264
bodegas@elpenitentesl.es
www.bodegaselpenitente.es

Cruz del Teide 2013 T

listán negro

86

Cruz del Teide Afrutado 2014 B

listán blanco

85

Tinto Tanganillo 2014 T

listán negro

85

BODEGAS VIÑÁTIGO

Cabo Verde, s/n
38440 La Guancha
(Santa Cruz de Tenerife)
☎: +34 922 828 768
Fax: +34 922 829 936
vinatigo@vinatigo.com
www.vinatigo.com

Viñátigo Baboso Negro 2013 T

100% baboso negro

88

Colour: light cherry. Nose: fruit liqueur notes, fragrant herbs, spicy, creamy oak. Palate: balanced, spicy, long, balsamic.

Viñátigo Ensamblaje 2013 T

baboso negro, negramoll, tintilla, vijariego negro

89

Colour: deep cherry. Nose: creamy oak, toasty, ripe fruit, balsamic herbs. Palate: balanced, spicy, long.

CÁNDIDO HERNÁNDEZ PÍO

Acentejo, 1
38370 La Matanza de Acentejo
(Santa Cruz de Tenerife)
☎: +34 922 513 288
Fax: +34 922 511 631
info@bodegaschp.es
www.bodegaschp.es

Calius 2014 T

listán negro, negramoll, castellana, vijariego negro

87

Colour: cherry, purple rim. Nose: red berry notes, floral, balsamic herbs. Palate: powerful, fresh, fruity.

FERRERA

Calvo Sotelo, 44
38550 Arafo (Santa Cruz de Tenerife)
☎: +34 649 487 835
Fax: +34 922 237 359
carmengloria@bodegasferrera.com
www.bodegasferrera.com

Ferrera 2014 B

85

Ferrera Legendario 2014 T

89

Colour: cherry, garnet rim. Nose: creamy oak, red berry notes, fresh fruit. Palate: flavourful, spicy.

MONJE

Camino Cruz de Leandro, 36
38359 El Sauzal
(Santa Cruz de Tenerife)
☎: +34 922 585 027
monje@bodegasmonje.com
www.bodegasmonje.com

Hollera Monje 2014 T Maceración Carbónica

87

Colour: cherry, purple rim. Nose: fresh fruit, red berry notes, floral. Palate: flavourful, fruity, good acidity.

MUSEO DE MALVASIA

Plaza de la Pila 5
38430 Icod de los Vinos
(Santa Cruz de Tenerife)
☎: +34 607 610 065

Catalina II Dulce 2013 B

100% malvasía

87

Colour: bright yellow. Nose: balsamic herbs, honeyed notes, floral, sweet spices. Palate: rich, fruity, powerful, flavourful, balanced.

Catalina II Semidulce 2013 B

100% malvasía

84

Don Tomás 6 meses 2013 T

tintilla, syrah

83

RICARDO GUTIÉRREZ DE SALAMANCA

Cº El Guincho, 140 Valle de Guerra
38240 La Laguna
(Santa Cruz de Tenerife)
☎: +34 658 893 860
Fax: +34 922 257 495
info@vinos1861.com
www.vinos1861.com

1861 2013 T Roble

listán negro

89

Colour: cherry, purple rim. Nose: ripe fruit, woody, grassy, earthy notes. Palate: flavourful, spicy, powerful.

1861 Malvasía Aromática 2013 B

malvasía

83

1861 Vendimia Seleccionada 2013 T
listán negro

90

Colour: ruby red. Nose: creamy oak, toasty, ripe fruit, balsamic herbs, scrubland. Palate: balanced, spicy, long.

TIERRA DE FRONTOS
Lomo Grande, 1- Los Blanquitos
38600 Granadilla de Abona
(Santa Cruz de Tenerife)
☎: +34 922 777 253
Fax: +34 922 777 246
bodega@frontos.es
www.frontos.es

Frontos 2014 RD
syrah, merlot

82

Frontos Semidulce 2014 B
listán blanco, moscatel

85

Tierra de Frontos 2014 T
syrah, merlot

82

Tierra de Frontos Baboso Negro 2014 T
100% baboso negro

91

Colour: bright cherry. Nose: ripe fruit, sweet spices, creamy oak. Palate: flavourful, fruity, round tannins, mineral.

VEGAS WINES
Guajara, 15 Las Vegas
Granadilla de Abona
(Santa Cruz de Tenerife)
☎: +34 922 732 173
vegaswinescanarias@gmail.com

Vegas Baboso Negro Vendimia Seleccionada 2014 T
100% baboso negro

88

Colour: cherry, purple rim. Nose: expressive, fresh fruit, red berry notes, floral, wild herbs, spicy. Palate: flavourful, fruity, good acidity.

Vegas Syrah Tintilla 2014 T
syrah, tintilla

87

Colour: cherry, purple rim. Nose: balsamic herbs, red berry notes. Palate: powerful, fruity.

Vegas Syrah Tintilla Baboso Negro 2014 T
syrah, tintilla, baboso negro

86

VINOS BLESSED
Molinillo, 15
38280 Tegueste
(Santa Cruz de Tenerife)
☎: +34 637 372 468
pablo@vinosblessed.com
www.vinosblessed.com

Blessed 2014 B
100% forastera gomera

87

Colour: bright straw. Nose: white flowers, fresh fruit, fragrant herbs. Palate: flavourful, fruity, good acidity, balanced.

Blessed 2014 T
100% tintilla

86

VINOS DE LA TIERRA

The number of "Vino de la Tierra" categories granted so far, 45, means the status is growing in importance, given that growers are only required to specify geographical origin, grape variety and alcohol content. For some, it means an easy way forward for their more experimental projects, difficult to be contemplated by the stern regulations of the designations of origin, as it is the case of vast autonomous regions such as La Mancha, Castilla y León or Extremadura. For the great majority, it is a category able to fostering vineyards with high quality potential, a broader varietal catalogue and therefore the opportunity to come up with truly singular wines, a sort of sideway entrance to the DO status.

The different "Vino de la Tierra" designations have been listed in alphabetical order.

In theory, the "Vino de la Tierra" status is one step below that of the DO, and it is the Spanish equivalent to the French "Vins de Pays", which pioneered worldwide this sort of category. In Spain, however, it has some unique characteristics. For example, the fact that the designation "Vino de la Tierra" is not always the ultimate goal, but it is rather used as a springboard to achieve the highly desired DO category. In addition, as it has happened in other countries, many producers have opted for this type of association with less stringent regulations that allow them greater freedom to produce wine. Therefore, in this section there is a bit of everything: from great wines to more simple and ordinary examples, a broad catalogue that works as a sort of testing (and tasting!) field for singularity as well as for new flavours and styles derived from the use of local, autochthonous varieties.

The new Spanish Ley del Vino (Wine Law) maintains the former status of "Vino de la Tierra", but establishes an intermediate step between this and the DO one. They are the so-called 'Vinos de Calidad con Indicación Geográfica' (Quality Wines with Geographical Indication), under which the region in question must remain for a minimum of five years.

In the light of the tasting carried out for this section, there is a steady improvement in the quality of these wines, as well as fewer misgivings on the part of the wineries about the idea of joining these associations.

VT / I.G.P. 3 RIBERAS

Granted by the administration at the end of 2008 for the wines produced and within the "3 Riberas" geographical indication. The different typologies are: rosé, white, red and noble wines.

VT / I.G.P. ABANILLA

This small wine region comprises the municipalities of Abanilla and Fortuna –in the eastern part of the province of Murcia– and some 1500 hectares, although most of its production is sold to the neighbouring DO Alicante. The region enjoys a hot, dry climate, limestone soils and low rainfall, features all that account for good quality prospects, although there are some differences to be found between the northern and the southern areas within it, given the different altitudes. The grape varieties allowed in the region for red winemaking are: bonicaire, cabernet sauvignon, forcallat tinta, garnacha tintorera, merlot, petit verdot, crujidera and syrah. For white wines, we find chardonnay, malvasía, moravia dulce, moscatel de grano menudo and sauvignon blanc.

VT / I.G.P. ALTIPLANO DE SIERRA NEVADA

With the goal to free Granada's geographical indication exclusively for the "Vino de Calidad" category, in 2009 the VT I.G.P.Norte de Granada changed its name to VT I.G.P.Altiplano de Sierra Nevada. The new geographical indication comprises 43 municipalities in the north of the province of Granada. The authorized grape varieties for white wine production in the region are chardonnay, baladí verdejo, airen, torrontés, palomino, pedro ximénez, macabeo and sauvignon blanc; also tempranillo, monastrell, garnacha tinta, cabernet franc, cabernet sauvignon, pinot noir, merlot, and syrah for red wines.

VT / I.G.P. BAILÉN

Bailén wine region comprises 350 hectares in some municipal districts within the province of Jaén but fairly close to La Mancha. Wines are made mainly from the grape variety known as "molinera de Bailén", that cannot be found anywhere else in the world, but also from other red grape varieties such as garnacha tinta, tempranillo and cabernet sauvignon, as well as the white pedro ximénez.

VT / I.G.P. BAJO ARAGÓN

The most "mediterranean" region within Aragón autonomous community, it borders three different provinces (Tarragona, Castellón and Teruel) and is divided in four areas: Campo de Belchite, Bajo Martín, Bajo Aragón and Matarraña. Soils are mainly clay and limestone in nature, very rich in minerals with high potash content. The climate is suitable for the right maturation of the grapes, with the added cooling effect of the 'Cierzo' (northerly wind), together with the day-night temperature contrast, just the perfect combination for the vines. The main varieties are garnacha (both red and white), although foreign grapes like syrah, cabernet sauvignon, merlot and chardonnay are also present, as well as tempranillo and cariñena.

VT / I.G.P. BARBANZA E IRIA

The last geographical indication to be granted to the autonomous region of Galicia back in 2007, Barbanza e Iria is located within the Ribera de la Ría de Arosa wine region, in the north of the province of Pontevedra. They make both red an white wines from with varieties such as albariño, caíño blanco, godello, loureiro blanco (also known as marqués), treixadura and torrontés (white); and brancellao, caíño tinto, espadeiro, loureiro tinto, mencía and susón (red).

VT / I.G.P. BETANZOS

Betanzos, in the province of La Coruña, became the second VT I.G.P.designation to be granted in Galicia. The vineyards is planted with local white varieties like blanco legítimo, Agudelo (godello) and jerez, as well as red grapes like garnacha, mencía and tempranillo.

VT / I.G.P. CÁDIZ

Located in the south of the province of Cádiz, a vast region with a long history of wine production, the "Vinos de la Tierra de Cádiz" comprises 15 municipalities still under the regulations of the DO regarding grape production, but not winemaking. The authorised white varieties are: garrido, palomino, chardonnay, moscatel, mantúa, perruno, macabeo, sauvignon blanc y pedro ximénez; as well as the red tempranillo, syrah, cabernet sauvignon, garnacha tinta, monastrel, merlot, tintilla de rota, petit verdot and cabernet franc.

VT / I.G.P. CAMPO DE CARTAGENA

Campo de Cartagena is a flatland region close to the Mediterranean Sea and surrounded by mountains of a moderate height. The vineyard surface ascribed to the VT I.G.P.is just 8 hectares. The climate is mediterranean bordering on an arid, desert type, with very hot summers, mild temperatures for the rest of the year, and low and occasional rainfall. The main varieties in the region are bonicaire, forcallat tinta, petit verdot, tempranillo, garnacha tintorera, crujidera, merlot, syrah and cabernet sauvignon (red); and chardonnay, malvasía, moravia dulce, moscatel de grano menudo and sauvignon blanc (white).

VT / I.G.P. CASTELLÓ

Located in the eastern part of Spain, on the Mediterranean coast, the geographical indication Vinos de la Tierra de Castelló is divided in two different areas: Alto Palancia –Alto Mijares, Sant Mateu and Les Useres–, and Vilafamés. The climatic conditions in this wine region are good to grow varieties such as tempranillo, monastrell, garnacha, garnacha tintorera, cabernet sauvignon, merlot and syrah (red), along with macabeo and merseguera (white).

VT / I.G.P. CASTILLA Y LEÓN

Another one of the regional 'macro-designations' for the wines produced in up to 317 municipalities within the autonomous region of Castilla y León. A continental climate with little rainfall, together with diverse soil patterns, are the most distinctive features of a region that can be divided into the Duero basin (part of the Spanish central high plateau) and the mountainous perimeter that surrounds it.

VT / I.G.P. CASTILLA

Castilla-La Mancha, a region that has the largest vineyard surface in the planet (600.000 hectares, equivalent to 6% of the world's total vineyard surface, and to half of Spain's) has been using this Vino de la Tierra label since 1999 (the year the status was granted) for wines produced outside its designations of origin. The main grape varieties are airén, albillo, chardonnay, macabeo (viura), malvar, sauvignon blanc, merseguera, moscatel de grano menudo, pardillo (marisancho), Pedro Ximénez and torrontés (white);and bobal, cabernet sauvignon, garnacha tinta, merlot, monastrell, petit verdot, syrah, tempranillo, cencibel (jacivera), coloraíllo, frasco, garnacha tintorera, moravia agria, moravia dulce (crujidera), negral (tinto basto) and tinto velasco (red).

VT / I.G.P. CÓRDOBA

It includes the wines produced in the province of Córdoba, with the exception of those bottled within the DO Montil-la-Moriles label. All in all, we are talking of some 300 hectares and red and rosé wines made from cabernet sauvignon, merlot, syrah, tempranillo, pinot noir and tintilla de Rota grape varieties.

VT / I.G.P. COSTA DE CANTABRIA

Wines produced in the Costa de Cantabria wine region as well as some inland valleys up to an altitude of 600 meters. The grape varieties used for white winemaking are godello, albillo, chardonnay, malvasía, ondarribi zuri, picapoll blanco and verdejo blanco; and just two for red wines: ondarribi beltza and verdejo negro. The region comprises some 8 hectares of vineyards.

VT / I.G.P. CUMBRES DE GUADALFEO

Formerly known as "Vino de la Tierra de Contraviesa-Alpujarra", this geographical indication is used for wines made in the wine region located in the western part of the Alpujarras, in a border territory between two provinces (Granada and Almería), two rivers (Guadalfeo and Andarax), and very close to the Mediterranean Sea. The grape varieties used for white wine production are montúa, chardonnay, sauvignon blanc, moscatel, jaén blanca, Pedro Ximénez, vijirego y perruno; for red wines, they have garnacha tinta, tempranillo, cabernet sauvignon, cabernet franc, merlot, pinot noir and syrah.

VT / I.G.P. DESIERTO DE ALMERÍA

Granted in the summer of 2003, the wine region comprises a diverse territory in the north of the province of Almería that includes the Tabernas Dessert as well as parts of the Sierra de Alhamilla, Sierra de Cabrera and the Cabo de Gata Natural Park. Harsh, climatic desert conditions follow a regular pattern of hot days and cooler nights that influence heavily the character of the resulting wines. The vineyard's average altitude is 525 meters. The varieties planted are chardonnay, moscatel, macabeo and sauvignon blanc (white); as well as tempranillo, cabernet sauvignon, monastrell, merlot, syrah and garnacha tinta (red).www.vinosdealmeria.es/zonas-viticolas/desierto-de-almeria

VT / I.G.P. EIVISSA

The production area includes the entire island of Ibiza (Eivissa), with the vineyards located in small valleys amongst the mountains –which are never higher than 500 meters– on clay-reddish soil covered by a thin limestone crust. Low rainfall levels and hot, humid summers are the most interesting climatic features. The authorized red varieties are monastrell, tempranillo, cabernet sauvignon, merlot and syrah; macabeo, parellada, malvasía, chardonnay and moscatel make up the white-grape catalogue.

VT / I.G.P. EXTREMADURA

It comprises all the municipalities within the provinces of Cáceres and Badajoz, made up of six different wine regions. In December 1990, the regional government approved the regulations submitted by the Comisión Interprofesional de Vinos de la Tierra de Extremadura, and approved its creation. The varieties used for the production of white wines are alarije, borba, cayetana blanca, chardonnay, chelva, malvar, viura, parellada, Pedro Ximénez and verdejo; for red wines, they have bobal, mazuela, monastrell, tempranillo, garnacha, graciano, merlot, syrah and cabernet sauvignon.

VT / I.G.P. FORMENTERA

This geographical indication comprises the wines produced in the island of Formentera. The dry, subtropical mediterranean climate, characterised by abundant sunshine hours and summers with high temperatures and humidity levels but little rainfall, evidently requires grape varieties well adapted to this type of weather. Red varieties are monastrell, fogoneu, tempranillo, cabernet sauvignon and merlot; malvasía, premsal blanco, chardonnay and viognier make up its white-grape catalogue.

VT / I.G.P. GÁLVEZ

Gálvez wine region, located in the province of Toledo, comprises nine municipalities: Cuerva, Gálvez, Guadamur, Menasalvas, Mazambraz, Polán, Pulgar, San Martín de Montalbán and Totanes. The authorized grape varieties are tempranillo and garnacha tinta.

VT / I.G.P. ILLA DE MENORCA

The island of Menorca, a Biosphere Reserve, has a singular topography of gentle slopes; marl soils with a complex substratum of limestone, sandstone and slate, a mediterranean climate and northerly winter winds are the most significant features from a viticultural point of view. The wines produces in the island should be made exclusively from white grape varieties like chardonnay, macabeo, malvasía, moscatel, parellada or moll; as for the red renderings, cabernet sauvignon, merlot, monastrell, tempranillo and syrah get clearly the upper hand.

VT / I.G.P. LADERAS DE GENIL

Formerly known (up to 2009) as VT I.G.P.Granada Suroeste, the label includes some 53 municipalities in the province of Granada. The region enjoys a unique microclimate very suitable for grape growing, given its low rainfall and the softening effect of the Mediterranean Sea. The white grape varieties used for wine production are vijiriego, macabeo, Pedro Ximénez, palomino, moscatel de Alejandría, chardonnay and sauvignon blanc; as well as the red garnacha tinta, perruna, tempranillo, cabernet sauvignon, merlot, syrah and pinot noir, predominantly.

VT / I.G.P. LAUJAR-ALPUJARRA

This wine region is located at an altitude of 800 to 1500 meters between the Sierra de Gádor and the Sierra Nevada Natural Park. It has some 800 hectares of vines grown on terraces. Soils are chalk soils poor in organic matter, rocky and with little depth. The climate is moderately continental, given the sea influence and its high night-day temperature differential. The predominant grape varieties are jaén blanco, macabeo, vijiriego, Pedro Ximénez, chardonay and moscatel de grano menudo (white); and cabernet sauvignon, merlot, monastrell, tempranillo, garnachas tinta and syrah (red). www.vinosdealmeria.es/bodegas/vino-de-la-tierra-laujar-alpujarra

VT / I.G.P. LIÉBANA

VT I.G.P.Liébana includes the municipalities of Potes, Pesagüero, Cabezón de Liébana, Camaleño, Castro Cillorigo y Vega de Liébana, all of them within the area of Liébana, located in the southwest of the Cantabria bordering with Asturias, León and Palencia. The authorized varieties are mencía, tempranillo, garnacha, garciano, merlot, syrah, pinot noir, albarín negro and cabernet sauvignon (red); and palomino, godello, verdejo, albillo, chardonnay and albarín blanco (white).

VT / I.G.P. LOS PALACIOS

Los Palacios is located in the south-western part of the province of Sevilla, by the lower area of the Guadalquivir river valley. The wines included in this VT I.G.P.are white wines made from airén, chardonnay, colombard and sauvignon blanc.

VT / I.G.P. MALLORCA

The production area of VT I.G.P.Mallorca includes all the municipalities within the island, which has predominantly limestone soils with abundant clay and sandstone, and a mediterranean climate with mild temperatures all-year-round. Red varieties present in the island are callet, manto negro, cabernet sauvignon, fogoneu, merlot, monastrell, syrah, tempranillo and pinot noir; along with the white prensal (moll), chardonnay, macabeo, malvasía, moscatel de Alejandría, moscatel de grano menudo, parellada, riesling and sauvignon blanc.

VT / I.G.P. NORTE DE ALMERÍA

The Vinos de la Tierra Norte de Almería label comprises four municipalities in the Norte de Almería area, right in the north of the province. They produce white, red and rosé wines from grape varieties such as airén, chardonnay, macabeo and sauvignon blanc (white); as well as cabernet sauvignon, merlot, monastrell, tempranillo and syrah for red winemaking and tempranillo and monastrell for rosé.

VT / I.G.P. POZOHONDO

The regulations for VT I.G.P.Pozoblanco were approved by the autonomous government of Castilla-La Mancha in the year 2000. It comprises the municipalities of Alcadozo, Peñas de San Pedro and Pozohondo, all of them in the province of Albacete.

VT / I.G.P. RIBERA DEL ANDARAX

The Ribera del Andarax wine region is located in the middle area of the Andarax river valley at an altitude of 700 to 900 meters. Soils are varied in structure, with abundant slate, clay and sand. It enjoys an extreme mediterranean climate, with low occasional rainfall and high average temperatures. The grape varieties present in the region are predominantly macabeo, chardonnay and sauvignon blanc (white); and cabernet sauvignon, merlot, syrah, garnacha, tempranillo, monastrell and pinot noir (red). www.vinosdealmeria.es/zonas-viticolas/ribera-de-andarax

VT / I.G.P. RIBERA DEL GÁLLEGO-CINCO VILLAS

Ribera del Gállego-Cinco Villas wine region is located in the territory along the Gállego river valley until it almost reaches the city of Zaragoza. Although small, its vineyards are shared between the provinces of Huesca and Zaragoza. Soils are mostly gravel in structure, which affords good drainage. The grape varieties used for wine production are garnacha, tempranillo, carbernet sauvignon and merlot (red), and mostly macabeo for white wines. www.vinosdelatierradearagon.es

VT / I.G.P. RIBERA DEL JILOCA

Ribera del Jiloca, located in the south-eastern part of Aragón along the Jiloca river valley, is a wine region with a great winemaking potential, given its geo-climatic conditions. Vines are mostly planted on slate terraces perched on the slopes of the Sistema Ibérico mountain range, at high altitude, something that affords wines of great quality and singularity. Vines are planted mostly on alluvial limestone terraces of ancient river beds. Garnacha is the predominant grape, followed by macabeo. A dry climate, abundant sunlight hours and cold winters are the features that account for the excellent quality of the local grapes.www.vinosdelatierradearagon.es/empresas/ribera_del_jiloca.php

VT / I.G.P. RIBERA DEL QUEILES

Up to sixteen municipalities from two different provinces (seven from Navarra and nine from Zaragoza) are part of the VT I.G.P.Ribera del Queiles. Wines are exclusively red, made from cabernet sauvignon, graciano, garnacha tinta, merlot, tempranillo and syrah. It has a regulating and controlling body (Comité Regulador de Control y Certificación) and so far just one winery. www.vinosdelatierradearagon.es

VT / I.G.P. SERRA DE TRAMUNTANA-COSTA NORD

Currently, this VT I.G.P.comprises 41,14 hectares an up to eighteen municipal districts in the island of Mallorca, between the cape of Formentor and the southwest coast of Andratx, with mainly brownish-grey and limestone soils. Single-variety wines from malvasía, moscatel, moll, parellada, macabeo, chardonnay and sauvignon blanc (white), as well as cabernet sauvignon, merlot, syrah, monastrell, tempranillo, callet and manto negro (red) stand out.

VT / I.G.P. SIERRA DE ALCARAZ

The Sierra del Alcaraz wine region comprises the municipal districts of Alcaraz, El Ballestero, El Bonillo, Povedilla, Robledo, and Viveros, located in the western part of the province of Albacete, bordering with Ciudad Real. The VT I.G.P.status was granted by the autonomous government of Castilla-La Mancha in the year 2000. The red varieties planted in the region are cabernet sauvignon, merlot, bobal, monastrell, garnacha tinta and garnacha tintorera; along with white moravia dulce, chardonnay, chelva, eva, alarije, malvar, borba, parellada, cayetana blanca and Pedro Ximénez.

VT / I.G.P. SIERRA DE LAS ESTANCIAS Y LOS FILABRES

Located in the namesake mountain region in the province of Almería, this VT I.G.P.was approved along with its regulations in 2008. The grape varieties planted in the region are airén, chardonnay, macabeo, sauvignon blanc and moscatel de grano menudo –also known as morisco–, all of them white; and red cabernet sauvignon, merlot, monastrell, tempranillo, syrah, garnacha tinta, pinot noir and petit verdot.

VT / I.G.P. SIERRA DEL NORTE DE SEVILLA

IThis region, located in the north of the province of Sevilla at the foothills of Sierra Morena, has a landscape of gentle hills and altitudes that range from 250 to almost 1000 metres. The climate in the region is mediterranean, with hot, dry summers, mild winters and a fairly high average rainfall. Since 1998, grape varieties such as tempranillo, garnacha tinta, cabernet sauvignon, cabernet franc, merlot, pinot noir, petit verdot and syrah (red); and chardonnay, Pedro Ximénez, colombard, sauvignon blanc, palomino and moscatel de Alejandría (white) have been planted in the region.

VT / I.G.P. SIERRA SUR DE JAÉN

In this VT I.G.P.there are some 400 hectares planted with vines, although a minor percentage are table grapes. The label includes wines made in the Sierra Sur de Jaén wine region. White wines are made from jaén blanca and chardonnay, and red from garnacha tinta, tempranillo, cabernet sauvignon, merlot, syrah and pinot noir.

VT / I.G.P. TORREPEROGIL

This geographical indication in the province of Jaén, whose regulations were approved in 2006, comprises 300 hectares in the area of La Loma, right in the centre of the province. The climate is mediterranean with continental influence, with cold winters and dry and hot summers. The wines are made mainly from garnacha tinta, syrah, cabernet sauvignon and tempranillo (red); and jaén blanco and Pedro Ximénez (white).

VT / I.G.P. VALDEJALÓN

Established in 1998, it comprises 36 municipal districts in the mid- and lower-Jalón river valley. The vines are planted on alluvial, brownish-grey limestone soils, with low annual average rainfall of some 350 mm. They grape varieties planted are white (macabeo, garnacha blanca, moscatel and airén) and red (garnacha, tempranillo, cabernet sauvignon, syrah, monastrell and merlot). www.vinodelatierravaldejalon.com

VT / I.G.P. VALLE DEL CINCA

Located in the southeast of the province of Huesca, almost bordering with Catalunya, Valle del Cinca is a traditional wine region that enjoys favourable climatic and soil conditions for vine growing: soils are mainly limestone and clay, and the average annual rainfall barely reaches 300 mm (irrigation is usually required). Grape varieties predominantly planted in the region are macabeo and chardonnay (white), along with garnacha tinta, tempranillo, cabernet sauvignon and merlot (red). www.vinosdelatierradearagon.es

VT / I.G.P. VALLE DEL MIÑO-OURENSE

This wine region is located in the north of the province of Ourense, along the Miño river valley. The authorized grape varieties are treixadura, torrontés, godello, albariño, loureira and palomino –also known as xerez– for white wines, and mencía, brancellao, mouratón, sousón, caíño and garnacha for reds.

VT / I.G.P. VALLES DE SADACIA

A designation created to include the wines made from the grape variety known as moscatel riojana, which was practically lost with the phylloxera bug and has been recuperated to produce both "vino de licor" and normal white moscatel. Depending on winemaking, the latter may either be dry, semi-dry or sweet. The vineyards that belong to this VT I.G.P.are mainly located in the south-western part of the region, in the Sadacia and Cidacos river valleys, overall a very suitable territory for vine growing purposes.

VT / I.G.P. VILLAVICIOSA DE CÓRDOBA

One of the most recent geographical indications granted by the autonomous government of Andalucía back in 2008, it includes white and sweet wines made in the Villaviciosa wine region. The authorized varieties are baladí verdejo, moscatel de Alejandría, palomino fino, palomino, Pedro Ximénez, airén, calagraño Jaén, torrontés and verdejo.

VT ALTIPLANO DE SIERRA NEVADA

BODEGA VERTIJANA

Paseo de Sierra Nevada, 7
18516 Policar (Granada)
☎: +34 605 074 459
vertijana@vertijana.com

Gentis 2014 T
garnacha, tempranillo

88

Colour: cherry, purple rim. Nose: powerfull, fruit preserve, wild herbs, earthy notes. Palate: powerful, fruity, unctuous.

BODEGAS CABALLO

Plaza del Horno, 18
41500 Alcalá de Guadaíra (Sevilla)
☎: +34 615 490 203
info@bodegascaballo.com
www.bodegascaballo.com

Guardián 2013 T
100% pinot noir

86

Pasio 2013 T
65% tempranillo, 35% syrah

85

Pasio 2013 T Roble
65% tempranillo, 35% syrah

86

BODEGAS MUÑANA

Ctra. Graena a La Peza, s/n
18517 Cortes y Graena (Granada)
☎: +34 958 670 715
Fax: +34 958 670 715
bodegasmunana@gmail.com
www.bodegasmunana.com

Delirio Joven de Muñana 2014 T
100% syrah

87

Colour: very deep cherry, purple rim. Nose: ripe fruit, floral, dried herbs, earthy notes. Palate: flavourful, fruity, fine bitter notes.

Delirio Rosado de Muñana 2014 RD
tempranillo, cabernet sauvignon, petit verdot

86

Muñana 3 Cepas 2010 T
syrah, cabernet sauvignon, merlot, petit verdot

89

Colour: deep cherry, purple rim. Nose: creamy oak, toasty, ripe fruit, balsamic herbs. Palate: balanced, spicy, long.

Muñana Petit Verdot 2009 T
petit verdot

87

Colour: bright cherry, garnet rim. Nose: balsamic herbs, tobacco, dried herbs. Palate: good structure, spicy, balsamic.

Muñana Rojo 2011 T
tempranillo, cabernet sauvignon, monastrell

89

Colour: bright cherry, garnet rim. Nose: ripe fruit, wild herbs, spicy. Palate: good structure, balanced, good acidity.

Mª AMPARO GARCÍA HINOJOSA

Isaac Albéniz 10 - 2º B
18181 Granada (Granada)
☎: +34 958 277 764
Fax: +34 958 277 764
info@anchuron.es
www.anchuron.es

Tejalín 2012 T
merlot, tempranillo

86

VT BAJO ARAGÓN

AMPRIUS LAGAR

Los Enebros, 74 - 2ª planta
44002 Teruel (Teruel)
☎: +34 978 623 077
pedro.casas@ampriuslagar.es
www.ampriuslagar.es

Lagar d'Amprius Chardonnay 2013 B
chardonnay

86

Lagar d'Amprius Garnacha 2012 T
garnacha

86

Lagar d'Amprius Gewürztraminer 2013 B
gewürztraminer

84

Lagar d'Amprius Syrah Garnacha 2010 T
syrah, garnacha

86

Lagar d'Amprius Syrah Garnacha 2012 T
65% syrah, 35% garnacha

85

BODEGAS CRIAL LLEDÓ

Arrabal de la Fuente, 23
44624 Lledó (Teruel)
☎: +34 978 891 909
Fax: +34 978 891 995
crial@bodegascrial.com
www.crial.es

Crial 2014 B
50% garnacha, 50% macabeo

85

Crial 2014 RD
garnacha

85

Crial 2014 T
garnacha, syrah, cabernet sauvignon

83

Crial Lledó 2011 TC
50% garnacha, 50% cabernet sauvignon

86

Les Roques de Benet 2011 T
60% garnacha, 25% syrah, 15% cabernet sauvignon

87

Colour: cherry, garnet rim. Nose: creamy oak, red berry notes, balanced. Palate: flavourful, spicy.

BODEGAS SIERRA DE GUARA

Fray Luis Urbano, 27
50002 Lascellas (Zaragoza)
☎: +34 976 461 056
Fax: +34 976 461 558
idrias@bodegassierradeguara.es
www.bodegassierradeguara.es

Evohé Garnacha Viñas Viejas 2014 T

88

Colour: cherry, purple rim. Nose: red berry notes, floral, balsamic herbs, earthy notes. Palate: powerful, fresh, fruity.

BODEGAS TEMPORE

Ctra. Zaragoza-Montalbán, s/n
50131 Lécera (Zaragoza)
☎: +34 976 835 040
info@bodegastempore.com
www.bodegastempore.com

Tempore Terrae Garnacha Finca Vasallo 2014 T
100% garnacha

83

Tempore Terrae Más de Aranda 2013 T
100% garnacha

84

Tempore Terrae Valdecastro 2014 T
100% tempranillo

85

COOPERATIVA DEL CAMPO SAN PEDRO

Avda. Reino de Aragón, 10
44623 Cretas (Teruel)
☎: +34 978 850 309
Fax: +34 978 850 309
info@cooperativasanpedro.es
www.cooperativasanpedro.es

Belví 2011 T
garnacha, tempranillo, syrah

78

Belví 2014 B
garnacha blanca

80

Belví 2014 RD
garnacha

83

DOMINIO MAESTRAZGO

Royal III, B12
44550 Alcorisa (Teruel)
☎: +34 978 840 642
Fax: +34 978 840 642
bodega@dominiomaestrazgo.com
www.dominiomaestrazgo.com

Dominio Maestrazgo 2012 T Roble
65% garnacha, 20% syrah, 15% tempranillo

90

Colour: bright cherry, garnet rim. Nose: balanced, expressive, ripe fruit, sweet spices, creamy oak, dried herbs. Palate: balanced, round tannins.

Dominio Maestrazgo Syrah 2011 T Barrica
100% syrah

87

Colour: black cherry, garnet rim. Nose: powerfull, warm, ripe fruit. Palate: correct, spicy.

Rex Deus 2010 T Roble
85% garnacha, 15% syrah

92

Colour: cherry, garnet rim. Nose: ripe fruit, cocoa bean, sweet spices, dried herbs, powerfull, tobacco. Palate: powerful, good structure, round tannins.

Santolea 2012 T
60% garnacha, 40% tempranillo

86

GRUPO MAGALIA

Avda. De Aragón 110
50710 Maella (Zaragoza)
☎: +34 976 638 004
Fax: +34 976 639 215
gerencia@magalia.org
www.magalia.org

Magalia 2014 B
garnacha blanca, macabeo

84

Magalia 2014 T
syrah, garnacha

86

Magalia Selección 2013 T
syrah, garnacha, merlot

87

Colour: very deep cherry, garnet rim. Nose: balsamic herbs, balanced, spicy, ripe fruit, fine reductive notes. Palate: full, flavourful, fine bitter notes.

IGV

N-211, KM 246,3
44600 Alcañiz (Teruel)
☎: +34 618 731 936
valdehueso@gmail.com

Viña Valdehueso 2014 RD
garnacha

82

Viña Valdehueso Garnacha 2014 T
garnacha

83

Viña Valdehueso Tempranillo 2014 T
tempranillo, garnacha

84

LETITVI

08290 Cerdanyola del Vallès
(Barcelona)
info@letitvi.com
www.letitvi.com

Próxima Parada 2013 T
syrah, garnacha

86

MAS DE TORUBIO

Plaza del Carmen, 4
44623 Cretas (Teruel)
☎: +34 669 214 845
Fax: +34 978 850 324
masdetorubio@hotmail.com

Cloteta 2013 T

garnacha peluda

88

Colour: light cherry. Nose: fruit expression, fruit liqueur notes, creamy oak. Palate: spicy, flavourful.

Xado 2013 T Roble

garnacha, cabernet sauvignon

84

Xado Blanco sobre Lías 2014 B

90% garnacha blanca, 10% sauvignon blanc

87

Colour: bright straw. Nose: white flowers, fine lees, dried herbs, mineral. Palate: flavourful, fruity, good acidity.

VENTA D'AUBERT

Ctra. Valderrobres a Arnes, Km. 28
44623 Cretas (Teruel)
☎: +34 978 769 021
Fax: +34 978 769 031
ventadaubert@gmx.net
www.ventadaubert.com

Dionus 2006 TR

60% cabernet sauvignon, 20% merlot, 20% cabernet franc

89

Colour: cherry, garnet rim. Nose: ripe fruit, old leather, tobacco, scrubland. Palate: correct, flavourful, spicy.

Venta D'Aubert 2009 T

48% syrah, 28% cabernet sauvignon, 20% cabernet franc, 4% merlot

89

Colour: dark-red cherry, garnet rim. Nose: dried herbs, old leather, tobacco, ripe fruit. Palate: correct, round tannins.

Venta D'Aubert Merlot 2010 T

100% merlot

92

Colour: cherry, garnet rim. Nose: balanced, complex, ripe fruit, spicy, fine reductive notes. Palate: good structure, flavourful, round tannins, balanced.

Venta D'Aubert Syrah 2006 T

100% syrah

90

Colour: deep cherry, garnet rim. Nose: spicy, old leather, waxy notes, ripe fruit. Palate: good structure, ripe fruit, long.

Venta D'Aubert Viognier 2014 B

100% viognier

90

Colour: bright straw. Nose: white flowers, fine lees, dried herbs, mineral. Palate: flavourful, fruity, good acidity, carbonic notes.

Ventus 2010 TC

46% cabernet sauvignon, 32% garnacha tintorera, 8% cabernet franc, 7% syrah, 8% monastrell

88

Colour: black cherry, garnet rim. Nose: balsamic herbs, balanced, earthy notes, old leather, scrubland. Palate: full, flavourful, round tannins.

VT BARBANZA E IRIA

BOAL DE AROUSA

Avda. de Compostela, 47
15900 Padrón (A Coruña)
☎: +34 981 811 110
adega@boaldearousa.com
www.boaldearousa.com

Albariño Boal de Arousa 2013 B

100% albariño

87

Colour: bright yellow. Nose: dried herbs, ripe fruit, sweet spices. Palate: flavourful, fruity, good finish.

ENTRE OS RIOS

Lugar de Entre os Rios, 2
15948 Pobra do Caramiñal (A Coruña)
☎: +34 607 817 876
adega@entreosrios.com
www.entreosrios.com

Altares de Posmarcos 2012 B

100% albariño

93

Colour: bright yellow. Nose: powerfull, candied fruit, citrus fruit, mineral. Palate: flavourful, long, spicy.

VT CÁDIZ

BODEGAS BARBADILLO

Luis de Eguilaz, 11
11540 Sanlúcar de Barrameda (Cádiz)
☎: +34 956 385 500
Fax: +34 956 385 501
barbadillo@barbadillo.com
www.barbadillo.com

Castillo de San Diego 2014 B

100% palomino

86

Gibalbín 2013 T

tempranillo, syrah, merlot, cabernet sauvignon, tintilla de rota

88

Colour: cherry, purple rim. Nose: ripe fruit, grassy, damp undergrowth. Palate: fine bitter notes, easy to drink.

Gibalbín 8 meses 2012 T

tempranillo, merlot, petit verdot

86

Maestrante 2014 B

100% palomino

84

CORTIJO DE JARA

Medina, 79
11402 Jerez de la Frontera (Cádiz)
☎: +34 956 338 163
Fax: +34 956 338 163
puertanueva@cortijodejara.es
www.cortijodejara.es

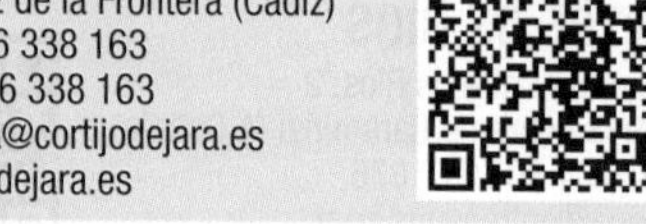

Cortijo de Jara 12 meses 2012 T

tempranillo, merlot, syrah

86

Cortijo de Jara 6 meses 2012 T

tempranillo, merlot, syrah

85

FINCA MONCLOA

Manuel María González, 12
11403 Jerez de la Frontera (Cádiz)
☎: +34 956 357 000
Fax: +34 956 357 043
nacional@gonzalezbyass.com
www.gonzalezbyass.com

Finca Moncloa 10 Barricas 2011 T

cabernet sauvignon, syrah, tintilla de rota

93

Colour: cherry, garnet rim. Nose: balanced, complex, ripe fruit, spicy, warm, balsamic herbs. Palate: good structure, flavourful, round tannins, balanced.

Finca Moncloa 2012 T

syrah, cabernet sauvignon, merlot, tintilla de rota, petit verdot

91

Colour: deep cherry, garnet rim. Nose: balanced, ripe fruit, scrubland, dried flowers, expressive. Palate: balanced, round tannins, spicy.

Tintilla de Rota de Finca Moncloa Dulce Natural 2012 T

100% tintilla de rota

92

Colour: cherry, garnet rim. Nose: fruit preserve, spicy, warm, fruit liqueur notes, balsamic herbs, expressive, elegant. Palate: powerful, flavourful, sweet, rich. Personality.

MIGUEL DOMECQ

Finca Torrecera, Ctra.
Jerez-La Ina Km 14,5
11595 Jerez de la Frontera (Cádiz)
☎: +34 856 030 073
Fax: +34 856 030 033
comercial@migueldomecq.com
www.migueldomecq.com

Alhocen Chardonnay 2013 B

100% chardonnay

88

Colour: bright yellow. Nose: ripe fruit, powerfull, toasty, aged wood nuances, pattiserie. Palate: flavourful, fruity, spicy, toasty, long.

Alhocen Selección Personal 2010 TR

syrah, merlot, cabernet sauvignon, tempranillo

89

Colour: pale ruby, brick rim edge. Nose: elegant, spicy, fine reductive notes, tobacco, ripe fruit. Palate: spicy, elegant, long.

Alhocen Syrah Merlot 2011 TR

syrah, merlot

87

Colour: very deep cherry, garnet rim. Nose: balsamic herbs, grassy, green pepper, ripe fruit. Palate: full, flavourful, round tannins.

Entrechuelos 2013 T Roble

tempranillo, cabernet sauvignon, syrah, merlot

85

Entrechuelos Chardonnay 2014 B

100% chardonnay

87

Colour: bright yellow. Nose: expressive, dried herbs, ripe fruit, spicy. Palate: flavourful, fruity, good acidity, balanced.

Entrechuelos Premium 2011 T
syrah, merlot, cabernet sauvignon, tempranillo

88

Colour: bright cherry. Nose: ripe fruit, sweet spices, creamy oak. Palate: flavourful, fruity, toasty.

Entrechuelos Tercer Año 2012 T
syrah, merlot, cabernet sauvignon, tempranillo

87

Colour: cherry, garnet rim. Nose: red berry notes, ripe fruit, spicy, creamy oak. Palate: flavourful, toasty, round tannins.

VT CAMPO DE CARTAGENA

BODEGAS SERRANO
Finca La Cabaña, 30 Pozo Estrecho
30594 Cartagena (Murcia)
☎: +34 968 556 298
Fax: +34 968 556 298
info@bodegasserrano.es
www.bodegasserrano.es

Darimus 2012 T Barrica
cabernet sauvignon, syrah

84

Galtea ESP
83

VT CASTELLÓN

BODEGA LES USERES
Calle Nueva, 23
12118 Les Useres (Castellón)
☎: +34 964 388 525
Fax: +34 964 388 526
info@bodegalesuseres.es
www.bodegalesuseres.com

33 Route 2012 T
tempranillo, bonicaire

87

Colour: bright cherry. Nose: ripe fruit, sweet spices, creamy oak. Palate: flavourful, fruity, toasty.

33 Route 2014 B
macabeo, chardonnay

87

Colour: bright straw. Nose: dried herbs, floral, fruit expression, earthy notes. Palate: powerful, flavourful, spicy.

33 Route 2014 RD
bonicaire, garnacha

85

86 Winegrowers 2012 TR
tempranillo, cabernet sauvignon

87

Colour: cherry, garnet rim. Nose: ripe fruit, spicy, creamy oak. Palate: powerful, flavourful, long, toasty.

BODEGA MAS DE RANDER
Ctra. Torreblanca-Vilanova, km. 2,5
12180 Benlloch (Castellón)
☎: +34 964 302 416
masderander@masderander.com
www.masderander.com

Syrah Mas de Rander 2012 T
syrah

87

Colour: bright cherry. Nose: ripe fruit, sweet spices, creamy oak. Palate: flavourful, fruity, toasty.

Temps Mas de Rander 2010 T
cabernet sauvignon, syrah, merlot

79

BODEGA VICENTE FLORS
Pda. Pou D'encalbo, s/n
12118 Les Useres (Castellón)
☎: +34 671 618 851
bodega@bodegaflors.com
www.bodegaflors.com

Clotàs 2011 T
90% tempranillo, 10% cabernet sauvignon

88

Colour: cherry, garnet rim. Nose: spicy, ripe fruit, balsamic herbs. Palate: flavourful, ripe fruit, good acidity, balanced.

Clotàs Monastrell 2011 T
monastrell

87

Colour: cherry, garnet rim. Nose: ripe fruit, fruit preserve, waxy notes, spicy. Palate: flavourful, spicy, balsamic.

El Dolcet del Clotàs Naturalmente Dulce 2013
50% monastrell, 50% garnacha

86

Flor de Clotàs 2011 T
tempranillo

87

Colour: cherry, garnet rim. Nose: spicy, ripe fruit, wild herbs, warm. Palate: flavourful, ripe fruit.

BODEGAS Y VIÑEDOS BARÓN D'ALBA

Partida Vilar La Call, 10
12118 Les Useres (Castellón)
☎: +34 964 767 306
barondalba@gmail.com
www.barondalba.com

Clos D'Esgarracordes 2012 T Barrica
garnacha, monastrell, tempranillo, merlot

89

Colour: cherry, garnet rim. Nose: ripe fruit, wild herbs, spicy. Palate: balanced, flavourful, long, spicy.

Clos D'Esgarracordes Colección Pelegri 2011 T
100% cabernet sauvignon

90

Colour: cherry, garnet rim. Nose: ripe fruit, wild herbs, earthy notes, spicy, balsamic herbs. Palate: balanced, flavourful, long, balsamic.

Clos D'Esgarracordes Dolç de Gloria Naturalmente Dulce 2012 B
100% macabeo

87

Colour: golden. Nose: powerfull, honeyed notes, candied fruit, fragrant herbs, acetaldehyde. Palate: flavourful, sweet, fresh, fruity, good acidity, long.

ILDUM VINARIUS

Escultor Maurat 22
12180 Cabanes (Castellón)
☎: +34 696 445 481
ildum@ildum.es
www.ildum.es

Bellmunt i Oliver Brut 2013 ESP
70% macabeo, 30% chardonnay

81

Bellmunt i Oliver Gran Brut 2013 BR
70% pinot noir, 30% chardonnay

83

Gallus Optimus 2013 T
merlot, cabernet sauvignon

84

Gallus Optimus Blanc 2014 B
macabeo, chardonnay, moscatel

81

VIÑEDOS Y BODEGAS MAYO GARCÍA

La Font 116
12192 Vilafamés (Castellón)
☎: +34 964 329 312
mail@mayogarcia.com
www.mayogarcia.com

Magnanimvs Rubí 2013 TC

86

VT CASTILLA

AGRÍCOLA CASA DE LA VIÑA

Ctra. La Solana Vva de los Infantes, Km. 15,2
13248 Alhambra (Ciudad Real)
☎: +34 926 696 044
bodega@bodegascasadelavina.com
www.bodegascasadelavina.com

Casa de la Viña 2011 T Barrica
tempranillo

86

Casa de la Viña Chardonnay 2014 B
chardonnay

85

Casa de la Viña Edición Limitada 2012 T
tempranillo

90

Colour: cherry, garnet rim. Nose: red berry notes, ripe fruit, spicy, creamy oak, complex. Palate: flavourful, toasty, round tannins.

Casa de la Viña Sauvignon Blanc 2014 B
sauvignon blanc

84

Casa de la Viña Syrah 2014 T
syrah

86

Casa de la Viña Tempranillo 2014 T
tempranillo

86

Colour: cherry, purple rim. Nose: powerfull, ripe fruit, spicy. Palate: powerful, fruity, unctuous.

ALENUR

Paseo de la Libertad 6 1º Izq.
02001 Albacete (Albacete)
☎: +34 967 247 001
Fax: +34 967 242 982
info@alenur.com
www.alenur.com

Alenur + 5 T
100% tempranillo

81

Alenur Coupage 2012 TC
85% tempranillo, 15% syrah

82

Colour: very deep cherry, garnet rim. Nose: balsamic herbs, overripe fruit, grassy. Palate: full, flavourful, spirituous.

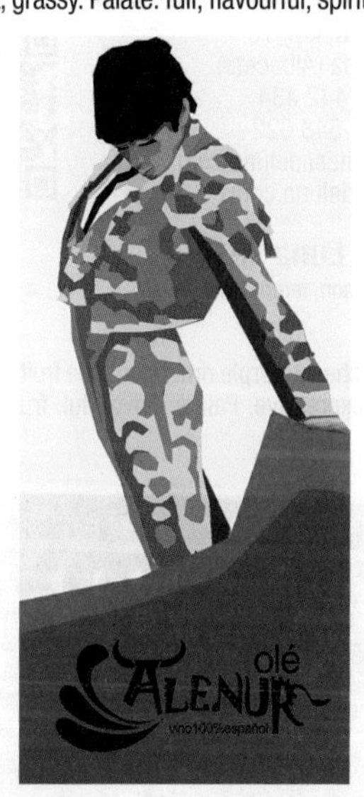

Alenur Tempranillo 2011 T
100% tempranillo

85

BODEGA CAMPOS DE DULCINEA

Garay, 1
45820 El Toboso (Toledo)
☎: +34 925 568 163
Fax: +34 925 568 163
camposdedulcinea@camposdedulcinea.es
www.camposdedulcinea.es

Campos de Dulcinea 2012 T
tempranillo

84 ♣

Campos de Dulcinea 2014 B
sauvignon blanc

83 ♣

Campos de Dulcinea 2014 RD
tempranillo

84 ♣

Campos de Dulcinea 2014 T
tempranillo, graciano

82 ♣

Campos de Dulcinea Tempranillo 2014 T
tempranillo
84

BODEGA DEHESA DE LUNA

Ctra. CM-3106, km. 16
02630 La Roda (Albacete)
☎: +34 967 442 434
Fax: +34 967 548 022
contacto@dehesadeluna.com
www.dehesadeluna.com

Dehesa de Luna 2013 T
cabernet sauvignon, tempranillo, syrah
88
Colour: bright cherry, purple rim. Nose: ripe fruit, sweet spices, creamy oak, expressive. Palate: flavourful, fruity, round tannins.

Dehesa de Luna Rosé 2014 RD
cabernet sauvignon
85

La Cañada del Navajo LCN Petit Verdot 2012 T
petit verdot
87
Colour: very deep cherry, garnet rim. Nose: expressive, balsamic herbs, balanced, toasty. Palate: flavourful, round tannins, fine bitter notes.

Luna Lunera Sauvignon Blanc 2014 B
sauvignon blanc
86

Luna Lunera Tempranillo 2014 T
tempranillo
84

BODEGA FAMILIA CONESA - PAGO GUIJOSO

Crta Ossa de Montiel - El Bonillo km 11
06210 El Bonillo (Murcia)
☎: +34 618 844 583
direccion@familiaconesa.com
www.familiaconesa.com

La Doncella de las Viñas 2013 T
tempranillo, syrah
87
Colour: garnet rim. Nose: ripe fruit, wild herbs, earthy notes. Palate: fruity, flavourful, spicy.

La Doncella de las Viñas 2014 B
chardonnay
86

La Doncella de las Viñas 2014 RD
syrah
85

BODEGA HACIENDA LA PRINCESA

Crta. San carlos del Valle;
Km 8; Apd. de Correos 281
13300 Valdepeñas (Ciudad Real)
☎: +34 638 335 185
haciendalaprincesa@telefonica.net
www.haciendalaprincesa.com

Hacienda La Princesa Chardonnay 2014 B
chardonnay
84

Hacienda La Princesa Gala 2011 T
tempranillo
88
Colour: cherry, garnet rim. Nose: ripe fruit, sweet spices, creamy oak. Palate: powerful, flavourful, spicy.

Hacienda La Princesa Sucunza 2011 TC
tempranillo, merlot
87
Colour: cherry, garnet rim. Nose: creamy oak, red berry notes, ripe fruit. Palate: flavourful, spicy.

BODEGA LOS ALJIBES

Finca Los Aljibes
02520 Chinchilla de Montearagón
(Albacete)
☎: +34 967 260 015
Fax: +34 967 261 450
info@fincalosaljibes.com
www.fincalosaljibes.com

Aljibes 2011 T
cabernet franc, merlot, cabernet sauvignon

86

Aljibes Cabernet Franc 2011 T
cabernet franc

88

Colour: very deep cherry, garnet rim. Nose: expressive, balsamic herbs, balanced, grassy. Palate: full, flavourful, round tannins.

Aljibes Petit Verdot 2011 T
petit verdot

88

Colour: bright cherry. Nose: ripe fruit, sweet spices, creamy oak, smoky. Palate: flavourful, fruity, toasty, round tannins.

Aljibes Syrah 2012 T
syrah

89

Colour: cherry, garnet rim. Nose: creamy oak, red berry notes, balanced, ripe fruit. Palate: flavourful, spicy, elegant.

La Galana Garnacha Tintorera 2012 TC
garnacha tintorera

88

Colour: very deep cherry, garnet rim. Nose: ripe fruit, raspberry, powerfull, scrubland. Palate: fruity, easy to drink, ripe fruit.

Selectus 2008 T
syrah, cabernet franc, cabernet sauvignon, merlot

90

Colour: dark-red cherry, garnet rim. Nose: smoky, aromatic coffee, toasty, ripe fruit, dried herbs. Palate: balanced, ripe fruit.

Viña Aljibes 2012 T
cabernet sauvignon, syrah, cabernet franc, tempranillo

84

Viña Aljibes 2014 B
sauvignon blanc, chardonnay

86

Viña Aljibes 2014 RD
syrah

88

Colour: rose, purple rim. Nose: red berry notes, floral, expressive. Palate: powerful, fruity, fresh, easy to drink.

BODEGA TRENZA

Avda. Matías Saenz Tejada,
s/n. Edif. Fuengirola Center
29640 Fuengirola (Málaga)
☎: +34 615 343 320
Fax: +34 952 588 467
info@bodegatrenza.com
www.bodegatrenza.com

Sedosa Aged in Oak 2013 T
tempranillo, syrah

84

Sedosa Tempranillo Syrah 2013 T
tempranillo, syrah

83

Sedosa Verdejo Sauvignon Blanc 2013 B
verdejo, sauvignon blanc

82

BODEGAS ANHELO

Jabalón, 14
13350 Moral de Calatraba
(Ciudad Real)
☎: +34 626 929 262
j.sanchez@bodegasanhelo.com
www.bodegasanhelo.com

Campo Anhelo Riesling 2014 B
100% riesling

87

Colour: bright straw. Nose: fresh fruit, fragrant herbs. Palate: flavourful, fruity, good acidity, balanced.

Campo Anhelo Tempranillo 2013 T Joven
100% tempranillo

86

Campo Anhelo Tempranillo 2013 T Roble
100% tempranillo

86

BODEGAS ARÚSPIDE

Ciriaco Cruz, 2
13300 Valdepeñas (Ciudad Real)
☎: +34 926 347 075
Fax: +34 926 347 875
info@aruspide.com
www.aruspide.com

Ágora 2013 T Roble
100% tempranillo

84

Ágora Ciento 69 2014 RD
syrah

84

Ágora Lágrima 2014 B
85% airén, 15% verdejo

83

Ágora Tempranillo 2014 T Maceración Carbónica
100% tempranillo

85

Ágora Viognier 2014 B Maceración Carbónica
100% viognier

83

Ardales 2013 T
100% tempranillo

85

Ardales 2014 B
100% verdejo

86

Autor de Arúspide Chardonnay 2012 B
100% chardonnay

86

Autor de Arúspide Tempranillo 2011 T
100% tempranillo

88

Colour: cherry, garnet rim. Nose: smoky, spicy, ripe fruit, fruit preserve. Palate: flavourful, smoky aftertaste, ripe fruit.

El Linze 2011 T
85% syrah, 15% tinto velasco

87

Colour: very deep cherry, garnet rim. Nose: fruit preserve, powerfull, violets, spicy. Palate: correct, easy to drink, round tannins.

Pura Savia 2013 T
100% tempranillo

87

Colour: cherry, garnet rim. Nose: balanced, medium intensity, ripe fruit, spicy. Palate: correct, balsamic, good acidity.

BODEGAS BARREDA

Ramalazo, 2
45880 Corral de Almaguer (Toledo)
☎: +34 915 435 387
Fax: +34 925 207 223
nacional@bodegas-barreda.com
www.bodegas-barreda.com

Torre de Barreda Amigos 2011 T
tempranillo, syrah, cabernet sauvignon

90

Colour: cherry, garnet rim. Nose: creamy oak, red berry notes, fresh fruit, fragrant herbs, expressive. Palate: flavourful, spicy, elegant.

Torre de Barreda Cabernet Sauvignon 2013 T
cabernet sauvignon

87

Colour: cherry, garnet rim. Nose: creamy oak, toasty, ripe fruit, balsamic herbs. Palate: spicy, long, powerful.

Torre de Barreda PañoFino 2013 T
tempranillo

91

Colour: deep cherry, purple rim. Nose: red berry notes, violet drops, sweet spices, creamy oak, expressive. Palate: powerful, flavourful, spicy, long.

Torre de Barreda Syrah 2012 T
syrah

89

Colour: cherry, garnet rim. Nose: creamy oak, red berry notes, balanced. Palate: flavourful, spicy, elegant.

Torre de Barreda Tempranillo 2012 T
tempranillo

88

Colour: bright cherry. Nose: ripe fruit, sweet spices, creamy oak, expressive. Palate: flavourful, fruity, round tannins.

BODEGAS CASAQUEMADA

13700 Argamasilla de Alba
(Ciudad Real)
☎: +34 628 621 187
casaquemada@casaquemada.es
www.casaquemada.es

Alba de Casa Quemada 2012 T
syrah

89

Colour: cherry, garnet rim. Nose: ripe fruit, fruit preserve, wild herbs, toasty. Palate: powerful, flavourful, spicy.

Anea de Casaquemada 2009 T
syrah

90

Colour: cherry, garnet rim. Nose: ripe fruit, wild herbs, earthy notes, spicy, balsamic herbs. Palate: balanced, flavourful, long, balsamic.

Brincho 2012 T
tempranillo

90

Colour: cherry, garnet rim. Nose: red berry notes, ripe fruit, spicy, creamy oak, complex. Palate: flavourful, toasty, round tannins, balanced.

Hacienda Casaquemada 2009 T
tempranillo

91

Colour: cherry, garnet rim. Nose: ripe fruit, spicy, creamy oak, balsamic herbs, balanced. Palate: flavourful, spicy, elegant.

BODEGAS CRIN ROJA

Paraje Mainetes
02651 Fuenteálamo (Albacete)
☎: +34 938 743 511
Fax: +34 938 737 204
info@crinroja.com
www.crinroja.com

Crin Roja Cabernet Sauvignon 2014 T Roble
cabernet sauvignon

84

Crin Roja Cabernet Sauvignon Syrah 2014 T Roble
cabernet sauvignon, syrah

86

Crin Roja Tempranillo 2014 T
100% tempranillo

82

Montal Cabernet Sauvignon Syrah 2014 T
85% cabernet sauvignon, 15% syrah

85

Montal Macabeo 2014 B
100% macabeo

85

Montal Tempranillo 2014 T
100% tempranillo

84

BODEGAS DEL MUNI

Ctra. de Lillo, 48
45310 Villatobas (Toledo)
☎: +34 925 152 511
Fax: +34 925 152 511
info@bodegasdelmuni.com
www.bodegasdelmuni.com

Corpus del Muni 2013 T Roble
tempranillo, syrah, garnacha, petit verdot

86

Corpus del Muni Blanca Selección 2014 B
verdejo, chardonnay, sauvignon blanc, riesling

87

Colour: bright yellow. Nose: citrus fruit, ripe fruit, fragrant herbs, floral, expressive. Palate: fresh, fruity, flavourful, balanced.

Corpus del Muni Lucía Selección 2010 TC
tempranillo

88

Colour: very deep cherry. Nose: toasty, ripe fruit, creamy oak. Palate: spicy, toasty, flavourful.

Corpus del Muni Selección Especial 2010 T
tempranillo

89

Colour: cherry, garnet rim. Nose: spicy, ripe fruit, balsamic herbs, balanced. Palate: flavourful, ripe fruit, spicy, long.

Corpus del Muni Vendimia Seleccionada 2014 T Joven
tempranillo, syrah, garnacha

88

Colour: cherry, purple rim. Nose: expressive, fresh fruit, red berry notes, floral. Palate: flavourful, fruity, good acidity.

BODEGAS EGUREN

Avda. del Cantábrico, s/n
01012 Vitoria-Gasteiz (Álava)
☎: +34 945 282 844
Fax: +34 945 271 319
info@egurenugarte.com
www.egurenugarte.com

Condado de Eguren Tempranillo 2013 T
100% tempranillo

84

Kame 2011 T
30% tempranillo, 35% cabernet sauvignon, 30% syrah, 5% petit verdot

88

Colour: cherry, garnet rim. Nose: creamy oak, red berry notes, balanced. Palate: flavourful, spicy, balanced.

Kame Muscat 2014 B
100% moscatel

86

Kame Verdejo 2014 B
100% verdejo

89

Colour: bright straw. Nose: white flowers, fresh fruit, fragrant herbs, expressive. Palate: flavourful, fruity, good acidity, balanced.

Mercedes Eguren Cabernet Sauvignon 2013 T
100% cabernet sauvignon

85

Mercedes Eguren Cabernet Sauvignon 2014 RD
cabernet sauvignon

87

Colour: rose, purple rim. Nose: floral, wild herbs, fruit expression, expressive. Palate: flavourful, complex, balanced.

Mercedes Eguren Sauvignon Blanc 2014 B
100% sauvignon blanc

86

Mercedes Eguren Shiraz Tempranillo 2013 T
50% syrah, 50% tempranillo

87

Colour: bright cherry. Nose: ripe fruit, sweet spices, creamy oak. Palate: flavourful, fruity, spicy, good finish.

Pazos de Eguren Tempranillo 2014 T
100% tempranillo

85

Reinares 2014 B
100% viura

83

Reinares 2014 RD
100% tempranillo

86

Reinares Tempranillo 2014 T
100% tempranillo

84

BODEGAS FERNANDO CASTRO

Paseo Castelar, 70
13730 Santa Cruz de Mudela
(Ciudad Real)
☎: +34 926 342 168
Fax: +34 926 349 029
info@bodegasfernandocastro.com
www.bodegasfernandocastro.com

Finca La Lomilla 2014 T
100% garnacha

86

Finca Las Virtudes Cabernet Sauvignon 2014 T
100% cabernet sauvignon

84

Finca Las Virtudes Chardonnay 2014 B
100% chardonnay

81

Finca Las Virtudes Merlot 2014 T
100% merlot

83

Finca Las Virtudes Sauvignon Blanc 2014 B
100% sauvignon blanc

82

Finca Las Virtudes Syrah 2014 T
100% syrah

85

BODEGAS FINCA LA ESTACADA

Ctra. N-400, Km. 103
16400 Tarancón (Cuenca)
☎: +34 969 327 099
Fax: +34 969 327 199
enologia@fincalaestacada.com
www.laestacada.com

Hello World Cabernet Franc 2014 T
cabernet franc

87

Colour: cherry, purple rim. Nose: expressive, fresh fruit, red berry notes, floral. Palate: flavourful, fruity, good acidity.

Hello World Petit Verdot 2014 T
petit verdot

86

Hello World Prieto Picudo 2014 T
prieto picudo

88

Colour: cherry, purple rim. Nose: fresh fruit, red berry notes, floral, expressive. Palate: flavourful, fruity, good acidity, balanced.

Secua Cabernet-Syrah 2010 T
cabernet sauvignon, syrah

88

Colour: very deep cherry, garnet rim. Nose: balsamic herbs, balanced, grassy. Palate: full, flavourful, long.

Secua Cabernet-Syrah 2011 T
cabernet sauvignon, syrah

90

Colour: cherry, garnet rim. Nose: ripe fruit, spicy, creamy oak, complex, balsamic herbs. Palate: flavourful, toasty, round tannins, balanced.

Secua Chardonnay Dulce 2014 B
chardonnay

86

BODEGAS HERMANOS RUBIO

Ctra. de Villamuelas, s/n
45740 Villasequilla (Toledo)
☎: +34 925 310 268
Fax: +34 925 325 133
info@bhrubio.com
www.bhrubio.com

Viña Alambrada 2014 B
airén

82

BODEGAS LAHOZ

Ctra. N-310 Tomelloso-Villarrobledo
Km. 108,5
13630 Socuéllamos (Ciudad Real)
☎: +34 926 699 083
Fax: +34 926 514 929
info@bodegaslahoz.com
www.bodegaslahoz.com

Recato Sauvignon Blanc Chardonay 2014 B
80% sauvignon blanc, 20% chardonnay

86

Recato Tempranillo 9 meses 2011 T Barrica
100% tempranillo

85

BODEGAS MAS QUE VINOS

Camino de los Molinos, s/n
45312 Cabañas de Yepes (Toledo)
☎: +34 925 122 281
Fax: +34 925 137 033
mqv@bodegasmasquevinos.com
www.bodegasmasquevinos.com

El Señorito 2011 T
100% tempranillo

92

Colour: cherry, garnet rim. Nose: red berry notes, ripe fruit, sweet spices, toasty. Palate: flavourful, spicy, elegant.

Ercavio 2014 B
100% airén

88

Colour: bright straw. Nose: white flowers, fresh fruit, fragrant herbs, expressive. Palate: flavourful, fruity, good acidity, balanced.

Ercavio 2014 RD
100% tempranillo

89

Colour: onion pink. Nose: elegant, red berry notes, floral, fragrant herbs. Palate: light-bodied, flavourful, good acidity, easy to drink.

Ercavio Selección Limitada 2011 T
100% tempranillo

89

Colour: cherry, garnet rim. Nose: creamy oak, red berry notes, balanced. Palate: flavourful, spicy, toasty.

Ercavio Tempranillo 2013 T Roble
100% tempranillo

87

Colour: bright cherry. Nose: ripe fruit, sweet spices, creamy oak. Palate: flavourful, fruity, toasty.

La Meseta 2010 T
tempranillo, syrah

89

Colour: cherry, garnet rim. Nose: creamy oak, red berry notes, fresh fruit, balanced. Palate: flavourful, spicy, elegant.

Perlas de Otoño Rosado BN
tempranillo, garnacha

88

Colour: coppery red. Nose: floral, jasmine, fragrant herbs, candied fruit. Palate: fresh, fruity, flavourful, correct.

BODEGAS MÁXIMO

Camino Viejo de Logroño, 26
01320 Oyón (Álava)
☎: +34 945 622 216
Fax: +34 945 622 315
maximo@bodegasmaximo.com
www.bodegasmaximo.com

Máximo Garnacha 2013 T
100% garnacha

86

Máximo Merlot 2012 T
100% merlot

83

Máximo Tempranillo 2013 T
100% tempranillo

84

Máximo Viura 2014 B
100% viura

84

BODEGAS MOISÉS CASAS

Victoria, 4
45830 Miguel Esteban (Toledo)
☎: +34 653 280 797
info@eccevinum.com
www.eccevinum.com

Ecce Vinum Coupage 2009 T Roble
65% merlot, 18% syrah, 17% cabernet sauvignon

86

Ecce Vinum Rosé de Aguja 2014 RD
100% tempranillo

86

Ecce Vinum Tempranillo 2011 T
100% tempranillo

87

Colour: cherry, garnet rim. Nose: creamy oak, red berry notes, fresh fruit. Palate: flavourful, spicy, easy to drink.

Ecce Vinum Tempranillo 2013 T
100% tempranillo

85

Ecce Vinum Viura 2013 B
100% viura

84

BODEGAS MONTALVO WILMOT

Ctra. Ruidera, km. 10,2
Finca Los Cerrillos
13710 Argamasilla de Alba
(Ciudad Real)
☎: +34 926 699 069
info@montalvowilmot.com
www.montalvowilmot.com

Montalvo Wilmot Cabernet de Familia 2007 T
100% cabernet sauvignon

88
Colour: ruby red. Nose: spicy, fine reductive notes, aged wood nuances, ripe fruit, balsamic herbs. Palate: spicy, fine tannins, balanced.

Montalvo Wilmot Colección Privada 2010 T Roble
75% tempranillo, 25% cabernet sauvignon

88
Colour: cherry, garnet rim. Nose: creamy oak, red berry notes, wild herbs. Palate: flavourful, spicy, long, correct.

Montalvo Wilmot Quintos de la Tejera 2014 T
100% tempranillo

86

Montalvo Wilmot Syrah 2013 T Roble
100% syrah

85

Montalvo Wilmot Tempranillo-Cabernet 2012 T Roble
75% tempranillo, 25% cabernet sauvignon

87
Colour: bright cherry. Nose: ripe fruit, sweet spices, creamy oak, lactic notes. Palate: flavourful, fruity, toasty.

BODEGAS MORALIA

Avda. de la Vendimia, 1
13350 Moral de Calatrava (Ciudad Real)
☎: +34 926 330 910
Fax: +34 926 319 523
bodegasmoralia@telefonica.net
www.bodegasmoralia.es

Moralia Merlot 2009 TR
merlot

85

Moralia Sensación 2014 B
verdejo

80

Moralia Tempranillo 2014 T
tempranillo

84

Moralia Troncal 2010 TR
tempranillo

86

Moralia Verdejo 2014 B
verdejo

82

BODEGAS MUREDA

Ctra. N-IV, Km. 184,1
13300 Valdepeñas (Ciudad Real)
☎: +34 926 318 058
Fax: +34 926 318 058
bmoreno@mureda.es
www.mureda.es

Mureda Chardonnay 2014 B
chardonnay

85 ♣

Mureda Estate Wine 2011 T
tempranillo

87
Colour: cherry, garnet rim. Nose: creamy oak, red berry notes, spicy. Palate: flavourful, spicy.

Mureda Sauvignon Blanc 2014 B
sauvignon blanc

85 ♣

Mureda Syrah 2014 T
syrah

88 ♣
Colour: cherry, purple rim. Nose: expressive, fresh fruit, red berry notes, floral. Palate: flavourful, fruity, good acidity.

BODEGAS NAVARRO LÓPEZ

Autovía Madrid - Cádiz, Km. 193
13200 Valdepeñas (Ciudad Real)
☎: +34 902 193 431
Fax: +34 902 193 432
laboratorio@navarrolopez.com
www.navarrolopez.com

Para Celsus 2014 T
tempranillo

87
Colour: cherry, purple rim. Nose: expressive, fresh fruit, red berry notes, floral. Palate: flavourful, fruity, good acidity.

Premium 1904 2012 T
tempranillo, syrah

88

Colour: cherry, garnet rim. Nose: ripe fruit, spicy, creamy oak. Palate: flavourful, toasty.

Premium 1904 2014 B
sauvignon blanc

86

Premium 1904 2014 B
chardonnay

88

Colour: bright straw. Nose: white flowers, candied fruit, citrus fruit, expressive. Palate: flavourful, fruity, good acidity, elegant.

Rojo Garnacha 2014 T
100% garnacha

86

Rojo Tempranillo 2014 T
100% tempranillo

87

Colour: cherry, purple rim. Nose: expressive, fresh fruit, red berry notes, floral. Palate: flavourful, fruity, good acidity.

Tierra Calar 2014 B
macabeo

85

Tierra Calar 2014 T
100% tempranillo

85

BODEGAS PÍO DEL RAMO

Ctra. Almanza, s/n
02652 Ontur (Albacete)
☎: +34 967 323 230
info@piodelramo.com
www.piodelramo.com

Pío 2011 TC
60% monastrell, 15% petit verdot, 15% syrah, 10% cabernet sauvignon

89

Colour: cherry, garnet rim. Nose: balanced, ripe fruit, spicy, creamy oak. Palate: good structure, flavourful, balanced.

Pío 2012 T Roble
60% monastrell, 25% syrah, 15% cabernet sauvignon

89

Colour: cherry, garnet rim. Nose: ripe fruit, fragrant herbs, spicy, toasty. Palate: powerful, flavourful, balanced.

Pío del Ramo Chardonnay 2013 BFB
100% chardonnay

85

Pío del Ramo Verdejo 2014 B
verdejo

82

Viña Betola 2013 T
70% monastrell, 15% syrah, 15% cabernet sauvignon

87

Colour: cherry, garnet rim. Nose: wild herbs, ripe fruit, spicy. Palate: powerful, flavourful, round.

BODEGAS REAL

Ctra. de Valdepeñas a Cozar Km. 12,800
13100 Montiel (Ciudad Real)
☎: +34 914 577 588
Fax: +34 914 577 210
comercial@bodegas-real.com
www.bodegas-real.com

Vega Ibor Garnacha Tintorera 2014 T
100% garnacha tintorera

86

Vega Ibor Merlot 2014 RD
100% merlot

84

Vega Ibor Tempranillo 2012 T Roble
100% tempranillo

86

Colour: cherry, garnet rim. Nose: smoky, spicy, ripe fruit. Palate: flavourful, ripe fruit, roasted-coffee aftertaste.

Vega Ibor Viura 2014 B
100% viura

81

BODEGAS RÍO NEGRO

Ctra. CM 1001, Km. 37,400
19230 Cogolludo (Guadalajara)
☎: +34 913 022 646
Fax: +34 917 660 019
info@fincarionegro.es
www.fincarionegro.es

Finca Río Negro 2011 T
tempranillo, syrah, merlot, cabernet sauvignon

91

Colour: cherry, garnet rim. Nose: expressive, spicy, earthy notes. Palate: flavourful, ripe fruit, long, good acidity, balanced.

BODEGAS SAN ISIDRO DE PEDRO MUÑOZ

13620 Pedro Muñoz (Ciudad Real)
☎: +34 926 586 057
Fax: +34 926 568 380
administracin@viacotos.com
www.viacotos.com

Carril de Cotos 2010 T Barrica
tempranillo

85

Carril de Cotos Airén 2014 B
airén

83

Carril de Cotos Cabernet Sauvignon 2011 T Barrica
cabernet sauvignon

84

Carril de Cotos Semidulce 2014 B
airén

82

Carril de Cotos Tempranillo 2013 T
tempranillo

86

BODEGAS SEÑORÍO DE YAGÜE

Camino de La Atalayuela, s/n
13300 Valdepeñas (Ciudad Real)
☎: +34 926 324 297
Fax: +34 926 321 416
info@senoriodeyague.com
www.senoriodeyague.com

Vineae ExpressiO VEO Chardonnay 2014 B
100% chardonnay

89

Colour: bright yellow. Nose: expressive, dried herbs, ripe fruit, spicy, dried flowers. Palate: flavourful, fruity, good acidity, balanced.

Vineae ExpressiO VEO Merlot 2014 T
100% merlot

86

BODEGAS VENTA MORALES

Paraje Casas Alfaqui, 1
03650 Pinoso (Alicante)
☎: +34 965 978 603
export@bodegasvolver.com
www.bodegasvolver.com

Venta Morales Tempranillo 2014 T
tempranillo

84

BODEGAS VERUM

Ctra. Argamasilla de Alba, km. 0,800
13700 Tomelloso (Ciudad Real)
☎: +34 926 511 404
Fax: +34 926 515 047
administracion@bodegasverum.com
www.bodegasverum.com

Verum Cabernet Sauvignon Tempranillo Merlot 2012 T Roble
77% tempranillo, 17% merlot, 6% cabernet sauvignon

85

Verum Merlot Tempranillo Cabernet Sauvignon 2011 TC
40% merlot, 40% tempranillo, 20% cabernet sauvignon

88

Colour: cherry, garnet rim. Nose: fine reductive notes, ripe fruit, spicy. Palate: spicy, long, toasty, balanced.

Verum Sauvignon Blanc Cuvée 1222 2013 B Barrica
sauvignon blanc

89

Colour: bright yellow. Nose: ripe fruit, powerfull, toasty, pattiserie, sweet spices. Palate: fruity, spicy, toasty, long, balanced.

Verum Sauvignon Blanc Gewürztraminer 2014 B
80% sauvignon blanc, 20% gewürztraminer

88

Colour: bright straw. Nose: white flowers, fresh fruit, fragrant herbs, tropical fruit. Palate: flavourful, fruity, balanced.

Verum Tempranillo Cabernet Franc 2014 RD
50% tempranillo, 50% cabernet franc

82

Verum Tempranillo V Reserva de Familia 2010 T
100% tempranillo

90

Colour: very deep cherry, garnet rim. Nose: expressive, complex, mineral, balsamic herbs, ripe fruit. Palate: full, flavourful, round tannins.

Verum Terra Airen de Pie Franco 2014 B
100% airén

86

Verum Vendimia Seleccionada Merlot 2010 T
100% merlot

89

Colour: cherry, garnet rim. Nose: ripe fruit, wild herbs, earthy notes, spicy. Palate: flavourful, long, balsamic, balanced.

BODEGAS VILLAVID

Niño Jesús, 25
16280 Villarta (Cuenca)
☎: +34 962 189 006
Fax: +34 962 189 125
export@villavid.com
www.villavid.com

Golden Bubbles of Villavid 2014 ESP
50% verdejo, 50% macabeo

86

Secret Bubbles of Villavid Rosado 2014 ESP

87

Colour: raspberry rose. Nose: floral, fragrant herbs, candied fruit. Palate: fresh, fruity, flavourful, sweet, balanced.

Villavid Bobal 2012 T Roble
100% bobal

85

Villavid Syrah 2012 T Roble
100% syrah

84

Villavid Tempranillo 2012 T Roble
100% tempranillo

84

Woman Soul of Villavid Semidulce 2014 B
50% verdejo, 50% macabeo

86

BODEGAS VIÑAS DEL CABRIEL

Olmedilla, s/n
16269 La Pesquera (Cuenca)
☎: +34 678 913 875
info@bodegasvinasdelcabriel.com
www.bodegasvinasdelcabriel.com

Renovatium "10 meses en Barrica" 2012 T
syrah, tempranillo

87

Colour: cherry, garnet rim. Nose: ripe fruit, spicy, creamy oak, complex. Palate: flavourful, toasty.

Renovatium "El Principio de Todo" 2013 T
bobal, tempranillo

85

BODEGAS VOLVER

Ctra de Pinoso a Fortuna
03650 Pinoso (Alicante)
☎: +34 965 978 603
export@bodegasvolver.com
www.bodegasvolver.com

Paso a Paso 2014 B
verdejo, macabeo

86

Paso a Paso Tempranillo 2014 T
tempranillo

88

Colour: cherry, purple rim. Nose: powerfull, ripe fruit, spicy. Palate: powerful, fruity, unctuous.

Paso a Paso Tempranillo Orgánico 2014 T
tempranillo

88

Colour: bright cherry. Nose: ripe fruit, sweet spices, expressive. Palate: flavourful, fruity, toasty.

BODEGAS Y VIÑEDOS CASA DEL VALLE

Ctra. de Yepes - Añover de Tajo,
Km. 47,700 - Finca Valdelagua
45313 Yepes (Toledo)
☎: +34 925 155 533
Fax: +34 925 147 019
casadelvalle@bodegasolarra.es
www.bodegacasadelvalle.es

Finca Valdelagua 2010 T
40% cabernet sauvignon, 40% syrah, 20% merlot

90

Colour: cherry, garnet rim. Nose: red berry notes, ripe fruit, spicy, creamy oak, complex. Palate: flavourful, toasty, round tannins, balanced.

Hacienda Casa del Valle Chardonnay 2014 B
100% chardonnay

85

Hacienda Casa del Valle Selección Especial 2012 T
cabernet sauvignon, syrah, merlot

86

Hacienda Casa del Valle Syrah 2012 T
100% syrah

85

BODEGAS Y VIÑEDOS CASTIBLANQUE

Isaac Peral, 19
13610 Campo de Criptana
(Ciudad Real)
☎: +34 926 589 147
Fax: +34 926 589 148
info@bodegascastiblanque.com
www.bodegascastiblanque.com

Baldor Old Vines 2009 T
100% cabernet sauvignon

86

Baldor Tradición Syrah 2011 T
100% syrah

87

Colour: bright cherry. Nose: ripe fruit, sweet spices, creamy oak. Palate: flavourful, fruity, toasty.

Ilex 2014 RD
100% syrah

85

Ilex 2014 T
50% garnacha, 50% tempranillo

85

Ilex Airén 2014 B
100% airén

80

Ilex Coupage 2012 T
50% syrah, 10% garnacha, 30% tempranillo, 10% cabernet sauvignon

85

Ilex Verdejo 2014 B
100% verdejo

82

BODEGAS Y VIÑEDOS PINUAGA

Ctra. N-301 Km. 95,5
45880 Corral de Almaguer (Toledo)
☎: +34 914 577 117
Fax: +34 914 577 117
info@bodegaspinuaga.com
www.bodegaspinuaga.com

Finca Salazar 2014 B
sauvignon blanc

87 ♣

Colour: bright straw. Nose: white flowers, fresh fruit, fragrant herbs. Palate: flavourful, fruity, good acidity.

Finca Salazar 2014 T
tempranillo

87 ♣

Colour: cherry, purple rim. Nose: expressive, fresh fruit, red berry notes, floral. Palate: flavourful, fruity, good acidity, balanced.

Pinuaga 10º Aniversario Edición Limitada 2012 T
tempranillo, merlot

89 ♣

Colour: deep cherry, purple rim. Nose: creamy oak, toasty, ripe fruit, balsamic herbs. Palate: balanced, spicy, long.

Pinuaga 200 Cepas 2011 T
tempranillo

90

Colour: cherry, garnet rim. Nose: balanced, complex, ripe fruit, spicy, fine reductive notes. Palate: good structure, flavourful, balanced.

Pinuaga Colección 2012 T
tempranillo

89 ♣

Colour: cherry, garnet rim. Nose: red berry notes, ripe fruit, spicy, creamy oak, complex. Palate: flavourful, toasty, balsamic.

Pinuaga La Senda 2013 T
80% merlot, 20% tempranillo

88

Colour: cherry, garnet rim. Nose: red berry notes, ripe fruit, wild herbs, mineral. Palate: flavourful, fresh, fruity, spicy.

Pinuaga Nature 2013 T
tempranillo

88

Colour: cherry, garnet rim. Nose: scrubland, ripe fruit, earthy notes, spicy. Palate: powerful, flavourful, long, spicy.

BODEGAS Y VIÑEDOS PONCE

Ctra. N-310
16230 Villanueva de la Jara (Cuenca)
☎: +34 677 434 523
bodegasponce@gmail.com

Depaula 2014 T
100% monastrell

90

Colour: cherry, purple rim. Nose: expressive, fresh fruit, red berry notes, floral, varietal. Palate: flavourful, fruity, good acidity.

BODEGAS Y VIÑEDOS TAVERA S.L.

45182 Arcicóllar (Toledo)
☎: +34 666 294 012
consuelo@bodegastavera.com
www.bodegastavera.com

3 Culturas 2014 B
100% chardonnay

85

Nereo Garnacha 2012 T
100% garnacha

86

Nereo Garnacha 2014 RD
100% garnacha

84

Nereo Syrah Tempranillo 2013 T
50% syrah, 50% tempranillo

84

Nereo Tempranillo Syrah Garnacha 2011 T
45% syrah, 45% tempranillo, 10% garnacha

87

Colour: bright cherry. Nose: ripe fruit, sweet spices, creamy oak, expressive. Palate: flavourful, fruity, toasty, round tannins.

BODEGAS YUNTERO

Pol. Ind., Ctra. Alcázar de San Juan s/n
13200 Manzanares (Ciudad Real)
☎: +34 926 610 309
Fax: +34 926 610 516
yuntero@yuntero.com
www.yuntero.com

Lazarillo 2014 B
verdejo

83

Lazarillo 2014 T Joven
tempranillo

84

BODEGAS ZIRIES

Menasalbas, 18
45120 San Pablo de los Montes (Toledo)
☎: +34 679 443 792
flequi@ziries.es
www.lobecasope.com

Navalegua 2013 T Barrica

89

Colour: deep cherry, purple rim. Nose: creamy oak, toasty, ripe fruit, balsamic herbs. Palate: spicy, long.

Navalegua 2014 T Barrica
garnacha

86

Ziries 2013 T
garnacha

88

Colour: bright cherry. Nose: ripe fruit, creamy oak, scrubland. Palate: flavourful, fruity, spicy.

CARRASCAS

Ctra. El Bonillo - Ossa de Montiel P.K. 11,4
02610 El Bonillo (Albacete)
☎: +34 967 965 880
info@carrascas.com
www.carrascas.com

Carrascas 2012 T
syrah, merlot, tempranillo, cabernet sauvignon

90

Colour: bright cherry. Nose: ripe fruit, sweet spices, creamy oak, expressive. Palate: flavourful, fruity, toasty, round tannins.

Carrascas 2013 B
viognier

91

Colour: bright straw. Nose: white flowers, fresh fruit, fragrant herbs, expressive. Palate: flavourful, fruity, good acidity, balanced.

Origen de Carrascas 2013 BFB
chardonnay

90

Colour: bright yellow. Nose: ripe fruit, powerfull, toasty, sweet spices. Palate: flavourful, fruity, spicy, toasty, sweetness.

Tiento de Carrascas 2012 T
merlot, cabernet sauvignon

92

Colour: cherry, garnet rim. Nose: creamy oak, balanced, ripe fruit, cocoa bean, earthy notes. Palate: flavourful, spicy, elegant.

CASA CARRIL CRUZADO

Ctra. Iniesta-Villagarcía del Llano km, 13
16236 Villagarcía del Llano (Cuenca)
☎: +34 967 571 154
Fax: +34 967 571 155
bodega@carrilcruzado.com
www.carrilcruzado.com

Carril Cruzado Chardonnay Sauvignon Blanc 2014 B
chardonnay, sauvignon blanc

85

Carril Cruzado Petit Verdot 2014 RD
petit verdot

85

Casa Carril Cruzado Multivarietal 2011 T
cabernet sauvignon, syrah, tempranillo, merlot, petit verdot

86

Casa Carril Cruzado Petit Verdot 2011 T
petit verdot

83

CASTILLO DE ARGUM

Ctra. Ossa de Montiel, Km. 1,200
02600 Villarrobledo (Albacete)
☎: +34 967 573 230
info@bodegaselcastillo.com
www.bodegaselcastillo.com

Argum 2014 B
sauvignon blanc

85

Argum Autor 2011 T Barrica
tempranillo, cabernet sauvignon, merlot

86

Castillo de Argum 2012 T Roble
tempranillo, cabernet sauvignon, merlot

85

Castillo de Argum 2013 T
cencibel

85

Castillo de Argum 2014 RD
cencibel

85 ♣

CONSTANTES VITALES

Plaza de Matute nº 12
28012 Madrid (Madrid)
☎: +34 609 079 980
info@miravinos.es
www.miravinos.es

Los Duelistas 2014 T
90% tempranillo, 10% graciano

89

Colour: bright cherry. Nose: ripe fruit, sweet spices, creamy oak. Palate: flavourful, fruity, toasty.

CORONADO, VINOS Y BODEGA

Ctra. San Isidro, s/n
16620 La Alberca de Záncara (Cuenca)
☎: +34 676 463 483
informacion@bodegascoronado.com
www.bodegascoronado.com

Charcón Sauvignon Blanc 2014 B
sauvignon blanc

86

Viña Charcón 2012 T Roble
cabernet sauvignon

86

Viña Charcón Selección 2012 T
cabernet sauvignon, petit verdot

86

COSECHEROS Y CRIADORES

Diputación, s/n
01320 Oyón (Álava)
☎: +34 945 601 944
Fax: +34 945 622 488
nacional@cosecherosycriadores.com
www.familiamartinezbujanda.com

Infinitus Cabernet Sauvignon 2014 T
cabernet sauvignon

86

Infinitus Cabernet Sauvignon Tempranillo 2013 T
cabernet sauvignon, tempranillo

85

Infinitus Gewürztraminer 2014 B
gewürztraminer

87

Colour: bright yellow. Nose: white flowers, fragrant herbs, ripe fruit, tropical fruit. Palate: fresh, fruity, easy to drink.

Infinitus Malbec 2014 T
malbec

88

Colour: cherry, purple rim. Nose: balsamic herbs, red berry notes, ripe fruit, balanced. Palate: flavourful, spicy, round.

Infinitus Merlot 2014 T
merlot

86

Infinitus Syrah 2014 T
syrah

87

Colour: cherry, purple rim. Nose: expressive, fresh fruit, red berry notes, floral, violets. Palate: flavourful, fruity, easy to drink.

Infinitus Tempranillo 2014 T
tempranillo

88

Colour: cherry, purple rim. Nose: red berry notes, ripe fruit, fragrant herbs, floral. Palate: powerful, flavourful, correct.

Infinitus Tempranillo Cabernet Franc 2014 RD
tempranillo, cabernet franc

87

Colour: brilliant rose. Nose: red berry notes, floral, expressive. Palate: fruity, fresh, easy to drink.

Infinitus Viura Chardonnay 2014 B
viura, chardonnay

85

DEHESA DE LOS LLANOS

Ctra. De Las Peñas de
San Pedro, km. 5,5
02006 Albacete (Albacete)
☎: +34 967 243 100
Fax: +34 967 243 093
info@dehesadelosllanos.es
www.dehesadelosllanos.es

Mazacruz 2012 T Roble
30% syrah, 27% tempranillo, 27% cabernet sauvignon, 16% merlot

88

Colour: cherry, purple rim. Nose: ripe fruit, sweet spices, scrubland. Palate: flavourful, spicy, powerful.

Mazacruz 2013 T
32% petit verdot, 32% tempranillo, 19% merlot, 17% syrah

87

Colour: cherry, purple rim. Nose: red berry notes, ripe fruit, wild herbs, spicy. Palate: powerful, flavourful, long.

Mazacruz 2014 B
60% sauvignon blanc, 40% verdejo

88

Colour: bright straw. Nose: white flowers, fresh fruit, fragrant herbs, expressive. Palate: flavourful, fruity, good acidity, balanced.

Mazacruz Cima 2010 T
44% cabernet sauvignon, 33% petit verdot, 11% merlot, 8% syrah, 4% graciano

87

Colour: cherry, garnet rim. Nose: smoky, spicy, ripe fruit. Palate: flavourful, smoky aftertaste, ripe fruit.

Mazacruz Selección 2011 T
50% cabernet sauvignon, 33% petit verdot, 17% syrah

90

Colour: very deep cherry, garnet rim. Nose: expressive, complex, balsamic herbs, ripe fruit. Palate: full, flavourful, round tannins, balanced.

DIONISOS - LA BODEGA DE LAS ESTRELLAS

13300 Valdepeñas (Ciudad Real)
☎: +34 926 313 248
dionisos@labodegadelasestrellas.com
www.labodegadelasestrellas.com

Dionisos 2014 B
75% airén, 25% macabeo

82

Dionisos Tempranillo 2012 T
100% tempranillo

87

Colour: cherry, garnet rim. Nose: red berry notes, ripe fruit, spicy, creamy oak. Palate: flavourful, toasty.

Ego Primus 2008 T
tempranillo, syrah

86

Flor de Rocío 2014 T Maceración Carbónica
100% syrah

78

Princesa de Tempranillo 2014 RD
100% tempranillo

86

Vinum Vitae 2007 TC
tempranillo

88

Colour: cherry, garnet rim. Nose: fine reductive notes, wet leather, ripe fruit. Palate: spicy, long, toasty.

DOMINIO DE EGUREN

Camino de San Pedro, s/n
01309 Páganos (Álava)
☎: +34 945 600 117
Fax: +34 945 600 590
info@eguren.com
www.eguren.com

Códice 2013 T
91

Colour: cherry, purple rim. Nose: ripe fruit, woody, roasted coffee. Palate: flavourful, spicy, powerful, good acidity.

DOMINIO DE PUNCTUM ORGANIC & BIODYNAMIC WINES

Ctra. N-301 km 162
16660 Las Pedroñeras (Cuenca)
☎: +34 912 959 998
Fax: +34 912 959 997
export@dominiodepunctum.com
www.dominiodepunctum.com

Dominio de Punctum 2014 RD
50% garnacha, 50% bobal

88

Colour: onion pink. Nose: elegant, red berry notes, floral, fragrant herbs. Palate: light-bodied, flavourful, good acidity, long, spicy.

Dominio de Punctum Sauvignon Blanc Semiseco 2014 B
100% sauvignon blanc

88

Colour: bright straw. Nose: white flowers, dried herbs, candied fruit, citrus fruit. Palate: flavourful, fruity, good acidity, round.

Dominio de Punctum Syrah 2014 T
100% syrah

87

Colour: cherry, purple rim. Nose: fresh fruit, red berry notes, floral, violets. Palate: flavourful, fruity, good acidity, easy to drink.

Dominio de Punctum Tempranillo Petit Verdot 2013 T Roble
70% tempranillo, 30% petit verdot

87

Colour: cherry, garnet rim. Nose: creamy oak, red berry notes, balanced. Palate: flavourful, spicy.

Dominio Punctum Tempranillo Petit Verdot 2014 T
70% tempranillo, 30% petit verdot

87

Colour: cherry, garnet rim. Nose: creamy oak, red berry notes, balanced. Palate: flavourful, spicy.

Finca Fabian 2014 RD
100% garnacha

86

Finca Fabian Chardonnay 2014 B
100% chardonnay

87

Colour: bright straw. Nose: white flowers, fresh fruit, fragrant herbs. Palate: flavourful, fruity, good acidity.

Finca Fabian Tempranillo 2014 T
100% tempranillo

86

EL PROGRESO SOC. COOPERATIVA DE CASTILLA LA MANCHA

Avda. de la Virgen, 89
13670 Villarubia de los Ojos
(Ciudad Real)
☎: +34 926 896 135
Fax: +34 926 896 135
administracion@bodegaselprogreso.com
www.bodegaselprogreso.com

Huertos de Palacio 2014 B
100% airén

83

Huertos de Palacio 2014 T
100% tempranillo
86

Huertos de Palacio 2014 T Roble
100% tempranillo
87
Colour: bright cherry. Nose: ripe fruit, sweet spices, creamy oak. Palate: flavourful, fruity, toasty.

Mi Chupito 2014 B
100% airén
78

ENCOMIENDA DE CERVERA

Arzobispo Cañizares, 1
13270 Almagro (Ciudad Real)
☎: +34 926 102 099
info@ecervera.com
www.encomiendadecervera.com

1758 Selección Petit Verdot 2009 T
petit verdot
88
Colour: bright cherry. Nose: sweet spices, creamy oak, fruit preserve. Palate: flavourful, fruity, toasty.

Maar de Cervera Cencibel 2013 TC
cencibel
86

Maar de Cervera Syrah 2011 T
syrah
87
Colour: bright cherry. Nose: ripe fruit, sweet spices, creamy oak. Palate: flavourful, fruity, toasty.

Señorío de Almagro 2010 T
syrah, tempranillo
86

Señorío de Almagro 2012 T
cabernet sauvignon, syrah, tempranillo, petit verdot
85

Vulcanus 2014 B
chardonnay, verdejo, sauvignon blanc
86

Vulcanus Alpha 2014 T
tempranillo
85

Vulcanus Multivarietal 2013 T
cabernet sauvignon, syrah, tempranillo
85

Vulcanus Selección 2013 T
cabernet sauvignon, syrah, tempranillo
84

FÉLIX SOLÍS

Autovía del Sur, Km. 199
13300 Valdepeñas (Ciudad Real)
☎: +34 926 322 400
Fax: +34 926 322 417
nfernandez@felixsolisavantis.com
www.felixsolisavantis.com

Consigna 2014 RD
tempranillo
83

Consigna Cabernet Sauvignon 2014 T
cabernet sauvignon
83

Consigna Chardonnay 2014 B
chardonnay
83

Consigna Merlot 2014 T
merlot
85

Consigna Sauvignon Blanc 2014 B
sauvignon blanc
84

Consigna Semidulce Airén 2014 B
airén
83

Consigna Shiraz 2014 T
syrah
84

Consigna Tempranillo 2014 T
tempranillo
85

Orquestra 2014 RD
tempranillo
84

Orquestra Cabernet Sauvignon 2014 T
cabernet sauvignon
85

Orquestra Chardonnay 2014 B
chardonnay
85

Orquestra Merlot 2014 T
merlot

86

Orquestra Tempranillo 2014 T
tempranillo

85

FINCA CASA ALARCÓN
Ctra. Montealegre del Castillo, km 4,5
02660 Caudete (Albacete)
☎: +34 965 828 266
Fax: +34 965 229 405
export@casalarcon.com
www.casalarcon.com

Blau 2011 T
100% monastrell

85

Casa Alarcón 2014 RD
100% syrah

85

Don Jaime 2011 T
tempranillo, cabernet sauvignon, petit verdot

86

Nea 2011 T
100% petit verdot

86

Tria 2011 T
100% syrah

86

FINCA CONSTANCIA
Camino del Bravo, s/n
45543 Otero (Toledo)
☎: +34 914 903 700
Fax: +34 916 612 124
lslara@gonzalezbyass.es
www.fincaconstancia.es

Altos de la Finca 2012 T
60% petit verdot, 40% syrah

92

Colour: cherry, garnet rim. Nose: balanced, ripe fruit, spicy, toasty, creamy oak. Palate: good structure, flavourful, round tannins, balanced.

Finca Constancia Graciano Parcela 12 2013 T
graciano

90

Colour: bright cherry. Nose: ripe fruit, sweet spices, creamy oak, expressive. Palate: flavourful, fruity, round tannins.

Finca Constancia Selección 2012 T
syrah, cabernet sauvignon, cabernet franc, petit verdot, graciano, tempranillo

89

Colour: bright cherry. Nose: ripe fruit, sweet spices, creamy oak, expressive. Palate: flavourful, fruity, toasty, round tannins.

Finca Constancia Selección 2013 T
syrah, cabernet sauvignon, petit verdot, tempranillo, graciano, cabernet franc

89

Colour: bright cherry. Nose: ripe fruit, sweet spices, creamy oak, expressive. Palate: flavourful, fruity, toasty.

Finca Constancia Tempranillo Parcela 23 2014 T
tempranillo

87

Colour: bright cherry. Nose: ripe fruit, sweet spices, creamy oak. Palate: flavourful, fruity, toasty.

Finca Constancia Verdejo Parcela 52 2014 B
verdejo

89

Colour: bright straw. Nose: white flowers, fresh fruit, fragrant herbs. Palate: flavourful, fruity, good acidity.

Fragantia Nº 6 2014 B
100% moscatel grano menudo

85

Fragantia Nº 9 Dulce Natural 2014 RD
100% syrah

85

FINCA EL REFUGIO
Ctra. Tomellosos-Socuéllamos, km. 14,6
13630 Socuéllamos (Ciudad Real)
☎: +34 629 512 478
info@fincaelrefugio.es
www.fincaelrefugio.es

Dominio del Prior Cabernet Sauvignon Merlot 2011 T
cabernet sauvignon, merlot

87 ♣

Colour: cherry, garnet rim. Nose: balsamic herbs, balanced, ripe fruit, spicy. Palate: full, flavourful, toasty.

Dominio del Prior Petit Verdot 2011 T
petit verdot

89 ♣

Colour: cherry, garnet rim. Nose: ripe fruit, spicy, creamy oak, complex. Palate: flavourful, toasty, round tannins, balanced.

Dominio del Prior Syrah 2011 T
syrah

88

Colour: bright cherry. Nose: ripe fruit, sweet spices, creamy oak, expressive. Palate: flavourful, fruity, round tannins.

Dominio del Prior Tempranillo 2011 T
tempranillo

86

Quorum de Finca El Refugio Private Collection 2011 T
tempranillo, petit verdot

90

Colour: cherry, garnet rim. Nose: ripe fruit, fragrant herbs, spicy, toasty, creamy oak, mineral. Palate: powerful, flavourful, balsamic, balanced.

FINCA LAS AGRUPADAS

Ctra. Ciudad Real-Murcia, km. 79,6
13300 Valdepeñas (Ciudad Real)
☎: +34 926 338 289
Fax: +34 926 338 534
finca@lasagrupadas.com
www.lasagrupadas.com

Finca Las Agrupadas 2013 T
80% tempranillo, 20% syrah

85

Finca Las Agrupadas Sauvignon Blanc 2014 B
85% sauvignon blanc, 15% airén

84

Semental 2012 T
60% garnacha, 40% monastrell

85

FINCA LORANQUE

Finca Loranque, s/n
45593 Bargas (Toledo)
☎: +34 669 476 849
fincaloranque@fincaloranque.com
www.fincaloranque.com

Finca Loranque Tempranillo Syrah 2009 T
syrah, tempranillo

84

Lacruz de Finca Loranque Cabernet Sauvignon 2011 T
cabernet sauvignon

89

Colour: cherry, garnet rim. Nose: creamy oak, red berry notes, balsamic herbs, fine reductive notes. Palate: flavourful, spicy, elegant.

Lacruz de Finca Loranque Syrah 2011 T
syrah

86

FINCA LOS ALIJARES

Ctra. 1927, km. 7
45180 Camarena (Toledo)
☎: +34 918 174 364
Fax: +34 918 174 364
gerencia@fincalosalijares.com
www.fincalosalijares.com

Finca Los Alijares 9 cotas 2013 T
merlot, syrah, tempranillo

86

Finca Los Alijares Graciano 2012 TC
100% graciano

87

Colour: cherry, garnet rim. Nose: fine reductive notes, ripe fruit, wild herbs. Palate: spicy, long, toasty.

Finca Los Alijares Graciano Autor 2013 T
100% graciano

88

Colour: bright cherry. Nose: ripe fruit, sweet spices, creamy oak. Palate: flavourful, fruity, toasty.

FINCA LOS MAJANARES

Casillas, 33
16611 Casas de Haro (Cuenca)
☎: +34 620 760 766
info@fincalosmajanares.com
www.bodegalosmajanares.es

Casa La Loma 2014 T Maceración Carbónica
syrah

87

Colour: cherry, purple rim. Nose: expressive, fresh fruit, red berry notes, floral. Palate: flavourful, fruity, good acidity, easy to drink.

Emperatriz Carretero 2014 RD
tempranillo

86

HAMMEKEN CELLARS

Calle de la Muela, 16
03730 Jávea (Alicante)
☎: +34 965 791 967
Fax: +34 966 461 471
cellars@hammekencellars.com
www.hammekencellars.com

Alma Gitana Old Vines Tempranillo 2013 T
tempranillo

86

Apanillo Tempranillo 2013 T
tempranillo

85

Capa Single Vineyard Tempranillo 2013 T
tempranillo

89

Colour: bright cherry. Nose: ripe fruit, sweet spices, creamy oak, expressive. Palate: flavourful, fruity, round tannins, balanced.

Capa Tempranillo 2014 T
tempranillo, syrah

85

Conde Pinel Oak Aged 2013 T Barrica
tempranillo

87

Colour: cherry, garnet rim. Nose: ripe fruit, fruit preserve, aged wood nuances, creamy oak. Palate: powerful, flavourful, correct.

Conde Pinel Tempranillo 2013 T
tempranillo

86

Conde Pinel Viura Verdejo 2014 B
viura, verdejo

84

El Paso del Lazo Tempranillo 2014 T
tempranillo

87

Colour: cherry, purple rim. Nose: floral, red berry notes, fragrant herbs. Palate: flavourful, fruity, good acidity.

El Paso del Lazo Viura Verdejo 2014 B
viura, verdejo

85

Flor del Montgó Tempranillo Organic 2013 T
tempranillo

87 ♣

Colour: deep cherry, purple rim. Nose: creamy oak, toasty, ripe fruit, balsamic herbs. Palate: balanced, spicy.

Montgo Tempranillo 2012 T
tempranillo

88

Colour: cherry, garnet rim. Nose: creamy oak, red berry notes, balanced. Palate: flavourful, spicy, balanced.

Picos del Montgó Tempranillo 2014 T
90% tempranillo, 10% syrah

86

LAZO BODEGAS Y VIÑEDOS

Finca La Zorrera, s/n
02436 Férez (Albacete)
☎: +34 622 766 900
info@lazotur.com
www.lazotur.com

Cabeza del Hierro 2011 T
50% monastrell, 10% syrah, 10% tempranillo, 10% petit verdot, 10% cabernet sauvignon, 10% bobal

87

Colour: cherry, garnet rim. Nose: fine reductive notes, wet leather, fruit preserve. Palate: spicy, long, toasty.

Fianza Selección Syrah 2011 T
syrah

88

Colour: cherry, garnet rim. Nose: fine reductive notes, aged wood nuances, ripe fruit. Palate: spicy, long, toasty.

Fianza Syrah 2011 T
syrah

85

Lacerta 2012 T
monastrell, bobal

88

Colour: bright cherry. Nose: ripe fruit, sweet spices, creamy oak, balsamic herbs. Palate: flavourful, fruity, toasty.

MANO A MANO

Ctra. CM-412, Km. 100
13248 Alhambra (Ciudad Real)
☎: +34 926 694 317
info@bodegamanoamano.com
www.bodegamanoamano.com

Manon 2013 T
100% tempranillo

88

Colour: cherry, garnet rim. Nose: creamy oak, red berry notes, balanced, sweet spices. Palate: flavourful, spicy, correct.

Venta la Ossa Syrah 2012 T
100% tempranillo

91

Colour: cherry, garnet rim. Nose: roasted coffee, smoky, spicy, ripe fruit. Palate: flavourful, smoky aftertaste, ripe fruit.

Venta la Ossa Tempranillo 2012 TC
100% tempranillo

93

Colour: bright cherry. Nose: ripe fruit, sweet spices, creamy oak, expressive. Palate: flavourful, fruity, round tannins.

MIGUEL A. AGUADO

Cantalejos, 2
45165 San Martín de Montalbán
(Toledo)
☎: +34 653 821 659
Fax: +34 925 417 206
info@bodegasmiguelaguado.com
www.bodegasmiguelaguado.com

Pasión de Castillo de Montalban 2011 ESP
macabeo

84

Pasión de Castillo de Montalban de Aguja RD
garnacha

83

San Martineño 2008 T
tempranillo

83

San Martineño 2008 TR
60% cabernet sauvignon, 40% garnacha

82

San Martineño 2014 B
macabeo

81

San Martineño 2014 RD
garnacha

84

San Martineño Garnacha 2013 T
garnacha

84

San Martineño Garnacha 2014 T
garnacha

84

San Martineño Tempranillo 2014 T
tempranillo

83

MONT REAGA

Ctra. N-420, Km. 333,200
16649 Monreal del Llano (Cuenca)
☎: +34 645 769 801
Fax: +34 967 182 518
mont-reaga@mont-reaga.com
www.mont-reaga.com

Blanco de Montreaga 2010 BFB
sauvignon blanc

90

Colour: bright yellow. Nose: ripe fruit, powerfull, toasty, aged wood nuances, pattiserie. Palate: flavourful, fruity, spicy, toasty, long, balanced.

Fata Morgana 2011 Tinto dulce
merlot

91

Colour: cherry, garnet rim. Nose: toasty, cocoa bean, creamy oak, fruit preserve, balanced. Palate: powerful, flavourful, spicy, long, balanced.

Isola de MontReaga 2014 B
80% verdejo, 20% moscatel

84

Isola de MontReaga 2014 T
tempranillo, syrah

85

Las Liras 2006 TGR
cabernet sauvignon

91

Colour: cherry, garnet rim. Nose: ripe fruit, wild herbs, earthy notes, spicy, balsamic herbs. Palate: balanced, flavourful, long, balsamic, fine tannins.

Mont Reaga La Espera 2008 T
70% cabernet sauvignon, 30% merlot

90

Colour: pale ruby, brick rim edge. Nose: elegant, spicy, fine reductive notes, tobacco. Palate: spicy, fine tannins, elegant, long.

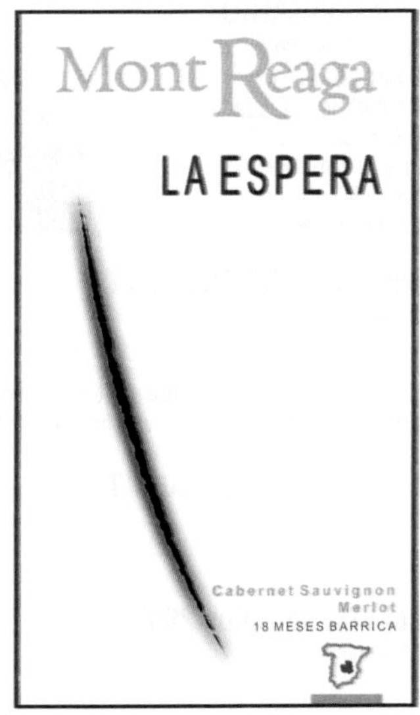

Montreaga Clásico 2005 T
syrah

88

Colour: deep cherry, brick rim edge. Nose: spicy, fine reductive notes, wet leather, aged wood nuances, fruit preserve. Palate: spicy, fine tannins, balanced.

MontReaga El Secreto 2004 T
cabernet sauvignon, syrah

90

Colour: pale ruby, brick rim edge. Nose: elegant, spicy, fine reductive notes, wild herbs, expressive. Palate: spicy, fine tannins, elegant, long.

MontReaga La Esencia 2008 T
syrah

91

Colour: very deep cherry, garnet rim. Nose: expressive, complex, mineral, balsamic herbs, ripe fruit. Palate: full, flavourful, round tannins, elegant.

Tempo 2011 T
cabernet sauvignon, syrah

88

Colour: very deep cherry, garnet rim. Nose: expressive, balsamic herbs, ripe fruit, complex. Palate: full, flavourful, round tannins.

MONTENOGARA, S.A.

Ctra. CM-4000 Km. 56,5
Pol Ind. Valle del Tajo
45685 Montearagón (Toledo)
☎: +34 925 865 434
Fax: +34 925 865 435
info@seleente.com
www.seleente.com

Seleente 2007 T
tempranillo, cabernet sauvignon, syrah, merlot, petit verdot

87

Colour: pale ruby, brick rim edge. Nose: spicy, fine reductive notes, wet leather, aged wood nuances, ripe fruit. Palate: spicy, fine tannins.

Seleente Colección Privada 2010 T
cabernet sauvignon, merlot, petit verdot

86

Seleente Vintage 2008 T
cabernet sauvignon, syrah, merlot, petit verdot

84

OSBORNE MALPICA DE TAJO

Ctra. Malpica - Pueblanueva, km. 6
45692 Malpica del Tajo (Toledo)
☎: +34 925 860 990
visitas.malpica@osborne.es
www.osborne.es

Solaz 2014 RD
85% syrah, 15% mencía

86

Solaz 2014 B
50% verdejo, 50% viura

82

Solaz Coupage 2013 T
50% syrah, 50% tempranillo

85

Solaz Tempranillo Cabernet Sauvignon 2013 T
50% tempranillo, 50% cabernet sauvignon

85

PAGO DE VALLEGARCÍA

Finca Vallegarcía, s/n
13194 Retuerta del Bullaque
(Ciudad Real)
☎: +34 925 421 407
Fax: +34 925 421 822
comercial@vallegarcia.com
www.vallegarcia.com

Hipperia 2011 T
50% cabernet sauvignon, 30% merlot, 10% cabernet franc, 10% petit verdot

92

Colour: deep cherry, purple rim. Nose: creamy oak, ripe fruit, balsamic herbs. Palate: balanced, spicy, long.

Petit Hipperia 2011 T
40% cabernet franc, 30% cabernet sauvignon, 20% merlot, 10% petit verdot

87

Colour: cherry, garnet rim. Nose: toasty, ripe fruit, balsamic herbs, grassy. Palate: balanced, spicy, long.

Vallegarcía Syrah 2011 T
100% syrah

92

Colour: very deep cherry, purple rim. Nose: characterful, ripe fruit, fruit preserve, powerfull. Palate: good structure, full, round tannins, fruity aftestaste.

Vallegarcía Viognier 2013 B
100% viognier

92

Colour: bright yellow. Nose: ripe fruit, powerfull, toasty, sweet spices. Palate: flavourful, fruity, spicy, toasty, long.

PAGO DEL VICARIO

Ctra. Ciudad Real - Porzuna,
CM-412 Km. 16
13196 Ciudad Real (Ciudad Real)
☎: +34 926 666 027
Fax: +34 926 666 029
info@pagodelvicario.com
www.pagodelvicario.com

Pago del Vicario 50-50 2010 T
tempranillo, cabernet sauvignon

88

Colour: cherry, garnet rim. Nose: ripe fruit, wild herbs, spicy, balsamic herbs. Palate: balanced, flavourful, balsamic.

Pago del Vicario 50-50 2011 T
tempranillo, cabernet sauvignon

86

Pago del Vicario Agios 2007 T
tempranillo, garnacha

86

Pago del Vicario Blanco de Tempranillo 2014 B
tempranillo

86

Pago del Vicario Corte Dulce 2007 B
chardonnay, sauvignon blanc

85

Pago del Vicario Merlot Dulce 2010 T
merlot

84

Pago del Vicario Monagós 2007 T
syrah, graciano

87

Colour: very deep cherry, garnet rim. Nose: balsamic herbs, ripe fruit, fine reductive notes. Palate: full, flavourful, round tannins.

Pago del Vicario Penta 2012 T
tempranillo, cabernet sauvignon, merlot, syrah, petit verdot

86

Pago del Vicario Petit Verdot 2014 RD
petit verdot

88

Colour: rose, purple rim. Nose: red berry notes, floral, fragrant herbs, expressive. Palate: powerful, fruity, fresh, balanced.

Pago del Vicario Talva 2014 B
chardonnay, sauvignon blanc

88

Colour: bright yellow. Nose: white flowers, dried herbs, mineral, ripe fruit, creamy oak. Palate: flavourful, fruity, round, spicy.

QUINTA DE AVES

Ctra. CR-5222, Km. 11,200
13350 Moral de Calatrava (Ciudad Real)
☎: +34 915 716 513
Fax: +34 915 716 511
yolanda.rosario@quintadeaves.es
www.quintadeaves.es

Alauda Moscatel Sauvignon 2013 B
50% moscatel, 50% sauvignon blanc

85

Búho Negro 2013 T
tempranillo, merlot, cabernet franc

85

Noctua Ensamblaje 2014 T
tempranillo, merlot, graciano, cabernet franc

86

Noctua Syrah 2014 T
100% syrah

87

Colour: cherry, purple rim. Nose: ripe fruit, violet drops, balsamic herbs. Palate: powerful, flavourful, good finish.

Otus 2014 T
tempranillo, merlot, graciano, cabernet franc

85

Quinto 2013 T
tempranillo

85

RODRÍGUEZ DE VERA

Ctra. de Pétrola, km. 3,2
02695 Chinchilla de Montearagón (Albacete)
☎: +34 696 168 873
info@rodriguezdevera.com
www.rodriguezdevera.com

Jumenta 2013 T Roble
merlot, garnacha tintorera

85

Rodríguez de Vera Chardonnay 2013 BFB
chardonnay

86

Sorrasca 2010 T

87

Colour: cherry, garnet rim. Nose: ripe fruit, wild herbs, earthy notes, spicy, balsamic herbs. Palate: flavourful, long, balsamic.

S.A.T. EL CASAR

CM 4006 pkm 50,900
45750 Huerta de Valdecarábanos (Toledo)
☎: +34 652 928 603
vegachicabodegas@gmail.com

Vegachica 2014 T Roble
100% syrah

85 ♣

SOC. COOP. AGRARIA SANTA QUITERIA, BODEGA TINTORALBA

Baltasar González Sáez, 34
02694 Higueruela (Albacete)
☎: +34 967 287 012
Fax: +34 967 287 031
direccion@tintoralba.com
www.tintoralba.com

Tintoralba Sauvgnon Blanc - Verdejo 2014 B
50% verdejo, 50% sauvignon blanc

86

TINEDO

Ctra. CM 3102, Km. 30
13630 Socuéllamos (Ciudad Real)
☎: +34 646 433 414
pvelasco@tinedo.com
www.tinedo.com

Cala N 1 2013 T
tempranillo, syrah, cabernet sauvignon

87 ♣

Colour: cherry, garnet rim. Nose: ripe fruit, toasty. Palate: powerful, toasty.

Cala N 2 2012 T
tempranillo, graciano, cabernet sauvignon

89

Colour: bright cherry. Nose: sweet spices, creamy oak, over-ripe fruit. Palate: flavourful, fruity, toasty, round tannins.

JA! 2014 T
tempranillo

88

Colour: cherry, purple rim. Nose: powerfull, ripe fruit, spicy. Palate: powerful, fruity, unctuous.

UNION CAMPESINA INIESTENSE

San Idefonso, 1
16235 Iniesta (Cuenca)
☎: +34 967 490 120
Fax: +34 967 490 777
aurora@cooperativauci.com
www.cooperativauci.com

Señorío de Iniesta 2013 RD
bobal

83

Señorío de Iniesta 2013 T
tempranillo, syrah

84

Señorío de Iniesta 2013 T
tempranillo, syrah, cabernet sauvignon

83

Señorío de Iniesta 2013 T
tempranillo, syrah, petit verdot

84

Señorío de Iniesta 2014 B
sauvignon blanc

84

Señorío de Iniesta 2014 RD
bobal

84

Señorío de Iniesta Tempranillo 2013 T
tempranillo

84

UVAS FELICES

Agullers, 7
08003 Barcelona (Barcelona)
☎: +34 902 327 777
www.vilaviniteca.es

Sospechoso 2012 T

88

Colour: cherry, purple rim. Nose: powerfull, ripe fruit, spicy. Palate: powerful, fruity, unctuous.

Sospechoso 2014 RD

88

Colour: onion pink. Nose: red berry notes, floral, fragrant herbs. Palate: light-bodied, flavourful, good acidity, spicy.

VINOS COLOMAN S.A.T.

Goya, 17
13620 Pedro Muñoz (Ciudad Real)
☎: +34 926 586 410
Fax: +34 926 586 656
coloman@satcoloman.com
www.satcoloman.com

Pedroteño 2014 T
tempranillo

85

Pedroteño Airén 2014 B
airén

83

VIÑA RUDA

Ctra de Alcázar, Km 0,5
13700 Tomelloso (Ciudad Real)
☎: +34 926 038 585
info@vinaruda.com
www.vinaruda.com

Ruda Casual Airen 2014 B
100% airén

84

Ruda Ensamblaje 2013 T
85% tempranillo, 15% syrah

86

Ruda Infusión 2014 T
100% tempranillo

85

VIÑEDOS BALMORAL

Mayor, 32 - 1º
02001 Albacete (Albacete)
☎: +34 967 508 382
Fax: +34 967 235 301
info@vinedosbalmoral.com
www.vinedosbalmoral.com

Edoné Cuvée de María 2011 ESP
chardonnay

84

Edoné Cuvée de María 2013 ESP
chardonnay

87

Colour: bright straw. Nose: fresh fruit, dried herbs, fine lees, floral. Palate: fresh, fruity, flavourful, good acidity.

Edoné Gran Cuvée Blanco 2010 ESP
chardonnay

85

Edoné Gran Cuvée Blanco 2012 ESP
chardonnay

88

Colour: bright yellow. Nose: fragrant herbs, ripe fruit, dry nuts, spicy. Palate: powerful, flavourful, ripe fruit.

Edoné Rosé Gran Cuvée 2012 ESP

86

Maravides 2012 T
27% syrah, 25% tempranillo, 25% merlot, 23% cabernet sauvignon

90

Colour: cherry, garnet rim. Nose: creamy oak, red berry notes, ripe fruit. Palate: flavourful, spicy, correct.

Maravides Chardonnay 2014 B
100% chardonnay

85

Maravides Mediterraneo 2013 T
100% tempranillo

87

Colour: deep cherry. Nose: ripe fruit, scrubland, toasty, smoky. Palate: spicy, long.

Maravides Syrah 2013 T
100% syrah

86

VIÑEDOS Y BODEGAS MUÑOZ

Ctra. Villarrubia, 11
45350 Noblejas (Toledo)
☎: +34 925 140 070
Fax: +34 925 141 334
info@bodegasmunoz.com
www.bodegasmunoz.com

Finca Muñoz Cepas Viejas 2010 T
tempranillo

91

Colour: cherry, garnet rim. Nose: ripe fruit, spicy, creamy oak, complex. Palate: flavourful, toasty, round tannins.

Finca Muñoz Reserva de Familia 2011 T Roble
tempranillo

89

Colour: deep cherry, garnet rim. Nose: balanced, cocoa bean, spicy, scrubland. Palate: good structure, ripe fruit, spicy, round tannins.

Legado Muñoz Chardonnay 2014 B
chardonnay

87

Colour: bright yellow. Nose: floral, ripe fruit, citrus fruit, wild herbs. Palate: powerful, flavourful, good finish.

Legado Muñoz Garnacha 2014 T
garnacha

85

Legado Muñoz Merlot 2012 T
merlot

87

Colour: cherry, garnet rim. Nose: ripe fruit, wild herbs, earthy notes, spicy, balsamic herbs. Palate: balanced, flavourful, long, balsamic.

Legado Muñoz Tempranillo 2014 T
tempranillo

86

VT CASTILLA Y LEÓN

ABADÍA RETUERTA

Ctra. N-122 Soria, km. 332,5
47340 Sardón de Duero (Valladolid)
☎: +34 983 680 314
Fax: +34 983 680 286
info@abadia-retuerta.es
www.abadia-retuerta.com

Abadía Retuerta Le Domaine 2014 B
60% sauvignon blanc, 40% verdejo

92

Colour: bright straw. Nose: fine lees, dried herbs, ripe fruit. Palate: flavourful, fruity, good acidity, round.

Abadía Retuerta Pago Garduña Syrah 2012 T
100% syrah

94

Colour: deep cherry, purple rim. Nose: expressive, red berry notes, ripe fruit, creamy oak, sweet spices, elegant. Palate: balanced, round tannins, spicy.

Abadía Retuerta Pago Negralada 2012 T
100% tempranillo

93

Colour: cherry, garnet rim. Nose: mineral, expressive, spicy. Palate: flavourful, ripe fruit, long, good acidity, balanced.

Abadía Retuerta Pago Valdebellón 2012 T
100% cabernet sauvignon

92

Colour: deep cherry, purple rim. Nose: creamy oak, toasty, ripe fruit, balsamic herbs. Palate: balanced, spicy, long.

Abadía Retuerta Petit Verdot PV 2012 T
100% petit verdot

93

Colour: cherry, garnet rim. Nose: smoky, spicy, ripe fruit. Palate: flavourful, smoky aftertaste, ripe fruit.

Abadía Retuerta Selección Especial 2011 T
75% tempranillo, 15% cabernet sauvignon, 10% syrah

90

Colour: bright cherry. Nose: ripe fruit, sweet spices, creamy oak, expressive. Palate: flavourful, fruity, toasty, round tannins.

AGRÍCOLA CASTELLANA - BODEGA CUATRO RAYAS

Ctra. Rodilana, s/n
47491 La Seca (Valladolid)
☎: +34 983 816 320
Fax: +34 983 816 562
info@cuatrorayas.org
www.cuatrorayas.org

Dolce Bianco Verdejo de Aguja 2014 Semidulce
verdejo

82

ALFREDO MAESTRO TEJERO

Avda. Escalona, 42
47300 Peñafiel (Valladolid)
☎: +34 687 786 742
Fax: +34 916 336 979
alfredo@alfredomaestro.com
www.alfredomaestro.com

46 Cepas 2014 T
100% merlot

88

Colour: cherry, purple rim. Nose: powerfull, spicy, overripe fruit. Palate: powerful, fruity, unctuous.

Amanda Rosado de Lágrima 2014 RD
100% garnacha tintorera
85

Castrillo de Duero 2013 T
100% tempranillo
90
Colour: cherry, garnet rim. Nose: ripe fruit, sweet spices, creamy oak. Palate: flavourful, fruity, round tannins.

El Marciano 2014 T
100% garnacha
92
Colour: deep cherry, purple rim. Nose: toasty, ripe fruit, balsamic herbs, wild herbs, mineral. Palate: balanced, spicy, long.

Lovamor 2014 B
100% albillo
88
Colour: bright yellow. Nose: dried herbs, faded flowers, slightly evolved, overripe fruit, dry nuts. Palate: ripe fruit, spirituous, fine bitter notes.

Viña Almate 2014 T
100% tempranillo
90
Colour: cherry, purple rim. Nose: expressive, fresh fruit, red berry notes. Palate: flavourful, fruity, good acidity, round tannins.

Viña Almate Finca La Guindalera 2013 T
tempranillo
91
Colour: cherry, garnet rim. Nose: ripe fruit, fruit liqueur notes, wild herbs, earthy notes, spicy. Palate: powerful, full, flavourful, balanced.

Viña Almate Finca La Olmera 2013 T
100% tempranillo
93
Colour: cherry, garnet rim. Nose: ripe fruit, spicy, creamy oak, mineral. Palate: flavourful, toasty, concentrated, round.

Viña Almate Garnacha 2013 T
100% garnacha
93
Colour: cherry, garnet rim. Nose: ripe fruit, wild herbs, earthy notes, spicy, balsamic herbs. Palate: balanced, flavourful, long, balsamic.

Viña Almate La Asperilla 2013 T
100% tempranillo
88
Colour: very deep cherry, garnet rim. Nose: complex, mineral, spicy, scrubland, balsamic herbs. Palate: full, flavourful, spicy, balsamic.

ALVAR DE DIOS HERNANDEZ
Zamora Nº8
47154 El Pego (Zamora)
eldelarecella@gmail.com

Vagüera 2013 B
90
Colour: bright yellow. Nose: faded flowers, dried herbs, spicy, expressive. Palate: fresh, balsamic, flavourful.

ÁLVAREZ DE TOLEDO VIÑEDOS Y GRUPO BODEGAS
Río Selmo, 8
24560 Toral de los Vados (León)
☎: +34 987 563 551
Fax: +34 987 563 532
admon@bodegasalvarezdetoledo.com
www.bodegasalvarezdetoledo.com

Marqués de Toro 2012 T
100% mencía
89
Colour: cherry, garnet rim. Nose: ripe fruit, wild herbs, earthy notes, spicy, balsamic herbs. Palate: flavourful, long, balsamic.

Señorío de la Antigua 2012 T
100% mencía
90
Colour: cherry, garnet rim. Nose: red berry notes, ripe fruit, fragrant herbs, spicy, toasty, creamy oak, mineral. Palate: powerful, flavourful, balsamic, balanced.

AVELINO VEGAS
Calvo Sotelo, 8
40460 Santiuste (Segovia)
☎: +34 921 596 002
Fax: +34 921 596 035
ana@avelinovegas.com
www.avelinovegas.com

Nicte 2014 RD
prieto picudo
89
Colour: rose, purple rim. Nose: floral, wild herbs, fruit expression, expressive. Palate: flavourful, complex, balanced.

Vegas 3 2013 T
tempranillo, cabernet sauvignon, merlot
86

AXIAL

Castillo de Capua Nº 10 nave 7
50197 Zaragoza (Zaragoza)
☎: +34 976 780 136
Fax: +34 976 303 035
info@axialvinos.com
www.axialvinos.com

La Granja 360 Verdejo Viura 2014 B

70% verdejo, 30% viura

82

BARCOLOBO

Basauri, 6 (Urb. La Florida)
28023 Aravaca (Madrid)
☎: +34 914 901 871
Fax: +34 916 620 430
info@barcolobo.com
www.barcolobo.com

Barcolobo 12 meses Barrica 2012 T

tempranillo, cabernet sauvignon, syrah

92

Colour: cherry, garnet rim. Nose: red berry notes, ripe fruit, spicy, creamy oak, complex. Palate: flavourful, toasty, round tannins.

Barcolobo La Rinconada 2014 T

tempranillo

88

Colour: cherry, purple rim. Nose: ripe fruit, roasted coffee. Palate: flavourful, spicy, powerful, unctuous.

Barcolobo Lacrimae Rerum 2014 RD

tempranillo

90

Colour: rose, purple rim. Nose: floral, wild herbs, fruit expression, expressive. Palate: flavourful, complex, balanced, elegant.

Barcolobo El Jaral 2012 T

tempranillo, cabernet sauvignon, syrah

93

Colour: cherry, garnet rim. Nose: red berry notes, spicy, creamy oak, expressive. Palate: flavourful, spicy, complex, balanced, elegant.

Barcolobo Verdejo 2013 B

verdejo

88

Colour: bright yellow. Nose: ripe fruit, powerfull, toasty, aged wood nuances, expressive. Palate: flavourful, fruity, spicy, toasty, long, balanced.

Barcolobo Verdejo 2014 B

verdejo

89

Colour: bright straw. Nose: white flowers, fresh fruit, fragrant herbs. Palate: flavourful, fruity, good acidity.

BELONDRADE

Quinta San Diego -
Camino del Puerto, s/n
47491 La Seca (Valladolid)
☎: +34 983 481 001
info@belondrade.com
www.belondrade.com

BELONDRADE Quinta Apolonia 2014 B

verdejo

91

Colour: bright straw. Nose: expressive, dried herbs, spicy, citrus fruit, fruit expression. Palate: flavourful, fruity, good acidity.

BELONDRADE Quinta Clarisa 2014 RD

tempranillo

88

Colour: rose, purple rim. Nose: red berry notes, floral. Palate: powerful, fruity.

BODEGA DE ALBERTO

Ctra. de Valdestillas, 2
47231 Serrada (Valladolid)
☎: +34 983 559 107
Fax: +34 983 559 084
info@dealberto.com
www.dealberto.com

CCCL 2009 T

tempranillo, cabernet sauvignon

88

Colour: cherry, garnet rim. Nose: ripe fruit, spicy, creamy oak, complex. Palate: flavourful, toasty, round tannins.

Finca Valdemoya 2011 T

tempranillo, cabernet sauvignon

87

Colour: cherry, garnet rim. Nose: ripe fruit, spicy, creamy oak. Palate: powerful, flavourful, toasty.

Finca Valdemoya 2014 RD

tempranillo

86

Finca Valdemoya Frizzante Tempranillo 2014 RD

100% tempranillo

87

Colour: brilliant rose. Nose: candied fruit, floral, rose petals, fragrant herbs, lactic notes. Palate: fresh, fruity, easy to drink, correct.

Finca Valdemoya Frizzante Verdejo 2014 B
100% verdejo

83

BODEGA DON JUAN DEL AGUILA

Real de Abajo, 100
05110 El Barraco (Ávila)
☎: +34 920 281 032
bodegadonjuandelaguila@gmail.com
www.donjuandelaguila.es

Gaznata 2013 T
garnacha

87

Colour: bright cherry, purple rim. Nose: red berry notes, earthy notes. Palate: fruity, easy to drink, correct, fruity aftestaste.

Gaznata 2014 RD
garnacha

83

Gaznata Concrete 2012 T
garnacha

87

Colour: cherry, garnet rim. Nose: ripe fruit, warm, characterful. Palate: ripe fruit, balsamic, round tannins.

Gaznata Finca Cipri 2013 T
garnacha

90

Colour: light cherry, garnet rim. Nose: ripe fruit, dried herbs. Palate: full, ripe fruit, long.

Gaznata Finca Mariano 2013 T
garnacha

88

Colour: cherry, garnet rim. Nose: ripe fruit, characterful, powerfull, warm. Palate: correct, ripe fruit, balsamic.

Gaznata Gredos 2010 T
garnacha

90

Colour: light cherry, garnet rim. Nose: expressive, balanced, ripe fruit, red berry notes, scrubland, mineral.

BODEGA EL ALBAR LURTON

Calle Nueva, 12
47491 La Seca (Valladolid)
☎: +34 983 034 030
Fax: +34 983 034 040
bodega@francoislurton.es
www.francoislurton.com

El Albar Lurton Barricas 2012 T

90

Colour: cherry, garnet rim. Nose: ripe fruit, wild herbs, earthy notes, spicy, balsamic herbs. Palate: balanced, flavourful, long, balsamic.

El Albar Lurton Excelencia 2009 T

92

Colour: deep cherry, garnet rim. Nose: aromatic coffee, spicy, ripe fruit. Palate: balanced, complex, good structure, full.

BODEGA EMINA RUEDA

Ctra. Medina del Campo - Olmedo, Km. 1,5
47290 Medina del Campo (Valladolid)
☎: +34 983 803 346
Fax: +34 902 430 189
emina@emina.es
www.eminarueda.es

Heredad de Emina Chardonnay 2014 B
chardonnay

86

Heredad Emina Gewürztraminer 2014 B
100% gewürztraminer

85

BODEGA FINCA CÁRDABA

Coto de Cárdaba, s/n
40314 Valtiendas (Segovia)
☎: +34 921 527 470
Fax: +34 921 527 470
info@fincacardaba.com
www.fincacardaba.com

Dominio Carmen 2014 T
tinta del país

85

Finca Cárdaba 2010 TC
tinta del país

88

Colour: cherry, purple rim. Nose: ripe fruit, roasted coffee. Palate: flavourful, spicy, powerful.

Finca Cárdaba Selección 2010 TR
tinta del país

91

Colour: cherry, garnet rim. Nose: ripe fruit, fragrant herbs, spicy, toasty, creamy oak, mineral. Palate: powerful, flavourful, balsamic, balanced.

BODEGA FINCA FUENTEGALANA

Ctra. M-501, Alcorcón - Plasencia, km. 65
05429 Navahondilla (Ávila)
☎: +34 646 843 231
info@fuentegalana.com
www.fuentegalana.com

Toros de Guisando Merlot 2010 T
merlot

89

Colour: very deep cherry, garnet rim. Nose: expressive, balsamic herbs, balanced. Palate: full, flavourful, round tannins.

Toros de Guisando Syrah 2009 T
syrah

85

Toros de Guisando Syrah 2010 T
100% syrah

88

Colour: very deep cherry, garnet rim. Nose: powerfull, ripe fruit, balanced, warm. Palate: fruity, flavourful, round tannins.

BODEGA MATARROMERA

Ctra. Renedo-Pesquera, Km. 30
47359 Valbuena de Duero (Valladolid)
☎: +34 983 683 315
Fax: +34 902 430 189
matarromera@matarromera.es
www.bodegamatarromera.es

Melior 3 2013 T
100% tempranillo

88

Colour: cherry, garnet rim. Nose: ripe fruit, spicy, creamy oak, balsamic herbs. Palate: flavourful, toasty, spicy.

BODEGA PAGO DE CALLEJO

Avda. del Cid, km. 16
09441 Sotillo de la Ribera (Burgos)
☎: +34 947 532 312
Fax: +34 947 532 304
callejo@bodegasfelixcallejo.com
www.bodegasfelixcallejo.com

El Lebrero 2013 B
albillo

89

Colour: bright yellow. Nose: expressive, dried herbs, ripe fruit, spicy, smoky. Palate: flavourful, fruity, good acidity, balanced.

Finca Valdelroble 2011 T Barrica
tempranillo, merlot, syrah

91 🍇

Colour: cherry, garnet rim. Nose: smoky, spicy, ripe fruit, scrubland. Palate: flavourful, ripe fruit.

BODEGAS ARRAYÁN

Gallarza, 9
28002 Madrid (Madrid)
☎: +34 916 633 131
Fax: +34 916 632 796
comercial@arrayan.es
www.arrayan.es

Garnacha de Arrayán 2013 T
garnacha

93

Colour: very deep cherry, garnet rim. Nose: expressive, complex, mineral, balsamic herbs, balanced. Palate: full, flavourful, round tannins.

BODEGAS CANOPY

Ctra. Toledo-Valmojado, km. 23
45180 Camarena (Toledo)
☎: +34 619 244 878
Fax: +34 925 283 680
achacon@bodegascanopy.com
www.bodegascanopy.com

KAOS 2010 TR
garnacha

90

Colour: bright cherry. Nose: ripe fruit, sweet spices, creamy oak, aromatic coffee. Palate: flavourful, toasty, round tannins.

BODEGAS CASTELO DE MEDINA

Ctra. CL-602, Km. 48
47465 Villaverde de Medina (Valladolid)
☎: +34 983 831 932
Fax: +34 983 831 857
info@castelodemedina.com
www.castelodemedina.com

Castelo Rosé 2014 RD
85% garnacha, 15% tempranillo

88

Colour: raspberry rose. Nose: floral, wild herbs, fruit expression, lactic notes. Palate: flavourful, balanced.

Syté 2010 T
60% syrah, 40% tempranillo

89

Colour: cherry, garnet rim. Nose: roasted coffee, smoky, spicy, ripe fruit. Palate: flavourful, smoky aftertaste, ripe fruit.

Vega Busiel 2011 T
60% syrah, 40% tempranillo

86

Viña Castelo 2014 RD
85% garnacha, 15% tempranillo

84

BODEGAS FRUTOS VILLAR
Ctra. Burgos-Portugal Km. 113,7
47270 Cigales (Valladolid)
☎: +34 983 586 868
Fax: +34 983 580 180
bodegasfrutosvillar@bodegasfrutosvillar.com
www.bodegasfrutosvillar.com

Don Frutos Verdejo 2014 B
100% verdejo

84

Tasco 2014 T
100% tempranillo

85

BODEGAS GARCÍA NIÑO
Avda. Julio, s/n
09410 Arandilla (Burgos)
☎: +34 636 970 508
Fax: +34 916 126 072
fernando@bodegasgarcianino.es
www.altorredondo.com

Altorredondo 2013 T
100% tempranillo

87

Colour: cherry, garnet rim. Nose: spicy, ripe fruit, creamy oak. Palate: flavourful, ripe fruit, correct.

Pago de Costalao 2011 TR
100% tempranillo

87

Colour: cherry, garnet rim. Nose: red berry notes, ripe fruit, spicy, creamy oak. Palate: flavourful, toasty.

BODEGAS GODELIA
Antigua Ctra. N-VI, NVI, Km. 403,5
24547 Pieros-Cacabelos (León)
☎: +34 987 546 279
Fax: +34 987 548 026
www.godelia.es

Libamus Tinto Dulce 2012 TC
mencía

87

Colour: cherry, garnet rim. Nose: fruit preserve, spicy, warm, fruit liqueur notes. Palate: powerful, flavourful, sweet, rich.

BODEGAS GRUPO YLLERA
Autovía A-6, Km. 173,5
47490 Rueda (Valladolid)
☎: +34 983 868 097
Fax: +34 983 868 177
grupoyllera@grupoyllera.com
www.grupoyllera.com

Cuvi 2013 T Roble
tempranillo

85

Yllera 12 meses 2012 TC
tempranillo

87

Colour: cherry, garnet rim. Nose: creamy oak, toasty, ripe fruit. Palate: flavourful, spicy.

Yllera Dominus 2011 TGR
tempranillo

92

Colour: cherry, garnet rim. Nose: ripe fruit, wild herbs, spicy, balsamic herbs. Palate: flavourful, long, balsamic.

Yllera Privée 2013 ESP
verdejo

83

Yllera Vendimia Seleccionada 2010 TR
tempranillo

90

Colour: ruby red. Nose: elegant, spicy, fine reductive notes, ripe fruit. Palate: spicy, long, flavourful.

Yllera Vendimia Seleccionada 2011 T
tempranillo

90

Colour: cherry, garnet rim. Nose: ripe fruit, spicy, creamy oak. Palate: flavourful, toasty, correct.

BODEGAS LEDA
Mayor, 48
47320 Tudela de Duero (Valladolid)
☎: +34 983 520 682
info@bodegasleda.com
www.bodegasleda.com

Leda Viñas Viejas 2012 T
100% tempranillo

91

Colour: cherry, garnet rim. Nose: ripe fruit, wild herbs, earthy notes, spicy, balsamic herbs. Palate: flavourful, long, balsamic, balanced.

Más de Leda 2012 T
100% tempranillo

89

Colour: very deep cherry. Nose: ripe fruit, sweet spices, creamy oak. Palate: flavourful, fruity, toasty.

BODEGAS MAURO
Ctra. Villaester, km. 1
47320 Tudela de Duero (Valladolid)
☎: +34 983 521 972
Fax: +34 983 521 973
comunicacion@bodegasmauro.com
www.bodegasmauro.com

Mauro 2013 T
90% tempranillo, 10% syrah

91

Colour: deep cherry. Nose: creamy oak, toasty, ripe fruit, balsamic herbs. Palate: balanced, spicy, long.

Mauro Vendimia Seleccionada 2011 T
100% tempranillo

92

Colour: cherry, garnet rim. Nose: red berry notes, ripe fruit, fragrant herbs, spicy, toasty, creamy oak, mineral. Palate: powerful, flavourful, balsamic, balanced.

PODIUM

Terreus 2012 T
100% tempranillo

96

Colour: cherry, garnet rim. Nose: balanced, complex, ripe fruit, spicy, balsamic herbs, earthy notes. Palate: good structure, flavourful, slightly dry, soft tannins, balanced.

BODEGAS MOCÉN
Arribas, 7-9
47490 Rueda (Valladolid)
☎: +34 983 868 533
Fax: +34 983 868 514
info@bodegasmocen.com
www.bodegasantano.com

Bravía 2014 T Roble
tempranillo

87

Colour: deep cherry, purple rim. Nose: creamy oak, toasty, ripe fruit, balsamic herbs. Palate: balanced, spicy, long.

Cobranza 2012 T
tempranillo

88

Colour: cherry, garnet rim. Nose: smoky, spicy, ripe fruit. Palate: flavourful, smoky aftertaste, ripe fruit.

Cobranza Vendimia Seleccionada 2012 T Roble
tempranillo

89

Colour: cherry, garnet rim. Nose: red berry notes, ripe fruit, spicy, creamy oak, complex. Palate: flavourful, toasty, round tannins.

BODEGAS PEÑASCAL
Ctra. Valladolid a Segovia
(N-601) km. 7,3
47140 Laguna de Duero (Valladolid)
☎: +34 983 546 080
Fax: +34 983 546 081
rrpp@vina-mayor.es
www.penascal.es

Cuesta del Aire Sauvignon Blanc Verdejo 2014 B
85% sauvignon blanc, 15% verdejo

84

Cuesta del Aire Tempranillo Shiraz 2014 RD
85% tempranillo, 15% syrah

86

Peñascal frizzante 5.5 B
84

Peñascal frizzante 5.5 2014 RD
82

Ponte Vecchio Moscato Frizzante B
84

Ponte Vecchio Moscato S/C RD
85

BODEGAS SANTA RUFINA
Pago Fuente La Teja. Pol. Ind. 3 - Parcela 102
47290 Cubillas de Santa Marta
(Valladolid)
☎: +34 983 585 202
Fax: +34 983 585 202
info@bodegassantarufina.com
www.bodegassantarufina.com

Bosque Real Cabernet 2012 T
100% cabernet sauvignon

82

Ultimatum Merlot 2012 T
100% merlot

80

BODEGAS TRITÓN

Pol.1 Parc. 146/148 Paraje Cantagrillos
49708 Villanueva de Campeán
(Zamora)
☎: +34 968 435 022
Fax: +34 968 716 051
info@orowines.com
www.orowines.com

Entresuelos 2012 T
100% tempranillo

89

Colour: cherry, purple rim. Nose: ripe fruit, cocoa bean, toasty. Palate: flavourful, spicy, powerful.

Entresuelos Tempranillo 2013 T
100% tempranillo

90

Colour: deep cherry, purple rim. Nose: creamy oak, toasty, ripe fruit, balsamic herbs. Palate: balanced, spicy, long.

Rejón 2011 T
100% tempranillo

93

Colour: cherry, garnet rim. Nose: ripe fruit, spicy, creamy oak, toasty. Palate: flavourful, toasty, concentrated, balanced.

Rejón 2012 T
100% tempranillo

94

Colour: cherry, garnet rim. Nose: ripe fruit, wild herbs, earthy notes, spicy, balsamic herbs, roasted coffee. Palate: flavourful, long, balsamic, balanced.

Tridente Mencía 2014 T
100% mencía

93

Colour: bright cherry. Nose: ripe fruit, sweet spices, creamy oak. Palate: flavourful, fruity, round tannins.

Tridente Prieto Picudo 2013 T
100% prieto picudo

91

Colour: cherry, purple rim. Nose: ripe fruit, woody, roasted coffee, varietal. Palate: flavourful, spicy, powerful, toasty.

Tridente Tempranillo 2012 T
100% tempranillo

92

Colour: cherry, garnet rim. Nose: ripe fruit, spicy, creamy oak, complex. Palate: flavourful, toasty, round tannins.

Tridente Tempranillo 2013 T
100% tempranillo

93

Colour: cherry, garnet rim. Nose: mineral, spicy, ripe fruit, toasty, creamy oak. Palate: flavourful, ripe fruit, long, good acidity, unctuous.

BODEGAS VEGA DE TERA

Bajura de los Carreteros, s/n
49624 Sitrama de Tera (Zamora)
☎: +34 606 411 428
contact@bodegasvegadetera.com
www.bodegasvegadetera.com

Vega de Tera 2013 T Roble
100% tempranillo

87

Colour: deep cherry, purple rim. Nose: creamy oak, ripe fruit, balsamic herbs. Palate: balanced, spicy, long.

Vega de Tera 2014 B
verdejo

88

Colour: straw. Nose: medium intensity, ripe fruit, wild herbs. Palate: correct, easy to drink, good finish.

Vega de Tera 2014 RD

86

Vega de Tera 2014 T
tempranillo

85

Vega de Tera 2014 T Roble
100% tempranillo

86

Vega de Tera Vendimia Seleccionada 12 meses 2012 T
tempranillo, prieto picudo

87

Colour: bright cherry, garnet rim. Nose: balanced, sweet spices, ripe fruit, dried herbs. Palate: flavourful, round tannins.

Vega de Tera Vendimia Seleccionada 24 meses 2011 T
tempranillo

88

Colour: cherry, garnet rim. Nose: creamy oak, balanced, ripe fruit. Palate: flavourful, spicy, correct, round tannins.

BODEGAS VETONÉ

Calle Arévalo, 5
05229 (Madrid)
☎: +34 619 654 812
vetone@vetone.es
www.vetone.es

Vetoné 2011 TC

80% tempranillo, 20% syrah, pinot noir

87

Colour: very deep cherry, garnet rim. Nose: powerfull, ripe fruit, fruit preserve, dried herbs, spicy, dark chocolate. Palate: fruity, round tannins.

BODEGAS VINOS DE LEÓN

Finca Monteleon
Valdevimbre (León)
☎: +34 987 209 712
Fax: +34 987 209 800
info@bodegasvinosdeleon.es
www.bodegasvinosdeleon.es

Palacio de León Cuvée 2011 T

100% tempranillo

88

Colour: bright cherry. Nose: ripe fruit, sweet spices, creamy oak, expressive. Palate: flavourful, fruity, toasty, round tannins.

Palacio de León Tempranillo 2013 T

100% tempranillo

84

BODEGAS VIZAR

Avda. Ramón Pradera, 14
47009 Valladolid (Valladolid)
☎: +34 983 682 690
Fax: +34 983 682 125
info@bodegasvizar.es
www.bodegasvizar.es

Vizar 12 meses 2010 T

85% tempranillo, 15% cabernet sauvignon

89

Colour: cherry, garnet rim. Nose: red berry notes, ripe fruit, spicy, creamy oak, complex. Palate: flavourful, toasty, round tannins.

Vizar Syrah 2010 T

100% syrah

89

Colour: deep cherry, garnet rim. Nose: creamy oak, sweet spices, characterful. Palate: balanced, powerful, long, spicy.

VIZAR

AÑADA: 2010
PARCELA: El Redondal
UVA: 100% Syrah
CRIANZA: 14 meses Roble Francés
ALCOHOL.: 13,5 %
PRODUCCIÓN: 3.000 botellas

BODEGAS VIZCARRA

Finca Chirri, s/n
09317 Mambrilla de Castrejón (Burgos)
☎: +34 947 540 340
Fax: +34 947 540 340
bodegas@vizcarra.es
www.vizcarra.es

Vizcarra Garnacha Selección Monovarietal 2013 T

100% garnacha

94

Colour: very deep cherry, purple rim. Nose: scrubland, spicy, ripe fruit. Palate: balanced, spicy, long, balsamic, fine tannins.

BODEGAS Y VIÑEDOS LA MEJORADA

Monasterio de La Mejorada
47410 Olmedo (Valladolid)
☎: +34 606 707 041
Fax: +34 983 483 071
contacto@lamejorada.es
www.lamejorada.es

La Mejorada Las Cercas 2011 T Roble

60% tempranillo, 40% syrah

92

Colour: bright cherry, garnet rim. Nose: complex, ripe fruit, balanced, spicy. Palate: good structure, flavourful, round tannins.

La Mejorada Las Norias 2009 T

tempranillo

93

Colour: cherry, garnet rim. Nose: ripe fruit, spicy, fine reductive notes. Palate: good structure, flavourful, round tannins, balanced.

La Mejorada Las Norias 2010 T Roble
tempranillo

93

Colour: cherry, garnet rim. Nose: smoky, spicy, ripe fruit. Palate: flavourful, smoky aftertaste, ripe fruit.

La Mejorada Tiento 2009 T

91

Colour: cherry, garnet rim. Nose: smoky, spicy, ripe fruit. Palate: flavourful, smoky aftertaste, ripe fruit.

La Mejorada Tiento 2011 T

93

Colour: bright cherry. Nose: ripe fruit, sweet spices, creamy oak. Palate: flavourful, fruity, toasty, round tannins.

Villalar Oro 2010 T Roble
100% tempranillo

89

Colour: cherry, garnet rim. Nose: creamy oak, red berry notes, fresh fruit, balanced. Palate: flavourful, spicy, round tannins.

Villalar Oro 2011 T Roble
tempranillo

90

Colour: bright cherry. Nose: ripe fruit, sweet spices, dark chocolate. Palate: toasty, round tannins, sweetness.

CLUNIA

Camino Torre, 1
09410 Coruña del Conde (Burgos)
☎: +34 607 185 951
Fax: +34 948 818 574
ppavez@principedeviana.com

Clunia Syrah 2012 T
syrah

91

Colour: bright cherry, garnet rim. Nose: ripe fruit, red berry notes, toasty, spicy. Palate: balanced, good structure, fruity.

Clunia Tempranillo 2011 T
100% tempranillo

93

Colour: cherry, garnet rim. Nose: red berry notes, ripe fruit, fragrant herbs, spicy, creamy oak, mineral. Palate: powerful, flavourful, balsamic, balanced.

Clunia Tempranillo 2012 T
100% tempranillo

91

Colour: bright cherry, garnet rim. Nose: ripe fruit, smoky, toasty. Palate: flavourful, spicy, powerful, round tannins.

🏆 PODIUM

Finca El Rincón de Clunia 2011 T
100% tempranillo

95

Colour: cherry, garnet rim. Nose: mineral, expressive, spicy. Palate: flavourful, ripe fruit, long, good acidity, balanced.

Finca El Rincón de Clunia 2012 T
100% tempranillo

94

Colour: cherry, garnet rim. Nose: complex, ripe fruit, spicy, mineral, creamy oak. Palate: good structure, flavourful, round tannins, balanced.

COMANDO G VITICULTORES

Avda. Constitución, 23
28640 Cadalso de los Vidrios (Madrid)
☎: +34 918 640 602
info@comandog.es
www.comandog.es

Rumbo al Norte 2013 T
100% garnacha

93

Colour: very deep cherry, garnet rim. Nose: expressive, complex, mineral, balsamic herbs. Palate: flavourful, round tannins, fine bitter notes, good acidity.

Tumba del Rey Moro 2013 T
100% garnacha

94

Colour: bright cherry. Nose: red berry notes, floral, grassy, balsamic herbs. Palate: flavourful, fine bitter notes, good acidity.

COMPAÑÍA DE VINOS MIGUEL MARTÍN

Ctra. Burgos - Portugal, Km. 101
47290 Cubillas de Santa María (Valladolid)
☎: +34 983 250 319
Fax: +34 983 250 929
comercial@ciadevinos.com
www.ciadevinos.com

Martín Verástegui 2008 BFB
100% verdejo

82

Martín Verástegui 2014 B
100% verdejo

84

Martín Verástegui 2014 RD
100% tempranillo

86

Martín Verástegui Vendimia Seleccionada 2006 TR
80% tempranillo, 20% garnacha

91

Colour: pale ruby, brick rim edge. Nose: elegant, spicy, fine reductive notes, tobacco. Palate: spicy, fine tannins, elegant, long.

Retola 12 Meses 2010 T

88

Colour: cherry, garnet rim. Nose: ripe fruit, spicy, creamy oak, complex. Palate: flavourful, toasty, long.

Retola 2014 RD
tempranillo, garnacha

84

Retola 6 meses 2013 T Barrica
100% tempranillo

87

Colour: cherry, purple rim. Nose: ripe fruit, roasted coffee, powerfull. Palate: flavourful, spicy.

Retola Verdejo 2014 B
100% verdejo

85

COMPAÑÍA DE VINOS TELMO RODRÍGUEZ

El Monte
01308 Lanciego (Álava)
☎: +34 945 628 315
Fax: +34 945 628 314
contact@telmorodriguez.com
www.telmorodriguez.com

PODIUM

Pegaso "Barrancos de Pizarra" 2012 T
garnacha

95

Colour: cherry, garnet rim. Nose: ripe fruit, wild herbs, earthy notes, spicy, balsamic herbs. Palate: balanced, flavourful, long, balsamic, elegant.

Pegaso "Granito" 2012 T
garnacha

93

Colour: ruby red. Nose: fruit liqueur notes, fragrant herbs, spicy, creamy oak, balsamic herbs, mineral. Palate: elegant, spicy, long, balanced.

DANILANDI

Constitución, 23
28640 Cadalso de los Vidrios (Madrid)
☎: +34 918 640 602
info@danilandi.com
www.danilandi.com

PODIUM

El Reventón 2013 T
garnacha

96

Colour: very deep cherry, garnet rim. Nose: complex, mineral, balsamic herbs, balanced, red berry notes. Palate: full, flavourful, round tannins.

Las Iruelas 2013 T

93

Colour: deep cherry. Nose: red berry notes, fruit expression, dried herbs, balsamic herbs. Palate: flavourful, good acidity, elegant.

DEHESA DE CADOZOS

José Bardasano Baos, 9 4º
28016 Madrid (Madrid)
☎: +34 915 280 134
Fax: +34 915 280 238
nmaranon@cadozos.com
www.cadozos.com

Cadozos 2011 T
tempranillo, pinot noir

91

Colour: cherry, garnet rim. Nose: ripe fruit, wild herbs, earthy notes, spicy, balsamic herbs. Palate: balanced, flavourful, long, balsamic.

Sayago 830 2011 TC
tempranillo, pinot noir

90

Colour: cherry, garnet rim. Nose: ripe fruit, fragrant herbs, spicy, toasty, creamy oak. Palate: powerful, flavourful, balsamic.

DOMINIO DOSTARES

24318 San Román de Bembibre (León)
☎: +34 987 514 550
Fax: +34 987 514 570
info@dominiodetares.com
www.dominiodostares.com

Cumal 2011 T
100% prieto picudo

93

Colour: deep cherry, purple rim. Nose: creamy oak, toasty, ripe fruit, balsamic herbs. Palate: balanced, spicy, long.

Estay 2011 T
100% prieto picudo

88

Colour: cherry, purple rim. Nose: ripe fruit, woody. Palate: flavourful, spicy, powerful.

Estay 2012 T
100% prieto picudo

87

Colour: bright cherry. Nose: sweet spices, creamy oak, fruit preserve. Palate: flavourful, fruity, toasty.

Tombú 2014 RD
100% prieto picudo

86

ERMITA DEL CONDE

Camino de la Torre, 1
09410 Coruña del Conde (Burgos)
☎: +34 690 738 388
Fax: +34 947 613 954
info@ermitadelconde.com
www.ermitadelconde.com

Ermita del Conde 2011 T
100% tempranillo

92

Colour: cherry, garnet rim. Nose: expressive, spicy, ripe fruit, complex. Palate: flavourful, ripe fruit, long, good acidity, balanced.

Ermita del Conde Albillo Centenario 2013 B
100% albillo

92

Colour: bright straw. Nose: fresh fruit, fragrant herbs, expressive, dried flowers. Palate: flavourful, fruity, good acidity, balanced, spicy.

Pago del Conde 2011 T
100% tempranillo

92

Colour: cherry, purple rim. Nose: ripe fruit, woody, roasted coffee. Palate: flavourful, spicy, powerful.

FINCA LAS CARABALLAS

Camino Velascálvaro, s/n
40400 Medina del Campo (Valladolid)
☎: +34 650 986 185
info@lascaraballas.com
www.lascaraballas.com

Finca Las Caraballas 2014 B
100% verdejo

90 ♣

Colour: bright yellow. Nose: expressive, dried herbs, ripe fruit, spicy. Palate: flavourful, fruity, good acidity, balanced.

FINCA TORREMILANOS

Finca Torremilanos
09400 Aranda de Duero (Burgos)
☎: +34 947 512 852
Fax: +34 947 508 044
reservas@torremilanos.com
www.torremilanos.com

Peñalba-López 2013 B

88 ♣

Colour: bright yellow. Nose: dried herbs, ripe fruit, spicy. Palate: flavourful, fruity, good acidity, balanced.

FORTUNA WINES

36207 Vigo (Pontevedra)
☎: +34 691 561 471
info@fortunawines.es
www.fortunawines.es

Alaia (4 Ever Alaia) 2012 T Roble
prieto picudo, tempranillo, mencía

86

GARNACHA ALTO ALBERCHE

Camino del Pimpollar, pol. 5 par. 17
05100 Navaluenga (Ávila)
☎: +34 616 416 542
sietenavas@hotmail.com
www.garnachaaltoalberche.com

7 Navas 2012 T Roble
garnacha

90

Colour: cherry, garnet rim. Nose: ripe fruit, scrubland, dried herbs, spicy. Palate: balanced, spicy.

7 Navas 2014 T
garnacha

89

Colour: cherry, purple rim. Nose: red berry notes, floral, balsamic herbs. Palate: powerful, fresh, fruity, easy to drink.

7 Navas Finca Catalino 2012 T
garnacha

92

Colour: very deep cherry, garnet rim. Nose: expressive, complex, mineral, balsamic herbs, balanced. Palate: full, flavourful, round tannins.

7 Navas Finca Faustina 2010 T
garnacha

92

Colour: cherry, garnet rim. Nose: mineral, expressive, spicy, dried herbs. Palate: flavourful, ripe fruit, long, good acidity, balanced, elegant.

7 Navas Selección 2011 T

91

Colour: cherry, garnet rim. Nose: ripe fruit, wild herbs, earthy notes, spicy, balsamic herbs. Palate: balanced, flavourful, long, balsamic.

GORDONZELLO

Alto de Santa Marina, s/n
24294 Gordoncillo (León)
☎: +34 987 758 030
Fax: +34 987 757 201
info@gordonzello.com
www.gordonzello.com

Antojo Dulce 2014 RD

prieto picudo

79

Dolca Semidulce 2014 B

verdejo

83

HACIENDA ZORITA MARQUÉS DE LA CONCORDIA FAMILY OF WINES

Crta Zamora-Fermoselle, Km 56
37115 Fermoselle (Zamora)
☎: +34 980 613 163
abasilio@unitedwineries.com
www.the-haciendas.com

Hacienda Zorita Magister 2011 T

60% tempranillo, 30% syrah, 10% merlot

92

Colour: cherry, garnet rim. Nose: red berry notes, ripe fruit, spicy, creamy oak, complex. Palate: flavourful, toasty, round tannins, balanced.

Hacienda Zorita Natural Reserve 2011 T

100% syrah

90

Colour: cherry, garnet rim. Nose: creamy oak, red berry notes, balanced. Palate: flavourful, spicy, elegant.

HEREDAD DE URUEÑA

Ctra. Toro a Medina de Rioseco, km 21,300
47862 Urueña (Valladolid)
☎: +34 915 610 894
Fax: +34 915 634 131
direccion@heredaduruena.com
www.heredaduruena.com

Forum Etiqueta Negra 2012 T

tinta del país, tinta de Toro

92

Colour: cherry, garnet rim. Nose: ripe fruit, spicy, toasty, creamy oak. Palate: powerful, flavourful, balsamic, balanced.

Santo Merlot 2012 T

85% merlot, 15% cabernet sauvignon

90

Colour: very deep cherry, garnet rim. Nose: balsamic herbs, ripe fruit, wild herbs, creamy oak. Palate: full, flavourful, balanced.

Santo Syrah 2012 T

100% syrah

90

Colour: bright cherry, purple rim. Nose: ripe fruit, sweet spices, creamy oak. Palate: flavourful, fruity, concentrated, balanced.

Santo Tempranillo 2012 T

100% tinta del país

89

Colour: deep cherry, purple rim. Nose: creamy oak, toasty, ripe fruit, balsamic herbs. Palate: balanced, spicy, long.

LAR DE MAÍA

47240 Valladolid (Valladolid)
☎: +34 650 986 098
info@lardemaia.com
www.lardemaia.com

Lar de Maía 2010 T

tempranillo, garnacha

86 ♣

MALDIVINAS

Polígono Industrial
Las Ventillas Nave 73A
05420 Sotillo de la Adrada (Ávila)
☎: +34 615 163 719
carlos@maldivinas.es
www.maldivinas.es

Combate 2014 B

albillo

92

Colour: bright straw. Nose: white flowers, fresh fruit, fragrant herbs, dry stone, balanced. Palate: flavourful, fruity, good acidity, balanced.

Doble Punta 2013 T

garnacha

89

Colour: light cherry. Nose: spicy, wild herbs, earthy notes, overripe fruit, fruit liqueur notes. Palate: powerful, flavourful, ripe fruit.

La Movida 2013 T

garnacha

93

Colour: cherry, garnet rim. Nose: fruit liqueur notes, fragrant herbs, spicy, floral, mineral. Palate: powerful, flavourful, fresh, balanced.

La Movida Granito 2013 T
garnacha

94

Colour: cherry, garnet rim. Nose: fragrant herbs, spicy, toasty, creamy oak, dry stone, red berry notes, fruit liqueur notes. Palate: powerful, flavourful, balsamic, balanced, elegant.

La Movida Laderas 2013 T
garnacha

92

Colour: light cherry. Nose: fruit expression, fruit liqueur notes, fragrant herbs, spicy, creamy oak. Palate: balanced, spicy, balsamic.

OSSIAN VIDES Y VINOS

Cordel de las Merinas s/n
40447 Nieva (Segovia)
☎: +34 983 878 020
ossian@ossian.es
www.ossian.es

Ossian 2013 BFB
100% verdejo

93

Colour: bright straw. Nose: white flowers, fine lees, dried herbs, ripe fruit, candied fruit, citrus fruit. Palate: flavourful, fruity, good acidity, elegant.

Ossian Capitel 2013 BFB
100% verdejo

92

Colour: bright yellow. Nose: ripe fruit, powerfull, toasty, aged wood nuances, pattiserie. Palate: flavourful, fruity, spicy, toasty, long.

Ossian Quintaluna 2014 B
100% verdejo

90

Colour: bright straw. Nose: white flowers, fresh fruit, fragrant herbs, expressive. Palate: flavourful, fruity, good acidity, balanced.

Ossian Verdling Dulce 2012 B
100% verdejo

93

Colour: bright straw. Nose: white flowers, candied fruit, balsamic herbs. Palate: rich, fruity, correct, elegant.

Ossian Verdling Trocken 2013 B
100% verdejo

91

Colour: bright straw. Nose: citrus fruit, fresh fruit, fragrant herbs, floral, balanced. Palate: fresh, fruity, balsamic.

PRIETO PARIENTE

San Judas, 6
47491 La Seca (Valladolid)
☎: +34 983 816 484
Fax: +34 983 816 600
info@prietopariente.com
www.prietopariente.com

El Origen de Prieto Pariente 2013 T
70% tempranillo, 20% garnacha, 10% cabernet sauvignon

89

Colour: bright cherry. Nose: ripe fruit, sweet spices, creamy oak, expressive. Palate: flavourful, fruity, toasty.

Prieto Pariente 2013 T
55% tempranillo, 45% garnacha

90

Colour: deep cherry, purple rim. Nose: creamy oak, toasty, ripe fruit, balsamic herbs. Palate: balanced, spicy, long, elegant.

Viognier de Prieto Pariente 2014 B
100% viognier

91

Colour: bright straw. Nose: white flowers, dried herbs, ripe fruit, citrus fruit, expressive. Palate: flavourful, fruity, good acidity, fine bitter notes, elegant.

QUINTA SARDONIA

Casa, s/n - Granja Sardón
47340 Sardón de Duero (Valladolid)
☎: +34 986 621 001
info@quintasardonia.com
www.terrasgauda.com

Quinta Sardonia QS 2011 T
tinto fino, cabernet sauvignon, petit verdot, syrah, malbec, cabernet franc

92

Colour: cherry, garnet rim. Nose: smoky, spicy, ripe fruit, dark chocolate, fruit preserve. Palate: flavourful, smoky aftertaste, ripe fruit.

Quinta Sardonia QS2 2012 T
tinto fino, cabernet sauvignon, petit verdot, malbec, syrah, merlot

90

Colour: bright cherry. Nose: sweet spices, creamy oak, overripe fruit. Palate: flavourful, fruity, toasty, round tannins.

RAMIRO WINE CELLAR

Camino Viejo de Simancas, km. 3,5
47008 Valladolid (Valladolid)
☎: +34 639 306 279
bodegasramiros@hotmail.com
www.ramirowinecellar.com

Ramiro's 2011 T
tempranillo

93

Colour: cherry, garnet rim. Nose: mineral, expressive, spicy, ripe fruit, balsamic herbs. Palate: flavourful, long, complex, balanced.

RODRÍGUEZ SANZO

Manuel Azaña, 11
47014 (Valladolid)
☎: +34 983 150 150
Fax: +34 983 150 151
comunicacion@valsanzo.com
www.rodriguezsanzo.com

Sanzo Tempranillo Frizzante 2014 RD
tempranillo

85

Sanzo Verdejo Frizzante 2014 B
100% verdejo

87

Colour: bright straw. Nose: white flowers, fresh fruit, fragrant herbs. Palate: flavourful, fruity, good acidity.

T * Sanzo 3 Tempranillos 2013 T
100% tempranillo

89

Colour: bright cherry. Nose: ripe fruit, sweet spices, creamy oak, warm. Palate: flavourful, fruity, round tannins.

VINOS DE ARGANZA

Río Ancares
24560 Toral de los Vados (León)
☎: +34 987 544 831
Fax: +34 987 563 532
admon@vinosdearganza.com
www.vinosdearganza.com

Lagar de Robla Premium 2013 T
100% mencía

90

Colour: cherry, garnet rim. Nose: sweet spices, creamy oak, ripe fruit, wild herbs. Palate: powerful, flavourful, easy to drink.

Terra Única Mencía 2013 T Roble
100% mencía

90

Colour: bright cherry, purple rim. Nose: red berry notes, ripe fruit, varietal, balsamic herbs. Palate: spicy, flavourful, long.

VINOS MALAPARTE

Crta. Cuellar – El Henar km 3,5
40200 Cuéllar (Segovia)
☎: +34 921 105 204
info@vinosmalaparte.es
www.vinosmalaparte.es

Las Lomas 2013 T
tempranillo, syrah

89

Colour: cherry, purple rim. Nose: ripe fruit, roasted coffee, sweet spices. Palate: flavourful, spicy, powerful.

VIÑAS DEL CÉNIT

Ctra. de Circunvalación, s/n
49708 Villanueva de Campeán
(Zamora)
☎: +34 980 569 346
aalberca@avanteselecta.com
www.vinasdelcenit.com

Venta Mazarrón 2013 T

91

Colour: deep cherry. Nose: creamy oak, toasty, ripe fruit, balsamic herbs. Palate: balanced, spicy, long, unctuous.

Villano 2013 T

100% tempranillo

91

Colour: bright cherry. Nose: ripe fruit, sweet spices, creamy oak, expressive. Palate: flavourful, fruity, toasty, round tannins.

VIÑEDOS DE LAS ACACIAS

Rio Selmo, 10
24560 Toral de los Vados (León)
☎: +34 987 544 831
Fax: +34 987 563 532
admon@vinosdearganza.com
www.palaciodearganza.com

Marqués de Montejos 2013 T

100% mencía

89

Colour: bright cherry, purple rim. Nose: ripe fruit, fruit preserve, balsamic herbs, sweet spices. Palate: powerful, flavourful, fine tannins.

Palacio de Arganza 2013 T

100% mencía

88

Colour: cherry, garnet rim. Nose: red berry notes, ripe fruit, spicy, creamy oak. Palate: flavourful, toasty.

Palacio de Arganza Cabernet Sauvignon Mencía 2012 T

cabernet sauvignon, mencía

89

Colour: cherry, garnet rim. Nose: ripe fruit, wild herbs, earthy notes, spicy, balsamic herbs. Palate: balanced, flavourful, long, balsamic, round tannins.

Señorío de Peñalba Selección 2013 T

100% mencía

88

Colour: bright cherry. Nose: ripe fruit, sweet spices, creamy oak, toasty. Palate: flavourful, fruity, toasty.

VIÑEDOS DE VILLAESTER

49800 Toro (Zamora)
☎: +34 948 645 008
Fax: +34 948 645 166
info@familiabelasco.com
www.familiabelasco.com

Avutarda 2013 T

tempranillo, cabernet sauvignon

87

Colour: bright cherry. Nose: ripe fruit, sweet spices, creamy oak. Palate: flavourful, fruity, toasty.

VT CASTILLA/CAMPO DE CALATRAVA

BODEGA AMANCIO MENCHERO

Legión, 27
13260 Bolaños de Calatrava
(Ciudad Real)
☎: +34 926 870 076
amanciomenchero@hotmail.com
www.vinos-menchero.com

Cuba 38 2014 T
tempranillo, cabernet sauvignon

84

Quarta Cabal 2014 B
airén

83

VT CÓRDOBA

NAVISA INDUSTRIAL VINÍCOLA ESPAÑOLA S.A.

Avda. José Padillo Delgado, s/n
14550 Montilla (Córdoba)
☎: +34 957 650 554
Fax: +34 957 651 747
abaena@navisa.es
www.navisa.es

Valpina 2013 TC
tempranillo, syrah, cabernet sauvignon

84

PÉREZ BARQUERO S.A.

Avda. Andalucía, 27
14550 Montilla (Córdoba)
☎: +34 957 650 500
Fax: +34 957 650 208
info@perezbarquero.com
www.perezbarquero.com

Casa Villa-Zevallos 2011 T Roble
tempranillo, syrah

82

Casa Villa-Zevallos S/C T
tempranillo, syrah

83

VT COSTA DE CANTABRIA

BODEGA NATES

Bº Llamosa, s/n
39761 Nates (Junta de Voto) (Cantabria)
☎: +34 616 111 907
comercial@bodegasnates.es
www.bodegasnates.es

Nates 2014 B
97% albariño, 3% godello

86

CASONA MICAELA

Barrio Henales
39880 Valle de Villa Verde (Cantabria)
☎: +34 638 934 429
casonamicaela@hotmail.com
www.casonamicaela.com

Casona Micaela 2014 B
75% albariño, 25% riesling

88
Colour: bright straw. Nose: fresh fruit, fragrant herbs, mineral. Palate: flavourful, fruity, good acidity, balanced.

Micaela Selección de Añada 2014 B
albariño, riesling

89
Colour: bright straw. Nose: fresh fruit, citrus fruit, floral, fragrant herbs. Palate: fresh, fruity.

VT CUMBRES DEL GUADALFEO

BODEGA GARCÍA DE VERDEVIQUE

Los García de Verdevique s/n
18439 Castaras (Granada)
☎: +34 958 957 025
info@bodegasgarciadeverdevique.com
www.bodegasgarciadeverdevique.com

Los García de Verdevique 2009 T
tempranillo, cabernet sauvignon, syrah

89
Colour: very deep cherry, garnet rim. Nose: ripe fruit, dried herbs, spicy, warm. Palate: ripe fruit, long, fine bitter notes.

DOMINIO BUENAVISTA - VINOS VELETA

Ctra. de Almería, s/n
18480 Ugíjar (Granada)
☎: +34 958 767 254
Fax: +34 958 990 226
info@dominiobuenavista.com
www.vinosveleta.com

Don Miguel Dulce 2009 T
60% cabernet sauvignon, 40% merlot

89

Colour: bright cherry, garnet rim. Nose: acetaldehyde, varnish, candied fruit, balsamic herbs. Palate: fruity, flavourful, sweet, balanced.

Nolados 2010 T
40% cabernet sauvignon, 40% cabernet franc, 20% tempranillo

89

Colour: deep cherry, purple rim. Nose: creamy oak, toasty, ripe fruit, balsamic herbs, complex. Palate: balanced, spicy, good finish.

Sweet Melodies Dulce Natural 2014 B
100% viognier

83

VT EIVISSA

CAN RICH

Camí de Sa Vorera, s/n
07820 Sant Antoni (Illes Balears)
☎: +34 971 803 377
Fax: +34 971 803 377
info@bodegascanrich.com
www.bodegascanrich.com

BES Can Rich 2014 RD
monastrell

79 ♣

Can Rich 2014 B
malvasía, chardonnay

87 ♣

Colour: bright yellow. Nose: ripe fruit, tropical fruit, white flowers. Palate: flavourful, fruity, ripe fruit, correct, fine bitter notes.

Can Rich 2014 RD
tempranillo, merlot

84 ♣

Can Rich Ereso 2014 BFB
malvasía

86 ♣

Can Rich Selección 2011 T
cabernet sauvignon, tempranillo, merlot

89 ♣

Colour: cherry, garnet rim. Nose: ripe fruit, wild herbs, earthy notes, spicy, balsamic herbs. Palate: balanced, flavourful, long, balsamic.

Lausos Cabernet Sauvignon 2008 T
cabernet sauvignon

90 ♣

Colour: dark-red cherry, orangey edge. Nose: ripe fruit, wild herbs, earthy notes, spicy, balsamic herbs, complex, tobacco. Palate: balanced, flavourful, long, balsamic.

Ros Fosc Tinto 2013 ESP
syrah

86

SA COVA

Bodega Sa Cova s/n
07816 Sant Mateu D'Albarca
(Illes Ballears)
☎: +34 971 187 046
Fax: +34 971 312 250
sacova@sacovaibiza.com
www.sacovaibiza.com

Sa Cova 9 2010 T

88

Colour: deep cherry, purple rim. Nose: creamy oak, toasty, ripe fruit, balsamic herbs. Palate: balanced, spicy, long.

Sa Cova Clot D'Albarca 2011 T
syrah, merlot

89

Colour: cherry, garnet rim. Nose: balanced, red berry notes, ripe fruit, dried herbs. Palate: fruity, balsamic, fine tannins.

Sa Cova Privat 2011 T

88

Colour: dark-red cherry, orangey edge. Nose: characterful, fruit preserve, spicy. Palate: spicy, balsamic, pruney.

VINOS CAN MAYMÓ

Casa Can Maymó
07816 Sant Mateu (Ibiza)
☎: +34 971 805 100
Fax: +34 971 805 100
info@bodegascanmaymo.com
www.bodegascanmaymo.com

Can Maymó 2011 T Barrica
tempranillo, merlot

87

Colour: deep cherry, garnet rim. Nose: balanced, expressive, ripe fruit, wild herbs, spicy. Palate: correct, round tannins.

Can Maymó 2014 B
malvasía, moscatel

84

Can Maymó 2014 RD
syrah, monastrell

86

Can Maymó Tradición 2012 T
monastrell

86

VT EXTREMADURA

BODEGA DE MIRABEL
Buenavista, 31
10220 Pago de San Clemente (Cáceres)
☎: +34 927 323 154
bodegademirabel@hotmail.com
es-es.facebook.com/pages/Bodega-de-Mirabel/192869280790808

Pagos de Mirabel 2013 T
100% garnacha

94

Colour: cherry, garnet rim. Nose: ripe fruit, wild herbs, earthy notes, spicy, balsamic herbs. Palate: balanced, flavourful, long, balsamic.

Tribel de Mirabel 2014 T
80% tempranillo, 20% cabernet sauvignon

88

Colour: cherry, purple rim. Nose: powerfull, ripe fruit, spicy, grassy. Palate: powerful, fruity, unctuous.

BODEGA SAN MARCOS

Ctra. Aceuchal, s/n
06200 Almendralejo (Badajoz)
☎: +34 924 670 410
Fax: +34 924 665 505
ventas@bodegasanmarcos.com
www.bodegasanmarcos.com

Jara de San Marcos Semidulce 2014 B
90% cayetana blanca, 10% moscatel

85

Jara de San Marcos Semidulce 2014 RD
100% syrah

84

BODEGAS CAÑALVA

Coto, 54
10136 Cañamero (Cáceres)
☎: +34 927 369 405
Fax: +34 927 369 405
info@bodegascanalva.com
www.bodegascanalva.com

Cañalva Coupage Especial 2010 TC
25% tempranillo, 25% cabernet sauvignon, 25% merlot, 25% syrah

87

Colour: cherry, garnet rim. Nose: fine reductive notes, aged wood nuances, ripe fruit. Palate: spicy, long, toasty.

Cañalva Macabeo 2014 B
100% macabeo

83

Cañalva Selección 2009 T
80% tempranillo, 20% cabernet sauvignon

87

Colour: cherry, garnet rim. Nose: ripe fruit, spicy, creamy oak, fine reductive notes. Palate: flavourful, toasty, round tannins.

Cañalva Tempranillo Cabernet Sauvignon 2013 T
50% tempranillo, 50% cabernet sauvignon

84

Fuente Cortijo 2010 TC
100% tempranillo

86

Luz 2014 B
macabeo, moscatel, verdejo

84

BODEGAS CARLOS PLAZA

Sol s/n
06196 Cortegana (Badajoz)
☎: +34 924 687 932
Fax: +34 924 667 569
export@bodegascarlosplaza.com
www.bodegascarlosplaza.com

Carlos Plaza 2011 T
70% tempranillo, 15% syrah, 15% merlot

87

Colour: cherry, garnet rim. Nose: creamy oak, toasty, ripe fruit, balsamic herbs. Palate: balanced, spicy, long.

Carlos Plaza 2014 B
100% pardina

82

Carlos Plaza 2014 T
90% tempranillo, 10% syrah

88

Colour: cherry, garnet rim. Nose: red berry notes, fruit liqueur notes, wild herbs, spicy. Palate: powerful, flavourful.

La Llave Roja 2011 T
70% tempranillo, 15% syrah, 15% merlot

87

Colour: bright cherry. Nose: ripe fruit, sweet spices, creamy oak. Palate: flavourful, fruity, toasty.

La Llave Roja 2014 T
90% tempranillo, 10% syrah

88

Colour: cherry, purple rim. Nose: lactic notes, raspberry, fragrant herbs. Palate: powerful, flavourful, concentrated, correct.

BODEGAS DE OCCIDENTE

Granados, 1 Bajo
06200 Almendralejo (Badajoz)
☎: +34 662 952 801
info@bodegasdeoccidente.es
www.bodegasdeoccidente.com

Buche 2013 T
tempranillo

88

Colour: bright cherry. Nose: ripe fruit, sweet spices, creamy oak. Palate: flavourful, fruity, round tannins.

Gran Buche 2011 TR
tempranillo

89

Colour: cherry, garnet rim. Nose: ripe fruit, spicy, creamy oak, complex. Palate: flavourful, toasty.

BODEGAS HABLA

Ctra. A-V, km. 259
10200 Trujillo (Cáceres)
☎: +34 927 659 180
Fax: +34 927 659 180
habla@bodegashabla.com
www.bodegashabla.com

Habla de la Tierra 2013 T
tempranillo, malbec, cabernet sauvignon, petit verdot, cabernet franc

87

Colour: cherry, purple rim. Nose: ripe fruit, balanced, scrubland. Palate: good structure, fruity, flavourful.

Habla de ti... 2014 B

90

Colour: bright straw. Nose: white flowers, fresh fruit, fragrant herbs. Palate: flavourful, fruity, good acidity, balanced.

Habla del Silencio 2013 T
syrah, cabernet sauvignon, tempranillo

89

Colour: very deep cherry, garnet rim. Nose: grassy, wild herbs, ripe fruit. Palate: powerful, round tannins.

BODEGAS LUIS GURPEGUI MUGA

Avda. Celso Muerza, 8
31560 San Adrián (Navarra)
☎: +34 948 670 050
Fax: +34 948 670 259
bodegas@gurpegui.es
www.gurpegui.es

El Hayedo 2014 T
tempranillo, garnacha

83

Pintoresco 2014 T
tempranillo

86

BODEGAS ORAN

Granados, 1
06200 Almendralejo (Badajoz)
☎: +34 662 952 801
info@bodegasoran.com
www.bodegasoran.com

Entremares Semidulce 2014 B
eva, pardina, cayetana blanca, montua

84

Entremares Semidulce 2014 RD
garnacha tintorera

85

Señorío de Orán 2013 T Roble
60% garnacha tintorera, 40% tempranillo

88

Colour: deep cherry, purple rim. Nose: creamy oak, toasty, ripe fruit, balsamic herbs. Palate: balanced, spicy, long.

BODEGAS RUIZ TORRES

Ctra. EX 116, km.33,8
10136 Cañamero (Cáceres)
☎: +34 927 369 027
Fax: +34 927 369 302
info@ruiztorres.com
www.ruiztorres.com

Cabernet Sauvignon de Bodegas Ruiz Torres 2010 T
100% cabernet sauvignon

87

Colour: very deep cherry, garnet rim. Nose: balanced, ripe fruit, grassy. Palate: full, flavourful, round tannins.

Syrah de Bodegas Ruiz Torres 2011 T
100% syrah

87

Colour: very deep cherry, garnet rim. Nose: complex, balsamic herbs, balanced. Palate: full, flavourful, round tannins.

Verdejo de Bodegas Ruiz Torres 2014 B
100% verdejo

84

BODEGAS TORIBIO

Luis Chamizo, 12 y 21
06310 Puebla de Sancho Pérez
(Badajoz)
☎: +34 924 551 449
Fax: +34 924 551 449
info@bodegastoribio.com
www.bodegastoribio.com

Mú + Madera 2013 T Roble
tempranillo, cabernet sauvignon, syrah

86

Mú 2013 T
tempranillo, macabeo

85

Mú 2014 B
eva, alarije, verdejo

84

Torivín Pi 2012 TC
tempranillo, cabernet sauvignon, syrah

88

Colour: bright cherry. Nose: ripe fruit, sweet spices, creamy oak. Palate: flavourful, fruity, toasty, round tannins.

COLOMA VIÑEDOS Y BODEGAS

Ctra. EX-363, km. 5,6
06170 Alvarado (Badajoz)
☎: +34 924 440 028
Fax: +34 924 440 409
coloma@bodegascoloma.com
www.bodegascoloma.com

Coloma Garnacha Roja 2012 T
100% garnacha roja

86

Coloma Muscat 2014 B
moscatel grano menudo

86

Coloma Pinot Noir 2014 RD
100% pinot noir

86

Coloma Selección Garnacha 2014 T Roble
100% garnacha

87

Colour: deep cherry, purple rim. Nose: creamy oak, toasty, ripe fruit, balsamic herbs. Palate: balanced, spicy, long.

Coloma Selección Graciano 2013 T Roble
100% graciano

85

Coloma Selección Merlot 2012 T Roble
100% merlot

85

MARQUÉS DE VALDUEZA

Fortuny, 19 1º Dcha
28010 Madrid (Madrid)
☎: +34 913 191 508
Fax: +34 913 084 034
contact@marquesdevaldueza.com
www.marquesdevaldueza.com

Marqués de Valdueza Etiqueta Roja 2011 T
44% cabernet sauvignon, 37% syrah, 19% merlot

83

Marqués de Valdueza Gran Vino de Guarda 2008 T
91% syrah, 9% cabernet sauvignon

91

Colour: cherry, garnet rim. Nose: ripe fruit, wild herbs, earthy notes, spicy, balsamic herbs, fine reductive notes. Palate: balanced, flavourful, long, balsamic.

MOSTOS CONCENTRADOS Y RECTIFICADOS

Ctra. Badajoz, 75
06200 Almendralejo (Badajoz)
☎: +34 924 677 337
Fax: +34 924 677 337
lolavargas@bodegasmcr.com
www.bodegasmcr.com

88 Cepas 2014 T
cabernet sauvignon, syrah, graciano, tempranillo

88

Colour: deep cherry, purple rim. Nose: powerfull, ripe fruit, wild herbs, spicy, characterful. Palate: balanced, round tannins.

Inés del Alma Mía 2014 B
chardonnay

90

Colour: bright yellow. Nose: white flowers, fine lees, dried herbs, ripe fruit, candied fruit, citrus fruit. Palate: flavourful, fruity, good acidity.

PAGO LOS BALANCINES

Paraje la Agraria, s/n
06475 Oliva de Mérida (Badajoz)
☎: +34 924 367 399
info@pagolosbalancines.com
www.pagolosbalancines.com

Balancines Gold 2013 T Roble

garnacha tintorera, syrah

88

Colour: deep cherry, purple rim. Nose: creamy oak, toasty, ripe fruit, balsamic herbs. Palate: balanced, spicy, long.

VIÑA PLACENTINA

Circunvalación sur – Urb. Haza del Obispo – Finca Pago de los Ángeles
10600 Plasencia (Cáceres)
☎: +34 927 116 250
Fax: +34 927 418 102
info@vinaplacentina.com
www.vinaplacentina.com

Viña Placentina Etiqueta Negra 2007 TR

100% cabernet sauvignon

85

Viña Placentina Etiqueta Roja 2011 TC

75% cabernet sauvignon, 25% merlot

82

Viña Placentina Finca Miraflores 2013 T

100% tempranillo

85

Viña Placentina Pago de los Ángeles 2005 TGR

100% cabernet sauvignon

84

ZALEO-VIÑAOLIVA

Pol. Ind., Las Plcadas II, Parcela 4-17
06200 Almendralejo (Badajoz)
☎: +34 924 677 321
Fax: +34 924 660 989
acoex@bme.es
www.zaleo.es

Zaleo Semidulce de Aguja Natural 2014 B

chardonnay

84

VT FORMENTERA

CAP DE BARBARIA

Ctra. de Cap de Barbaria, km. 5,8
Apartado de correus 380.
07860 Sant Francesc (Formentera)
☎: +34 934 950 956
Fax: +34 934 951 027
info@capdebarbaria.com
www.capdebarbaria.com

Cap de Barbaria 2010 T

cabernet sauvignon, merlot, monastrell, fogoneu

92

Colour: cherry, garnet rim. Nose: ripe fruit, wild herbs, earthy notes, spicy, balsamic herbs. Palate: balanced, flavourful, long, balsamic.

Cap de Barbaria 24 2011 TR

cabernet sauvignon, merlot, monastrell, fogoneu

93

Colour: cherry, garnet rim. Nose: expressive, spicy, earthy notes, wild herbs. Palate: flavourful, ripe fruit, long, good acidity, balanced.

Ophiusa 2012 T

cabernet sauvignon, merlot, monastrell, fogoneu

89

Colour: cherry, garnet rim. Nose: dried herbs, spicy, earthy notes. Palate: flavourful, ripe fruit, balsamic.

TERRAMOLL

Ctra. de La Mola Km. 15.2 – El Pilar de La Mola
07872 Formentera (Illes Balears)
☎: +34 971 327 293
Fax: +34 971 327 293
info@terramoll.es
www.terramoll.es

Es Monestir 2012 TC

monastrell

92

Colour: cherry, garnet rim. Nose: ripe fruit, wild herbs, earthy notes, spicy, balsamic herbs. Palate: balanced, flavourful, long, balsamic.

Rosa de Mar 2014 RD

merlot, cabernet sauvignon, monastrell

86

Savina 2014 B

viognier, moscatel grano menudo, malvasía, garnacha blanca

88

Colour: bright straw. Nose: white flowers, fresh fruit, fragrant herbs. Palate: flavourful, fruity, good acidity.

Terramoll Primus 2008 TC

90

Colour: pale ruby, brick rim edge. Nose: elegant, spicy, fine reductive notes, tobacco. Palate: spicy, fine tannins, elegant, long.

VT ILLA DE MENORCA

CELLER SOLANO DE MENORCA

Cugullonet Nou
07712 Sant Climent - Mahón
(Illes Balears)
☎: +34 607 242 510
saforana@saforana.com
www.saforana.com

Sa Forana 2013 T

cabernet sauvignon, ull de llebre, merlot

88

Colour: deep cherry. Nose: ripe fruit, sweet spices, creamy oak, scrubland. Palate: flavourful, fruity, toasty.

FINCA SA CUDIA

Cos de Gracia, 7
07702 Mahón (Illes Balears)
☎: +34 686 361 445
Fax: +34 971 353 607
fincasacudia@gmail.com
www.vinyasacudia.com

Sa Cudía 2014 B

100% malvasía

90

Colour: bright yellow. Nose: expressive, dried herbs, ripe fruit, spicy. Palate: flavourful, fruity, good acidity, balanced.

FINCA SA MARJALETA

Camí d'Alpare, s/n
07760 Ciutadella de Menorca
(Illes Balears)
☎: +34 971 385 737
Fax: +34 971 385 737
marjaleta@telefonica.net
www.marjaleta.com

iamontanum 2012 T

92,5% syrah, 7,5% tempranillo

91

Colour: cherry, garnet rim. Nose: ripe fruit, balsamic herbs, earthy notes, spicy. Palate: spicy, long, toasty.

iamontanum 2013 T

90% syrah, 10% tempranillo

90

Colour: cherry, purple rim. Nose: ripe fruit, roasted coffee. Palate: flavourful, spicy, powerful.

iamontanum 2014 B

viognier

89

Colour: bright straw. Nose: white flowers, ripe fruit, balanced, citrus fruit. Palate: rich, flavourful, fruity.

VT LADERAS DEL GENIL

BODEGAS SEÑORÍO DE NEVADA

Ctra. de Cónchar, s/n
18659 Villamena (Granada)
☎: +34 958 777 092
Fax: +34 958 107 367
info@senoriodenevada.es
www.senoriodenevada.es

Señorío de Nevada 2014 B

viognier

88

Colour: bright yellow. Nose: dried herbs, ripe fruit, spicy. Palate: flavourful, fruity, good acidity.

Señorío de Nevada 2014 RD

garnacha

87

Colour: light cherry, bright. Nose: red berry notes, ripe fruit, fragrant herbs, balanced. Palate: balanced.

Viña Dauro 2013 T Roble

syrah

85

VT MALLORCA

4 KILOS VINÍCOLA

1ª Volta, 168 Puigverd
07200 Felanitx (Illes Balears)
☎: +34 971 580 523
Fax: +34 971 580 523
fgrimalt@4kilos.com
www.4kilos.com

12 volts 2013 T

fogoneu,

91

Colour: cherry, garnet rim. Nose: ripe fruit, wild herbs, earthy notes, spicy, balsamic herbs. Palate: balanced, flavourful, long, balsamic.

4 Kilos 2013 T

93

Colour: ruby red. Nose: wild herbs, balsamic herbs, floral, fresh fruit, spicy. Palate: flavourful, good acidity, light-bodied, balanced, elegant.

ANA VINS

Camí Vell de Muro s/n
07350 Binissalem (Illes Balears)
☎: +34 971 511 719
info@ana-vins.com
www.ana-vins.com

Ana Blanc 2014 B

chardonnay, prensal, moscatel

89

Colour: bright straw. Nose: fresh fruit, expressive, dried flowers, wild herbs. Palate: flavourful, good acidity, balanced.

Ana Negre 2012 T

callet, cabernet sauvignon, tempranillo, merlot, syrah

90

Colour: light cherry. Nose: medium intensity, scrubland, dried herbs, spicy. Palate: balanced, easy to drink, ripe fruit.

Ana Rosat 2014 RD

manto negro, callet, merlot, syrah

89

Colour: onion pink. Nose: elegant, red berry notes, floral, fragrant herbs. Palate: flavourful, good acidity, long, ripe fruit, fine bitter notes.

Ana Selecció 2012 T

manto negro, merlot, syrah, callet, cabernet sauvignon, tempranillo

91

Colour: bright cherry. Nose: toasty, ripe fruit, balsamic herbs. Palate: balanced, spicy, long, flavourful, good structure.

ARMERO I ADROVER

Camada Real s/n
07200 Mallorca (Illes Ballears)
☎: +34 971 827 103
Fax: +34 971 580 305
luisarmero@armeroiadrover.com
www.armeroiadrover.com

Armero Adrover Chardonnay Prensal 2014 B

87

Colour: bright straw. Nose: white flowers, fresh fruit, fragrant herbs. Palate: fruity, good acidity, balanced, easy to drink.

BINIGRAU

Fiol, 33
07143 Biniali (Illes Balears)
☎: +34 971 512 023
Fax: +34 971 886 495
info@binigrau.es
www.binigrau.es

B Selecció 2011 T

80% manto negro, callet, 20% merlot

92

Colour: cherry, garnet rim. Nose: elegant, creamy oak, spicy, scrubland, ripe fruit. Palate: balanced, round tannins, balsamic.

Chardonnay Binigrau 2014 BFB

chardonnay

91

Colour: bright straw. Nose: white flowers, ripe fruit, sweet spices. Palate: flavourful, fruity, good acidity, round.

Dolç Binigrau 2010 T

manto negro, merlot

88

Colour: cherry, garnet rim. Nose: fruit preserve, spicy, warm, fruit liqueur notes. Palate: powerful, flavourful, sweet, rich.

E - Binigrau 2014 RD

50% manto negro, 50% merlot

87

Colour: rose, purple rim. Nose: floral, red berry notes, ripe fruit, characterful. Palate: powerful, fruity, flavourful.

E - Binigrau 2014 T

50% manto negro, 50% merlot

90 

Colour: cherry, purple rim. Nose: red berry notes, balsamic herbs, ripe fruit. Palate: powerful, fruity, flavourful, balsamic.

Nou Nat 2014 B

60% prensal, 40% chardonnay

92

Colour: bright straw. Nose: white flowers, fine lees, dried herbs, ripe fruit, citrus fruit. Palate: flavourful, fruity, good acidity, elegant.

Obac' 13 2013 TC

manto negro, callet, merlot, syrah, cabernet sauvignon

90

Colour: bright cherry, garnet rim. Nose: ripe fruit, spicy, earthy notes, scrubland. Palate: flavourful, spicy, easy to drink, balsamic.

BODEGA BINIAGUAL

Llogaret de Biniagual, Cami de Muro s/n
07350 Binissalem (Mallorca)
☎: +34 689 183 954
Fax: +34 971 886 108
info@bodegabiniagual.com
www.bodegabiniagual.com

Sant Gall 2011 TC

manto negro, syrah, cabernet sauvignon

87

Colour: cherry, garnet rim. Nose: red berry notes, fresh fruit, balanced. Palate: spicy, easy to drink, balanced.

BODEGA CASTELL MIQUEL

Ctra. Alaró-Lloseta, Km. 8,7
07340 Alaró (Baleares)
☎: +34 971 510 698
Fax: +34 971 510 669
info@castellmiquel.com
www.castellmiquel.com

Monte Sion 2010 T

38% syrah, 33% sauvignon blanc, 13% merlot, 9% monastrell, 7% tempranillo

88

Colour: dark-red cherry, orangey edge. Nose: toasty, ripe fruit, balsamic herbs, warm. Palate: balanced, spicy, long.

Stairway to Heaven Cabernet Sauvignon 2011 TR
100% cabernet sauvignon

88

Colour: bright cherry. Nose: scrubland, dried herbs, spicy, characterful, ripe fruit. Palate: balanced, warm, balsamic.

Stairway to Heaven Shiraz 2010 TR
syrah

87

Colour: cherry, garnet rim. Nose: warm, dried herbs, spicy. Palate: fruity, easy to drink.

BODEGA MESQUIDA MORA

Camí Pas des Frare, s/n
(Antigua Ctra. PorreresSant Joan)
07260 Porreres (Illes Balears)
☎: +34 971 647 106
Fax: +34 971 168 205
info@mesquidamora.com
www.mesquidamora.com

Acrollam Blanc 2014 B
prensal, chardonnay

87

Colour: bright yellow. Nose: dried herbs, faded flowers, characterful, ripe fruit. Palate: flavourful, balanced, fine bitter notes.

Sincronía 2014 T
callet, manto negro, cabernet sauvignon, merlot, syrah

89

Colour: bright cherry, garnet rim. Nose: scrubland, ripe fruit. Palate: spicy, balanced, balsamic.

Sòtil 2013 T
callet

89

Colour: bright cherry, purple rim. Nose: expressive, characterful, earthy notes, ripe fruit. Palate: balanced, good acidity, good finish.

BODEGAS ÁNGEL

Ctra. Sta María - Santa Eugenia, km. 4,8
07320 Santa María del Camí
(Illes Balears)
☎: +34 971 621 638
Fax: +34 971 621 638
info@bodegasangel.com
www.bodegasangel.com

Ángel Blanc de Blanca 2014 B
prensal, chardonnay, viognier

87

Colour: bright yellow. Nose: white flowers, ripe fruit, balanced. Palate: correct, fine bitter notes, good acidity.

Ángel Cabernet Sauvignon 2011 T
cabernet sauvignon

88

Colour: cherry, garnet rim. Nose: medium intensity, dried herbs, ripe fruit, spicy. Palate: fruity, flavourful.

Ángel Lau Rosa 2014 RD
manto negro, merlot

86

Ángel Negre 2013 T Barrica
manto negro, merlot, cabernet sauvignon

89

Colour: light cherry, garnet rim. Nose: medium intensity, scrubland, spicy, ripe fruit. Palate: balanced, good acidity.

Ángel Viognier 2013 BFB
viognier

87

Colour: bright yellow. Nose: toasty, spicy, ripe fruit. Palate: correct, flavourful, toasty.

BODEGAS JOSÉ L. FERRER

Conquistador, 103
07350 Binissalem (Illes Balears)
☎: +34 971 511 050
Fax: +34 971 870 084
info@vinosferrer.com
www.vinosferrer.com

José L. Ferrer DUES Syrah Callet 2013 T
syrah, callet

88

Colour: light cherry, garnet rim. Nose: earthy notes, wild herbs, spicy. Palate: easy to drink, correct.

BODEGAS SON PUIG S.L.

Finca Son Puig, s/n
07194 Puigpunyent (Illes Balears)
☎: +34 971 614 184
Fax: +34 971 614 184
info@sonpuig.com
www.sonpuig.com

Son Puig Callet i Ull de Llebre 2014 T
callet, tempranillo

85

Sonpuig 2014 BFB
chardonnay, prensal, sauvignon blanc

88

Colour: bright straw. Nose: toasty, ripe fruit, spicy. Palate: flavourful, fruity, rich, toasty.

Sonpuig Blanc D'Estiu 2014 B
prensal, chardonnay, sauvignon blanc

88

Colour: bright straw. Nose: faded flowers, dried herbs, balanced. Palate: flavourful, fresh, ripe fruit.

Sonpuig Estiu 2014 T
tempranillo, callet, merlot, cabernet sauvignon

86

Sonpuig Prensal 2014 B
prensal

87

Colour: bright straw. Nose: medium intensity, ripe fruit, dried herbs. Palate: correct, easy to drink, flavourful, fine bitter notes.

BODEGUES MACIÀ BATLE
Camí Coanegra, s/n
07320 Santa María del Camí
(Illes Balears)
☎: +34 971 140 014
Fax: +34 971 140 086
correo@maciabatle.com
www.maciabatle.com

Piedra Papel Tijera 2014 B
65% prensal, 25% chardonnay, 10% moscatel

86

CA'N VERDURA VITICULTORS
S'Era, 6
07350 Binissalem (Illes Balears)
☎: +34 695 817 038
tomeuverdura@gmail.com

L'Origen 2012 T
89

Colour: light cherry. Nose: cocoa bean, ripe fruit, spicy. Palate: good structure, flavourful, sweet tannins.

CELLERS UNIÓ
43206 Reus (Tarragona)
☎: +34 977 330 055
Fax: +34 977 330 070
info@cellersunio.com
www.cellersunio.com

Roua Mediterranea Blanc de Blancs 2014 B
macabeo, prensal

89

Colour: bright straw. Nose: fragrant herbs, ripe fruit. Palate: balanced, fine bitter notes, good acidity.

Roua Mediterranea Negre Selecció Especial 2013 T
manto negro, cabernet sauvignon, merlot

87

Colour: light cherry, garnet rim. Nose: wild herbs, spicy, varnish. Palate: fruity, fine bitter notes, correct.

COMERCIAL GRUPO FREIXENET
Joan Sala, 2
08770 Sant Sadurní D'Anoia
(Barcelona)
☎: +34 938 917 000
Fax: +34 938 183 095
freixenet@freixenet.es
www.freixenet.es

Susana Sempre 2013 T Roble
88

Colour: cherry, garnet rim. Nose: red berry notes, ripe fruit, fragrant herbs, spicy, toasty. Palate: flavourful, balsamic, balanced.

Susana Sempre 2014 B
86

FINCA SON BORDILS
Ctra. Inca - Sineu, Km. 4,1
07300 Inca (Illes Balears)
☎: +34 971 182 200
Fax: +34 971 182 202
info@sonbordils.es
www.sonbordils.es

Finca Son Bordils Blanc de raïm Blanc 2014 B
prensal

91

Colour: bright straw. Nose: dried herbs, ripe fruit, dried flowers, expressive. Palate: flavourful, fruity, good acidity, elegant.

Finca Son Bordils Cabernet Sauvignon 2008 T
cabernet sauvignon

89

Colour: bright cherry, orangey edge. Nose: ripe fruit, wild herbs, earthy notes, spicy, balsamic herbs. Palate: balanced, flavourful, long, balsamic, powerful.

Finca Son Bordils Chardonnay 2014 B
88,3% chardonnay, 7,5% riesling, 4,2% viognier

90

Colour: bright straw. Nose: white flowers, fresh fruit, fragrant herbs, expressive. Palate: flavourful, fruity, good acidity, balanced.

Finca Son Bordils Merlot 2008 T
94% merlot, 6% manto negro

90

Colour: bright cherry, orangey edge. Nose: balanced, expressive, varietal, scrubland. Palate: round tannins, spicy, balsamic, long.

Finca Son Bordils Muscat 2014 B
moscatel grano menudo

89

Colour: bright yellow. Nose: varietal, fresh, white flowers, expressive. Palate: fruity, flavourful, easy to drink.

Finca Son Bordils Negre Magnum LA108 2008 T
63% merlot, 33% cabernet sauvignon, 4% manto negro

90

Colour: deep cherry, orangey edge. Nose: spicy, balsamic herbs, tobacco, ripe fruit. Palate: good structure, flavourful, round tannins, balanced.

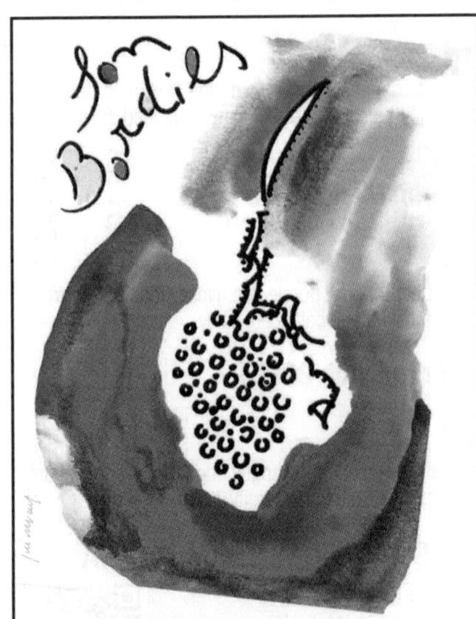

Finca Son Bordils Rosat 2014 RD
51,7% monastrell, 48,3% merlot

89

Colour: onion pink. Nose: elegant, red berry notes, floral, fragrant herbs. Palate: light-bodied, flavourful, good acidity, long, spicy.

Finca Son Bordils Syrah 2008 T
syrah

87

Colour: bright cherry. Nose: ripe fruit, sweet spices, expressive. Palate: flavourful, fruity, toasty, round tannins.

Finca Son Bordils Syrah Magnum 2007 T
syrah

88

Colour: light cherry. Nose: toasty, smoky, spicy. Palate: correct, balanced, ripe fruit.

Son Bordils Cabernet Sauvignon Magnum 1,5 l 2007 T
cabernet sauvignon

90

Colour: bright cherry, orangey edge. Nose: spicy, tobacco, dried herbs, ripe fruit, fruit preserve. Palate: good structure, flavourful.

Son Bordils Merlot Magnum 1,5 l 2007 T
merlot

91

Colour: dark-red cherry, orangey edge. Nose: fruit liqueur notes, scrubland, old leather. Palate: balanced, spicy, long, good acidity.

GALMÉS I RIBOT

Ctra. Santa Margalida - Petra
07450 Santa Margalida (Illes Balears)
☎: +34 678 847 830
vins@galmesiribot.com
www.galmesiribot.com

Margalida 2014 B
chardonnay, prensal

86

Petit Som 2012 T
cabernet sauvignon, merlot, callet, fogoneu

87

Colour: bright cherry. Nose: ripe fruit, balsamic herbs, spicy. Palate: balanced, spicy, long.

Petjades 2013 T
gorgollassa

87

Colour: light cherry. Nose: expressive, characterful, wet leather, ripe fruit. Palate: balanced, easy to drink, ripe fruit, balsamic.

Som 2010 T
merlot, callet, fogoneu

89

Colour: cherry, garnet rim. Nose: ripe fruit, wild herbs, earthy notes, spicy, balsamic herbs. Palate: balanced, flavourful, long, balsamic.

Som Blanc 2014 B
giró ros
88
Colour: bright straw. Nose: balanced, fragrant herbs, dried flowers, medium intensity. Palate: flavourful, ripe fruit, balanced.

Som Selecció Catalina 2010 T
merlot
90
Colour: bright cherry, garnet rim. Nose: scrubland, spicy, characterful, ripe fruit. Palate: balanced, round, round tannins.

SON CAMPANER

Cami de Son Campaner, Sancellas
07140 Sencelles (Illes Balears)
☎: +34 971 870 004
info@soncampaner.es
www.soncampaner.es

Son Campaner Athos 2012 T
merlot, manto negro, cabernet sauvignon
90
Colour: cherry, garnet rim. Nose: powerfull, warm, characterful, spicy, ripe fruit. Palate: flavourful, good structure, round tannins.

Son Campaner Blanc de Blancs 2014 B
macabeo, prensal
88
Colour: bright straw. Nose: fresh fruit, fragrant herbs, expressive. Palate: flavourful, fruity, good acidity, balanced.

Son Campaner Blanc de Negres 2014 RD
cabernet sauvignon, syrah
86

Son Campaner Merlot 2012 T
merlot
90
Colour: very deep cherry, garnet rim. Nose: expressive, complex, balsamic herbs, balanced, earthy notes. Palate: full, flavourful, round tannins.

Son Campaner Pálido 2014 B
cabernet sauvignon, syrah, macabeo
86

Son Campaner Terra Rossa 2012 T
manto negro, cabernet sauvignon, merlot
91
Colour: cherry, garnet rim. Nose: ripe fruit, wild herbs, earthy notes, spicy, balsamic herbs. Palate: balanced, flavourful, long, balsamic.

SON PRIM PETIT

Ctra. Inca - Sencelles, Km. 4,9
07014 Sencelles (Balears)
☎: +34 971 872 758
correo@sonprim.com
www.sonprim.com

Cup Son Prim 2012 T Barrica
merlot, cabernet sauvignon, syrah
91
Colour: deep cherry, purple rim. Nose: creamy oak, toasty, ripe fruit, balsamic herbs. Palate: balanced, spicy, long.

Son Prim Cabernet Sauvignon 2012 T
cabernet sauvignon
91
Colour: cherry, garnet rim. Nose: ripe fruit, wild herbs, earthy notes, spicy, balsamic herbs. Palate: balanced, flavourful, long, balsamic.

Son Prim Merlot 2012 T
merlot
89
Colour: deep cherry, purple rim. Nose: toasty, ripe fruit, balsamic herbs. Palate: balanced, spicy.

Son Prim Syrah 2012 T
syrah
88
Colour: dark-red cherry, orangey edge. Nose: spicy, characterful, warm, ripe fruit. Palate: fruity, spicy, good acidity.

VINOS Y VIÑEDOS TRAMUNTANA

Jesús, 13 Baja
07003 Palma de Mallor (Baleares)

Ca'N Xanet 2012 T
91
Colour: cherry, garnet rim. Nose: ripe fruit, spicy, creamy oak, complex. Palate: flavourful, toasty.

Cadmo 2012 T
92
Colour: bright cherry. Nose: ripe fruit, sweet spices, creamy oak. Palate: flavourful, fruity, toasty, round tannins.

Cumas 2012 T
manto negro

94

Colour: light cherry, garnet rim. Nose: ripe fruit, scrubland, spicy, elegant. Palate: complex, flavourful, fruity, fine tannins.

Sibila 2012 T

91

Colour: light cherry. Nose: fruit liqueur notes, fragrant herbs, creamy oak. Palate: spicy, long, toasty.

VINS MIQUEL GELABERT
Salas, 50
07500 Manacor (Illes Balears)
☎: +34 971 821 444
info@vinsmiquelgelabert.com
www.vinsmiquelgelabert.com

Dolç de Sa Vall 2013 B
moscatel

88

Colour: bright yellow. Nose: balsamic herbs, honeyed notes, floral, sweet spices, expressive. Palate: rich, fruity, flavourful.

Dolç Martina 2013
riesling, chardonnay

93

Colour: bright golden. Nose: honeyed notes, candied fruit, citrus fruit, faded flowers, expressive. Palate: full, flavourful, complex.

VINS NADAL
Ramón Llull, 2
07350 Binissalem (Illes Balears)
☎: +34 971 511 058
Fax: +34 971 870 150
albaflor@vinsnadal.es
www.vinsnadal.es

Blanc 110 Vins Nadal 2014 B
chardonnay

85

Coupage 110 Vins Nadal 2010 T Barrica
manto negro, cabernet sauvignon, merlot, syrah

90

Colour: cherry, garnet rim. Nose: fruit preserve, aged wood nuances, toasty, scrubland. Palate: flavourful, round tannins, long, balanced, powerful.

Merlot 110 Vins Nadal 2007 T Barrica
merlot

85

Rosat 110 Vins Nadal 2014 RD
manto negro

87

Colour: rose, purple rim. Nose: red berry notes, floral, expressive, lactic notes. Palate: powerful, fruity, fresh.

VINYA SON ALEGRE
#N/D
#N/D #N/D (#N/D)
☎: +34 606 401 408
sinesolesileo@hotmail.es
www.vinyasonalegre.com

Cocó Barber 2014 B
malvasía, chardonnay

86

S'Antigor Negre 2012 T
cabernet sauvignon, merlot

86

S'Aragall Blau 2014 RD
merlot, syrah, cabernet sauvignon

86

VINYES MORTITX
Ctra. Pollença Lluc, Km. 10,9
07315 Escorca (Illes Balears)
☎: +34 971 182 339
Fax: +34 871 100 053
info@vinyesmortitx.com
www.vinyesmortitx.com

L'Ergull de Mortitx 2012 BFB
malvasía, chardonnay, moscatel

87

Colour: bright yellow. Nose: powerfull, toasty, aged wood nuances, pattiserie. Palate: flavourful, fruity, spicy, toasty, long.

L'U Blanc 2012 BFB
malvasía, chardonnay

88

Colour: bright yellow. Nose: ripe fruit, toasty, aged wood nuances, warm. Palate: flavourful, fruity, spicy, toasty, long.

L'U Negre 2011 T
syrah, merlot, tempranillo, cabernet sauvignon

90

Colour: cherry, garnet rim. Nose: ripe fruit, wild herbs, earthy notes, spicy, balsamic herbs. Palate: balanced, flavourful, long, balsamic, round tannins.

Mortitx Blanc 2014 B
malvasía, moscatel, chardonnay

86

Mortitx Negre 2012 T
merlot, syrah, tempranillo, cabernet sauvignon, monastrell

87

Colour: deep cherry, purple rim. Nose: toasty, ripe fruit, balsamic herbs. Palate: balanced, spicy, long, easy to drink.

Mortitx Syrah 2010 T
syrah

88

Colour: very deep cherry, garnet rim. Nose: ripe fruit, toasty, smoky, scrubland, dried herbs. Palate: good structure, flavourful.

Rodal Pla de Mortitx 2011 T
syrah, merlot, cabernet sauvignon, tempranillo

89

Colour: very deep cherry, garnet rim. Nose: expressive, balsamic herbs, balanced, earthy notes. Palate: full, flavourful, round tannins.

VT RIBERA DEL ANDARAX

BODEGA ÁNFORA

Barranco del Obispo, 1
04729 Enix (Almería)
☎: +34 629 131 370
Fax: +34 950 341 614
info@fincaanfora.com
www.fincaanfora.com

Vega Enix Calidón 2009 T
merlot, cabernet sauvignon, syrah, garnacha, monastrell

89

Colour: cherry, garnet rim. Nose: balanced, complex, ripe fruit, spicy, fine reductive notes. Palate: flavourful, round tannins, balanced.

Vega Enix Monteneo 2011 T
garnacha, monastrell

88

Colour: cherry, garnet rim. Nose: wild herbs, spicy, fruit preserve. Palate: flavourful, balsamic.

Vega Enix Santys 2010 T
syrah, garnacha

91

Colour: very deep cherry, garnet rim. Nose: expressive, complex, mineral, balsamic herbs, balanced. Palate: full, flavourful, round tannins.

Vega Enix Xolair 2010 T
merlot

90

Colour: deep cherry. Nose: creamy oak, toasty, ripe fruit, balsamic herbs. Palate: balanced, spicy, long.

VT RIBERA DEL GÁLLEGO-CINCO VILLAS

BODEGAS EJEANAS

Avda. Cosculluela, 23
50600 Ejea de los Caballeros (Zaragoza)
☎: +34 976 663 770
Fax: +34 976 663 770
pilar@bodegasejeanas.com
www.bodegasejeanas.com

Un Garnacha 2011 T Roble
garnacha

85

Un Garnacha Plus 2007 TR
garnacha
88
Colour: pale ruby, brick rim edge. Nose: elegant, spicy, fine reductive notes, tobacco. Palate: spicy, fine tannins, elegant, long.

Un Tempranillo Garnacha 2011 T
tempranillo, garnacha
86

Uva Nocturna Merlot 2013 T
100% merlot
87
Colour: dark-red cherry. Nose: fruit liqueur notes, scrubland, spicy, medium intensity. Palate: ripe fruit, correct.

Uva Nocturna Syrah 2012 T
100% syrah
85

Vega de Luchán 2014 RD
cabernet sauvignon, merlot
85

Vega de Luchán Tempranillo 2009 T Barrica
tempranillo, cabernet sauvignon
84

EDRA BODEGA Y VIÑEDOS
Ctra A - 132, km 26
22800 Ayerbe (Huesca)
☎: +34 679 420 455
edra@bodega-edra.com
www.bodega-edra.com

Edra Merlot Syrah 2010 T
merlot, syrah
89
Colour: cherry, garnet rim. Nose: ripe fruit, wild herbs, spicy, balsamic herbs. Palate: flavourful, long, balsamic.

Edra Xtra Syrah 2010 T
syrah
90
Colour: cherry, garnet rim. Nose: red berry notes, ripe fruit, spicy, creamy oak, complex. Palate: flavourful, toasty, round tannins.

VT RIBERA DEL JILOCA

VINAE MURERI
Ctra. Murero-Atea - Finca La Moratilla
50366 Murero (Zaragoza)
☎: +34 976 808 033
info@vinaemureri.com
www.vinaemureri.com

Murero 18 meses 2009 T
87
Colour: pale ruby, brick rim edge. Nose: spicy, fine reductive notes, wet leather, aged wood nuances. Palate: spicy, fine tannins, balanced.

Muret Azul 2012 T
85

Muret Oro 2010 T
100% garnacha
84

Muret Vidadillo 2014 T
84

Pizarra Blanca 2014 B
83

Xiloca 2014 T
84

VT RIBERA DEL QUEILES

BODEGA DEL JARDÍN
San Juan, 14
31520 Cascante (Navarra)
☎: +34 948 850 055
info@bodegadeljardin.es
www.bodegadeljardin.es

1 Pulso 2011 T
85% tempranillo, 15% merlot
88
Colour: cherry, garnet rim. Nose: ripe fruit, wild herbs, spicy, slightly evolved. Palate: powerful, flavourful, balanced.

2 Pulso 2011 T
40% tempranillo, 40% merlot, 20% cabernet sauvignon
87
Colour: cherry, garnet rim. Nose: ripe fruit, spicy, creamy oak. Palate: flavourful, toasty, correct.

EDRA BODEGA Y VIÑEDOS

Ctra A - 132, km 26
22800 Ayerbe (Huesca)
☎: +34 679 420 455
edra@bodega-edra.com
www.bodega-edra.com

Edra Grullas de Paso 2011 T

garnacha, tempranillo, merlot, cabernet sauvignon

87

Colour: cherry, garnet rim. Nose: creamy oak, red berry notes, balanced. Palate: flavourful, spicy, long.

GUELBENZU

Paraje La Lombana s/n
50513 Vierlas (Zaragoza)
☎: +34 948 202 200
Fax: +34 948 202 202
info@taninia.com
www.guelbenzu.com

Guelbenzu Azul 2011 T

merlot, tempranillo, cabernet sauvignon

89

Colour: cherry, garnet rim. Nose: creamy oak, red berry notes, spicy, fine reductive notes. Palate: flavourful, spicy.

Guelbenzu Evo 2010 T

cabernet sauvignon, merlot, tempranillo

89

Colour: cherry, garnet rim. Nose: ripe fruit, spicy, creamy oak, complex. Palate: flavourful, toasty, round tannins.

Guelbenzu Lautus 2005 T

tempranillo, cabernet sauvignon, merlot, garnacha

90

Colour: ruby red, brick rim edge. Nose: elegant, spicy, fine reductive notes, tobacco. Palate: spicy, fine tannins, elegant, long.

Guelbenzu Vierlas 2012 T

syrah, merlot, graciano

86

VT VALDEJALÓN

THE GARAGE WINE

La Quimera del Oro 30 3D
50019 Zaragoza (Zaragoza)
☎: +34 669 148 771
info@thegaragewine.com
www.thegaragewine.com

Botijo Rojo 2011 T Roble

garnacha

88

Colour: cherry, purple rim. Nose: ripe fruit, woody, roasted coffee. Palate: flavourful, spicy, powerful.

Botijo Rojo 2013 T

garnacha

86

Estrambótico 2012 T

garnacha

90

Colour: bright cherry. Nose: ripe fruit, sweet spices, creamy oak, expressive. Palate: flavourful, toasty, ripe fruit.

Frontonio 2011 T Fermentado en Barrica

garnacha

92

Colour: cherry, garnet rim. Nose: ripe fruit, wild herbs, earthy notes, spicy, balsamic herbs. Palate: balanced, flavourful, long, balsamic.

Microcósmico 2014 B

macabeo

89

Colour: bright yellow. Nose: expressive, dried herbs, ripe fruit, spicy. Palate: flavourful, fruity, good acidity, balanced.

Telescópico 2014 B

macabeo, garnacha blanca, viognier

91

Colour: bright yellow. Nose: white flowers, fine lees, ripe fruit, citrus fruit, fragrant herbs. Palate: flavourful, fruity, good acidity, elegant.

TABLE WINES / WINE

Just outside the "Vino de Calidad" status, we find the "Vino de Mesa" ("Table Wine") category, which are those not included in any of the other categories (not even in the "Vino de la Tierra" one, regarded as "Vino de Mesa" by the Ley del Vino ("Wine Law"). The present editions of our Guide has up to 41 table wines rated as excellent, something which is quite telling, and force us to a change of mind in regard to the popular prejudice against this category, traditionally related –almost exclusively– to bulk, cheap wines.

In this section we include wines made in geographical areas that do not belong to any designation of origin (DO as such) or association of Vino de la Tierra, although most of them come indeed from wines regions with some vine growing and winemaking tradition.

We do not pretend to come up with a comprehensive account of the usually overlooked vinos de mesa (table wines), but to enumerate here some Spanish wines that were bottled with no geographic label whatsoever.

The wineries are listed alphabetically within their Autonomous regions. The reader will discover some singular wines of –in some cases– excellent quality that could be of interest to those on the look out for novelties or alternative products to bring onto their tables.

ALAN DE VAL

San Roque, 36
32350 A Rua de Valdeorras (Ourense)
☎: +34 988 310 431
Fax: +34 988 682 640
alandeval@alandeval.com
www.alandeval.com

Alan de Val Rosé 2014 RD

100% brancellao

85

ALEMANY I CORRIO

Melió, 78
08720 Vilafranca del Penedès (Barcelona)
☎: +34 938 180 949
sotlefriec@sotlefriec.com
www.alemany-corrio.com

El Microscopi 2013 T

merlot, cariñena, cabernet sauvignon

89

Colour: very deep cherry, purple rim. Nose: expressive, balanced, scrubland, spicy. Palate: correct, balanced.

ARCHS

Major, 9
43713 Lletger (Sant Jaume dels Domenys) (Tarragona)
☎: +34 605 228 760
info@archscellers.com
www.archscellers.com

Archs – Merlot Parc del Foix 2014 T

merlot

81

Archs – Xarel·lo 1953 2014 B

xarel.lo

86

ATTIS BODEGAS Y VIÑEDOS

Lg. Morouzos, 16D - Dena
36967 Meaño (Pontevedra)
☎: +34 986 744 790
administracion@attisbyv.com
www.attisbyv.com

Sitta Dulce Nana 2013 B

100% albariño

93

Colour: bright yellow. Nose: pungent, saline, dried herbs, citrus fruit, ripe fruit, wild herbs. Palate: powerful, flavourful, spicy, balanced, elegant. Personality.

Sitta Laranxa 2014 B

90

Colour: bright golden. Nose: faded flowers, ripe fruit, citrus fruit, dried herbs. Palate: fresh, flavourful, spicy, balsamic.

Sitta Pereiras 2013 B

100% albariño

91

Colour: bright yellow. Nose: citrus fruit, ripe fruit, balsamic herbs, floral, candied fruit. Palate: fresh, fruity, elegant, balanced.

BODEGA ALISTE

Pza. de España, 4
49520 Figueruela de Abajo (Zamora)
☎: +34 676 986 570
javier@hacedordevino.com
www.vinosdealiste.com

Geijo 2014 BFB

50% viura, 30% verdejo, 20% chardonnay

87

Colour: bright yellow. Nose: dried herbs, ripe fruit, spicy, earthy notes. Palate: flavourful, fruity, good acidity.

Marina de Aliste 2013 T

90% tempranillo, 10% syrah

91

Colour: cherry, garnet rim. Nose: ripe fruit, wild herbs, earthy notes, spicy, balsamic herbs. Palate: balanced, flavourful, long, balsamic.

BODEGA CAMPOS DE DULCINEA

Garay, 1
45820 El Toboso (Toledo)
☎: +34 925 568 163
Fax: +34 925 568 163
camposdedulcinea@camposdedulcinea.es
www.camposdedulcinea.es

Campos de Dulcinea 2014 ESP

macabeo

85 ♣

BODEGA CASTELL MIQUEL

Ctra. Alaró-Lloseta, Km. 8,7
07340 Alaró (Baleares)
☎: +34 971 510 698
Fax: +34 971 510 669
info@castellmiquel.com
www.castellmiquel.com

Stairway to Heaven 2014 RD

50% syrah, 50% cabernet sauvignon

86

Stairway to Heaven Sauvignon Blanc 2014 B
100% sauvignon blanc

87

Colour: bright straw. Nose: fresh fruit, fragrant herbs, expressive, varietal. Palate: flavourful, fruity, good acidity, balanced.

BODEGA JESÚS ROMERO
Martín I, nº1-2ªH
44415 Rubielos de Mora (Teruel)
☎: +34 659 917 677
juanvi.alcaniz@gmail.com
www.bodegajesusromero.com

Rubus 2014 T
garnacha, syrah, tempranillo

84

Rubus Quercus 2014 T
garnacha, syrah

88

Colour: bright cherry. Nose: ripe fruit, sweet spices, creamy oak, expressive. Palate: flavourful, fruity, toasty, round tannins.

BODEGA KIENINGER
Los Frontones, 67
29400 Ronda (Málaga)
☎: +34 952 879 554
martin@bodegakieninger.com
www.bodegakieninger.com

7 Vin Blaufraenkisch 2013 T
100% blaufraenkisch

91

Colour: deep cherry, purple rim. Nose: medium intensity, wild herbs, spicy, ripe fruit. Palate: ripe fruit, round tannins.

7 Vin Zweigelt 2013 TC
100% zweigelt

89

Colour: deep cherry, purple rim. Nose: dried herbs, ripe fruit, spicy. Palate: correct, balanced, easy to drink, good finish.

BODEGA MAS DE RANDER
Ctra. Torreblanca-Vilanova, km. 2,5
12180 Benlloch (Castellón)
☎: +34 964 302 416
masderander@masderander.com
www.masderander.com

Mistela Tinta de Rander Vino de Licor 2014 T
moscatel de alejandría, moscatel grano menudo, moscatel hamburgo

87

Colour: bright cherry, garnet rim. Nose: acetaldehyde, varnish, candied fruit, expressive. Palate: fruity, flavourful, sweet.

BODEGA PARDO TOLOSA
Villatoya, 26
02215 Alborea (Albacete)
☎: +34 963 517 067
Fax: +34 963 517 091
export@bodegapardotolosa.com
www.bodegapardotolosa.com

Mizaran Macabeo 2014 B
100% macabeo

85

Sensibel 2013 T
tempranillo, bobal

79

Sensibel 2014 B
macabeo

83

Sensibel 2014 RD
bobal

70

BODEGA RUA
Campo Grande, 97
32350 A Rua de Valdeorras (Ourense)
☎: +34 988 310 607
Fax: +34 988 312 016
market@cooperativarua.com
www.cooperativarua.com

Amavia 2014 B
godello

87

Colour: bright straw. Nose: dried herbs, faded flowers, ripe fruit, slightly evolved. Palate: ripe fruit, thin.

BODEGA SIESTO
Calle La Fuente, 14
49152 Sanzoles (Zamora)
☎: +34 657 689 542
contacto@bodegasiesto.com
www.bodegasiesto.com

Siesto 2013 T
bruñal, tempranillo, cabernet sauvignon

88

Colour: cherry, garnet rim. Nose: ripe fruit, wild herbs, earthy notes, spicy, balsamic herbs. Palate: balanced, flavourful, long, balsamic.

BODEGA SOLEDAD

Ctra. Tarancón, s/n
16411 Fuente de Pedro Naharro (Cuenca)
☎: +34 969 125 039
Fax: +34 969 125 907
asv@bodegasoledad.com
www.bodegasoledad.com

Kruberg Chardonnay 2013 B
chardonnay

80

Kruberg Syrah 2014 T
syrah

82

BODEGA VICENTE FLORS

Pda. Pou D'encalbo, s/n
12118 Les Useres (Castellón)
☎: +34 671 618 851
bodega@bodegaflors.com
www.bodegaflors.com

Clotàs 2010 T
85% tempranillo, 15% cabernet sauvignon

89

Colour: cherry, garnet rim. Nose: fine reductive notes, spicy, scrubland. Palate: spicy, long, toasty, correct.

BODEGAS AVANCIA

Parque Empresarial a Raña, 7
32300 O Barco de Valdeorras (Ourense)
☎: +34 952 504 706
Fax: +34 951 284 796
avancia@jorgeordonez.es
www.grupojorgeordonez.com

Avancia Rosé 2014 RD
100% mencía

89

Colour: rose, purple rim. Nose: red berry notes, floral, expressive. Palate: powerful, fruity, fresh, good acidity.

BODEGAS BRECA

Ctra. Monasterio de Piedra, s/n
50219 Munébrega (Zaragoza)
☎: +34 952 504 706
Fax: +34 951 284 796
breca@jorgeordonez.es
www.grupojorgeordonez.com

Garnacha de Fuego 2014 RD
90% garnacha, 10% viura

88

Colour: brilliant rose. Nose: red berry notes, floral. Palate: powerful, fruity.

Garnacha de Fuego 2014 T
100% garnacha

88

Colour: bright cherry, cherry, garnet rim. Nose: sweet spices, creamy oak, overripe fruit. Palate: flavourful, fruity, toasty, round tannins.

BODEGAS CABALLO

Plaza del Horno, 18
41500 Alcalá de Guadaíra (Sevilla)
☎: +34 615 490 203
info@bodegascaballo.com
www.bodegascaballo.com

Blanka 2014 B
100% riesling

87 ♣

Colour: bright yellow. Nose: white flowers, citrus fruit, ripe fruit. Palate: flavourful, fruity, fine bitter notes.

BODEGAS EJEANAS

Avda. Cosculluela, 23
50600 Ejea de los Caballeros (Zaragoza)
☎: +34 976 663 770
Fax: +34 976 663 770
pilar@bodegasejeanas.com
www.bodegasejeanas.com

Uva Nocturna 2014 B
chardonnay, verdejo, moscatel

86

Vega de Luchán Moscatel 2014 B
14,5% moscatel, verdejo

87

Colour: bright yellow. Nose: balsamic herbs, honeyed notes, floral, sweet spices, expressive. Palate: fruity, powerful, flavourful, fine bitter notes.

BODEGAS FONTEDEI

Doctor Horcajadas, 10
18570 Deifontes (Granada)
☎: +34 958 407 957
info@bodegasfontedei.es
www.bodegasfontedei.es

Garnata 2012 T
58% garnacha, 29% merlot, 13% syrah

87

Colour: deep cherry, purple rim. Nose: creamy oak, toasty, ripe fruit, balsamic herbs, fruit preserve. Palate: balanced, spicy, long.

Prado Negro 2012 T
57% cabernet sauvignon, 25% cabernet sauvignon, 18% merlot

86

BODEGAS GUTIÉRREZ DE LA VEGA

Les Quintanes, 1
03792 Parcent (Alicante)
☎: +34 966 403 871
info@bodegasgutierrezdelavega.es
www.bodegasgutierrezdelavega.es

Casta Diva Cosecha Dorada 2014 B
moscatel

91

Colour: bright yellow. Nose: white flowers, candied fruit, honeyed notes, fragrant herbs. Palate: fresh, fruity, balsamic, balanced.

Casta Diva Cosecha Miel Dulce 2013 B
moscatel

94

Colour: bright yellow. Nose: balsamic herbs, honeyed notes, floral, sweet spices, expressive. Palate: rich, fruity, powerful, flavourful, elegant.

PODIUM

Casta Diva Reserva Real Dulce 2002 B Reserva
moscatel

98

Colour: golden. Nose: powerfull, honeyed notes, candied fruit, fragrant herbs, acetaldehyde, sweet spices. Palate: flavourful, sweet, fresh, fruity, good acidity, long.

Furtiva Lágrima Dulce 2014 B
moscatel

92

Colour: bright yellow. Nose: honeyed notes, floral, sweet spices, expressive. Palate: rich, fruity, powerful, flavourful.

Imagine 2012 T
giró

91

Colour: cherry, garnet rim. Nose: ripe fruit, wild herbs, earthy notes, spicy, balsamic herbs. Palate: balanced, flavourful, long, balsamic.

Monte Diva Crianza Biológica 2013 MZ
moscatel

89

Colour: bright yellow. Nose: flor yeasts, lees reduction notes, pungent, ripe fruit, aged wood nuances. Palate: good acidity, spicy, long.

Príncipe de Salinas 2010 TC
monastrell

87

Colour: cherry, garnet rim. Nose: fine reductive notes, wild herbs, spicy. Palate: spicy, long, toasty.

PODIUM

Recóndita Armonía 1987 T
monastrell

95

Colour: mahogany. Nose: acetaldehyde, varnish, candied fruit, pattiserie, sweet spices. Palate: fruity, flavourful, sweet, balanced, elegant.

PODIUM

Recóndita Armonía 1978 Dulce T
monastrell

98

Colour: mahogany. Nose: fruit preserve, dry nuts, acetaldehyde, spicy, creamy oak, expressive. Palate: powerful, flavourful, spicy, long, balsamic, balanced, elegant.

PODIUM

Recóndita Armonía 1979 Dulce T
monastrell

96

Colour: mahogany. Nose: ripe fruit, fruit liqueur notes, spicy, acetaldehyde, sweet spices, dry nuts. Palate: powerful, rich, flavourful, sweet, elegant, balanced.

PODIUM

Recóndita Armonía Dulce 1985 T
monastrell

95

Colour: light mahogany. Nose: powerfull, complex, dry nuts, toasty, acetaldehyde, varnish, spicy. Palate: rich, long, fine solera notes, spicy, round, sweet, elegant.

Recóndita Armonía Dulce 2013 T
monastrell

92

Colour: cherry, garnet rim. Nose: fruit preserve, spicy, fruit liqueur notes. Palate: powerful, flavourful, sweet, rich, balanced.

Rojo y Negro 2010 T
giró

88

Colour: cherry, garnet rim. Nose: complex, ripe fruit, spicy, fine reductive notes. Palate: good structure, flavourful, round tannins, balanced.

Ulises 2012 T
giró, monastrell, syrah

87

Colour: deep cherry. Nose: creamy oak, toasty, ripe fruit, grassy. Palate: balanced, spicy, long.

BODEGAS HACIENDA DEL CARCHE

Ctra. del Carche, Km. 8,3
30520 Jumilla (Murcia)
☎: +34 968 975 942
info@haciendadelcarche.com
www.haciendadelcarche.com

Escarche Dulce
monastrell

85

BODEGAS LAHOZ

Ctra. N-310 Tomelloso-Villarrobledo
Km. 108,5
13630 Socuéllamos (Ciudad Real)
☎: +34 926 699 083
Fax: +34 926 514 929
info@bodegaslahoz.com
www.bodegaslahoz.com

Sol de Lahoz 2014 B
95% airén, 5% sauvignon blanc

82

Sol de Lahoz 2014 T
100% tempranillo

80

BODEGAS MÁLAGA VIRGEN

Autovía A-92, Km. 132
29520 Fuente de Piedra (Málaga)
☎: +34 952 319 454
Fax: +34 952 359 819
bodegas@bodegasmalagavirgen.com
www.bodegasmalagavirgen.com

Moscatel Naranja B
moscatel

86

BODEGAS MARCOS MIÑAMBRES

Camino de Pobladura, s/n
24234 Villamañán (León)
☎: +34 987 767 038
satvined@picos.com

Los Silvares 2013 B Roble
85

M. Miñambres Albarín S/C B
82

M. Miñambres s/c RD
cencibel, prieto picudo

80

M. Miñambres S/C T
82

BODEGAS MARQUÉS DE VIZHOJA

Finca La Moreira s/n
36438 Cequeliños - Arbo (Pontevedra)
☎: +34 986 665 825
Fax: +34 986 665 960
marquesdevizhoja@marquesdevizhoja.com
www.marquesdevizhoja.com

Finca Lobeira 2014 B
100% albariño

88

Colour: bright straw. Nose: white flowers, fine lees, dried herbs. Palate: flavourful, fruity, good acidity, round.

Marqués de Vizhoja 2014 B
85

BODEGAS PÁEZ MORILLA

Avda. Medina Sidonia, 20
11406 Jerez de la Frontera (Cádiz)
☎: +34 956 181 717
Fax: +34 956 181 534
bodegas@paezmorilla.com
www.paezmorilla.com

Risa de Aguja B
moscatel de alejandría

84

Tierra Blanca Semidulce 2014 B
85

BODEGAS SERRANO

Finca La Cabaña, 30 Pozo Estrecho
30594 Cartagena (Murcia)
☎: +34 968 556 298
Fax: +34 968 556 298
info@bodegasserrano.es
www.bodegasserrano.es

Darimus Syrah Dulce 2014 T
syrah

89

Colour: cherry, garnet rim. Nose: fruit preserve, spicy, warm, fruit liqueur notes. Palate: powerful, flavourful, sweet, rich, balanced.

Viña Galtea Moscatel Semiseco 2014 B
moscatel

84

BODEGAS SIERRA DE GUARA

Fray Luis Urbano, 27
50002 Lascellas (Zaragoza)
☎: +34 976 461 056
Fax: +34 976 461 558
idrias@bodegassierradeguara.es
www.bodegassierradeguara.es

Idrias Chardonnay batonage sobre lías 2014 B

88

Colour: bright straw. Nose: white flowers, fine lees, dried herbs. Palate: flavourful, fruity, good acidity, round.

Idrias 2014 B

85

Idrias 2014 RD

87

Colour: rose, purple rim. Nose: red berry notes, floral, expressive. Palate: powerful, fruity, fresh.

Idrias Abiego 2013 T

88

Colour: cherry, garnet rim. Nose: creamy oak, toasty, ripe fruit, balsamic herbs. Palate: balanced, spicy, long.

Idrias Sevil 2008 T

87

Colour: cherry, garnet rim. Nose: ripe fruit, old leather, tobacco. Palate: correct, flavourful, spicy, fine bitter notes.

BODEGAS TORRES

Miguel Torres i Carbó, 6
08720 Vilafranca del Penedès
(Barcelona)
☎: +34 938 177 400
Fax: +34 938 177 444
mailadmin@torres.es
www.torres.com

Floralis Moscatel Oro de Licor Moscatel

moscatel de alejandría

85

BODEGAS VALDECUEVAS

Ctra. Rueda- Nava del Rey, Km 2,5
47490 Rueda (Valladolid)
☎: +34 983 034 356
Fax: +34 983 034 356
bodega@valdecuevas.es
www.valdecuevas.es

Diwine Frizzante B

83

BODEGAS VICENTE GANDÍA

Ctra. Cheste a Godelleta, s/n
46370 Chiva (Valencia)
☎: +34 962 524 242
Fax: +34 962 524 243
info@vicentegandia.com
www.vicentegandia.es

Hoya de Cadenas Organic Tempranillo 2013 T

100% tempranillo

85 ♣

Hoya de Cadenas Organic Verdejo 2014 B

100% verdejo

85 ♣

Sandara Blanco ESP

verdejo, sauvignon blanc, viura

82

Sandara Rosado ESP

100% bobal

82

Sandara Tinto ESP

bobal, monastrell, cabernet sauvignon

82

Vicente Gandía Organic Tempranillo 2014 T

100% tempranillo

86 ♣

Vicente Gandía Organic Verdejo 2014 B

100% verdejo

86 ♣

Whatever it Takes by David Bowie 2012 T

100% syrah

86

Whatever it Takes by George Clooney 2012 T

100% cabernet sauvignon

85

Whatever it Takes by Pierce Brosnan 2012 T

100% tempranillo

86

BODEGAS Y VIÑEDOS CASTIBLANQUE

Isaac Peral, 19
13610 Campo de Criptana
(Ciudad Real)
☎: +34 926 589 147
Fax: +34 926 589 148
info@bodegascastiblanque.com
www.bodegascastiblanque.com

Amá Garnacha S/C T Roble
100% garnacha

85

Baldor Tradición Chardonnay 2013 BFB
100% chardonnay

88

Colour: bright yellow. Nose: ripe fruit, powerfull, toasty, aged wood nuances. Palate: flavourful, fruity, spicy, toasty.

Lagar de Ensancha s/c T
48% tempranillo, 36% cabernet sauvignon, 16% syrah

79

Solamente 2014 RD
100% syrah

85

Solamente S/C B
50% verdejo, 50% airén

83

Solamente s/c T
80% syrah, 20% tempranillo

83

Zumo de Amor s/c T
50% syrah, 50% tempranillo

83

BODEGAS Y VIÑEDOS CERRO DEL ÁGUILA

Avda. de Toledo, 23
45127 Las Ventas con Peña Aguilera
(Toledo)
☎: +34 625 443 153
bodegascerrodelaguila@gmail.com

Malabra 2013 T
garnacha, cencibel

90

Colour: deep cherry, purple rim. Nose: creamy oak, toasty, ripe fruit, balsamic herbs. Palate: balanced, spicy, long, elegant.

Puerto Carbonero 2013 T
garnacha

92

Colour: light cherry, garnet rim. Nose: expressive, complex, mineral, balsamic herbs, balanced. Palate: full, flavourful, round tannins. Personality.

Vereda del Lobo 2013 T
garnacha, otras

91

Colour: light cherry, garnet rim. Nose: fruit liqueur notes, spicy, wild herbs, expressive. Palate: powerful, flavourful, good structure.

BODEGAS Y VIÑEDOS GARAY

Avda. de Sevilla, 76
21700 La Palma del Condado (Huelva)
☎: +34 617 423 368
mario@bodegasgaray.com
www.bodegasgaray.com

Garay BLEU 2014 B
100% zalema

89

Colour: bright golden. Nose: complex, balanced, faded flowers, spicy. Palate: rich, flavourful, long, fine bitter notes.

Garay RED 2014 B
100% zalema

87

Colour: golden. Nose: creamy oak, sweet spices. Palate: ripe fruit, correct, balanced.

CAVAS DEL AMPURDÁN

Pza. del Carme, 1
17491 Perelada (Girona)
☎: +34 972 538 011
Fax: +34 972 538 277
perelada@castilloperelada.com
www.blancpescador.com

Blanc Pescador Premium Blanco de aguja
67% xarel.lo, 33% chardonnay

84

Blanc Pescador Verdejo Vino de aguja B
90% verdejo, 10% sauvignon blanc

83

Blanc Pescador Vino de aguja B
60% macabeo, 20% parellada, 20% xarel.lo

82

Cresta Azul de Aguja B
60% moscatel, 30% xarel.lo, 10% parellada

83

Cresta Rosa Premium Rosado de aguja
85% pinot noir, 15% syrah

84

Cresta Rosa Vino de Aguja RD
70% tempranillo, 25% merlot, 5% cabernet sauvignon

82

Rosé Pescador Rosado de aguja
40% trepat, 30% merlot, 15% garnacha, 15% tempranillo

83

CELLER COOPERATIU D'ESPOLLA

Ctra. Roses, s/n
17753 Espolla (Gerona)
☎: +34 972 563 178
Fax: +34 972 563 178
info@celleresspolla.com
www.celleresspolla.com

Babalà Vi Blanc Simpàtic 2014 B
cariñena blanca, moscatel de alejandría

84

Negre Jove 2014 T
lladoner blanco, lladoner roig, lladoner

86

Vins de Postal - Bassedes 2011 T
lladoner

91

Colour: light cherry. Nose: fruit expression, fragrant herbs, spicy, creamy oak. Palate: balanced, elegant, spicy.

Vins de Postal – El Beurac 2013 B
lladoner

90

Colour: bright yellow. Nose: ripe fruit, toasty, pattiserie. Palate: flavourful, fruity, spicy, toasty, long.

Vins de Postal – La Cardonera 2013 B
cariñena blanca

91

Colour: bright straw. Nose: ripe fruit, sweet spices, creamy oak. Palate: flavourful, complex, rich, balanced.

Vinya Orlina Negre 2014 T
lladoner, cariñena

85

CELLER LA VINYETA

Ctra. de Mollet de Peralada
a Masarac, s/n
17752 Mollet de Peralada (Girona)
☎: +34 630 405 118
celler@lavinyeta.es
www.lavinyeta.es

Mig Mig 2012 T
marselan, garnacha gris

88

Colour: very deep cherry, garnet rim. Nose: powerfull, fruit preserve, dark chocolate. Palate: powerful, long, balsamic, round tannins.

Sereno 2009 Solera
garnacha gris

90

Colour: light mahogany. Nose: acetaldehyde, pungent, varnish, aged wood nuances, creamy oak. Palate: powerful, flavourful, spicy, long, balanced.

CLOS DELS CIMS

Avda. Royal, 308
08474 Gualba (Barcelona)
☎: +34 678 889 808
romerolluis@hotmail.com
www.closdelscims.blogspot.com

Clos dels Cims 2014 T
100% syrah

88 🌿

Colour: light cherry, garnet rim. Nose: fruit liqueur notes, fragrant herbs, floral, violets, mineral. Palate: fruity, flavourful, balsamic.

CLOT DE LES SOLERES

Heretat Ferrer de La Vall
08784 Piera (Balcelona)
☎: +34 644 223 075
clotdelessoleres@gmail.com

Clot de Les Soleres 2014 RD

81 🌿

Clot de Les Soleres Cabernet Sauvignon 2011 T
cabernet sauvignon

70 🌿

Clot de Les Soleres dulce 2013 RD
cabernet sauvignon

85 🌿

Clot de Les Soleres Macabeo 2013 B
macabeo

89

Colour: bright straw. Nose: dried herbs, faded flowers, ripe fruit, slightly evolved. Palate: ripe fruit, spicy.

Clot de Les Soleres Semidulce 2012 RD
cabernet sauvignon

83

Clot de Les Soleres Xarel.lo 2014 B
xarel.lo

88

Colour: bright straw. Nose: white flowers, fine lees, dried herbs, citrus fruit, ripe fruit. Palate: flavourful, fruity, good acidity, round.

COMPAÑÍA DE VINOS LA ZORRA

San Pedro, s/n
37610 Mogarraz (Salamanca)
☎: +34 609 392 591
Fax: +34 923 418 018
estanverdes@vinoslazorra.es
www.vinoslazorra.es

8 Virgenes Serranas 2014 B
palomino, moscatel, rufete blenco

93

Colour: bright straw. Nose: white flowers, fresh fruit, fragrant herbs. Palate: flavourful, fruity, good acidity, balanced.

COMPAÑÍA DE VINOS MIGUEL MARTÍN

Ctra. Burgos - Portugal, Km. 101
47290 Cubillas de Santa María (Valladolid)
☎: +34 983 250 319
Fax: +34 983 250 929
comercial@ciadevinos.com
www.ciadevinos.com

Martín Verástegui Dulce B
pedro ximénez

89

Colour: old gold, amber rim. Nose: honeyed notes, floral, sweet spices. Palate: rich, fruity, powerful, flavourful.

CORTIJO DE LAS MONJAS

Estación de Parchite, 104
29400 Ronda (Málaga)
☎: +34 913 878 612
www.haciendas-espana.com

Ándalus Petit Verdot 2006 T

90

Colour: cherry, garnet rim. Nose: ripe fruit, wild herbs, earthy notes, spicy, balsamic herbs. Palate: balanced, flavourful, long, balsamic.

COSTADOR TERROIRS MEDITERRANIS

43002 Vila-Seca El Molar (Tarragona)
☎: +34 657 397 375
info@costador.net
www.costador.net

1954 Xarel.lo 2014 B
100% xarel.lo

88

Colour: coppery red. Nose: dried flowers, dry nuts. Palate: flavourful, full, correct, fine bitter notes, good acidity.

La Fassina Pinot Radical Biodinàmic 2014 T
100% pinot noir

89

Colour: light cherry. Nose: fruit liqueur notes, fragrant herbs, spicy, creamy oak. Palate: spicy, long, toasty, balsamic.

La Presa Romana 1905 2014 B
100% macabeo

89

Colour: straw, pale. Nose: ripe fruit, balanced, dried herbs, dried flowers, expressive. Palate: flavourful, fruity, fine bitter notes.

COTO DE GOMARIZ

Barro de Gomariz s/n
32429 Leiro (Ourense)
☎: +34 988 488 741
Fax: +34 988 488 174
mmontoto@cotodegomariz.com
www.cotodegomariz.com

VX Cuvée Caco 2008 T
sousón, caiño longo, caiño da terra, carabuñeira, mencía

89

Colour: cherry, garnet rim. Nose: smoky, spicy, ripe fruit, toasty. Palate: flavourful, smoky aftertaste, ripe fruit, good structure.

VX Cuvée Primo 2007 T
sausón, caiño longo, caiño da terra, carabuñeira, mencía

91

Colour: cherry, garnet rim. Nose: red berry notes, fresh fruit, balanced, wild herbs. Palate: flavourful, spicy, balanced.

DANIEL RAMOS

San Pedro de Alcántara, 1
05270 El Tiemblo (Ávila)
☎: +34 687 410 952
dvrcru@gmail.com
www.daniel-ramos.es

Zerberos Dair 2013 T
garnacha

91

Colour: light cherry. Nose: fruit liqueur notes, fragrant herbs, spicy, creamy oak. Palate: balanced, elegant, spicy, long, toasty.

Zerberos Viento Zephyros 2013 B Roble
albillo, sauvignon blanc

89

Colour: bright yellow. Nose: dried herbs, spicy, fruit liqueur notes, slightly evolved. Palate: flavourful, fruity, good acidity, balanced.

Kπ Amphorae 2013 T
garnacha

89

Colour: bright cherry. Nose: sweet spices, creamy oak, fruit liqueur notes. Palate: flavourful, fruity, balanced.

Kπ Rosé 2012 RD
garnacha

91

Colour: onion pink. Nose: elegant, red berry notes, floral, fragrant herbs. Palate: light-bodied, flavourful, good acidity, long, spicy.

Kπ White 2014 B
sauvignon blanc

90

Colour: golden. Nose: ripe fruit, wild herbs, dry stone, faded flowers. Palate: powerful, flavourful, rich, fine bitter notes.

DOMINIO DEL BENDITO

Pza. Santo Domingo, 8
49800 Toro (Zamora)
☎: +34 980 693 306
Fax: +34 980 694 991
info@bodegadominiodelbendito.es
www.bodegadominiodelbendito.es

La Chispa Negra Dulce 2009 T
tinta de Toro

91

Colour: cherry, garnet rim. Nose: fruit preserve, spicy, warm, fruit liqueur notes. Palate: powerful, flavourful, sweet, rich.

EDRA BODEGA Y VIÑEDOS

Ctra A - 132, km 26
22800 Ayerbe (Huesca)
☎: +34 679 420 455
edra@bodega-edra.com
www.bodega-edra.com

Edra Blancoluz 2013 B
viognier

88

Colour: bright yellow. Nose: ripe fruit, spicy, dry nuts, citrus fruit, wild herbs. Palate: powerful, flavourful, long.

EL ESCOCÉS VOLANTE

Barrio La Rosa Bajo, 16
50300 Calatayud (Zaragoza)
☎: +34 637 511 133
info@escocesvolante.es
www.escocesvolante.es

Mandat Opus Caña Andrea 2014 T
95% garnacha, 5% morrastel, bobal

92

Colour: cherry, garnet rim. Nose: ripe fruit, wild herbs, balsamic herbs, dry stone. Palate: balanced, flavourful, long, balsamic.

Mandat Opus Carramainas 2014 B
85% macabeo, 15% otras

89

Colour: bright yellow. Nose: candied fruit, dried herbs. Palate: flavourful, fruity.

ENVINATE

Gran Vía, 2 1ºC
27600 Sarría (Lugo)
☎: +34 682 207 160
asesoria@envinate.es
www.envinate.com

Albahra 2014 T
garnacha tintorera

91

Colour: cherry, garnet rim. Nose: medium intensity, balsamic herbs, ripe fruit, fruit liqueur notes. Palate: powerful, flavourful, mineral, balanced.

Puzzle 2014 T
garnacha, touriga nacional, monastrell

89

Colour: cherry, purple rim. Nose: powerfull, ripe fruit, spicy, dried herbs. Palate: fruity, flavourful, balanced.

T Amarela 2014 T
trincadeira preta

93

Colour: cherry, garnet rim. Nose: fresh fruit, balanced, red berry notes, ripe fruit, creamy oak. Palate: flavourful, spicy, elegant.

Táganan 2014 B
malvasía, marmajuelo, albillo, vijariego blanco, gual, listán blanco

92

Colour: bright straw. Nose: dried herbs, faded flowers, smoky, spicy, saline. Palate: fresh, fruity, balsamic.

Táganan 2014 T
negramoll, listán negro, baboso negro, vijariego negro, malvasía negra

92

Colour: cherry, garnet rim. Nose: smoky, damp earth, balsamic herbs. Palate: flavourful, complex, good acidity, balanced.

Táganan Parcela Amogoje 2014 B
malvasía, marmajuelo, forastera, albillo, vijariego blanco, gual

93

Colour: bright yellow. Nose: balsamic herbs, faded flowers, mineral, candied fruit. Palate: flavourful, good acidity, spicy, mineral, balanced.

Táganan Parcela Margaelagua 2014 T
negramoll, listán negro, baboso negro, vijariego negro, malvasía negra, moscatel negra

92

Colour: light cherry. Nose: floral, wild herbs, red berry notes, fruit liqueur notes. Palate: balanced, powerful, flavourful.

EQUIPO NAVAZOS

11403 Jerez de la Frontera (Cádiz)
equipo@navazos.com
www.equiponavazos.com

PODIUM

La Bota de Florpower nº57 MMXII 2012 B

95

Colour: bright yellow. Nose: dried herbs, candied fruit, fruit preserve, iodine notes. Palate: complex.

PODIUM

Navazos Niepoort 2014 B

95

Colour: bright straw. Nose: faded flowers, candied fruit, saline. Palate: full, good acidity.

FINCA VALLDOSERA

Masia Les Garrigues, s/n
08734 Olèrdola (Barcelona)
☎: +34 938 143 047
Fax: +34 938 935 590
general@fincavalldosera.com
www.fincavalldosera.com

Finca Valldosera Subirat Parent 2013 B
100% subirat parent

88

Colour: bright yellow. Nose: expressive, ripe fruit, spicy, faded flowers. Palate: flavourful, fruity, good acidity, balanced.

Finca Valldosera Syrah Merlot 2013 RD
syrah, merlot

85

Finca Valldosera Syrah Merlot Cabernet 2013 T
syrah, merlot, cabernet sauvignon

86

Finca Valldosera Xarel.lo 2013 B
xarel.lo

88

Colour: bright straw. Nose: white flowers, fresh fruit, fragrant herbs, expressive. Palate: flavourful, fruity, good acidity, balanced.

GONZALO CELAYETA WINES

Barrandón, 6
31390 Olite (Navarra)
☎: +34 620 208 817
info@gonzalocelayetawines.com
www.gonzalocelayetawines.com

Pura Maturana 2013 B
maturana blanca

87

Colour: bright yellow. Nose: ripe fruit, powerfull, toasty, aged wood nuances, dried herbs. Palate: flavourful, fruity, spicy, long.

GUY ANDERSON WINES LTD.

Ctra. N-2 km. 341
50172 Alfajarin (Zaragoza)
☎: +34 976 140 473
Fax: +34 976 140 268
chris@guyandersonwines.co.uk
www.guyandersonwines.co.uk

El Burro Garnacha 2013 T
100% garnacha

88

Colour: deep cherry, purple rim. Nose: creamy oak, toasty, ripe fruit, balsamic herbs. Palate: balanced, spicy, long.

El Burro Garnacha 2014 T
garnacha

87

Colour: cherry, purple rim. Nose: powerfull, ripe fruit, spicy. Palate: powerful, fruity, unctuous.

HENOBA
Virtudes, 13
13340 Albaladejo (Ciudad Real)
☎: +34 629 849 634
info@lagardebesada.com
www.lagardebesada.com

Henoba Vino de Autor 2012 T
tempranillo

86

HERETAT ANTIGUA, CASA SICILIA 1707
Paraje Alcaydias, 4
03660 Novelda (Alicante)
☎: +34 965 605 385
Fax: +34 965 604 763
administracin@casasicilia1707.es
www.casacesilia.com

Ad Gaude 2009 TR
monastrell, syrah, petit verdot

89

Colour: cherry, garnet rim. Nose: roasted coffee, smoky, spicy, ripe fruit. Palate: flavourful, smoky aftertaste, ripe fruit, full.

JAVIER SANZ VITICULTOR
San Judas, 2
47491 La Seca (Valladolid)
☎: +34 983 816 669
info@bodegajaviersanz.com
www.bodegajaviersanz.com

V Dulce de Invierno Vendimia Tardía B
80% verdejo, 20% moscatel

91

Colour: bright golden. Nose: candied fruit, honeyed notes, floral, sweet spices. Palate: balanced, flavourful, unctuous.

JORGE ORDÓÑEZ & CO
Bartolome Esteban Murillo, 11
29700 Velez-Málaga (Málaga)
☎: +34 952 504 706
Fax: +34 951 284 796
info@jorgeordonez.es
www.grupojorgeordonez.com

Botani Dulce ESP
100% moscatel de alejandría

87

Colour: bright straw. Nose: candied fruit, white flowers, fragrant herbs. Palate: fresh, fruity, flavourful, sweet.

Botani Seco 2014 ESP
100% moscatel de alejandría

89

Colour: bright straw. Nose: floral, fragrant herbs, candied fruit, citrus fruit. Palate: fresh, fruity, flavourful.

LA CALANDRIA. PURA GARNACHA
Camino de Aspra, s/n
31521 Murchante (Navarra)
☎: +34 610 438 879
remacha@lacalandria.org
www.puragarnacha.com

Tierga 2010 T
garnacha

90

Colour: cherry, garnet rim. Nose: creamy oak, ripe fruit, balsamic herbs. Palate: spicy, long, balanced.

MAS COMTAL
Mas Comtal, 1
08793 Avinyonet del Penedès
(Barcelona)
☎: +34 938 970 052
Fax: +34 938 970 591
mascomtal@mascomtal.com
www.mascomtal.com

Antistiana Incrocio Manzoni 2013 B
Incroccio manzoni

90

Colour: bright yellow. Nose: powerfull, citrus fruit, ripe fruit, wild herbs. Palate: powerful, flavourful, fine bitter notes.

PODIUM

Lyric Vino de Licor Dulce Vino de Licor Gran Reserva
merlot

95

Colour: mahogany. Nose: spicy, creamy oak, roasted almonds, varnish, acetaldehyde, pungent. Palate: powerful, flavourful, spicy, long, balanced, elegant.

Mas Comtal Pizzicato Frizzante 2014 RD
moscatel

85

MAS DE LA CAÇADORA

Avinguda de la Ctra., 9
43777 Els Guiamets (Tarragona)
☎: +34 656 336 877
masdelacasadora@yahoo.es
www.masdelacasadora.com

Brugent 2013 B

xarel.lo, garnacha blanca, macabeo

92

Colour: bright straw. Nose: white flowers, fine lees, dried herbs, ripe fruit, wild herbs, mineral. Palate: flavourful, fruity, good acidity, elegant.

Rosa La Guapa 2011 T

90% cariñena, 5% merlot, 5% garnacha

93

Colour: deep cherry, garnet rim. Nose: spicy, warm, scrubland, ripe fruit. Palate: balanced, ripe fruit, long.

Rosa la Guapa 2014 B

90% garnacha blanca, 10% moscatel de alejandría

89

Colour: bright yellow. Nose: expressive, dried herbs, ripe fruit, spicy, honeyed notes. Palate: flavourful, fruity, good acidity.

MAS DE LA REAL DE SELLA

Calle Sella, 42
03570 Villajoyosa (Alicante)
☎: +34 699 308 250
info@masdelarealdesella.es
www.masdelarealdesella.es

Mas de Sella Carreró 2010 TR

garnacha, cabernet franc, marselan, syrah, cabernet sauvignon

92

Colour: cherry, garnet rim. Nose: spicy, earthy notes, scrubland. Palate: flavourful, ripe fruit, long, good acidity, balanced.

Mas de Sella Selección 2012 T

garnacha, cabernet franc, marselan, syrah, cabernet sauvignon

90

Colour: very deep cherry, garnet rim. Nose: expressive, balsamic herbs, balanced, waxy notes. Palate: full, flavourful, round tannins.

MUSTIGUILLO VIÑEDOS Y BODEGA

Ctra. N-330 km. 196
46300 Utiel (Valencia)
☎: +34 962 168 260
Fax: +34 962 168 259
info@bodegamustiguillo.com
www.bodegamustiguillo.com

Mestizaje 2014 B

60% merseguera, 40% viognier, malvasía

91

Colour: bright yellow. Nose: dried herbs, ripe fruit, spicy. Palate: flavourful, fruity, good acidity, balanced.

NIÑO DE LA SALINA

Corredera s/n
29330 Almargen (Málaga)
☎: +34 952 182 608
Fax: +34 952 182 609
info@fontalbacapote.es
www.fontalbacapote.es

Al Fresco 2014 B

sauvignon blanc

86

Al Fresco 2014 RD

garnacha

86

Al Fresco Dulce 2014 T

syrah

84

PAGO DE ALMARAES

Ctra. de Fonelas, Km. 1,5
18510 Benalúa de Guadix (Granada)
☎: +34 958 348 752
info@bodegaspagodealmaraes.es
www.bodegaspagodealmaraes.es

Almaraes 2013 T Roble

100% syrah

80

Elvira 2014 B

100% vijiriego

83

Mencal 2014 B

95% moscatel de alejandría, 5% chardonnay, sauvignon blanc

86

Mil Años un Reino Frizzante 2014 B

100% moscatel

84

Mil Años un Reino Frizzante 2014 RD
syrah, tempranillo, merlot, cabernet sauvignon, cabernet franc

84

Ribera del Farbes 2014 T
syrah, tempranillo, cabernet sauvignon, cabernet franc

85

PAGO DE LA ROGATIVA
Paraje de La Rogativa. Finca "Casas de Alfaro" Polígono 30 Parcela 9
30440 Moratalla (Murcia)
☎: +34 615 689 083
info@pagodelarogativa.es
www.pagodelarogativa.es

Viñedo de la Rogativa 2012 T
90

Colour: bright cherry. Nose: ripe fruit, sweet spices, creamy oak, expressive. Palate: flavourful, fruity, round tannins.

PAGO DE THARSYS
Ctra. Nacional III, km. 274
46340 Requena (Valencia)
☎: +34 962 303 354
Fax: +34 962 329 000
pagodetharsys@pagodetharsys.com
www.pagodetharsys.com

Pago de Tharsys Selección Bodega 2004 T
90% merlot, 10% cabernet franc

90

Colour: pale ruby, brick rim edge. Nose: spicy, fine reductive notes, wet leather, aged wood nuances, fruit liqueur notes. Palate: spicy, fine tannins, balanced.

Pago de Tharsys Nuestro Bobal 2010 T
85% bobal, 15% cabernet franc

86

Pago de Tharsys Vendimia Nocturna 2014 B
albariño

88 ♣

Colour: bright straw. Nose: fresh fruit, white flowers, balsamic herbs, expressive. Palate: powerful, flavourful, long, spicy.

PAGO DIANA
Pago Diana, Manso Sant Mateu s/n
17464 Sant Jordi Desvalls (Girona)
☎: +34 666 395 251
info@pagodiana.com
www.pagodiana.com

Ninfas 2012 B
verdejo, gewürztraminer

75

PALACIO DE CANEDO
La Iglesia, s/n
24546 Canedo (León)
☎: +34 987 563 366
Fax: +34 987 567 000
info@pradaatope.es
www.pradaatope.es

Pardoxin Dulce Natural 2011 B
godello

91

Colour: bright yellow. Nose: balsamic herbs, honeyed notes, floral, sweet spices, expressive. Palate: rich, fruity, powerful, flavourful, elegant.

PARDAS
Finca Can Comas, s/n
08775 Torrelavit (Barcelona)
☎: +34 938 995 005
pardas@cancomas.com
www.cellerpardas.com

Pardas Sumoll Rosat 2014 RD
88

Colour: rose, purple rim. Nose: red berry notes, floral, expressive. Palate: powerful, fruity, fresh.

PÉREZ CARAMÉS
Peña Picón, s/n
24500 Villafranca del Bierzo (León)
☎: +34 987 540 197
enoturismo@perezcarames.com
www.perezcarames.com

Casar de Santa Inés 2013 T
47% merlot, 30% tempranillo, 17% pinot noir, 6% mencía

84 ♣

Casar de Santa Inés Pi9 1999 T
100% pinot noir

85 ♣

ROSELL MIR
Bario El Rebato s/n
08739 Subirats (Barcelona)
☎: +34 938 911 354
infoceller@rosellmir.com
www.rosellmir.com

Pla de la Creu 2014 B
xarel.lo

85

Pla de la Creu 2014 RD
syrah, merlot

84

Pla de la Creu Negre 2012 T
cabernet sauvignon, merlot

85

SEÑORÍO DE VALDESNEROS
Avda. La Paz, 4
34230 Torquemada (Palencia)
☎: +34 979 800 545
Fax: +34 979 800 545
sv@bodegasvaldesneros.com
www.bodegasvaldesneros.com

Amantia Naturalmente Dulce 2012 T
tempranillo

88

Colour: coppery red, bright. Nose: balanced, powerfull, dried fruit, floral. Palate: correct, long, easy to drink.

SEXTO ELEMENTO
C/Caliches, 13
46310 Venta del Moro (Valencia)
☎: +34 637 414 137
bodega@@vinosextoelemento.com
www.vinosextoelemento.com

6º Elemento 2012 T
100% bobal

92

Colour: cherry, garnet rim. Nose: ripe fruit, wild herbs, earthy notes, spicy, balsamic herbs. Palate: balanced, flavourful, long, balsamic, elegant.

SISTEMA VINARI
Antiga Ctra. de Manacor, 168
07200 Felanitx (Islas Baleares)
☎: +34 650 131 472
eloi@sistemavinari.com
www.sistemavinari.com

Chateau Paquita 2013 T
45% callet, 30% manto negro, 25% monastrell

90

Colour: light cherry, purple rim. Nose: characterful, expressive, red berry notes, faded flowers. Palate: balanced, spicy, easy to drink.

TERRUÑOS ÚNICOS
Plaza de España, 19
45211 Recas (Toledo)
☎: +34 925 522 979
Fax: +34 925 522 978
terrunosunicos@gmail.com

Galbana Vino de Parcela 2012 T
tempranillo

89

Colour: bright cherry. Nose: sweet spices, creamy oak, candied fruit, overripe fruit. Palate: flavourful, fruity, toasty, round tannins.

La Bicicleta 2011 T
tempranillo

91

Colour: very deep cherry, garnet rim. Nose: wild herbs, pungent, characterful, ripe fruit. Palate: good structure, full, powerful, powerful tannins.

TRESGE WINERY
Calle A, 12
02200 Casas Ibañez (Albacete)
☎: +34 676 599 583
gratias@gratiaswines.com
www.gratiaswines.com

Gratias Blanc 2014 B
100% tardana

88

Colour: bright yellow. Nose: expressive, dried herbs, ripe fruit, spicy. Palate: flavourful, fruity, good acidity, balanced.

Gratias Máximas 2013 T
100% bobal

89

Colour: bright cherry. Nose: ripe fruit, sweet spices, creamy oak, wild herbs. Palate: flavourful, fruity, toasty.

Gratias Rosé 2014 RD
100% bobal

86

UVADEVIDA
Cañuelo, 8
45180 Camarena (Toledo)
☎: +34 667 252 158
uvadevida@uvadevida.com
www.uvadevida.com

Latitud 40 (Etiqueta Color) 2013 T

89

Colour: very deep cherry. Nose: expressive, complex, mineral, balsamic herbs, fruit preserve. Palate: full, flavourful, spicy.

Latitud 40 (Etiqueta Oro) 2012 T
100% graciano

90

Colour: cherry, garnet rim. Nose: ripe fruit, spicy, fine reductive notes, balsamic herbs. Palate: good structure, flavourful, balanced, powerful.

VINOS DON ANGEL

Camino Adais 6A
38789 Puntagorda (La PAlma)
donangel@don-angel.net
www.don-angel.net

Don Angel 2014 RD
tempranillo, verdejo

83

Don Angel Angelayo 2007 T
cabernet sauvignon, tempranillo, listán prieto

88

Colour: pale ruby, brick rim edge. Nose: spicy, fine reductive notes, wet leather, aged wood nuances, fruit liqueur notes. Palate: spicy, fine tannins, balanced.

Don Angel Angelayo 2008 T
cabernet sauvignon, tempranillo, listán prieto

86

Don Angel Blanco Doña 2014 B
verdejo, sauvignon blanc

84

Don Angel Tintórico 2008 T
cabernet sauvignon, tempranillo

87

Colour: cherry, garnet rim. Nose: smoky, spicy, ripe fruit, warm. Palate: flavourful, smoky aftertaste, ripe fruit.

Don Angel Tintórico 2009 T
cabernet sauvignon, tempranillo

83

Don Angel Tintórico 2010 T
cabernet sauvignon, tempranillo, garnacha

88

Colour: cherry, garnet rim. Nose: fine reductive notes, wet leather, aged wood nuances. Palate: spicy, long, toasty.

VINS DEL COMTAT

Turballos, 11
03820 Cocentaina (Alicante)
☎: +34 965 593 194
Fax: +34 965 593 590
vinsdelcomtat@gmail.com
www.vinsdelcomtat.com

Viognier de Vins del Comtat 2014 B
100% viognier

85

VINS DEL TROS

Major, 12
43782 Vilalba dels Arcs (Tarragona)
☎: +34 605 096 447
info@vinsdeltros.com
www.vinsdeltros.com

Morenillo Àmfora 2013 T
morenillo

87

Colour: deep cherry, purple rim. Nose: balanced, ripe fruit, wild herbs, spicy. Palate: correct, balsamic.

VINYES MORTITX

Ctra. Pollença Lluc, Km. 10,9
07315 Escorca (Illes Balears)
☎: +34 971 182 339
Fax: +34 871 100 053
info@vinyesmortitx.com
www.vinyesmortitx.com

Dolç de Gel Mortitx 2012 B
moscatel, riesling, malvasía

89

Colour: golden. Nose: powerfull, honeyed notes, candied fruit, acetaldehyde. Palate: flavourful, sweet, fresh, fruity, good acidity, long.

VIÑAS EL REGAJAL

Antigua Ctra. Andalucía, Km. 50,5
28300 Aranjuez (Madrid)
☎: +34 913 078 903
Fax: +34 913 576 312
reservas@elregajal.es
www.elregajal.es

Galia 2012 T
tinto fino, garnacha

93

Colour: deep cherry, garnet rim. Nose: balanced, expressive, spicy, cocoa bean, ripe fruit, balsamic herbs. Palate: spicy, ripe fruit, long, round tannins.

VIÑEDOS Y BODEGAS MAYO GARCÍA

La Font 116
12192 Vilafamés (Castellón)
☎: +34 964 329 312
mail@mayogarcia.com
www.mayogarcia.com

Magnanimvs Platino Vino de Autor sc T
86

VIÑEDOS Y BODEGAS PAGOS DE NONA

☎: +34 650 986 185
info@pagosdenona.com
www.pagosdenona.com

La Chá Pieros 2014 T
mencía
90 🌱
Colour: cherry, purple rim. Nose: red berry notes, floral, balsamic herbs. Palate: fresh, fruity, good acidity.

Mil Razas 2014 RD
82 🌱

Santyuste 2014 B
verdejo
88 🌱
Colour: bright straw. Nose: dried herbs, faded flowers, slightly evolved, overripe fruit. Palate: ripe fruit, sweetness, good acidity.

VIÑOS DE ENCOSTAS

Florentino López Cuevillas, 6 1ºA
32500 O Carballiño (Ourense)
☎: +34 988 101 733
Fax: +34 988 488 174
miguel@losvinosdemiguel.com
www.xlsebio.es

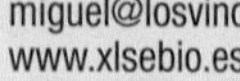

O Con 2013 B
albariño
93
Colour: bright yellow. Nose: white flowers, fine lees, dried herbs, ripe fruit, citrus fruit. Palate: flavourful, fruity, good acidity, elegant.

SPARKLING WINES-TRADITIONAL METHOD

All the wines included in this section are made by the so-called traditional method of a second fermentation in the bottle, the same one used in Cava –and Champagne– production, but in areas outside those ascribed to Cava or any other Spanish DO. They represent a tiny part of all the sparkling wines made in Spain and their figures and quality are understandably far away from those of Cava.

BODEGAS EL INICIO

San Vicente, 22
47300 Peñafiel (Valladolid)
☎: +34 947 515 884
Fax: +34 947 515 886
info@bodegaselinicio.com
www.bodegaselinicio.com

Vis a Vis 2014 B
100% verdejo

83

BODEGAS GRUPO YLLERA

Autovía A-6, Km. 173,5
47490 Rueda (Valladolid)
☎: +34 983 868 097
Fax: +34 983 868 177
grupoyllera@grupoyllera.com
www.grupoyllera.com

Yllera 5.5 Rosé Frizzante 2014 ESP
verdejo, tempranillo

86

Yllera 5.5 Verdejo Frizzante Semidulce 2014 ESP
verdejo

87

Colour: bright straw. Nose: floral, fragrant herbs, candied fruit. Palate: fresh, fruity, flavourful, sweet, easy to drink.

FREIXENET

Joan Sala, 2
08770 Sant Sadurní D'Anoia (Barcelona)
☎: +34 938 917 000
Fax: +34 938 183 095
freixenet@freixenet.es
www.freixenet.es

Freixenet Mía Moscato B

86

Freixenet Mía Moscato RD

85

MENADE

Ctra. Rueda Nava del Rey, km. 1
47490 Rueda (Valladolid)
☎: +34 983 103 223
Fax: +34 983 816 561
info@menade.es
www.menade.es

Duo Menade ESP

90

Colour: salmon, bright. Nose: fine lees, floral, ripe fruit, expressive. Palate: flavourful, long, fine bitter notes, fine bead.

PALACIO DE CANEDO

La Iglesia, s/n
24546 Canedo (León)
☎: +34 987 563 366
Fax: +34 987 567 000
info@pradaatope.es
www.pradaatope.es

Xamprada 2009 ESP Reserva
godello, chardonnay

84

Xamprada Extra Brut Ecológico 2011 ESP
godello, chardonnay

83

Xamprada Extra Brut Rosado 2013 ESP
mencía, godello

80

Xamprada Rosado Semiseco 2013 ESP
mencía, godello

80

Xamprada Semiseco 2012 ESP
godello, chardonnay

82

RAVENTÓS I BLANC

Plaça del Roure, s/n
08770 Sant Sadurní D'Anoia (Barcelona)
☎: +34 938 183 262
Fax: +34 938 912 500
raventos@raventos.com
www.raventos.com

PODIUM

Enoteca Personal Manuel Raventos 1998 BN

96

Colour: bright golden. Nose: fine lees, dry nuts, fragrant herbs, complex. Palate: powerful, flavourful, good acidity, fine bead, fine bitter notes.

PODIUM

Enoteca Personal Manuel Raventos 1999 BN

96

Colour: bright golden. Nose: dry nuts, fragrant herbs, complex, fine lees, macerated fruit. Palate: powerful, flavourful, good acidity, fine bead, fine bitter notes.

🏆 PODIUM

Enoteca Personal Manuel Raventos 20 Anys 1996 ESP

97

Colour: bright golden. Nose: fine lees, fragrant herbs, characterful, ripe fruit, dry nuts, elegant. Palate: flavourful, fine bead, fine bitter notes, smoky aftertaste.

🏆 PODIUM

Enoteca Personal Manuel Raventos 2000 BN

96

Colour: bright golden. Nose: dry nuts, fragrant herbs, complex, fine lees, sweet spices. Palate: powerful, flavourful, good acidity, fine bead, fine bitter notes.

🏆 PODIUM

Enoteca Personal Manuel Raventos Magnum 2002 BN

96

Colour: bright golden. Nose: dry nuts, fragrant herbs, complex. Palate: powerful, flavourful, good acidity, fine bead, fine bitter notes.

L'Hereu 2013 ESP

macabeo, xarel.lo, parellada

90

Colour: bright straw. Nose: floral, fragrant herbs. Palate: flavourful, good acidity, fine bead.

Manuel Raventos 2007 ESP

80% xarel.lo, 20% parellada

94

Colour: bright golden. Nose: fine lees, dry nuts, fragrant herbs, complex, toasty. Palate: powerful, flavourful, good acidity, fine bead, fine bitter notes.

Raventós i Blanc De La Finca 2012 ESP

xarel.lo, macabeo, parellada

91

Colour: bright straw. Nose: dried herbs, fine lees, floral, candied fruit. Palate: fruity, flavourful, good acidity.

Raventós i Blanc De La Finca Magnum 2012 ESP

xarel.lo, macabeo, parellada

92

Colour: bright straw. Nose: fresh fruit, dried herbs, fine lees, floral. Palate: fresh, fruity, flavourful, good acidity.

Raventós i Blanc De Nit 2013 ESP

macabeo, xarel.lo, parellada, monastrell

89

Colour: bright straw. Nose: fresh fruit, dried herbs, fine lees, floral. Palate: fresh, fruity, flavourful, good acidity.

INDEXES

ECOLOGICAL WINES

WINERIES

WINES

D

E

F

WINERIES **PAGE**

WINERIES	PAGE

C

WINERIES	PAGE

WINERIES	PAGE

WINERIES	PAGE

D

WINERIES PAGE

Q

R

S

S

T

WINES PAGE

A

WINES PAGE

WINES PAGE

WINES PAGE

WINES	PAGE

WINES	PAGE

WINES	PAGE

B

WINES | PAGE

D

WINES	PAGE

G

WINES PAGE

I

J

WINES PAGE

WINES PAGE

M

WINES PAGE

P

S

WINES PAGE

T

WINES PAGE

WINES PAGE

WINES PAGE

WINES PAGE

WINES	PAGE

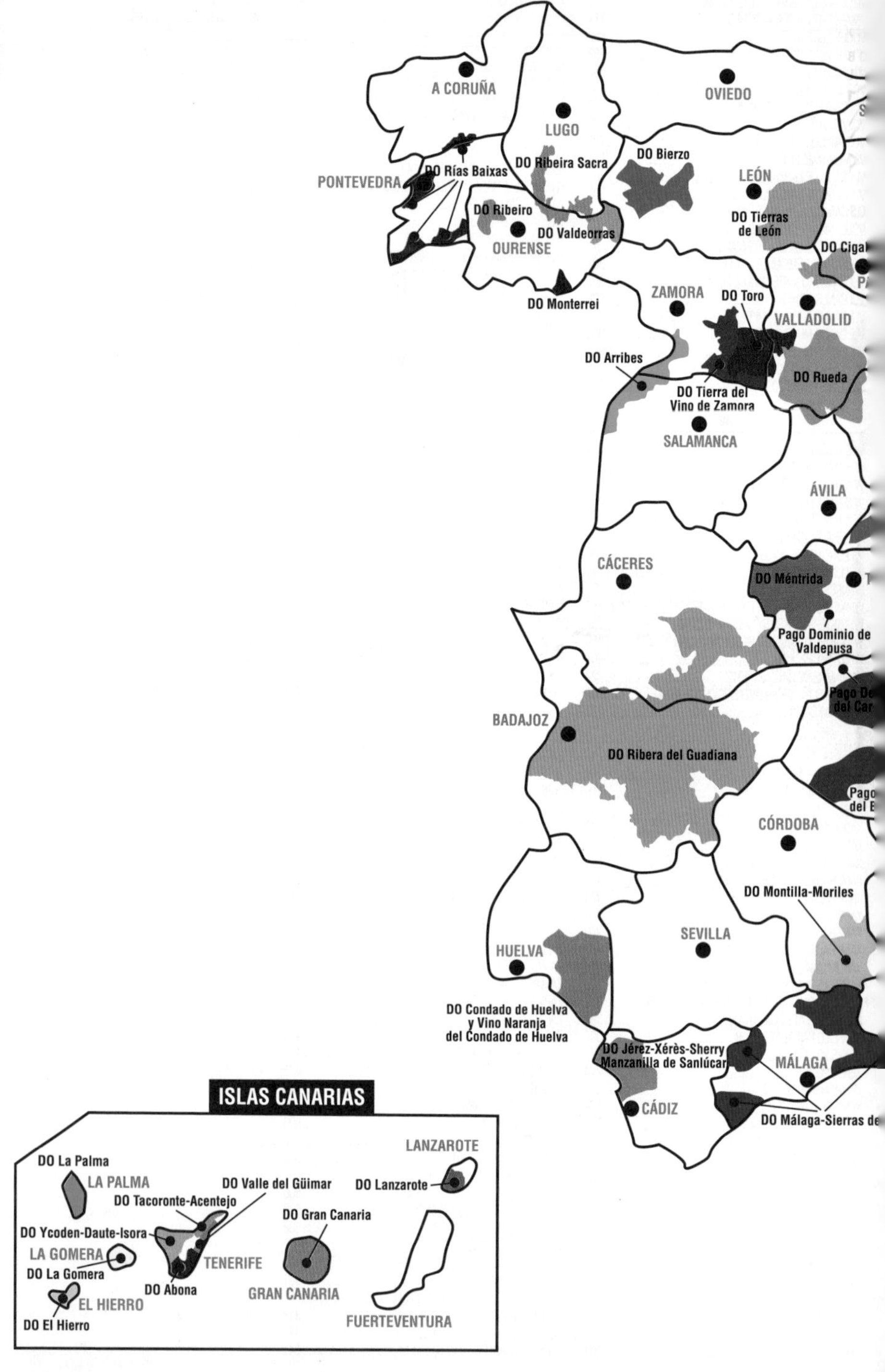
A CORUÑA
LUGO
OVIEDO
DO Bierzo
LEÓN
DO Ribeira Sacra
DO Rías Baixas
PONTEVEDRA
DO Ribeiro
DO Valdeorras
OURENSE
DO Tierras de León
DO Monterrei
ZAMORA
DO Toro
VALLADOLID
DO Arribes
DO Rueda
DO Tierra del Vino de Zamora
SALAMANCA
ÁVILA
CÁCERES
DO Méntrida
Pago Dominio de Valdepusa
BADAJOZ
DO Ribera del Guadiana
CÓRDOBA
DO Montilla-Moriles
SEVILLA
HUELVA
DO Condado de Huelva y Vino Naranja del Condado de Huelva
DO Jérez-Xérès-Sherry Manzanilla de Sanlúcar
MÁLAGA
CÁDIZ
ISLAS CANARIAS
DO La Palma
LA PALMA
DO Valle del Güimar
DO Lanzarote
LANZAROTE
DO Tacoronte-Acentejo
DO Gran Canaria
DO Ycoden-Daute-Isora
LA GOMERA
DO La Gomera
TENERIFE
DO Abona
GRAN CANARIA
EL HIERRO
DO El Hierro
FUERTEVENTURA

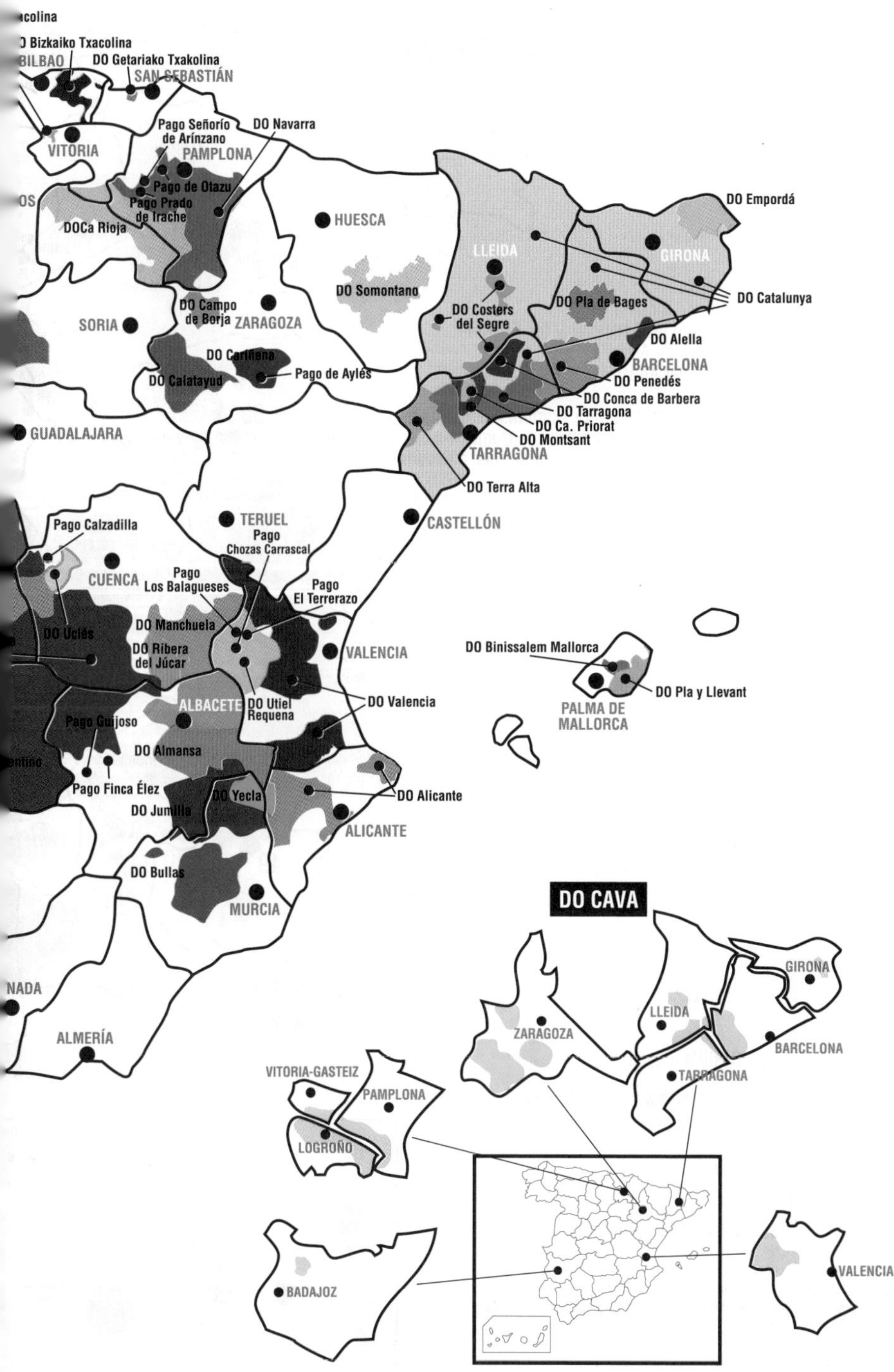

MAP OF THE DO´S IN SPAIN AND VINOS DE PAGO

ANDALUCÍA
1 - Norte de Almería
2 - Sierra de las Estancias y los Filabres
3 - Desierto de Almería
4 - Ribera del Andarax
5 - Laujar-Alpujarra
6 - Contraviesa-Alpujarra/Cumbres de Guadalfeo
7 - Granada Suroeste/Laderas de Genil
8 - Norte de Granada/Altiplano de Sierra Nevada
9 - Sierra Sur de Jaén
10 - Bailén
11 - Torreperogil
12 - Córdoba
13 - Villaviciosa de Córdoba
14 - Sierra Norte de Sevilla
15 - Los Palacios
16 - Cádiz

ARAGÓN
17 - Ribera del Gállego-Cinco Villas
18 - Ribera del Jiloca
19 - Valdejalón
20 - Bajo Aragón
21 - Valle del Cinca

CANTABRIA
22 - Liébana
23 - Costa de Cantabria

CASTILLA-LA MANCHA
24 - Castilla
25 - Pozohondo
26 - Sierra de Alcaraz
27 - Gálvez

CASTILLA Y LEÓN
28 - Castilla y León

EXTREMADURA
29 - Extremadura

GALICIA
30 - Betanzos
31 - Barbanza e Iria
32 - Val Do Miño-Ourense

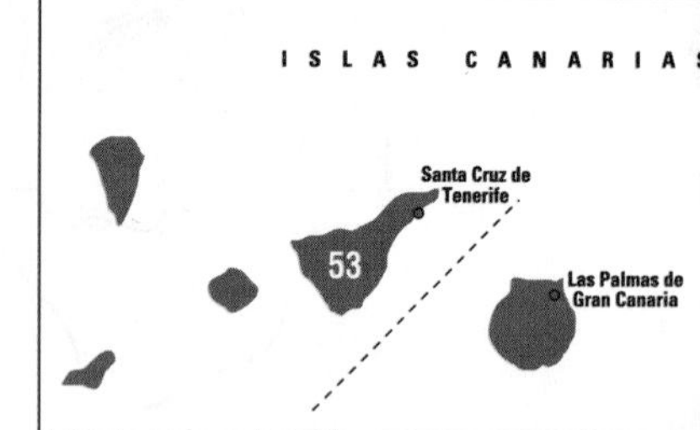

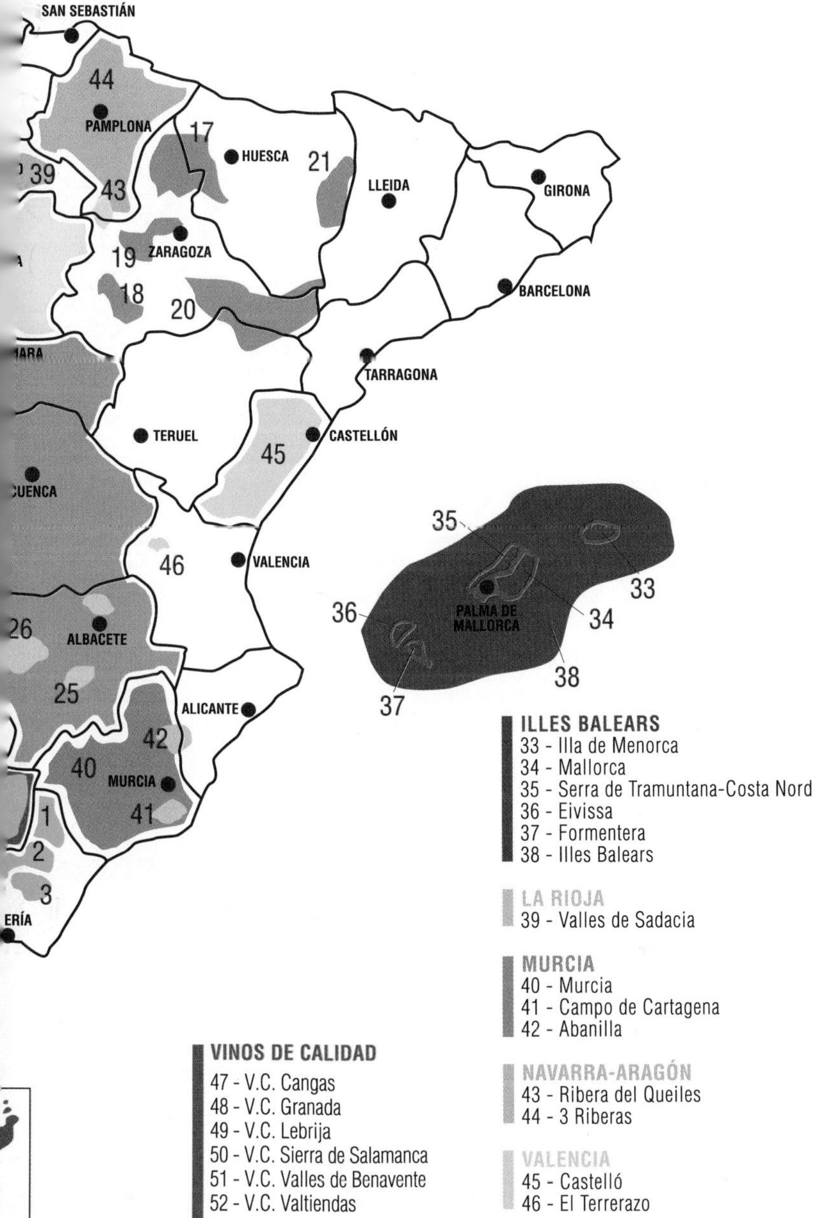

ILLES BALEARS
33 - Illa de Menorca
34 - Mallorca
35 - Serra de Tramuntana-Costa Nord
36 - Eivissa
37 - Formentera
38 - Illes Balears

LA RIOJA
39 - Valles de Sadacia

MURCIA
40 - Murcia
41 - Campo de Cartagena
42 - Abanilla

NAVARRA-ARAGÓN
43 - Ribera del Queiles
44 - 3 Riberas

VALENCIA
45 - Castelló
46 - El Terrerazo

VINOS DE CALIDAD
47 - V.C. Cangas
48 - V.C. Granada
49 - V.C. Lebrija
50 - V.C. Sierra de Salamanca
51 - V.C. Valles de Benavente
52 - V.C. Valtiendas
53 - V.C. Islas Canarias